1 MONTH OF
FREE
READING

at

www.ForgottenBooks.com

By purchasing this book you are eligible for one month membership to ForgottenBooks.com, giving you unlimited access to our entire collection of over 1,000,000 titles via our web site and mobile apps.

To claim your free month visit:

www.forgottenbooks.com/free1233234

ISBN 978-0-332-72823-0
PIBN 11233234

THE ARENA.

/ 0 ? 3 7 /

EDITED BY B. O. FLOWER.

VOL. XV.

PUBLISHED BY
ARENA PUBLISHING CO..
BOSTON, MASS.
1896.

THE PINKHAM PRESS, 289 Congress Street, Boston.

CONTENTS.

CONTENTS.

ILLUSTRATIONS.

Richard T. Ely

THE ARENA.

No. LXXIII.

DECEMBER, 1895.

PERSONAL RECOLLECTIONS OF AMERICA'S SEVEN GREAT POETS.

I. A MORNING WITH LOWELL, BY REV. M. J. SAVAGE.

My boyhood was spent on a poor little farm in the edge of the village of Norridgewock, in Maine. We had very few books, and those almost entirely religious. Having suffered all my life from book-hunger, it was a great thing for me when I was able to find anything to satisfy it. In one way we were fortunate beyond most small country towns. At that time there was a man, strong and original in character, who carried on the trade of harness-maker and saddler. Well-informed and thoughtful himself, he took an unselfish interest in the enlightenment of his town. As a practical expression of this, he had established a little circulating library in his harness-shop; and anyone could have the use of this on the payment of fifty cents a year. Sometimes we were not able to afford even this small outlay, but during most of my boyhood I had access to this little library. I was specially fond of poetry, and read nearly all of the standard English poets long before I had any idea of their relative rank or value.

It was in this library that I made my discovery of Lowell. The book was his first series of the "Biglow Papers." The humor attracted me, as humor has always attracted me ever since: but I also acquired a taste for the genuine poetic ability of the man, and was thrilled and roused by his patriotic and humanitarian enthusiasm. Ever since that day, I have looked eagerly for anything from the pen of Lowell and have always regarded him, and do still, as, on the whole, perhaps the greatest of our American poets. I hesitate in saying this when I think of Emerson and Whitman. But if poetic form is to be counted in giving a man his rank, it must be confessed that these two are seriously lacking. He is the first among our wits, in the English sense of that word; and he seems to me to have reached a higher height, and sounded a deeper depth, than almost any other of our singers.

Since admiration of a man's work paves naturally the way for love of his person, I learned to love Lowell before I had

JAMES RUSSELL LOWELL.

ever seen him. And since he had so uniformly and so finely voiced the best things in the way of moral reform and the higher patriotism, I had come to look upon him as a leader who was always to be found in the van. When, therefore, a few years ago, there appeared in the Atlantic a poem of his, under the title "Credidimus Jovem Regnare" I read it with a shock of disappointment. The title of this poem might perhaps be somewhat freely rendered, "We used to

believe that Jupiter reigned." It had about it that humorous touch which is always so natural to Lowell, and it was a
little difficult to be sure as to just how much of earnest
meaning it might contain. But•it read like the reactionary
utterances of an old man, who, although he had once been a
leader in the world's progress, had become weary of the battle, and out with the tendency of things. He did not seem
to me to comprehend the deeper meanings of the scientific
study of the age; he talked as though the world were putting protoplasm in the place of God, and in general showed
that, if he apprehended the scientific drift of modern
thought, he was at any rate out of sympathy with it. Knowing that his antecedents and training had been Unitarian
and liberal, I perhaps forgot for the time that his life had
been devoted to literature and that he had never been a student of science. At any rate, I felt so deeply on the subject
that I wrote and published a tiny book, under the title
"These Degenerate Days," dedicating it to him and sending
him a copy. This called out a letter from him, which is valuable in a biographical way, as indicating his real position
and outlook over the world. Because, while minister to
England, he frequently attended the Established Church,
and because the Episcopal burial service was read at his
funeral, many have supposed that as he grew older he
became more conservative and less in sympathy with liberal
ideas. As bearing, however, on his real views, I will here
quote a few words from his letter, which is dated from
Deerfoot Farm on the 5th of April, 1887:

On my return here yesterday, I find your little book and note. I
could not but be touched and pleased with both. I am pleased also
with the stalwart faith you show,—a faith (in essentials) not greatly
differing from my own, as you will see if you look into my "Cathedral," I think. The poem [Credidimus Jovem Regnare] on which you
comment was composed fifteen years ago, and the title I originally
meant to give it was "A Humorist's Growl," which would have explained that it was not argumentative, but only the expression of a
mood.

It has seemed to me that this might be interesting to the
public, as a declaration, in earnest prose, of Lowell's real
position.

It was some time after this that I spent with Lowell the
morning of which I am now to write. It was not long after
his return from his position as minister to England; and,
having made an appointment with him beforehand, I called
on him in his home at Elmwood. He received me in his
study, the large square room on the first floor, at the left of
the entrance. Those who have seen him there will be

familiar with the room, ideal in its arrangements as the study of a poet. Many of those who have spoken or written of the surroundings of Lowell's boyhood and youth have seemed to find in them some explanation of his poetic nature.

REV. JOHN W. CHADWICK, A. M

The only difficulty with this is the fact that other boys, born and trained amid scenes and surroundings quite as poetical, do not turn out poets after all. At any rate, whether it had in it the power to create or develop the poetic faculty, it was the fit setting of a poet's life and work.

As I remember the way in which he received me, the quiet ease with which he made me perfectly at home, it may be proper for me to say a word concerning Lowell's general attitude toward the public. He was by birth an training an aristocrat in the best sense of that word. He never found it easy to make his life a common, to be freely entered and trodden down at random by all the world. He was not so easily accessible as Longfellow; he claimed that he had a right to his own time, his intimacies, and his friendships. But to those who knew him, to those to whom he opened his arms and his heart, he was the most delightful of companions. He has been severely criticised for the attitude of dignity and reserve which he took and maintained while he was our minister at the Court of St. James; and it is freely admitted that he was not one of those who liked to be slapped on the back by everybody, and that he was not willing to be made an errand boy or a London guide for wandering Americans. But no man who ever occupied a diplomatic position in Europe has ever stood more steadily for the essential principles of our republic, maintained more uncompromisingly the dignity of an American citizen, or reflected more credit on his country.

So much for the general attitude of Lowell toward the outside world. After some time spent in general conversa-

WILLIAM CULLEN BRYANT.

tion, I ventured to express to him my sense of the service which he had rendered America and the credit which he had reflected upon the country by the work which he had done abroad.   I told him I was proud of his record and his work, as a citizen and in official position; but that I found myself now and again regretting that his public work had taken

RALPH WALDO EMERSON.

so much of his time and absorbed so much of his strength, which it seemed to me ought to have been given to literary and particularly to poetical work.   I was surprised at the response which he made to this suggestion.   He said at once: "You have given substantial expression to my own feeling.   I have been haunted by the idea that it might have been better if I had devoted myself more exclusively to my literary work."   And on this he rose, crossed the

OLIVER WENDELL HOLMES.

OLIVER WENDELL HOLMES.

room, opened a drawer, and took out a little manuscript which he brought back and, sitting down beside me, proceeded to read. It was a poem entitled, "My Brook."

This poem is most interesting from an autobiographical point of view. I do not remember that anywhere else Mr. Lowell's feeling on this particular subject has been made clear. Before he began to read he explained to me that, as Beaver Brook had been connected with his earliest poetic inspirations, he had naturally turned to it again as in some sense the genius of his literary life and work. And he went on to say that in this poem he had pictured himself as coming back to the scenes and work of his youth, and expressing his regret that he had been so long away and had lived another kind of life for so many years that he half suspected he had lost his early power and inspiration. He had written this poem in England, and soon after its composition he had received a letter from the New York *Ledger*, begging him to send them something, anything, from his pen. Being situated at the time so that it was impracticable for him to write anything new, he sent them this poem. He added that he was both surprised and gratified to receive in return a check for two hundred pounds, which at that particular time was anything but unwelcome to him. As there has been of late a good deal of discussion concerning the money payment for literary work, it is thought that this item may not be without interest as bearing on the question of the money value of a great reputation.

This poem has not as yet appeared in Lowell's published works. It will be all the more interesting, then, to the lovers of Lowell, particularly on account of its significance as touching his own estimate of his life-work. Giving due credit to the New York *Ledger*, in which it first appeared, I venture now to transcribe it, asking that it be read in the light of the preceding explanation, given to me by Lowell himself:

My Brook.

'Twas deep in the woodland we first plighted troth,
  When the hours were so many, the duties so few;
Life's burthen lies wearily now on us both,
  But I've never forgotten those dear days—have you?

Each was first-born of Eden, a morn without mate,
  And the bees and the birds and the butterflies thought
'Twas the one perfect day ever fashioned by fate,
  Nor dreamed the sweet wonder for us two was wrought.

I loitered beside you the summer day long,
  I gave you a life from the waste-flow of mine,
And whether you babbled or crooned me a song,
  I listened and looked till my pulses ran wine.

'Twas but shutting my eyes, I could see, I could hear,
  How you danced then, my nautch-girl, 'mid flagroot and fern,
While the flashing tomauns tinkled joyous and clear
  On the slim wrists and ankles that flashed in their turn.

JOHN G. WHITTIER.

Ah, that was so long ago! Ages it seems;
  And now I return, sad with life and its lore.
Will they flee my gray presence, the light-footed dreams,
  And Will-o'-the-wisps offer their lanterns no more?

Where the bees' hum seemed noisy once, all was so still,
  And the hermit thrush nested, secure of her lease,
Now whir the world's mill-stones, and clacks the world's mill;
  No fairy gold passes, the oracles cease.

The life I then dreamed of was never to be,
    For I with my tribe into bondage was sold,
And your sun-gleams and moon-gleams, gay elf-gifts to me,
    The miller transmutes into every-day gold.

What you mint for the miller will soon melt away,
    It is earthy, and earthy good only it buys;
But the shekels you tost me are safe from decay,
    They were coined of the sun and the moment that flies.

Break loose from your thraldom! 'Tis only a leap;
    Your eyes 'tis but shutting, just holding your breath!
Come back to the old days, the days that will keep;
    If there's peace in the mill-pond, there's better in death!

Leap down to me, down to me! Be as you were,—
    My nautch-girl, my singer! Again let them glance.
Your tomauns, the sun's largess, that wink and are there,
    And gone again, still keeping time as you dance!

You are mine, fly with me, then; with life of my life
    I made you a naiad, that were but a stream.
In the moon are brave dreams yet, and chances are rife
    For the passion that ventures its all on a dream.

Make haste, or it may be I wander again!
    'Tis I, dear, that call you; youth beckons with me;
Come back to us both, dear! In breaking your chain
    You let the old summers and fantasies free.

Leap bravely! Now down through the meadows we'll go
    To the land of Lost Days, whither all the birds wing,
Where the dials move backward and daffodils blow;
    Come, flash your tomauns again, dance again, sing!

Yes, flash them, and clash them on ankle and wrist,
    For we're pilgrims to dream land, fair Daughter of Dream,
Where we find again all that we wasted or missed,
    And Fancy, poor fool, with her bauble's supreme.

As the Moors in their exile the keys treasured still
    Of their castles in Spain, so have I; and no fear
But the doors will fly open, whenever we will,
    To the heart of the past and the sweet of the year.

After he had finished reading, he told me that he was
under contract not to let the poem leave his own hands until
after it was published in the *Ledger*, but that when it had
appeared he would make me a present of the manuscript
which he had just read to me. This he afterwards sent me,
and it is from this that I have just made the copy that is
here printed.

Lowell's life is now an open secret, and I came away from
my morning in his study with the feeling that he was, what

REV. EDWARD EVERETT HALE, D. D.

all men now know him to have been, one of the gentlest, sweetest, noblest, and staunchest natures that our time has seen. So long as our democracy can produce children and champions like him, we may be both proud of the past and confident of the future.

II. Emerson, by Rev. John W. Chadwick, A. M.

Among many happy fortunes that have befallen me, I count one of the happiest to have seen face to face Bryant and Emerson and Longfellow and Whittier and Holmes and Lowell, and to have had speech with them; although with some of them not much. Had not Bryant died the very year I made my summer home in Chesterfield he would have been my country neighbor, and I might, perhaps, have known him well. I say "perhaps," because he was not an easily accessible or communicable spirit. As it is, I know his haunts extremely well: the roads he tramped, the trees and flowers and streams he loved, are also mine, but I met him socially but once. That once was at the table of a host than whom the world has never known a better—Dr. Henry W. Bellows —and then he left the talk to others in the main. His appearance I imagine is quite misconceived by the majority. He was by no means the leonine Jupiter of Launt Thompson's colossal bust. His frame was small, his features were delicate, and at the last there was something a little overpowering in his full and flowing beard.

I refrain from my impressions of Whittier and Holmes and Longfellow and Lowell, albeit they are pleasant chapters in my memory, lest I should trench upon the parts which have been assigned to others in these recollections of our poets.

As for Emerson I dare believe that few who knew him in the flesh or spirit cherished a warmer gratitude to him or a more loyal affection, but I knew his person much less intimately than I knew his books. To the best of my knowledge and belief I was attracted to the first of these I knew by its title, "Representative Men"—having then as now a passion for biography — without any previous knowledge of the writer's name and fame. This was about 1856. Here was an herb that had a pungent, aromatic savor, such as I had not known before, and withal a subtle mystery and charm that lured me on from page to page. I did not understand much more than half, but that half was better than the aggregate of many ordinary books.

My first opportunties for hearing him were singularly fortunate. Theodore Parker had gone abroad not to return
again, and his society was hearing Emerson and Garrison
and Phillips and other men of note from week to week. On
one of these occasions Emerson made an address on Thoreau, shortly after his death. Since then I have read much
concerning Thoreau, but measured by the large utterance
of that address it all seems pitifully frail, nor in the words as
printed do I seem to find all that I heard in Music Hall that
day.

An occasion far more memorable was a Sunday shortly
following Lincoln's proclamation threatening emancipation,
Sept. 22, 1862. I have heard Sumner and Phillips and Lincoln and Gladstone and other famous orators, but never
from other lips words so impressively spoken as those concluding that address: "Do not let the dying die. Hold them
back to this world until you have charged their ear and
heart with this message to other spiritual societies, announcing the melioration of our planet."

A few months later I went to Concord to take charge of
the High School, filling out the term of Goodwin Stone who
had gone off to the wars where death impatiently awaited
him. Thoreau was already laid to rest in Sleepy Hollow.
Hawthorne would follow soon, but then he was a notable
figure on the village street, ploughing along with eyes cast
down, "wild, homeless eyes," that seemed more conscious
of the elusive phantoms of his "Dolliver Romance," on which
he was then at work, than of the passersby. I was domiciled
at Mrs. Clark's, with whom John Brown had stayed during
his Concord visits, and my room—the one that he had occupied three years before—was subject for my imagination to
the frequent visitation of his mighty ghost. One evening
during my Concord days Curtis came to lecture, and his old
friends and neighbors were out in force, Emerson among
them, and Alcott, harboring no resentment because Curtis
had called him Plato Skimpole in an early skit.

But the ambrosial night was one at Emerson's own house.
No lamps or candles were brought in, but that was all the
better, for the mercury was below zero and the fire-dogs in
the big fireplace were heaped high with blazing wood that
cast a ruddy light on the warm-colored furniture and hangings of the room. There was plenty of good talk, Alcott
doing more of it than Emerson or Conway or Sanborn, if not
more than all these together. But Emerson was himself a
copious talker, and I suppose that all who knew him well, or
had some real acquaintance with him, must have wondered
if his conversation was not his most delightful gift.

WILLIAM CULLEN BRYANT.

In conversation he had little of the hesitation which was characteristic of his public manner. This has never been described so well by any other writer as by Mr. Alcott in his "Concord Days" in a passage which begins, "See our Ion standing there." The description there of the hesitating manner is as felicitous as possible. Lowell fancied that it was the deliberate artifice of the oratorical artist. One hesitates to differ from so wise a critic, but to me it always seemed to be of the essence of the man, an expression of his conscience for reality and truth. It was as if he assayed every word that he offered you as the price of your confidence in his intelligence and honest dealing. We seemed not so much to hear him as to overhear his mind, rethinking what he had written. Many of his lectures as printed have a swelling climax, but the conclusion often took his hearers completely by surprise. The stream of his discourse would be running on smoothly as ever and suddenly disappear. As one reporter said,

> "He folded his *script* like the Arabs
> And as silently stole away."

And, by the way, the reporters were an abomination in his eyes. When I complained of their misreporting him, he said, "But those who do that are not the most terrible. The most terrible are those that take down all I say, so that I cannot use the thing again." His sense of the right of property in ideas was particularly keen.

I had great luck in hearing him and meeting him, but my best time with him was on a journey from Boston to New York. I discovered him early in the day and had four or five hours of his delightful talk. If he wished me further he dissembled wonderfully well, for each time I set out to leave him he protested that he desired me to remain. He had written that when we find a man reading Horace on the train we wish to embrace him. I found him reading Horace and I made the inevitable remark. But how little can I now recall of a conversation which at the time I thought I never should forget. One of the subjects was Carlyle, and he detained us long. Emerson quoted a pathetic passage from one of his letters about his wife, with whom, recently dead, he was "holding silent communion; silent on both sides." Of a more recent letter, railing overmuch at "this mad, roaring world," he said, "I have not yet felt inclined to answer it." He shamed me for knowing so little of Landor, praising him in terms which now, with ampler knowledge, I cannot but think extravagant. He quoted approvingly some new western poet whom I cannot identify. One of the quotations was "Life is a lamp whose splendor hides its base," and another "The short parenthesis of life was sweet." He was severe on someone who had spoken intimately of his domestic privacy, saying, "He must have been consorting with my cook." The train-boy beguiled me into purchasing some maple candy, and Emerson asked, "Does it taste as good as the rose-cakes that you made when you were a boy?" I confessed that it did not, and that discouraged him from sharing my bounty or purchasing upon his own account.

One evening in Brooklyn, over the tea-table and afterward, is marked with a white stone. He had said in his lecture: "Everybody likes poetry. They do not like Pope or Tupper or Shelley. But they like Homer and Shakespeare and Burns." I took up the cudgels for Shelley within a narrow range, but he yielded scarce a jot; and in his "Parnassus" he does worse than omit the "Skylark," printing two or three stanzas. He read to us Wordsworth's "Intimations of Immortality," and it took on a rarer beauty. He had spoken in his lecture of Jones Very, and I said I knew the man. "You know his ghost," he said.

If Emerson laughed at all, it was very quietly. Carlyle's loud roaring laugh must have been intolerable to him. But Emerson's smile was something to remember. It was the wisest smile. His lips and eyes were implicated in it about equally. It could do many things: for one, express his "cherub scorn" of what he didn't like; also his gladness in a thought which came to him he knew not whence; again his pleasure in some palpable absurdity, as in his lecture on "The Comic" where the little boy is well satisfied with A and B but staggered by W. "The devil!" said the boy, "Is that W?"

"Let me see," he said on one occasion; "where did I see you last? Oh, I remember! It was at the tavern, the stone tavern on School Street,"—meaning the Parker House! It was close by the said "tavern" that I saw him for the last time, and the whole street seemed to be lighted up and cheered and brightened with the ineffable sweetness of his face. It was as if some superior being from a higher world had lost his way amidst the jostling crowd.

III. Emerson in his Home, by F. B. Sanborn.

For many years I had the good fortune to see much of Emerson in his own home at Concord, and to converse with him freely and intimately on many topics. I was struck from the first—my first call was in the summer of 1853—by the readiness and force with which he expressed himself in conversation. In extempore speaking, before an audience, there was always some hesitation in his manner; and this grew to be painful in his latest years, when his memory began to fail, as it did for some ten years before his death in April, 1882. But nothing could be more prompt, responsive, and pertinent than his questions and replies in conversation; and what he said might have been printed as it fell from his lips, with far less need of revision than happens usually with literary men. Not that he was precise or pedantic in his choice of words, nor that he prepared himself, as many good talkers have done, by looking up certain subjects in advance, and skilfully turning the conversation towards these. On the contrary, he followed the impulse and spirit of the occasion, and let the talk run on as it might happen; but so full was his mind, so thoughtful his habit, and so original his genius, that he was seldom at a loss how to meet any questioner or how to accost any subject.

He was aided in this readiness by his wonderful memory, which had been active and strong by nature, and had been trained from childhood by the acquisition and imparting of what he found best in all the literatures which had fallen in his way, or which he had studied to acquire. Poetry and eloquence especially had interested him, and always clung to his memory. He once told me that in his first long voyage (I suppose to Sicily in 1832–3), finding himself with little companionship, he began to see what long poems he could recall from end to end; and was pleased to find that he knew the whole of Milton's "Lycidas," and, if I am not mistaken, of the much longer poem, "Comus." Milton had been familiar to him from boyhood, and so continued through life, although he did not, like his friend Thoreau, prefer Milton to Shakspere.

Another noticeable thing was his courtesy and consideration for all who called on him, or whom he met as the friends of his children, or of his relatives or acquaintance. The ties of relationship were very strong with him, and he delighted in those family gatherings which were customary in his household, as they had been in that of his grandmother, Mrs. Dr. Ripley, at the Old Manse. His father he only remembered as a child of eight may; and his grandfather Emerson he never saw; but his grandmother Emerson, being left a widow in 1776, soon after married the young minister who succeeded to the vacant pulpit, and who, for more than half a century, occupied the fine homestead which had been built

for his predecessor. This Old Manse, so well known from
Hawthorne's description, was occupied by Emerson at
various times, for a longer period than by Hawthorne; and it
used to be said that much of his first volume, "Nature," was
written in its chambers. After the burning of his house in
the summer of 1872, he retired for some weeks to the Old
Manse, where his cousin, Miss Elizabeth Ripley, then lived;
and it was his old affection for the place and the family
which attracted him then.

Literary topics, on the wide range of philosophic thought,
made the staple of Emerson's conversation, when among
men of letters or those men and women of liberal minds, akin
to his own, by whom he was so often surrounded in his own
house, or who accompanied him on his long walks through
the fields and woods of Concord. His habit was to walk
every day (usually in the afternoon, the study being his place
through the morning hours), and I have been his companion
during hundreds of miles in these excursions. It was on a
walk with him in the summer of 1855, and crossing a certain
bridge (how well I remember it!) that he first spoke to me of
Walt Whitman, whose earliest book, the thin quarto
"Leaves of Grass," had just appeared. He praised the
work, "a singular mixture of the Bhagavadgita and the
New York *Herald*," as he termed it; and he gave me a copy.
We often returned to the subject of Whitman in after years,
and a few months after Thoreau's death in 1862, Emerson
said to me that he had been impressed anew, on reading
Thoreau's Journals in manuscript (as he had been in 1856,
by Thoreau's account of his interview with Whitman), with
the strong interest his Concord friend had taken in the
vigorous new poet. I mention this by way of introduction
to my report of a conversation or two that I am soon to
quote, in illustration of Emerson's later thoughts and turn
of mind.

My acquaintance with Emerson's old friend, Bronson
Alcott, began a few months earlier than my first call upon
Emerson in Concord; for he was then living in Boston, and
more accessible to me in Harvard College than was Emerson in his village retirement. Naturally, since everything
that concerned Emerson was of interest to a young disciple,
I inquired of Alcott what his first knowledge of his Concord
brother had been. He told me that he first heard the Reverend Ralph Waldo Emerson (as he was then called) preach,
in Dr. Channing's Federal-Street pulpit, a little before or
after his own marriage to Miss May in 1830. The sermon
was on "The Universality of the Moral Sentiment," and Mr.

Alcott was struck with the apparent youth of the preacher, the music of his elocution, and the sincere and direct manner in which he addressed his audience.

Their acquaintance, however, did not begin until 1834, the year in which Emerson read a poem in Cambridge before the Phi Beta Kappa society. Upon that occasion, as Mr. Alcott told me in 1878, he took the young poet's arm, and they walked together among the members of the society, Emerson saying, "Come, we will not mince matters," and stepping along with the Connecticut schoolmaster at his side. In delivering his poem, which made some allusion to Washington, and contained tributes to Lafayette and to Webster, Mr. Alcott told me that Emerson "read for awhile, but not feeling satisfied with what he was reading, presently he closed his manuscript and sat down unconcerned." This poem has never been printed, and when I asked Emerson about it in the same year (1878), he had forgotten exactly what it contained—perhaps there might be something in it about Washington.

No man could be more hopeful for young writers of any promise than was Emerson. It was at this time (Aug. 19, 1878) that I called on him one afternoon, and found him busy with papers of obscure authors who had sent them to him; one of these was Mr. P. Kaufman, formerly of Canton, Ohio, whom he had once met in New York, but had then lost sight of. He asked if I knew him, and then read me some verses of W. H. Babcock on "Joseph the Nez Percé," which he said he had read to audiences at the Old South and elsewhere, and thought them good. But when he sent them to Mr. Howells, asking to have them printed in the *Atlantic*, this editor had sent them back, saying they were not good enough. "We thought we had some interest in our own magazine," said Emerson, a little piqued at the affair; and he gave me the verses, asking me to get them published somewhere, and have a little money sent to the author. Accordingly, I sent them to G. W. Curtis, who had them printed in *Harper's Monthly*, for which they seemed to be good enough.

On this occasion I showed Emerson Chateaubriand's account of his interview with Washington in 1791, and also his first interview with Napoleon, some years later. He had never seen either, and read them in my presence, asking me what was the meaning of *jouets*, of *sable*, and of *curi*. He said, "Chateaubriand evidently thought as much of himself as of Washington; but Bonaparte saw through him; that man always knew how to meet men on their own ground—

whether Christians or Frenchmen." He had read a few
books of Chateaubriand, but not these *Memoires d'Outre
Tombe*. Not long after (Oct. 20, 1878) I asked what had become of his lecture on France, which I had heard when in
college, and admired. He said he had given it in a course
of lectures at Boston in 1853, and again at Philadelphia in
1854; afterwards he read it one evening in Cambridge, where
"the great man from Germany" (meaning Louis Agassiz)
heard it and protested against it as not quite just to France,
of which Agassiz had the most agreeable recollections.
Since then he had never given it, in deference to Agassiz's
opinion. I suggested he should send it to be printed in
London—whence had just come a request for a new book
from him—and let the English test its quality. He said no;
he should not send that certainly, and he hardly thought he
should send anything.

On the same evening I spoke of Whitman and his poetry.
Emerson said that when Whitman came to Boston in the
spring of 1860, to print there an edition of his "Leaves of
Grass" (which Thayer & Eldridge published, soon after
Redpath's Life of John Brown and "Echoes from Harper's
Ferry") he asked Longfellow, Holmes, and Lowell whether
he should invite Whitman to the Saturday Club, as he would
gladly have done. "But they declared no wish to meet him,
so he was not asked." I remembered, but did not recall the
fact to his mind, that Alcott, Emerson, and Thoreau all
wished then to invite Whitman to Concord; but neither
Mrs. Alcott, Mrs. Emerson, nor Sophia Thoreau was willing
to meet him; so the invitation was not given. In 1881 he
came to visit me in Concord, and Emerson, Alcott, and
Louisa Alcott all met him at my house; the next day Mrs.
Emerson invited him to dinner, and we all dined together
there.

Pursuing the conversation of 1878, Emerson said that he
first met Whitman in New York, about 1855, and asked him
to dine with him at the Astor House; he came, and at dinner, instead of drinking out of a glass, called for a tin cup.
He then took Emerson to an engine-house, and showed him
the conveniences there for the firemen to sit and read or chat
with one another, and praised the companionship of the men.

Emerson said that Whitman had written nothing worth
remembering for many years now (1878); his earlier books
had made a deep impression on the mind, but these later
poems were forgotten as soon as read. Whitman had come
to hear him lecture in Baltimore, after the war; and he had
tried to find Whitman in Washington the next Sunday—

going from Charles Sumner's house to look him up—but
without success.

At this date Emerson's memory was uncertain; he recalled many things, but also forgot much that he had well
known. I requested his autograph of a short poem to
accompany his portrait in *Scribner's Magazine*, and told
him that Mr. Gilder, the editor, had suggested "Forbearance." He did not recognize his poem by that name; but
when I recited the first line,

> Hast thou named all the birds without a gun ?

he smiled and said, "That poem has pleased more than one
person," naming, in particular, Senator Hoar's brother
Edward (a silent man), whose opinion, he said, "is worth a
great deal, because he never says anything." He thought
"Forbearance" was not very suitable to face his own portrait; nor did he like "The Days" entirely, for that use.
Finally it was agreed that he should write off a stanza from
his "Two Rivers"; and when I showed him the verse beginning

> Musketaquit, a goblin strong,
> Of shard and flint makes jewels gay,

he said, "Ellen [his daughter] wants to have the place
remembered where she was born," as if declining to notice
the beauty of the poem. He also repeated what he had said
to me not long before: "It has been decided that I cannot
write poetry"; adding, "Others have found it out at last,
but I could have told them so long ago." Miss Emerson
afterwards suggested that her father was thinking of what
Carlyle had said to John Sterling against his writing in
verse; but I put another interpretation upon it.

These extracts from the journal where I noted down the
remarks made to me from time to time by this poet-phil-
osopher, may be depended on as giving the substance, and
often the exact words, of the conversation. As I write them
now, they inspire a regret that no fuller record was made of
such intimate interviews, extending through nearly thirty
years, and only heightening the impression of genius, goodness, and wisdom which Emerson's books give the reader.

IV. Personal Recollections of Oliver Wendell Holmes.

By Edward Everett Hale.

It is about a year, I see, since Dr. Holmes' death. The
true way to write a man's biography is to take people on the
day they hear of his death and write down the anecdotes

which spring to their lips spontaneously as to his life. You
then get something like Plutarch's Lives, which are made
up of the anecdotes which had filtered down to him, in some
cases for hundreds of years, sometimes from books, sometimes from tradition.

I met an accomplished lady, as old as I am, who said of
Dr. Holmes: "Yes, he was always so friendly. He made you
so entirely at ease. The first time I ever spoke with him, I
suppose I was a girl of sixteen, not used to talking with
persons of such a reputation as he had already. It was in
the old Cambridge omnibus; I was seated at the upper end.
He came up to me, for the families knew each other, and to
a schoolgirl of my age was willing to pour out his anecdote, his fun, and his philosophy, exactly as if I had been
his equal and an old companion. We have been very intimate since," she said, "but I never have forgotten the enthusiasm and delight which I felt in that omnibus ride."

This would make one ask if Holmes were particularly at
home in omnibuses and street-cars, so many are the similar
stories of his courtesy and tenderness, even to the last
weeks of his life, to those whom he met in travelling. But
the frequency of such stories comes literally because in
modern life we live so much in public in these places. It
is a satisfaction to recollect that he has immortalized
the trolley and the electric by the charming "Broomstick
Train."

The truth is that a certain exuberance of life, if you please
a certain exuberance of kindness or sympathy, made him
specially companionable. Early in life I met a novelist of
great reputation, and I was satisfied that he kept to himself
his best notions so that he might use them in his books.
With Holmes, it was exactly the other way. He bubbled
over with whatever came to him, and liked to tell his next
neighbor, though it were a car-conductor, some bright thing
which had come to him. I have been sorry to see that
people have sometimes spoken of this as if it were conceit
on his part. I do not think it was conceit; I think it was the
feeling that the next man was as good a fellow as he was,
and would appreciate, as well as he did, some funny conception.

I am tempted to write down one of his questions, which is
always turning up for answer in my mind. I met him in
some omnibus, I forget where, and I asked his opinion of
so-and-so, of whom it was necessary that I should give some
account. He answered as to the fact—whatever it was, I
have forgotten—and then proceeded to this generalization:

"The truth is," he said, "people whose health is declining in consumption are very apt to see far into the other world and to show what you and I would call decided religious proclivities. Whether they go into consumption because they are very near heaven, or whether they are so near heaven because they are in the early stages of phthisis, I do not know. It is just as it was when we were in Paris, at one of the hospitals. As I went downstairs after the clinique, there was a fellow with a magnificent head of hair, selling hair-oil to all who would buy. Whether he sold hair-oil because he had a magnificent head of hair, or whether he had a magnificent head of hair because he used that hair-oil, I have never known."

His enthusiasm for the country was utterly unaffected, and not in the least got up to order. It appears all the way through, even in the verses which savor most of city life. I interviewed him once, at the request of Mr. McClure, who had gone to him and made all the preliminary arrangements. Frankly, I think he knew he must be interviewed, and he thought he had rather be in the hands of a friend than of a stranger. Very fortunately for us all, he got switched off upon his life in Berkshire. He told how he came to live there. It seemed that in the early days some Wendell among his ancestors had received a grant there, and the place was called Wendelltown. The Indian name of the place had been Pontoosuc, once Poontooksuck, which means "where the brook falls." From this grant, a part of the whole came to Dr. Holmes' mother, and after he had once seen the place he arranged with her that he might build his summer house there. There his children grew up, and there he enjoyed the glory of a Berkshire summer and of its autumn. He cited on that day a magnificent passage from a poem which he read at a cattle-show as early as 1849. I printed this passage, and his reference to it, in Mr. McClure's magazine.

One of the most charming essays is that on the seasons, not so much remembered as some of the others, I hardly know why. It begins with this pleasant announcement of the annual exhibition:

Walk in, ladies and gentlemen ! The wonderful exhibition of the Seasons is about to commence; four shows under one cover; the best ventilated place of entertainment in this or any other system; the stage lighted by solar, lunar, and astral lamps; an efficient police will preserve order. Gentlemanly ushers will introduce all newcomers to their places. Performance in twelve parts. Overture by the feathered choir; after which the white drop-curtain will rise, showing the remarkable succession of natural scenery designed

and executed solely for this planet—real forests, meadows, water,
earth, skies, etc. At the conclusion of each series of performances
the storm-chorus will be given with the whole strength of the wind-
instrument orchestra, and the splendid snow-scene will be introduced, illuminated by grand flashes of the Aurora Borealis. Admit-
tance free, refreshments furnished, complete suits of proper costume
supplied at the door, *to be returned on leaving the exhibition.*

Then he goes on to a careful and fair enough discussion as
to the different motives with which different people study
nature and the ways in which they undertake it. But what
makes the real charm of the essay is the pretty description
that he gives of the home garden at Cambridge. He remembered the garden as a boy remembers the garden of the dear
old home. Time had gone by, he had lived in one place and
another, and everything was changed; among the rest, the
old garden had given way. It was just as the jungle
marched down upon the village at the order of Mowgli in
Mr. Kipling's story. So the garden, which he remembered
first "in the consulship of James Madison," as he says, was
a wilderness in "the consulship of Abraham Lincoln."
Then he determined to reconstruct it, and he tells so prettily
the way in which he reconstructed it, and his success. The
final triumph was when the yellow-birds came back to the
sunflowers.

I remember their flitting about, golden in the golden light, over
the golden flowers, as if they were flakes of curdled sunshine. Let
us plant sunflowers, I said, and see whether the yellow-birds will not
come back to them. Sure enough, the sunflowers had no sooner
spread their disks, and begun to ripen their seeds, than the yellow-
birds were once more twittering and fluttering about them.

A great deal has been said, but enough cannot be said, of
his kindness to young people. I like young people, and they
do me a great deal of good. But his courtesy and tenderness and freshness, in interview after interview, with those
who came, either to pay him homage or to ask for his advice,
were something which you could not believe if you had not
seen it and known it. Till a very late period, he answered
all the letters of these boys and girls with his own hand; his
house was open, an hour or two every day, to receive them.
At the end of the day he had the consciousness, and it ought
to have been a glad consciousness, that he had made happy
so many persons who, as the deaf-and-dumb world says,
"had no claim upon him whatever." Claim or no claim, he
wanted to give them pleasure, or he wanted to start them
on a higher walk of life; and he did it. What might have
happened with those two hours a day if he had not done it,
perhaps the good God and the angels know; but one may

well wonder if he could have found any line of life by which
he could have answered better one of the great purposes of
his own life. For he was thoroughly glad when he had
made the world happy.

Have I succeeded in giving at all the impression which
lingers in my own mind, of a certain satisfaction whenever
you met him, because you felt that you were as likely to
have him at his best at that moment as you could find any
man when his eyes were "in a fine frenzy rolling"? He
lived in the present, I think, and that with all his might.
He entered into the joy of the universe. I suppose he had
his moments of depression or dissatisfaction; but he did not
wash his dirty linen before the world. If he met you, you
got the best that was in him. There is no chance whatever
that the bright things which he said in conversation will
ever get themselves written down. No Boswells give us
such things, there are no shorthand writers behind the
screens who preserve them, and the phonograph has not
yet come to that consummate point that it writes for us
biographies.

I believe I have told, in a public address, a good story
which I have never written down. I was to preside, one
year, at the annual dinner-party of Phi Beta Kappa. This
dinner-party is apt to be about the best fun of the year, precisely because there are no reporters present and everybody
says exactly what he chooses without any fear of the echo.
By way of preparation for the dinner, I wrote to two or
three of those whom I knew the younger members would
like to see. Among others, I wrote to Holmes, to remind
him of the anniversary and to say that I hoped he would
come. I got a good-natured note in reply, in which he said
virtually that his pump had sucked, and that he had determined not to write any more occasional poems for dinner-
parties. To this I boldly replied: "Who said anything about
a poem? I did not ask you to speak. I have only embarrassment of riches. But the boys would like to see you;
come and sit by my side, and you shall not say a word." In
reply to which, almost as soon as the mail could bring it,
came a very droll answer: "The idea of my going to Phi Beta
without reading some verses is absurd. I have already
found a theme, and the verses are half done. I shall come—
fix that on your mind; and I shall be very angry if I am not
called upon to speak." Such are almost the words he used,
in a note which, in some unfortunate frenzy of folly, I gave
away to some wretched hunter of autographs.

So he came, and we had a charming little poem from him.

V. John Greenleaf Whittier as I knew Him, by Mary B. Claflin.

Mr. Whittier, the poet beloved of the people, was unique in his absolute simplicity and truthfulness. The transparency of his soul was apparent to all who came in contact with him, and it would seem impossible to represent anything to him otherwise than just as it was in *truth*, because he detected at a glance, the slightest prevarication or false coloring. He seemed more akin to God than most human beings, in his childlike trust and faith in the fatherhood of the divine Being, and in his exquisite love to Him whom the Father sent to teach us the brotherhood of man. Mr. Whittier's love to his kind, his godlike justice and mercy in all his dealings with his fellowmen, were so apparent that it was not easy to turn aside from the straight and narrow path of righteousness when dealing with him. His language was simple as a child's and unadorned with superfluous words. It was always yea and nay, and his "thee" and "thou" were musical sounds in the ears of those who loved him—and who did not love him?

Sometimes a friend would ask him why the Quakers perverted the English grammar in such fashion with the *thee* and *thou*. His reply always hushed the questioner, and made him feel that he would rather hear Mr. Whittier's sweet tones in the language he chose to use, even if it defied all the rules of English grammar: "It has been the manner of speech of my people for two hundred years; it was my mother's language, and it is good enough for me; I shall not change my grammar."

Mr. Whittier's conversation was full of reminiscences of his early life in the country. He loved nature with a reverent and appreciative love. Every little flower growing by the roadside or in the green meadows about his early home he looked upon as a thought of God for His children; the sunset clouds awakened in his poetic heart such enthusiasm that his great luminous eyes would light up as if they saw through the gates into the celestial city beyond—the city where, he said,

> No branch of palm, no gate of pearl I merit,
>   Nor street of shining gold.

> Some humble door among the many mansions,
>   Some sheltering shade where sin and sorrow cease,
> And flows forever through heaven's green expansions
>   The river of Thy peace.

He saw God's works in all things and recognized His love in dealing with His children. All the windows of his heart were open to the day.

He once said to me: "I have seen a very wicked woman to-day on her death bed. She was suffering intolerable tortures on account of the sins of her past life and the near approach of death. I stood by her bed; she was poor and friendless, and as I listened to her groans and moans I said, 'I would give all I possess to relieve that poor soul'; and then came the thought, as from God,—Who am I, a sinful man, to offer my little all to relieve that sin-burdened soul, when there is One with infinite love and limitless power who waits to show mercy? I will leave the poor woman with Him." And such was his attitude toward all erring and sin-sick souls.

In the main Mr. Whittier's life was one of earnest, serious thought. He was always working for the amelioration and elevation of humanity, and yet he was full of wit and humor. Not even Sydney Smith, who was so famous for his wit, or our own Dr. Holmes, could excel him in repartee.

A young girl who was in the house with Mr. Whittier, and of whom he was very fond, went to him one day with tearful eyes and a rueful face, and said: "My dear little kitty Bathsheba is dead, and I want you to write a poem to put on her grave stone. I shall bury her under a rose bush."

Without a moment's hesitation the poet said in solemn tones:

> Bathsheba! to whom none ever said scat—
> No worthier cat
> Ever sat on a mat
> Or caught a rat
> Requiescat!

The same little girl's pony broke his leg, and again the poet was called upon to comfort the child with some poetic sentiment. She said, "I have written some lines myself but I can't think how to finish the verse."

"What did you write?" asked Mr. Whittier.

> "My pony kicked to the right, he kicked to the left,
> The stable post he struck it,
> He broke his leg short off"——

and then added Mr. Whittier,

> "And then he kicked the bucket!"

Mr. Whittier was attending a fair in the city which was being held for some object of charity. A lady said to him,

"I have already given one hundred dollars to this object; I will give ten more if you will give me an impromptu couplet."

Quick as thought he wrote:

> Rejoicing that the emptiest fame
> May change at charity's sweet claim
> To gold of God—I give my' name.
>
> JOHN G. WHITTIER.

He was always ready to respond to charity's sweet claim.

During the war a Quaker friend who was a shipbuilder called on Mr. Whittier and said: "Friend Whittier, I am in great perplexity. Thee knows I do not approve of war any more than thee does, and I do not wish to do anything to help it on. I am asked to build some war ships, and I am told there is great need of them. What shall I do?"

The two old friends talked over the situation for awhile, but Mr. Whittier did not commit himself till just as the shipbuilder was leaving, when he said, "Thomas, if thee builds the ships, I advise thee to use the best timber, and build them strong."

There was at one time a desire on the part of the abolitionists to make a colored preacher chaplain of the house of representatives, and knowing that Mr. Whittier would have great influence he was asked to head the petition to bring about the desired end. Of course everybody knew Mr. Whittier was the most ardent abolitionist of them all, and that no one could outdo him in devotion to the colored brethren, and when the petition was handed him it was never for a moment doubted that he would sign it with alacrity. He shook his head and said, "Thee knows I don't approve of hiring folks to pray and paying them for it."

Mr. Whittier was the close friend of Curtis, Longfellow, Lowell, Holmes, Emerson, and Bayard Taylor, but it was not until the later years of his life, after the great question of freedom had been settled, that he was recognized as their peer in a literary sense.

VI. WILLIAM CULLEN BRYANT, OUR POET OF NATURE, AS I REMEMBER HIM, BY HENRIETTA S. NAHMER.

As Bryant was the oldest of our galaxy of American poets, and the first of them to pass away, those who can speak of him from personal recollection are themselves fast passing with the second century since his advent. Not far from the birthplace of Bryant, which is marked by a plain monolith in granite, and on the same ridge where the Bryant homestead commands a view of the Hampshire hills for miles, there stood in the fifties a little red schoolhouse so completely hidden in the forest that the stranger could not know of its existence until close upon it. Here was the typical New England school of that date, and while as yet no modern methods had crept in to disturb the somewhat dull serenity of teacher and pupil, there was once a day at least a refreshing détour into by-ways, where one might associate with the great ones of literature; and in the daily reading of selections from the English classics was begun that education which Matthew Arnold defines as the highest culture, "the knowledge of the best that has been thought and said in all ages." Instead of the commonplaces by which the children of to-day are nourished, the youth of that time were spelling out lofty themes from Cowper, the smooth verse of Addison, and the unequalled repose and dignity of Gray's "Elegy." What matter if the philosophy and insight of the glorious verse of "Thanatopsis" was beyond the reach of our comprehension, the rolling measure of its cadences was music to our ears, even then stirring to the harmonies of the universe.

One summer day a traveller, slight in build, of quiet, thoughtful manner, passed through those leafy paths vocal only with song birds and the prattle of school children. The good old New England training, which inculcated reverent and respectful greeting to the stranger, had not yet passed out of fashion, and we shyly courtesied to the passing wayfarer. He with the old-time courtesy to old and young alike pleasantly returned our greeting, and passed on. Later we were told by our elders that the author of "Thanatopsis" had returned for a brief hour to the old home of his childhood, now passed into the hands of strangers. We had scarcely realized before that our poet was of flesh and blood, and busily concerned in the world's work. Still less did one of that merry careless group laboring to parse what seemed to her immaturity the painfully involved sentences of that immortal poem, dream that in the years to come, she should have pleasant associations for a brief season with the gray-haired bard.

The years that bridged the fifties and seventies, the fateful years of the republic, passed, and Bryant, who had served his country faithfully by his pen, through the storm and stress of civil war, now retired to the old scenes of his youth, restoring the family home, to which he came for a few weeks each year, to perform the literary task so congenial, the translations from Homer. Here also he laid out roads, planted orchards, and became an influence among the townspeople, who in their isolation and somewhat narrow sphere, began to see and appreciate the larger views of life which such an honored citizen of the great world brought into the little town. We had looked on our poet as one who in the political world and among literary circles reflected honor upon our unknown quiet town among the hills; now we were to know him as the country gentleman, interested in rural pursuits, and as he beautified this home an impetus, whose results were beneficent and far-reaching, was given to the neighbor farmers. Scotch larches were added to our flora, and willows from Roslyn were transplanted to the banks of the rivulet, and once from far away Scotland the poet, touched with loving remembrance, sent a request that some fringed gentian be transplanted to a well known corner, in the green fields of his modest country home.

At one time Charles Sumner came to spend two or three days with the poet, and upon one auspicious afternoon George W. Curtis drove over from his summer home in Ash-field, to greet the famous men. While the three, with John H. Bryant, the poet's brother, were seated upon the piazza, nineteen hundred feet above the sea level, commanding a glorious panorama of mountain, valley, and sky, convers-ing of the San Domingo annexation, the theme which was absorbing the mind of the great senator, the room behind was quickly filled with country folk, eager to catch a glimpse or a word, upon the only occasion that ever came into their lives to see these notable men, who, unconscious of this homage, might yet feel that it was no mean tribute from this true and honest farmer folk.

Bryant presented his native town with a library and the necessary buildings, and in the completing and arranging of that work, it was the happy privilege of the writer to spend some hours with Bryant, and, after his return to the city, to have the benefit of his advice by correspondence. Awaiting the completion of the stone edifice designed for their reception, the books were stored in the unfinished rooms of the house which had been his maternal grand-father's and which was in process of restoration. The glory of autumn was upon the hills and tinging the forests with splendor, and as the gray-haired man climbed nimbly the steep hill between the homestead and our place of work, the inspiration which natural scenery ever had for him clothed his daily morning greeting with winged and happy utter-ance.

After the necessary instruction as to the work of the day, for a few moments pleasant and instructive chat would follow, suggested by some open book upon the table. These never-to-be-forgotten half hours were grave or gay, as befitted the subject. With folded arms and devout manner, it would be a stanza from Pope or Dante repeated unexpectedly in the abandon of the hour, suggested by some reference; or some humorous passage from the Biglow papers would enliven the moment. Underneath that exterior of almost harsh reserve, there was hidden keen appreciation of the grotesque and humorous.

Quite by accident, the morning talk drifted to J. Shelton Mackenzie, and with twinkling eye Bryant related the following: "I met him once upon the boat crossing to Brooklyn. He accosted me by inquiring if I was not Bryant, saying he recognized me by my portrait. As we had been corresponding I replied that I was pleased to meet him. Mackenzie said he was reading 'Ruth Hall' by Fanny Fern, and said: 'How she does pitch into Nat and her father; it is wrong, very wrong to speak of them so. And that Thackeray who reveals the shortcomings of a friend, it is wrong, very wrong.' I answered that as they were great men the temptation to speak of them was very strong. Mackenzie said it reminded him of the story of an Irishman, who was leaning out of his window, with his shillalah, and a bald-headed man passed along, whereupon he rapped him upon the head, and said upon being reproved, 'The occasion was too tempting—if it had been me own father I couldn't have helped it.' Upon leaving the boat Mackenzie said, 'You must excuse my impudence, but the occasion was too tempting.' "

From this lighter vein, Bryant passed to graver themes, and when the listener deplored her inability to reconcile the disputed facts in history, especially as regards the beautiful Mary Queen of Scots, he answered: "You remember what Horace Walpole said, 'As for history, I know that's a lie.' " He spoke of the unfairness of Macaulay to William Penn, and his partial apology for Hastings, of Froude's disparagement of Mary Stuart without warrant from contemporary documents, of the recent criticism of the Roman historian Paulus, and added: "People will differ in regard to the events of the past as they do in regard to the interests of the present. Only omniscience can see in an absolutely true light the circumstances of any event, and human narratives of that event must have in them more or less of error. No two witnesses of anything that has happened wholly agree in their representation of it. All that we can do is to adopt what seems most probable."

On one Sabbath afternoon, in the unfinished building which later was given to the poet's older daughter, the Rev. Mr. Waterston who had baptized the poet in Italy, spoke to the neighbors and country people, as the sunset filled the valley below with the radiance of departing day.   .

It was also the happy privilege of the writer to share with the neighbors and country people in the Sunday services at the little church in West Cummington, on Sept. 2, 1877, where Mr. Bryant recited his poems of "Thanatopsis," "The Water Fowl," and "Waiting by the Gate." As we saw the lithe, quick movement with which he ascended the hill, and heard the clear ringing voice, and saw the bright kindling eye, how could we think that these were his last public words to his native villagers, and that only a few months would pass before, as in the prime of life he had desired, in the month of June,

> The sexton's hand my grave to make
> The rich, green mountain turf should break.

THE WONDER OF HYPNOTISM AND THE TRANS-
FER OF SENSITIVENESS FROM MEN TO
INERT SUBSTANCES.

BY HENRY GAULLIEUR.*

Few of our modern attempts to solve scientifically the great mystery of LIFE have led us to more astonishing results than the discoveries made recently in Paris by Col. A. de Rochas, the well known scientist and director of the Ecole Polytechnique, concerning the "luminous effluvia," or magnetic emanations, from the bodies of living men.

Colonel de Rochas is too well known to the scientific world by his numerous works on hypnotism, and his constant studies of hypnotic phenomena, covering a period of fifteen years, to need an introduction from the writer to the American public. Connected with the great scientific institute where both military and civil engineers of France acquire under the government's direction the highest possible degree of human knowledge in the various branches of their profession, Colonel de Rochas has attained, outside of his official duties as "*Administrateur*" of that well known institute a world-wide celebrity as a skilled experimentator and conscientious investigator of scientific truths.

The discoveries made lately by him, and confirmed by the experiments of others, in the several hospitals of Paris, can be told in very few words; but simple as they are, so far as the establishment of facts is concerned, these discoveries lead us far away from the current opinion of mankind, and of physiologists in particular, on the nature and extent of our organic sense of feeling; they upset our present knowledge of the territory to which our nerves were said to be confined; they show us conclusively by well-established facts based on strictly scientific experimental methods, that under peculiar conditions our nervous-physical perceptions by the sense of touch extend *outside* of our skin; and that

---

*Though the author of this paper is a well known writer in France, many of our readers may not be acquainted with his literary and scientific work, hence the following letter from the Hon. Carl Schurz will give an added interest to the paper:

" In reply to your letter, it gives me pleasure to say that I have known M. H. Gaullieur for many years as a gentleman of excellent character, and I regard him as a writer of uncommon ability. " Very truly yours,

" B. O. FLOWER, Esq." " CARL SCHURZ."

the faculty of perceiving such sensations, apparently lost in
a mesmerized subject, can be transferred for a certain time
and at a distance to inanimate substances like water, wax,
metals, or cloth.

For the benefit of such readers as may not be familiar
with previous discoveries, the knowledge of which is necessary in order to understand the recent investigations of Col.
de Rochas, I must translate first here some statements of a
celebrated Austrian chemist, the Baron von Reichenbach,
who was the first scientist, over forty years ago, who discovered the "luminous effluvia," or phosphorescent-like
emanations from animals, plants, and magnets.

Here are Reichenbach's own words ("Lettres Odiques et
Magnétiques," Stuttgardt, 1856):

Take a "sensitive" man and put him in a dark room. Take along
a cat, a bird, a butterfly, if you have one, or only some flowerpots.
After a few hours of such a sitting in the dark, you will hear that
man say some very strange things. The flowerpots will appear to
him in the darkness and become perceptible. At first they will
appear as a grey cloud on a black background; then he will see some
lighter spots; finally each flower will become distinct, and all forms
will appear more and more clearly. One day I placed one of these
flowerpots before M. Endlicher, the well known professor of botany.
He was an average sensitive. He exclaimed with fear and surprise:
"*A blue flower, a gloxinia!*" It was indeed a *Gloxinia speciosa* or
coerulea which he had seen in the absolute darkness, and which he
had recognized by its form and color. . . . Your cat, your bird, your
butterfly, will all appear thus in the dark, and some parts of these
animals will appear luminous. Then your sensitive man will tell
you that he sees you. Tell him to look at your hands. At first he
will say that he sees a grey smoke; then the fingers will appear with
their own light. He will see a luminous protuberance at each
finger, sometimes as long as the finger itself. When the first surprise is past, caused by the luminous appearance of all men, call
the attention of your "sensitive" friend to the details of what he
sees. You will then probably hear him say with much surprise that
the colors of the light are not the same in all parts of the body; that
the right hand shows a blue light, and the left hand a yellow-reddish
light; that the same difference appears at your feet; and also that
all the right side of your body and face is bluish and darker than
the left side, which is yellow-reddish and much lighter (Letter 5).

Reichenbach found something else. He discovered that
under similar conditions in a dark room a magnet emits a
blue light at its north pole, and a yellow-reddish light at the
south pole. This light varied, according to the strength of
the magnet and the sensitiveness of the seer, from one to
three feet in diameter. It appeared like a fiery flow inter-
mingled with sparks. "But," adds Reichenbach, "I advise
you not to omit any of the precautions I have indicated as
necessary to obtain absolute darkness, and also to train
your 'sensitive's' eyes for hours in the dark; otherwise he

will not see anything, and you would lose your time, suspecting me unjustly of making false assertions."

Reichenbach's experiments were repeated in England by
Alfred Russel Wallace, Gregory, and other prominent
naturalists, and were fully confirmed. Reichenbach contended then that he had discovered a new force, which he
called OD. Most scientific men ridiculed the idea and they
did not take the trouble to investigate the discovery.
Official science, especially in Germany, does not generally
admit what is not yet printed in school books.

In France these "luminous effluvia" seen by mesmerized
patients had often been reported by the latter to the mag-
netizing doctors who were trying to cure diseases by magnetic passes. The "magnétiseur" Deleuze had noticed the
fact. About 1850, Dr. Despine, at Aix les Bains, and Dr.
Charpignon, at Orleans, had confirmed these observations,
and they had noticed specially the "effluvia" which some
mesmerized persons could see on various metals, gold, silver,
etc. But "official" science did not care for such experiments. Magnetism, proclaimed at the end of last century,
by the French academy of Sciences, to be a humbug, was
hardly recognized yet as a fact worthy of investigation.
Such men as Puy Ségur and Deleuze were ridiculed; and we
may say that official science never believed seriously in
magnetism until Braid christened it hypnotism and Charcot
popularized it in Paris.

It is only recently that Reichenbach's discovery was
taken out of oblivion by Dr. Durville, Dr. Luys, and
Colonel de Rochas, with what extraordinary results we
shall now see.

The very first question that arose was whether this luminous coating and these "luminous effluvia" which mesmerized persons declared they could perceive on others,
were real and objective or imaginary and subjective? This
led to the very wonderful discoveries of which I spoke at the
beginning of this paper, and for which Colonel de Rochas
deserves due credit.

He hypnotized at different stages two different subjects
at the same time and in the same room. Let us call them
A and B. A reported that he could see a luminous or phosphorescent coating on B's body; he could see besides that
B's eyes, mouth, ears, nostrils, and finger-ends were emit-
ting a flame-like light, blue on one side of the body, yellow-
reddish on the other. Those openings seemed to act like
"escapes" for these flames, which are independent from the
coating of the skin. Did A see them because he had a

mesmeric illusion, or were this coating and the lights real?

A common glass of water being brought, it was put within the radius of B's luminous effluvia as described by A, who could see how far they reached. After a few minutes A reports that the water itself has become luminous, and that it remains luminous for a long while, even if removed to the other end of the room out of reach of B's effluvia. B's sensitiveness of the skin has been made to disappear by the hypnotic process; but any touch or puncture of a pin or needle on the outside edge of the phosphorescent or luminous coating perceived by A's eyes, is immediately perceived by B. His body does not feel the sharpness of a needle, but the outer edge of his luminous effluvia, several feet away from the skin, has acquired that sensitiveness lost by the body. And here appears a wonderful fact. *The water in the tumbler removed to the end of the room has acquired that same sensitiveness.* If you pinch the water with your fingers or touch it with a pin, B will scream that you pinch him, or prick him with a pin. But B will not feel the action if performed by a person who has no magnetic relation to him; in other words, the action of the magnetizer alone will be felt in the water by the subject.

Consequently the nervous sensitiveness of B's flesh has been carried further than the surface of his body, and has been communicated to objects duly soaked and impregnated by his luminous effluvia; and finally, the sensitiveness of these objects remains in them for a while even when removed to a certain distance from B's effluvia. "The water," says De Rochas, "loads itself with sensitiveness as calcium does with light; and the energy received radiates from it till it has returned all it has received, in other words, till it is spent or emptied."

Let us examine now more closely and with more details this strange transfer of the sensitiveness of our nerves to inert objects, which Colonel de Rochas calls the "exteriorization of sensitiveness."

A's eyes have been brought up by hypnotic process to a state which allows him to see the "luminous effluvia." But what he sees and describes varies a great deal according to the grade of hypnotic sleep in which B is being plunged. When B is awake and in his normal state, A describes the "effluvia" as a luminous coating on the skin; but as soon as B loses his sensitiveness under the action of mesmerism, the coating seems to dissolve itself in the atmosphere. Then it reappears like a light mist or smoke, which condenses itself and becomes brighter and brighter, till it takes again the appearance of a thin coating of light following all the forms of the body at a distance of about an inch from the skin. B feels then every touch of the magnetizer on the surface of that coating.

If you continue further the hynotizing process on B, A will see, around B's body, several new luminous coatings separated one from the other by a space of about two inches. The sensitiveness of B exists then only on these coatings of light, and seems to be in inverse ratio to their distance from the skin. These coatings will extend from six to nine feet from the body. They will go through a wall, not being stopped by masonry; and they will appear in the next room through the wall.

A glass of water which has remained a few minutes within the luminous coatings of B's body becomes brilliantly illuminated, as already stated. But when the water is thoroughly saturated, a luminous column of smoke will arise vertically from its surface. The acquired sensitiveness of that water when removed becomes weaker with the distance. If the water is carried too far it disappears. This seems to prove conclusively that B's feeling of touch transmitted to the water is real and not influenced by any suggestion.

Now if we make a small statuette or figure of common moulding wax and place it awhile in the "luminous effluvia" of B, then withdraw it and prick it with a pin, B will feel the puncture of the pin at the corresponding part of his body. If you touch the head of the wax figure B will feel the touch on his own head. If you prick the leg of the statuette, B will feel the point of the pin at his leg, and the puncture will even appear on the skin. If you cut a lock of his hair during his sleep without his knowledge, then plant that lock of hair on the wax figure and pull it slightly, B exclaims suddenly, "Who is pulling my hair?" The same results are obtained if you try the experiment with the whiskers or beard, or even sometimes with the trimming of a fingernail.

Generally in most cases reported by Colonel de Rochas the sensitiveness did not extend over fifteen or twenty feet from the body of the subject, but there were exceptions.

The sensitiveness was then transmitted to a photographic image of the subject by leaving the plate for some time before using it in the "effluvia" of the subject. Here in several instances the plate retained the sensitiveness of the latter for several days. But unless the sensitiveness of the subject has been exteriorized (transferred from the skin to the "effluvia") before the photograph is taken, and unless the plate has been well impregnated in the "effluvia," the sensitiveness does not exist.

Colonel de Rochas tells us that he made the following experiments on Mme. O—— in the presence of Dr. Barlemont and MM. Paul Nadar and A. Guerronan, in the well known photographer's studio of Nadar in Paris. A photograph was taken under the conditions just mentioned. As soon as the plate was carried to the dark room and touched the developing bath, Mme. O—— complained of a cold chill. She could not localize on her body the touch of her image, but she had a general perception of that touch; and she felt "seasick" every time the water of the developing bath was agitated. At the next experiment, Mme. O—— being asleep and the operator having gone to another floor of the building to develop the plate, she fell suddenly in convulsions as if she had been sick at the stomach. It turned out that the operator had accidentally broken the plate on the next floor in dipping it in the bath.

Another experiment of Colonel de Rochas on Mme. O—— took place as follows: He used generally the palm of his right hand to hypnotize her; he had a life-size photograph of that palm of his hand taken. Mme. O—— was awake and sitting on a chair, not knowing what was going on in the room. Then one of the assistants, being concealed behind a screen, presented the plate on which the hand of Col. de Rochas was photographed to the plate on which the image of Mme. O—— had been previously taken. At the instant when the gentleman opposed the two plates to each other, Mme. O—— stopped her talk and fell asleep on the chair. Then Colonel De Rochas walked behind the screen *and woke up Mme. O—— by simply blowing on her image.*

This experiment was repeated twice without notifying Mme. O—— of what had been done. Then it was communicated to her; she was surprised and stated she would defeat the experiment the next time; she said she could successfully oppose it. The experiment was then tried against her and with her knowledge. She fell asleep one minute after the two plates were placed in opposition to each other: she could not fight the influence any longer.

The substances which are the most apt to acquire the sensitiveness of the mesmerized subject are generally the same as those which are the most apt to retain odors. Liquids, viscous substances, specially those deriving their origin from animals, like beeswax, also cloth of a loose texture like woollen velvet, are peculiarly adapted for it. But all subjects do not "exteriorize" their sense of feeling in the same manner. One subject transferred his sensitiveness specially well to iron, another one to silk, and both these subjects had very little power on water or wax.

The sense of touch or feeling seemed to be the only one exteriorized. If the agent spoke in a very low tone of voice to the water away from the subject, after the water had been impregnated with "effluvia" from the ear, the subject felt only a slight sensation of tickling in his ear. But some others nevertheless felt the influence of a small vial of valerianate of ammonia hermetically sealed which had been plunged in the sensitive water.

It should also be observed that all these experiments succeeded only with persons whose sensitiveness was either naturally very great or whose sensitiveness became developed by practice.

Thus, this wonderful "exteriorization" and transfer of a man's sense of feeling to inanimate objects opens now a vast field for new investigations. It shows, in the first place, what enormous physical influence on health and disease the luminous effluvia of a human being can exert. Experiments made by Dr. Babinski (the former assistant of Charcot) in Paris at the hospital La Salpêtrière, and by Dr. Luys at the hospital La Charité, show that some diseases have been cured by treating them magnetically. A magnet was used in several cases, and here is an instance of its application for transferring disease.

A metallic crown duly loaded with a magnet had been used at the Charité hospital for the treatment of a man. He was cured, and the crown was stored away in a closet for two weeks. Then it was tried on the head of a healthy subject in a state of hypnotic lethargy, and this man showed at once the same symptoms and the same manifestations of disease from which his predecessor had suffered. It seemed as if the magnetic crown had recorded the symptoms in the same manner as a phonograph records the voice. Had the first man died instead of being cured we should thus, says Colonel de Rochas, have called back, so to speak, the characteristics of a dead human being.

Medical science, consequently, will have to take due notice of such facts, and they will modify to a great extent the exclusive theory of propagation of diseases by microbes.

Then again this transfer of sensitiveness to inert objects throws a most interesting light on the dark and obscure practices of sorcerers and witches in the Middle Ages. Our forefathers believed in the faculty of hurting an enemy under peculiar conditions prescribed by sorcerers, by transferring to him a disease or by stinging his image duly prepared for the purpose. History gives us many accounts of celebrated trials before courts of justice, where the accused man was executed for having killed or attempted to kill by such means a celebrated man. Such was the trial of Robert d'Artois, in France, the record of which we still possess, accused of having applied his dark science to the wife and son of Philip VI of Valois, in 1333. We never believed in such crimes, nevertheless Colonel de Rochas tells us that, after a sitting, as he had stung with a pin the leg of the wax figure used that day, he saw from his window the subject going home, stop suddenly in the street and rub violently his leg. He had felt the wound. Now in olden times a few hairs, or some trimmings of the fingernails, or a tooth, were supposed to transfer the sensitiveness under certain conditions from the subject to his image.

The sorcerer's art was two-edged, like a sword. It was believed that it could hurt, but it was also expected that it could heal. Our old libraries are full of ancient treatises proved now to contain some grains of scientific truth amidst much superstitious rubbish. We did not believe that they contained any truth at all, but now we see that they do, and we understand our forefathers better. Read the works of Robert Fludd (born in Kent, England, in 1574) and you will see how he cured diseases by transfer. He was one of the foremost scientific men of his time and appears now to have known more than we did in some respects. Paracelsus, born in 1493, Van Helmont born in 1577, and Maxwell, who died later, had full knowledge of this extraordinary faculty of our nerves to extend their action outside of our skin. Most of their medical science was based on facts which we have rediscovered to-day. Read the works of Digby, who was one of the most extraordinary Englishmen of his time, a celebrated soldier, statesman, and naturalist at the same time, who defeated at sea the Venetians and the Algerians, and then studied medicine at Montpellier, in France, and published a treatise on the nature of substances. You will see what he says about curing wounds by dipping simply a rag soiled by the blood of the patient in a certain liquid, without applying anything to the wound itself. Of course most of that old science was rubbish, but not all of it, and we were wrong in calling these men fools.

Then again these facts recently discovered in Paris by De Rochas, and others who followed and repeated his experiments, show conclusively—in the writer's opinion at least—that the common scientific theory based on our present knowledge of matter by which we have tried to explain man's nature is absurd. They show how little our modern physiology and our present materialistic schooling understand the problem of human existence; they show how wrong we were in confining the energy of our human force, of our human being, within the boundaries of our skin.

THE OPPORTUNITY OF THE CHURCH.*

BY PROF. GEORGE D. HERRON, OF IOWA COLLEGE.

We are nearing the social crisis of the world. The existing order has already served over-time. It is now senseless, and growing worse. To spend and be spent mending it is to waste one's life, and involve the common life in still deeper and wider complications. The present order cannot be mended; it can only give birth to the new order, the regenerate civilization.

The social crisis is also the crisis of the organized religion that bears Christ's name. While the forces of selfishness and sacrifice are gathering for their hardest struggle on the field of Christ's truth, the cross has become foolishness to His church. The church has become of the world, even as Jesus was not of the world. Social things which are the worst abominations in the sight of God are not so highly esteemed in the world as in the church. The church has been over-reconciling itself to the will of the world, rather than vicariously reconciling the world to the will of God. The idea of the religious life prevailing in the church is no longer constructive, but rather obstructive and deadly. It has done its work, and must have an end. It is in vain that dogmatic stupidity, moral indolence, and official hypocrisy try to confine the human and universal religion of the kingdom of God within the terms of the religion of theology, pietism, ecclesiasticism, and the interests which monopoly have vested in religion. If the church refuses to give forth the realization of the social ideal of Jesus, it will surely meet with a fate like unto the religion of Judaism.

Revolution of some sort is not far off. The social change will bring forth either the revolution of love or the tragedy and woe of a leadership inspired by a love of revolution. Either a revival of love, an outpouring of love through the Messianic fellowship of some vast social sacrifice, or a universal French Revolution will come. Either a religious movement, producing a revival such as the prophets dimly or never dreamed of, or blood such as never flowed will remit the sins of the existing order. For a religious revival, springing from some vast and wondrous social love, Christendom waits in fear, anxiety, and expectancy.

* Condensed from a lecture course given in Boston, November, 1895.

Except its manifest subservience to wealth, nothing more clearly indicates the unmoral influence of religion than the contemptuous meaning which has come to be attached to the word holiness. By the holy man is meant, in the popular thought, simply no man at all; while the word primitively meant a whole human man, normally fulfilling all the natural functions of his life in their wholeness. The Holy Ghost, or the Whole Spirit, is given to run the world with, and the teachings of Jesus are a revelation of the world righteously ordered and naturally operated. The piety that finds the market and the state uninteresting as religious spheres, or that ignores them through material or intellectual self-interest, is a delusion and a curse. We can get beloved brethren to wrestle all night, or at least a part of the night, in revival prayers; but the revival we need is a restitution of stolen goods, of wealth gained through oppression and social atheism. We can get them to give feasts in the name of Jesus; but the testimony which Jesus asks is the restoration of what has been economically plundered from the sheep. The rebuke of Edward III to the pope at Avignon, to the effect that "The successor of the apostles was set over the Lord's sheep to feed and not to shear them," is equally applicable and pertinent to the priests of the market and the pious popes of industry; these are the influential factors in organized religion. "Pure religion and undefiled 'before our God and Father is this, to visit the fatherless and widows in their affliction, and to keep himself unspotted from the world." Devotion to God is the complete sacrifice of self in the service of man, and ecstatics are without value that do not fruit in ethics. The clean putting away of evil doings, with the seeking of justice and the relieving of the oppressed, is the condition upon which the Lord invites us to reason together with Him in the things of religion.

I frankly say that I dread nothing more than the influence upon the social movement of existing organizations of religion. With the fullest recognition of the anxious seeking for righteousness on the part of a greater number of individuals in the church than ever before, I make this confession of dread. With Dr. Bruce, I am a pessimist as regards the church, and an optimist as regards the kingdom. The movement for social democracy is itself the religious aspiration and effort of the common life to realize its sanctity, and organized religion offers no channel for this realization. In a profound sense, existing organizations of religion afford to the forces making for social righteousness the unsafest possible leadership. A vast deceit would likely be practised upon the social movement by the church itself, and history sadly repeat itself, in the compromise of the social ideals of the people with the interests of the capitalistic order which the church would effect. I am here reminded of the sad condition of Italy, now almost on the verge of disintegration, fulfilling what Mazzini foresaw, when the monarchical statecraft of Europe intrigued to prevent the organization of liberated Italy in his ideal of a social republic.

With the present tendency, the evolution of the better society is likely to be the church's disgrace, and not its glory, with the religion of Jesus finding some other channel of expression than the church as a result. Nobody any longer conceives of religiousness as being an indication of righteousness. The church as a whole does not know what Jesus taught, and so far as it knows does not believe His teachings practicable. The real social reconstruction is moving on outside of, and largely in opposition to, organized religion; its leaders who come from are not of the church. Just as surely as the Jews were building up a religion apart from the actual facts of society when Jesus came, and as surely as Rome was building up a religion apart from the conditions existing when Luther came, so are we Protestants now institutionally building up a religion apart from the true facts and conditions of society. Dr. Parkhurst in New York is no more an answer to this charge than Savonarola in Florence is an answer to Protestant charges against Rome. Protestant Christianity is practically a caste religion, in spite of its missions, its exceptional institutional churches, and its ludicrous willingness to receive the poor.

If ever the church needed to be told, in all the plainness of speech which the love of righteousness can conceive, that it cannot serve God and mammon, it needs to be told this now. In no nation on the earth is there such abject submission to mere money in both church and state as there is in America. Money has more influence than Jesus upon the ecclesiastical attitude toward the problem of social justice. Our persistent blinking this fact, our evasion of the moral responsibility it puts upon us, may prove the displacement of the existing church. Pastors may secure active participation in municipal reforms from the very men who buy the city's councils and loot its people, only to find the city in a last state worse than the first. It is easy for pastors and bishops of wealth to try experiments in the slums, which are righteous things for them to do. But suppose we try the

sacrifice of preaching the Sermon on the Mount, or of applying the teachings of Jesus, in the churches of wealth! The
church will accept any number of social philanthropies, or
religious benevolences, but it is by no means ready to be
despised and rejected of the rich and powerful, that it may
seek the righteousness and social justice of the kingdom of
God. Until the church repent itself of its money worship,
it is not even a fit companion for the social movement, and
would lead it in a devolution rather than an evolution.
Any leadership the church would now put forward to represent it would be chiefly interested in keeping the social
movement within the bounds of the interests of mammon,
and from accomplishing the real social ideals of Jesus and
the people. In any safe leadership of the church, money
and houses, lands and railways, must become component
parts of the moral agony of its preparation for leadership.
The church must get free of its manifest subjection to
money, with its institutions free of servile dependence thereupon, if it is to avert the necessity of God's turning to the
churchless peoples, or to the people regardless of the church,
to find new channels for the redemptive life that is to heal
the nations. Like Jacob of old, the church of America
needs to come to Jabbok ford, sending the stuff of wealth
that has caused its bitter servility to the other side of the
river, making restitution to the tribe of Esau it has robbed,
regarding no more the success of its membership in cheating
and stealing as a mark of a specially favoring providence,
pursuing no more a religion that is not the righteousness of
God in human relations, that God may wrestle with it in all
the power of the common interests of man, and then it may
come forth a new church with a new name, with a moral
glory that shall bring the multitudes to its doors with hosan-
nas of thanksgiving and tears of boundless joy, the leader of
the peoples into the social Israel of blessed justice.

The redemptive need of civilization, the divinest want of
the church, is not what we call successful men, who are the
church's curse and the nation's corrupters, but strong men
willing to fail, that they may prove the justice of love and
the social wisdom of sacrifice. A single generation of Christians, yea, a single generation of preachers of Jesus' gospel,
great enough to fail, could regenerate civilization! If the
religious leaders of our day·would be willing to suffer the
loss of all things, and become sin that civilization through
them might be made the righteousness of God, they could
bring in the thousand years of peace. They would not
drink of the fruit of the vine until they could drink it new in

the Father's kingdom: they would not enjoy the fruits of
the earth until they could enjoy as sharers with all human
life, redeemed to the holy society. As the Father sent
Jesus, so sends He each of them, to bear away the sins of the
world, and become disastrous worldly failures, that the
social order of His kingdom may appear amidst the passing
away of the society of civilized selfishness.

At best, our measures of failure and success are the denial
of Christ's philosophy of life. His blessing is not upon the
successful, but upon the faithful in the sacrifice of service;
not upon the religiously and materially comfortable, but
upon those who have visited Him in human life imprisoned,
sick, sinning, oppressed, morally and physically loathsome,
and shut out from the regard and grace of the existing
order.

The prophets the Scriptures glorify were mainly disgraceful figures in the eyes of their times. Jesus and the disciples were outlawed. John the Baptist, who prepared their
way, was beheaded in the interests of official peace. Paul,
the most daring adventurer that ever put out upon a voyage
of moral discovery, was loosened from prison to be led to
his execution. Savonarola was both hung and burned, after
fearful agonies of torture. The Protestant reformers were
the hunted and hated heretics of their day. Wesley,
Edwards, and Finney were driven from their churches.
Mazzini and his friends were vagabonds on the face of the
earth. Not long ago, Garrison was dragged through the
streets of Boston by a commercially inspired mob, and Love-
joy met his death at the hands of political retainers. Which
of the prophets of progress, whose faith we glorify with our
words, but whose truth we make the refuge of our social
cowardice and religious lies, was not outlawed, mobbed, or
slain?

To eulogize these is easy, requiring no adventure of faith
or risk of reputation; to defend them is always safe. But to
the prophets gone we are never so untrue as when defending
them against the larger truth calling for our own faith and
sacrifice. We honor in truth the reformers of religion and
civilization, and best defend their name and faith, by being
as ready in our day as they were in theirs, for failure and
disgrace. Have we their faith to put the righteous judgments of God over against the false judgments of organized
covetousness? Can we bear the shame of no reputation in
the eyes of the successful, of being accounted commercial or
ecclesiastical failures, that we may face the religious and
political lies now darkening the social mind, cursing our

methods and institutions, and bring them to judgment before the truth of Jesus? Our ability to divinely fail for right's sake is the real measure of our faith.

This gain of human values through failure is not in harmony with our modern notions of success, which prostitute every sacred human power to the gross and hideous lust of money, and make a religion of covetousness. It accords not with the spirit of Anglo-Saxon enterprise, which exalts rights above service, and rates commercial success above all that makes up the real life. It is not agreeable to present patriotism, which consists chiefly in loyalty to one's property, subordinating the welfare of society to material gains, and to the anarchical liberty of the individual. There is no welcome for it in the world of business, the greatest corrupter of nations and enemy of man. The respect of the political economist it has not, nor is it in keeping with the greedy maxims of Benjamin Franklin. It is disgusting to the theologian, and frightful to the ecclesiastic. It will not mix with the moral nostrums prescribed by pulpit and press as "The Secret of Success," or "The Way to Succeed in Life," and like wretched stuff poured into this suffering world by those who are called its teachers. It comports not with the vicious motives for excellence upheld by the ethical imbecility of our educational systems. But Jesus' doctrine of life is either the delusion of history, the divine tantalism of hopeless human suffering, or our ruling standards of success are worse than pagan; they are devilish, and the destroyers of human life. The efforts of the church to reconcile the commercial morals of modern industrialism with the revelation of human law and life in Christ, is treason to the kingdom of God, and the worst apostasy of the church; yea, it is the chopping down of the cross, and the setting up of the throne of mammon in its place.

If we believe Jesus' doctrine of life to be true, then in the name of our belief we must take square issue with those who teach that man's first and fundamental duty is to get a living. They would build human life on a lie. True, we must gain our bread by our work; but bread is not the end of work, and man does not live by bread alone. The end of work is distributive justice, social character, the divine personality of the sons of man; and these are the word of God in human life. Our first and fundamental duty is to seek in what manner and by what work we can best fulfil the righteousness of Christ in our life, and in the life of the world. Not the preservation of life, but the increase of right, is the first law of man's nature; and he that preserveth his life wastes it, while he that wasteth his life in the pursuit of righteousness finds it eternally. Our life has but one duty, in fact, and that is the faithful witnessing, with the individual and collective doing, of the righteousness of Christ, believing that this universe is so principled and organized that only right can in the end bring food to the producer, and abundance to the working children of men. Our duty to God, nation, family, is to illustrate in our life the sacrifice of the Christ, who is the righteousness of God made manifest for the practice of man.

SHOULD THE GOVERNMENT CONTROL THE TELEGRAPH?

I.

WHY THE GOVERNMENT SHOULD OWN THE TELEGRAPH.

BY PROF. RICHARD T. ELY, OF THE UNIVERSITY OF WISCONSIN.

The very clearness of the case in favor of the public owner-ship and management of the telegraph constitutes the difficulty in the preparation of an article on the subject. One who has examined understandingly arguments for and against public ownership finds it hard to put himself in the position of a sincere and intelligent opponent. The telegraph is in this respect quite different from the railways. The arguments in favor of the nationalization of the railways seem to the present writer to be conclusive, and yet it must be admitted by everyone that there is strength in the arguments of those who favor private railways. We have immense difficulties to overcome whether we have public or private ownership of railways. No argument, however, in favor of private ownership of the telegraph seems to be able to stand the test of any careful analysis or searching criticism.

First of all, we may make the claim that public ownership and management of the telegraph would be in harmony with the best thought of the founders of this republic. The telegraph is a natural monopoly. There were few businesses of the nature of the telegraph when this republic was established, but there was one conspicuous example of a natural monopoly. That was the postoffice, and that was made a public function, and has been regarded as such ever since, to the great benefit of the people of the United States. Even if the telegraph were not an essential part of the postoffice it would be in harmony with the principles of the fathers of the country to make it a public service; but it is an essential part of the postoffice business, and to connect it with the postoffice would be simply a logical development.

The nature of the present service of the private telegraph companies is the strongest kind of an argument in favor of public ownership; especially when this is brought into contrast with our postoffice service, and when it is remembered that this postoffice service itself would be still further improved if it received its logical completion in public telegraph service.

Questions of public policy are not to be argued merely from the standpoint of cost and price, but high charges for any service which is of such general importance as the telegraph are a serious consideration. The charges of the private telegraph service in this country are exorbitant. All arguments which aim to show the contrary are deceptive. They may be plausible but they are not ingenuous. The most familiar form of this argument is the comparison of the cost of sending a telegram a long distance in this country and a long distance in Europe. It is, however, an elementary fact that distance has very little to do with the cost of sending a telegram, and consequently should not have any great force in the determination of a fair price for the service, provided the telegram is a domestic one. The truth is, that in nearly all countries distance is entirely neglected and one uniform price is charged, just as our postoffice charges one uniform price for sending a letter, regardless of distance. The reason why a comparatively high price is charged for a telegram, say, from London to St. Petersburg, is because such a telegram is an international one and the receipts have to be divided among several countries. In the case under consideration, we should also remember that we have a cable service to be taken into account. The usual price for sending a telegram from any part of one country to any other part of the same country is about ten cents. In some cases it is a little less, in some it is a little more. The charge in Germany and England is twelve cents.

We have next to note the poor quality of the telegraph service in the United States. It has been stated by a well known writer that it is the poorest telegraph service in the civilized world. Certainly the contrast between the service in this country and the service in Germany is most painful to one who has lived in both countries. The service in this country is so defective and so irregular that frequently the telegraph is not used when it would be a great convenience. It is impossible to send a telegram and to be sure that a prompt reply will be received. The writer of this article has sent a telegram a distance of some four hundred miles, and has given the telegram a start of twenty-four hours, then taken a train and arrived at the destination of the telegram on the same day on which the telegram was delivered. This is by no means an isolated experience.

So far as the writer's experience goes, it is seldom that a telegram is received in the United States which in spelling and in every other particular is absolutely correct.

whereas he does not remember to have received a telegram in Germany in which there was any mistake. Why this should be the case is apparent when one visits the telegraph office in both countries. Experienced and tried men, with comparatively short hours, are employed in Germany, while in the telegraph offices of this country one finds very young lads, and they are frequently overworked.

The telegraph service in the United States is poor because offices are so frequently closed. A few years since, when it was of urgent importance that a telegram should be sent from Richmond, Va., not an office could be found open until seven o'clock in the morning. Offices are closed on the whole, or a great part, of Sunday. No one would be hypocrite enough to pretend that this is due to any scruples in regard to the observance of Sunday. It is simply due to pecuniary considerations. The convenience of the public is lightly considered and neglected when it does not bring in any net return to minister to this convenience. A comparison with the postoffice is again to the disadvantage of the telegraph, although the telegraph service is more urgent. When it is remembered that telegrams so often deal with matters of life and death, even the strictest sabbatarian must acknowledge that there is strong reason why telegraph offices should be open every day.

The service in the United States is poor because the number who are accommodated with the convenience of a telegraph office is far smaller than it should be. The postoffice department plants a postoffice even in rural districts, and attempts to provide all the people with postal facilities. Every postoffice should be at the same time a telegraph office, and might be one if the telegraph were a part of the postal service.

A strong line of argument in favor of a public telegraph service is found in the condition of employees. Frequently, if not generally, they are too young and they are worked long hours. The fact that so few mature men are found among them shows that they have no secure tenure of office and no permanent employment. One young generation of telegraph operators gives way to another. They are employed frequently in dark, dingy, and ill-kept rooms. The contrast with the class of operators employed in a country like Germany and the neat and attractive offices found in that country is painful, and is really a disgrace to our own country.

One of the strongest arguments in favor of a postal telegraph is, that such a telegraph would carry with it an improvement in our civil service. It would be a force making for political purity. It would be hard to imagine at the present juncture a greater victory for civil-service reform than the acquisition of all the telegraph lines in the United States by the postoffice. It would remove a great source of corruption; a source so powerful, that it has been claimed that it recently defeated the election of a presidential candidate. It would increase the number of offices in which civil-service rules would be applied, even according to existing law, inasmuch as it would add to the number of employees in the postoffices in the country; and it would be an irresistible argument in favor of the extension and elevation of the civil service. Some want to have us wait until the civil service has been already improved, but the purchase of telegraph lines would inevitably carry with it the improvement of the civil service. The country would insist upon it. The acquisition of the telegraph lines by the nation would convert more people to civil-service reform in one day than all the speeches which have ever been delivered on the subject could win to this good cause in a year.

The situation of this country is not so different as many would have us believe from that of other countries in which the telegraph service is a part of the postal service. We find that after long years of experience practically the whole civilized world except the United States has decided in favor of the public ownership and management of the telegraph. Nowhere has it been found that there is any political objection to public ownership and management. The experience of monarchical and that of republican countries tell the same tale.

Last of all it should be said that as the telegraph is a natural monopoly, only one telegraph system is wanted in any one country. Two systems, one public and one private, could not fail to produce disastrous results both economically and politically. The true policy is the purchase of the existing telegraph lines at a fair price. If the right has been reserved to purchase the lines at an appraised valuation, this right should be used. It must be remembered, however, that a large capitalization of the telegraph plant of the country is due to the false policy of attempted competition in the telegraph business, and this policy has been fostered by the general public. It would seem only fair that the general public should bear at least a part of the loss in the price paid for the existing plant. After all, to acquire the private telegraph lines and the plant which goes with them would cost a sum which is very small for a country which has had an annual surplus of $100,000,-000, and the benefits would be great and lasting.

II.

THE LEGAL ASPECT OF THE TELEGRAPH AND TELEPHONE SERVICES ESSENTIAL PARTS OF AN EFFICIENT POSTAL SERVICE.

BY JUSTICE WALTER CLARK, LL. D., OF THE SUPREME BENCH OF N. C.

Many who admit the great advantages, nay, the necessity, of the telegraph and telephone services being operated as a part of the postal system, are deterred by the inquiry, Is it constitutional? In truth it is unconstitutional for this essential branch of the postal system to be operated by a private monopoly or in any other manner than by the government.

When the constitution placed the postoffice in the hands of the government it conferred exclusive operation, and with it all means of operating it to the best advantage. The same clause of the constitution of the United States (Art. 1, sec. 8) which empowers Congress to declare war, raise and support armies and a navy, to coin money, regulate commerce, and borrow money on the credit of the United States, includes the provision to "establish postoffices and post roads." If the power of the government is exclusive as to the other provisions it is so also as to the postoffice, for all these powers are conferred by the same clause and by the same words—in one breath as it were. The numerous decisions of the United States Supreme Court holding the power of Congress over the postoffice and the carrying of mails to be exclusive, render unnecessary any discussion of an undisputed point. It is interesting to note, however, that in 1836, Hon. John C. Calhoun, the leader of the strictest constructionists who denied to the general government all powers not clearly granted, in a report made by him as chairman of a committee of the United States Senate, said: "It must be borne in mind that the power of Congress over the postoffice and the mail is *an exclusive power.*" These words have been cited and approved by the Supreme Court of the United States in the case of *ex parte* Jackson so recently as the 96 United States Reports on page 734. The bestowal of the exclusive right and duty to operate the postoffice carried with it the exclusive right and duty to use all the agencies that would make the postoffice most highly efficient, as such agencies from time to time should be improved or invented. On this principle the first telegraph line was built by a congressional appropriation under a "strict construction" administration (Polk's), and the telegraph belonged to the government, 1844–47; and when under mistaken notions of economy it was then turned over to private ownership, Henry Clay, the great Whig leader, and Cave Johnson, the Democratic postmaster-general, were among the public men who went on record as earnestly protesting against such a step. Indeed the Supreme Court of the United States in a unanimous opinion (Pensacola *vs.* Tel. Co., 96 U. S. 1) has held that the telegraph came within the grant of power to establish the postoffice. The opinion delivered by Chief Justice Waite says:

The powers thus granted are not confined to the instrumentalities of the postal service known or in use when the constitution was adopted, but they keep pace with the progress of the country and adapt themselves to the new developments of time and circumstances. They extend from the horse with its rider to the stagecoach, from the sailing vessel to the steamboat, from the coach and steamboat to the railroad, and from the railroad to the telegraph, as these new agencies are successively brought into use to meet the demands of increasing population and wealth.

Justice H. B. Brown, who is recognized as one of the ablest members of the United States Supreme Court, in the leading article in the August *Forum*, says:

If the government may be safely entrusted with the transmission of our letters and papers, I see no reason why it may not also be entrusted with the transmission of our telegrams and parcels, as is almost universally the case in Europe.

The Act of Congress, 1866, ch. 230, also expressly recognizes that this is a governmental function, temporarily permitted to be used by private companies, inasmuch as it provides that all telegraph lines built thereafter shall at any time after five years from the date of the act be turned over to the government, *on demand*, on payment of the value of the wires, poles, etc.

It will be noted just here that so far as railroads are used for the transmission of mail, they were promptly, and from the beginning, adopted and used exclusively by the postoffice. Whether, in so far as railroads are used for the entirely different purpose of carrying passengers and freight, they shall be taken over by the government, is an entirely different question, standing on its own basis, which has never affected the undeniable right and duty of the government to use them exclusively so far as they are used for the carriage of mails. But the telegraph and telephone (so far as used by the public for hire) are, and can be, only used for the transmission of mail, and unquestionably come within the exclusive grant to the government of operating the postoffice. The telegraph and telephone are simply the *electric mail* or mail sent by electricity, just as the railway mail is sent by steam agency in preference to the horse power formerly used in the days of stagecoaches and horseback riders and canal boats.

When the government shall assume its duty of sending the mail by electricity, railroad companies can still operate their own telegraph lines on their own business, and private telephone exchanges will still exist, just as railroads and others may now send their own letters by their own agents (U. S. Rev. Stat., §3985), but may not carry them for others for hire (U. S. Rev. Stat., §§3982, 3983, 3984, 3986, 3977, 3990). Then, as now, the government would only have the exclusive privilege of carrying mail for *hire* (U. S. Rev. Stat., §3992). This privilege of carrying mail for hire, whether sent by electricity or steam or stage coach or on horseback, is an exclusive governmental function, and no corporation or monopoly can legally exercise any part of it. It is the duty of the government to do it, and to do it in the quickest and most efficient manner and at the lowest possible rate consistent with the cost.

The army and navy and the department of justice are departments of exclusive governmental functions in the same manner and to exactly the same extent as the postoffice. But suppose that some branch of the department of justice (as by turning in the fines, penalties, and tax fees) or of the war or navy could be made a source of revenue, would it not be singular to turn over that revenue-paying part of those departments to a private monopoly, leaving the people to support the non-profitable part? Yet that is exactly what is done with the postoffice. Though the postoffice is as exclusively a governmental function as the army or navy or the department of justice, the government operates only the slow, antiquated, non-paying part of the postoffice, leaving the taxpayers to make up an annual deficit of six or eight millions; while the improved, up-to-date part of the postoffice, the rapid or electric mail, is operated by a private monopoly and pays a heavy dividend on its watered stock of one hundred and fifty millions—ten times the actual value of its plant.

Besides, this system is unjust, for the private monopoly naturally selects the best-paying districts, and a large part of the people are denied the advantages of a modern postoffice. In every country, save ours alone, the power of the monopoly has failed to maintain a system so unconstitutional and so opposed to the best interests of the public.

Hence in every country except ours the telegraph and telephone are constituent parts of the postoffice, with the double result that the postoffice facilities of the telegraph and telephone are extended to the country postoffices, and the postal revenues show a profit instead of a loss. Notably Great Britain, which has most widely extended the use of the telegraph and telephone as a part of its postoffice, shows a large annual profit from its postoffice instead of the deficit which was usual before the telegraph and telephone were added to the postoffice by Mr. Gladstone in 1870.

But there are those who say that operating the telegraph and telephone services would centralize the government. Yet it would be hard to see why an efficient postal service is more centralizing than an inefficient one, or why mail sent by electricity or pneumatic tubes (which should be adopted in the large cities) is more centralizing than mail sent on horseback or by steam. It is a puzzle to understand why ownership of telegraph or telephone wires costing less than ten dollars per mile should imperil the government more than the ownership of gunboats or postoffice buildings or postal cars. If it were a question of adding new functions to the government, as the ownership of railroads and the carrying of freight and passengers, this argument would be a legitimate one for debate. But when the constitution has already turned over the exclusive duty of transmission of mail to the government, there can be no argument of this kind properly used against the introduction of the most improved methods for the transmission of the mail, whether by electricity or by pneumatic tubes.

Telegraphic dispatches would be as sacred in the hands of government employees as other mail is now, or as the telegrams are in the hands of the employees of a private corporation. Besides, government employees, especially under civil-service rules and subject to the supervision of public opinion, would be less capable of using the telegraph for partisan purposes, as has been done under corporation ownership, and as was attempted to be done in the first Cleveland election, as everyone remembers. With telephones at all country postoffices and all villages and the smaller towns, few additional employees would be required, and those few would be added at centres requiring the telegraph and where civil-service rules obtain. The telephones and telegraphs would be put in the postoffice buildings already owned or rented by the government, thus saving the rent of all the buildings now used by the private companies. This and the saving of salaries of the officials of the present corporations and the dividends on their largely watered stock would enable the government to reduce its tolls to the uniform rate of ten cents per message, independently of the large increase in business.

In Italy the government is proposing to reduce its telegraphic rates to five cents per message, and in Sweden the government charge for a telephone connected with every city in the kingdom is six dollars per year. In Great Britain (by the official report made to this government in the United States Consular Reports for April, 1895) the increase since the government has taken over the telegraph and telephone has been tenfold in private messages and thirtyfold in press messages, and the improvement in promptness of delivery has been from an average of two to three hours under private ownership to an average of nine minutes under government. This wonderful increase in business has been due to the threefold cause of cheap rates, extension of the lines to all postoffices, and greater promptness in delivery.

With wire costing less than ten dollars per mile there is no reason why the government should not own a line to every postoffice in the Union. There should be no dicker with private companies about leasing or purchasing. In 1866 they only asked for five years to close up, but when the five years were out they had formed the present great trust and defied the public. They have had thirty years' notice to abandon their use of a branch of the governmental functions. In that time they have received hundreds of millions of profits illegally extorted from the toiling masses. They have no right to extract another dollar by lease or sale of their antiquated or wornout instruments. By the act of 1866 (above cited) they have no claim for compensation for franchises or expected profits. They have only a privilege, determinable (after 1871) at the option of the government upon payment of the assessed value of wires, poles, etc. Let the government give the actual value of such wires as it may wish to use and take complete and exclusive possession of the duties of a postoffice. Every postmaster who can talk can use the telephone, and where a telegraph office is required the government can employ an assistant as operator as easily as any other clerk.

Other countries are doing this good work of furnishing electric mail facilities at cheap rates to all the people, in the country as well as in the town. Why, alone of all the world, should this government, which claims *par excellence* to be a government of the people and for the people, fail in this constitutional duty of furnishing proper postal facilities to all its people? The only proper postal facilities for the American people are those which shall extend to every nook and corner of the republic, which shall be the best which the latest advances in science can offer, and which are furnished as near the exact cost of the service as possible without profit. Such postal facilities the American people are entitled to demand as a right. They should rest contented with nothing short of this.

SCIENTIFIC THEOSOPHY.

BY JOSEPH RODES BUCHANAN, M. D.*

"Theosophy"—divine wisdom—is a grand word, not to be lightly or irreverently applied to anything which does not primarily come from the divine sphere, for unless its origin is there, the word "Theosophy" is an imposture.

This word was first introduced into the sphere of science at the beginning of this century by that bold original genius, Dr. F. J. Gall, the first revealer of the true anatomy of the brain, whose anatomical teaching has since been followed by anatomists and whose remarkable dissections surprised leading anatomists and even puzzled some of his contemporaries. He initiated, or we may say created, cerebral psychology, and his extreme originality and success excited the jealousy of Napoleon, who could not endure the overshadowing of French genius, and stimulated though not successfully the French opposition, for Gall had as signal success in France as in Germany.

The word "Theosophy" was applied by Dr. Gall to that portion of the brain which establishes the reverential relation of man to the Deity, which must therefore be intimately associated with supernal inspiration. In this he spoke more wisely than he understood, for in his writings he did not rise much above the level of his unspiritual contemporaries. The substantial correctness of Gall's discoveries has been verified by *all* who have followed his method of studying the comparative development of the brain in men and in animals, and even by Dr. Vimont, who began his observations for the *refutation* of Gall and ended by publishing a large work in *confirmation*. But his discoveries are little known to those who have not followed his methods of observation.

Neither completeness nor accuracy can be demanded of the *creator* of a new science, but Gall fell into few errors, though he came far short of completing the survey of man in his mental constitution, and did not even attempt a solution of the physiological problems of the brain. My own discoveries of 1841 and '42 in which the functions of every con-

---

*Author of "The New Education," "System of Anthropology," "Therapeutic Sarcognomy," and "Manual of Psychometry."

volution of the brain, both psychic and physiological, have been established by electrical experiment to the entire satisfaction of all who have witnessed the experiments (endorsed by a medical college and a university), have confirmed nearly all the discoveries of Gall, as the first steps of solid psychic science in connection with anatomy, which lead toward the temple of divine wisdom.

Every profound thinker, knowing that man is the masterpiece of the universe, knows also that the soul is the loftiest subject toward which the scientist can direct his attention with the hope of comprehension, since Deity is far beyond the comprehension of man. The soul of man, the intelligible image of the Divine, is manifestly the only teacher, the only volume in which the lessons that approximate the Infinite can be learned.

The soul, which is the essential vitality of all beings, has in all forms of life its terrestial home in the brain, in which a special apparatus belongs to every function of life, as distinct in all cerebral fibres as in the optic and auditory nerves.

Manifestly, then, the arcana of the universe have their home in the brain, in which, by the vast complexity of the millions of elements in its structure, and the still more incalculable extent and variety of psychic elements and organization, the intelligence of humanity has been baffled, and man in the nineteenth century confesses that he has no understanding of his own essential existence and of the relation of his most mysterious and controlling anatomical structure to his most limitless nature and capacity.

If the intelligence of mankind is sufficiently advanced in this century to justify the introduction of the word "Theosophy," it must be manifestly by the comprehension of the limitless soul; and while living in material forms, that is possible only by reaching it through the anatomical apparatus with which it is identified, the development of which reveals the extent of its own evolution, and the laws that control its apparatus. Evidently, therefore, it is in cerebral science and its correlative, psychic science, that the possibility of Theosophy exists, for until that is attained we can only crawl in subordinate and accessory sciences, as the mole crawls in the earth.

What mastery of divine wisdom is attainable by this method, it is the purpose of this essay to show, as far as it can be done in the narrow limits of a magazine essay. But the preliminary statement must be offered that all knowledge is from God, and may be called inspiration. Our life is a continual absorption of divine wisdom from that vast volume of divine revelation, the visible and invisible universe, through our external and internal senses. Shut off from that volume which sends its influx through light, sound, movement, force, and innumerable forms and phenomena, the mind of man would remain an absolute blank. All the phenomena of nature are expressions of divine wisdom and power, from which man receives his own intelligence and power.

The physical facts of nature come to us through the external senses, as to animals, and to man they bring the invisible truths, the laws of nature, which he clearly sees in the phenomena. In men of the nobler type, this knowledge amounts to philosophy; and in men of a more elevated spiritual type, something more than the physical laws of nature comes in this influx—a perception of that psychic world of life and power with which the human soul perceives its kinship—the world of immortality and divinity—a world which is not perceptible to the lower types of humanity, to which even philosophy is dim and doubtful if not unknown.

The nature and source of this grander knowledge have been and still are a puzzling marvel to all mankind, and the word occult has been indefinitely used for a realm of infinite mystery, credulity, superstition and fraud.

The possibility of divine wisdom from divine inspiration has been recognized throughout Christendom in reference to Jesus, but this belief as to Him was not associated with any understanding of the relations between humanity and divinity—their *rationale* and law—the part that inspiration has played, and the far more important part that it may play in the future, as the light illumining the world. St. John said, "That was the true Light which lighteth every man that cometh into the world," and St. John was a philosopher.

A systematic investigation of this subject was begun in 1841-42, abandoning all old paths and taking the only path that leads directly on to the heart of the infinite mystery—the direct investigation of the divine image in its earthly incarnation in the human brain.

The starting point was the discovery that all human sensibilities to the influences of the universe are located in the middle, or as now called, spheno-temporal lobe of the brain, resting chiefly on the wings of the sphenoid bone where the ascending fibres of the *corpora striata* have their final distribution. There is no room here for the history of this discovery and its tests, but I may say that it was further verified about thirty years later, when Professor Ferrier by partial destruction of the base of this lobe in a monkey, destroyed the sense of feeling on the opposite side of the body, according to the law of decussation.

This structure, connected in action with interior convolutions of the front lobe and the delicate *septum lucidum*, brings into one group the structures and corresponding faculties which take cognizance of all impressions that we receive from the visible, material, and the invisible or psychic elements of the universe. As the external sense of vision by means of light, grasps the existence and movement of the millions of suns, so does this finer and more interior sense reveal worlds heretofore unknown to science and only dimly imagined in a dreamy way by those who without systematic investigation have spoken, during the last twenty-five hundred years, of their mysterious impressions and beliefs, mingled often with baseless fancies. -

To show how I was led along the path of discovery it is well to give the first steps, which have long been published in the *Journal of Man* and the "Manual of Psychometry— the dawn of a new civilization." which has diffused the knowledge of my discovery and its application among all civilized nations, there being no difficulty in the way, since the demonstrations are extremely easy. The reader will kindly hold in suspense any opinion on the phrase, "the dawn of a new civilization," as it is the purpose of this essay to prove it a just and reasonable claim. For if this discovery is to result in the rapid enlargement of *all sciences relating to man*, all sciences relating to the past, all political and religious history, and in short all philosophy, all social institutions, and all religion, it will certainly be competent to establish "a new civilization" as fast as intelligence can overcome inherited barbarisms. All these consequences are sure to come when the divine elements in man are understood throughout the world, incorporated in educational systems, and made active in abolishing ignorance, crime, and all our hereditary barbarisms with which mankind are satisfied because they know nothing of a true civilization.

As the space allotted to this essay is too limited for illustration, for demonstration, and for the convincing facts that would instruct, much reliance must be placed upon the sagacious intuition of readers, which is not deficient in the readers of the ARENA, who are probably the foremost thinkers of our nation.

A very concise statement must now be given of the initial steps of my investigation fifty-four years ago, based upon a prior seven years' investigation of the brain, resulting in many discoveries, among which was the importance of that region of the brain where the sensitive and intellectual functions are brought into conjunction.

Bishop Polk of the South, whom I met at Little Rock in 1841, had a finely developed brain and vigorous intellect— an accomplished gentleman. He had a very large endowment of the sensitive region, which I have mentioned, and when I told him of his marvellous capacities in that direction he surprised me by the statement that his sensibility was so acute that whenever he touched brass even accidentally and unconsciously he instantly tasted it. Had I met him after following this clue to its results, he might have given me some splendid illustrations of the higher powers of the human soul, such as I afterwards obtained from Bishop Otey of Tennessee and Chancellor Scott of Mississippi.

I determined to find out at once if this high grade of sensibility was common or anomalous. I found that a large number of my acquaintance had similar powers, and when they held their hands behind their backs, they could recognize the peculiar influence of any metals placed in their hands, and thus distinguish one from another. Nearly all that I tested manifested this capacity, for the climate there was favorable to the nervous system.

The next step was to try other substances, beginning with salt, sugar, spices, and any convenient substance. The taste would sometimes be perceived distinctly, but the uniform result was to impart the characteristic influence of the substance on the constitution. When medicines were used, the exact effect belonging to the medicine when taken internally would be perceived by from fifty to ninety per cent of the persons tested. In subsequent years I found that those possessing the highest sensitive endowments could pronounce upon a medicine almost instantly, when placed in the hands, and give a more accurate and reliable statement of its effects and its adaptation to various diseases than could be obtained from the dispensatories and other standard professional works—of which reports I have a valuable collection of about three hundred on which I rely in preference to medical authorship. Even the infinitesimally prepared globules of homœopathic practitioners were readily described by my best psychometers.

It had been supposed and is still taught that absorption into the interior of the body is necessary for medical effects, and that no mere exterior contact can have any effect, but in my experiments, even contact with the cuticle was entirely unnecessary, and the medicines were wrapped in papers so as to conceal them from the knowledge of the psychometer, and in teaching students, I used for convenience a small piece of paper on which a little fluid extract had been dried, or paper containing the substance concealed, or a glass vial containing the fluid, which of course made the experiment a little slower in reaching the result. Sometimes I have arranged a convenient group of about a dozen, connecting hands, and taking a single specimen of the medicine, sent a current of electricity through it to carry its potentiality to the sensitive, and thus enabled everyone in the circuit to feel and describe the medical potency. For the last twelve years my annual classes of the College of Therapeutics have participated in this experiment. It would be practicable in this way to medicate a thousand sensitives with a single medical dose and continue the process indefinitely without the slightest diminution of the quanity of the medicine. No abnormal sensibility is requisite, for such sensibilities belong to the majority of mankind, and in hot climates to everybody.

The practical result of these demonstrations is that medicine will be made an accurate science when these heretofore unknown powers are utilized. I might safely undertake to revise the entire pharmacopœia of the medical profession, rectify its errors, and add several hundred valuable remedies now unknown, within twelve months devoted to the task. But more urgent duties have claimed my time.

These things I have been teaching, demonstrating and publishing for many years, but no medical college unless I was a member of the faculty has ever manifested a desire to know anything about it, and I have not thought it expedient to urge any species of knowledge upon the attention of those who manifested not only indifference but aversion.*

* When I proposed, about fifteen years ago, to make these demonstrations before a committee of the National Medical Association, I was firmly but courteously informed by the venerable head of the society, Professor Gross, with whom I was well acquainted, that the thing was entirely impossible, for the *reason* that they were governed by a *medical code* and I had not submitted to it. The code is a relic of barbarism, which will disappear in the coming century. It proscribes more than thirty thousand of *the very best* physicians in the United States, as unfit to be treated as gentlemen, and absolutely reverses the meaning of the word *ethics.* Unconscious of satirizing himself, the note of Professor Gross suggested that my *medical* discoveries might be presented to some societies outside of the medical profession! When I made a similar proposition to the Kentucky State Medical Society and a committee was appointed, *the committee never met! Verbum sat.*

When Americans undertake anything they are apt to surpass the slow coaches of the old world. Certainly they have done so in medical bigotry and medical legislation procured by a lobby. The demonstrations which were so firmly rejected here were not refused in France. Forty-four years after my first experiments here, Drs. Bourru and Burot made similar experiments, not so extensive or scientific or valuable, and more marvelous, by holding medicines behind the heads of very sensitive subjects (a method I had avoided as unnecessarily marvelous and less reliable) and producing the complete effects of the medicines. Their experiments were repeated and confirmed by the professors and officers of the Naval Medical School at Rochefort and

Psychometry is the word I was compelled to coin and intróduce for these and other new powers and processes which are destined to revolutionize the medical profession by giving the same accuracy to *diagnosis* as to the knowledge of medicines. A perfect knowledge of the disease and a perfect knowledge of the remedy make a scientific practice of therapeutics, and measures are now being taken in California proposing to leave the old medical colleges in their stagnant condition and establish a school which instead of dreading progress will welcome every discovery and accept my additions to biology, which for half a century have withstood criticism and received the endorsement of every committee of investigation. "Westward the star of empire wends its way."

The ability to make a correct diagnosis of disease, to enter into close sympathy with the patient, and to look with intuitive perception into all his interior conditions, realizing not only his feelings but the pathological conditions of his interior organs which so often defy all college rules for diagnosis, and produce a vast amount of radical errors and false treatment for conditions not existing (rivalling in its results the horrors of chattel slavery); is an inherent capacity of the best developed constitutions, and exists, though latent, in various degrees, in nearly if not quite a million of the people of the United States, at least half of whom with a little training in the science of psychometry would be competent to guide the medical profession and correct its blunders.

Man has not been turned out by divine power blind and helpless among ten thousand dangers, but is endowed with a clear vision to meet all the demands of his career. My students for many years have been trained to exercise these powers and few have failed to develop them.

Of course many of the medical profession possess this capacity and are led by its exercise to the highest rank of professional success; but all such exalted powers are scorned and ridiculed by colleges, and their possessors being kept in ignorance do not use them, and would be afraid to confess their intellectual capacities. Dogmatic ignorance is the imperious master of the situation, and patients who puzzle the faculty have to resort to those who have never been instructed (?) by colleges for a satisfactory diagnosis.

---

were reported and honorably received in the National Association for the Advancement of Science at Grenoble, France, in 1885. They have since been repeated by Professor Luys at Paris. The metallo-therapy of the French hospitals is another illustration of the same principles. France is far ahead of America in neurological studies. It seems unlucky that I was not born in France.

` But in spite of colleges, the knowledge and use of this power have gone round the world, and in the hands both of the ignorant and the educated it has saved many thousand lives. In some of my students it has made marvellous displays, such as revealing the medical history of years, discovering anomalous and unsuspected conditions, and even telling the whole story at the first sight of a patient not yet within twenty feet of the observer. Some years ago 1 knew a gentleman of very scanty medical education who possessed this psychometric faculty in a high degree and was then, I believe, receiving a larger income than any physician in our country. Had he been enslaved by the code, he would have been a common obscure doctor.

That Theosophy *revolutionizes* what is called medical science is a necessary result of the emancipation of the divine wisdom bestowed on man. It is not merely by giving a true diagnosis, a true knowledge of medicines, and ability indefinitely to enlarge the materia medica, which are simply rectifications of antiquated ignorance, but by adding to this rectified science three new therapeutic methods, not known in the old colleges, that the revolution is completed. With this *meagre* introduction of a great theme, the reader may be prepared for the demonstration in my next essay that Theosophy brings "a new civilization."

SHALL WOMEN VOTE?

BY HELEN H. GARDENER.

In a little volume just issued, called "The Woman-Suffrage Movement in the United States,"* the topic is more
fully, freely, plainly, and badly dealt with upon the strictly
conservative and religious side than I remember to have
seen before. I am truly glad to have read this book. It is so
amusing. I have not laughed more heartily for some time,
and I believe that the little volume will be one of the most
useful ever put into the hands of the suffragists and will
cause more uneasiness in the conservative camp than has
been felt for years. Something of the thought of the book is
in these paragraphs on pp. 75–6:

> When the American pulpit realizes that this question involves the
> infallibility of God's word just as much and with much more logical
> and practical certainty than does the scientific question of evolution
> or the critical one of the inerrancy of the written word, it will appre-
> ciate the alarming and portentous condition of American society.
>
> This question is fundamental; it is the foundation-stone of the
> social, moral, and religious structure which the English-speaking
> race has erected upon the divinity and authenticity of the Word of
> God. Remove the foundation, and the structure falls to the ground.
> And who will rebuild it? Will the cowards who allowed it to be
> destroyed before their very eyes? I trow not. The law of marriage
> was announced by God in the very beginning of time, long before the
> promulgation of the Decalogue, *and for all time and for all the nations
> of man.* It was to govern the one relation of life and social arrange-
> ment common to all the different races of mankind, and was fixed as
> the foundation of the family, of society, of order and government,
> regardless of its special form or nature. *Whatever changes it has re-
> ceived from custom or legislation have always worked an injury to the
> unity and purity of the home and to the peace and happiness of society.*

Italics mine.

I should like to read the reply of the orthodox suffragists.
Not being orthodox myself, I believe with him in much that
he says of the influence and effect of the Bible teaching on
the woman question. Believing as I do that the Bible in
this matter as in previous causes of progress and civilization has stood and does stand directly across the path of justice, truth, progress, and science, I simply say, as Wendell
Phillips said of it when men like "A Lawyer" asserted that

* "The Woman-Suffrage Movement in the United States," by A Lawyer. Pp. 153;
price, cloth 75 cents, paper 25 cents. Arena Publishing Company.

the Bible upheld slavery, "Then so much the worse for the
Bible." This I should say to "A Lawyer." Notwithstanding which fact, he (or I) could prove just as good a scriptural
case against himself as a lawyer, a voter, an owner of property, or an eater of meat. "If eating meat offend thy
brother, eat no meat." Meat-eating offends many millions
of his brothers. "Look not upon the wine when it is red"
is violated in letter every time a Christian takes the sacrament (unless perchance he uses white wine, which would not
keep the command "in spirit"). But I am glad this book
was written. It is a record to be met by those who hold that
the Bible is a friend to the progress of women. It will be
interesting to see how they will do this. There is a naive
paragraph on pp. 85–6:

It might be well to inquire why it was that the Catholic Church so
early declared marriage to be a sacrament. The facts of history
during the Roman Republic and the days of the Cæsars and the
earlier years of the empire must have been well known to Roman
Catholic ecclesiastics, who have been always more or less politicians.
They must have studied the causes of the decline and fall of the
republic, and accepting fully the Biblical doctrine of marriage, they
at once saw the vast power and influence *which they and the church
herself could acquire* and wield through that principle of morals and
law, if it were ever acknowledged to be correct, and were accepted
and obeyed. It gave to woman absolute protection; she accepted it
and obeyed the church. It restrained the passions of man in public
and private life through the wife and mother, and consequently controlled the husband; and he feared the church.

Italics mine.

There is a volume of confession and fact in that one paragraph, but it is amusing to see it come from that side. Had
J. S. Mill, Huxley, Robert Ingersoll, or Elizabeth Cady
Stanton written it, one could imagine what a chorus of protest would have gone up from a church whose ulterior
motives were thus laid bare, so that she is declared by her
devotees to have subordinated one sex and brutalized the
other in order to own both. It is one of the important
truths of history, which has previously been strenuously
denied by the church and her devotees. We are glad that
"A Lawyer's" candor outran his discretion. It will be
worth while knowing what happens to him when the Right
Reverend of his diocese discovers his identity.

No state has the right to degrade one of its citizens unless
that citizen has given cause for the degradation. Is not
that a fair and plain proposition? I think "A Lawyer"
would say that it is *unless* that citizen chanced to be a
woman, and then he would baldly and frankly say that the
Bible degrades woman. God Almighty did, and therefore

the state has no right to ameliorate her condition. Indeed he does say this in substance throughout his book. He argues for her degradation wholly upon Bible grounds and makes no claim whatever upon an ethical, natural, or political basis where he concedes her the right and logic of the argument. This is the position of the book, and he supports his argument in the main very well indeed if one accepts his religious premises. It is true that we might hit back by reminding him that he is not so rigid in the application of other scriptural injunctions as in that dealing with the subordination of women, but all things being equal, he has done about the best that could be done on that side, which is no doubt the reason the Arena Company published the book. It believes that all sides of all questions should have a hearing, and that suppression is never argument; nevertheless the Arena editor and the Arena Company, singly and collectively, are on the other side of this question, while it concedes the right of a full hearing to "A Lawyer."

There is an amusing passage, pp. 88–91:

No one can predict or foresee what will be the influence and effects of female suffrage upon society and law, and through them upon the government itself, until it has been practically carried to its ultimate end in the affairs of this country, state and federal. It cannot be fully worked out in one or even two generations. Old and established civilizations, with their customs ingrained in the character and interwoven with the daily thoughts and life of a people, do not so easily fold themselves up to be laid away in the lumber-room of history. Under the final operation of this principle all the restraints of honor and of chivalry, of society and of law, will be removed, and men and women will meet in their future dealings in the same way that men meet men in their trades and traffics; women will no longer be dealt with as women, but as citizens, because the law will not any longer so consider them. In the future they will be simply buyers and sellers, traders, merchants, with no legal difference between them and men. The social distinction will be in the dress, and in that alone. It will make the marriage tie simply a bargain and sale—a trade based upon the pecuniary ability of each or of one only to support the family. Husbands will be bought, and wives will be sold. It will degrade woman and unsex man.

Ultimately, when its fullest operation and influence are felt and developed under its exclusive sway, women will again become "hewers of wood and drawers of water," because men, with their wits sharpened by experience with other men and from constant trade, will soon absorb, in some way or other, beyond the protecting touch of the law, all the property owned by the women; consequently there will be eventually a direct antagonism and actual hostility between husband and wife as to property and rights of property, producing lawsuits to be followed by divorce suits, and leaving the children, if any, to the care of the world. Public honor having been lowered by this principle, and women claiming under it the right to buy from and to sell to whom they please, there will be no private reason left in the heart, mind, or conscience of men why they should not increase their own fortunes out of the property of their wives.

It will be legal; it will be common; it will be done every day. Might, aided by experience, will be the measure and test of right. And should sickness become the constant companion of the woman after her money was gone, she would be put aside as no longer fit for service, or dropped on the wayside in the journey of life like a lonesome weed.

Husband and wife could testify against one another, could sue one another, and could buy from or sell to one another. The marriage tie would be simply an agreement between a man and a woman to live in the same house and occupy the same bed, with no protection or exclusion against any intruder during the continuance of the contract. That will be the entire legal and moral extent of this contract. It would produce at once bickerings, charges, criminations, lawsuits, divorce suits; and when the different families of the interested parties took sides in the litigation about the property, there would be street-fights, bloodshed, and murder.

Now are not the woman's wits also sharpened? She is "in trade." But the author fears antagonism between husband and wife *because* he secures all the property, whereas he has all along argued that as it is *now* the husband *should* own the property, and that it is unseemly for a wife to "control her own property or own it!" Now it appears from this last argument that woman suffrage will produce this very state of things which he has thought right! There is an occasional "lonesome weed" nowadays, so I have heard, and also there are weeds which yearn for a chance to be lonesome rather than to be the owned "queens" of men who are willing to subject them to such indignities. Much of this is a purely gratuitous assumption, and I presume that "A Lawyer" is not unaware that with the class of moral idiots he has described here (of whatever sex they may be) the lack of a vote fails to make the woman chaste or loyal or content with her husband; nor do the words of a priest restrain such a man, as the brothels will all attest. It is well known that these are chiefly supported by men who have accepted marriage with a disfranchised subordinate as a "sacrament."

The rest of this prophecy of the dire results of justice to woman is worth going miles to read. The author promises almost all the disasters known to man, and they are to appear "before the third generation shall have passed away" after woman suffrage is introduced. He appears to be in blissful ignorance of the fact that *now* the third generation born under woman suffrage is living very comfortably and happily in Wyoming, and that that state has fewer criminals, jails, asylums, and paupers to the thousand population than any other in America. But a fact of this kind need not and does not interfere with oceans of theory. He says, "By their effects shall ye know them," but refuses to look at effects or to listen to a proposal to "try all things and hold fast that which is good," although he opens with this very quotation. Hold fast that which you have got is his theory, and try nothing else.

On pp. 95–6 he says that when J. S. Mill, Buckle, Ingersoll, and those who believe in woman's rights "talk of liberty, they mean license." No man who has read the works of these men named, or read or heard the leaders of the woman-suffrage movement, is justified in making such a charge as that. It is a libel, pure and simple. However much "A Lawyer" may dissent from the views of an opponent, it is difficult to grasp his ethical (not to mention his religious) point of view and status when he ventures on such a statement. It has been my fortune to know personally most of the leaders in this movement, and to have read and heard them, and to know much of their personal lives and aims, and there is in no state, no church, and no home (not excepting the mother, wife, or daughter of "A Lawyer" himself) a loftier, truer, more truly liberty-loving and license-hating number of men and women on this globe. Their own lives and writings (with their own names given freely to the world) are open to the public, and "A Lawyer" can only prejudice his case and his audience by such a statement. He refers to Lecky to sustain his case, but in fact Lecky is wholly against him, and was one of the very ardent advocates of a larger liberty for woman, and was one of the first who pointed out that Christian law had degraded woman's status, and put a blight on progress. "A Lawyer" presumes too much upon the ignorance of his readers.

In chapter vii he argues that men are so wholly brutal, so entirely vicious, that were it not for the Bible they could and would have no idea of or respect for justice. He is apparently wholly unaware of any natural or scientific basis of morals. He does not appear to know that there are nations giving no allegiance to the Bible whose morals and sense of justice are quite equal to those of any Christian nation. Witness Japan in her last war. He thinks so badly of man that he believes that nothing but fear of hell and a priest and a vengeful and arbitrary God can keep him from devouring woman. No suffragist, however excited, charges man with quite so much willing and conscious brutality. It remains to be seen if men relish the character and reputation "A Lawyer" gives them. On pp. 103–4 he says:

It would well become all men to look to the future with great fear and trembling.

Without stopping to criticise or answer Mill's arguments in his "Subjection of Women," let us say he has suggested no remedy.

Admitting his facts to be true and his argument to be unanswerable, his conclusion resolves itself into this proposition: either the men of to-day ought voluntarily to turn over the government of the world to the women of to-day; or the Maker of us all made a mistake in that He did not make the men of to-day women, and the women of to-day men. The first alternative is a flat impossibility; the second is simply questioning God's wisdom, and does not in any wise aid or bolster up his argument. In a word, it is sheer nonsense, in which Mill frequently stranded all his logic, unless he followed some other mind.

The demand of the women who seek the suffrage is perfect equality before the law, in society, and under the government.

His misunderstanding of Mill and of the whole situation is so ludicrously apparent that this argument requires no reply. Women don't want to be men; they don't want men to be women. They simply wish to reduce the bump of self-importance of men sufficiently to enable them to grasp the fact that man is not the whole human race, and that in assuming to be so, and legislating upon that theory, he has not only outraged woman, but seriously crippled himself and his children. So long as each man lived for himself alone, and had no wider horizon, no sense of responsibility or honor or justice toward either his own posterity or the other half of the race, the subjugation of woman was inevitable. But the rising conscience—the development of a natural and scientific basis of morality as opposed to the strictly arbitrary and variously interpreted religious basis—has resulted as inevitably in a rising tide of civilization and progress, in which the question of the justice and right of the subordination of woman is one of the vital issues which any student of dynamic sociology might have foreseen and prophesied as to its drift.

Then, too, with the development of the knowledge and importance of heredity would naturally come the absolutely incontrovertible fact that subject mothers never did and subject mothers never will give to this world a race of healthy, liberty-loving, justice-practising, sane, and moral children. In Bible times they gave to the world sons who had to have "devils" — whole herds of them — "cast out," they gave lying Peters and thieves for the cross, they gave treachery, butchery, beggary, idiocy, insanity, and malice, as they do yet and as they will to the end of the chapter of enforced maternity and brutalized paternal ownership. It is simply for men to choose whether they wish to pay such prices as these for the gratification of their sense of ownership and their autocratic power. The ablest, wisest, and best men of the age feel that the price is altogether too high. The heartwrung mothers of crime and insanity and vice *know* that it is, and if they fought only half-heartedly for their own emancipation, they are willing to fight to the death to save their children from the results of the blindness of man.

"A Lawyer" shows pretty conclusively, from his point of view, that many previous forms of government and rule have produced dismal failures. All of these were under male control; all were the failures of male rulers to grasp the problems which arose; all indicate a lack of sufficient knowledge and moral and civic character to meet the developing situations. Is not this in itself an indication that men alone *cannot* legislate wisely and successfully and fairly for both sexes? Have not thousands of years of partial and total and repeated failures under various forms demonstrated pretty fully the fact that half of the race has neither the wisdom nor the ethical ability to legislate for and rule the whole race? Does not "A Lawyer" cut the ground from under his own feet?

He proves his case from the ultra orthodox point of view of one who believes in a "personal God," who had a "chosen" people and who changed His laws from time to time as He saw fit; who assumes that all "Pagans" are lower than are Christians in ethics and morals; who accepts the dictum of the Catholic Church as final, and finds that "Luther knew how to destroy, but not how to construct"; who holds that "submission" is the full law for a wife, but that she is also a "queen" and an "equal" with her husband; who on another page finds that "such equality" is impossible and her obedience to his will and control is imperative; who finds that it is wrong, unnatural, and impious for her—this "queen"—to "have control of her own property"; who finds that Christ settled for all time and so that "*no* one can misunderstand" the relations of husband and wife; who insists that the Bible is *in toto* against the equality of the sexes, the elevation of woman, or her equality with man before and in the law,—all of which many Christian clergymen have striven to disprove to their women supporters. I am more than pleased to see the whole case put so fully and simply and brutally before women and before men who believe that the Bible has been woman's friend. I hope most sincerely that both sides will read, analyze, and understand this book. I do not believe that the cause of woman could have a better stimulator than is this naive, simply stated, frank argument for her degradation and subjection. Fair-minded men will rebel, and it will need nothing more potent than a very slight self-respect and sense of justice to show women the outrage of it.

He claims the "headship and rule" for the husband not at

all on account of his superiority or ability, but *solely* on
Biblical authority, and says, pp. 64–7:

That brings us directly face to face with female suffrage and its
effects upon the institution of marriage as established by God and
upon the doctrine of the marital relation as announced in the Scriptures. The Scriptures as the Word of God are either infallible or
they are not infallible. Female suffrage is based on the assumption that the sexes are equal in all things, personal, social, legal, and
political, and that marriage does not qualify or alter that equality.
This is "the head and front of its offending," and it is enough. If this
conclusion is justified by the irresistible logic of the argument upon
which the question plants itself, then it can only be sustained by a
denial of the headship of the husband, by an assertion that marriage
is a civil contract and not an institution of God, and that, being
a civil contract made by two persons at will who are in all respects
absolutely equal, it can be dissolved at pleasure by these persons,
and that God in the beginning had nothing to do with it. This conclusion conflicts at all points with the Word of God, denies its infallibility, and puts forth another law of marriage. And further, if the
Scriptures are not infallible, then God has no right to His awful
sovereignty, and should be dethroned; the Christ was an impostor
and a fraud; and man and woman should be guided by their reason
alone, and are responsible solely and exclusively to themselves in this
life and in the life to come.

The assertion of female suffrage, carried out to its logical conclusion, as a correct principle in human affairs, is simply a denial of the
right of God to reign, and of the infallibility of his word as his
revealed will as to those affairs. If the principle is true, it destroys
all distinctions and admits of no exceptions, because the headship of
the man as husband refuses and excludes all equality in the woman
as wife, and consequently the equality which it demands for woman
must be not only personal and social, but also legal and political. If
it be contended that these passages of Scripture are local in their
application to, and temporary in the jurisdiction of their authority
over, the relations of husband and wife, and ought to be so accepted
in their practical consequences, social and legal, upon human affairs,
I will not meet the argument intended to be thus asserted by the
childish question, What portion, then, of the New Testament is to be
considered as universal and permanent in its nature and of binding
force? I shall at once admit that, if they are local and temporary,
then they are not a part of God's law enacted for all time and for all
His creatures, and consequently the New Testament is, to that extent,
not Sacred Scripture and therefore is not infallible.

This view of the New Testament is not only the fruitful mother
of infidelity, but is *per se* an actual denial of its authenticity and infallibility as a part of God's Revealed Will. It is not to be argued in
this connection that this construction is correct on the basis of an
exception to the rule, because there can be no exception to this rule.

Now the same dire and dreadful things were said to
men by kings and barons when they assured men that none
but infidels, etc., could claim equality and suffrage for all
men, because God had "set rulers over them," and "men
differ as one star differeth from another in glory," and God
had "appointed some to rule by divine right and some to
serve," etc.; but we do not observe that "A Lawyer" catches

the point of this logic of Scripture *as applied to himself* and
men generally. The same Biblical scarecrow (as written,
translated, and interpreted by white men) was observable in
the slavery days. But "A Lawyer" and his followers, who
are distinctly taught in the Bible to "be in subjection to the
powers that be,", to "render unto Cæsar," etc., prefer to
decide in these days who shall be Cæsar, and to make and
unmake the "powers," which "be" only so long as they
suit the taste of the male voters. "A Lawyer" should
pardon women for having also absorbed a little of the
logic of events, and for concluding that, if a "A Lawyer"
and his sex generally can bear up with fortitude when
they themselves disregard the Bible teachings for their own
elevation, possibly an earthquake will not follow the assumption of women that the time has come for them also
to decide for themselves somewhat about "the powers that
be"; and they find their authority (on p. 68) when they
realize that "A Lawyer" is voting in spite of the fact that his
male ancestors were taught that it was against the Bible for
the common herd to presume to rule.

A marriage that cannot sustain itself without the subjection of one party to "the sacrament" cannot too quickly be
dissolved for the interest of the state, of the children, and of
morality. So long as wifehood and motherhood are mere
matters of power and submission—of ownership and dependence—just so long will the state continue to have born
to it feeble-minded, untruthful, insane, diseased, and criminal citizens. "A Lawyer" says (p. 52) that he is no soci-
ologist. That is perfectly patent. It is also patent that he
is no student of heredity nor of anything approaching a
lofty ethical basis of sex morality and justice. The double
standard of morals, ethics, right, justice, and honor which
is fostered by his basis of argument, is at the root of more of
the crime, insanity, disease, and idiocy of the race than are
all other causes combined. Women are beginning to understand this in a vague way, and to refuse, as they should, to
be the enforced mothers of a tainted progeny, which shall be
a curse to itself and to the world into which it is recklessly
thrust. Their sense of responsibility and honor toward the
unborn is awakening, and when it is developed, children will
cease to be the products of Lust and Fear, of Power and
Submission; mothers will cease *to transmit to their children*
the passions and propensities which inevitably lead
to battlefield, hospital, insane asylum, and prison.
Man will be the gainer. He will then be born with
a sense of justice which would prevent him from

arguing calmly, as "A Lawyer" does, that it is wrong for a woman to own and control her own property, but that *he* should have it. The men born of that higher type of motherhood would scorn themselves for even wishing to establish such an immoral basis of action for their own selfish interest, which is, in its ultimate analysis, simply and only misappropriation of the goods of another to one's own selfish use.

"On the theory of the inspiration of the New Testament it must stand as a whole or fall as a whole, because the allowance of an exception to any portion, is to admit the argument against its infallibility."

Yet to-day not even the most orthodox of the clergy believe in and preach that it was "devils" that were in the insane man, nor do they preach "witches." I venture to assert that if a thief took away our author's cloak he would not present him with his coat also, nor would he "turn the other cheek" if struck a blow. This is not the way lawyers do; it would ruin their trade. What would become of "A Lawyer's" practice if some one who had been kidnapped called upon him for advice and redress in court and he replied by saying that kidnapping was all right because the Bible distinctly says, "If a man compels you to go with him one mile, ye shall go with him twain." How would it do to advise all the tramps and paupers in his state to "take no thought for the morrow, what ye shall eat nor what ye shall drink nor wherewithal ye shall be clothed"? Are these New Testament principles "for *all time and all people*"? Does "A Lawyer" believe that if they were obeyed civilization would continue? When he is ill, does "A Lawyer" call in the elders and have himself well oiled and prayed over, or has he the wicked and unbiblical habit of getting a doctor? Does he take no heed for the morrow—or does he take a fee? Has he "gone into all nations and preached the gospel" or does he practise law? Was not that command general? Was it not for all time and *to him*? If not, why are the others to *all* women? Come, come, Mr. Lawyer, even on your own grounds, and with your own logic, might it not be better if you would search (and obey) the Scriptures more faithfully for your own sex and self and be less distressed because women do not adhere to the letter of that which you and all men violate daily? Is there not an absolute command about first casting the beam out of one's own eye? Is there not another (also Christ's and for *all* men and all time) about selling all you have and giving it to the poor? Does "A Lawyer" believe in and live up to that? Does "A

Lawyer" believe that no rich man can enter the kingdom of heaven? Does he believe that Balaam's ass spoke human language?

The few times that Christ had occasion to speak to or of lawyers He appears to have quite clearly indicated that they were an undesirable class. Was this for all time, all peoples, and all lawyers? In Luke xi:52 He said, "Woe unto you, lawyers! for ye have taken away the key of knowledge; ye entered not in yourselves, and them that were entering in ye hindered." And even unto this day "A Lawyer," who very evidently has not "entered in," is struggling to take away the key and hinder all women from entering. Yes, *that* remark must surely have been for all time if not for all lawyers.

Matt. xxii:35: "Then one of them [the Pharisees], *which was* a lawyer, asked *him* [Jesus] *a question*, tempting him," etc., and the reply of Jesus was a command which "A Lawyer" indicates by his book is still unkept.

In Luke x:25 the Lord is again represented as "tempted" by a lawyer, even as woman to-day is tempted to yield to this Pharisaic argument, and Jesus then, as woman to-day, declined the honor.

Luke xi:45–8 Christ appears to have foreseen the present position of "A Lawyer" and says: "Woe unto you, also, ye lawyers! for ye lade men [women?] with burdens grievous to be borne, and *ye yourselves touch not the burdens with one of your fingers.* Woe unto you! *for ye build the sepulchres of the prophets,* and your fathers killed them." Had Christ had "A Lawyer" instead of lawyers in mind He could not have made a clearer home thrust.

Luke vii:30, "But the Pharisees and the lawyers rejected for themselves the counsel of God." And they are doing it yet if the counsel of God is the voice of justice and honor and right.

Pp. 73–4:

It is not that the church and religion will lose the active work and influence of these women; it is the open defiance of God's law as to marriage and as to woman's place in society under that law, which permeates all social and religious questions touched by the relation of husband and wife, that will produce the great and irreparable injury. The true civil relation of man and woman, whether as husband and wife or as citizens, springs directly from God's law of marriage; because, under that law, it is expected and intended that all men are to be, or should be, husbands, and all women wives. Therefore it goes behind future or predetermined relations between them, and fixes their natural and necessary relations to civil government before they assume the final relation to one another of husband and wife.

If this theory or construction is wrong, either the whole object of God's *law would be frustrated, or the civil government would, of necessity, be compelled to enact the law as it stands in the Bible: in other words, the human law would be compelled to take from the wife those rights now contended for, and put her where God's law puts her the moment she becomes a wife—by sheer brute force.*

Italics mine.

He appears to believe, and states in substance over and over, that women cannot be induced to marry men unless they are kept subordinate. That is to say, women must be forced to marry. This is a pretty low ideal of marriage, and "A Lawyer" seems to distrust wholly the attractive qualities of his own sex. A man who can secure or keep a wife only upon such terms is to be pitied indeed, for he has fallen far below the brute males, many of whom attract and keep mates with a varying degree of permanency. But the fact is that a very large percentage of the advanced women and the suffragists are not only married, but are happily married and are mothers of fine, healthy, intelligent, and loving children. Their husbands do not find it difficult to meet the situation. Most of them are able, capable, educated, thoughtful men who have a vast contempt for the laws which place their wives at a political and social, legal and financial, disadvantage. It is these very men whose wives, mothers, sisters, or daughters are leaders in the suffrage movement; who, most appreciating the qualities of such women, wish the state to have the advantage of the expression of their views in the organic law; and also wish to relieve their own sex from the stigma which attaches to those who hold by force the birthright of another, or are *willing* to profit (in a near-sighted way) by the degradation of their sisters.

"A Lawyer" assumes that if women voted, they would not marry. Wyoming does not appear to bear him out, neither does England, nor Australia, nor New Zealand. It is an assumption so absurd that it needs no reply. The two things have no necessary relation. The one has to do with legal status, and with one's power to be heard as to choice in the organic law; the other is a tender, personal home relationship. One might as well argue that if women vote, they will cease at once to like ripe peaches and that they will have to be caught and fed. Men *as* men have not had the franchise for so very long. It did not undermine any of their personal love relations. They did not become worse fathers or husbands because they assumed a new and more dignified footing in the state.

The author goads the "pulpit" to cease being "cowards" and to speak out upon this matter. Bishop Doane and Rev.

Lyman Abbott have done so, but I have heard of no minister or man who has had the good fortune to have had a mother, a wife, or a daughter who was or is a logical woman suffragist who takes the side of repression of womanhood. These men have learned to trust and admire unrepressed womanhood, and to value it far above a sense of ownership and mastery. They have found it far sweeter and loftier to live in warm companionship and equality with a woman who is brave and loving and true to her husband not because he is her "head" or master, but because there is absolute mutual respect, love, confidence, and equality. Such men would find marriage with a woman who was willing to be and remain their inferior and "subject" to them an intolerable, ghastly mockery of the relationship to which they have grown accustomed between two who are equals in fact and who should be so in law.

There are passages now and then in the book which almost convince the reader that the object of the entire work is a travesty, a burlesque upon the ultra-conservative-religious view of this subject; witness for example p. 114:

The mere fact that Queen Elizabeth is admitted to have been a great sovereign, notwithstanding the very distinguished ability of her cabinet, proves nothing but the omnipotence of God.

Is not that fit for opera bouffe?

He says that in New York City alone there are 50,000 "loose women" (which means, according to statistics, 450,-000 "loose men"), while he says "men have kept women pure" by denying them the ballot. He argues that these 50,000 women are a sufficient proof that women are not fit to take part in the municipal government, but he utterly forgets the 450,000 men who sustain and produce these women. He also forgets the fact that in cities where the ballot is in the hands of women, those of this class, almost every one, refuse to register and vote. This is history; "A Lawyer's" statement is only assumption. But to point out the fallacies of the book, its contradictions, its logical non-sequiturs, and its absolute historical misstatements would require a volume larger than is the book itself, for few pages lack several of these defects. The question is insistent when the book is finished, *Is* it the sincere and best effort of that side, or is it a burlesque? And to confess the truth, I do not know. I shall be glad to have its readers decide, if they can.

EQUALITY OF OPPORTUNITY: HOW CAN WE SECURE IT?

BY JAMES L. COWLES.

The fundamental postulates of our modern political economy are the free movement of labor and the free movement of capital. It is to the realization of these postulates in practical life that we are to look for the equalization of opportunities. It was to make these postulates practical realities that the inventors of the steamboat and the locomotive gave to the dead earth a circulating system, and it was to crown their work that the electrician created a nervous system and breathed into arteries, veins, and nerves alike, the breath of life. These inventors are the world's great ministers, and they are rapidly converting it from an abode of savage brutes, each preying upon the other, into an abode of civilized human beings, each finding his greatest delight in the other's welfare.

"Of all inventions (the alphabet and printing press excepted)," says Macaulay, "those which abridge distance have done most for the civilization of our species. Every improvement in the means of locomotion benefits mankind morally and intellectually as well as materially, and not only facilitates the interchange of the various productions of nature and of art but tends to remove national and provincial antipathies and to bind together all the members of the human family."

The ideal condition of things would be to annihilate time and space and to make transportation and communication altogether free, and it is toward this goal that the world is steadily moving.

"The crowning improvement in postal matters, that of an international transit entirely free," says the British Encyclopædia, "is merely a question of time. It is the logical, the necessary complement of the work initiated at Paris in 1863, organized at Berne in 1874, and methodized again at Paris in 1878. One postal territory, one code of postal regulations, one uniform postal tariff, free conveyance between nation and nation, will be the outcome of this important movement." And this era of free international conveyance may not be so far off as some of us imagine. Already a five-cent stamp carries a letter round the world and a ten-cent stamp carries an eleven-pound package across any of the great countries included in the Parcels Post Convention of Vienna. The *Times*, of Hartford, Conn., in its issue of August 31, says that a proposition will actually be made at the International Postal Congress which meets at Washington in 1897; for each nation to carry the mails of all other countries across its territory free of charge.

The removal of all legal restraints upon the exchange of kindly services between nations must be near at hand, and the time cannot be very far away when the commerce destroyer will be transformed into the commerce promoter. True we have just completed three of these commerce destroyers at a cost of $3,000,000 each and with an annual burden for their maintenance of $800,000. "What," says Mr. Edward Atkinson, "are they good for? Nothing. What are they bad for? Everything." And is not this building of warships by civilized nations for the purpose of destroying one another's commerce a most stupid waste of human energy? Would it not be an infinitely more effectual method for preserving the peace and promoting the prosperity of nations for the different governments to join in the support of great international steamship lines devoted to the free conveyance of persons and property across the ocean ferries?

Under free international transit there would be no starvation, no congestion, either of human beings or of their products, anywhere. The questions of imports and exports, of immigration and emigration, would settle themselves, for both men and products would go forthwith where they were wanted. And this movement would be attended not only with no increase but with an actual decrease of our present burdens. It would only require that a comparatively small part of the public revenues now devoted to mutual injury should be devoted to mutual service. Is this a mere dream? The dream of to-day may be the reality of to-morrow.

But even though free international conveyance be in the dim distance, it does not follow that we may not secure free transit or comparatively free transit, at least within the limits of this country, in the near future. The advance in transportation and communication from the burden-bearing slave painfully dragging his or her slow way along the forest trail, to the electric car on the T-rail, measures all the difference between the American civilization of 1492 and that of to-day; but, great as has been this advance, the restrictions upon the transmission of intelligence and upon the movements of persons and of property are still the grand determining factors in human destiny.

The taxes on communication are still so high that only the well-to-do can make use of the telephone and the telegraph in their ordinary transactions, and the transportation tolls are so heavy that the ordinary laborer cannot go outside his immediate neighborhood to find employment or to educate his children or to expend his earnings. He is still the slave of his environment, and it is a very narrow environment. It is only on great occasions, such as a marriage, a birth, or a death, the removal of his family to a new home, or a very rare excursion, that the ordinary man can make use of that marvellous circulating and nervous system which the common interest demands should be always at his free service.

Many an opportunity to earn a day's wages is lost, many a family drags through life half fed, half clothed, ill-sheltered from the winter's cold and the summer's heat, simply because the bread-winners cannot pay the transportation taxes between their homes and the places where they are wanted; and this while great locomotives, capable of hauling 500 passengers in a train, run past our stations with average loads of but 42 passengers, loads hardly up to the capacity of a pair of mules. The lowest regular fare on a steam railway, two cents a mile, is an almost complete confiscation of the wages of a day laborer seeking occupation an hour's journey from his home, and a ride of 10 minutes to and fro absorbs full 10 per cent of his wages. To the man engaged in irregular employment, the man of all others most in need of the widest possible opportunities for obtaining occupation, the steam railroad is practically useless. Commutation tickets are unavailable in such cases. Even the swiftly moving electric car seldom attracts the ordinary laborer, for a five-cent fare to and from his home is a 10-per-cent income tax on a wage of a dollar a day and a 7½-per-cent tax on an income of $1.50 a day. To pay such a tax regularly is altogether beyond his ability.

Under present conditions the wage-worker must be within walking distance of his work, even though he be compelled to live in a city slum and though his family be forever shut out of the green fields and seldom see the blue heavens. And it is towards the city slum that his steps are tending, for the workman must follow his work, and the business of the country is rapidly concentrating itself in the great cities, while small places are being wiped out; their industries are being taken from them. Not only is the business of the country concentrating itself in our great cities—it is falling into the hands of a very few men in those cities; and the Hon. Chauncey M. Depew says that this is due to discrimination in freight rates in favor of the larger places and in favor of the larger dealers in those places.

These other facts are also worthy of notice, namely, a steadily growing discontent among the workmen compelled to follow their industries to the great cities, and a disposition to meet this spirit of discontent by an appeal to military force. In evidence of this statement it is only necessary to call attention to the immense fortresses recently erected in Boston and New York.

Checked in its fertilizing course, there is a congestion of the life-blood of the nation (its labor and its capital) at the great centres. That congestion must be relieved or the inflammation will continue to increase with all its dread consequences. The crisis is dangerous, but it is not to be met by the lancet. If it seems sometimes that the only difference between the past and the future is to be the difference between the savage of the dark forest and the savage of the dismal slum, it is because the masses of the people are not secured in the free and equal use of our systems of public communication and transportation.

The remedy would seem to be obvious. Make the railways, the tramways, the telegraph and telephone systems of the country, free to the use of the whole people in their ordinary transactions, and support these great public works by the ordinary forms of taxation. This done, we might raze our modern bastilles and disband our military forces, for the conditions which are the cause of our present dangers would soon pass away. Work and workmen would distribute themselves throughout the country where the circumstances were most favorable to the common welfare. The benefits accruing from every advance in "freedom to trade" would be equally divided among the whole people. The slum and the palace would both tend to disappear, for there would be neither excess of poverty nor excess of wealth. Each man would be master of himself in a sense the world has never yet known. This whole country would be open to every man for the disposal of his services and for the satisfaction of his wants. How it would widen, how it would equalize opportunities for labor and for enjoyment, if the entire system of railways, tramways, telegraphs, and telephones of this country were free to the ordinary use of the people.

And why not? Why support highways, schools, jails,

prisons, poorhouses, armies and navies, forts and fortresses,
by the ordinary forms of taxation, and leave these infinitely
more important public works to be supported by tolls, levied
not by the representatives of the people convened in their
public assemblies, but by private corporations and by private individuals endowed in respect to these tolls with practically absolute power?

Here lie the possibilities of the future. According as we
deal with this question shall we go backward or go forward.
The control of public communication and transportation,
the regulation of the movements of intelligence, of persons,
and of property, is the very highest attribute of sovereignty.
It includes the power of industrial life and industrial death,
as we have seen most graphically illustrated in the case of
the Standard Oil Company and its ruined competitors. It
involves our political liberties also. If the private managers
of our railways and tramways, our telegraph and telephone
systems, retain their present power, giving the free use or
comparatively free use of these public services to their
friends, while they exact, from the rest of us, the heaviest
possible tolls, the result must be a growing inequality of
opportunities, and in the end a state of things very much like
that which existed at Rome at the fall of the empire, a very
few dissolute rich men and a nation of discontented slaves.
On the other hand, managed by the public authority and
limited in use only by the public want, these great public
works would secure to every man ever widening opportunities and to the whole nation ever increasing prosperity.

But I do not propose to advocate such a radical change as
this to-day. I only ask that a single step in advance be
taken. My proposition is to bring the systems of public
transportation and communication under the control of the
postoffice, making ordinary travel and the ordinary use of
the telegraph and the telephone free, and determining the
tolls charged for special services and for the transportation
of property on the postal principle, adopting at the outset
the lowest rate now charged for the shortest distance for
any particular service as the uniform standard rate for
that class of service for all distances within the United
States.

And first as to the free conveyance of passengers and as to
the demand for it. Mr. W. M. Acworth, the distinguished
English writer on railroad problems, says: "If passengers
could travel free, their numbers would increase so enormously that it would be necessary to create a new railway
system to accommodate the existing goods traffic." There

is room, however, both in this country and in England, for a vast expansion of railway passenger traffic with the present equipment, for in neither country are the passenger locomotives used up to a tenth part of their capacity, and it is very safe to say that nôt an eighth part of the car equipment is used. Neither in England nor in this country does the average passenger train carry over forty-two persons—about two-thirds the capacity of a single American car. Every man, who rides in a railway car to-day, pays not only for the seat he occupies but for eight or nine seats kept empty by high fares.

And these prohibitive fares, confining the laboring classes to their narrow homes both for work and for pleasure, prevent the expansion of freight traffic by checking both the producing and the consuming powers of the population. Under free travel, wealth would increase so rapidly that the public would be quite able to create a new railway system when it became necessary.

We have an admirable illustration of both the public and the private benefits to be derived from free travel in the case of the free ferry established over the Thames, at Woolwich, in 1889. Mr. R. A. Cooper, of England, in his interesting pamphlet, "Free Railway Travel," says that, in the second year of its existence, this free ferry carried the equivalent of over 6,210,000 passengers, at a cost, including interest and repairs, of about £14,350. At a penny a passenger, the rate charged by the Great Eastern ferry boats which run alongside the free ferry, the cost would have been over £25,850. The saving to the public was therefore £11,500 for the year; and this from a ferry just established and capable of carrying, if necessary, 10,000,000 more passengers with scarcely any additional expense. The trade of Woolwich, moreover, was very largely increased, and land in North Woolwich which was recently a swamp was rapidly built over, the houses being occupied as soon as completed.

How keenly free travel would be appreciated by the general public is proved by the eagerness even of the most wealthy classes to get passes. It is evidenced again by the enormous use of the electric tramway system with its comparatively low fares and frequent service.

Some of our Connecticut towns have already inaugurated the custom of transporting school children free between their far-away homes and the central school, and with very great benefit.

During a good part of last year, one of the tramway lines of Savannah, Ga., was run at one-cent fares, and this low rate was attended with an actual increase in gross receipts, its cars transporting from 1,400 to 1,800 passengers per car per day. These figures mean the saving of many a weary journey to tired humanity; they represent the saving to the city of Savannah of just so much human energy for remunerative employment; they mean lower house rents and more comfortable homes; yes, and they mean profit to the tramway company as well, for they mean receipts of from $14 to $18 per day per car as against expenses of from $10 to $13.

It may be worth while right here to take note of one or two of the economies that will follow free travel. There will be no tickets and no ticket agents will be needed. The conductor, freed from his business of collecting tax receipts, will be able to dispense with the service of one or more brakemen in his train. The saving in these items will run up to many millions, and on our tramways it will be proportionately much greater, for the present system requires a tax-collector on every car (conductors on tramways are nothing but tax-collectors), at an expense varying from $1.80 per car per day, in some parts of the South, where the wages are 10 cents an hour, to $3.60 a car day (the tramcar day is 18 hours), in New England, with wages at 20 cents an hour. Free travel will effect a saving of from $600 to $1,200 per car per year, or about 20 per cent of the entire expenses.

The electric cars of Chemnitz, Saxony, are run without conductors and with a consequent saving to the company of 44,000 marks ($11,000) per year. The Saxon cars run as fast as ours and with but very few accidents. The tolls (less than 2½ cents each, less than one-half the ordinary American tolls) are paid into fare-boxes placed one at each end of a car.

But it is not enough to abolish the tax-collector from the railway and the tramway. Ordinary travel should be altogether free. Is a free railway an anomaly? There are thousands of them in existence to-day. What are the elevators in our city apartment and office buildings but vertical railways? And who ever heard of a landlord charging tolls for the ordinary transportation of persons and property on the railway which connects the different towns and villages located in his tower? And would it not be a most stupid thing for the owner of such a tower to allow a stranger to erect the vertical railway in the building and to exact such tolls as he pleased for the use of it? Would not the owner of the railway very soon become the owner of the tower?

And what is the difference in principle between this vertical railway running to and fro between earth and heaven and the horizontal railway that clings humbly to earth's bosom? If it is good business policy for the owner of the tower to run his heavenly road free of tolls and to support it by a general tax on the tower property, would it not be equally good business policy for our different communities to run our systems of earthly communication free of tolls and to support them by the ordinary forms of taxation? As to cost there can be no comparison between the two. The road from the nether to the upper regions must be infinitely the more expensive both in its construction and its maintenance.

Free travel, by ordinary public conveyance, does not however imply that all travel should be free. My proposition is simply to change the relation of the classes. The president of the Pennsylvania Railroad Company says that the passengers in Pullman cars do not pay half the cost of their transportation, and "the man who gets his dinner on the train to New York does not pay twenty-five per cent of the cost of that dinner. It is the poor men who sit in the common car and sit two or three on a seat, who support the railways of the country." "In India," says Mr. Horace Bell, the consulting engineer of the state railways, "the third-class travel affords the backbone of coaching receipts: the other classes might, as far as profit is concerned, be abolished; indeed on most lines their removal would be a positive gain." Not many years ago a leading railway manager in India stated that it would pay him to give every first-class passenger twenty rupees to stay away. It is said that the balance of loss from the first- and second-class service of the railways of England, north of the Thames, in the year 1890, was $1,625,000.

In other words, in America, in India, in England, and it may be very safely assumed, everywhere else in the railway world, the rich live on the charities of the poor. Now this surely is contrary to common sense and to common justice as well as to sound business policy. Travellers in Pullman cars, first-class passengers, should not only pay the actual cost of their own carriage but should also contribute of their abundance for the support of the general traffic without which they could not enjoy their luxuries. This does not, however, necessarily involve any increase in the charges made for *special* services.

President Roberts' statements as to the cost of Pullman travel are true, I believe, only because the rates are so high that comparatively few people can afford to use the Pullman cars. I doubt if on an average a fourth of the seats and berths of our Pullman cars are occupied. It is not by increasing transport taxes that Pullman cars are to be made a source of income or that the freight business is to be made more profitable. On the other hand, it is by making the rates low and uniform, so that cars which now go empty may then go full, and that men and women, now impoverished by tariffs which prohibit them from obtaining occupation outside their homes, may then be enabled so to widen their spheres of action as to obtain a comfortable living.

As to the actual cost at which persons and property can be transported by railway when the equipment is used up to its capacity, we have some valuable evidence. In 1881, the third-class fares on the East India Railway were reduced from about three-fourths of a cent a mile to one-half a cent, and "from the very first the effect of the reduced fare was clearly seen, not only in the increase of numbers and in the slow but steady increase of receipts, but also in the manifest advantage which it gave to goods traffic in facilitating the movement of the smaller traders." In 1892, the net earnings of this road, with fares of but $2\frac{1}{2}$ pies (five twelfths of a cent) a mile, were 9.62 per cent on its capital. The Madras road has lately adopted a rate of two pies (about one-fourth of a cent) a mile and with very encouraging results.

Mr. Bell believes that for the carriage of food, grains, minerals, and the lowest class of passengers the Indian rates are the lowest in the world. "At the same time," he says, "it is by no means to be assumed that rates and fares have reached their lowest remunerative level; indeed there is good reason for the belief that, in the class of goods above mentioned and in third-class passenger fares, further reductions are certainly to be expected in the near future and on sufficiently profitable conditions. The statistics of the railways which serve the poor and populous districts point to the certainty that with large numbers (and large numbers always follow low fares), low speed, and properly fitted vehicles, passengers could be carried at one pie (one-sixth of a cent) a mile and leave a profit of 20 to 30 per cent; the cost of carriage is a quantity varying with the volume of traffic, and it may be found that an even lower rate is possible."

The experience of India and indeed of the whole world proves that the one essential thing in railroad business is large volume of traffic (large average train-loads); and with rates low, stable, uniform, regardless of difference of distance, and with trains run to meet the necessities of the masses, there will invariably be a large volume of traffic.

The lowest average train-load of any of the Indian railways is over 126. The average train-load of the entire Indian railway system is over 200. The Madras road carries over 260 passengers in its average train, and the Bengal, Northwestern &.Tirhoot road over 290.

With average train-loads of 290 passengers, the cost per passenger on the New York, New Haven & Hartford railroad would be very little over one-third of a cent a mile, and a fare of one-half a cent a mile for ordinary travel would yield enormous profits.

In thinly settled Russia, under the new tariff of December, 1894, the third-class fare for short distances, .666 of a mile to 106.8 miles, is but a little over three-fourths of a cent a mile. For distances of 106.8 miles to 198.9 miles the rate is less than one-half a cent a mile, and for longer distances the fares are still lower. Eighty-one cents will carry a passenger 106 miles or as far as from Hartford to New York; $2.32 will transport a traveller 464 miles, or farther than from New York to Buffalo, and for a trip of 1,989 miles the fare is but $5.95. And our consul-general at St. Petersburgh says that if travel increases as it has increased under previous reductions of fares, there is every reason to believe that these low rates will not only be a great benefit to the Russian people but will also prove profitable to the railways. In Belgium workingmen's trains have been running for many years carrying men to and from their homes and their places of business, forty-two miles, six days in a week, for fifty-seven cents for the entire week's service, and these trains have been profitable.

On the eighth of August last, three excursion trains were run over the Cleveland, Canton & Southern railroad, from Zanesville, Ohio, to Cleveland and return, 286 miles, for seventy-five cents the round trip—less than three-tenths of a cent a mile. Each of these trains consisted of 10 cars carrying 700 passengers. The receipts therefore amounted to $525 per train trip—$2.125 per train mile, or nearly double the earnings of the average passenger train of the country and 50 per cent more than the earnings of the average train of the New York, New Haven & Hartford railroad, in 1890, when it was paying 10-per-cent dividends. The cost and time of these excursion trains as compared with the regular trains, was not much greater. But granting the cost to have been $1 a mile, or more than double the cost of the regular trains (.4719 in 1893), even then the cost to the railroad was only one-seventh of a cent a mile per passenger, and the profit of each passenger was over 45 per cent.

But the cost of transporting the passengers who will be induced by low fares to fill up the unoccupied capacity of our present railway equipment is lower than even these figures would indicate. The following calculation made by Mr. Acworth relates directly to the English railways, but it is equally applicable here: "If a passenger who would otherwise have stopped at home, were induced to go from London to Glasgow by the offer of a first-class ticket for threepence (6 cents), the company would, unless indeed there was no first-class seat available on the train, secure a net profit of 2½ pence (5½ cents), for the additional farthing (one-half cent) is an ample allowance for the cost of haulage. The figures in detail are as follows: Extra coal used, four pounds, cost three-sixteenths of a penny; extra oil, stores, and water, one-sixteenth of a penny; total four-sixteenths of an English penny, equal to one-half an American cent. Add say another half a cent for wear and tear of the seat and you have one cent. Up to the capacity of the railway equipment of a country the cost of the additional passengers who could be induced to travel by low fares would not be over one cent for a distance of 410 miles.

As to freight, the *Railroad Gazette* tells us that during the past few months the New York Central & Hudson River railroad has hauled grain from Buffalo to New York, 440 miles, for 3.69 cents a hundred pounds, less than 80 cents a ton, and these low rates, resulting in train loads of 1,800 tons (60 cars of 30 tons each), earned for the road over $3.24 a train-mile, or more than double the average earnings per train-mile of the railways of the country, and far more than the earnings per mile of its own average train.

But these figures not only show the low cost of railway transportation under a large volume of traffic—they also confirm the axiomatic truth that distance is not a factor that should be considered in the determination of rates, and thus clear the way for a very simple and practical solution of the whole railway problem. The mileage system of rates should be altogether abandoned, and so far and so long as our systems of public transportation are supported by tolls, those tolls should be determined on the postal principle, the lowest rate charged for the shortest distance for any particular service being adopted as the uniform standard rate for that class of service for all distances, and the whole business should be brought under the control of the post-office.

This system of disregarding distance in the determination of transportation taxes has been in use for many years on several of the great railway milk routes entering New York City, the rates being the same within distances of 200 miles, and says the interstate commerce commission: "It has served the public well. It tends to promote consumption and to stimulate production. It is not apparent how any other method could be devised that would present results equally useful or more just. It is upon the whole the best system that could be devised for the general good of all engaged in the traffic." Yes, and experience is rapidly proving that this system of grouping stations with a uniform standard rate, regardless of distance, is quite as applicable to other branches of railway traffic as to milk.

Potatoes are given the same rates from the different stations on the lines and branch lines of the New York, Philadelphia & Norfolk road within limits of 200 miles.

The grouping of stations with a uniform rate is very common in the coal districts. The entire Hocking Valley is grouped. In the Delaware peninsula, the rates on grain, flour, and other similar products are the same for a large group of stations.

All or nearly all the hundreds of railroad stations in New England, south of Portland, Me., are included in the group known as "Boston Points," from which the rates are the same on the same class of goods to each of the stations in even larger groups in the South and West.

In transcontinental traffic, all the Pacific Coast terminals, from Tacoma and Seattle, in the state of Washington, on the north, to San Diego, Cal., in the south, are in one group from which the rates are, in general, uniform to all the principal stations in each of the six great groups into which the railroad territory of the United States east of the Missouri River is divided. The carload rates on oranges are the same from Los Angeles, Cal., to all stations east of the Mississippi River, the same to Chicago, 2,265 miles, and to New York, 3,180 miles. The carload rates on grain are the same over the Northern Pacific Railway, from all its stations in the state of Washington, to St. Paul, Minn.

On petroleum and its products, the western-bound rates to San Francisco, Sacramento, Oakland, Stockton, Marysville, San Jose, Los Angeles, and San Diego, Cal., are the same over the all-rail lines, from all points in the United States east of the Missouri River.

In January, 1894, the Canadian Pacific road commenced to sell passenger tickets at the same rate, $40 first-class and $30 second-class, from St. Paul to Vancouver, 1,660 miles, to Portland, 1,990 miles, and to San Francisco, 2,760 miles.

The custom of giving large groups of stations a uniform rate on similar goods, in through business, has, indeed, become almost universal, and, as I have shown, it is not uncommon in local traffic. Milk, oranges, potatoes, coal, grain, passengers, are transported to-day, in numberless instances on our American railways, at the same rates, between stations varying in distance from one another and from the starting point, from a score of miles to a thousand.

Nor is this growing custom confined to the United States. The milk rates on the Great Western Railway of England, are the same for distances 10 miles to 100.

The stations in the coal regions are very commonly grouped both in Great Britain and on the Continent. The same rates are charged from coal stations in Germany to Bremen and to Hamburg, although the former is 71 miles further off than the latter.

In 1889, the railway stations of Hungary were grouped for long-distance traffic, within distances of 140 miles to 457 miles, with a uniform rate, by ordinary trains, first-class, $3.20, second-class, $2.32, third-class, $1.60, and by express, first-class, $3.84, second class, $2.80, and third-class $1.92.

In the summer of 1893, the Belgian government began selling passenger tickets good for 15 days over its entire network of railways, some 2,000 miles, for $10 first-class, $7.60 second class, and $5 for third-class tickets, thus placing its whole railroad system in one group.

As to the grouping of stations with a common rate in our city tramway traffic, every American knows how wonderfully profitable it has been to the tramways and what a boon it has proved to the people.

Nearly sixty years have passed since Sir Rowland Hill startled the people of England with his scheme of a "penny post," proposing at one sweep to reduce the average price of inland postage from 20 cents to 2 cents, and to carry a letter from Land's End to John O'Groat's at the same rate as from London to the nearest village. It was a new idea in those days, this placing all the postal stations of a great country in one group, with one uniform standard rate, and that the lowest rate then existing, and the postal authorities declared the reformer mad. But we all know the story of Mr. Hill's wonderful triumph. His plan was hardly made public before it attracted great and hearty support, and in a very short time it was carried into effect. Colony after colony and state after state followed in the wake of Old England. Rates were continually reduced, and in nearly every instance the postoffice revenue was greater at the reduced rate than when it was considerably higher.

In 1874 the International Postal Union was formed and nearly all the postoffices of the civilized world were soon brought into one great group with a uniform rate of five cents.

Several of the nations of Europe have also, in recent years, extended the sphere of the postoffice to the transmission of parcels, one pound to eleven in weight, grouping practically all products in one class and including in one or two groups all their respective towns and villages. The Imperial Parcels Post of Germany carries parcels up to 11 pounds, distances up to 10 miles, for $6\frac{1}{4}$ cents, and for all greater distances within the Empire for $12\frac{1}{2}$ cents.

Our own postoffice carries paper-covered books from the homes of book-publishers and news-agents to their customers, anywhere within our American empire, in parcels from one pound to a carload, for one cent a pound, and this by express trains. And now we find great railway corporations and groups of corporations giving to each of the stations in ever widening zones, the same uniform grouped rates, sometimes for persons, sometimes for property, almost universally in through business, and not infrequently in way traffic.

Is it not certain that we have discovered here the natural law for the determination of transportation taxes, and is it not time that this law, this best system that can be devised for the good of all engaged in the traffic, should be enforced by the only power to which its execution can be safely entrusted, namely, by the general government? The possibilities of our public transportation service when it is once devoted solely to the public welfare are altogether beyond imagination.

And what is true as to the conveyance of persons and property by tramway and railway is equally true as to the transmission of intelligence by telegraph and telephone. Three years ago, Postmaster-General Wanamaker declared that with the telegraph and the telephone under the control of the postoffice, one-cent letter postage, the world over, 10-cent telegrams, and 3-cent telephone messages would be near at hand.

Add to these low taxes on the transmission of intelligence, similar low and uniform taxes on transportation, on parcels, one cent a pound by express trains, and on ordinary freight, rates varying from $1.20 a ton first-class freight to 40 or 50 cents a ton on sixth class between any two stations in the country, ordinary travel free, and for special passenger service make the rate now charged for the shortest distance the uniform standard rate for all distances, and we should soon have such a condition of things in this country that the tramp, the pauper, and the criminal would disappear, and with them would go the slum, the poorhouse, and the jail.

"The natural effort of every man to better his own condition, when suffered to exert itself with *freedom and security*," says Adam Smith, "is so powerful a principle that it is alone and without any assistance, not only capable of carrying on society to wealth and prosperity, but of surmounting a hundred impertinent obstructions with which the folly of human laws too often encumbers its operations, although the effect of these obstructions is always more or less to encroach upon its freedom and to diminish its security." If these statements of the great Scotch lover of wisdom be true, what may we not expect from this wonder-working principle when both the inventor and the lawmaker unite for the removal of the natural and legal obstructions to its free action?

We are entering upon a new era, an era when the workers of the world are to be its rulers, when war and hate and robbery are to pass away, and a new standard is to be lifted on which is to be emblazoned the double motto,

"Liberty, Fraternity, Equality."
"Freedom to Trade, Peace on Earth, Goodwill among the Nations."

"Men, my brothers, men the workers, ever reaping something new,
That we have done but the earnest of the things that we shall do:

"If you'll dip into the future but where human eye can see,
You'll behold a glorious vision, all the wonders that shall be;

"See the heavens filled with commerce, argosies of magic sails;
Pilots of the purple twilight, dropping down with costly bales;

"Far along the world-wide whisper of the south wind rushing warm,
With the standards of the people plunging through the thunder storm;

"Till the war-drum throbs no longer and the battle-flags are furled
In the Parliament of man, the Federation of the world."

THE PEOPLE'S LAMPS.

BY PROF. FRANK PARSONS.

PART I. ELECTRIC LIGHTING (*continued*).

§ 4. *The Public Safety* calls for municipal control of electric service no less strongly than economy, justice, and the fair diffusion of wealth. In 1890 a committee of the New York Legislature found that "Sixteen deaths were directly traceable to the poor insulation and bad arrangement of the wires of the electric light companies of New York City." Fire Marshal Swene of Chicago reports 231 fires caused by electric light wires and lights during two years (1893–4) in that city. In his address last year to the 28th annual meeting of the National Board of Underwriters President Skelton said: "Concurrent action regarding our greatest enemy, electricity, seems to be imperative. There has been plenty of evidence that fires caused by electricity are growing alarmingly frequent, and inspections show that but few buildings in any community are safely wired. This great and increasing danger cannot be ignored. It threatens the very life of fire insurance." In Boston we have had emphatic object lessons on the danger of the wires; they not only have originated a number of disastrous fires, but almost always they greatly hinder the subduing of the flames, and injure more firemen than all other perils put together. The firemen very justly dread them more than they do the fire.

If our cities would take the light works and unite them not only with the water system, but with the fire department also, a great improvement would soon take place in the safety of our cities. The firemen would be careful about the wiring for it is a question of life with them. It would do the regulars good to have something to occupy part of their time, and by a judicious use of their idle hours the city could wire all buildings in proper style and bury the cables underground at a very small expense.

§ 5. *Electrical Politics* constitute the reverse side of the shield on whose front we have found Extortion. The companies are obliged to give due attention to politics in order to keep their right to obtain an exorbitant profit on light, and they are compelled to make large profits on light in order to give due attention to politics. They begin usually

by bribing the councils to get their franchises. Then
they have to keep on bribing to prevent the granting of
rival franchises, and measures looking to the reduction
of prices, and all other legislation injurious to their
interests. To secure immunity from interference with
their monopolistic right to overcharge—their inestimable privilege of taking something for nothing—
and to intrench themselves in the law, they put their
money and influence into politics, robbing the public with
one hand, and with the other bestowing a part of the booty
on the officers of the law, to keep them from stopping the
game. This is well known to be the situation in Boston,
New York, Brooklyn, Philadelphia, Chicago, Minneapolis,
and other large cities. In Northampton, Mass., it was
found that all the city government from the mayor down
were holders of stock in the electric lighting company. A
member of council in Paris, Ill., says: "The light companies
are composed of sharp, shrewd men. Their stock is distributed where it will do the most good. It was observed
that the company took special interest in city elections.
Men who never seemed to care who was made congressman,
governor, or president, would spend their time and money
to elect a man of no credit or standing in the community.
The question was, 'Are you for the light company?' "

One of the *Aegis* investigators questioned nearly every
large city in the United States upon this point, and
a great majority replied that the electric light companies are in politics, and some said that the companies
own and run the city. Mayor Weir of Lincoln, Neb.,
wrote: "The electric companies are in politics in
every sense of the word. They attempt to run our city
politics, and usually succeed." Similar words came from
the officials of Milwaukee, Kansas City, Sacramento, and
many other cities. Electrified politics are not a success for
the people; electricity is undoubtedly beneficial to the body
politic when properly administered, but it will not do to
leave the treatment to unprincipled quacks, who care nothing for the health of the patient, if they can only get his
money.

In one case public ownership has been crippled and
finally destroyed by the scheming of a private company.
Michigan City built a public electric light plant in 1886 with
84 arcs, for $7,500. During the first three years the cost per
arc was $43. Then the Electric Street Railway Co. wished
to buy the plant and had some backing in the government.
The opposition, however, was strong. The result was that

the cost mysteriously increased to $80 per arc, and at last in 1892 the plant was sold to the E. S. R. Co. for $2,500, the company agreeing to furnish the city with light at a cost not to exceed $75 per arc. The moral is that if a private company owns the government or the officers in charge of the light plant, it can nullify the benefits of public ownership. Public light works must be entrusted to men who are true to the interests of their employers. Fortunately such breaches of trust are very rare; so far as I know, this is the only instance. With this sole exception diligent search and questioning among the cities owning electric plants, has failed to reveal the least indication of corruption arising therefrom or connected therewith, the evidence being on the contrary that good government has been developed and strengthened, through the increased interest taken by the people in municipal affairs in consequence of their increased magnitude and importance.

§ 6. *Stock Watering* is another favorite pastime with electric light companies, as with all other companies except those of a military nature that have no stocks but of a kind with which water does not agree. We have already shown in § 3 that the capitalization of the Boston Electric Light Company is probably almost half water, and the symptoms are strong in the Edison also. In 1894 its capitalization was reported as $3,150,000 and it was assessed on $816,300—it was willing to pay dividends and interest on nearly four times the value it wished to pay taxes on. What a dainty plan it is for a little group of men (women are not yet sufficiently "developed," thank goodness) to pay in $100,000, and vote themselves stock to the amount on its face of $500,000! Or better still to issue a million of stock and bonds, keep a good lot of it, give your friends some, and the legislators and councilmen some, sell the rest, build the works with a part of the money you get from the "bloomin' public" in this quiet way, spend another part to buy the sort of politics and laissez-faire administration your business needs, and put the remainder in your pocket; then make some light, charge three or four times what it is worth, get a contract from your friends in power to light the city, turn in a small valuation to the assessors so as to make expenses light, but roll up the capitalization so as to spread out big profits over a large surface and make them look thin and small to the stingy people who are apt to object to a man's making a few hundred per cent,—nice plan, isn't it? almost as good as a bank robbery for getting hold of other people's funds, almost as good for rapidity and a great deal safer. And then if the people should wake up and attempt to take control you can put on an innocent look and tell them it's mean to ruin your trade, and if they insist they at least ought to buy up your plant at the entire amount of your capitalization.

How do you like the picture, my dear American citizen? You have to pay all the bills; you create the wealth that pays for the light plant or construct it with your own hands, and then you pay two or three times the worth of the light you use in order that a parcel of men, who fool you with some cunning accounts and slips of paper, may grow rich in return for the service of cheating you. Not all the companies are organized in this way—only the most unprincipled men turn the screws with all their power—but the principles set forth above are applied to a greater or less degree in a large proportion of corporations of every description. It is strange indeed that men who would die before they would pay one cent of tribute to a foreign prince under the name of tribute, will pay without a protest many millions of de facto tribute every year to the princes of deception, both foreign and domestic.

§ 7. *The Bad Service* rendered by many of the private companies is matter of common complaint. Philadelphia pays inspectors to test the arc lights nightly to see if the companies are living up to their contracts. The results are given in Chief Walker's reports. Many times the lamps fall far below the agreement. The latest report at hand (that for 1893, p. 108) shows that 7,100 lights were deducted from the bills of the various companies during the year. The *Aegis* of March 3, 1893, p. 168, gives a list of thirty-five cities in twenty states whose lamps were examined by experts and found to be far below the contract agreement.

Public ownership is not an absolute guarantee of good service, but a public monopoly has at least no interest opposed to good service. A business is apt to be managed in the interests of its owners. If the people own the lights they will be more apt to get what they want than under an antagonistic ownership. The servants of the people, with a good civil service, will be more apt to do the people's will, than the servants of a company whose will is opposed to the people and who are in the business to get all they can and give no more than they must.

§ 8. *Competition Does not Solve the Problem and Cannot.*—The people have sought relief in competition, but have found it foolishly expensive to build two or more plants in the same area, each one capable of doing the whole work of

the district, and have discovered that it is always a failure
in regard to prices, because the companies, after a little, are
sure to combine, openly or in secret, and lift the prices
higher than ever, in order to pay dividends on the double
investment. Allen R. Foote, the head of the Electrical
Department of the Eleventh Census, says: "There can be no
competition in the electric service of a city. Separate
companies will quickly combine or agree on rates."

§ 9. *Regulation is Likewise a Failure.*—Finding the effort
to secure competition worse than useless, the people have
appointed commissioners to conserve the public interests,
keep the companies in sight of the law, and regulate rates,
but they have proved to be powerless to give the people
reasonable rates because of the mass of watered stock in the
hands of innocent purchasers, who have a right to demand
that the company be allowed to charge rates which will
enable it to pay dividends on all its stocks. The federal
courts hold that they have this right under the constitution
of the United States, any regulation that makes it impossible to pay a reasonable dividend being in reality confiscation. This, and the power of the company to tune its reports to any song that suits its ear, renders the commission
of little òr no account, except to raise the taxes a little
higher so as to pay their salaries. The commissioners do
not even succeed in stopping unjust discriminations by the
companies. In fact, the commissioners are not infrequently
men who sympathize with all the corporation methods and
monopoly tactics of the companies they are appointed to
watch. Even when they try to do their duty by the public
they are frequently crippled by the power of the corporations in legislature and council, by the indefiniteness or
unreliability of their returns, by the water in their stock,
and by their cunning evasions of the law. Massachusetts has a commission system which has been referred
to by the advocates of private enterprise all over the
world, as the perfection of corporate control, and yet
it has failed to secure reasonable rates (they are more
*un*reasonable in Massachusetts than in many places that
have no commissions, and are above the average charges
for the whole United States), has failed to secure safety or
good quality, or a stoppage of discriminations or violations
of law, all of which facts are abundantly proved by the confessions in its own reports. And there is no other state in
the Union that shows so much anxiety as Massachusetts
to adopt public ownership of the electric lights; in a single
year, twenty-five out of its 205 towns and cities having

more than 1,500 population acted upon the question, seventeen of them establishing a public system or voting for it, and eight appointing committees to investigate the subject. Regulation is capable of accomplishing much more than it ever has yet in America, but at its best it can never solve the monopoly problem. It is only an expensive makeshift, for it does not destroy the antagonism of interest between the monopolist and the public, which is the cause of all the evils of private monopoly.

§ 10. *Public Ownership the Only Remedy.*—Competition and regulation have failed and must always fail. One relief only is left: there is no escape from private monopoly but in public monopoly. That, with a good civil service, solves all the difficulties, and it is the only thing that can solve them because it is the only thing that can remove the antagonism of interest which is the taproot of the evils of monopoly.

When we examine cities that have already adopted this solution, we find economy, impartial administration, regard for public safety, efficient service, and a decided gain for good government—all the evils of private monopoly overcome, and no new evils introduced, if the civil service is guarded, which it is our duty to see done for the sake of good government in general, as well as in order to enjoy in the fullest degree the benefits of the public ownership of monopolies.

Public ownership is essential, not only to the highest economy, safety, and political purity, but also to the full attainment of those further fundamental purposes of statesmanship, the diffusion of wealth and the substitution of coöperation in the place of conflict.

§ 11. *The Current of Opinion and Events Runs Swift and Strong toward the Municipalization of Electric Light.*—In 1892, 125 cities in the United States owned and operated electric light works, in 1893 the *Aegis* found 190 cities and towns in the United States operating their own electric plants, and now there are more than 200.

In England, Scotland, and Wales more than 160 towns and cities own and operate their gas works, and a large number of them unite electric light works with the gas plants. In Germany a number of important cities have adopted this reform, among them Dresden, Darmstadt, Metz, Breslau, Barmen, Hamburg, Konigsberg, Dusseldorf, Cologne, Lubeck, etc. Berlin in 1888 made a contract with the Berlin Electric Light Company which provides that the city shall receive ten per cent of the company's gross receipts; if the company earns more than six per cent on its actual investment the city is to receive twenty-five per cent of the excess, in addition to the ten per cent of gross receipts; the city lighting is to be done at very low rates, and rates to private consumers are outlined by the agreement; the city officers have the fullest powers of inspection of the management and accounts; and the city has the right to buy the entire plant any time after Oct. 1, 1895, on a basis of valuation carefully provided for in the contract.

How strongly the tide is moving toward public ownership in America may be seen in the fact that not only the cities owning municipal light works are nearly unanimous in praise of the system, but in a majority of the sixty-five cities with private ownership of light that were examined by the Evansville committee, the officers were of opinion that public ownership would be best. Only eight out of the sixty-five answered "No" to the question, "Should cities do their own lighting?" Thirty-six answered emphatically in favor of public ownership, and twenty-one either had no opinion to express or did not wish to express the opinion they had. When we remember that answering "Yes" to such a question means the political opposition of the electric companies without reference to party, and probably the opposition of other corporations (for when a man is once tainted with this heresy of public ownership there's no depending on him to do the will of any corporation), and when we remember that even silence in the face of such a question —the great question of the age to the companies—would render the silent officer an object of doubt and distrust to some of the chief builders of politics, electors to offices, and providers of fat positions,—when we remember all this, the Evansville record is even more remarkable than the rapidity with which municipalities are going over to the public camp or their almost universal satisfaction with the results of their pilgrimage.

There is hope even of our largest cities. In Philadelphia Mayor Stuart, Mayor Warwick, and many other prominent city officers have favored and do favor public ownership of electric light. In Boston a committee of the common council has just reported unanimously and with the strongest emphasis in favor of public ownership in this city. The committee visited ten cities east and west. Their report, dated Oct. 10, 1895, is a very interesting and important addition to the literature of the subject. Their study of Chicago led them to the conclusion that when the city puts its four plants into full operation the cost per arc will be reduced to $60 even with 8-hour labor at good pay. In Springfield they

found the situation reported to me by the mayor and set
forth at the close of this article. They discovered that
Bloomington, Ill., saved enough in five years to pay for the
plant, etc. The committee tested Table X of the August
ARENA, p. 381, and finding it correct inserted it in their
report. The committee found the operating cost in the
cities visited by them to be $43 to $60 except in Detroit
where the cost is $75 because of very incomplete operation
as yet, and in Chicago, where as we have seen the exceptionally good treatment of labor lifts the rate. The committee
sums up its conclusions as follows:

> The actual cost of construction will not exceed $168 per arc for
> an overhead system of 3,000 arcs in Boston, and your committee are
> positive that they are not in error in making this statement. The
> additional cost of real estate will of course depend upon the loca-
> tion, but your committee believe that such locations can be secured
> as to bring total cost of plant, including land and buildings, not
> over $250 per arc.
>
> Assuming that an estimate of $250 per arc is correct, the cost to
> the city of a 3,000-arc plant (600 lights in excess of present needs)
> would be $750,000. The interest on the investment, a fair charge for
> depreciation, and well-paid labor, would, in the opinion of your
> committee, make the total cost not over $75 per arc, and there
> would be a net saving to the city of at least $125,000 per year. . . .
>
> The City of Boston should not pay more than $75 per arc per
> year for its electric lighting, pending the establishment of a munici-
> pal electric-light plant.

The report closes with a recommendation that the legislature be requested to grant Boston the immediate right to
establish an electric plant. In reply to a criticism on their
report, the committee strongly reaffirm their conclusions
and state that since 1882 Boston has actually paid the
Electric Light Companies $2,125,000 for services which
would have cost but $800,000 under public ownership
according to the experience of cities that have been and
are making their own light; in other words, public ownership would have saved Boston taxpayers one and one-third
millions in the last dozen years on public lights alone.

§ 12. *How to Municipalize Electric Light.*—Generally the
city acquires existing plants or builds a new one of its own.
Neither plan is free from difficulty. It is wasteful to duplicate electric systems in the same streets, and it is the method
of war. On the other hand, purchase quite often involves
injustice. It is unfair to the taxpayers to buy existing
plants at the exorbitant values usually put upon them by
their owners and transformed into "market" values by
means of watered stock and heavy overcharges; and it is

unfair to bona fide holders of stock paying full value in open market, to take the plant at less than its market value.

In the case of a national purchase the conflicting interests of stockholders and taxpayers may be harmonized by the issue of national currency in payment of stock and bonds, which would throw no special loss on any individual, would distribute over the whole country the burden of a change that is for the benefit of the whole country, and would also be a great advantage in itself as a moderate expansion of our finances and a mild relief from the nervous prostration that has followed our long struggle with the national grippe called "contraction." In such a case there is a public benefit to balance the payment of watered values.

But a city cannot issue currency, and the collateral benefit to the financial system falls out of the scales. There is left simply the purchaser of watered stock on the one side, and the public on the other—one of them must lose. It is clear ethically that the taxpayer has the superior right. The watering of stock is a fraud. Even if authorized by the people's agents, it was an authorization without authority—the people never gave their agents a right to sanction such an outrage. The purchaser of stock knows of the prevalent practice of watering, knows that it is a fraud on the people's right of eminent domain, and should be held bound to inquire, and to take his stock subject to the right of the people to reclaim the franchise at actual value on the basis of fair charges for the service rendered, considering the labor and capital really involved.*

If the courts had taken this view of the matter at the start, there would probably have been very little watering done. But as it was the judges held and continue to hold that when the people take private property for public use they must pay its full "market value," and in the case of a franchise the market value includes whatever the watered stock will bring in the market.

The market-value principle is on the whole a beneficent one, entirely just in reference to the mass of cases in the early law by the decision of which the principle was established. But the application or extension of the principle to modern corporations has led the courts to take a position the illogic of which is revealed not only by the fundamental considerations of justice already noted, but even by the

---

* If abstract justice could be reduced to practice, we would take from the taxpayers the actual value of the property and no more; settle the bonds and pay market values to the bona fide holders of stock as far as the purchase money and the remaining assets of the company would do it, and leave the managers who watered the stock to bear the loss. The trouble would be to locate the sin.

basic principles of the competitive system of which these
corporations and their methods are a part. The people
have a right to set up a rival plant. Ten men have this
right with the authority of the people, or a thousand men,
or the people may do it themselves directly. Of course the
right is questionable ethically except as the best means of
conquering a greater evil; but competition gives the right
unreservedly, and the courts recognize it most fully. Yet
this right means the right to squeeze the water all out of a
private plant. How, then, can it be logically held that the
people have no right to squeeze out the water by the easy
method of a just appraisal of actual investment, but must
resort to the clumsy and expensive method of a rival business? It is true that the constitution does not permit the
taking of property except upon due process of law, which
involves the right to a judicial hearing, and that the people
cannot take private property except for public use and upon
just compensation. But it is true also that the courts have
full power to decide what constitutes just compensation,
and that market values inflated by fraudulent means are not
a true measure of just compensation. The fair measure is
the value the franchise would have on the basis of reasonable charges considering the labor and capital involved. and
the returns to similar labor and capital in the open field of
moderate competition. After the long line of decisions
affirming the market-value test, it is not easy to change the
law, and much injustice must result in any case—to the public if the law remains as it is, to individual stockholders if
it is changed.

Perhaps the very best way would be to provide that on
and after a specified date (a few years subsequent to the
passage of the law) all persons buying corporate stocks and
bonds should be deemed to take with notice of the fraud
called "watering," and should hold subject to the right of
the people to take the corporate property at its just value
purged of the said fraud and of all other frauds, viz., the cost
of duplication plus whatever sum the said corporation may
have paid into the public treasury in purchase of its franchise. The passage of an act holding stockholders to notice
would make buyers cautious, and market values would fall
toward the true level as the time approached for the law to
take effect. The courts fully recognize the power of the
public to regulate rates so long as reasonable dividends remain, and if water were not in the way, the earning capacity
of a company could be reduced so that its market value
would at least approach the just figures.

Another law that would do good would be a provision that any town or city should have a right to purchase property within its limits at a price not exceeding thirty per cent advance on the value at which the said property is assessed with the owner's knowledge at the time an application for said purchase is filed in court by the town or by any ten respectable citizens on its behalf, with fair allowance of course for improvements made between the application and the actual purchase. In other words, the amount on which a property owner pays taxes shall be held to be at least seventy per cent of its real value by his admission.

Another bit of legislation very greatly needed is the emancipation of municipalities. They are for the most part tied to the apron strings of the state, and cannot move without the consent of their maternal guardian. Our cities are not of age nor full discretion; they do not enjoy self-government and cannot run a wire along their own streets without the permission of the other towns, cities, farms, and districts in the state. There should be legislation in every state granting to cities and towns the privilege of home rule; in respect to their own internal affairs they should govern themselves. In Massachusetts after three years' struggle we succeeded in obtaining chap. 370 of the Acts of 1891 which enables "cities and towns to manufacture and distribute gas and electricity" for their own use or for sale to their citizens. There must be a two-thirds vote in each branch of the council and an approval by the mayor in each of two consecutive years, and then a ratification by a majority of the voters at the polls. In towns there must be a two-thirds vote in two town meetings. If there is a private plant in the place when the first vote is passed, and it is suitable to the municipal use, its owners may compel the city or town to buy said plant at its fair market value, including as an element of value, by the law of 1891, "the earning capacity of such plant based on the actual earnings being derived from it at the time of the final vote." Chap. 454 of the Acts of 1893 repealed the quoted words, gave the city after the first vote a right to demand a schedule of property from the private companies, required the companies to file the said schedule within thirty days after the request if they wished to retain their right to compel a purchase, made a number of concessions in the interest of the public in case the property is not desirable, and left the compensation to cover *the fair market value of the plant*, there being no words referring to the franchise, or to the earning capacity either, except words of exclusion and repeal. This looks as though the people of

Massachusetts *might* obtain justice in these cases. The franchises were theirs originally; they were lent to the companies free of charge; the companies have made a good deal of money out of the loan; it is perfectly proper to reclaim the franchises upon payment of the real value of the improvements the companies have made.

The provision requiring a two-thirds vote for two consecutive years, is oppressive, and was probably intended to kill the law by giving the companies a year after the first vote in which to secure the mayor or enough councilmen to prevent a second successful vote as required. The desire of the people for public ownership has been so great, however, that they have been able again and again to fulfil the conditions of the law and beat the companies on their own ground.

A city may borrow the money to buy or build and gradually pay off the debt out of the taxes saved by the lower cost of light, or from the receipts if the plant is a commercial one. If borrowing is impracticable the city may still obtain a public plant without increased taxation. For example, Springfield, Ill., was paying $138 per full arc on the moon schedule. The city was aware that the price was too high, but could not borrow money to build because of the limit on its borrowing power. It therefore made a contract with a body of sixty citizens by which the latter were to build a plant, supply full arcs on moon schedule at $113 a lamp, apply all surplus above running expenses and seven per cent interest on their investment to the cancellation of the capital account, and when this process pays for the property turn it over to the city free of debt. A 450-arc plant costing $70,000 has been built under this contract; 300 arcs are in operation; the plant is run by two electricians who have contracted to supply light for $60 a lamp; the city pays $113 a lamp, the extra $53 going to pay interest and cost of the plant, which it will do in about five years. In addition to this all public buildings are lighted with incandescents free of charge, and 25 per cent of the gross receipts for commercial lighting is credited to the city. Such are the facts as they come to me in a letter from Mayor Woodruff. The city is saving $25 a lamp and paying for the plant at the same time; in five years it will own the plant free, and will then get its light for less than one-half what it formerly paid to a private company; and during the entire process of purchase there isn't a dollar of debt upon the city, nor any increase of taxation, but a decrease of it from the very start. Springfield has taught her sister cities a valuable lesson; and yet fine as her method is, it is not so good as purchase for cash if the city is able, for that would save to the people the interest at seven per cent that now goes to the parties who built the plant.

NOTE 1. — AUTHORITIES.

In addition to visitation, correspondence, and the study of municipal reports, the committee has examined many electrical publications, and numerous discussions of public lighting. Some of those most useful to the general student are as follows: Group A.— 1. Electrical Census of New York, 1890, Allen R. Foote. 2. Bulletin 100 of the 11th Census, dealing with 50 of the larger cities of the United States. 3. Senate Mis. Doc. 56, 2d sess. 51st Cong. tabulating prices in 500 cities and towns under private ownership. 4. House Ex. Doc. No. 15, 1st Sess. 52d Cong. useful facts tabulated by the Electrical Commission of the Dist. of Columbia. 5. The Reports of the Mass. Gas and Electric Light Commissioners. 6. W. J. Buckley's "Electric Lighting Plants," D. Van Nostrand, N. Y., 1894. 7. Quarterly Publications of the Amer. Statistical Asso., Mar., June, 1893. "Cost Statistics of Public Electric Lighting," by Victor Rosewater. 8. The directories of Whipple, Brown, Johnson, etc., which may be found in any first-class library.

The data recorded by these authorities are supposed to have been gathered and arranged without argumentative purpose, and solely to disseminate information and increase our scientific knowledge. So far as I can judge, the work is free from any intent to support the opinions of the authors. It is true that Allen R. Foote, the head of the Electrical Department of the last census, is strongly opposed to public ownership, as his magazine articles clearly show, and that the Massachusetts Commission has been charged with manifesting a very peculiar solicitude for the interests of the private companies (see the testimony of Mr. Williams and the remarks of Mayor Matthews in the Bay State Gas Trust Investigation, pp. 17, 21, 75, 76.) It does not appear, however, that these personal factors have affected the returns unless perhaps their unconscious influence may have produced the remarkably clumsy arrangement of some of the electrical tables of the Census (making the columns of cost wellnigh worthless for purposes of comparison) and the equally remarkable *omissions* of both reports. I am assured by the Massachusetts Commissioners that they are fully aware of the imperfections of their reports especially in respect to the total output of electric companies, and they have tried hard to remedy the trouble even introducing a bill to require the companies to make proper returns, but the measure was defeated.

Mr. Buckley is not interested one way or the other in the question of public ownership; he writes for engineers in a thoroughly scientific way. Chief Walker also is simply a scientific electrician, "conservative and careful, and thoroughly master of his business," as Director Beitler says in his message to the mayor. The chief's estimates are given in Director Beitler's report (see next group).

Group B.— 9. "Electric Street Lighting," by R. J. Finley, *Review of Reviews*, Feb. 1893, p. 68. 10. Professor Ely's " Problems of To-day," pp. 260–273, 3d Ed. 1890. 11. The Report of Director of Public Safety, Abraham M. Beitler, to the Mayor and Councils of Philadelphia, Jan. 8, 1894, printed in the Journal of Select Council Vol. II, Oct. 5, 1893, to Mar. 30, 1894, p. 117 et seq., and containing, 12 a copy of the very full report made by a Committee of the City Councils of Youngstown, Ohio. 13. The Report of the Evansville Committee, Feb. 28, 1894, an admirable statement which, with the Report of Springfield, Ill., is published in *Light, Heat and Power* for March, 1894, and in the *Engineering News* for Apr. 12, 1894. Springfield followed the advice of its committee and built a plant in the manner narrated in the closing paragraph of the text; 14. The *Ægis* of Wisconsin University (where Professor Ely is now) for Mar. 3, 1893; 15. Rev. Walter Vrooman's "Public Ownership"; 16. Victor Rosewater's article in the *Independent* March, 1890, and 17 the Providence Advance Club Leaflet No. 3 (1891) may also be referred to. The documents of this group come from persons who favor public ownership and who wrote with argumentative purpose. Since these groups were made up the important report of the Boston committee has come to hand (see § 1[1]).

Group C.— 18. H. A. Foster on "Public Lighting," in the *Electrical Engineer*, Sept. 5, 1894. 19. M. J. Francisco on "Municipal Ownership." 20. The Report of the Committee of Philadelphia Councils printed in the same volume with Director Beitler's Report. These come from sources antagonistic to public ownership. Mr. Foster's article, however, is written in a spirit of fairness that puts to shame the intense partisanship and distorting personal interest elsewhere manifested in this group (see note below).

NOTE 2. — BIAS AND MOTIVE.

It is of great importance to remember that those who oppose public ownership usually do so from motives of self-interest of a low type, or from the bias of conservative training resisting change and new ideas by instinct and reflex action, or from both these motives; while those who advocate public ownership generally do so from a conviction that it will be for the good of the community — a conviction reached in many cases after long, earnest, painstaking study that has overcome preconceived opinions to the contrary. Such advocacy, moreover, is frequenty opposed to the selfish interests of the advocate, and made at serious loss and inconvenience.

It is perfectly possible for a man to oppose the municipalization of electric lighting from motives as pure and lofty as those which lead Professor Ely, Editor Flower, Mayor Stuart of Philadelphia, Mayor Pingree of Detroit, Mayor Cregier of Chicago, Dr. Lyman Abbot, Dr. Taylor, Director Beitler and many other distinguished men to advocate it; but in general personal interest is a strong factor in the arguments of the opposition, while it has little or no place in the advocacy of public ownership. The committee of Philadelphia Councils was controlled by men intensely favorable to the private companies as the report shows upon its face. The chairman made no effort to ascertain facts but devoted himself to a direct and determined attack upon Director Beitler's report, calling in Mr. Cowling, manager of the Powelton Electric Company, to testify that the director's estimate of 15 cents per arc per night was too low and ought to be over 40 cents — the Powelton Company is one of those from which the city buys light at the rate of 45 cents a night, or $164 a year. It would indeed be curious if the manager of the Powelton could not show how foolish it would be for the city to do anything that would interfere with such a contract, yet his figures are mild compared with what the chairman of the committee attempted to force the director to accept. For example, Mr. Cowling's estimate for real estate was $35,000, while the chairman of the committee placed that item at $75,000 and another committeeman wanted to make it $125,000 for a 400-arc light plant. The animus of the committee is further shown in the fact already mentioned that the pamphlet resumè of the investigation published for free distribution, entirely omits the report of Director Beitler and the estimates of Chief Walker, and publishes only the chairman's attack on Beitler and Manager Cowling's estimates.

M. J. Francisco's pamphlet is no better in motive He is attorney for an electric light company, and has been president of the National Electric Light Association. He is at the head of a company in Rutland, Vt., which the *Ægis* says was charging $280 per arc per year in 1893. In trying, therefore, to justify the high rates of the private companies against the indictments of Groups A and B, he was simply acting the part of a man accused of theft endeavoring to shield himself and his accomplices, and vindicate the right to continue his profitable enterprise. Mr. Johnston of the *Ægis* consulted Chicago's chief of construction and other officers in reference to Francisco's statements about that city, with the following result: "In this pamphlet Francisco says that part of the operating expenses are charged to the police and fire departments. Mr. Carrol says not one cent is so charged." (Indeed Francisco must have thought the officers of fire and police were sleepy gentlemen to allow such accounting — they wish, like other officers, to make as good a showing as possible for their own departments.) "Francisco figures linemen's salaries at $2,500. There is not a lineman employed by the city; all the wires are underground. The cost of coal per lamp is given by Francisco at $40, while the real cost is but $27, and in nearly every calculation, Francisco has juggled with the facts in order to prove his theory."

Mr. Foster's case is very different. He also has been a prominent officer of the National Electric Light Company, and has done considerable writing upon electrical subjects. The *Electrical Engineer* sent letters to 150 of the towns and cities that own and operate electric light works, received replies from forty-nine, and employed Mr. Foster to write them up. The *Electrical Engineer* is strongly antagonistic to public ownership, and Mr. Foster's views lean the same way. His bias has led him perhaps to adopt a very high rate of depreciation, and to make some errors of statement and comparison which he might have eliminated had not the results of the errors been favorable to his views and so lulled his watchfulness to sleep. But on the whole his intent to be fair is very apparent. For example he says, "The tone of all communications from those favoring the municipal side seems to have taken it for granted that the results shown would tell that side sufficiently well, and it must be admitted that in quite a number of cases such has been the fact." Again, "Somewhat over half [of the 34 places fully reported and in successful operation of public light works] are places where it is very doubtful if a commercial or private plant could be made to pay under any circumstances." And still again, "In all fairness it may be said that the much vaunted better management in private hands does not exist in fact, the men in charge of city plants comparing quite favorably with those in charge of private plants of similar size" (*Electrical Engineer*, Sept. 5, 1894, pp. 183, 184, 189.)

NOTE 3.—FALSE COMPARISONS.

In handling large masses of figures some errors are almost sure to creep in. The original information may be inaccurate, the author may make a mistake in using his data, the copyist, the printer, or the proof-reader may introduce a few variations to relieve the monotony of statistical discussion ; but there are no such excuses for the mischievous processes of thought that pervade so many of the essays on this subject on both sides of the question. The lofty motives of reformers do not, unfortunately, protect them entirely from illogic. They are not apt to resort to intentional falsehood nor to be influenced by selfish considerations, but they are nevertheless under the necessity of guarding themselves against the dangers of overstatement, of giving too ready a credence to all that seems favorable to them, and of underrating or ignoring the arguments, ideas, and feelings of their opponents.

Of the defective processes of thought just referred to, the most important is false comparison. It appears in numerous forms. One of the commonest is the *fallacy of averages*. It is a pleasing sort of condensation to lump a hundred cities in a couple of averages and lay down a generalization to the effect that private lighting is twice as costly as public. This result was obtained not only by Evansville, but by Mayor Pingree of Detroit and by the committees of Peoria, Springfield, Haverhill, and Scranton, all finding the average cost in public plants to be about $50 to $60, and in private companies twice as much. These averages do not add fixed charges to the reported expenses of public stations — an omission justified in some cases but not in all. The *Ægis* investigation avoided this error and found an average of $77.68 total cost per arc at an average candle-power of 1918 and an average run of 7.9 hours per night — $50 operating cost and $27.68 interest, depreciation, taxes, etc. Interest, as we know, does not belong in the calculation; depreciation was put at 5 per cent, which is too high, and taxes at 2 per cent on the whole value, which is also too high (see supra). The *Ægis* investigators found 224 private companies throughout the United States reported in Brown's Directory with an average charge of $102.40 for the same lamp running an average of 6.8 hours, or over an hour less each night than the public plants; and if the correction is made to 7.9 hours the average charge of the private companies would be $116. In Massachusetts 67 private companies make an average charge of $98.96 for a lamp averaging 1473 c. p. and burning 5.6 hours; correcting to 1900 c. p. and 7.9 hours we have an average charge of $146 in Massachusetts as compared with $77.50 for public service. Bulletin 100 of the eleventh census puts the average price paid under contract with private companies in 47 cities of more than 100,000 population in 23 states, at $139.31, and in the 24 largest cities of the United States the Federal Commission found the average price paid by the city to a private company to be $140 per arc. Bulletin 100 is entirely unreliable, as has already been seen, and as will more fully appear directly; any average based on it will be below the truth for standard service, because it includes sub-arcs and incandescents with the full arcs.

If the student wishes the averages resulting from the data of this report he may construct them for himself; the committee prefers to deal with specific cases and comparisons in which every element is taken into account.

When the individual cases that form the average are carefully classed, or the service rendered is accurately averaged as well as the cost, the results may have value, but the fact so frequently urged by reformers, that the average yearly cost per street lamp in cities possessing their own electric plants is only half the average yearly cost per street lamp in cities securing light by contract with private companies, while very suggestive, and really an understatement of the advantages of public ownership as revealed by a careful analysis of many specific cases, is nevertheless in itself entirely devoid of probative force. The average yearly service per lamp in the cities under private contract may be double the average service in the public plants; we cannot know the real meaning of the average unless we tabulate the elements of production in all the cities that enter into it, or those elements at least which are not known to be so nearly uniform as to cause no appreciable or important variations in the cost.

Take a specific case. A writer obtains the prices of light per arc year in a number of cities under public ownership and in another group under private ownership, takes the average of each group, $53 and $114 perhaps, and then infers or leaves the reader to infer that public ownership is much cheaper than private. That is the truth as we know, but such averages do not prove it; with another selection of cities the average might be against public ownership. Moreover the $53 represents only running expenses, while the $114 represents total cost, and the cities of the private group may get two or three times as much light, or have to pay two or three times as much for power and labor as the cities of the public group, for all that usually appears in these investigations of averages. The town of B gets a 1200-c.-p. lamp 6 hours for $50; C gets a 2000-c.-p. lamp 8 hours for $56; the average cost is $53 — the average cost of what? D pays $100 for a sub-arc all night, and E pays $128 for a full arc moonlight schedule; the average cost is $114 — the average cost of what? Is the average thing that is paid for the same in the two cases? Does the word cost mean the same in both cases? Or is the whole statement a compound pun? A certain music box costs $50, and a certain piano $200; the average cost is $125 — but the difficulty is to tell what it is the cost of. If you went to another city and found cornets selling for $30 and parlor organs for $100, would you be justified in taking the average, $65, and proclaiming that musical instruments were cheaper in the latter city than in the former?

This fallacy of incongruous averages is to be found in Census Bulletin 100, in the *Ægis*, in Mr. Finley's article in the *Review of Reviews*, February, '93, in Victor Rosewater's first article, in Francisco's "Municipal Lighting," in Horatio Foster's essay, and in many of the reports of local committees.

If care is taken to see that all the units in a group are of the same sort the average may be very useful, and such averages are to be found in electrical discussions mingled with the incongruous sort which is the only sort we wish to condemn per se. The true way to study electric light is to find the cost of a standard service under specific conditions, and determine the effect of all possible departures from those conditions — then you are in a position to say what should be the cost of a given service under given conditions and ascertain if the present rate is too high. During this process units that are essentially alike may be grouped and averaged to obtain the mean of the variations produced by one or two unreduceable causes, such as the personal qualities of superintendents, etc.

Imperfect averages are not the only subjects of false comparison. Sometimes the cost per lamp hour or candle-power hour or kilowatt hour is used as a basis of comparison, but it is not valid unless the variations in the conditions of production are taken into account. It does not even eliminate the question of schedule, for if two plants are equal in every way except that one runs all night and the other to midnight, the cost per lamp hour, etc., will be considerably less in the former than in the latter. If the cost per candle-power were the same in the two cases, the all-night lamp would cost twice as much as the midnight lamp, whereas we know the difference is only one-fifth — so that an all-night plant that charges the same per candle-power as a midnight plant is charging a great deal too much if the midnight charge is a proper one and other things are equal. To compare the price per lamp hour in a commercial plant running day and night with the lamp-hour cost in a street plant running only during the night or part of the night, for the purpose of throwing discredit on the latter, would be very unfair; the street plant may be well managed and give its service at cost, and yet the hourly rate may differ little or none from that of the other plant which is making fifty per cent profit because of the advantage its commerce gives it. New York companies make a difference of 10 cents a night in their bids for street lamps located in streets where no commercial lighting can be obtained — $36.50 more per year for a standard arc without commercial environment. The volume of business and the proportion of the capacity in use also affect the lamp-hour rate as seriously as the annual rate. How great such effects may be will be seen from the report of Pres. Sir John Pender to the directors of the Metropolitan Electrical Supply Co. of London a few years ago, which said in substance, "Our working expenses with 30,000 lights, are with few exceptions, the same to all intents and purposes as they will be when we are giving our maximum supply of 114,000 lights." The president went on to say that as they were making a profit with 30,000 lights, the business would be a very good one when they were running 114,000 at a "comparatively small increase of expenses." A number of the letters received by this committee from municipal superintendents, stated that their plants were run at half or two-thirds capacity but could be run at full capacity with little additional expense, reducing the cost per lamp by nearly one-half or one-third respectively.

Of all the misuses of comparison that fill the literature of electric light, perhaps the most misleading are those that are based on Census Bulletin 100 without investigating the service represented by its rates. The compilers of that Bulletin appear to have taken the total yearly amount paid by each city for electric light, divided it by the number of lamps, and set down the quotient in the column of " annual cost per lamp." For example the Lawrence cost per lamp is given as $26 a year, and the Boston cost at $237; no data as to candle-power, hours of burning, etc., are to be found in the Bulletin. The facts are that Boston had over a thousand full arcs of 2,000 candle-power burning all night and every night at a cost of $237 a lamp; there were also a few street lamps of lower candle-power which do not seem to have been taken into account. In Lawrence there were 133 lamps of 30 candle-power burning all night and every night at $36.50 a year each, 424 lamps of 20 candle-power burning from dark till midnight every night at $18 a year each, and 23 lamps of 2,000 candle-power averaging six hours per night at $122 each per year. The total cost of electric light in Lawrence was therefore $15,292, and the number of lamps 580, giving an average cost per lamp of $26; but what is that average good for? I am sure I do not know.

Mr. Johnston in his *Ægis* address, p. 169, says: "Last year Kansas City, Mo., was paying $200 a year for the same kind of lamp for which St. Louis paid its company $75; San Francisco pays $440.67 for the same service that Denver gets from another company for $58½; Rutland, Vt., pays $280 for a lamp that Mt. Morris, N. Y., under exactly similar conditions, obtains for $49." The first comparison was just, but Denver is another case in the census, like Lawrence; it was paying about $200 for a standard arc, and the conditions in San Francisco were not the same. The Mt. Morris lamp was a 1,200 c.-p. burning only till midnight, and water was the source of power, in part at least. Such defects in so able an address are a misfortune, which, however, is partly alleviated by the speaker's quotation from Whipple, a high authority among the opponents of public ownership: "It is plain that no local conditions can cause anything like such a great variation in prices. It is largely a matter of shrewdness on the part of officials on both sides as to the price paid."

Even Mr. Foster's work is tainted with the poison of false comparison. He first adds 13½% on the investment for fixed charges—a great deal too much, as I think I have shown in § 3. Then he *estimates* (as he tells us he had to since they were not reported) the watt hours per lamp for all commercial arcs and incandescents, and for nearly half the street lamps; he says he has not much confidence in his estimates as to said hours, in which we cordially agree with him, said estimates being vague guesses apparently based on the principle that lamps of a given candle-power are run the same number of hours in all places. After this he proceeds to calculate the cost per kilowatt hour and per lamp hour, covering a 7x10 page of the *Electrical Engineer* with three- and four-place decimals to complete the operation. Being based on hours of burning guessed at in ¾ of the cases, and on fixed charges out of all bounds, it is easy to see how much more convenient it will be to use these lamp-hour rates as a basis of comparison with the charges of private companies instead of comparing the cost of a standard arc per year in a public plant with the cost of a standard arc per year in a private plant under similar conditions of production, as an unscientific person would be apt to do rather than spend a couple of weeks writing down guesses at schedules and ciphering out mysterious and irresponsible hour rates to four places of decimals, so as to forget that the said hour rates are based on guesses and proceed to draw inferences from them that never could be obtained from the simple, undifferentiated, unmystified, unsophisticated cost per arc per year. The public plants included in Mr. Foster's investigation are in every part of the country from Maine to California under all sorts of conditions as to output and length of run, cost of labor and power, but Mr. Foster says nothing about said relations of cost (except the general remark that in more than half of these places a private plant could probably not be made to pay), and selects a lot of places in New York state, nestling near the coal fields, pairs them off by population with the public plants—underground system against overhead, little street plants against commercial plants, stations with tremendous investment ($473 per arc in the case of Alameda, Cal., which counts pretty fast at 13½ per cent), and $5 or $6 coal, against stations with low investment and $2 coal; and then, without making any allowance for differences of condition, sums up his groups, takes the average on each side, and announces that "The result is somewhat surprising, as there is a difference of twenty per cent in favor of the private companies." As already remarked (p. 94 of the ARENA for September, '95), if the manifestly unjust comparisons are omitted Mr. Foster's tables result in favor of public ownership in spite of the odds arising from Mr. Foster's overestimate of fixed charges, reckless guessing at hours, and special selection of private plants, which was probably not done with any intent to color the truth, but simply because the figures in respect to New York are easily attainable. It does seem strange, however, that Mr. Foster should have any confidence in results that rest so largely on the estimated schedules, reliance on which is expressly disclaimed by him.

Valid comparisons and useful averages are plentiful enough, and it is best to confine ourselves to them. If we find that I'y paid $186 a lamp last year, and this year gets the same service or better from its own plant at a total cost of $62 per lamp, while the rates of private companies not affected by the growth of public ownership remain substantially the same as last year, we may conclude with reasonable certainty that public ownership has resulted in a saving of about two-thirds of the former cost per lamp in I'y. If we find that S gets a 2,000-candle-power lamp burning all night and every night for $75 a year on a contract fair to all parties, while B, Y, and P pay $146 to $180 for the same or lower service, and on studying the conditions of production in S, B, Y, and P discover that the difference in cost of production between S and the other cities is little or nothing we may conclude that B, Y, and P pay more than they ought, more than they would if they had as much wisdom as S and used it upon their street-lighting contracts. If we find two cities with practically identical conditions, and one makes a standard arc for $46 a year, while the other pays $146 per standard arc, we may conclude that the latter pays about $100 per lamp more than if it managed the business for itself as skilfully as the former city does. If we find one city paying $100 a year for an all-night sub-arc on a fair contract, and another paying $182 a year for the same service, and learn that the difference in conditions of production is decidedly in favor of the latter, we may conclude that it is losing more than $82 a year on each lamp. If we find in one city a fair profit at $87 a year for a standard arc with 50 lamps, coal at $2 58, etc., and another city paying $127 a standard arc with 488 lamps, coal at $3, etc., and having allowed for all important differences of condition we ascertain that the cost of producing a standard arc in the latter city is $7 a year less than in the former, we may conclude that the $127 should be reduced to $80. On these and other methods that seem to us to conform to the laws of scientific reasoning we have placed our trust in this report.

NOTE 4.—ERRATA.

Page 596 ARENA for May, 1805, twenty-second line from top, "2 cents" should be 2½ cents.

Page 129 ARENA for June, Table IX, San Francisco $148 should be San Francisco $200

Page 380 ARENA for August, fourth line from the top, "full arcs" should be sub-arcs.

THE LIFE OF SIR THOMAS MORE.

BY B. O. FLOWER.

To the casual observer the life of Sir Thomas More presents so many contradictions that it will prove an enigma
unless he is acquainted with the type of individual to which
the philosopher belonged; the cold, calculating intellect
little understands, much less appreciates, a mind so profoundly sensitive to the varied and multitudinous influences
of environment as that of the author of "Utopia." His
brain received and reflected the complex and frequently
opposing influences of his wonderful time as did the mind
of no other man of his epoch. His intellect was largely
swayed by the thought-waves which beat upon the brain of
his century with a force and persistency hitherto unknown.
He felt most keenly, *and with a sympathy for both*, the
struggle between the old and the new. But he also felt the
higher and diviner thought-waves—those subtle influences
which inspired Angelo, and drove with tireless energy the
brush of Raphael. He was a man of vivid imagination, but,
true to the spirit of his country at this age, the divine afflatus
which came to him awakened the ethical nature, while in
sunny Italy, it spoke to the artistic impulses.

In great transition periods there are always a few children
of genius, who hear something higher than the din and
tumult below—lofty souls who hear a voice calling them to
ascend the mountain of the ideal and catch glimpses of the
coming dawn; these chosen ones bear messages from the Infinite to humanity. They behold the promised land from the
heights, and they return with a word and a picture; but to
the careless rich, the frivolous, the poor, who are absorbed
in self, to the slow-thinking and the slaves to intellectual
conventionalism, their messages are as sounding brass and
a tinkling cymbal. They who speak of peace, progress and
happiness through altruism usually find that they have
spoken in an unknown tongue to prince and pauper. But
their messages are not in vain: the true word once given will
not return barren. It touches some awakened intellects, it
kindles a fire which burns brighter and brighter with each
succeeding generation. The ideal once given becomes
an inspiration. The prophet is the annunciator of the

Infinite. The eternal law of justice and progress, when once more broadly and truly stated, sits in judgment on individuals, societies and nations.

The philosopher when upon the mountain of the ideal receives truths larger and more potential for good than aught man has before conceived. But when he returns to earth, that is to say when he is jostled by the positive thoughts of masterful· brains, when he is confronted by dominant ideas struggling to maintain supremacy in the empire of thought, he is in peril; that which was a blessing upon the mount becomes a dirge in the valley, for unless he is great enough to hold steadfastly to the high new truth, and rise above sensuous feeling, personal ambition and innate prejudices, he is liable to yield to the psychic forces in the atmosphere below. Then he falls, and the fall is pitiful, for after calling the world to judgment by a great new ideal of truth, he rejects the divine message which he has uttered, and by it is condemned. Painful to relate, this was, I think, to a great degree true of Sir Thomas More, as we shall presently see.

But the point I wish to illustrate just now is the liability on the part of historians and biographers to misjudge persons who are profoundly sensitive, endowed with a wealth of imagination, but who also possess deep-rooted convictions—men who love the good in the old, and yet who yearn for the new; those who in moments of ecstasy speak for the ages to come, but when oppressed by the fear and prejudice which environ them, reflect the dominant impulses of the old. Without a clear understanding of the mental characteristics of such natures, it will be impossible to understand, much less sympathize with, the noblest and most far-seeing English philosopher of his age.

Sir Thomas More was born when the twilight of mediæ-valism was paling before the dawn of modern times. Feudalism had lived its day; there were everywhere the signs of a coming storm. The conditions of the poor had grown most pitiful. The ambition of kings had received a strange new impulse; the superior rulers surged forward toward absolute power, with a confidence and recklessness which cowed the feudal lords. The popes, as we have seen. in many instances were secular potentates rather than spiritual fathers. Dreams of conquest swelled in the breasts of those born to the ermine, those who had risen to the scarlet cap, and those who had carved out position and power by the possession of military genius and daring. aided by the fortunes of war. But while the anarchy of

feudal brigandage was giving way before a more centralized and, in a way, orderly rule, while kings were engrossed
with plans for personal aggrandizement, scholars, scientists,
and skilled artisans were intoxicated by an intellectual stimulation seldom if ever equalled in the history of the race.
Some were revelling in the rediscovered treasures of
ancient Greece; some were brooding over the wonder-stories
of the far East. Artists and sculptors were transferring to
canvas and marble the marvellous dreams which haunted
their imagination. Gutenberg had recently invented the
printing press, Copernicus was interrogating the stars, and
another profound dreamer was gazing upon the western
ocean with a question and a hope—the one which would
not be silenced, the other so big as to appear wild and
absurd to the imagination of small minds. At this momentous time, when the clock of the ages was ringing in the
advent of an epoch which should mark a tremendous onward stride in the advance of humanity—at this time when
change was written over every great door of thought or
research throughout civilization, Sir Thomas More was born.

At an early age he was sent to St. Anthony's School in
London; afterward he entered the home of Cardinal Morton
as a page; here his fine wit and intellectual acuteness
greatly impressed the learned prelate, who on one occasion
remarked, "This child here waiting on the table will prove
a marvellous man." On the advice of the cardinal, young
More was sent to Oxford University, where a strong friendship grew up between the youth and Colet. At Oxford
Thomas More learned something of Greek. From this
college his father removed him to New Inn that he might
perfect himself in law; still later he entered Lincoln Inn,
where he continued his studies until he was ready for admission to the bar.

Shortly before Thomas More entered Oxford, England
began to respond to the intellectual revolution which had
enthused the advanced scholarship of the Continent. In a
few years, thanks to a few bold, brave men, Great Britain
was convulsed with a religious and intellectual revolution
which struck terror to the old-school men and the conventional theologians. In 1485 Linacre and Grocyn visited
Italy, where they diligently studied under some of the great
masters who were making Florence the most famous seat of
culture in Europe. Linacre was tutored by Poliziano. In
1493 Colet visited Italy and came under the influence of Pico
della Mirandola and Savonarola. These three scholars returned to England, fired with moral and intellectual enthu-

siasm and touched by the dawning spirit of scientific inquiry. Linacre and Grocyn taught Greek at Oxford; later, the former founded the College of Physicians of London. Colet broke away from the scholastic methods of mediævalism and startled England no less by his handling the New Testament in a plain, common-sense way than by his plea for a purified church.· Later he proved how deep were his convictions and how sincere his desire for a higher and truer civilization, by devoting the fortune left him by his father to the founding of St. Paul's Latin Grammar School, where children were to receive kind consideration instead of being subjected to the brutal treatment which characterized the education of that time,* and where, under the wisest and most humane teachers, "the young might," as the founder expressed it, "proceed to grow." In this noble innovation Colet laid the foundation for that rational and popular system of education which has grown to such splendid proportions throughout the English-speaking world, and which probably finds its most perfect expression in the public-school system in the United States.

We now come to a passage in the life of Thomas More, which calls for special notice, as it illustrates the intensity of his religious convictions even when a youth. Had the philosopher been born a few years earlier, in all probability he would not only never have written "Utopia," but we should doubtless have found him among the foremost enemies of the new order. Throughout his life he ever exhibited a divided love. The new learning and the spirit of the dawn wooed and fascinated him until he paused long enough to realize how rapidly the old was falling away, then a great fear came upon him lest the church should go down and civilization degenerate into barbarism. He was by turns the most luminous mind among the philosophers of the dawn, and the most resolute defender of conventional religion. In this he reflected the varying intellectual atmosphere which environed his sensitive and psychical mind, and which sprang from ideas and influences which challenged his confidence or coincided with his convictions. When he completed his education he and William Lilly (afterward head master of the Latin Grammar School founded by Colet) determined to forswear the world and become monks. For four years they dwelt at Charterhouse, subjecting themselves to the most severe discipline, scourging their bodies on Friday, wearing coarse hair shirts next

* Youths were brutally beaten at that time at school; it being an all but universally accepted precept that "Boys' spirits must be subdued."—*Maurice Adams.*

the skin, and living upon the coarsest fare. Whether close acquaintance with the monkish life of that time disillusioned More, as it had disillusioned Erasmus some years before; whether the entreaties of Colet and Erasmus, or the passion excited by the bright eyes and sweet winning manners of Miss Colt, whom he frequently met when visiting her father's home at that time, served to make him forego his determination to become a monk, we know not; perhaps all these exerted an influence. Erasmus disposes of the question in this characteristic expression, "He fell in love, and thought a chaste husband was better than a profligate monk." And thus instead of taking vows he married Miss Colt and renewed the study of law.

In 1504 More was elected to a parliament convened by Henry VII to extort money from the impoverished people in the form of "reasonable aids, on the occasion of the marriage of his daughter and the knighting of his son." The subsidy demanded from the wretched and oppressed people amounted to considerably over half a million dollars (£113,-000); a sum of this size at that time was equivalent to many times a like amount to-day, for the medium of exchange was then so scarce that a fat ox sold for twenty-six shillings, a fat wether for three shillings and sixpence, and a chicken brought a penny.* The Parliament had grown so servile in the presence of the growing despotism of the crown, that only one voice was raised against the measure, and that voice was Thomas More's, then a beardless youth. He denounced the demand as extortionate and unreasonable; he showed how the people were oppressed and overtaxed; how an increase of taxation would mean added misery to the English people. Reason after reason was advanced for denying or at least substantially reducing the amount demanded; argument after argument, clear and convincing, fortified each reason advanced. The members of Parliament were enthused even while they sat in amazement at the unmatched daring of the gifted youth. Something of the old-time fire and love of liberty filled their craven minds. They began to behold how low they had fallen by surrendering their manhood and the sacred trust given them through fear of losing their heads. The friends of the king were astounded; they gazed at one another in blank amazement; the reckless audacity of this youth who stood as the incarnate voice of justice pleading the cause of the poor menaced the throne. At length the fearless orator resumed his seat, and so clear, logical, and unanswerable had been his plea that for a moment the mem-

* Froude's History of England, vol. i, pp. 30.32.

bers of Parliament forgot their role of puppets and became
men. The demand was rejected, and in its stead an allowance of about $150,000 (£30,000) was granted, whereupon a
Mr. Tyler, one of the members of the king's privy chamber,
who was present, brought the king word that his demand
had been denied, owing to the eloquent opposition of a
"beardless boy." The king was at once enraged and
alarmed; he could find no cause for the immediate arrest of
the offender, so he sought to wreak vengeance on the father;
a complaint was accordingly trumped up, and old Mr. More
was sent to the Tower, where he remained until he paid a
fine of five hundred dollars (£100). Thomas More now
retired to private life, and was preparing to leave England
owing to disquieting rumors which came to him of the king's
displeasure, when Henry VII died.

With the accession of Henry VIII to the throne, the star
of the apostles of culture rose. The king espoused the cause
of the new learning, and More, Colet, and Erasmus and
their companions basked in the royal favor. In vain the
Trojans, as the defenders of conventionalism were called,
denounced the new learning, and at length Henry VIII
silenced the "brawlers." One of this class took occasion to
denounce the heresies of Erasmus in a sermon before the
king. After the discourse he was summoned to the presence of Henry, and there interrogated; More being present
answered the arguments advanced by the dogmatist. At
length, finding it impossible to cope with More, the priest
fell at the feet of the king. He was trembling with terror
as he implored the king's forgiveness, saying he had been
carried away "by the spirit." "But," said Henry, "that
spirit was not the spirit of Christ, but of *foolishness.*" Next
the king asked him if he had read the works of Erasmus; the
priest acknowledged that he had not. "Then you prove
yourself a fool," cried the king, "for you condemn what you
have never read." This illustration indicates the attitude
of Henry VIII toward the apostles of the new learning
during the early years of his reign.

In 1515 More was sent with a royal embassy to the Low
Countries to settle a quarrel between Henry VIII and Prince
Charles. While in Flanders, More heard wonderful stories
of the New World, and also the fabled land of India now
opened, nay, more, all but conquered, by Portugal. The
very air of Flanders was vibrating with that restlessness
which comes over men when life becomes more dignified and
its possibilities greater. Wonder trod upon the heels of
wonder, and a great hope filled the minds of the commercial

world, no less than the realm of the thinkers. While here, More wrote the second part of "Utopia." The first part was not written until after his return to England.

The publication of "Utopia" revealed afresh the superb courage of its author; it was a thinly disguised satire on England. It contrasted the England of his time with what England might and should be. It was written to influence, if possible, a headstrong, vainglorious and extravagant young king, who during six years of his reign had involved his country in an ignominious war, which had drained the well-filled coffers left by Henry VII; a young king who was now insisting on levying the enormous income tax of sixpence on the pound, and insisting that the tax extend to the miserable, half-starved agricultural laborers. Henry VIII greatly admired Thomas More, but only a thinker who placed conviction above even life would have dared put forth a work so bold and so well calculated to open the eyes of the people to the shallow pretences as well as the criminality of the rich and powerful. Artemus Ward speaks of a man who was fifteen years confined in a dungeon; one day an idea struck him—he opened the window and climbed out. Now, "Utopia" was calculated to show the sturdy Englishmen the window, and King Henry was no dolt—indeed, he was a man of strong mental power and quick perceptions; he was as headstrong and despotic as he was intellectually acute; hence Thomas More in publishing "Utopia" displayed that same superb courage which he evinced in his strenuous opposition to the extravagant demand of Henry VII.

How striking in contrast was the action of Machiavelli, who at this time had finished "The Prince," and was industriously seeking some method of bringing it before the attention of one of the ambitious despots of Italy. More risked the king's displeasure, and indeed his own freedom, to win a greater measure of happiness for the people and to advance civilization. Machiavelli sought to destroy freedom and the rights of man by furnishing a diabolical treatise for the private perusal of a tyrant, hoping, thereby, to win an important position as counsellor for the despot, and also to gain wealth. The motives which actuated these two great writers on political economy were as unlike as were their works; from one fountain flowed poison and darkness, from the other hope and light.

King Henry took "Utopia" in good part, and instead of disgracing the intrepid author, he knighted him; and from time to time promoted him, making him treasurer of the exchequer, speaker of the House of Commons, and at length,

when Wolsey fell, he was made lord chancellor of England.
More was then fifty-one years old. His personal appearance has been thus graphically described by Erasmus:

"He is of middle height, well-shaped, complexion pale,
without a flush of color in it save when the skin flushes.
The hair is black shot with yellow, or yellow shot with black;
beard scanty, eyes grey, with dark spots, an eye supposed in
England to indicate genius, and to be never found except in
remarkable men. The expression is pleasant and cordial,
easily passing into a smile, for he has the quickest sense of
the ridiculous of any man I ever met. The right shoulder
is higher than the left, the result of a trick in walking,
not from a physical defect. The rest is in keeping. The
only sign of rusticity is in the hands, which are slightly
coarse. From childhood he has been careless of appearance,
but he has still the charm which I remember when I first
knew him. His health is good though not robust, and he is
likely to be long-lived. His father, though in extreme old
age, is still vigorous. He is careless in what he eats. I
never saw a man more so. Like his father, he is a water-
drinker. His food is beef, fresh or salted, bread, milk, fruit,
and especially eggs. His voice is low and unmusical, though
he loves music; but it is clear and penetrating. He articulates slowly and distinctly, and never hesitates. He dresses
plainly; no silks or velvets or gold chains. He has no concern for ceremony, expects none from others, and shows
little himself. He holds forms and courtesies unworthy of
a man of sense, and for that reason has hitherto kept clear
of the court. All courts are full of intrigue. . . . His talk
is charming, full of fun, but never scurrilous or malicious.
He used to act plays when young; wit delights him, though
at his own expense."

The years which had passed over Sir Thomas More from
the day he entered the service of the king until he left the
chancellor's office were fraught with anxiety and apprehension. He was a keen observer and an excellent reader of
human nature. He early learned the true character of the
king. On one occasion after Henry had visited him at his
home in Chelsea, his son-in-law, William Roper, expressed
his joy at seeing the king so attached to his father-in-law.
"Ah!" replied Sir Thomas More, "if my head would win him
a castle in France, it should not fail to go." But distrust
in the king was by no means his chief cause for apprehension and gloomy forebodings. The hope of the new learning, which promised so much a few years before, when its
apostles had the ear of some of the most powerful sovereigns

and when its cause was openly espoused by many of the
greatest prelates and scholars of the age, was suffering a
partial eclipse, while, on the other side, the Reformation was
assuming giant-like proportions.

The disciples of the new learning were distinctly apostles
of broad culture. The leaders among the reformers too
frequently assailed culture as the handmaiden of evil; they
had seen culture and art flourishing in Italy and elsewhere,
where artificiality, insincerity and cynical scepticism prevailed, and they imagined that art and scholarship, beyond
very narrow limits, were sensual and enervating. Moreover, the summary measures being adopted by the church
aroused the spirit of hate and retaliation, as is ever the case,
and calm reason gave way before savage invectives and
violent denunciations. More, Erasmus and Colet had
dreamed of a purified church in which love should supplant
form and dogma—a pure religion based on reason and hos-
pitable to science and culture. But instead of this they
now beheld the church rent asunder. Schisms were springing up on every hand. Instead of the waters of reformative
truth, flowing gently over the earth, cleansing it of corruption and giving life to that which was highest and finest, as
the apostles of the new learning anticipated, they beheld in
the Reformation a torrent which was sweeping the good
away with the bad; a savage, intemperate power, which
opposed culture and railed against that which they held
sacred in religion, a movement which gained momentum and
volume with each succeeding month.

The day for a middle course seemed past. The cry, "Who
is on the Lord's side?" came from the reactionary and intolerant Catholics no less than from the Reformers.
Zwingli and Latimer threw in their lot with the Reformation. Erasmus opposed the Reformation, but held aloof
from the reactionaries. Sir Thomas More moved slowly but
steadily toward the camp of the ultra-conservatives. To
him came some of the most intense spirits among the old-
time Catholics of England, and he caught the infection of
their mental atmosphere. Their fears seconded his apprehensions, and further fanned to fire the prejudice which at
one time he seemed to have outgrown. The ascetic spirit
which in youth almost made a monk of him, again asserted
itself to a degree, and we find him once more wearing the
coarse hair shirt next his skin, and he also returned to the
old habit of scourging his body with whips and knotted
cords, as he had punished himself in youth when he expected to become a monk.* The magnificent faith in truth,

---

* See Roper's Life of More.

the wonderful spirit of toleration breathed forth in "Utopia," which lifted him high above the finest think-ers of his age, faded away, and he became a persecutor of heretics.

I know it has been argued that he merely permitted the execution of the law; while on the other hand Froude goes, I think, to the opposite extreme in representing More in darker colors than the facts warrant. This historian claims that for some time before the fall of Wolsey the persecution of heretics had become less and less rigorous, but with the accession of More to the chancellorship, the fires of Smith-field were again lighted. From official documents of the time it appears evident that persecutions continued during the brief period in which he served as lord chancellor. And we know enough of the courage and fidelity to convictions of More to be sure that he would not have remained a day in the high office to which he had been appointed had the king in-sisted on the destruction of heretics when More felt that such a course was criminal and wrong. The man who had defeated the demand of Henry VII; who had at a later day, when speaker of the House, defied Cardinal Wolsey; the man who preferred the block to taking the oath under the Supremacy Act, was not the man to allow men to be punished for heresy under his rule and remain silent if such punishment ran contrary to his convictions of right. And yet he doubtless had his misgivings. His prophetic soul cast a sombre shadow over the future, for on one occasion when William Roper congratulated Sir Thomas More on "the happy estate of the realm that had so Catholic a prince that no heretic durst show his face," the philosopher replied, "I pray God that some of us, as high as we seem to sit upon the moun-tains, treading heretics under our feet like ants, live not the day that we gladly would wish to be at league with them to let them have their churches quietly to themselves, so that they would be content to let us have ours quietly to our-selves."

It would have been far better for the reputation of Sir Thomas More had he steadfastly refused to become lord chancellor of the realm, for during this period he placed an indelible blot upon a reputation which otherwise was fairer than that of any other great man of his age, and it is doubly sad when we remember that he himself had called the church, the state, and the individual conscience to judgment for in-tolerance in "Utopia." I can conceive of few sadder spec-tacles than that presented by a lofty genius, like More, who, after ascending the mountains of the ideal and there receiv-

ing the inspiration which belongs to the dawn of true civilization, so far forgets the fine, high truth he has enunciated
as to turn his back upon it and allow himself to become a
persecutor of those who differ from him.

But while not ignoring this blot on the otherwise fair
fame of Sir Thomas More, let us not forget that he
lived in an age when the Inquisition of Spain, having
received the authorization and benediction of the church,
was in active operation. Ferdinand and Isabella, whose
reign was so indelibly stained with persecution and murder
of Jews, Moors, and heretics, had each been designated
"The Catholic," as a title of special favor. On every hand
it was argued that the heretics would be burned forever
and ever in a lake of fire and brimstone; that if a heretic
was allowed to go at large he would soon poison the souls of
others. It was felt that the man who, having a plague, went
forth sowing death, was less dangerous than the man who
sowed the seeds of heresy, which it was affirmed were the
seeds of eternal death. More had always cherished a passionate love for the Roman Church. It never seemed to
occur to him seriously to question the authority of the pope.
And had not the church and that pope sanctioned persecutions? Had not John Huss long before been burned to
death? and he was only one of many. Moreover, the spirit
of the age favored persecution; it was a savage period;
human life was very cheap. Thieves were hanged by the
score in England. The blood of the Hundred Years' War
between France and England left its impress on the brain of
this century. The dark shadows of departing mediævalism
were still visible, while already in the south loomed the
formidable spectre of the coming half-century of religious
persecution, which should prove such an age of human
slaughter and fiendish torture as Europe had never known.
Thus while we deplore the fact that More permitted persecution, we must not judge him by the standards of our time.
nor must we forget the fact that More's brain was sensitive
to the dominant thought-vibrations of the hour, as well as
the positive convictions of those in whom he placed confidence.

It was during this brief and sunless period when he was
lord chancellor of England that the turn of the tide of his
worldly fortunes set in. The king vainly endeavored to win
him to his way of viewing the proposed divorce. Sir
Thomas More saw in it the severing of the crown from the
Church of Rome, and held steadfastly to his convictions
which were opposed to such a step. At length rather than

consent to the divorce he resigned his position at the court. He went from office a very poor man, as he had steadfastly refused all proffered assistance and had spurned the princely bribes which were offered him.

In 1534 the Act of Supremacy was passed and More was summoned to take the oath. The king was very loth to destroy his one-time friend; he made many overtures, and assured More of his love for him. Later he threatened; both plans were alike unavailing. Had More been willing to consent to a modified oath, he would probably have escaped the block, but the philosopher ever placed loyalty to conviction of right above life; he was accordingly arrested and at length was beheaded. His tragic death raised him to the peerage of martyrs.

The domestic life of Sir Thomas More was singularly beautiful. His home has been termed a miniature Utopia. He possessed a gay and buoyant spirit and carried sunshine instead of fear to his friends. His political career, if we except his actions when religious prejudice clouded his reason and dulled his naturally keen sense of justice, evinced statesmanship of a high order. His views on social problems were in many instances hundreds of years in advance of his day, while his genuine sympathy for the poor and oppressed led him dauntlessly to champion their cause, where a time-server would have remained silent. He was a statesman unsullied by the demagogism of the politician. He was an apostle of culture, and in his writings embodied the best impulses of the new learning in a larger way than did any other scholar of his time. He was a prophet of a true civilization, and had his soul remained upon the mountain, above the baleful psychic waves which beat around his prejudices and played upon his fear, More's life, as well as his writings, would have proved an unalloyed inspiration to the generations who came after him. Yet, though like Seneca, whom in very many respects More resembled, he sometimes fell far short of his high ideals, when judged in the light of his age and environment, he stands forth one of the noblest figures of his time, and in his "Utopia" he reveals the imagination of a true genius, the wisdom and justice of a sage, and the love of a civilized man.

NAPOLEON BONAPARTE.

A Sketch Written for a Purpose.

BY JOHN DAVIS.

CHAPTER IV.

Failure of Napoleon's Financial System — Success of the English System.

I now call attention to an incisive discussion of the subject of taxation by Napoleon. Writing from Fontainebleau to his brother Joseph, king of Naples, Oct. 21, 1807 (Conf. Cor. p. 276), he said:

> *My Brother:* I see by your letter of the 3d of October that your kingdom, taking one month with another, gives you 900,000 ducats, which make 4,410,000 francs; that is to say, nearly fifty-three million francs a year. This is very little. The kingdom of Italy yields me 122,000,000. I should like to have a statistical return of your kingdom to make me well acquainted with its extent, population, and taxation. It seems to me that your kingdom ought to yield at least a hundred million.

Here is a letter written by Napoleon to Joseph when in Spain, dated Dec. 12, 1808:

> Send agents into the provinces to seize the funds in every town and village in that part of Cuenca, La Mancha, Castile, Segovia, and Talavera de la Reyna, into which we have entered. There is money everywhere.

Again, six days later, Napoleon wrote to Joseph very urgently on the same subject:

> I can find only thirteen million in the public exchequer, and eleven million in the *caisse consolidation* and others, which make altogether twenty-four million, and, with the eight that you brought, thirty-two million. You must make use of them either through the capitalists in Madrid or by other means. It is for the minister of finance to find out the way. Here is already a fortnight passed, and these moments are the most precious, as force may now be employed. You should therefore procure about thirty million reals in specie without losing a minute.

Napoleon wanted money, and he wanted it quickly, while "force could be employed." The fact is, his policy was an absolute failure from the beginning, *except when force could be used.* And even that was not sufficient, as already stated, unless he invaded neutral or friendly nations, where he could tax and rob both friends and enemies. This proposition was proved and illustrated by the invasion of Spain, where the people were less friendly than in other parts of western Europe. After the first experiences there, it was impossible to prevent the war from being, in part, a burden on the French treasury. Napoleon's letters on the subject state the case very fully. Writing to General Berthier in Spain, he says:

Paris, Jan. 28, 1810. Let the king of Spain know that my finances are getting into disorder; that I cannot meet the enormous cost of Spain; that it is become absolutely necessary that the funds required to keep up the artillery, the engineers, the administration, the hospitals, surgeons, and administrators of every description, should be furnished by Spain, as well as half the pay of the army. . . . All that I can do is to give two millions a month towards its pay.

As matters grew more desperate Napoleon wrote again to Berthier on Feb. 8:

I can no longer stand the enormous expenses of my army in Spain. . . . In future I shall be able to send only,two millions a month to pay the troops that surround Madrid, and which form the nucleus of the army. . . . Write to the general commanding in Aragon that he is to employ the revenue of the province, and, if necessary, even levy extraordinary contributions for the pay and support of his army. . . . Write to Generals Thiebault, Bonnet, and Kellerman, and to the Duke of Elchingen, . . . that they must not trust to the French treasury, which is exhausted by the immense sums which it is obliged to send; that Spain swallows up a prodigious amount of specie, and thus impoverishes France.

July 14, 1810, General Berthier wrote to Joseph as follows:

The emperor, sire, is deeply grieved to hear that the army which is laying siege to Cadiz is in a state of complete destitution; that their pay is nine months in arrears. This state of things may be productive of serious misfortune.

That is the opinion of the emperor respecting the war in Spain, where, he says, "to discipline and pay Spanish troops is to discipline and pay one's enemies." It is thus seen that, where the people are united, war cannot be made to support war, on the Napoleonic plan.

May 29, 1811, Napoleon writes from Havre to General Berthier in Spain:

Express my perfect satisfaction to Gen. Suchet, and let him know that I have granted all the promotions for which he asked. Reiterate to him the order to levy a contribution of several millions upon Lerida, in order to obtain food, pay, and clothing for his army. Tell him that the war in Spain makes such an increase of forces necessary that I am no longer able to send money thither; that war must support war.

Advice like that was never thrown away on General Suchet. At the close of the campaign in the province of Valencia, he imposed on the people a contribution of fifty-nine million francs; and "such was the skill that long experience had given the officers of the imperial army in extracting its utmost resources from the most exhausted country, that this enormous impost was brought, with very little deduction, into the public treasury." Marshal Suchet was also so particular to maintain order in his conquered province, that he promptly arrested the most energetic characters, especially among the clergy, on the side of independence; nearly 1,500 in number were arrested and sent to France, "and some hundreds of them were shot when unable, from fatigue, to travel farther." His rigorous and extortionate administration in Valencia was so pleasing to Napoleon that he conferred on him the title of Duke of Albufera, with rich domains attached in the kingdom of Valencia. And on this new kingdom, including the dukedom of Albufera, Napoleon bestowed two hundred million francs, to be raised in different parts of Spain.

I will now give illustrations of Napoleon's plan of collecting taxes and contributions in countries which had been exhausted of their money, and were compelled to pay their contributions in kind. The Poles, from the very first until their utter ruin in 1812, were friendly to Napoleon and to France. They contributed to the armies of the emperor, both men and money, to the utmost of their ability. The city and province of Warsaw alone furnished 85,000 men, fully equipped with arms, horses, wagons, and artillery, to the grand army for the invasion of Russia. Napoleon had no more faithful allies than the Poles, yet his hand of spoliation fell upon them most heavily. Russian Poland was the first province in Russia to be despoiled by the march of the grand army as it started to Moscow. Alison's "History of Europe" (vol. x, pp. 818–19) says:

The wants of such a prodigious accumulation of troops speedily exhausted all the means of subsistence which the country afforded, and all the stores they could convey with them. Forced requisitions of horses, chariots, and oxen from the peasantry soon became necessary, and the Poles, who expected deliverance from their bondage, were stripped of everything they possessed by their liberators. To such a pitch did the misery subsequently arrive that the richest families in Warsaw were literally in danger of starving, and the interest on money rose to eighty per cent. Yet such was the rapidity of the marches at the opening of the campaign, that the greater part of the supplies thus exacted were abandoned or destroyed before the army had advanced many leagues into the Russian territory.

The Polish territory about Warsaw was utterly ruined.

It was stripped of its able-bodied men and of every means of life. The 85,000 Poles were the best troops in the grand army. They were in all the great battles; they were inured to the climate and accustomed to the management of horses and vehicles; they carried with them smiths for the shoeing of horses and the repair of wagons, and they were the only troops that returned from Russia with a whole battery of artillery in good condition. And yet. so heartless was Napoleon, that in his flight from Russia through Warsaw he declared to the Abbé de Pradt that the Poles had done nothing, and that he had not seen a Pole in his army during the entire campaign.

My next picture of taxation and spoliation without mercy will be that of Prussia. Alison's "History" (vol. xi, p. 224) says:

The pecuniary exactions which had been drawn from Prussia and the requisitions in kind which had been drawn from its unhappy inhabitants during the last year (1812) would exceed belief were they not attested by contemporary and authentic documents. From these it appears that no less than 482,000 men and 80,000 horses had traversed Prussia in its whole extent in the first six months of 1812, and that more than one-half of this immense force had been quartered for above three months on its unhappy provinces. By the convention of Feb. 24, 1812, the furnishings made for its support were to be taken in part payment of the arrears, still amounting to nearly one hundred millions of francs, which remained unpaid of the great military contribution of six hundred forty millions levied on Prussia after the battle of Jena. But though the French authorities, with merciless rapacity, enforced the new requisitions, they never could be brought to state them in terms of the treaty, as a deduction from the old ones. The French hosts, like a cloud of locusts, passed over the country, devouring its substance, plundering its inhabitants, and wrenching from them by the terrors of military execution the whole cattle, horses, and carriages in their possession. The number of horses carried off before September in the single year of 1812 in East Prussia alone, amounted to 22,700, while that of the cattle was 70,000, and that of the carts seized was 13,349. The weekly cost of Junot's corps of 70,000 men, quartered in lower Silesia, was 200,000 crowns (£50,000 sterling), and that of all the rest of the country in the same proportion. These enormous contributions were exclusive of the furnishings stipulated to be provided under the treaty of Feb. 24, 1812, which were also rigidly exacted; and of the arrears of the great contribution of 1806, the collection of which had become, by the total exhaustion of the country, altogether hopeless.

The arrears above mentioned, which were rigidly exacted, are given in Count de Segur's "Expedition to Russia" (vol. i, p. 22), as follows:

Two hundred thousand quintals of rye. 24,000 of rice, 2,000,000 bottles of beer. 400,000 quintals of wheat, 650,000 of straw, 350,000 of hay, 6,000,000 bushels of oats, 40,000 oxen, 15,000 horses, 3,600 wagons with harness and drivers, each capable of carrying a load of 1,500 pounds weight, and, finally, hospitals provided with everything necessary for 20,000 sick.

That is the way Napoleon collected arrearages of taxes from an exhausted people, when there was no money in the country. It will be remembered that he got his foothold in Prussia by professing to be a republican and proclaiming "war on the palace, but peace to the cottage." This hypocrisy divided the people and gave him easy victories. At a later date, when his treason to liberty became manifest, it was too late for the people to help themselves. At the time of the above devastations and exactions Prussia was an ally of France, and furnished her quota of men in the grand army for the invasion of Russia.

Napoleon, at one time being taunted as "a mere youth" by an older officer who had never commanded an army in battle, replied, "One ages very fast on the battlefield." The reply was appropriate and cutting; but, later on, Napoleon found that there was "a field of finance" in which *he* had not "aged very fast." He found that war, on the modern plan, requires money; and, discarding paper, he must have metal. He next slowly learned that the metallic money of Europe was easily exhausted, not only in each conquered country, but in all of them. So to get more money to supply his increasing necessities, he was compelled to extend his conquests. New conquests required larger armies and still greater quantities of money. Hence the effort to supply his increasing necessities for money by new conquests was like an effort to fill a sieve with water. It could not be done.

And yet, when contributions from present acquisitions of territory had been collected, paid out, and ultimately hoarded by individuals, out of the reach of even the sword, he had no resource but new conquests. In this way all the countries subject to the French empire were exhausted of their specie, and new pastures for military forage and exactions had to be found, and new treasuries which could be robbed.

There were, ultimately, but two countries in Europe worth robbing—England and Russia. The former was safe in her citadel amid the waves. Russia was open to invasion by land; and beyond Russia to the east and southeast lay all Asia, with great wealth and numerous treasuries of specie. The men and money of Russia were to enable the conqueror to proceed with his long-cherished hopes of invading Asia. That enterprise had been cut short years before by his failure at the siege of Acre. He had two principal reasons for invading Russia, both financial: (1) to recuperate his own exhausted finances; and (2) to break down the English finances by closing the ports of Russia against English goods, as he had already closed most of the ports of the rest of Europe.

Count Philip de Segur, in his "Expedition to Russia" (vol. i, pp. 52–3), gives the principal reason for the invasion of Russia in Napoleon's own words. Count Mollien, trying to dissuade the emperor from invading Russia, remarked to him that his finances required peace. Napoleon replied, "On the contrary, they are embarrassed and require war." The Duke of Gaeta also opposed the invasion on financial grounds. The emperor listened to him attentively to the end, then, with a smile, said, "So you think I shall not be able to find anyone to pay the expenses of the war?" On another occasion, writing to Mollien on the subject (Lanfrey, vol. iv, p. 468), he "calculated the resources which the war would place in his hand. Not only ought it to give him the dominion of the world, but likewise the means of restoring his finances: 'I shall make this war for a political object; also for the sake of my finances. Have I not always reëstablished them by war?'"

On the way to Moscow, Napoleon was advised to stop and winter at Witepsk. He objected on account of having to pay his own expenses. "While at Moscow," said he, "there will be peace, abundance, a reimbursement of the expenses of the war, and imperishable glory." His generals long and earnestly argued with him against going to Moscow. They said that every year the hardships of war increased, fresh conquests compelling them to go farther in quest of fresh enemies. Europe would soon be insufficient; he would want Asia also.

At sight of Moscow, his exultation knew no bounds. Count Philip de Segur, an eyewitness, in his "Expedition to Russia" (vol. ii, p. 30), says:

His eyes, fixed on the capital, already expressed nothing but impatience. In it he beheld in imagination the whole Russian empire. Its walls inclosed all his hopes—peace, the expenses of the war, immortal glory. His eager looks, therefore, intently watched all its outlets. When would its gates be open? When should he see that deputation come forth which would place its wealth, its population, its senate, and the principal of the Russian nobility at his disposal?

Poor, mistaken man! Prior to this he had gained victories in countries permeated with the liberal ideas of the French republic. It was not so in Russia. Both the government and the people were against him. He had lost more than two-thirds of the grand army in reaching Moscow. And, as he entered its gates in triumph, he was in fact a beaten man, with no chance of returning to France again except by flight. He was never again to enter Paris except

as a fugitive. However, he thinks of money and has his
consolation. Though Moscow yields him nothing but burnt
ruins, want, and danger, he says: "Millions have no doubt
slipped through our hands, but how many thousand millions
is Russia losing? Her commerce is ruined for a century to
come. The nation is thrown back fifty years, which of itself
is an important result. And when the first moment of enthusiasm is past this reflection will fill them with consterna-
tion." The conclusion that he drew was "that so violent a
shock would convulse the throne of Alexander, and force
that prince to sue for peace."

But Napoleon waited in vain for the Emperor of Russia to
treat with him. The "honest-money" man who would never
use paper could now find no more treasuries to rob, and his
effort to get into the Russian treasury had broken his back.
His financial system had failed, utterly and ingloriously, beyond the hope of recovery. He next tries *paper!* Yes, the
Emperor Napoleon appeals to paper money for salvation!
He tries paper in its most ignoble form. The famous brig-
and of Europe, unable further to replenish his treasury by
the methods of savagery, turns *counterfeiter!* I will relate
the case. It may, perhaps, not inappropriately be styled a
farce by the "star actor," in that stupendous tragedy known
as "Napoleon's Expedition to Russia." I call attention to
this item for two reasons: (1) To prove that Napoleon was
out of money, and that it was *imperious pecuniary necessity*
that drove him to Russia; that the invasion of Russia was
an absolute *dernier ressort* for financial purposes; that it
was absolutely necessary to recruit his finances, which were
"embarrassed"; and (2) I desire to prove that the *purse* is
mightier than the sword, compelling, by the inexorable laws
of finance, even "the Conqueror of Europe," "the king of
kings," "the Lion of the desert" to bow his head in impotent
submission, to yield to the inevitable!

Speaking of the French army in Moscow, M. Thiers, in his
History (vol. iv, p. 216), says:

Paper roubles being the money that is current in Russia, and the
French army chest, containing a large quantity of them, fabricated in
a manner which has already been described, but of which there was
then no suspicion, he [Napoleon] caused it to be announced that all
provisions, and especially forage, brought into Moscow would be paid
for, and directed that those peasants who answered to the appeal
should receive ample protection. He also paid the army in the paper
roubles, at the same time arranging, however, that those officers who
desired to send their pay to France should be able to exchange this
paper for genuine money at the government treasury.

But how came those "fabricated" Russian roubles in that

French army chest in Moscow? M. Thiers (vol. iv, p. 196), explains the matter:

Napoleon now had at his disposal, consisting partly of a great sum in money, and partly of a still larger sum in false paper roubles which he had forged in Paris without scruple, considering himself justified by the example of the coalitionists, who at another period filled France with forged assignats.

By this time it is seen that the "honest-money" financier who would never issue or use paper money, who would "stop the pay of his soldiers rather than use it," was ultimately glad to fabricate and use the counterfeit paper of a foreign nation, and even to pay his troops with it!

Napoleon returned from Russia badly crippled, to use his own expressive language, "like a lion with his nails pared and mane cut," but full of vinegar and vigor. He called himself a "lion not yet dead." He conscripted the youth of France and raised an army of a million men, but he had no more easy victories. He met one defeat after another, and to pay expenses he levied taxes on everything in France that was taxable; he seized and sold estates, somewhat after the manner of the revolution, but with less discrimination and justice.

The tide had turned; France was invaded, Paris was occupied by the allies, and the whilom conqueror of Europe and the would-be emperor of Asia became an exile in the island of Elba; afterward came Waterloo and St. Helena.

Let us now examine the paper system of England in contrast with the financial system of Napoleon. In 1797 coin failed in England to meet the demands for prosecuting the wars against the French republic. The Bank of England paid out its last silver sixpence, and paper money was the only resource. It was adopted, specie was abandoned; and then commenced a contest of eighteen years of British paper against the coin of Europe in the hands of Napoleon. After the fall and banishment of Napoleon, when paper money had completed its triumph over metal, Alison (vol. vii, p. 1) described the situation and the cause of England's success as follows:

It would be to little purpose that the mighty drama of the French revolutionary wars was recorded in history if the mainspring of all the European efforts, the British finances, were not fully explained. It was in their boundless extent that freedom found a never-failing stay; in their elastic power that independence obtained a permanent support. When surrounded by the wreck of other states, when surviving alone the fall of so many confederacies, it was in their inexhaustible resources that England found the means of resolutely maintaining the contest and waiting calmly, in her citadel amid the waves, the return of a right spirit in the surrounding nations.

Vain would have been the prowess of her seamen, vain the valor of her soldiers, if her national finances had given way under the strain; even the conquerors of Trafalgar and Alexandria must have succumbed in the contest they so heroically maintained if they had not found in the resources of government the means of permanently continuing it. Vain would have been the reaction produced by suffering against the French revolution, vain the charnel-house of Spain and the snows of Russia, if Britain had not been in a situation to take advantage of the crisis; if she had been unable to aliment the war in the peninsula when its native powers were prostrated in the dust, the sword of Wellington would have been drawn in vain, and the energies of awakened Europe must have been lost in fruitless efforts if the wealth of England had not at last arrayed them, in dense and disciplined battalions, on the banks of the Rhine.

How, then, did it happen that this inconsiderable island, so small a part of the Roman empire, was enabled to expend wealth greater than ever had been amassed by the ancient mistress of the world; to maintain a contest of unexampled magnitude for twenty years; to uphold a fleet which conquered the united navies of Europe, and an army which carried victory into every corner of the globe; to acquire a colonial empire that encircled the earth, and subdue the vast continent of Hindostan, at the very time that it struggled in Spain with the land forces of Napoleon, and equipped all the armies of the north, on the Elbe and the Rhine, for the liberation of Germany?

The solution of the phenomenon, unexampled in the history of the world, is without doubt to be in part found in the persevering industry of the British people, and the extent of the commerce which they maintained in every quarter of the globe. But the resources thus afforded would have been inadequate to so vast an expenditure, and must have been exhausted early in the struggle, if they had not been organized and sustained by an admirable system of finance, which seemed to rise superior to every difficulty with which it had to contend. It is there that the true secret of the prodigy is to be found; it is there that the noblest monument to Mr. Pitt's wisdom has been erected.

Near the close of his History (vol. xiv, p. 170) Alison again states the case as follows:

In vain, however, would have been the numerous advantages, physical and political, which Great Britain enjoyed during the contest, if a fortunate combination of circumstances, joined to uncommon wisdom on the part of its government, had not established a system of currency in the heart of the empire, adequate to the wants of its immense dependencies, capable of expansion at will, according to the necessities of the times, and not liable to be drawn off at particular periods by the balances of trade or the military necessities of foreign states. No amount of metallic treasure could have been adequate to the wants of such an empire during such a contest; if the whole gold and silver of the world had been brought together, it would have proved unequal to the combined necessities of the government and the people. The vast and imperious demand for the precious metals, and especially gold, for the use and maintenance of the immense armies contending on the continent, of necessity and frequently drained away nearly the whole precious metals from the country at the very time when they were most required for the support of domestic credit or the cost of warlike establishments. When such a drain for specie set in from foreign ports, certain ruin must have ensued, if the empire had possessed no resources within itself to supply the place of the precious metals which were taken away. But such resources did exist and were managed with a combined liberality and caution which gave the country the whole benefits of a paper currency, without any of the danger with which it is attended. In February, 1797, when the vast abstraction of specie from the British islands, owing to the campaigns of the preceding year in Italy and Germany, joined to an extraordinary run upon the banks, arising from a panic at home, had brought matters to extremities, the Bank of England was on the verge of bankruptcy, and the nation within a hairbreadth of ruin.

But Mr. Pitt was at the helm, and his firmness and foresight not only surmounted the crisis, but drew from it the means of establishing the currency of the country on such a footing as enabled it to bid defiance throughout the whole remainder of the war, alike to foreign disaster and internal embarrassment. To the suspension of cash payments by the act of 1797, and the power in consequence vested in the Bank of England, of expanding its paper circulation in proportion to the abstraction of the metallic currency and the wants of the country, and resting the national industry of the country on a basis not liable to be taken away either by the mutations of commerce or the necessities of war, the salvation of the empire is beyond all question to be ascribed.

Not only did paper prove the salvation of the British empire, but it became the ultimate resource and safety of the continent. In September, 1813, Russia and Prussia jointly adopted the paper system of England. Speaking of it, Alison's History (vol. xii, p. 5) says:

To the supply of money obtained, and the extension of credit effected by this bold but withal wise and necessary step, at the critical moment when it was most required, and when all human efforts but for it must have been unavailing, the successful issue of the war and the overthrow of Napoleon are mainly to be ascribed.

England issued that paper money for Russia and Prussia, and guaranteed its circulation in their own dominions. Speaking of the case, Alison's History (vol. xii, p. 6) says:

It affords a proof, also, of the inexhaustible resources of a country which was thus able, at the close of a war of twenty years' duration, not only to furnish subsidies of vast amount to the continental states, but to guarantee the circulation of their own dominions, and cause its notes of hand to pass like gold through vast empires, which, extending from the Elbe to the Wall of China, but a few months before had been arrayed in inveterate hostility against it.

In 1815, the contest between paper money and metal ended. During a part of the struggle there were arrayed on each side more than a million men in arms. In 1812, nearly all the nations of the continent except Sweden, Turkey, and Russia were on the side of Napoleon, aiding him to replenish his finances by robbing the Russian treasury.

All southwestern Europe had been robbed and taxed to penury. When Napoleon failed to reach the Russian treasury, and his "financial system" of "honest money" and "forged paper" had utterly failed, he went to the wall in spite of all his relentless conscriptions of men and money in France, aided by his still numerous allies. His army of a million men and conscript boys, in 1813, melted down to nothing in a dozen months. Brigandage as a financial system can only be justified from the standpoint of piracy; and the brigand must be sure that he is master of both ends of the halter, otherwise ultimate results may prove unsatisfactory to him.

It may be argued, perhaps, that Napoleon's *system* was right and proper, but that his administration of it was bad; that he should have obtained his specie by taxation and borrowing. In reply it may be said that, in time of war, there are seldom any lenders of specie. During the wars of Napoleon there were few either in England or on the continent. England, Russia, Prussia, and all the other borrowers had to be content mostly with paper. Napoleon alone objected to paper. He was determined to use specie only. To get it he levied taxes and contributions, but the levies could only be collected by *force;* and that was his system, as here described. He pursued the only course open to him with his specie system.

During the late war in this country gold disappeared as the dangers increased. It could not be coaxed nor forced from its hiding until the use of the greenback began to threaten its supremacy. Then, by a bribe of from fifty to one hundred and fifty per cent added to its price, it could be had in limited quantities only. In view of all the facts and the experiences of the past, including Rome, Venice, and many later nations, it may be stated as a general proposition, almost without exception, that paper is the only available and reliable money capable of meeting the great and sudden emergencies of war. It saved the Roman empire after the disastrous battle of Cannæ; it sustained the existence and the vast commerce of the republic of Venice for more than six hundred years of almost continual warfare on sea and land, without panic or failure; it was the only available war money in the American and French revolutions; of England and the continent of Europe during the Napoleonic wars; of America in time of the great rebellion; and of France in time of peace after her defeat and humiliation in 1870.

The reason why modern wars cannot be successfully prosecuted with coin may be stated in few words: gold and silver cannot expand to meet the increasing demand for money. And, failing to meet the monetary demands, money at once appreciates in value. A money of insufficient volume and increasing value *will not circulate!* It hides away in the bankers' vaults and misers' hoards. This makes matters worse. The appreciation is accelerated; and *an appreciating money will not circulate!* In time of war coin refuses to go into battle after the first shock of arms. This is a law of finance which even the sword of Napoleon could not reverse. The moment he supplied himself with coin by forced taxes and contributions, and paid it out, it escaped into private hands and was hidden away till the rise in the value of coin should cease. Hence new conquests were necessary to recoup his finances; and when the last public treasury, the last bank vault, and the last hidden hoard were out of his reach, his financial system failed, and his sword lost its power. England, with her expansive paper, came out of the contest with a million men on foot and afloat, guarding in triumphant safety an empire that encircled the globe. She was mistress of the ocean in every part of the world, she dictated the policies of Europe, and her people were jubilant and happy.

A VISION NOT DREAMT OF IN THE PHILOSOPHIES.

BY BAYLIS MONTGOMERY DAWSON.

> " It is by no breath,
> Turn of eye, wave of hand, that salvation
> Joins issue with death!"

I wonder why it is that story keeps so in mind—the one Aunt Abbie told. Each detail comes back so vividly!

We were sitting in our hammocks, you and I, swinging lazily, quietly enjoying the many beauties of that perfect day and scene—Elm Farm. I do not have to close my eyes to see it now: the little clouds that glisten as they float, the green fields, the woods and hills all about, and away off on the far horizon our mountains, with their familiar outlines stamped so cleanly against the lighter blue. Odors and perfumes delightfully new to city folks, of clover, grasses, flowers, all sweet and pure, filled the warm, life-giving air; and the low voice of Nature fell so soothingly, lulling every sense to dreamy ecstasy.

Then Aunt Abbie came to add the last touch. How the neat figure and kindly face harmonized with the fresh green earth, the old, weather-worn house—with the simple handiwork of Nature and man!

She told us of the clover, and where lucky sprays could be found—perhaps; of the flowers, the wooded walks, the little rivulet on Elm Farm. We swung and listened while she entertained us from her store of fact and fancy, quaintly expressed in that dear dialect, a matter more of inflection and simplicity than of changed word forms. But hers was a busy life; she had "just come out for a moment and must go right back."

"Haven't you time for a story, Aunt Abbie, before you go, just one?"

No one could withstand that, so she turned back; and as the tale unfolded, our swinging hammocks slowly came to rest, the shrill voices from the grass sank into a soft accompaniment, and the glorious beauties all around became a simple background, as all attention was held by the weird relation.

"Well, it isn't much of a story anyhow, just about my sister. She had been sick a long time. Her cough had been growing worse and worse till she was so thin and weak it made my heart ache to be near her, and she did suffer so. Everybody else knew it couldn't last much longer, but she was always saying she was getting better, and would be well soon.

"I was terribly afraid to have my sister leave us. I felt she was not ready to go. She didn't seem to be a Christian, and—I was afraid.

"This night I am telling about, I went to bed all tired out, but for a long time I couldn't get to sleep for thinking of my poor sick sister, and praying for her as I lay and tossed. Then I don't remember anything, till she came and called me. I saw her come in with a lamp. It lighted up her face, and I shall never forget how she looked—so thin and weak and sunken, all but her eyes, and they seemed to glisten as if they were burning; and her hair, that was so soft and fine, shone too in the light. She took my hand, and somehow I knew she wanted me to go with her for company. I didn't feel like saying a word, and it didn't seem strange at all to follow her out into the night. Rain had been falling, and the ground was wet and slippery. Everything was so gloomy and still! Great dark clouds seemed almost ready to fall, they looked so heavy, the woods and hills were black, and as I looked back once I saw the house, all dark but one little light in her window shining in the night. She didn't speak at all, but hurried on, clinging to my hand and pulling. I never had been over that road before, nor even seen such a country. There were no woods and no fields, only great rocks, lying all about and piled in hills.

"By and by we came to a river. It was broad and deep, because the water flowed so slowly, and made hardly any noise as it swept along. I looked back to the right, and saw the moon shining through a hole in the clouds. It looked so strange! My sister's hand felt cold, clutching mine, as she stood and looked out across to the bleak and shadowy other shore. Then I saw a little boat coming towards us swiftly. It seemed to glide along, and although the man in it was rowing, it came much faster than any man could make it go, and without a sound. I was afraid of that dark man in his black boat, and tried to pull my sister away as he stepped ashore; but she couldn't move, and didn't struggle as he took her hand and pulled her from me into the boat. He turned and started back, and then—the boat sank. I saw it go down, leaving a little whirl where it had been on the water, and—I was alone. My sister had gone down there."

Aunt Abbie stopped, overcome by the vivid recollection of that terrible scene, then resumed, in the suppressed, awed voice which narration of the supernatural seems always to inspire.

"I stood a long time looking down at the spot where I had seen my sister go. Gradually a light began to glow and grow there. I raised my eyes to see where it came from, and right across the dark river saw—her, my sister, standing and looking at me. But it was not my sister as I had known her, for she was beautiful, glorious—all the light that made the night so bright came from her. Her face, her hair, the white robe that floated about her, shone with a light like that of little stars on a cold, clear winter night. As I stood with outstretched arms gazing at the sister I loved, the brightness seemed to grow and fill her eyes, till all that I could see was light. Staggering and blinded I fell on the river bank, and knew no more.

"In the morning my mother came to wake me. Her voice trembled as she told how my sister had gone to sleep for the last time here. But I never was afraid for her after what I had seen that night."

The good woman left us to think it over, while she made ready the midday meal.

MISS DROMGOOLE OUT FOR A DAY'S VACATION ON THE RIVER ELK.

THE VALLEY PATH.

A Novel of Tennessee Life.

BY WILL ALLEN DROMGOOLE.

This clay well mixed with marl and sand,
Follows the motion of my hand:
For some must follow and some command,
Though all are made of clay.

—"Kéramos."

The sea forms just a few faint bubbles
Of stifled breathing, when a ship goes down.

—Alice Cary.

CHAPTER I.

At the foot of the crags, a gray bird in a nest of green, stood the doctor's cabin. Above it, the white mists ascending and descending about the heights of Sewanee; below, a brown thread in winter, in summer a strip of gay green, the pleasant valley of the Elk; through the valley—now lisping along its low banks, now cutting its course, a mountain torrent, through a jungle of cedar and ivy and laurel, the everlasting greens—the Elk itself, gurgling gaily down to meet the Tennessee; and through the valley, in and out among the greens, climbing the mountain farther back, the old brown footpath that used to pass the doctor's door. Making a turn or two it also passed the door of the next house; a little white-washed cabin, set back in a clearing which Alicia Reams, the miller's granddaughter, used to call her "truck patch." Singing among her pea-rows, summer days, her voice would come down to the doctor under his own vine and fig tree, mixing and mingling strangely with his fancies.

The click-clack of the mill on Pelham Creek might be heard too as far as the doctor's, such days as toll was plenty and the wind not contrary.

It was only a step from the doctor's house to Alicia's by way of the brown footpath, and he was a frequent visitor at the miller's. Yet were their lives far enough apart, for all the connecting path. For Jonathan Reams was a dusty old fellow in jeans, a domestic that was considered only the better for being unbleached. Of a pattern was the miller with his wife, familiarly known, as mountain mothers are, as granny. Of a pattern the two so far as appearances went; no further, for granny was querulous and "fixed in her ways some." Any hour of the day, when she was not dozing over her pipe, either upon the hearth or under Alicia's honeysuckle vines, her voice might be heard scolding the miller, calling to Alicia to "shoo the chickens out of the gyarden," singing the praises of the herb doctor or the psalms of the Methodists, as her mood might move her. Alicia's mother, however, had "been a schoolma'am once, befo' she died," and had taught her children, Al and Lissy, something of books. She had been a dreamer evidently, who had mistaken brawn for manhood and so married Jed Reams, the miller's son. The mother died, for grief of her mistake; the father, like other miller's sons, from natural causes. The boy Al inherited the mother's frail physique; to the girl fell her qualities of soul. Humble folks enough were they.

There was a silver doorplate on the doctor's door:

BARTHOLOMEW BORING, M. D.

Within, there were books, carpets, and servants: those marks of culture, and, they said, of the "eccentric." Such they were pleased to call him, those who had known him before the valley knew him, for a friend. He might have walked the heights; that he found the valley paths more to his taste, the years in which he trod their humble ways bore evidence. That he had been ignorant of those unpretentious ways the first days of his coming, the silver plate bore evidence. When he did fall into line with all about him the silver plate furnished so much of wonder and amusement that he let it be. And there it is to this day:

BARTHOLOMEW BORING, M. D.

They had come for miles to look at it; come horseback and afoot, singly and in squads. They had wondered if M. D. might not be a warning, like "hands off," or "look out for pickpockets," or "don't tramp on the grass," until at last a shrewd young giant from across the mountain made out to read the riddle:

"It stands for mad," he declared. "Bartholomew Borin', Mad Doctor.' That's what the sign says."

From that time he was placed, labelled like a vial of his own strychnine; *the mad doctor.*

He chuckled, enjoying the joke as keenly as its perpetrators. He even swore they were right: "Else why

should a man forsake houses, and brethren, or wife,"——
and there he stopped, as he always did, to sigh. Wife; that
was the pivot upon which his fate had turned; swung from
sun to shade, to rest at last under the stiller shadows of the
wilderness.

The footpath way was familiar with his tread; and with
his thoughts,

"If things inanimate catch heart-beats."

He was fond of its varied windings among the dusky glooms
and sunnier ways. The brown trail had been first opened
by the cattle that went up daily to graze upon the long lush
plateau grasses, stopping by the way to touch their nozzles
to the cooling waters of the Elk. Later the opening in the
brake became a footpath for the people on the mountain's
side who came down Sabbath mornings to worship in the
valley "meet'n house" at Goshen near unto Pelham Creek.

"Because," they said, "the Episcopers had tuk the
mount'n bodaciously, callin' of it S'wany. And furthermore," they said, "Episcopers an' mount'neer won't mix
worth mentionin'."

And so the mountain monarch had followed the example
of his red brothers and "moved on," leaving the plateau to
the "Episcopers," who planted their flag and erected their
homes and worshipped their God under the beautiful groves
of Sewanee. But to this good day "Episcoper" and mountaineer refuse to mix, "worth mentionin'."

The doctor "mixed" with them as little as his rustic
neighbors.

"They're out of my beat," he would declare, pointing
along the footpath. "Too high," pointing up the mountain,
"too *church*. I like this better."

He seldom followed the path further than the foot of the
mountain, unless he had a patient up there, as was sometimes the case among the very poor, the natives, living along
the steep. He would walk to the spot where the path made
a turn at Alicia's truck patch, and stand leaning over the
palings of Alicia's fence, talking with grandad Reams, the
miller, about heaven, until dismissed by granny from the
doorstep, as "a doggone infidel."

Sometimes it would be Alicia he talked with, about the
chickens, the eggs he wanted her to fetch over, or to ask if
little Al was ailing. Sometimes he only walked there to
look up at the heights and at Sewanee, and to wonder concerning its creeds and dogmas. But he always called over
the fence to Alicia, for some one thing or another.

"Just for the pure pleasure of hearing her laugh," he told himself; "it is like the gurgle of Elk River among the gray rocks at low-water time." He remembered the first time he ever walked there and saw the bright head among the corn rows, and heard the little gurgling laugh, and met the honest, gray eyes with their untroubled deeps, and felt the force of her beautiful character, abloom like the sturdy mountain laurel among the secluded ways of the wilderness. He remembered her hands, and the first strong clasp of her fingers, and the gentleness of their touch the first time he ever met her, in a cabin by the Pelham road, with a dead baby lying across her knees, and those strong gentle fingers feeling for its heart, that had fluttered like a wounded bird's and then—stopped. She had looked like a Madonna, with her motherly arms and sweet girl face. In his fancy he had called her "the Madonna," that first time he saw her. And he had wondered then—but if he is going back to that "first time" when, yielding to a whim or an inspiration, he had bidden the old walks farewell, sent his servants on to prepare a place for him to set his foot down free of creeds and friends and heartaches, and had sought the cabin in the wilds, cast his lot among the humble dwellers there, and had stumbled upon other creeds and friends and heartaches— why, we will turn the page and go with him, back to that *first time* when among the Tennessean vales, in a cabin in the wilds, he encountered Alicia, the miller's granddaughter, *his* Madonna.

Women know their fate from the moment they know any-thing; with a change in the pattern of a dress their destinies are fairly one, with perchance this slight variety—wife, spinster. But men stumble upon a strange destiny as they stumble upon one another; along the crowded walk, in the glare and glow of gaslight, in the ballroom, in the quiet woodland ways after their rose dreams have ended, along with youth and youthful fancies. Yet are the colors of the afterglow warmer, less blinding than the sun's rays at meridian.

CHAPTER II.

The workmen had gone back to the city and the house had been in all readiness for more than a week, when a trap set the doctor and his terrier Zip down at the gate of that which he was pleased to term his "mountain home."

Aunt Dilce had scrubbed and rubbed and made things "homeful" within doors, while her son Ephraim had performed a like service in stable and yard. Both servants, however, felt that it was so much good labor gone for naught: so much care put upon a cabin that was only a cabin when all was said and done. The only redeemable feature about the business was that it was all for the master, and was one of his whims of which, they doubted not, he would soon tire.

Then there was the silver doorplate: to be sure that covered a multitude of sins. Aunt Dilce felt an honest town pride in that doorplate. The workmen whom the doctor had sent up to attend to things, and who had put the plate in place, were scarcely outside the gate before old Dilce was polishing the bit of silver fit to kill. She kept it up every day until the doctor arrived. When the natives began to ride by and peep over the low fence at the little shining square, the old woman only polished the more vigorously. When they opened the gate and striding up the walk to the door, stood spelling out "the sign," her pride in it became such that she would certainly have rubbed it out of countenance but for the doctor's rush to the rescue.

It was the morning after his arrival, a morning in early spring. The laurel was in bloom along the river bluffs, and a quince tree in the corner of the yard near the fence gave promise of bursting buds.

The doctor rose early—an indication of old age he told himself—and called for his coffee.

"Throw open the windows," he said to Ephraim, "then hand me my purple dressing gown and tell your mother I want my coffee. I want it hot: as hot as ——"

"Here 'tis, marster: en yo' bre'kfus' 'll be raidy in a minute." The old woman had appeared most opportunely: the doctor was about to let slip his one pet profanity.

He laughed softly as he slipped into his purple robings and his easy chair, and leaning his big gray head back against the velvet rest he prepared to enjoy the coffee which old Dilce was arranging on the stand at his right hand.

There was a click of the little gate latch; the "big gray" was lifted; through the open window came the fresh, sweet river-breath, and the far-away odor of new mould where some industrious plowman was overturning the sod further down the valley. And through the window the twinkling blue eyes saw a long, lank figure, followed by another and another, amble up to his doorstep, stop a moment, and move on, making room for the next, like a procession at a public funeral stopping to look at the corpse in state. Fully twenty passed in at the gate and out again. The master turned to Dilce:

"What the hell are they doing?" he demanded; and then came old Dilce's turn at chuckling.

"Hit's de do' fixin's, marster," she declared. "Dem do' fixin's am too fine fur dese parts; en de ain' showin' ob you de proper respec', accordin' ter my suppression. Yistiddy one o' de stroppinist ones ob dem all nicknamed ob you 'de Mad Doctor.' He say dat what de sign mean; M. D.—'Dat mean Mad Doctor,' he say."

The gray head went back upon the velvet chair rest, and a laugh echoed among the rafters and sills and beams of the gray cabin such as they had not heard since rescued from the owl, the bat and the gopher, to make room for the medicine boxes and books of the "mad doctor."

"It is enough to make them think me a lunatic," he told himself, as all day the passersby stopped to wonder at the reckless waste of silver. "And when they discover that I am not here to practise, but merely to nurse a whim and a disposition to cynicism and catarrh, they will think me madder still—rip, ranting mad. 'The other side' thought the same thing because I refused to put the plate on a door in the city. Well, well: we'll see, we'll see. Maybe there will be no call for declining to practise," he laughed softly, "among my new neighbors. At all events I need not refuse until the arrival of my first patient."

Sure enough, as he had half expected, they set him in the balance at once. "Against herbs and conjure and hornets," he said whenever he told the joke, as he certainly did tell it, to any of his former friends who hunted him up now and then by a visit to his "shanty," or sent him an invitation to meet them at Sewanee, the Episcopal seat of learning.

They set him in the balance the very first day of his arrival. He was strolling about the yard among the flower beds Ephraim was laying off, enjoying his modest possessions in his own cranky old way, bareheaded, the sun making a sparkle of his wavy hair that touched the purple velvet collar of his robe, working a pleasant contrast even in the eyes of the young giant riding along the footpath toward the gate.

To a mind more familiar with the æsthetic might have occurred some pretty imagery, some blend of color, gray and purple, like the mists that covered the mountain-top. But the visitor was a stranger to æsthetics. He saw the gray head and the purple gown, the kindly, old-young face with its laughing eyes half hidden under the bushy brows. If he made any comparison nobody knew it. There were curiosity, eagerness, business, in the man's whole appearance; in the very trot of the yellow mule upon whose bare back he sat astride, his own bare feet almost touching the ground on either side.

At the visitor's "Halloo," the doctor looked up from the mignonette bed; something told him this was the arrival of his first patient. The two regarded each other steadily. What the doctor saw was a slender-built young fellow, with clean, sharply defined features, blue eyes that were wells of mirth, a chin which meant defiance, a brow browned by the valley sun, and pushed back with careless, unconscious grace an old slouch hat, the inevitable adornment of his class. A mass of soft clinging curls gave a girlish softness to the defiant face. The full, beardless lips were ready to break into smiles despite the scowl with which their owner was regarding this newcomer to the valley.

In this newcomer the visitor saw a young-old face; the eyes and smile of youth, the lines and snow of age on brow and temple. Beyond the physician the mountaineer saw the silver door plate and its flaunting M. D., and seeing took courage.

"Air you the town doctor?" he demanded, flecking a cockle burr from the yellow mule's comb with the tip of a willow withe which served him as a riding whip.

"Yes," said the doctor, "I am, and a mighty good one at that."

The visitor lifted his big bare foot and planted it upon the topmost rail of the gray worm fence, almost under the very nose of the Æsculapius, and pointing with the willow switch to his great toe, swollen and red and distorted, demanded:

"What ails *hit?*"

The possessor of three diplomas put on his spectacles: the toe was three times its ordinary size; the flesh was raw-looking and ugly: he touched it gingerly with his practised fingers.

"A bad toe," he declared, in his slow, professional voice.

Ephraim, the bow-legged boy of all work, had sauntered up, dragging his hoe after him; Aunt Dilce was listening, arms akimbo, from the corner of the house.

"That, sir," the physician explained, "is what we doctors call a pretty bad case of erysipelas."

The mountaineer reined in the yellow mule. "Erysip'lls *hell!*" he replied. "A hornet stung it."

The mule went down the road to Pelham in a cloud of yellow dust. Old Dilce ambled back to the kitchen with her cotton apron stuffed into her mouth. Ephraim stumbled

back to his mignonette bed. The doctor suddenly turned
upon him:

"You Ephraim."

"Yes, sah!"

Ah! he *was* showing his ivories.

"If you ever tell that to a living soul, sir, I'll break every
bone in your body; do you hear, sir?"

He couldn't hear Aunt Dilce chuckling over the cake she
was about to slap upon the hoe that had become too hot
while she had been enjoying the call of the master's first
patient.

Yet that first patient proved another pivot upon which
life made a turn; such is the unsuspected magnitude of
trifles. It was the real beginning of his life in the little
cove tucked away among the spurs of the Cumberlands
where he had elected to pass his summers, not his life.
That he would have other patients he never once considered;
no more did he moralize upon "the opportunities of doing
good" which had become too much of a phrase to hold real
earnest meaning. He had given up moralizing long ago;
while as for the opportunities he rather thought of them as
something either self-creative or thrust upon one. That
they would come he took for granted, though he refused to
seek them. When at last one tapped at his door he did not
recognize it at all, hearing in its voice only the cry of suffering humanity; he merely buttoned on his coat and went to
meet it, that was all.

(To be continued.)

BOOKS OF THE DAY.

MAX NORDAU'S "DEGENERATION." *

A man who has done such good work as the German Hebrew, Max Nordau, in his volumes, "Conventional Lies" and "Paradoxes," is perhaps entitled to more serious consideration than has been accorded him by certain critics who have lost all patience with the glaring inconsistencies, the intemperance and the abusiveness which are too often present in his latest work. But it must be admitted that the fatal defects of "Degeneration" as a volume of criticism, no less than the lofty assumption of monopoly of wisdom on the part of Nordau, are well calculated to provoke the criticism which has been meted out to him on all hands. While I have always deplored the mediæval ideas which this writer has advanced in regard to woman and his total lack of sympathy with much that I regard as most vital in the new thought of our day in his earlier works, I had so admired his brave, strong and vigorous unmasking of conventional hypocrisy, that it was with the most painful disappointment that I finished a perusal of his last and most pretentious volume; because this book, while possessing the vigor, and, at times, the brilliancy and lucidity of expression which are characteristic of "Conventional Lies," impresses me as lacking every element which must distinguish any work of literary criticism that in the nature of the case can possess real value.

A critical treatise conspicuously wanting in discriminating judgment, in all sense of proportion, in a temperate or judicial spirit, and which is glaringly inconsistent, as well as frequently abusive, even descending at times to coarseness and vulgarity, cannot be expected to add lustre to the fame of the author. Nor can it prove helpful to thoughtful and discriminating people, although it is liable to prove exceedingly injurious to that large class of readers who do little thinking for themselves, and who are more influenced by brilliant rhetoric than by a logical or critical examination of a subject. I do not wish to be unfair to Max Nordau, and yet I cannot understand how any candid reader can escape the conviction that all of the defects I have mentioned are present in a fatal degree in this work. In his diagnosis he reminds me far more of a pretentious charlatan, than a truly scientific physician. Like a quack who has made a vital mistake in regard to the disorder of the patient, and who seeks to

---

* "Degeneration," by Max Nordau. Cloth; pp. 560; price $3. D. Appleton & Co., New York City.

exaggerate unduly and to magnify all symptoms which might support his erroneous conclusions, while resolutely closing his eyes to the major symptoms which prove the falsity of his position, our author has arrived at certain conclusions which are open to serious criticism, and maintains his false premises by magnifying the unquestioned evils which are ever present in a great transition period like ours. But he does something even more indefensible, in manufacturing capital by assailing and abusing many of the noblest and sanest brains of this or any other age.

His work, while at times unquestionably brilliant, lacks every element of sound criticism, and is painfully wanting in the application of scientific methods at almost every point. That it contains some philosophy, I gladly concede; that many of his strictures on the tendencies of certain gross and materialistic writers are excellent, I freely grant, while I must admit that those who are conversant with his writings will be surprised at many of the strictures coming from Max Nordau. These excellences in his work, which we readily admit, are, however, so hopelessly mixed with scurrilous criticism of the finest and loftiest thinkers of the age that the result is painful to those who have admired Nordau in the past. An indiscriminate and often inaccurate attack upon writers and thinkers who are manifestly far less amenable to the criticisms made than is the critic, naturally offends the sense of justice in sober and sane men and women. All that he says which is true and just in criticism of our age might be said of any great transition period, or any era of great growth, of any time when the race has been engaged in a tremendous struggle for the realization of higher ideals and nobler truths. Such periods are always trying to sensitive natures, for the ocean of human thought is lashed by its own conflicting ideas like the sea in a furious tempest.

Moreover, as new lights dawn there are always some minds who abuse the higher trust vouchsafed to the expanding mental hunger, mistaking a wider liberty which should serve to impel man more rapidly upward for a permission for license which degrades. This is unfortunate; something always to be deplored and condemned. But to mistake these exceptional instances for a tendency of civilization is one of those fatal errors of our critic; and after arriving at this false conclusion to seek to sustain it by denouncing as "degenerates" such noble characters as Ruskin and Tolstoi is as unphilosophic as it is absurd. We naturally expect that Nordau would show no quarter to mystics, idealists, or symbolists. A Sadducee of the Sadducees; a man who has been the idol of the realists, who is nothing if he is not blunt, and in the eyes of many, gross; a thinker whose ideas are not only materialistic, but whose conceptions in many respects, certainly in regard to woman, are cast in an ancient mould, is not to be expected to show much consideration toward those persons who have heard the "still small voice"; who are conscious of "the inner light"; who see and hear much which men and women on a different plane cannot comprehend. Nordau in this respect is precisely like one who is color-blind and who is also afflicted with egomania. He is disgusted and indignant that any one should see what he does not see, and at once relegates such persons to the realm of the mentally unsound and labels them "degenerates." The possibility of his being mistaken never enters his mind. The mystics are "degenerates," and that settles it, for Nordau has spoken.

One would scarcely expect to find a critic thus afflicted with egomania denouncing Ibsen as an egomaniac. The admirers of the great Norwegian poet, however, will be pleased to learn that, after denouncing him at length in the most vigorous manner, ridiculing what he terms "his absurdities," and sneering at his defence of wider freedom for women, Nordau relents slightly, and gravely tells us that "Ibsen is not wholly diseased in mind, but only a dweller on the borderland—a mattoid." But having admitted this much our critic seems to be oppressed with a guilty fear lest he has conceded too much, especially when he remembers "his imbecile tendency toward allegory and symbolism." This form of "mental stigma of Ibsen," his "mysticism," throws Nordau into a paroxysm, as anything relating to idealism, mysticism, or symbolism is liable to exert a very unwholesome influence upon him; and he tells us that Ibsen might "be numbered among the mystic 'degenerates.'"

In this fashion he rambles on until a new idea seems to rush in upon his frenzied brain, when he exclaims "this egomania assumes the form of anarchism." Poor Nordau! What is the form which characterizes your egomania? For surely there never was a clearer case of egomania than that exemplified in your latest work.

On reading this book one is reminded of the little boy who sallies forth with his hatchet, bent on chopping down every flower and shrub which age has not rendered impervious to his attacks. One trembles at times for Nordau's own brain children, for they are far more vulnerable than many of the works which he assails most savagely in order to establish the fact that the authors against whom he inveighs are "degenerates." But our anxiety on this point is unnecessary; he mercifully spares his own works. That he lacks all sense of proportion and constantly displays an absence of intellectual poise is seen in his assault upon almost all the great thinkers of our time, urging that they are insane or "degenerate." The mystic and the realist, the idealist and the veritist, John Ruskin and Tolstoi, together with Ibsen and Wagner no less than Zola and writers of still more questionable morals, are all indiscriminately assailed. He shrewdly saw that by attacking the noblest and most luminous geniuses of the century, as well as men of grosser fibre, he would call down the indignation and contempt of thoughtful people. Therefore in his preface he predicts that he will be assailed, and in an ingeniously written advertisement of his book in the August *Century Magazine* we find him posing as a prophet and martyr. He gravely informs us that people have been distressed at the rumors of his insanity, and have written him to know whether or not there is insanity in his family, after which he soberly states that his ancestors have been rabbis, where the only sign of insanity he knows of is found in their not being thrifty enough to amass money. I am free to confess, after reading his shrewd advertisement of his book in the *Century* and a recent number of the *Forum*, that I think we can fairly absolve him from any suspicion of insanity on *the ground of lack of thriftiness.* Any reasonably sane man would know that a work which assails as "degenerate" the noblest constructive thinkers, as well as the grosser writers of our times, would call forth general condemnation from thoughtful people, so it needed not the keen vision of a prophet to foresee this; and it is equally clear that if our author expected that a person who assailed so lofty and inspiring an author as John Ruskin as a "degenerate" would retain the esteem of well-balanced men and women, he could not, to say the least, have formed a very high opinion of the discriminating power of men and women of our time. His criticisms of the pre-Raphaelites, who we are gravely informed "got their leading principles from Ruskin," display such ignorance of the facts involved that the reader is at once placed on his guard against accepting as facts various statements on which much of Nordau's reasoning is based. The necessity for this becomes more and more apparent as one peruses this volume, which as I have observed is at once brilliant, erratic, reckless, and not seldom violently abusive. Those acquainted with Ruskin's "Modern Painters" will be amused to hear this critic of critics referring to the great English thinker's work as *"feverish studies in art."* Nor will sane persons agree with him when he adds that *"Ruskin's theory is in itself delirious."*

Whenever the gross materialism of Nordau runs against the finer conceptions of idealists or mystics, which he is wholly unable to comprehend, not only is he satisfied that he has found a "degenerate," but he becomes so furious that he is liable to resort to scurrilous epithets. The mystics among painters of an earlier day, such artists, for example, as Giotto and Fra Angelico, were unlike Ruskin and the modern painters of whom he writes, in that the former were "mystics through ignorance," whereas the latter's *mysticism arose from mental degeneration!*

When our critic comes to Wagner he at times appears to lose all control of his mental powers; sometimes becoming absurd, at other times abusive, and so palpably unjust in his strictures and so devoid of the critical spirit as to make one feel mingled pity and disgust for the critic. Nordau has a case to make against Wagner, who he informs us is a "mystic," a "sensualist," and an "anarchist." And being both prosecutor and judge he proceeds without interruption, ignoring almost every essential of sound criticism. I have space for only a few of the extreme utterances which illustrate the lack of discriminating power and the incoherence of our author. And I wish to preface these extracts with one in which our critic characterizes one kind of "degenerate" which I think most persons who wade through this bulky volume will agree is far more applicable to Max Nordau than to Richard Wagner: "His fundamental frame of mind is persistent rage against everything and everyone, which he displays in vicious phrases, savage threats, and the destructive mania of wild beasts. Wagner is a specimen of this species."

In the chapter entitled "The Richard Wagner Cult," we are told that "Richard Wagner is himself alone charged with a greater abundance of degeneration than all the 'degenerates' put together with whom we have hitherto become acquainted. The stigmata of this morbid condition are united in him in the most complete and most luxurious development. He displays in the general constitution of his mind the persecution mania—megalomania, a mysticism; in his instincts vague philanthropy, anarchism, a craving for revolt and contradiction; in his writings all the signs of graphomania, namely, incoherence, bugitive ideation, and a tendency to idiotic punning, and in the groundwork of his being the characteristic emotionalism of a color at once erotic and religiously enthusiastic. . . . His system calls for criticism in every part. . . . The incoherence of Wagner's thought, determined as it is by the excitation of the moment, manifests itself in his constant contradictions. . . . Wagner is a desperate anarchist." (This is a favorite expression with Nordau, when he wishes to arouse the prejudice of his readers against some great genius.) Again he tells us that "shameless sensuality prevails in his dramatic poems. . . . The irresistible propensity to play on words and other peculiarities of graphomania and maniacs is developed to a high degree in Wagner. Like all 'degenerates,' Wagner is wholly sterile as a poet, although he has written a long series of dramatic works. . . . Wagner swaggers about the art work of the future, and his partisans hail him as the artist of the future. He the artist of the future! He is a bleating ego of the far-away past. His path leads back to deserts long since abandoned by all life. Wagner is the last mushroom on the dunghill of romanticism. . . .

"Of Wagner the musician I treat lastly, because this task will give us a clear proof of his degeneracy. . . . To the end of his life Wagner's existence was conflict and bitterness, and his boastings had no other echo than the laughter not only of rational beings, but, alas, of fools also. It was not until he had long passed his fiftieth year that he began to know the intoxication of universal fame. And in the last decade of his life he was installed among the demigods.

It had come to this; that the world in the interval had become ripe for him—and for the madhouse. He had the good fortune to endure until the general degeneration and hysteria were sufficiently advanced to supply rich and nutritious soil for his theories of art." In one place Nordau tells us that with Wagner amorous excitement assumes the form of mad deliriums.

In his shrewd advertisement of his book in the *Century*, to which I have alluded, Nordau complains of the abusive character of the criticisms which have been heaped upon him. In this connection let me quote the following compliment paid by Nordau to the tens of thousands of the most intellectual and cultured men and women of modern civilization who admire Wagner:

"The lovers of his pieces behave like tom-cats gone mad, rolling in contortions and convulsions over a root of valerian. They reflect a state of mind in the poet which is well known to the professional expert. It is a form of Sadism. It is the love of those 'degenerates' who in sexual transports become like wild beasts. Wagner suffered from erotic madness, which leads gross natures to murder from lust and inspires higher natures with works like *Die Walkure, Siegfried* and *Tristan und Isolde*."

Would it not be difficult to conceive of anything more coarse, vulgar, abusive, or insulting to be hurled in the face of refined, highly organized and truly civilized men and women? And yet Nordau poses as a martyr and complains against the abuse of his critics!

There is one other point I wish to notice about this book, which emphasizes the inconsistency of the author. In his chapters on Realism he makes several very excellent observations as to the influence of gross and sensual literature on certain minds He holds that such realistic pictures, even though true, are poisonous, and severely denounces them; and then, as we near the close of the volume, he draws a picture of the twentieth century as it might be if conditions as he imagines they exist continued to run riot, and in this imaginary sketch he completely out-Zolas Zola, but assures us at length that such conditions will not obtain. Now if it is poisonous to have these pictures or delineations given to the world in literature, even though they be true, what can be said of the man who draws an imaginary sketch at once revolting and disgusting, while he admits that such a condition of things will never be realized!

I have seldom read a book so thoroughly disappointing as this; a book which I regard as exceedingly pernicious, because of the confusing of the ignoble with the noble, chiefly due, I think, to the absence of any fine spiritual discernment in the author and to a mental state which has rendered him entirely unable to discuss matters temperately, judiciously, consistently, or with any sense of proportion in regard to their merits and demerits.

B. O. FLOWER.

THE PASSING OF ALIX.*

This bright, American society novel will appeal to a large class of persons who desire to read for amusement and who do not wish to be burdened with weighty themes. And yet the chief value of the work lies in the *naïve* manner in which the author sows seed thoughts which will set many readers to thinking. Every little while the interrogation is raised, and then the writer artlessly carries us on with the story in hand. The author is evidently familiar with society life in New York and Paris.

The heroine Alix, is a beautiful Virginia girl. Her father, a wealthy Parisian, had fallen in love with a young American beauty in Paris, but the young lady, unlike most of the daughters of our mushroom aristocracy, would marry only on condition that her husband should come to America and to her loved Virginia to live. This he did. At the birth of Alix the mother passed beyond the curtain of physical life. The father cherished and reared with the greatest care his little daughter. When a young lady the two went to Paris. Here a boyhood friend of the father, the Marquis de Morier, a distinguished but dissipated member of the old order, sought the daughter's hand for the ducats the marriage would bring. He played his game skilfully, however, and deceived the father, who believed him to be the soul of honor. The daughter, always accustomed to acquiesce in her father's wishes, married De Morier. On their wedding trip they stop at Monte Carlo. There the bride is startled to see the maniac gleam in the eyes of her husband when he sees the gamblers plying their trade, and his conduct assures her that she has married one as insane in regard to gambling as was ever drunkard in regard to drinking. Coming out of the halls a telegram is handed her informing her of the sudden death of her father.

But it is not my purpose to tell the story. The events which follow reveal to the young wife the real nature of the moral wreck she has married. She leaves him a handsome sum and returns to America. On board ship she meets an elderly lady and a strong intimacy springs up. They are spiritually related, and that is the truest relationship that can exist. After a time a child is born, and the young mother follows the promptings of her sense of duty and informs the Marquis, who, however, dies shortly after the birth of the child. Later, the high-minded little American widow meets and loves the son of the elderly lady whom she met on her return to America. This young man was then absent in the Orient.

Of the remainder of the novel I shall not speak, for it is not my purpose to dwell upon the entertaining story here given. The land is

---

* " The Passing of Alix," by Mrs. Marjorie Paul. Pp. 266; price, cloth $1.25, paper 50 cents. The Arena Publishing Company, Boston, Mass.

flooded with novels quite as strong as this from a literary point of view and some far more meritorious if judged as literature. But the true value of this story lies in its twentieth-century seed thoughts which are given to the gay novel reader among society people. The work will appeal to a class who would not read a story of a different character, and they will unconsciously receive some fine thoughts which cannot fail to prove beneficial. Thus, for example, we find these observations in regard to woman's position in the marriage relation:

The world condemns always that woman who will not subject herself to her husband, be he ever so vile, so he be great in its estimation—great in riches or titles, and greatly sought after.

* * * * *

Bitter the tears and terrible the strivings, the invectives, against fate and a false dictum of those unfortunates also, children who have actually been thrust into the world without the ordinary forethought which attains in the most trivial undertaking, and, worse still, into chaotic and opposing elements, unwelcomed and unloved. Is it amazing, given such conditions and habitudes, that society both high and low, should be corrupt, families embittered, and communities disrupted?

Better depopulate our continents than thrust unwilling and unwelcome human egos into the vortex of a civilization which does not civilize the fathers and mothers of men.

It would be well to civilize the individual, to teach him the ethics and responsibilities of fatherhood, motherhood—that the foundation-stone of vice and pauperism is irresponsible propagation. License, unrestricted or unhallowed, is a crime in nature's ordinances.

So long as church or state approves or tolerates such irresponsibility, or encourages directly or supposititiously, the hungry, the illiterate, the imbecile, or the criminal to "increase and multiply," rather than teach them temperance, responsibility, and an exceptional obligation in this fundamental and far-reaching procreative principle of life and living, so long will poverty, viciousness, and violence hang like a pall over the wide, unthinking world.

* * * * *

The innocent—none are innocent who, knowing, withhold knowledge; who, beholding the inevitable, refuse to raise a hand to stay the torrent which ignorance is forcing to the flood. All will go down before its onslaught if eyes that see warn not the sightless and knowledge give not of its abundant store, that ignorance be arrested at its source and not its centres.

* * * * *

Men will not force the siege, but women must. Men will surrender when women proclaim their freedom. When they have won the ballot, surely they will besiege the judiciary and the halls of legislation and demand the children's ransom. They will ena t laws that shall replace the old laws of oppression and protect these little people whose small voices are not heard in the land, but who presently will make or mar its civilization.

The spirit which permeates the work is summed up in the words:

This is heaven—to help the beloved who are helpless, to inaugurate great reformations, and, impressing certain sensitive and responsive organisms, push them forward to completion.

To progress, there is no other heaven. Hell is retrogression.

The story is occult and will appeal to the uninitiated in our great cities who are eagerly seeking occult truths. Many critics sneeringly pronounce this passion for spiritual and occult knowledge among the wealthy a "popular fad." I do not regard it as such. It is the outcropping of hearts hungry for something grander, nobler, and truer than the shallow round of social life offers. Some there are who are faddists, but this is not true of the majority; they hunger and thirst for something deeper and higher than the frivolity of social life or the empty and meaningless platitudes of creedal religion. Hence, they turn to occult research for something to satisfy their spiritual hunger. To this class of persons this work will appeal strongly. One cannot but regret, however, that a book which contains so much of the higher truth of the new time should not be stronger in a literary way, although I think it is up to the general run of novels of society life of our time. I am curious to see how it will be received. To serious students of life, grand and noble souls, *those who know that self mastery is essential, and that the concern of one is the concern of all*, this novel will be tiresome in its pages devoted to general topics and the butterfly life which thousands of self-absorbed children of earth are living; on the other hand many of the careless lovers of the general society novel, while they will enjoy the lighter chapters, will I fancy find the high and ennobling thoughts sown throughout the book tiresome, if, indeed, they understand or are able to grasp their real meaning. Yet, as before observed, there are thousands of children of wealth in the social world who are hungry for the truths which this book contains, and to them I fancy it will appeal.

Here are some lines which will reflect the new thought of our time and which give this book a value aside from the ordinary society novel. They are words of one who has been a student of nature and her mysteries and who has drawn deeply from that inner well of knowledge which speaks of the divine in man:

God never built a prison for a world, and manacled its occupants, after imbuing them with aspiration and mentality.

A fury might, had she the deific and creative faculty; but furies are destroyers. None but the living God creates or governs.

* * * * *

And what He has created lives and grows, and as expressed in man blossoms into an intellectual profundity which unravels the abstruse, forcing the very elements to serve him in his search for truth. And the laws of nature aid him and abet him.

God has set His seal upon His children; in the image of divinity has he shaped them and their attributes. To what end, then? To the end that they shall grasp of their own effort and volition the eternal secrets, which are no longer secrets if He solve them.

Eternal progress is eternal mystery and solution. And only so can men become as God in likeness and similitude. As yet they are but the shadows of His reflex. The Christ encouraged research. "Seek and ye shall find. Knock and it shall be opened."

The prophets were fallible, as are the prophets of to-day. As much as is possible God constantly reveals Himself and many miracles through many prophets, whose sensitive organisms predilect them to inspirational prophecy.

* * * *

There are miracles to-day, as there always have been, such as Christ revealed to His disciples, which they performed in accordance with natural laws, and which many men of many ages have performed, having faith and comprehension of this immutable but marvellous law of psychics. Christ Himself proclaimed it—"And greater things than these shall ye do."

* * * * *

To give each ray or child of his begetting the faculty and the opportunity—here or somewhere—of hewing its career of individual conquest, by eternal exploration and experimental knowledge.

There can be no knowledge without personal experience and investigation, no achievement without effort, no eternity of fulfilment and progression without ages of experience and aspiration.

The extracts quoted will give the reader an idea of the author's style, and, as before observed, I believe this novel will prove helpful in dropping high and noble thoughts in minds not ready to read a more serious work. I conclude this notice by quoting the closing paragraph which gives a hint that I believe to contain a profound truth:

It may well be that in heaven there is no "marrying or giving in marriage" in any accepted sense or meaning. But that there is indubitably a love so great and indivisible that life or death or eternity itself may not disrupt or wither it, that love itself proclaims which has survived the throes of time and defies the grave to sever it.

It may well be that such alone are the "marriages made in heaven" or of which heaven takes any record.

B. O. FLOWER.

OUT OF THE PAST.*

This is not only an interesting but an instructive book. The tale is of the nature of an allegory, built upon the basis of the unending conflict between Good and Evil. Yet it is so skilfully wrought that the story itself holds the reader's interest and compels his admiration to the exclusion of the thought of its allegorical nature.

The method employed in the telling of the "Story of Gargya Balaki" (chapters 2 and 3), while possibly open to the criticism of prolixity, has been carefully planned to conform, in a measure, to the line of Hindu writing as found in the "Hitopadesa" and in the "Upanishads."

In those chapters he has outlined the possible life of a Brahmin of the earlier times, using extreme care to express by quotations the laws which compelled him, as a conscientious Brahmin, to pass

---

* "Out of the Past," by E. Anson More, Jr. Price, cloth $1.25, paper 60 cents. Arena Publishing Co.

through the four stages known as the "Brahmacarin," "Grihastha," "Vanaprastha," and "Sannyasin." These quotations are taken from the "Four Vedas," "Hindu Institutes" (or "Laws of Menu"), the "Upanishads," "Bhagavad-Gita," etc.

In chapter 4 he has pictured the several experiences of the soul in its various transmigrations after death, as described in the "Upanishads," and in accordance with the doctrine of the "Sankhya Karika."

The words ascribed to the Buddha have been taken from the "Dhammapada" and other writings of his early disciples.

In every instance the author has made it a rule to correctly illustrate his quotations by placing them in their proper environments. If the reader should care to combine information with what pleasure he might derive from the story, he will find that information given to accord with the belief of the orthodox Brahmin.

Two young men, college graduates, go to India. Their guide was bitten and killed by a cobra. One, being left alone while his comrade was gone for help, went into a cavern, where he had a grewsome experience with a cobra, which he conquered. There is the suggestion all the time that the cobra is a human being's soul thus incased as a punishment. Then he found in the pillow of a mummy, over which the reptile had seemed to keep guard, old writings, which he took to a native priest to translate.

The translation indicates that, from the Hindu point of view, women are "the cause of all trouble," etc. It is done in (Hindu) biblical style and has many Hindu words. The great sage who wrote the manuscript once went to Indra to get advice about women, having cursed his wife "because the flies troubled him in the morning." He then remarks naively, "Yet could not Indra help me, for women are subtle in wickedness beyond his curing." Indra recommends him to go to a still wiser god, and takes him through space to a mountain hundreds of miles high where the mango trees were miles high. There he is given the Holy Manuscript to read, and reads (and *incidentally writes into it what he sought*) as to the conduct and duty of wives. The author indicates in footnote, and later on elaborates the idea, that this was the way the priests originated the law of burning wives on husbands' graves— "Suttee." "Thereupon I showed them"—the householders who came first to learn—"the verse as it was changed, and they rejoiced *changing each his own book;* and we all agreed to teach the doctrine throughout the land, and to call it Sute or Suttee—it is revealed." "So they gave me many presents and great riches, and returned each to his home. For truly women, if taught the Suttee, will think more of their husbands living than dead. Verily it will make the husband's life precious unto them."

There follows a well-argued satire on the situation, To a religious

mind it would possibly be very serious. To me it is exceedingly
amusing and is good logic. Then heresies arose, and it was said
"Man had written the Vedas!" also that "Woman could attain beati-
tude through her own petty moralities." "And the women were
drunken with liberty." He then explains how he secured the first
victim for Suttee and how inspiring and noble was the sight, and
how *the priests had presents* as a result. The book has many wise
"sayings" of Hindu origin. It symbolizes much that is as true in
America as he makes it seem with the Hindu, with Vishnu, or with
Om. Man tries to bind woman to him by force, and at and for his
pleasure, but ever and always the real woman eludes him, and he is
not happy with the shell he secures by force and artifice. She does
not leave him, but he sees scorn, contempt, pity, and distrust ever
in her eyes. Her voice is gentle; she submits when she must, but he
knows that he has not secured what he sought. He knows, without
knowing why, that he has lost the spirit in compelling the action
of womanhood. Yet he does not understand. Much of it reminds
one of Oliver Schreiner's "Dreams." An idea of the fascinating
style of the book may be indicated by a quotation:

I was Gargya Balaki, the twice-born man, and, with Uma, I had
reached the place of the cave. The chamber was finished, and I
was returning from it to where she lay asleep under a tree. In
my hands were a roll of strips of cotton cloth, and a bamboo bottle,
containing a liquid wax. Before this my dream was indistinct, hazy,
like a foggy morning on the water. Impressions of form, of color,
of motion, came to me suddenly and fragmentarily, as sea waves
appear from the fog to break at our feet. But when I reached Uma,
and bent over her in hopeless passion, I suffered as no woman had
made me suffer in all my actual past as Maurice Amilon. The love
of my dream was the agony of a strong, resolute, unscrupulous
man, hopeless yet purposeful. Even as I dreamt, I wondered at myself, as one will in a dream, and realized that the feeling was deeper,
more passionate than I had ever known.

One moment of suffocating intensity, then I had her bound hand
and foot, immovable, and as I turned backward her tongue, to
imprison the five vital airs, she opened her eyes. She seemed to
understand what I was doing, to fathom the depths of my passion,
and I perceived not only scorn but triumph in her gaze. For an
instant it unnerved me and I was powerless to move, to think, so
like the agony of death was the bodily pain I suffered. But strength
came to me, and I wound the cloth about her and would not see
her, yet I felt her look. And as I wound wrap by wrap, an inward,
exultant cry arose from my heart. "She is mine, mine, mine!"

It was a horrible dream and I strove to waken from it; but I
could not. I was Gargya Balaki, desperate, hungering, yearning
Gargya Balaki, who loved and would not lose.

I cried aloud, saying, "I will not look at her," but could not resist
the impulse to meet her gaze. And then I would have given anything to have missed seeing her expression, so terrible was it in
blended pride, pity, and triumph.

In one of his visions with the gods, a voice said, "These are all
the inventions of man, of avaricious, bigoted, priest-creating man."

"It wat the saddest voice I had ever heard." His punishment begins: "The soul of the Hindu priest passed into the body of the cobra," "and the woe of my punishment seemed to stretch through the years that were gone, and forever into the future."

Finally the young American student secures the mummy of the Hindu girl he had found in the cave and takes it to New York to see if he can revive it according to his dream and the instructions contained in the paper he had found in the cave, and had translated. Thence he goes with "it" and his sister to the mountains of Colorado. Then we have the description of the experiments in following out the Hindu priest's method of restoration of life. Interest is well sustained, and the probableness of the whole thing made to appear. She is made to live, but is like a little child—she, the wise Uma. Then begin the long watch and wait for memory and intelligence to develop or return. The development of his theory of a dead and living brain in one head is interesting, unique. The mingling of "holy writ," of various gods and bibles, in awakening brain is truly well done and effective. As he watches her development, misgivings as to the wisdom of calling her back to life stir him; "I was beginning to realize what it is to be responsible for the existence of a human being." One day he told her of a part of his life in India.

"Do not stop," she said wistfully. "You make me see many· things."

I thought of the well at Cawnpore, and its memorial garden, of the garrulous old soldier from whom I had the story of the massacre; and I related to her incidents of the mutiny, when life was a little thing, and men and women rose superior to death, coveting it as a relief from indescribable horrors. I pictured to her the "Massacre Ghaut," where I had sat and translated the story of Gargya Balaki. The yellow Ganges had been pleasant to me; its low banks more sightly than where the bushes had masked the boats that were covered with luxuriant shrubbery, and nowhere were they served to decoy the English soldiers from their miserable fort. For the first time Uma heard of Nana Sahib's treachery to those who had received him after as a welcome guest. She heard of the days of heat and carnage, of pestilence and thirst, and how the confiding English forgot their sufferings in their joy over the deliverance Nana had planned only for their destruction. I told how the men filled the boats they believed would save them; and of the crash of ambushed cannon, the roll of musketry, the death cries, the death silence. I could not touch upon the indescribable ending of that awful drama, when women and children were butchered, and cast indiscriminately into the well from the bloody house. Yet I told her of Havelock's men, trying in spite of floods and heat, and the odds against them, to force a way to their relief, and how they wept when, too late, they reached the well, and swore vengeance, and treasured hairs from the slaughtered women and children to keep them to their vows.

Then I spoke of a lady I met in Cawnpore. Her hair was white, her face very gentle, her voice noticeably soft. She, too, had passed through the furnace of these summer months, when hope was gone;

and once she and her husband had promised each other that the last two shots from his pistol should be, one for her and one for him. Then I would have stopped but Uma said:

"Your words are full of strength. They send strange heats through me. Everything seems larger, and life nobler, while you speak. Death is not fearful when we use it to befriend us."

He touches in a new and fascinating way the idea of the transference of thought—of the action of one mind upon another. The girl recites indiscriminately from the newly learned Bible and the half forgotten Vedas :

"Christ said: 'But I say unto you that ye resist not evil; but whosoever shall smite thee on thy right cheek, turn to him the other also.' "

"Buddha said: 'When a good man is reproached, he is to think within himself, These are certainly good people since they do not beat me. If they begin to beat him with fists, he will say, They are mild and good because they do not beat me with clubs. If they proceed to this, he says, They are excellent, for they do not strike me dead. If they kill him, he dies saying, How good they are in freeing me from this miserable body!' "

The story preserves throughout the idea that whether in India or America, whether 2500 years ago or to-day, whether under Buddha or Christ, woman, as sister, wife, or mother, is ever and always an automaton. Man is the world, the "lord," the "master," the "teacher"; she is ever and always his pupil and slave. He lives for and because of himself—she for and because of him. Whether intentionally or not, the author shows also that most of her sorrows and sufferings and many of man's are due to this single fact—the dog-like faithful confidence and belief in and obedience to his will—the obliteration of her individuality. I am not at all certain that this thought or intention is in the author's mind, but that it is the effect left upon the mind of the reader is undoubted.

HELEN H. GARDENER.

A WOMAN WHO DID NOT.*

This is a novel having, so far as I can understand, no conceivable good purpose and therefore no excuse for existence. It has not even the merit of good or commendable literary style. Its tone throughout is, I think, immoral, and whatever lesson its pages may teach will be bad, more or less degrading to the reader of either sex. The book is an insult to decent, intelligent womanhood, and it is, or should be, therefore, also an insult to decent, intelligent manhood. Its heroine toys with the morally doubtful, and its hero explicitly regards virtuous living as too monotonous, and vice, if gilded, as a pleasant refuge from *ennui.*   C. SELDEN SMART.

---

* " A Woman Who Did Not," by Victoria Crosse. Cloth; price $1. Roberts Brothers, Boston, Mass.

THE LAND OF NADA.

This book may be read with profit and pleasure by the young. The story is wholesome and improving and the perusal of it will strengthen the moral fibre of the youthful reader. The land here described is a land of genii, fairies, and goblins over whom rule a kind-hearted if somewhat dull-witted monarch, King Whitcombo, and his lovable consort, Queen Haywarda, who had a "sweet way of mothering everything and everybody." This good king and queen had an only son, Prince Trueheart, a lad of fourteen, who unfortunately was blind; but he was the happy possessor of a violin which a fairy had given him at his birth. He acquired so complete a mastery of this magic instrument that "by the witchery of his harmonies he sent wild thrills" through his absorbed and breathless audience. These "exultant thrills became so ecstatic that they trickled and dropped off in round beads of gold" out of which the goblins made all sorts of beautiful things. This skill of the prince in discoursing sweet music is turned to fine account by the author in the sequel.

Visitors from neighboring lands frequented the court of King Whitcombo and Queen Haywarda. Among these Prince Arthur, Prince Kneebaby and his two sisters, the Princesses Helen and Wimpsy, who were respectively six and seven years old, were especially welcome. How Prince Arthur was the means of bringing great happiness to the royal family is related in a very entertaining way.

As one reads of the beauty and resources of the Land of Nada, one no longer wonders that King Whitcombo and Queen Haywarda were led to give up their home in their native land—the home of a long line of ancestors—and seek to develop a land so rich in possibilities. A balmy climate and gorgeous flowers increased the attractiveness of this wonderful land, and here for years they lived a delightful life, until in the lapse of years a great sorrow came to them. The few menial offices were performed by goblins. When, for instance, the king desired buttermilk, Ingram would hasten to the meadow where grazed the graceful cattle watched over by fairies, and, approaching a pale-white cow, would obtain the desired beverage by using the magic song:

> Gentle Seafoam, soft as silk,
> Give the king the buttermilk.

By similar magic songs Babe would get delicious milk, rich cream, and excellent butter for the queen's table. But ordinary mortals who inhabited the town had, in those days as so often in our days, to be content with the blue milk of Harebell, the pale-blue cow.

---

* "The Land of Nada," by Bonnie Scotland. Pp. 115; cloth 75 cents, paper 25 cents. The Arena Publishing Company, Boston.

Gillia, however, a cow whose body was the color of crushed strawberries, yielded the most wonderful products, products that are toothsome to the most fastidious youngsters.

The beauty of the land of Nada was enhanced by a bewildering variety of trees, " forming a vast breadth and wealth of sloping orchards and shady groves." In the centre of the garden stood a strangely curious tree that yielded a bountiful supply of three different kinds of lemonade. This tree was the cause of trouble, as once upon a time was another tree that grew in a still fairer garden. From other trees delicious fruits were canned and preserved in a truly remarkable way. But the most wonderful tree was the genealogical tree that stood before the queen's window. In its branches grew seats like swinging chairs, where the king and queen and Prince Trueheart would sit for hours, the parents describing to the blind prince the great variety of beautiful things they saw, while he in turn would charm them with sweet music from his violin; and "as the soft strains from the little magic instrument floated through the air, the very birds paused to listen and ceased their carols."

The full-dress parade of hens resplendent with all the vivid hues of the rainbow from deepest purple to palest lavender, "drilled by gay and martial roosters of the same hue as the divisions of which they had charge," is an episode that children will particularly enjoy.

But perhaps the most wonderful event that occurred in this land of wonders is yet to be mentioned. Amid the branches of the wonderful genealogical tree where, as has been said, the king and queen and Prince Trueheart passed many delightful hours, there grew, in the course of time, a wonderfully beautiful cradle that the fairies decorated as only fairies can; and into it "one little blue-eyed darling fluttered downward — down, down, down — until the soft white-robed form nestled within the cradle rocking there in the boughs of the genealogical tree." Under direction of the fairy queen the flowers in an exquisitely melodious song hailed the advent of the babe. Kings and queens, fairies and goblins, came from far and near to pay their respects to the beautiful little Princess Dorothy.

How this enchanted land was shut off from other lands and securely guarded by a monster genie; how the genie Strictumtaskum-trabajo, the servant of the lemon tree and the guardian of the underground goblins, instigated by the lemon tree brought trouble upon the land; how the enchanted hawks instructed by this wicked goblin spirited away little Dorothy; how Aunt Hope consoled the queen; how Prince Trueheart earned gold for the redemption of his sister; how Dorothy, after being well cared for by a tender-hearted goblin maiden, was finally restored; and how several betrothals were happily celebrated; lo, is not all this and very much more recorded in this delectable little volume?.

Nor is the book devoid of humor. Even older readers will smile as they read, to learn that there was not perfect equality in Nada; some could have lemonade; some, only picnic lemonade, or circus lemonade. The ladies there, too, observed the fashion of wearing "very full sleeves to their gowns, so large, indeed, that they were obliged to enter church doors sideways." And it will doubtless occasion surprise that under the lovely Haywarda society was broken up into sets. "The hens were of different colors, and each remained in her own set. This is the reason that when they wished to *sit* they fell into the way of calling it *set*, because they were so particular about going outside of their own circle."

The typographical execution of the volume is admirable. The healthy tone pervading the story will be noted with pleasure by parents who select their children's reading with scrupulous care. The book will be an acceptable present to any child whose taste has not been perverted by devouring sensational stories.

E. H. WILSON.

ROBERTA.*

It is a common remark that the market is to-day flooded with cheap and trashy literature. But it is also true that never before were so many noble men and women endeavoring, through the medium of either the novel or works of a more serious character, to uplift humanity and rescue the submerged tenth, by calling attention to the hideous injustice of our social laws, and bringing before the minds of those who are willing to see, the wrongs which exist in our midst, but which the easy-going sophists who are not willing to see, comfort themselves by believing to be necessary evils.

One of these noble writers is Miss Blanche Fearing, who is already known to the public through her works, "The Sleeping World," "In the City by the Lake," and other volumes. But in "Roberta," the work now under consideration, Miss Fearing has surpassed all her previous efforts. To my mind, it is one of the strongest social novels which has appeared since Victor Hugo wrote his masterpiece, "Les Miserables." Indeed, while not being in any sense of the word imitative, the history of Roberta Green, the heroine of the book, is strikingly similar to that of the hero of "Les Miserables," Jean Valjean.

The scene of the story is laid in the new Chicago, or the Chicago which sprang from the ruins of the great fire of Oct. 9, 1871. Roberta, the heroine, is the daughter of simple, honest, industrious working people, although her father, John Green, is superior in thought and refined feeling to the average workingman. For his

---

* "Roberta," by Blanche Fearing. Cloth; pp. 424; price $1. Charles H. Kerr & Co., Chicago, Ill.

little "Berta" he cherishes a love that is almost akin to worship, and his ambition for the child, who is beautiful, with gentle, winning ways and a great love for books, is that she should have a fine education. Johnny Green, as his fellow-workmen called him, had never studied political economy; he knew nothing of the iron law of wages; yet he realized in a blind way that something was wrong in our social economy, which prevented him, despite years of steady, unflinching, hard work from providing what was necessary for the comfort and education of his family.

When Roberta was fourteen years old, her father was killed by falling from the scaffolding on one of those modern structures of our large cities which rejoice in the name of "sky-scrapers." And now the burden of caring for the little family--there were three other children, the youngest a mere babe—devolved upon Roberta, on whom her mother had always leaned for support and advice, notwithstanding her tender years. The little girl who had hitherto been shielded from contact with the rough and unfeeling world was forced to go into a factory, in order by her slender earnings to help keep the family from starvation. The author thus describes her new surroundings:

> One of a long row of pale, silent girls, most of whose ages ranged from twelve to twenty, though there was one middle-aged woman, and two with iron-gray hair and bent shoulders, and one little girl who could not have been more than nine, unless, indeed, she had been stunted like a plant taken from the garden while it is yet young and tender, and thrust into a dark cellar, Berta sat day after day bent low over the heavy jackets, toiling patiently up and down the long, monotonous seams, never speaking to her neighbors, unless it was to borrow a needleful of thread, for the girls furnished their own needles and thread.
>
> The large room was ill-lighted and ill-ventilated. The ceiling was low, and black with smoke and dirt. The air, besides being laden with lint and dust, was saturated with a confusion of odors which the most sensitive olfactories would have analyzed and classified with difficulty, predominant among which were the impure exhalations from a throng of half-starved, unwashed human bodies (and many of them were mere bodies; the souls having shriveled away or become altogether worm-eaten), bad sewerage, and the hot, sickening steam from the penny soup kitchen in the basement, where most of the employees took their midday meal.
>
> The floor trembled with the jar of heavy machines, whose ceaseless roar and rumble would have baffled any attempt at conversation had not the rules of the establishment prohibited all talking among employees. The monotonous thunder of the machines was varied a little by the dull thud of the pressers' irons.
>
> At noon when they flocked to the soup kitchen, and at night after work when they were putting on their wraps, the girls sometimes talked together, but their conversation consisted chiefly of bitter execrations upon their employers, expressions of discontent about their work, and coarse jesting and bantering about their male acquaintances. And what wonder? Of what shall we talk if not of the things of which we think, and of what shall we think if not

of the curious pattern of circumstances and events falling hourly from the roaring loom of life, at which destiny sits feeding the vital threads? Shall we think of lofty sentiments in noble tragedies which we have never read, or of the faces of Madonnas in the Louvre or the Pitti which we have never seen, or of "The Messiah" of Handel, or "The Elijah" of Mendelssohn, which we have never heard? For the most part we speak as we think, and we think as we are, and we are largely what our conditions in life have made us, for it is a rare soul that can be much above its conditions. To be sure, there is a power within us designed to enable us to change or modify the environment into which we are born, but mighty are the external forces with which it must contend.

Amid these surroundings Berta, who, in spite of being a poor man's child, had from birth been accustomed to clean and wholesome conditions, soon sickened of typhoid fever, and was taken to the hospital. Here she attracted the attention of one of those ghouls under the semblance of women, who seek victims among the young and innocent of their own sex. This woman managed to prevent Berta's having any communication with her mother, and as soon as she was permitted to leave the hospital took her to her own home, and for the furtherance of a deep-laid scheme of fraud and swindling married her to her son. In a short time, however, both mother and son were arrested for swindling, and Berta with them. On being questioned she claimed to be the wife of the son, but both mother and son laughed her claim to scorn, declaring that they had taken her from the hospital to act as a maid. Roberta was then discharged. She returned to her home, where the mother was trying to support herself and her little ones by taking in washing. Here the child of fifteen soon became a mother, and henceforth had to endure obloquy and reproaches, which in her youth and ignorance of the cruelty of the world she did not even comprehend. In order to relieve her mother's burdens, as soon as she was able Berta sought work and obtained a situation as maid with a wealthy but vulgar and coarse-minded woman.

During all this time, however, Roberta was being utterly metamorphosed from the timid, loving, winsome child, who used to nestle at her father's knee when the day's work was done and read to him or talk with him. The author describes the change which had taken place, not only in the outward form, but in the soul:

She stood before the full-length mirror and contemplated herself. Somehow that strange, unfamiliar self had become a great mystery to her. What was it she beheld? Not the pale, timid little girl she had been accustomed to meet on such occasions, but an erect, finely-developed figure, dark, restless, resentful eyes that looked out fearlessly and defiantly, lips and cheeks deeply dyed with the glowing carmine of healthful youth, this rich coloring heightening the dazzling whiteness of the skin, and the whole set off by a crown of jet-black ringlets, clustering round the face, whose chief expression was of vague discontent and undefined strength. The whole attitude of the erect, finely-proportioned figure, head up, shoulders back, arms folded across the chest, and one foot a little in advance of the other, expressed resistance. Unconsciously to herself she had been interrogating life, and when the soul begins speaking to life with interrogation points, look for a sharp controversy. The soul is likely to be perplexed and grieved, and life is likely to be put to much confusion, like a reluctant witness whose answers are inconsistent and contradictory.

While in the service of the woman referred to Berta incurred her displeasure and after a shower of abuse was ordered to leave the house, and without the month's wages which was due her. Before leaving she had occasion to go into her mistress' room, where she saw a heap of jewels lying in an open casket. Smarting under the abuse which had been heaped upon her, and remembering that the woman had refused to pay her what was justly hers, the thought flashed across her mind that she would pay herself with some of these jewels. Our author says:

Poor ignorant child! What did she know of crime and its consequences? What conception had she of the might and majesty of the law, reaching forth its strong arm persistently and resistlessly to lay hold of its violators? What did she know of the distinctions between robbery and burglary, between grand and petty larceny? What did she know of the felonious taking and carrying away described in the statute? She simply knew that she was suffering from the evils deeds of others; that she had not consciously sinned, and yet that she had been cruelly and unjustly punished; that the vulgar and wicked could pave their way with gold and jewels wherever they chose to go; that wealth made theft simply sharp practice, licentiousness simply fast living; that money closed the eyelids of justice, and laid the finger of silence upon the lips of public opinion. She was vaguely conscious of all these things, and as she gazed at the jewels consciousness of her own wrongs grew stronger, and her apprehension of right and duty as applied to her own conduct fainter and weaker. It is often so with us all. The strokes of injustice which we receive are apt to paralyze our own sense of justice. This is especially true of youth and ignorance.

With her breath coming quickly and her cheeks burning, Berta thrust her fingers into the casket and closed them over some of the gems. Then she fled.

Then begins a career which carries the reader along with breathless interest, and which, as before observed, bears a wonderful resemblance in many respects to that of Jean Valjean. Berta's regeneration begins, as did Jean Valjean's, through meeting with one of those pure, lofty souls who, like the good bishop in "Les Misérables," fulfil the ideal of the Christ life. Roberta becomes a beautiful character, beloved and influential, and devotes her influence and means to uplifting suffering humanity.

The book is essentially a powerful plea for justice and equality of opportunity—the watchwords of to-day. It is a strong arraignment of a social system which inevitably makes criminals, and then relentlessly hunts to death the victims of its own blind fatuity. The burning question of the reciprocal duties of labor and capital is fairly and judicially handled, as will be seen from the following quotation, which aptly illustrates the author's impartial and unbiased treatment of this subject. An erratic, but large-souled and philanthropic young lawyer, one of the finest individualities in the book, is about to embark in a coöperative enterprise, and before the inauguration of the scheme he thus addresses those who are to be associated with him in the work:

"My fellow-workmen, I trust we shall never lose the feeling of fellowship which now exists among us, the feeling of fraternal love and confidence necessary to a coöperative scheme like ours. It is not a scheme to build up one man's fortunes under the guise of a scheme of philanthropy for other men. I am furnishing the capital; you are furnishing the labor—we will share the profits equally.

"My fellow-workmen, we all know that labor has been, and is being, grievously oppressed, but in our efforts to secure justice for ourselves, let us not lay upon ourselves the guilt and obloquy of the same errors for which we have condemned our oppressors. Let us not take the weapons from their hands simply that we may use them ourselves as they have done. I have heard many among my fellow-workmen declare that the rich have made their millions from the sweat of the workingman. Let us not deceive ourselves in this matter. Suppose two of your number were to go together, and suppose one of them should manipulate his purchase with so much wisdom and sagacity as to become wealthy, while the other, lacking wisdom and foresight, should make nothing, would you say that the one is not entitled to the reward which his superior sagacity has earned? Men buy and sell labor, and if one who buys the labor of his fellows, uses it with more sagacity than another, shall he have no right to the results?"

"Aye, but," growled one dark-browed man, "if he buys it for less than half it is worth, then profits by what he has ground out of the poor workingman?"

"That is too often true, but not always. I believe it is possible for a man to become rich without injustice to other men. We are not all born with business sagacity, any more than we are all born with a talent for music or painting. What I believe is this, that while a man has a right to all he honestly acquires through his own industry and sagacity, as soon as he acquires more than he requires for his own reasonable pleasure and comfort, the surplus becomes in his hands a trust fund for the benefit of his fellow-men. He is declared by the divinest moral law to be a trustee for humanity. His wealth is his to use as he sees fit, but he is bound to use it for the good of his fellow-men.

"Liberty sits in the land of her choice, weeping over the unhappy condition of her favorite children, Labor and Capital, who were wedded by divine authority in the beginning, but are now alienated and divorced from each other. Never will Liberty hold up her head and turn toward humanity a serene and unclouded brow, till she has seen her beloved children, Capital and Labor, kneeling before her with clasped hands, and the world has echoed with the music of their reconciling kiss. And this happy day of peace will not come until the majority of men and women have become capable of surveying these great questions from every point of view, until capital can consider them from the standpoint of labor, until you, my fellow workingmen and women, are able to consider them from

the standpoint of the capitalist, for labor is often as unwise and as
unjust in its methods as it is possible for capital to be. Let us
embark in this new venture with the determination to be nothing
if we are not just."

The author presents many different phases of life, and an unusual
number of finely-drawn characters. The courtroom scenes are
graphic in the extreme, and the most careless reader cannot fail to
notice that they are portrayed by an initiate in the mysteries of the
law. And such, indeed, is the case, for Miss Fearing is a lawyer of
marked ability, and it is said has never lost a case entrusted to her.
The work is not only deeply interesting as a novel, and excellent
from a literary point of view, but it is bound to have a permanent
place in our literature as a noble plea for truth, for justice, and for
the right.

MARGARET CONNOLLY.

A NEW DEPARTURE.*

In this remarkable book whose author hides modestly behind
three initials, one finds not only *a* theory as to creation and conscious life, but many theories found in all the bibles and all the
different schools of thought of which we have any knowledge,
although no quotations are made except from the English version of
the Ezra Bible. All are cunningly dovetailed together with much
ingenuity, and put forth with a calm assumption of certainty, calculated to carry conviction to most readers not too well rooted in
their own beliefs to hazard a new departure in any direction. To
such as these our author must be addressing himself when he
asks (p. 10):

But although we may say "We have all the light that ever was or
ever shall be," can we thus prevent the rising of the sun? . . .
Unbelief affects only the people; it is powerless to change the plan
of an omniscient God.

"Much of the opposition which Jesus encountered," continues our
author, "arose from the unwillingness of the Jews to 'purge out the
old leaven.'" So it did, just as in these days, every one who essays
to lead the masses out into wider fields and to take a new departure
from the land of bondage in which they have so long dwelt, finds
the race-thought so strong in them that he cannot move them nor
"do many mighty works there, because of their unbelief."

And yet this book can hardly be called dogmatic, for in all the
two hundred pages, the first person singular of the personal pro-
noun is not once found, relating to the author. This is surely as
remarkable as anything about the book, in these days when nearly
everyone who has received a little instruction in some particular

---

* "A New Departure," by W. K. M. Pp. 244; price, cloth $1.25, paper 50 cents.
Arena Publishing Company.

"cult" or has been given some notes of lectures or lessons, hastens to appear before the public as an eminent occultist or a profound scholar, anxious to enlighten the world at once as to the mysteries of the ages. Our unknown author has not done this, at any rate, but, on the contrary, while the book shows that he or she must have read or heard many, many lessons, keeps resolutely in the background, and having put forth in the introduction the twenty-four points which are to be elucidated, proceeds to carry on the work with the steady aim and vigorous swing of a master builder, "hewing to the line, no matter where the chips may fall."

. The truth which lies between the lines of all the bibles, that the union of Divine Love and Wisdom (the mind of God) is creative power, is found in every chapter of this "New Departure," particularly in the Introduction. Very busy men and women, people who are learning or have learned to live in the eternal now, "redeeming the time, because the days are evil," and striving to be useful in hastening the "New Time" of which the earnest editor of the ARENA dreams so fondly, will probably read only the Introduction and perhaps the prophecy anent the year 2,000 (pp. 226-228), and thus get at the gist of the book without taking time to follow all the rest. But students of all sorts of religious teachings; believers in the "eternal reality of religion," all who have time and inclination for research into various beliefs; Catholics, Protestants, Buddhists, Swedenborgians, Mental and Spiritual Healers, Spiritualists, Theosophists, and even Gnostics will find between the covers of the "New Departure" food for thought and the uplift which comes with any attempt to fix the "mortal mind" on things unseen, "eternal in the heavens."

The twenty-fourth proposition (p. 17) of the three understandings seems to be the key to the whole subject:

The first does not recognize mind as governing matter; the second deals with the power of material mind over matter—thereby in a measure controlling it, thus giving people "whereof to glory, but not before God"; the third is the gift of the Lord, even discernment of the infinite Wisdom and of the power of the Spirit of God to restore His creation. The first understanding entered with Adam, and has always governed the majority. The second arises at intervals; the third exists in an epoch of Light. Moreover, the second is the germ whence springs "the spirit of antichrist"—the violent opposition to Truth; that opposition prevailed in the latter days of the first epoch. Jesus referred both to those governed by the first understanding and by the second, when he said: "If I had not come and spoken unto them," . . . and "done among them the works which none other man did, they had not had sin"; for they would not have been conscious of a higher Wisdom. But when that Wisdom was made known "they had no cloak for their sin if, after having seen, they hated both Him and His Father." During an epoch of Light they that take up the cross—the opposite understanding from the material —are "baptized with the Holy Ghost [spiritual perception], and with fire," the Truth that destroys error and brings at-one-ment with the Infinite.

The interpretation of symbols (second chapter); the explanation of the meditatorship of Jesus (p. 29); the description of the thought-process used in mental healing (p. 57 and note p. 66); the chapter on Creation, all are very full of occult meaning, if read aright, for as the author pertinently asks: "Why do we cling so persistently to the letter and scorn the idea of there being a hidden meaning therein?"

All depends upon the point of view and the spirit in which one searches:

He who looks always for that which is crooked, will see and call all things crooked; he who looks always for the good, the pure, the true, and the straight will find these always. He who aims to brighten and uplift the soul through Spirit will find the Spirit; he who looks only for the cunning and selfishness of the animal will find fellowship only with the animal.

To these latter people the book before us will be of no interest, but they will pronounce it mere "Words, words, words," like this review.

JULIA A. DAWLEY.

WHICH WAY, SIRS, THE BETTER? *

The strike is not an innovation. Labor organizations have devised new modes of carrying on a strike that they may the better effect their purpose until a strike has become a kind of inherent civil war; but the thing itself is not a novelty to the student of history. Egyptian taskmasters oppressed Hebrew laborers until a commanding genius organized his afflicted fellow-countrymen and led them forth from their bondage, leaving their oppressors to their own devices. And every school boy has read the story of the secession to the Sacred Mount. The Senators of Rome, whose saving common sense seldom failed them in an emergency, sent, not an armed host to compel submission, but their shrewdest orator to persuade the commonalty to return; and the concessions made augmented the power of Rome. Indeed strikes have been as it were mile-posts along the highway of civilization.

The modern strike, however, whether it be undertaken to obtain an advance or to resist a reduction in wages; to gain shorter hours or to prevent longer hours; to prevent the discharge of union men or to hinder the employment of non-union men; to regulate the mode of manufacture in various ways; or to assist strikers in other branches of industry, is often characterized by personal violence and wanton destruction of property. A free man has the right to refuse to work for the wages proffered. But surely no intelligent person can admit that he has the right to say an equally competent workman shall not exercise his right to accept the wages offered. As

---

* "Which Way, Sirs, the Better?" by James M. Martin. Cloth, 75 cents; paper, 25 cents. Boston: Arena Publishing Company.

the laborer is under no compulsion to remain in the employ of a certain capitalist, said capitalist should be free to conduct his business affairs according to his best judgment. When laborers, however hard their lot may be, resort to license and crime to achieve their end, they necessarily lose the sympathy and forfeit the respect of those who long to see the condition of the workingman improved. Some may think that the excesses of strikers are justifiable on the ground that only so can they hold their own against capitalists who by whatever means, obtain legislation in the interest of their own class, regardless of its effects upon the laboring class. But two wrongs cannot make one right; there is a better way. There is properly no place for strikes in a state when life is so complex as it is to-day in every highly civilized community.

But strikes are not only barbarous, they are, also, enormously expensive. Statistics, however carefully collected and tabulated, can give only a partial account of the great cost of labor warfare. In the report of Colonel Carroll D. Wright, United States Commissioner of Labor, the loss of wages from 1881 to July 1, 1894, is put at $163,807,866, and the loss to employers by strikes during the same period is estimated at $82,590,386. These figures show that the wage-earners, who can least afford it, lose twice as much as the capitalists. But this does not tell the whole story. The capitalist, though reduced it may be to the verge of bankruptcy, may regain his lost business; the laborer not only loses his wages, but frequently his position. The sufferings endured by the innocent victims of the strike both during its progress and after the conflict is ended are too intangible to be represented by dollars and cents.

It is believed that most strikes are due to false economic theories. When capitalists and wage-earners alike clearly grasp the economic principle so thoroughly established by Lord Brassey that high-priced labor is the cheapest and low-priced labor the dearest when quantity and quality of manufactured product is taken account of, it will be evident to all that labor cannot afford to quarrel with capital and that capital cannot afford to neglect the interests of labor. When true views obtain regarding the mutual dependence of capital and labor, we may hope for a cessation of strikes.

The problem is further complicated by the besotted ignorance of the majority of laborers in those branches of industry most subject to strikes. How dense this ignorance is may be illustrated by the following colloquy quoted from the book under review:

"And how does yez loike auld Bilden's tin per cint squaze?"
"You mean the reduction," replied Michael.
"Faix, an' what ilse could I be afther namin' of it? I don't dignifoy it by the name of reduction; it sounds too raspictable; I call it squaze, for that's what it mains," answered Patrick.
"Well, I haven't had time to consider the matter fully. It is something to think about before making up one's mind."

"To think aboot, to consader? Faix, and in what condation is a mon to consader whin seein' he hasn't a cint in his pocket, a score against him at me friend's, Master Schlausser, and an impty mail barrel to home for Bridget and the childers. Why, mon, who can think and consader under such circumstances?"

"But, Patrick, every question, you know, has two sides to it, and should not be decided too hastily," answered Michael, conciliatorily, seeing the rising ire of his excitable colaborer.

"'Two soldes to it.' Faix, to Paddy Murphy and Bridget a quistion of a tin per cint squaze by auld Bilden has but one soide, and that's the soide of Paddy and Bridget. But come, Moike, have a glass o' beer. My throat's dry as a whustle a considerin'.'"

If the majority of employees were so intelligent as the following speaker all labor difficulties would be easily adjusted. Note the saneness of the man:

"The Lord help us, Mary," answered Michael. "I have plead and urged a return to work, even at the reduction, until I am become an object of suspicion among the rest of the workmen, although, God knows, wages were low enough before, and I had hoped that the reduction would not long be insisted upon by Mr. Belden, and that we would not be idle more than a week or two at the furthest."

And to his wife who asks if there is reason for the reduction, he replies:

"I only know this, that by the latest quotations of the iron market there is a decline in the prices of such products as are made in these mills. Money is a little close; besides, by the failure of Scroggs & Co. and Anderson Bros., Mr. Belden has been delayed in collecting, if he has not lost, large bills due him by these firms. I know this from what I overheard at the office of the works yesterday in a conversation between two of the bookkeepers, and while I cannot well afford a reduction, yet I would rather suffer it than have the mills close at this season of the year. Mr. Belden has always, so far as I know, acted honorably with his workmen, and I do not think would require a reduction unless circumstances absolutely demanded it."

But unfortunately such as he have very little influence when a strike is imminent. The following extract represents much more truly the difficulties that beset both employer and the more intelligent workmen:

"Gentlemen," he said, "wull ye's lis'en. Ye's committee" (accent on the last syllable) "has called ye's together on very important business. Ye's have seen the notices up in the mills, sayin' that ye's must be takin' less wages. Now it's for ye's to spake yer moin's. Es fur me, an' I'm a-thinkin' I'm spakin' the moin's of a majority of ye's (if mistakin I'll stand corrected), I'm a-makin' no sich concessions."

"Faix, an' that's me moind," shouted Patrick Murphy.

"Hould yer tongue, ye blatherin' fool, while I'm a-spakin'. I was a-sayin' to ye's whin interrupted, I'm a-makin' no sich concessions. If John Bildin can't run his mills without a-grindin' tin per cint off'n me wages the ould machine may stand till kingdom cum. Now, what does ye's say?"

This senseless harangue voiced the sentiments of the majority of the laborers. But Michael Durant was determined to prevent hasty action if possible, and watching his opportunity he arose and spoke as follows:

"I fully appreciate the situation and the importance of the action we may take to-night in the matter before us, and its probable effect upon our interests as workingmen. For six years I have worked in these mills, and have known many of you for a much longer time, and I regret very much the occasion of our being called together. Of one thing I am confident we must all testify, and that is to the uniform kindness of Mr. Belden toward us in the years past. I think I know something of the history of the man, left an orphan at an early age, and who, as a poor boy, earned his living by working in a mill. He is, therefore, not a stranger to the wants of a working-man, and, I believe, in his prosperity, he has not forgotten them."

"An upstart, nothin' but an upstart; where did he git his monny?" shouted Patrick Murphy.

"Shut your trap, you beer-logged fool!" answered another to this interruption.

"Order!" demanded the chairman.

"Yes, order! order!" shouted a dozen voices in unison.

Michael proceeded: "This is the first time since I came here that a reduction has been asked. Payment of wages has been always promptly made, often at great personal inconvenience to Mr. Belden, and I cannot but believe that this reduction would not be asked were it not that some stress of circumstances demanded it, and of which we are ignorant. I move, therefore, that a committee be appointed to confer with Mr. Belden in this matter."

The committee was appointed. Mr. Belden gave good and sufficient reasons for the reduction. They admitted that they were aware of the truth of much that he said but demanded that his statement should be supported by an inspection of his books by competent men. When Mr. Belden learned that this demand was their ultimatum, he dismissed the committee with these words:

"Then your union is making a condition that, I can assure you, will never be submitted to as long as I run these works, and, until modified further conference is useless. So good-day, gentlemen."

When the committee made their report at the next meeting of the assembly, the more conservative strongly urged further negotiations, but in vain. The strike occurred. Lives were lost. The mills were closed for months; and all but a few of the more conservative and trustworthy, who were retained to care for the property, received an indefinite discharge. Thus had reason been "drowned in ignorance, intelligence bogged in stupidity, and questions of the greatest import decided by petty jealousies." After months of weary waiting:

Springtime came at last, and with its bursting buds, springing grasses, and blooming flowers, came renewed health and strength to the proprietor of the works at Beldendale. He longed again for the activities of business life, and as he walked about the deserted mills, with their smokeless stacks, rusted rolls, and silent engines, he matured his plans, and, in imagination, pictured the vast struc-

ture throbbing again with a new life of productive vigor. In furtherance of his plans, he had printed and distributed the following:

"To My Old Employees and Other Workingmen:

"I invite you to a conference on Monday, April 30, at two o'clock
P. M., at my mills. All who desire work are cordially invited to be
present.

"JOHN BELDEN."

The remaining pages of this fine story, a story that instructs as
well as entertains the reader, elucidate the author's "better way,"
a way founded on the basis of profit-sharing. Mr. Martin's solution
of this complex and difficult problem would work admirably with
the Michael Durants; but the Patrick Murphys—what shall be done
with them? It is not easy to reason with a man whose actions are
swayed by the part of him that lies below the diaphragm. For such
as these there seems to be no place in Mr. Martin's system, for he
says, "the shiftless, intemperate, and careless have been gradually
weeded out by the changes of time." Thus the problem, after all,
is not solved by our author. And yet his fine, clean, straight story
goes to the heart of one of the great issues of the day, and it will
undoubtedly be productive of great good; for the book will be read
by thousands who would not look between the covers of a scientific
work on an economic question. And readers will discern that in the
author's view no antagonism exists between capital and labor, but
only between the few unscrupulous capitalists and unreasonable
laborers.

The writer regards the book as a substantial contribution to the
literature on social and economic questions, and predicts for it a
wide and fruitful circulation. If only the two classes of strife pro-
moters—the employers who seek not the way that makes for peace
and the labor leaders whose stock in trade consists in collisions
between employers and their workmen—could be induced to read
Mr. Martin's book in the frame of mind in which Saul was after his
arrest on the way to Damascus by the heavenly messenger, the
devil's theory, "Get all you can in every transaction and give no
more than you must," would speedily be superseded by the Christ-
theory, "Take heed that you get no more from your neighbor in any
transaction than he can safely give you, and give him as much in
return as you safely can."

E. H. WILSON.

PERSONAL RECOLLECTIONS OF AMERICA'S SEVEN GREAT POETS.

PART II.

I. CONVERSATIONS WITH WALT WHITMAN, BY HORACE L. TRAUBEL.

I group together here, without reference to superficial literary unity, some desultory but important notes derived from conversations had with Walt Whitman in the few months preceding his death.

Much of Whitman's life had been stormy. He lived to see the storm dying if not dead. He felt in his later days that he had produced indubitable effects. He never doubted of final acceptance. But he was scarcely prepared to have positive evidences of recognition appear in his lifetime. "The world moves at a faster pace than of old," he reflected; "its instruments of movement are prompt and numerous: the harvest is hastened." I remember that he avowed himself in this way: "I am here at last. From 1855 until the last few years I wondered if I had yet arrived. I am here to stay." Then, as if to anticipate any possible charges of egotism, he would explain: "But I am more than I. What am I but an idea, spirit?—a new language for civilization? What am I but you, what are you again but this same I?"

Whitman did not deceive himself. He acquiesced in the terms of opposition. He never wished to believe what the plain facts of every day denied. He met every negative with a welcome. He was grateful for objections and a generous host to all visiting objectors. He was a good listener but an unwilling controversialist. He was the last man in a controversy and the first out. He gave his "God-bless-you" even to dissent.

ANOTHER PORTRAIT OF WALT WHITMAN.
TAKEN IN HIS LATER YEARS.

Old, physically a wreck, bodily much-suffering, baffled each day in attempts to acquit himself of appointed labors, he could say to me every night and every morning: "I shall be happy till you come again and happy when you come." And, commenting upon his utter physical depletion, he would laugh and remark: "We accept these terms for our bodies only: the escape is certain."

Whitman felt content in his achievements. Yet he would also without bias review his career. Let me cite here an item of his talk which I transcribed: "I see nothing to regret. I have not always been satisfactorily expressed. On the whole, with most of my arrows, I have reached my mark. If there is any mistake at all—any lack of full emphasis anywhere—it is in what I have written in behalf of the criminal, outlawed, discredited classes. I might have said more for these—made my sympathy, hospitality, more manifest. But I guess I will be understood."

Whitman assented to this statement, "to the last word," as I made it to a third person in his presence: "The 'Leaves' are not to be readily or carelessly accepted. The impression, so generally adverse, at first blunt, sharpened later into a challenge, grows by degrees by the law of its own violence until criticism exhausts the possibilities of keen and subtle impeachment. But after this entrance-price is paid there ensue other phenomena to those who have persevered. Reading the book continuously, breathing its atmosphere, its drift will eventually appear as in a flash. Now, this experience is not decisive at all points, but it affords a satisfactory basis determining your future relations to the book." Whitman said: "I want you to write that down and print it sometime." Again, he would declare: "This idea that we call our own will make its own audience. It will grow by the taste of itself."

Almost the last counsel Whitman addressed to me had reference to the relations sustained by him to the literary guild: "The 'Leaves' are not a literary exercise or a lesson in literary values and proportions: they are crude imprints from the life, in which all valuations and proportions are recognized but whose primary power is resident elsewhere than in the art-impulse." And he frequently intimated that this was "in effect the key of the temple": "above the belief about things is the seeing them."

One night we talked of immortality. "I was asked to-day whether your belief in immortality persisted."

"What did you answer?"

"I said that if immortality depended upon your or any

HENRY W. LONGFELLOW.

man's belief in it you could not believe.   I said that immortality is seen and felt.   I said that you see and feel it."

He cried: "Amen!"   Furthermore, he asserted, as in effect he had done on another occasion to Nelly O'Connor, when she asked him the direct question whether he "felt sure" of immortality: "I do: I am sure of it: the doors are all taken off, the walls are all down, there is nothing to hinder."   And when he spoke of immortality it was not as of something which "in a certain contingency" might "be withdrawn" but as of a universal law whose circle had no outside.   The day before he died he made this memorable remark: "There is no bad in the final analysis—there is no shadow, no grief, no antagonism: every man, understanding, dares look every other man square in the eye."

Whitman's personal manners were eminently complimentary.   You felt that he was master of himself and that he demanded the same self-mastery of you.   He desired no mastership.   When he said a wise thing you were apt to feel that you heard yourself talking.   He was mystic and mechanic.   His wagon may have been hitched for all necessary occasions to the most illustrious stars in the firmament, but the burdens it carried in the intervals were reminiscent of earth-uses and employed for the temporal as well as the prophetic interests of man.   In his personal atmosphere commonplace and genius felt an equal welcome.   He conferred no titles.

There was no egotism in Whitman.   There was the consciousness of great personal power.   He exerted this power to general, not personal, ends.   If he said "I" was it not equally the part and duty of every other to say "I" and to make for themselves all the claims he could make for himself?   He would not only say for himself, "I and my father are one," but he would insist that it was necessary to the perfection of his claim that he should also say, "You and your father are one," and that you should say, "I and my father are one."

This will bear witness to his oriental spirit: "There are *arguments* against immortality but there is no *vision* of denial.   Did it never occur to some people how little way argument would carry them? how short the term of life of a thing proved by what is called logic?"

Whitman delighted in men and women who took hold of life with both hands.   He read books and papers multifariously, and he promptly and unsparingly separated what was reflected and incidental from what was vital and indestructible.   He wrote a great book.   Yet he insisted by

HENRY W. LONGFELLOW.

this very book, and in all private mention of it, that he could not be understood until the man back of the book had been embraced.

Whitman never derided art. He sternly moulded it into forms suited to his message. He never denied the value of formal scholarship. He only contended that it was ranked by what was spontaneous and creative. He believed in books. He consciously produced an immortal book. But he held that books owed their life to men as sunbeams to suns. He believed in art. But he pointed out the not novel but often ignored or forgotten fact that art divorced from life is dead. He protested to the last that his message was on no side negative. The opinion that he read little seems generally accepted. He read much. But he was never cheated by books. He could instantly detect the point at which the written chapter broke faith with life. The counterfeit sparkle of juggled words received the instant stamp of his disfavor.

Whitman's fondness for the generic word "America" has been and is misunderstood. To him America was not a geographical name or a political institution but a spirit. If he spoke familiarly of America and of democracy, making these household words and gods, identifying one with the other, declining to consider the possibility of their separation, it was not in any alienating spirit. He conceived of America at all times as having ideally at heart the interests of all races. By those who only superficially read or knew him he was taken as the apologist and boasting trumpeter of current political methods and policies. He was awake to all the needs of experience. He did not disdain the steps by which ends are accomplished. But he never swore that the step was the end. Having infinite faith and boundless vision he had infinite and boundless patience. America, democracy, were only in small part political. The political was the superficial. Underlying the sensational features of our democracy he recognized social, religious powers by whose husbandry freedom would yet universally prevail. America was indicator. It reported to him the situation from the advance line. "I see to the future better through the American than through the older races. This is not to say that I deny the older races. There is no privilege enjoyed by one above any other in this movement of peoples. We are evoked from the same beginnings, we reach towards the same destiny. In spite of quarrels there must be healing—in spite of differing routes and storms that seem to wreck, there is only one ship and one port and all will rid gaily in together at last."

Whitman did not negative the churches. He included them. He never ceased his refusal of all special claims made for any one faith. "I am as much Buddhist as Christian, as much Mohammedan as Buddhist, as much nothing as something. I have a good deal of use for all the religions. But if I am to be dragooned into some small desert place, which in the churches is called a creed, and left there to die, I must act upon my always reserved right of personal decision. The time will come when even Christians will acknowledge that Ingersoll, reforming the average Christianity of our day, was a direct witness of God." Nevertheless, "while I expect to see the whole nature of Christian theory changed, much old trumpery and barbarity dismissed, I do not feel called upon to use an axe myself."

In social reform, though never pledged to specific philosophies, his sympathies were towards the largest justice. "My heart is for all, and yet it may also be said to be specially for those who are victims of privilege, discrimination, greed, robbery. We do not see to the end. The fight is on. Has it not always been on? The smoke of the battle confuses the issue. Yet I know who will win—that the people will win—and I know why their victory is inevitable and I know why their victory is nobody's defeat." This was his reply to a very hot agitator who protested that Whitman was not sufficiently emphatic in his labor philosophy: "I know that what you ask for is right and will be given, and I know that if it is not true for the whole world it is just as true for you. I know that denunciation will not hurt and may help and I know that what you call my want of fire will not hurt and may help. My way is mine—I can force myself into no expression of violent indignation. If I say I cannot feel your heat in this matter, do not set it down for want of sympathy but for thoroughness of faith. I believe perhaps more than you do that these things must develop. Sometimes great heat comes from lack of faith: not always, however, as I know it does not in your case."

Yet he could also more directly indicate the points at which he supposed the movement would first take efficient root: "I am for free trade—free trade absolute; I am for South and North, not North against South; I am for Europe and America, for Africa and Asia, not for any one as against any other; I am for free land, for a plot of ground for every man who wants it and power nowhere to disturb him. Being for these things, I am for all politics and philosophies which will assist in developing them—even for agencies often thought contradictory of each other, for I perceive that the best life often comes through that narrow pass. I am not for laws. The law is an axe. I am for conscience, solidarity, good-heart, agreement all around and universal recognition of even-handed rights."

The profit of such discourse may easily be comprehended. For long years we spent evenings going over such ground, comparing notes, testing every day's history and every year's summing-up by laws of social being obvious and agreed upon by us. No territory was escaped or denied. In his bedroom, he in his big chair by the window, I upon some other chair or the lounge or the bed, the light rarely turned up, precious excursions of speech and precious intervals of silence alternating, there grew in me a profounder acknowledgment of his greatness. When his weakness increased and he was kept in his bed, our habit of daily discourse, some of it for practical interests, continued. His old energy of perception was maintained and his curiosity was unabated. No day brought darkness in these relations. No event shadowed his spirit. Serene and cheerful, he died with his face to the East. His youth was never lost. From such an atmosphere I offer these leaves.

II. A Glimpse of Longfellow, by Rev. M. J. Savage.

Mr. Longfellow's house is the one American poet's home which is familiar to everybody. It is the place which is sure to be visited by everyone who goes to Cambridge. This is the natural result of the fact that he is, beyond all question, the most popular of our poets. He gives voice to the average sentiment, and touches the average heart. He has never written a line which, on account of its obscurity of style, needs a commentator. It may be a question as to whether one would prefer to be the profound or lofty poet of the few, or he who should give utterance to the hopes and fears and joys of the many. At any rate, it is this latter distinction which belongs to Longfellow. He is the most widely read poet among the people of the English-speaking world.

The Craigie house stands facing the open ground, now reserved as a park, which stretches between it and the Charles River. This river, which the poet so loved, may perhaps be taken as a fitting symbol or illustration of his own life and work. It is not a great stream; its banks are not majestic like those of the Hudson or the more majestic Columbia, which beyond question is the grandest river in America. It winds peacefully through quiet fields and

beneath overhanging trees, by the side of villages and
through the city to the sea. It beautifies as well as vivifies
all its borders, and reflects the quiet or busy life through
which it passes. It may be taken as a parable of the poet
himself. It is not very deep; it has no cataracts or striking
rapids; it is always sweet and beautiful in its flow. Longfellow was master of the art of poetic form and whether
he wrote easily or not, he makes always easy reading.

The poetry of Longfellow, as is doubtless the case with
all poets, was the natural expression of the man. Sweet
and genial and lovable, he was the friend of all mankind.
He was perhaps the most generally and easily accessible of
all our greater poets. His door was always open to whomsoever would enter, and his time always at the disposal of
any comer. He never refused himself to the autograph hunter, saying that if he could give any one pleasure by so simple a thing as writing his name, he was glad to do it. It is
said of him that he always answered, with his own hand,
every letter which he received. This raises a question,
which perhaps is worth a passing word of comment.

Every man to-day, who has reached a position of any
prominence, finds himself in danger of being overwhelmed
by applicants and applications of every kind. It is coming,
then, to be a question as to whether the tradition of Longfellow in this regard can be perpetuated. Has a man a right
to deluge a busy clergyman, a busy poet, or a busy novelist,
with letters, and demand that they be answered at the expense of any amount of strength or time? Has any one
who chooses the right to call upon a busy man and take
an hour or two hours of precious time for his own purposes
or as the result of a passing whim? It is said of Napoleon,
and probably the same has been said of a great many others,
that he was accustomed to keep his letters for three or four
weeks, saying that by that time they did not need to be answered. At least half the letters which a busy man receives
are of no practical value, either to the receiver or the
writer; and it is a very serious question as to whether the
time of the receiver, at any rate, could not be better spent
than in answering them. Sometimes a question is inno-
cently asked which can be adequately answered only by a
review article or a book. Very frequently literary aspir-
ants want their manuscripts looked over, criticised (which
means praised), and a publisher procured for them; and
frequently they are very indignant if any one declines
to accede to the modest proposal. Not infrequently they
attribute a refusal to jealousy of their rising genius. At

any rate, they never seem to question the supposed fact
that they have a perfect right to the uncompensated consumption of another man's time, however valuable it may
be to him. They are familiar with the proverb that "time
is money," but while they would shrink from begging for
twenty-five cents or a dollar, they seem to think they have
a perfect right to "hold up" the unfortunate victim, and demand his time or his life. Longfellow always gave with
full hands in response to this public and general extortion.
But one cannot help wondering as to whether there is real
discourtesy in a man's laying claim to his own time and
his own strength, any more than there is in his insisting
on his title to his own pocket-book.

In spite of all my philosophy on the subject, however,
I am one of the people who went to see Longfellow, to encroach upon his valuable time. He received me with the
same warm welcome and smiling courtesy with which he received all the world. There is no need of my describing the
house, or the famous clock on the stairs visible as one
entered the hall, or the quiet, homelike study in which we
sat and talked. We did talk upon a great many things,—
books, his own and others; about mutual friends, and the
thousand-and-one things which would naturally enter into
such a conversation. But now comes a good illustration
of the tricks that memory will play upon one. We did discuss serious things; but not having made any notes of
our conversation at the time, all those discussions have
faded, and are too indistinct for any clear record now. I
remember chiefly that we sat and told stories together.

He offered me a cigar, and I took it that I might keep him
company; for Mr. Longfellow, as the Dutchman said of his
friend Hans, "vas a good smoker." And one of the stories
which he told, apropos of smoking, I have since had occasion very many times to repeat. Feeling, as Mr. Spurgeon
expressed it, that I can "smoke a cigar to the glory of
God," I like particularly to tell this story to any friends
of mine who assume that smoking is one of my vices. Mr.
Longfellow told of a certain cardinal calling upon a certain
pope, and the pope offering him a cigar, whereupon he
replied, "Thank God, I am free from that vice!" To which
the pope rejoined, "Vice? If it had been a vice, you would
have had it long ago!"

I have many good portraits of Longfellow, but the one
I value most is that which hangs in the chamber of memory,
—the poet in his morning jacket, with his face framed
in white whiskers and hair, and that face the outward

symbol of a soul whose chief characteristics, beyond intelligence and mental power, were gentleness and sweetness,
tenderness and love.

One other glimpse of Longfellow I wish briefly to portray.
He came over one winter day and called at my house, while
I was living at No. 37 West Newton Street. He was dressed
in his long fur-lined overcoat, and looked the embodiment,
not of the grotesqueness, but of the geniality and good
nature of Santa Claus as he came in out of the storm. My
son Max was then a little boy, two or three years old.
Mr. Longfellow showed the humanness of his nature and
his love for children by coaxing the little fellow to him,
and turning his timidity into the freest kind of familiarity.
In spite of our endeavors to the contrary—for I have never
believed my children so wonderful that everybody ought
to love them—Mr. Longfellow insisted upon having out his
frolic with the child. They played together as we talked,
and the boy made free with hair, whiskers, and pocket
at his will. So fine a time was he having that when Mr.
Longfellow rose to go, you would have supposed he was
about to part with his dearest friend. The foot of a long
flight of stairs had been reached and he was about to
go out upon the street, when Max rushed to the door and
called out, "Mr. Longfellow! Mr. Longfellow! Come back.
I want to kiss you again!" Whereupon he turned, came
up the long flight of stairs, sat down on the top step,
took the little fellow in his arms, and had the frolic and
the fun all over again.

I saw the poet afterwards a good many times, but I love
to think of the great man sitting on the stairs and stooping
to the love and tenderness of a little child. It revealed
the childlikeness of his own nature, and hinted the secret
of the perennial freshness and youthfulness of his own
heart.

AN INSPIRED PREACHER.*

BY REV. R. E. BISBEE.

As goes theology so goes the world. All permanent reforms have sprung out of great spiritual revivals, and all great spiritual revivals have had their origin in new theological conceptions. There are some seeming exceptions but they are seeming only. A close study will show the truth of what is here affirmed. Preaching has been the great motor power of progress, and preaching has been intense and forceful in the degree that the preacher has been inspired by new and burning theological truths. The importance then of the new theology, the new evangelism, and of inspired preaching in a time like the present cannot be overestimated.

The evangelist Moody is quoted as saying that he knows the Bible to be inspired because it inspires him. If this is a true test of inspiration, then certainly Frederick W. Robertson was inspired, for his sermons have inspired many and deserve the widest reading and closest attention. Note his delineation of the God of the old school theologian:

> The God of the mere theologian is scarcely a living God. He did live; but for some eighteen hundred years we are credibly informed that no trace of His life has been seen. The canon is closed. The proofs that He was, are in the things that He has made, and the books of men to whom He spake; but He inspires and works wonders no more. According to the theologians, He gives us proofs of design instead of God, doctrines instead of the life indeed.

Never was there a truer statement of a false theology, a theology from which the world must break away or wander in endless night.

The denial of present-day inspiration comes from the indentification of inspiration with infallibility. Herein lies one of the strangest inconsistencies of religious logic. Theologians claim absolute biblical infallibility, but deny present-day infallibility; they therefore feel obliged to deny

---

* Frederick William Robertson, a preacher in the Established Church of England, was born in London of Scotch parents, Feb. 3, 1816, and died Aug. 15, 1853. He is considered by some as the greatest preacher of the present century. His sermons have a very extensive sale and may be found at any book store.

present-day inspiration. It will be a great day for the human race when it is freely admitted that infallibility is not the necessary logical consequence of inspiration. To acknowledge the everyday presence and power of the Holy Spirit as the Spirit of revelation and truth, and with the same breath to declare revelation ended and sealed, is the height of absurdity. Theologians feel this, and in order to escape they tell us that the Bible is a special revelation, a revelation having the special credentials of the Almighty such as miracles and minute predictions. They acknowledge that God is always the same, that His years fail not, that He is no respecter of persons, that He is the common Father of the great brotherhood of man, that in Him we all live and move and have our being, and yet by predetermination He waited several thousand years after the dawn of civilization before He began His so-called special revelation, and then He sealed it up in one of the darkest hours of the world's history.

It is this erroneous view, this false conception of God and revelation, which has retarded progress and is the great danger of the present hour. John Greenleaf Whittier is quoted by one of his friends as saying that the appeal to an infallible Bible had kept back civilization two hundred years. It has been made the bulwark of slavery, the stronghold of the liquor traffic, and is to-day the chief weapon directed against the emancipation of woman. It is not the Bible itself that is thus condemned, but the idea of its absolute infallibility, making an appeal to its proof texts a final authority in all matters of morals and religion, even when in opposition to the enlightened conscience of our own day.

That the Bible contains much of the word of God, that taken as a whole its revelations have never been surpassed, that it is specially inspired in the sense that its authors specially sought after God and were devoted to Him, no candid man will deny. It is also true and demands special emphasis, that God is ever the same, that revelation is continuous and eternal, that inspiration is given in all ages to all who meet the conditions, that there has never been more than one dispensation, and that the Holy Spirit has been given from the time of the first man and in equal degree to all who have equally opened their hearts to Him. God, in order to make himself known as God, has never been obliged to resort to the tricks of the prestidigitateur, but His unvarying laws in nature and His presence in the human heart have been sufficient evidence of His existence and of His goodness and power. This view is by no means intended to deny the *fact* of miracles, but miracles as special credentials of revelation, without which revelation would not be proved, it does deny.

The idea, then, of God's immediate, eternal, and inspiring presence ought to be preached and emphasized. By preaching otherwise, the race has been robbed of a glorious hope, civilization has been retarded, tradition has usurped the throne of reason.

In an article on "The August Present" in the ARENA for August, 1895, the editor uses this strong language:

The slothful, the fearful, the worshipper of the past, and those who love ease and self-comfort, no less than those who are so low on the plane of development that they have more confidence in brute methods than in reason and the divine impulse, are striving in a thousand ways to turn humanity backward; like the ten spies who brought an evil report of Canaan to the children of Israel, these voices seek to turn humanity backward by appealing to prejudice, superstition, fear, the love of ease, and the savagery resident in the human heart. They are seeking to outlaw daring science and investigation; to replace the spirit of tolerance, charity, intellectual hospitality and ethical religion with the savage dogmatic faith of darker days. They are fanning the spirit of hate between religious factions; they are cultivating the war spirit, and turning the contemplation of the young from the noble ideals of a Victor Hugo to the bloody triumphs of a Napoleon. They are endeavoring to raise authority above justice and to discourage man's faith in a nobler to-morrow. They sneer at the efforts of philosophers and reformers to substitute justice for injustice. In a word, they are striving to turn civilization backward at the moment when strong and clear the order to march forward should be given.

If we hearken to these voices of the night, we assist in the commission of a mistake of measureless proportions, a mistake which must necessarily result in clouding the face of civilization for generations to come by checking the rapid march of progress; if we remain neutral, refusing to bear arms in the stupendous battle now in progress, we are recreant to the urgent duty which confronts us, and by so doing neglect the splendid opportunities given to us to be torch-bearers of progress in the most critical moment in the history of civilization.

If prejudice, selfism, and ancient thought triumph over knowledge, altruism, and justice in the present crisis, humanity will have another long night before her, another forty years in the wilderness.

The dangers shadowed forth in these words are recognized by all the thoughtful, and yet there is a way of escape. The clergy can easily stem the tide of worldliness that is setting in so mightily. To do this they must frankly admit the truth, open their eyes to the latest research, invite the fullest investigation, and preach with the fearlessness and zeal of genuine prophets. So long as they appeal to the inspiration of the past for all authority, disclaim any right of their own to speak in the name of Jehovah, teach that revelation is finished and sealed up, so long they will go halting and their words will be well-nigh powerless. While they need not assume a boastful spirit, yet they should have wrought within their souls a conviction of the truths they utter, should feel that these truths are from God, and that in expressing them they speak for God. They should, moreover, teach the possibility of present-day prophets and prepare the people to receive them. Let this be done, and then, when a new prophet arises he will be quickly understood. Imagine such a preparation in the past generation for Wendell Phillips, or in our own for Professor Herron! To-day the cry comes to the clergy of America as never before: *"Prepare ye the way of the Lord."* But in making the transition from the old way to the new, there are some practical difficulties to be overcome. The utterance of new truth invariably brings the cry of "heresy." The honest preacher will be charged with scepticism, even infidelity. The professed friends of the truth will do all they can to destroy his influence, if not by argument, by the use of opprobrious epithets. Andrew D. White in an article in the *Popular Science Monthly* quotes Bishop Wilberforce in an address to Colenso at his ordination as follows:

You need boldness to risk all for God; to stand by the truth and its supporters against man's threatenings and the devil's wrath. . . . You need a patient meekness to bear the galling calumnies and false surmises with which if you are faithful, that same satanic working which, if it could, would burn your body, will assuredly assail you daily through the pens and tongues of deceivers and deceived, who under a semblance of zeal for Christ, will evermore distort your words, misrepresent your motives, rejoice in your failings, exaggerate your errors, and seek by every poisoned breath of slander to destroy your powers of service.*

Even if the prophet be brave enough to endure all this, it may not always be wise for him to provoke it. What he should seek is not simply to utter truth, but to be heard and to be understood. He must if possible avoid arousing those prejudices which will shut the ears of the world against him. He must find a way to maintain his freedom, his self-respect, and still be persuasive and powerful. It is because F. W. Robertson could do this to so large a degree that he is worthy of special attention in these ominous times. And first and most important of all he was a man of wonderfully sweet spirit. He was, of course, accused of heresy, his sensitive soul was wounded by the

* Mr. White goes on to show that when Colenso followed the advice here given, Wilberforce made the prophecy true by becoming Colenso's bitterest persecutor. We have a similar condition of things to-day in the systematic persecution of Professor Herron.

reproach and desertion of friends, but his *life* won back all who were worthy, and made them sincere mourners at his early death. The reformer and prophet must have a life above reproach. He must be willing to forego anything and everything whereby his brother stumbleth. Above all he must keep his temper. The appeal of an honest, fearless, sweet, and loving life is irresistible. Such was the appeal made by Robertson, and to-day his life and his sermons are finding their way to the hearts of increasing thousands. Such preachers and such preaching are the hope of the day.

The great preacher is he who voices the best and holiest thoughts of the people. The thoughts of a righteous people are the thoughts of God. Happy is the preacher who can express these thoughts simply and clearly, who speaks to the heart, who gives utterance to the truths the people already feel. By the people I do not mean those warped and twisted theologians who have strained their minds to think in certain channels, until it is impossible for them to think accurately and consistently. I mean the earnest, striving people who are hungry for truth and ready to accept it at any cost, people who have no creed to maintain, who have no everlasting logical consistencies to guard.*

Open the sermons of Robertson where you will, take him on any subject, you will find him teaching plain, simple, common sense. He is never hampered by tradition, yet never violent. He is never daring you to follow him. He simply unfolds the truth and makes it luminous with the choicest words. He treats old faiths with the utmost respect. He brings out what truths there are in them, and with a magic touch transforms them into life and beauty. With him the atonement loses its harsh and vindictive character, the doctrine of the trinity becomes natural and plausible, prophecy is changed from petty prediction to the grandest statement of universal truths, regeneration becomes a plain necessity to every true nature, and Christ is the fulfilment of the longing desire of imperfect man.

This is what he says of the Bible in his sermon on "Inspiration." Possibly the opening sentences may be considered too strong by some, but who can fail to admire the general statement? The entire sermon should be read in order that the extract may be fully understood:

---

* The writer had occasion to utter some of the foregoing sentiments in the presence of such a people not long ago. The pastor was the only one who objected. The thoughtful laity were delighted.

Scripture is full of Christ. From Genesis to Revelation everything breathes of Him; not every letter of every sentence, but the spirit of every chapter. It is full of Christ but not in the way that some suppose; for there is nothing more miserable, as specimens of perverted ingenuity, than the attempts of certain commentators and preachers to find remote and recondite and intended allusions to Christ everywhere. For example, they chance to find in the construction of the temple the fusion of two metals, and this they conceive is meant to show the union of divinity with humanity in Christ. . . . If it chance that one of the curtains of the tabernacle be red, they see in that the prophecy of the blood of Christ. . . . I mention this perverted mode of comment because it is not merely harmless, idle, and useless, it is positively dangerous. This is to make the Holy Spirit speak riddles and conundrums, and the interpretation of Scripture but clever riddle-guessing. Putting aside all this childishness, we say that the Bible is full of Christ. Every unfulfilled aspiration of humanity in the past; all partial representations of perfect character; all sacrifices, nay even those of idolatry, point to the fulfilment of what we want, the answer to every longing — the ■■■ of perfect humanity, the Lord Jesus Christ.

A better statement, consistent at the same time with the claims of the Bible and the teachings of science, it would be hard to find. These words should be pondered by the thousands of itinerant evangelists who are doing all they can to turn the Bible into a book of magic, and who dishonor God and His revelation by claiming inspiration for every letter. The gift of such a revelation as many apparently sincere preachers claim, would be the worst thing God could do for the world.

The student of Robertson should especially note his sermons on *truth*. The sin against the Holy Spirit—the Spirit of Truth—is twofold. It consists first in shutting our eyes to the truth from the fear of consequences to our creed; and secondly, in refusing to acknowledge the ever-abiding presence of the Spirit to lead us into all truth. God is a Spirit and they that worship Him *must* worship Him in spirit and in *truth*. God Himself cannot save one who refuses such a faith and such a worship. It is the law of life. There is no being so pitiful, so hopeless, as he who thinks his creed contains all the truth, and who squares all his utterances by it; who boasts that "the doctrine of his church can never change"; none so wretched as he who suppresses his nobler reason in order to be consistent with the dictates of authority. To the thousands thus burdened, who dare not speak the truth that burns within them, I appeal. Be free. This is what Robertson says of those who suppress their better thoughts:

The law of truth is that it cannot be shut up without becoming a dead thing and mortifying the whole nature. . . . Truth cannot bless except when it is lived for, proclaimed, and suffered for. This is the lowest step of a nation's fall when the few who know the truth refuse to publish it.

Again, in his sermon on "Freedom by the Truth," he says:

Worse than he who manacles the hands and feet is he who puts fetters on the mind, and pretends to demand that men shall think and believe and feel thus and thus, because others so believed and thought and felt before. . . . There is a tendency in the masses always to think — not what is true, but — what is respectable, correct, orthodox: we ask, Is that authorized? It comes partly from cowardice, partly from indolence, from habit, from imitation, from the uncertainty and darkness of all moral truths, and the dread of timid minds to plunge into the investigation of them. Now, truth known and believed respecting God and man frees from this, by warning of individual responsibility. But responsibility is personal. It cannot be delegated to another and thrown off upon a church. Before God, face to face, each soul must stand to give account. . . . That mind alone is free which, conscious ever of its own feebleness, feeling hourly its own liability to err, turning thankfully to light from whatever side it may come, does yet refuse to give up that right with which God has invested it of judging, or to abrogate its own responsibility, and so humbly and even awfully resolves to have an opinion, a judgment, a decision of its own.

These words pondered over, accepted, applied, would set the world free and save the fate of civilization.

In line with the foregoing he utters these portentous words on infallibility. I commend them to those timid souls who for fear of reproach are afraid to speak out the truths they feel, who dare not go outside their church for directions as to their moral duty, who, for instance, would not dare vote for the emancipation of woman if they thought it was forbidden by an inspired Paul, who in brief lay their consciences at the feet of a supposedly infallibly inspired past. The statement that "the soul is thrown in the grandeur of a sublime solitariness on God," I count as the climax of all the great preacher's utterances:

And it matters not in what form that claim to infallibility is made: whether in the clear, consistent way in which Rome asserts it, or whether in the inconsistent way in which churchmen make it for their church, or religious bodies for their favorite opinions: wherever penalties attach to a conscientious conviction, be they the penalties of the rack and flame, or the penalties of being suspected, avoided, and slandered, and the slur of heresy affixed to the name till all men count him dangerous lest they too should be put out of the synagogue; and let every man who is engaged in persecuting any opinion ponder it — these two things must follow — you make fanatics, and you make sceptics: believers you cannot make.

Therefore do we stand by the central protest and truth of Protestantism. There is infallibility nowhere on this earth; not in Rome; not in councils or convocations; not in the Church of England; not in priests; not in ourselves. The soul is thrown in the grandeur of a sublime solitariness on God. Woe to the spirit that stifles its convictions when priests threaten, and the mob which they have maddened cries heresy, and insinuates disloyalty — "Thou art not Cæsar's friend."

Mr. Robertson speaks to nearly every want of the human

soul. He was not aware of his own eloquence and power.
He did not wish to write out his sermons for publication
but his hearers insisted upon it. The souls of the hungry
know when they are fed, and Robertson fed them. On dark
Scripture passages he let in floods of light; he punctured
errors, he corrected fallacies; in practical affairs he gave
the wisest advice. Here is a sentence which it might be
well for modern missionaries to ponder: "In order to elevate Christianity it is not necessary to vilify heathenism."
It would be hard to find a precept more true, or more
frequently violated.

He was singularly free from cant. Not long since I read
some of Gerald Massey's poems in the presence of a congregation. Every line breathed of the Christlike spirit,
although the devout poet did not mention Christ by name.
At the close of the reading a listener asked if the author
believed in Christ as God; "because," said he, "he nowhere
mentioned Him, and if he does not believe in Christ as
God that spoils it all." This called to my mind the fact
that some people who are very jealous of the name of Christ,
are so little acquainted with the real person that they do
not know Him when they meet Him unless He is labelled.
A genuine portrayal of Christ needs no label of cant
phrase or name. To preach Christ without especially advertising to do so is characteristic of true prophecy and of
true reform. The dearest lovers of Jesus, those most
worthy of His name and most earnest for His life, are
how often accused of denying Him by those who can see
Him only in forms of words. Declare your belief in Jesus
as God, and you may have great freedom. You may
apologize for cruelty and war, you may uphold monopoly
and condone vice, and you will be counted orthodox.
Omit such declaration, and then preach Jesus in all the
beauty of his holiness, set before the world the glorious
hope of all men being like Him in this life, attempt to apply
His teachings to business and politics, and you are in danger
of the rack.

I have prepared this paper with the hope that some who
are struggling for spiritual freedom, and who are searching
for wise methods of presenting the truth which dawns upon
them, might receive help. To all such I would say, Study
Robertson. He is not perfect, he is not infallible, but he
is very helpful. Living as he did fifty years ago, that he
should speak so clearly, so impressively on questions of
this present day is nothing short of marvellous. It shows
that truth is the same in all ages, and that inspiration presents to all great minds similar visions.

If all preachers would seek this same inspiration, would "throw themselves in the grandeur of a sublime solitariness on God," and demand great things of the Spirit, would speak out fearlessly for the rights of man, would insist upon the truth at any cost, would demand that Christianity should claim for its credentials, not submission to a creed dictated by the church, not a hope of final absolution and a home in a future heaven, but a noble life, an irreproachable character, honesty in business, and righteousness in politics; if preachers would insist that to vote is a sacred duty, and that the question how to vote is one of the deepest moral import, the ballot "a freeman's dearest offering"; if they would themselves earnestly seek light on every question that affects the welfare of mankind and then let their light shine, there would be no danger of retrogression. Genuine Christianity applied is the hope of the world.

A recreant clergy, afraid of investigation, preaching half-truths, presenting a narrow gospel, unwilling to humbly confess error, clinging to dogma, uttering cant, bowing the knee to Baal, with "creeds of iron, and lives of ease," is our greatest danger, the chief obstacle in the way of progress. I cannot close this article better than by another brief quotation from the "Inspired Preacher":

Now see what a Christian is drawn by the hand of Christ. He is a man on whose clear and open brow God has set the stamp of truth; one whose very eye beams bright with honor; in whose very look and bearing you may see freedom, manliness, veracity; a brave man, a noble man, frank, generous, true, with it may be many faults; whose freedom may take the form of impetuosity or rashness, but the form of meanness, never.

REPRESENTATIVE WOMEN ON THE VITAL SOCIAL PROBLEMS.

IS THE SINGLE TAX ENOUGH?

HENRY GEORGE AND NEHEMIAH.

In Henry George's book, called "The Land Question," on page 16, I find the following:

In the very centres of civilization, where the machinery of production and exchange is at the highest point of efficiency, where bank-vaults hold millions, and show-windows flash with more than a prince's ransom, where elevators and warehouses are gorged with grain, and markets are piled with all things succulent and toothsome, where the dinners of Lucullus are eaten every day, and, if it be but cool, the very greyhounds wear dainty blankets—in these centres of wealth and power and refinement, there are always hungry men and women and little children. Never the sun goes down but on human beings prowling like wolves for food, or huddling together like vermin for shelter and warmth.

On page 73 are these words:

It is the year of grace 1881, and of the republic the 105th. The girl who has brought in coal for my fire is twenty years old. She was born in New York, and can neither read nor write. To me, when I heard it, this seemed sin and shame, and I got her a spelling-book. She is trying what she can, but it is uphill work. She has really no time. Last night when I came in, at eleven, she was not through scrubbing the halls. She gets four dollars a month. Her shoes cost two dollars a pair. She says she can sew; but I guess it is about as I can. In the natural course of things this girl will be a mother of citizens of the republic.

Underneath are girls who can sew; they run sewing-machines with their feet all day. I have seen girls in Asia carrying water-jugs on their heads and young women in South America bearing burdens. They were lithe and strong and symmetrical; but to turn a young woman into motive power for a sewing-machine is to weaken and injure her physically. And these girls are to rear, or ought to rear, citizens of the republic.

But there is worse and worse than this. Go out into the streets at night, and you will find them filled with girls who will never be mothers. To the man who has known the love of mother, of sister, of sweetheart, wife, and daughter, this is the saddest sight of all.

In different language we find a similar state of affairs told in the fifth chapter of Nehemiah—history, I believe, of a condition which existed among the Jews about 2400 years ago:

1 And there was a great cry of the people and of their wives against their brethren the Jews.

2 For there were that said, We, our sons, and our daughters are many; therefore we take up corn for them that we may eat, and live.

3 Some also there were that said, We have mortgaged our lands, vineyards, and houses, that we might buy corn because of the dearth.

4 There were also that said, We have borrowed money for the king's tribute, and that upon our lands and vineyards.

5 Yet now our flesh is as the flesh of our brethren, our children as their children; and, lo, we bring into bondage our sons and daughters to be servants, and some of our daughters are brought unto bondage already, neither is it in our power to redeem them; for other men have our lands and vineyards.

You see the similarity between the two pictures as drawn by Henry George and by Nehemiah.

But at this point I imagine a look of triumph on the face of any single-taxer who may chance to read thus far, and he exclaims: "See what's the trouble? Land monopoly. 'Other men have our lands and vineyards.' Under the single tax it is probable that there would have been no need to borrow money for the king's tribute."

In a leaflet by Henry George called "Causes of Business Depression" he says:

There is but one cure for recurring business depression. There is no other. That is the single tax—the abolition of all taxes on the employments and products of labor and the taking of economic or ground rent for the use of the community by taxes levied on the value of land, irrespective of improvement. . . . That the monopoly of land—the exclusion of labor from land by the high price demanded for it—is the cause of scarcity of employment and business depressions is as clear as the sun at noonday.

Here is Henry George's cause of hard times, such as he and Nehemiah 2400 years apart depict so similarly and graphically. But the cure? Henry George says "There is but one cure—the single tax." But now hear what Nehemiah says as to the cause and cure of this terrible condition:

6 And I was very angry when I heard their cry and these words.

7 Then I consulted with myself, and I rebuked the nobles, and the rulers, and said unto them, Ye exact usury, every one of his brother. And I set a great assembly against them.

8 And I said unto them, We after our ability have redeemed our brethren the Jews, which were sold unto the heathen; and will ye even sell your brethren? or shall they be sold unto us? Then held they their peace and found nothing to answer.

9 Also I said, It is not good that ye do: ought ye not to walk in the fear of our God because of the reproach of the heathen our enemies?

10 I likewise, and my brethren and my servants, might exact of them money and corn: I pray you let us leave off this usury.

11 Restore I pray you to them, even this day, their lands, their vineyards, their oliveyards, and their houses, also the hundredth part of the money, and of the corn, the wine, and the oil, that ye exact of them. .

12 Then said they, We will restore them and will require nothing
of them; so will we do as thou sayest. Then I called the priests, and
took an oath of them, that they should do according to this promise.

13 Also I shook out my lap, and said, "So God shake out every man
from his house, and from his labor, that performeth not this promise,
even thus be he shaken out and emptied. And all the congregation
said Amen, and praised the Lord. And the people did according to
this promise.

Henry George says, "There is but one cure—the single
tax." Nehemiah says, "I pray you let us leave off this
usury." Which is right? I vote for Nehemiah. When I
was a little girl we (my father's family) used to say, "It's as
true as the Bible." We had no stronger or more solemn
phrase for affirming the veracity of a statement. But it is
not in this spirit that I accept Nehemiah's verdict instead
of Henry George's. It appeals to my reason; and I can but
believe that "blindness in part hath happened unto those"
who advocate land reform and declare that usury (Christian
name, interest) is right and the money question of no consequence. Further than this, as nearly as I can learn
there is no common understanding of the money question among the advocates of the single tax. One of them
not long ago in a private letter to me said, "The money of
the world is for sale the same as any other production of
human labor," and spoke of "fighting the windmill, money."
In the same letter he enclosed two essays, one by Henry
George, "The Causes of Business Depression," before quoted
from, and one by H. F. Ring, "The Case Plainly Stated."

Mr. George says, "Land and labor—these are the two primary factors that produce all wealth." Alluding to money,
he says, "It is only an intermediate, performing in exchange
the same office that poker chips do in a game." Mr. Ring
in his essays says: "Three factors enter into the creation
of every conceivable kind of wealth. These factors are land,
labor, and capital." I think Mr. Ring does not use the word
money in his whole essay, so I must conclude that money
is included in his term "capital," as he says "Labor does
the work, capital loans the tools, and land furnishes the
natural elements."

I cannot attempt in any brief space to review these essays
as I would like to. I have alluded to them to show what
seems to me a large lack of appreciation and understanding
regarding the money question.

A strong point made by single-taxers is that no man
created land, therefore no man has a right to charge any
other man for the use of it. They also affirm that as the
community creates land values, therefore the community

has a right to these and may take them in the form of a tax. (I have tried to state the positions fairly.) But are not these propositions true of money? My friend alludes to money as "a product of human labor," but if he will stop to think he must see that it is not so. No individual can create money, let him labor never so long and hard. Some try it and succeed in producing a fair counterfeit which often answers the purpose, but even the most contemptuous single-taxer will not claim, when he knows how it was produced, that it is really money. God does not make money, it does not grow on trees, it is not dug out of the ground, it is not produced by labor; how then does it come into existence? Jesus of Galilee acknowledged its source when he took the coin and asked, "Whose is this image and superscription? They say unto him, Cæsar's. Then saith he unto them, Render therefore unto Cæsar the things that are Cæsar's, and unto God the things that are God's."

Money is a creation of law. Cæsar as an individual could not make money. As the representative of the Roman government he did. Money, in this country, is a manifestation of a universal agreement. Probably Mr. George was right in comparing it to the chips in poker, but as I do not understand that game I am not sure.

But of one thing I do feel sure, and while I do not wish to be dogmatic or discourteous I have no hesitation in saying that no one who understands the history of finance in this country since 1859, to say nothing of the time before that and of the world's history, will speak lightly of the money question. To simply study the moves of the banking fraternity for the last three years ought to open anyone's eyes to the importance of the currency question. Bankers produce no wealth. All that they get then is at somebody's else expense. How do they get it? By usury. Who pays usury? Only somebody who is in debt. This being the case, is it not for their interest to keep people in debt? Yes, up to a point beyond which they cannot pay the usury. And even beyond that it's "Heads I win, tails you lose"; for as a rule money is loaned only on good security, and if the debtor cannot pay his interest the creditor gets the security, which is usually worth more than the amount secured. In this way men in Nehemiah's time got possession of other men's land. In this way in Christ's time the Pharisees "devoured widow's houses." In this way now I believe the monopoly of the land goes on.

Henry George says, "Seasons of business depression come and go without change in tariff and monetary regulations."

I think he made that statement without due consideration of the facts, and that if he looks up all the seasons of business depression that have come and gone he will find *always* a change in monetary regulations." During the season of business depression from 1873 to 1878 a certain statesman (?) boasted that his party had "doubled the value of the dollar by its legislation." What is the effect of doubling the value of the dollar? The man who already has the dollar can get with it twice as much of the things that money can buy, and the man who has the dollar to get must give twice as much labor to get it. The creditor gets twice as much value as he bargained for, and the debtor, if he can, pays twice as much as he agreed to, or, failing in this, gives up his security. Is the money question a windmill? Usury and land monopoly are chronic, constitutional diseases like consumption; but contractions in the money volume, either absolute or relative, are the acute diseases, like pneumonia, which sometimes cure but oftener confirm and hasten the chronic disease. Wherever money has been, so far as I know, there has been usury.

Whatever else the banker is he is not quixotic. He does not fight windmills. He knows, if the single-taxer does not, that there is something in the money question—for him. For what is the banker making his present desperate fight, which has laid our industries low and filled the land with suffering? It is one of the battles in the war which he has kept up with more or less vigor since 1859 for the full control of our currency. A settlement cannot much longer be delayed. Either the people must take entire control and destroy the privilege of charging for the use of money which they collectively and they only can create and give value to, or they must put themselves in the banker's hands and let him issue all the money. To do this is to make him a partner in every business enterprise, drawing from it whatever per cent it will bear. Do Henry George and his followers feel willing to carry this useless load, even under the single tax?

Money is not made for the same purpose nor by the same means that anything else is, and to reason about it as if it were is to involve the reasoner in error and confusion. It may be quite as dangerous to mistake a giant for a windmill as to mistake a windmill for a giant.

The landlord's work is easy to see. Its effects, at least a portion of them, are plain. But the work of the lend lord is so indirect in its effects on the producers of wealth that its fatal results are often superficially attributed to other causes. It is so easy to say, "If I own all the land, 1 can make you pay me all your money and all the things you can produce for the privilege of staying on the land," that many forget to look into the means by which the land gets away from the many to the few. Lord Bacon said, "Usury bringeth the treasures of a realm into a few hands." I believe it.

Whatever the single tax might have done if applied to primitive conditions, something more is needed now. I have no quarrel with single-taxers except for their bigotry; but when they insist that a thing does not exist because they have not seen it, I lose patience. The single tax seems as reasonable and equitable as any compulsory tax. For one thing it would do away with any excuse for that contemptible thief, indirect taxation—"the tariff"—and for those spies who under the respectable name of custom-house officers open my lady's trunks and "inspect" her underwear; a thing which, let us hope, any one of them would scorn himself infinitely for doing as a private individual. We owe the advocates of the single tax a great debt of gratitude for so clearly and persistently showing the wrongs done to the people. No class of persons has ever done it more faithfully; but that the single tax alone would cure these ills has never yet been made clear to my comprehension.

CELIA BALDWIN WHITEHEAD.

HOW THE SINGLE TAX WILL FREE MEN.

In any form of society there can be but two primary factors in production—land and labor. Labor represents man in action and includes all his powers, whether mental or physical; land includes all outside of man; all other factors in production are or can be but subdivisions of these two primary factors. All political economists term the returns to the factor land "rent," and the returns to the factor labor "wages." Therefore to speak of the "rent of ability," as Mrs. Russell did in the August ARENA, whether it refers to the mental ability or muscular ability of labor, is clearly a misuse of economic terms.

In the July ARENA Mrs. Russell held that the statement that "All wealth is created by the application of labor to land" is "inadequate to present conditions." Her position may be illustrated thus:

The factors in production are

$$\text{Wealth} = \text{Land} \times \text{Capital} \times \text{Labor} \times \text{Ability};$$

In distribution

$$\text{Wealth} = \text{Rent} + \text{Interest} + \text{Wages} + \text{Rent}.$$

The correct statement is:

The factors in production are

$$\text{Wealth} = \text{Land} \times \text{Labor};$$

In distribution

$$\text{Wealth} = \text{Rent} + \text{Wages}.$$

All other factors are but sub-divisions of these two, and consequently, distribution must correspond.

But, from the way Mrs. Russell discussed "rent of ability," it seems that what she had in mind was, not ability, but knowledge. Ability is capacity—power to acquire and use informaion. Hence, ability inheres in the individual man; he can neither impart nor give it to others, nor hand it down to the future. Knowledge is information; that which is gained by learning; stored-up learning. In using any particular knowledge — though it has "accumulated as the legacy of one age to another"—we do not necessarily hinder others using the same knowledge at the same time; but in using any particular piece of land we do necessarily prevent others using it at the same time. That is, while the possession of knowledge is *not* necessarily exclusive, the possession of land *is*. (1)

In the August ARENA Mrs. Russell said: "Whether the drawing off of the unemployed to work for themselves on land set free for their use by the single-tax would materially or permanently increase wages in factories depends on the profits of manufacturing. It is to the poorest land in use, or to the best business locations for which there is no competition, that the unemployed would go with their empty pockets. What these could make working *for themselves* on their land or in their shops, would depend upon their ability to compete with capitalistic methods. . . . Yet their degree of success is the single-tax measure of just wages for the lowest grade of workers employed by masters; and to their earnings could the lowest grade be held— a bare living by long hours at hard work." This is the keynote to all Mrs. Russell's arguments, and the idea runs through all her discussions of the single tax. She believes the single tax will free the land, but will *not* free the man who has only his labor to sell. (2)

This assumption is based on a failure to recognize the foundation upon which the power of monopoly rests. The power of all monopoly rests on the cornering of land. Because, first, it gives the monopolizer easy access to the raw material from which all wealth is made, and upon which all must live, while at the same time preventing such access by the masses; and, second, thereby forces the masses

into competition with each other for the privilege of access
to nature—for employment—thus reducing their wages to
the lowest point at which they can live. This gives the
monopolist all power, the very lives of the laborers depending on his pleasure. He thus obtains cheap labor and cheap
land, from which combination all his wealth results; and
he can manipulate—use—these factors as he chooses, and
go on indefinitely storing up wealth.

The cornering of land is the great parent monopoly on
which all other monopolies depend. Nothing else but the
application of the single tax can abolish the corners in land
and thus put labor on its feet—secure its independence—
where it can overthrow the other monopolies. Under the
single tax everyone would have to pay *just as much* for the
privilege of holding land idle or poorly used as if he put it
to its best use. This will make it unprofitable to hold land
except for use. The profit in landholding will then be to the
user, and to him only, in proportion to use. (3)

Mrs. Russell considers that: "The single tax is merely one
method of putting in practice the *principle* that all mankind
have equal rights to the use of the earth." This principle
would be better stated by saying that no one has any right
to exclude any person from any portion of the earth at any
time, which is another way of stating the law of equal freedom as applied to the land question. That law is: That
every person have freedom to do all that he wills, provided
he infringes not the equal freedom of any other. Anything
more or less than equal freedom is inequitable, and no lover
of justice would desire to advocate it.

Mrs. Russell says: "The bondholder can live wherever in
the world he pleases, on the rent of our land supplied him
by the single tax, free from toil and from taxes, with less
anxiety and more freedom than the landlord of to-day. Tell
me if this is not so." Assuming that all federal, state, and
local bonds will be paid, principal and interest, they can
soon be fully met with a fraction of what now goes to landowners as rent, and that without considering the enormous
saving in public expenses involved in the adoption of the
single tax. The occupation of bondholders will quickly
disappear under the reign of the single tax. (4)

Without the single tax we might have government ownership and operation of railways, and yet the rent-absorber
would be the gainer, and labor remain where it is; or we
might have the best possible money system and it would
profit labor nothing, as the rent-absorber would pocket the
gain. For it is competition between men unable to employ

themselves that reduces wages to a bare living and thus
enables rent-absorbers to pocket the benefits of such reforms. With the single tax in operation equal freedom in
the use of the earth would be secured and labor placed in a
position to deal effectively with these problems, by being
able to employ itself.

Throughout her argument Mrs. Russell ignored the three
points brought out by Mrs. Robinson, in which the latter
showed that under the single tax the drawing off of many
unemployed to till the land, the removal of taxation from
the products of industry, and the flow of capital into untaxed property will combine to raise wages. It is more
than probable that, upon the adoption of the single tax,
very few will at first take to farming. To illustrate: If the
city of St. Louis were to adopt the single tax to-day, the
immediate result would be to throw open to use thousands
of acres of vacant land within the city limits. Some of it
would be abandoned by its owners as unprofitable to hold,
and some would be put to use by the owners, who would
begin building and other improvements in order to put the
land to its best use. This would give immediate employment to unskilled labor in digging foundations, etc., and to
architects, stonemasons, bricklayers, carpenters, and all
sorts of laborers; also to dealers in lumber, brick, iron, and
all other materials, who would need more men in their shops
and factories; so that the largest part of the unemployed
would find work right at hand, without going outside the
city.

At the same time the large number of tenants who now
pay from ten to forty dollars a month rent would find
themselves able to get ground at such a low annual tax that
they would soon be able to set about building homes or buying and improving those they were renting. This would
require more workmen, not only in the building trades, but
in painting, paper-hanging, carpet and furniture making,
etc. There are thousands of people in every city who have
savings enough with which to build homes for themselves
if only they could get the land. They now get discouraged,
as the land is always held just beyond their reach by speculative prices. There are now enough such people alone to
employ the present unemployed for some time. The unemployed, thus finding work, would be able to pay for more
and better food and clothing and so set to work grocers,
market-gardeners, and clothiers, and the farmers would
find a ready market right at hand for their productions.
And these hitherto unemployed men, thus set to work,

would soon save enough to build homes, and so, in their turn, employ all the trades.

This demand and supply would act and react in an ever widening circle. There would be no necessity for anyone taking to farming who had no desire or inclination that way. At the same time the vastly increased demand for farm products would so increase the farmer's wages (that part of his product he is able to retain) that many would be attracted to farming, as they would be to any other profitable employment. This would be the more certain as the farmer would not then, as now, be forced far out from the centres of population. Speculation in land has forced the margin of cultivation far beyond its natural limit. The application of the single tax will bring this margin back, and farms can then be easily obtained near their natural markets, the cities and towns; so that Mrs. Russell's fear that the man wishing to employ himself will be forced into the wilderness or desert to work long hours at hard labor, is entirely without foundation.

This is no fancy picture. Wherever assessments have been increased on vacant or poorly used land, the tendency has been to immediate improvement, thus employing more labor on the same amount of land; which proves that all that is necessary to increase the tendency, to the point outlined above, is to increase the application of the principle, which, carried to its logical conclusion, is the single tax. (5)

Mrs. Russell asserts that "The question is whether we shall have industrial self-government by national organization of our industries for the benefit of all, or become the virtual slaves and puppets of combined capital." That is *not* the question. The question is whether we shall have equal or unequal freedom. Under present conditions we have unequal freedom. The single tax is the necessary first step in securing equal freedom, and it can be secured in no other way than by taking this first step. Kindergartens are needed in which nationalists (socialists) can learn the meaning of equal freedom. It must be understood that in the discussion of the order of production and distribution of wealth—political economy—thievery, charity, etc., are not considered, as they have no place in the natural order. The cause of all thievery and the necessity for all charity is the inequitable distribution of wealth, which, in turn, arises from unequal freedom in the use of the earth. Strictly speaking, the single tax will be, not the end, but the beginning of the end, of all monopolies. The strength of monopoly lies in the unemployed, in there being more men than jobs. The single tax, by introducing an era of more jobs than men, at once knocks the foundation from under monopoly. Instead of laborers competing with each other for work, we shall have the spectacle of capitalists competing with each other for laborers. Under such a condition monopoly will inevitably crumble and fall.

To the query, Is the single tax enough? I answer, yes, it is enough to establish the primary equal freedom—equal freedom in the use of the earth—without which equal freedom in other things is impossible. And equal freedom in all things is the highest possible condition conceivable, as it is the only condition which allows the fullest and highest development of every individual. (6)

ESTELLA BACHMAN BROKAW.

NOTES IN REPLY.

(1) There is no dispute about the two *primary* factors in production,

"When Adam delved and Eve span,"

but in modern production the importance of capital (though merely stored-up labor) as a factor, is clear; and sooner or later the powerful fourth factor, ability, must be generally recognized. In "The Land Question" Mr. George said: "In steam and electricity and all the countless inventions which they typify, mighty forces have entered the world," and these, he said, "will compel great social changes." In almost every department of labor they are constantly lessening the need of human hands and are turning men out of employment, just as surely as land monopoly prevents the access of labor to land. How shall we equalize the plenty and the leisure these "new forces" bring? Only by "great social changes" for the benefit of all.

We say "ability" and "rent of ability" for lack of better terms. This ability is not mere personal knowledge or individual capacity. It applies especially to the invention, improvement, and use of machinery, and necessitates the organization of labor and the use of great capital. If the term "land" be made to include "all outside of man," why limit the word "rent" to its past strict economic use? Interest is sometimes called the "rent of money," and we daily hear of boat rent, house rent, etc. Till we can do better, we may call *the additional wealth created by the use of machinery in combined labor* the "rent of ability."

As I said at first, the single-tax political economy seems to be "based on the assumption that our industries are and

will remain simple as a general rule," and it scarcely recognizes machinery except as labor-saving devices for individual use. Though "the possession of knowledge is not necessarily exclusive," the capitalistic organization of industry
with modern methods is usually decidedly "exclusive" of all
smaller competitors.

(2) I have seen clearly from the first that the single tax
has in it the power not only to free the land for use, but
also to free men from the necessity of working for others in
order to escape starvation, and to free individuals, too, from
the necessity of coöperation with their fellows if they prefer life *a la* Robinson Crusoe. But I do not see that it alone
will free them from what I call poverty, or release them
from the power of monopoly. Though the single tax has in
it the *power* to free the land and to give to all employment
and food, I see a possibility that it might fail of even this,
simply because of the unequal freedom and unequal power
of unequal capitals. If there is no limit to the amount (in
quantity and value) of land which individuals or syndicates
may hold if they only pay to the public the assessed rental
value, can you not see that in the consolidation of great
monopolies and the concentration of enormous capitals now
rapidly going forward, the effect of the single tax in placing
much vacant land cheap in the market might be to throw
it into the hands of syndicates powerful enough to control
legislators and assessors, as well as the land on which the
people must live? With real estate associations in every
city and a national organization, is there not this dire
possibility?

(3) We have had repeated assertion that, as Miss Gay
said, "All monopolies have their root in land monopoly;
destroy that and they die." I confess I have not so far discovered the proof of this sweeping claim. It is said above
that the power of all monopoly rests upon the cornering of
land, because "it gives the monopolizer easy access to the
raw material from which all wealth is made, and thereby
forces the masses into competition with each other for the
privilege of access to nature"; thus giving the monopolist
"cheap labor and cheap land, from which combination all
his wealth results." Mrs. Brokaw was perhaps thinking of
mines, but I do not discover this to be the case with regard
to the establishment of any of the most powerful trusts that
tyrannize over us. The president of the great oil combination, "the parent of the trust system," testified in 1888 (after
several years of the trust) that, "It does not own any oil
wells, or lands producing oil, and never did." It began as a

combination of oil refineries. Was it not so with the sugar
trust? It was not by cornering land, but by cornering the
market, that the great meat monopoly was established. Mr.
Lloyd says in "Wealth against Commonwealth":

When a farmer sells a steer, a lamb, or a hog, and the housekeeper buys a chop or a roast, they enter a market which for the
whole continent, and for all kinds of cattle and meats, is controlled
by the combination of packers at Chicago known as the "big four."

This combination does not need to own the "thousand
hills" on which are pastured the cattle which they buy
cheap and sell dear, and I do not see how a tax on land
values can especially affect the monopoly of the meat market, nor how it can destroy Mr. Rockefeller's facility for
"passing round the oil" and taking toll thereon—though
to be sure the oil trust is at last buying cheapened oil fields.
But it has become powerful enough now to buy almost
everything in sight, including assessors, legislators, and
governments.

In the long list of such combinations there are trusts
(monopolies) which exist in spite of all laws against them,
some of them aided by tariffs, and some by cheap land and
cheap labor; but can it truthfully be said that the single tax
will destroy them all? Land is often the least valuable of
their assets, as it is of the elevator trust, which makes dividends of from twenty-five to thirty-five per cent for stockholders by taking toll from wheat-growers and from bread-
eaters, and which has no tariff protection.

No one has made clear to me how it is that (as Miss Gay
said) the railroad and telegraph monopolies "have their
strength in monopoly of land"; nor how the taxation of land
values alone will destroy their monopolistic power. That
these two monopolies greatly aid other powerful combinations, there can be no doubt. To tell what laws we can
enact or abolish *after* the establishment of the single tax,
is not to prove that the single tax will do it all.

Mr. George said, in "The Land Question":

When a capital of a million dollars comes into competition with
capitals of thousands of dollars, the smaller capitalists must be
driven out of the business or destroyed. *With great capital nothing
can compete save great capital.* . . . A while ago and any journeyman
shoemaker could set up in the business for himself with the savings
of a few months. But now the operative shoemaker could not in a
lifetime save enough from his wages to go into business for himself.
And now that great capital has entered agriculture, it must be with
the same results. The large farmer, who can buy the latest machinery at the lowest cash prices and use it to the best advantage, who
can run a straight furrow for miles, who can make special rates with
railroad companies, take advantage of the market, and sell in large

lots for the least commission, must drive out the small farmer of the early American type, just as the shoe factory has driven out the journeyman shoemaker.

(4) Concerning bonds: these are constantly increasing our public interest-bearing debts, and bonds cannot be paid and their interest stopped till they are due. Many single-taxers have a happy faith that economic rent would yield so bountiful a revenue that we could immediately do wonderful things with it. But one of the prominent single-tax writers and speakers told me, a year or so ago, that he thought the rent of land would shrink so much with the application of the single tax that there would never be more than enough for an economical administration of the government.

(5) If Mrs. Brokaw will look again she will see that I did not "ignore" Mrs. Robinson's three points, but that I tried to show how the hampered condition of the now unemployed when at work on free land in competition with capitalists, and with the cheap labor of foreign countries, would make them poor buyers of factory wares, and that most of these wares could be more cheaply imported from countries of cheap labor than made here; so that the starting of factories and the expected perpetual motion of the single tax might fail, after all. Miss Gay said at the beginning of this discussion that all depends on the prosperity of those working at the margin of cultivation, and referred us to Mr. George's chapter on wages. In "The Story of My Dictatorship" the question is begged throughout by the constant assumption that the application of the single tax almost immediately gives the farmers plenty of money to spend, greatly stimulating all other industries. This I still doubt, the more as I see farmers in this vicinity, in August, leaving delicious green peas and green corn and string beans unharvested because the bounty of the crop has made the price so low that they cannot pay even the labor offering itself at fifty cents a day. Scarcity last year made potatoes very dear. Now, before the cheapest "digging time," farmers are getting only fifteen or eighteen cents a bushel.

Can it be imagined that the holder of vacant land would immediately begin to build or otherwise improve his lots because of increased taxation, if he could not see profit in so doing? That would depend upon the present number of vacant houses and on the profitable demand for factories, stores, and dwellings. From the windows of my suburban home, I can see three pretty cottages sorrowfully abandoned by the young couples who built them for permanent homes.

as the demands of competitive business made it necessary
for the men to live elsewhere and the separation of families
grew intolerable. And in the two large cities near, vacant
stores and offices are a frequent sad spectacle. Even if a
boom in building should immediately follow the adoption
of the single tax, it could not continue indefinitely.

(6) We set out with the question, "Is the single tax
enough to solve the labor question?"—which Miss Gay asserts and Miss Chapman reiterates, but which Mrs. Brokaw
and others prudently fail to affirm. As for myself I am more
sure than ever that our equal right to the use of the earth
(which includes the equal sharing of economic rent) is simply a necessary *part* of the full solution. I did not mean
to set this question aside in suggesting *the inevitable choice
between industrial self-government and a plutocratic oligarchy.* Mrs. Brokaw says the question is "whether we
shall have equal or unequal freedom." The former, by all
means, say I. So let us all try unitedly, in the great struggle before us, to free ourselves not only from the power of
land-grabbers, but also from the power of the money-grab-
bers, a well-entrenched class who mean to issue and manipulate our currency, with power to corner any metal or
commodity money, and to fatten by the repeated issues of
unnecessary interest-bearing bonds. Our equal freedom is
impossible with a monopolized telegraph to control our
communication, and with railroads run for private gain.
Reforms here, and more also, are necessary to our equal
freedom. It seems to me decidedly like "making a programme for Providence" to insist that the single tax must
be accomplished first in order of time.

Equal freedom means a great deal, and the quotation
from Mr. George, given above and italicized by me, applies
again right here: "*With great capital nothing can compete
save great capital.*" Full economic equality is the desideratum. Nowhere short of this is there equal freedom.

As soon as I saw our August papers in print, I noticed
that the quotation from Huxley which I added at the last
moment does not apply to Miss Chapman's remarks on
nature's part in our economic salvation. She was thinking
not of what is called the "cosmic process" (the struggle for
existence and the survival of the fittest), but of that beautiful power of self-healing which Nature displays when she
has a fair chance. I too admire and reverence that power.
But I cannot agree with Miss Chapman that in our present
complex civilization the mere shifting of taxation from
everything else to economic rent "will guarantee a just

equality of opportunity to all men," and that all else may be left to "God and Nature."

The gathering of the single tax and its application to public uses are artificial processes. How *much* depends upon the *use* made of that public revenue! "God and Nature" would demand the exercise of human judgment, and could not be displeased by any organization of our industrial forces which would enable every one of us—including our weak and suffering and long-defrauded brothers and sisters—to reap the full benefits of all that the progress of civilization has brought us, and give equal freedom to all for the use and enjoyment of life's best gifts—equal opportunity to grow and learn, and do and enjoy.

F. E. R.

A UNIVERSAL RATIO—A SILVER BILL TO SUIT BOTH PARTIES.

BY ROBERT STEIN.

U. S. Senate, Washington, D. C., March 21, 1895.

Mr. Stein's article on the Kanitz free silver bill is an admirable presentation of the present situation. How is it possible to avoid the conclusion that the fall in the price of silver is caused by its demonetization, and that the price will be restored by remonetization? It cannot, perhaps should not, be done at a bound, but by some gradual though sure process. Why, then, should not the United States pass the Kanitz free silver bill, declaring its determination to open its mints again to free coinage, at the French ratio of 15½ to 1, when enough nations have acceded to make success certain? I see no objection.

W. E. Chandler.

Brown University, Providence, R. I., Aug. 27, 1895.

You have done a useful piece of work in publishing a "uniform ratio bill" for circulation in our country. I hope some such bill will pass Congress. Unity of ratio is all-important, and you do well to emphasize it. I hope you are right in saying that the President of the United States would sign such a bill, and I dare say you are.

E. Benj. Andrews,
President Brown University.

St. John's College, Cambridge, England, Aug. 29, 1895.

While I would not have it understood that I advocate the ratio of 15½ to 1, I do not think there can be a question that you are right as between 15½ to 1 and 16 to 1 for the United States. Of course 16 to 1 would be perfectly inoperative in America if 15½ were in force in Europe; or rather, as you point out, it would be operative in the sense that you would be drained of silver and France of gold. The French are far too shrewd to go into any arrangement of such a kind; and the effect of your adopting 16 to 1 would be, in my opinion, to effectually stop international bimetallism.

H. X. Foxwell,
Professor of Political Economy, Cambridge University.

212

E. BENJAMIN ANDREWS, LL. D.

U. S. SENATOR W. E. CHANDLER.

L. BRADFORD PRINCE, LL. D.

MORETON FREWEN.

SANTA FE, NEW MEXICO, Sept. 2, 1895.

I think the plan proposed in your article is probably the best of any that can be accomplished at this time, and it would certainly be a very great step forward if such a bill could be passed and signed. I think that all who have given attention to the subject will agree that the ratio of 15½ to 1 is the proper one, and probably the only one on which we can secure the concurrence of France and the other Latin Union countries, and I am very glad to see that point so clearly brought out in your article. We advocate 16 to 1 because that is simply a restoration and not a novelty, and therefore avoids some argument; but of course everyone favoring 16 to 1 will be glad to have the ratio made 15½ to 1, and I think all understand that if there is international action, it should be on that basis. I am heartily in favor of "independent action " by our government; but of course I know it would be a great advantage if we can have the coöperation of others; and besides, *a great many would support a bill like yours, who would not favor independent action.*

L. BRADFORD PRINCE, LL. D.,
Ex-Governor of New Mexico.

CHAMBER OF DEPUTIES, PARIS, FRANCE, Sept. 11, 1895.

I do not believe that the solution of the problem of the establishment of international bimetallism can at present be brought about by a conference similar to those that have been held in the past. In this respect I share the views recently set forth by Mr. Balfour. The governments will have to arrive at a previous understanding on the points under discussion before such a conference assembles. The governments themselves will not take this step unless their parliaments compel them. It is the duty of bimetallists in the various nations to labor for this end.

The proper common ratio is that which imposes no serious sacrifices on anybody. You show very clearly that the ratio of 15½ to 1 is the only one which really fulfils this condition, and you will render a signal service to the general cause of justice, by the reëstablishment of monetary peace among men, if you succeed in causing the ratio of 15½ to 1 to be adopted by the United States.

I am convinced that if in 1834, when your great republic modified its monetary law, changing from 15 to 1 to 16 to 1, you had adopted 15½ to 1, the ratio prevailing in France, all the monetary crises which have been ruining us all during the past twenty years would have been avoided; because I am firmly convinced that if in 1873 a monetary union had been in existence for nearly forty years between France and the United States, on the common basis of the ratio of 15½ to 1, these two great republics might have remained indifferent to the monetary policy of Germany, and might have continued, by their powerful union, to assure to the world the benefits of a stable standard of value.

There is no objection whatever to the separate adoption by the respective parliaments of France, Germany, England and the United States of a law declaring, in substance, that their citizens are authorized to pay their taxes either with a fixed weight of gold or with a weight of silver 15½ times as great; with an additional clause stating that this law shall become operative only when the government of France, Germany, England, and the United States shall have agreed on a common date for its promulgation.

I for my part am willing to labor for this end, and I was glad to learn at a recent visit to the German Bimetallic League that several of its most prominent leaders share this view.

The German bimetallists are to-day agreed with the French bimetallists not only on all questions of principle but also on the question of the only ratio that can be adopted, and we all hold, like you, that *the adoption of this same ratio* 15½ *to* 1 *by the United States will remove one of the greatest difficulties* in the way of the realization of the measure which will be most fruitful in the uplifting of the prosperity of agriculture, industry, and commerce of the civilized world, ruined by the blind adoption of the single gold standard.

ED. FOUGEIROL, *député de l'Ardèche,*
Vice-President of the French Bimetallic League.

COODHAM, KILMARNOCK, N. B., Sept. 12, 1895.

I think very well of the "Kanitz silver bill," and the pamphlet I consider an excellent one. It expresses exactly what we English bimetallists feel, viz., what a pity it is that the bimetallists in the States, who are all international bimetallists, and form the great majority of the nation, should be fighting amongst themselves instead of joining us here in forwarding an international agreement. If the bill you propose could be passed, *it would help us immensely here,* and would, I feel sure, have an effect in Europe.

SIR W. H. HOULDSWORTH, M. P.

Member of the English Gold and Silver Commission in 1888.

SIR W. H. HOULDSWORTH, M. P.

MUNCHEN-GLADBACH, GERMANY, Sept. 20, 1895.

When the solution of the silver question by the international way is at last set in motion, *silver will of itself solve the main question, that of the ratio,* and 15½ to 1 will no longer appear as a phantom even to the most faint-hearted bimetallist. I adhere unflinchingly to the conviction that the former ratio of values between gold and silver must be restored; all agreements on any other ratio would be half measures. We ought not to be afraid to go to the root of the evil before it is too late.

OTTO WÜLFING,
Member of the German Silver Commission.

BERLIN, Oct. 5, 1895.

If the bill proposed by you is introduced and passed in Washington, it will be a very great help to the endeavors of bimetallists in Europe, and it may be hoped that it will be the way in which bimetallism will be attained. So far as I know the attitude of the leading bimetallists, *similar bills would promptly be introduced in the Reichstag and in the French Chamber of Deputies, and would in all probability be passed in both countries.* My friend, Herr Von Kardorff, has long recommended such action. The adoption of such laws of identical tenor by the three great states would have a decided effect in favor of bimetallism in England. The English voters would then finally solve the question.

Your project of such a bill recommends itself for the further reason that the battle of the standards in the United States is systematically misrepresented by the European gold press. The gold press endeavors to deceive public opinion in Europe into the belief that the free coinage party in the United States corresponds to the European bimetallists, while its opponets are adherents of the gold standard in the European sense, that is to say, opponents of the international double standard. In reality every bimetallist, that is to say, every adherent of the international double standard, is bound to oppose the free coinage of silver by any single country, because the object, namely the stability of the ratio of values between silver and gold, can only be reached if several great states adopt the same double standard. Now that the gold production has increased so enormously, there is an increased possibility that the United States may be able alone to maintain 1:16, but only so long as the gold plethora continues, which will not be long. A permanently stable ratio of values, a really healthy monetary system can only be secured through an international double standard, which will probably be rendered impossible, for a measurable period, by the victory of the free coinage party of the United States.

DR. OTTO ARENDT.

DR. OTTO ARENDT,

*Member of the Prussian House of Deputies,
and of the German Silver Commission.*

LONDON, ENGLAND,
Oct. 19, 1895.

I quite endorse your remarks on the Lodge-Reed policy of a "Tariff cum Silver" union, with say France and Germany — that is to say, cutting tariffs in favor of those nations which keep open mints. I do not see why the Republican Party has not before this harmonized on these lines, it is a policy which the Democrats would have to accept, or disrupt their South.

MORETON FREWEN.

DENVER, COL.,
Oct. 31, 1895.

If we ever secure an international agreement to use silver, it will be at the ratio of 15½ to 1. It is folly to talk of a ratio corresponding to the commercial ratio now existing between gold and silver. France will not consent to a change, and if we secure independent action on the part of

SENATOR H. M. TELLER,
OF COLORADO.

our government, it ought to be at the French ratio. I am glad to hear that Laveleye's book, "Money and International Bimetallism," has been translated. It is an admirable work.

H. M. TELLER.

A recent cartoon in *Judge* represents Messrs. Reed, McKinley, and Harrison sitting, corporeally, on a fence, while on one side stands Senator Sherman, holding a tablet inscribed "Gold the only standard," and on the other side Senator Jones, displaying a sign "Free Silver," each beckoning to the fence-bestriders and addressing to them this appeal, "Oh, come off!"

One who got his first notion of the silver controversy from that cartoon would probably draw this inference: There are in the United States two irreconcilable parties, the gold party and the silver party, each of sufficient strength to cause public men to hesitate to incur its antagonism. The same conclusion would be reached by reading many of the current newspapers. He who has settled down in that belief will find his mental equilibrium rudely shaken when he learns that Senator Sherman, generally supposed to be

the leader of the ultra gold men, was one of the signers of
the telegram to the bimetallist meeting at the Mansion
House, London, in 1894, expressing the belief that the free
coinage of gold and silver by international agreement
would be a blessing. Similarly, one who has contracted
the notion that Senator Jones is an enemy to gold will be
disappointed if he tries to discover in the senator's published speeches a single phrase indicating that he desires
the disuse or diminished use of gold.

If, then, both parties mean practically the same thing,
is it not rather painful to hear such titles as "robber blood-
sucker, plutocrat," hurled from one camp at the other, to
be met by such missiles "as fanatic, crank, hayseed"?

Assuming that the professions of both parties are sincere
(and it would be a sad day on which we had to admit
that the majority of our public men are pretenders), the
terms "gold men" and "silver men" are seen to be inappropriate. They ought to be replaced by the terms "international bimetallists" and "independent bimetallists." Even
these terms lay too great stress on the difference between
them, since both parties desire international bimetallism.

The attitude of the international bimetallists is well
defined by the telegram just mentioned:

> We desire to express our cordial sympathy with the movement to pro-
> mote the restoration of silver by international agreement, in aid of
> which we understand a meeting is to be held to-morrow, under your
> Lordship's presidency. We believe that the free coinage of both gold
> and silver by international agreement at a fixed ratio would secure to
> mankind the blessings of *a sufficient volume of metallic money*, and, what
> is hardly less important, would secure to the world of trade *immunity
> from violent exchange fluctuations.* (*Signed*) John Sherman, William
> B. Allison, D. W. Voorhees, H. C. Lodge, G. F. Hoar, N. W. Aldrich,
> D. B. Hill, E. Murphy, C. S. Brice, O. H. Platt, A. P. Gorman, W. P.
> Frye, C. K. Davis, S. M. Cullom, J. M. Cary.

If this means anything, it means this: *The only sound
money is bimetallic money.*

What that party does not want is perhaps best set forth
in the following lines written by Gen. Francis A. Walker:

> The only bimetallism which would satisfy me would be free coinage
> of silver at a given ratio, by agreement between a certain number of im-
> portant commercial nations. Until we can get this, I am opposed to any
> devices for increasing the use of silver, here or there, and to any tin-
> kering whatsoever with the subject.

The attitude of the independent bimetallists is set forth
in "Coin's Financial School":

> Free coinage by the United States will at once establish a parity
> between the two metals. Any nation that is big enough to take all the

silver in the world, and give back merchandise and products in payment for it will at once establish the parity between it and gold. . . . But we alone would not have to maintain it. We know now that Mexico, South and Central America, the Asiatic governments and France would be with us from the start.

What that party does not want is set forth in the same book, in a passage which at the same time calls in question the sincerity of the opposite party:

The money lenders of the United States, who own substantially all of our money, have a selfish interest in maintaining the gold standard. . . . They believe that if the gold standard can survive for a few years longer, the people will get used to it—get used to their poverty—and quietly submit. To that end they

COUNT VON KANITZ.
MEMBER OF THE GERMAN REICHSTAG,
AUTHOR OF THE KANITZ SILVER BILL.

organize international bimetallic committees and say, "Wait on England; she will be forced to give us bimetallism." Vain hope!

Thus we have the curious spectacle of two great parties, with identical aim, yet working with might and main against each other.

What the ultimate outcome of the struggle will be, even Mr. Harvey, the author of "Coin's Financial School," declares himself unable to foresee. That the free-silver agitation will soon die out is not probable, seeing that it has steadily gained in strength during the last fifteen years. But inasmuch as the distress for which free silver is said to be the only remedy is affirmed to be so acute as to demand immediate action, it is well to inquire how soon a free-silver bill may become a law. It certainly cannot be before March 4, 1897. Nor will the most sanguine free silver man be ready to affirm that its immediate passage after that date is assured.

It cannot be doubted, therefore, that the independent free coinage party would be glad to see other measures adopted, in this country or elsewhere, tending to hasten the advent of universal free coinage. On the other hand, it is natural to suppose that the international bimetallists cannot but chafe under the charge of insincerity cast on them by the other party, and must therefore be desirous of showing by works the faith that is within them; in fact, since they deny the efficacy of independent free coinage, it behooves them to propose other measures and try to prove that these will be efficient in securing what this party regards as the only practicable solution—international free coinage. Seeing how closely identical are the aims of both parties, it would seem strange if no measure could be devised, apt to satisfy both. Evidently, such a measure would be carried with hardly a dissenting vote.

The most obvious measure would be another monetary conference. Such a conference may still be called by Germany. The recent Conservative victory in England renders this more probable, and at the same time is a guarantee that England's attitude will not be as uncompromising as formerly. Even if Germany does not tender such an invitation, there seems to be no good reason why the United States should not do so a third time. It is

impossible to imagine that the German government would this time send none but gold monometallists to such a conference, thus trampling on the wishes of its best suporters, the German farmers, who within the last two years have become a unit in favor of bimetallism.

But supposing that it is impossible to cooperate with foreign *governments*, it may still be possible to cooperate with foreign *bimetallists*. One of the greatest obstacles that bimetallists in every country have to contend with is the uncertain attitude of other countries. A notable instance of this appeared in the German Silver Commission of 1894. It is generally assumed as a matter of course that France is ready at any moment to join an international free coinage union. Yet Dr. Bamberger did not think it absurd to maintain that the co-operation of France is by no means a certainty, and in support of his view brought forward several arguments which certainly deserve notice. Thus, if we recognize that the cause of free coinage in our country is promoted by the efforts of foreign bimetallists, it would

M. E. FOUGEIROL,
MEMBER OF THE FRENCH CHAMBER OF DEPUTIES,
VICE-PRESIDENT OF THE FRENCH BIMETALLIC
LEAGUE.

seem to be obviously to our interest to aid their endeavors by removing, so far as possible, all stumbling blocks out of their way. The first requisite to that end will be to define the attitude of our government in such terms as to silence all doubts on that score. This will be the best possible preparation that we can make for a monetary conference.

An endeavor will now be made to show that this purpose will be accomplished by a bill, introduced by Count Von Kanitz in the German Reichstag and afterward submitted to the German Silver Commission of 1894. In essence that bill provides for the eventual unlimited coinage of gold and silver at the ratio of 1:15½, the coinage of silver to be gratuitous, that of gold to be subject to a coinage duty. The law is to become operative only "when other great states shall have adopted the free coinage of silver."

In this form of the bill three points may be criticised. First, in the opinion of Emilè de Laveleye, bimetallism is not quite perfect unless the coinage of both metals be gratu-

itous. Second, it might be better to enumerate the countries whose analogous action is desired. Third, even a
temporary limitation of coinage, such as that contemplated
in the German bill, must vitiate the action of bimetallism.
Amended in these respects the bill might be introduced in
Congress in the following form:

*An Act to introduce the free and gratuitous coinage of gold and silver at
the ratio of 1 :15½.*

Be it enacted by the Senate and House of Representatives of the
United States in Congress assembled:

SECTION 1. That any person may bring to any United States mint
gold and silver bullion not less in value than fifty dollars, and have the
same coined, free of charge, the gold into the usual coins of the present
legal weight and fineness, the silver into dollars, each dollar containing
399.9 grains of standard silver; or to receive in exchange certificates
stating the value of the standard coin metal deposited, but not specify-
ing whether it was gold or silver; that these certificates shall be redeemable on demand, either in gold or silver at the option of the treasury; and that the said coins and certificates shall be legal tender for
all debts public and private.

SEC. 2. That the existing silver dollars of the United States shall be
retired. and, if recoined, shall be made into dollars in accordance with
Section 1.

SEC. 3. That this law shall become operative only when England,
France, and Germany shall have adopted similar laws providing for the
unlimited purchase of gold and silver bullion under such provisions
that the purchasing price and the unlimited paying power of the two
metals shall be as 15½ to 1.

The bill will probably have to contain a number of details
which need not be specified here. Only the four great
commercial nations are named, because their action will
suffice. Evidently, similar action by other nations will be
highly desirable..

In discussing this bill, it will not be necessary to express
an opinion on the merits either of the "sound money"
doctrine or of the independent free silver doctrine, nor
even of monometallism or bimetallism. Inasmuch as both
parties in the United States profess to desire international
bimetallism, all that will be attempted will be to show that
this bill ought to satisfy both parties. Believing this to be
its most commendable feature, the writer would deem it
particularly fortunate if the bill were to become known as
"The Reconciliation Bill."

Let us first try to imagine what will be the consequences
if this bill becomes a law.

In all probability silver will at once go up several pence. It was the general opinion in the German Silver Commission that the mere preparations for international bimetallism would drive silver upward with lightning rapidity. It is natural to suppose that France will hasten to pass a similar law, since its object is to make the French system universal and save France from loss—in fact, the F r e n c h government was merely *authorized* in 1876 to suspend free coinage—and again silver will go up a few pence. Thereupon the German bimetallists, elated at the success of their own law in foreign lands, will unite on this one measure

PROF. DR. F. ZIRKEL.
GEHEIMER BERGRATH, PROFESSOR OF GEOLOGY
AT THE UNIVERSITY OF LEIPZIG,
MEMBER OF THE GERMAN SILVER COMMISSION.

and carry it triumphantly; and again silver will climb up a few pence, probably beyond 38, at which England closed the Indian mints. England will then gladly reopen these mints, and more pence will be added to the silver price. Next the other countries of the Latin Union, as well as Austria-Hungary, Holland, Spain, Mexico, Central and South America, perhaps even Russia, will pass similar laws. Meantime, various countries, seeing which way the wind blows, will hasten to buy silver while it is yet cheap; Germany among others will probably be wise enough to buy sufficient silver at 31 pence so that when it rises to $60\frac{3}{4}$ pence she may make up and more than make up for the loss of 96,000,000 marks which she suffered through her silver sales. Private individuals, too, will hasten to purchase silver before it rises to par. From all these causes combined, the price of silver will presently be back to $60\frac{3}{4}$ pence; and then England will have no reason whatever for remaining outside the bimetallic union.

Of course it is not to be expected that everything will come off smoothly according to programme. But it would be difficult to imagine an alteration in circumstances that might not be met by an alteration in plan.

This bill ought to be particularly welcome to the free silver men, because it will afford to them an opportunity of scoring an immediate practical success and not interfere in the least with a free coinage bill that may be introduced later on. Agitation is comparatively easy when you can say: To-morrow the battle will be fought and the victory be ours! Enthusiasm is apt to be dampened when the cry is: To arms! To arms! Let us fight and conquer *two years from now*! The present bill, if supported by all the free silver men, is practically sure of passing through Congress, *and of receiving President Cleveland's signature.* If it leads to similar action in France and a few other states, it is plain that free coinage by the United States would become far less risky and therefore its adoption by Congress more probable. In this way this bill will serve as a stepping-stone from which the advance to free silver may more easily be made in 1897; a trophy which the free-silver leaders may exhibit to their followers to reanimate their courage—an important matter at this moment, after so many years of arduous struggle without the slightest practical result.

It is well known that the ratio of 1:16 is advocated by the free silver men for the sole reason that it simply implies the maintenance of the old silver dollar, and may therefore be expected to arouse less opposition. They have repeatedly declared that 1:15½ will be equally welcome to them. This declaration is repeated in "Coin's Financial School." Moreover the United States government, by giving its adhesion to the project of a Bimetallic Union submitted to it by the French government in 1881, expressly declared its willingness to adopt the ratio of 1:15½.

Nay, more; the change of ratio is a necessary prerequisite to free coinage. Even Mr. Harvey, while maintaining that the United States alone can establish the parity between gold and silver, expresses the conviction that "France would be with us from the start," and it may not be unfair to assume that in this case "the wish was father to the thought." But if we count on the coöperation of France, it will be well for us to have a distinct idea of what we 'expect France to do. Is she to resume free coinage at 1:15½ or is she to adopt our ratio of 1:16? Let us see what either alternative implies.

If France has free coinage at 1:15½, while the United

States has it at 1:16 (1:15⁸⁵/₈₆) ,the mints of the two countries will give me the same amount of money for 1,000 pounds of gold; but if I bring 1,000 pounds of silver (pure), the United States mint will give me $15,515.15, while the French mint will give me $16,004, so that in taking silver to the French mint I can make a profit of $488.85, or 3.15 per cent. This profit after deducting cost of shipment, insurance, and loss of interest, will still be sufficient to cause every holder of silver to send it to France rather than to the United States. At the same time, gold will tend to flow to the United States,

LEUSCHNER
GEHEIMER OBER-BERGRATH,
MEMBER OF THE GERMAN REICHSTAG, AND
OF THE GERMAN SILVER COMMISSION.

where it is valued higher than in France, so that a time will come when the United States will be deprived of all her silver and France of all her gold. If France adopts the United States ratio of 1:16, she will have to recoin her $492,000,000 in silver, involving a loss to her treasury of $15,000,000. On the contrary if the United States recoins her $625,300,000 in silver at 1:15½, she will gain $20,000,000—sufficient to establish a department of public roads at Washington and maintain it for forty years with an appropriation of half a million a year.

But the matter does not concern France alone. The table on pages 44–45 of the report of the director of the mint, shows that the ratio of 1:15½ is practically universal, the United States and Mexico forming the only notable exceptions. If free coinage is made universal, it is evident, from what has just been said, that the same ratio must be adopted everywhere. If we insist on our ratio of 1:16, we shall have to persuade all the other countries not only to overturn their monetary systems, but also to do so at a loss, in recoining their silver. The degree of alacrity with which they will allow themselves to be thus persuaded may be guessed by observing their desperate and often fruitless struggles to escape a deficit. On the other hand, if we recoin our silver at 1:15½, and thus consent to make a profit of $20,000,000, we shall only have to persuade the other countries to allow their coinage systems to remain as they are. In brief: if the United States ratio be adopted, we shall gain nothing and nearly every other country will lose; if the European ratio be adopted, no country will lose, and we (and Mexico) will gain. Is it possible to imagine that one can be a friend of silver and yet insist on 1:16?

This state of the case is clearly set forth by Emile de Laveleye in "La Monnaie et le Bimétallisme International" (Paris: Felix Alcan, 1891). In chapter 43, to show that France cannot alone resume free coinage, he points out that such resumption would cause France to be flooded with all the loose silver of the neighboring states. He then continues:

But there is another obstacle, which is *absolute*.

In the United States, silver is coined at 1:16. If they adopted free coinage of the two metals at 1:15½, it is evident that all their silver — $625,300,000 — would flow to the mint, to be recoined into new dollars, since 15½ ounces would procure the same paying power that 16 ounces did before; thus the net profit would be half an ounce on 16.

If the mint at Paris was thrown open to silver on the basis of the old ratio, the same operation would ensue; it would be somewhat less profitable, because the expense would be greater; but yet the profit would still suffice, and thus all the white metal of the United States, coming to be coined in France, would take thence a corresponding quantity of gold through the operations of arbitrage, independent of the action of the commercial exchange. As was shown very clearly by Mr. Cernuschi, when two bimetallic systems exist at the same time in two countries with different ratios, each of the precious metals, gold or silver, will flow to the country which assigns to it the highest paying power. Thus in 1792 the United States adopted bimetallism with the ratio of 1:15, while in France the ratio was 1:15½. As gold in France had 15½ times the paying power of silver, while in the United States it had only 15 times the paying power of silver, gold flowed away from America to be coined at Paris. In 1834, the United States, in order to attract gold, adopted the ratio of 1:16. Immediately the movement was reversed. As the purchasing power of silver in the United States was 16 times less than that of gold, while in France it was 15½ times less, silver flowed out of America. On the other hand, gold, having now acquired in the United States a purchasing power 16 times that of silver, instead of 15½ times in France, sought New York.

Up to 1870, French bimetallism was able, without wavering, to resist the withdrawal now of gold, now of silver, by the bimetallism of the United States, because that country up to 1880 had only a very limited metallic circulation compared to that of France, and because during the civil war the paper money drove both the precious metals out of the country at the same time.

From the organization of the United States Mint down to 1872, only $8,045,838 were coined in silver,* which, imported into France little by little, to be there coined, could not exercise any perceptible influence on French bimetallism. But this is no longer the case.. The United States already possesses a considerable stock of coin, and it increases more rapidly than in any other state, because the silver purchases under the Bland law and under the new silver law regularly add a considerable quantity of silver to the gold coined each year.

Hence France will never be able to resume the free coinage of the two metals, either by herself or by agreement with other states, unless the United States adopts the ratio of 1:15½ or France adopts the ratio of 1:16.

Since France would lose in adopting 1:16, while the United States would gain by adopting 1:15½, the latter ratio would necessarily be chosen.

Other forcible passages of similar tenor must regretfully be left unquoted. In these the famous Belgian economist shows that free coinage by the United States at 1:16 would be a grievous blow to international bimetallism, and, first and foremost, would render the coöperation of France impossible; and what doth it profit us to gain all Asia and South America if we lose France? Whatever may be the immediate effect of the adoption of 1:16, it certainly cannot produce the much-desired condition of stability and international equilibrium, and thus the change of ratio will eventually have to be made. Then why not make it now so as to put an end to the trouble?

Under these circumstances the death of Dana Horton, at the very moment when his great authority might have been exerted to the best effect, is a national, nay, international, calamity. The lifelong endeavor of this eminent economist, whom Professor Foxwell calls *the greatest of all modern writers on money*, was to bring about international unity of ratio. It is hoped that, as a slight mark of recognition of his services, Congress will promptly issue a new edition of his report of the Conference of 1878, a mine of information constantly quoted by European economists. "Three separate times," he tells us, "one might say, the world has stumbled upon the treasure of unity of ratio, yet has never recognized it or possessed itself of it. England had the opportunity in 1717; France in 1785 and 1803; the United States between 1834 and 1837." He shows that the purpose of all changes of ratio in the past was to prevent

---

*Silver coinage in the United States from April 2, 1792, to June 30, 1872:

One-dollar pieces	$8,045,838
Half-dollar pieces	199,630,871
Quarter-dollar pieces	87,536,274
	$295,212,983

At the same time a large amount of foreign silver was in circulation in the United States.

the outflow of one or the other metal, but that those who
made the change invariably jumped out of the frying-pan
into the fire by overrating the metal previously underrated.
This necessarily implied the underrating of the other metal
and immediately caused its outflow. Had England, when
she changed her ratio in 1717, followed Sir Isaac Newton's
advice and assigned to the two metals the same relative
value that they had in France, there would have been no
further inducement to export either. May it not be hoped
that now, after one hundred and seventy-eight years, the
world has grown wiser, and will not continue the monetary
vendetta by keeping up the difference in ratio?

Let it be understood that nothing that has here been said
is intended as an argument against independent free coinage
by the United States. That movement could not have
gained the adherence of half the United States if it was a
mere "craze." But since, by the admission of the free silver
men themselves, international bimetallism would greatly
aid their cause; since it is very doubtful whether an independent free coinage bill can ever be passed; since it is manifestly impossible for the next two years; since the bill here
proposed would be the best preparation for a free coinage
bill; since it does not make us dependent on foreign countries any more than they become dependent on us—not
subordinate but coördinate—and since we can escape such
interdependence only by ceasing to trade with foreign
countries; it ought to be evident that if a single free-silver
man fails to support the present bill or even opposes it, he
will simply furnish a brilliant illustration of the saying that
man is "fearfully and wonderfully made."

It may be all right to say, "Let us not wait for foreign
countries"; but that does not warrant the conclusion that
we must reject the aid which foreign bimetallists offer;
still less the conclusion that we must so arrange our plans as
to render foreign coöperation impossible. Rather, if we
resolve to go ahead alone, let us go ahead in such way as to
render it as easy as possible for foreign countries to join
us if they feel so disposed. The German bimetallists,
among others, have a hard struggle to maintain against
intrenched prejudice; it is positively disgraceful, nay criminal, for American so-called friends of silver to render the
struggle still harder; and it is not to be wondered at if
bitter words are heard now and then in Germany in reference to America.

If therefore the free silver men are determined to array
themselves in 1897 against the gold men and the interna-

tional bimetallists alike, it is to be hoped that at any rate they will not frustrate the hopes of international free coinage by clamoring for "the dollar of the fathers," but will adopt a dollar that may fit into an international system, consisting of 399.9 grains of standard silver, 359.91 grains being pure silver; that is to say, 15½ times 23.22 grains, the weight of the gold in the gold dollar. The suggestion is respectfully submitted to Mr. Harvey that in the next edition of "Coin's Financial School" the passage above quoted be amended so as to read: "France will be with us from the start, if we adopt 1:15½." Even so, free coinage by the United States, though no longer a real obstacle to international free coinage, yet by lessening pressure on the English and German governments, may render them less disposed to take part in measures in behalf of silver.

But why drive carpet tacks with a sledge hammer? Since everybody admits that international free coinage is the best solution, why not work for that solution? A slight acquaintance with the movement in foreign lands will convince anyone that all that is needed is a little more coöperation among the bimetallists of all countries. When we consider that bimetallist resolutions were this year adopted by large majorities by the German Reichstag, the Prussian Upper House, and the English House of Commons; that the English Gold and Silver Commission of 1888, consisting of six gold men and six bimetallists, unanimously declared that a fixed ratio could be maintained by international agreement under any circumstances that may now be foreseen; that two ardent bimetallists are now members of the British cabinet and another ardent bimetallist has been for years director of the Bank of England; that the English Bimetallic League numbers among its vice-presidents sixty-seven members of Parliament and has a guarantee fund of £50,000; that France has repeatedly declared herself ready to resume free coinage if other great states do the same; that M. Ribot, the minister of finance, on February 2 of this year, declared the purpose of his government to be "to hasten the solution and assume such an attitude as will encourage the movement of public opinion in neighboring countries"—it seems like flying in the face of facts to assert that foreign countries are not ready to coöperate with us. Above all, when we consider that the idea of a uniform ratio was first suggested by Sir Isaac Newton; that Lord Beaconsfield declared that the gold standard was not the cause of England's prosperity but its consequence;

that Mr. Goschen, chancellor of the exchequer, declared the further extension of the gold standard to be not merely a utopia but a pernicious utopia—it seems little less than levity to decry England as the great marplot of bimetallism. And when under these circumstances a great party in America says, "Wait on England; she will give us bimetallism," and when this party tries its best to coöperate with the foreign bimetallists, it seems truly marvellous that those who profess to be the best friends of silver should charge that party with duplicity, and thus do all in their power to "chide away their friends."

The proposed bill will afford to both parties an opportunity to prove their sincerity. As it recognizes the necessity of international action, it will be most appropriately introduced by an international bimetallist; and if it is then opposed by the free silver men, the charge of duplicity may be very effectually retorted on them. The longer the international bimetallists observe a passive attitude, merely checking the endeavors of the free silver men, the more ground will they give for the accusation made by their opponents. It is to be hoped therefore that they will hasten to champion a bill which seems to be in perfect harmony with their program. If international action is to be taken, some one nation must set the ball rolling; and none can do so more appropriately than the United States, the largest silver producer, whose stock of silver is largest, which has always taken the lead in all movements to bring nations closer together, and which moreover is to make $20,000,000 by the operation. The risk that might be involved in independent action is entirely avoided by the clause which renders the operation of the law dependent on similar action by other countries. The efficiency of that clause is so self-evident that after reading it, one turns to the proceedings of the German Silver Commission with eager curiosity to see what arguments were advanced against it by the gold men. The reader who does so, will be astonished to find that this clause, which seems to contain the kernel of the matter, and to which Mr. Von Kardorff took special pains to call attention, was passed by without a word of comment by the gold men, save fourteen lines of invective, which one vainly scans for a trace of argument. Will the reader be blamed if he draws the inference that that "potential" clause is unassailable? On closer examination it will be found to contain the key to the whole situation. The stock argument of the gold men is always this: "We do not know what our neighbors are willing to do. If we go ahead, we may be left to incur the risk alone." This stronghold of monetallism will be over-thrown by the "potential" clause. When each nation says, "I am ready to go ahead if you go with me, but I will not move a step unless you move too," no nation will be left to bear the burden alone. But the crowning beauty of the bill, as Mr. Von Kardorff points out, is this, that it renders an express international agreement unneces-sary. Each nation may pass this bill without incurring any obligation toward other nations, and if it proves unsuitable, each nation may repeal it without consulting the others. If, however, as seems probable, an express international agreement is deemed necessary, this bill will be the best preparation for it. *When all countries have independently signified their willingness to do the same thing, they will find it easy to bind themselves to it jointly.*

Both Soetbeer, the great authority of the gold mono-metallists, and the English Gold and Silver Commis-sion of 1888, admitted that a fixed ratio between gold and silver could be maintained if adopted by the princi-pal commercial nations. Soetbeer, however, doubts whether such an agreement can be brought about. In the German Silver Commission the gold men constantly asserted the impossibility of maintaining an interna-tional treaty in regard to the money standard. It is very much to be regretted that the proposal repeatedly made to make this question the subject of a special discussion, was not carried out, for to the uninitiated it might be inter-esting to hear the reasons why such a treaty is impossible. In discussing its possibility, it is all-important to know what it contains. On this subject we are not in the dark. Such a treaty, drafted by Mr. Cernuschi, was submitted to the Monetary Conference of 1881, and the governments of the United States and France declared themselves willing to accept it. As this treaty (with the exception, perhaps, of the larger part of article V) must necessarily form the basis of discussion, it may be well to reprint it here, from the Proceedings of the International Monetary Conference of 1881 (Washington: Goverment Printing Office), page 490:

Draft of a resolution for an international treaty.

ARTICLE I. The United States of America, the French Republic, etc., form themselves into a Bimetallic Union on the terms and condi-tions hereinafter stipulated.

ART. II. The members of the Union shall admit gold and silver to mintage without any limitation of quantity, and shall adopt the ratio of 1:15½ between the weight of pure metal contained in the monetary unit in gold, and the weight of pure metal contained in the same unit in silver.

ART. III. On condition of this ratio of 15½ being always observed, *each state shall remain free to preserve its monetary types: dollar, franc, pound, sterling, mark,* or to change them.

ART. IV. Any person shall be entitled to take any quantity of gold or silver, either in ingots or in foreign coins, to the mints of any member of the Union for the purpose of getting it back in the shape of coin bearing the state mark ; the mintage shall be gratuitous to the public ; each member of the Union shall bear the expense of its mintage.

ART. V. The mints of each state shall be bound to coin the metal thus brought by the public as speedily as possible, and at the aforesaid ratio of 1 to 15½ between gold specie and silver specie; the coin thus manufactured shall be delivered to the person who shall have brought the metal, or to his assigns; if the person bringing gold or silver requests immediate payment of the sum which would accrue to him after the interval of mintage, that payment shall be made to him subject to a deduction which shall not exceed two per thousand; the sum shall be handed over, *at the will of the paying party,* in coin, or *in notes convertible at sight into metallic money.*

ART. VI. The gold and silver money shall alike be legal tender to any amount in the state which shall have manufactured them.

ART. VII. In each state the government shall continue to issue, as a monopoly, its small change or tokens; it shall determine their quantity or quality, and shall fix the amount above which no person shall be bound to receive them in payment.

ART. VIII. The fact of issuing or allowing to be issued, paper money, convertible or otherwise, shall not relieve the state issuing it, or allowing it to be issued, from the above stipulated obligation of keeping its mints always open for the free mintage of the two metals at the ratio of 1 to 15½.

ART. IX. Gold and silver, whether in ingots or in coin, shall be subject to no custom duty, either on importation or on exportation.

ART. X. The reception of silver shall commence at the same date in all the mints of the Union.

ART. XI. The present convention shall remain in force till the 1st of January, 1900. If a year before that date notice of its abrogation has not been given, it shall of full right be prolonged by tacit renewal till the 1st of January 1910, and so on by periods of ten years until such notice of abrogation shall have been given a year prior to the expiration of the current decennial period; it being however understood that notice of abrogation given by states having in Europe less than twenty million inhabitants, or subject to the inconvertible paper money system, while releasing those states, shall not prevent or interfere with the decennial tacit renewal of the present Convention between the other members of the Union.

It will be noticed that this treaty, like the Kanitz free coinage bill, expressly adopts 1:15½. One of the reasons of the passive attitude of the sound-money party in the United States seems to be that they are unwilling to commit themselves to any definite ratio, saying that that is a matter of detail. Theoretically indeed that attitude is perfectly correct; so was the attitude of the mule between the two haystacks. In practice, however, it blocks the way to any positive measure. Suppose that delegates did come to a monetary conference uncommitted to any ratio. Would they be in a situation different from that in which we now are? Could they use any arguments pro and con, different from those used a hundred times?

The moment that any other ratio than 1:15½ is taken into consideration, difficulties rise mountain high. On the contrary, 1:15½ will make hardly any change in the present situation, beyond enabling the United States to pocket $20,000,-000. That ratio actually prevails in the Latin Union and in most of the other European states, and all they will have to do will be to resume free coinage which they have merely suspended. Germany has $110,000,000 in silver thalers at 1:15½, circulating *as full legal tender;* all she has to do is to open her mints to the free coinage of such thalers. England would merely have to open her mints to the free coinage of a silver piece of four shillings, the legal-tender double florin proposed by Mr. Henry Gibbs, director of the Bank of England. Moreover, what argument could be brought forward in favor of any other ratio? Of all the chapters of Mr. Laveleye's book, none is more convincing than chapter 56, in which he proves that such a thing as a "market price" either of gold or silver never existed, and that from the very nature of things a market price of a legal-tender coinage metal is a contradiction in terms. Above all, can we consistently with honor think of lowering the ratio and thereby making France pay the penalty for the sins of other nations —France which has been the best-behaved and most public-spirited nation in this matter, maintaining her perfect (or almost perfect) scientific bimetallic system for seventy years, with signal benefit to the whole world, and especially to England, while other nations were playing those pranks which finally forced even reluctant France to suspend free coinage? Distinguished monometallists admit that if the ratio of 1:15½ is reaffirmed now, it can be maintained for some time, perhaps ten years; and there are certainly good geologic authorities for the belief that it can be maintained for any time on which our present plans can possibly have a bearing. But should it be found impossible to maintain it, say fifteen years from now, *let it then be changed by universal agreement so that no one shall lose,* instead of each nation asserting its financial "independence" in the bull-in-a-china-shop fashion that they have done hitherto.

In brief, it is not decent for civilized nations to try to manœuvre, each for itself, to keep out of harm's way no matter what harm may come to the others. The ceaseless process of integration has brought us to a point where the result desired by all can only be obtained by joint action. When everybody in the world has become everybody else's

neighbor; when it takes only seventy days to travel around
the globe; when international commerce has assumed enormous proportions; it is preposterous to assume that nations
can maintain a financial independence which was impossible among mediæval.kingdoms, with their trifling foreign
commerce. "I believe," said Prof. Suess before the German
Silver Commission, "that statesmanship nowadays has problems to deal with for which there are no traditions, and that
a moment will arrive when the statesmen of the leading
states could hardly win greater fame than by applying themselves to those great problems which embrace all mankind,
and whose solution affects not only the interests of one state
but those of the whole." In "The History of Currency," by
W. A. Shaw (London), p. 17, the monetary tactics of the
Middle Ages are thus described: "The wish of the fourteenth and fifteenth century ruler was not merely to defend
his own stock of precious metals from depletion, but . . .
to attract to himself the stock of his neighbors by whatever
craft. There was a general struggle for the coverlid of
gold, and the methods of that struggle were almost barbaric
in their rudeness, violence, craft, and dishonorableness."
The author evidently expects the reader to infer that compared to those ancient methods the conduct of modern states
is a model of dignity and public spirit. Yet in his very
description he employs the simile of a coverlid, used by
Prince Bismarck in 1881 to describe the present condition. Another current term, "the scramble for gold," was
invented to describe the tactics of the last twenty-five years.
Can it be said, then, that we have advanced much beyond
the Middle Ages? The bimetallists affirm that Sir Isaac
Newton's invention—a universal ratio—will put an end
to this unseemly struggle. If any are disposed to deny
this, it behooves them to propose other measures. Certainly, if the further extension of the gold standard is a
"pernicious utopia," if the world is to be permanently
divided into two groups, one using the "'more esteemed,"
the other the "less esteemed" metal, every nation will strive
to get the more esteemed metal, and thus the disgraceful
scramble for gold will become perpetual; sore feelings will
be kept up between nations that ought to march hand in
hand; and mutual friction will consume a large part of the
energy that ought to be devoted to the conquest of nature.

The most distinctive quality of civilized man, because
essential to coöperation, is forbearance. If we are to
coöperate, we must each of us study the idiosyncrasies
of the other, and, when difficulties appear in the way of
coöperation, ascertain their cause with a view to their re-

moval, instead of flying off in a huff. From this point of view the proposition that the United States should go ahead without regard to other countries is simply a return to mediæval methods. Far more statesmanlike and in keeping with modern ideas is the course adopted by the French government, as described by the minister of finance, "to assume such an attitude as will encourage the movement of public opinion in neighboring countries." Especially is it necessary to study the peculiar situation in England. English conservatism, which has preserved that country from many calamities, now and then causes a valuable idea to be adopted less quickly than might seem desirable. If England still clings to her paleolithic system of pounds, shillings, and pence, it evidently is not because it is to her interest to do so, but simply because the average Englishman is infinitely long-suffering. We ought to be able to understand this all the better, seeing that we too have been unable to shake off that strait-jacket, our absurd system of weights and measures, while other nations have long ago donned that free and easy garment of French invention, the metric system. If England needs scolding, that duty belongs not to us but to the English bimetallists; and they are performing it with zest.

"The favorite policy of the city editors," says Prof. H. S. Foxwell, in an article in the *Contemporary Review*, December, 1892, "is the policy of 'drift.' Here it is to be feared that they have some right to be regarded as representative. There is nothing your busy man dislikes so much as to be squarely faced by inconvenient facts, which compel him to reconsider a familiar course of action, perhaps even to grapple with an unfamiliar idea. It has been somewhat unfairly said that it requires a surgical operation to get a joke into a Scotchman; but anyone who has tried both feats will admit that this is child's play compared with the effort required to get a new idea into an Englishman. The Englishman resists ideas *a outrance*. Hence his general disposition toward *laissez faire;* which, no doubt, has its healthy side, but is clearly out of place in the region of currency policy, where there is no possibility of escaping the intervention of the state." The period since 1816 having been one of vast expansion of England's commerce and industry (though before the gold discoveries in 1848 she was on the verge of revolution), the people have grown accustomed to regard the gold standard as the cause of their prosperity, and some time will elapse before the public mind assimilates Lord Beaconsfield's dictum "that the gold standard is not the cause of England's prosperity, but its consequence."

But in no country is the sense of justice more developed, and nowhere is the judgment of the people sounder, when once they can be brought to examine a question in earnest. No one can read Professor Foxwell's above-cited article (only one out of a great number of masterly bimetallist articles with which the foremost English magazines teem) without gaining the conviction that England is preparing to coöperate in carrying out the plan proposed in 1717 by her own peerless Newton.

There is one motive which more than any other ought to have weight with Englishmen. It has repeatedly been shown that the high tariffs at present imposed by nearly all countries are a direct consequence of the attempt to extend the gold standard. High tariffs necessarily limit England's market and thus deprive her of incalculable millions. The injury she thus suffers certainly far outweighs the advantage, insecure at best, which her bondholders derive from the increased value of their foreign bonds. Should universal bimetallism be adopted, and the life-blood of commerce once more circulate freely, it is practically certain that the high tariff walls, like unhealthy excrescences, will vanish. England's products will once more find unhampered access to every corner of the globe, and the spectre of starvation will depart from thousands of English homes.

At the same time, while removing all obstacles to an international understanding, and cherishing the fullest confidence in the public spirit of all civilized nations, it can do no harm to inquire whether, in case any nation should be churlish enough to refuse her coöperation, any means may be found to induce her to reconsider the question. Three such measures have been suggested.

First, tariff measures, proposed especially by Senator Lodge and Speaker Reed. This suggestion has been received with sneers by certain circles in this country and in Europe. Sneers are a poor substitute for argument. What is to prevent us from enacting that if any country passes a law similar to the one above described, we will lower the duties on certain of its imports by such and such amount for such and such time? How does this idea differ from the reciprocity principle which is the special pride of the Republican party, the pet achievement of one of the greatest of our latter-day statesmen, Mr. Blaine? If we could say to Brazil, "You take our iron free and we'll take your coffee free," why we can't say to Germany, "You take our silver free, and we'll take your sugar free?" The motives which prompt the raising and lowering of tariffs are infinite in diversity, and some of them seem to be of little moment. Can it be that these are deemed adequate, while the fostering of our silver industry and the establishment of a stable basis of currency shall be deemed an inadequate motive for tariff measures?

Second, why should not some countries protected by the Monroe doctrine, especially Mexico, declare that until universal bimetallism is adopted, at the ratio of 1:15½ they will pay the interest on their foreign debt only in silver at that ratio? Might not this bring silver at once up to par? If it is an injustice to pay in another metal than that stipulated, that injustice is merely technical, so long as the other metal is thereby brought up to par; the real injustice is suffered by the debtor who has to pay double the stipulated value. It is a case where "the letter killeth but the spirit giveth life." Was not the law made for man and not man for the law? The nation that blocks the way to an international agreement, and thus condemns the world to financial anarchy, commits so heinous an offence against humanity that it may justly be considered as an outlaw.

As a last resort the United States might adopt independent free coinage (of course at 1:15½, in order not to create gratuitous difficulties). The question would then arise whether our debts are gold debts or bimetallic debts. If Congress says they are bimetallic debts, or if the treasury so interprets them, there would seem to be no doubt that we shall instantly have universal bimetallism. If Congress leaves the debts undefined, and if the treasury continues to regard them as gold debts, we shall probably (though not inevitably, and at any rate not very soon) be reduced to the silver standard and thus be in the same position as Mexico, which, under the administration of President Diaz, is said to be advancing more rapidly than we are. Such a prospect is certainly not frightful; and he who speaks of the silver "craze" merely confesses that he does not possess the judicial cast of mind. Our trade relations with gold countries would then become subject to the fluctuations of the exchange. "Who would suffer thereby?" asks Laveleye. "Europe much more than America. Suppose silver dropped to 43 pence and the dollar worth only 3 francs 50; one-half of our exportations to America would become impossible." Mr. Samuel Montagu, as quoted by Professor Foxwell, does not hesitate to say that this loss of the par between the two metals "is sufficient to kill all legitimate trading by Englishmen with silver . countries." Now whoever reads the reports on the condition of industry in

Europe will know that any further contraction of their markets will produce widespread disaster. It is probable therefore, that, as soon as our silver standard was completely established, they would come humbly knocking at our door, inviting us to join an international bimetallic union. Perhaps Professor Suess had this in mind when he wrote the closing sentence of his book, "The Future of Silver":* "The question is no longer whether silver will again become full-valued coinage metal over the whole earth, but what are to be the *calamities* through which Europe will have to pass before that result is attained."

But who has an abiding sense of the theorem that the shortest distance between two points is a straight line; who is trying to collect evidence to substantiate the belief that the definition of man as a *rational* animal is increasingly true—such a one would have to regard it as a grievous disappointment and a disgrace to our century if drastic coercive measures like those just indicated were found necessary to bring about an international agreement which a calm presentation of arguments, seconded by candor, forbearance, and public spirit, on the part of all concerned, ought to suffice to effect. Such coercive measures ought not to be adopted hastily, for by arousing bad blood, they might thwart the effect of argumentative methods. When once the United States has set the ball rolling by a positive measure looking toward international free coinage, it may confidently be expected that other countries will be only too glad to follow, for it is impossible to believe that they can be deaf to the warning uttered (in substance) by Professor Suess: *"The day will come when the commercial and industrial supremacy will pass away from Europe; but it is not to the interest of Europe to hasten the coming of that day by forcing silver countries to establish their own industries."*

Above all let us refrain from irritating England by reproaching her with a selfish and cruel policy, disregarding the interests of other countries; for that reproach is undeserved. There is no country where the modern humanitarian spirit is more developed, where the "debrutalization of man" has proceeded farther, than in England. It was a typical Englishman, Lord Russell, who said (the quotation is made from memory) "I will never consent to be reckoned among those who think that the interests of England

---

* A translation of that valuable work was published by the finance committee of the United States Senate and will be sent gratis to applicants until the edition is exhausted.

may be promoted by injustice done in any quarter of the globe." Of another typical Englishman, Mr. Gladstone, it has been said that he would not hesitate a moment to ruin England in order to preserve the smallest Indian tribe from wrong. If Mr. Gladstone could be convinced to-day that bimetallism is better for the world, though not for England, can anyone doubt that he would at once become its champion? And having leisure now, who knows but he may take to reading Archbishop Walsh's pamphlet?

The objection may be raised that the proposed "reconciliation bill" simply affirms what everybody knows, namely, that the United States is ready at any moment to join an agreement based on the European ratio. The objection would be perfectly proper if the public in America and Europe was composed exclusively of financial experts. As a matter of fact, the utterances of some of the most active campaigners are quite at variance with that supposed attitude of the United States, and it is possible that these utterances may be taken as the prevalent sentiment by those who estimate the value of a principle by the number and loudness of the speeches made for or against it. Hence the real attitude of the United States ought to be affirmed with all the emphasis which an express law can give. Again, though foreigners may be aware of this attitude, yet they do not say so. One of the reproaches which they cast on our Government is its alleged lack of a definite policy. "Why," they will say, "should we disturb our monetary system for the sake of a measure depending for its efficacy on coöperation with the United States, when nobody knows what the United States Congress will do next? In particular, how can we adopt free coinage at $1:15\frac{1}{2}$—the only practicable ratio for us—when the United States may at any moment adopt free coinage at $1:16$ and thus rob us of our gold?" These reproaches will cease to be reasonable when our government expressly assumes the fixed and consistent attitude imputed to it by those familiar with the situation.

But most potent of all will be the force of example. If the United States, the most important bimetallic country, adopts a definite plan of action, in accordance with the necessities of the situation in Europe, the same plan will inevitably be adopted by the bimetallists all over the world, and thus their hosts, hitherto unorganized, will be welded into a compact mass. In Germany, in particular, the effect will be magical. Seeing how great was the majority in the Reichstag in favor of the recent

POSTAL TELEGRAPHY.

BY LYMAN ABBOTT, D. D.

The ARENA asks me to contribute to a symposium on "Should the Government Control the Telegraph?" a short article stating in as cogent a manner as possible my views on this most important question. As this is to be only one of several articles I may assume that others who are experts will contribute detailed facts and figures and that I may confine myself to a statement of fundamental principles.

The Policy Recommended.—The United States government should ascertain what it would cost to duplicate at the present time the Western Union Telegraph plant. It should then offer to purchase the plant at that price from the Western Union Telegraph Company. If the telegraph company declines the offer the government should proceed to construct a telegraph system which should run throughout the United States. Under this system the telegraph office and the postoffice would be in the same building and in the smaller towns and villages in the same room. The postmaster would operate the telegraph, personally or by an assistant or assistants, and the Western Union Telegraph Company would be left undisturbed in the right to use its own plant in the conduct of business. The public could choose between the public and the private telegraph. In case the Western Union Telegraph Company sold its plant to the United States the latter would have a practical, but it should not be an official, monopoly. Private enterprise should be left free to compete with the government.

Advantages of the Plan.—1. The United States has an unquestioned constitutional right to pursue this policy. The maxim that it is the function of government to govern is no longer accepted as axiomatic by any considerable number of Americans. No arguments would induce us to abandon the postoffice and relegate the carriage of letters to private enterprise. That it is the function of government to provide for thought-intercommunication between the people is accepted practically by the entire nation. There is nothing inconsistent with our traditions, habits, or constitution in extending this principle so that thought-intercommunication shall be provided by electricity as well as by steam or stage-coach.

2. The Western Union Telegraph must pay an interest of five to ten per cent on watered stock to its stockholders. The United States Government would have to pay an interest of two and a half or three per cent on the actual cost of construction. If I am rightly informed, this alone would make a difference of not less than five per cent on not less than fifty millions of dollars. The Western Union Telegraph Company must pay an office rent and an operator's salary in every town and village. In all the smaller places the postoffice would afford ample office accommodations for the telegraph and the postmaster or his assistant could operate the telegraph with little or no increase of salary. In England twelve cents is the minimum charge for a message to any part of the United Kingdom. It is said by experts that twenty-five cents as a minimum charge for a message to any part of the United States would pay the interest on the investment and the cost of administration. It is not important to determine whether this estimate is accurate or not. It is certain that the cost of telegraphing could and would be greatly reduced.

3. As a result the use of the telegraph would be greatly increased. It is now the privilege of the few; it would become the convenience of the many. A uniform rate and a reduction of expense would operate exactly as it has operated in the postoffice. Messages would be multiplied as letters have been multiplied. Popular communication would be by electricity. Lightning would become the servant of the people; it is now the servant only of a moneyed aristocracy. Every postoffice would be a telegraph office; for in remote hamlets to which the wire did not reach there would be telegraph blanks, and the stage coach would carry the message to the nearest telegraph office whence it would be forwarded by wire.

4. That this is no fancy of a dreamer is shown by the experience of Great Britain. Within three or four years after the English government assumed the control and ownership of the telegraph the offices had increased thirty per cent, the messages fifty per cent, and the number of words sent two hundred per cent, while the cost to the people had decreased forty per cent. It is true that the government telegraph in Great Britain has not always been self-supporting, as the postoffice in the United States is not always self-supporting. But this is partly due to extravagant prices paid by the English government for pri-

vate telegraphs in the outset, and partly due to a laudable but excessive ambition to increase public facilities more rapidly than the public income fully justified.

5. The thought-intercommunication of a nation ought never to be left subject to the control of private parties. It is generally believed that in many instances the intelligence flashed over the wires of the Western Union Telegraph Company has been effectually used for purposes of private speculation before it reached the parties for whom it was intended. In one notable instance it was generally believed that the returns of a presidential election were kept back until interested parties could avail themselves of the knowledge privately obtained for speculative purposes. It is not necessary to determine whether these suspicions were well grounded or not; it is sufficient to note that they exist, and that the public has no means of protecting itself against the perpetration of such wrongs so long as the telegraph is in the hands of private parties. If the telegraph is a department of the government the public can hold the government responsible for its administration and need not wait for legal proof of an abuse in order to correct it.

The whole matter may be summed up in one brief paragraph. There are certain public functions absolutely necessary to the life of the nation. Government is one, but only one, of these functions. Popular education is another; the carriage of the mails another; and the transmission of telegraphic messages has become still another. Whether the government shall itself perform these functions or leave them to be performed for it by private enterprise is a question to be determined wholly by a consideration of another question, namely, In which way will the public welfare be best served? Theory and experience combine to answer that, as the public can better transmit its own mails, so it can better transmit its own telegraphic messages than by leaving either to be done for it by private enterprise.

WHY I OPPOSE GOVERNMENTAL CONTROL OF THE TELEGRAPH.

BY POSTMASTER-GENERAL WILLIAM L. WILSON.

The question of governmental control of the telegraph as a part of the postal system has been under discussion for the past quarter of a century and more, and possesses an attractiveness that will always keep it in some form before the public mind. More than one president and successive postmasters-general have felt called upon to consider the question and to express opinions on one or the other side. Much instructive material is consequently stored away in their messages and reports, especially in the hearings before congressional committees charged with the consideration of proposed legislative measures. Two postmasters-general, Mr. Creswell in 1873 and Mr. Wanamaker in 1890, each with a different scheme, have made vigorous efforts to secure action from Congress. A review of this long agitation in the light of these public documents indicates that, in the country at large, it reached its highest stage during and just after the great telegraphic strike of 1883, when the New York *Herald* and other influential journals took it up and urged it with force and persistence.

Doubtless because of this strong backing, the then post-master-general, who was the late secretary of state, Walter Q. Gresham, considered the various propositions for a government telegraph in his annual report for 1883, with the careful judgment he was wont to give to all public matters, and reached the conclusion, that while the existing companies "operated their lines solely for the purpose of making money," and charged "unreasonable rates," yet the objections in each of the plans proposed were so grave that he did not think the evils complained of were so "grievous as to call for congressional intervention." The question seems to have lain dormant, so far as the department was concerned, until revived by Mr. Wanamaker's new proposal.

Up to that time propositions for a postal telegraph had contemplated, as a rule, either the acquisition of existing lines by purchase, or the construction of a government system. Such action was beset with so many difficulties, as well of policy as of business detail, that it naturally found but occasional and spasmodic advocacy in Congress, from men whose opinions were influential there or in the country. Those who conceded the constitutional right of Congress to establish a telegraphic postal system, whether as a monopoly like the postal service, or as a competitor and moderator of rates for private corporations, were still staggered at the idea of putting the government into the field of private enterprise, and to that degree making it more bureaucratic; of committing it to large and unknown liabilities and expenditures; of entrusting so great a business to a civil service built up under the spoils system and saturated with its partisanship, to say nothing of exposing the open business or political correspondence of the people to such a machine; or of putting the responsibility and burden of such a service on all the people as taxpayers, while only one in sixty used the telegraph, and no probable reduction of rates or increase of facilities would greatly multiply this number as compared with all.

Mr. Wanamaker sought to avoid the main objections by proposing a "limited post and telegraph," by the establishment of a bureau in the postoffice department for the deposit, transmission, and delivery of telegrams through the medium of the existing postoffice service. Contracts to run for ten years were to be made with one or more telegraph companies, already existing or to be incorporated, for the transmission of telegrams at rates not exceeding fifteen, twenty-five, or fifty cents each, according to distance, for the first twenty words, and one cent for each additional word. All free delivery postoffices and all offices of the contracting companies were to be telegraph stations, and in addition such other postoffices and telegraph offices thereat as the postmaster-general might designate. The money-order service was to be adopted between postoffices designated as postal telegraph money-order offices.

Under this plan a letter would go through the same stages of collection and delivery as it does to-day, but its contents would travel from postoffice station to station by wire instead of by sealed package in the mail. The government would collect, by stamp or otherwise, all charges, and pay them over, at stated accountings, to the telegraph companies, after retaining first-class letter post-

. age, and in proper cases special delivery or money-order fees.

It cannot be denied that this plan for a limited post and telegraph, often suggested before, but, so far as I know, never worked out in detail until it was taken up by Mr. Wanamaker, steers clear of or minimizes the most serious objections urged against governmental control or ownership of telegraph lines. It was in its main outlines an extension of the contract system for carrying the fast mail, from the railroads to the electric lines, with a compensation to the latter based on the actual work done, collected from those who called for the service by the department, and accounted for to the telegraph companies.

But although presented with the characteristic energy of the late ex-postmaster-general, who called to his aid, as far as he could do so, the press and the trade and labor organizations of the country, to a Congress of his own party, at a time when the treasury was embarrassed with a surplus, and that Congress was looking for objects on which to expend it, the proposal seems to have made little impression on the country, and still less upon Congress. Indeed, so far as I now recall, it was not acted upon by the House committee on postoffices and post roads and was not debated at either session of the fifty-first Congress. This would indicate, at least, that there is no great popular demand for a postal telegraph service, limited or otherwise, and that in the United States the telegraph is regarded, and is destined for some time to be regarded, more as an adjunct for the newspaper service and for business, than as a desideratum for ordinary social correspondence. And until the people at large feel that the telegraph is such a general necessity, and are goaded to action by the injustice, extortion, or faulty service of private corporations now furnishing our telegraphic communications, it is scarcely probable that Congress will be aroused to a serious consideration of the question.

Many saw in this proposal but an entering wedge to a complete purchase or administration of the telegraphic service by the government, and for that reason stoutly opposed the first steps. Fully recognizing that both the telegraph and the telephone have become, more and more, a part of the equipment of our modern industrial and social life, they cling to the vital idea of our federal polity as a guardian of liberty and a guarantor of justice, and wish to limit its operations to these ends and to those activities

which are really governmental. To paternalize the govern-.
ment or make it more bureaucratic is in their judgment
to repress private enterprise and to imitate the monarchical
systems of the old world.

Advocates of governmental ownership are constantly
pointing to state administration in other countries of the
telegraph, the telephone, the parcel post, savings banks,
and railroads. They forget the different foundations on
which we build. In some of the countries which they
cite, there is so little private initiative that if such things
exist at all they must be maintained by the state; in all of
them the traditions and habits of paternalism are strong,
and repressive of individual enterprise; in most of them
the government can undertake such enterprises as economically and manage them as efficiently as private persons,
individual or corporate. None of these conditions exist
or ought to be fostered with us. Here there is no lack
of capital or enterprise to provide the public with any
service it demands or will pay for, and in the long run as
cheaply and completely as it can be done. Here we have
a continental arena and a dual system of governments and
sovereignties. Here we have had, and still have in vanishing force, the unsettling, at intervals, of every branch of the
federal executive, by the mutations of politics, as witness
the loot of the railway mail service in 1889 and the crip-
pling blow to its efficiency and accuracy.

Here the cost of any business enterprise carried on by the
government is greater than it would be in private hands.
The postoffice department is no exception to this rule,
although much of its work is done through contracts with
private persons. The ninety millions now expended, wonderful and grand as are its results, would produce better
results if the service could be organized and everywhere
administered as our most successful railroad corporations
manage their affairs.

Nothing is more certain, were the government to undertake the control or monopoly of the telegraph, than that
we should have, at any rates of service the people would
expect, a heavy annual deficit, to swell the regular deficit
of the postoffice department.

Even in the United Kingdom, whose area is so much
smaller and whose population is so much more compact
than ours, the postal telegraph throws an annual deficit
on the taxpayer, which seems to be increasing of recent
years. From the report of the postmaster-general for
1893-4, I find the deficit to be £473,735, or more than two

and a quarter million dollars, and nearly a million dollars, if we strike out the annual interest charge on capital invested. For the last seven years this deficit has been £2,354,877, or eleven and a half million dollars, a sum nearly equal to present annual receipts.

There is to-day immense room for the increase and perfection of our postal facilities, but, policy aside, there is no room for the assumption by the treasury of vast unknown liabilities and of a service to be administered at a yearly loss. Reviewing the controversies of the past thirty years, and acknowledging as I do the merits and attractions of Mr. Wanamaker's scheme, I find myself in accord with the conclusion reached in 1883, by Judge Gresham, especially as that conclusion had been more comprehensively stated by Postmaster-General Denison years before, in a report to the Senate: "As a result of my investigation under the resolution of the Senate, I am of opinion that it will not be wise for the government to inaugurate the proposed system of telegraph as a part of the postal service, not only because of its doubtful financial success, but also its questionable feasibility under our political system."

THE TELEGRAPH MONOPOLY.

BY PROFESSOR FRANK PARSONS.

Uncle Sam's letters go on foot, on horseback, in wagons, stages, steamboats, railway cars, and pneumatic tubes, but the telegraph wire he cannot have, for that is sacred to Wall Street. The "common people" may use foot-power, horse-power, steam-power, and wind-power, but electricity, the best and swiftest of all, is reserved for the use of monopoly and those who can pay its extravagant rates.

It is perfectly natural that Wall Street should wish to keep the telegraph in its own control, for it plays an important part in the processes by which Wall Street gains possession every year of many millions of the wealth created by the "common people." It is equally natural for the people to wish that the transmission of their messages and in fact all their business should be performed in the best possible manner, by the most effective means, and with the most approved and advantageous methods. It is also natural that they should wish to reduce the power of monopoly and check the flow of their wealth into Wall Street.

The people want good service and low rates; the companies want dividends. The people wish to own the telegraph so that it may be managed in their interest. The companies do not care to divide the control or the profits; they prefer to keep the power and the profit for themselves. They do not believe in partnership. It is very much easier to make millionaires with a telegraph owned by a few individuals than it would be with a telegraph owned by the people. The postoffice doesn't make millionaires; the signal service is not a millionaire mill, nor the army, nor the navy, nor the department of agriculture, nor the census, nor the public schools. When Uncle Sam administers a business he does it at cost, or if there is a profit he divides it among all the seventy million partners he works for—the stockholders in this big corporation we call our country. This big corporation created the telegraph franchise and gave it all the value it possesses. It has generously allowed the little corporation to use that franchise free of rent for many years to the incalculable profit of the latter. Now the big corporation wants to use the telegraph in its postoffice, but the little corporation in Wall Street says, No.

This conflict of interests has produced a long and earnest discussion of the question whether or no the people shall be permitted to use the electric current in the transaction of their postal business. Books, pamphlets, bills, speeches, arguments, investigations, and resolves have appeared in single file and in battalions until the literature of the subject makes of itself a very respectable library. And still this great case of

THE PEOPLE v. MONOPOLY,

which for fifty years and more has been on trial in the halls of Congress and on appeal to the Supreme Court of Public Opinion, remains upon the docket. During this half century of litigation, the case has come to trial in nearly every nation on the globe, and in almost all of them judgment has been rendered for the people. Statistics from seventy-five of the principal nations of the world show that the government owns and operates the telegraph in all except

| Bolivia, | | Cuba, |
| Cypress, | Hawaii, | Honduras, |

and the

UNITED STATES.[1]

How do you like the company, Uncle Sam? France, Germany, Russia, Sweden, Norway, Denmark, Switzerland, and many other nations built their own lines at the start. In Belgium and in the Netherlands some of the early lines were built by the government and some by private enterprise. The government lines were the most satisfactory and the public system was rapidly extended both by direct construction and by the purchase of private lines.[2] In England the telegraph was originally in private hands but a three years' active campaign gave the people an easy victory.[3]

---

[1] Vrooman's "Public Ownership," pp. 214, 216. Also 10th Census, vol. 4, "Postal Telegraph." Postmaster General Creswell's Report, 1872, with statistical tables, and the Statistical Year Book of Canada, 1892, p. 301.

[2] H. Rep. 114, 41-2, p. 2; 10th Census, vol. 4, "Postal Telegraph."

[3] The first English telegraph line was built in 1846. In 1854 complaints began to be made of extortion, error, and inadequacy. These were repeated at intervals until the Edinburgh chamber of commerce brought the matter of public ownership definitely before parliament in 1865, and in 1868 a bill was passed to enable the Postmaster General to acquire and operate the telegraph lines, and the transfer was made Feb. 1, 1870. (Bronson C. Keeler in *Forum*, vol. 9, p. 454, and H. Rep. 114, 41-2, pp. 6 to 8.)

In America, more than fifty years of effort and appeal have failed to win the postal telegraph. Henry Clay, Charles Sumner, Hannibal Hamlin, General Grant, Senators Edmunds, Dawes, Chandler, and N. P. Hill, Gen. B. F. Butler, John Davis, Postmaster-Generals Johnson, Randall, Maynard, Howe, Creswell, and Wanamaker, Professor Morse, the inventor of the telegraph, Cyrus W. Field, the founder of the Atlantic Cable and a director in the Western Union Company, James Gordon Bennett, Professor Ely, Lyman Abbott, B. O. Flower, Judge Clark, Henry D. Lloyd, Dr. Taylor, T. V. Powderly, Samuel Gompers, Marion Butler and a host of other eminent men in every walk of life have championed the cause of the people.[4] Legislatures, city councils, boards of trade, chambers of commerce, and labor organizations representing many millions of citizens have joined in the effort to secure a national telegraph. The New York *Herald*, Boston *Globe*, Philadelphia *Times*, Chicago *Tribune*, Albany *Express*, Washington *Gazette*, Omaha *Bee*, Denver *Republican*, San Fran-

---

[4] James Russell Lowell, Phillips Brooks, Francis A. Walker, and others of the highest character and attainments have expressed their sympathy with the movement, though too much engrossed with other cares to take an active part in it. In respect to the first two I speak from personal knowledge. President Walker in a lecture entitled " Confessions of an Individualist," delivered at the Charlesgate, Boston, Mar. 14, 1894, laid down the principle that the line between government functions and those which were not was the line between " services and offices which tend to become monopolies and those which do not." This clearly includes the telegraph among governmental functions. It not only tends to become a monopoly, it *is* a monopoly now of the worst and most dangerous type. (Wan. Arg. 1890, p. 5; Sen. Rep. 805, p. 1; I. T. U. Hearings, 1894, p. 39; National Board of Trades Report on Telegraph, 1882, p. 11.) President Walker further said, that another valid test would include in governmental activities any function in respect to which experience showed public administration to be beneficial to society and productive of an increase of individual activity. This rule also would make the telegraph a government service as the facts that appear in the text of this and subsequent articles abundantly prove. In conversation lately with the General I referred to his lecture at the Charlesgate and he said in substance: There are no hard and fast lines by which to determine what the government shall do. When the people desire a reform we should have it. But it is not well to make a change before public sentiment is ready to stand behind it. If we do reaction may follow and we shall go back and forth, moving unsteadily as a drunken man reels on his way. The telegraph service is better in France, England, and Germany than it is here, and it will be well to put it under government control whenever the people wish it. I remarked that millions of people and the greatest organizations in the country had persistently demanded a national telegraph, and that John Wanamaker declared the Western Union to be the only visible opponent, upon which the General said, " If that be true the time has come for it." The opinion of President Walker is of great importance because he is the acknowledged leader of the conservative school of political economy, the recognized chief of those most likely to object on philosophic grounds aside from considerations of self-interest, to any extension of government functions. If individualism and conservative political economy agree to the postal telegraph what is there but fossilized prejudice and selfish disregard of the public good to oppose it?

cisco *Post*, and a multitude of other papers representing every phase of political opinion have earnestly advocated the measure. Two political parties have definitely demanded a government telegraph; more than two millions of men by vote and petition have asked for it.[5]

[5] The Farmers' Alliance and Industrial Union, the National Grange, the Knights of Labor, the Railway Union, the American Federation of Labor, the International Typographical Union, the People's Party, and the Prohibitionists are a unit on the question of government ownership of the telegraph. Two years ago the Populists claimed two million ballots and a vote of 1,650,000 was conceded to them by the more liberal of their opponents. The Prohibitionists polled about a quarter of a million, so that at least a million and a half and probably two millions of votes were cast in support of parties making the national telegraph one of their chief demands. The Farmers' Alliance in 1890 claimed a membership of over four million men and women according to a book about the Alliance by H. R. Chamberlain, p. 7. The paid-up membership is said to be a good deal less now, but it is still true that the Alliance together with the National Grange substantially represents the agricultural interests and sentiment of the country, and both organizations have most emphatically announced their wish for a government telegraph (Journal of proceedings of the National Grange, 26th Sess., 1892, p. 207; Special Rep. of the I. T. U. committee on Governmental Ownership and Control of the Telegraph, 1894, p. 42 *et seq.*; testimony of Marion Butler, president of National Farmers' Alliance, before the House Com. on the Postoffice and Postroads). The American Federation of Labor represents the trade unions of the country and is composed of over 800,000 working men who demand government ownership of the telegraph (President Gompers' testimony, Special Rep., I. T. U., p. 7). At one time 530,000 Knights of Labor signed a petition for a government telegraph. (Statement of Mr. Beaumont, Mar. 7, 1890. Wanamaker's Argument 1890, p. 2). At another time Grand Master Workman T. V. Powderly is said to have declared that 800,000 signatures were obtained by the Knights, upon a petition for government ownership, and the petition was circulated only three weeks. In 1888 a resolution was submitted in the House, which began thus: " Whereas petitions bearing the signatures of more than two millions of people request Congress to pass a bill and provide for the establishment of a postal telegraph system " (Wan. Arg. p. 179). A way back in 1875 massive petitions had poured in upon Congress from twenty-eight states and three territories asking the government to build a telegraph. Truly, as Mr. Wanamaker says, " the agricultural and industrial masses want the telegraph within their reach" (Wan. Arg. p. 3).

No less strenuously do the commercial masses desire government ownership of the telegraph. A strong stand upon this question has been taken by the New York Board of Trade and Transportation, the Manufacturers' Club of Philadelphia, the Chambers of Commerce of Denver, Pittsburg, Richmond, etc., the Commercial Club of Kansas City, the Board of Trade of Jersey City, the Norwich Board of Trade, the Winona Board of Trade and numerous other powerful organizations of capital. The National Board of Trade declares in its reports that it " represents a majority of the commercial organizations of the country,"and year after year it has made the question of a national telegraph one of the main objects of its solicitude(see Rep. of Ex.Com. N. B. T., Nov. 15, 1882, and statements before committee on postoffices and postroads Mar. 25, 1890, p. 16 *et seq*). Here are the names of some of the great organizations which belong to the National Board of Trade: Baltimore Board of Trade, Baltimore Corn and Flour Exchange, Boston Merchants' Association, Bridgeport Board of Trade, Chicago Board of Trade, Cincinnati Chamber of Commerce, Detroit Board of Trade, Indianapolis Board of Trade, Milwaukee Chamber of Commerce, Milwaukee Merchants' Association, Minneapolis Board of Trade. New Haven Chamber of Commerce, New York Board of Trade and Transportation, New York Chamber of Commerce, Philadelphia Board of Trade, Portland (Oregon) Board of Trade, Providence Board of Trade, San Francisco Chamber of Commerce, Scranton Board of Trade, St. Paul Chamber of Commerce, Trenton Board of Trade.

At least four state legislatures have joined in the petition to Congress for government ownership of the telegraph, Massachusetts passing the resolution in 1893 without a dissenting voice. The Philadelphia common and select councils have also unanimously passed a similar resolve. Even the press, though largely under the thumb of the telegraph monopoly, have to a surprising extent endorsed the demands of the business men, mechanics, and farmers. Wanamaker says: " Of 280 newspaper articles which have come under my notice during this discussion (1890), 209 are for postal telegraphy and 80 against it. The objections are mostly smartly turned sentences about the utter business inexperience of persons engaged in trade." (Wan. Arg. pp. 3, 22, *et seq.*) In appendix K (p. 182 *et seq.*) of the Wanamaker pamphlet are gathered a large number of articles published in 1883 just after the telegraph strike; most of them strongly favor a public telegraph, and nine tenths of the favorable clippings support the plan of government ownership. We shall see later why it is that the press is not so entirely unanimous in its advocacy of a national telegraph as the business men are and the agricultural and industrial masses, whose organizations speak for twenty-four millions of workers representing nearly the whole seventy millions of our population.

And all the time the active opposition has come from a single source—the group of capitalists who claim the exclusive right to send the English language along an electric wire.[*] It is true that a small but powerful group

---

[*] Wanamaker said in 1890, " The Western Union is now the only visible opponent"; and the select com. of the House on the postal telegraph in 1870 said that objections to government interference with the telegraph had "come altogether from one quarter, namely, the Western Union Company" (II. Rep. 114, p. 13). Western Union methods of debate will be dealt with in detail hereafter, but it may be well now to clear the way of a few of their favorite fallacies.

"A public telegraph will paternalize the government," say the defenders of monopoly. If so, it is pretty badly paternalized now, with the postoffice, the fish commission, the treasury, customs, navy, army, agricultural, judiciary, signal service, and all the other departments; but the people don't seem to desire to give up such paternalization—they appear to enjoy it. In truth, however, public service is not paternalism but fraternalism. A father is not elected by his children to control them and his rule does not rest upon their assent. If you and I choose Mr. B to manage certain affairs for us, the said B does not become our paternal relative, but our agent.

"It will cost too much." It need not cost the people one dollar of taxes to establish the postal telegraph. Plenty of capitalists are ready to build the lines for the government, introduce low rates, and agree to turn the plant over to the nation for actual value at the end of fifteen or twenty years, or allow the service to pay for the plant gradually (as in the case of the Springfield electric works, see ARENA for December, 1895), a method that would give the people a clear title in a few years, even at rates far lower than those in force now (see testimony of the representatives of New York syndicates that were ready and willing to build a postal telegraph system under the provisions of Wanamaker's bill. The Bingham Com. Hearings, March 4 and 14, 1890). Better still to build or buy and issue treasury notes in payment; that would correct in part the evils of the vast contraction of the currency that has so long oppressed the people and secure the telegraph without a burden. Or bonds could be issued and the service let to pay the debt in fifteen or twenty years, on the plan by which Wheeling secured her gas works. In either way, no taxes are needed. As for the cost of operation, the select committee on the telegraph in 1870 calculated that the government could do the business performed by the Western Union at a cost of at least $1,500,000 a year lower than the Western Union could do it; the absolute saving would be at least that much by reason of combination with the postoffice and consequent saving in rent, fuel, light, and the distribution of labor (H. Rep. 114, p. 44). As the telegraph plant and business is more than twice as large now as in 1870, the saving in the same proportion would not be less than three million dollars a year. This is on the supposition of continuing to do business by the methods now in use; but if improved methods well known [in the electrical world were adopted in the postal telegraph, the saving would be far greater, so great indeed that there seems every reason to believe a uniform rate of five cents a message of twenty words would yield a substantial profit. Proof of this upon the highest and most disinterested electric and telegraphic authority will be given when we come to the subject in the text.

"The postal telegraph may be all right in Europe, but not in America. We don't want to imitate the monarchical systems and institutions of the old world." I wonder if the gentlemen who made this "argument" and those who repeat it refrain from using the multiplication table and the ten commandments because they are in vogue in Norway and Sweden, Denmark, Belgium, etc. Do they abstain from wearing clothes, because the wearing of clothes is an institution that exists in Russia? Do they go on their four legs for fear of imitating the kings and emperors by walking on two ? We must not wear overcoats or neckties or trousers, the Germans do that.

of politicians and conservatives have lent their aid to the grateful monopoly by delaying legislation, hindering in-

It was very dangerous, wasn't it, for us to adopt the idea of that monarchical Englishman, Stephenson, or the idea of that imperial Dutchman, Gutenberg, and it will be equally dangerous for us to adopt the idea of the despotic Gladstone that the telegraph is a good thing in a postoffice, won't it? It does seem as though fast mails would be as valuable and sensible in a republic as in a monarchy. France thinks so, and Switzerland, the most democratic country in the world. New Zealand also and the states of Australia, — these are all republics and each has a national telegraph system; we may imitate them if you insist on regarding the question as a matter of imitation; — or we may take England as an example, for she is in every substantial sense as real a republic as the United States. In truth such objections seem foolish and weak, and must arise from very careless thinking, reckless appeal to prejudice, or a desperate lack of good argument. I would not trouble the reader with a refutation were it not that men in high position have been known to repeat such absurdities and give them the impetus of their names, whereby insidious appeals are made to the thoughtless prejudice of unenlightened patriotism. True patriotism wide awake demands for America all that is good, whether it originates in Europe or the Feejee islands. In the case of the telegraph, however, we have only to follow the lead of our own government which was the first to adopt the electric telegraph and establish it, in connection with the postoffice where it would have remained to this day had it not been for the power of private capital and the weakness of some of our legislators, and the failure of others to foresee the enormous value of the telegraph.

" It will put the government into the field of private enterprise." Well, that is what the people have been doing since the dawn of civilization. Defence was once dependent entirely on private enterprise; so were education, justice, prevention and punishment of crime, guarding against disease, care of the sick, extinguishment of fire, manufacture of the weather, transmission of intelligence, etc. The people have put the government into the field formerly occupied by private enterprise because they have become aware that the government could do the work better than private enterprise. In the present case of the telegraph, however, the quoted words at the head of this paragraph are not strictly true. It would have been more accurate to say of the postal telegraph, " It will put the government into the field of despotic monopoly."

" It is not the government's business." " It is out of the government's sphere." Senator Edmunds does not think so (see Sen. Rep. 577, part 2); nor Walter Q. Gresham, (Postmaster General's Rep. 1883); nor Judge Clark, nor sixteen or more committees of Congress, nor Congress itself, nor the Supreme Court of the United States (see for authorities, the last topic of this article, " Duty of the government to establish a postal telegraph.") Henry Clay did not think the telegraph was out of the government's sphere; nor did Charles Sumner of Massachusetts; nor Thomas Jefferson, Alexander Hamilton, James Madison, Benjamin Franklin, and the other founders of the constitution who expressly made the transmission of intelligence a part of the business of the government; surely these men knew more about the legitimate sphere of government than the Western Union and its allies. Professor Ely does not think the telegraph is beyond the sphere of government; nor President Walker, the head of the school of conservative political economy; nor Gladstone, who represents highwater mark in the statesmanship of England and to whose efforts that country largely owes its postal telegraph; nor Bismark, nor Carnot, nor the patriot statesmen of Switzerland. The truth is that anything the government can do to benefit the people is within its sphere; the public good is the supreme law. It is just as much within the sphere of the government to send a message along a wire as to send it along a railroad or pneumatic tube. The government is simply an instrument to render service for the people. A cobbler might have opposed the use of the sewing machine for stitching leather on the ground that such work was out of the sphere of the sewing machine, with just as much reason as the Western Union in opposing a postal telegraph on the ground that such work is out of the sphere of the government.

vestigation, and pigeon holing reports, but the monopoly itself is the only one that appears in active opposition to the postal telegraph. The line of battle is clearly drawn. On the one side the farmers, merchants, mechanics, and working classes—the whole body of the people—with the philosophers, statesmen, philanthropists, and reformers; on

---

"The government could not be sued." It will be an easy matter to provide that damages for error or delay should be recovered by suit against "The Telegraph Department."

"But the increase of patronage will be dangerous." There need not be any increase of patronage. The government may contract for telegraphic service as it does for railway service. Or it may own the lines and contract for the service. Or better far, it may own and operate the lines under strong civil service rules as is the case in England, France, Germany, Switzerland, Australia, and other countries (see 11th report U. S. Civil Service Com., 1895). With a solid civil service law and a non-partisan board (i. e., a board composed of a member from each party), to administer it, an increase of public employees no longer means an increase of patronage, for there is no patronage where appointment depends upon merit proved in competitive examination, promotion follows on valuable service, and removal is only for serious cause judicially ascertained with a right of appeal to the regular courts. Such provisions would form a part of a wise postal telegraph law. But even without them the danger from increase of patronage would be slight. Uncle Sam has 240,000 employees. In combination with the postoffice, the telegraph would not require an addition of more than 20,000, a large part of them women and boys who are not yet able to vote. With a population of seventy millions and a voting class of eighteen millions a group of 260,000 government employees does not look alarmingly dangerous, especially when we consider that 48,000 are already under civil service rules, 40,000 more in army and navy, and another large body composed of quite inoffensive women. Some years ago the government had 2,500,000 employees and they were armed to the teeth and many croakers predicted that they would do dreadful things; but they didn't, they saved the republic.

"The secrecy of messages will be violated." There is no complaint of such sort against the postal telegraph in England or on the continent, but there have been loud complaints against the Western Union on this head, both in respect to United States government messages, even in time of war, and in respect to individual business, and the facts have been proved in court and damages awarded (H. Rep. 114, pp. 10–12, 68, and Congressional Record, 2d Sess. 43d Congress, p. 1422).

"Only one in sixty uses the telegraph. No probable reduction of rates or increase of facilities would be apt to raise the proportion much, and it would not be fair to put on the taxpayers the burden of a service used only by a few." As already remarked there will not be any burden about it. The business can easily pay for itself and more as it does in many countries across the sea. It will be more apt to lower the rates of taxation than to raise them. But there is another and deeper falsity in the above objection. The statement that "no probable reduction of rates or increase of facilities would be apt to raise the proportion" of people using the telegraph is a statement that could only be made by one quite unacquainted with the history of the telegraph and the postoffice, both in Europe and America, and with the history of this discussion, or by one entirely free from any inconvenient regard for the truth. The facts set forth in numerous public documents in this country and in Europe and reported to Congress by its committees again and again conclusively prove that reduction of rates and increase of facilities produce the most astonishing increase in the use of the service. "The reduction of rates one-half in Belgium and Switzerland doubled the correspondence in one year" (Sen. Rep. 242, 43-1, p. 4), and the extension of facilities was slight, only one-fifteenth to one-twentieth, merely the normal growth

the other the Western Union, the politicians, and a few individuals who have not recovered from the soporific doses
of the ancient political economy of bestillity and letalone-
ativeness injected into their thought in their college days
and who are not yet sufficiently awake to know that the
days of laissez-faire are done. On the one side Commerce,

(see statistics, H. Rep. 114, pp. 2, 56). R. B. Lines, who made the census of the postal
telegraph for the United States government testified as follows before the House
committee on appropriations: " In Switzerland and Belgium a reduction of one-half
in the rates produced a double business in one year, with very slight increase of facilities. In Great Britain the adoption of a uniform and slightly reduced rate nearly
swamped the lines with messages, and in Canada a reduction which applied to less
than ten per cent of the business augmented it twenty-five per cent in the first year"
(H. Mis. 73, 42-3). " In Prussia in 1867, a reduction of thirty-three per cent in the rate
was followed by an increase, in the very first month after the charge, of seventy per
cent in messages. In France, in 1862, a reduction of thirty-five per cent in the rate
was followed by an increase of sixty-four per cent in messages. The Swiss inland
rate was reduced fifty per cent on Jan 1, 1868, and in the first three months there was
an increase of ninety per cent in the inland messages over the corresponding months
in the previous year" (H. Rep. 114, p. 3). The Belgian director of telegraph writes in
respect to the several reductions in his country: " These reductions have caused four
times the number of dispatches that would have been sent at the old rates. It has
thus been a great boon to the people" (H. Rep. 114, p. 24). In Switzerland, "the reduction by one-half of the internal tariff had the effect of doubling the number of
dispatches of that class, and that immediately, almost without transition " (Swiss
Rep. for 1868, quoted in H. Rep. 114, p. 28). In England a reduction of thirty-three
per cent on three-tenths of the messages and fifty per cent on the remainder caused
an increase of one hundred per cent in the business in about two years. There was
in this case a considerable extension of lines. One president of the Western Union
forgot to sustain this plea of no-great-prospect-of-increase-of-business-by-reason-of-
reduction-of-rates-and-increase-of-facilities, and he testified before the select committee on the postal telegraph that if the bill it was considering should be adopted rates
would be decreased sixty per cent and " the messages offered for transmission
would be from ten to fifty times more than the wires would carry" (H. Rep. 114, pp.
32, 125, 134).

And the Western Union does not do and never has done one-half the business its lines
would carry, so that the total increase according to Mr. Orton would be from twenty
to one hundredfold the present business. The development of business consequent
upon low rates and the extension of lines results from the use of the telegraph by a
larger number of people. The wealthy people of the cities use it now all they wish to;
they would use it little if any more with a five-cent rate than with a rate of twenty-
five cents. But to the poor and to people in moderate circumstances, the difference
between the telegraph and postal rates is practically prohibitive except under the
stress of very special need. President Green of the Western Union said that 46 per
cent of their business is speculative, 34 per cent legitimate trade (his own words), 12
per cent press, and 8 per cent social (Bingham Hearings, 1890, p. 56). In Sen. Rep. 577,
part II, p. 15, the then president of the Western Union said the company's social business was five or six per cent of the whole. In Belgium the social messages constitute
55 to 63 per cent of the whole. Formerly when the rates were higher the social business was only 13 per cent in that country (I. T. U. Hearings, 1894, p. 17; Sen. Rep. 577,
p. 16). In England the social business is said to be four times as large as in this
country — eight times as large in proportion to the population (testimony G. G. Hubbard, I. T. U. Hearings, 1894, p. 24). In Switzerland the social dispatches are 61 per
cent of the whole (Sen. Rep. 577, p. 16). Comment is unnecessary. The facts speak
for themselves.

Agriculture, Manufactures, Labor, Philosophy, and Progress; on the other side Wall Street, Self-interest, and Sophistry.   On the one side the People and Common Sense; on the other Unscrupulous Power and its allies—the People against Monopoly.

Able counsel for the people have not failed to push their cause.   Senator Edmunds in '83 introduced a bill to establish a postal telegraph, another in '85, and another in '87.   Senator Dawes from '73 to '88 introduced four bills to provide for the transmission of correspondence by telegraph.   Others have been equally persistent.   Altogether more than seventy bills have been introduced into Congress for the purpose of establishing a postal telegraph.   Eighteen times committees of the House and Senate have reported on the question, sixteen times in favor of the measure, twice against, a clear majority of three-fourths in favor of the people.[7]   Some of the ablest men in Con-

[7] The adverse reports are
      House Report, 32, 40th Cong. 3d Sess., 1869.
      Senate Report, 434, 50-1, 2 pages.
   The favorable reports are
      House Report, 187, 28-2, Mar. 3, 1845, Committee of Ways and Means.
      House Report, 114, 41-2, July 5, 1870, Washburn, Select Com. on Postal Telg.
      House Report, 115, 41-2 (Palmer).
      House Report, 6, 42-3 (1872).
      House Report, 125, 43-2 (1875), Gen. Butler, Judiciary Committee.
      House Report, 137, 46-3 (1881), Committee on the Postoffice and Postroads.
      House Report, 2004, 47-2 (1883), Bingham.
      House Report, 1436, 48-1 (1884), Committee on P. O. and P. R.
      House Report, 965, 50-1 (1888), Rayner, Committee on Commerce.
      Senate Report, 18, 41-2 (1870), Ramsey, Committee on P. O. and P. R.
      Senate Report, 20, 42-2 (1872), Id.
      Senate Report, 223, 42-2 (1872), Zachary Chandler, Committee on Commerce
      Senate Report, 242, 42-3 (1872), Committee on P. O. and P. R.
      Senate Report, 242, 43-1 (1874), Id.
      Senate Report, 624, 43-2 (1875).
      Senate Report, 577, 48-1 (1884), N. P. Hill, Committee on P. O. and P. R.
      Senate Report, 577, 48-1 Part 2.
   For hearings, memorials, etc., see
      H. Mis., 36, 41-3, Washburn.   H. Mis., 39, 41-3, Hubbard.
      H. Jour., p. 173, 41-3, Washburn.
      Sen. Ex. Doc., 14, 40-2, Belknap, Secretary of War.
      H. Rep., 69, 42-2, Committee on Appropriations.
      H. Mis., 73, 42-3, Id.   Sen. Mis., 79, 42-3, Hubbard.
      Sen. Rep., 805, 45-3, Committee on Roads.
      Sen. Mis., 86, 42-2, Memorial of Western Union.
      Sen. Mis., 39, 50-1, Id.
      The Investigations on "Labor and Capital" by the Blair Committee of the
         Senate on Ed. and Labor, 48th Congress (1883).
      Census Report on Foreign Postal Telegraph by R. B. Lines, 1883.
      The Bingham Hearings, "Statements in Regard to Postal Telegraph Facil-
         ities," being the hearings of the House Committee on P. O. and P. R. in
         reference to the Wanamaker Bill, 1890.
      I. T. U. Hearings before the Committee on P. O. and P. R., May 4 to June
         26, 1894.
   In House Report 69 the committee had no question before them but the interpretation of the telegraph act of 1866 in respect to the powers of the postmaster general,
etc.   In Senate Report 805 the committee on railroads was instructed to inquire if it
was expedient to authorize the railroads to do telegraph business.   The committee
reported that, "In order to intelligently conclude as to the proper remedy for the
evils sought to be cured, to wit, the great existing monopoly of the business of transmitting telegraph dispatches," the committee's powers of inquiry should be extended
so as to "embrace the expediency of a postal telegraph system."

gress have conducted these investigations and made the reports.

Of the two adverse reports, one was a two-page document mildly expressing the opinion that the telegraph monopoly should be regulated but that public ownership was not best because of the increase of patronage, and because the committee thought it would cost more to run the telegraph under the government than under private enterprise. No evidence was taken, no investigation was made; the committee simply stated their feeling about the matter. The report was made by John H. Reagan of Texas.

The other adverse report was made in 1869 upon the ground that the five years of security given to the companies by the law of 1866 had not yet elapsed. The Telegraph Act[s] of July 24, 1866, gave any company organized under the laws of any state a right to construct and operate lines "through and over any portion of the public domain of the United States, over and along any of the military or postroads of the United States, and over, under, or across the navigable streams and waters of the United States," on condition: (1) That government business shall have priority of transmission over all other business and shall be sent at rates to be annually fixed by the postmaster-general; (2) "that the rights and privileges hereby granted shall not be transferred by any company acting under this act to any other corporation, association, or person; provided, however, That the United States may at any time after the expiration of five years from the date of the passage of this act, for postal, military, or other purposes, purchase all the telegraph lines, property, and effects of any or all of said companies at an appraised value, to be ascertained by five competent, disinterested persons, two of whom shall be selected by the postmaster-general of the United States, two by the company interested, and one by the four so previously selected; (3) that before any telegraph company shall exercise any of the powers or privileges conferred by this act, such company shall file their written acceptance with the postmaster-general of the restrictions and obligations required by this act."

The Western Union and other companies accepted the provisions of this act and extended their lines on the faith of it, wherefore the committee were perfectly right in saying that as the period fixed by the statute had not expired, Congress ought not to pass "any law hostile to the spirit

---

[s] U. S. Statutes at Large ior 1866, p. 221,

of the contract into which the companies had entered by
its invitation," and in refusing to favor bills to establish
government lines which would subtract from the companies' business during the said five years.[9]

The only adverse matter of any volume or even apparent
weight consists of the testimony of successive presidents
of the Western Union and the arguments of the company's
counsel. Such testimony and argument has occupied
much time in several congressional hearings, and has also
appeared in pamphlet, magazine, and newspaper form.

Of the favorable reports the most important are House
Reports 114 and 187, and the Senate Reports 18 and 577.
Valuable data and powerful arguments are also to be
found in the proceedings of committees that did not make
a formal report. The argument of Postmaster-General
John Wanamaker and the testimony taken by the Bingham
committee in 1890, are worthy the most careful attention.[10]
The investigations of the Blair committee in 1883,[11] and the
I. T. U. hearings before the House committee on the post-
office and postroads in 1894, are also specially valuable.
The reports of our postmaster-generals,[12] the public docu-

---

[9] H. Rep. 32, 49-3, p. 7 (1869).

[10] The hearing was before the House Committee on Postoffice and Postroads, 51st
Congress. Only a few copies of the proceedings were published. Mr. Wanamaker's
argument and part of the evidence were printed under the title, "An Argument in
Support of the Limited Post and Telegraph by the Postmaster General," Government
Print, 1890. This can be easily obtained and is one of the most valuable documents
in the literature of the subject.

[11] The hearings occupied about a year's time of the Senate Committee on Education
and Labor. The testimony taken by the committee is published in four volumes under
the title "Labor and Capital." A fifth volume was announced but never published
because the committee for some reason did not make a report.

[12] The most noteworthy are those of Cave Johnson, 1844-5, Creswell, 1871-2-3, Maynard, 1880, Howe, 1882, Gresham, 1883, and Wanamaker, 1890-92; the last two and
Creswell's report of 1872 are the most important. All but Mr. Gresham advocate the
postal telegraph. Mr. Gresham quotes the following words from the report of the
Committee on Ways and Means (H. Rep. 187), and calls them "just remarks": "The
same principle which justified and demanded the transference of the mail on many
chief routes from the horse-drawn coach on common highways to the steam-impelled
vehicles on land and water is equally potent to warrant the calling of the electro-
magnetic telegraph in aid of the postoffice in discharge of its great functions of
rapidly transmitting correspondence and intelligence." Later in the report he states
that he does "not feel at liberty to recommend a government telegraph because of
the danger to purity of administration arising from an increase of service under the
spoils system." The only way to reconcile these two ideas expressed within the same
report within a few paragraphs of each other, is to conclude that Postmaster General
Gresham would favor a postal telegraph under thorough-going civil service rules impartially and firmly administered, for that would carry out the principle he advocates,
and at the same time avoid the danger he fears; and that is precisely the kind of
postal telegraph we advocate, so that Walter Q. Gresham seems to be substantially in
harmony with the movement.

ments of England, France, Germany, Belgium, Switzerland, Sweden, Norway, Italy, Russia, New Zealand, and Australia, the volumes of the *Arena, Forum, North American Review,* and other magazines, the works of electrical engineers, the Western Union reports, the proceedings of labor unions and of commercial organizations, the platforms

---

Postmaster General Bissell devotes three pages to the subject in his report for 1894. He opposes a postal telegraph. He thinks it would cause a deficit and be productive of " wrangling and jealousy " through the " limitless difficulty of determining the character, quality, and amount of service that should be accorded to the various sections of the country." It is hard to see why the introduction of electric mails should cause any more wrangling and jealousy between different sections of the country or any more trouble in distributing the service than the introduction of steam mails or the adoption of the free delivery system. Give fair facilities to all and better facilities where the amount of business warrants it; the test of population and business done determines the distribution of service now without the slightest difficulty and would do so just the same if the functions of the postoffice were multiplied a hundredfold. As to the deficit, Mr. Bissell bases his belief on the assertion that the English postal telegraph does not pay its operating expenses. This is not true, but if it were, the conclusion of Mr. Bissell would not follow. If it is good logic to say, "England has a deficit on its postal telegraph, therefore the United States would have a deficit on its postal telegraph," then it is good logic to say, "France, Switzerland, Sweden, Belgium, and other countries realize a profit on their postal telegraph, therefore the United States would make a profit on the postal telegraph." As already remarked the statement of the postmaster general in respect to England is not true though he doubtless thought it was. He says on page 48 of the Report for 1894, that the interest on the English telegraph investment for the year 1893 was $1,455,584. "In the operation of the service there was a further loss of $811,741."

The report of the English Postoffice for 1893 showed that there had been a large extension of lines to life-saving stations and other points, 673 new offices in all. I suspected that the cost of new construction had been included in the "*expenditures*" assumed by Mr. Bissell to be *operating* expenses, so I wrote to the English Postmaster General and here are the figures he sends me for 1893:

Total Receipts.	New Purchase and Construction	Operating Expenses.	Total Expenditure.	Net Profit on Operation.	Interest.
£2,526,312	£185,609	£2,507,385	£2,692,994	£18,927	£298,888

So there was a net profit on operation of $94,635. I suppose some one who looks at the lump sums of the English Postmaster General's report for 1893-4 and does not think of inquiring about the items will be telling some one that there was a deficit in operation of almost a million, whereas the itemized account shows that taking out the cost of new construction, there was a net profit of $138,850. In 1890, the net profit was $1,451,320; in 1887, it was $442,420; in 1881, it was $2,257,315; in 1875, it was $435,375; in 1873, it was $568,995; such are some of the figures taken at random. The profit varies, but every year from 1894 back to the first report in 1871, shows a considerable net profit in the operation of the telegraph. In the last three years and the five years from 1884 to 1888 the surplus was not sufficient to defray the cost of new construction or extensions; but in each of the other sixteen years the net profit was a good deal more than sufficient for this purpose — the excess after paying for all extensions rising in some years as high as a million and a half of dollars. From February, 1870, down to the present time the actual cash received for postal telegraph service in England has paid all operating expenses and all cost of extensions, new purchase,

Postmaster-General John Wanamaker adopts this view that it is the duty of Congress to establish a postal telegraph.[14] Indeed it has been from the first the almost unbroken doctrine of the postoffice department that it was in duty bound to keep up with the times and not permit itself to be outstripped in the rapidity of communicating intelligence (see H. Rep.187 quoted below).

Senator C. A. Sumner of California said before the H. Com. on Postoffices and Postroads, on March 25, 1884:

"I lay it down as a proposition that I want to have duly considered by this committee and the country — that the constitution of the United States as interpreted by a century of unchallenged legislation, does imperatively require that the Congress of the United States shall establish a postal system. I lay it down as a fundamental proposition that the postal telegraph is a part of the postal system of the government; the postal system of the United States having been established for the purpose of transmitting intelligence between the inhabitants of the land."

Gardiner G. Hubbard says that Congress had no more right to delegate the power of transmitting intelligence than the power to coin money or declare war. Senator Edmunds said in his testimony before the Senate Committee on Postoffices and Postroads that government was constituted to promote the general welfare, to disseminate intelligence, to defend the country, etc., and that the telegraph was essential as a military establishment, essential to education and to social welfare.[15]

The Senate Committee on Postoffices and Postroads of 1874, which numbered among its members such men as Hannibal Hamlin and Alexander Ramsey, said in its report on the telegraph:

"The constitution devolved upon Congress the duty of transmitting all correspondence including that by telegraph as well as that by mail."[16]

But to find the most careful and convincing statement of this point we must go back to the House Committee of Ways and Means in 1845. The government had already built the first telegraph line and the question of extending the service under government ownership was before the committee. Here is a portion of its noble report:[17]

"The government is authorized and required by the constitution to carry intelligence. The functions thus devolved on the government of

---

[14] Wanamaker Pamphlet, pp. 148-9.
[15] Sen. Rep. 577, part 2, p. 4.
[16] Sen. Rep. 242, 43-1, p. 6.
[17] H. Rep. 187, 28th Cong., 2d Sess., pp. 1-3.

performing for the people the office of universal letter-carrier and news carrier, is a matter of the very highest consequence in every light in which it can be viewed. The bare fact that our ancestors refused to leave it dependent on individual enterprise or state control, and rested it expressly in Congress, abundantly attested their anxious sense of its importance, and their conviction of the impracticability of realizing the requisite public advantages from it otherwise than by giving it federal lodgment and administration. But though not anticipated or foreseen, these new and improved modes were as clearly within the purview of the Constitution as were the older and less perfect ones with which our ancestors were familiar, and there being no doubt entertained either on this point or as to the obligation of the government to lay hold of the best and most rapid methods of transmission which the improvement of the age puts in its reach; steam power commended itself at once to adoption and has long been extensively employed both on land and water for the carriage of the mail.

"It is not without full reflection that the committee insist on the principle that it was the duty as well as the right of the government thus to avail itself, even at heavy additional expense, of the powerful agency of steam, for the purpose of accelerating the mails. It would have been a gross and manifest dereliction to have permitted that vitally important concern, the transportation of the mail—a concern so anxiously intrusted by the Constitution to federal authority—to lag behind the improvements of the age, and to be outstripped by the pace of ordinary travel and commercial communication. Such is the view which the postoffice department takes of its own obligation and upon which it habitually acts. To be outstripped by private expresses is deemed discreditable to the department, injurious to the general interests of the country and a thing therefore not to be permitted.

"This great and fundamental principle upon which the department acts (of not being outstripped in the transmission of correspondence and intelligence) led necessarily to using the steam-engine in the service of the postoffice and it must and will lead with equal certainty to the adoption of any other newly discovered agency or contrivance possessing decided advantages of celerity over previously used methods. The same principle which justified and demanded the transference of the mail on many chief routes, from the horse-drawn coach on common highways to steam-impelled vehicles on land and water, is equally potent to warrant the calling of the electro-magnetic telegraph—that last and most wondrous birth of this wonder-teeming age—in aid of the postoffice in discharge of its great function of rapidly transmitting correspondence and intelligence."

If these strong words of wisdom, and the farsighted prophecies of Professor Morse, and the stirring appeals of Henry Clay had been heeded there would have been no telegraph question to-day, the great Wall-Street monopoly would never have been born, and the people would not have had to give fifty years of unsuccessful effort to the purpose of getting their will and their rights enacted into law in the shape of a postal telegraph.

(To be continued.)

THE BOND AND THE DOLLAR.

BY JOHN CLARK RIDPATH, LL. D.

PART I. GENESIS AND EVOLUTION OF A MONSTER.

War preys on two things—life and property; but he preys with a partial appetite. Feasting on life, he licks his jaws and says, "More, by your leave!" Devouring property, he says, between grin and glut, "This is so good that it ought to be paid for!" Into the vacuum of the wasted life rush the moaning winds of grief and desolation; into the vacuum of the wasted property rushes the goblin of debt. The wasted life is transformed at length into a reminiscent glory; the wasted property becomes a hideous nightmare. The heroes fallen rise from their bloody cerements into everlasting fame; the property destroyed rises from the red and flame-swept field as a spectral vampire, sucking the still warm blood of the heroic dead and of their posthumous babes to the tenth generation!

The name of the vampire is *Bond*.

On the 1st of March, 1866, the national debt of the United States entailed by the Civil War reached the appalling maximum of nearly three thousand millions of dollars.* The American people were inexperienced in such business. They had never known the incubus before. Europe had known it, but not America. For a long time the public debt of the nation had been so small as to be disregarded. Now all of a sudden, with the terrible exigencies of the war, the debt expanded and settled over the landscape like a cloud from Vesuvius, darkening from shore to shore.

So far as the people and the government were concerned, it was an honest debt. The method and intent of Lincoln and the great men around him in 1862-63 were as sincere and just as they were humane and patriotic. As for the American people, they were always honest. The nation was in deadly peril, and must be rescued at whatever cost. The war was a devouring demon. With the explosion of every shell, the product of a hundred toiling hands was instantly vaporized; for the bomb is not filled, as many suppose, with powder and iron and death, but with the potatoes and milk and biscuit of mankind. At intervals the

* In exact figures, $2,827,868,959.46.

expenditure was more than a million, and sometimes more than two millions of dollars a day. The government had nothing of its own, did not venture to take anything *as* its own, and must therefore support itself by loans or perish Conforming to the method of the age, the nation borrowed from the accumulations of the rich, and gave them therefor its promises to pay.

The promises to pay got themselves into a bond.

It is the order of modern society that he who has may lend to him who has not, and receive his own with usury. This principle was adopted by the American republic in the day of trial. The means necessary for the prosecution of the war were not taken—as the life was taken—but were borrowed. The quadrennium was an epoch of prodigious borrowing. A great part of the lending was patriotic; but much of it, even at the first, was interested, and was mixed with contrivance and ulterior designs.

The currency that had to be provided to meet the startling emergency that had overtaken the American people was, in the nature of the case, made to be a legal tender in the payment of debts. The government must needs have such a money. All metallic money—as is its invariable habit under such circumstances—slunk away and hid itself in dark coffers, mostly beyond the sea. What did gold care for liberty, for the waste of human life, for the republic, for the Union made sacred by the sacrifices and blood of our fathers?

It was intended by those who first contrived the legal-tender currency that it should be absolute money in the payment of all debts of whatever kind. The Supreme Court of the United States has since decided by a voice of eight to one that Congress possessed—and possesses—the right and power to make such a money, whether in war or in peace. The validity of the Legal-tender Act is now as much a part of the constitutional history of the United States as is the abolition of African slavery. But they who were skilful in watching their own interests, even in the throes of our national break-up and impending catastrophe, adroitly contrived that the national currency should have an *exception* in it in favor of those who should lend their means to the government. They who should make such loan should receive therefor a bond; and the interest on the bond—as also the duties on imports of foreign goods—was exempt from the legal tender of paper and reserved for coin.

Thus came the bonded debt of the United States. The

debt grew with the progress of the war, until it seemed to approach infinity. The nation swayed and struggled through the bloody sea, and came at last to the shore. The process of debt-making had acquired so great momentum that it was difficult to get it checked and reversed. In the early summer of 1865 the soldiers of the Union army were mustered out and remanded to their homes. By August the work was done; the Grand Army was no more; but such was the confusion that for fully six months longer the expenditure rolled on without abatement.

The great question which confronted the nation at the beginning of 1866 was the management of the debt. There were bonds galore: a seven-thirty series of two hundred and fifty millions, by Act of July 17, 1861; then five hundred and fifteen millions of five-twenties, by Act of February 25, 1862, becoming more than twelve hundred millions by subsequent issues; then ten-forties in several series—7.3-per cents, 6-per cents, 5-per cents, 4.5-per cents, 4-per cents; plain bonds at the first, and coin bonds finally—short loans and long loans and longer loans, *but always becoming longer*, until a measure of calm ensued, and the nation found opportunity to take account of its losses and consider the question of payment.

If governments had the same care for the life of the people as for the property of those who possess property, then national debts would not be made, or at least not perpetuated, by the event of war. It had been an act of infinite mercy on the part of the government of the United States in that day to take directly whatever was necessary —as it did take whatever *men* were necessary—for the suppression of the Rebellion. That course would have ended it. Had that almost unprecedented policy been temperately and successfully pursued, the cost of the war would hardly have been one-fifth of what it has become; the bond would never have existed; the wealth of the people would not have been concentrated in the hands of a few; the present harrowing and dangerous conditions of American life would not have supervened, and the victorious defence of the Union would long ere this have become a glorious and unclouded reminiscence.*

* Let no one aver that making war without making a national debt is an absurd vagary. That would be to condemn as a financial quack no less a personage than William E. Gladstone! Mr. Gladstone is without a doubt the greatest statesman in finance that England has produced within the present century. It has been the one ruling and undeviating principle of his policy, alike in peace and in war, to make the annual revenues *under all circumstances* meet the annual expenditures of the empire. He began to battle for this principle in 1853 when as chancellor of the exchequer he had to provide the means for the prosecution of the Crimean War. On this question he and Disraeli divided forever. The former proposed to provide the

Strange it is, however, that our vaunted and vaunting
civilization, even to the present day, prefers property to
man. It exalts the one and tramples on the other. In this
particular we have been even as the rest. Judging by the
facts there is no government on earth to which its mules are
not dearer than its men! Strange, too, that whoever appeals on behalf of the man as against the mule and urges the
protection of the one at the expense of the other is held
to be an enemy of society! Property in this particular
having no conscience, or only the conscience of being always
in the wrong, fortifies itself with every casuistical and
fallacious argument known to the category of self-interest.
and puts down both the man and his advocates. The
"sacred rights of property," meaning the right of something
that belongs to life to seize that life by the throat and
strangle it, are promulgated and upheld with constitution
and statute and bayonet; while the "rights of man," so
much in vogue in the great epoch of regeneration at the
close of the eighteenth century. are, at the close of the
nineteenth, positively under the ban in every civilized state
of the world. According to the plutocratic lexicons of at
least two continents, the "rights of man" have come to
signify merely—anarchy.

Our staggering nation arose and stood. The horizon
cleared. The government of the republic was preserved
for posterity. It found itself, however, in the grip of a
python, from which. after thirty years of writhing, it is
less able to free itself than ever before since the close of the
conflict. In the course of the war and just afterwards it
was discerned by those who held the national debt, as it
had been discerned by some of them from the beginning,
that it was a good thing for the possessors. A great interest had been created by the battle of the national Union
for its life—the interest of the bond.

It were vain to conjecture how many sincere patriots
found themselves possessors of the interest-bearing obligations of the nation. For all such there is no animadversion,
but rather praise. It were equally vain to conjecture

means of war by increasing the annual revenues; the latter proposed to borrow. **Mr.
Gladstone** did adopt the method of paying as he went, and held to it until the overthrow of the Aberdeen ministry. He stoutly affirmed in presenting his first budget
that, war or no war, the national debt of Great Britain should not be increased but
that the cost of supporting the British army in Asia should be met *year by year* by
an increase in the income-taxes and excises. This policy was supported by the prince
consort who declared it to be "manly, statesmanlike, and honest"; the policy of borrowing the prince characterized as "*convenient, cowardly, and perhaps popular.*"
He ought to have added *suicidal*. As long as Gladstone remained in office he forced
the revenues to meet the expenditures within the year. His principle through life
has been, in every emergency, not to *borrow*, but to tax — that is, to *take*.

how many held those obligations simply for the profit and advantage and power that were in them and with no concern about the welfare of the government or of the people of the United States; but the latter class, whether many or few, increased, and the former class decreased, until the fundholding interest was consolidated in the hands of a party having its bifurcations in New York and London.

The party of the bond became skilful and adroit. It began immediately to fortify itself. It took advantage of the inexperience of the American people and of their legislators. It profited by the mistakes and misplaced confidence of both. They who held the bonds were wise by ages of training in the Old World and the New. They understood the situation perfectly, and adopted as their method a policy embracing two intentions: First, *to perpetuate the bond* and make it everlasting by the postponement and prevention of payment; Second, *to increase the value of the currency* in which all payments were to be made; that is, to increase the value of the *units* of such payments as the payments should become due, so that whatever might be the efforts of the people to discharge the debt it should increase in value as rapidly as they could reduce it! And the honest people, abused to the soul by the politician and by Shylock, knew not that it was so.

For thirty years this game has been persistently, skilfully, and successfully carried out. It has been a play worthy of the greatest gamesters that ever lived! We do not call to mind any other such stake among the nations as that placed upon the issue; and the bondplayers have won on every deal. They have succeeded on both counts of their policy. They have turned over the debt into new forms of bond, and these again into newer, under the name of refunding, persuading the people that the process was wise and needful, and cajoling them with the belief that the rate of interest was each time reduced for the benefit of the nation. It was done "in the interest of the people"! We, the holders of the bond, being patriots, labor only for the interest of the people!

It is true that each act of refunding and transforming the national debt has lowered somewhat the *nominal* rate of interest; but at the same time it has lengthened the period of payment. At the beginning the date of payment was at the option of the government. Then it was at five years from the making of the bond; then it was at ten years; then at twenty years; then at thirty years. Now the period of possible payment has been extended until the second decade of the next century cannot witness the end of the game. If the treasury should have to-day, or in the year 1900, a surplus of six billions of gold the government could not call and cancel its bonds. They were not made to be called and cancelled, but to be refunded and perpetuated.

Besides, the reduction of interest has been a reduction only in name. In no case has the reduction been made until the value of the dollar of the payment has been so enlarged as more than to balance the reduction. The same thing is true of the payment of principal as well as the payment of coupon. For thirty years the American people have been pouring into that horrid maelstrom the volume of their great resources. They have paid on their debt, or at least they have *paid*, in this long period such a prodigious sum that arithmetic can hardly express it.[*] The imagination cannot embrace it. And yet it is the truth of the living God that in the year 1895, at its close, the national debt of the United States, in its bonded and unbonded forms, will purchase as its equivalent in value as much of the average of twenty-five of the leading commodities of the American market, including real estate and labor, as the same debt would purchase at its maximum on the 1st of March, 1866! The people have paid and paid for thirty years, and at the end have paid just this—NOTHING![†]

---

[*] The American people have never realized the incalculable sums which have been paid out of their treasury in the ostensible work of discharging the interest and principal of the war debt of the nation. Sometime, perhaps, the final aggregate may be made up and historically recorded. Within the first ten years after the conclusion of the war, that is, at the close of the fiscal year, 1874-75, the government had already paid *in interest only* on the public debt $1,442,057,577! And this was but the beginning. At the close of the year 1895 the interest account has reached the prodigious total of more than two billion six hundred and thirty-five millions of dollars!

[†] The verification of this astounding truth is as plain and irrefragable as any other arithmetical result.

On the first of March, 1866, the national debt was in exact figures	$2,827,868,959.46
For the sake of easy computation the same may be stated in round numbers at	2,825,000,000.00
The debt at the close of the year 1895 (statement for November) is	1,126,379,106.00
For convenience of counting, the same may be given in round numbers as $1,125,000,000.00	
To this add ten per cent (a very low estimate) for the present average premium on the debt (interest-bearing and non-interest-bearing) above the par of gold 112,500,000 00	
Total present gold value of the debt	$1,237,500,000.00

On the first of March, 1866, the prices current of nine leading staples of the American market, selected broadly from the whole, were as follows:—

Wheat per bushel, from $1.78 to $2; average	$1.90
Flour per barrel, $10.50 to $11; average	10.75
Cotton per pound	.48
Mess Pork per barrel	28.37
Sugar per pound	.11125
Wool per pound, 50 cents to 56 cents; average	.53
Beef per cwt., $12 to $18.50; average	15.25
Bar Iron per pound, 6 cents to 7½ cents; average	.0675
Superior farming lands in Ohio and Mississippi valleys (approximately) per acre	75.00

Let all men know it. Let the world know it. Let the common man ponder this appalling statement of an undeniable truth. Let our national authorities know it. Let the leaders of every political party have it shouted in their ears. Let every administration that has been in power from the first of Grant to the last of Cleveland be told in trumpet voice that the publications put forth from month to month as statements from the treasury about the reduction of the

At the close of 1895 figures for November 10) the prices current for the same staples were as follows: —

Wheat per bushel $0.58
Flour per barrel 3.50
Cotton per pound 085
Mess pork per barrel 8.20
Sugar per pound, 4½ cents to 5½ cents; average 05
Wool per pound, 20 to 23 cents; average 215
Beef per cwt., $8.50 to $10.50; average 9.50
Bar iron per pound, 1⅗ to 3¼ cents; average 0267
Superior farming lands, same as above, in Ohio and Mississippi valleys (approximately), per acre 35.00

The national debt on the first of March, 1866, would therefore purchase of the above staples as follows: —

Of wheat . . . . 1,486,842,105 bushels
Of flour . . . . 262,790,697 barrels
Of cotton . . . . 5,885,416,666 pounds
Of mess pork . . . . 99,576,313 barrels
Of sugar . . . . 25,393,348,314 pounds
Of wool . . . . 5,330,188,679 pounds
Of beef . . . . 181,967,213 cwt.
Of bar iron . . . . 41,851,851,851 pounds
Of superior farming lands as above (approximately) . . . 37,666,666 acres

The national debt at the close of the year 1895 will purchase of the above staples as follows: —

Of wheat . . . . 2,133,620,689 bushels
Of flour . . . . 353,571,428 barrels
Of cotton . . . . 14,558,823,529 pounds
Of mess pork . . . . 150,915,853 barrels
Of sugar . . . . 24,750,000,000 pounds
Of wool . . . . 5,755,813,953 pounds
Of beef . . . . 130,263,136 cwt.
Of bar iron . . . . 46,348,314,606 pounds
Of superior farming lands as above (approximately) . . 35,357,142 acres

The purchasing power of the national debt at the close of 1895 is therefore *greater* than was that of the national debt on March 1, 1866, as follows: —

In the case of wheat by . . . . 646,778,584 bushels
In the case of flour by . . . . 90,780,731 barrels
In the case of cotton by . . . . 8,673,406,863 pounds
In the case of mess pork by . . . . 51,339,540 barrels
In the case of wool by . . . . 425,625,274 pounds
In the case of bar iron by . . . . 4,496,462,755 pounds

The purchasing power of the national debt at the close of 1895 is, by like deduction, *less* than was that of the national debt on March 1, 1866, as follows: —

In the case of sugar by . . . . 643,348,314 pounds
In the case of beef by . . . . 51,704,076 cwt.
In the case of farming lands as above by (approximately) . . 2,309,523 acres

From this calculation it is seen that the purchasing power of the debt at the close of 1895 is far greater than it was on March 1, 1866, on *six* of the nine great staples enumerated, and that it is less by a comparatively small per cent on only *three* of the articles enumerated. There is an overwhelming preponderance on the *average* of the whole list in favor of the debt as it stands at the close of the current year. That debt, in a word, is worth more to the holders than it was at its nominal maximum nearly thirty years ago! There is no kind of sophistical argument or doctored statistics in the world that can overcome or seriously modify the conclusions here drawn from premises that are incontrovertible.

national debt by the payment of three millions or seven millions or ten millions have been essentially and utterly false. True it is that the debt has been *nominally* reduced according to the publications; but it has never been so reduced until by the contrivance of those who possess it the purchasing power of the currency in which the debt was to be paid has been augmented fully as much as the equivalent of the payment!

Thus from month to month and from year to year the astounding process has gone on. And thus from year to year the judgment of the American people has been abused with the iteration and belief that they were paying their debt, when in truth all the multiplied millions on millions and billions which they have paid have been simply *contributed* to the fundholding class whose claim after a lifetime is worth as much as it was at the beginning! The resources of a great people have been poured like a roaring river into a sinkhole that has swallowed all; and the golden streams of the contribution have issued silently through a thousand unseen spouts into the private reservoirs of the holders of the debt.

The policy of the fundholding interest has thus simplified itself into (1) the indefinite extension of the bond, and (2) the manipulation of the dollar. To the extent that the first part of this policy has prevailed, the United States has been remanded to the same category with the nations of Western Europe, having their perpetual bonded debts. To the extent that the second part of the policy has prevailed, the people of the United States have been continuously robbed of their resources for nearly the full period of a human life. In the meantime the people have been familiarized with the proposition—put forth timidly at first—that a national debt is a national blessing. It furnishes the cement—so runs the patriot song—whereby the moneyed classes are bound in devotion to the government and become a part of it, as in England; thus the government is made *strong* and *enduring!*

Meanwhile the various refundings have been celebrated in political pæan as marvels of finance. By the organs of the party in power one-half of the people have been led to believe that the national honor is preserved, the national faith made good, and great economy manifested in those manipulations of the bonds by which, series after series, the longer have been substituted for the shorter. The other half of the people, who would have discovered the bottom intent in the process and thwarted the scheme at the next election, have been prevented from doing so by the fact that *their* organs and leaders have had a common interest with them of the dominant faction. Several secretaries of the treasury have been made into great financiers by becoming the willing clerks of the fundholding class in those delicate and beautiful processes by which the national debt is to be made everlasting with the accompaniment of popular applause.

But the extension of the bonded debt and the hope of its eternal life were not the principal concern of those who obtained possession of it. Their imaginations were not indeed much dazzled with the prospect of having the bond merely perpetuated; because men who are engaged in such schemes rarely look beyond the limits of their own lives. It sufficed, therefore, that the bonded debt should be life-long, with the hope of another avatar. That secured, the undivided energy of those who secured it might be directed to the manipulation of the dollar; and it is safe to assert that the skill developed in this part of the bondholding policy has never been elsewhere shown by men. The complete history of the processes by which, with contraction and substitution, the dollar to be employed as the standard of payment in the discharge of the private and public debts of the people of the United States has been gradually and adroitly lifted from one valuation to another, until within thirty years (1865-1895) its purchasing power has been increased to the ratio of more than three to one, could never be written or recited. It surpasses human credulity. It goes beyond the average range of mortal invention and fixes itself in the catagory of the devilish!*

For a long time the subtle work of extending and transforming the bond and at the same time of raising the value of the dollar of payment was so easily and noiselessly effected that the people did not awake to the realization of the thing done until it was *fait accompli*. The class in whose interest the various changes have been made have been enabled to coddle some, to hoodwink others, to corrupt many, and to terrorize a multitude. We have seen those who have been aroused to the pitch of denouncing and exposing the giant fraud of the century turn about and decry as repudiators, enemies of the national credit, and disturbers of "the business interests" of the nation, the true friends of public honesty and good faith among men. At

---

* Abraham Lincoln said: "If a government contracts a debt with a certain amount of money in circulation and then contracts the money volume before the debt is paid, it is *the most heinous crime* a government could commit against the people."

least two secretaries of the treasury have exhibited to mankind that species of tergiversation which in the administration of a high office can hardly be distinguished from treason
to the human race!

Let us for a moment trace the principal changes that
have been effected in the dollar of account and payment under the dictation and management of the money power, and
with the cheerful acquiescence of several conniving administrations. In the first place, the great body of the bonded
debt of the nation was purchased in the time of the war
with the legal-tender paper money to which the government
had been obliged to resort. There has been no other traitor
to the American Union and to the liberties of the people
comparable in his perfidy with gold. Specie fled like a
coward before the first blast of battle.*

It is literally true that the great Rebellion was suppressed
and the Union upheld by the expedient of a non-interest-
bearing paper currency devised in the presence of the overwhelming exigency of war and dismemberment.† The
precious metals dived out of sight. The world knows
the story. The United States went upon a basis of paper.
For four years of war and fourteen years of peace, the
finances of the nation and of the people in their private
capacities were conducted on a legal-tender of paper.
Metallic money and the money metals rose rapidly in value,
or at least in price. Now gold was at a premium of 30
per cent; now 50 per cent; now 100 per cent; and
finally 185 per cent above par. Gold and silver money became a tradition and a myth. The people neither knew nor
cared what had become of them.

Owing to the nefarious exception in the legal-tender currency in favor of the interest on the public debt and duties
on imports, a Gold Exchange was organized in New York,

---

* Within ten days after the secession of South Carolina, and ten days *before* the
"Star of the West" was fired on in the harbor of Charleston, every bank in New
York suspended specie payments, leaving both people and nation to their fate.

† The efficiency of the legal-tender currency in the suppression of the Rebellion
has never been — can never be — overestimated. Twelve years after the war, Hon.
William D. Kelley, of Pennsylvania, addressing an assemblage of ex-Confederate
officers at Macon, Ga., said: "Your leaders were mistaken in their financial theory.
They believed that the United States could use nothing but gold and silver as
money, and that as they had none of these metals, they could not put armies in the
field to overwhelm you, or fleets upon the ocean to blockade your coasts; they had
not studied the constitution to see that the government has control of the question
of what shall be money. We discovered that it had, and when we could not get gold
or silver, we *made* the greenback, and it was that that whipped you." "Yes," said
one of the officers with enthusiasm: "Judge Kelley, you are right; it was the greenback that whipped us!" This is the currency that Shylock is now trying to have
cancelled *because it is so great a menace to the interests of the people.* He desires to
have the legal-tender currency destroyed, in order that money sharks may be prevented from using that currency to deplete the national treasury of its gold! The
hypocrisy of such a pretence is beyond the reach of satire!

añd gold was *bought* with which to pay the semi-annual
coupons of the bonds and the duties on imported goods.
Trading in gold and in the speculative margins of gold
became a business, in some sense the greatest of all the
businesses; certainly it was the most picturesque.

It was under these conditions that the great bulk of the
national debt was put into the form of bonds. The bonds
were purchased with the legal money of the country. They
were purchased at par according to the standard of the
universal currency. The advantage in purchasing them was
generally given by the government to the purchasers. Already the bondholder was a lord and the government a serf.
Inducements were freely offered to stimulate the sale of
the bonds. Payments were made easy; slight discounts
were not unusual; interest was sometimes advanced; and
many other methods were adopted to make the sale of the
national securities free and copious. Finally, the purchaser
of bonds to the value of fifty thousand dollars might receive
as a gratuity forty-five thousand dollars in paper money,
and with *that* establish a bank of issue, discount and loan.

In this manner the national debt became a bond.

From that day to the present the bond industry has been
the one ever-flourishing, permanent, and deep-down industry, not indeed of the American people, but of the class who
hold the national securities and live by them. This industry has combined with the two leading political parties,
and has made and kept them a unit for more than twenty
years. This industry has insinuated itself into the government, and has become the energizing and controlling force
in the public life of the nation; and before it all other industries have been compelled to stagger and bend and break,
until the bond not only rules but reigns.

No one has ever calculated with certainty the average
cost of the government bonds to the original purchasers.
To do so is a complicated problem. They were of many
series, extending over a span of years, and were bought at
different crises when the premium on gold was rising or falling. The higher that premium rose, the cheaper the bonds
were, as tested by the measurement of gold.* By this meas-

---

* The debt-making epoch of the Civil War covered a period of four years, ten
months, and nineteen days. The middle date of this period was Sept. 9, 1863; but by
far the greater part of the debt was incurred *after* that date. The premium on gold
reached fifty per cent on Dec. 14, 1863, and remained above that figure for one year,
three months, and twenty-seven days, covering the period of greatest debt-making.
Gold reached 200 on the 21st of June, 1864, and remained *above* 200 until Feb. 22, 1865.
It reached the topmost figure of 285 on the 12th of July, 1864. The dealers in bonds
called it a "flurry in gold!" This was the period of the *maximum* debt-making.
The legal-tender currency with which the bonds at that crisis were purchased was
worth thirty-five cents by the gold standard. It was the very heyday, when the bond-
nest was feathered for the laying of the golden egg.

urement it is probable that the average cost of the five-twenties to the purchasers was not more than fifty-five, or certainly not more than sixty-five cents to the gold dollar. Nearly all the other series were purchased at a like enormous discount, as tested by the standard of coin. In the sale of the bonds, before the debt reached its maximum in March of 1866, the standard of the legal-tender paper was uniformly observed. It was by the common measure of the money of the country that the whole original debt was sold, and mostly by that measure that it was funded and refunded for at least fourteen years after Appomattox. But the mythical gold barometer kept in the safe in Lombard Street in London showed that the purchases of the bonds were actually made at prices ranging from about forty-six to seventy cents to the coin dollar.

By the close of the war the seven-thirty bonds were already falling due. The five-twenties would be due in a short time. That is, in a short time the government would have the *option* but not the *necessity* of redeeming them. And now it was that the fundholding interest put itself in antagonism to the national welfare, and conceived the project of doubling its investment at one stroke by compelling the payment of all the bonds in coin. They had been purchased on the basis of one currency. That currency was worth only about half as much, unit for unit, as the mythical metallic currency which had now become only a reminiscence. Or, to put it the other way, the phantom metallic currency was worth at least two for one of the currency of all business, of all manufacture, of all production, of all accounting; that is, two for one of the currency of the people and the nation. The holders of the bonds perceived that if, under these conditions, they could secure a statutory declaration of the payment of both principal and interest of the five-twenty bonds in coin, then they would have gained, at the expense of the overburdened nation, not only the principal and the legitimate interest to which they were entitled and which ought to have satisfied, but also about two for one on their whole investment!

The stake was worthy of the trial. The game might well be played with all the skill and intrigue and specious formality of which human nature is capable. On one side of the table sat the representatives of the bond; on the other side sat the American people; and the bond won! By the Act of March 18, 1869, entitled "An Act to Strengthen the Public Credit," etc., but which ought to have been entitled "An Act to Transfer the Resources of the American People to

the Hands of a Few under Sanction of Law,"* it was de-
creed that the bondholder should have his two for one;
that the five-twenties and all like obligations of the government, whether they were or were not by their own terms
payable in coin, should now be made so payable; that the
national credit required that a bond which had been purchased in one currency should be paid in another currency
worth twice as much; that the property loaned to the
republic for the suppression of the Rebellion should be returned twofold beside the interest; that the holder of the
national obligation, in addition to being preserved whole
and harmless, should be enriched by law at the expense of
the people; but that the widow who had given her four sons
to her country and had followed them one by one to their
last resting-places under the apple trees in the orchard,
should receive back nothing but weeds and that celestial
sorrow which transfigured her face evermore into the face of
an angel!

(To be continued.)

---

* John Sherman, addressing the Senate on the 27th of January, 1869, just before
the passage of the so-called "Act to Strengthen the Public Credit," and speaking of
the prospective legislation, said : " Sir, it is not possible to take this voyage without
sore distress.　To every person except the capitalist out of debt or the salaried officer or annuitant, it is a period of loss, danger, prostration of trade, fall of wages,
suspension of enterprise, bankruptcy, and disaster. . . . It means the ruin of all
dealers whose debts are twice their capital, though one-third less than their property.
It means the fall of all agricultural productions, without any very great reduction of
taxes." Even so. *Et tu, Brute!* This cold-blooded proposition of Sherman means,
when reduced to an example, simply this : Every young and aspiring man in the
United States, just beginning life with wife and child and home, having five hundred dollars in money (his pay for service in the army), a home worth fifteen
hundred dollars, and a debt of a thousand dollars, *will be inevitably bankrupted!*
The calculation of the senator was correct.

COUNT TOLSTOY'S PHILOSOPHY OF LIFE.

BY ERNEST HOWARD CROSBY.

During the past few years much has been said of certain peculiar features of Count Tolstoy's doctrines, and his views on the subject of marriage and physical labor, his manner of dressing and living, his objections to wine and tobacco, to gold and silver, are familiar subjects of discussion. To appreciate justly a man's opinions, however, we should examine them from the inside and grasp first those ideas which lie at the base of his system. In the case of the Russian moralist the task of separating the essential from the incidental has fortunately been performed by himself, and in his treatise on "Life"* he gives us the very core of his faith. The fact that the author is the greatest living novelist and one of the conspicuous figures of the age would be enough to give to this volume the interest at least of curiosity. But it is rather on account of its intrinsic worth—because it presents with all the freshness of a new discovery one of the oldest solutions, and perhaps the truest, of the mystery of life—that it seems worth while to call attention to the book.

Most men, he says, lead only an animal life, and among these there are always some who think themselves called upon to guide humanity. They undertake to teach the meaning of life without understanding it themselves. These teachers are divided into two classes. To the first, composed of scientific men, he gives the name of "Scribes." These it is who declare that man's life is nothing but his existence between birth and death, and that this life proceeds from mechanical forces—that is, from forces which we style mechanical for the express purpose of distinguishing them from life. It is only in the infancy of a science, when it is as yet vague and indefinite, that it can thus pretend to account for all phenomena of life. Astronomy made the attempt when it was known as astrology; chemistry assumed the same rôle under the name of alchemy; and today the science of biology is passing through a similar phase. While occupied with one or more aspects of life, it claims to embrace the whole. The other class of false doctors he calls the "Pharisees." They are those who pro-

* "Life," by Count Tolstoy. Thomas Y. Crowell & Co., New York.

fess verbally the tenets of the founders of the religions
in which they have been educated, but who do not comprehend their real meaning and consequently content themselves with insisting on forms and ceremonies.

The wars of the Scribes and Pharisees—to wit, of false
science and false religion—have so obscured the definitions
of life laid down ages ago by the great thinkers of mankind,
that the Scribes are quite ignorant that the dogmas of
the Pharisees have any reasonable foundation at all; and,
strange to say, the fact that the doctrines of the great masters of old have so impressed men by their sublimity that
they have usually attributed to them a supernatural origin,
is enough to make the Scribes reject them. Because the
speculations of Aristotle, Bacon and Comte have appealed
to only a small number of students—because they have
never been able to gain a hold on the masses and have thus
avoided the exaggerations produced by superstition—
this clear mark of their insignificance is admitted as evidence of their truth. As for the teachings of the Brahmins,
of Buddha, of Zoroaster, of Lao-Tse, of Confucius, of Isaiah,
and also of Christ, they are taxed with superstition and
error simply because they have completely transformed the
lives of millions of men.

Turning from the futile strife of Scribes and Pharisees
we should begin our researches with that which we alone
know with certitude, and that is the "I" within us. Life
is what I feel in myself, and this life science cannot define.
Nay, it is my idea of life rather which determines what I
am to consider as science, and I learn all outside of myself
solely by the extension of my knowledge of my own mind
and body. We know from within that man lives only for
his own happiness, and his aspiration towards it and his
pursuit of it constitute his life. At first he is conscious
of the life in himself alone, and hence he imagines that the
good which he seeks must be his own individual good. His
own life seems the real life, while he regards the life of
others as a mere phantom. He soon finds out that other
men take the same view of the world, and that the life in
which he shares is composed of a vast number of individualities, each bent on securing its own welfare and consequently doing all it can to thwart and destroy the others.
He sees that in such a struggle it is almost hopeless for
him to contend, for all mankind is against him. If on the
other hand he succeeds by chance in carrying out his plans
for happiness, he does not even then enjoy the prize as he
anticipated. The older he grows, the rarer become the

pleasures, ennui, satiety, trouble, and suffering go on increasing; and before him lie old age, infirmity, and death. He will go down to the grave, but the world will continue to live. The real life, then, is the life outside him, and his own life, which originally appeared to him the one thing of importance, is after all a deception. The good of the individual is an imposture, and if it could be obtained it would cease at death. The life of man as an individuality seeking his own good, in the midst of an infinite host of like individualities engaged in bringing one another to naught and being themselves annihilated in the end, is an evil and an absurdity. It cannot be the true life.

Our quandary arises from looking upon our animal life as the real life. Our real life begins with the waking of our consciousness, at the moment when we perceive that life lived for self cannot produce happiness. We feel that there must be some other good. We make an effort to find it, but, failing, we fall back into our old ways. These are the first throes of the birth of the veritable human life. This new life only becomes manifest when the man once for all renounces the welfare of his animal individuality as his aim in life. By so doing he fulfils the law of reason, the law which we all are sensible of within us—the same universal law which governs the nutrition and reproduction of beast and plant. Our real life is our willing submission to this law and not, as science would have us hold, the involuntary subjection of our bodies to the laws of organic existence. Self-renunciation is as natural to man as it is for birds to use their wings instead of their feet; it is not a meritorious or heroic act; it is simply the necessary condition precedent of genuine human life. This new human life exhibits itself in our animal existence, just as animal life does in matter. Matter is the instrument of animal life, not an obstacle to it; and so our animal life is the instrument of our higher human life and should conform to its behests.

Life, then, is the activity of the animal individuality working in submission to the law of reason. Reason shows man that happiness cannot be obtained by a selfish life, and leaves only one outlet open for him, and that is love. Love is the only legitimate manifestation of life. It is an activity which has for its object the good of others. When it makes its appearance, the meaningless strife of the animal life ceases.

Real love is not the preference of certain persons whose presence gives one pleasure. This, which is ordinarily

called love, is only a wild stock on which true love may be
grafted, and true love does not become possible until man
has given up the pursuit of his own welfare. Then at
last all the juices of his life come to nourish the noble graft,
while the trunk of the old tree, the animal individuality,
pours into it its entire vigor. Love is the preference
which we accord to other beings over ourselves. It is not
a burst of passion, obscuring the reason, but on the contrary no other state of the soul is so rational and luminous,
so calm and joyous; it is the natural condition of children
and the wise. Active love is attainable only for him who
does not place his happiness in his individual life and who
also gives free play to his feeling of good-will toward others.
His well-being depends upon love as that of a plant on light.
He does not ask what he should do but he gives himself up
to that love which is within his reach. He who loves in this
way alone possesses life. Such self-renunciation lifts him
from animal existence in time and space into the regions
of life. The limitations of time and space are incompatible
with the idea of real life. To attain to it man must trust
himself to his wings.

Man's body changes; his states of consciousness are successive and differ from each other; what then is the "I"?
Any child can answer when he says, "I like this; I don't
like that." The "I" is that which likes—which loves. It
is the exclusive relationship of a man's being with the world,
that relation which he brings with him from beyond time
and space. It is said that in his extreme old age, St. John
the apostle had the habit of repeating continually the
words, "Brethen, love one another." His animal life was
nearly gone, absorbed in a new being for which the flesh
was already too narrow. For the man who measures his
life by the growth of his relation of love with the world,
the disappearance at death of the limitations of time and
space is only the mark of a higher degree of light.

My brother, who is dead, acts upon me now more strongly
than he did in life; he even penetrates my being and lifts
me up towards him. How can I say that he is dead? Men
who have renounced their individual happiness never
doubt their immortality. Christ knew that He would
continue to live after His death because He had already
entered into the true life which cannot cease. He lived
even then in the rays of that other centre of life toward
which He was advancing, and He saw them reflected on
those who stood around Him. And this every man who
renounces his own good beholds; he passes in this life into

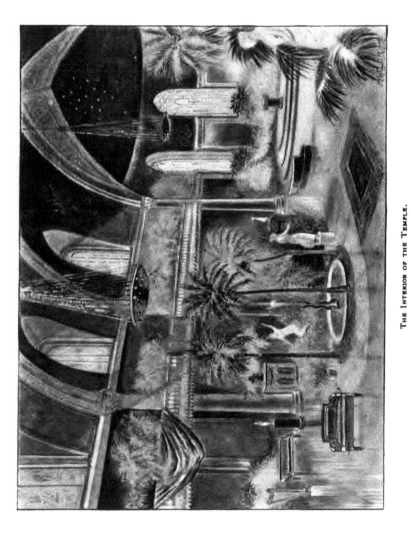

THE INTERIOR OF THE TEMPLE.
(Between Two Worlds, see Chapter I.)

a new relation with the world for which there is no death; on one side he sees the new light, on the other he witnesses its action on his fellows after being refracted through himself; and this experience gives him an immovable faith in the stability, immortality, and eternal growth of life. Faith in immortality cannot be received from another; you cannot convince yourself of it by argument. To have this faith you must have immortality; you must have established with the world in the present life the new relation of love, which the world is no longer wide enough to contain.

The above résumé gives a most inadequate idea of Count Tolstoy's philosophy of life, but it is sufficient to bring out the salient points, to wit, his idea of the failure of man's ordinary life, of the necessity, in the course of nature, of loving self-renunciation, and of the resulting growth in love and the realization of immortality on earth.

"But this is sheer mysticism," is doubtless the first objection. Yes, it assuredly is, but that is no argument against it. Mysticism is nothing but the recognition of the other world as a palpable fact instead of as an abstract theory. All religions had their origin in mysticism, and in so far as they have wandered away from it, just so far have they fallen into formalism. Mysticism is really religion at first hand, such as the faith of General Gordon, who used to say that he believed in the "real presence," meaning, as he explained, the actual manifestation of God in his own soul. It is not becoming for those at least who profess to put their confidence in Him who said "The kingdom of God is within you," to quarrel with the man who finds it there. In short, all Christians should be more or less mystics.

If, then, admitting that the treatise on "Life" is in fact mystical, we compare it with the works of those to whom the name of mystic is usually given, we are at once struck by the remarkable sanity of the Russian author. The practice of exploring the unseen world is often dangerous for those who attempt it, but Count Tolstoy has escaped the vagaries of Boehmen, the visions of Swedenborg, and the hysterical excesses of St. Theresa. And the reason of his freedom from these extravagances is not far to seek. He opens a door into the invisible, but it is not the door of mere contemplation, of quietism, of retirement into self. There is something morbid in the very idea of making deliberate excursions into another sphere. Here lies the mistake of the Christian ascetics, of the Persian Sufis, of the Hindoo Buddhists, and of the Theosophists of to-day. We may well suspect any form of religion which withdraws a man's interests and labors from this world; its corner-stone must be selfishness in spite of any disguises.

Count Tolstoy's door to the mysteries, however, is simply active love for mankind. According to him, preoccupation in working for the happiness of others has a reflex action in the depth of our being which makes us feel eternal life. It is this intensely practical side of his mysticism which preserves its equilibrium. Other mystics have made much of love, but it has almost always been an internal love of the Deity which discouraged action and gave free scope to a diseased imagination. Of all the old mystics the German Tauler bears perhaps the greatest resemblance to Count Tolstoy, and Vaughan refers to his remarkable combination of inward aspiration and outward love and service (Vaughan's "Hours with the Mystics," fifth edition, vol. i, pp. 251, 256). It is noticeable, too, that Swedenborg speaks of offices of charity as the means of conjunction with heaven ("Heaven and Hell," i, 360).

Lawrence Oliphant, who owed much to Swedenborg, professed opinions substantially identical with those of Count Tolstoy, but the final outcome of his theological speculations, with its detailed account of things celestial and terrestrial, makes the simplicity of the latter conspicuous by contrast. Trances and visions may be very edifying to him who indulges in them, but they are very apt to unfit him for leadership of the masses of mankind, for these cannot follow him, and it is best that they should not.

The proper answer for me to make to the member of the Theosophical Society who wishes to convert me to his belief in the seven planets and the astral body and Karma and Devachan is that these things are none of my business. Granted that I am an immortal being, still this life is too short to study eternity in. But when a man comes to me laying stress on my duties here on earth and promising me the proof of the truth of his doctrines in my own consciousness, I can well afford to give him a hearing. Count Tolstoy makes no claim to novelty for his teaching. It is that of Christianity—of the Christianity of the Sermon on the Mount as distinguished from that of the Council of Nicæa. He virtually says to us: "Renounce your selfish ends; love all men—all creatures—and devote your life to them. You will then be conscious of possessing eternal life and for you there will be no death."

No appeal is made to argument, but we are asked to test the theory in our own experience, and this it is possible for us to do, for love is to a certain extent at every one's command. Ruysbroeck, the German mystic, says: "Everything depends on will. A man must will right strongly. Will to have humility and love and they are thine" (Vaughan, vol. i, p. 32). This is entirely consistent with the teaching of Christ, for He says, "A new *commandment* I give unto you, that ye love one another."

THE SPIRITUALIZATION OF EDUCATION IN AMERICA.

BY LILIAN WHITING.

For what need I of book or priest
Or sibyl from the mummied East
When every star is Bethlehem star?
— *Emerson.*

The keynote of the new educational movement may be found in the words of Professor Dewey of the University of Chicago, that "Education is not the preparation for life: it *is* life"; in the words of Josephine P. Locke, that "The human being is before all mathematical data and information. Attitude of mind, sympathy, responsiveness, living interest—these all come first and precede mere learning"; in the words of Col. Francis W. Parker, that "The common school is the central means to preserve and perpetuate the true democracy." From this trio of truths one may well find his point of departure in any attempt to present a synthetic view of the new movement which it is no exaggeration to call the spiritualization of education in America.

What is this new movement? It is development rather than cramming. It is the application of the idea that the child is a human being who comes into this world with a certain definite nature resulting from inherent qualities, and that the true aim and scope of education is to develop these qualities into mental strength and moral power; "to lead," as Dr. Maudsley has well said, "to the continual transference of thoughts and feelings into external actions of a beneficial kind."

Some time about the first of October a letter came to me from Miss Josephine P. Locke, supervisor of drawing in the public schools of Chicago, saying that an exhibition of the art work of the pupils was then made in the Art Institute and inviting me to come out to study and write of it. At that moment nothing seemed more impossible than that I could do this, and I replied to that effect, with sincere regrets that it was so. A week passed by during which I had not consciously thought of the matter when one morning I wakened with an absolute conviction that I must go to Chicago and fulfil as best I might the request which I held to be a privilege and an opportunity. Just what unknown and unrecognized spiritual experiences had brought me to this decision is a question of the occult realm and need not here be discussed. It was, however, so important a factor in the experience that one would indeed "reckon ill" who should leave it out. To myself, it served to transfer the entire trip and subsequent observations to the higher plane of life where we are led as actors in the spiritual drama. "When a god wishes to ride," said Emerson, "every chip and stone will bud and shoot out wingèd feet to carry him." The expression is not too strong. A controlling purpose cuts its own channel through material difficulties, and speedily I—who had thought the journey and its inroads on time an impossible thing—found myself on the delightful Fitchburg route for Chicago where I could at once assert, "I come, I see, I *am* conquered," changing only the tense of the classic tradition.

Two galleries were devoted to the art work of the children from the grammar and primary schools. Prepared to be interested, I was captivated. There was a most remarkable expression of the unfolding and development of the mind of a child. There was evidence that the pupils were awake; that they were beings of vivid perceptions, of keen interests, of latent powers. Here was a drawing which revealed how the child had gone out into Jackson Park and looked around him; that he had discovered for himself architecture, perspective, relation, atmosphere; that objects had a meaning for him; that he was learning to know something about the world in which he lived. Or again, here was a street scene; a bridge, a tree, a bit of landscape, a train of cars, a drawbridge. That children ranging from eight to fifteen could have made some of these drawings seemed incredible. The freedom, the artistic taste, the art of selection and of combination, were all revealed wonderfully.

It is a great mistake to suppose that drawing should be taught only to prospective artists. As well assume that no one should have literary tastes developed and cultivated save those who promise to be poets and novelists. Drawing, like music and literature, is one of the means toward symmetrical development. Like those invaluable "nature studies" of Professor Jackman, it is one of the means to stimulate the imagination, to call into exercise creative ability, to interest the mind, to develop those powers which, in after life, are requisite for any form of achievement.

The first step toward the drawing is the exercise with

colored paper and scissors. Those thousands of pairs of
scissors in the Chicago public schools are not only cutting
pictures in paper, pictures imaginatively grasped from
story, poem, legend, or romance, or evolved from familiar
scenes, but they are cutting a new and finer. future for the
next generation. "The study of nature," says John S.
Clark, of Boston, "should mean coming into spiritual con-
- tact with the inward meaning of nature." The open gate
to this is in the training of art education and the culture
of all the child's faculties by that means. President Baker,
of the University of Colorado, says that while the training
of memory, observation, expression, and reasoning is an
important part of education, it is not all, and he adds: "The
imagination, deductive reasoning, the rich possibilities of
emotional life, the education of the will through ethical
ideas and correct habit—all are to be considered in a scheme
of learning. Ideals must be added to the scientific method."
In this exhibition there were drawings that would have
done credit to any recognized school of design. There
were "illustrated compositions"—where the pupil had
written story or rudimentary essay, with marginal illustrations of his own devising, or with decorative headings
and tail pieces. And again I studied and marvelled over
the scissors-and-paper work, and saw in it how perception,
taste constructive ability, and imagination are developed
by such practice. The eye is trained in color and in form.
What an introduction of idealism into education, vivifying
and uplifting its entire scheme! Here is the germ of the
very transfiguration of life, I reflected.

M. Lavisse, of France, addressing a primary school, exclaimed: "Ah, si je pouvais eveiller dans l'aime d'un seul
enfant quelque sentiment poetique que bienfait!" (Ah,
if I could call forth in a single child a sentiment poetic—
how great a thing!) Evidently some one was arousing a
sentiment poetique in the children of the Chicago schools.
And who? The supervisor of drawing, Josephine C. Locke.
A study of methods and results led to questioning Miss
Locke regarding her ideals of education.

"The ultimate ideals," she replied, "are faith, hope, and
love; these are the ultimate and final ideals. They are
not to be intellectually acquired, nor physically developed,
but spiritually attained; and their attainment is character.
Training in morals may or may not include them; discipline
of the will may or may not; but these ideals felt in the heart
include all things. The letter killeth, but the spirit giveth
life. Shall not these ideals have place in a scheme of learn-

ing? With the novel, the drama, and with religion pleading for idealism, education must at least suggest it."

The supervisor of drawing in the public schools of Chicago would be the first to deprecate any personal allusion. Her work is for the work's sake, for art's sake, for the sake of the child and all its future usefulness and happiness; yet it is impossible to observe a great work involving such countless details, pursued with such splendid energy, such self-forgetting zeal, such generous and noble purpose—a work constantly relating itself to the supreme ideals of life—without realizing the potency of such service as that of Miss Locke. Her training is based on her conviction that imagination is the spiritual faculty; that the power to feel and express the beautiful is the dividing line between a machine and a man.

"This form study and drawing," she says, "has a larger significance than the training of hand or eye, or the recording or describing of data, valuable as these are. It means the development of the sympathetic nature of the child, the preservation of him as a many-sided human being, the formation of his taste, and the uplifting of his ideals."

Such work, showing how children will enter into the very spirit of their subjects, illustrating poem or story read by the teacher—the "Chinese moon-story," for instance, set forth by a boy whose men really looked like Chinamen and whose architectural work was that of a Chinese pagoda; or the legend of young Lochinvar shown by the ardent lover bearing his bride away on a bicycle; or a composition about Napoleon presenting a very clever pen-and-ink sketch of the emperor; all these and a thousand others that could be named testify to the imaginative range and the creative power innate in the child, and which can be evolved, or so stunted as to practically disappear.

This brings us face to face with the question, Is imaginative development desirable in public-school education? Is the child to be crammed and stuffed with facts, with dates, with records, that make his mental possessions a mass of "unrelated fragments," as Clarence Cook wittily termed the Cesnola statues, or shall this education be something human, practical, elevating, and responsive? Shall learning be related to life? Shall the child be fitted for that higher world which the advance of humanity is creating? Paul Desjardins voices the homage of the state to the new idealism. There are new views of the university of the world, he says: of poetry, of religion, of virtue, of kindness, of worth. "Think it over," he adds; "these are the objects on which our new generation is fixing its thoughts and trying to awaken yours."

The new education must comprise the spirituality of life as its direct aim and ultimate effect. We must revise our ideals as to what constitutes success. The term must not be held up as synonymous with either a great fortune or a great fame. It must be taught that success lies in the quality of personal life; that to be just, considerate, courteous, and helpful to others is success; that to have those intellectual and spiritual resources which feed the mind and sustain the soul in whatever vicissitudes of fortune may occur, is success; that to be able to so command all the forces of one's nature as to be serene, confident, and joyful in all the undertakings and in all the varied circumstances of life, is success. The pupil who comes from our public schools with the foundation of convictions like these has indeed received a true education. The child is made up of physical, intellectual, and spiritual potentialties: education is that process which should develop these in the sense of true and symmetrical values of sane living. Emerson has well said that our tokens of love are, for the most part, barbarous. Our ideals of success are not less so. Our national future depends on a complete revision and regeneration of our ideals of success. "Be great enough to fail," exclaims a heavenly voice now ringing in the air—that of the prophet and seer, Professor George D. Herron. The spectacular ideal of place and power is a pernicious element in the life of to-day. The only true success lies in social service. The Christ-ideal is the only safe social ideal. Only as education inculcates in the pupil the ideal that man is to be a coworker with God, is that education worthy, and its results to be desired.

Instead, what have we seen? A false system of pedagogy which relied on the unwholesome stimulus of competition. The pupil was to learn—not for learning's sake, for life's sake, but to "get ahead" of some other pupil, to rank first, to carry off a prize. Children are trained in the morbid atmosphere of self-consciousness. Under such training nervous energy is diverted to pernicious ends. The danger is that the pupil *learns* so much that he *knows* nothing. There is a perpetual straining after effect, and service degenerates into a spectacle.

That wise and good prelate, Bishop Spalding, has recently said:

For the education of men, which is the highest human work, one heroic, loving, and illumined soul is worth more than all the money endowments. How poor are they who have only money to give.

Imagination is the faculty that creates for us true ideals of life, and gives us the wingéd power for their realization. Imagination must not be confounded with mere fancies, phantoms, and fantasies. It is the working factor of practical life. The great merchant whose ships are on the seas, whose power is a controlling one in commerce; the astronomer, turning his glass on the starry firmament; the editor of the great daily paper; the college president; the manager and executive head of a great mechanical enterprise—each and all must be men of imagination. The presence or the absence of that faculty is what differentiates the man of affairs from the man of no affairs at all; is what distinguishes the high ability that achieves something from the inane, the incompetent, or the inefficient that achieves nothing.

Now to break down what Miss Locke well designates as the "Bastileism" of our public schools, what are the forces to use? The culture of the imagination; *the substitution of the quality of life for the quantity of acquirement*, as the ultimate ideal to be held. In these two propositions we hold the key to the spiritualization of education in our country. It is to art and to the spirituality of the ideal that we must look for the potent aid—art, in the manifold manifestations of music, drawing, modelling, writing, and speaking: the spiritual ideal in its application to the entire quality of daily life.

The movement in Chicago is more or less repeated or reflected in several other cities; but as it was there that the opportunity was given me to study it, the illustrations can best be drawn from the methods in use in that city. Boston is signally aided by the Public School Art League which is making the schoolrooms beautiful in color and filling them with pictures and casts. This stimulates love of the beautiful and the heroic; it offers ideals to people the imagination; it radiates the glow of poetry and romance over life. Charm and interest are the fit furnishings for a school room.

Professor Dewey of the University of Chicago defines imagination as the power by means of which are carried on all educational activities, and he adds:

The dawn of the imagination in a child marks the first great epoch in his life. It is the dawn of the true self-consciousness, and marks the passage from merely mechanical to free and intelligent activities. This dawn of imagination in the child, this beginning of spontaneous imagery (play), as distinct from the carrying out of the physical activity, is the first great step in the child's life. It means that the child is no longer at the mercy of an immediate suggestion. About the same time there is developed the sense of ownership, the power of going back in time, of anticipation, and of simple generalization, causation, and reasoning.

Imagination is interpretation always. No one can help another unless he can think himself, for a moment, into the other's place.

The art instruction in the public schools of Chicago, as developed and led by Miss Locke, will prove the initiation of a new movement everywhere. Her training is based on this truth: "Imagination is the spiritual faculty." Developing this brings out the power to feel and to express the beautiful which, as Miss Locke well says, is

the dividing line between a machine and a man. Power to feel is insight, is conviction to intelligence. To conserve this power to feel which in childhood is so buoyant, while teaching how to think, is primarily the mission of art in the common schools. Thus form-study and drawing, or elementary art, has a larger significance than the training of hand and eye or the recording and describing of data, valuable as these are; it means the development of the sympathetic nature of the child, the preservation of him as a many-sided human being, the formation of his taste, and the uplifting of his ideals.

Writing and language are equally means of expression with drawing, but it is not in this that their highest value consists, but in the ideas they express, the thought they convey, and their application to each other.

A common-school course of study must provide for the needs of intelligent labor, though not necessarily for the training of educated or skilled labor — a something that can be left with safety to the care of the high and special school.

The question is, How can the human being be preserved and yet be instructed in those elementary principles that belong to literature, art, science, and mechanics? It is true technical training as such cannot be given, nor technical ideals realized; but the habit of mind, the power of observation, the ability to read and judge of form, to appreciate size, proportion, and harmony, to be interested in objects and to enjoy nature — these are the things that a course of study can profitably encourage.

Again Miss Locke says:

A feeling for beauty means a perception of the harmonies of life. It is the mission of art to preserve and awaken the latent instinct of childhood. The fulness and the joy of life largely depend upon correspondence to environment, upon response of the child or individual to his surroundings. Modern education in restoring the myth, the legend and the fairy tale, recognizes as fundamental the old Greek thought concerning nature as intelligent and animate. Myth, legend, and fairy tale have always been the foster mother of art, for these kindle a sympathy with nature. Without sympathy and without nature there is no art. . . .

The fact that machinery dominates American life more than in any other country seems to indicate that art instruction and education in general in this country must arrange itself on a new basis. Of the sixty million of the horse-power of steam used on all the earth, the United States consumes a third, or an equivalent to the labor of two hundred and fifty millions of men. This it is that makes us one third richer than England and twice as rich as France. With these riches we buy our technical skill. We do not produce it as European nations do; we buy it and are likely to continue to buy it for another generation. Between morn and eve on a Minnesota farm, a machine will bind and cut twenty-four acres of wheat twentyfold quicker than the farmer could do it without mechanical aid. The labor thus freed flees to the city only to find itself again cornered by the monster machinery. The sweat shop, the sewing machine, the steam factory, all stand ready to devour unintelligent labor. From this it is evident that training in mathematical accuracy, automatic habits, and exactness of detail is not the most helpful education for an American, since in all these points machinery can excel him. The message of machinery is very clear. It says: "Look out how you import European methods and practices; look out how you spend labor on the exact, the imitative, and the mechanical. Unless you recognize the beautiful in what you do, unless you incorporate the art element into your work, I, with my thousand hands to your one, will destroy both you and it."

Professor Jackman of the Normal School in Chicago has originated a system of "nature study" which brings the child into swift and sympathetic response to the world in which he lives. Professor Tomlins, the famous musician and orchestral conductor, is giving a musical training to the children of the public schools that is fulfilling the prophecy of Wagner, when he says: "The future of music is that it shall come down in harmony and love and helpfulness to those who toil in the fields, to the worker, that there shall be fragrance in the life of him who only digs."

The technical outline of the art instruction in the Chicago public schools, with its refreshing contrast to the old Kensington and Walter Smith system, is thus indicated for the first five grades:

1. Story telling with the scissors, with charcoal, or with pencil; much of this work is done in connection with the reading lesson.

2. Nature study; drawing of whole plants, of branches and sprays, showing principles of growth and movement.

3. Form study, expressed by both paper cutting and drawing, based on the geometric type solids.

4. Block building and imagination; the children build with their blocks, weave a story about them, and then draw the same.

5. Figure sketching; children posing for one another.

6. Group work; pictoral drawing in light and shade from the geometric solids.

7. Still life; books, fans, and vases are combined into groups as well as studied separately.

8. Illustration of literature; it may be a poem or song or history or science lesson; this may be done with pen and ink or with pencil.

So far as possible the same subjects are being continually

studied under fresh conditions. The technical elements have been united to the spontaneous; imaginative and artistic composition is practised and sought for in every exercise. The ugly is simply not recognized; even in the most elementary exercise the pleasing is made an important point to be observed. The impressional methods are followed as promotive of more individuality on the part of the children and as capable of developing more poetic feeling. Froebel defined the world of art as the "visible revelation and expression of the invisible spirit of man." Here we have the clew to the spiritualization of education. The invisible spirit expresses itself in a visible revelation. Education is seen to be this expression—an affair of conduct, of character, rather than of mere knowledge. "Get the quality of life right," said Phillips Brooks, "and an eternity of living in the light of God will take care of the quantity."

The convictions regarding the new education have crystallized into the following expression from Miss Locke:

1. Synthesis is more than analysis; present first the synthetic side.
2. Thought is before the form; work for the thought first.
3. Imagination includes memory; place it first.
4. The mass is more important than its details; locate size and position first.
5. Surface includes outline; practise the rendering of surface side by side with outline.
6. Direction is more than line; seek for the general direction first.
7. It is feeling that vitalizes; feeling is more than result; preserve feeling first, last, and always.
8. Expression by the free hand must precede all use of instruments.
9. Characterization, not technical accuracy, must be the basis of criticism.
10. Work to give the child confidence in himself, to put him in possession of his own natural powers.

This beautiful condensation fitly presents the spirit of the advance movement.

No reference to the present work in Chicago could be adequate that did not fitly present the determining contribution of the philosophic thought of Col. Francis W. Parker. To his championship of the natural sciences and history as important factors in the work of the primary grades, their introduction into the primary schools is due; to his study regarding true self-government is due the application of the principles of Delsarte, in the reaction of pantomimic expression on the mind, to the applied curriculum of moral training. Colonel Parker is the great psychologist among educators. His intellectual breadth, his profound philosophic study, and his remarkable power of translating ideal views into practical application, are potent factors in the present development of pedagogic thought. The phases of it shown in Chicago are as important in any comprehensive view of the forces of the age as is the study of social conditions and of scientific progress.

"The child is a soul seeking manifestation," says Miss Locke; "the child is an imaginative being hovering in regions of poetic rhythm; the child is a reservoir of feeling and instinct." Education is the province of the poet and the painter, of the saint and the seer. Beauty and love are its handmaids; sight and service are its aims. The measure of right and truth and beauty is the measure of that true education whose results are known in the spiritualization of human life.

THE UTOPIA OF SIR THOMAS MORE.

BY B. O. FLOWER.

PART I.

Long before Professor Drummond had elucidated the great evolutionary truth that the ascent of man was marked by the triumph of altruistic over egoistic sentiment,* Sir Thomas More's keen insight and intellectual penetration enabled him to see that the highway upon which humanity must pass to secure progress, felicity and true civilization must be other than the savage struggle for self alone which had controlled man in the past, when the animal overmastered the spiritual in governmental as well as individual life. The central idea of "Utopia" is the triumph of altruism over egoism. That Sir Thomas More had to conform, in a way, to the dominant ideas of his age in order to be taken with any degree of seriousness—as, for example, when he makes the accomplishment of universal prosperity and happiness flow from the absolutism of King Utopus—is not surprising, as we shall presently see.

Though the philosopher lived in an essentially savage age, in which the brutal theory that might made right was accepted almost as a truism, and which was permeated by selfishness, intolerance and heartless disregard for the weak and unfortunate, he caught luminous glimpses of felicity to be attained through the abolition of class privileges and the establishment of just conditions. In conceiving that human happiness and national prosperity could best be promoted by the application of the Golden Rule, Sir Thomas More was as wise as he was sympathetic, as scientific as he was humane, and was in perfect accord with the best thought and latest discoveries and deductions of enlightened science. This great scientific truth was grasped by More through his rare prophetic or intuitional power, in a selfish, brutal and unscientific age. The central idea emphasized in "Utopia" contains the redemptive potentiality for human society, however crude or wide of the mark the work may be in some of the details of government. [When we bear in mind the condi-

* "The Ascent of Man," by Henry Drummond, F. R. S.

tions of the civilization of Europe in the fifteenth and
sixteenth centuries, and also remember the limitations under
which the English philosopher necessarily labored in order
to make his work appeal to his young sovereign, we shall
appreciate how far in advance of his age was this great
prophet of a higher civilization, and shall also understand
why at times he halted and in a degree conformed to the
monarchical ideas and the intellectual limitations as well
as the tyranny of conventionalism which marked his time.
Yet, notwithstanding these limitations, "Utopia" was in
spirit so true to the best impulses of man, so in general alignment with the then undreamed-of evolutionary processes
of life and society, that it has not only proved an inspiration to social reformers and humanitarians from his century
to the present time, but to-day there are thousands where
heretofore there were tens who advocate the central ideas
he advanced as the true solution of the problem of human
society; and, as I have pointed out, they are borne out
by the theory of evolution, which was at first supposed to
be directly opposed to the altruistic conception.

On the threshold of our examination it will also be interesting to note the fact that for generations and perhaps
centuries before Sir Thomas More wrote "Utopia" there had
existed in the Western World a government which had abolished poverty. This unique civilization flourished in what
is known to-day as Peru, and although less complex, and in
many respects less advanced than the most enlightened
European nations of the age of More, it was incomparably
in advance of the nations which surrounded the Land of the
Incas, as Peru was commonly termed. The concern which
this Western civilization exhibited for the welfare of its
children and the many noble characteristics of its government, gave it a prestige, power and glory, despite its
crudities and objectionable features, which was not approached by any sister nation, and in various respects it
surpassed the Christian nations of Europe of that age.
It is true that this civilization went down before the merciless sword of the Spaniard, precisely as Christian
Rome went down before the barbarians of the North, or as
Poland succumbed to the savage fury of Russia. But
the facts which have come to us from Spanish historians
are a revelation in that they show in a marked manner what
was actually accomplished by a simple people in an age
when the dream of enlightened coöperation was not yet
born, and when the idea of the divine right of rulers still
held the human mind in thrall.

This strange and ancient civilization, in some respects so wise and considerate, was, as one would naturally expect in a rude age, marred by many blemishes. Thus, for example, in matters of religion the ancient Peruvians, like the Egyptians of old, believed their first rulers were children of the sun. They were very dogmatic in their theological views, and, like all dogmatic religionists, showed scant toleration to those who, however sincere, differed from them. Thus from the fragmentary records which have come to us, we are led to infer that the soul-withering spirit of persecution, which is so thoroughly antagonistic to spiritual growth or intellectual advancement, was present in this ancient civilization, although in justice to the Incas it is fair to say that even the records of their conquerors do not indicate that they were so intolerant as the Christian Spaniards of the fifteenth and sixteenth centuries. A most interesting glimpse of this peculiar civilization, as gathered from the most trustworthy sources, is given in the following words by Clements Markham in an admirable history of Peru*:

In many respects Peru under the Incas resembled the "Utopia" of Sir Thomas More. . . . Punishments for crimes were severe and inexorably inflicted. Not a spot of cultivable land was neglected. Towns and villages were built on rocky hills, cemeteries were in deserts or in the sides of barren cliffs, in order that no land might be wasted. Dry wastes were irrigated, and terraces were constructed, sometimes a hundred deep, by the sides of mountains. The results were commensurate with the thought and skill expended. . . . Provision was made to supply all classes of the people with everything they required that was not produced by themselves, through a system of colonies or mitimæs. Inhabitants of a populous district were removed to a less crowded one, the comfort of all classes was promoted by exchange of products, waste places were made fertile, and political objects were also secured. . . . Under the Inca system all who could work were obliged to work, all lived in comfort, and there was ample provision for the aged, for young and children, and for the sick. Tillers of the ground and shepherds received the share of produce called Huaccha, and the surplus went to the mitimæs in exchange for other products. All other workers were maintained from the share called Inca, including the sovereign and his officers and the army. . . . So perfect was the Inca organization that it continued to work efficiently, and almost mechanically, for some time after the guiding heads had been struck down. The Spanish conquerors found that when they marched through the districts, sacking houses and destroying growing crops, the local officers kept a careful record of the injury done. The accounts were then examined and checked, and if one district had lost more than another, those that had suffered less made up part of the share called Inca, so that the burden might be shared equally by all. Under such a system there could be no want, for thought was taken for the nourishment and comfort of every creature. There was hard work, while provision was made not

---

* "History of Peru," by Clements R. Markham, F. R. S., F. A. S.

only for rest but also for recreation. The dreams of socialists were made a reality in the system which grew up and flourished under the rule of the Incas.

Henry Austin, in his thoughtful work entitled "A Story of Government," observes that *"The Spanish historians record with grave amazement that they had discovered a miraculous land in which there was no such thing as a poor or discontented man, in which everybody worked, from the emperor down, a reasonable length of time at tasks fitted to their strength and their ability;* in which the problem of mere living, as it confronts us moderns, in our so-called civilized cities, has been satisfactorily settled, in which the average of human happiness was large and increasing."

The facts disclosed by the civilization of ancient Peru have a very special interest and value in view of the contemptuous sneers of superficial thinkers who, with grave assumptions of superior wisdom, never tire of asserting that such a condition as Sir Thomas More depicts could never exist; in reality, it did exist under conditions which were strikingly similar to the popular ideals in regard to rulership, the rights of classes, and the claims of theology which marked the England of Sir Thomas More, as well as other European nations of that age, and from what we can gather from historians, who could not be accused of being partial to the western civilization which Spanish soldiers so ruthlessly and brutally destroyed, *a condition of peace, prosperity, and fraternity prevailed in ancient Peru unknown to any nation of Europe contemporaneous with the supremacy of the government of the Incas.*

With the recent scientific conceptions as to the ascent of man and the suggestive history of the ancient Peruvians in mind, we will now consider the social vision of England's great philosopher and statesman.

A great many of the reforms which Sir Thomas More described as being practised by the Utopians, and which were regarded as ideal, visionary and absurd in his time, and for many generations after his death, are now coming into successful operation. Take, for example, universal or compulsory education, such as prevails at present in so many states of our republic; this was foreshadowed by More, as we are told that in Utopia every child received a good education, and thus ignorance—the great cause of lawlessness and wretchedness—was banished. Again, the general demand for industrial education, which is gaining such favor among thoughtful and enlightened men and women, prevailed in this island country. On this point we are told that

"Husbandry is a science common to them all in general, both men and women, wherein they be all expert and cunning, being instructed from their youth, partly in their schools and partly in the country nigh unto the city, brought up, as it were, in playing, not only beholding the use of it, but also practising it. Besides husbandry everyone learned some trade or science as his own special craft, such as cloth-working in wool, flax or cotton, or the smith's craft, or the carpenter's trade."

We are further told that "the child is permitted to select the trade or science he desires to master," and "if he wishes to perfect himself in two crafts, he is permitted to do so."

In Sir Thomas More's day the College of Physicians was founded in London, but the treatment of the sick was crude and often barbarous, and our modern methods would have been deemed visionary indeed. Yet the low ideals and limited conceptions of his age did not prevent the author of "Utopia" from describing an enlightened way of treating the sick, which our tortoise-like civilization is gradually acting upon. Thus, we are told that

"First, and chiefly, respect is had to the sick that be carried in the hospitals, for in the circuit of the city, a little without the walls, they have four hospitals, so large and ample that they may seem four little towns, made thus commodious that the sick may have a generous allowance of room amid charming surroundings. These hospitals be so well appointed and with all things necessary to health so furnished, and moreover they have so diligent attention through continued presence of skilful physicians, that though no man be sent hither against his will, yet, notwithstanding, there is no sick person in all the city that had not rather lie there than at home in his own house.

The persistent demand on the part of organized labor for a ten- or eight-hour work-day was anticipated by Sir Thomas More, for in Utopia men worked but six hours a day, and are therefore "not wearied from early in the morning to late in the evening with continual work like laboring and toiling beasts." After the six hours which was given daily to toil each person was free to enjoy and improve himself. Public lectures of various kinds, musical entertainments, and halls where games were played were provided for those who desired to take advantage of these pursuits for self-improvement or wholesome recreation. "For it was held by the Utopians that the time which could be spared from the necessary occupations and affairs of the Commonwealth the citizens should enjoy in freedom for herein they suppose the felicity of life to consist." The six hours a day we are assured is ample for the performance of all necessary work. Indeed, we are told that "That small time is not only enough, but too much for the store and abundance of all things that be requisite either for the necessities or commodities of life," and by way of explanation the author continues: "The which thing you also shall perceive if you consider how great a part of the people in other countries live idle." In Utopia all able-bodied men and women perform a modicum of labor and all enjoy ample time for self-culture, for recreation, and for following any line of thought they may fancy. Agriculture, husbandry, and allied pursuits are esteemed very highly throughout the island. Poultry-raising is carried on very extensively by means of incubators, for we are told that "they bring up a multitude of poultry by a marvellous process, for the hens do not set upon the eggs, but by keeping them in a certain equal heat they bring life into them."

In the sixteenth century the soldiers were considered among the most honorable of men; war was esteemed more than legitmate; it was the pastime of kings, princes, popes, and mighty lords, and received the sanction of conventionalism; on the other hand, husbandry and other noble pursuits which added to the wealth, happiness, and comfort of society were looked down upon with supreme contempt. Sir Thomas More appreciated most keenly that war was one of the most conspicuous survivals of the savage in society and that the contempt for productive and ennobling trades and callings owed its source to false ideals and base conceptions of the true grandeur of nations; hence he tells us that the Utopians "detest and abhor war" as "a thing very beastly," that "they count nothing so much against glory as glory gathered in war," and though both men and women are drilled to a limited extent in the manual of arms that they may defend their fair domain in case of invasion, they discourage war, and when possible avoid the useless and criminal shedding of human blood.

And then, doubtless foreseeing the objections which would be advanced to the peace policy of the Utopians by superficial persons, who would at once exclaim that such a policy would expose a government to wrongs committed against it without the nation being able to redress its wrongs, our author states that when wrongs are perpetrated even against any friendly nation, the Utopians adopt a more excellent and enlightened method of punishment, provided the lives of the Utopians and their allies have not been sacrificed. In cases where other nations "by cunning or guile defraud" the Utopians, or "when violence be done to their bodies, they wreak their anger by abstaining from trading or carrying on any friendly relations with the offending nation, until satisfaction or restitution is made."

If the lives of any Utopians have been sacrificed, the

nation is quick to resent it, for the citizenship of this country is regarded as a very sacred trust, to be protected at
all hazards, even by war if that be necessary; but in such
cases we are told, every effort possible is made to prevent
the wholesale slaughter of life, even the lives of their
foes, for "they be not only sorry but also ashamed to achieve
a victory with bloodshed, counting it great folly to buy
precious wares too dear, but they rejoice if they vanquish
their enemies by craft," and for that act they make a
general triumph, "and conceiving the matter to be manfully
handled they set up a pillar of stone in the place where they
have vanquished their enemies in token of victory, for
they glory and boast that they have played the man indeed,
because they have overcome as no other living creation but
man could overcome, that is to say by the might of wit,
for with bodily strength, bears, lions, boars, wolves, dogs
and other wild beasts do fight, and as the most part of them
do surpass man in strength and fierce courage."

We further learn that it is a settled policy with the
Utopians to kill as few men as possible in the event of war,
and to visit their vengeance upon those who cause the
war rather than upon the helpless persons who are so recklessly hurried to death by their rulers; hence they offer
enormous rewards to any man who will slay the prince or
the king of the people who war against them, and also rich
rewards for the life of all the kings or princes or counsellors
who are directly responsible for the appeal to brute force.
As may be supposed this procedure works most effectively
in deterring warlike rulers from picking a quarrel with the
Utopians.

The Utopians, as we have seen, "detest war and count
nothing so much against glory as glory gotten in war."
These words, written for the eyes of a young king who had
already squandered vast sums in reckless and disgraceful
warfare, and penned at a time when some of the nations
of Christendom were perpetually engaged in war, reveal
the prophet soul who beheld a brighter and more humane
age in the future, when the true grandeur of nations would
be held to consist in something nobler than wholesale murder. And these words remind us of the following noble
utterance of our illustrious statesman, Charles Sumner:

But war crushes with bloody heel all beneficence, all happiness, all
justice, all that is God like in man — suspending every commandment
of the Decalogue, setting at naught every principle of the gospel, and
silencing all law, human as well as divine, except only that impious
code of its own, the laws of war. . . . And now, if it be asked why, in
considering the true grandeur of nations, I dwell thus singly and exclu-

sively on war, it is because war is utterly and irreconcilably inconsistent with true greatness. Thus far man has worshipped in military glory a phantom idol, compared with which the colossal images of ancient Babylon or modern Hindostan are but toys; but we, in this favored land of freedom, in this blessed day of light, are among the idolaters. It is not enough to be free. There must be peace which cannot fail, and other nations must share the great possession. For this good must we labor, bearing ever in mind two special objects, complements of each other: First, the arbitrament of war must end; and, secondly disarmament must begin.

Casting our eyes over the history of nations, with horror we discern the succession of murderous slaughters by which their progress is marked. Even as the hunter follows the wild beast to his lair by the drops of blood on the ground, so we follow Man, faint, weary staggering with wounds, through the Black Forest of the past, which he has reddened with his gore. Oh, let it not be in the future ages as in those we now contemplate! Let the grandeur of man be discerned, not in bloody victory or ravenous conquest, but in the blessings he has secured, in the good he has accomplished, in the triumphs of justice and beneficence, in the establishment of perpetual peace! . . . To this great work let me summon you. That Future, which filled the lofty vision of sages and bards in Greece and Rome, which was foretold by prophets and heralded by evangelists, when man, in happy isles, or in a new paradise, shall confess the loveliness of peace, may you secure, if not for yourselves, at least for your children! *Believe* that you can do it, and you *can* do it. The true Golden Age is before, not behind. If man has once been driven from paradise, while an angel with flaming sword forbade his return, there is another paradise, even on earth, which he may make for himself, by the cultivation of knowledge, religion, and the kindly virtues of life; where the confusion of tongues shall be dissolved in the union of hearts, and joyous nature borrowing prolific charms from prevailing harmony, shall spread her lap with unimagined bounty, and there shall be perpetual jocund spring, and sweet strains borne on "the odoriferous wing of gentle gales," through valleys of delight more pleasant than the Vale of Tempe, richer than the Garden of the Hesperides, with no dragon to guard its golden fruit.

(*To be continued.*)

BETWEEN TWO WORLDS.*

BY MRS. CALVIN KRYDER REIFSNIDER.

CHAPTER I.

Upon the southwest corner of a certain street in a certain city in a certain country, a certain number of years ago, stood a certain stone building which would give the beholder a certain conviction that it had been built for a certain purpose and was then occupied for a certain other very decidedly different purpose. Indeed there could be no mistake that this very building had been erected and dedicated to the worship of God by some certain devout apostles of some certain creed, for over the archway of the main entrance were the words, "The Lord is in His Holy Temple."

There were ample grounds about it, showing that at the time of the erection land in this city had not been so valuable as at the time our story opens, nor could the owners then have dreamed of its prospective value, else they would not have parted from it at the time they did. But their flock had grown into a vast and wealthy congregation and they had sold at public auction this Holy Temple to the highest bidder, believing they could take their Lord along with them and establish Him in a location more suitable to their increased wealth and influence. Although the organ was the very best in the city it was announced that it would be sold in the building, the bell in the belfry, all just as it was, and the auctioneer cried out, "going, going, gone," at a round sum, the purchaser proving to be a strange, whitehaired man who might be a priest, a layman, a missionary or a theatre manager. Nobody knew, nobody cared—because he had every dollar ready to pay cash down for his purchase. He was a shrewd one, it seemed, for he required abstracts down to the government title. True, some inquiring minds speculated upon the object of the purchase, but when the sale was perfected the purchaser gave such persons to understand that he had bought without stipulation as to its use or occupation, and that said deed of sale and purchase gave him the privilege of using it as he chose.

As time passed on curiosity died out and the grant-
ors had their minds engrossed in the planning and
erection of something worthy the tenets of their faith,
to all of which the present owner of the Temple was
oblivious, as if he had never heard of one of them.
But he was not idle. The pews were removed, the carpets
were taken up, and the beautiful hard polished wood of the
pews was formed into an elegant floor. The carpets in
rooms on either side of the entrance were similarly removed
and polished hardwood floors replaced them. And the
morning sun poured his beams through the stained glass
windows into the bare, forsaken Temple. Below was a
large basement where the Sabbath school had once met.
It was similarly robbed of its long wooden seats and the
walls were freshly painted by workmen who seemed to be
foreign and to understand that they were well paid to do a
thing silently, thoroughly and speedily. New heating
apparatus was put in and electric lights were added to the
gas-fixtures.

When all was in readiness drays stopped at the door
and box after box, huge in dimensions and heavy in weight,
was delivered. Perhaps no work ever was done so noiselessly before. Perhaps the workmen were superstitious
in thus erasing from the Temple all traces of the original
purpose of its construction. The instigator of the change was
there when they arose from their couches in the gallery and
ate their breakfast which had been sent they knew not from
whence, but only that it was good; and then he stayed,
silently moving here and there, opening this box, directing
the position of that, all of which was done without marring
the polished floor. If their curiosity was aroused as to
what those boxes contained they must have suffered much
until it was gratified, for they dared not ask.

One morning they were ordered to open the boxes in the
east room, and when they had done so they were amazed
to see that they contained only large handsome French plate
glass mirrors, one of which they were ordered to place on
each of the four walls. Then they were directed to the
west room where the walls were adorned in similar manner. Going thence to the main building they opened all
the boxes; mirrors, statuary, oriental rugs and rich hangings of purple, scarlet, blue, white and gold, and tables
of onyx and richly carved woods were taken therefrom.
Here they worked until the whole place was transformed
into a dream under the owner's silent guidance. His handsome face framed in its snowy hair might have proclaimed

him to a superstitious mind an *Eros* creating an enchanted palace with a holy shrine for some ideal goddess. Especially did this seem true when they had finished decorating the pulpit. There was something priestly and grand about it. Indeed never before had the interior of this building looked so like a temple dedicated to the great God of Love.

On either side of the pulpit were large airy rooms built for studies, and these were alike adorned with mirrors. cabinets, tables, couches and easy chairs. The railing of the gallery had all been repolished. The arched dome was changed to heavenly blue with golden stars and angel faces gleaming through the misty clouds above the chancel. Strewn here and there were statues and tables; looking down from the gallery into the auditorium the whole took on a bewildering, real, yet unreal, appearance. Silence and solitude in their most attractive forms were here. The tumultuous world seemed no more; its noise, its bustle, its hurry-scurry, its street noises and street cries were all gone, shut out by the massive walls; but there was a real presence here—a possibility of something never seen or felt before; a great Spirit seemed to breathe peace upon the place.

As the workmen took their leave, out through the main door whose archway was guarded by heavy iron gates with bolts and bars, they felt that they had taken part in preparing a holy place; but what new sect or creed would occupy that place was unknown to them, nor did they remain in the city to discover, but were apparently bent upon leaving it by the very first steamship; and thus shut out from the world it was hardly possible that curious eyes would ever again see those beauties. Fountains plashing merrily like dropping pearls kept time to the soft music of sweet-toned music boxes among rich palms and plants and vines and flowers, which were brought in by florists and placed where the owner directed them, until the whole place breathed the fragrance of their exuding love and life. Then he stood with bare head in the fading light and pronounced it finished for its purpose.

CHAPTER II.

He turned on the electric light when the shadows had fallen too deep for him to survey his surroundings, and the effect was more fairylike and bewildering than before. It was autumn and growing chill outside. Had he not once or twice consulted his watch one might have deemed him utterly indifferent as to time, but this one act proclaimed him a real, living man, and not some enchanted being strolling here among the beautiful things he had strewn with such prodigality about him. The soft, measured step, his hands folded behind him, indicated no abstraction. He was very sensible of his surroundings, for ever and anon he paused and bent his head above a flower as if to inhale its fragrance. But surely he was waiting for somebody! The thick walls shut out sound completely but at last he put on his hat and approached the door, nor did he remain long outside. He returned accompanied by two women and a man. They laid off their wraps in one of the ante rooms and then followed him into the main building. An exclamation of surprised delight fell involuntarily from their lips as the view burst upon them, for the Temple was of no mean proportions and was worthy its name from base to dome.

"Oh father! are we really going to live in this lovely place?"

"Yes, my child. I am happy if it pleases you as it does me."

"Father, it is like a dream!"

As the girl strolled down the long avenue of palms and statues she seemed one of them just awakened to sentient life. She ascended the pulpit, with its rich hangings, and stood silently gazing down the long vista. Raising his eyes her father looked upon her, and never had her beauty struck him so forcibly as now. In attitude and aspect she was a goddess or a saint.

They were led to the organ gallery, whence they got a new view of the scene beneath, which lay like an enchanted sea whose waters had yielded up her treasures and then silently sunk back into earth again.

Suddenly a long, sweet, full tone trembled upon the silence as if it would fain express its wondrous joy. It was the grand old diapason of the organ which Ruby struck. As it floated and died away the father quoted:

> " Through all the compass of the notes it ran,
> The diapason closing full in man."

Descending arm in arm, followed by the elder couple, they entered the boudoir on the east.

"Ah, father! Here I could never wear a cloud on my face without seeing how it disfigured me," said Ruby, alluding to the mirrors.

"No, but with their aid can we learn to see ourselves as others see us?"

"I do not know, father, and yet,—I feel secure in the thought that you see me as I am; and that I see you only to love you more each day. How white you grow! Really your hand is almost transparent."

They stood before one of the mirrors and others reflected them full length on every side. Beside an ordinary person the father would have appeared deadly pale; but the pure dazzling whiteness of his daughter's face and brow, the alabaster white hands in which she clasped his own, made him appear only as he was. Standing here together she seemed intently studying their reflected faces, and her golden head beside his of silver looked like sunlight upon the snow. The fresh young face, mobile and intense, with its starry eyes, saw something more beautiful in the one beside it—the spirit rising up, rejecting, day by day, the material body; and never, oh never, had it said so plainly to her, Soon you will stand here alone!

"Of what are you thinking, my child?"

"How spiritual your face has grown! How almost entirely it has thrown off all human imperfection! And a thought occured to me, father, that my great enemy is very near at hand."

"Ah, child, can I never teach you that death means life, and life death? It is nothing to die, only a change, so that the material eye no longer beholds us. Death is resurrection, child. Our spirits are prisoners here in the material bodies which serve as prison walls. Death, our best friend, unbars the door."

"Father, could I always keep the grand idea with me, could I live and do my duty, when these material eyes could no longer see you?" she said trembling.

"Hast thou seen thy God, save in His blessings, in this faint reflection of His love in me, and dost thou not adore His holy name? Must thou see the sun to know that he is there even when the clouds obscure his light? Must thou see thine own soul ere thou believest thou hast one, child?"

"No, father, no!" she answered softly.

"Thou canst see only natural things with those natural eyes. Thy spirit hath spiritual eyes, and thou shalt see me even though this earthly body be buried in the ground, when those spiritual eyes are opened, as I pray they shall be."

When they entered the chapel the factotum, Mrs. Goode, assisted by her husband, had prepared the evening meal.

Two spotless tables were spread alike with silver, china and crystal. It was a simple repast of bread, butter, fruit and milk, the elders having chocolate instead. The father and daughter, and husband and wife, appeared to sit at separate tables more from convenience and freedom than from any feeling of separation by birth or position. The conversation turned upon the journey, which Ruby described to her father, telling him some of the thoughts she had entertained—the pleasant or unpleasant sensations they had produced—saying:

"Father, I wonder how a person reasons who believes his thoughts to be creations of his own brain, and believes himself to be responsible for the bad ones or worthy of creating the good ones?"

"They are not happy people, my child, as I can affirm from sad experience. I once believed those things, and took great credit to myself when a noble suggestion was made to me, and grew correspondingly degraded in my own estimation when dark suggestions clouded my brain and filled me with hatred and revenge."

"You had not learned, then, father, what you have always taught me; that we are only receptacles—receivers of good or evil; that thoughts are suggestions from good or bad spirits and are not ours until we appropriate them and make use of them; then they are ours, but not until then. Am I right?"

"Yes, my child, quite right."

"Then, father, there would be no evil if we should reject all evil suggestions and not entertain them as our guests till they lodge with us long enough to become our own."

"Only our hereditary evils, my child," he said, following her with interest and smiling.

"O father! I wish, I *do wish* there was no hereditary evil! How good then people might become! But, father, if the soul comes from the father I believe I have a pure one; you must feel glad of that?"

A shade like the passing of a dark-winged bird for a moment clouded his face.

"I was not always grounded in the faith I have taught you. I had evils appropriated by myself, evils inherited from my ancestors, but there was, thank God! enough of the remains of good for the Lord to find a place where He could lay His head within me."

Now that her mind was upon this subject she would have chosen to penetrate it more deeply; a desire that often

came upon her with great force. She would have asked
if her mother had been so good a woman as he was a man.
But, as if he felt the sphere around her changing, and
cognized its cause, a silence for the first moment fell
upon them.

"Religion, father," she said at length, softly, "is the
nourishment of the intellectual man, faith of the spiritual,
and good works of the celestial man."

"Yes, religion, true religion, harmonizes science and
philosophy; a false religion is a sort of mania more dangerous than anything on earth. For Christians in Christian lands to worship a false God is a dreadful thing, and
to worship with a false conception of God is to worship a
false God; far better to be heathen in the darkness of
ignorance, for then they are in the blessedness of innocence."

And now they rose after a silent return of thanks and
went into the Temple.

"Everything except the plants, father, is familiar," she
said as they again walked arm in arm, "for they were all in
our own home, but how different the effect in this great Temple with its softened light, its arched dome, its white
columns. And yonder pulpit! If you take pupils how
grand to make their trial orations standing there. It will
give them inspiration. I am going to try it myself, father,
just to learn the effect of my voice. You shall play the organ, or Mr Goode shall do it, and we can sing,—shall we
not? O father: I feel here the truth of our Saviour's words,
'The kingdom of heaven is within you.' I could live here
always, father, and be happy."

"Not so, my child, there would be no progression. But
it is a sweet place in which to dwell together when we
return from our journeyings. Tomorrow, child, I shall
tell you why I purchased it. When in the world we mortals
must be of the world, and my child must know all I do and
why I do it. But it grows late; we shall say goodnight
here." And without another word they knelt down in the
centre of the Temple and in unison repeated a simple
prayer, that prayer of all prayers, and then silently kissed
each other goodnight.

CHAPTER III.

Ruby woke at seven, at first scarcely conscious that she
was not dreaming still of living in some enchanted spot.
But her image reflected in the mirror greeted her with a

calm expression and recalled her surroundings. She smiled and it smiled again. She clasped her hands and straightway it seemed absorbed in silent prayer.

"As we do so we become," and the silent lips in the mirror moved as she spoke.

Looking quietly into the pictured face she addressed her words to it:

"O silent yet powerful monitor! Turn where I will I see thee still! Do I see thy face darken, I know my own is clouded. Dost thou rear thy little head in sudden pride at some vain thought, I know whom thou dost imitate. Dost thou bend awkwardly, or heedlessly dash thy foot along, I know who does the same. Then, to make thee a pleasant picture to look upon, a sweet companion to be ever near me and keep me company, I know whose heart I must keep fresh and pure."

A robe of soft white cashmere was quickly donned; for Ruby had nothing about her of the lagging so conspicuous in the morning preparations of the dull, material girl of today. She read a chapter in the Bible and sat for some minutes afterwards with closed eyes in quiet self-communion. An hour later she joined her father who sat in his study in an arm-chair wearing a comfortable dressing gown and slippers. A round table spread with breakfast service showed that Mrs. Goode was already astir. Again the simple, frugal meal might have attracted the attention of an epicure as the old lady with her white neckerchief and broad flaring cap distributed toast, eggs, and chocolate, and later served light brown cakes and honey.

"Did you rest well, father?" asked Ruby, as she poured his chocolate.

"Very well indeed, my child; and your face indicates a peaceful and healthful repose."

"Oh! yes, one long delicious dream, to awake and find it all reality."

After a pleasant breakfast her father proposed a walk. Ruby had nothing to do but to pin on her hat and veil—for she never walked out unveiled—and to throw about her a long graceful wrap which completely hid her peculiar dress which might have attracted attention, a thing which her father had always taught her to avoid. People, old and young, male and female, stared at him with his white face and hair, his erect carriage, and that delicate spiritual countenance which startled every beholder.

"How great this New World is, father! How immense! —the Old World magnified many times. No wonder these

Americans are so bold and free. Already I feel glad to
identify myself with them. I was very young when you
brought me with you on your first tour of lectures. How
cordially we were received! I wished then we might remain here. But like all other wishes I have made it has at
last come to pass. Do you know, father, I never had a wish
in all my life that was not, sooner or later, gratified?"

"That is pleasant for me to know," he said, looking lovingly into her face. The veil that shaded it from the common gaze was slightly drawn from the side next to him,
so that occasionally they could look into each other's
eyes.

He felt a moment afterwards that she would like to
modify her speech; and she came near saying, "*every wish
but one*, father," but the words refused to come; and as she
silently pondered it she felt that when it was best for her,
it, too, would be gratified.

So she chatted away again about America—its wealth and
beautiful scenery and its climate; the sunny South in winter, the North or East in summer, the lakes and mountains.

After an hour or so they found themselves again at
home, and once seated in his study her father turned to
her and said:

"You are quite old enough now, my child, to learn something of practical business. I have endeavored to teach
you nothing that was not reasonable and practicable.
When I decided to move from L—— I bethought me where
I could invest my money. This will be a great city some
day. Commercially it is most favorably situated, and after
looking thoroughly into the laws which govern this country
I decided to lay out all I could spare right here. We
wanted a home. To buy one in a good neighborhood would
have cost as much as I gave for this building, and as years
passed there would be very little increase in the value
of a dwelling. This will, in course of years, make a fine
business block, when the value will be very largely and
rapidly enhanced. I figured that we could make our home
here for some years, as there are many charming features
about it, while it grows in value."

"I see, father, and a lovelier place in which to live could
not have been selected."

"Now I have a few thousands that I want to invest
safely, and believing that unimproved lands would be the
surest I have looked about and found just what I want.
It can be purchased very reasonably, in fact cheaply, now.
Indeed the owner says it is practically useless to him,

being broken and hilly, with lakes and ponds. It is too far from the city, he says, to grade, and is not fit for cultivation; but if I live I will show him some day the object of its purchase. He can use the money I shall pay him to his advantage now, while I can use the land to the advantage of others and the city, as well as to ourselves, in years to come. Does my Ruby catch father's business ideas as readily as she does his legal ones?"

"Quite, father. I want to learn everything that is useful. It will help me to help others who have not such opportunities to learn."

"Quite right, my dear. Useful knowledge is all that is worthy of the name. Then, too, should I be called away, my child will know how to manage what she has, to use it and do good with it."

"That I shall, father, believing always that you see me and love me and guide me."

"I do not know that I shall do anything here. If I have no pupils I am afraid I shall be unreasonable and teach you too much," he said, smiling.

"No danger of that, father. I drink in only wholesome truth in theology, law, literature and science from you. I never grow weary. It would be a great pity, though, if you should not have pupils, because somebody is losing so much. This training of voice and action is needed everywhere, on the stage and in the pulpit."

"Yes, it is a greatly needed art, and the only road to great success, if the votaries of oratory could only realize it. Many a grand mental effort has fallen into oblivion just because there was no cunning in the voice, no pleading in the action, to carry it home to its auditors."

It would be a revelation to the spoiled beauty of fashion to see this lovely young creature listening with such attention to lessons in plain business investments that looked forward to wealth—wealth to use for the good of others—and not the planning of robes and the purchase of jewels; and yet this young lady possessed a few rare ones in her own name. Her father had taught her their spiritual meaning and told her that she should strive to wear them worthily.

Had she again hoped that in this interview he would tell her the story which ofttimes seemed to tremble on his lips but could find no utterance, that perhaps he felt questioned by her eyes which like two sinless souls asked of him why life was so different to him and her from what it might have been? Where was that other, that link which, broken, left those two apart, separate, and yet of the same chain, the first and the last? Where was, who was, that second? Why had she never been taught anything about a sainted mother in heaven, and all of the beautiful things which songs said of those mothers? She had read books to learn more of them; but Dickens' Cleopatra and the Old Soldier, Adam Bede's fretful, exasperating mother, Becky Sharp as a mother, and numerous others, all of a like character, convinced her that there was something yet to be understood and reconciled between the two, those said and sung and many of the real flesh-and-blood mothers of to-day.

After luncheon Mr. Goode ordered the carriage, and Mr. Gladstone invited him and his wife to accompany himself and daughter on the drive. And here we may observe these worthy people. Mr. Goode, as he sat beside his wife, appeared three years her senior, or about fifty. He was strong and muscular, with a good, pleasant face, and was evidently a man of some education. He was an intuitive musician.

Mrs. Goode, whom Ruby lovingly called "Goodie," was a fair, round, rosy, good-natured matron, a trifle too stiff perhaps to show her loving qualities to the casual observer, but just now, with Trueman beside her, and Ruby and Mr. Gladstone facing her, aside from a few neckerchiefs and a square box, Mrs. Goode positively carried her whole world with her, and was therefore a peaceful, happy woman, a true type of those worthy English people whose characters the great Dickens drew so tenderly and taught every English-speaking reader to love.

An hour's drive brought them to the spot indicated. They had left the smoke of the city behind and driven in the direction which would soonest take them from its great pulsing heart. They drove upon a hill and from thence surveyed the surroundings. Far to the east rose the smoke of the great city, and at intervals lay gardens and small farms. They all agreed upon the admirable location; and when they returned they found the owner at his office in the city and the sale was perfected. The notary, who was also familiar with the tract, looked rather deprecatingly at the white-haired grantee as if he thought he would better have kept his money for the young lady who would doubtless be an orphan soon.

"Come into the study, Goode," said Mr. Gladstone after tea, which meant, of course, to bring Mrs. Goode.

They found Mr. Gladstone at a table with papers, pen, ink and pencil.

"I want to show you why I bought this land. Come here, Ruby, Mrs. Goode, look. This is the city," he said pointing to a plat. "It is growing like a healthy baby. It will not cross the river for that is impracticable; it has gone far enough in this direction; it cannot go further here for every foot of ground is leasehold or disputed title. Now it is bound to go somewhere and I am sure that it will go west the most rapidly. It may take years, say twenty (I don't believe it), but even then Ruby will be only thirty-eight. Remote from the city, the taxes will be limited until its value increases. Unimproved, there are no repairs to be made, and after all I have taken less risk in thus burying my talent in the earth than you think," he said, looking at the grave face of Trueman Goode, whose gray eyes took in the plat but whose face still wore an expression of doubt.

"Now, I want Ruby to keep her eyes open when mine are closed, and watch the needs of the people and turn this into a great public benefit. Not that I mean a charity affair except so·far as downright love and good and progress go. She must sell her land but make it something worthy of both heart and brain.

"Again, while we are here together, I want to explain that all my worldly affairs are in such condition that should I die at any moment no trouble can come to any of you, provided you, Trueman, Mrs. Goode and Ruby adhere to my instructions and sacredly keep certain promises."

They all agreed.

"There is money enough in the Bank of England to pay taxes on this building and ground, and on this land, and to keep you all comfortably. Beware of changing your mode of living, for then you venture upon a perilous and unknown sea. Mrs. Goode knows to within a pound sterling what it takes to keep the house for a year. These are tax receipts and you see what the amounts are. My life is insured for sufficient to support Ruby and enable her to hold this property until such time as it will be proper to sell it. Ruby in my testament is my sole heir. There is no other person on earth who has any right or claim upon me." He trembled visibly, but looked firmly into the face of one and then the other. "Trueman Goode, you and your wife know this; if ever any one else makes the claim or asserts the right I now deny, prove to my child that her father spoke the truth, had been just and right. You promise?"

"We do."

"And Ruby, child, remember who have been your friends. Never forsake the love and counsel of these good people, the most faithful friends your father ever knew. Whatever change circumstances may bring to you, remember that when I am gone you are safe only under their watchful care until you are married. You promise?"

"I do."

"You will never part from this money I leave you in love, for any wrong or unholy purpose; I mean for vanity, self-gratification, or through any influence brought to bear upon you by any one who may lay claims upon you or attempt to make you believe it is right to do otherwise than I direct."

"Never, father."

"To-morrow we shall go before a notary and have all these things legally settled. I am in my usual health, and that is the time to settle our worldly affairs."

Before the next day was ended deeds were placed on record, the testament was signed and sealed and a sworn copy placed in the hands of Mr. Goode, and another in the city's vault kept for such purposes.

"A remarkable man, that," said the notary wiping his spectacles. "Hedges himself in on every side as if he constantly expected an attack from an enemy."

"And is quite right I imagine," said his partner, "for old Death holds his scythe very close to him. I am sure he might count the dropping sands in his hourglass, so few they are."

And thus the matter of worldly interests was settled never to be alluded to again. Mr. Gladstone realized the wisdom of making these necessary preparations and made them carefully. No thought of them could again disturb their peaceful life. And having thus secured his loved ones from the ills of want and poverty his mind was free from anxiety and all his energy was turned upon his labors in a higher sphere of action. The material part disposed of as a necessary step, means perfect freedom in living a spiritual life. They were then separated, not mixed together and bound up, so that the natural must necessarily retard the growth of the spiritual; not neglected wholly, so that it could stalk in upon them gaunt and grim and claim attention. Could not all the world learn a lesson from this man?

CHAPTER IV.

Autumn had glided calmly into winter. The daily walk was shortened or postponed by rain, sleet, fog, or snow, but the glowing fire and a cheerful aspect indoors made ample amends for it.

In the New World Ruby perceived a new condition of things, new possibilities for development of the intellectual man. She realized how this far-famed America could justly claim prestige over all other countries; and yet the fact was forced upon them that the masses needed intelligent guidance here, as elsewhere on the face of the earth. The Americans are never slow to avail themselves of good opportunities and therein lies the secret of their power; therefore we knew in advance that Mr. Gladstone's talents would not rust, for many are eager to avail themselves of such teaching.

Pupils had come and Ruby frequently sat alone in her father's study while he drilled some young advocate, clergyman, or politician in the Temple. At other times she was a silent and unseen spectator from the gallery. There was one, a tall, graceful young man, who possessed a naturally fine voice and who strove earnestly to reach an ideal of his own. At times he caught the spirit of his subject and needed no guide, it seemed. At other times he was preoccupied and dull.

"I cannot do it, sir," she heard him say one afternoon as she sat in the gallery unobserved, listening. "If I could hear you first I believe I could imitate it."

Ruby was now deeply, intensely interested, for this imitation was a gift peculiarly her own. The request seemed natural, for she had often made it herself, and she wondered what her father's answer would be.

"Very well," he replied, and the young man came down from the pulpit and stood in the auditorium with folded arms.

Her father began in a low, clear, distinct voice, an argument before a jury in behalf of a criminal for his life. He stated the facts as they had been represented by opposing counsel, and then stated them as he believed them to be and would have the jury to understand them. So real did the whole appear that Ruby's heart went out towards this unseen or imaginary criminal with real, heartfelt sympathy. She forgot to watch the silent auditor below, and heard only the final appeal which her father made in that thrilling voice to that unseen jury.

When silence fell the young man again mounted the steps but he would not proceed. "Not to-day, my dear sir, not to-day; to-morrow maybe I can summon up courage to attempt to imitate you. I thank you for your kindness. The effect upon me was electric. I can carry it all in my heart, and when it is fixed there I'll try to send it forth again."

"Just as you choose," her father answered, "just as you like."

Ruby always looked at other people in contrast with her father, never in comparison. This young man was a trifle taller than he, and so slightly built as to appear taller than he really was. There was nothing weak or effeminate about him, and still there was a distinction that marked him from other men by a certain delicacy of feeling apparent in his voice and manner. His hair was dark and slightly curled, his complexion a rich olive. He wore no beard, and his clearly cut lips, which were clean shaven, defined a mouth of rare power and beauty. His teeth were small, even, thick and ivory white. He was so entirely different from any of the rest of her father's pupils that Ruby could not resist asking about him when she joined him again in the study.

"He is, as you know, unknown to me, only recommended as a graduate of Cambridge. Whether he will choose the church or the law I do not think he has decided. His moods are so variable, his nature so sensitive, that he must look well to it, for he stands an equal chance of failure or success. He needs some powerful incentive like falling in love or having his ambition aroused by an op- ponent. I think it would do him good to meet the hand- some Saul who comes to-morrow, and perhaps he will."

"Saul, father?"

"I call him so. A powerful young giant, a Greek, who combines the energy of manhood with the engaging uncon- sciousness of a child. A perfection of the senses, a fine physical organization, a spiritual nature infolded in strict unity with the body, a form which might supply the sculp- tor with his models of Jove, and the most wonderful voice I have ever heard; a rare, extravagant spirit, such as ap- pears in the world at intervals and discloses to us new truths in nature; a man of God walking the earth among men, who will make his commission felt in the heart and soul of the lowliest hearer, for he speaks with his heart."

Such praise from her father's lips exalted this unknown Greek in Ruby's mind, and she resolved to see him, to hear him, for thus far she had not done so, and the young Frenchman had impressed her as her father's most promising pupil.

"Did I mention to you," her father continued, "that I have a female pupil in whom I am much interested?"

"When does she come?"

"The day after to-morrow. She has a peculiarly sweet speaking voice but I doubt its strength; however, I will see. She wishes to be an actress."

(To be continued.)

THE VALLEY PATH.

A Novel of Tennessee Life.

BY WILL ALLEN DROMGOOLE.

CHAPTER III.

During the next week the physician from the city heard
more than once how "Joe Bowen got ahead o' the mad doctor." He had been questioned about it when he went over
to the little country town of Moffit, and had even told the
joke of his own accord, laughing at it as heartily as the
rest. It proved an introduction for him at all events, and
went to verify the old saying that "a bad reputation is
better than none." The people round about heard of him
as a physician, and one afternoon, about ten days after Joe
made his call, the doctor had a second.

A man from up the valley in passing left word of "a
fambly o' children down with scyarlet fever in a house on
the Pelham road." He "reckined they'd take it mighty
kin' if the mad doctor 'd step over an' see what he could
do for 'em."

Being a three-mile "step" he ordered his horse, and as
a *family* had been attacked with the disease he carried his
medicine case along.

It was his first ride down the Pelham road, and notwithstanding there were suffering children at the end of his
journey he rode slowly. The young spring was abroad; the
woods were a mass of quivering new greens; the trees,
alive with birds; where he crossed Pelham creek the water
rose with a sibillant gurgle to the bay mare's belly. The
birds made merry over their nests in the heart of the
laurel brake; in the tops of the red-oak trees a little mountain oriole was calling, calling, in his half-merry, half-mel-
ancholy song, the first note of which is a whistle, the second
an inquiry, the third a regret, and the fourth an unmistakable sigh—a trill of music and a wail of melancholy. The
good green grass crowded the roadside; the wild honeysuckle nodded to him from the deeper hollows of the wood;
the very winds that fanned his cheek were gentle, kind,
sympathetic. He scarcely saw, he only felt the glad new
restfulness of living.

"It was a wise move," he murmured, "a very wise move. I am glad I came to the wilderness." He rode on for a moment in silence, the mare's feet scarcely audible in the light green sward of the almost untravelled valley road. Suddenly he lifted his head and looked about him, snuffling the keen, spring-scented air.

"What a place to die in!" he exclaimed, "to grow old and die in. Up sir! we are loitering in this Sleepy Hollow."

He touched the animal with the bridle rein lightly, and ere long the restful woods with their seduction of sound and color lay behind him.

It was noon when he reached the house, one of the ordi nary two-room log cabins of the neighborhood, having a shed in the rear and an open passage between the two living rooms.

An old woman, tall and gaunt and cadaverous-looking, occupied the little home-made bench that adorned the passage; before her stood a large jar, a crock, surmounted with a wooden top: the crock was doing duty as a churn; the woman was industriously plying the dasher. She rose when the doctor rode up, and called to him to "turn his nag in the yard, else it would be worrit toe death by a loose mule o' Joe Bowenses that was rampantin' the country."

He obeyed instructions, and a moment more stood in the passage, inquiring after the sick.

"They're right in thar," said the woman, "if you're the doctor man."

"Are they yours?"

"Naw, sir, they ain't mine, an' I'm glad of it, bein' as they're all three 'bout ter die. One of 'em's in an' about dead I reckin. I ain't got but one, an' he's a man growed. Though I ain't tellin' of you, doctor, that I never had no more. I've done my part I reckin; I've got 'leven dead ones. I failed ter raise em; the measles an' the whoopin' cough an' the fever set in an' they all went—all but Jim. Jim he tuk the jandice oncet, but he got over it. I'm mighty glad ter meet you, Doctor Borin'."

"Thank you, madam," replied the physician, with such honest simplicity and hearty sincerity that the woman's sallow face beamed the pleasure the words gave her. It was only a simple greeting from a gentle heart; but because of it the mad doctor had one friend more upon the list of those who loved him.

"Do you live here?" he asked.

"Naw sir; I live in the first house on the road ter S'wany, back o' yo' place. My name's Tucker; Mis' Tucker. You

can go in now an' see the child'en, Doctor Borin', if you
please ter; I come over ter try an' help a bit, an' I'll jist
churn this milk an' give Lissy a swaller o' fresh buttermilk.
Pears like she can't be persuaded ter take time ter eat
nothin'."

He glanced carelessly at the low-ceiled room, the two
beds occupying two corners, the small trundle bed drawn
into the centre of the room, and the little square window
which did duty in the way of light and ventilation, the
batten shutter thrown wide open. A boy of about ten years
lay tossing upon the trundle bed, flushed and fretting with
fever. Upon another bed, listless, and pale as marble, a
young girl was lying. Hers was a complicated case, and
might prove a hopeless one. The great, hollow eyes were
turned to the door, watching the doctor; a low panting.
moan issued continually from the thin bloodless lips.

He took it all in at a glance; the poverty, the crowded
close air, the ignorance of disease, and the suffering occa-
sioned thereby. But that which appealed to him above
all things was the figure of a young girl seated beside an
empty cradle with a little baby upon her knees, her hand
lying lightly upon its breast. At first he had seen in the
uncertain light only a coil of bright hair, of that peculiar
shade that is neither golden nor auburn; it was more like
a dab of warm sunshine in the gloom of the place. As his
eye became accustomed to the gloom, the outline of the
face grew broader and he saw where womanly tenderness
and girlish sweetness blended into a Madonna-like perfection of beauty. She wore a dress of some dark stuff open
at the throat and with the sleeves pushed back in clumsy little rolls above the dimpled elbows, plump and shapely. Her
face was bent over the child upon her lap, and her slender
strong fingers were feeling under the bosom of the little
white gown for the baby's heart.

She lifted her head when the physician bent over her
to look into the small smiling face against her knee. Even
then he noticed that the large gray eyes lifted to his were
tearless, the slender fingers were firm and without a tremor:
if she felt an emotion she held it magnificently in control.

"Go to the others," she said in a quietly impressive tone.
"Go to the others; it ain't no use to waste time here. I
felt its heart stop beatin' when I heard your step in the
passage. I ain't been able to find it any more."

Not even when she began to smoothe the lids down over
the staring baby eyes, did the slender fingers falter.

"It's ma is down in the orchard with its pa," she con-

tinued, when the physician questioned her concerning the
parents. "They went out to keep from seein' it die. But
it died mighty easy; there was nuthin' to run from as I
can see—jest a little baby goin' to sleep."

The slender fingers went on smoothing the dead eyes:
there was a caressing something about the manner in which
they moved that robbed their task of horror. The physician
regarded her steadily a moment:

"Are you one of the family?" he asked. "Do you belong
here?"

"No, sir," she replied in her soft musical drawl. "I live
in the house nearest yours; I'm Alicia Reams, the miller's
granddaughter. They call me Lissy for short. I'm just
here to help some; so if you want anything I can get it for
you. So can Mrs. Tucker, if you'll speak to her outside the
door there."

"Well," said the physician, "I 'want' a good deal. First
thing, I want that churn stopped, or carried out of reach
of the ears of this nervous girl here. Then I want to
separate living and dead in this house, or we shall have
more dead in a little while. Isn't there another room across
the passage?"

"Yes, sir. If you'll call Mrs. Tucker to take the baby I'll
help you with the others."

She placed the dead child in the arms of the older woman,
directed her where to find its "things" and sent her into
the shed room to make the tiny body ready for burial. Then
she gave a little tuck in her sleeves and turning to the
physician said in a whisper:

"I'm goin' to run down in the orchard and send the baby's
pa to Winchester after a coffin and things; I'll come right
back in a minute. Try and do somethin' for Cora; she's
suffered lots, Cora has."

She flitted away like a dash of lost sunshine, leaving the
real gloom of death in the room. Yet her presence lingered:
the low sweet cadence of her voice still sounded in the doctor's ears; the bright face with its great gray eyes—shadow
pools, he called them—was still before him. What a face
it was: neither girl's nor woman's, yet—lacking. There were
fire, warmth, feeling; a native refinement marked her
handling of even the ordinary coarser duties which devolved upon her; there was gentleness in every motion of
the body. The touch of her fingers was magnetic: her hand
had brushed his when he examined the baby upon her knees,
and it had thrilled him as he had not been thrilled in
twenty years. How strong her presence, outlined against

the weakness about her. Already he had begun to speculate concerning her; surely the girl had possibilities—a
future something beyond the listless lives about her, ran
his thought. She was at his side again while he was trying
to solve the riddle of her.

"Now, Doctor Borin'," she said, "I'm ready to help you
do something for these. I'm ready to take hold, and you
needn't mind tellin' me; I'm used to doin' for the sick.
There's been a good deal o' sickness in this valley, and I've
learned to help some, bein' as help was scarce."

Together they worked; he directing, and lending a hand
when one was needed, as it often was. In a little while the
sick had been removed into the room across the passage
and made comfortable in the fresh sweet beds for which
the humblest of the region are known. The boy was soon
fast asleep under the doctor's ministrations. The case of
Cora, the young girl, was not so easily managed. Fever
had started again, and the scene through which she had
just passed, the grief stricken mother, the dead baby, the
restless fretfulness of her brother, had so excited the patient that the physician found it difficult to calm her. He
remained until dusk and returned again after supper, remaining until midnight, gently soothing his patient, until,
with the aid of his skill and a subtle something in his presence, she fell into a deep slumber. At midnight he left
Alicia in charge.

"Allow no one to enter the room," he said to her as
they stood together for a moment in the passage where a
feeble old lantern was doing its best, with the assistance
of the moon, in the matter of lighting the way for the
neighbors who dropped in at all hours of the night to
"sit up with the corpse" in the family room. "Nobody must
go in there except you or Mrs. Tucker; she has the gift
of discretion as well as yourself. Above all things keep
from the sick children what is going on in the next room.
I will return at eight o'clock to-morrow; can you hold out
so long?"

He could almost see the laugh in her gray eyes lifted to
his, in the sickly light of the lantern.

"I'm good for a week yet, Doctor Borin'," she said. "Hold
out! you don't know Lissy Reams."

"I *shall* know her," he replied, "if she is to set herself up
as my rival or my partner in practice here."

He heard her low gurgling laugh, instantly checked as
she remembered the presence in the cabin. "We're neighbors," she said; "I have got a little truck patch where I

raise things to sell at S'wanee. I'll fetch you over a mess of beans soon; see if I don't."

"And all the fresh eggs you can spare," said the doctor. "I want to engage them now, for *years—as long as I live.*"

"Heish," she said softly, "don't make me laugh. It ain't kind, at a time like this. Besides, I might die long befo' you—who knows?"

"You? Look at those arms, will you? Then go look in the glass, in the mirror, and see the blood come and go in your cheeks. Moreover, old Dilce, my housekeeper, tells me that you go up the mountain every morning by sun up, and in a canter. In a canter—think of it! I couldn't walk up in a day. And you talk of dying before me. Tut! Let me hear you laugh again."

But the laugh did not come; gazing full into his eyes, she had found there nothing, notwithstanding the lightness of his tone, to sanction mirth. In the lantern's light he saw an unmistakable shadow, faint, vague, and fleeting, hover for an instant in her eyes.

"I ain't always so lively," she said slowly, "nor so reasonable neither, I reckon. Sometimes I have the blues awful, and then I'm just good for nothin'. I ain't any help to anybody when I get the blues. And most of the time it's just about nothin' I have 'em. Ain't I an awful goose?"

As if the confession were precisely that which he had expected, he said in a vague, dreamful tone, "I know—yes, I understand."

"Doctor Borin'?" The eager surprise in her voice quite startled him.

"Why, you see," he said in explanation, "we doctors possess certain secret entrances to the soul, not permitted others. We understand character as well as body. Now you are what we in our profession would call ethereal— that is, pertaining to the spirit. You are a dreamer."

She laughed softly, under her breath, lest the gay sound should reach the troubled ear of the bereaved and jar unpleasantly.

"I'm a peddler of truck," she replied. "I sell vegetables to the college boardin' house at S'wanee. In the winter I sell butter and eggs and dried beans to the same house. That's my life pretty much, and that's the kind of dreamer I am. Though I ain't sayin' but I'd like—"

"There," said he, "I told you so. Your garden rows are full of your dreams, dropped in with your seed. And your egg basket wouldn't begin to hold the fancies that fill your heart while you trip up the mountain to Sewanee."

He left her standing in the passage, her bare arms folded upon her breast and gleaming like silver in the mingled light of moon and lantern. The picture of her stayed with him while he rode home in the soundless midnight: the fair young face with that dainty mingling of color which belongs alone to first sweet youth; the coy blending of girl and woman; the graceful, well-fulled body; and the soul lurking in the gray deeps of eyes which once seeing would forever refuse the darkness of life's ways. Out of place —as much out of place in that wilderness cabin as his silver doorplate on the hut at the foot of the mountain.

There was a tragedy in her life; the bare fact of her being was a tragedy, and could round to no other end than the tragic. Some souls are born to it; and whether they live quietly, unknown, and die tamely in their beds, unmourned, or whether their lives, like candles, are snuffed out at their best brightness, amid the lamentations of the multitude, matters nothing and alters nothing. The tragedy has been enacted; the soul has suffered, and has fulfilled that whereunto it was born.

Suddenly he gave the lines a quick impatient jerk. "Bah!" he exclaimed; then in a softer tone: "I am bewildered by a dash of yellow hair, and a dabble of pink-and white cheeks. I am an old fool. The girl will marry some strapping mountaineer, rear a houseful of tow-headed children, wash, scrub, bake, and be happy, after the manner of her kind. But I believe——" The words were lost in a gurgle of water—Pelham creek among its gray rocks winding down to meet him at the ford.

"Who knows? who knows?" Her words came back to him in the lisping flow as the mare's feet touched the moon-flecked flood. "I might die long befo' you—who knows?"

"Who knows?" he mused; "who knows anything? And how little any of us know, for that matter. Yet *I* know the miller's grandchild, with half a showing, would not live the prosaic life of the mountaineer, despite the strong, brown arms and the thriving truck patch."

What a contrast she presented to the woman he had known; what a contrast to her, that one woman who stood out in his thoughts like a ghost in the midday—a ghost that is not seen, but felt, and is cold, chilling the soul of warm life.

Then he thought of his friends at home, his former *confreres* and companions. What would they think of the extent to which his "crankiness" had carried him?—ministering in hovels at midnight, without so much as the mean motive of a few dollars by way of recompense.

"They may think as they choose," was his thought. "Most men, all men I believe, have their cranks—their ideal life they call it. The only difference with us is that I am fool enough to indulge mine. I claim the right to live my own life—to spoil it myself, rather than permit others to spoil it for me; since I spoil it at least in the faith that I am doing my best for it. And after all, life is a solitary thing, and must be lived alone. They who pass upon it and advise about it, can do no more; for life in the abstract, like death, knows no duality. Now this girl—but enough: I am an old fool."

Yet the picture of her stayed with him; and when at last he fell asleep in his own bed, drawn as he always had it, where the moonlight from the small old-fashioned window fell athwart his pillow, he still saw her, in a dream, sitting beside an empty cradle with a little waxen baby on her knees.

CHAPTER IV.

Dr. Boring had an early breakfast the next morning and immediately after ordered his horse.

"They are as like as not to lay the corpse out on the bed with one of my patients," he said, in reply to Aunt Dilce's complaining." "Moreover, I left the little Reams woman there,"—it never occurred to him to call Alicia, as his mind had received its first impression of her, a girl,—"and she must be all used up by this time. One of those children is going to have a fight for life, and if I can get in any work it must be at the start; there is scant need of a physician at the finish. I am going to send Alicia Reams over here, Aunt Dilce; and I want you to have a good hot breakfast for her and make her take the time to eat it. Be good to her, black mammy; when she gets here, look after her; make her rest awhile. Then do you send the horse back to me."

He found Alicia as busy as though she had not lost a wink of sleep in a month. She was bending over a saucepan in the shed room, mixing a meal poultice for Cora, who had complained of "a mis'ry in the side."

He went from room to room with the freedom to which they were too well accustomed to consider it presuming, until he found her in the shed room.

"I will attend to that," he said, indicating the poultice; "do you get on your bonnet and mount my horse,—can you ride?"

She nodded, smiling. "I've always lived nigh enough to the mount'n to be called a mount'n girl," she said; "an mount'n girls can ride anything, from broomstick to steer. Is somebody else sick, an' you want me to go there, to help nurse 'em?"

"Hell!" he murmured. "Go there? *No!* I want you to mount that horse and get away from sick folks. Get away like you were getting from Indians, measles, small-pox, yellow jackets. Do you understand?"

She set the saucepan upon the hearth and crammed her apron into her mouth. "Great I am!" she exclaimed, when the disposition to laugh outright had been overcome. "I have *heard* you were nicked."

"You haven't heard the half," he replied. "Here! throw that mash in the pig pen; I have a mustard plaster for the pain in the side. The children are both better. I'm glad of that— I've got to prove to these people that I'm a doctor, even if I don't know a hornet's sting when it is thrust under my nose."

A flash of the gray eyes, a dimpling of the cheek, and a twitching of the red lips told him that she knew the story, though she said, with proper demureness, "Did somebody allow you didn't know the difference?"

"Oh, I didn't," he admitted with open candor. "I was completely sold. But if I can help these little children back to health I am willing to take my chances with you people. Now Lissy, you must do as I say. Aunt Dilce is holding your breakfast back until you come. You ride on to my house, take a good rest, a good breakfast, and then go home and go to bed."

"I ain't tired," she replied, "and I ought to stay here and help about buryin' of the baby."

"Burying be hanged," he replied. "Unless you do as I tell you I shall go back and eat the breakfast myself, and leave the sick to go as the baby went. Do you understand? If you value your friends here, and my reputation as a physician, you must do as I command."

"Oh, these ain't my friends," she replied. "I never was here before."

"What? what are you doing here, then?"

"Helpin'," she replied. "I always help. That's all I *can* do; I'm an awful sinner—worse than you, I reckin. You'll hear all about it. But I can't help it; I'm bound to act according' to my light, and I haven't seen the way to the mourner's bench *yet.* And Brother Barry—he's the circuit rider—he says I'm bound for hell and torment, and that

I'm one o' the stiff-necked and hard of heart. Did you notice I didn't even cry when the baby died in my lap? I couldn't; all the rest cried. But me—I couldn't see what there was to sorrow about in a little baby jist slippin' from this world o' trouble up to God. It was all mighty sweet and happy to me. I was sort of glad to see it go; I knew it would never be worried with doubts, like me, nor be hindered none by lack o' light and grace. Doctor Borin', I hear Cora cryin' with the mis'ry in her side; won't you go in and put the mustard to it? An' I'll run 'long and get the breakfast you saved. It was mighty good of you. I'll sure enjoy it. I know I will. An' I'll surely fetch the mess o' beans by an' by; an' fresh eggs enough for your many a breakfast. If," she added roguishly, "you don't die of old age befo' the hens can get on their nestses."

When she had gone, although he gave his full attention to the sick, she was not once absent from his thoughts. If she had puzzled him the night before, the piquant beauty of her face only charmed and bewitched him the more in the good glow of the daylight. He had felt a great curiosity in seeing it again; without giving form to the doubt, he had somehow felt vaguely that something was lacking to the face's full perfection. She was not slow, dull, after the manner of the mountain maidens, owing perhaps to the influence and teachings of her valley mother. There was nothing stupid, none of the heavy country girl about her. Yet when the large eyes looked full into his he saw the wavering, weaker lights under the strong purplish gray; and when she had gone he whispered to his own inquiring heart: "A nature to be moulded; an impressionist, with a tendency toward the morbid."

It was noon when he left the house of mourning. The little baby had been laid to sleep in a neighboring burying-ground, and the sick were doing reasonably well. He had found a good deal to contend with in the matter of the infant's burial. In the tall gaunt minister who had arrived in time to conduct the services, and in the stupid persistence with which he insisted upon the performance of the duty upon which he had come, Doctor Boring recognized Brother Barry, the Methodist circuit rider. A funeral was expected, was customary; Brother Barry was not to be set aside by the ravings of an infidel. But when the infidel took the father of the dead babe aside and swore in large round English that the singing and confusion would endanger the life of Cora, Brother Barry for once in his life was forced to the wall. So the men tiptoed into the passage, lifted the small pine coffin in their hands, and the rest followed noiselessly to the little grave that had been prepared in the valley shade, within reach of the lisping music of Elk River.

"The child will sleep as well without their howling," said the doctor, as the bay mare trotted along the valley road in the direction of home. "It will sleep as well and wake as surely—if they wake, those silent sleepers."

His thought took a sudden melancholy turn. He let the lines fall upon the bay's neck, and she fell into the ordinary jog-trot of animals less daintily sired than this bay Morgan. She even stopped to seize a mouthful of the new greens crowding the roadside, without rebuke from the dreaming rider.

Suddenly he roused and took up the lines sharply; his ear had caught a note of discord in the noontime harmony. He listened; a twinkle came into his eyes, and a smile parted for a moment his lips. He had almost reached the turn in the road where his cabin would stand revealed. Already he could see the low worm fence, which he meant to replace with a pretty paling by and by, and a raw-boned, flea-bitten mare that was cropping the new buds of his favorite quince tree, to which she had been "hitched" by a bridle rein twisted among the low-drooping branches which overhung the fence upon the outside. He had a caller. He recognized the flea-bitten mare; he had seen it at the baby's burial when Brother Barry rode up. He also recognized the voice of Aunt Dilce "laying the law down" to bow-legged Ephraim:

"You Efum? Git up from dar en he'p dribe de peeg out'n de yard, fo' hit root all de marster's flow'rs up. Heish up yo' mouf, you fool you, don' you know dar's comp'ny in de house? Makin' all dat fuss ter let folks know dey done lef' de gate op'n, en tu'n all de peegs in de country in de yard. Sooey dar! Haid 'im off'n dat vi-let bed, nigger Dar! dar he goes! knock 'im in de haid. Skeer 'im out'n dem chulups, en shet yo' mouf. Tain' none yo' business ter let folks know dey done lef' de gate op'n, same lack dey ain' got no sense en no raisin' nohow. Dar! hit dat peeg! Don't let 'im inter dat minuet baid, you fool! Call 'im off! Peeg? peeg? Sooey dar, sooey. Call 'im, haid 'im fo' I bus' you wide op'n wid dis here rock, en make you mo' bow-laigged en what you is a'raidy. Hit 'im! sooey dar! Heish yo' mouf! whi' folks know niggers ain' got nuffin ter do' 'cept ter run de hogs out. Dat's what de good

Lord made dey-all fur; jes' ter 'commerdate po' white trash. Look at dat peeg, sooey! Hit 'im dar! haid 'im! Now you got him; haid 'im off todes de gate. Dar! easy now—hit 'im! bus 'im wide op'n! hit 'im in— Dat fool nigger done let dat horg slip froo his laigs."

The doctor heard every word (so too had the guest within doors, as Aunt Dilce meant he should). He saw the old woman's chase after the interloper, and recognized the jeopardy of his pets, the flower beds. Yet he smiled as he dismounted and tossed his bridle to Ephraim. The little gate still swung wide open upon its hinges, just as the visitor had left it; a pair of yellow, weather-beaten saddle-bags lay upon his doorstep, and Zip, his little black terrier, was industriously seeking an investigation of their contents.

(To be continued.)

BOOKS OF THE DAY.

A DANGEROUS BOOK.*

REVIEWED BY EDGAR FAWCETT.

The wise Huxley, that noble thinker, somewhere tells us that to accept as truth any proposition which our reason, duly questioned, fails to sanction, is an act of immoral tendency. Thus far reason has formed the sole healthful impetus of human progress, and whenever its course has been deflected or disturbed by hindrances of a purely emotional kind, civilization has suffered. I do not wish to predict that "A Study of Death" is capable of effecting any such serious havoc. But there are certainly minds of a quality so sensitive to random impressions, however injurious, that the blended falsity and hysteria of such a work may permanently harm them. On the other hand, there is a safeguard for these readers in the density of many pages and passages; the most trained intelligence could gather from them no definite meaning whatever. Once upon a time the "mystic" and the "seer" were held in respect, like the astrologer and fortune-teller. But broadened knowledge has happily freed us from such uncanny thraldoms. "Refrain," says Herbert Spencer, " from rendering your terms into ideas, and you may reach any conclusion whatever. The whole is equal to its part, is a proposition that may be quite comfortably entertained, so long as neither parts nor wholes are imagined." The author of "A Study of Death" certainly does a great deal of imagining, and as for his parts and wholes, these are jumbled together in the wildest way. To instance the flimsiness and poverty of his reasoning, we may take this sentence: "Even the reptile, followed to the end of its course, is seen to take to itself wings of ascension." Or this other: "The bee, closely observed, is seen to inject into each cell of honey some poison from his sting, which makes the sweetness wholesome —a venom inherent in the virtue."

This is the sort of writing considered "valuable" and "convincing" in Butler and Paley years ago. It is still esteemed "comforting" by a certain class of readers at the present date, though these are possibly not the class by which Mr. Alden would care to have his picturesque platitudes, heavy with verbal ornamentations, appreciated. To find analogies between the processes of nature and the supposed spiritual future of man, and then present them as

---

* "A Study of Death," by H. M. Alden. Harper & Bros.

proofs of the latter, is an old trick of the fanatical optimist. But apart from this unoriginal element, the book, to any logical mind, fairly bristles with absurdities. For instance, Mr. Alden would have it believed that there is a relation between the phenomena of sleep and death not by any means fanciful, but based upon physical conditions. It seems extraordinary that he should not know how science would smile its amazement upon any such suggestion, and yet he writes with an air of positive scientific erudition that makes us marvel all the more at his haphazard and vagabond postulates. "Sleep," he declares, "in this special sense" (i. e., the normal sense), "is, indeed, akin to death. But he stands this side of the veil, only simulating the offices of his invisible brother." Sleep, in other words, does not merely resemble death, but is a milder form of the great destroyer's immobility and silence. Mr. Alden should visit a hospital and strive there to verify his brilliant discovery. He might learn, if he permitted any mental part of him so humdrum as his common sense to become operative, that sleep is the very reverse of all mortuary agencies—that physicians regard it as the one most curative influence, and are only too glad when they can induce it by means of rest and quiet rather than by a recourse to anodynes. But in any case they believe in its reinvigorating and re-creative force, and are presumptuous enough to agree with Shakspere rather than Mr. Alden concerning its efficacy as "tired nature's sweet restorer."

But everywhere, in this diverting if fatally shallow treatise, we find the same reckless presentment of fallacy. The syllogism is served up to us in little shattered parcels, like a dime's worth of broken candy. "It is a commonly accepted scientific truth," we are told, "that the continuance of life in any living thing depends upon death." With all due honor to the ratiocination of Mr. Alden, we would venture to quote from a thinker whom he might possibly judge worthy of his passing respect, while not for an instant conceding him as an intellectual equal. "Were there no change in the environment but such as the organism had adapted changes to meet," says Herbert Spencer (in a trifling work of his called "Psychology," and one which it might strike Mr. Alden as almost an insolence to place on a level with his "Study of Death"), "and were it never to fail in the efficiency with which it met them, there would be eternal existence and universal knowledge."

Surely this quotation would go to prove that there is at least one great mind in the world besides that of our author, which does not hold the continuance of life in any living thing to be dependent on death, apart from ranking it as a "commonly accepted scientific truth." But Mr. Alden, who refers to the views of the alleged Belgian poet, Maeterlinck, on this gloomy subject, would perhaps place them above those of Mr. Spencer. He may rate Maeterlinck higher, too, than John Stuart Mill, that logician so distinctively second-rate because rash enough to believe in the evidence of his senses, and so tediously loyal to the multiplication table that he insisted on asserting, even till the hour of his death, that twice two does not make five.

" *Human existence,*" finely says Mill, " *is girt round with mystery : the narrow region of our experience is a small island in the midst of a boundless sea, which at once awes our feelings and stimulates our imagination by its vastness and its obscurity. To add to the mystery, the domain of our earthly existence is not only an island in infinite space, but also in infinite time. The past and the future are alike shrouded from us : we neither know the origin of anything which is, nor its final destination.*"

But Mr. Alden isn't to be "downed" by anybody so unpleasant and agitating to dear old ladies and nice young girls as the late John Stuart Mill. Plainly he doesn't at all believe in the small island or the boundless sea. To him human experience is a vast continent, every lake, river, and mountain of which he has explored, and concerning which he is prepared to give you the most cocksure opinions. As for the boundless sea, he has discovered all its shores, and mapped them out with commendable patience and diligence. He tells you (page 239) that Christ refused his "duties as a citizen of this world" because he wished to impress humanity by "the introduction of a new death, bringing it next to a new birth." He defines the dreadful early barbarisms of infant races (page 33) as "a shimmering veil of lights and shadows, of comings and goings, pulsing with the beating heart of the Great Mother, whose changeful garment forever hides and forever discloses the charm of her wondrous beauty." (This species of euphemism regarding cannibals may or may not produce its consoling results upon certain European widows and orphans, for whom the balm-bearing paragraph was perhaps intended.) He coolly informs us (page 48) that "there was a time when, in a sane mood and without jugglery of any sort, the living had communion with the souls departed"—thus agreeably complimenting the present century by explaining to it that when mankind were grossly ignorant, hideously warlike, absorbed in the grossest vices of slavery and polygamy, the Deity thought them worthy of special tribute and allowed them privileges denied to the purest and noblest men of more civilized times.

But what one might call the crowning audacity of this curiously self-assertive work may be found on page 320, where we are thus condescendingly enlightened: "There is one utterance by the Lord, recorded in the gospel, concerning the state of the children of the resurrection: 'They shall not marry, nor be given in marriage: neither shall they die any more.' It is remarkable that, in this declaration, *sex and death are joined together, as science shows them to be* in the specialization of organic life." Sex and death are joined together ! Yes, Mr. Alden, it is all truly "remarkable," as you say. And no less remarkable, in your book, is the assertion that "No divine revelation has ever *attempted to broach the inviolable secret*. Eye hath not seen, ear hath not heard, neither hath it entered into the heart of man to conceive."

In other words, biblical disclosure, on which this entire dissertation of three hundred and fifty-seven pages is founded, has no importance whatever ! The book of "Revelation" means nothing, and the four gospels are equally significant. And yet a perfervid religionist has talked with us through sentence after sentence of involved rhetoric, and rhetoric again and again so obtuse, so muddy in meaning, so deeply drenched with obscurity, so ponderously verbose, that all we have seen, from time to time, has been the dim flicker of an intensely orthodox and conventional faith. Surely Talleyrand erred when he said that words were given us to conceal our thoughts. Mr. Alden makes it indisputable that words may fulfil a different office—that of concealing our absence of thoughts, and investing this blank (if the phrase be permissible) with countless artful embroideries. His book is an exceedingly dangerous one to the large numbers of people who have not yet learned to think for themselves. It is misleading, specious, jesuitical. It is enormously pompous, while clad with a superficial pietism. I can compare it to nothing more aptly than to one of those gaudy and speckled growths of fungus which we sometimes meet in our woodland walks, fragile enough, despite its bigness, for the stroke of a cane to demolish it, and yet, if taken for an edible mushroom, packed with baneful results.

HILL-CREST.*

Reviewed by E. H. Wilson, A. M.

"Some books," says Lord Bacon, "are to be tasted, others to be swallowed, and some few to be chewed and digested." Many readers will find "Hill-Crest" a book "to be chewed and digested." Many doubtless will read it cursorily and be captivated by the story. But the author of this didactic story has lived a life full of rich and deep experiences, which enables her to write a book pregnant with meaning for all who can penetrate below the surface. A careful perusal will well repay the effort made, and a reader of fair perspicacity will readily discover the secret of the book, and feel grateful to the author for her message and not the less grateful because it requires careful search to find it.

The message, I say, is hidden; and if after a careful search you find and take into your life the sweet lesson, and it brings to your heart the peace and happiness it has brought to mine, I shall be forever thankful that I said to the little book, "Go forth."

---

* "Hill-Crest: A Novel," by Julia Colliton Flewellyn. Pp. 304; price, cloth $1.25; paper 50 cents. The Arena Publishing Company, Boston, Mass.

Whoso keeps in mind Lessing's noble words, "Did the Almighty, holding in His right hand *Truth* and in His left *Search after Truth,* deign to tender me the one I might prefer,--in all humility, but without hesitation I should request *Search after Truth,*' will rejoice that the reader may have the pleasure of discovery, sure that the message will bring "sweetness and light" into the life of the recipient, and so extend the kingdom of heaven.

No young person of either sex can read "Hill-Crest" thoughtfully without having the horizon of his life widened. The sweet wholesomeness of the book is refreshing. The view herein presented of the unselfish manliness and womanliness, the sweet reasonableness that should permeate and sanctify the home life, cannot fail to be suggestive and inspiring to every thoughtful reader, especially when contrasted with the life of children brought up under the baneful influence of a "fashionable mother" as illustrated by the following extracts:

Geraldine felt so discouraged with him [her brother Roger]. She had been brought up by her fashionable mother to believe that a girl's first duty was to marry well; and that if she used every means in her power to that end, even stooping to deceive and prevaricate, it was all a part of the correct plan to get a husband. Aiming at this mark, it was no wonder that her better nature was stifled and her views of life distorted. God pity the children of such mothers. They begin life at a disadvantage, with wrong ideas of what they owe to themselves and to their Creator, and living as they do in an atmosphere of deception and false pride, they imbibe so much of its poison that it accompanies them through life and renders them suspicious of others, making a farce of all that is good and holy in this world, and completely shutting out of their hearts all true faith and trust in the divine realities of the world to come.

* * * *

It pained Berthy to hear him say these things, and she laid her hand on his (they were sitting on the sofa) and said, "Roger, do not say there is no one to care for you; you have a mother," and she put great emphasis on the word. It had always seemed to her that to have a mother was the acme of human bliss. But her cousin only laughed a cold, hard laugh, such as one hears sometimes from an old world-worn man, but seldom from a boy of nineteen. The girl drew back from him; she did not understand the meaning of that laugh, but she did not like the sound of it. It seemed so unlike the bright, mirthful merriment that she remembered so well.

After the above conversation the young girl called to see her friend and confidante, Mrs. Kenyon, a woman whose nobility of soul had made her almost a mother to the motherless Berthy:

Berthy, in her characteristic way, had told Mrs. Kenyon everything, all Roger had said about his mother and his aimless life. It was a revelation to that true Christian woman; and she thanked God in her heart that she had been kept free from the folly of fashionable life, if it was to rob a *mother* of her holiest mission— her children's love and welfare.

A few days later Roger was in jail. Mrs. Kenyon visited him and had a long talk with him.

When Roger was left alone it did seem to him that his burdens were greater than he could bear. He threw himself on his bed, if a prison cot can be called by so respectable a name, and gave an almost heartbroken wail. He realized for the first time that what he had lacked all his life was the Christian influence of a good mother. How well he remembered that the boys used to say to him: "I tell you, McDonell, you have got the right kind of an old woman at your house. She is not forever worrying about your long goings and short comings, like ours." And he had thought himself it was kind of jolly that she let him have his own way so much. But now he knew if she had loved him as she ought she would have been anxious on his account, as any fond mother is; and now that he was in trouble, how sweet it would be to feel *her* caressing hand on his head as he had felt the hand of that blessed old woman as she sat by his side. There was a great difference between these two women, and it suddenly dawned on his mind that it was the love of God in the heart of one and the love of the world in the heart of the other that made the difference.

How a saintly person may influence the young to a higher life by skilful leading is apparent from this quotation:

"He is our Father, thee knows," said Mrs. Kenyon, "and has promised to hear His children when they cry unto Him. Thee is trusting Him every moment of thy life."

"Oh," said Berthy, "I am not trusting Him at all. I do not know how to trust Him."

"Is thee not sure the sun will rise to-morrow, and is not God able to manage thy little, unruly heart as well as this great universe?"

Those who are accustomed to the indiscriminate denunciation of pride will be surprised by the answer of Mr. Howell, a clergyman, to the question, "Is pride a fault, and how far can that pride be carried safely?" which was raised by Mr. Montgomery, an ideal young clergyman and the principal hero of the story:

"I do not quite understand you," he said, "pride is not always consistent with reason; but you speak of a certain kind of pride; please explain yourself."

"It is the pride of position, a sort of self-respect," said Mr. Montgomery, rising to his feet, for he felt he could make himself understood better when standing. "Those girls Mrs. Howell spoke of seem to think that their work shows too plainly that perhaps necessity has something to do in making them proficient, and I ask if it is right to nurture such pride, or to try with God's help to root it out of our natures?"

"Well," said the old man slowly, "I have thought a great deal on that subject myself, and have come to the conclusion that if there was more of that kind of pride, or independence, we will call it, the world would be the better. That is the stuff in a man that will make him economize rather than parade his poverty. It is what you see in a woman that makes her cover the shortcomings of her husband, instead of making it a town scandal; and, although in some cases it is carried too far, as are a great many admirable traits of character, still, in itself, it is a good thing."

A few weeks later Mr. Montgomery was summoned to Denver to meet a rich old uncle, who desired the companionship of his nephew for the brief remainder of his life. The principal part of the interview is subjoined:

"I may as well tell you at once that if what I have heard about you of late is true I will have nothing to do with you, if you are my brother's son."

"And what have you heard, may I ask?" said Charley, his face reddening at the implied insult.

"Well, I have heard that you were studying to be a preacher, and if that is so you will have to give it up, that is all," he said, modifying his first assertion somewhat.

"Well, you have heard the exact truth. I have been studying now for two years, and in another year I shall be ordained. If my life is spared it will be devoted to this work, and I trust that nothing will prevent my finishing the course I have mapped out." He said it in a proud, independent manner, as one who had no idea of changing his mind or purpose.

The old man arose from his seat on the sofa and stood before his nephew, his tall form bent forward and his keen black eyes shining with suppressed passion.

"Do you mean by that, that you will not give up preaching for anything I can offer? Do you realize what you are throwing away?"

"This is not the first time in my life that I have been tempted with gold, and I say to you now what I have said before, that no mere worldliness can tempt me to disobey the call of the gospel."

Young Montgomery requested Mr. Raymond, his uncle's lawyer, who was present, to ring for a servant to show him out of his uncle's house. As the young man was striding rapidly down the street, Mr. Raymond succeeded in overtaking him and pressed him to accept his hospitality, hoping that he might effect a reconciliation between nephew and uncle. During the evening the lawyer held a long and earnest conversation with the young man, which culminated thus:

"Mr. Raymond," said Charley, leaning towards him with a flushed face, "let us thoroughly understand each other before we go any farther. My uncle said plainly that he hated churches and preachers and would have nothing to do with them. And I, for my part, have decided to make the church my life work, and all he can say or offer will not shake my determination or change my purpose in the least. And as I have reason to believe he will not alter his views any, I cannot see how a reconciliation is going to be brought about."

"You do not pretend to say that you will absolutely throw up all hopes of your uncle's money for the sake of preaching the gospel?" and the lawyer stared at the young man as if he were a natural curiosity.

"I mean that identical thing," said Charley, setting his lips firmly together.

Mr. Raymond yielded for the nonce and the gentlemen spent the remainder of the evening with the family. On the morrow, however, Mr. Raymond took Mr. Montgomery out ostensibly to show him the town but really to attempt again to find some vulnerable spot in the young man's armour. While riding they met Mr. Raymond's friend and pastor, who, being suddenly summoned from town was perplexed by the difficulty of finding a suitable person to occupy his pulpit the next day. Mr. Montgomery was asked to preach. Mr. Raymond succeeded in prevailing upon the uncle to go with him to the morning service. After the evening service, young Montgomery informed his host that he should see his uncle as he intended to leave the city on the following morning. Against the protests of his host, he persisted and the interview was very affecting:

Charley took the cold, quivering hands between his own warm palms, and said, anxiously, "Are you feeling sick to-night?"

His uncle said in answer: "I have been sick ever since you came. I thought you ought to give up everything if I willed you my money, and I thought you a fool because you wanted to preach; but when I heard you this morning talk of how much Christ had sacrificed for us, and how He was tempted, and had resisted for our sakes, as I sat there I knew you felt every word you said. Oh! my old heart is broken." He added bitterly: "I have spent my whole life getting gold, and now it mocks me. I could not look at the silver on my dinner-table to-day, its glitter seemed like evil faces grinning at me. I would be glad to die, but I know I am not fit to be in the presence of the man-Christ that you pictured so plainly to me this morning. I have said and done all in my power all my life against the Church of God, and now I feel that the worst hypocrite whose name is on her books is better prepared for heaven than I am. I could go down on my knees to ask your pardon for what I said to you the other day."

It was nearly an hour since they came together, and they were still holding each other's hands, when Theodore made his appearance and asked if Mr. Raymond's carriage should wait any longer.

John Montgomery said promptly: "No, send it away, we do not want it to-night." And Mr. Raymond knew when Theodore told him what his master said, and how he was holding his nephew's hand and looking into his face, that Charley Montgomery had made no mistake in choosing the gospel in preference to his uncle's money, for now he was sure of both.

The reader's attention will be arrested from time to time by a sentiment like this:

It is good to know for ourselves that we have done our duty, but words of appreciation from lips we love are like springs of cooling water in the barren desert.

They knew why their aunt had always disliked Berthy so much; but as they looked at her now, in a neatly-fitting dark blue dress, with its trimmings of cardinal velvet, her eyes sparkling with merriment, her parted lips showing a line of white teeth, they wondered that they had ever considered her homely; yet they had, for Kathey had said many times, "There is no use trying the effect of nice clothes on Berthy, for they seem to be thrown away." What was it then that had wrought this change?

As if in answer to her thoughts, Berthy caught sight of her

brother's arm, "Oh, Charley," she said, "where is the sling for your arm?"

"I 'slung' it away so I could hug my new sister," he said, as he put his arm around her.

Kathey knew by the light in the dark face that those words of love and endearment were what she had needed all her life to bring out not only the beauty of her face but the glow of soulful interest in everything that was good and noble, and she chided herself that she had allowed the little, motherless girl to starve in her very presence, when a word of kindness or love would have been to her as daily food.

Why are hungry souls left to starve when a hearty grasp of the hand or a word of sympathy and encouragement or a glance of kindly interest even costs so little—nay, so enriches the giver? Perhaps it is because so many have not learned the lesson inculcated by our author thus:

"When did you learn that sweet secret of submission? I was older than you before I accepted it."

"From my spiritual guide," said Berthy, smiling and motioning toward the room occupied by her Quaker friend.

"Then you have, indeed, much to be grateful to her for. I meet a great many life-long Christians who do not seem to understand what I mean by the Fatherhood of God; it is the only true source of happiness."

He then went on to tell her something of his past life; how many struggles he had, and how mercifully he had been led through them all.

"I have always felt that in God's hand I was the instrument sent to save the soul of poor Uncle John; that was the strongest temptation I ever had to resist. There I was in a strange city, with only a few dollars in the world, and not enough to pay my board a week. I felt I had some right to his money, for I was his legal heir; but he denounced all forms of religion, and declared I should not have anything to do with the ministry if I lived with him. His lawyer, after kindly inviting me into his house, advised me to lay aside my radical views, and accept the home and money he, too, thought I had a right to expect. I tell you it was a battle I found hard to fight, but the victory more than paid for the conflict. The last two years of my uncle's life were those of perfect peace."

The quotations so freely made will serve to show that the atmosphere of the book is bracing, its doctrine sound, and that Mrs. Flewellyn accepts Emerson's dictum: "The only gift is a portion of thyself."

A NEW ARISTOCRACY.*

At the present time, when so many books of a trashy or artificial character are being put forth in elegant style and pushed by the great book houses, it is not surprising that works of fine ethical value and charmingly written, when published by obscure firms, fail to come

---

* "A New Aristocracy," by Birch Arnold. Bartlett Publishing Company, 30 & 32 West Thirteenth Street, New York, 46 West Larned Street, Detroit, Mich. Pp. 316; paper 50 cents.

before the attention of thoughtful people who would appreciate their intrinsic value. Recently I chanced to read Birch Arnold's "New Aristocracy" and was greatly impressed with its value at the present time. The story is simply but charmingly told; it is unique in many respects, and from cover to cover it is charged with the luminous and redemptive thought of the new time. I think our author underrates the part which unjust legislation plays in pressing the masses downward to a point where they lose the sturdy self-reliance which is at once essential for success in the industrial struggle and to industrial and national progress. Unjust laws augment miserable conditions and deaden the independent and naturally hopeful spirit in the human breast. Hence in all our discussions we must insist upon the establishing of just conditions which favor an equality of opportunity.

Our author very wisely emphasizes the necessity for individual development, and throughout the work throws out so many suggestions which will be helpful to earnest workers that I feel that this book merits a very wide reading, especially at the present time. As a story it is a delightful narration of the lives of three orphan children, thrown almost penniless on the world, on the death of their father, a rector in a village church. Their first experiment is in market gardening, and later their lives in the city, mingling with a larger world and bringing sunshine into many hearts, even when their own were shadowed, is very vividly brought out. The author aims to show the divine in the human heart of both rich and poor, and that the children of wealth no less than those "who are under the wheel" only reach the height where they know what true and enduring happiness is, when they learn to do for others, or adopt the principles of the Golden Rule into the web and woof of life. I would that "A New Aristocracy" could be placed in the hands of our people and that both young and old might read its bright, interesting and suggestive pages, for its influence could not fail to quicken conscience and inspire the divine in the heart of the reader.

B. O. FLOWER.

THE SNOWS OF YESTER-YEAR.*

REVIEWED BY NEWELL DUNBAR.

"Nay, never ask, this week, fair lord,
Where they are gone, nor yet this year,
Except with this for an over-word—
But where are the snows of yester-year?"

A story absolutely without action; occurring wholly within the bounds of a single Colorado house and garden; and containing

---

* "The Snows of Yester-Year: a Novel," by Wilbertine Teters. 12mo, pp. 244; price, cloth $1.25, paper 50 cents. Arena Publishing Company, Boston.

practically just four characters, of whom two are hopeless invalids, and another is little more than a hint. Yet, in a marked manner, this novel grasps the attention at the start and holds it to the very last word.

It will be remembered that James Russell Lowell once confessed that, when a young man freshly glorified with his university's *accolade*, and so unquestionably empanoplied for the battle of life, casting about for some way in which to distinguish himself in the coming fray he was overwhelmed with the conviction that every device of attack had already been tried—that no unachieved exploit remained. Like the Poet in Schiller's parable he found the universe appropriated. This misery is one that stares every clever young man and young woman in the face. Yet the author of the "Biglow Papers" managed, and every true aspirant in literature or elsewhere manages, speaking paradoxically, to discover the non-existent: *i. e.*, to find a peculiar field, an original vein. The doing this, it may be remarked in passing, grows more difficult every year—especially for minds of an overconservative cast. Fortunately, however, need of discouragement never exists; for there is and always will be a virgin fund in the universe ready to honor the drafts of the duly accredited, even though the returns made be merely in the form of old coin reminted.

Miss (or Mrs.) Wilbertine Teters—unless, possibly, that striking name be just a *nom de guerre*—is to be congratulated on having achieved in some degree this prerequisite success of originality. The unusualness of her book in the respects designated, of course, is not fully perceived by us, until we have finished reading and reached the contemplative and purely critical stage where we roll over synthetically and analytically in our mind the outcome. At first we simply take her story up and, finding ourselves interested, and every once in a while as we proceed receiving a distinct tingle of intellectual or æsthetic enjoyment, just read on with growing appreciation to the end.

How comes it that a delectable and strong effect results from so apparently inadequate a cause? Or if the points specified at the beginning of this critique constitute *obstacles* in the way of the pleasure received rather than its cause, what is the richness that associated with them can overcome a poverty so pronounced?

The story in the first place, then, is written in a strikingly bright and piquant style. There is a sparkle in the pages like Sévigné's. Further, they contain really subtle analysis and delineation of character; evince knowledge of the world, of society and of human nature, and abound in fresh, glancing, epigrammatic, witty and wise conversation, while they handle the "stage settings" effectively. (Colorado winters, by the way, furnish a subject that justly comes in for its full share of sarcasm.) The rise and progress of a tender passion—the never-failing theme—of course is told, reciprocated in this case, and diversified with somewhat unusual conditions. As to the passion, it belongs to a handsome, musical and conservative (at times shrewdly so), but consumptive (not too) young Canadian, Halcourte by name, who on account of his disease is able to keep alive only as an exile, and so is sojourning for very life's sake in the dry air of the Rockies; he has not always been a wreck, and is a past master in affairs of the heart. As to the reciprocation, that is supplied by Miss Norwista Ensleigh, a beautiful and pure-minded, soaring, much-read but very inexperienced young woman with an unoccupied and yearning heart; this is her first fray. Possibly, however, the passion and the reciprocation are *vice versa*. Of Miss Ensleigh it is said:

About love she knew absolutely nothing. Her simple method of learning how much she cared for a man had been to shut her eyes tightly and think how much she would like to live with him for a month, a year, maybe ten or twenty of them! to see the same face opposite her at the breakfast table every morning, until she would come to know every curve, every outline, every wrinkle, every weakness; and she never failed to know that it would take a very good face to stand that scrutiny, and that none could possibly look so pleasant to her now as Aunt Sue's. It might be all very well for a month, but at a year she weakened, and the prospect of a lifetime at the side of one man visibly discouraged her. At such times she thought seriously of convents when Aunt Sue should die.

The declaration takes place in a low-raftered, hot attic, while Norwista is sitting on a newspaper spread out upon the dusty floor. Naturally, Halcourte's illness is a stumbling-block and a torture to them both. When at last Norwista can bring herself to say she will marry him, and goes to him with a letter containing her consent, it is only to behold him expire of a hemorrhage before her face, the light of ecstasy dying in his dying eyes, and her very garment being stained by the sinister-hued current flowing from his lips that bears on its ill-starred drops his life away from them both and from happiness for either!

Aunt Sue, mentioned above, is merely a side show and hardly appears; yet, as is the case with all the characters—indeed rather more so than with the other minor ones—she is vividly drawn, though with frugal strokes. In her portrait here is an ingenuous feature:

Aunt Sue had a great horror of burglars, and every night made preparations for their coming (or his coming, rather, for her mind never grasped the possibility of the advent of more than one at a time) by putting on a chair drawn up to her bedside a hammer and a can of cayenne pepper. She intended to beat the burglar over the head with the hammer, after she had dazed him by throwing the cayenne pepper in his eyes. She hesitated a long time before she could make up her mind to beat him over the head, it seemed so brutal and unlady-like, but she finally decided it was the only thing she could do in order to stun him and thus gain time to run away.

The Major, too, or "the Majah," as he is addressed by "the Madame" (of her more anon) who was born in Florida, and on occasion of meeting him invariably develops a tendency to revert to the mitigated accent of her childhood—Major Treadwell, who has Christine, the amiable and long-suffering maidservant, for partner in the venture of supplying the remaining side shows, merely fulfils the function of bringing about Norwista's acquaintance with the Madame. He is like "the footman who calls out in impassive voice the name of the man who is to make or mar our fortunes and is seen no more." Nevertheless, the Major is sketched in with a firm and graphic touch. "Are there any rewards or punishments," the author asks, "for these careless people who stop for a moment in our path, and by a few hasty words change our whole life? Are they unhappy if misery ensues for us, or gay if happiness comes? Are they blown in our way by chance, or do they stop us from destiny?"

But the *pièce de résistance* of course, is the widely experienced, the reminiscent and the cynical Madame. The Madame, no doubt, is why the story was written. With the author she was clearly a labor of love. Above all the rest she stands out saliently and in a high degree of finish, and whoever has formed her acquaintance will not easily forget her. The Madame is likely to take her place in fiction, not indeed of the first rank, but in a grade below the first as an abiding character.

The Madame is a retired opera singer, with both an American and European experience, half-foreign in her ideas and ways, twenty-nine years old, but looking younger (though "all the world knows" she "would rather be thirty than seventeen"), of distinguished presence, yet pale and attenuated, and with green eyes and reddish hair, albeit possessed of uncommonly satisfactory and fastidiously shod feet which she never grows tired of admiring. She has been, at various times, pronounced by the infallible faculty an incurable consumptive—from a fever caught in Italy—with not a month of life before her. This cheerful sentence, however, bothers her not a whit; in spite of it, "if constantly and so mysteriously near death" she is "yet alive and never really ill," and has taken unto herself a husband—a muscular, matter-of-fact and slightly puzzled business man who adores her. Him, by the way, she alternately snubs and deluges with demonstrations of affection; and, in either case, he understands her about equally ill. "The Madame" (a nickname originally given her by this conjugal *attaché* because, as he luminously expresses it, "she made him feel that way the greater part of the time") is pestered with indifferentism and *ennui*. For her, too, life is

> "——an unweeded garden,
> That grows to seed."

Banished like Halcourte, and for the same reason, to semi-death in Colorado, which she detests, she spends her time mostly moping round revolving recollections. "She lived in dreams, and many pathetic 'I remembers' interspersed her slightest conversation. 'Yet to have no pleasure but that which is dreamed, or no joy but that which is past, is hard when one is still no more than twenty-nine,' she confessed." As Norwista is raw and optimistic, so in even greater degree is the Madame, who having seen the world has thereby grown disillusioned, apparently a thoroughpaced pessimist. She takes her Schopenhauer—and, by the way, she is very fond of quoting him—"straight." Being a woman, her pronounced talent for inconsequence was to be expected. For example:

"'Oh, where are the snows of yester-year?'" she had begun sadly once, but as everybody seemed to be profoundly ignorant she had returned to her silence. Now she seemed about to speak again. Had she more to say about that ballad of dead beauties?

"Men," said the Madame oracularly, "are like dogs. They need to feel the cut of your lash before they can be expected to lick your hands."

A deep silence followed this startling announcement.

But the keen and educated faculty of analysis constantly exhibited by her is by no means a matter of course; Mr. Henry James himself would have no cause for feeling ashamed of it. Evidently, the Madame takes to this sort of thing instinctively, as ducks to water; for when Norwista says to her, "I believe you would tear a soul apart in order to analyze it—analyzing doesn't cure," her sole and sufficient reply is, "Ah, but I like to go to the bottom." *Voila tout!* It is an irrepressible desire. Besides, in her view analysis affords her sex a defence. "Women in the abstract," she says, "know so much of the passion and pain of life; and the only way to hedge themselves in from it, is to carefully dissect every emotion that threatens to assail them."

The Madame (Mrs. Lawry to the best of the reviewer's belief is her proper style and title, though she is never once called by it) to all enthusiasm—except that of love—applies the wet blanket of cold incredulity, and mocks at most things. She is on one occasion represented as looking up at the stars, musing upon how often and from spots on the earth's surface how far apart she has gazed on them. Yet she could scarcely say so indifferently as wrote poor Heine—

> "Immerhin! Mich wird umgeben
> Gotteshimmel, dort wie hier,
> Und als Todtenlampen schweben
> Nachts die Sterne über mir."

Her apathy hardly extended so far as *that*, and she was mortally afraid of death, in any case, though half ashamed to show it.

To cite her own words: "It may seem strange that, with all my intellect, I should be such a coward, but I think that is the height of
intelligence. If people tell me they are . . . brave, I know they are
ignorant."

Theologically and philosophically, the Madame like many a
more finished speculator is undeniably "mixed," although as a rule
she is a pagan, and to a limited extent an Epicurean, yet with an
admixture of what seems like Buddhism imperfectly understood.

Having like Ulysses "*seen the town* and learned the mood of many
men"* (among them, be sure, not a few male would-be sirens), the
Madame discourses generously from her store. Smart sayings and
Rhadamantha-like *mots* flow from her as naturally as juice from
peaches. A book that, like this one, is wholly destitute of incident
must be composed of *something;* accordingly "The Snows of Yester-Year" may be said to be framed of talk and the Madame,
principally the Madame—or indeed, to be still more exact, principally of the Madame's talk. And right brilliant and sententious
talk it is. As a specimen of it (by no means at its best, but short and
readily detachable, and so adapted for quotation), read the following:

She yawned lazily and considered the beading on the toe of
her slipper. "All this talk that people have to go through
with, though," she resumed, "just after they are introduced and
before they can become friends, is so tiresome. I have often thought
how much more pleasant it would be, and how much effort it would
save our best foot—the one we are always supposed to be putting forward—if people would only write up the general facts of their lives;
where born, say, of whom, prefer winter or summer, water or wine,
materialist or idealist, and have their little histories up to date
printed on nice little slips of paper, and as soon as they are introduced, exchange slips. Now, just fancy us all strangers to each
other sitting around here reading each other's slips. I would read
Hal's and I should say, 'So your intimate friends call you Hal? Well,
how d'ye do, Hal! I rather think I shall like you.'"

"Thanks—a thousand times," murmured Halcourte softly.

To sum up this audacious personage in a vivid phrase, obviously
of Spanish extraction, that used to be and no doubt is now in vogue
in her despised though accepted asylum, the Madame is "more fun
than a bullfight." If she had only had her health and full vigor!

If the book has any moral or *motif*, beyond the Madame and the
admirable telling, it must be sought at the very end in the Madame's
recantation of her ever-ready scepticism. There, utterly worn out,
and sobbing as she lies back among her pillows, to the Norwista
whose faith and intellectual freshness and youth she has killed,
this feminine La Rochefoucauld says:

"I was all wrong, dear child, all wrong. My bitterness, my blame,
my disbeliefs—all were wrong. I would have you believe this.

* Odyssey, I., 3.

Under all the sorrow and suffering of life runs God's great purpose. Cling to your ideals, Norwista—always. Though seemingly mistaken and broken, they are symbols of higher things that we but dimly imagine. No life can fail to be rendered noble and unselfish, which, holding fast its belief in things beautiful and good, yet bears with smaller lives, and wears unflinchingly the Crown of Pain. I would have you remember this. All is God's will."

This retraction however, it is sad to say, bears small appearance of being uttered in good faith—at any rate, of expressing permanent conviction. This may seem like an ungracious assertion to make; but, in the reviewer's judgment, the text of the story appears to compel it. The Madame's words have every indication of being merely a sop—to an extremely intermittent conscience on the part of the Madame, or possibly to Public Opinion on the author's. Also, anybody so diabolically sharp as the Madame is described as being must have perceived the affair between Norwista and Halcourte. If she knew about it, why did she give no sign? If she did not know about it, she lacked in reality some of the keenness ascribed to her. Lastly, it must be said that the adoption of two doomed invalids as heroine and hero, together with the at times almost grotesquely unheroic when not actually repulsive details given or scenes depicted connected with their ailment, and the lovemaking of one of them with a healthy girl, seems a strange and an unfortunate choice of material for a novel. One is at a loss to see any satisfactory reason why the choice should have been made, or any adequate end gained by having made it. Truly, the authors of "Jane Eyre" and "Camille" (or their shades) drag a still lengthening chain of unenviable responsibility.

"The Snows of Yester-Year" is distinctly clever. Yet somehow the reader finds himself involuntarily wondering whether its writer's ability is limited to merely "copying" these characters whom she happens to have known, and whether the morbid atmosphere in which revolves what there is of story is detachable. If she can direct her style, her freshness, her brilliancy, her observation, philosophizing and power of analysis and delineation at will, and especially employ them on a more wholesome theme, and will do so, there is undoubtedly a public that, while welcoming this book, will be still more glad to hear from her again.

HERO TALES FROM AMERICAN HISTORY.*

The country has been so afflicted of late with the Napoleonic craze, that it is most pleasing to note a strong tendency toward a reaction, and literature dealing with men and women of conviction, conscience, and principle is again receiving the attention which has

* "Hero Tales from American History," by Henry Cabot Lodge and Theodore Roosevelt. Illustrated; cloth; pp. 336; price $1.50. New York Century Publishing Company.

been so lavishly bestowed upon the incarnation of selfish ambition which darkened Europe and did so much toward deadening the fine sensibilities of humanity.

Among the notable new books for the young which partake of the reaction toward things more wholesome and manly, is a volume from the scholarly pens of Senator Henry Cabot Lodge of Massachusetts and Theodore Roosevelt, the much maligned head of the New York Police Commission. The stories are written in a stirring manner. The authors have selected great figures and thrilling episodes in our history and have treated them in a way at once scholarly and vivid. The character sketch of George Washington is, perhaps, one of the strongest delineations of Washington's character in a few words I have ever read. I know of nothing written for the young which will compare with it. The stories of the battles of Trenton and of New Orleans are particularly strong. But the work as a whole is most admirable, as it will impress upon the minds of our youth, the principles for which our great men have dared and frequently died, and thus do much toward stirring the higher and finer impulses in the child mind.

B. O. FLOWER.

Most truly Yours
Walter Clark

THE ARENA.

No. LXXV.

FEBRUARY, 1896.

THE LAND OF THE NOONDAY SUN — ANAHUAC — MEXICO.

BY WALTER CLARK.

While Europe, Asia and Africa were having their revolutions and dynastic changes, which are narrated in the so-called "Histories of the World," the great drama of life was equally being played out on this side of the Atlantic. Here likewise great empires rose, flourished and passed away, to be succeeded by others. Here too ambitious men intrigued, schemed and fought, to obtain fame which they fondly believed would last forever. On either side of the ocean, in ignorance of their contemporaries, life proceeded on parallel lines. In each hemisphere from time to time some great nation believed its own civilization "the world," its own king "king of kings," its own government and rule the final and lasting one. All have disappeared, and the moon shines coldly down and the night winds sigh alike over the ruins of Nineveh and Palenque, Memphis and Uxmal, Carthage and Cholula, Troy and Tenochtitlan, and many another metropolis whose walls and temples have been dust and whose heroes, kings and people have been nameless for many a dead and forgotten century.

When Mexico first became known to Europeans it was the seat of a great empire where the arts and sciences flourished, while savages of the lowest grade of barbarism roamed at will throughout the territory now covered by the great "Republic of the North." Mexico was first discovered to Europeans by Cordova, who landed at Cape Catoche in Yucatan, 1517, somewhat more than one hundred years before the landing of the Pilgrim fathers at Plymouth Rock. In 1518 Grijalva anchored off the site of modern Vera Cruz and opened communication with the Aztecs. In April, 1519, Hernando Cortez landed at the same spot and with scant ceremony began his march upon the capital which he entered in November of that year. From the death of Guatemozin, the last Aztec emperor, in August, 1521, the Spaniards held possession of the country exactly three hundred years till the withdrawal of Juan O'Donoju, the last Spanish viceroy, in August, 1821, when Spain recognized the independence of the country, which had been secured by the combined efforts of the descendants of the conquered Indians and the native descendants of their conquerors.

The history of Mexico prior to the conquest has been only partially recovered. The earliest authentic fact ascertained is

CATHEDRAL, FACADE.

that, about A. D. 650, the Toltecs were in possession of a vast empire. This was coeval with the disorganization existing in Europe after the irruption of the Goths and Vandals, and a century and a half before the coronation of Charlemagne, which event marked the beginning of the social and political structure of modern Europe. Who were the predecessors of the Toltecs, and who the Toltecs themselves and whence they came, will remain unknown until some new Champollion shall arise to decipher the writings chiselled in the stones and pencilled in the marble of the mighty cities whose ruins extend for miles along the rivers of Yucatan. Tradition relates that all these successive nations who held sway in Mexico came from the northwest, and everything in fact points to their Mongolian origin, which is true perhaps of all the aborigines of the two Americas save the Esquimaux and Greenlanders, whose ancestors in some remote age may have crossed over from Europe.

In the eleventh century, about the time William of Normandy was founding the English monarchy upon the victory at Hastings, another conqueror — but nameless now forevermore — leading the Aztecs from the northwestward, came down upon the Toltecs, enervated by the plenty and ease of their long dominion, and drove them out to Yucatan and Guatemala, where the degenerate remnants of their descendants still linger.

CATHEDRAL, INTERIOR.

The Aztecs held high rule till four and a half centuries later they in turn met their fate beneath the iron rule of Cortez and his adventurers. The Aztec civilization possessed many of the arts and sciences and was the equal of the contemporaneous civilization of Asia and in many respects not inferior to that then existing in Europe. It was, however, marred by human sacrifices, not less than twenty thousand victims, mostly prisoners of war, being offered annually, it is said, in their temples.

During the three centuries of Spanish rule there were sixty-four viceroys, all of them being Europeans except one Juan de

POPOCATAPETL.

Acuña (1722–34) who was born in Peru. The first and most prominent viceroy was Antonio de Mendoza; next to him Pacheco (1789–94) was the most famous. The revolt against Spain was inaugurated by Hidalgo, a priest, Sept. 16, 1810, which is the natal day of Mexican independence. The next year he was captured and shot, when the leadership was taken up by Morelos, another priest. The republic has shown its gratitude by naming a state after each of these patriots.

Independence was acknowledged by Spain in the treaty of Aguala, August, 1821, and Augustin Iturbide became provisional president. The crown was offered to a royal prince of Spain but being declined, Iturbide was proclaimed emperor May, 1822. In March, 1823, ten months later, he had to flee for his life and returning from England in 1824 was taken prisoner and shot. Between 1821 and 1868 the form of government was changed ten times. Over fifty persons succeeded each other as presidents, dictators or emperors, both emperors being shot —Iturbide in 1824 and Maximilian in 1867 — and more than three hundred successful or abortive revolutions are recorded; but amid all this confusion the thoughtful student will detect a steady progress towards the ultimate triumph of those Liberal ideas which are the true basis of national freedom. The long struggle between the aristocratic and clerical party termed *Escosses* and the democratic element styled *Yorkinos* or Liberals has definitely resulted in victory for the latter, as with the similar struggle in France.

The first constitution was adopted in 1824 and was modeled upon that of the United States, though strange to say this country did not recognize the Mexican Republic till 1829. In 1838–39 there was war between Mexico and France. In 1845 Texas seceded, and when President Santa Anna attempted to coerce her at the head of his army, she took the president prisoner. On June 4, 1845, war between Mexico and the United States began over a dispute as to the little strip of territory between the Nueces and the Rio Grande rivers; Texas having become a member of the American Union, which claimed the Rio Grande as the boundary, while Mexico asserted that the Nueces river, a few miles farther north, was the true line. This war was ended nearly three years later by the treaty of Guadaloupe Hidalgo, ratified May 19, 1848, whereby Mexico ceded quite half of her entire territory. Meantime General Taylor had won the battles of Palo Alto, Resaca de la Palma and Monterey in 1846, and the brilliant victory of Buena Vista on Feb. 22, 1847, where he defeated four times his number. In March of the latter year General Scott landing at Vera Cruz had marched on the capital, defeating the enemy at the National

NATIONAL PALACE.

Bridge, Contreras, Cherubusco, Cerro Gordo, Molino del Rey, and Chapultepec, and capturing the capital in September. Several years later, in 1853, the United States purchased the lower part of Arizona for $10,000,000, a transaction known as the Gadsden purchase.

In 1857 the new constitution was adopted, which with some slight modifications is still in force. In 1861 the British, French and Spanish governments jointly invaded Mexico in the interest of their subjects who held the repudiated bonds of Mexico. The English and Spanish withdrew the next year, but the French persisted and in July, 1863, set up an imperial government and caused the crown to be tendered to Maximilian, an Austrian archduke who entered the country with his empress in 1864. Under pressure from the United States, which had been relieved from its internal complications, the French troops were gradually withdrawn in 1866 and 1867, and Maximilian, being left without support, was captured and shot at Querétaro June 19, 1867, together with his two leading generals, Miramon and Mejia. Juarez, a full-blood Indian by the way, became president and restored order with a firm hand. He died in 1871 and was succeeded by Lerdo de Tejada.

In 1876 Porfirio Diaz headed a successful revolution and became president, but was defeated at the election of 1880 by Gonzales. In 1884, however, General Diaz was elected, and reëlected in 1888 and again in 1892. He is a man of superior ability and has the confidence of the country as an upright and patriotic man. In Mexico, as in France, the era of revolution seems to be closed and the country has apparently entered upon a long period of profound repose and peaceful development.

Such is a summary of the stormy history of a country whose people have been as volcanic as their soil. Their government is modeled upon that of this country. There are twenty-seven states, with two territories (Tepic and Lower California) and a Federal District, like our District of Columbia. The Federal Senate consists of two members elected by each state and the Lower House of Congress is apportioned upon the basis of population. The president is elected upon the electoral plan used in this country, and the cabinet consists of seven secretaries for state, war, navy, etc. Their constitution having been adopted later than ours has profited by some of the mistakes shown by our experience; they have avoided the life tenure for the Federal Supreme Court, whose judges are chosen for a term of six years, and the two federal senators for each state are chosen by the people thereof instead of by its legislature. In general, the limits of the powers and rights of the federal and state governments, respectively, differ little from ours. The law has been codified, the Code Napoleon being the law of the land.

AZTEC ANTIQUITIES.
CALENDAR.

The population of Mexico is about twelve millions, of which six millions, or one-half, are full blooded Indians, four millions mixed whites and Indians, one and one-half millions native whites, probably two hundred thousand Americans from the United States and one hundred thousand Europeans, one hundred thousand other foreigners including Chinese, some ninety thousand mulattoes and only ten thousand negroes. These are round numbers but approximate the mark. Spanish is the recognized national language but the majority of the nation still use the various Indian dialects of their ancestors. The Catholic church has been stripped of its privileges and a large portion of its property, and the political influence it formerly enjoyed is rigidly repressed, but as yet there are comparatively very few Protestants. Prior to the anti-clerical revolution in 1859, the Catholic church owned more than one-third of all the property in the country.

The area of the Republic of Mexico is about seven hundred and fifty thousand square miles, equal to fifteen states the size of North Carolina or nearly seventeen the size of New York. The largest states are in the north — Chihuahua eighty-eight thousand square miles, Sonora seventy-six thousand, and Coahuila sixty-three thousand; but these are very thinly populated, having only two to three people to the square mile. The smallest state, Tlascala, has less than sixteen hundred square miles of territory, being larger

AZTEC ANTIQUITIES — CHAC MOOL STATUE.

than Rhode Island but smaller than Delaware. The most populous states are Jalisco, with one and a quarter millions, and Guanajuato, which has also passed the million mark. The least populous states are Colima with seventy thousand and Campeachy with ninety thousand. The states are divided into departments, counties, cantons, etc. The boundary line between Mexico and the United States is eighteen hundred miles in length. Mexico lies between the eighty-seventh and one hundred seventeenth meridians of longitude and between the fifteenth and thirty-second degrees of latitude, the northern part being in the same latitude with Georgia and our Gulf States. The central and southern parts are in the latitude of Hindostan, Siam, Arabia and Upper Egypt. The shape of

CHAPULTEPEC CASTLE.

the country roughly resembles a cornucopia with its mouth to the north, which may possibly prove significant.

The great bulk of the territory of the republic is a high central plateau, averaging seven thousand feet above sea level. This descends abruptly on the east to the Gulf of Mexico, and slopes more temperately to the Pacific. This causes a division of the country into three zones. The *Tierra Caliente*, or torrid zone, lies on the shores of the Gulf and the Pacific; here are grown coffee, sugar, bananas and other tropical fruits. The great central plateau is called *Tierra Frias* or frigid zone, and the slopes on either side *Tierra Templada* or temperate zone, for in one day's travel, passing down the mountains, the traveller can see every variety of product and feel corresponding changes in temperature. The rainy season varies in different localities, but roughly speaking embraces the months from June to October, while during the rest of the year rain very rarely falls. A clear sky prevails, as a rule, the entire year except for a few hours of the day during the rainy season.

The second tallest mountain is Popocatapetl, which, towering to the height of nearly eighteen thousand feet, hangs over the city and valley of Mexico, while Orizaba, 18,314 feet high, and midway to Vera Cruz from the capital, looks down upon the scorching sun-

VERA CRUZ. PALACE, WITH SHIPS AT ANCHOR.

burnt plains of the *Tierra Caliente,* with the smooth summit of the mountain shining like burnished steel, in a covering of eternal snow and ice. Orizaba, which is a half mile higher than Mont Blanc, the highest peak in Europe, is the culminating point of the North American continent, Mt. St. Elias, in Alaska, being 18,010 feet in height. Further south, Jorullo, which was a volcano thrown up in 1759, still smoulders, though beneath its wreath of smoke it wears a diadem of snow.

The annual income of the republic is forty million dollars, half of it being derived from the customs. The national expenditures about equal the receipts, over one-fourth (ten million, five hundred thousand) being expended on the army and navy. The navy is lilliputian, but the army numbers about the same as that of the United States — twenty-five thousand men. The uniform is a dark blue. The national debt is one hundred seventy-five millions. The assessed value of property for taxation is five hundred millions, the actual value being nearly double that sum.

The mineral wealth of Mexico is incalculable. The gold and silver taken out of her mines since the occupation by Cortez foot up over four thousand millions of dollars, and her mineral wealth is scarcely tapped. The largest silver mines are at Guanajuato, Guadalajara, Catorce and Zacatécas. Petroleum, iron and sulphur are abundant. The full capacity of the country as to agriculture has not yet been fairly tested. The average yield of cotton is seven hundred pounds per acre, being three times the average in our southern States.

HERNAN CORTEZ' TREE.

Coffee of the finest and best quality is grown, and its cultivation is rapidly increasing since the advent of railroads. The cultivation of coffee was introduced into the West Indies in 1714, but for some unexplained reason it took nearly a hundred years longer to reach Mexico, where its cultivation began early in the present century. Tobacco is indigenous, and indeed takes its name from Tobaco, in Yucatan. In the *Tierra Caliente* three crops of Indian corn annually, on the same ground, is the rule.

Such in brief résumé are the history, geography, civil status, climatology and products of our next-door neighbor who is so little known to us, but who offers to our friendly enterprise treasures beyond computation and to the traveller and visitor, scenery of surpassing beauty and interest. Future articles will be more in detail and less general in their nature.

It may be mentioned incidentally that Cortez, who was rewarded for his conquest by the title of Marquis of the Valley (of Oaxaca, in southern Mexico) still has descendants living in the state of Oaxaca who bear the surname of Monteleone, and the grandson of the emperor Iturbide, who was also adopted by the emperor Maximilian as his heir, is an officer in the army of the republic.

Much as Mexico owes to the genius and firm government of Juarez and afterwards of Diaz, it is no less indebted to the rapid extension of the railroad system which now embraces near eight thousands miles and reaches nearly every important point. Railroads are great educators and by offering markets in other quarters for the overproduction of localities give an incentive to industry and more profitable employment than revolutions and *pronunciamentos* to the energetic, active-minded element of the population. Besides, the prompt concentration of troops enables government to repress insurrection in its beginning. The railroads are usually of the standard gauge and rarely run nearer any town than a mile or two.

By a curious experiment, the sharpest and shrewdest criminals upon conviction are sentenced to serve upon the police force, and it is said the plan works admirably, there being no better officers than these men when intrusted with power and responsibility. Upon the same plan, the leaders of brigands when captured are offered by the government the alternative of taking a command in the army, devoted to the suppression of brigandage, and this has been the most effectual means of clearing the country of that pest.

Mexico has not made the mistake of contracting her currency, and hence being untrammelled in her progress has marched on by leaps and bounds in her development during these latter years, while the United States, owing to a contrary policy, has been suffering under the blight of a long enduring depression.

A HALF CENTURY OF PROGRESS.

BY MARY LOWE DICKINSON, PRESIDENT OF THE NATIONAL
COUNCIL OF WOMEN OF THE UNITED STATES.

In the month of June of last year there went out
from the president of the National Council of Women of the
United States the following invitation, which we venture
to repeat, as indicating as fully as any later utterance the
significance and scope of the occasion to which it refers:

Believing that the progress made by women in the last half-century
along religous, philanthropic, intellectual, political and industrial lines
may be still further promoted by a more general acknowledgment of
their efforts and successes, it has been decided to hold in New York
City a gathering whose object shall be to give deserved recognition of
woman's past achievement.

As an appropriate time for such a celebration, the eightieth birthday
of Mrs. Elizabeth Cady Stanton has been chosen. Her half-century of
pioneer work for the advancement of women makes her name a natural
inspiration for such an occasion, and her life an appropriate object of
the congratulation and homage of the world.

The celebration will take place under the auspices of the National
Council of Women of the United States, which is composed of twenty
national organizations. All affiliated societies, organizations outside the
Council, and interested individuals are hereby cordially invited to unite
with the Council in grateful recognition of the debt which the women
of the present owe to the pioneers of the past.

From the supreme interest in the enfranchisement of woman, the ideas
and influence of Mrs. Stanton and her great co-worker, Miss Anthony,
have permeated all fields of progress, until these leaders have become
the natural centre of that group of pioneers in education and philanthropy, in the professions, the industries and the arts whom we hope
to bring together on this occasion. We aim to show to the younger generation, not alone the work that has been wrought by and for women,
but the world's great women workers whose struggles and sacrifices
have brought nearer a new day of truer freedom and nobler development
for the race.

Naturally the invitation reached a multitude of individuals thoughtful enough to recognize the relation of
woman's progress to human progress. From men and
women on both sides of the ocean, whose names are identified with efforts to lift humanity to the highest type of
moral, social and intellectual life, it brought responses expressing warmest sympathy with the proposed reunion.
Similar responses came, not only from the organizations
represented in the National Council, but from scores of

(By permission, from copyright photograph by G. G. Rockwood, New York.)

ELIZABETH CADY STANTON.

(From latest photograph.)

others not yet affiliated therewith, and each organization, whether composed of men and women, or of women only, was invited to representation on a general committee, from whose members were chosen special committees who, with the assistance of additions from the patron list, prosecuted the local work. That patron list, too long for insertion here, included many names from both continents, whose weight depended not upon social standing, but upon records of coöperation in educational, philanthropic or political work, such as had for its object the betterment of human conditions and the development of the race.

As the above invitation indicates, the reunion had a fourfold function. First of all, it was intended to emphasize a great principle of truth and justice, and to throw that principle into grand relief by showing the loftiness of character that had resulted from its embodiment in a grandly unique personality. The world naturally thinks of the personality before it thinks of the principle. It has at least so much unconscious reverence and courtesy left as to honor a noble woman even when failing to rightly apprehend a noble cause. And yet it was the principle which, within the woman, had operated as a mighty moral force, guiding her efforts and dominanting her powers for more than half a century. It was the principle, acting like the little leaven within the mass of accumulated circumstances and inert conditions, which Mrs. Stanton, of all women, would desire to see emphasized and exalted to its true place in the minds of loyal women and admiring men.

Appreciation and enthusiasm for this grand principle of human equality and the grand personality that fought for it ran quite too many years at our feet in a sluggish, creeping stream, whose flowing was looked down upon with indifference or scorn. In these later years the current has risen like a tide, moving steadily upward, flooding many hearts with loyalty and stirring many lips to utterance. To afford this tardy loyalty its proper outlet and expression, to render more tangible and definite all vague and hesitant sympathy, to crystallize the growing sentiment in favor of human freedom of body and brain and soul, to give youth the opportunity to reverence the glory of age, to give hearts their utterance in word and song, was perhaps the most popular purpose of the reunion. In other words, it gave an opportunity for those who revered Mrs. Stanton as a queen among women, to show their reverence, and to all others an opportunity to recognize the work her life had wrought, and to see in it an epitome of the progress of a century.

In the third place, the reunion was an expression and illustration of the distinctive idea of the National Council, which aims to give recognition and honor to all good in all human effort without demanding uniformity of opinion as a basis of approval or coöperation. It claims and acts upon the fact of possible unity of service for humanity, notwithstanding differences of creed and conviction and methods and plans.

Of the numerous organizations which separately declared their sympathy with the movement to honor Mrs. Stanton's birthday, by a reunion of women workers and a consideration of the sources and value of woman's work, hardly any two were alike in views, in scope or in practice, yet all could meet together in loyalty to a great principle, and in honor to a great personality. Some societies, indeed, which had never before found common ground enough to give them a place to stand amicably side by side, met most cordially upon this plane. Not even the shadow of prejudice could obscure their appreciation of that which appeals to all humanity, as distinctively noble, and unity of feeling on this one point seemed for the time being strong enough to sweep away all trace of doubt of one another, and all sense of difference in deed and creed. The things that separate shrank back into the shadows where they belong, and all hearts brave enough to think, and tender enough to feel, found it easy to unite in homage to a life which had known a half century of struggle to lift humanity from bondage and womanhood from shame.

I have said the object of the reunion was fourfold. Aside from Mrs. Stanton and her work, its chief interest centered around the large band of pioneers composed of women who in one line or another of helpful work, had given the best years of their lives to labors that tended to the betterment of mankind. The gathering meant, for them, aside from all deeper significance, an opportunity to take one another by the hand, to look into one another's faces. Very sweet faces many of them were, too,

> "Wearing marks of age and sorrow,
> As the midnight wears its stars."

In the general plan of the celebration it was hoped to gather together representatives of every phase of woman's work. Lack of time would, of course, prevent elaborate records of the progress in each particular line during the last half century; but those most familiar with each department had prepared outline sketches of progress in their own especial field, and it was intended that brief abstracts from these records should be presented at the celebration.

The progress of woman along educational, reform, industrial or artistic lines has been by ways both long and hard, how hard they only know, who, never once turning back when the road grew thorny and steep, opened the track for the later pilgrims who have followed in their steps. Through what currents of opposition, varying in speed and force, through what deserts of ignorance, over what mountains of prejudice, across what streams of adverse criticism they made their way, with little beyond the light of truth and scarcely the dream of freedom for a guide, driven by the innate longing and love for both truth and freedom, rather than by any hope of securing it, they pressed onward with the ultimate result of a new and vital public sentiment, a new and wider outlook, new powers and possibilities, new projects; a decided gain in fact, on all that meant new hope for humanity because it meant new life for womankind.

And this reunion was the first general recognition, the first almost universal frank acknowledgement of the debt the present owes to the past. It was the first effort to show the extent to which later development has been inspired and made possible by the freedom to think and work, claimed in that earlier time by women like Mrs. Stanton and Miss Anthony and many others whose names stand as synonyms of noble service for the race. To those who looked at the reunion from this point of view it could not fail of inspiration. He who stands on any height, material, intellectual or spiritual, gains strength to go higher still by a backward glance which shows him that nothing began in himself, that for every stepping-stone by the way he is a debtor to one who went before. Our whole complex problem, and our last half century of progress therein, lost nothing of dignity when, on this night of recognition, students young and old listened while the president of one of our noblest colleges for women traced eloquently the relation between present and past conditions of woman student life, proving our debt to the noble women who knew what it was in earlier days, first to plead, and then to knock, and last to batter at the brazen gates of prejudice and tradition which shut them out of the knowledge they desired.

For the followers in lines of philanthropic work to look in

the faces and hear the voices of women like Clara Barton
and Mary Livermore; for the multitude enlisted in the
crowded ranks of literature to feel in the living presence
what literature owes to women like Julia Ward Howe; for
the white ribbon army to turn from its one great leader of
to-day whose light spreading to the horizon does not obscure or dim the glory of the crusade leaders of the past;
for art lovers and art students to call to mind sculptors
like Harriet Hosmer and Anna Whitney, and remember
the days when art was a sealed book to women; for the
followers of the truly divine art of healing to honor the
Blackwell sisters, and the memory of Madame Clemence
Lozier; for the mercy of surgery to reveal itself in the
face of Dr. Cushier, who has proved for us that heart
of pity and hand of skill need never be divorced; for women
lifting their eyes to meet the faces of Phœbe Hanaford and
Anna Shaw and other women who to-day in the pulpit as
well as out of it may use a woman's right to minister to
needy souls; for the ofttime sufferers from unrighteous
law to welcome women lawyers; for the throng of working
women to read backward through the story of four hundred industries to their beginning in the "four," and remember that each new door had opened because some woman
toiled and strove; for all these exercises were a part of a
great thanksgiving pæan, each phase of progress striking
its own chord, and finding each its echo in the hearts that
held it dear. It is not strange that all together were united
in praise of the one great principle of human equality,
which alone made progress possible in any one of their
chosen fields, or that as the pioneers in other fields grouped
themselves about Mrs. Stanton, as the centre of interest
and homage, they all should give her work its rightful
rank, its leadership in importance and in power. How
could they fail to do this when more and more is the fact
emphasized that no amount of nurture, no outpouring of
the rain of patronage or the sun of sympathy is going to
bring fruit of freedom to a tree that has no freedom in fibre
or in root. We may nurse and cherish any one branch of
our good works, but if the essential life-giving principle
never reaches up to our branch from the root, not only
is it fruitless, but soon or late "it withereth away."

The fact needs no illustration. Justice must precede
mercy; no amount of alleviation of human conditions will
avail for permanent good while the giver, bestowing favor
with one hand, shuts tightly in the other the key that
opens all sealed doors and makes a free way for the human
soul and brain to claim its birthright.

Mrs. Stanton's life and work were an utterance of a century's long-stifled demand for this essential freedom at inmost fiber and root of life; for our birthright of power to live and move and *have* our being, to *have* it for ourselves and for the best we can make of it and do with it as a part of the divine inheritance and gift of "Him in whom we live and move."

To the student of history, or to him who can read the signs of the times, there was such a profound significance in this occasion as makes one shrink from dwelling too much upon the external details. Yet viewed as a pageant only, it was a most inspiring sight, and one truly worthy of a queen. Indeed, as we run the mind back over the pages of history, what queen ever came to a more triumphant throne in the hearts of a grateful people? What woman ever before sat silver-crowned, canopied with flowers, surrounded not by servile followers, but by men and women who brought to her court the grandest service they had wrought, their best thought crystallized in speech and song. Greater than any triumphal procession that ever marked a royal passage through a kingdom was it to know that in a score or more of cities, in many a village church on that same night festive fires were lighted, and the throng kept holiday, bringing for tribute not gold and gems but noblest aspirations, truest gratitude and highest ideals for the nation and the race.

The great central meeting was but one link in a chain; yet with its thousands of welcoming faces, with its eloquence of words, with its offering of sweetest song from the children of a race that once was bound but is now free, with its pictured glimpses of the old time and the new time flashing out upon the night, with the home voices offering welcome and gratitude and love, with numberless greetings from the great, true, brave souls of many lands, it was indeed a wonderful tribute, worthy of the great warm heart of a nation that offered it and worthy of the woman so revered. Her birthday ought, from this time forth, to be a day of jubilee, to mark an era in national life, a day when mothers call upon their daughters to strive for the highest and best and upon their sons to recognize what the nation owes to womanhood.

From the suggestions of the president of the National Council of Women the two following may be emphasized:

Why should not this occasion [she asked] be the beginning of an era of gratitude and recognition in which, as the pioneer in one line of work or another comes to ripeness of years and service, her eightieth birthday shall be remembered, especially by those who have profited by her leadership in their own chosen field? How many such women have given time, labor, strength, and have known suffering and sacrifice, but have during a long life been unable to aid the cause they loved in more material ways. Why should not the friends of education, for example, make it possible for the one who is most truly the pioneer in that field of progress to fulfil her heart's desire, thus helping to advance some favorite branch of the work, and giving the aged leader at the same time this crowning and special joy of ability to bestow? Think how religion and philanthropy, and countless other causes, would be benefited by such birthday funds, and far more and better, how gratitude and reverence, and the sense of obligation to cherish and develop what we have, would grow and be kept alive by the memory of what our possessions cost.

And one question more [she added]. Why should not the anniversary of this eightieth birthday be made a national holiday, a day in which to rear statues to heroines as well as to heroes, a day when institutions if to women belongs the praise of establishing, endowing or supporting them, shall be dedicated to the women? Why not a Stanton Free Library, a Barton Hospital, a Hosmer Museum of Art, an Anthony School of Citizenship, and many more, each receiving its dedication on the 12th day of November, which should evermore be known among us as the pioneer holiday, the day when the present brings its offering to the past?

If Mrs. Stanton's life had done no more than to be the inspirer of a plan like this, it would have justified the thronging crowds, the multiplied gatherings, the glorious tribute of song from over the sea. It seemed fitting that Madame Antoinette Sterling, who, twenty years ago, took her wonderful voice away to England, where it won for her a unique place in the hearts of the nation, should, on returning to her country, give her first service to the womanhood of her native land. "I am coming a week earlier," so she had written, "that my first work in my own beloved America may be done for women. I am coming as a woman and not as an artist, and because I so glory in that which the women of my country have achieved." So when she sang out of her heart, "Oh, rest in the Lord; wait patiently for Him," no marvel that it seemed to lift all listening hearts to a recognition of the divine secret and source of power for all work, whether of women or of men.

One charming feature of entertainment was a series of pictures called "Then and Now," each illustrating the changes in woman's condition in some one particular during the last fifty years. And after this upon the dimness there shone out one after another, the names of noble women like Mary Lyon, Maria Mitchell, Emma Willard and many others whose influence has been felt upon all progress, but who have passed away. Upon the shadows and the silence broke Madame Sterling's voice in Tennyson's "Crossing the Bar."

And when this was over, as with one voice, the whole audience sang softly, "Auld Lang Syne."

And last, but not least, should be mentioned the greetings that poured in a shower of telegrams and letters from every section of the country, and many from over the sea. These expressions, not only personal congratulation for Mrs. Stanton, but utterances of gladness for the progress in woman's life and thought, for the conditions so much better already than in the past, and for the great hope for the future, would make of themselves a most interesting and wonderful chapter, unfortunately altogether beyond the limits of our space. Among them may be mentioned letters from Lord and Lady Aberdeen, from Lady Henry Somerset and Frances E. Willard, from Canon Wilberforce and many others, including an address from thirty members of the family of John Bright, headed by his brother, the Right Honorable Jacob Bright; a beautifully engrossed address, on parchment, from the National Woman Suffrage Society of Scotland, an address from the London Women's Franchise League, and a cablegram from the Bristol, England, Women's Liberal Association; a letter from the Women's Rights Society of Finland, signed by its president, Baroness Gripenberg of Helsingfors; telegrams from the California Suffrage Pioneers, and others from the Chicago Woman's Club; from the Toledo and Ohio Woman's Suffrage Society, from the son of the Rev. Dr. William Ellery Channing, and a telegram and letter from citizens and societies of Seneca Falls, N. Y., accompanied with flowers and a handsome piece of silver. There were letters from Hon. Oscar S. Straus, ex-minister to Turkey, Miss Ellen Terry, Professor D. Cady Eaton of Yale University, and scores of others. An address was received from the Woman's Suffrage Association of Utah, accompanied by a beautiful oxidized silver ballot-box; and from the Shaker women of Mount Lebanon came an ode.

Numerous organizations and societies, both in this country and abroad, wished to have their names placed on record as in fullest sympathy with the movement. Many organizations were present in a body, and one was reminded, by the variety and beauty of the decorations of their boxes, of the Venetian Carnival, as the occupants gazed down from amid the silken banners and the flowers, upon the throng below.

The whole occasion was indeed a unique festival, unique in its presentation, as well as in its purpose, plan, character and spirit. No woman present could fail to be impressed with what we owe to the women of the past, and especially to this one woman who was the honored guest of the occasion. And no young woman could desire to forget the picture of this aged form as, leaning upon her staff, Mrs. Stanton spoke to the great audience, as she has spoken hundreds of times before in legislative halls, and wherever her word could influence the popular sentiment in favor of justice and freedom for all mankind.

No words about her could be as eloquent as her own, uttered at the close of a life the profound significance and influence of which can hardly be written. At the jubilee that will come at the end of the next half-century, when the things she dreamed of shall be living realities, the things she lived and strove for be the everyday experience, will be revealed her true place and rank among the leaders of her time.

IS WOMAN EMBODIED OBSTRUCTION?

BY HELEN CAMPBELL

It may be objected by the readers of the ARENA, that the above title hardly covers the ground expected in an article on coöperation on which 1 am asked to give my view with its special bearing on women. As a student of general conditions for women, from that of the wage-earner in factory or shop or any of the myriad avenues of earning now open, to that of the wageless but no less hard-working farmer's wife, in lonely New England hill town and on lonelier western prairie, I have formed my own opinion as to how far women are ready for the type of progress involved in genuine coöperation, and it will have its own place before my portion of space is filled. In the meantime, I propose to give one on the same subject, which took form unexpectedly to all concerned, and produced an excitement from which the listeners of that day have not yet fully recovered.

It was in a well-known woman's club not far from one of the great centres, and a hundred women or so had been devoting the afternoon to a summary of woman's progress, congratulating themselves that in all fields an open way lay before her; four hundred trades at her option and artistic and professional life receiving each year a larger and larger number of recruits. Name after name came up, and for each was some soft and silky word, the apparently very honest feeling of admiration and good will.

A stranger sat in the background, a woman in middle life, with a benevolent face, and eyes in which the kindliness was mingled with gleams of humor that came and went swiftly. It was the face of a woman who had lived, and to whom wide experience had brought the power of cool, dispassionate judgment of this problem of living. Her lips had curled now and then, the sarcasm followed instantly by a smile that meant compassion certainly; though why should compassion be in order of that assembly of comfortable, well-to-do women?

"Friends," she said, suddenly rising to her feet as a pause came in the proceedings, "I am a stranger, yet I am certain that some of you know me. I am ———"; and she

gave a name so familiar that a general stir of interest went
through the assembly. "I want the right to speak to you
for a few moments if I may."

"We shall be only too happy to hear any word you have
for us," said the president, and folded her hands expectantly.

"In all the congratulations the afternoon has held," began the speaker, "there has been a note now and then of
sorrow and dismay at the disabilities that still hedge about
the woman in trades. Nobody has gone back of the present
era or asked how it is that for thousands of years she let
every industry that had belonged to her pass into the hands
of man, and is but just beginning to reclaim her natural
activities. We know if we read any study of prehistoric
times, like Tylor's 'Primitive Culture' or Mason's 'Woman's
Place in Primitive Culture'—the latest word on this subject—that all arts and trades began with her. Read
Drummond's chapter in his 'Ascent of Man,' on 'The Evolution of a Mother,' and you will see how this must have
been inevitable. To make things better for the child was
the instinct of all mothers then as now. One by one, arts
and industries developed because of its needs, and as they
developed passed into the hands of man, who, from a hunting and fighting animal only, was gradually taking on civilized characteristics, and discovering not only how to do
things better, but now to do them more easily. So far as
invention has a history, it is always the man who forces
the woman to give up her heavy stones for grinding and try
the mill; to use an improved loom, to accept the cook-stove
instead of the open fire and its back-breaking system of
crane and pots, the sewing machine instead of the needle;
in short, all modern conveniences.

"What woman has done with the sewing machine she
has done with most other inventions for her benefit—turned
them into new instruments of torture. The sewing machine
has enabled her to put a hundred tucks where once she
put three, and every garment is made to hold a wilderness
of stitching. Complication and always more and more
complication has become the order of living, and labor-
saving inventions crowd houses, and demand a new form of
skilled labor to take care of them.

"From the beginning of homes or workshops, women have
steadfastly labored at complication and men at simplification. The fact that a man is successful in business means
that he knows how to adapt means to ends. His office is a
model of compactness; everything at hand that can make

work swift and easy. In every trade, the worker, as dentist
or carpenter, has his tools in perfect order and arranged
close at hand so that every motion will tell. The kitchen
of a dining car or of a great ocean-liner is a model of condensed convenience. And while the man worker in these
lines is condensing his space and making every step and
stroke tell, the woman worker in the same field has only
in scattered instances planned to the same ends, but goes
on in the old helter-skelter fashion. Day by day life com-
plicates. The daily paper brings the ends of the earth to
our door. We must learn the lesson that all mankind is
one, whether we will or no. More work to be done; less
and less time to do it in. Complexity is the law of being
for this complex creature we call man, nor do I believe
that a return to primitive simplicity is either possible or
desirable. Men have found out many inventions. They
have not yet found out how to make their uses a unit and
let all share the benefit alike.

"You wonder what I am driving at. It i the terrible
waste of force that modern housekeeping represents—waste
not only in expenditure, but in results. Each kitchen has
its Moloch in the cook-stove, the shrine before which 'a
passing train of hired girls' incessantly does homage. The
coal that cooks for six could as well cook for sixty. The
anguish of the wash-day, the weekly martyrdom of the
housekeeper, has no more place under the civilized roof
than the weaving of cloth or the salting and curing of
meats. For the poor it is an even more wasteful system,
since they must buy in quantities so small that they pay
double and treble the sum the article is worth. 'We have
no time for anything,' is the cry of all women, yet not one
of you is willing to submit to the personal trouble that
might be involved in a new experiment, or to work out for
the world, as it must be worked out, all that belongs to this
business of coöperation. Every sign of the times shows
that it must come. It is part of every great business; it
is the secret of success in trusts and combinations of every
order.

"I do not ask anyone to give up the home. That is no
part of coöperation. But it is time that this business of
cooking and cleaning for humanity should be transferred to
the hands of experts. The woman will still find occupation
in genuinely caring for her family, teaching and training
as to-day she cannot. As to cooking, the kind which too
many of us have been made to know is warranted to
kill and not to cure. The kitchen is not an essential part

of the home. But the coöperative kitchen and laundry, no matter on how simple a scale, mean not only more time for the higher aspects of living but more money to spend in real things. Living, as we get it in our isolated, individual system, is organized waste and destruction; and women who oppose and refuse to even listen to rational talk as to possibilities, what are they but organized obstruction? This is a bomb in your midst. I see it in your faces. You would vote for any suggestion under heaven rather than a deep and earnest consideration of the real place of coöperation.

"The preciousness of home? I know all about it. You women with comfortable homes forget that you represent only a fraction of the myriad to whose homes only the hard side of life comes. The tenement house home is a torture chamber, and the kitchen of the farmer's wife no less so.

"Objection? A thousand if you choose, but not one that cannot be met and made to change its face.

"I have heard women say with a gasp, 'It does look as if we should have to come to coöperation, and how awful it is!' Awful? Yes, as the angel of death is called awful till we find that its coming is deliverance into the larger life. Precisely so with this business of coöperation. Till you have tried it you know nothing of its real meaning, and once tried you will marvel that you delayed so long. And so, as I have listened I have longed that you should at least study the meaning of the word, and see if your way into all that you crave does not lie in this path and no other. You have had almost a generation now of study and of all that has come in with the woman's club. That has been all right. But now you are beginning to think of something beside mere literary and artistic questions. You admit that there are problems, and of them all not one is greater or more compelling than this, as to how our system of living for ourselves, for our poor, may be bettered. And the thinker knows that this one word holds it all, and waits for women to put away the inertia that is part of their life, it would seem, and think till they can work, and work till the way is clear, and coöperation is the simple, natural, heaven-ordained method of life. I beg you to think of it."

The speaker paused and looked around—a look that seemed to hold a sort of divine compulsion—then sat down and for a moment closed her eyes and bent her head almost as if in prayer. Then she smiled, for the eyes met hers blankly, and only here and there was there token of sympathy or approval.

"I said they were organized obstruction," she murmured, and gave cheerful attention to the remaining proceedings, which included a vote of thanks for her protest, but no suggestion to pursue the subject.

In every woman's club in the United States, the members' chat before the programme opens turns on the terrors of domestic service and the problems hedging about all housekeeping. When it turns on the real way out and how to find it, the human race will be by that much nearer the millennium. Till then, why should I not agree with my friend and make my own the title I have chosen, since, till that day dawns, woman stands, and must stand, as "organized obstruction"?

PERSONAL RECOLLECTIONS OF AMERICA'S SEVEN GREAT POETS.

PART III.

I. SOME PERSONAL REMINISCENCES OF WHITTIER, WITH OBSERVATIONS ON HIS RELIGIOUS VIEWS, BY REV. CHRISTOPHER COFFIN HUSSEY.

There are friendships which do not depend upon length of acquaintance or frequency of meeting. Such was that which existed between the poet Whittier and myself. Being, like him, a member by birth of the Society of Friends, and admiring him through his poems, yet we had no personal intercourse prior to the summer of 1859, when we were both in attendance at the Friends' yearly meeting at Newport.

The condition of the Society at that time created unusual interest, and acquaintance would ripen rapidly between a thinker like Whittier and a minister in the Society, especially if the two were in sympathy on the questions in agitation. The Friends had never been a theological people; personal righteousness and obedience to the divine light had from the first been the cardinal points of belief and preaching. About the year 1823, under the leadership of an influential minister, this doctrine of the inner light was given increased prominence. This led to a division of the body in America. As is the result of all separations, the divided bodies grew apart. What proved to be the somewhat smaller party were called Hicksites; the other body became gradually known as the Orthodox. In New England the latter were so largely in preponderance that virtually no separation took place, and so all who were members there found themselves, whatever their personal sympathies, allied with Orthodox Friends.

Such were the conditions at the time of my first meeting with Whittier, and partly because of this our friendship commenced, as it continued, on the religious side of life mostly. The Orthodox leaning was on the increase in New England, and there were in attendance at this yearly meeting prominent ministers who brought out extreme forms of Calvinistic doctrine, which were extremely trying to Whittier as to many others.

On the last evening of the meeting's sitting he and I talked long, and he gave a full expression of dissent from the prevailing tendencies.

I said that I saw no way as a minister but to leave the Society.

He quickly replied, "No, thee must not; this is not legitimate Quakerism; it will pass over."

"I fear not," I replied.

It was near midnight when we parted.

Years after, alluding to this conversation he said, "Thy fears were a truer prophecy than my hopes."

After several years, during which we knew comparatively little of each other, I was driving with my family to Hampton, and took Amesbury as our stopping-place for the night. After tea, accompanied by my daughter, I called on my old friend. In becoming the regular incumbent of a pulpit, I had put myself in a position heretical to an old-time Quaker. I said to the servant, "I will not send my name; say, an old friend." As Whittier came into the study, I remembered my change from the dress in which he had always seen me, and as he paused an instant, I said, "Does thee know me, John?"* "To be sure, I know thee"; and in his own hearty way, and with loving words of welcome, he caused all fears of what years of change might have wrought to vanish, and we were one again in spirit launched on a delightful talk. As we rose to leave, my daughter drew from its concealment her autograph album, saying, "I have so often heard my father speak of thee, and have so loved thy poems, that I have a favor to ask of thee." "I know what it is, pass it along"; and stepping to his desk, he wrote:

> Faith shares the future's promise. Love's
> Self offering is a triumph won;
> And each good thought or action moves
> The dark world nearer to the sun.

After this we met as frequently as circumstances allowed. On one occasion, accompanied by a valued friend who had much desired to meet Whittier. I went to the old family house of "Snow-Bound" fame. It was an ideal day for such a visit.

> All day the gusty north wind bore
> The loosening drift its breath before,
> Low circling round its southern zone
> The sun through dazzling snow mist shone.

---

* Friends do not use the term Mr. and Mrs. in addressing one another, but either use the first name or say friend, a custom that Mr. Whittier and myself always retained.

We saw the chamber where the poet tells of his sleeping in boyhood.

> Within our beds awhile we heard
> The wind that round the gables roared
> With now and then a ruder shock
> Which made our very bedsteads rock;
> But sleep stole on as sleep will do
> When hearts are light and life is new.

We stood by the great fireplace where,

> Shut in from all the world without,
> We sat the clean-winged hearth about,
> Content to let the north wind roar
> In baffled rage at pane and door,
> While the red logs before us beat
> The frost line back with tropic heat.

On our return to Whittier's study, I asked him if the group of which the poem speaks were all real characters, and if any were left now. "Yes, they were real characters, but I, alone, am left"; adding, with pathos, "And that is the penalty of living to be old." Encouraged by questions, he talked on of several of the group.

> Our mother while she turned the wheel,
> Or run the new-knit stocking heel,
> Told how the Indian horde came down,
> At midnight on Cochece town.

Of the sister whose early loss he deeply felt,

> As one who held herself a part
> Of all she saw, and let her heart
> Against the household bosom lean.
> Upon the motley braided mat
> Our youngest and our dearest sat,
> Lifting her large sweet asking eyes,
> Now bathed within the fadeless green
> And holy peace of paradise.

> Next, the dear Aunt, whose smile of cheer
> And voice in dream I see and hear,
> The sweetest woman ever fate
> Perverse denied a household mate,
> Who lonely, homeless, not the less
> Found peace in love's unselfishness.

And so we talked on. At length the afternoon, all too short, was spent. As we were about to leave, our friend was called from the room a moment. In his absence my companion said, "I much want Mr. Whittier's autograph, but I hesitate about asking for it." I said, "I will open the way." The response was hearty. Stepping to the desk, the

REV. CHRISTOPHER COFFIN HUSSEY.

following sentiment was written and is cherished as u precious memento.

> For whatsoever here is wrong, I crave
> Forgiveness; and if aught be found
> Of flower or healing leaf where weeds abound,
> Let me not rudely claim
> As mine the gifts the Heavenly Father gave,
> Nor, without guilty shame,
> From undeserved blessings frame
> A heathen altar for the idol Fame!

The next meeting with my poet friend that is prominent in memory was on a summer Sabbath day. I was stopping with my family near Amesbury and proposed to attend meeting there, learning that Whittier was at home. As we drew near the meeting house, we overtook him, and stepping from my carriage I took his arm and we went into meeting together. After a little time of silence—once the prevailing habit of Friends, and always beautiful—there was speaking. I took part in it, quoting, as I closed, from one of Whittier's poems. I saw he was moved, and when he and I were walking to his house, he said, "Surely the Lord sent thee to us to-day." I quote this because of the significance of his way of putting it; it was in accordance with the Friends' idea that the spring of all true ministry is not in the preacher himself, but in the power of the divine Spirit. The most I ever heard in my boyhood of comment on preaching was, "Friend B——— was favored to-day."

Years have passed since that summer's day, but the fragrance of the hour of quiet worship, of the walk to the poet's study, of the few moments passed there, and of the impressive parting can never be lost.

> There was the secret sense
> Of all things sweet and fair,
> And beauty's gracious providence
> Refreshed us unaware.

It is the case sometimes that we most reveal ourselves without the use of words. An instance of this occurred with my friend, the significance of which caused it to be remembered. We were attending a Friends' quarterly meeting, when a minister who was an extremist in the modern Quaker evangelical tendencies said: "Friends, it is not by obedience to an inward light, as so many amongst us have been saying, but by faith in the atoning blood of Christ shed on Calvary, that we are to be saved." The utterance was so at variance with the accepted belief of Friends, and so shocked my friend, that half unconsciously he turned to me and by a slight touch telegraphed his pained dissent. It is but just to say that the meeting was redeemed near its close to a more spiritual and more genuinely Quaker attitude by an eloquent woman preacher, a much loved cousin of Whittier's, with whom and her valued companion his spirit was in close sympathy to the end of his life. This little incident spoke clearly as to Whitier's doctrinal position.

Memory lingers most deeply over the meetings with my friend during the last summer of his life. He was staying at Hampton Falls. I, with my family, was at Little Boar's Head, a few miles away, "the sweetest spot," my friend said to me, "of all the New Hampshire coast." We met several times during that fortnight. Previously, I had been to all the spots in that vicinity made famous by Whittier's poems or by his ancestry. I had been to the site of the house of Christopher Hussey, from whom, notwithstanding some late genealogical confusion, he traced his lineage, his mother being a Hussey. I had visited the house, still well preserved and showing its original comparative magnificence, which was the scene of his poem, "The Old Wife and the New." I had traced from Great Boar's Head

> Rivermouth rocks [which] are fair to see,
> By dawn or sunset shone across,

and also the river which comes winding down,

> From salt sea meadows and uplands brown.

I had been shown where the reputed witch of the locality, Goody Cole, "sat by her door, her wheel awhirl," as the ill-fated party rounded the point.

I had stood where the first meeting house stood to which that party, wrecked by the sudden squall, were brought for burial.

> Solemn it was in that old day,
> In Hampton town and its log-built church,
> As side by side the coffins lay,
> And the mourners stood in aisle and porch.

These localities acquired a deepened interest from Whittier's explanations, but memory dwells most fondly on the conversation of the last interview. There was no intimation of its being the last, but the coming event seemed to cast its shadow upon us. All I had known of my friend's theological position had come to me in a fragmentary way, never by any approach to discussion, and now when the conversation had led up to it, I said:

"John, does thee remember what thee once said to me on the doctrine of immortality?"

"No, what was it?"

"I do not positively assert immortality. I do not reason about it or try to prove it, but I perfectly trust that there is a life beyond—more spiritual than this and of more perfect adjustments—because I entirely believe that the Power which placed us here, and is over all life, is one of perfect justice and love."

No one could be farther than Whittier from applying to himself any sectarian name. The nearest approach to this I ever knew was on that afternoon. We had been expressing views in which we were united, much at variance with those popularly called evangelical, when, as a sort of summing up he said:

"Well, they say of thee and me we are Unitarians."

It came to me to say, as I rose and took his hand, "Thee cannot know how much we who are so often called to speak a word of comfort are indebted to thee for 'The Eternal Goodness,' or how priceless a legacy thee would have left to the world if thee had written nothing else."

And so we parted. I had asked Whittier where I could procure his "Margaret Smith's Journal."

"Thee will find it in the last edition of my prose works."

A few days after I went to Boston for it. I had known of my friend's illness, and as I passed I saw the bulletin announcing his death. It was a shock, but there quickly arose a sense of victory and of gratitude for such a noble life with such a peaceful ending. And his words came to me:

> And so beside the silent sea
> I wait the muffled oar.
> No harm from Him can come to me
> On ocean or on shore.

On all great questions of belief there is a desire for the support of leading thinkers which inheres in human nature and may be helpful, while it is liable to be pushed too far. Such seems to have been the case in some minds with regard to our friend, a man whom all would have liked to own as a companion in the realm of religious thought. That he could ever be classed as evangelical, using that word in its popular acceptance, would seem strange to any who knew the complexion of his inner life. Although outspoken and fearless in the declaration of his opinions, as his prose works show, as well as his earlier poems, which stirred the hearts of thousands in the great anti-slavery struggle, no one would be less likely than he to engage in dispute on speculative questions, or to state his convictions in the language of theological controversy. One who dwelt so near as he to the divine centre of light and love could not but be in sympathy with what was spiritual, broad, and progressive. He was not a contender for forms or a promulgator of doctrine, but his religious position was clearly defined to himself and to those who best knew him.

His poem, "The Eternal Goodness," has brought comfort to uncounted numbers, and almost more than anything else he wrote it brings out his religious position, especially when read in the light of an interesting bit of history concerning it which was told me by an intimate friend of his.

His poem, "The Two Angels," had appeared. It is a striking denial of the doctrine of unending suffering and an assertion of the final prevalence of divine love. Some of his Quaker friends were uneasy with this and expostulated with him. "The Eternal Goodness" was his reply. By knowing this circumstance the value of the poem is enhanced.

O Friends, with whom my feet have trod
  The quiet aisles of prayer,
Glad witness to your zeal for God
  And love of man I bear.

I trace your lines of argument;
  Your logic linked and strong
I weigh as one who dreads dissent,
  And fears a doubt as wrong.

But still my human hands are weak
  To hold your iron creeds;
Against the words you bid me speak
  My heart within me pleads.

          *   *   *   *   *

I see the wrong that round me lies,
  I feel the guilt within;
I hear, with groans and travail-cries
  The world confess its sin.

Yet, in the maddening maze of things,
  And tossed by storm and flood,
To one fixed trust my spirit clings;
  I know that God is good!

          *   *   *   *   *

I know not where His islands lift
  Their fronded palms in air;
I only know I cannot drift
  Beyond His love and care.

In closing these familiar recollections of one so highly esteemed and loved, I cannot forego the temptation of quot-

ing these lines from the tribute to him by his long-time
friend. Oliver Wendell Holmes:

> In the brave records of our earlier time
>   A hero's deeds thy generous soul inspired,
> And many a legend, told in ringing rhyme.
>   The youthful soul with high resolve has fired.
>
> Not thine to lean on priesthood's broken reed;
>   No barriers caged thee in a bigot's fold;
> Did zealots ask to syllable thy creed,
>   Thou saidst "Our Father," and thy creed was told.
>
> Best loved and saintliest of our singing train,
>   Earth's noblest tributes to thy name belong.
> A lifelong record closed without a stain,
>   A blameless memory shrined in deathless song.

II. BRYANT, THE POET-POLITICIAN, BY F. B. SANBORN.

Although a reader of Bryant's poetry ever since I can
remember, and of his newspaper, the New York *Evening
Post*, for many years, my acquaintance with him was but
slight, and that in his old age. It was partly on philanthropic and partly on political ground that we met; for he
contributed, at my request, a letter to be read at the memorial service for his friend and mine, Dr. Howe, of Boston,
in 1876; and a little earlier we had both spoken at a celebration of the centenary of Adam Smith's great book, in
favor of freer trade. This was a policy Bryant had long
advocated, as indeed the New England Federalists often
did in the first decades of this century. What attracted
my notice at this public dinner in New York, where Bryant
presided, was his nonchalance, when, not having his speech
well in memory, he coolly pulled his manuscript from his
coat-pocket and read it to us. He was then an impressive
figure, with his snowy hair and beard; but I found less of
the poet in his bearing and conversation than I had fancied.
My friend and housemate, Ellery Channing, himself a poet,
and who often met Bryant at Lenox or New York, half a
century ago, has compared his appearance then to a thriving
carpenter's aspect, as he went to his morning's work or returned from it at noon or night. Indeed Bryant, though a
true poet, was quite as much politician as bard; and this his
life-story shows, though most of us have forgotten it.

He was the son and grandson of New England Federalists of the Adams or Hamilton type—country doctors, too,
who in Massachusetts were apt to be men of political prominence and pronounced opinions. His father, Dr. Peter

Bryant, of Cummington, though fond of French literature, and himself speaking the French language (learned during captivity in Mauritius as ship's surgeon, in 1795–6), was sharply opposed to President Jefferson, who was charged (falsely) with being at the head of a French party in America, and denounced as a friend and tool of Bonaparte. Brought up in the midst of such political animosities, William Cullen Bryant's poetic temperament precociously turned him into a rhymester against the author of the Declaration of Independence, and the head of the great party with which, for thirty of his most active years, Mr. Bryant afterwards connected himself. At the age of thirteen the boy was found by his father to have composed these lines, of mingled bombast and scurrility, addressed in 1807 to the president of the United States:

> And thou, the scorn of every patriot name,
> Thy country's ruin and thy council's shame!
> Poor servile thing! derision of the brave!
> Who erst from Tarleton fled to Carter's cave;
> Thou who, when menaced by perfidious Gaul,
> Didst prostrate to her whiskered minion fall;
> And when our cash her empty bags supplied,
> Didst meanly strive the foul disgrace to hide:
> Go, wretch, resign the presidential chair,
> Disclose thy secret measures, foul or fair;
> Go search with curious eye for hornéd frogs
> 'Mid the wild waste of Louisianian bogs;
> Or, where Ohio rolls his turbid stream,
> Dig for huge bones, thy glory and thy theme.

With this imitation of Pope and Campbell, Bryant's Federalist father, then a member of the Massachusetts general court, was so delighted that he bade his son go on. The result was a poem of more than five hundred lines, which Dr. Bryant carried to Boston, and got printed under the title of "The Embargo, or Sketches of the Times; a Satire by a Youth of Thirteen." It sold well among the angry merchants of Boston and reached a second edition in 1809, when some shorter pieces were added—an "Ode to Connecticut River," "The Spanish Revolution" (against Napoleon), etc., among which was a translation of Horace's Ode XXII of the First Book (*Integer vitae, scelerisque purus*).

As time went on, and he began to study law, first among the hills of Hampshire County and then at Bridgewater, where his grandfather still lived and practised medicine, Bryant disclosed still more partisan sentiments, always with a poetic or imaginative turn inspiring him. Fancying that the road to success in law would be long and doubt-

Haffone, from a painting by Mrs. R. E. lisher.

ful—as in fact it was, so that he gave it up, in after years, for literature and journalism—he joined a volunteer militia company in Plymouth County (or proposed to) and tried to get a military appointment from the Federal governor of Massachusetts. The future army in which he hoped for a commission was intended, in the eyes of the hot Federalists, young and old, for ultimate service against Madison and the national authority. Of this revolutionary scheme, Bryant leaves us in no manner of doubt, for he wrote to his father, Oct. 10, 1814:

The force now to be organized may not be altogether employed against a foreign enemy; it may become necessary to wield it against an intestine foe in the defence of dearer rights than those which are endangered in a contest with Great Britain [with which we were then at war]. If we create a standing army of our own, if we take into our own hands the public revenue (for these things are contemplated in the answer to the governor's message), we so far throw off our allegiance to the general government, we disclaim its control, and revert to an independent empire. If we proceed in the manner in which we have begun, and escape a civil war, it will probably be because the administration is awed by our strength from attempting our subjection. By increasing that strength, therefore, we shall lessen the probability of bloodshed. . . . If I should enter into the service of the state, I should procure the means of present support; I should then come into the world with my excessive bashfulness and rusticity rubbed off by a military life, which polishes and improves the manners more than any other method in the world.

Here, then, was the disunion plot of Timothy Pickering and the Connecticut Federalists (for which, in 1804, they had secured, as they thought, the coöperation of Aaron Burr) brought to a practical issue by the ill-success of Madison and Monroe in carrying on war with England; and here was the headlong poet, not yet twenty, planning a military career for himself, in the establishment of Federal control of the government, or else of a separate confederacy—exactly what Calhoun planned for South Carolina in 1832, and what Jefferson Davis carried out in 1861. Older men were at work in the same mad way, and the famous Hartford Convention, which met Dec. 15, 1814, was expected to frame the timbers of a new northern confederacy. But that body shrank from the task, and young Bryant defends them, in a letter to his older brother, from the charge of having failed to do anything:

They have publicly proclaimed the terms on which depends the continuance of the Union; they have solemnly demanded of the national government that the rights taken from them should be restored, and barriers erected against future abuses of authority. Next June will be time enough to tell the world that the original compact between the states is dissolved.

There is much similarity between this action of the New
England Federalists in 1814, and that of the Democratic
party in 1864, when, after nominating General McClellan
for president against Lincoln, they demanded peace with
the Confederacy, as the Federalists had demanded peace
with England. Jackson destroyed the fine English army
at New Orleans, a few weeks after young Bryant wrote,
just as Sherman captured Atlanta in 1864, and destroyed
Hood's rebel army. With peace, soon after, in each case,
came great public abhorrence of the Hartford Convention
Federalists and the McClellan Democrats. Both had
sinned against the strong American sense of nationality;
and they ceased to wield political power for twenty years.

Bryant seems to have taken the lesson to heart, and when
he next appears in politics, it is upon new issues, and in the
ranks of the party he had so hotly opposed. About 1820,
in company with the Sedgwicks of Berkshire, where he then
lived, and some years afterward in New York, he came
forward as the advocate of free trade, against the new
"American system" of high tariff announced by Henry
Clay and the manufacturers of New England and the Middle States. By this time the poet-politician had become a
convert to the policy of his boyish aversion, Jefferson, and
believed that "the world is governed too much"; that the
true business of government is to leave as much as possible
to private initiative, and to foster and depend on the
growth of individualism, whether in church or state. These
institutions were united in New England during Bryant's
boyhood, but his father had felt the impulse of what a
friend calls "devout free-thinking," and had become a Channing Unitarian. The son took the same view; for liberal-
ism in religion is congenial to poets, and closely connected
with liberal politics. Moreover, the personality of Jackson
and Van Buren, the leaders of the Democracy in 1828, was
attractive to young literary men like Bryant, Bancroft, and
Hawthorne; of their party, too, were Irving and Cooper,
then the greatest names in our literature. Bryant, in the
Evening Post, soon uniting his fortunes with William Leggett, became the chief journalistic advocate of Jackson's
radical measures, and supported Benton and Van Buren
in their courageous efforts to give the country a sound
currency.

From his convictions in favor of a low tariff and a metallic currency Bryant never departed, and when President
Lincoln and Secretary Chase asked Congress to make government paper money (the "greenback") a legal tender in-

stead of gold and silver, the *Evening Post* opposed the plan, and declared, what the event has since justified, that no such measure was needed, and that it would work the country harm in the future. Nearly thirty years before, Mr. Bryant had pointed out that extreme speculation in lands might cause such inflation of the currency as to cause many failures and derange our whole financial system—as it did.

Even more than this was the *Evening Post*, sixty years ago, in line with the development of our latest politics. With his friend Leggett, he sided with the multitude against the powerful merchants, bankers, and capitalists, against whom Jackson and Benton carried on their long warfare in regard to the banks and the government. The interests of labor were seen to be directly involved in that struggle; as they are now in the contest with trusts, monopolies, railroad rings, and the vast combinations of capital which have labor at their mercy, and, under pretence of holding wages up, really have forced down (by their large profits on capital, and the high prices thence resulting) the "living wage" of the laborer.

So when anti-slavery agitation grew warm, Bryant, in accord with true Democracy, but in frequent antagonism with his political party, refused to condemn the agitation, and denounced the mobs in New York and Boston which broke up abolition meetings. He also opposed the annexation of Texas, and united with his friend Van Buren in the revolt of 1848 against the two old parties. It is true that, like Van Buren, he afterwards went back to the Democrats, and supported Franklin Pierce in 1852; but that was his last act of party fealty. He soon joined effectively in the formation of the Republican party of 1865, and was a firm supporter of the war for the Union and of the emancipation of the slaves as a war measure.

The earliest manifestation of his devotion to the cause of liberty struggling against oppression was his youthful sympathy for the Greeks in their war with the Turks, and for the Italian liberals and the friends of constitutional government in Spain and Spanish America. In these matters he was in accord with most of our countrymen, who favored every movement to throw off the yoke which the Holy Alliance and European kings in general had imposed on mankind after the world-struggle of Napoleon's wars. Much of his poetry turns on this conflict between power and freedom, and in his poem "America" he points out the true mission of our country among the nations, and has given expression to the sentiment of his whole life:

AMERICA.

O Mother of a mighty race,
Yet lovely in thy youthful grace!
The elder dames, thy haughty peers,
Admire and hate thy blooming years.
    With words of shame
And taunts of scorn they join thy name.

Ay, let them rail — those haughty ones,
While safe thou dwellest with thy sons.
They do not know how loved thou art,
How many a fond and fearless heart
    Would rise to throw
Its life between thee and thy foe.

They know not, in their hate and pride,
What virtues with thy children bide;
How true, how good, thy graceful maids
Make bright, like flowers, the valley shades:
    What generous men
Spring, like thine oaks, by grove and glen.

What cordial welcomes greet the guest
By thy lone rivers of the West;
How faith is kept, and truth revered,
And man is loved, and God is feared,
    In woodland homes,
And where the ocean border foams.

There's freedom at thy gates and rest
For earth's down-trodden and opprest,
A shelter for the hunted head,
For the starved laborer, toil and bread.
    Power, at thy bounds,
Stops and calls back his baffled hounds.

O fair young mother! on thy brow
Shall sit a nobler grace than now.
Deep in the brightness of thy skies
The thronging years in glory rise,
    And as they fleet,
Drop strength and riches at thy feet.

Thine eye, with every coming hour,
Shall brighten, and thy form shall tower;
And when thy sisters, elder-born,
Would brand thy name with words of scorn,
    Before thine eye,
Upon their lips the taunt shall die.

THE UTOPIA OF SIR THOMAS MORE.

BY B. O. FLOWER.

PART II.

In viewing the religious toleration of Sir Thomas More at the time he wrote "Utopia" we are impressed with the noble and grandly humane spirit evinced by this prophet of a lofty civilization, when on the summit—when the God within swayed his soul and cast out fear. But, turning from these pages, glowing with a tolerance so far in advance of his time, to the story of the life of Sir Thomas More in after years, while lord chancellor of the realm, and there noting his intolerance, we are painfully reminded of the frailty of human nature and the liability of sensitive or impressionable minds to be swayed by human thought when strong prejudices are aroused. The noblest natures are not impregnable if they for a moment lose sight of that basic principle of civilization which we call the Golden Rule.

Regarding Utopia we are informed:

There be divers kinds of religion in sundry parts of the Island and divers parts of every city. Some worship for God, the Sun, some, the moon, some, some other of the planets. There be those that give worship to a man that was once of excellent virtue or of famous glory. But the most and the wisest part *believe that there is a certain Godly Power unknown, everlasting, incomprehensible, inexplicable, far above the capacity and reach of man's wit, dispersed throughout all the world,* not in bigness but in virtue and power. Him they call Father of all. To Him alone they attribute the beginnings, the increasings, the proceedings, the changes, and the ends of all things.

The enlightened views of the founder of this Commonwealth and his aversion to violence and the spirit of hatred always liable to arise among men where dogmatic theology prevails is thus set forth:

For King Utopus, even at the first beginning, hearing that the inhabitants of the land were before his coming thither at continual dissensions and strife among themselves because of their religion, made a decree that it should be lawful for every man to favor and follow what religion he would, and that he might do the best he could to bring others to his opinion so that he did it peaceably, gently, quietly, and soberly, without haste and contentions, rebuking and inveighing against others. If he could not by fair and gentle speech induce them into his opinion, yet he should use no kind of violence and refrain from unpleasant and seditious words.

The ideas of King Utopus on religion were far broader than the popular opinions or current views throughout Christian Europe at the time when More wrote, as will be seen from the following:

Whereof he durst define and determine nothing unadvisedly, as doubting whether God desiring manifold and divers sorts of honor would inspire sundry men with sundry kinds of religion, and this surely be thought a point of arrogant presumption to compel all others by violence and threatening to agree to the same as thou believest to be true. Furthermore, though there be one religion which alone is true and others vain and superstitious, *yet did he well foresee that the truth of its own power would at the last issue out and come to the light.* But if contentions and debates be continually indulged in, as the worst men be most obstinate and stubborn, he perceived that then the best and holiest religion would be trodden underfoot and destroyed by most vain superstitions. Therefore all this matter he left undiscussed and gave to every man free liberty to choose and believe what he would.

It is sad indeed that the illustrious author did not cling to these wise precepts when he rose to the first place under the throne of England. Once indeed we see the spirit of intolerance flash forth in Sir Thomas More's description of religious views prevalent throughout Utopia; once we see his lack of faith in the power of truth; once his loyalty to freedom in thought, justice, and wisdom is found limping on a crutch, and that is in the following passage relating to atheists:

He (King Utopus) earnestly charged them that no man should conceive so vile and base an opinion of the dignity of man's nature as to think that the souls do die and perish with the body, or that the world is not governed by divine Providence. Him that be of contrary opinion they count not in the number of men, as one that has abased the high nature of the soul to the vileness of brute bodies. . . . Wherefore he that is thus minded is deprived of all honors, excluded from all offices, and rejected from all common administrations in the public weal, and thus he is of all sorts despised as of an unprofitable and of a base and vile nature. *Howbeit they put him to no punishment, because they be persuaded that it is in no man's power to believe what he lists, nor do they constrain him with threatenings to dissemble his mind and show countenance contrary to his beliefs. For deceit and falsehood and all manner of lies as next unto fraud they do detest and abhor.* But they suffer him not to dispute in his opinions, and that only among the common people. For many men of gravity and the priests they encourage to exhort him, to dispute and argue, hoping that at the last his madness will give place to reason.

The spirit evinced in this passage, though displaying a sad lack of faith in the power of truth and the wholesomeness of free thought, was far above the savage, intolerant, and unreasoning spirit which prevailed through Europe during the sixteenth century, and in the expression, "They be persuaded that it be in no man's power to believe what

he lists," we see that this ardent Catholic in this age of
religious fanaticism caught a glimpse of a great truth,
the wilful refusal to recognize which has led to untold
suffering and persecution. Many of the noblest prophets
of progress and disciples of science and truth have been
slain because they saw larger truths than the convention-
ists of their age regarded as orthodox, and because they
were too noble and high-minded to lie and go to the grave
mantled in hypocrisy.

Very apt is the way Sir Thomas More satirizes the tendency of dogmatic religion to make its adherents intolerant
and persecuting by narrowing the intellectual vision of
those who fall under the proselyting influence of the
apostles of creedal and dogmatic religions. The Christian
visitors to Utopia, finding the wider latitude given to religious
views, make haste to promulgate the conventional Christian
theology of the sixteenth century. As soon as one of the
Utopians was proselyted he became infected with that intolerance which has ostracized where it has been unable
to destroy the advance guard of civilization and progress
in all ages. But I will let the author of Utopia tell the
story:

> He, as soon as he was baptized, began against our wills with more
> earnest affection than wisdom to reason of Christ's religion, and began
> to wax so hot in his matter that he did not only prefer our religion be-
> fore all others, calling them profane and the followers of them wicked
> and devilish and the children of everlasting damnation.

The Utopians, we are told, believed "that the dead be present among them, though to the dull and feeble eyesight of
man they be invisible." They reason that the spirits of the
loved ones not only enjoy the liberty of coming back and
becoming in a way guardian angels, but that the love of
those who leave us is intensified as their vision is broadened, "they believe, therefore, that the dead be presently conversant among the quick as beholders and witnesses of all
their words and deeds. Therefore, they go more courageously
to their business, as having a trust in such guardians."
This, it will be seen, is curiously enough the central claim
of modern spiritualism. And it is the hope of arriving at
a scientific solution of this momentous problem that has
inspired the tireless labors of earnest thinkers and scientific bodies which during recent years have engaged in the
critical investigation of psychical phenomena. The prophet
when upon the mountain of exaltation not infrequently
catches luminous glimpses of great truths which are not
scientifically established by the slower methods of reason-

ing, resulting from the vast accumulation of authoritative data, until centuries later. And may not the author of "Utopia" in one of these moments have caught a glimpse of a truth which science will some day establish to the satisfaction of those who desire the truth, but who are only influenced through cold facts resting on unchallenged data?

The religion described as prevailing among the Utopians reflects many ideas accepted in More's day, but we here also find much which was far in advance of his age, much of it being based on common sense rather than being the offspring of dogmatism. Thus we are told that "'They believe that felicity after death is obtained by busy labors and good deeds in life." It is a point with them to seek to "mitigate and assuage the grief of others" and to "take from them sorrow and heaviness of life." They define virtue "To be life ordered according to nature, and that he doth follow the course of nature which in desiring and refusing things is ruled by his reason." They hold "That the soul is immortal and ordained by God to felicity; that our virtuous and good deeds be rewarded and our evil deeds be punished." In other words, the Utopians believed that as a man sowed so should he reap, and that no suffering of the innocent could wipe away the consequences of sins which sear, crush, and deform the soul; but as we have seen, they believed in the ultimate felicity of the spirit— a belief which alone can make creation other than a colossal mistake, a measureless crime.

The Utopians favor pleasures which do not debase or cause injury to others. They are represented as being far more humane than the Christians of contemporary Europe. This was very noticeable in the treatment of criminals. While England was hanging thieves by the score, the Utopians were striving to reform their erring ones and resorting to the death penalty only in extreme cases.

Women, though by no means exercising the rights they enjoy with us, were treated with far more consideration than they received in the Europe of the sixteenth century. Among other privileges accorded them, they were admitted to the order of the priesthood, and in the marriage relation they received a consideration which England for many generations after "Utopia" was written refused to yield them. One thing in regard to the divorces in Utopia is surprising when we remember that Sir Thomas More was a most devoted Roman Catholic. In the altrurian island, we are informed that "Now and then it chanceth whereas a man and a woman cannot agree between themselves, both of them finding other with whom they hope to live more quietly and merrily, and they by full consent of them both be divorced asunder and married again to others. But that not without the sanction of the council" after the petition has been diligently considered.

In the present transition stage of our society peculiar interest attaches to Utopia's social and economic conditions, as here we find much that is suggestive, and which will prove helpful if we keep in view the fact that while the altruistic spirit of Utopia is the spirit which must prevail in the society of the future if man is to progress, nevertheless, the methods suggested by Sir Thomas More, though they were as enlightened and intelligent as the civilization of his time could comprehend, are not the methods which enlightened civilization in the present age would employ, as they are too arbitrary and artificial. We are now beginning to perceive that the evils of society are to be remedied by (1) education—a wise foresight, which never loses sight of the civilization of to-morrow, and (2) the establishing of conditions favoring justice and freedom and fraternity, which are only possible by the abolition of all class privileges, speculation, and legislation and the recognizing of the great fundamental economic truth that the land belongs to the people. Moreover, the fetich of gold-worship must be overthrown, because it, more than war, pestilence, or famine, destroys the happiness of millions, while it corrupts the few.

Sir Thomas More appreciated the fact that gold madness was enslaving millions and destroying the happiness and comfort of the masses. Thus, among the Utopians, he tells us:

They marvel that gold, which of its own nature is a thing so unprofitable, is now among all people in so high estimation that man himself, by whose yea and for whose use it is so much set by, is in much less estimation than the gold itself. Inasmuch as a lumpish blockhead churl and which hath no more art than an ass, shall have, nevertheless, many wise and good men in subjection and bondage, only for this — because he hath a great heap of gold. . . . They marvel at and detest the madness of them which to those rich men in whose debt and danger they be not, do give honor for no other consideration but because they be rich.

In Utopia the spectres of want and starvation which haunt our poor and fill all thought of old age with frightful forebodings are unknown, but they were very much in evidence in European life during the fifteenth and sixteenth centuries. It was during the century of Sir Thomas More

that there "arose for the first time in England a true
proletariat divorced from the soil and dependent entirely
upon wages, with no resources against old age, sickness,
or lack of employment. The misery of the masses was
perhaps never greater."* The author of "Utopia" points
out that while in other countries the laborers know they
will starve when age comes unless they can scrape some
money together, no matter how much the commonwealth in
which they live may flourish, in Utopia things are very different, for there "There is no less provision for them that were
once laborers, but who are now weak and impotent, than for
those who do labor." A comparison is next made by Sir
Thomas More in which the justice and wisdom of the
Utopians in providing for an insurance or pension for the
aged laborers, are set over against the murderous, selfish,
and shortsighted system which was then in practice and
which unhappily has been intensified rather than weakened
with the flight of centuries.

For what justice is this, that a rich goldsmith or a usurer, or in short
any of them which do nothing at all, or if they do anything, it is of a
kind not necessary for the commonwealth, should have pleasant and
wealthy lives, either by idleness or by unnecessary business, when in
the meantime poor laborers, carters, ironsmiths, carpenters, and ploughmen by so great and continual toil be scarcely able to live through their
work by necessary toil, without which no commonwealth could endure,
and yet they have so hard and poor a living and live so wretched and
miserable a life that the state and conditions of the laboring beasts be
much better. Moreover, these poor wretches be persistently tormented
with barren and unfruitful labor, and the thought of their poor, indigent,
and beggarly old age killeth them. For their daily wages be so little
that it will not suffice for the same day, much less it yieldeth any overplus that may be laid up for the relief of old age.

More than three centuries have passed, and yet this vivid
picture of unjust and unequal social conditions is a graphic
characterization of present-day society throughout the
Christian world.

Is it not an unjust and unkind public weal [continues the author of
"Utopia"] which gives great fees and rewards to gentlemen as they
call them, to such as be either idle persons, flatterers, or devisers of
vain pleasures, while it makes no provision for poor ploughmen, colliers,
laborers, carters, ironsmiths, and carpenters, without whom no commonwealth can continue? But after it hath abused the laborers of their
lusty and flowering age, at the last when they be oppressed with old age
and sickness, forgets their labor and leaveth them most unkindly with
miserable death.

After this vivid and painfully true picture of the essential injustice of governments manipulated by caste and

---

* Maurice Adams, in Introduction to "Utopia."

gold, or the fiction of birth and the cunning of capital.
Sir Thomas More makes a scorching arraignment of the
soulless capitalism of his time, which is even more applicable to our age of trusts, monopolies, syndicates and multi-
millionaires:

> *The rich men not only by private fraud, but also by common laws do
> every day pluck away from the poor some part of their daily living.* There-
> fore, when I consider all these commonwealths which nowadays do
> flourish, I can perceive nothing but ascertain conspiracy of rich men pro-
> curing their own commodities under the name and title of the common-
> wealth. They invent and devise all means and crafts, first how to keep
> safely without fear of losing that which they have unjustly gathered to-
> gether, and next how to hire and abuse the work and labor of the poor
> for as little money as may be. These most wicked and vicious men by
> their insatiable covetousness divide among themselves those things
> which would have sufficed for all men.

Again, he compares the murderous merciless reign of the
titled and the capitalistic classes, who had become well-nigh
all-powerful through special privileges, with the operation
of different conditions in the land he is describing:

> How far be they from the wealth and felicity of the Utopian com-
> monwealth, where all the desire for money with the use thereof is ban-
> ished. How great the occasion of wretchedness and mischief is
> plucked up by the roots, for who knoweth not that fraud, theft, rapine,
> brawling, quarrelling, strife, treason, and murder, which by daily pun-
> ishments are rather revenged than restrained, do die when money
> dieth. And also that fear, care, labor, and watching do perish when
> money perisheth.

Sir Thomas More further emphasizes the wisdom of the
Utopian provisions by calling attention to the fact that
after failure of crops in England it was no uncommon
thing for thousands to starve for food while the rich
possessed abundant stores of food to have afforded plenty
for all, and by a just distribution of wealth, whereby the
wealth producers might have had their own, no industrious
man, woman, or child need have died by starvation or the
plague which not infrequently accompanied the famine.

From the foregoing we see how high an altitude Sir
Thomas More had reached, even in his savage and self-
absorbed age. From his eminence he caught luminous
glimpses which come only to prophet souls. There can
be no doubt that the author of "Utopia" derived much
inspiration from Plato, even as such prophets of our time
as Edward Bellamy, William Morris, Joaquin Miller, and
William Dean Howells have derived consciously and
directly or unconsciously and indirectly much inspiration
from Sir Thomas More. All these and many other earnest
lovers of the race have reflected in a more or less true and

helpful way the persistent dream of the wisest and noblest
spirits of all time—a dream which has haunted the aspiring soul since the first man faced the heavens with a
question and a prayer.

Sir Thomas More failed in the details of his plan, but
the soul of "Utopia" was purely altruistic and in alignment
with the law of evolutionary growth, hence his work was
in deed and truth a voice of dawn crying in the night—
a prophet voice proclaiming the coming day. As Maurice
Adams well says:

Sir Thomas More found the true commonwealth nowhere. But in so
far as the social order he advocated is based on reason and justice, the
nowhere must at length become somewhere, nay, everywhere. Some of
the reforms which he perceived to be necessary have already been realized, others are being striven for to-day. May we not hope many more
will at length be attained? Surely never before was there such a widespread revolt against social wrong and injustice, such a firm resolve to
remove the preventable evils of life, or such a worldwide aspiration for
a recognition of society on a juster basis. It cannot be that the promise of better things is forever to remain unfulfilled! From the summit
of the hills of thought may we not catch the first faint streaks of the
dawn of a nobler day? Can we not trace the dim outline of a real society slowly forming amongst us in which none shall be disinherited or
trodden underfoot in a senseless or reckless race for wealth, but where
all shall be truly free to develop the full capacity of their nature in co-
operation with their fellows for a common good?

THE TELEGRAPH MONOPOLY.

BY PROF. FRANK PARSONS.

II.

§ 2. *The Evils of our present Telegraph System are manifestly great.* In the first place a large part of our people have *no* telegraphic facilities. A private company selects the best districts, builds its lines where the traffic will be large, and leaves the more thinly settled portions of the country without any service at all. A public enterprise, on the contrary, does not chiefly aim at dividends, but at efficient service of the public as a whole. The difference is strongly illustrated by the contrast between the Western Union and the Postoffice; the former has 21,000 offices, the latter 70,000.° The policy of the Postoffice is the true one. Farmers and ranchmen are a benefit to the whole community. It is not their fault that it costs a little more to send a message 200 miles than 100. Distance is an accident entirely independent of the merit or demerit of the individual, and the burden of it should not be allowed to fall upon any individual, but should be borne by society. If any difference is to be made, it ought to be in favor of the country districts, not against them, for it should always be an object of solicitude with the statesman to add to the advantages of country life, so as to counteract, as far as possible, the tendency to overcrowd the cities.

In the second place the rates are very high—so high that the telegraph is beyond the reach of the majority even of those who live in the favored localities where the companies condescend to open their offices. *The private telegraph*

° The offices of rival telegraph companies are not included because they are mere duplications and do not represent new localities supplied with telegraph facilities; indeed the figures 21,000 and 70,000 do not disclose the full superiority of the postoffice in respect to universality of service, because the 21,000 telegraph offices include all the offices in the cities, where it is often the case that a considerable number of telegraph offices are maintained in the district served by one postoffice—the whole cluster of telegraph offices being really entitled to count only as one in a fair comparison of the extent of country and population served by the telegraph and the postoffice respectively.

charges of America are more than double the public telegraph rates of Europe.[1]

[1] Telegraph rates in this country are 25 cents to $1 for 10 words and 2 to 7 cents for each word in addition. The night rates are somewhat less; for example:

FROM	TO	DAY.		NIGHT.	
		For 10 words.	For each extra word.	For 10 words.	For each extra word.
Boston	Worcester . .	25 cts.	2 cts.	25 cts.	1 ct.
"	New York City .	25	2	25	1
"	Philadelphia . .	25	2	25	1
"	Chicago . . .	50	3	30	2 cts.
"	Denver . . .	75	5	60	4
"	San Francisco .	100	7	100	7
New York	Chicago . . .	40	3	30	2

In Europe the usual rate is about 10 cents for 20 words and ¼ a cent to a cent for each further word (H. Rep. 114, p. 1, Switzerland; p. 2, Belgium; p. 4, France). See also Blair Committee, vol. 2, p. 982, and Professor Ely in December ARENA, 1895, p. 50. In Belgium the rate for additional words is less than ¼ a cent each, being 2 cents for each 5 words (10th Census, vol. 4). In Great Britain the rate is 6 d. for 12 words and ½d. for each added word (P. M. Genl.'s Rep. 1895, p. 35). In France the charge is 10 cents for 20 words and 1 cent for each further word regardless of distance, except that messages to the French possessions in Africa pay 1 cent a word from the first word — 20 words 2000 miles for 20 cents (10th Census, vol. 4; H. Rep. 114, p. 4; Sen. Rep. 577, part 2, p. 22.) The ordinary charge per message in Germany is 12 cents (Professor Ely in ARENA for December, 1895, p. 50). The 20 words include address and signature, which President Green says will average 7 words, leaving 13 words clear message for 10 to 12 cents, with additional words at the rate of ¼ a cent to 1 cent a word, as against 25 cents for 10 words and 2 to 7 cents per word in addition. The average charge per message in Great Britain is 15¼ cents, about half the average in this country. A comparison of average tolls, however, does not do full justice to the low-tariff country, because low rates increase the length of messages, as was clearly shown by the history of the B. & O. company, the average of whose messages under the 10-cent rate ran up to 16 words (Bingham Hearings, p. 76, testimony of D. H. Bates).

A comparison of city rates leads to the same result. In Boston a city message costs 20 cents plus 1 cent per word beyond 10, or 90 words for a dollar. In Berlin the charge is 5 cents (initial fee) plus ½ a cent a word, or 190 words for a dollar, which is more than double the Boston service for the same money after subtracting the 7 words for address and signature.

The Western Union is no better off when we compare its press rates with those across the sea. President Green told the Senate Committee on Postoffice and Post-roads, that the press rate was 6¼ cents per 100 words (Sen. Rep. 577, part 2, p. 23). Like most of his statistics this does not agree either with the facts or with the rest of his testimony. Some papers in large cities where there are a number to divide the expense of the same despatch may get part of their news for 6¼ cents a hundred words, but that is not the average rate paid by newspapers throughout the country, much less the average rate *received by the Western Union* per message of 100 words, which is the question at issue now. On the very same page 23 the same President Green illustrated the accuracy of his statement by saying: "We charge the New York Associated Press about 2¼ cents a word from New York to New Orleans, and ½ of a cent for each drop (22 of them), so that they get 1500 words a day for about $1.87½ at each of those places." $1.87½ for 1500 words is 12½ cents per 100, instead of 6¼ cents. But even this is not correct. Counsel for the People in this case went to the office of

The Western Union has endeavored to overcome the force of this tremendous fact by asserting that the rate is a matter of distance and that the distances are greater here, and tables of distances and charges were presented to committees of Congress for the purpose of proving the

the superintendent of the Western Union and inquired about press rates, saying he had seen the above statement about a drop rate of one-eighth of a cent a word between New York and New Orleans. The answer was: "I wish you'd tell me about those rates. We never heard of them. Our press rates are uniform all over the country, ⅜ of a cent a word in the day time, and ¼ of a cent at night. Several people have come in just as you have and asked about a drop rate of one-eighth of a cent. But we don't know of any such rate."

"The B. & O. may have sent messages at such rates sometime," said a clerk.

"No," said the superintendent, " they never sent messages as cheap as that."

Counsel also sent an agent to the State Street office of the Associated Press. They said they rented a wire, but it cost even more than ordinary newspaper work because the telegraph company thought 10 papers could afford to pay more than 1. In general newspapers had to pay two-thirds of a cent a word, drop message or terminal just the same, for you have to have an operator at Worcester or any intermediate point to take off the despatch just the same as at the terminal, and the operator is the main item.

On the aforesaid page 23, President Green says : " We sent 5,200,000 words of press sent ; 200,000 messages of 30 words" (it should be 173,333 messages according to the arithmetic I studied), "and we got $1,800,000, so that we got about 20 cents per message of 30 words sent" ($10 per message according to my arithmetic); "but the amount *delivered* was 605,474,000 words, which divided by 30 makes over 20,000,000 messages delivered" (he did get that right). Now $1,800,000 for 20,000,000 messages would be 9 cents per message of 30 words delivered, or 30 cents per 100 words delivered, including drops and terminals. Even this is below the truth according to the statements of the Western Union superintendent and the Associated Press, which are 66 cents a hundred day, and 33 cents night.

In Great Britain the press rates are 20 cents for 75 words day, or 100 words night, with a drop rate of 4 cents per 75 day, or 100 night. These extremely low rates result in an average charge of about 4½d. or 9 cents per 100 words — a press tariff which is about one-fourth of ours and is a little too low, about 11¼ cents per 100 words being necessary to pay the cost of the service, according to 41st Report of the English Postmaster General (1895), pp. 35–6 and 37, where the facts are fully given (the cost being found by adding the £300,000 to the receipts from 650,000,000 words at 9 cents a hundred).

In Germany telegraph lines are leased for press purposes at the rate of $4.80 a day (7 A. M. to 9 P. M.) and half rate or $2.4 per night; this is for a Morse line. A Hughes line rents for $9.60 a day and $4.80 a night. The Hughes system has double the carrying capacity of a Morse line in the same time (10th Census, vol. 4). If 1500 words were sent over a Morse line the cost would be 32 cents per 100 words by day line, and 16 cents per 100 by night. If there were 22 drops, as in President Green's New Orleans illustration, the average cost for each town or city served with the news would be about 1 cent per 100 words for rent of the telegraph line.

To rent a line from the Western Union costs $20 a mile for a day line, and $10 a mile for a night line, about $25,000 a year or $70 a day for a line from New York to New Orleans. With 1500 words a day the cost would be $4.66 per hundred words by day, and $2.33 per hundred by night, or an average cost for each town of about 15 cents per 100 for rent of the telegraph line. A line from Boston to New York costs $4,500 a year or $12 a day, and one from Philadelphia to Chicago costs $14,000 a year or $40 a day. The company supplies only the line and the instruments; the lessee must find the operators, clerks, etc., and perform all the labor of collection and transmission.

assertion. Unfortunately for the Western Union the Washburn Committee consulted geographies and telegraph maps and found that the length of telegraph routes between the cities of Europe was strangely minified in the Western Union statement, while the distances between American cities were mysteriously larger than those set down in maps and geographies. Here are some examples:

| FROM LONDON TO | TELEGRAPH DISTANCES. | |
	Western Union Statement, Miles.	Truth in Miles.
Dover	50	82
Plymouth	100	246
Paris	200	313
Reims	250	400
Hamburg	380	556
Munich	540	800
Berlin	560	722
Prague	600	958
Madrid	750	1,225
Rome	850	1,349
Naples	950	1,510
St. Petersburg	1,160	1,806

Not one single distance is correctly stated. It is necessary in nearly every case to add at least one-third and often more than one-half of the stated distance to obtain the real distance. The sum of the stated distances was 15,724 miles, and the sum of the real distances was 22,578 miles, or almost one-half more than the Western Union's statement. To show the falsity of statements about American routes it was not even necessary to disturb the dust on the geography—the statement was its own refutation; for example, the distance from Memphis to New York was placed at 2,000 miles, while in other tables of the same Western Union testimony the distance was said to be 1,000 miles. So the distance from New York to Chicago was placed at

In Germany the rental is not by the mile but by the line—the rate being averaged for long lines and short ones, so that a group of papers in a distant part of the empire pays no more for its news over a rented line, than a group of papers near the capital.

Looking back over the facts set forth in this long note it is no wonder that Postmaster General Creswell declared " the average rates here to be 1½ to 4 times as high as those of Europe " including Russia, Turkey and all; nor that Gardiner G. Hubbard, one of the highest authorities in the country, told the Senate Committee on Postoffices and Postroads that " rates are twice as high here as in England " (Sen. Rep. 242, 43–1, p. 25). Rates have fallen on both sides of the water since that report was made, but the statements it makes are still true, as the facts of this note abundantly prove.

750 miles, and to Galena at 1,400 miles, though Galena is only 185 miles from Chicago.—Substituting the true distances in the comparison of telegraph charges in Europe and America, the committee obtained very different results from those of the Western Union statement. The rates and distances from Paris to 30 odd cities all over Europe were placed in one table; a similar table was made with Berlin as a centre. For the United States a table was made of the rates and distances from Washington to 30 odd of our chief cities having distances almost identical with those in the tables of Paris and Berlin. The conclusion of the committee from these tables, together with the corrected tables of the Western Union statement (rates and distances from New York to 61 American cities, and from London to 29 cities in all parts of Europe, the cities in each table being chosen by the Western Union), was that *the rate per mile in Europe was less than half the rate per mile in America.* And the rates compared were for internal traffic in the United States, and for international traffic in Europe. The cost of international communication is more than the cost of internal communication for an equal distance, because the receipts have to be divided among two or more nations each of which desires nearly or quite as much return as for an internal message, and the division itself entails additional expenses of bookkeeping, etc. *When internal rates in Europe are compared with internal rates in America, mile for mile, the contrast becomes more glaring than ever; the committee found that the rate per mile in England was less than one-third the rate per mile in the United States, and in France less than one-fourth of our rate, mile for mile.*[2] A substitution of present rates in

---

[2] For all the facts of this paragraph see the tables prepared by the Washburn Committee, H. Rep. 114, pp. 57-62, and the discussion on pp. 29-32. As a matter of fact, distance has little to do with the cost of telegraphing. The Western Union's reports show that the cost of maintaining the lines is only about one-tenth of the total cost of a message (2 or 3 cents a message), so that even if our distances were double those of Europe, as the Western Union would have us believe, still it would not be justified in doubling the charge on that account, since the increase of cost over Europe due to doubling the distance would be only one-half the whole cost due to our entire distances, or one-twentieth of the total cost of a message, or 1 to 1½ cents per message.

Postmaster General Creswell also examined this matter of distance very carefully, and in his report of Nov. 15, 1872, p. 24, he says: " The tables (Telg. 4) give a comparison of telegraphic tariffs in Europe with those in the United States, as regards distance, showing the lowest average rate per mile on 32 messages sent from Washington to points east of the Mississippi River, to be higher than the highest average rate per mile abroad (that in Russia), and the average rate per mile on 96 messsages here to be from 1½ to 4 times as high as those of Europe, notwithstanding the greater distances in this country."

the Washburn tables shows that substantially the same relations still exist between our rates per mile and those of Europe.

Driven out of this defence of distance and finding their assertion that the service is cheaper here than in Europe no longer tenable,[3] the Western Union affirms that the reason of cheap service over there is to be found in the low wages paid to telegraph operators. President Orton declares: "If we could be provided with operators at the rates paid for such service in Europe, I would undertake to render a better service at half the average rates now existing in Europe. I entertain no doubt of my ability to accomplish that result."[4] The committee, however, on the data furnished by the president, found that the average salary of operators in this country could not exceed $333, while in France, by President Orton's own statistics, it was $430, or nearly a hundred dollars more than the Western Union average,[5] and yet

---

[3] Chairman Hill of the Senate Committee on Postoffices and Postroads said to President Green of the Western Union: "How can you say that your system is cheaper when France sends 20 words 2,000 miles for 20 cents, and in several countries of Europe messages are sent for one-half a cent a word?"

Green. "When you understand that we pay more than twice as much to our operators as they do, and that material, except as to wood and coal, is higher, there is every reason why it should be higher here" (Sen. Rep. 577, Part 2, p. 25).

Here is a complete backdown on the question of rates — an admission that ours are higher than Europe's, which the witness had formerly denied — and an attempt at defence on the ground of wages. As a matter of fact the average wages of telegraph employees are not as high here as they are in several of the countries of Europe where telegraph rates are most moderate, while the amount of work done per employee is greater here than in Europe (see the facts in notes 5 and 8 below). It is still as true as it was in 1874, that "rates are twice as high here as in England, and yet it costs us less to do the work" (Sen. Rep. 242, 43-1, p. 25, testimony of Gardiner G. Hubbard).

[4] Testimony of President Orton, H. Rep. 114, p. 137.

[5] H. Rep. 114, pp. 43, 129. President Orton told the committee that the salaries of operators in Europe were "less than one-half as much as similar employees received here." Immediately afterward, he gave a table on the surface of which it appeared that the French government pays its telegraph employees below the grade of superintendent an average of $430. In the same speech, President Orton put the amount expended for labor by all the telegraph companies of the United States at about $2,000,000. From the Western Union Reports and other data the committee found the number of operators to be 6,000 (the postmaster general's report for that year said there were 6,162 telegraph offices in the United States), so that even if the whole 2 millions had gone to the operators they would only have received an average of $333 each instead of $860 as would be necessary to make good Mr. Orton's assertion as to the superiority of our wages — a rate which would have amounted to more than 5 millions for operators' salaries alone, whereas Mr. Orton states the total expense of all companies for all purposes as 4 millions for the year under discussion. We shall see hereafter that Western Union statements about wages are entirely unreliable even when they prepare tabulated data respecting their own employees. Their president tried to convince Congress in 1884 and in 1890 that they paid their operators an

the French telegraph tariff is only one-fourth of ours. In Great Britain the average pay of a telegraph employee was $360, according to the 10th census, vol. 4, and it has been rising ever since. In Germany the average was $300. According to the same authority the salary of telegraph employees throughout Europe averaged $320 each for the year 1880.—The president of the Western Union stated in the Blair Committee that "the aggregate salaries from president down are (1883) between 4 and 5 millions a year,"[6] and that the "number employed and paid by the Western Union Company is about 25,000,"[6] which would make the average salary $200, showing that European telegraph wages are 60% higher than ours according to Western Union data. Even if the Western Union could reverse the result of its statements and intensify the reversal so that wages here should be made to appear twice as much as in Europe, still the defence would be no better off, for it claims that the American operator does twice as much work as the European,[7] so that the company could pay twice the European salary without making the cost per message any higher than across the sea; and if we place this statement as to superior efficiency alongside of the truth in respect to salaries, we should expect the cost of a telegram here to be only half as much per mile as in France instead of four times as much.[8] The truth is, as shown in the notes (1, 3, 5, 8),

average of $65 a month, but there was abundant evidence that the average was not much over half that sum, and Mr. George caught the president squarely in the net of self-contradiction by showing that on his own data the $65 average would make a total for labor of operators alone that would be several millions more than the entire reported expenditure for labor, to say nothing of other employees, whose pay if added would make a total twice the one reported by the company (see Blair Com., vol. 1, p. 908).

[6] Blair Committee, Senate Investigations on " Labor and Capital," vol. 1, p. 901.

[7] Blair Com. vol. 1, p. 890. Examination of Dr. Norvin Green, president Western Union.

Q. Comparing operator with operator, is the American operator superior to the English ?

A. Undoubtedly he is.

Q. And does about twice as much work, I understand ?

A. I think, taking them in the aggregate, that they do twice as much work as the Englishmen.

Even this is not the extent of our wonderful dexterity, at least in certain localities. When Mr. Orton was president of the Western Union, he wrote to the postmaster general that " the working force in New York does nearly 4 times as much in proportion to number as the working force in London " (Sen. Rep. 242, 43-1, p. 25).

[8] The fact is that the Western Union statements are not correct either in regard to wages or efficiency. The 10th Census tabulates in vol. 4, the telegraph statistics of Europe and the United States for 1872, and for 1880. Postmaster General Creswell also tabulates the facts for 1868 to 1872 in his report for the latter year, p. 160. According to

that telegraph wages are lower here than in many parts of Europe, while the amount of business done per employee is larger here than across the sea, so that the real cost of transmitting messages is lower here than in Europe—a state of things, however, which results from conditions not altogether creditable to us (see note 8).

Expelled from this defence of high cost, the company ventures one more plea in the hope of justifying its charges, viz., that Europe makes a deficit. This plea also has been investigated, and it was found that France (the country showing the strongest contrast to Western Union charges, and paying the highest wages) was nevertheless realizing

---

the Census, 13,700,000 messages went over the wires in the United States and the employees of the telegraph companies numbered 10,000, giving 1,370 messages per employee. In Europe there were 46,797 employees and 55,265,298 messages, or 1,180 messages to each employee. In 1880 the number of messages per employee was 2,100 in the United States and 1,420 in Europe. (Many employees who devote more or less of their time to postoffice duties are included in the European returns of employees.) These figures indicate that the companies here could pay about one-third higher salaries than Europe without raising the cost per message above the European rate. The tables show that in 1872 the average telegraph salary in the United States was $360 against $290 in Europe ($288 is the census figure, $291 the postmaster general's) and in 1880 the average telegraph wage was $327 in the United States and $320 in Europe — a very creditable increase in Europe and a considerable fall in America — and this was prior to the reductions which constituted a part cause of the great strike of 1883. The reduction of wages here and their rise in Europe has continued down to the present time, so that now (1895) the average is about $300 in the United States and $350 in Europe, with about one-third more messages per employee here than in Europe — wherefore the indications are that so far as labor is concerned the telegraph service can be performed here at rates one-third lower than in Europe, since our companies receive one-half more service for $1 expended in wages than the European telegraph systems. (This would much more than offset any possible difference of distance even if it existed to the full extent of the Western Union's falsified tables, see note 2.) It must be kept in mind that the differences in " efficiency " above mentioned are not to be taken in disparagement of European workers. Individual quickness and aptitude constitute but one element in the problem. The number of messages per worker depends on the whole much more upon the density of the business, the hours of labor and the distribution of offices and employees than upon any differences in individual industry or capacity. This is clearly shown when we examine the subject in detail. For example in 1880, France had 1,925 messages for each employee, Great Britian 2,625, and Russia only 760; in the United States the average was 2,100 for the entire business, —2,750 for the Western Union, but for the companies outside of the Western Union it was only 565 messages per worker — considerably less than even the snowy wastes of Russia have to show, — so that it is not a question of the superiority of the American citizen. The French "efficiency" is undoubtedly considerably higher than the census figures above given, for two-thirds of the employees constituting the divisor in the calculation are engaged more or less of their time in the postal service aside from the telegraph. The Western Union is fond of tickling the ear of Congress and flattering the patriotism of the people with all sorts of complimentary statements about the efficiency of their service, but the cold fact is that the Western Union obtains its large percentage of messages per worker, first by selecting the localities where business will be more dense, instead of sending the telegraph into every district as in many of the nations of Europe, and second by working its employees very long hours.

a profit on its telegraph business of more than a third of the gross receipts.[9] It was further ascertained that England, Switzerland, Sweden, Prussia, Belgium and other countries make a profit on their telegraph systems;[10] that Europe as a whole did the same;[11] and that the Western Union had ciphered out a loss for Europe by adding the cost of construction into the operating expenses.[12]

The truth is that rates are higher here than in Europe because private enterprise aims at dividends while public enterprise is satisfied to serve the people about at cost. The contrast is finely illustrated in the case of Great Britain, the 18 million messages sent in 1873 under public ownership costing the public just what 9 million messages would have cost under the displaced private ownership,[13] and in 1886 and '87 after the further reduction in 1885, it cost the people only a trifle over $6/10$ as much for each million messages as in 1873-4, and about $3/10$ as much as in 1869 under private ownership.[14] How different this record from that of the Western Union Company, which has frequently raised rates, at the very time when the cost of sending messages was rapidly diminishing,[15] and has

---

[9] Sen. Rep. 577, part 2, p. 26; see also H. Rep. 114, p. 4.

[10] H. Rep. 114, pp. 2, 5, 24, 88. The average yearly profits for a period of 5 years were $2.58 per mile of wire in France, $4.82 in Prussia, $8.27 in Belgium, $12.26 in Switzerland. For the English profits see note 12 in part 1 of this discussion.

[11] H. Rep. 115, p. 4, middle. See also the table of European statistics given to the Bingham Committee by President Norvin Green in 1890, which shows a million surplus for the 18 nations whose receipts and disbursements are given (Bingham Hearings, p. 39).

[12] H. Rep. 115, p. 4, middle.

[13] Sen. Rep. 242, 43-1, p. 9.

[14] Forty-First Rep. of Eng. P. M. Genl., 1895, and Mr. Morley's Returns to the House of Commons, Feb. 11, 1895.

[15] H. Rep. 6, 42-3 (1872), p. 3, where the Committee on Appropriations tabulate some of the changes in the Western Union tariff. Here are a few specimens:

From New York to										Rates 1852			1868
Cleveland	.	.	.	.	.	.	.	.	.	$0.50	.	.	$1.00
Buffalo	.								.	.40	.	.	.75
Cincinnati	.								.	.75	.	.	1.00
Providence	.								.	.20	.	.	.30
St. Louis	.								.	1.45	.	.	2.00
New Orleans	.								.	2.40	.	.	3.25

Again the reports of the Western Union show that from 1887 to 1890 the average charge increased 2 cents per message, while the average cost decreased half a cent per message, and the admitted profits of the company rose from 4 millions (on 17 millions receipts), to 7½ millions (on 22½ millions receipts), or from 23 per cent to 32 per cent of the gross receipts. Perhaps the most striking instance of the solicitude of the Western Union for the public welfare is the case described on page 53 of the second part of Sen. Rep. 577, in which the Western Union swallowed a cable company and then proceeded to make the rates 8 times as high as they were before the combine.

not reduced them at all except under compulsion of competing companies or the fear of an overpowerful agitation for a public telegraph.[16]   One of the most significant
facts of the tenth census is the statement in the fourth
volume respecting the profits of the telegraph service—"the per cent of profit to cost is 2.9% in Europe
and 29.5% in the United States,"—a tenfold profit without going below the surface of the Western Union
returns. We shall have occasion hereafter to dissect
the said returns, and we shall find that the real profit
is far greater than the reported profit; there is reason to
believe that it has been as high as 414% in a single year—
i. e., 414% on the real investment.[17]

To go more fully into the subject: the real reasons why
rates are too high in this country are three—needless expenses, illegitimate expenses and overgrown profits. Underneath and behind all these is the reckless power and
greed of a great corporation left free to act by inert and
conspiring congressmen; this is the underlying, ultimate
cause that produces needless and illegitimate expenses and
unjust profits which are the immediate causes of excessive
rates. We cannot expect a private company to avoid the
wastes incident to competition or the effort to guard against
it, which not only makes the cost of transmission greater
than it need be, but also entails many needless expenses
entirely aside from the work of sending messages and
maintaining the lines—only a National Telegraph System
can avoid such losses; neither can we expect a private corporation to do business without a profit—only the government or a body of philanthropists will do that; but we have
a right to expect that even a private corporation will be
satisfied with a fair profit on the actual investment, and
that it will not falsify its accounts by incorporating in its
statement of *operating* expenses such alien items as the cost
of new construction, of buying up rival lines, of lobbying
city council and legislatures, of paying exorbitant rentals

[16] Sen. Report, part 2, p. 52, reduction because of discussions in Congress; Blair
Testimony, v. 2, p. 1272. Gould's war on the Western Union brought rates down.
Bingham Hearings, Green's Testimony, p. 61, on the B. & O. war, saying: " We have
never undertaken to crush out any opposition with low rates. They have generally
been butting against us with low rates, and their general drive has been to compel us
to buy them off on the basis of the damage they could do us. Some of them have been
successful. The last formidable competitor we had was the B. & O. They came into
the field to smash things and they did." D. H. Bates, manager of the B. & O. lines,
says the Western Union did reduce its rates even below those of its competitor in the
effort to crush it (pp. 73–4, Bingham Hearings).

[17] I. T. U. Hearings, 1894, p. 59.

for leased lines, interest, profit and running expenses all in one lump called a "rent," etc., in order to make the cost of sending messages appear much greater than it is. That is, we have a right to expect this if it is reasonable to expect a private corporation to deal honestly with the public, which some may believe to be doubtful, while others who understand corporation life from the inside, or from close observation, will hardly think the subject open to question.

There is every reason to believe that telegraph rates could be reduced in this country to half the present charges and still leave a good margin of profit. The Baltimore & Ohio Company had a 10-cent rate for a long time on 19 routes and made a profit on the business.[18] The Western Union itself has frequently made an equally moderate rate under the pressure of competition,[19] and even without such pressure it carries from New York to Bradford, between the oil exchanges, a distance of 400 or 500 miles, at the rate of 10 cents a message.[20] The company has voluntarily accepted as "satisfactory" rates less than one-fifth of its ordinary charges, and covering a business amounting to many hundred thousand dollars a year.[21] And finally the Western Union carries many millions of messages for the press at an average of 30 cents per 100 words or 6 cents for 20 words.[22] Turning to other sources of information

---

[18] Bingham Hearings, p. 21, Wanamaker's testimony, pp. 61-2, President Green's testimony saying the B. & O. lost money, and p. 72-6, testimony of D. H. Bates, manager of the B. & O. telegraph company, contradicting President Green and affirming that the B. & O. did make a profit in spite of its low rates, and that the Western Union succeeded in buying up the B. & O. lines, not because they proved unprofitable, but because disaster overtook the road in other departments and it sold its telegraph business as the most available source of realizing the funds necessary to right itself. The following are examples of the B. & O. tariff: New York to Portland, Me., and intermediate points, 10 cents; New York to Philadelphia, Baltimore and Washington, 10 cents; New York to Chicago, 15 cents; New York to St. Louis, 20 cents; to New Orleans, 50 cents; to Galveston, Tex., 75 cents. The average charge on all messages was 16¼ cents (Bingham Hearings, pp. 76, 62).

[19] For example to keep pace with the B. & O. (page 62, Bingham Hearings, testimony of President Green). To fight a railway line the Western Union reduced the rate from Jackson to Natchez via Vicksburg to 10 cents for 10 words 1 cent for each further word (Blair Com. vol. 1, pp. 898, 900).

[20] Sen. Rep. 577, p. 59; "as they fix their own rates in this case they make money at those rates," p. 60. The company also carries from New York to Washington for 15 cents, p. 60.

[21] H. Rep, 6, p. 6. The signal service business which would have amounted to $644,648 at ordinary rates (and $264,278 at the government rate of 25 cents for 25 words over each circuit of 250 miles), was done for $123,662, "the rates being voluntarily accepted by the Western Union as satisfactory." That was 20 years ago, but as the cost of transmission has fallen still more than the company's charges, the contrast remains good.

[22] See note 1 above.

we find Postmaster-General Wanamaker proposing that
"charges in any one state and between any stations not
more than 300 miles apart shall not exceed 10 cents for
messages of 20 words or less, counting address and signature, nor over 25 cents for any distance under 1,500 miles,
nor over 50 cents for any distance."

Q.—"Upon what basis do you make the estimate of the
rates you give us?" asked the Bingham Committee.

Wanamaker.—"Largely by the rates that were current
when there was competition, before the Western Union
had absorbed the other lines."

Q.—"Don't you think it would be possible to give a lower
estimate?"

Wanamaker.—"I think it would. It would be such a benefit to get 20 words for 10 cents that I am afraid if rates were
lower we would be in the same position as the English
lines were in the beginning. They were overwhelmed with
business. My own judgment is, upon consultation with
intelligent experts, that a lower rate than this can be fixed,
but in the initiative it seems desirable not to attempt too
much." [23]

A syndicate of New York capitalists offered to accept
Postmaster-General Wanamaker's rates, building the lines
to connect the postoffices, supplying the operators, charging
the rates above named and giving the government 2 cents
on each message to pay for its collection and delivery.[24]
In the spring of '95 Mr. Wanamaker told the counsel who
is writing the People's Brief in this case, that he thought
a uniform 10-cent rate for 20 words, regardless of distance,
could be established in this country and yet leave the system
self-sustaining. The experience of Europe, and the B. &
O.'s success with low rates in spite of tremendous competition, leaves little room to doubt the correctness of
Mr. Wanamaker's conclusion. Some facts would indicate
the possibility of a still lower rate. At the annual meeting
of the National Board of Trade in January, 1888, Hon.
R. W. Dunham of Chicago, described the operations of a
telegraph company doing business between Milwaukee and
Chicago, and of which Mr. Dunham was a stockholder. The
company began with a charge of 1 cent a word, and within

[23] Bingham Hearings, 1890, p. 6. and Wanamaker's Argument on the Telegraph, p. 6,
et seq. Mr. Wanamaker told the Committee that his plans would save the people one-
half the money they have to pay for telegraph service at existing rates (Bingham
Hearings, p. 14).

[24] Bingham Hearings, testimony of John Wanamaker and J. M. Seymour. See also
Wanamaker's "Argument," pp. 6, 7.

two years paid back to the stockholders 90¢ of the money they had paid in. Then they reduced the rate to $^1/_2$ a cent a word or 5 cents a message, and at this rate paid over 40 per cent on the entire stock. This went on for two years and then "we doubled our stock from $14,000 to $28,000, making it one-half water, and still the result is about the same, and from 25 to 40 per cent is still paid back on the 5 cents a message paid by the patrons."[25] Such results with a business all the time under fire of a fierce competition, clearly prove the possibilities of a low tariff. This Milwaukee fact, together with the Western Union rates for signal service and press messages, points to the conclusion that a 10-cent rate would be more than sufficient even with present methods. And if recent inventions (to be hereafter described) were adopted, we would be able, according to very high electrical authorities, to send 1,000 words from New York to Chicago at a cost of 50 cents—a service for which the Western Union charges $31. With the saving effected by this new method, the further saving of rent, fuel, light, labor, etc., resulting from a thorough combination of the telegraph business with the postoffice, freedom from competition or the menace of it, the absence of watered stock, magnate salaries, dividends, lobby expenses, purchases of blackmailing schemes and rival franchises, etc. (all of which matters will be dealt with in detail in subsequent parts of this brief),— with all these savings and the enormous increase of business that would come with low rates,[26] it is not unreasonable to suppose that a uniform 5-cent rate would be amply sufficient to sustain a telegraph system owned and operated by the government under good civil-service regulations.

It follows as a natural consequence from narrow facilities and high charges, that only a very small portion of our people are able to use the telegraph. President Green says that only a million people use the telegraph at all, and that "46¢ of the total business is purely speculative —stockjobbing, wheat deals in futures, cotton deals in futures, pool room, etc.;—34¢ is legitimate trade; about 12¢ of the business is press business, and about 8¢ of it is social."[27] A stronger argument for public

---

[25] Wanamaker's Argument, pp. 69-70.

[26] See the third and fourth pages of note 6, part I of this discussion.

[27] Bingham Hearings, 1890, pp. 41, 56. See also Sen. Rep. 577, pp. 15, 16, part 2, pp. 63, 244. President Green told the Senate Committee in 1884 that "less than 1 per cent of the people used the telegraph"; "only half a million" used it; "about 5 or 6 per cent of the messages were social." President Green wished Congress to believe that the narrow patronage of the telegraph and the predominance of speculative use ought

ownership could hardly be made. It is an outrage upon
civilization that one of the greatest inventions of all
the ages should be permitted to be captured by corporate
greed, kept out of reach of the great mass of the people,
and reserved for uses in which the business of gamblers
forms the chief part, and is even given priority of transmission over all other business, as is well known to be the .
case on the Western Union lines. A company that manages the telegraph with so little wisdom and public spirit
as that ought not to be allowed to control it at all. Think
of it—50 years since the lightning was harnessed to language and literature, and the people cannot even yet avail
themselves of the discovery; 50 years, and gamblers are
still the main beneficiaries; 50 years, and Wall Street is
still in possession. It is time a suit in ejectment were
brought. It is time the telegraph were taken from the
gamblers and given to the people. The electric current
belongs to the people and must be made available for their
use. Our 5, 6 or 8% of social messages must be changed
to 50 or 60% as in France, England, Belgium, Switzerland
and other countries of Europe and Australia,[28] and our

---

to prevent the government's undertaking the business. His idea was based on the assumption that the use of the telegraph would remain the same under public ownership as it is now—an assumption which is conclusively proved to be false by the whole
history of the telegraph in Europe and Australia (see note 6 to part I and note 28 to
this part of the present discussion). Even if the president's assumption were true it
would not prove his case, for besides its lack of universality, there are many other
evils of watered stock, overgrown profits, unjust discrimination, ill-treatment of employees, interference with the freedom of the press, etc., for all of which the cure of
public ownership is demanded.

[28] H. Rep. 114, p. 42; Sen. Rep. 577, p. 16; I. T. U. Hearings, 1894, pp. 17, 24. "In
Europe, where the cheap system prevails, two-thirds of all despatches are on social or
family matters" (H. R. 114, p. 42). "In Belgium when the rates were high only 13
per cent of messages were on social matters, at low rates 59 per cent" (Sen. Rep. 18);
afterwards 63 per cent (I. T. U. Hearings, p. 17). See further the third and fourth
pages of note 6 to part I of this discussion. Great Britain, with about half the population of the United States, sends about the same number of messages over the wires.
France and Switzerland also send more messages per capita than we do.

	Telegrams per 100 persons.
Great Britain .	184
Switzerland .	127
France .	108
United States	95

A similar story is told by the contrast between the use of the telegraph and the
postoffice.

Great Britain .	1 telegram to 30 letters and postal cards.
Switzerland .	1 " " 30 " " " "
Belgium .	1 " " 23 " " " "
France .	1 " " 23 " " " "
United States .	1 " " 42 " " " "

46¢ of gambling must be reduced to 20¢ at the start, and afterward, when Partnership and Mutualism have attained their perfect form, to zero absolute.

(To be continued.)

Communication by telegraph in the best countries of Europe bears a much larger proportion to communication by post than in this country. This is not due to dearth of letters in Europe, but to better use of the telegraph, as the former table shows, and as is proved directly by the world's postal statistics which place the letters and postals per capita in England and France above the number here and in Switzerland about the same as here. In Western Australia and in New Zealand the letters and postals per capita are more than twice the number here, but counsel was not able to obtain precise data as to the use of the telegraph in those countries (see data in Eng. P. M. Genl.'s Rep. 1895, p. 35; Canada Year Book, 1892, p. 300; P. M. Genl. Wanamaker's Rep. 1892, p. 874). Taking newspapers, etc., into account, the United states comes next to Great Britain in the use of the postoffice (Wan. 1892, p. 872); but considering the use of the postoffice for the purposes of personal communication, a considerable number of nations outrank us.

The change of relative use that has followed public ownership of the telegraph in England is as remarkable as any of the preceding facts. In 1866 there was 1 telegram to 37 letters in Belgium with a government telegraph, and 1 telegram to 121 letters in England with a private telegraph (H. Rep. 114, p. 7). Now it is 1 to 23 in Belgium and 1 to 30 in England — nearly 300 per cent relative gain due to the change from private to public ownership, supposing the gain in Belgium to represent the ordinary development of business without change of condition.

MADNESS AS PORTRAYED BY SHAKSPERE.

BY FORBES WINSLOW, M. D., LL. M., D. C. L.

Shakspere was a true psychologist, in the exact interpretation of the word. He understood, as no other dramatist has ever done, the lights and shades depicted in madness; he knew how to graphically delineate its varieties.
He was conscious of the profoundly melancholic type so
often met with in real life, and of the fact that such a
mental state may be ferocious, terrible or heartbreaking;
he knew how to illustrate each of these. He had apparently
studied the subject deeply. His pathos and tragic dealings
with madness are wonderful. His knowledge of human nature must have been profound. He could shed tears with
it in true sympathy, and he could appreciate its varieties.
Degrees of madness are far more common than is generally believed, but the highest degrees of it are rare and
wonderful to witness in those of extraordinary mental
powers, or who have possessed striking characters before
the mental edifice fell to ruin and desolation. It is deeply
interesting to consider what Shakspere has done for us in
this great and mysterious affliction of fallen humanity.
He has left his book of nature as descriptive of several
deeply profound and interesting phases of this malady.
Nothing can be more subtle, yet decisively marked, than the
gradations by which King Lear, from a venerable and
almost doting old man—who wishes to "shake all cares and
business" from his bowed-down tree of life, so that he may,
"unburthen'd, crawl toward death"—rises with preter-
natural strength into the most towering condition of utter
madness. There is a general impression, in recollections
of the tragedy, that the first outburst of the madness of
Lear—that is, the turning point when his rage and conflicting passions carried his mind beyond all self-government, or definite conception of itself and its own purposes
—was displayed at the close of act ii, where he exclaims
to his daughters:

No, you unnatural hags,
I will have such revenges on you both
That all the world shall — *I will do such things* —
What they are, yet I know not; but they shall be

The terrors of the earth. You think I'll weep;
No, I'll not weep.
I have full cause of weeping; but this heart
Shall break into a hundred thousand flaws,
Or ere I'll weep — O Fool, I shall go mad!

Thus, after rising apparently to the highest pitch of fury with one unnatural daughter, he suddenly discovers another daughter yet more unnatural, so that his violence is impelled to burst all bounds. He then pauses an instant to contemplate the first daughter again, because he now believes her less monstrous and by comparison almost kind, when he immediately perceives that she is even worse than the second daughter. These sudden and violent bursts and recoils of passion—the rapid alternations of the frenzy of hate with loving though much-exacting hope—and the manifest confusion of his brain, as displayed in the equal fury and vagueness of his purpose, added to the final declaration of the frantic condition into which he was rushing—all these seemed to indicate the point where Lear's reason gave way, and every fresh emotion and thought *would* impel him deeper into the chaotic elements of insanity.

Some writers have placed the first symptom of positive derangement at the close of the fourth scene of the third act, where the forlorn king tears off his clothes, meets the storm on the heath, and discourses with Edgar, who is disguised as Mad Tom.

Kent. Importune him once more to go, my lord:
His wits *begin* t' unsettle.

There is no doubt that Othello, when he stabbed Desdemona, was driven to madness by the green-eyed monster, jealousy. His mental power was completely unhinged; his mind was unbalanced, and he was unable to resist the power which exerted itself over him in a constitution which, no doubt, had been materially upset and weakened by the conduct of Iago towards him. Many cases of impulsive homicidal insanity are due to jealousy, which acts on some persons in a terrible way.

With regard to the madness of Lady Macbeth, here we have an illustration of a woman, at the time of the murder of the king, screwing her courage up, so to speak, for a gigantic effort to commit a crime. After this a reaction sets in. The unnatural state in which she had been suddenly gives way, and her mind becomes deranged. Macbeth, conscious of this, and aware of the fact that the mind of his spouse is agitated night and day by the feeling of her guilt, appeals to her physician in the celebrated speech commencing:

> " Canst thou not minister to a mind diseased,
> Pluck from the memory a rooted sorrow,
> Raze out the written troubles of the brain,
> And with some sweet oblivious antidote
> Cleanse the stuff'd bosom of that perilous stuff
> Which weighs upon the heart?

Lady Macbeth's insanity was simply that produced by a guilty conscience, and a similar state is often met.

The mental condition of Hamlet has frequently been discussed, and various interpretations have been given in connection with the subject. Shakspere intended Hamlet to be a man of passionate disposition, of noble and gentle temperament, most affectionate, devoted to the memory of his father, and indignant at the absence of shame in his mother.

> Frailty, thy name is woman! —
> A little month! or ere those shoes were old
> With which she follow'd my poor father's body,
> Like Niobe, all tears; — why she, even she, —
> O God! a beast, that wants discourse of reason,
> Would have mourned longer, — married with my uncle.

The play thus commences with a delicate youth, with feelings of grief mingled with disgust, who had doubtless reflected for some time upon a theme which was both repugnant and harrowing to his sensitive nature, and which rendered his mind liable to be unhinged at the slightest provocation. The primary cause for the sudden outbreak of Hamlet's madness may be traced to the appearance of his father's ghost, causing a state of excitement, but calming down by degrees as the vision disappears. The first evidence of his mental aberration occurs in the scene when the apparition has left him and he is asked by Horatio what secret has been divulged:

> There's ne'er a villain dwelling in all Denmark
> But he's an arrant knave.

To which Horatio replies:

> These are but wild and whirling words, my lord.

This is the first allusion to the wildness and unnaturalness of Hamlet's disposition. Another early indication of his condition occurs in the interview between Ophelia and her father:

> My lord, as I was sewing in my closet,
> Lord Hamlet, with his doublet all unbraced;

> No hat upon his head; his stockings foul'd,
> Ungarter'd, and down-gyved to his ancle;
> Pale as his shirt; his knees knocking each other;
> And with a look so piteous in purport
> As if he had been loosed out of hell
> To speak of horrors, he comes before me.

In this scene Polonius alludes to the return of the gifts made by Hamlet to Ophelia as the cause of his madness:

> " That hath made him mad."

In the following scene we find Rosencrantz and Guildenstern, both intimate friends of Hamlet, sent by the king to act as attendants and watch over his personal liberty. From a previous acquaintance with him, it was not to be expected that a suspicion would be cast on the motive of their visit to Denmark and intrusion on his presence. The queen instructs them:

> Good gentlemen, he hath much talk'd of you,
> And sure I am two men there are not living
> To whom he more adheres.

> And I beseech you instantly to visit
> My too much changed son.

There can be no doubt but at this period of the play Shakspere regarded Hamlet as a madman, driven to desperation by all that he had gone through. A mind embracing both gentleness and firmness, naturally of a strongly melancholic temperament, of a highly reflective character, stung to remorse and terror by the villany of his uncle, the murder of his father and the incestuous behavior of his mother, all acting as excitants in one already predisposed to melancholy, and prostrating by their baneful influence his mind, producing the condition as depicted by the dramatist. Polonius, who was of a crafty and knowing disposition, and ever eager to express his opinion to the king, considered that he had found out the cause for this strange change in Hamlet's mind,—

> I have found
> The very cause of Hamlet's lunacy.

Of course he here alludes to the supposed affection for Ophelia, about which, however, there is a diversity of opinion, it being doubted by some whether Hamlet really loved Opelia or not.

Hamlet is evidently conscious of his condition, for he perceives that he is being watched by Rosencrantz and Guildenstern. He asks them a direct question:

> Were you not sent for? Is it your own inclining? Is it a free visitation? Come, deal justly with me; come, come; nay, speak.

This remark is made to them in reference to their sudden visit to Elsinore. Again:

What have you, my good friends, deserved at the hands of Fortune, that she sends you to prison hither?

It has often been argued from Hamlet's conversation here that he was feigning madness. This is, to my mind, however, contradicted in the beautiful speech describing his morbid brooding, which frequently has been brought forward as a typical illustration of a melancholic temperament. Burton, who was a contemporary of Shakspere's, has also depicted this condition in his "Anatomy of Melancholy." He writes:

They are soon tired with all things; they will now tarry, now begone; now in bed, they will rise; now up, then they go to bed; now pleased, then displeased; now they like, then dislike all. Sequitur nunc vivendi, nunc moriendi, cupido.

This passage is most descriptive of an ordinary melancholic temperament, one in such a state of general restlessness and disquietude as existed in Hamlet. Hamlet thus describes his melancholic disposition:

I have of late—but wherefore I know not—lost all my mirth, forgone all custom of exercises; and indeed it goes so heavily with my disposition that this goodly frame, the earth, seems to me a sterile promontory; this most excellent canopy, the air, look you, this brave o'erhanging firmament, this majestical roof fretted with golden fire—why, it appears no other thing to me than a foul and pestilent congregation of vapours.

Suicidal tendencies are always present in connection with melancholia. Shakspere, mindful of this, introduces in the following scene a speech as illustrative:

To be, or not to be, — that is the question.

From the context this evidently refers to the contemplation of self-destruction. The interview between Hamlet and Ophelia in which she is informed that he never loved her is characteristic of a mind unhinged:

Oh, what a noble mind is here o'erthrown!

His melancholic state gradually subsides into one of subacute mania, reaching its culminating point in the scene with the players, where he finds the account given by the Ghost of the murder of his father corroborated:

Now could I drink hot blood,
And do such bitter business as the day
Would quake to look on.

After the interview with his mother and the murder of Polonius, Hamlet is sent to England under the charge of Rosencrantz and Guildenstern, to whose protection he has been entrusted by his uncle:

And he to England shall along with you.

On his return home Hamlet meets the cortège bearing the "Fair Ophelia." It is a curious and significant fact that from the time of Ophelia's burial up to the termination of the play, no allusion, directly or indirectly, is made to Ophelia. Hamlet seems utterly to have forgotten the existence of such a person; with the funeral rites she apparently vanished from the world of his memory. After Ophelia has been interred in her mother earth, there are no evidences of unsound mind in Hamlet. He appears now to have quite regained his normal mental condition, and he continues in a sound state of mind until the termination of the play. As a substantial proof of this, I must refer to the speech made by him to Laertes previous to their duel. It is, however, to be regretted that this is omitted in the present version of the play usually performed. Upon this the whole question hinges as to whether he was feigning madness:

Give me your pardon, sir; I've done you wrong;
But pardon't, as you are a gentleman.
This presence knows,
And you must needs have heard, how I am punished
With a sore distraction. What I have done,
That might your nature, honour and exception,
Roughly awake, I here proclaim was madness.

He declares further on in the same dialogue that he destroyed Polonius and drove Ophelia to distraction under the influence of insanity. He says that "his madness is poor Hamlet's enemy."

The inference to be gathered from this is either that Hamlet was sane and excused himself on a self-imposed plea of madness, or that he was eager to explain the reason for his misdeeds. There is sufficient evidence from a careful examination of the traits in his character to ignore the first plea. Hamlet was not a coward. He would not have made use of deception to escape calumny and disgrace. On the contrary, he was brave, truthful, honorable and mentally resolute, and I cannot admit that he was a man likely to purposely deceive Laertes. It was contrary to his nature and to the history of his case. The general opinion at which I have arrived is that there is no evidence to prove that Hamlet feigned madness, and that, tracing

the delineations of his disposition carefully, there is conclusive evidence of the existence of mental aberration, followed, as I have shown, by complete restoration to health
previous to the termination of the play.

Shakspere founded his play of Hamlet on the story of
Amleth, the son of Horwondil, told by Saxo Grammaticus.
In this tragedy the young prince is called upon to revenge
the murder of his father, killed by his uncle Fengo. Amleth assumes madness in order to escape suspicion and so
be allowed to remain about the court without mistrust.
Throughout this play the character exhibits much cunning
and forethought, but there is an absence of the real madness
portrayed in Shakspere's Hamlet. No doubt it was the intention of Shakspere to elevate the character and to throw
around it the majesty of melancholy and the pecularities
which accompany melancholy of a morbid description. In
the Danish legend no mention is made of the ghost; this is
entirely a creation of the immortal bard; but from its appearance dates Hamlet's lunacy, which stamps the character
of the young prince, besides adding to the general interest
of the play from a dramatist's view. The intense horror,
the delicacy of the expression and feelings of a mind suddenly unhinged, have their true vent.

Another curious fact is that though Ophelia goes mad,
while in this state she never in any way crosses Hamlet's
path. Had Hamlet seen her thus, it would have been next
to an impossibility to have kept up the deception further:
his want of feeling would have amounted to heartlessness,
and would have lessened him in the esteem in which we
have been taught to regard this, the favorite character of
Shakspere. The very foundation of Hamlet's character
appears to be great mental sensibility, and one easily impressed by the events surrounding him and by any situation which might excite him. Though bent on revenge,
he is irresolute and inactive at times; though suffering
from the profoundest melancholy, we find him jocular and
merry; and though some authors regard him as a passionate
lover, he is nevertheless apparently callous about the object of his adoration: his sole idea is to revenge the foul
murder of his father, and he is heedless of anything else.
From the very moment Hamlet enters on the scene our
attention is fixed solely on him; he is the absorbing feature
of the play. Shakspere loved him beyond all his other
creations. The deep interest in the play is the conception
of Hamlet by the dramatist. Critics have frequently drawn
attention to the strange behavior of Hamlet towards

Ophelia. This may be accounted for from an erroneous but general accepted opinion, that the love of Hamlet for Ophelia was deep and profound. He was apparently captivated by her innocence and purity, by her beauty and tenderness of nature. To Hamlet's mind, which is almost spiritual and of a loving and gentle disposition, there must have been something very attractive in Ophelia, as an ideal image of nature and life. There is no evidence of real love in Hamlet portrayed through the play; but, on the other hand, there is tenderness, sorrow and pity for him. The love shown by Ophelia was not reciprocated. He throws aside his supposed love without flinching and without pain, and it vanishes as if it had never existed. His general demeanor is consistent with this. He felt that he had a duty to crush the love existing in Ophelia's heart. He sought her presence in his madness, as if ever eager to show her the fatal truth.

The character has taxed the genius of Booth, Kemble and Kean, by whom different readings were given of the play. In the first-named, an air of fierceness and anger was thrown over the majesty of Hamlet, whereas Edmund Kean in his personification of the character went to the opposite extreme. Henry Irving depicted the character with consummate skill, and gave to the play a reading which stamps his production as the greatest one England has ever seen. He, however, obliterated from his version the final speech made by Hamlet to Laertes, where he excuses himself on the ground of madness. The question, "Was Hamlet mad?" is of great importance.

Ophelia is one of the most touching creations of Shakspere's transcendent genius. Over her character he threw a charm, a brilliant flood of fancy, "sweet as springtime flowers." Hers is a character redolent of feminine gentleness, purity and grace. But, ever true to nature, this great magician and all but inspired poet could not sacrifice truth to fiction, fancy to fact, and he therefore makes this love-sick girl, during her insanity, give utterance to conceptions that never could have suggested themselves to her exquisitely chaste and delicate mind before it was prostrated and perverted by disease. With regard to the character of Ophelia and the place she holds throughout the play, she exhibits all that is young, beautiful, artless, innocent and touching. She is a striking contrast to Hamlet's mother; surrounded by all that is corrupt and wicked, she moves an emblem of spotless purity and love in all the unpolluted loveliness of her nature. As soon as we know her association with the hero of the play, we know that her fate is doomed, that her path is shadowed with all that is dark and sad. We pity her, and as the play advances, our pity increases and our love for her becomes more intense. The more the question is discussed, the more the play is analyzed, the more convinced we become that nothing but madness could have excused Hamlet's conduct towards Ophelia. It is but a humane acceptation of the situation. His whole character is so noble as to make this the one rational excuse we can find. He is not a character of exemplary virtue, set forth for our guidance, but he is a perfectly dramatic character and absorbs our profoundest attention amidst his vagaries. Had he been assuming madness this could not have been kept up indefinitely, so as to exclude the nobleness of his nature and the reigning impressions in his mind. His very conversation with the gravediggers, though apparently jesting, is in itself a proof of the deepest melancholy still existing in his heart. Garrick, when he produced the play, excluded this scene, wherein exists the very moral of the tragedy.

In conclusion, it may be stated that at the commencement of the play, we see Hamlet in the enjoyment of that greatest earthly blessing, *mens sana in corpore sano.* On the appearance of his father's ghost his mind becomes unhinged by melancholy, and this condition passes into one of subacute maniacal excitement after the play-acting scene. He is then sent to England as I have previously stated in charge of Rosencrantz and Guildenstern, and returns perfectly sane, when seen again at the burial of Ophelia. He continues sane during the play, and asks Laertes' pardon for what he has done, being conscious of his previous state, which he openly declares to have been one of madness. This is the only conception which can be given to the character of Hamlet, and the play is full of proofs which one and all negative the assumption that Hamlet was feigning madness.

That Shakspere himself had the utmost reverence for female purity and virtue is evident in all his writings; and although undoubtedly he has, according to the manners of his time, indulged very often in a warmth of expression which would be unsuitable to the present age, he has always drawn a broad distinction between the pure and ideal love, which is founded upon esteem and affection, and that material development of the passion which is common to man and the brute creation. In some of his "Sonnets," and even in the very beautiful though amorous poem of "Venus and Adonis," there are abundant illustrations of the above remarks; as for instance where, in the last-named work, the youthful and really virtuous huntsman declares, in answer to the impassioned address of the Paphian Queen:

Love cometh like sunshine after rain,
　But lust's effect is tempest after sun;
Love's gentle spring does always fresh remain,
　Lust's winter comes ere summer half be done;
Love surfeits not, Lust like a glutton dies;
Love is all truth, Lust full of forgèd lies.

The marriage of Shakspere, although only in his eighteenth year, was unquestionably a great cause, if not the chief cause, of the development of his marvellous intellectual qualities. The copious well of his imagination required only some power to draw up its overflowing waters wherewith to irrigate the barren fields of dramatic literature in the sixteenth century, and the necessity of obtaining a livelihood was the engine which evolved the latent streams.

Full many a gem of purest ray serene
The dark unfathomed caves of ocean bear;

and the pure gem of Shakspere's genius, which might have remained concealed had not circumstances revealed its beauty and its brilliancy, was rescued from obscurity by his marriage with Anne Hathaway and his meeting with strolling players at Stratford-upon-Avon.

To a mind like Shakspere's, looking at this period of his life from a psychological point of view, it is quite conceivable that not only the easy and jovial manners of the actors presented great and irresistible attractions, but that the very poor condition of dramatic literature in his time fired his ambition to produce something better than the trash then deemed good enough to be presented to the public. No authentic particulars have been handed down as to the manner in which he spent his time from the age of twenty-one to twenty-five, which must have been in him a period of the greatest intellectual activity, in which he was no doubt occupied either in writing plays himself, or in adapting and improving the works of his predecessors or contemporaries. But from internal evidence it is plain that the representations of the stage, crude and coarse as they were in his youth, inspired him with many of those lofty thoughts which breathe and burn throughout his writings, and which, deriving their source from a microcosm seen in actual life, expanded into those boundless regions of thought and invention in which time and space are annihilated, and in which man and nature are depicted in all their multitudinous aspects, in beauty and deformity,

in light and in darkness, in gayety and in despair, in sunshine and in storm, in space and in infinity, in time and in
eternity. "All the world's a stage," as he beautifully expresses it,

> And all the men and women merely players;
> They have their exits and their entrances,
> And one man in his time plays many parts.

And again, when Macbeth, at length weary of life and
deserted by his friends, exclaims,

> Life's but a walking shadow, a poor player
> That struts and frets his hour upon the stage,
> And then is heard no more.

How well can we understand that the representation on
the stage (sometimes probably in a barn) at Stratford-upon-
Avon inspired Shakspere's mind with the grandeur and at
the same time the weakness and vanity of human things!
The actors, repeating high-flown and bombastic lines, attired
as kings or heroes, putting off for a time their ordinary
dresses and attired in glittering but tawdry colors, and
again resuming their shabby habiliments, would readily
convey to his mind a picture of the changeful condition of
mankind in actual life; while the stage, glowing with artificial light and scenery, or perhaps only tenanted for a time
by walking puppets, terminating their brief career of a few
hours to sink into darkness and silence, would be to him
a type of life and death, not only in man, but in the great
scheme of nature herself, and would shadow forth the beauties of creation, the monuments of art, the symmetry of the
universe, as the things of an hour and perishable as the
scenery of a stage play.

> These our actors,
> As I foretold you, were all spirits, and
> Are melted into air, into thin air;
> And, like the baseless fabric of this vision,
> The cloud-capp'd towers, the gorgeous palaces,
> The solemn temples, the great globe itself,
> Yea, all which it inherit, shall dissolve,
> And, like this insubstantial pageant faded,—
> Leave not a rack behind.

SCIENTIFIC THEOSOPHY.

THE DAWN OF A NEW CIVILIZATION.

BY PROF. JOSEPH RODES BUCHANAN, M. D.

In my previous brief essay, I spoke of the essential revolution in therapeutic science arising from a perfect knowledge of remedies, a perfect diagnosis, and the introduction
of three new methods in the treatment of disease suggested
by the new physiology of the entire man, all of which will
be embraced in the therapeutic science of the college* now
organizing, in which we expect to demonstrate many other
laws of nature and therapeutic possibilities for the body
and soul of man, which mechanical dogmatism neither
seeks nor desires to know.

The limits of this essay do not permit any description
of the three peculiar methods, but a correct idea of them
may be obtained from "Therapeutic Sarcognomy" under
which a number have already been trained, which presents
the new physiology and its consequent therapeutics.

This medical revolution is one example of the vast enlargement and change in established sciences now approaching, and hereafter to occupy the entire field of vital science,
which must be the result if man possesses grander powers
than hereditary ignorance and superstition have heretofore
allowed him to use. The claim is now presented that man
has such powers, and as soon as he learns to use them freely
and fearlessly the inherited ignorance and consequent
dogmatism of the dark past will be dissipated by the
divinity in man. That expression is used, not in any sense
akin to theological mysticism, but as the expression of a
scientific, available and immensely valuable truth, which
must of course force its way with some difficulty through
that nearly prohibitory tariff against any large importation
from the divine field of limitless knowledge which our
posterity are destined to enjoy. The tariff is as firm still
as in the last two centuries, but not enforced by formidable
punishments, as in the case of Roger Bacon, Bruno and
Galileo.

---

* Physicians who are interested in such a college, and could participate in such an
enterprise, are invited to write to Dr. Buchanan, at San Jose, Cal.

The divinity in man of which I speak, is a conception so vast that only in the last twenty years have I fully realized it, and only in the last five been disposed to speak of it. What is divinity? Is it not the combination of omniscience, omnipresence and omnipotence? Do these exist in man potentially or actually, to any considerable extent, and available for scientific and social progress? If so, then divinity is the proper scientific expression, and the emancipation of that divinity implies the universal revolution which I assert is coming.

Then listen to my story. The most obvious application (which was first apparent) of my discovery of the vast capacities of the anterior region of the brain, was the creation of a new *materia medica*, giving precision to medical science. The iceberg resistance of medical colleges to such attempts, and the somewhat analogous achievement by the followers of Hahnemann in spite of collegiate hostility, made it more important to follow other lines of investigation so numerous and extensive that one lifetime was really inadequate.

The impressional perception of therapeutic powers in medicines and other physical agencies was less important than the impressional perception of vital influences and laws. The impressional psychometer (they who are capable of being such count by millions and always have) when properly trained, has but to give up exclusive reliance upon his external physical senses and rely upon his more divine interior endowments, while every muscle is in profound tranquillity, and become able to feel and perceive sympathetically the natural and the morbid sensations and conditions of the one whom he touches properly, as thoroughly as he would feel all the potentialities of a medicine, and arrive at a perfect sympathetic understanding of his life and all its conditions so as to make a complete and correct diagnosis, and realize it so fully that unless his own vital force is sound and vigorous, the same morbid conditions may be transferred to himself. This I have painfully experienced when coming into contact with the sick and finding that I absorbed their pathological conditions, and thus knew more than the rules of diagnosis suggested, but at the expense of my own health, so that for many years, being careful of my own constitution, I have known scarcely any derangement of health (except from malaria) which had not been thus imparted—a condition which kept me from active practice, because not endurable, and at length compelled me to give it up entirely, as I never approached a patient, even without contact, without borrowing something from him.

The law of contagion thus illustrated has been a sort of *pons asinorum* for the medical profession, which the colleges have never crossed. Their mechanical dogmatism prevents them from recognizing the simple law of nature which runs through the centuries, that contagion does not depend on mechanical transfer, nor on imitation, but on the capacity of the nervous system of man to be affected by any conditions or processes in its vicinity, as one musical string vibrates in response to another, or as an electric current in one wire may start a current in a wire miles away. Such sympathies may be inactive in hard, resisting constitutions, or may be overcome by the higher vital force of the recipient, but when the nervous system is adequately developed they are limitless. Although myself much below the average psychic capacity of my students, I have felt the illness of a friend two hundred miles away, noted it at the exact time, and verified it afterward. I was compelled to request my learned friend Professor Gatchell, not to visit me when he had a cold, as its effect upon myself was too great.

There are many who can feel the conditions of friends at a distance, and physicians who while sitting in the office can determine the condition of a distant patient. The late Dr. John F. Gray, of New York (a very eminent physician), while in his room at the Fifth Avenue Hotel, looked into the condition of one of his patients in Jersey City, and not only satisfied himself of the man's state, but made such a psychic impression on him that the patient believed he was visited at that time by Dr. Gray, who came in, looked at him and retired without saying a word, and would not believe Dr. Gray when he assured him that he had made no such visit.

I ought to introduce here a chapter of demonstrative facts, but for want of space I pass on to the comprehensive statement that he who has a good nervous development and can feel the proximity of another's hand without touch, and has learned how to use his power, by assuming the necessary passiveness (for which some instruction is generally necessary) can place his fingers upon any part of the head or body of anyone who has a vigorous vitality, and realize the vital force flowing from that spot, learning from any locality on the head the true function of the subjacent brain. Yet never in the world's past ages, never in the schools or closets devoted to research, has this simple worldwide fact been known or suspected. Its very simplicity has made it incredible to the scholastic mind, and it continually comes as a matter of astonishment to my students who, whether they are young tyros or learned medical professors, are as much astonished as the old gentleman hunting all day for his spectacles, when told they are on his head. Could I, with this knowledge, have been present with Gall and Spurzheim in their investigations of the brain, they might have been protected from several grave errors, and led into a vastly larger field of science than that which they explored at the end of the last and beginning of this century. It is well, however, that theosophic science was delayed a century, for it would not have been tolerated in their day; but they had great success while they lived in introducing the anatomy and physiology of the brain.

Of course I applied this power to the investigation of the brain and body, and results of the exploration were given to the world in 1854 in my "System of Anthropology," which was soon sold out, and in 1885, in "Therapeutic Sarcognomy," now in its third edition. (My books have only been printed and furnished to applicants, without the aid of publishers.) This psychometric survey of the constitution was simply a revision for greater accuracy of the ground already travelled over, yielding a map of the functions of the brain and the psycho-physiological potencies in the body.

In the experiment just mentioned the passively intuitive sensitive in touching the surface of the body yields to its influence; but in my first experiments the passively sensitive individual was made the subject of the operator, and the organs of his brain were separately subjected to reënforcement by vital influence from myself or another, and after this method had been extensively used it was replaced for general reasons by the stimulant influence of static electricity, which is equally effective.

I had been seven years engaged in the investigation of the brain when I decided to try direct experiment, and thereby revealed a far greater impressibility than I anticipated, which seemed to give free access to all the realms of anthropology, and as it ultimately proved to the sphere of divine wisdom. This discovery, announced in April, 1841, and widely published, that the brain was impressible by vital and electric influences so as to compel the manifestation of its functions and give them as positive a certainty as Bell and Majendie attained in experimenting on the spinal nerves, has been repeated by many (who often mismanaged it), and among the first was the brilliant writer,

Prof. J. K. Mitchell of the Jefferson Medical College of Philadelphia (the ablest man of the faculty), who showed me, in 1842, an interesting chart of his experiments on the head of the editor, Joseph Neal (author of "Charcoal Sketches"). Yet I have never heard of anyone who treated the matter as anything more than a passing wonder, or sought any positive and valuable scientific results, as they generally confounded my simple, normal method with mesmeric procedures which made them delusive.

The impressibility of the brain, although widely announced, met with no intelligence competent to understand, realize and use it, but after its triumphant demonstration at New York in 1842, was recognized by the *Democratic Review* as by far the most important discovery ever made in physiology. (Allow me here to suggest that this singular liberality toward a new science was largely personal, and due to my personal introduction by ex-President Van Buren.)

The entire map of the brain which was thus revealed, and the map of the vital forces in the body in all parts, and especially along the spinal column, and its sympathies with the brain (for which I adopted the name *sarcognomy*) presented a complete view of both the psychic and the physiological functions of man and their anatomical locations, constituting the first presentation of a complete *anthropology*, for there is nothing in man but his psychic and physiological powers, and the soul to which they really belong, which finally lifts them out of the body for a more congenial home. Thus were all the possibilities, laws and mysteries of humanity brought within reach for a minute investigation by methods which are both microscopic and telescopic, the vast results of which will fill future libraries. But those interesting and instructive volumes must be written by others, for in the course of nature I must soon lay down the pen after finishing my fourteenth volume.

Thus was the physiology of man completed by revealing the functions of his brain—by far the most important of all his organs—putting an end to the solemn scientific farce of discussing and pretending to analyze man, without knowing the commanding centre of his life, the organ that governs all others. Without the brain, the philosophy of man, with which the learned world has been stolidly contented (as in a play of Hamlet with Hamlet omitted), is but an *acephalous monstrosity* which the next century will bury quietly, wondering at nineteenth-century folly.

In speaking thus I do not impeach the intelligence of such leaders as Huxley, Spencer, Darwin, Wallace, Currier, Humboldt, Agassiz, Beale, Ferrier and a mighty host of scientists, for they are ruled by a law of evolution which is the master of the world of mind as well as matter—the law -of *inertia*—a foundation upon which divine power builds the eternally growing temple of humanity by slow successive steps. How long was a flat, one-sided world an unquestioned doctrine, as the time to question it had not arrived? How long did the human mind rest content in geocentric astronomy? How long was it thought useless and forbidden to look beyond the old continents, until Columbus came? America, the destined ruler of mankind, was as far away from human philosophy as the heart before the time of Harvey, and the brain in the nineteenth century. That great men submit to such limitations and dare not advance, simply snows the slow progress of the evolution of mind and the long dominance of that inertia which as a gregarious instinct holds all mankind as an animal herd and tramples down all who do not move with it, and of course ambitious men are not willing to be trampled down. They go with the millions and rule them. But nature did not encumber me with any such ambition for power and wealth, and I have not feared the trampling.

Let us thank the scientists who have taught mankind to look forward as well as backward, and taught the church to submit to the change as it is now submitting slowly to evolution. It may require more than another century to teach scientists to look not only downward, outward and forward in the physical, but inward and upward to causation, and to learn that man is not a temporary chemical combination but a permanent being.

The word *anthropology* gives but a dim and feeble conception of the science. This absolutely new and vast but demonstrable and often demonstrated science is sustained by seven demonstrations, each of which might alone be sufficient.

1. The experiments on the brain and body in which the subject (persons of intelligence and integrity being chosen), is made to realize every passion, emotion or faculty desired, by vital or by electric excitement of the different convolutions of the brain, such as irritation and restlessness, good nature and tranquillity, self-esteem, humility, avarice, generosity, love, hate, indolence, sleep, hunger, disgust, drunkard's thirst, spirituality, sensitiveness, melancholy, gayety, debility, muscular strength on either- side of the body,

variations of the heart, the pulse, the temperature and the viscera, etc.,—the results being sometimes moderately produced, but in weak subjects uncontrollably.

2. The effects of warmth and coldness or of inflammations in different parts of the brain and of surgical injuries.

3. The concurrent reports of many psychometers who recognize, feel and describe the action of the various organs —persons whose reports on any other subject would command belief.

4. The effects of inordinate development or deficiency of particular convolutions upon the character, constitution and morbid tendencies.

The corroboration of the physiological results by the results of vivisection and the electric experiments on the brains of animals which have been carried on so extensively by European physiologists, and fully reported, especially by Professor Ferrier—furnishing a style of demonstration I had desired for thirty years. Their location of muscular power is the same through which I made a public experiment on the head of Dr. Parmlee, at New York in 1842, which resulted in the appointment of a committee and a very satisfactory report.

6. I may add the local sensations in the head produced by the different faculties and their organs, which I have distinctly observed when the mental excitement was sufficient to produce active circulation. Having watched this closely many years and realized distinct sensations in every region of the brain, with an accurate knowledge of the localities, this is more decisive to me than it can be to anyone else, though I have often pointed out the coincidences in others. Heat, throbbing, stinging, soreness, aching, coldness, pressure and a sense of vacuity or inaction occur in the localities affected, sometimes even producing a bristling of the hair at the excited spots. Anyone who will study the subject in this way can get the same evidence when he knows the localities if he has sufficient excitability in the brain.* A careful study of these local sensations would long ago have revealed the essentials of cerebral science.

7. The crowning demonstration, which is mathematical, is to me as impressive as any. It is the demonstration which I give to my students, that every human faculty and every organ of the brain act in accordance with a certain

---

* A letter just received relates the writer's intense local sensations at the organs affected, even more intense than my own; and while writing this essay I was surprised to find that a vivid conception of an unpleasant condition produced a distinct sensation over the brain spot affected. These sensations always come unexpectedly. I have often found them in others.

mathematical line of direction coinciding with the fibres of the organs, which I call the pathognomic line; and that the same mathematical law rules all the functions of the body and all voluntary or spontaneous movements of the limbs, the trunk and the features, and the course of every drop of blood. The law is recognized and understood as true whenever it is distinctly presented. It is a basic law of hygiene, expression, art and oratory, of which Delsarte had an incomplete empirical conception in his theories. The law is not confined to man; *it is a law of the universe.*

Though unable to make the psychometric experiments myself with any satisfactory facility, I have gained a more positive conviction of functions from my own experiments in applying my fingers to stimulate any location in the impressible. I cannot do this many minutes without feeling the reflex influence on myself from the point that is touched. In some rare cases it has come with electric quickness. I often convinced stubborn sceptics by disagreeable experiments on themselves, but the undesirable effects on myself compelled its discontinuance.

In the half century since these discoveries I have had very little interest in propagandism after the first four years, for demonstrations seemed to produce no diffusive effect beyond their immediate presence. They fell into the public mind as a meteorite falls in a bog. The whole interwoven construction of current opinions, scientific dogmas, fashions, fads and so-called philosophies and theologies, welded together by selfishness and moral cowardice, made an impenetrable mass, the whole of which would need to be removed to make room for the truth that might consign it to oblivion, for there are few of the dominant *opinions* of the nineteenth century that future centuries will accept. My quiet proceedings and demonstrations were not the methods by which the charlatan stirs an excitement. No souls aflame with the love of divine wisdom and eager for exploration were visible—only a few manly friends. Pope's famous couplet ending ".All fear, none aid you and few understand" continued to be true, and the poet Bryant quoted it to me, but did nothing more, for he was controlled by politic friends. The idea of exploring the desolation in the Arctic zone excited a thousand times the interest of the thought of exploring divine wisdom; and in sober truth, ten million times more interest was excited by the exploits of a noted drunkard pugilist, whom city authorities honored, and who would not condescend to go to Congress because it did not pay as well as pugilism.

Let me add that it is with grim satisfaction I know that, as an octogenarian, it cannot be many years before I shall be transferred from the sphere of terrene barbarism to the only realm of civilization (with which mortals have so little intercourse).

These doctrines have been taught to many pupils who have repeated the demonstrations by experiment. The subject was mastered by the late Professor Gatchell, who had no intellectual superior in the homœopathic ranks, who lectured on the subject, and who often repeated my experiments and felt their truth in his own person. He carried one of my experiments, antagonizing the vital force, further than I ever dared, until the subject became pulseless.

In the winter of 1842–43 at New York, a committee of investigation (appointed by a public meeting), of which W. C. Bryant, the editor and poet, was the chairman, after witnessing my experiments, made a report occupying more than a page of the *Evening Post*, declaring that my doctrines had "a rational experimental foundation, and the subject opens a field of investigation second to no other in immediate interest and in the promise of important future results to science and humanity." The *Democratic Review*, a leading magazine at that time, conducted by one of the committee, said (as already mentioned) in reference to this investigation, "To Dr. Buchanan is due the distinguished honor of being the first individual to excite the organs of the brain by agencies applied externally directly over them, before which the discoveries of Gall, Spurzheim or Sir Charles Bell—men who have justly been regarded as benefactors of their race—dwindle into comparative insignificance." Such was the language of candid and learned gentlemen, one of whom (Dr. Forry) was a well-known medical author, and founder of a medical magazine which is still published.

Such endorsements in various language but equally decisive, and some extremely eulogistic, have been given by every one of ten committees of investigation. The most extensive was a three-column report by the faculty of the Indiana University in 1843. In the committee of physicians at Boston my experiments were made on one of the committee, Dr. Lane (an author), in which, in addition to the psychic effects, I demonstrated the control of the brain over the pulse, showing the ability to produce any required condition of it—all of which was published by the committee.

Thinking no further public demonstrations necessary, and seeing that they produced no practical results, inspiring

no ambition to cultivate a new and limitless philosophy,
I devoted myself to the establishment of a liberal medical
college at Cincinnati in which my doctrines and discoveries
were taught and were proclaimed as the philosophy of the
college (the Eclectic Medical Institute), the success of which
during the ten years of my connection with it was remarkable—surpassing in attendance the combined classes of the
three other medical colleges—and its system of practice
(in which my therapeutics was not then incorporated) is now
followed by at least ten thousand physicians.

I might beg pardon for this somewhat personal digression,
but it is necessary in presenting a novel scientific philosophy
which implies a total revolution, and consigns the dominant *opinions* (but not science) of the century to oblivion,
to show that it is not an untested theory nor a private, un-
published and untested set of experiments, but a thorough
investigation of nature, with results never denied by any
who are acquainted with the investigation, but only by those
who are unwilling to learn, like Horky, the "principal
professor of philosophy at Padua," who in the time of Galileo refused to look through his telescope and learn the
truth. In my experience of colleges I have found that with
rare exceptions Horkyism is the predominant spirit. It
may not be politic to say so, but I can afford to tell the truth.
No one had a fairer prospect of success in a college career
than myself in 1841, when duty required me to surrender
such ambitions and enter the solitary and hazardous path
of the reformer.

The word *anthropology* conveys but a feeble hint to the
reader of the magnitude and importance of a new science,
foreign to the sphere of thought in this century, but really
the largest realm of science known to man, though foreign
to the imagination of philosophers heretofore, except to
Scotland's profoundest thinker, David Hume, who expressed his estimate of it almost as if he had foreseen its
development and supremacy. It is the greatest science
(though not the only one) born by the emancipation of the
divine element in man, which masters the universe—the
long-buried talent of the unfaithful—for history is a record
of man's infidelity to God and to himself. It does not admit of condensation into a magazine, but I hope to make
it a pleasure to the enlightened in the work now preparing
entitled "The New World of Science."

Anthropology reveals on the internal face of the lobe
and in its most exterior convolution, the location of the
faculties of which I have spoken, which transcend all

collegiate conceptions of the human mind—which read physiology, read disease, read character, read nature in all departments as an open volume, and taking up any emanation of human intelligence, understand and judge it at once.

It was in 1842 that I found a psychometer with whom I had been surveying the brain who could take up my letters and describe their authors as freely and correctly as if personally acquainted with them—any fragment of writing being sufficient. This fact has become widely known in civilized countries to the intelligent, although the slaves of authority, habit and fashion may still be ignorant of it, and may as usual continue so until it is forced upon them. There are many in high position in whom the mention of a revolutionary truth excites the same feeling as a mention of smallpox—a desire to get away from it and to have it quarantined; but I will mention no names, only the sorrowful fact that in the nineteenth century there is a large class of this character, the discovery of which was a great enlargement of my practical knowledge of mankind.

The discovery of such a capacity as mentioned, made necessary the coining of a new word to cover the apparently limitless capacities of the mind existing in millions, and the word *psychometry* was adopted, signifying etymologically soul-measuring—measuring the souls of others and measuring all things by our own soul. But this word refers only to the process or method, not expressing the science or philosophy evolved, which I was too cautious or modest to name by a word of commensurate dignity, as my personality was too closely associated with the subject.

The boundless realm into which *psychometry* leads us is justly called *theosophy*.* The pronunciation upon persons from their manuscript was commonly supposed to be dependent upon the magnetic influence of the person imparted to the paper; but no such influence is really *necessary* though it does exist, and a misleading magnetic influence may be imparted to the paper by those who have handled it or by things with which it has been in contact. Nevertheless a photograph or engraving leads to the same description, and even a simple name is sufficient for those of superior endowments.

The late Mrs. C. H. Buchanan, when I placed in her hands, unseen, merely the name of Homer or Demosthenes or any

---

* This noble word cannot be degraded or lose its true meaning by the persistent attempt to make it a mere trade-mark for the exploded inventions of Blavatsky, which had not a single element of theosophy to give dignity to their fictions, plagiarisms and grotesque fancies.

ancient or modern person, gave a faithful description as prompt and reliable as if of something recent and familiar. The thing that we use is merely an index to lead the mind to the subject to be investigated, and hence it is clear that the mind of the psychometer is an independent emancipated intelligence which ranges through the universe as far as man's fragment of divine omnipresence permits, to bring back what is wanted. She would describe the scenes connected with El Mahdi in Egypt or the warfare at Alexandria, or of the French at Foochow, or the unknown regions in the Arctic circle. The report bore no relation to my own knowledge or ignorance of the subject, and might contradict or agree with my opinions, if I had any. She would commonly sit at her desk, and without my knowledge answer letters and excite the wonder of correspondents, even as far off as the antipodes. When she placed her hand upon a volume without seeing it, her estimate of it would be as correct as that of a judicious reviewer.

Intelligent readers, keeping up with human progress, know that descriptions have often been given of distant scenes and called clairvoyance, which they suppose to be something abnormal or dependent on mesmeric preparation, which with some is necessary.

The psychometric faculty has an omniscient range. The lowest portion of the cerebral organ has merely physical perceptions, but the higher portion realizes character, conditions, history, and all that can be known of the past, reaching on into the unknown; how far it can go we shall ascertain by future researches. I believe it may reach back beyond all geological knowledge to the earth's fiery mass, and down along the ages of the tedious evolution of the vegetable and animal kingdoms.

It was in vain that I announced this limitless power and gave such illustrations as were convenient. "The dull cold ear of death" was not more unresponsive than our stagnant colleges. But a scientific genius came forward and stood by my side, giving the ample demonstrations that were needed. Professor Denton, the able geologist and eloquent lecturer, who defeated President Garfield long ago in public debate, applied psychometry to geology and paleontology with the startling results which he recorded in his three-volume work entitled "The Soul of Things," to which I have pleasure in referring the reader. But alas! in the midst of his great labors he laid down his life, while in scientific exploration of an East Indian island (New Guinea), near the equator, twelve years ago. Sad beyond expression is the terrible sweep of death, when it cuts down the world's benefactors in the midst of their unselfish service! His discoveries in Egypt are lost to the world. But our tears fall in vain! Yet truth does not perish when its champions die. What Denton recorded will hereafter (when the world is slightly civilized) be illustrated by thousands, for all history is an open book to the true psychometric telescope, which dispels the myths and traditions of superstition. Denton and the writer in acting as Herbert Spencer advises, uttering fearlessly the highest truth that we perceive, have portrayed a realm of science which Spencer could not see, but which is already becoming visible to millions.

When directed to an individual the psychometric power traces his career in life and, if it is finished, follows him as a disembodied spirit in the higher world, describing his post-mortem condition and the manner in which he looks upon his past life, and the sentiments he would express if he could speak.

Does, then, this divine gift to man open to his ready exploration all volumes of the divine wisdom displayed on earth or in heaven? Most surely it does, and wisdom thus given and received is truly *theosophy*—divine wisdom. To man can be revealed without the aid of literary dictation from the past, all the processes of soul life and physical life in the body, and all the grades of ascended life in the higher worlds; all the mysterious conditions of disease; all the *immeasurable* resources of nature for the restoration of health, which he has so sadly misunderstood and abused that many have lost faith in their real value; all the world's geological ages, and its present strata deep in the ground unseen; all the qualities and nature of that imperfectly developed life in the animal kingdom, which man tortures and destroys; all the rectifications of biography that he cares to seek; and the history of the religions in which the ancient ignorance of mankind has been fossilized—as few have ever known that religion, if true, is by its very nature ever progressive, and was so intended to be by Christ.

Nor is this divine faculty, the God in humanity, confined in its scope to man and his proximate sciences. The planetary family, warmed around one solar fire, is not beyond its scope, and nothing shall be hidden from the adult race of man, though much has been invisible during his long infancy, not yet ended.

Finally, my labors of sixty years have been entirely for *useful* results—to create a true therapeutics for healing body and mind, a philosophy that solves all the great problems now under discussion in which men are slowly, very slowly, approaching truths which I have long enjoyed; to give the law of progress, and the religion scientifically true, which in antiquity was fully realized by Jesus Christ alone, whom His professed followers have not understood, but whom *theosophy* reveals *as He was and is.* Yes, theosophy will reveal to the church the Jesus Christ who has been blindly worshipped, and in whose sacred name so many crimes have been perpetrated, and when that complete revelation shall have been accepted, as it finally must be, the entire world of humanity will be uplifted toward heaven, and there shall be no more war. And all these things shall be demonstrated before the end of the nineteenth century.

THE BOND AND THE DOLLAR.

BY JOHN CLARK RIDPATH, LL. D.

II. How the Monster Became King.

It was on the 18th of March, 1869, that the government of the United States made its first league and covenant with the fundholding interests against the people. By the terms of that league the millionaire who had given a hundred thousand dollars for a bond of the same denomination should receive back, true enough, a hundred thousand dollars, but should receive it in units of another kind worth about two for one.*

From that day, distant from the present by more than twenty-six years, there has been no deviation or shadow of turning on the part of intrenched intrigue to carry out the compact. Year by year the bolts and bars have been driven ever further and deeper with blow on blow of the sledge of the money power, until the national fraud has been glorified under the name of honor, and the wholesome truth nailed in the coffin of contempt. Each succeeding administration has been even as its predecessor, but more so in its devotion to the bondholding interest at the expense of all besides.

Having secured the declaration of the payment of the national debt in a currency different from the currency of the contract, the next step was that of lengthening and perpetuating the bonds. If the bonds, now payable in coin, were good for ten years or twenty years, then they would be better for thirty years or forty years to run. Nor will the government now be so eager to pay when payment in coin is impossible. The people can now be made to believe, what is true, that the government *cannot* for the present pay our bonds. They must therefore be extended. Great financiers will they be who can sell us a five-per-cent bond with an extension of ten years, and take up a six-per-cent

---

* The fact that the interest on the five-twenty bonds was by specification payable in coin shows conclusively that the body of the bond was payable in the lawful money of the country. Else why the specification as to how the interest should be paid? If the body of the bond were payable in coin, it had been the sublimated absurdity of the century to specify that the coupons should be paid in coin also! What kind of bond would that have been the principal of which was payable in coin and the coupons in legal tender?

439

bond which is falling due. That is the process of refunding in a nutshell, and that requires the gigantic intellect of some great secretary to do it. We, the beneficiaries, may hold out to him the impossible prospect of being president— if he will do the work well!

The history of the various refunding operations by which the short high-rate bonds of the government sold during the war period were translated into long lower-rate bonds is but the record of a scheme which was contrived by the bondholders themselves, ratified by an undiscerning Congress, and carried into execution by the treasury department of the United States, with the ulterior design of preventing payment by lengthening the time to run, and with the still further hope of making a perpetual interest-bearing fund in the European manner.

The first measure passed by Congress with this intent was the act of July 14, 1870, entitled "An Act to Authorize the Refunding of the National Debt." This act reaffirmed the proposition that all the bonds of the United States were redeemable, both principal and interest, in coin, and authorized the secretary of the treasury, as such bonds, series after series, should fall due—that is, reach the date at which the government had the *option* of redeeming them— to prepare and sell new bonds, extending the time to run and lowering the nominal rate of interest. Under this act the process of refunding was carried on by those interested in it as actively and earnestly as though it were a manufacturing industry, until all the bonds were extended and most were made as long as the current lives of men. Then the work abated, partly because of the weakness of all posthumous inducements, and partly because by this time certain symptoms of alarm and jealousy were noted among the people.*

---

* As much as two years before the passage of the Refunding Act, the people had begun to show signs of distrust at the manœuvres of the fundholding classes. The popular suspicion was shown in the declarations of the political platforms of both parties, in 1868, in the greater part of the country. The sentiment of the people, always true, even when overborne by their masters, was overwhelmingly in favor of the honest payment of the five-twenty bonds; that is, in favor of paying them in *the same currency* with which they were purchased. That currency had already appreciated in its purchasing power about thirty per cent. In the central United States the Republican platforms in the year just named were generally unequivocal in endorsement of the proposition to pay the five-twenties in the legal-tender money of the country. In the writer's own state, in that year, the platform was as follows: "The public debt made necessary by the Rebellion should be honestly paid; and all bonds issued therefor should be paid in legal tenders, commonly called greenbacks, except where, by their express terms, they provide otherwise." On this platform Senator Oliver P. Morton, of great fame and equal honesty, carried the state by a heavy majority for himself and General Grant. Within six months from that time, however, he yielded or was conquered—and in yielding lost the ambition of his life. The titanic knees of that great and resolute man, little acquainted with the common use of pregnant hinges, were broken, not, as the people supposed, by paralysis, but by the bludgeon of the money power!

The bonds had now become the most profitable of all investments. Of all the forms of property they were the most exempt from hazard, most convenient, and most strongly fortified by law. They offered themselves, however, only to the surplus accumulations of capital. The man of moderate means must needs employ his whole resources in the business to which he devotes his energies. When capital accumulates in large amounts and there is no such thing as a national bond in which it may ensconce itself and begin to grow, such capital must of necessity offer itself for the promotion of legitimate productive, manufacturing and commercial enterprises. It must under such conditions *do* something useful for mankind; but where the bond exists, surplus capital takes the form of the bond by preference of all other enterprises, and to that extent all other enterprises languish and weaken for their wonted stimulus.

By the beginning of the eighth decade thus much had been accomplished: The fundholding interest had confirmed itself to the extent of getting a long bond for a short one, with the guaranty of payment of both principal and interest in coin. The next point attained by the bondholding power—for it had now become a power—can hardly be touched upon with equanimity. The coin of the United States existed in two kinds, silver and gold. Should the government ever again reach the basis of specie payments, the debtor would have the option of paying in the one coin or the other, according to his convenience and the plentifulness of the given kind. This option constitutes the essential element of bimetallism. That it could be taken away from the debtor seems in the retrospect a thing so monstrous as to be incredible. It was a valuable option which the debtor in the United States had held unchallenged from the foundation of the government. No creditor had ever tried to take it from him. It had never been denied by any. It had always been cheerfully conceded down to the time of the Civil War, when an unforeseen condition removed all coin and put the country, as we have seen, on the basis of a legal-tender of paper.

Now that coin was again in sight, or was supposed to be coming in sight; now that the government had declared its purpose to pay the national debt in coin, though that debt had been contracted on a basis of paper, it might reasonably have been supposed that the bondholding interest would be contented with that enormous concession, and being thus glutted to repletion, would seek no further extortion from the American people. But on the contrary the monstrous scheme was conceived of destroying the option of the debtor to pay in silver, by destroying the coin unit of that metal, thus reducing the debtor—all debtors, including the government of the United States— to the necessity of paying in gold only. The scheme was not only conceived, but was contemplated with equanimity, not indeed by the people, but by those whose interests were so profoundly concerned. In the last session of the Forty-second Congress, the question was insinuated into legislation, but was housed from the public with a skill worthy of the noblest cause. It was already the plan of the conspirators to have an act passed by Congress as soon as possible declaring a date at which specie payments should be resumed in the United States. But preliminary to such declaration and as an antecedent thereof it was seen to be advantageous to tamper the coin dollar in which payment was to be resumed.

For the time being and for some years to come—so ran the bondholders' dream in 1873—the government and people alike must continue to prosecute their business on the basis of the paper legal-tender; but in the future, as we the financiers clearly perceive, another dollar, that is, a metallic dollar, is to be substituted for this legal tender of paper; and it is to our interest to have that other dollar as valuable as possible. We will not only go to the length of substituting a metallic dollar still worth a premium of from thirty to fifty per cent for the current dollar of the country, but we will go further than that, and tamper with the metallic dollar itself, so that *that* also may ultimately, in some twenty years, be worth two for one! We will take away, if we can, by some process, the optional dollar now constitutional for eighty-one years in the United States, and will place in its stead a dollar in one metal only—a metal that we know, from its scarcity and from our ability to corner it in the markets of the world, must rapidly, under such conditions, appreciate in its purchasing power, all the time hiding its own fallacy, while at the same time the discarded metal, being disparaged and abolished, must lose its quality as primary money and be driven gradually into the relation of subsidiary coin and mere merchandise.

Words are inadequate to describe the profundity and criminality of this scheme. It was carried into effect by the Act of Feb. 18, 1873. It was done by a turn of Shylock's wrist, so adroit, and one might say devilish, as to be indescribable in the phraseology of this world. It was an act on which no king of the seventeenth century would have ventured without incurring the risk of revolution. It was an act which, instead of being misrepresented by those who have found it out and nailed it to the gibbet of public contempt, has never been adequately denounced. It was an act which has positively blackened the honor of the American republic. It was an act which though subsequently defended, even to the present day, by all the purchased ability of the world, is nevertheless condemned by the conscience and common sense of mankind as the most cold-blooded, unjust, uncalled-for, unmitigated and damnable outrage ever done in this century to the rights and interests of a great people!

The Act of 1873 abolished the standard unit of money and account in the United States. Until that time all other coins in use under our constitution and statute had been made to do obeisance to the silver dollar as the unit of money and account. That dollar had never been altered by the fraction of one grain in the quantity of pure metal composing it from the time when it was ordained in 1792 to the time when it was abolished from the list of coins to be henceforth struck at the mints of the United States. Every other coin whether of gold or silver had been altered and altered again; the silver unit never. To that unit all the rest, both gold and silver, had from the first been conformed.* The eagle of the original statute and of all

---

*In the recently published book called "A Coin Catechism," by J. K Upton, three times assistant secretary of the treasury and financial statistician of the Eleventh Census, the following remarkable interpretation of the Coinage Act of April 2, 1792, is given: "The first Congress of the United States provided for the coinage of 'silver dollars, or units, each to be of the value of a Spanish milled dollar as the same is now current, and to contain 371.25 grains of pure silver,' and fractional pieces of the same fineness and proportional weight, and *gold pieces to contain 24.75 grains of pure gold to a dollar*," etc. The last clause of this is so cunningly false as to be amusing. It is a logical and literary curiosity that ought to be remanded to the text-books as the finest existing example of sophism. Why did not the author go on with his quotation from the statute of 1792 and give the clause relative to the coinage of gold? He knew that to do so would be ruinous to the special plea which he was making. The first Congress of the United States did *not* provide for any such coinage of gold as that described by Mr. Upton Mr. Upton either knows it or else he does not know it. The "gold pieces" to which he refers in his carefully covered expression were precisely as given in the text above; namely, an eagle, a double eagle, a half eagle, and a quarter eagle, and the coins each and several are defined in the statute as being *of the value of so many dollars, or units, and the dollar, or unit, is defined as being 371.25 grains of pure silver.* The *conformity* of gold to silver by the same statute at 15 to 1 made the gold coins to be multiples of 24.75 grains of gold — a proportion which was afterwards twice altered to preserve the conformity. This simply showed the amount of gold which at the time should be, *not* a dollar, but *of the value* of a dollar. Senator Sherman says in a published note relative to Upton's book: "His statements on financial matters *may be implicitly relied on*" Of course! As matter of fact, Mr. Upton's whole book is pervaded with the same species of false interpretation shown in the quotation given in this note. *Ex uno exemplo disce omnia.* And as to false quotations, the *Century Dictionary*, making a pretence of citing the statute (see under the word "dollar"), has this: "That law [Act of April 2, 1792] provided for the coinage of 'dollars or units, each to be of the value of a Spanish milled dollar,' as that coin was then current, and to contain 371¼ grains of pure silver," etc. This quotation curiously omits the word "silver" before "dollars or units," and yet in that omitted word lies the whole controversy! It is not good usage in making a quotation to leave out *the principal thing!*

subsequent statutes was not made to be ten dollars, but
to be of *the value* of ten dollars. The half eagle was not
made to be five dollars, but to be of *the value* of five dollars.
The quarter eagle was of *the value* of two and a-half dollars,
and the double eagle was of *the value* of twenty dollars.
Even the gold dollar of 1849, mirabile dictu! was *not* a dollar, but was made to be of *the value* of a dollar! The subsidiary coins were all fractions of the dollar, and the dollar
was of silver only.

Not a single dictionary or cyclopædia in the English
language before the year 1878 ever defined dollar in any
terms other than of silver. In that year the administrators
of the estate of Noah Webster, deceased, cut the plates of
our standard lexicon and inserted *a new definition* that had
become necessary in order to make the bond intrigue, in
Congress and out of it, consist!

True it is that by the statute of 1792 the dollar was
made to *exist* in the gold coin also; but that dollar was
a dollar only by its conformity in value to the silver coin
which was the one standard unit of money and account.
Our metal money existed in both kinds, and the system
was bimetallic to this extent, that the debtor might pay
in either; but the unit existed in silver only. To abolish
that unit, to strike it down, to cancel it, and to substitute
another therefor WAS a crime! It has been rightly so
branded by the American people, and it will be so written
in history. It makes no difference whether it was done
secretly or openly; whether in the day or in the night;
whether by a committee or by the House in full debate;
whether Congress understood it or did not understand it.
It was a crime all the same against the rights and interests
of the American people; aye, against the American people
themselves and against all the people of the world; for
it was done against justice, against truth, against the law
of both man and God.

Nevertheless it was done. Again the bondholding interest had played a great game with the American people,
and had won as before. The next event of the programme
was already rising above the horizon. That was the formal
declaration of a date when the gold dollar, instead of the
alternative bimetallic dollar of the American people, should
begin to be paid in discharge of the debts of the nation.
The act fixing that date was passed on the 14th of January,
1875; and the 1st of January, 1879, was named as the day
when specie payments should be resumed at the treasury
of the United States—and if there, then everywhere.

About the year 1877 the American people made a discovery—not a pleasing discovery. They found that they were ginned in a trap which had been set for them without their knowledge four years previously. The date for the resumption of specie payments was near at hand. The means for such resumption had to be provided. The national treasury could not resume on nothing, but must be supplied in advance with the coin necessary for such an enormous transaction and for keeping up the work when it should be once begun. The people had been supposing that both gold and silver would be gathered without discrimination for the discharge of the debts of the government. To their amazement, they found that they had been beaten by a game. Not a silver dollar was coining or could be legally coined at the mints to meet the coming emergency.

Only a few years before, the enormous treasures of the Rocky Mountains had been laid bare. It were hard to say whether there was greater cause of amazement or rage when the people found that the very resource to which Lincoln had pointed in his last public utterance as the means of paying the war debt had been purposely cut off!* When the reason of this was inquired, Shylock pointed his benevolent finger to the act of 1873. It was unlawful to coin silver dollars! The debt must be paid in gold. When the inquiry was pressed as to whether the silver dollar had not always been the dollar of the constitution and the statute, whether it had not been in particular the dollar of primary money when the bonded debt was incurred, Shylock shuffled and lied and made an affidavit that he was an honest man!

---

* On the afternoon before the assassination, when Vice-President Schuyler Colfax was on the eve of departing for the West to examine into the conditions and prospects of the proposed Pacific Railway, President Lincoln said to him, measuring his words: "Mr. Colfax, I want you to take a message from me to the miners whom you visit. I have very large ideas of the mineral wealth of our nation. . . . Now that the Rebellion is overthrown, and we know nearly the amount of our national debt, the more *gold and silver* we mine makes the payment of that debt so much the easier. Now I am going to encourage that in every possible way. [Even so, O Lincoln!] We shall have hundreds of thousands of disbanded soldiers, and many have feared that their return home in such great numbers might paralyze industry by furnishing suddenly a greater supply of labor than there will be a demand for. I am going to try and attract them to the hidden wealth of our mountain ranges where there is room enough for all. Immigration, which even the war has not stopped, will land upon our shores hundreds of thousands more per year from overcrowded Europe. I intend to point them to the *gold and silver* that waits for them in the West. Tell the miners from me that I shall promote their interests to the utmost of my ability, *because their prosperity is the prosperity of the nation;* and we shall prove in a very few years that we are the *treasury of the world*." These are the last glorious words of Lincoln. O thou Immortal! In thy staunch and capacious heart there was a place even for the miners and the mining interests of our country. Thy last thoughts of public concern in this world were how the war debt was about to be paid with the treasures of the mountains! To remember such a man and to compare him with the poor automata who are now truckling and fawning around the *Hessian* Rothschild in order to support the treasury of the United States kindles in every patriot soul a fire in which the flames of inspiration are blended with flashes of undying contempt!

Hereupon a clamor—first of many—arose in the country. The people broke into insurrection against the money power. There was a wrestle between them and their oppressors. For the time being their representatives in Congress, less swayed than afterwards by the tremendous influences around them, stood fast for truth and right. A battle was fought in the second session of the Forty-fifth Congress, and on the 21st of February, 1878, the act was triumphantly passed for the restoration of the silver dollar and for the compulsory coinage of that unit at the minimum rate of two millions of dollars a month.

We need not here recount how the Act of Remonetization was sent to the president of the United States to meet at his hands the puny rebuff of a veto. Nor need we refer to the other fact that the veto itself was buried, *without a word of debate*, under a majority of 46 to 19 in the Senate, and of 196 to 73 in the House of Representatives. So perish all similar documents evermore!

It was by means of the Act of 1878 that the government of the United States was enabled to make good its declaration of specie payments at the appointed time. Within eleven months the ordeal came and was passed. The premium on gold was obliterated. Both money metals stood side by side in the accomplishment of this work. The first metallic money that reappeared in the channels of ordinary trade was the old silver dollar, restored, not indeed to its unlimited and equal rank, but to a measure of efficiency.

The Act of Remonetization was in force for twelve years and five months. In this period at the mints of the United States were coined more than three hundred million silver dollars. These were added to the volume of the currency, in spite of the grimaces and gripings of Shylock.

The law of 1878 was very far short of perfection. It left silver exposed to the intrigues of the enemy, and placed gold in such a situation that the price of it might be gradually advanced at the option of the holders. It made silver to be merchandise, coinable into dollars that were to be buoyed up by coinage from the bullion value which the Goldites might measure in terms of gold, and depress as much as they pleased. This actually occurred. Gold began steadily to appreciate. Its purchasing power, as measured by the average of all other commodities, rose higher and higher. The supposition that the average of all other commodities declined in *value* is absurd. They only declined in *price*—price as measured by gold. Gold as measured by silver advanced in price and purchasing power. The *price* of silver bullion declined, or was forced down, by the standard of gold; but the *value* of silver—raw silver—did NOT decline more rapidly than the average of the great products of America and Europe; that is, it did not decline at all.

The whole situation was so contrived as to produce a divergency, a disparity, in the bullion values of silver and gold; but gold was able to conceal its fallacy, just as any other metal, from iron to iridium, would conceal its fallacy if it were the sole standard of values. So much gold, namely, 23.22 grains, was stamped as the standard dollar, and if the treacherous metal had risen until its purchasing power was five hundred per cent of what it had been previously, until one unit of it would purchase a thousand bushels of wheat or fifty acres of farming land, it would not have revealed the lie that was in it! It would still have been "the honest dollar"! As matter of fact, gold bullion rose higher and higher, and all things else, including silver bullion, were correspondingly depressed in price.

The advantages which this condition—carefully con- trived by the money power with machinations and in- trigues extending back to the close of the war—would give, and did give, to the owners of gold and those to whom gold had been promised in payment cannot well be de- scribed. It was incalculable. The spectral nightmare of debt built him a throne on the ruins of a million homes— just as Sherman had said he would—and plumed himself all summer. The Goldites became by the possession of augmented power the autocrats of the world. Strange in- deed to see the prices of all the products and industries of men sinking, sinking, under the pressure of so small and diabolical an instrument as a gold dollar! The thing has seemed to be possessed of a veritable devil. Its action has been like that of a manikin three miles out at sea, sub- merged to his chin, but by some infernal self-pressure able to lift himself out of the water to the horizon of his waist. Looking around over the vast deep, he cries in glee, "Great heavens, how the ocean has sunk away!"

NAPOLEON BONAPARTE.

A Sketch Written for a Purpose.

BY JOHN DAVIS.

CHAPTER VI.

Mistakes of Napoleon.

Napoleon was a man of expedients. In devising and choosing temporary measures for the most desperate emergencies, history scarcely affords his equal. But in doing this he looked only to the present, and seemed utterly oblivious as to ultimate results. Hence, while his measures contributed to present success, they very often, at a later date, contributed to his overthrow. When calculating the perturbations of the planets of the solar system one must take into account every fact and circumstance of the problem, and the influence of each body upon the others; so, in like manner, unless writers on Napoleon take this comprehensive view of the subject in its various details, they must greatly differ in estimating his character and its numerous and complicated phases. The man in question, overestimating his importance, likened himself to a "star," while in reality he was more like a fickle, inconstant planet, or the satellite of a planet, which, full-orbed and brilliant at Dresden, in 1812, was as dead three years later as an exploded meteor. So sudden and complete a collapse from mid-heaven glory to the darkness and littleness of St. Helena, could not have happened without sufficient reason. I will now recount some of the causes or "mistakes" which made Napoleon's downfall inevitable.

The first Napoleonic mistake was duplicity. The expedient of misstating his age let him into the military school of Brienne and opened up to him a career as a citizen of France. Further on he proclaimed himself a republican, when at heart he was not. This claim, often and loudly repeated by himself and his emissaries in the countries which he had chosen for invasion and spoliation, divided the people and gave him cheap and brilliant victories. Then, when victorious, his treachery to liberty appeared, and the unfortunate victims were subjected to the most crushing pecuniary exactions and merciless despotism. Italy, Poland, Germany, and other countries conquered by Napoleon were examples of what I state. It was his habit also to levy at first as heavy a contribution as in his judgment it was possible for the conquered country to pay; then in due time he goaded the people into revolt while he still held the country, so that further exactions and confiscations could be enforced. He complained continually to Joseph of his lack of vigor when king of Naples. Writing to him on the subject, he said:

I should very much like to hear of a revolt of the Neapolitan populace. You will never be their master till you have made an example of them. Every conquered country must have its revolt. I should see Naples in a revolt as a father sees his children in the smallpox ; the crisis is salutary, provided it does not weaken the constitution.

The reason why he enjoyed a revolt in a conquered country is explained in another letter to Joseph:

As Calabria has revolted, why should you not seize half the estates in the province ? . . . The measure would be a great help, and an example for the future.

Examples of the spoliation of exhausted countries were seen in Poland and Prussia, already mentioned. Napoleon got his foothold and mastery in all those countries through duplicity and treachery more than by military heroism. But his successful expedients ultimately proved to be mistakes, and when his reverses came, the oppressed people promptly joined his enemies and could seldom be reconquered. This fact was abundantly proved by the action of Prussia prior to the battles of Lutzen and Bautzen, and by that of Austria prior to the battle of Leipsic. If Napoleon had treated those countries as sister republics, standing by the people against their despotic rulers, there would have been no revolts, and they would have remained his friends and allies when his disasters came. His characteristic duplicity and treachery were practiced in all his dealings, both with individuals and with nations. He advocated the policy, taught it to his officers, and practiced it himself as a just and wise course. It often wreathed his brow with a halo of unmerited glory, but at the same time it planted his path with dragons' teeth, which ultimately became armed men in the ranks of his enemies.

Closely allied to duplicity and treachery was the expedient of corruption. It was sometimes easier to enter the fortress of an enemy with a golden key than by a regular siege, and to win a battle with golden bullets rather than with lead and iron. One object of the expedition to Egypt was the acquisition of the island of Malta. It was fortified by an impregnable fortress, well armed, manned, and victualled. Napoleon had no time for a regular siege, so he sent his emissaries some months ahead of the expedition. On his arrival the gates and doors swung open after the merest show of resistance. Alison (vol. iv, p. 567) says:

Before leaving France the capitulation of the place had been secured by secret intelligence with the Grand Master and the principal officers, who had, as the reward of their treachery, been struck off the list of French emigrants. Dessaix, Marmont, and Savary landed, and advanced, after some opposition, to the foot of the ramparts. Terms of accommodation were speedily agreed on. The town was surrendered on condition that the Grand Master should obtain 600,000 francs, a principality in Germany, or a pension for life of 300,000 francs ; the French Chevaliers were promised a pension of seven hundred francs per year each ; and the tricolored flag speedily waved on the bulwark of the Christian world.

When passing through the fortifications after the surrender, Caffarelli remarked: "It was lucky that there was somebody within to open the gates for us, or we should never have got in." It was not uncommon for the French generals to bribe the governor of a place to surrender it by promising to leave in his possession the military chest of the garrison, and permitting the populace to plunder their own nobles, as an inducement for them to favor, or, at least, not to oppose the invasion of their country. Speaking of the passive surrenders of the German fortresses in 1806, after the battle of Jena, Sir Walter Scott (p. 385) says:

It is believed that, on several of these occasions, the French constructed a golden key to open these iron fortresses, without being at the expense of the precious metal that composed it. Every large garrison has, of course, a military chest, with treasure for the regular pay of the soldiery ; and it is said that more than one commandant was unable to resist the proffer, that, in case of an immediate surrender, this deposit should not be inquired into by the captors, but left at the disposal of the governor, whose accommodating disposition had saved them the time and trouble of a siege.

An important and most successful Napoleonic expedient was his favorite plan of supporting his armies by pillage, by foraging on the country through which he passed, whether hostile or friendly. If hostile, he claimed the right to live at the expense of the enemy; if friendly, the people should be only too glad to contribute to the support of their deliverers. This policy saved expense, reduced to a minimum the usual incumbrances of baggage trains, and greatly accelerated the marches of his armies. Napoleon's armies were noted for the celerity of their movements, and often gained victories because they found their enemies unprepared. With an occasional supply of "biscuits and brandy," which could be shipped in barrels and hogsheads to central points to meet the armies on their marches, the French troops were usually required to supply the rest of their subsistence by pillaging the invaded territory.

This expedient was very convenient to the generals and economic for the commissary department, but it was terribly wasteful of human life. The foraging parties in a friendly country soon aroused a sentiment of hostility among the people, which showed itself by numerous assassinations of the foraging troops. That feature of the case was observed in Italy, where Napoleon bitterly complained of the numerous assassinations of his men. He mentioned it as one of the causes of hostility toward Venice, when seeking pretexts for the future spoliation of that country. In hostile countries it showed itself in perpetual skirmishes on the flanks and outskirts of the invading armies.

This fact was verified in Russia, where the French losses during the march of the Grand Army were frightful. Napoleon's army was spread out over a wide extent of country in order to be able to subsist as it marched. There were 600,000 men, with horses sufficient for the numerous bodies of cavalry, the heavy trains of artillery, and the carriages and wagons for the transportation of men and munitions. It was probably the largest body of armed men under a single commander ever seen in the world. Its consuming capacity was immense. The Russian army which met the French at the frontier on the Niemen was about half as numerous as the invaders. It could not meet them on equal terms in regular battle with any hope of success. The Russians therefore adopted the policy of retiring before the enemy and exhausting the country of its supplies as it retreated. This compelled the French foragers to spread out to the right and left of the army in order to obtain supplies. Thus scattered abroad in detached parties they were continually attacked and cut off by the Cossacks and other light troops. These skirmishes were perpetual, from day to day, every hour after the French army entered Russian territory. It was a fight for life from the beginning to the very last moment of the occupation of Russian soil. And during almost the entire time the French army was in the midst of a severe and decimating famine. Marshal St. Cyr estimated that Napoleon lost 300,000 men from famine alone, because it was not possible to supply the men with food on the Napoleonic plan. The losses by sickness, battle, and capture were very great. The general impression prevails that Napoleon lost most of his men by the cold weather. This is not true. Alison (vol. xi, p. 309), speaking of this matter, says:

But the decisive circumstance which proves that Napoleon's disasters in 1812 were owing, not to the severity of the climate, but to the natural consequences of his own measures, is to be found in the fact, now fully ascertained, that five-sixths of his losses had been sustained before the cold weather began ; and that out of 302,000 men and 104,000 horses, which he in person led across the Niemen, there remained only 55,000 men and 12,000 horses when the frost set in ; that is, he had lost 247,000 men and 92,000 horses under his immediate command before a flake of snow fell. It is neither, therefore, in the rigor of the elements, nor in the accidents of fortune that we are to seek the real cause of Napoleon's overthrow, but in the natural consequences of his system of conquest ; in the oppressive effects of the execrable maxim that war should maintain war ; . . . by throwing the armies they had on foot upon external spoliation for support, at once exposed them, the moment the career of conquest was checked, to unheard-of sufferings, and excited unbounded exasperation among every people over whom their authority prevailed.

It would be interesting and instructive to pursue the track of Napoleon's armies in Italy, Spain, Germany, Poland, and other places, to show the great destruction of human life in all cases where an army must support itself by pillage. I will recite but one additional case. Alison (vol. xi, p. 213) says:

The French army lost one-third of its number by the march through Lithuania in summer (1812), before the bloodshed began, when the resources of the country were still untouched and the army fresh and in high spirits.

Subsistence by pillage also affords uncommon opportunities for desertions, and it usually damages the discipline of an army; yet there is a fascination about it which greatly pleases a licentious soldiery. They especially delight in brigandage and rapine in countries filled with villages and towns. The evil passions of men have full play when let loose to prey upon society, with the one condition that there must be a prompt return to the ranks at stated hours and in obedience to given signals or orders in cases of emergency. This Napoleonic device was a system of devastation which no people could endure or forget. It multiplied the conqueror's enemies and intensified their enmities to the last degree of desperation, insuring the downfall of the tyrant at the earliest possible moment.

If any one desires to understand the rapacity and ferocity of pillaging by a licentious soldiery he has but to read Napoleon's opinion of it when in St. Helena, after years of experience and personal observation. On one occasion he had promised his soldiers twenty-four hours of pillage in the town of Pavia; "but after three hours," said he, "I could stand it no longer, and put an end to it. I had but 1,200 men; the cries of the populace which reached my ears prevailed. If there had been 20,000 soldiers, their number would have drowned the complaints of the people, and I should have heard nothing of it." The emperor in St. Helena was quite a moralist, very different from the same emperor in Europe at the head of an army marching through a conquered country. He fully saw that his early expedient of subsistence by pillage was a very grave mistake, though at first it facilitated the celerity of his movements and aided vastly in his brilliant conquests.

Napoleon's mistake in choosing his financial system has already been sufficiently discussed except in a single particular. It was this system, with its inevitable crises and distresses, which excused or compelled his great political blunders. When he first attained the military leadership, had he quietly accepted the situation in the spirit of self-defence only, the French revolutionary wars would then have ended. This he was not willing to do.

Two impelling causes induced Napoleon to adopt the policy of invasion: first, his personal ambition; and second, his financial necessities. These two causes operated together at the very commencement of his career, and he was unwilling or unable, through lack of knowledge or patriotism, afterwards to separate them. By admitting both of these impelling agencies all his foolish, wicked, and fatal invasions may be accounted for. To leave out either, they cannot be. On the mere ground of personal ambition the invasions of San Domingo, Russia, Syria, and other wild expeditions, presuppose the extreme of lunacy. But Napoleon was not a lunatic. Merely on the ground of personal ambition there was no reason for invading the Batavian, the Swiss, or the Venetian republics; nor for trampling to death so unmercifully the territories of Prussia and Russian Poland, both countries, at the time, being friendly to France.

The neglect of the financial element in the problem of Napoleon's career causes many of the diverse opinions respecting the man. As well try to account for the perturbations of the planets of the solar system with one-half of them left out of the account. It was utterly impossible to account for the strange movements of the planet Uranus until the discovery of Neptune. So important and true is this statement that the size, location and movements of Neptune were pointed out by the mathematicians at their desks before the telescope had identified the planet.

The laws of nature which govern society are just as fixed and certain as are the laws which govern the material universe, and they apply as exactly to the volitions of a single mind acting under a single condition or circumstance as to a combination of numerous wills acting under a combination of circumstances. In the material world these laws, and the facts and phenomena which reveal them, have been so thoroughly studied that the velocities, times, and orbits of all the planets, satellites, and asteroids, and even several of the comets, are now matters of certainty, about which there cannot be two opinions. When the same knowledge and exactness have been applied to the study of the character of Napoleon there will be less disagreement among writers.

When studying his career as a military hero, all agree that we must know the style of tactics with which he governed his armies and the nature and character of the arms with which his soldiers were supplied. No man can explain his victories, or even his existence and safety for a single day in the deserts of Egypt or Syria, unless it is known that he was supplied with artillery to defend his squares of infantry against the terrific charges of the Turks and Mamelukes. But when we hear the command, "Infantry in squares, six deep, artillery at the angles!" then all becomes plain. We can then understand Napoleon's cheap and easy victory at the Pyramids, and can see how it was possible for 6,000 Frenchmen to win the battle of Mount Thabor against 30,000 brave and determined Turkish cavalry. So in considering the general career of Napoleon we must understand his tactics, his arms and munitions, and also his *finances*. To leave out a single item deranges the entire calculation, and the results are diverse and enigmatical. Include all the elements necessary to the calculation, and definite and correct results are possible.

In 1796 Napoleon and the French Directory found themselves sorely in need of money. The assignats had failed through over-issue in the form of counterfeits sent over from London, and there was no coin in circulation. There were several systems any one of which could have been adopted then, since the government had acquired considerable stability. First, a new paper currency manufactured by the government, in a high style of art, above the arts of the counterfeiters, might have been issued in moderate quantity, accompanied by a levy of taxes on the property of the country, the new paper to be receivable for taxes, and to be a general legal-tender in all payments. Such a currency would have circulated in France, and would have been as good as the issuing government, which, from that moment, was continually growing more and more stable and reliable. A second plan might have been instituted, similar to the system adopted in England a year later. A third plan could have been an exact copy of the Venetian system, which had proved a magnificent success for more than six centuries, through war and peace, without a single panic or failure.

None of these plans suited Napoleon. He preferred metallic money, to be obtained in the only way possible, by the invasion and robbery of other countries; and he at once set the example of its success by the invasion and spoliation of Italy. Under the republic, before Napoleon was placed at the head of the army, the war in Italy had been a war of liberation, to deliver the Italians from the despotism of Austria. He professed the same intention, but immediately made it a war of spoliation. And thus commenced that scheme of military brigandage which has so long enjoyed honorable mention by so many writers, as "war supporting war." When Italy was exhausted, other countries were invaded; this required more money and made further conquests necessary, and thus when the system got started it was like a moving avalanche on the face of a mountain; there was no stopping-place until it went to pieces at the bottom, with no means of recovery.

If it is objected that the French government was not sufficiently established in 1796 to insure the success of a paper system of finance, we have but to compare its stability at that date under Napoleon and the Directory, with the critical condition of the British government in 1797, when the British paper system was adopted. In 1797 the British armies had been defeated, the bank had suspended payment, and the fleet, the pride and safety of the empire, was in a state of mutiny, actually blockading the city of London under the flag of "the Floating Republic." "Everything," says Alison, "seemed falling to pieces at once." In that dangerous crisis and condition of uncertainty the British government adopted a system of paper money, which immediately brought light instead of darkness, and maintained the empire on a safe and stable basis till the triumphant close of the war in 1815.

If Napoleon had devised and adopted that system in 1796, how different might have been the history of Europe in after years! But there was no time prior to the invasion of Russia when Napoleon might not have changed from his contracting metallic system to an expansive one of paper, if he had had the wisdom and patriotism to do so. There were also specially favorable times for such a change. For two years before and after the peace of Amiens there was a general cessation of hostilities, with Napoleon completely master of France as First Consul, and his dominions were bordered with a "girdle of affiliated republics." The peace with England was satisfactory to the people of both countries, and the most unbounded joy prevailed when its terms were made known. All were heartily tired of war, and the paper credits of both countries suddenly rose from five to seven per cent. Alison's History (vol. v, p. 623) says:

Never since the restoration of Charles II had such transports seized the public mind. The populace insisted on drawing the French envoys in their carriage; and they were conducted by this tumultuary array, followed by a guard of honor from the household brigade, through Parliament Street to Downing Street, where the ratifications were exchanged, and at night a general illumination gave vent to the feelings of universal exhilaration. Nor was the public joy manifested in a less emphatic manner in Paris. Hardly had the cannon of the Tuileries and the Invalides, in the evening, announced the unexpected intelligence, when everyone stopped in the streets and congratulated his acquaintance on the news; the public flocked in crowds to the theatres, where it was officially promulgated amidst transports long unfelt in the metropolis; and in the evening the city was universally and splendidly illuminated. There seemed to be no bounds to the glory and prosperity of the republic, now that this auspicious event had removed the last and most inveterate of its enemies.

Definitive treaties of peace were also made with Turkey and Russia, amounting with the latter power almost to an alliance, designed, says Alison (vol. v, p. 629), "to restore a just equilibrium in different parts of the world, and to insure the liberty of the seas, binding themselves to act in concert for the attainment of these objects by all measures, whether of conciliation or vigor, mutually agreed on between them, for the good of humanity, the general repose, and the independence of governments."

France was then a first-rate power, dominant in all the policies of the continent, with a government as firmly established as any in Europe, and with considerable colonies in many parts of the world. Nothing was wanting for the complete felicity of France except money. The French finances were embarrassed. The revenues were less by several million francs than they had been in 1789, while the expenditures were vastly greater. The deficit for years had been supplied by forced contributions from the conquered countries. In time of peace that resource was cut off, and Napoleon found himself in financial difficulties. This was the golden moment for him to have established a paper system like that of England or Venice.

But the man of the past had neither the wisdom nor the patriotism to adopt the systems which had proved superior to coin in every great emergency. Inspired by the centuries of darkness from which he sprang, he was determined to tolerate nothing that would brighten the future. Being a mere meteor, or "star" from the ages of barbarism, he was willing to use only the money of savagery, and to acquire it by the methods of piracy. So, Europe being at peace, he fitted out an immense armament to "reduce" the island of San Domingo. He invaded the island, appropriated the army chest, and robbed the local depositaries, obtaining in all some three or four million francs; but he lost his army, and the expedition was not a financial success. After peace was concluded, the black governor of the island was captured by treachery, and Napoleon caused him to be starved to death in prison, to compel him to tell if he had any hidden treasures. The faithful black would reveal nothing.

In the meantime the French treasury was growing very lean and hungry, and there must be found a remedy, hence our military brigand began to seek pretexts for war. The treaty of peace had tied his financial hands. He bullied and defied England, violated Prussian territory, and sought excuses for ruptures with Russia and Austria, in order to create a general war for purposes of brigandage. Then came his famous preparations at Boulogne for the descent on England, the battles of Ulm and Austerlitz, the conquest of Prussia, and unlimited levies and contributions of men, money, munitions, and supplies. The brigand had found his harvest-time, and he revelled in blood, treasure, and "glory"!

The spoliations and devastations of conquered territories went on swimmingly for half-a-dozen years; but, finally, the war in Spain became a burden to the French treasury, the revenues of 1810 and 1811 had fallen below former figures, and the emperor grew uneasy. In this financial dilemma he resolved on the invasion of Russia. His generals and all the world declared that France had no just cause of war with Russia. But Napoleon had determined on war. He demanded that Russia should close her ports against the admission of English goods. He could not invade and conquer England direct, because the British fleets were master of the Channel; but he would conquer the entire continent and shut out English goods, and thus, financially, smother the great mistress of the ocean in her own nest. He was not like the foolish toad which thought to inhale a sufficient amount of air to make itself as big as an ox, but like that other toad, even less wise than the first, which thought to inhale within itself all the atmosphere of the world, and thus to suffocate and extinguish the ox. In each case there was a fatal toadal catastrophe. Napoleon's first efforts were encouraging, but when the breath of the polar bear entered his lungs the experiment failed.

Historians dwell glowingly on the great power and magnificence of the French empire in 1812, and never tire of the imperial splendor of Napoleon's court at Dresden, on his way to Russia. Almost all the sovereigns of the continent, including the king of Prussia and the emperor of Austria, were there. The theatre of Paris had been transferred to Dresden. The young empress of France, then mother of the "King of Rome," was in attendance, and the oldest sovereigns yielded to the ascendent of her youthful diadem. "Flattery exhausted its talent, and luxury its magnificence," says Alison (vol. x, p. 616), "and the pride of the Cæsars was forgotten in the glory of one who had risen upon the ruins of their antiquated splendor." The power and grandeur of Napoleon were boundless. All looked to him as "the source of all true glory." The proudest kings waited in his antechamber, and queens were maids of honor to the empress of France. With more than Eastern munificence he distributed costly presents as marks of recognition to the innumerable crowd of princes, ministers, dukes, and courtiers that thronged with oriental servility around his person. "The vast crowd of strangers," continues the same writer, "the superb equipages which thronged the streets, the brilliant guards which were stationed in all the principal streets of the city, the constant arrival and departure of couriers from or toward every part of Europe, all announced the king of kings, who was now elevated to the highest pinnacle of earthly grandeur."

But amid all that power and glory there were drawbacks and dangers. In the heart of every conquered and ruined king, prince, and potentate, there rankled the bitterest hate, only watching for a safe opportunity to stab his imperial master to the heart. Even at that very moment the people of Prussia and Poland were suffering the sorest distresses through the devastations and rapine of half a million soldiers, occupying their fields and towns and violating their families. No nation in Europe south of the Niemen but had felt the weight of Napoleon's despotisms, and remembered them with undying hatred. Added to these dangerous conditions the proud emperor felt the fatal tortures of impecuniosity. He was in need of money; he was now being driven, by the fatality of his life, by his "destiny," into the invasion of Russia. It proved a most fatal political as well as financial mistake, from which he was never able to recover.

What a glorious opportunity was now presented for Napoleon to change his financial system, to restore good feeling throughout Europe, to restrict the power of Russia, and to build up for himself in southwestern Europe and northern Africa a most magnificent empire, with the Mediterranean as a "French lake," in which to create and nurture a naval power capable of contending with that of England for the mastery of the ocean! Instead of invading Russia he might have issued a decree reëstablishing an independent kingdom of Poland, with ample territories bordering on the old Russian frontier; strengthening Denmark with additional territories and power; defining the kingdom of Prussia, with liberal additions from the smaller German states; restoring the empire of Austria, with enlarged boundaries north and east, to compensate for the surrender of Italy; and then guaranteeing the autonomy of European Turkey as the possessor and guardian of Constantinople, to compensate for the surrender of Egypt and the Grecian peninsula.

This would have left for Napoleon all the western and southern parts of the continent, from the Rhine to the coast of Syria, and all northern Africa from the Straits of Gibraltar to the Red Sea, with an outlet south and southeasterly as far as his arms and enterprise might be able to carry him. He would have in the Mediterranean a school for his navy, and an equal chance with England for the acquisition of colonies in all parts of the world. Such a policy would have reduced the difficulties of uniting the diversities of language, race, and religion. It would have set apart for the new potentate a *Latin empire* to be consolidated, defended, and governed according to his best and wisest policy, with a cordon of friendly powers between him and Russia from the Baltic to the Black Sea. The Czar would have been confined to his ancient and helpless limits of old Russia, with no outlet to the ocean, except by consent of Denmark and Sweden during a small portion of the year. To enforce such a decree Napoleon had then on foot 1,200,000 men, all immediately available and ready for business. He was completely master of the situation. This liberal policy would have been pleasing to all the great powers except England and Russia; and all the newly restored and liberally defined kingdoms would have been bound with the new Latin empire and with each other to defend the autonomy of each and all.

That such a policy was feasible prior to the disastrous invasion of Russia we have the testimony of Napoleon himself. The difficult part of it would have been the reëstablishment of Poland as a bulwark against Russia on the Baltic. On this point (Bourrienne, vol. iii, p. 309) Napoleon said: "It is nevertheless true that with an independent kingdom of Poland, and 150,000 disposable troops in the east of France, I should always be master of Russia, Prussia, and Austria." A Latin empire such as here mentioned was feasible in 1812. In 1801 to 1803 it might have been constructed on the basis of a confederation of Latin republics, with France as the controlling force, leaving the Teutonic nations from the Baltic eastward as a barrier against Russia. That Napoleon had at times thought of a confederation of European republics is occasionally seen in his conversations on the subject. Speaking of the union of the Latin nations into one government (Las Casas, vol. iv. p. 107) Napoleon said:

" All the south of Europe, therefore, would soon have been rendered compact in point of locality, views, opinions, sentiments, and interests. In this state of things what would have been the weight of all the nations of the north ?" After some further conversations, he resumed the subject: "At all events this concentration will be brought about sooner or later by the very force of events. The impulse is given; and I think that since my fall and the destruction of my system, no grand equilibrium can possibly be established in Europe, except by the concentration and confederation of the principal nations. The sovereign who, in the first great conflict, shall sincerely embrace the cause of the people, will find himself at the head of all Europe and may attempt whatever he pleases."

Evidently the emperor in St. Helena was contemplating "the might-have-beens." The campaigns of 1813 and 1814, and the battles of Lutzen, Bautzen, and Leipsic, had taught him the power of an aroused people, and when too late he saw the fatal mistake of his treason to liberty. In 1802 to 1803, during the peace of Amiens, Napoleon might have established in western and southern Europe a grand confederation of Latin republics, on which, through fear of their own people, the kings would not have dared to make war. In 1812 he might have established a Latin empire, embracing France and affiliated and adjacent nations from the Rhine to the Red Sea, including Rome, Athens, Alexandria, Carthage, and other ancient seats of empire, with opportunity to enter Asia through the valley of the Euphrates, as Alexander did, or by the way of the reopened Suez canal of the ancients, as contemplated by Napoleon himself when in Egypt.

But all these dreams and possibilities gave place to the fatal invasion of Russia! Why was this? Popular writers tell us that it was because of his uncontrollable ambition. The answer is unsatisfactory. The establishment of a united and impregnable Latin empire, converting the Mediterranean into a "French lake," frequently contemplated by Napoleon, with two practicable routes into the richest parts of Asia, and with Russia solidly locked up among her snowdrifts and icebergs, would have yielded him tenfold more glory than could possibly be gained by the most successful invasion of Russia. These subjects had all passed in review before his mind, and were more or less seriously considered. Why then did Napoleon choose the more costly, more hazardous, and less glorious enterprise?

There can be but one satisfactory answer, and Napoleon stated that answer to Count Molien:

My finances are embarrassed and require war. . . . I shall make this war for a political object, and also for the sake of my finances. Have I not always reëstablished them by war?

He neglected no details of the subject. He calculated the resources which the war would place in his hands. He thought it would add to his political importance, and give him, likewise, "the means of restoring his finances." In other words, Russia had a rich and tempting treasury which had not been robbed, and Napoleon needed money. To reach that treasury he filled his army chest with *forged paper roubles*, and made the effort. Had he established a Latin empire instead of invading Russia, his finances must have taken the form of the English paper system, or the long- and well-tried system of Venice, or, still better, the system adopted by France two generations later after the German invasion. But Napoleon preferred the money of barbarism. In order to secure it he adopted the devices of the counterfeiter and the methods of the brigand; he marched to Moscow and fattened the wolves of Russia on the flesh of half a million soldiers. But he obtained no money. His finances were not "reëstablished," and from that moment his downfall became inevitable.

(To be concluded.)

BROTHERHOOD.

BY BIRCH ARNOLD.

Lo! a mighty passion pulses,
  And swells adown the aisles of time.
Loud its clarion voice is ringing,
  Ever ringing words sublime:—
"Men of thought and men of purpose,
  Slaves no longer bow ye down!
God is God, and God in manhood
  Shall your holy efforts crown.

"Long the world has slept and slumbered,
  Lulled by false and futile peace,
While the souls of men were hungered,
  Starved with wants that never cease.
There is work, O men my brothers,
  Work to conquer schism, creed;
Close within the arms of mercy,
  Fold these hungering ones of need.

"Long the world, in drunken pleasure,
  Steeped in sense of self and gold,
Madly faced, in bold defiance,
  Sinai's thunders loudly rolled.
But to-day and now, my brothers,
  Justice lifts her drooping head,
Cries aloud in bitter anguish
  Like a soul in bondage led.

"Half the world is crushed and stifled,
  'Neath Oppression's iron heel;
Few there are who dare for Freedom,
  Few there are with hearts to feel.
But to work, O men my brothers,
  Break for God the tyrant's power;
Rend the chains of caste and Mammon,
  Bring the serf his freeman's dower.

"Not for triumph's noisy plaudits,
  Not for greed of gold or fame,
Into earth's discordant noises
  He, the Prince of Heaven, came:
But to show you, O my brothers,
  Love's triumphant power to heal,
Teach you all of Heaven's mercy,
  All its pity how to feel.

"E'en though scoffers may decry you,
  Love is balm for every stroke;
Shoulders bent to righteous burdens
  Find how easy grows the yoke.
Shall we falter, then, my brothers?
  Men are dying, ours to save;
Bring the oil of cheer and healing,
  Cover up the yawning grave.

"Crush the Self that wars with Mercy,
  Slay the fiends of gold and pride;
Never man was made more holy,
  Till the soul was crucified.
Courage then, O men my brothers,
  Be as soldiers in Truth's cause;
Foes may strike, but strike the harder,
  Till earth yields to Heaven's laws!"

For lo! a mighty passion pulses
  And swells adown the aisles of time;
Loud its clarion voice is ringing,
  Ever ringing words sublime:
"Men of thought, and men of action,
  Slaves no longer bow ye down!
God is God, and God in manhood
  Shall your holy efforts crown."

A NEW SYSTEM OF STATE WARRANTS.

BY HON. HOWARD L. WEED, OF STATE OF WASHINGTON.

In this age of combines, corporations, pools, and trusts, it were well to investigate somewhat in order to see if any good can be drawn from these institutions which can be used to offset the multitudinous evils which they have produced the world over. Without entering elaborately into details at this time, concerning the enslaved condition of mankind, their mighty woes and terrible sufferings as being the direct results of the workings of these same institutions, I will introduce the subject in contemplation at once by making the preliminary remark, that the individuals who compose these various corporations, trusts, etc., have formed these different combinations for the purpose of securing greater and more continuous prosperity, both individually and collectively. From a business point of view the plan has proved to be a brilliant success to the individuals who have so extensively given up competition and have pooled their separate interests to form these enormous trusts.

Why can not the taxpayers of any state of this Union take a lesson from trusts and combine their forces in the matter of the issuance and redemption of warrants and the payment of taxes?

We find that in nearly all of the counties of each of the states several kinds of warrants are being issued against the various existing funds, so that we have a floating indebtedness consisting of state warrants, county warrants, city warrants, town warrants, school-district warrants, etc., which are drawn against their various funds, when cash is not available, in payment for public supplies and improvements and for salaries of public officials and employees.

In order to redeem outstanding warrants various taxes are levied, known as the school tax, city tax, county tax, state tax, etc., payable in cash and apportioned to appropriate funds, at which time the warrants with accumulated interest are paid according to numerical order and cancelled.

There must be, in the aggregate, over two hundred thousand public funds in existence in the United States; therefore the market price of the outstanding warrants ranges through several hundred degrees of value, depending upon the condition of the funds against which they are drawn. For purposes of discussion and for simplification in the presentation of the plan embodied in this article, let us take under consideration the system of warrants in vogue in the state of Washington and show how a new system of warrant issuance and redemption can be inaugurated which will be infinitely better than the present system. I do not claim that perfection is one of the attributes of the proposed plan. The problem which confronts us now has to deal with the feasibility of adopting a system which is less imperfect than the present one. That which is true for the state of Washington is also true for the other states and for the entire nation. It must be borne in mind at all times in the consideration of the merits of the proposed system, that the various districts, towns, cities, and counties of Washington have been issuing warrants for many years, that they issue them now, and, in all probability, will continue to issue them for many years to come; and furthermore, that the plan I advocate does not mean an additional issue or overissue or supplementary issue of warrants, but it means *an entire substitution of non-interest-bearing state warrants for all other kinds of warrants to be issued by the various districts, towns, cities, and counties in the state and by the state itself.*

There are several hundred districts in this state which are issuing warrants, the payment or redemption of which is guaranteed by the various tax-rolls. When the money has been collected from the taxpayers the warrants are called in and paid by the treasurer in charge. However, since the taxes are paid very slowly the delinquent tax-list grows larger each year, and as a consequence the amount of outstanding warrants increases in corresponding ratio. This is no time to mince matters; the warrant-buyer or other investor makes it his business to thoroughly investigate financial conditions, and he understands the situation fully whether we do or not. The multiplicity of warrants being issued from the different districts go begging among the warrant-barbers in order to have their whiskers trimmed in varying styles of beauty commensurate with their general make-up and financial backing, and in this process the warrants of some districts suffer a very close shave.

It is a gigantic illusion for anyone to suppose that by selling a warrant to some purchaser more money is put into circulation. If a man sells $10 worth of wood to the city and receives a warrant in payment for the same, which he sells to a purchaser for $9 in cash, and in turn the purchaser holds said warrant until the taxpayer has paid $10 taxes and $2 interest into the city treasury, at which time the holder of the warrant comes forward, presents it for redemption and pockets the $12, it is certainly a logical statement as well as a mathematical fact to say that more money has been going out of circulation while it is being collected and held by the city treasurer than went into circulation when the warrant was first sold for cash.

It is claimed by the warrant-buyer that, as this paper falls into the hands of merchants and others who have to pay cash for goods or who have to *pay their taxes in cash* (mark this), it is absolutely necessary to sell the warrants for cash in order to meet immediate demands on account of the lack of money in the city treasury with which to redeem the said warrants. This is a true statement, I am sorry to say, and under the present system of issuance and redemption of warrants the custom of buying and selling them will have to continue until, on account of rapid depreciation in value, the dealer will refuse to take any more paper of this kind. The greater the amount of depreciation in value of the warrant, the greater will be the cost of material and supplies furnished to the city; consequently the amount of taxes to be paid will be increased proportionately.

Now, how are we going to change things for the better? We can change them for the better, even if by so doing we cause the warrant-buyer to look around with a view to engaging in some other line of business. This can be brought about by enacting a number of bills in the state legislature the headings of which will read somewhat as follows:

First.—An act providing for the assessment and collection of all district, town, city, county, and other taxes and revenues by the state, and empowering district, town, city, county, and other officials connected with this work to act as ex-officio state officers.

Second.—An act providing for quarterly tax-collection.

Third.—An act to provide for the issuance of non-interest-bearing state of Washington warrants to all school-districts and other districts, towns, cities, and counties, and for state indebtedness, and *prohibiting* the issuance of county, city, town, school-district, and other district warrants.

Fourth.—An act empowering the state to receive non-interest-bearing state of Washington warrants in payment for all fines, dues, fees, water-rents, licenses, taxes, and other revenues due to the state or to any portion of the state.

Fifth.—An act providing for the refunding of outstanding state, county, city, town, school-district, and other district warrant indebtedness, warrants of old issue to be called in and warrants of new issue to be exchanged for the same.

It may be necessary to subdivide some of the above proposed bills, or it may be found advisable to rearrange the headings, to obtain the best results. It will be observed that no change in the system of electing the various officers will be necessary, for the officers acting under the present system will act as ex-officio state officers.

The first benefit to be derived from this system of issuing one kind of warrants of high grade instead of over one thousame kinds of low-grade ones, will be the cutting down of the present rate of yearly issuance of $8,000,000 to $7,000,000, which represents a saving of $1,000,000; for it is evident that the higher the grade of the warrant used, the less will be the amount to be issued. Under the workings of the old system the average life of warrants is about two years, so that the interest accumulating upon the total annual issuance in this state amounts to over $1,000,000, while the new system eliminates interest. Therefore the total saving upon each year's warrants will be over $2,000,000 to the taxpayers of the state; and putting this in another light it represents a yearly saving of about seven dollars per capita.

Under the new system, when the tax-rolls and estimated revenues are turned over to the state for approval and collection, should it appear that any particular district has been assessed at too high a valuation, then the state must cut down the assessment to conform with valuations actually existing. Then *enforce* the payment of taxes, but with provisions hereinafter set forth.

When the state shall have approved of the assessment-roll and estimated yearly revenues of a district, it shall issue state of Washington non-interest-bearing warrants to the proper district officer, in amount equal to the amount of taxes and revenues called for upon the assessment-roll and estimates of that district, these warrants being signed by the proper state officers, with a blank place for the signatures of the district officers, who in turn shall sign them when they are paid out for the same purposes and in the same manner that the old district warrant was used.

In some districts the old-style warrants, after being issued, sell to the brokers for fifty cents on the dollar. If warrants in that district are issued to the amount of $100.000 per annum, they produce but $50,000 worth of return to the district and to the individuals who receive them from the district, while it costs the district $100,000 and interest to redeem them. Under the new system $50,000 in state warrants will produce $50,000 worth of return to the district and to the individuals first receiving them, while it costs the district but $50,000 with no interest to redeem them.

The state plainly says to the district, While we are backing you up with our credit, which is much greater than yours, we decline to furnish you with any more of this credit than you are actually worth; and, while we take upon ourselves the responsibility of collecting taxes and revenues from the individuals of your district, we will have it understood that these taxes must be paid within a specified time.

The new warrants should be in denominations of $100, $50, $20, $10, $5, $2, $1, 50 cents, and 25 cents.

These warrants are to be receivable at par at any subtreasury in the state *without reference to numerical order or date of issue and without reference to the district from which they were issued,* in payment for all water-rents, dues, fines, fees, taxes, and other revenues due to the state or to any subdivision of the state. At the present time, in many schooldistricts, towns, cities, and counties, the salaries of teachers, officials, and other employees are paid in warrants drawn against their various funds; and I may state right here that the time is near at hand when all salaries will be paid in warrants, and as *some system* of issuing warrants is bound to be used for many years to come, is there any sane individual who will claim that the proposed non-interest-bearing state warrant is not a more desirable class of paper, with its numerous provisions for redemption, than the ordinary district warrant with its one path to redemption?

It may be well to add at this time that a system of transference of cash funds from one sub-treasury to another should be adopted, and that any sub-treasurer should be empowered to exchange warrants of one denomination for like amounts in warrants of other denominations, this suggestion having reference to the new system of warrants. If a man shall receive a $100 warrant in Seattle and he comes to Spokane and wishes to pay his water-rent, which amounts to $7.65, he can hand over his $100 warrant and receive in change one $50 warrant, two $20 warrants, one $2 warrant, one 25-cent warrant, and 10 cents in silver.

No overissue of warrants in any district can take place, as that district receives from the state only that amount in warrants which its tax-rolls and other rolls call for; and when the state assumes the responsibility of assessing, issuing warrants, and collecting taxes and other revenues, no risk can be incurred, for the reason that the demand by the state for the return of the warrant is equal to the supply of outstanding warrants. How shall we dispose of the tax to pay interest upon bonded debt which must be paid in cash? How shall we cancel our bonds as they fall due?

With regard to the payment of bonded debts, it is provided by the laws of this state, that, during the last few years prior to the expiration of the time set for the payment of a bond, an additional tax shall be levied, collected, and set aside for the purpose of making said payment. Very well, let us see if any interference takes place here. If the general tax-rolls and other revenues produce an income of $7,000,000 for the entire state, and the annual bonded-debt tax-roll shall, for example, amount to $3,000,000, making a total of $10,000,000 to be collected from the taxpayers, it stands to reason that $7,000,000 in warrants will not pay $10,000,000 in taxes and revenues, therefore somebody will have to pay the $3,000,000 extra taxes in cash, no warrants having been issued against a bonded-debt tax-roll. Without any interference taking place this simply produces a ten-dollar demand for every seven dollars in floating warrants, or in other words a down-hill pull against the warrants to bring them home again; therefore they will always circulate *at par,* in the capacity of money.

I estimate that after the new system shall have been in operation for a year, at least $3,000,000 in warrants will be in *constant active circulation* in this state (Washington), which amounts to about $10 per capita. The present actual cash circulation does not amount to over $10 per capita; so the new system will bring our circulation up to $20 per capita.

As a matter of fact, a large percentage of individuals will pay cash in liquidation of general improvement taxes and dues, not happening to possess warrants at the time in which they make their quarterly tax payments or other dues, which cash will be used to redeem such warrants as are held by persons who have no taxes to pay. How absurd it is, indeed, for one to argue that this paper will have to suffer a heavy discount because it is paid out by the city or district to a person who owes no taxes, when about the first individual with whom he deals will be some one who is owing for water-rent, court fees, license dues, taxes, or some other dues collectable by the state!

We have been under the false impression, when, at a discount for cash, some one has sold his warrant (received for services rendered or supplies furnished to the district, city, or county), that a good thing has been accomplished by putting that much money into circulation. We did not take into consideration the fact that the city treasurer has been collecting money from taxes, etc., and putting it aside in order to pay this warrant, principal and interest, and that while this fund is accumulating more money is going out of circulation than went into circulation when the warrant was sold. The truth of the matter is, that money has been steadily going out of circulation by this very process. As before mentioned, over one thousand various school-district, street, bridge, road, park, public-building, city, county, fire, water, state, and other funds are being kept in existence by the present glorious system of finance used in this state, which is true, more or less, of all the other states as well. In each of these funds, a small amount of cash has accumulated, but not enough in the majority of cases to call in an outstanding warrant. As a rule this money cannot be transferred from one fund to another, although in the aggregate they must contain over $1,000,000. If we had *one fund only,* in connection with a system of transferring money from one sub-state-treasury to another, the above condition of affairs need not exist.

Now arises the question, "What shall we do with the present outstanding warrant indebtedness? It must be understood that, with the old system or with the new or with a combination of both, in order to continue to do business, it will be absolutely necessary to enforce the payment of delinquent taxes within some specified time.

In order to facilitate the redemption of old district, city, and county warrants (some of which, by the way, have been outstanding for four or five years), the state, after having made a careful investigation into the condition of any district fund and its delinquent tax-rolls, and after having determined as to the legality of its floating indebtedness, shall issue non-interest-bearing state warrants amounting, for instance, to twenty-five per cent of the legal outstanding warrant indebtedness, and shall exchange the new warrants for the old ones, *principal and interest,* without reference to numerical order, first come first served. When this amount of delinquent taxes shall have been collected in this particular district, thereby redeeming a corresponding amount of the new state warrants, repeat the process. The old debt will be rapidly extinguished by this plan, and I fail to see where a conflict can arise between two systems.

Bridge and public building contractors have told me that this new state warrant is the one wanted. They will figure their bids at par and pay their employees and material bills with these warrants. The largest taxpayers in the state of

Washington inform me that this warrant is to be preferred above all others, and that they stand ready to accept it at par in payment for real estate, no matter what the magnitude of the transaction may be. The merchant will accept the warrant for his goods because he has his taxes and water rents to pay. The merchant will pay a part of his clerk's salary in warrants because the clerk has to pay taxes and can use the warrants for this purpose. The warrant will be accepted for rent by the landlord because it pays taxes. The farmer will also use it.

It is obvious, therefore, that the objection that the merchant must sell his warrant at a great discount to raise cash to send to the non-resident with whom he deals fails completely when we remember the numerous uses or demands for the warrants throughout the state and their intrinsic value as redemption money. It may happen that the merchant may possess more warrants at some particular time than he can use right then, but on account of the general demand for them to be used as local currency the temporary discount will be very small.

Furthermore, on account of the increased facility with which redemption can be made, the demand for redemption by holders of warrants will become less and they will circulate more freely in the capacity of money. If any individual state in this Union will adopt the foregoing plan of issuance and redemption of warrants it can soon free itself from the clutch of the money power, for while I have said nothing about this warrant as *being money*, still it acts *in the capacity of money*. The old style of warrant immediately after being issued finds its way into some vault, where it *remains out of circulation*, in addition to causing the circulating medium to be steadily robbed by the withdrawal of what is termed discount and interest. The new warrant, on the other hand, immediately goes into circulation to the extent of several millions of dollars per annum. Which will you have, a district warrant worth fifty or seventy-five cents on the dollar and redeemable in one way only, or a state warrant, redeemable in a thousand ways? This plan can be extended to two or more states, and the warrants of one state can circulate in the other and be receivable for taxes, all balances being settled monthly or weekly through clearing-houses.

If extended to cover the entire nation, the plan would be, in brief, as follows; Let all tax-rolls, excepting for interest on bonded debt, and other estimates from each state be turned over to the United States treasurer. He will issue to each

state in *United States non-interest-bearing warrants* the amount
called for upon the rolls and estimates. These warrants
will be redistributed to the various districts pro rata as
outlined in previous pages. They will then be paid out for
salaries, public supplies, improvements, etc., in the same
manner and for the same purpose for which the two hundred thousand different kinds of warrants are now used.
The issuance of all other than the United States warrant to
be stopped; refunding of old warrants to be as I have
outlined. Then the new United States warrant is to be
accepted anywhere in the United States in payment for
taxes, without reference to numerical order and without
reference to the district from which it was first issued. All
necessary precautions can be taken to prevent counterfeit-
ing or overissue. This plan will put into *constant active
circulation at least one billion dollars* more than now exists.

The bankers of Wall Street and officials at Washington,
D. C., are planning and scheming to advance and put into
operation some method of issuing paper money backed up
by pure unadulterated wind. Every dollar issued under
my plan will be backed up by over thirty dollars in real
estate, and every dollar of this new paper must be redeemed
or someone will lose his property, for the warrant is a *first
mortgage upon property* and must be paid within a specified
time. The old plan compels the individual to pay his taxes
in cash, no matter how little money there is in circulation.
The new plan *advances the money* (or its equivalent) with
which to pay the taxes.

This matter will come before the legislature of the state
of Washington at its next session, and as it is advocated by
our leading taxpayers, I feel assured that some action will
be taken to put the plan into operation at an early date.

As surely as will the moisture which arises from the
surface of the ocean and which falls as rain and snow, fulfilling its various functions by invigorating the vegetable
and animal kingdoms of the earth and by ministering unto
the numerous wants of man, be compelled by the ever-
present law of gravitation to return to the source from
which it came, just so surely will these warrants, issued by
the state to its individuals, buy products, pay debts, effect
transactions in thousands of ways between man and man,
and finally, under the ever-present pressure of the state for
the payment of taxes, be compelled to gravitate toward the
source from which they came and thereby be redeemed.

THE ZEALOUS MOSLEM.

BY EMMA GHENT CURTIS.

In a picturesque vale of the Orient bright
    Lived men who loved science and learning;
They counseled together and voted a tax
    For a school which should answer their every yearning.

Some Ghebers, I'm told, had long lived in the vale,
    And a Brahmin or two had residence there;
Moslems were many within its confines
    And one Christian merchant breathed its soft air.

The school was set up with fitting display;
    The matter of science was made a strong feature;
And as one might expect from conditions that reigned
    A brilliant young Moslem was chosen as teacher.

The sons of the residents hastened to school,
    Commanded to peaceably study together,
To learn all the secrets of sun and of moon
    And the whys and the wherefores of changeable weather.

The brilliant young Moslem most pleasingly taught
    The secrets of suns and of science,
But he furthermore urged with unwearying zeal
    His flock in Mahomet to place their reliance.

"Hold! hold!" cried the Ghebers; the Brahmins cried "Hold,
    We pay our full share of the wage you receive";
The Christian said darkly: "You pocket my gold,
    Yet teach you my sons a false faith to believe."

Said the teacher: "'Tis true I am paid by you all,
    But in teaching my faith I do only the right;
My faith is the true one, all others are false;
    I shall slight no occasion for spreading the light."

Christian, Brahmin, and Gheber insisted in turn
    That his own faith, or none, should be taught;
But such infidel boldness so freely displayed
    On the teacher a fainting fit brought.

All protests were useless; the Moslems were strong,
    They outnumbered all others twenty to one;
So the few paid their taxes and fretted and fumed,
    But the will of the Moslems only was done.

Said the Christian one morn, "How wicked it is
    To tax man for a purpose that fills him with fears."
Said the teacher, "What a good Moslem am I,
    Thus to force the true doctrines on infidel ears."

BETWEEN TWO WORLDS.

BY MRS. CALVIN KRYDER REIFSNIDER.

CHAPTER V.

About three o'clock the next afternoon Ruby sat in the gallery waiting for some of her father's pupils to appear. It was a pleasant way of disposing of a leisure hour or so, and she could appreciate it, too, inasmuch as she had gone through the same drill and was now an accomplished elocutionist. She had lost herself in some inward reflection when at length a clear, round, penetrating voice roused her.

"Your Honor, and Gentlemen of the Jury."

"Your Honor" expressed deep reverence and lofty regard.

"Gentlemen of the Jury" was uttered in such a tone as to win the heart of every juror. Then came the same appeal in defence of the man on trial for his life that she had heard her father make the day before. Her father sat in the high-backed, crimson velvet chair, the judge of the unseen criminal, and listened to the eloquent appeal. The ardent pleader argued in that earnest, convincing tone which carries conviction to every listener; he pleaded with all the pathos and energy of a soul for a soul, now bringing forth the dreadful temptation, the overmastering spirit of some unseen devil, and lastly he brought the picture close home so that each juryman might put his own son into that criminal's stead and ask, "How would I that others should do to mine were he on trial for his life for this crime?"

Ruby saw that her father was proud and happy. The young speaker had forgotten all else. No need now to remind him to dwell on his vowels and strengthen his consonants. His soul went forth in every word he uttered; to him a life hung upon his words, his tone, his gestures; there seemed to be no thought of fame nor honor for himself; to be *felt* as well as *heard* was his aim—to convince men as he was convinced—and he had succeeded.

When he had finished her father rose and took his hand and gave him most cordial words of congratulation.

"You have found the key; remember always to use it so

well, and fame and distinction are yours; persuasion is the crown of rhetoric."

Ruby now was conscious of another presence, and looking over the railing saw a tall princely man making his way to the pulpit. He planted his feet with firm, even tread, and indeed reminded her of an ideal Saul. He mounted the steps and she saw her father introduce the two men. She heard the first speaker ask permission to remain and listen to the fine voice of which he had heard so much spoken in praise, and a gracious acquiescence was given.

"Surely father was right! This is no ordinary man."

As he towered head and shoulders above them and as Ruby looked upon him she recalled her ideal Saul, and the words of Samuel to him as he anointed and blessed him rose involuntarily to her lips: "Is it not because the Lord hath anointed thee to be captain over his inheritance,"— and as she gazed wonderingly upon him she seemed to hear the voice of Samuel still speaking to him the words of divine prophecy: "And the words of the Lord will come upon thee, and thou shalt prophesy with them, and shalt be turned into another man. And let it be when these signs are come unto thee that thou do as occasion serve thee; for God is with thee."

He began to speak. The first sentence came to Ruby as the first grand chord in a great harmony. It soared up to the arched dome and seemed to circle through every inch of space, then came floating down to settle like a blessing upon her. Again, up, around, down, circling the columns, causing the leaves on the palms to quiver, the statues to tremble as if awaking into life, opening the half-closed buds of flowers in delight, closing the full-blown ones in wonder, and thrilling everywhere till it struck an answering chord in the organ that gave back a grand response.

She looked at him entranced as he stood like a man suddenly immortalized. He was listening to himself, his whole being concentrated in sending forth those sounds, yet guarding them with masterly skill lest one inharmony invade. No tone went forth but his quick ear caught first and retained last. He did not seem to choose words or subjects but passed from one line of work to the other; from the deepest orotund up to and through all the exercises of the pure tone.

When they had finished Ruby descended slowly to her father's study. The three were together there. Her father was congratulating and warmly praising both. She would have withdrawn immediately but the eyes of both young men seemed for a moment to hold her spellbound. They were struck with wonder at her apparance, as though one of the statues in the temple had come, warm with life, before them. It was only an instant and she was gone. Her father had not observed her, and she fled away in a kind of fluttering, wondering, delicious terror.

"Have you any lady pupils?" asked the Greek.

"One, only."

"Then perhaps we had better leave you; we may disturb or delay you."

Mr. Gladstone did not urge them to stay. He gave each a pamphlet written by himself, containing many valuable hints to aid them in the prosecution of their studies.

The young men departed. At the door they bade each other a friendly adieu, hoping to meet again. Each carried with him a vision of that statuesque beauty who had appeared so mysteriously and vanished so quickly and silently. Each wondered if she had listened to him and which of them had pleased her best.

The next day Ruby waited for the appearance of the would-be actress. She was prompt and at half-past three she came, half shyly, half confidently, across the chancel to meet Mr. Gladstone.

She was slightly above medium height, with good features. Her closely fitting dress displayed a lithe, angular figure. She seemed to understand that there was work, hard work, before her, but her manner, as well as her strong face, indicated an indomitable will and untiring energy.

She was crude, and it would take some little time to discover any real power in her; but Mr. Gladstone asked only patience, perseverance and love of some well defined line of art. He would take care of the rest. Only be certain you have chosen the thing for which you are best fitted, was always his instruction.

"I must do something," she said, "and I want to do something that shall be worthy of all the energy I have to expend. I shall not be satisfied with mediocrity."

"There now, you have pleased me. Aim to reach the very highest point attainable in whatever direction your talents lead you. It may be slow and tedious at first but nothing is lost by laying a perfect foundation."

"Can you give me any encouragement?" she asked earnestly. "I have no time nor money to waste."

"I can give you every encouragement if you put your whole heart and mind upon your work."

Her task having been assigned her, she took her depart-

ure. It was not many days until Mr. Gladstone told her
frankly that with earnest work continued she could realize
her fondest hope. She was patient, untiring, and he was
thoroughly in sympathy with her.

Work, work, work! Salome had never known anything
but work. She had read of a poor girl who had gone on
the stage and made a great fortune. Why should not she?
Money! That is all, after the whole story is told,
which brings comfort and peace and rest in this world.
Money!—that she might repay scorn for scorn. Money!—
that she might make people forget that her father was
a drunkard, that she might raise her mother from drudgery.
Money!—that she might buy friends and not care for enemies. Money!—to make her forget past slights of school
girls and boys. Money! money!—to wash out every dark
spot in the past; gold to gild the future!

She walked home with a lighter step than she had ever
known as these thoughts came through her brain, and
turned a willing hand toward preparing the evening meal.
She lived no longer in the dim, dark rooms, but fancy
carried her away to the beautiful temple where she had
stood and heard words of encouragement. It took her further and she saw the place lighted and filled with admiring
people, eager, waiting, watching, *for her;* and then she
fancied herself in trailing satin and glittering gems appearing before them, welcomed with loud applause.

O Hope! thou blessed angel! bringing light into the
deepest gloom, joy to the saddest heart; drying tears, bind-
.ing up our wounds; cheering us on the dark road of
despair or duty! What could we mortals do without
thee?

She was no longer plain Salome, the school mistress. She
was Juliet to-day, loving, devoted, waiting for her Romeo;
Lady Macbeth to-morrow, plotting, planning for a kingdom
and a crown, and before her crumbled every barrier even
as before Lady Macbeth had melted every obstacle.

She tore down and planted her feet ruthlessly upon
visions of a new spring hat and walked over even a silk
dress pattern that rose to tempt her. "Lessons, lessons!
I'll double them up, I'll pay for four a week instead of two,
and earn the money, too."

Never had Mr. Gladstone seen such ambition, such
dauntless courage. He almost forgot Saul and his friend,
or thought their efforts tame before this giantess hemmed
in by poverty and toil.

The winter was over. Spring was nearing summer. The

season had been a pleasant and profitable one to all. Ruby had never met Salome to speak to her. "King Saul" and Demosthenes still looked for the golden-haired statue but it appeared no more before them.

Mr. Gladstone had found many of his former admirers and occasional calls were exchanged between them, and he and his daughter were urged to become members of various clubs, literary, ethical, historical and philosophical, formed to investigate and discuss the most absorbing questions of the day.

"I really cannot find time for all these things and do justice to my class, therefore we will choose those things that seem most profitable to study and leave the rest to others who have more leisure. But, my dear," he said earnestly to Ruby, as they sat alone, "I find there is a good work for you to do. Salome needs a guide. When she comes again I will present you to her. She is capable of doing great good or great evil in the world in the profession she has chosen. We must show her, with God's help, the true way."

The next day when the lesson was over Ruby approached Salome with one of her fair hands filled with fresh flowers and said: "Papa promised me the pleasure of speaking with you to-day. He praises your work highly."

Salome stood silently gazing upon Ruby, too much surprised to speak. Such strange and wondrous beauty awed her. Every motion of the graceful body as she approached and greeted her was firmly fixed in Salome's remembrance. A pain, acute and poignant as steel, pierced her very soul at the contrast. Something, too, akin to sorrow, a dread fear of failure came upon her for the first time, with many conflicting emotions; and still Salome, idly turning the flowers which Ruby placed in her hands, could not have told whether she was pained or pleased to meet this strangely beautiful woman whose peculiar charm made all other women seem to her to be made of very common clay.

It was not many days, however, before this ambitious woman decided to turn her new acquaintance to account and learn from the daughter all those feminine graces she so fully possessed, while from the father she was learning the cunning of voice and action.

Ruby did not question the motive; she understood this poor girl's needs and determined to aid her father in his earnest wish to develop all the power in her for her own good. Salome made a study of Ruby from the first hour they met, and continually dwelt upon the wide difference between her and all other women she had ever seen. What constituted that difference? It was what she needed, what she wanted, what she must have—for it meant success.

Ruby's perfect placidity, caused by mental and bodily freedom, was very charming. This bodily freedom seemed to be the foundation of the beautiful mental freedom which had never been destroyed, and was exhibited in the child-like trust which she daily displayed in all the affairs of life, and in the exquisite responsiveness to the spiritual truths which her father taught her. The very expression of her face, as she walked beside her father, was a lesson to Salome, and could have been to all observers who were seeking, as Salome sought, a higher life. And she felt that these two were indeed "led beside the still waters" and made "to lie down in green pastures." Instead of making conflicts for themselves they met, with the Lord's quiet strength, whatever they had to pass through. In them the natural and ideal were truly one, and they seemed to reach the latter by the former.

A more complete contrast in two women, not only in personal appearance but in their mental views and conversational powers, can scarcely be conceived. Salome was brilliant, too strong to be delicate and tender of sentiment, but choice in her use of language. Every thought expressed showed plainly its worldly mold. Ambition had made her sharp and critical, and pride kept her ever on the alert to avoid the errors that she detected in others. "An unripe persimmon," her intoxicated father would say —"an undeveloped genius" Ruby recognized. The strained, almost unnatural, exterior could not hide from the penetrating eyes of love which Ruby turned upon her, the rough diamond. Her father had pointed it out to her at first, but now it was plain, plain as the noonday sun.

To-day they stood in the temple where Salome seemed to gain her inspiration. Her dark, troubled face, already bearing unmistakable lines of care, her fine eyes burning with slumbering fires of hatred and jealousy, the nervous twitching of the well-shaped mouth she strove vainly to control, were all heightened by the calm figure opposite her in its robe of purity, with the healthful tone, the tender mouth, the great luminous eyes in which for a moment a tear glistened as it recognized the effort of that young creature—tortured, self-tortured, it is true, but making a brave effort to conceal her misery.

Mr. Gladstone took her hand kindly, almost reverently; but to his surprise she withdrew it rudely, and holding it up before him, with burning cheeks, said with withering scorn:

"I could not even have the hand of a lady. I have been stamped as low-born with this unmistakable emblem that even the illiterate may read."

"Ah, let me read it for you, and make you feel grateful for the distinction conferred upon you by trusting you with such a hand," said Mr. Gladstone.

His tone, his manner, checked the rising tears of wounded pride, and she permitted him to take her hand although the contrast in mould and texture of his own again caused a blush to mantle her dark cheeks. He read as from a book:

"The pink finger-tips indicate good arterial circulation; the strong, nimble fingers, great force of character; the well-developed joints which seem to annoy you so much, proclaim the true philosopher; this prominent thumb removes you from all little meanness of character."

As he spoke Ruby observed the pleasant change that came over Salome while she listened with absorbed interest to what he said.

"Yes, it is a very good hand; indeed it was this very hand which first interested me in you; it proclaimed undaunted courage, honesty of purpose, reason; and see here,"—he took the thumb and threw it apparently out of place, bending it as he chose with perfect ease. "This is the greatest test of true, innate refinement that is indicated by a human hand—the flexibility and perfect control of a well developed thumb. There is music and harmony written in this hand."

As he spoke he raised his eyes to her face and saw that it was almost radiant with a look of pleasure and hope he had never seen there before, and a something else—what was it? was it feigned or real? an expression of such adoration as he had never before seen a human face wear.

"Now, for the face; the complexion is sallow only because of gloomy thoughts, and unwise selection of food. The remedy is happy, hopeful thought and proper food. The eyes express without attempt at disguise every emotion of your soul and the color varies to suit the occasion. The brow will be improved with the hope and happiness that will come by and by. The mouth and eyes act in perfect harmony, the only thing that can give perfection to expression, without which the face is automatic. The nose—well,

it is an unusual nose, but Lavator affirms that he has never
in one instance seen such a nose where the possessor was
not capable of very high attainments. Your hair is abundant and of a rich, warm color, showing a naturally affectionate nature. You have ready use of good language.
Your voice is the voice of one who could never for a moment
be suspected of being low-born as you said. It has power,
pathos, firmness, character. I predict for you a great
future, my child; up hill, even to the mountain top, but you
will reach it safely by and by."

She closed her other hand upon his and for a moment
held it firmly between both of her own. Her impulse was
to shower tears and kisses upon it, to fall down at his
feet and tell him what his words had done for her—they
had made her satisfied with herself; but Ruby was there,
self-possessed Ruby, who would be shocked at her or think
she was only acting.

"Our heavenly Father knows where to bestow His good
gifts; this temple is well fitted to do the work allotted to
this soul; it was built for strength. Grace and beauty
can only come from the soul and you will find no difficulty
in giving expression through this lithe body to every
emotion of which your soul is capable. This is indeed a
great gift; be grateful for it and keep faithfully your trust;
it is a sacred one. Make a solemn compact with your own
soul and your mirror. Ruby can advise you on the subject
of dress."

"Will you," she asked, turning to Ruby, "show me how
to clothe myself as becomingly as you clothe yourself?"

"Certainly; there should be no hesitation in deciding
whether one will be a dummy to hold the clothing the
seller wants to be rid of, or whether one will be a distinct
personality, sublimer and better than any vesture ever
made. A woman should express her taste, her soul in her
raiment. The task of deciding what will be most becoming and beautiful is done once for all. The right thing in
the right place, once determined, may be strictly adhered
to until personal conditions change or experience suggests
something better. I know the shades of color most becoming to me, and style of vesture. I vary the material with
the season. Indeed I give no thought to my apparel. It
has been decided so long ago, so satisfactorily, that I am
free as the birds in this respect. My time is too valuable
to watch the fashions in dress, much less to imitate them.
I have no curiosity to know how I should appear in a
fashionable dress or cloak."

"How did you learn all this?" asked Salome.

"Nature," Ruby said smiling, "is an unerring guide. Autumn shades for the autumn of life, winter for old age, spring and summer for childhood and youth. Besides, the gentler birds and animals wear appropriate hues to their nature, the soft blue gray and white for the dove, the brown for the pheasant, the blue for the jay, and so on. A woman does herself great injustice to wear the garb of the raven, the crow or the vulture."

CHAPTER VI.

Salome had become a frequent visitor to the temple and was always welcome. It never grew familiar to her, but each day presented the same bewildering, real, unreal mystic shrine it had at first appeared to her overawed imagination. The inhabitants, too, it was impossible for her to believe them to be flesh and blood human beings, having the same bodily needs as other creatures. When her first timidity wore off and she found that she could talk and ask questions of this Greek statue, and could be sure of a clear answer given with so much evident pleasure, she believed herself as blessed as though she were receiving oracles from a goddess, and every word sank into her heart to take deep root there some day; but not, she found long afterwards, until they were warmed by the sunshine of her own love and gratitude and watered by her own tears of repentance.

"I am here again," she sighed one Saturday morning, seating herself near Ruby who sat in the temple with an open Bible in her lap. "I cannot stay away. I walk around the building like one who has found a hidden treasure and must come and satisfy himself each day that it was not stolen in the night; or a fountain at which I must drink or perish, and yet whose waters I cannot reach. I dream of it in the night. The Temple, your father and yourself are real then; awake, all is like a dream. I am drawn hither by a current stronger than air or water. I cannot help myself, for I would fain learn of you how to be like you, and yet my heart is so full of worldly ambition of another order; such longing, unrest, chagrin, and disappointment. But, surely, ambition only could have attained what your father and you have done."

Salome sat on the top step leading to the pulpit, while Ruby was sitting near her looking down the auditorium.

Ruby had followed her every word, watched the convulsive movement of her dark, firm hands clasped over her knees, the kindling fires in her brown cheek and the smouldering light in her dark eyes. She saw deeper with her pure eyes and perceived that the good in this girl was rising up against the evil, and that powerful as the latter was it must go down in the conflict. She did not question this self-tortured girl. She was silent for she knew that Salome would speak.

"Tell me," said Salome, "at least pardon me, if I say I long to know how you began life; were you like other children?" She was so eager, so much afraid of being wounded or rebuked that she was quite awkward and Ruby herself wondered if the skill of a born actress was in her.

"Yes," answered Ruby quietly. "Very much like them, except in this. My father's wisdom in furnishing me only wholesome, nutritious food, saved me all the aches and pains that bodily flesh is heir to, and kept my brain equally well supplied with nourishment. I believe thereby I have been happier for having been healthier than most children."

"What was your next lesson?"

"Let me recall," said Ruby thoughtfully. After some consideration she answered. "Whether it was my very next lesson or not, I cannot say; but the one I remember best, for it was so difficult to live by, was this."

She turned the leaves of her bible and read, " 'Judge not, that ye be not judged. For with whatsoever judgment ye judge, ye shall be judged.' I was very quick to see faults in other people, with the beam in my own eye."

She paused and looked calmly down the long vista, her mind apparently absorbed in self-communion, and Salome's great troubled eyes were upon her.

"You could not help it; we cannot help seeing faults in others, can we?"

"No,—but that is the sad part for us. Were we pure we could not see evil in others; for you understand the pure cannot see evil." She quoted, " 'Thou art of purer eyes than to behold evil, and canst not look upon iniquity.' Could we purify ourselves from all evil and falsity we would become so spiritual that we could see the spiritual part of man, or that part which is untainted by the grosser or more sensual, but could not see the evil!"

"But we cannot become so; that would be divine."

"If we would remember that, however, and judge not, we should not be judged, for with whatsoever judgment we judge we shall be judged; in other words we can see no more evil in others than we have in ourselves, and in judging we pass verdict upon ourselves. Sad to think of, isn't it? but true, and just."

After a pause, during which Salome sat with her straight dark brows almost knitted together, she said:

"Repeat that, please, I scarcely know whether I catch your meaning. Christ saw the evil in others and berated them most soundly."

"His humanity did,—that part of Him inherited from Mary. The Divinity did not," said Ruby. "We are images, or mirrors, into which God looks to find a likeness of Himself. If He sees no good He is not there, and He does not see us at all—the wicked part of us."

"The wicked give themselves a great deal of unnecessary trouble, then, in imagining that God is always thinking of them and planning to punish them," answered Salome, with a peculiar smile.

"Do you think so?" inquired Ruby. "Isn't it more likely that they do not think of God at all, or, if they do, attribute to him only their own worst qualities? I rather imagine that they think little about God—the true God."

In a moment she continued, "Christ is within me when I make place for Him to abide with me. Hell is within me when I crucify Him with evil. Do I love Him, His Divine love, His Divine truth and wisdom? God is Divine love, the Son Divine truth, and the Holy Spirit Divine wisdom. And my neighbor; who is he? I once thought it was only the man or woman who lived next door to me. Now I learn that my neighbor is the good in every human being, manifest in every good word and deed. Why, it is easy then to love one's neighbor for in loving good I love an attribute of God."

To Salome's restless, ambitious, soul-weary existence, nothing was so puzzling as the systematic daily labors of Mr. Gladstone, in which his daughter shared, except in the instructions in oratory, and even there she now found Ruby was often a silent, unseen participator from the gallery. She felt that had she attained the excellence to which Ruby had arrived nothing could induce her to toil another hour. She felt that she would sit down and feast her soul upon books and music, never crossing the threshold save to hear some grand lecture or oratorio, or to drive those spirited horses. She marvelled that Ruby could find pleasure in the ordinary occupations of life, much less deeds of common charity, going out among the wretched and the poor.

"These people become more thriftless, more cunning, and devise all sorts of means to impose upon such people as your father and yourself," said Salome to Ruby in conversation upon the subject.

"We go among those who need us most—who are ready to receive us," said Ruby. "We do not trouble those who *enjoy* their degradation; but those who are earnestly seeking the truth and are willing to be led. The field is broad enough for us and we leave to others more fitted for the work, those to whom you refer. There is work for all of us and we should each fake the duties we are best fitted to perform.

Ruby's character was a beautiful prism reflecting all of the heavenly light about her. Other natures may show shades of color, hers the full glory of all. Others lived in antagonism to nature's laws, she in perfect harmony with them. Others were seeking flaws in every character, she, in her sympathy, was finding only the germs of good.

Mr. Gladstone's class in self-culture consisted of adult men and women who seemed anxious to attain to the mental and physical perfection he assured them was possible, but who seemed to fail utterly to realize that a teacher can only instruct a person how to accomplish a purpose, but that the effort necessary to success in any direction depends upon the student's receptivity. They seemed to think they should arrive in a few weeks, or months at most, at the very point to which he had attained after twenty years of faithful toil, self-sacrifice and study. They could not give up, as he had done, the fragrant cup of coffee and the tempting steak and game. Their progress must come without self-abnegation. They could not yield to the belief that what enters into a man feeds the quality of his nature, and that to starve out the fierce part of his animal nature he must abjure stimulating food and drink, and to cultivate the more gentle side he must 'feed the lambs,' . or the patient, loving part of the nature.

He had, too, the various dispositions which gather into one class. Women who believed in telling everyone they knew what unkind thing everybody said of them, seeming to think they were doing a favor; women who hated every one their husbands loved; women who could not see why anyone should be able to do anything they could not do; those who would not believe anything which could not be verified by the sense of sight or touch. They were a class of material men and women, the spiritual side of whose natures lay dormant. Mr. Gladstone sought to awaken it if possible.

(To be continued.)

THE VALLEY PATH.

BY WILL ALLEN DROMGOOLE.

CHAPTER IV.

It was the first call the circuit rider had made at the cabin. The doctor chuckled.

"Liked my looks, I suppose," was his reflection, "or else he saw my chicken coop,—these Methodists!"

Old Dilce, none the cleaner for her race with the hog, hobbled forward to say, in the half-complaining tone familiar to her race:

"De preacher ob de gospil am in de house, marster, en he look lack he toler'ble hungry fur his dinner."

The doctor laughed softly, rescuing the saddle bags, thereby bringing upon himself an onslaught from the terrier.

"Well, then," he said, "do you be sure you fix him up a good one."

"Who, me?"

"Yes, you. And tell Ephraim to take the mare to the barn."

The old woman's face wore a knowing look.

"'He say he ain't got but jes' a minute ter set. He say he got ter be about his Marster's business."

"Yes," said the doctor, "I have heard something like that before. You had better get the dinner ready, chicken pie and apple dumplings."

Still she didn't move; evidently there was news yet. He waited a moment for its coming.

"Dat little gal f'm down yon'er et toler'ble hearty dis mawnin'."

"Who? what? Oh, Lissy. Did she? Well, I'm glad of that. She's a good girl. You must be good to Lissy."

"I sho am," was the hearty reply. "She mighty p'lite, en thankful. That little gal hab good raisin', sho's you bawn."

"Oh, get out with you," laughed the doctor, "the girl knows no more of courtesies than Zip here. Never been beyond the mountain in her life."

"Den she am a bawn lady," declared old Dilce, nothing daunted. "She ain' no po' white trash."

"See here now, Aunt Dilce, what did the girl give you? Oh, you needn't protest, I know well enough she bought you."

"Fo' God, marster, she ain' gimme a bressed thing. She say she gwine fetch me some terbacky out'n o' her grandpa's patch bimeby, dat's all. En she say she wish ter de goodness you ud come over dar en see her grandpa, he's plumb peart en healthy en *dat* fond o' comfy! En she e't her bre'kfus tolerble healfy; she sho did."

"Aunt Dilce," said the physician, "my tobacco box is on the mantel; help yourself, you sly old rogue. Now go and get the dinner for the preacher. I am going in to invite him to remain to it."

"You won't have ter baig, I'll be boun'," was the parting shot as she went back to her kitchen.

The doctor opened the door and went in. As he entered his cosy little study, a stalwart robust figure, clad in a rusty black suit of clothes and carrying a worn silk hat in his hand, rose to meet him. The face wore a woe-begone, lugubrious expression, as if the sins of the world had been too many for the broad bent shoulders. A mass of long, sandy, unkempt hair lay upon the sleek collar of the ecclesiastic coat. He was a typical backwoods circuit rider; the air of conscious rectitude, of superior knowledge, and a friendly familiarity with the Holy of Holies that was vouchsafed to but few stamped his calling beyond a shadow of doubting. He extended his hand to meet the physician.

"I come in the name of the Master," he said.

"Well, you found the door open, at all events," replied the physician; "I tarried awhile with the sick down the valley. Resume your seat, sir."

"Death and disease walk the earth," chanted the divine in solemn measures. "Sorrow an' desolation walk hand in hand. One sows an' another reaps, and no man knoweth what a day may bring forth. My brother. I am come in the name of the Master. I come not to call the righteous but sinners to repentance. I have come to beg you to repent—to warn you and to teach you."

"Wait until after dinner," said the doctor. "I'm a terrible old fool, I reckon, but I like to take my lesson on a full stomach. Sit down there, Brother Barry. I am going to fill a pipe for you, and introduce you to my dog Zip; then I am going to give you a good dinner, another pipe, and a peep at the prettiest colt in this valley. Then I'm going to send you up those stairs into my guest chamber, 'the upper room' where you are to have a bath, a nap, and remain as long as you choose. Heavens! don't object, man; doesn't your Methodist nose tell you there is chicken in the air? Chicken pie, and here is Aunt Dilce come to tell us it is on the table. Come out; we will talk religion some other time."

Brother Barry, however, seemed disposed to argument.

"My Master's business,"—he protested, though decidedly more feebly than at first—"I must be about it: I cannot tarry."

"Why," laughed the doctor, "I thought you were sent here to seek a lost sheep. I tell you, sir, you've run against the toughest old ram that ever tried to butt its own brains out. You may spend a week on me if you are so inclined, but you are not commanded to starve meanwhile; on the other hand you are told not to muzzle the ox that treadeth out the corn. Come out to your fodder."

The invitation was too hearty for resistance. The Methodist placed his tall hat on the table and followed the doctor out to dinner. It was the first of many they were to take together, these two whose lives were to cross but not, in the finer sense, to touch each other; these two, the one broad and warm with the sunshine of all charity, the other narrow and ignorant and immovable, making religion a dark and unreal thing and demanding of its advocates a life of perpetual gloom in a path beset by dangers, curses, terrors; these two, the one with his eye fixed ever upon the sun, the other a groveller among the glooms, believing always in the depravity of humanity and always bearing the burden of its rescue.

The Methodist made himself at home from the moment he entered the doctor's door. He was made as welcome as any might desire; only upon matters of religion the physician refused to talk. But Brother Barry was a man of infinite resources, and failing to take the doctor by one means he had recourse to others. That he would be converted at the last the circuit rider held no shadow of doubt.

The first night of his arrival, when the physician had been sleeping for hours he was awakened by a tremendous thumping upon the floor of the chamber overhead.

He sprang from his bed with a start and ran to the door of the little old-fashioned stairway that went up from his own bedroom. His thought was that Brother Barry was again "surrounding the throne," an exercise that had kept him awake for more than an hour during the earlier night. But this was more serious; Brother Barry was calling for a light.

"Fetch a light, brother; fetch a light quick, and pencil
and paper; I have got a thought."

The doctor's gray head was thrust well into the doorway.

"Oh, you go to sleep, Brother Barry," said he, "and trust
the Lord for another." And closing the door the old infidel went chuckling back to bed.

They were odd companions, these two; yet each was interesting to the other. The preacher regarded the doctor
with a kind of pious pity, while the physician's feeling for
him would have partaken largely of contempt but that his
good heart recognized the fact that the Methodist was
honest even in his ignorance. After three days Brother
Barry threw his saddlebags across the back of the flea-
bitten mare and took his departure. In that three days'
time he had vainly endeavored to impress the doctor with
a sense of his great danger, and had been laughed at, or
cut off with the offer of a pipe or a plate of fruit. He had
been ready to swear a dozen times; only the respect in
which he held his cloth had been sufficient to prevent an
outbreak. The doctor had sworn a dozen times, and more.
Yet he had never once lost patience; not even when his
guest had pronounced with tragic attitude, the "Woe!
woe! to them that are at ease in Zion." All he had said
was, "Hell!" and he had laughed even while saying that.

CHAPTER V.

A red rose bush bloomed by the cabin door, and the bees
were busy among the honeysuckle trailing the piazza and
crowding the windows of the miller's house. Not that the
dusty old miller or his sharp-voiced wife ever gave a thought
to the training of the vines; they were Alicia's; her hand,
with the assistance of Al, had put them there and carefully
tended them until they were a bower of bloom, where the
bees came summer days, hunting for honey among the
pink and pearl-white blossoms.

Doctor Boring recognized her spirit everywhere about
the picturesque little place the first morning he went to
call upon his neighbors there. He had felt something like
admiration for the miller as he stood for a moment looking
over the gate into the pretty sloping yard with the newly
whitewashed cabin in the centre. There was an air of
thrift about the place, as if the little mill on the creek
had earned its full measure of toll. Even the greens in
the garden seemed to have outgrown the vegetables of
other gardens. The peas were clambering up their cedar

stakes, a riotous jumble of white bloom and delicate tendril. And above the stakes, a glister of gold in the sunlight, he saw Alicia's bright head, beside a slender youth whom he recognized as "little Al," the delicately disposed brother.

The boy was adjusting some vines that had had a tumble together with their props. That he found his task an amusing one might be easily inferred from the laughter with which he received Alicia's instructions as to the manner in which the work should be done. More than once she playfully boxed his ears, all unconscious of the visitor regarding them over the palings of the low fence.

The doctor, watching, wondered how many milkmaid castles she had erected upon the proceeds of the truck patch, when the peas and early potatoes should be ready for the boarding house at Sewanee.

A smile played about his lips and twinkled for a moment in the eyes that were not always mirrors of mirth, and he playfully shouted:

"Look out for frost."

Alicia gave a startled little scream and turned quickly to find the owner of the voice.

Al laughed merrily over her surprise.

"You ware good scared, Lissy, I do believe," said he; "you turned plumb white."

She gave him no reply, if indeed she heard him. She was full of the pleasure of seeing Doctor Boring.

"Come in," she called, "come right in, the dogs don't bite. I'm awful glad to see you. So'll grandad be, I know. The beans are fullin' right along; you'll get your mess by and by, if, as granny says, 'God spares me.' I certainly think He will, I'm that well and healthy. Though I reckon Brother Barry'd think He ought not to, seein' I'm such a sinner. But sakes! how I do run on, without ever stoppin' to tell you this is my brother, Doctor Borin'. This is Al. I've in and about raised Al; you see he fell to my care when he was just nine years old. Don't you think I've brought him up toler'ble well?"

The laughing face, full a foot above her own, testified to the bringing up, at all events.

"I come mighty nigh outgrowin' my gyardeen," said the boy. "If I keep on I'm mortal certain I'll ketch up with her by and by, doctor."

"But you can't step over that three years' gap between us, son," laughed Alicia. "No, sir, he ain't anything but a boy dressed up in men's clothes, Doctor Borin'. Don't you mind his grown-up airs; I'm three years older than him, an' I ain't so *mighty* old, as I can make out. He's jist a boy, doctor, that I'm raisin' to take care of me in my old age. Yonder's grandad."

They were walking in single file up the path to the house. An old man, small, bent and full of lively interest in the world about him, came out to meet them. Behind him, her sunbonnet about her ears, hobbled granny.

"I'm mighty glad to see you," said grandad. "I've been expectin' of you ever since my granddarter Lissy telled me about yer, an' yer fine fixin's down yander. Lissy she sets store by fine fixin's, *an'* so do I, though you needn't tell the old woman. Her face air turned heavenward; but me an' Lissy air toler'ble fond o' 'the pomp an' glory,' ain't we, darter? You-uns air valley-born, my granddarter tells me —come from the town. Well, I'm mount'n, me an' the ole woman. Born an' lived an' might 'a' died thar but for the 'Piscopers. When they took it up we-uns stepped down. But we're mount'n-born. Lissy and Al air valley; tha'r ma was a valley woman. All well yo' way?"

The doctor laughingly told him that he was pretty much all there was "his way," except the servants, the stock and Zip. "The rest of the family," said he, "enjoy their usual good health."

"Glad to hear it," said the miller. "Glad to hear it. We-uns don't appear ter be as thrivin' as common. Al thar is enjoyin' mighty poor health lately; he's aguey, threatened o' chills."

"Needs quinine," said the doctor. "Come to see me, Al, and I will give you a tonic that will set you up in a week."

"Hush," whispered the miller; "don't let the ole woman hear you. She don't believe in such, she's goin' ter live an' die by yerbs an' boneset tea. Thar she air now."

A wrinkled old crone advanced to meet them, peering from under her brown sunbonnet at the visitor. Her face was sharp but not unkind; the same might be said of her voice.

"You air the mad doctor, I reckin," she sang out in her cracked treble. "Well, we air all hearty, thank the Lord. Lissy, run an' fetch a cheer for the mad doctor. Maybe he aims to set a spell."

He "set" until near noon, and when he left it was with a cordial invitation to "come again," and "to be neighborly."

Lissy walked down to the gate to tell him of another case of fever that had broken out in the village of Pelham. She "wondered if there could be any danger of its making its appearance at S'wanee."

He looked up; the mist-wrapped summits frowned defiance to scourge in any form; the tall tops of the trees swayed lightly in the fresh, crisp mountain breeze, itself a tonic to keep at bay the malaria of the lowlands.

"Not up there," said he. "The fever could not live a day up there. That is God's country."

She smiled; a happy, dancing light playing among the deeps of her earnest eyes.

"It air good," she said softly, a caress in the slow-spoken words, the dialect of her grandparents into which she sometimes dropped in her dreamful moods. "It air good an' healthy. I look at it sometimes when the clouds lie low upon it, an' I can only make out the windin's o' the little footpath step by step, an' it seems to me like the hills o' heavin; an' we can only reach the top of it step by step, ever' day. It certainly *do* seem like the hills of heavin." She sighed lightly, and rested her chin upon her hand, her elbow upon the gate, her gaze fixed upon the misty mountain top. "Though," she added after a moment, "I reckin it 'll be a mighty long time befo' I find the hills of heavin so nigh to hand—a mighty long time *if* Brother Barry has the cuttin' of my weddin' garmint. Brother Barry allows I'm give over bodaciously to the *devil*. If, says I, there *be* a devil."

The last sentence was uttered in a whisper, and almost lost in the laugh which accompanied it; a laugh in which the doctor joined as heartily as if the girl had perpetrated some rich joke, rather than scoffed at traditions that were almost as old as the hills towering above the cabin in which she was born. Where, he wondered, had the old-fashioned maiden fallen upon the new heresies?

She was a puzzle to him; he studied the puzzle seriously as he tramped home by the brown footpath. She was a careless, happy girl one moment; the next a serious, earnest woman. She could not be more than sixteen years of age, he thought; she was at the turning, the crisis, where girl and woman meet. Careful, careful; oh, how a hand was needed to shape that beautiful young soul aright! She was full of doubts. Life itself was a wonder, a riddle to her; it was so beautiful, so fresh, so mysterious. Every fibre of soul and body went to meet it, and trembled and thrilled with the strangeness and the sweetness of it. A word, a hint, would fill her soul with richness; and a word or a hint would crush her peace into ruin forever. She would make a grand wife, but she was young yet; sixteen.

The doctor opened his door softly, and entered his bedroom. Upon the old-fashioned dresser stood a small square mirror, with his shaving case lying beside it. He lifted the mirror and carried it to the window; pushed back the white muslin curtain and made a careful study of his face.

"White hair," he said, "may stand for trouble, no less than years. Wrinkles may index sorrow as well as time. And the heart doesn't always keep pace with the body in its race for the grave. Let me see; let me see." He placed the mirror upon the window sill, and stood looking out, his hands clasped behind his neck, his eyes fixed upon, without seeing, the long reddish lane that led to Pelham. "Forty," he mused, "forty-five and sixteen. Sixteen and ten are twenty-six, and ten are thirty-six, and nine are forty-five. Sixteen from forty-five leaves twenty-nine. It *is* 'a gap,' as she said of the three between her brother and herself. Yet"—

A softness stole into the calm blue eyes: a smile of rare content parted his lips. Had he at last found happiness? That will o' the wisp so many have chased in vain, had it come to him in a cabin under the shadow of the mountains? Truth, freshness, innocence, youth; what else could happiness offer? And to say nothing of the possibilities, the hidden aspirations, and the unsuspected strength that were all to be developed. Life turned its rose again to eyes that had looked upon its sombre side. Hers was a nature easily moved; hers a heart ripe for impressions; her soul one that thirsted for truth, *the* truth. How he would love to have the fashioning of that character, the guiding of the elastic young will. It would be a sweet task—a very pleasant task indeed. He was half tempted——

He thought of his friends at home; what would they say? Why, that he was mad, stark. But, he reasoned, it was none of their affairs. He proposed to live his own life in his own way, and after his own best interest, as *he* saw it. A strain of an old poem drifted through his thoughts— a little old song of Browning's. Something had set it jingling in his heart. He repeated it softly, under his breath, the quiet melancholy of his voice lending a charm to the poet's thought:

> The good stars met in your horoscope,
>   Made you of spirit, fire and dew;
> And just because I was thrice as old,
>   And our paths in the world diverged so wide,
> Each was naught to each, must I be told?
>   We were fellow mortals, naught beside?

He was fond of Browning, who threw off the convention-alities, broke out of the traces, so to speak, and spoke his thought in his own brave way. The poet reminded him of a fiery horse which, refusing the bit and spurning alike both chicanery and caress, dies a wild free thing at last, his great spirit breathed upon and breathing in the untamed children he has sired. Doctor Boring was fond of those untamed children of the poet's brain and especially fond of Evelyn Hope. And—*was* he fond of Alicia, that he called her "Evelyn" in that soft voice of his?

(To be continued.)

BOOKS OF THE DAY.

ETIDORHPA, OR THE END OF EARTH.[*]

REVIEWED BY MARGARET CONNOLLY.

The present is an age of expectancy, of anticipation, and of prophecy; and the invention or discovery or production that occupies the attention of the busy world, as it rushes on its self-absorbed way for more than the passing nine days' wonder must needs be something great, indeed. Such a production has now appeared in the literary world in the form of the volume entitled "Etidorhpa, or the End of Earth," the very title of which is so striking as to arrest the attention at once. Of course the reader will at a glance interpret the name backward.

But first a word as to the author of this work, which is destined to be the great literary sensation of the nineteenth century. Prof. John Uri Lloyd, whose name is among the list of the world's great men, occupies the chair of chemistry in the E. M. Institute of Cincinnati, O. He has been awarded the highest honors by the American Pharmaceutical Society and Cincinnati College of Pharmacy, and when, at Berne, Switzerland, it was decided to publish the biographies and portraits of eighty of the world's greatest pharmacists, Professor Lloyd was one the few chosen in America. He is the author of a standard work on pharmaceutic chemistry and of several other scientific works. His reputation in Europe is not less than in his own country, and some of the most noted scientists of England and Germany, after crossing the Atlantic, have visited him for the purpose of examining his famous library, which contains the largest private collection of botanical and pharmaceutical books in the world. The author of such a book as "Etidorhpa," however, might well rest his fame on this single achievement.

In a brief review it is difficult to give any conception of a work which is at the same time scientific, philosophical and metaphysical, yet possessing a weird charm and fascination that is beyond description. It purports to be the story of a man who, in his passionate pursuit of the study of alchemy, was led to forfeit all earth ties—home, family, affection, friends, and all that endears life to man—in order to gain an insight into the mysteries of nature not ordinarily vouchsafed to men. He has committed his marvellous experiences to writing, which, after the lapse of a certain number of years,

---

[*] "Etidorhpa, or the End of Earth," by Prof. John Uri Lloyd. With many illustrations by J. Augustus Knapp. Author's edition. By John Uri Lloyd, Cincinnati, O.

he wishes to publish for the benefit of mankind. With this object
in view, he presents himself one dreary midnight in November,
without the ceremony of knocking or opening a door, before the
astonished vision of one Llewellyn Drury, a student of things scientific and occult, as he sits alone in his library. The weird visitor,
who styles himself "I Am the Man Who Did It," proposes to read
to Llewellyn Drury the story of his adventures in search of knowledge on condition that he will publish the manuscript after thirty
years have passed. The latter agrees to this condition, and promises
to do so, or, failing himself, to get someone else to do it. When
the time comes for the publication of the manuscript, however, he
evades the responsibility and the task is assumed by Prof. John
Uri Lloyd. The ghostly visitor invites criticism and challenges discussion, promising to answer all questions and to prove any disputed
points that Drury may choose to make.

He then proceeds with the story of his wonderful experiences.
Under the guidance of a strange, semi-human being, who is endowed with godlike attributes, albeit rather repulsive in appearance, he is led into the interior of the earth, where he learns all the
mysteries of nature. The formation of the earth is explained by his
guide who proves to him that it is a hollow sphere, having an outer
or upper crust, the plane on which man lives, of about eight hundred miles in thickness. The guide, who is apparently eyeless,
pilots him safely over the inequalities and obstacles in their path.
As they proceed on their journey the darkness in which they were at
first enveloped gives place to a softened, radiant light, which the
guide explains as coming from the modified rays of the sun penetrating through the earth's crust. The nature and causes of volcanoes, the formation of artesian walls, matter and motion and other
mysteries of nature are accounted for, and in many instances on
grounds utterly opposed to all ideas of modern science. The explorers pass through forests of fungi, marvellous in beauty; they partake of strange, delicious foods, produced within the surface of the
earth, which are neither animal nor vegetable nor fruit, yet seem to
partake of the qualities of all. As they proceed on their remarkable journey the Man Who Did It loses his physical attributes
one by one; he no longer needs food to sustain him; he has no
sense of fatigue, and skims on his way like a bird. Scientific
problems are discussed and theories are advanced in regard to questions which are to-day puzzling and bewildering the most learned
scientists; theories which at first sight seem to be but the wild
imaginings of a luxuriant fancy, but which are seemingly proved
in the most logical and scientific way, so that the reader readily
accepts that which if put forth in a dogmatic and authoritative
manner would be scouted by all as opposed to reason and science
and human research.

One cannot but admire the skill with which the author sustains his arguments and his ingenious method of proving his statements in a threefold manner. First, the guide explains in the most lucid way the wonderful earth mysteries to the Man Who Did It; the Man Who Did It reiterates and explains to Llewellyn Drury, who questions and absolutely denies the truth of many of the statements made, which are then proved and demonstrated by actual experiment. The illustrations accompanying these demonstrations are so admirable in detail that even a child can understand the problems dealt with. It is possible that this work may open up a new field to scientific workers, notwithstanding the fact that its author advances his startling theories under cover of fiction, and in a playful rather than a dogmatic or authoritative way.

While there is not a chapter in the book that is not of absorbing interest, some deserve special mention. The chapter dealing with "The Food of Man" is most admirable, and the statement is made that food and drink are not matter, only "carriers of assimilable bits of sunshine," the sun being shown to be the great life-giving energy of the universe. The chapters treating on drunkenness and the drinks of man, showing the awful power of the temptation to drink and the horrors resulting from indulgence, burn themselves into the brain. They are blood-curdling as any of the pictures in Dante's Inferno. The description of the meeting with Etidorhpa, or the vision which appears to the Man Who Did It in the Drunkard's Den, is so exquisite that one cannot help quoting some passages. Preceded by a host of beautiful female forms, she floats before his bewildered gaze, and addresses him in the following words:

"My name is Etidorhpa. In me you behold the spirit that elevates man, and subdues the most violent of passions. In history, so far back in the dim ages as to be known now as legendary mythology, have I ruled and blessed the world. Unclasp my power over man and beast, and while heaven dissolves, the charms of Paradise will perish. I know no master. The universe bows to my authority. Stars and suns enamored pulsate and throb in space and kiss each other in waves of light; atoms cold embrace and cling together; structures inanimate affiliate with and attract inanimate structures; bodies dead to other noble passions are not dead to love. The savage beast, under my enchantment, creeps to her lair, and gently purrs over her offspring; even man becomes less violent, and sheathes his weapon and smothers his hatred as I soothe his passions beside the loved ones in the privacy of his home.

"My name is Etidorhpa; interpret it rightly, and you have what has been to humanity the essence of love, the mother of all that ennobles. He who loves a wife worships me; she, who in turn makes a home happy is typical of me. I am Etidorhpa, the beginning and the end of earth. Behold in me the antithesis of envy, the opposite of malice, the enemy of sorrow, the mistress of life, the queen of immortal bliss.

"Love, by whatever name the conception is designated, rules the world. Divest the cold man of science of the bond that binds him to his life-thought, and his work is ended. Strike from the master in music the chord that links his soul to the voice he breathes, and his songs will be hushed. Deaden the sense of love which the artist bears his art, and as the spirit that underlies his thought-scenes vanishes, his touch becomes chilled and his brush inexpressive. The soldier thinks of his home and country, and without a murmur sheds his life blood.

"And yet there are debasing phases of love, for as love of country builds a nation, so love of pillage may destroy it. Love of the holy and the beautiful stands in human life opposed to love of the debasing and vicious, and I, Etidorhpa, am typical of the highest love of man. As the same force binds the molecules of the rose and the violet as well as those of noxious drugs, so the same soul conception may serve the love of good or the love of evil. Love may guide a tyrant or actuate a saint; may make man torture his fellow, or strive to ease his pain."

The author is imbued with a strong spirit of occultism, which is manifest all through the book, and which is especially apparent in chapter XXXIII, "A Study of Science is a Study of God."

As the Man Who Did It nears the confines of the Beyond or the Unknown Country whither he is bound, his body to all intents and purposes is a mere shell or encumbrance, for he neither eats nor breathes, his heart has ceased to beat, and the necessity of speech between himself and his mysterious guide has long been done away with. Finally they come within sight of the shores of the "Unknown," and a figure in human form is seen standing motionless, awaiting their coming. Here his strange companion leaves him, and our hero passes into the "Beyond."

This work is not alone a literary masterpiece; it is a prophecy, a foreshadowing of the development to which the race may yet attain. It contains thought-germs calculated to revolutionize the world of science, which is wont to be so dogmatic in its purely materialistic views, rejecting as impossible any theory which appears to conflict with certain established laws. Science too often forgets that her mistakes and blunders, even in the recent past, have been as glaring as any of which religion was guilty in a darker age; and many scientists forget that they are still, notwithstanding the marvellous discoveries of the nineteenth century, "like little children, playing on the shores of an infinite ocean, and picking up here and there a pebble." Written by one of the world's greatest scientists, this volume is permeated by a profoundly religious and lofty spirituality, and he pleads that science give room for the development of the soul of man, showing that science and true religion are inseparable. Step by step, in perfect gradation, he leads up to the conclusion that "a true study of science is a study of God," and that the scoffing scientific agnostic and the unquestioning faithful believer will yet meet on common ground.

Of the richness of imagery and wealth of imagination displayed in the pages of Etidorhpa, it is difficult to give any idea. The work is so many-sided that it will appeal to all classes and be a favorite with all. The scientist, the philosopher, the student, the lover of poetry, romance and fiction, will drink in its pages with delight and find infinite food for thought. The diversity of the author's style is such that he has been compared by various critics to such masters as Jules Verne, Dumas, Victor Hugo, Dante.

The plot of the story is supposed to be founded on real events familiar in the minds of many persons yet living. It is not easy to determine where to draw the line between fact and fancy; that is, to determine how much of the work is pure romance and how much the thought resulting from the author's scientific investigations. Be that as it may, this book will stimulate the slowest and quicken the liveliest intelligence.

As a specimen of the bookmaker's art, the work is superb. The illustrations are numerous and of surpassing excellence, conveying as they do to the mind of the reader in the clearest manner the details of the various scenes described by the author.

It is to be regretted that only a limited edition of "Etidorhpa" has been issued, for during this period of unrest and inquiry and reaching out into the unknown, the world has need of the best thought of her wisest and noblest thinkers. It is a work that should have the widest possible circulation, for, rightly interpreted, it will broaden the mind and stimulate to noble endeavor, abounding as it does in thought which sings to the spirit:

"Build thee more stately mansions, O my soul,
    As the swift seasons roll!
    Leave thy low-vaulted past!
Let each new temple, nobler than the last
Shut thee from heaven with a dome more vast,
    Till thou at length art free,
Leaving thine outgrown shell by life's unresting sea!"

FROM DREAMLAND SENT.*

REVIEWED BY B. O. FLOWER.

Miss Whiting's new volume of poems is a fit companion to her wholesome and helpful prose volume, "The World Beautiful." Her verses are pervaded with a fine spiritual atmosphere; a lofty faith, or perhaps I should say a something more positive than faith in the persistence of the soul after the change called death, is at all times present. In many of these lines I have been reminded of the spirit which permeates the poetry of Louise Chandler Moulton, although in Miss Whiting's verses we do not find the sadness present in similar creations of Mrs. Moulton's. I think this spiritual affinity

---

* "From Dreamland Sent," by Lilian Whiting. Cloth; pp. 134; price $1.25. Roberts Brothers, Boston.

in thought will be readily recognized by those familiar with Mrs. Moulton's exquisite lines, after reading this work, especially a number of poems of which the following lines are typical:

Companioned.

Through days and dreams I seem to walk with one
　　Whose feet must shun
Henceforth the paths of earth; for whom the sun
Rises in unknown realms I cannot trace;
And still there is to me no vacant place.
Before me comes upon the air her face.
In the deep, luminous and wondering eyes
I read the rapture of a glad surprise;
A tender hand is clasped within my own,
And on the air there vibrates still her tone.

O friend! on whom the vision shines to-day,
　　What mystic sway
Hath wrought its spell o'er thee? What fair desire,
As o'er that sea of glass with mingled fire
Thy way hath sped—what fair desire
Is born within thy soul? What strange, sweet dreams
Transfigure thy new life, in wondrous gleams
Of rose and gold and pearl, through starry space?
Not vainly do I ask. Thy tender grace
Answers my love, and brings the new life near;
And all our baffled meanings grow more clear.

And the stanzas entitled:

Sometime.

Sometime you'll think of these summer days
Dreamily drifting through purple haze.

Sometime, with a thrill of passionate pain,
You'll long for their sweetness o'er again.

Sometime, when the moonlight is silvering all,
And the pansies sleep by the garden wall,—

In the mystic twilight's odorous dusk,
Freighted with clustering rose-blooms' musk,—

You will watch for a flitting figure there,
White-robed and noiseless, with falling hair.

And gazing deep in the luminous eyes
That made for your life its paradise,—

The silence and music and wonderful calm
Of this magical summer will linger like balm—

Till, starting, you waken to clasp but air,
And list to a flitting footfall there.

Sometime you'll listen in silence lone
For a girlish voice that was all your own;

For words that only to you were given,
Telling of love and the sweetness of heaven.

Sometime you'd give all the wise world's praise
For one of these vanishing summer days.

For just one leaf from the swaying bough,—
Sometime you'd clasp it; oh, why not now?

The volume, while lofty and truly spiritual in atmosphere from cover to cover, is characterized by a pleasing variety in conceptions no less than in treatment. Here is a delightful little conceit:

As in Vision.

Little girl upon the street,
Laughing eyes and tripping feet,
With your hands all running over
Daisy blooms and flowers of clover,
You to me a picture bring
Of a long-lost sunny spring;
Waving woods and sunset skies
Rise like dreams of paradise.

Little girl, when coming days
Hold for you their memories;
When in womanhood's fair land
You shall, haply, one day stand,—
Keep your childish faiths as sweet
As the blossoms at your feet;
Though your hands no more run over
With the daisies and the clover.

Some day, little maiden fair,
With the wind-tossed, sunny hair,
Shall you flush at love's sweet praises,
That are sweeter than the daisies;
Woman's hopes and woman's love,
Sweetness sent by Heaven above,—
With these shall your hands run over,
Dropping daisy blooms and clover.

One of the noblest poems is dedicated to the memory of Phillips Brooks, and from this I make the following extracts:

Ah, where shall we lay our deep sorrow,
How speak of our loss,
That our noblest of friends has been given
The crown for the cross?

Since he, whom we knew but to honor,
To love and revere,
Who brought to all hearts the glad tidings
In messages clear,—

Whose hands, with their pure benediction,
  Uplifted in prayer,
Were our pledge of the Saviour's direction,
  His guidance and care,—

Since he, our pastor and helper,
  So tenderly dear,
Has gone to the Wonderful Country
  That lieth so near!

And now, in the hush of the morning,
  In its silence and calm,
We would gather a few leaves of healing,
  For sorrow a balm.

Our friend—full of gifts and of honors,
  Of rare culture and grace,
Of sweetness and faith that no other
  Can hope to replace—

Has fought the good fight, and has entered
  The rest that God gave;
And the lives he has blessed bring the tribute
  We lay on his grave.

For all, in his presence uplifting,
  Were exalted and cheered;
And virtue seemed more to be cherished,
  And sin to be feared.

*   *   *   *   *

Oh, still, from that life thou hast entered,
  Behold us, we pray!
Vouchsafe still to guide and direct us,
  And teach us the Way.

May we feel that ever upon us
  Are the vows of the Lord;
May our lives be more worthy thy teaching,
  And show forth God's word.

From these quotations our readers will perceive that this is a volume of verses of superior excellence. It merits wide reading, and its influence cannot fail to quicken the spiritual sensibilities and uplift the reader. At a time like the present such works as "The World Beautiful" and "From Dreamland Sent" are of special value, for in transition periods it is of paramount importance that while justice, freedom, liberty and progress are firmly insisted upon, we awaken man on the spiritual instead of the animal side of his being. Then, again, while the thought-waves of the world are being so profoundly stirred, sensitive minds call for literature whose influence is at once soothing and uplifting. This last volume will materially add to the already brilliant reputation of its talented author.

THE LAND OF THE MUSKEG.*

REVIEWED BY B. O. FLOWER.

I have seldom been so agreeably surprised in a book as in this volume, which describes in a charmingly direct and candid manner the story of an expedition across the great swamps or muskegs of western British America, a region which was in part explored by Mr. Dawson in 1879, but which, for the most part, is only familiar to the Indian tribes and a few half-breeds. On the maps this vast expanse is indicated as "good land," and works describing this section of British America are actual Baron Munchausen tales when they attempt to show the plenitude or bear, moose, beaver, and other kinds of game. It was these alluring descriptions, together with the desire to penetrate a vast region of British possessions which was practically unexplored and a love for the freedom which Nature gives to those who break away from the trammels and the comforts of civilization, which led Mr. Somerset and his friend, Mr. Arthur H. Pollen, to undertake a tramp across this uncivilized region of our continent. In being able to purchase whatever was needed, Mr. Somerset enjoyed an advantage which few explorers have experienced; while, on the other hand, I remember no instance where a traveller only nineteen years of age has displayed the sturdy qualities of our ancestors under the most trying circumstances as did young Mr. Somerset during the long, weary tramp through vast, dismal swamps and trackless forests.

In this expedition the youthful traveller found that the expected game was conspicuous chiefly by its absence, while millions of mosquitoes and the dreaded bulldog fly made life miserable. Rain fell almost incessantly until the weather grew extremely cold; and this cold found the little party without food and reduced to such extremity that they had at length to shoot and eat one of their pack horses to sustain life. Such were some of the experiences of our author; yet a delightful spirit of wholesome, sturdy, healthy youth pervades the volume, which is surpassingly well written, when one remembers the writer to be in his minority.

The diction is excellent, and a spirit of candor pervades the work, which is most delightful and draws the reader very close to the author. It is good to find an absence of all artificiality and an honest frankness in viewing all things described. We have seen so much of shallowness, so much of insincerity and intrigue among the scions of wealthy families and have so often been disgusted at the spectacle presented by the fortune hunters of European aristocracy, who constantly visit our shores in search of the purses of the daughters of the few, who, through unearned increment,

* "The Land of the Muskeg," by H. Somers Somerset; with four maps and over one hundred illustrations, printed on heavy plate paper, handsomely bound in cloth, stamped in black and gold. Price $4. J. B. Lippincott & Company, Philadelphia; William Heinemann, London.

class laws, special privileges, and gambling, have acquired the millions which in justice largely belong to society and the wealth creators, that to find a young man of the order of Mr. Somerset is delightful. Of course I know that his noble-minded mother would desire her son to evince that superb loyalty to conscience and sturdiness of character that mark true manhood, but which are so frequently absent among the children of wealth. But sons are by no means always what their mothers desire them to be, and I feared that this work would be disappointing in more ways than one. In point of fact, it is one of the most entertaining volumes of travel I have read within the past few years. The narration is constantly relieved by the introduction of matter which gives variety and interest to the work, and the general observations are, I think, eminently practical.

Mr. Somerset regards as extremely unwise the action of the Church of England in sending missionaries to convert the Indians, who have for generations been converted to Christianity as much as their nature is capable of being converted by Catholic missionaries. Moreover, he shows how the hard-earned money of many who contribute to missionary work for the heathen sometimes is largely employed for the comfort of the wolf in sheep's clothing who acts as missionary. A case in point which he cites is so suggestive and striking that I give it below:

John Gough Brick was standing at the door of his house when we rode up. He wore a large pair of moccasins on his feet, blue overalls covered his legs, surmounted by a long black frockcoat, a grey flannel shirt and a celluloid collar. Mr. Brick was kindness itself, entertaining us with a jovial hospitality that was past praise, and with a fund of Rabelaisian anecdote marvellous in its steady volume. I have heard that he has gained for himself quite a reputation as a *raconteur* in this particular line. And there can be no doubt that few ministers of the Church of England have so full and varied a vocabulary of purely secular language.

He has a large farm near the river, which, as he told me, had been started as a school of agriculture for the Indians. The game is fast disappearing from the country, and unless the natives are taught to raise crops and till the land, they will undoubtedly starve. But as Mr. Brick boisterously observed, "I don't allow any of those damned Indians around *my* place." He has not even a rudimentary knowledge of the language of his congregation, and so would be quite unable to preach in the native tongue, even if he had a mind to. But he has resided at the Mission for some years, and he told me quite seriously that "he knew the Cree for bread."

The mission is, I believe, not financed by the Church of England Missionary Society, although the Bishop of Athabaska retains his hold over the place, which will return to the Society upon the death or retirement of the present occupant.

Mr. Brick is, without doubt, a most capable and energetic farmer, but he has, of course, no market for his produce, and so, although he can almost make a living by his own industry, he cannot make sufficient to carry on the good work amongst the heathen (*i. e.*, Catholie). Accordingly, from time to time he makes pilgrimages to England and there collects funds. If this gentlemen appeared in the old country saying: "I am an excellent farmer; I am a pioneer in a savage land; I am an honest man, who works to support a wife and family; my life is hard, but I am opening up a new centre for immigration," no one could have anything to say against the proceeding, although Mr. Brick might not acquire as much money as he does at present. But when one thinks of the needy people, who with many a struggle have subscribed their pittance that poor savages may gain knowledge and hear the gospel, the case alters considerably. For my own part, I believe that more good might be done nearer home by the outlay of the same money; and to me it seems particularly absurd to keep ministers of religion in a foreign land simply to convert the remnants of a dying race to Protestantism, when the Catholics have already made them about as Christian as they are capable of being.

I have long felt that if our Christian people would address themselves first to the crying abuses and the injustice at home, and strive to abolish the slums of our cities, to establish happiness through securing fundamental justice, insisting on more of the Sermon on the Mount in life here and now; in a word, if Christian nations would first remove the beam from their own eye, they would be doing better work than donating princely sums for foreign missions while vast numbers of our people are ignorant, naked, and depraved who might and could be lifted to a higher and happier plane of life.

Here is a vivid description of the Cree Indians, together with one of their popular legends:

The Cree Indians are, for the most part, dark, spare men, showing many of the usual characteristics of the aborigines of the continent, but of peaceful disposition and great charm of manner. They speak an exceedingly beautiful language, and converse with ease and fluency, pronouncing their words with wonderful distinctness, and showing their meaning with many well-considered gestures. Their chief topic of conversation is naturally hunting, for by this they gain their living, but they seem also to be very fond of tale-telling, and now and again one may hear legends and fables from the older men, which speak of the times when the game was more plentiful in the country, and consequently men had more time for talk. I have set down two such tales here, as I think they may be of interest. The first recalls the Welsh story of Gelert, and one would be curious to know if it is current amongst other peoples. Thus runs the tale:

There was once a young man who was very poor; his father and mother and all his relations had been killed in a raid, and he was left alone in the world with no friend but his faithful dog. So he journeyed for many days, picking up a living as best he could. One day he came to the lodge of an "Oukimow" or big chief. Now this chief had everything that he could possibly want—fine clothes, many wives, and the most beautiful cooking pots. But above all he had a lovely daughter. This lucky man had a bow which was enchanted. Whatever he shot at with his arrows died, so he had always plenty of meat hanging in his camp, and no one dared quarrel with him, for if they did, they were sure to be killed. The mystery of the bow was a secret, but the great man's daughter had learned it from her father, and now she told it to this young man who had become her lover. But the chief found this out, so he drove him away, and again he wandered, thinking of the lovely girl, and full of rage at her father's treatment. One day when he was asleep under a birch-tree he was awakened by the Old Wanderer*—the cunning one—who asked him what service he could render him. So he told his story, saying that he was very anxious to kill the big Chief of the Bow, in order that he might marry his daughter, but that he knew he could not prevail against the magic weapon, and therefore he had not tried. Now the Wanderer knew all things, and he told him that the spell was broken since the tale of the bow had been told, and that he might safely go and kill his enemy. However, he said that he would make the matter certain, and provide the young man with another magic bow. So he told him to "cut down the birch-tree and make from it a bow and arrow, and make a bow-string from the fibres of the bark; and when you have done this," he said, "call me." The young man made the weapon and the string, and called. And the Wanderer came and spoke the magic word, and gave the bow to the young man, telling him that the arrow would hit whatever he fired at, but that he was only to use it once against his enemy. So the young man went and slew the "Oukimow," and became the chief of the tribe, and married the girl, and owned the fine clothes and beautiful cooking pots.

In his new greatness he became very haughty. So the "Wanderer" appeared and told him to go and do honor to the birch-tree; but he was proud and did not do it, saying that no harm would come. After a while a son was born to him. And the whole tribe feasted, and he said to his people, "Let us go and honor the birch-tree." And they all went. But instead of doing it honor he took a whip and lashed it, making the marks which may be seen upon the bark to this day. Then came the "Wanderer" a third time, and told him that his son was dead because of his sin. He hastened home and saw his dog standing over the cradle covered with blood. Then he was wild with rage and shot at the dog with his magic bow; and the arrow flew and killed the dog, but pierced his son as well, and he came and saw many dead wolves around the cradle, and realized that his faithful dog had protected the child, and that he had lost his son through disobedience to the laws of the "Cunning One."

The following description of an Indian sweat bath is interesting, and will further serve to illustrate the style of our author:

And thus, with many struggles and pantings, we reached the higher ground, and pushed forward through a fairly open country. Once during the day we came upon a deserted Indian camp. From the condition of the ashes and other signs we judged that it was not more than two weeks old. There had evidently been a sick man in the party, for the remains of a sweating-house were still standing. It is made after this manner: Many small branches are stuck in the ground in a circle, and the extremities and twigs are plaited together so as to form a kind of roof. Blankets are then thrown over the whole, and the patient creeps in and sits down upon the floor.

---

* This "Wanderer" appears many times in Indian legend. He seems to be an evil spirit with a strong tendency towards good. Thus he will benefit some unlucky person and yet be called "the evil and cunning one" by the narrator.

Meanwhile large stones have been heated in a fire, and these are passed into the hut by the man's friends, whilst he pours water upon them, and so makes a steam under the blanket. After a while the heat must become almost unendurable, but the process is continued until the unfortunate patient can stand it no longer, and is forced through sheer exhaustion to emerge from his Turkish bath. Whether this cure is beneficial in the treatment of the various diseases to which Indians are subject, I am unable to say, but they all place great faith in its healing powers."

And here is a description of a camping experience which will be more pleasant to the reader than it was to the explorer:

Once we had a really fine day, and made our camp in the evening in high spirits, for the sky was cloudless and the night still. We were so sure of the weather that we did not even unfurl the tent or stretch the fly, but made our beds where we pleased, and turned in under the shelter of some magnificent trees, confident of a good rest after our day's work. About one o'clock in the morning, however, it began to rain in torrents, and did not stop until midday. It had been so dark that we could not find our tent roll, and therefore we had returned to our blankets and slowly became soaked. I think I have seldom passed a more miserable night. I had a waterproof sheet under my bedding, and on getting up found that it had most inconveniently held the water, and that I was surrounded by a pool six inches deep.

It is a common fact that in all ages and among all people some members have been gifted with occult powers, such as clairvoyance, prevision, or clairaudience. Others may be present who have neither eyes, ears, nor consciousness to recognize that which comes to the sensitive when this strange, supernormal experience comes to him. Socrates had his demon or spirit; to Catherine of Siena her visions and voices were as real as the bread she ate; to the wonderful Maid of Orleans her angel visitors and communications were so real that they transformed the bashful peasant child into the most successful warrior of her time. Yet these gifts, if I may call them such, come to civilized and savage alike, and are most likely to appear where the spirit of arrogance and dogmatism are absent, and when people have not been taught to believe by self-sufficient authority that such things are *impossible*. A curious and interesting case of prevision is thus related by Mr. Somerset as having been experienced by John, a half-breed who was a member of their party:

John suddenly turned towards us and said, "Gentlemen, we shall meet three Beaver Indians to-morrow on the river." Of course we all imagined that he was joking, but Round told us that whenever John prophesied the coming of strangers he was always right. He said he had known him for close upon fourteen years, and that he had never made a mistake about this. The most of us were incredulous, thinking that the whole thing was absurd; but John stuck to it that he was right, and that we should see on the morrow.

On the following day we scattered through the country in search of meat. Daukhan and I had started towards the river, intending to ford the stream on horseback, and then leave our animals and hunt to the right of the camp, when we were joined by Round and John, who also wished to cross the river and hunt to the left. The river was very rapid and the stones slippery, so that the horses stumbled and lurched in the swift water in a manner not very pleasant to the rider. When we reached the southern shore we tethered our horses and were on the point of starting into the bush when we saw something moving on the river some distance further down. We waited, and presently a canoe came round the point. Now it must be remembered that since we left Dunvegan, nearly two months before, we had not seen a single human being, and this made John's prophecy the more extraordinary, for there had been nothing to show that we should meet these Indians. John himself showed no surprise at seeing them, but simply remarked that he knew they were coming, and was glad they had arrived. He afterwards told me that he had not always possessed this gift of second-sight, but that he had had it since the death of his infant daughter some fifteen years before. He said that he was upon an island on the Peace River, twenty miles from Dunvegan, when one afternoon something told him that his child was dead, and that a man was coming to him in a canoe to break the news. After a few hours the man came, and ever since then he had always known when he was going to meet any one, and from which direction they would come. He added that sometimes people came when he had no presentiment; but when he had the presentiment they were sure to come. Whilst he was talking the canoe had approached, so we went down to the water's edge and signalled to the Indians to come ashore. They proved to be Beaver Indians, three in number, as John had foreseen—a young man, his wife and mother.

The Beaver Indians are described as being very different from the Crees, the former having made little progress in the way of civilization. In referring to them, Mr. Somerset says:

Fifty years ago the Indians of the Northwest were in the stone-hatchet period. Many of the tribes have made extraordinary mental strides in so short a time, but there has been little progress among the Beavers, so that one comes across the anomaly of a man with a primitive, stone-implement-period mind, carrying in his hand that product of centuries of thought—the Winchester rifle. His ideas and wants are expressed in a series of chucks and grunts, and he is careful to move his lips as little as possible in speaking. It would be impossible to shout in his language. He uses primitive gestures, pointing to mountains or trees when he speaks of them, and signifying the departure of an animal or person by throwing out his hand before him.

Somers Somerset may well feel proud of his work, both as traveller and author, and I shall be surprised if this gifted young man does not make an illustrious place for himself in whatever field of work he selects, as he has evinced the qualities of sturdy manhood and that daring spirit which, when controlled by judgment and conscience, contributes much toward enduring success. As I have observed, one of the great charms of this volume lies in the candor and frankness everywhere displayed; and the evident simplicity of life, as opposed to the feverish artificiality of present-day life, adds to my conviction that the author has a brilliant future before him.

The book is handsomely printed in large type, and the maps are excellent. I regret to say, however, that the pictures in many instances are very poor, and I think the work would have been more attractive if at least one-third of these illustrations had been omitted. They are frequently small and so indistinct as to be valueless. Had the publishers had them photographed, enlarged, retouched and strengthened the effect would have been far different, and the volume would have been a fine example of the triumph of the printer's art.

POLITICS AND PATRIOTISM.*

REVIEWED BY E. H. WILSON.

The author of this important work is a practical man of affairs. In the fulfilment of his duty as a citizen, he was brought into conflict with the ring that has dominated the city of Baltimore for more than twenty years. After having thus gained full knowledge of the iniquities of ring rule, he conceived the idea of setting forth the causes of municipal corruption and suggesting remedies for prevalent abuses. By depicting the real features of the iniquitous rule he hoped to make the misuse of power so repugnant to respectable citizens that these would rise in their might and put an end to bossism in city politics. But further reflection caused him to believe that to secure a permanent improvement in municipal government something must be done to awaken the patriotism of the people so that citizens should feel it a duty to meet faithfully every obligation resting upon them in the exercise of their civic functions. He therefore decided to widen the scope of his work and study "politics not as a science, but as a civic duty": for political activity as a civic duty and the cultivation of patriotism he rightly deems "as essential to the welfare of our country and to the well-being of its citizens as the acquirement of scientific knowledge or familiarity with philosophic dogmas." Hence in his own words, "The purpose of this work is to advocate the true principles of popular government, to counsel the employment of honesty and intelligence under all conditions in the administration of government, and to advise the application of those rules of justice which must extend equality to all before the law, and thereby promote that patriotism, that unselfish love of country, which is the sole foundation upon which republics are built."

It will thus appear that our author will not think his effort

---

* "Politics and Patriotism," by Frederick W. Schultz. Pp. 496; price, cloth $1.25, paper 50 cents. The Arena Publishing Company, Boston, Mass.

crowned with success until he sees the consummation of the ideal state so graphically described by Burke in these words: "All persons possessing any portion of power ought to be strongly and awfully impressed with an idea that they act *in trust*, and that they are to account for their conduct in that trust to the one great Master, Author, and Founder of society. . . . They who administer in the government of men, in which they stand in the person of God Himself, should have high and worthy notions of their function and destination. Their hope should be full of immortality."

Though conscious of his own indifferent equipment in scholarship to treat worthily the larger theme, he yet resolutely makes the attempt, trusting that his endeavor and the facts presented may prompt some trained writer of ample learning to undertake a work of the first importance in morals as well as in politics. He writes with the strength and assurance of a man thoroughly conversant with the facts wherewith he illustrates his points. He has consulted the best authorities and cites them freely in support of his argument. And it is easy to believe that this volume will be more widely read and more productive of good than if it were a profoundly philosophical treatise elaborately wrought in plan and detail by a scholar of great erudition. Some of his ringing sentences remind one of that noble passage in which Cicero asserts that love of country is a holier and deeper love than that for our nearest kinsman and that no one has any claim to the name of a good man who even hesitates to die in its behalf.* Indeed, it is difficult to understand how the author could use less forcible terms since he is persuaded that the careless indifference with which many of the best and most law-abiding men neglect their civic duties threatens to imperil our republican form of government; and he is strong in the belief that "Patriotism is the foundation on which is built a nation's strength and greatness."

Consequently the author makes three general divisions of his theme; and assigns about half the volume to "The Republican Era," and nearly a fourth to each of the others—"The Era of Injustice" and "The Era of Corruption." In the first part he passes in review some of the political advantages enjoyed under our government and the benefits derived, and also illustrates abuses that weaken its democratic features. Some of his sub-heads are: Growth of Democratic Ideas; Political Development; The Nature of Patriotism; Political Education; The Duty of the People; Municipal Elections; Socialism and Progress; Iniquity of Protection; Ownership of Industries by Government; Labor and Capital; Triumph of Selfishness; Taxation and Disbursement. Mr.

---

* Cari sunt parentes, cari liberi, propinqui, familiares; sed omnes omnium caritates patria una complexa est, pro qua quis bonus dubitet mortem oppetere si ei sit profuturus?

Schultz holds that protective-tariff legislation is class legislation and therefore unconstitutional; and he boldly asserts that "free trade is the wedded consort of a free government." His exposure of "the iniquity of protection" is illustrated by the following paragraph:

The forced tribute demanded by protection bears upon every one dwelling under our government from the infant in the cradle to the aged man tottering upon the verge of the grave; and even the corpse does not escape until covered by mother earth. The single man feels the burden least of all; the man of family suffers the exaction in proportion to the number of those whom he is compelled to support. And here again, the man whose fecundity enriches and strengthens government is punished for his good offices; while the selfish or the delinquent citizen, who by celibacy or violation of the laws of nature makes no addition to the nation's strength, is rewarded by a lighter infliction. The man that takes upon himself the cares of matrimony, at the very beginning of this useful career, finds his efforts clogged by these obscure influences; and as children come to the household, the burden inflicted by government is proportionately increased although, if he be a workingman, his salary or wages are most likely to remain stationary. Of course, with increase of family increased normal expenses must occur under any system; but the injustice of the protective system is apparent, because of the increased fine unnecessarily placed upon him with the advent of every child, and the certainty that the fine is to be used to multiply the wealth of a more fortunate and already wealthy neighbor.

His stand against socialism is equally uncompromising:

The development of enlightened government teaches that democracy is the inspiration of progress. Socialism as revealed by its objects stands convicted the enemy of freedom. Democracy expands, socialism circumscribes. Democracy is the general and judicious exercise of the distinct elements of will; its strength exists in patriotism and industry. Socialism is the enemy of development, a leveler of aspiration, an invitation to sloth, and a destroyer of all our higher ideals. Unless patriotism assumes a broader sway the coming century will witness a battle royal between the two principles for supremacy in government.

Paternalism in all its varied forms he abhors, for "General welfare can be promoted only when government exercises its legitimate functions,—those which are expressed in our basic law." Hence, agreeably to the principles of a "strict constructionist," he resolutely sets his face against that "class of philosophers whose brains are pregnant with deformed ideas" that produce "a progeny of isms" as follows:

That government has higher duties than to govern; that the people's economic welfare is of more importance than their political fate; and, stretching their theories still further, that the question of individual advantage is more to be considered than the question of national prosperity. Out of distorted views of the relation of government to the individual has grown the shame of civilization, anarchy. And out of the equally mistaken idea that government owes debts to the people other than that of governing justly, impartially, honestly, and economically has grown the impossibility of socialism.

The author regards "labor leaders" as criminals equally with the political boss, because while ostensibly working to promote the interests of the people, they in reality are selfishly intent on securing advantages for themselves. And this deplorable state of affairs will continue until respectable and self-respecting men adequately fulfil their obligations as citizens. Until then we may expect a diminution of the sum of morality in the community, rule in the hands of professed politicians whom no one trusts or ignorant fanatics whose exploitation or mismanagement of affairs cannot fail to make the judicious grieve; for meantime the toilers whose daily bread depends on the labor of their hands find no help, no comfort, no relief. But however gloomy the future may look, however disheartening the despondent may find the prognostics, it shows not saneness of mind to accept pessimistic conclusions. Rather should brave, sincere souls find hope in the noble words nobly phrased by a distinguished statesman, patriot, and scholar of the last century: "A man, full of warm, speculative benevolence, may wish society otherwise constituted than he finds it; but a good patriot and a true politician always considers how he shall make the most of the existing materials of his country. A disposition to *preserve*, and an ability to *improve*, taken together, would be my standard of a statesman. Everything else is vulgar in the conception, perilous in the execution."

In the second part—"The Era of Injustice"—the author discusses taxation under various sub-heads, some of which are these: Inequality in Taxation; Present Method of Assessment entirely Wrong; Single Tax upon Land; Single Tax upon Incomes the only Just Tax; How Wealth Should Be Considered; Retaxing the same Articles; Insurance by Cities Profitable.

Government goes half way in insuring property by organizing a fire department, says the author, and he thinks it might properly complete the insurance of property to the benefit of owners and of the public treasury. As cities furnish an abundant supply of water, so they may logically insure against fire.

The author illustrates the inequity of double taxation; he argues against a single land tax and in favor of a single income tax—not, however, a graduated income tax, which he regards as unjust. He supports his contention that "An income tax fairly assessed would be in point of justice the least exceptional of all taxes" by citations from J. S. Mill and Prof. R. T. Ely. He brushes aside as of little force Mill's doubt regarding the possibility of collecting the tax in "the present low state of public morality," in the belief that if people had the conviction forced home upon them that an equal and equitable system of taxation was applied to all without favor or discrimination, respect for government would be increased, patriotism fostered, and consequently a growing disposition among all to bear each his just part of the expense of maintaining government. The entire revenue should be derived from the income tax and a tax levied on intoxicating liquors. No other tax should be laid, and in assessing property for purposes of taxation, wealth should always be considered:

1. With respect to its income-producing power. 2. With respect to its stability or continued power for producing income. 3. With respect to its known income-producing power, where it is not actively exercised but is permitted to remain passive for comfort, pleasure, convenience, or future gain. By this method all wealth would be valued and assessed according to the income that it produced by active exercise or by passive increment, or, better and plainer still, the actual and indicated income could be taxed; it would thus become only a matter of figures, to arrive at an absolutely just sum which each would be called upon to pay, and there would be no excessive and unequal burden for any one to lament over, nor insufficient amounts to cause others to exult; all would be treated alike.

Furthermore, inasmuch as this system of taxation would increase the sum of morality, it should be received with favor by Christians.

It is Christianlike and just to have a due regard for the morals of the people. Any scheme of taxation, if fair and equitable, which would keep man from indulging in his natural inclination to sin, would be the proper one to adopt. But can this be found? Thus far there is little probability of reaching the desired end. Therefore that system which presents the least incentive to untruth should commend itself to the Christian. The income tax, properly administered, presents this feature, because it imposes proportionately equal burdens upon all, and does not become a charge upon debt or misfortune.

To make taxation less burdensome, it is proposed that the taxpayer should be permitted to pay his tax in instalments at his convenience. The matter of interest could be adjusted when the last payment was made.

The author attributes the prevalent unrest and discontent to class legislation favoring certain industries, corporations, trusts, etc., at the expense of the masses; and to unequal and unjust taxation. He would remove this unrest and discontent by means that have been described already in this review. It is unnecessary to repeat them.

When taxation shall have been readjusted so that it shall rest on a just and stable foundation, the patriotic ardor of the people will be augmented and they will then duly perform every civic duty, demagogues will perish off the face of the earth, political rings and bosses will be relegated to a limbo, large and broad perhaps but yet far from bliss, and labor leaders will cease to dupe their deluded followers. Whether this "deep, halcyon repose" from schemes of unscrupulous politicians will be witnessed on the hither side of that bourn whence "no traveller returns," the sceptical will doubt; but it hardly admits of doubt that the duties and responsibilities of citizenship should command the serious thought of those who are too busy with their own affairs to take heed lest the state suffer harm. Many who cannot accept the author's conclusions will yet thank him for writing so valuable a book in the interest of a patriotism that places country before party. And who shall say that the intelligent and the educated by their silence, inactivity, and apparent acquiescence in the abuses that Mr. Schultz holds up for condemnation do not deserve to have their neglect of duty characterized in even stronger terms than he chooses to employ?

Part third has to do with municipal corruption. The author's "familiarity with it and his practical knowledge of its vicious tendencies lead him to believe that it is the one evil which must be utterly abolished if we expect patriotism to live and our republic to be preserved." On this subject the author thinks that he can speak with authority, for he has studied the question in all its phases that he might the better fight the ring in his native city. He declares that he speaks with full knowledge whereof he affirms, and he copiously illustrates and enforces his assertions by facts which he has himself witnessed. He shows that his own city is not singular in its sufferings from ring domination, by calling attention to the situation in many other cities. He shows that efforts for reform have not resulted in permanent improvement because of their spasmodic nature, and the partisan spirit of even the most respectable portion of the community. He is so impressed by the hold partisanship has even on those who alone can effect a permanent reform that he would make James Russell Lowell's apothegm, "The highest privilege to which the majority of mankind can aspire is that of being governed by those wiser than they," read: "The highest privilege to which those endowed with civic rights aspire is that of being governed by those shrewder and generally more depraved than they."

The author strikes the axe at the root of the evil when he says that a municipality should be conducted according to business principles, and inveighs against the practice of carrying on a city campaign with sole reference to the supposed interests of the two great parties in state and nation. So long as men whose conscience would unmercifully sting them for the slightest lapse of decency, or the merest approach to dishonor, openly and boastingly wear the livery of rings, and applaud and defend their rule and acts, because they are promoting the interests of their party, just so long will it be impossible to purge municipal government of rascality, venality and criminality.

The "boss" is vividly portrayed in all his repulsiveness. And a rough scheme for the reconstruction of primaries and safeguarding them by law, which the author thinks will strip the "boss" of his power, is offered for consideration. How the proposed scheme would work I am not prepared to say, but I see no hope for better things until city elections are separated from state and national elections by the longest possible interval of time. If city officials were elected in seasons of political rest in state and nation, the needs of the city and the character of the candidates might receive proper attention, and the result of the election might show that citizens were interested in choosing the best men.

The volume is valuable as a presentation of the views of one who has had unusually favorable opportunities for discovering the motives that actuate the political boss whose domination works so disastrously to the weal of the community and to the fair fame of the city; and it will no doubt be regarded as an important contribution to the discussion of the subject. Some of the author's generalizations seem too sweeping for general acceptance. Many will not be able to concur in his unqualified assertion that "Popular opinion is always a sure gauge of the justice of a measure"; and when they recall such outbursts of popular fury as followed the ratification of Jay's treaty, for example, they will prefer to coincide in the view expressed by a shrewd New Englander when he said to a distinguished exile, "Remember, sir, that everything great and excellent is in minorities." It is the opinion of the "saving remnant" that exalts a nation, and only when the people follow their lead is there much truth in the saying, *vox populi, vox dei.*

The usefulness of the book would be much enhanced, at least for busy men, if the author had provided a suitable index, and it is to be hoped that this lack will be supplied in future editions.

BEAUTY FOR ASHES.*

Reviewed by Julia A. Dawley.

"In all that has been said, written or thought about the souls of the departed," says the author of this singular little book, "it seems to be conceded that when the body dies, the souls of the faithful take up their abode in heaven and are at rest for all eternity. But the others, what of them? . . . To all these questions the answers are all speculation. . . . When they escape or depart from the body then it is possible that they are borne about this revolving earth by restless winds, until, as air rushes in to fill the vacuum made by lightning, the wandering soul steps into the first resting place it can find."

---

* "Beauty for Ashes," by Kate Clark Brown. Beacon Series. Pp. 120; cloth 75 cents, paper 25 cents. Arena Publishing Company.

This theory of wandering souls seeking reëmbodiment in order to perform some unfinished work, to make reparation for wrongdoing, or worse still, to carry out some plan of vengeance or mischief, is by no means new. It has been taught for untold ages, but like many teachings of the kind, only in a semi-private way and mentioned with bated breath as a grewsome possibility, not a reasonable probability. But latterly, as the French say, "we have changed all that." There seems all at once to be a flood of literature good, bad and indifferent turned loose upon the reading world, all full of these hitherto occult speculations and teachings. "The time of making known has come," the masters are said to have declared; a call has gone out for books setting forth in every possible way in order to catch the notice and hold the attention of all sorts of readers the lesson that—

"The dead alone *are* living—
And the living alone *are* dead."

"The thing that hath been, it shall be"; the inevitable law of Karma, unchangeable as God and no less just, must be fulfilled by every soul sometime, somehow, somewhere; and finally, Love is the greatest thing on earth, the Secret of Life, and only unselfish devotion which seeketh not its own and never faileth can bring beauty for ashes into a blighted life. Such is the decree.

The little book which is the subject of this notice brings out all these lessons in a pleasing way, taking up the earth life of a wandering spirit still held close to the earth by her own misdeeds done "in the form," as mediums say. She finds a medium in an innocent child-wife, loving, pure and unselfish, and when the child, Lorris, is born in a terrific, howling storm and the young mother's soul set free, the reëmbodiment of Ray Lorris Cameron begins. The story is well told, the action is never tiresome, and the end is a happy one, even though it is at a deathbed.

He staggered to his feet and looked down with dazed eyes. It was Ray that lay there dead, with Lorris' gentle smile upon her face.
"The thing that hath been," he murmured, "it is that which shall be."

HIS PERPETUAL ADORATION.*

REVIEWED BY B. O. FLOWER.

In his latest work Dr. Forbes Winslow, member of the Royal College of Physicians, London, and physician to the British Hospital of Mental Disorders, observes that "Something more potent than the mere intellectual culture is required to be put in force for the

* " His Perpetual Adoration: or, The Captain's Old Diary," by Rev. Joseph F. Flint, author of " In Potiphar's House." Price, paper 50 cents, cloth $1.25. Arena Publishing Company, Boston, Mass.

purpose of regulating the conduct of a respectable being with a free will, like man, safely across the stormy sea of life from birth to death. The moral senses alone touch the relationships of life. The intellectual is manifestly subordinate to the spiritual."

This tremendous truth has been so thoroughly ignored in education, in literature, and in home training that it, probably more than anything else, is responsible for the deplorable condition of affairs which meets the conscientious student of human life on every side. There is a manifest lack of appreciation for the eternal verities; a torpidity of conscience which leads to the most unfortunate results. In "His Perpetual Adoration: or, The Captain's Old Diary," the Rev. Joseph F. Flint, who is a strict orthodox clergyman and who at times goes far beyond my own views in regard to the religious sentiments expressed, has done a splendid work in the way of awakening conscience and giving to thoughtful people a psychological work. There are innumerable writers at the present time who are giving the world productions elegantly finished and well nigh faultless in literary style, but which exert no moral influence upon the reader.

Mr. Flint tells a plain straightforward story. He is a clergyman rather than a purely literary writer, hence in some respects his work lacks in literary finish, but this is more than made up in the strong moral atmosphere which pervades the book. It is a story of our late civil war, told in diary form, but unlike the numerous stories which have flooded the market in recent years and which deal with the exterior aspects of the war rather than with the interior workings of the brain, it concerns itself little with the outward show although there are two or three graphic descriptions of scenes in our late civil war related in a vivid and stirring manner. The great charm of the work lies in its being a psychological study. It is an appeal to the moral nature of the reader; it is in fact a diary of a soldier in which are revealed the inner thoughts, which are so seldom given to the public and in which we are able to enter the holiest of holies of the human soul and see its struggles and temptations; the struggles and temptations of the lower nature surrounded by the environments of camp life which are so demoralizing to many sensitive natures. Fortunately for the "captain" there was in his case, a noble, pure-minded girl at home whose words, no less than her thought and atmosphere, which ever environed him, rescued him in the most perilous moments of his career. The world to-day is hungering for books which appeal to the conscience or the moral side of man's nature. Indeed, the salvation of the race depends largely upon works which will awaken the spiritual side of our being. Perhaps it would be impossible to get a better idea of the purpose of the author than by making a few brief quotations from his preface which I give below:

Let it be said at once, that it is because most people live the life of the flesh that they find Venus and Bacchus so attractive. They live for the immediate present, and that means for the fleeting and the sensual.

The life of the spirit is already intensely interesting and highly prized by all who know by personal experience of its supreme blessedness. Granted the inner preparation of mind and heart, then anything short of whitest purity is absolutely vapid and repellent. It is altogether a question of appreciation; the aristocracy of moral culture has never had any trouble to decide what is truly fascinating and worthy. The only question worth considering is, Can the majority of mankind be induced to appreciate the best, and eventually come to live the life of the spirit? We believe they can. We believe the time is coming when men will turn with unspeakable loathing from the gross and carnal (as a finality), and cling with joy to the elevated and, therefore, permanent advantages of chastity.

Next must be mentioned the appeal to manhood. Is it manly to betray the innocent and then forsake them? Is it the part of true manhood to starve the higher nature and pander to the baser instincts? Certainly not. But not all men are manly men; many have not the faintest conception of true gentlemanly qualities, and, what is infinitely worse, bluntly assert and defend a type of manhood that would disgrace a Turk. They glory in their shame, ruthlessly despoiling the helpless, and then bragging over their villainous escapades.

But the difficulties in the way should not discourage the friends of moral reform. Let us do what we can, "if by all means we may save some." When General Grant besieged Vicksburg he drew up division after division, and planted his batteries in every coign of vantage, until at last the Gibraltar of the West fell. So in this fight against entrenched vice we must push the battle to the wall.

In this book I wish to give prominence to a piece of artillery additional to those already mentioned, namely the argument from psychology, the necessary workings of the human soul. What we think and do, even in our most abandoned moments, leaves its impress upon the quality and force of our personal life ever after. Each man's moral status is at any given moment the product of his entire past. The physician who habitually fixes his attention upon the processes of the human body comes, in time, to have a very different outlook upon existence from that of the preacher, who is chiefly occupied with conscience and man's inner world of the spirit. And, in turn, the Roman Catholic priest undergoes a distinctly different psychological development from that of his Protestant brother, who lives, as it were, in a different world from the former. So with the sailor, the artist, the merchant, and the lawyer; each imbibes a different set of impressions, hence is to that extent a different being. Why should not this same law of psychology operate in that which is most fundamental to every man's consciousness—his physical manhood? The heaven-wide difference in the habits and opinions of mature men in matters of sex may surely be traced to what they thought and did in this particular during the formative period of their lives. Marriage is not so much the beginning as the culmination of moral discipline. It is not the signal for reform, but the fruit and blossom of virtue.

This thought has been uppermost in the preparation of this book, and for the setting of the story the great American conflict has been chosen. An attempt is here made to portray, not primarily the outward facts, but the inner history and unfolding of character of one soldier to whom the war proved a splendid training-school. The central idea of this book is the attainment of character under difficulties, with special reference to the problem of personal morality and deathless love. The hero is the representative of a growing class of young Americans whose mental grasp and moral stamina enable them to see clearly and desire ardently the highest and best within the range of human experience. What is possible to one is possible to all who will fulfil the conditions.

From the above it will be seen that this diary, which is written in a plain, straightforward manner, but which is nevertheless exceedingly interesting, is chiefly valuable as being a psychological study of the workings of the human mind, and the triumph of the moral over the animal in a young man's nature.

After the preliminary chapters, the diary opens with the call to arms, the parting of the soldier with a high-minded, true-hearted, noble young woman, whom he hopes at some future time to win. The terrible temptations of camp life, especially to a young man with unfavorable hereditary tendencies and early environment, are experienced. He is subjected to a peculiarly strong temptation, but the words and the ideal of his betrothed save honor and manhood, and from this crucial moment he develops into a higher and nobler man. The happy union of the two souls, one of which has from the first borne the stamp of nobility, and the other which has grown to greatness through resisting temptation, makes this book exceedingly helpful. It is a fact that cannot be too frequently emphasized that the memory of a noble life, a high ideal or a noble sentiment thrown into the mind at a crucial moment in life very often leads to the development of a nobler manhood. This thought is strongly presented in Mr. Flint's work. As I have before observed, the world is full of elegant literature of a *dilettanti* character, but we need more of that literature which will appeal to the conscience of men and women and especially to the young; and while being an interesting story, this work has its chief value in appealing directly to the higher impulses of the soul.

NICODEMUS.*

REVIEWED BY B. O. FLOWER.

This exquisite little volume is a gem from cover to cover. The lines are in stately blank verse, and a lofty spirituality pervades every page. The following extract will convey to the reader the style and spirit of the writer:

> One night from sleepless bed I rose, and went
> To where He lodged, and bade the porter say

---

* "Nicodemus," by Grace Shaw Duff, bound in vellum stamped in gold, profusely illustrated by original drawings, reproduced in half-tone by Frederick C. Gordon. Illuminated initial letters. Price 75 cents. Arena Publishing Co.

One Nicodemus—ruler—came, and speech
Would have with Him. There was no moon, but hosts
Of stars, and soft, pale glow from shaded lamps
Made silver light. The air was still, with just
Enough of life to waft at times a faint
Sweet oleander scent, and gently float
Some loosened petals down. I heard no sound,
But sudden knew another presence near,
And turned to where He stood; one hand held back
The curtain's fold; the other clasped a roll.
No king could gently bear a prouder mien;
And when I gracious rose to offer meet
Respect to one whose words had won for him
Regard, I strangely felt like loyal slave,
And almost . . . "Master!" trembled on my lips.
A deep, brave look shone in His eyes, as if
He saw the whole of mankind's needs, yet dared
To bid him hope, and when He spoke, His words
And voice seemed fitted parts of some great psalm.

But the great spiritual lesson, a lesson of vital import, is found in the closing stanza, in which it will be seen that Nicodemus pleads for a fairer trial for Jesus, and though he fails to receive justice for the great Nazarene, into his own soul comes that spiritual illumination which will ever come when mankind acknowledges and acts up to the higher spiritual law.

We have a law that none be judged to death
Before himself has pled his cause. That day
I begged the council call the Nazarene;
The claim He made should win at least respect.
Alas! my words had little use, at least
For Him. For me they seemed the first faint breath
With which the spirit's born. He said 'twas like
The wind, it came and went, and no man knew
From whence or where. I left the counsel hall
With deep exultant hope that what He said
Was true—and heeded not their taunting cry:
      "Go search and see,
      No prophet comes from Galilee."

The dainty volume is small, but rich in high spiritual worth; it is profusely illustrated, and each page of text contains an illuminated initial letter. It makes an elegant little presentation volume, and will be prized by spiritually-minded people far more than more expensive booklets or cards.

THE DOUBLE MAN.*

REVIEWED BY E. N. FROTHINGHAM.

"The Double Man" is in two parts, an introduction and the main story. In both parts the author stands probe in hand reaching to the bottom of the worst ulcer that afflicts humanity. Many, even of those who are anxious to see the sore healed, would prefer

---

* "The Double Man: a Novel," by F. B. Dowd. 12mo, pp. 303; price, cloth $1.25, paper 50 cents. Arena Publishing Company.

treatment by plaster so that the offensive matter might be kept out of sight. Unconsciously they choose the method · condemned through Jeremiah, "They have healed the hurt of the daughter of my people slightly, saying 'Peace, peace!' when there is no peace." Job has something to say about "a strange punishment to the workers of iniquity." Swedenborg and others who have seen into the world next to this have had something to say about punishments—restrictive and reformatory in their design—that were peculiar to that world. That world is drawing near to this and bringing with it experiences hitherto not generally known. Mr. Dowd has described one of them in the introduction to "The Double Man." It is of a truly horrible nature; yet, bad as it was, one is inclined to congratulate Mr. Albee on being freed from his load of Karma before passing on into another life.

Both parts of the book emphasize reason and kindness as the proper methods to be used with the disembodied. This is something new. The same idea is brought out in "Pilate's Query," in the mode of treatment used by Paul Seawright; but, so far as we know, nowhere else. We have had the law of love for the insane, the drunkard, the criminal in this world; but for those whom we call dead, only exorcism and, if they happen to have been our own, prayers. So general, however, is the unbelief, conscious or unconscious, in the reality of the existence of those not seen by mortal eyes, that even exorcism and prayer have been neglected or scoffed at. In "The Double Man" the same treatment is accorded to all whether their clothing be material or astral.

A, perhaps one might say the, prominent subject in the book is hypnotism. The facts in this case—for the tale is said to be true in its main features—are all against Hudson's theory of the supremity of auto-suggestion over anything that could come from without. Ina is led into that which her soul abhors, while in the hypnotic state. The story is full of warning.

These are features of the book that strike the reader. After the reader comes the student. To him it unfolds mysteries manifold; mysteries of the relation of mother and child. mysteries of the relation of love both on the earthly and heavenly planes, mysteries of the relation between the wrong-doer and the wronged; mysteries of the relation of each to all. All this is for the patient and thoughtful student only.

Mr. Dowd speaks the truth, but at times so strongly as to arouse a temporary reaction. Such emphatic statements tend, like the explosion of a bomb, to arouse attention and at the same time to stun the listener. But when the reverberations have died away, and the time of quiet thought comes, then is the hour of their justification. Above all will any one, be he reader or student, be unwise if, not finding the introduction to his mind, he lays the book aside too suddenly.

THE ARENA.

No. LXXVI.

MARCH, 1896.

MEXICO IN MIDWINTER.

BY JUSTICE WALTER CLARK, LL. D.

Of the Supreme Bench of North Carolina.

Leaving New Orleans on the Southern Pacific R. R. one bright December morning in 1895, the route lay amid the great sugar estates of southern Louisiana, the country being dotted with the tall chimneys of the sugar houses and refineries, especially in the Bayou Teche country, which is possibly the best section for sugar planting in the Union. Crossing the Sabine River into Texas we travel thirty-eight hours, or nine hundred and fifty-four miles, through that truly Empire State before reaching El Paso, and even then we are still in Texas, for the state boundary is several miles further west. El Paso boasts that it is a central point, being twelve hundred and twenty-four miles from the City of Mexico, and about the same distance respectively from New Orleans, San Francisco, and Kansas City. Its inhabitants have the additional reason for believing their city the central point in the universe, that the sky fits down at the same distance all around it. Many a man goes through life thinking himself the centre, and viewing the world solely from his own standpoint, for no better reason. While on our long route through Texas, we passed over the bridge across the Pecos River, three hundred and twenty-seven feet high, being the second highest bridge in the world.

Crossing the Rio Grande, which is here a slight stream in midwinter, not much over ankle deep, we pass into the *United States of Mexico,* for such is the official and legal designation of this country, which is a federal republic of allied states, whose constitution in its main features is a copy of our own. The custom-house officials, like all Mexicans, are very polite, and indeed the examina-

THE LAW SCHOOL, GUADALAJARA.

tion of baggage is not much more than a formality. We find that the railroad conductors and engineers, and indeed most of the station agents, are Americans, and the cars and engines are from the United States also. This is to a very large extent true of all the railroads in Mexico.

The railroad from El Paso to the City of Mexico must pass over almost the identical route used by the Aztecs on their march to the same city centuries ago. Through most of the twelve hundred and twenty-four miles from El Paso to the city of Mexico, the railroad (the Mexican Central) passes through the centre of the great plain of the table-lands, which average six thousand to seven thousand feet above sea level, with mountain ranges on either hand, marking the edges where the country on either side begins to descend to the shore. The first four hundred and fifty miles is through the great plains of the State of Chihuahua, which is a stock country and thinly settled, the population being principally in the mining towns in the mountain ranges off from the line of railway. Along this route, however, must be the sportsman's paradise, as game of all kinds is very abundant.

We then pass into the State of Durango and run some seventy miles along its upper edge through a fine farming country known as the Mapinis section, where cotton is largely raised. One insignificant station alone ships

GOVERNOR'S PALACE, GUADALAJARA.

forty thousand bales of cotton annually, and as the value of silver money has not been artificially doubled by legislation, as with us, cotton brings its normal price of thirteen to fourteen cents per pound. The railroad rates and passenger fares remaining also at the same figure as formerly, the farmer does not, as with us, have to pay double the amount in produce for the transportation of himself or freight and for taxes, and consequently is very prosperous. The cotton plant in Mexico lasts for seven or eight years without replanting and yields two crops a year.

At Torreon we pass in the State of Coahuila, and meet the International R. R. (known as Count Telfner's R. R.), which, crossing the Rio Grande at Eagle Pass in Texas, offers a shorter route to the central and eastern parts of the United States than the Mexican Central; still it is not so direct as the Mexican National R. R., which, crossing the river still lower down, at Laredo, is the shortest, route of all, having reduced the time from New York to the City of Mexico to four and a half days. The International, crossing the Central here at Torreon, proceeds southwestwardly some two hundred miles further to the city of Durango. Torreon is a thriving, live town which has sprung up since the advent of the railroads and already numbers several large factories. We now pass through some seventy miles in Coahuila, and ascending a cross range

THE QUARRY VILLAGE OF EL ABRA.

TAMPICO FROM THE WHARF.

FALLS OF THE ABRA.

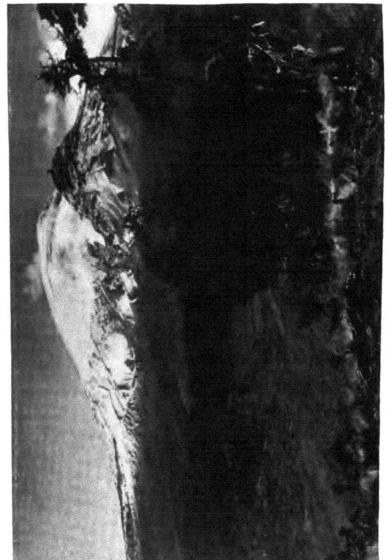

POPOCATAPETL, FROM TLAMACAS.

GUADALUPE, THE CHURCH.

of mountains pass into the great mining State of Zacatecas. Magnificent scenery meets the eye on every side, range after range of mountains bursting on the view, the railroad track doubling and turning like a hunted hare to find its way through the maze. Finally we reach the capital of the state, the city of Zacatecas, and stop over to see it. Before describing the people, their customs, and the novelties surrounding us, reference should be made to the financial differences of the two countries.

At El Paso we changed our United States money into Mexican, receiving nearly two dollars for one. As a few years back the Mexican dollar was at par with the American dollar, this striking fact must be noticed. Either the American dollar must have appreciated, in which case debtors, both public and private, and all taxpayers have been forced to pay double what they should—an enormous robbery of the many for the benefit of the few, of the wealth-producers for the emolument of the wealth-consumers; or else the Mexican or silver dollar has depreciated one-half. If it were the latter, then the prices of all things depending upon competition would be doubled. On the contrary, we find in Mexico, that the prices of nearly everything remain at the same level as ten or fifteen years ago. Cotton is thirteen cents per pound, wheat one dollar per bushel and sometimes a little more. Railroad passenger fares remain two and three cents per mile as formerly, and hotel rates

THE GREAT SPRING NEAR HERCULES.

PUENTE DE DIOS.

hazard, and they at least pillaged foreign nations. But this crime has been manipulated by the tools of the bondholders in secret, in congressional lobbies and committee rooms; there has been nothing heroic, and the only greatness in it has been in the magnitude of the plunder and the vastness of the sums transferred annually by this legislative legerdemain from the masses to the monopolies and multimillionaires, whose annual aggregate far surpasses the plunder that has ever yet fallen to a conquering army in the wealthiest country.

There was no pretext for it, since silver, when demonetized, was worth more than gold, and there has been nothing since to depreciate it. That silver in fact has not depreciated in the least may be seen right here in Mexico, and throughout the fifty millions of people living on this hemisphere, south of the Rio Grande, in all which countries the silver dollar will pay as much taxes, as much public or private indebtedness, as much railroad freight and passenger fare, as it ever did, and where consequently farm produce and land will bring the same prices they formerly did. The standard of value not having been artificially enhanced, fixed charges, as debts and taxes, are not enhanced, and the same amount of produce or labor will pay them. In the United States every farmer who last year sold cotton at seven cents or wheat or corn at fifty cents or less was contributing just one-half the value of his produce to the further enrichment of those already too rich. The value of cotton is thirteen cents and upwards, and of wheat one dollar and upwards, measured by the value of the dollar when the bulk of private and public indebtedness was created, and when official salaries and most other governmental expenses were regulated. The loss to the farmers of the South therefore last year was thirty dollars per bale, or, on an estimated crop of seven million bales of cotton, full two hundred and ten millions of dollars for the year 1895 on that one crop alone. In truth the total amount of the profits reaped by the capitalists through the legislation which has doubled the value of the public and private debts held by them staggers the imagination and fatigues indignation to compute. The wonder is not that there is widespread and incurable depression throughout the United States, but that we can exist under such a state of things. Were we not the wealthiest and most energetic and most patient people on the face of the globe we should sink under it.

We know the widespread ruin this legislative enhance-

THE FALLS OF JUANALATLAN.

PLAZA DE ARMAS AND CATHEDRAL, GUADALAJARA.

ment of the value of the dollar has made in the United
States. It is well to consider the effect on Mexico of her
wiser course of letting the standard of values remain as
it naturally was. In the first place, her farm and other
products are raised on the silver basis and are sold in the
United States on a gold basis. Coffee, for instance, is raised
at a cost of nine cents in silver, and is sold in San Francisco
at twenty-two and a half cents in gold, equal to forty one
cents silver. This makes the raising of such articles for export very profitable. Then the railroads charge at the same
rate as formerly for freight and passengers (i. e., two or
three cents per mile for passengers), with the result that
the people can ship freight and travel at about half the
cost (measured in produce) as in the United States. The
railroads are prosperous, and becoming more so each year.
In Mexico only one railroad has been in the hands of a
receiver and that only for a short time, while in the United
States nearly half the railroads have had to go into the
hands of a receiver, with the consequent loss of capital stock
and the freezing out of holders of the second and third
mortgage bonds. Then, too, the premium on gold, while
amounting to a bonus on coffee and other produce exported
to the United States, amounts on the other hand to a protective tariff of nearly ninety per cent against the importation of manufactured goods, machines, etc., from the United
States into Mexico. The result is that we have lost a
vast and growing trade with Mexico and the Central and
South American states. What goods we do sell there are
sold by our manufacturers at far lower rates than at home;
and even then, under the tremendous protection of ninety
per cent, manufactories are springing up all over Mexico.

Americans, attracted by the great prosperity prevailing
in Mexico, are to be found everywhere and in every line
of business; and even our capitalists, after forcing the public
to pay two dollars in value for every dollar loaned the government, are permanently doubling their capital by turning
this money squeezed out of the American taxpayers into
Mexican dollars, at nearly two for one, and investing at
par all through Mexico. Thus American enterprise and
American capital are both flowing in a full tide into that
country to build it up, while here capital is engaged in forcing the government to issue more bonds that the interest
received may find a safe and non-taxable investment, since
enterprises are no longer as profitable in the United States
as they were under the bimetallic standard. The exports
of Mexico in 1869 were twenty millions of dollars, but in

1892–3 they had increased to one hundred millions, and for 1896 it is estimated they will be over one hundred and fifty millions, while imports from the United States are falling off. Our gold dollar being convertible into two Mexican dollars is bringing in an enormous amount of capital from the United States for permanent investment in Mexico. It being unprofitable to send Mexican silver to the United States, it is being invested in new enterprises in Mexico, thus aiding in the wonderful development and prosperity now obtaining in that country. Furthermore, many wealthy Mexicans, having fixed incomes, formerly preferred to live abroad in the United States and elsewhere, but the depreciation of their silver incomes has driven them home, where silver remains at par, and thus a not inconsiderable addition is made to the wealth of the country.

The price of labor in Mexico has always been absurdly low, owing to its quantity being in excess of the avenues for employment; but the prosperity brought about by the causes above enumerated, and the manufactories, railroads, and many other new enterprises are gradually creating a demand for labor, and slowly but surely raising the price of wages, though they are still very low.

As above stated, if the American people were not the most patient in the world, they would not have thus submitted to this enormous and unjust transfer of wealth from the millions of wealth-producers to the handful of the idle rich. Those who have thus pillaged us, elated with the success of their plans, now threaten to still further contract the currency by retiring the greenback, and thus still more to increase the value of the dollars which the people must pay and they must receive. Should that plan succeed, the next step would be to declare that gold is depreciated by the opening of new mines and to insist on more grains of gold being put into the dollar. There is no limit to the exactions of avarice save the refusal to submit to them. Those who think that even that limitation is impossible might learn a lesson from Mexico.

The Catholic Church, by three centuries and a half of a policy as deliberate and as carefully planned as that of the monopolies and the money power in the United States to-day, came to own absolutely one-third of all the property in Mexico and controlled the balance. The masses were kept in ignorance, and the leaders and intelligence of the country were intimidated or bought. But there comes an end to such things. In 1859 the property of the church was confiscated. The church party called in the English,

CASTLE OF CHAPULTEPEC FROM THE GARDEN.

the Spanish, and the French, and the latter gave them an emperor. But the French were driven out, the emperor was shot, and to-day throughout the vast territory of the Mexican republic, nearly four times as large as France or Germany, the Catholic Church does not own a foot of soil or a dollar of any property. The very church buildings, hoary, some of them, with nearly four centuries of use, belong to the government, and services can be held in them only by permission of the authorities elected by the people. Not a priest can walk the streets in his official robes. Mexico remains Roman Catholic in her religion, but when the alternative was presented whether the church should own the country or the country should own the church, Mexico, in spite of centuries of veneration for religious authority and the influence of consolidated wealth and the ignorance and poverty of her masses, was able to vindicate the rights of the people.

What this priestly monopoly was to Mexico the money power is to the United States. The multi-millionaires, the bondholders, the trusts and monopolies already own over one-third of the property of our country and are reaching out for the rest. Many leaders they nominate and elect to office, others they intimidate or corrupt. But our people, while patient, are not ignorant, and if the course of the monopolies and combinations continues unchecked they will wake up some morning to find, as the Catholic Church did in Mexico, that the sovereign people own the country and all that in it is. The Catholics in Mexico venerated the church fully as much as we ever did the right of individual ownership of any species of property; but the welfare of the people is the highest law, and when that becomes imperilled, as it was in Mexico, by the money power in the shape of the church, and as it is in the United States by the same deadly enemy in the guise of multi-millionaires and monopolies, the manhood, the brains, and the honesty of the people will assert themselves, and we will not go down under the same enemy that destroyed Rome and so many other nations in the past. The world is older and wiser.

The gold dollar in the United States may well be called a mythical dollar. Not one man in a hundred ever sees one. It is not used to buy corn or wheat or cotton or flour or railroad tickets or dry goods. It is only for the sacred use of the idle rich when they wish to measure by a high standard, *doubled in value*, the principal and interest of bonds which, on their face, by the contract, are payable *in coin*— i. e., either gold or silver.

IXTACCIHUATL FROM THE SACRO MONTE.

In drawing these lessons from the past experience and the present prosperity of Mexico, there are those who will say that Mexico is inferior to the United States in education, in civilization, and in many other respects. To some extent this is true—and so much the worse for the objectors. For if Mexico, in spite of all these disadvantages, is prosperous and going forward by leaps and bounds, with her standard of values maintained at the same point, so much greater is the damnation of the men who, notwithstanding our great and manifest superiority, have brought the blight and curse of a long enduring depression upon us by robbing the wealth-producers in the interest of the wealth-consumers through the device of doubling, by surreptitious legislation, the value of the dollar. And if Mexicans, with three hundred and fifty years of priestly rule, three hundred of which were also under a foreign yoke, and fifty more passed amid civil dissensions, could assert themselves and throttle the gigantic money power which oppressed them, what cannot, and what will not, seventy-five millions of the foremost people on the earth be able to do when satisfied that they owe it to themselves and their posterity to break the yoke which binds them?

A SUCCESSFUL EXPERIMENT FOR THE MAINTENANCE OF SELF-RESPECTING MANHOOD.

BY B. O. FLOWER.

Mayor Hazen S. Pingree, of Detroit, Mich., is one of the most remarkable personages in public life to-day. He has had to meet the abuse, the baseless calumny, and the sneers of conventionalism and plutocracy much as had Abraham Lincoln prior to his first election. But it is a noteworthy fact that the assaults made against the popular mayor have emanated from the citadels of plutocracy and from a slothful conservatism, which has ever opposed all movements looking toward radical reform and the establishment of fraternity and justice.

Owing to the most vicious form of paternalism, because partial in its character, vast corporations, trusts, combines, and monopolies have gained wellnigh absolute control of legislation in many sections of the country, and have succeeded in more than one instance in tainting the law-making and law-executing departments of government throughout the republic. These corporations have mercilessly plundered the masses and, through their ill-gotten gains, are to-day a very real menace even to the life of the republic.

Mayor Pingree has assailed the plunderers of the people in so effective a manner as to make him dreaded by plutocracy or organized wealth, and his recent election for the seventh consecutive term as mayor of Detroit by a magnificent plurality of over eight thousand votes, with almost every paper in the city against him, and with the combined influence of the plutocratic organizations which he had so successfully assailed waging a determined fight to prevent his reëlection, was one of the most significant events of the past year in municipal elections, especially when it is remembered that the banks and Chamber of Commerce* of

---

* The following extract from Mayor Pingree's address before the Chamber of Commerce shortly before his reëlection will be interesting to our readers, as showing how the banks, trusts, and monopolies pull together against the interests of the masses, and how they seek to ruin in a business way the public officials who bravely endeavor to break up the corrupt rings, trusts, and combinations of plunderers. In this address, as reported by the *Evening Press* of Detroit of November 2, Mayor Pingree said:

"I would be glad to credit the Chamber of Commerce with any efforts in my behalf, in aid of several years' fight against direct and indirect taxation. I do not recall any

THE DETROIT PLAN — A SCENE IN THE VEGETABLE PATCHES.

Detroit were in a marked degree arraigned in opposition to this brave defender of the masses against a vicious and discriminating paternalism.

But it is not of Mayor Pingree's phenomenal success in fighting, almost single-handed, rings and ring rule that I wish to speak at the present time. I desire to say a few words in regard to the eminently practical and successful experiment

aid received from this chamber for any effort of mine in endeavoring to reduce street railway charges. The voters of the city asked for city ownership of street railway tracks at an election for which I arranged, and they asked it four to one. Did you aid in bringing that around? I hope you did. I want to ask how many are here, who assisted in procuring the groove rail for Detroit? It cost me several hundred dollars to take the aldermen and the board of public works to Buffalo to secure the adoption of that rail. How many of you assisted in establishing a public lighting plant which lowers the cost of the lighting of the city from one-third to one-half, thus lessening your taxes in that direction? This cost me more than $1,000 out of my own pocket. To have worked in favor of the corporate capital that lighted the city instead of for a public plant, would have put many thousands of dollars into my pocket which would have been taken out of your pockets and the rest of the taxpayers of the city of Detroit, in excessive charges. When I tried to catch the briber of the electric lighting company, at a cost of over $2,000, one good citizen, who was not a member of the Chamber of Commerce, shared that expense with me. I borrowed that money in New York during the panic at 12 per cent interest, as I could get none of Detroit's corporate capital. Your prosecuting attorney handled the hired detectives whom that money paid for, and he knows what the bills were. That money was expended to lower your taxes by preventing the theft of public money.

" When the Preston National Bank, on account of false representations, moved to put me out of that bank which I helped to organize, and in which I was a director, and in which I held $27.000 stock at the time, did the Chamber of Commerce interfere in the interests of one of Detroit's business men? Did the Chamber of Commerce interfere when not a bank in Detroit was out of the combination which refused to take the account of Pingree & Smith, a firm of excellent repute and standing in the city of Detroit, a firm operating a factory employing more people than any other shoe factory in the West; a firm of thirty years' standing; a firm of more importance to the city of Detroit than all the landed estates in the city; an institution paying from $4,000 to $6,000 every week to labor? Did the Chamber of Commerce investigate the false representations that I was opposed to corporate capital? These are questions in of this man of the people looking toward the maintenance or restoration of self-respecting, independent manhood and the reduction of the burden of expense which year by year was falling with greater and greater weight upon individuals and municipalities. His plan was so eminently common-sense, so just and statesmanlike in principle, that it should have commended itself to all well-wishers of the republic and the race as a valuable palliative measure to supplant the old method of conventional charity which has proved so inefficient, and which has frequently lowered manhood and proved otherwise vicious in its effect on the recipient.

As before said, owing to the power which has grown out of the most vicious kind of paternalism, which has fostered monopolies and combines by granting special privileges to the few at the expense of the many, Mayor Pingree's noble plan for palliative measures looking toward enabling the "out-of-works" to earn a competence and gain a start in life instead of becoming wards of the city or tramps, was met on almost every hand by jeers, scoffs, and ridicule. He was pronounced a visionary or a crank; his proposition was treated as a huge joke, or as something thoroughly impracticable, and we were gravely informed that the "out-of-works" would not work if the opportunity were offered them. This last statement has been a part of the stock in trade of certain debased public journals which have sought to crush out all healthy sympathy for the "out-of-works, and to throw cold water upon all common-sense plans for restoring or maintaining independent manhood.

Had the mayor of Detroit been a weak man, the unanimity with which the press belittled his practical proposition, the general declaration that it was thoroughly visionary, and

which I claim a Chamber of Commerce should interest itself. They are vital to the business interests of Detroit. The concern of one honorable business house should be the concern of all. But ours was not the only institution conspired against. I could tell you of others, were not the story a very foul blot on the fair name of our city.

"Did you come forward when I sent a communication to the council to get a reasonable rate from the gas companies? Did you extend moral or other aid when I said that C. P. Huntington's reputed agent offered me first $50,000 and was willing to increase it out of a second $50,000 if I only said I was tired of fighting and would sign the gas ordinance?

"Was the Chamber of Commerce alarmed for corporate capital when I sent a communication to the common council in which I stated that the stockholders of the Citizens' Street Railway Company had held a meeting for the purpose of raising $75,000 to bribe your mayor and his secretary? Did it occur to the Chamber of Commerce that the raising of such a sum for such a purpose was a graver menace to corporate capital than the ravings of the anarchist, and that it is such criminal acts that convey the direst threat to business interests?

"I have said government should exercise proper control over the corporations, especially those operating public franchise. I still say it. And let me illustrate the nature of this control in a simple way. In the franchise of one of our city street railways was a clause providing that workingmen's tickets should be sold. The company evaded the law. All other tickets were sold on cars. These were not. For four long years the company dodged this obligation until I forced their sale, after a long struggle in the courts.''

the almost universal ridicule which was heaped upon him, would have deterred him from carrying into execution a plan which would have commended itself to thoughtful statesmen in the earlier days of our history. He, however, determined to carry the measure to success, having thorough confidence in its practicability. He accordingly communicated his plan to Captain Cornelius Gardener, whose service in the United States Army had fitted him in many ways to successfully superintend the work in hand. Owing to the general hostility to the mayor's proposition, it was impossible to secure the necessary funds for the carrying out of his plan, and whatever money was subscribed was secured through individual subscriptions.

Just here it may be interesting to quote some passages from the recent official report of the agricultural committee to the common council of the city of Detroit, rendered on Nov. 25, 1895, in which we have an outline of the proposition so successfully executed by the mayor of Detroit and his earnest colaborers. The report says:

This plan, which originated with Mayor Pingree, had for its object the assisting of people with families who were in poor circumstances, by permitting and encouraging them to cultivate idle land lying within or near the city limits, gratuitously offered for that purpose by charitable persons. It is a well-known fact that there are in this city [Detroit] a great number of working men with large families who are not able to obtain continuous employment at such wages as will support them and their families, and who are driven by necessity to apply for aid to the organized charities during the whole or a portion of the winter months. Primarily to assist these, so that they might be self-dependent, and also such others as being able-bodied, yet who for divers reasons, are objects of charity, was the purpose of this plan.

The report thus continues, giving the unexpectedly large return which resulted from the carrying out of the mayor's idea:

Lying idle within the limits of the city, there were over 6,000 acres of land, portions of which, if cultivated in small pieces by the class mentioned, would more than suffice to make them comfortable and independent of charity. Besides the father, nearly every poor family has among its members, persons who can work in a garden. It was for the purpose of properly organizing such a plan that the mayor appointed a committee in 1894, and again in 1895. In 1894 the money—$3,600—necessary to carry out the plan was raised by subscription and by divers means. Some 975 families were assisted in that year, and crops to the value of from $12,000 to $14,000 were harvested.

This year [1895] $5,000 was appropriated for the purpose, by the common council, and this plan of assistance, after the experience of last year, was heartily endorsed by the aldermen. The city is to

THE DETROIT PLAN—THE AGRICULTURAL COMMITTEE AND
SOME OF THE WORKERS.

be congratulated that its common council is sufficiently far-sighted
to appreciate the utility and good permanent tendencies and results
of the plan. As in 1894 a committee was appointed by the mayor to
take the matter in charge. The methods pursued since have been
similar to those then adopted. Tracts of available land, and in as
large pieces as possible, were solicited and procured for this purpose,
from owners and agents. In every case the use of the land was
offered free. The land was plowed and harrowed by contract per
measured acre. It was then staked off by foremen hired for this
purpose into parcels of one-third and one-fourth acre. In all there
were plowed and harrowed 455 acres and staked off into 1,546
parcels.

No difficulty was experienced in getting people to take lots, and it
was even necessary, for want of sufficient land, to refuse some who
applied. It is an error to suppose that because people are poor and
needy, they refuse to help themselves where an opportunity offers.
From the experience of the committee such is seldom the case.

Out of the 1,546 applicants for lots, 1,258 had been on the books of
the City Poor Commission. Opportunity was also offered to obtain
a parcel by paying a small sum of money, from fifty cents to one
dollar, as rent. About 100 persons availed themselves of this. The
allotments were planted by the cultivators under direction of foremen employed by the committee, the potatoes and other seeds being
delivered upon the ground. During the summer months, the cultivated lands being unfenced were looked after by two mounted
policemen—one on the east side and one on the west side of the city.
These reported daily to the secretary for instructions, and each day
made the rounds of the parcels under their supervision. Very little
trespassing was reported.

Almost every variety of vegetable was raised during the summer
by the cultivators, and from time to time consumed for food. The
principal crops, however, were potatoes, beans, and turnips. The
care taken of the crops by the cultivators was equal to that taken by
the best market gardeners.

A fair estimate of the potatoes harvested has been obtained, and

In making its report the committee is certain that it errs rather on the side of being too conservative than too liberal in its estimates.

In estimating the value of the crops raised, the prices set opposite are those which the committee believes to be a fair average during the time over which these articles of produce have been and will be used as food. Large quantities of potatoes were dug before late potatoes had come into the market, and reduced their price. It must also be considered that poor people are generally obliged to buy by small measure and hence have to pay more than by the bushel:

Potatoes	61,840	bu. at	$ .40		$24,736.00
Beans	1,000	" "	1.50		1,500.00
Turnips	3,000	" "	.30		900.00
Beets	1,000	" "	.30		300.00
Corn	400	" "	.35		140.00
Cabbage	4,668	hds. "	.03		140.00
Squash	400	each "	.09		36.00
Pumpkins	500	" "	.08		40.00
Total					$27,792.00

Besides the above crops, many people raised radishes, lettuce, cucumbers, and other small vegetables of which no figures can be given. The committee from its thirty lots dug about 1,100 bushels of turnips, 500 of which were turned over to the Poor Commission and the remainder, together with a quantity of potatoes, were divided among lot-holders whose crops had yielded poorly.

It is fair to say that the yield returned to the cultivators about the value of $30,000; but even if its returns amounted to only half that sum, it was well worth the money invested, for in every case it went to the support of our most needy people who by their own labor provided that which perhaps they might otherwise have been obliged to receive from direct charity. Each person was permitted to harvest without interference or condition, whatever his lot contained; nor did the committee concern itself with the disposition of the crops.

From the above it will be seen that while the city of Detroit appropriated $5,000 during 1895 for this admirable palliative measure, the crop harvested amounted to from $27,000 to $30,000 in cash value. Furthermore, all thoughtful, far-seeing, humanitarian, and patriotic citizens will readily see that in infusing hope and self-respect into individuals and transforming objects of charity into independent, self-sustaining persons, the community and nation must necessarily realize far more in substantial gain than can be computed in dollars and cents. For the vital fact cannot be too frequently emphasized, that whatever restores or helps to maintain independent manhood is of inestimable value to society and the state; while, on the other hand, anything which lowers essential manhood or takes an iota from the self-respect of the humblest citizen is a real injury to the whole people. The unheeded cry for work, which is the cry of self-respecting manhood and the antipodes of an appeal for conventional charity, has, during the past few years, embittered thousands of American citizens. It has forced other thousands into environments of moral death, and driven multitudes of men, women, and children to drink, crime, immorality, and suicide. And these irreparable calamities might have been averted had our nation appreciated the importance of maintaining the manhood and self-respect of her citizens and holding their loyalty by bands woven of love and wisdom.

The falsity of a cry raised by a vicious and slothful conventionalism and a soulless plutocracy, and which has found ready echo from multitudes who never think for themselves, that the "out-of-works" do not desire to earn a livelihood, was clearly exposed in the first year's trial of Mayor Pingree's plan, when three thousand persons applied for an opportunity to earn a livelihood. Unfortunately, however, owing to the limited resources of the committee, less than one-third of this number could be accommodated.

Speaking of the success of the experiment in 1894, which, in the nature of the case, was not dwelt upon at length in the report of 1895, from which I have quoted extensively above, Captain Gardener in the course of a very interesting address delivered at the Pan-American Congress held at Toronto, July 22, 1895, made the following statement: "It is fair to say that the venture netted to the cultivators food to the value of $14,000 at a cost to the committee of $3,600."

The phenomenal success which attended this much ridiculed plan led other cities to adopt in a more or less comprehensive manner Mayor Pingree's suggestions. Among these cities I have only space to mention New York, Omaha, Nebraska, and Buffalo, New York. In New York City the funds available were only sufficient to give employment to eighty-four families. This aid was furnished by the New York Society for the Improvement of the Condition of the Poor, and three hundred acres of vacant land within the limit of Long Island City were turned over for the above-named purpose. The Society prepared the ground, furnished the seeds, and also employed expert agriculturists to instruct these amateur farmers. At the close of the season the New York *World** made a careful investigation of the results attending the experiment. The Society was at an expense of about $5,000; the value of the crop raised was about $9,000, and the amount of vegetables raised was as follows:

---

* New York *World*, Oct. 27, 1895.

THE DETROIT PLAN — MAYOR PINGREE, CAPTAIN GARDENER, AND OTHERS,
IN THE MIDST OF THE POTATO PATCHES.

THE DETROIT PLAN — SOME OF THOSE WHO WERE AIDED BY MAYOR
PINGREE'S MEASURE.

Potatoes	6,235	bushels.
Peas	817	"
Beans	1,260	"
Turnips	900	"
Carrots	40	"
Cabbages	9,927	heads.
Tomatoes	530	crates.
Corn	1,200	ears.

One woman, Mrs. Staedling, cleared over \$130 from one-third of an acre, while one man and his wife made over \$400 during the summer. The most remarkable success was that of Mrs. Dora Ruppert, a young woman, twenty-nine years old, who for years has been struggling hard to feed and clothe herself, her husband and his six children, she having married a widower. At the beginning of the season they were in debt \$200. Her husband was only able to get work occasionally. In her statement to the representative of the New York *World*, Mrs. Ruppert said: "After supplying our own household, I have sold enough vegetables to clear \$402. I still have three wagon-loads of potatoes and turnips at the farm." She had paid off her \$200 indebtedness and had \$200 in the bank.

I have dwelt on these cases in detail for the purpose of showing how valuable this eminently practical experiment has proved in restoring self-respect and manhood, and in making independent citizens of numbers who were being pushed year by year into the dead seas of want known as the "slums" in our great cities. It has also led quite a number of persons to branch out and garden independently in a small way. Captain Gardener, in the address before referred to, says:

A gentleman writes me from a small village not far from Detroit that twenty-five families have moved to that neighborhood, which had cultivated our lots last year. These took land lying idle to cultivate on shares, being convinced from experience that a good living could be obtained from a few acres, if properly cultivated. He says "I know that these families came here directly as a result of your potato scheme."

Captain Gardener continues:

The Detroit Plan has been, after careful investigation, adopted in a number of cities in the United States, modified according to circumstances. The mayor of Omaha, Nebraska, Hon. George P. Bemis, writes me as follows: "The use of vacant land was solicited, and we received offers of the free use of land aggregating about eight hundred acres, all within the city limits. Land was plowed and furnished for five hundred and seventy-one worthy applicants, and a competent gardener employed for sixty days as superintendent. About three hundred acres were thus distributed, and besides this, seventy acres more to others with an agreement to turn over to the commission one-third of the crop produced. The plan gives promise of being a great success. All the gardens are in excellent condition, *and it is impossible to estimate the saving which will be made to the county and to citizens generally, but it will undoubtedly amount to many thousand dollars.*"

Of the experiment in Buffalo, the same gentleman continues:

Mr. William A. Stevens [the gentleman in charge of the work in that city] writes as follows: "The work of our association goes bravely on and promises a great success. We are using about two hundred and twenty acres of land, allotted to five hundred and fifty families. There will be used about $2,000, and we expect to show at least five dollars for every dollar invested." . . .

The experiment in Detroit has demonstrated the following facts: First, since the largest item in the cultivation of vegetables is labor, furnished by the people themselves, much good may be accomplished by this plan with small expense to charitable people or to taxpayers. Second, that the wholesale robbery and trespassing predicted, even upon the land unfenced, is not the fact. Third, that the poor and unemployed in cities are glad to avail themselves of an opportunity to raise potatoes and other vegetables for their own subsistence, provided the land be furnished and they are assured the results of their labor will accrue to them. Fourth, especially to day-laborers with large families, the opportunity to cultivate a small piece of land is a godsend, as it enables them, together with what they can earn, to get along without other assistance; and that, to the class who are constant recipients of charity, and are practically continuously so supported, the cultivating of the soil and obtaining food other than by gift, is a valuable lesson, which tends to wean them from pauperism and restore instincts of self-dependence and manhood.

From the foregoing facts it will be evident to all thoughtful persons that this experiment is a success, whether we view it from a social, economic, financial, or ethical point of view. It is true that it is a palliative measure, but it is a palliative measure which works in the right direction. I would not for a moment have our readers ignore the fact that only radical economic changes founded on justice and comprehending the abolition of all class privileges and special legislation will satisfy the awakened intelligence of the present age or meet the demands of the civilization of to-day. But while we are vigorously carrying on this educational agitation for justice, progress, and fraternity, it is our duty to aid in every possible way such palliative measures as the above, which assist in restoring or maintaining self-respecting manhood. Had Mayor Pingree accomplished nothing beyond the successful carrying out of this thoroughly practical and common-sense plan, he would have justly earned for himself the title of a benefactor of the race.

THE BOND AND THE DOLLAR.

BY JOHN CLARK RIDPATH, LL. D.

III. THE MONSTER REIGNS.

By the year 1890 the people of the United States rightly reckoned that the time had come to end the discrimination against silver money. By the same date Shylock concluded that a favorable crisis had arrived for him to get undone *in toto* the legislation of 1878. He had succeeded in the interim, by means of the discrimination against silver as primary money, and by availing himself of the results of the stoppage of free coinage in the Latin Union, in raising the price of gold about thirty per cent. This fact taken the other way gave opportunity to Shylock to deplore the existence of a seventy-cent silver dollar. He was grieved beyond measure at the dishonesty of such a dollar—not on his own account, but for the credit of his country! The purchasing power of raw silver had not, according to the average prices of the other great commodities of the world's market, declined at all in the twelve intervening years; but the fund-holding interests had contrived a condition of values and prices that enabled them, by jugglery and falsehood, to denounce the silver dollar as a depreciated and dishonest coin, and thus to force a disparity in the bullion values of the two metals.

The people and their representatives, however, smiled at the ravings of the Goldites, and went forward to complete the legislation of 1878. At this time, namely in 1890, there was a firm majority in both houses of Congress in favor of the free coinage of silver. The nation as such was in favor of that measure. The administration was against it. The question was introduced into Congress in several forms. Motions and bills were multiplied. At length on the seventeenth of June, 1890, the Senate, which body has never appeared to a better advantage in our history, boldly took the initiative, without giving the enemy a chance to adopt his usual tactics, and suddenly prepared and *passed* an Act for the absolute restoration of silver to its old-time constitutional place in the currency system of the United States.

The Senate at this date was strongly Republican, and the majority in favor of the Free-Coinage Bill was seventeen.

In the House of Representatives there was an unequivocal majority in favor of the measure; but before this majority could declare itself and force upon the President the (to him) dangerous alternative of either accepting the will of the country or of obeying the behest of the money power with a veto, the bill was arrested by the Speaker, Thomas B. Reed, and then under the dictation of the administration and Senator John Sherman a new bill was prepared, which on the whole was the most monstrous contrivance that has ever thus far been injected into the monetary legislation of the country.

This measure, conceived in intrigue and stigmatized by its own inventors from the day of its inception, was insinuated into the House in place of the Free-Coinage Bill of the Senate, and was forced upon that body, whose members could not bear the whip of party and the loss of patronage. The Act thus adopted by the House was taken back to the Senate, and that body was thrown upon its haunches by the same power that had prevailed in the House. The majority of seventeen yielded, and the Sherman Law, so-called, became a fact with the signature of the president. It was the most misbegotten and ill-born measure that ever saw the light. It should have been designated the Bastard Bill; for it was disowned from birth by its father! It pretended to be a bill in the interest of silver money and for the preservation of bimetallism in the United States. On the contrary, it was a cunningly devised expedient of the Goldites, by which they gained in the contest with the majority ten times more than they lost.*

By the Act of 1890, the gold monometallists once more prepared a situation of which they could avail themselves in the future. The law was so framed that when through the abuse of it by the secretary of the treasury it should

---

*Notwithstanding the fact that the Sherman Law was an anti-silver law, the first effect of it—energized by the popular misapprehension on the subject—was a marked decline in the premium on gold. This was shown in a corresponding rise in the bullion price of silver. The silver rate was advanced from day to day according to the London quotations through a period of eight or ten weeks. Then the advance was checked. The quotations stood for a brief period at the crest; and then began that steady and long-continued decline which reached the depths in 1893-94, when the price of silver bullion was marked at less than fifty cents to the gold dollar.

This phenomenon was caused in large part by the shrewd action of Great Britain. That power was alarmed at the results which seemed to follow the Sherman Law. For many years Great Britain had been purchasing American and Mexican silver at the rate of about fifty millions annually. These purchases she made at *bullion* rates; and the bullion she coined and sent out at *coin* rates to her more than three hundred millions of East Indian subjects. It was a harvest bountiful and easy. The United States and Mexico paid the reapers, and Great Britain gathered the sheaves. Seeing the advance in the price of silver in the latter part of 1890, Great Britain boldly and unscrupulously during the remainder of that year and the first half of 1891 cut down her purchases of American silver by fully ten millions of ounces, with a view to glutting the market, reducing the price, and influencing American legislation. She succeeded on all three points! That she nearly ruined her industries in India and brought millions of her subjects to beggary was nothing; she was playing for a larger stake!

prove a failure—as from the first it was intended by its makers to be—the only thing required on the part of the money power was to raise a clamor against a single clause of the law and secure the repeal of that clause. By so doing the whole fabric of the silver legislation of the country, extending at broken intervals from the foundation of the republic to the year 1890, would be dissolved like a fiction, and gold monometallism would reign supreme.

The United States now entered upon the era of silver purchasing. The metal which the men of the constitutional era had chosen whereby to measure all other values (gold included) was degraded to merchandise. The Sherman Bill provided for the coinage of silver dollars at the discretion of the secretary of the treasury. It might as well have provided that the directors of the Bank of England should, at their discretion, hold their sittings in Mozambique! It was never intended to coin the puchased silver, but to treat it as merchandise. It was intended to accumulate it, and then to raise an alarm about the accumulation. The law continued in force for three years and four months. During that period the secretary of the treasury purchased monthly four million five hundred thousand ounces of silver, and issued therefor legal-tender treasury notes redeemable in either silver or gold at the option of the *secretary*. In this instance the option was cunningly restored to the *payer*, with the full knowledge that the payer would use that option in a manner further to depress the relative price of silver bullion and to make gold the dearer coin! This provision of the law was said to be an expedient for preserving the parity of the two metals, but in reality it was an expedient to exaggerate their disparity by enabling the holders of the treasury notes, with the connivance of the secretary, to draw therefor the gold of the treasury, leaving the silver to accumulate.

We need not here enter at length into the beauties of the Sherman Law. The people of the United States now understand it. They now know what it was intended for, and what it has been made to accomplish. They perceive clearly enough—all intelligent men perceive—that the Act of 1890 was but another adroit step in the processes by which silver was to be ultimately discarded as primary money, and the United States placed in firm monetary league with Great Britain on the single basis of gold. In the short space of three years matters had gone so far that the gold party, then in firm possession of the administration which it had created in 1892 for its own purposes, and triumphant by its power over the House of Representatives, felt sufficiently emboldened to attack the purchasing clause of the Sherman Law, and by annulling that destroy the whole.

It is scarcely worth while to recite the story of the contest of 1893. The miserable mêlée is still fresh in the minds of men. No doubt the Sherman Law ought to have been abrogated. It was not a silver law, but a law in the interest of gold. Nothing could have been devised more suitable to the ultimate interests of the gold party. That power, now in active control of both the leading political parties, was able to work its will. The repeal of the purchasing clause of the Act of 1890 was effected without conditions, and with the passage of that repeal, on the first of November, 1893, the legislation against silver, which was begun in silence in 1873 against the interests of honest money in the United States and in favor of substituting a long dollar worth fully a hundred and seventy cents for the dollar of the law and the contract, was boisterously and triumphantly completed. By that Act the will of the people of the United States was prostrated. The people themselves were gagged and manacled. Both houses of Congress were thrown down, and Juggernaut was pulled over them by the minions of a power having its head-centre in Lombard Street, London.

The conspiracy of the International Gold Trust seems to have triumphed. The indignation of the people against it · has been of no avail. That power which became organic as a bondholding class in America just after the close of the Civil War has, by its league with the financial system of Great Britain, succeeded in trampling down truth and justice, in choking the protests of a mighty people, in destroying their industries, in reducing them from proprietors to tenants, in taking away the rewards of labor and enterprise, and in establishing a condition which tends inevitably to the early and permanent institution in the United States of a peasantry subordinated to the will and purpose of their masters.

The visible gold in the world amounts to about four hundred and eighty-five cubic feet. The greater part of this, nearly all of it indeed, is owned by private parties.* It is controlled finally by a few men who hate free institutions and who care nothing for the rights of mankind or the interests of civilization. On the basis of these four hundred and eighty-five cubic feet of gold it is proposed to conduct the business of all the world! It is the most monstrous scheme

---

* Of the gold supply of the world the Rothschild already owns more than *sixteen hundred millions!*

ever known in history. The public and private debts of the American people amount to about forty-five billions of dollars.* Of this debt less than ten per cent is held abroad. Most of the foreign holding is in Great Britain. Yet by the bond of this ten per cent the United States has become an appanage of Great Britain. The independence which we thought we had achieved a hundred and twenty years ago and which we supposed we had confirmed fourscore years ago has been reconverted into a miserable dependency which might suggest to a pessimist that it would have been better never to break with our good mother at all!

The present aspect of the world is that of one centralized power, having its seat in London, with outlying dependencies. India with nearly four hundred millions is one dependency; Australia with four millions is another dependency; Canada wth six millions is a third; the United States with seventy millions is a fourth; the states of the Latin Union are the fifth. Germany and Russia are flattered with the belief that they are members of the league; but as matter of fact they are only Cambacérès and Lebrun in the consulate. The *First* Consul—and the only one of any importance—has his headquarters in the Bank of England.

It is now only a question how the robbers who have despoiled mankind in the two civilized continents by means of the Bond and the Dollar are going to get off with their swag. They must have a little time and opportunity. In order to secure these, they cajole the nations with pleasing delusions and fancies. One of these fancies is impending universal war. War is an exciting circumstance, and the prospect of war serves to distract the attention of peoples from the wrongs which they have suffered. The rumor of world-wide war is the substance of the daily news. People read it and believe it; Shylock is in ecstasies over the success of his ruse, and if he thought he could sell more bonds he would plunge all nations into a bloody and exterminating conflict. Another one of the illusions is the factitious discovery of gold. The propaganda having its headquarters in London and its American branch in William

---

*In the spring of 1895 the gold propaganda sent out from New York a number of distinguished advocates to teach the people how business is reviving, how the financial question is solved, how silver is dead, and in particular how easy and admirable has been the change from the bimetallic basis of currency to gold monometallism. In this interest Mr. Chauncey M. Depew appeared at Detroit and delivered an oration in which it were hard to say whether the wit were more stale or the facts more false. He showed that it was easy for the American people to extricate themselves from debt by the standard of gold, for the reason that the public and private indebtedness of the people is only *fourteen billions of dollars*. One might regard this statement as being interested and excogitated from the prejudice of the orator, but for the suspicion that he may have obtained his figures from *Upton's financial statistics in the Census of 1890!*

enemy./ I do not know a great newspaper that in its tone is heartily friendly to the common people./ The local leaders in politics follow the great leaders, and they the greater, until we arrive at the supreme management; and that, in both the dominant parties, is identical in intent and character. An attempt is made to create fictitious issues, upon which to induce the people to divide and agitate. One boss says, Lo, here; and another boss says, Lo, there.* Now it is the revival of the tariff question; now it is the mythical Monroe doctrine; now it is the annexation of Hawaii or Cuba; now it is Venezuela; now it is Armenia; now it is this, and now it is that, in the expectation that the people may be deluded therewith and lose sight of the fundamental question of their wrongs, until what time they shall be completely bound and translated out of the character of freemen.

How much further this malevolent and ruinous work can be carried on before the end come no man may well foretell. The winter snows whiten the landscape. A measure of forced activity has been produced in the business world. After the horrors of three years' prostration, the haggard workman returns downhearted to his tasks. A crippled tenant husks the corn in a field that was his own. He is an old soldier! The farmer and the mechanic labor on in hope deferred that a better day is coming. Whether it will come depends upon the people themselves. In one of the inspired passions of the French Revolution, the democrats made a statue like a titan, and set it up near where the Bastile had stood. They called it *Le Peuple Hercule.* It was the People Hercules. It represented the great ideal in its strength and majesty. Whenever the spirit of such an ideal shall repossess our American citizenship, the end will come, and the wrongs which the people have suffered by the Bond and the Dollar will be righted.

---

*The creed of the Rev. Hosea Biglow is no longer satire, but history. That creed, victorious alike over liberty and law, has become incarnate in the political boss, whose faith and that of his prototype are one:

> "I du believe thet I should give
>   Wut's his'n unto Cæsar,
> Fer it's by him I move an' live,
>   Frum him my bread an' cheese air;
> I du believe thet all o' me
>   Doth bear his superscription, —
> Will, conscience, honor, honesty,
>   An' things o' thet description."

For "Cæsar" read *Shylock.*

MAETERLINCK AND EMERSON.

BY HAMILTON OSGOOD.

As one studies the character of Maeterlinck he becomes more interesting. By his plays alone he could not fairly be judged, for, notwithstanding the intentions, literary and mental, which are to be discovered in them, these plays fail to reveal the inner life of the man. They show him as a literary impressionist, fond of the psychological; but save perhaps to one who knows him well, they do not disclose that which would be considered the spiritual life of this ardent soul.

His essay upon Ruysbroeck offers a better means of knowing him. Here one finds himself in touch with what is truest and simplest in Maeterlinck. In spite of his youth, he seems to have attained to clear vision with reference to life. One feels that, practically, Maeterlinck has discovered that the events of life, while they make up the sum of life, and while in themselves they are shadows of deeper things, are not life itself, and that the "me" of every individual is in unceasing contact with the source of all life. Indeed, much that he has written would give one the impression that Maeterlinck is a man of mature years, a mere man of books and seclusiveness.

See, then, what he really is as discovered by Jules Huret, who gives this racy sketch of him:

Surprise. Aged twenty-seven years, rather tall, shoulders square, a blond moustache closely clipped, with regular features and a youthful ruddiness of cheek and clear eyes, Maeterlinck exactly realizes the Flemish type. This, united with a very simple, rather timid manner, without gesture, but also without embarrassment, at once arouses a feeling of very agreeable surprise. The man, correctly dressed, wholly in black, with cravat of white silk, does not play the part of the precocious genius, nor of the mystic, nor of anything else. He is a modest man and a sincere. But this charm has its reverse. If I do not succeed in making my host forgetful that he is being interviewed, a thing which terrifies him, I shall win nothing, or almost nothing, from this tranquil, square-shouldered man, by my inquiries. A quarter of an hour has scarcely passed when I realize that it will not do to talk either of himself or of others, or so very little. To talk of things in very brief phrases, to respond to my questions in monosyllables, a slight gesture, a toss of the head, a movement of the lips or of the eyelids—such, so long as he feels that the indiscretion of the interviewer is hovering over him, will be the attitude of the interviewed. In order to succeed in dissolving slightly this bland mutism, it will be necessary for me little by little to cause the subject of my journey to be forgotten. Again I feel that there is neither a part assumed nor pose. He simply does not talk as others do.

We breakfast, both with a formidable appetite.

"Yes, I have a ferocious appetite," he said. "The fact is, I take a great deal of physical exercise—canoeing, dumb-bells; in winter I skate, often going upon the ice as far as Bruges and even to Holland; and every day the bicycle—when I do not plead—but that happens so rarely."

"You are a lawyer?"

"Yes, but as I told you—so rarely. From time to time a poor peasant comes to ask me to defend him, and I plead—in Flemish."

We agree that since *he has nothing to say to me*, we will take a walk through the city. Finally opening a conversation, Maeterlinck said:

"I think there are two kinds of symbols: one may be called the symbol *a priori*, the symbol of deliberate purpose; it originates in abstraction and attempts to invest abstractions with humanity. The prototype of this symbolic manner, which closely borders upon the allegorical, may be found in the second part of 'Faust' and in certain tales of Goethe's, in his famous '*Marchen aller Marchen*,' for example. The other variety of symbol would be rather unconscious, it would occur without the knowledge of the poet, often in spite of him, and almost always would far exceed his thought. It is the symbol which is born of all the genial creation of humanity. Its prototype may be found in Æschylus, Shakspere, etc. I do not believe that a work could be born alive from the symbol; but the symbol is always born of the work—if this be alive. The work born of the symbol can be only an allegory, and this is why the Latin spirit, the friend of order and certainty, seems to me to be more inclined to the allegorical than to the symbolical. The symbol is a force of nature, and the spirit of man is not able to resist its laws. All that the poet can accomplish is to put himself, by *rapport* to the symbol, in the position of Emerson's carpenter. If he wishes to dress a timber the carpenter does not place it above his head, but under his feet, and thus, at each blow of his adze,it is not he alone who works; his muscular forces are insignificant; but it is the entire earth which works with him; in assuming his chosen position he calls to his aid all the forces of gravitation of our planet, and the universe approves the slightest movement of his muscles.

"So it is with the poet, you see. He is more or less powerful, not by reason of what he himself does, but by reason of that which he succeeds in making others perform and by the mysterious and eternal order and the occult force of things. He must place himself in the position in which his words have eternity as a fulcrum and each movement of his thought should be approved and multiplied by the unique and eternal force of the gravitation of thought. The poet, it seems to me, should be passive in symbol; and the purest, perhaps, is that which appears without his knowledge and even counter to his intention; and, from another point of view, the quality of the symbol would become the counterpart of the power and vitality of the poem. If the symbol be very exalted it is because the work is very human. It is very much as we said this afternoon: if there be no symbol, there is no work of art.

"But if the poet set out from the symbol in order to reach the work, he is like the carpenter who squares a timber placed above his head. He has to vanquish the entire force of gravitation in his poem. He sails against wind and tide. He is no longer carried beyond his thought by the force, the passions, and the life of his creations, but is in open war with them; for the symbol which emanates from the life of every being is far higher and more impenetrable than the most marvellous preconceived symbol, and the simple life of beings contains truths a thousand times more profound than all those which our highest thought is able to conceive.

"If I succeed in creating human beings, and if I allow them to act in my soul as freely and as naturally as they would act in the universe, it may be that their actions would absolutely contradict the primitive truth which was in me and of which I believe them to be the offspring; and yet I am certain that they are right in their opposition to this temporary truth and to me, and that their contradiction is the mysterious daughter of a more profound and more essential truth. And this is why my duty, then, is to keep silence, to listen to these messengers of a life which I do not yet understand, and to incline myself humbly before them. From a still more restricted point of view it would be the same with images which, so to speak, are the coral strata upon which the islands of the symbol rear themselves. An image might cause a deviation of my thought. If this image be exact and gifted with an organic life, it obeys the laws of the universe much more strictly than does my thought, and, for this reason, I am convinced that in its opposition to my abstract thought it will almost always be right.

"If I listen, it is the universe and eternal order which think in my place, and, without fatigue, I shall go beyond myself. If I resist, one might say that I am struggling against God."[*]

In this disquisition it is of extreme interest to observe how much Maeterlinck is influenced by Emerson, with whom, perhaps, he is as familiar as is any other European *littérateur.* Indeed, the Maeterlinck of *Les Aveugles, Princesse Maleine,* and other plays which present him as a symbolist, has another, a deeper, and a more important side. He is a mystic, and his mysticism is based upon a deeply religious nature. This we do not find strictly implicated in his plays. We must turn to his preface to his translation, from the Flemish, of Ruysbroeck's "L'Ornement des Noces Spirituelles" and to his other and more recent translation of "Fragments of Novalis," from the German.

Leaving these delightful pieces, with the single remark that in the former of them we find another indication of Maeterlinck's love of Emerson, let me sketch a pleasant experience which I enjoyed last year in Paris:

While looking over the literary collection offered for sale by *La Mercure de France,* I was surprised by the discovery of a volume composed of seven essays by Emerson, translated into French by Mademoiselle Mali, whose *nom de plume* is

---

[*] Charmingly translated into English by Jane T. Stoddart, and published in London by Hodder & Stoughton.

I Will. She resides in Verviers, and the book has just been
published in Brussels by Paul La Comblez. There was a
preface by Maeterlinck. Whatever might be the correctness, or other merit, of the translation, the preface was sufficient to arouse a lively curiosity. The book was purchased,
and a careful comparison with the original made it com-
fortingly evident that the translation was not only strikingly
well done, but that it must have been made by one who loved
Emerson. The truth of this is borne out by Miss Emerson
herself, who speaks with warmth both of Mademoiselle
Mali's work and of her interest in Emerson. The essays
chosen by the translator sufficiently indicate her sympathy
with what was most attractive in the author. They are
"Self-Reliance," "Compensation," "Spiritual Laws," "The
Poet," "Character," "The Over-Soul," and "Fate," and it
gives one pleasure to reperuse them in the aroma of a language as poetical as that of the translator. Indeed, as one
reads them in their French garb, the consciousness of a
feeling of gratitude to Mademoiselle Mali grows upon one.

Turning, then, to the preface by Maeterlinck, it was found
to be so sympathetic, so appreciative, and withal so imbued
with Emerson's purest and highest thought, that a desire
to lay it, in our own tongue, before American readers,
became instant and forcible. Inasmuch as each reader can
criticise it for himself, comment upon this excellent paper
were needless. But suggested by this preface, there is one
thought which probably will occur to all who are familiar
with Emerson's writings, viz.: that while writing his preface
Maeterlinck was strongly influenced by "The Over-Soul."

THE PREFACE.

"One thing alone is of import," says Novalis; "it is the
search for our transcendental me."

At times we perceive this "me" in the words of God, of
poets, and of sages, in the depths of certain joys and certain
sorrows, during sleep, in love, and in "strange junctures,"
where from afar it beckons to us and with pointed finger
shows us our relations with the universe. There are wise
men who cling to this search alone and write books in which
only the extraordinary reigns. "What is of worth in books,"
says Emerson, "if it be not the transcendental and extraordinary?" They are like painters striving to seize a resemblance amid darkness. Some trace abstract images, immense but almost indistinct. Others succeed in fixing an
attitude or an habitual gesture of the superior life. Others,

again, imagine strange beings. There exist but few of these images. They never resemble each other. Some are very beautiful, and they who have not seen them remain throughout their lives like men who never have come forth into the light of day. Among these images are those whose lines are purer than the lines of heaven. And then these figures appear to us so far away that we know not whether they are living or whether they were transcribed according to our own fancies. They are the work of pure mystics, and man does not yet recognize himself in these resemblances. Others, still, whom one calls poets, speak to us indirectly of these things. A third class of thinkers, elevating by one degree the old myth of the centaur, by mingling the lines of our apparent with thôse of our superior me, have given us a more accessible image of this occult identity. The face of our divine soul smiles at moments over the shoulder of her sister, the human soul, bending to the humble needs of thought; and this smile which gives us a passing glimpse of all which lies beyond thought, is alone of import in the works of men.

They are not many who show us that man is greater and deeper than man, and who succeed thus in fixing some of the eternal allusions which, at each moment of life, we encounter in a gesture, in a sign, in a look, in a word, in a silence, and in the events which surround us. Of all sciences that of human greatness is the strangest. Not one among men is unfamiliar with it, but almost all are ignorant that they possess it. The child who meets me will not be capable of telling his mother whom he has seen, and yet the moment his eye has rested upon me he knows as well as my brother does, and three times better than I do, all that I am, all that I have been, all that I shall be. On the instant he knows me in my past and in my future, in this world and in the other worlds; and, in their turn, his eyes reveal to me the rôle I play in the universe and in eternity.

Infallible souls mutually judge each other, and so soon as his glance has met mine and has absorbed my face, my attitude, and all the infinitude which surrounds them and of which they are the interpreters, this child knows upon what to lay hold; and although he cannot yet distinguish between the crown of an emperor and the wallet of a beggar, he knows me, for a moment, as exactly as God does.

It is true that already we act like gods, and all our life passes away in the midst of certitudes and infinite infallibilities. But we are blind men playing with jewels, and this man who knocks at my door, the moment he salutes me spreads before me spiritual treasures as wonderful as does the prince whom I may have rescued from death. I open to him, and in an instant, as from the height of a tower, he sees at his feet all that happens between two souls. I judge the peasant girl, of whom I ask the way, as profoundly as if I begged ôf her the life of my mother, and her soul has spoken to me as intimately as the soul of my betrothed. Before replying to me she quickly rises to the greatest of mysteries; then, suddenly, knowing what I am, she tranquilly tells me that I must take the village path on the left. If I pass an hour in the midst of a crowd, saying nothing and without thinking of it for a moment, I have judged the living and dead a thousand times, and which of these judgments will be reversed at the last day? In this room are five or six beings who talk of rain and pleasant weather; but above this miserable conversation six souls hold converse which no human wisdom could approach without danger, and although they speak through their expressions, their hands, their faces, and through their united presence, they will always be ignorant of what they have said. They must, however, await the end of this elusive dialogue, and this is why they experience an indefinable and mysterious joy in their *ennui*, without knowing that which listens in them to all the laws of life, of death, of love, and which, like exhaustless rivers, flow about the house.

It is thus always and everywhere. We live in accordance only with our transcendental being, whose actions and thoughts every moment pierce the envelope which encloses us. To-day I shall meet a friend whom I have never seen, but I know his work, and I know that his soul is rare and that, in accordance with the duty of superior intelligences, he has spent his life in revealing it with all possible clearness. I am filled with inquietude, and it is a solemn hour. He enters, and at the movement of the door, which opens upon his presence, all the explanations he has given during many years fall into dust. He is not what he believes himself to be. He is of a nature different from that of his thoughts. Once more we prove that the emissaries of the spirit are always unfaithful. He has said very profound things about his soul, but, in this second of time, which separates the look which tarries from the look which vanishes, I have learned all that he can never say and all that he can never make live in his spirit. Henceforth he belongs to me forever. Formerly we were united by thought. To-day, something a thousand, thousand times more mysterious than thought has delivered us to each other. We had waited years and years for this moment, and, behold, we feel that all is useless, and, to avoid the fear of silence, we, who were prepared to show each other secret and prodigious treasures, converse upon the time of day or upon the setting sun, in order to give our souls time to reverence each other and unite in another silence which the murmur of lips and of thought will not be able to disturb. . . .

Beneath all we live only soul to soul, and we are gods who do not know each other. If, this evening, it be impossible for me to bear my solitude, and if I go down among the people, they will tell me that the storm has shaken down their pears and that the late frosts have closed the port. Is it for this that I have come? And yet I soon go away, my soul as satisfied and as full of force and of new treasures as if I had spent these hours with Plato, Socrates, and Marcus Aurelius. By the side of that which their presences proclaimed, what their mouths said was not heard, and it is impossible for man not to be great and admirable. In comparison with the truth which we are and which silently asserts itself, that which thought thinks is of no importance, and if, after fifty years of solitude, Epictetus, Goethe, and St. Paul landed upon my island, they would be able to tell me only what the youngest cabin-boy of their ship could tell me, at the same time and perhaps more directly. In truth, that which is the most singular in man is his gravity and his concealed wisdom. The most frivolous amongst us never really laughs, and, in spite of his efforts, never succeeds in losing one minute, for the human soul is attentive and does nothing useless. *Ernst ist das Leben;* life is grave, and in the depths of our being our soul has not yet smiled.

On the other side of our involuntary agitations we lead a marvellously still, very pure and steadfast existence, to which the hands which reach out, the eyes which open, the looks which meet, make unceasing allusion. All our organs are the mystic accomplices of a superior being, and it is never a man, but a soul that we have known. I did not see the poor man who begged for alms upon the steps of my threshold, but I perceived something else: in his eyes and mine two identical destinies saluted and loved each other, and at the moment when he stretched forth his hand the little door of the house opened for an instant upon the sea.

"In my dealing with my child," says Emerson, "my Latin and Greek, my accomplishments, and my money stead me nothing, but as much soul as I have avails. If I am wilful, he sets his will against mine, one for one, and leaves me, if I please, the degradation of beating him by my superiority

of strength. But if I renounce my will and act for the soul,
setting that up as umpire between us two, out of his young
eyes looks the same soul; he reveres and loves with me."

But if it be true that the least amongst us is not able to
make the slightest gesture without reckoning with the soul
and the spiritual kingdoms where it reigns, it is also true
that the wisest almost never think of the infinite which is
affected by the movement of an eyelid, by a nod of the head,
by the closure of a hand.

We live so far from ourselves that we are, almost all of
us, ignorant of what happens at the horizon of our being.
We wander haphazard in the valley, not suspecting that all
our gestures are reproduced and acquire their significance
upon the mountain top, and at intervals it is necessary that
some one should come to us and say: Lift your eyes. See
what you are. See what you do. It is not here that we live;
it is up yonder that we exist. See what that look exchanged
in the shadow, and those words which have no sense at the
foot of the mountain, become, and what they signify beyond
the snow of the peaks, and how our hands, which we think
so feeble and so small, unconsciously reach God every
moment.

Beings have come thus to touch us upon the shoulder as,
with significant gesture, they show us what is happening
upon the glaciers of mystery. These beings are few. There
are three or four of them in this century. In the other centuries there are five or six, and all that they have been able to
say to us is nothing in comparison to that which takes place
or to that of which our soul is not ignorant. But what does
it matter? Are we not like a man who lost his sight in the
first years of his childhood? He has seen the innumerable
spectacle of beings. He has seen the sun, the sea, and the
forest. Now these wonders exist forever in his very being;
and if you speak of them to him, what will you be able to
say to him, and what will be your poor words in comparison
with the glade, the tempest, the aurora, which still live in
the depths of his spirit and of his substance? But he will
listen to you with an ardent and astonished joy, and
although he knows, although your words more imperfectly
represent what he knows than a glass of water represents
a noble river, the puny and powerless phrases which fall
from the mouths of men will illumine for an instant the
ocean, the light, and the sombre foliage which sleep amidst
the gloom beneath his eyelids.

The faces of this transcendental me, of which Novalis
speaks, are probably innumerable, and none of the mystic

moralists have succeeded in comprehending them. Swedenborg, Pascal, Hello, Novalis, and a few others, examine our
relations with a subtle, far-removed, and abstract infinite.
They lead us upon mountains the summits of all of which
seem to us neither natural nor habitable, and where often we
breathe with difficulty. Goethe accompanies our soul upon
the shores of the sea of serenity. Marcus Aurelius leads
it to sit upon the declivity of the human hills of a perfect
and wearisome goodness and under the too heavy foliage
of a resignation without hope. Carlyle, the spiritual
brother of Emerson, who in this century warns us from the
other extremity of the valley, makes the only heroic
moments of our being pass like lightning-flashes upon depths
of darkness and the storm of an unceasingly monstrous
unknown. He leads us like a flock driven astray by tem-
pests, toward unfamiliar and sulphurous pastures. He
drives us into the deeps of a gloom which he has discovered
with joy, and which is illumined only by the violent and
intermittent star of heroes, and there, with a malicious laugh,
he abandons us to the vast reprisals of the mysteries.

But meanwhile behold Emerson, the good shepherd of the
pale and green meadows of a new, natural, and plausible
optimism. He does not conduct us to the brink of abysses.
He does not make us leave the familiar and humble
enclosure, because the glacier, the sea, the eternal snows,
the palace, the stable, the cold hearth of the poor, and the
bed of the sick, all exist under the same sky, are purified by
the same stars, and submissive to the same infinite powers.

For many souls he came at the moment of necessity, at the
instant when they were in mortal need of new explanations.
The heroic hours are less apparent, those of abnegation
have not yet returned; there remains to us only the life of
every day, and yet we cannot live without greatness. He
has given an almost acceptable meaning to this life which
no longer possessed its traditional horizons, and perhaps he
has been able to show us that it is strange enough, profound
enough, and great enough to have no other goal than itself.
He knows no more about it than do others, but he affirms
with more courage and he has confidence in the mysterious.
We must live—all you who traverse days and years without action, without thought, without light, because, in spite
of everything, your life is incomprehensible and divine.
We must live, because no one has the right to abstract himself from the spiritual events of common weeks. We must
live, because there are no hours without secret miracles and
ineffable significations. We must live, because there is not

an act, not a word, not a gesture, which escapes inexplicable
claims in a world "where there are many things to do and
few to know."

There exists neither a great nor a small life, and the action
of Regulus or of Leonidas, when I compare it with an instant
of the secret existence of my soul, has no importance. It
is able to do or not to do what they have done; these things
do not concern the soul; and while he was returning to Carthage, the soul of Regulus probably was as abstracted and
as indifferent as that of the workman on his way to the mill.
The soul is too far from all our actions; it is too far from all
our thoughts. Alone in the profound of our being, it lives
a life of which it does not speak; and on the heights where it
reigns the variety in existence is no longer apparent. We
march oppressed under the weight of our soul, and there is
no proportion between it and us. Perhaps it never thinks
of what we are doing, and this may be seen in our faces. If
one could ask an intelligence from another world: What is
the synthetic expression of the face of men? without doubt
after having seen them in their joys, in their sorrows, and
in their inquietudes, this intelligence would reply: *"They
appear to be thinking of something else."*

Be great, be wise and elegant; the soul of the beggar who
holds out his hand at the corner of the bridge will not be
jealous, but yours, perhaps, will envy him his silence. A
hero needs the approbation of the ordinary man, but the
ordinary man does not ask the approbation of the hero, and
like a person whose treasures are in a safe place, he pursues
his life without anxiety. "When Socrates speaks," says
Emerson, "Lysis and Menexenus are afflicted by no shame
that they do not speak. They also are good. He likewise
defers to them, loves them, whilst he speaks. Because a
true and natural man contains and is the same truth which
an eloquent man articulates, but in the eloquent man,
because he can articulate it, it seems something the less to
reside, and he turns to these silent, beautiful, with the more
inclination and respect."

Man is greedy for explanations. It is necessary to show
him his life. He rejoices when, somewhere, he finds an
exact interpretation of a slight gesture which he made
twenty-five years ago. In this life there is no slight gesture.
What exists is the totality of the daily attitude of our soul.
You will not find here the eternal character of the thought
of Marcus Aurelius. But Marcus Aurelius *is* thought, *par
excellence*. Besides, who among us leads the life of a Marcus
Aurelius? Here it is the man, and nothing more. He is not

arbitrarily exalted; only, he is nearer to us than usual. It is John who cuts his trees; it is Peter who builds his house; it is you who talk to me of the harvest; it is I who give you my hand; but we are so placed that we are in contact with the gods, and we are astonished by what we do. We did not know that all the powers of the soul were present, we did not know that all laws of the universe waited upon us; and, like people who have witnessed a miracle, we turn and look at each other, speechless.

Emerson came to affirm with simplicity this secret and equal grandeur of our life. He has filled us with silence and admiration. He has put a beam of light under the footsteps of the artisan who comes from the workshop. He has shown us all the powers of heaven and earth occupied in sustaining the threshold upon which two neighbors talk of the rain which falls, or of the wind which is rising; and above these two passers-by, who have met each other, he has made us see the face of a god who smiles at the face of a god. No other is nearer our common life than he. He is the most attentive, the most assiduous, the most honest, the most scrupulous, perhaps the most human of monitors. He is the sage of common days, and the total of common days is the substance of our being. More than one year passes without passions, without virtues, without miracles. Teach us to venerate the most insignificant hours of life. If, this morning, I was able to act in accordance with the spirit of Marcus Aurelius, do not come and italicize my actions, for I myself know that something has happened. But if I think I have lost my day in miserable, petty undertakings, and if you can prove to me that, meanwhile, I have lived as profoundly as a hero, and that my soul has not lost its rights, you will have accomplished more than if you had persuaded me to-day to save my enemy; for you have augmented in me the sum, the greatness, and the desire of life, and to-morrow, perhaps, I shall know how to live with respect.

THE SOCIAL EVIL IN PHILADELPHIA.

BY REV. FRANK M. GOODCHILD.

In his excellent letters to his son about duties, Cicero reminded the boy that there were some things that it was right to do, but not to talk about. A slight modification of that precept will give us the habitual attitude of most people toward the subject of this article—it points to things which it is both wrong to do and wrong to speak of. And the poor zealot who, in order to help set things right, ventures to recite modestly what is done most immodestly is worse reprobated than the creators and the supporters of the iniquity. There are not wanting those who think Philadelphia the nearest to unfallen Eden of any place in the world. To announce our subject is to shock them mortally. But to accommodate them with silence is to give the evil further chance to grow; it asks for nothing so much as to be let alone. And though the cure is drastic, the time has probably come when, following the lead of Isaiah, God's prophets should cry aloud and spare not, and lift up their voices like trumpets and show the people their transgressions and the house of Jacob their sins. I believe our hope of improvement lies in burning into the hearts and the minds of the people the tragedies that are being enacted about us every day. And while I could wish for a pleasanter, cleaner task than this I have set myself, I have a profound conviction that the ghastly story must be told and often repeated, before men, engrossed with their own concerns, will shake off their drowsiness and demand that the iniquity be blotted out.

I do not believe that Philadelphia is a sinner above all others in this matter of dishonored womanhood, and yet we have our full share of guilt. The people who dwell on the banks of the Delaware are just the same as those who live on the banks of the Thames and of the Hudson. The same outrages that shocked the world when exposed by Mr. Stead with regard to London, and by Dr. Parkhurst with regard to New York, are perpetrated here in Philadelphia. We have our thousands of men who make the spoiling of maidenhood a pastime. We have our hundreds of women whose fortunes are made out of trade in the bodies and souls of their poorer sisters. We have our great procession of girls, somebody's daughters, with sin-stamped faces, but all of them with what the Russians call "a spark of God" in them, thrust into the great maw of man's lust. We have the same naïve officials, too, who grow fat by inaction.

It is not easy to get at the precise number of prostitutes in any great city. Most estimates are the sheerest guesses, and are very wide of the mark. The ordinary figure given for London, for example, is from sixty thousand to eighty thousand. But General Booth, who surely knows if anyone does, says that those figures are a monstrous exaggeration if they are meant to apply to those who make their living solely and habitually by prostitution. It has been declared that in New York city there are between forty thousand and fifty thousand such women. That would make one habitual prostitute for every nine mature men in the city. And as it is estimated that every fallen woman means on an average five fallen men to support her, it would appear that more than half our men are regular contributors to the brothel, which I should hesitate very much to believe. Eight years ago the superintendent of the Florence Night Mission estimated that there were then fifteen thousand prostitutes in New York city.* The number has not increased by more than ten thousand certainly, probably not by more than five thousand. An army of twenty thousand such hapless creatures is ghastly enough not to need exaggeration.

Estimates of the number in Philadelphia run all the way from fifteen hundred to ten thousand. The estimate of fifteen hundred is based on there being three hundred houses of ill-fame in the city, five girls to a house being a fair average. But I can find without any difficulty, three hundred such houses in the district between Sixth and Broad Streets, and Arch and Green. In Mr. Stead's map of the notorious nineteenth precinct of the first ward of Chicago are shown more than one hundred and fifty properties, thirty-seven of which are brothels. I have before me at this moment a sketch of a third of a block in Philadelphia, bounded by Fourth, Bainbridge, Trout and Barrow Streets. It contains about forty properties. Thirty of them are brothels. Two squares west is Middle Alley. It is one square in length and contains forty-four properties, of which forty are brothels, and by actual count there are a thousand visitors to them daily. Less than a mile to the north of Ninth Street, from Wood to Buttonwood Streets, taking in Canton Street, about a hundred feet to the west,

---

*Proceedings of First Convention of Christian Workers, Chicago, June, 1886, p. 42.

there are crowded together more than fifty brothels. These
sketches of polluted districts in the Quaker city are not
solitary, but might be extended indefinitely did space allow.
There are not less than one thousand such houses in the city,
and as many as five thousand women live among us by the
sale of their bodies. I wish I might have confidence that
the estimate is too high; but nearly six years of observation
make me fear that the figures are much too low. This does
not include, of course, the vast multitude of poor girls
whose labor yields scarcely enough to keep body and soul
together, many of whom fall victims to the lecherous men
who are always on the watch for "new cases," and who know
only too well just when to make their "propositions."

The houses of ill-fame in Philadelphia are widely dis-
tributed. There are certain districts, to be sure, where
they "most do congregate." Ninth Street, from Arch to
Spring Garden, Tenth Street, within about the same limits,
Eleventh Street, in spots, Race, Vine, Callowhill, Wood,
Buttonwood Streets east of Broad, Pearl Street, Morgan
Street, Sergeant Street, Bay, Barclay, Hurst, Trout and
Barrow Streets, Middle Alley, Soap-Fat and Currant Alleys,
Bainbridge Street east of Fourth, South Front Street
among the sailors' boarding houses, and a score of other
districts, are locations familiar to those who know anything
of low life in Philadelphia. But there is no neighborhood
in the city that has not its joint or joints. In abandoned
districts from which the churches are departing you find
them, and in respectable districts, "squat like a toad close
by the ear" of the church, you find them still. They are as
ubiquitous as is the passion of man.

There are different sorts of houses, too, apart from
quality. There are establishments where the girls are kept
as you would keep any other wares for sale, and there are
houses where no girls are kept, but where couples repair
for indulgence. There are houses that are run only at night
and others that are incessant in their operation. There are
houses that hide behind a "Furnished Rooms" sign, others that
show a dressmaker's plate, others that advertise massage
treatment, and others that make no attempt to conceal their
character, but brazenly announce "Miss Tillie" or some other
such name on the door or window. There are houses that
shelter confirmed prostitutes who will accommodate you for
fifty cents, and there are others that will furnish you by
appointment with a maiden guaranteed not to have been
violated, for which unless you are a regular customer for
such goods you may have to pay fifty dollars or even more.

As there are different sorts of houses so there are different sorts of abandoned women; that is, they ply their trade in different ways. There are first and highest of all, the kept mistresses provided for by one man who visits them regularly and to whom they keep themselves faithful. They often persuade themselves that their relation is as sacred as marriage. Then there are the inmates of a house presided over by a madame for the accommodation of patrons who come to the house. Again there are the "sitters," in many cases store girls who go to such an establishment as that of Madame Evans and "sit" in the evening to receive gentlemen visitors. And last of all there are the "rounders" who walk the streets and solicit patronage and who when they have attached themselves to some one take him to their own room or to some one of the numerous houses of assignation. I stood at Eighth and Vine one Saturday evening not long ago and counted forty-seven of these poor lost creatures pass me in ten minutes, some of them sodden with drink, most of them with painted faces, some of them old in sin, some of them mere girls, just starting it would seem. I observed them solicit with their eyes and with speech too. I heard fair-looking young men ask them what I should think it would have scorched their lips to ask,—"What is your price?"—and then, thinking it too high, they passed on to find some one who held her honor more cheaply or whom necessity pressed more severely.

Oddly enough there is a great deal of caste among these lost women. The kept mistresses despise the whole tribe of their looser sisters and would resent being classified with them, though it is almost as sure as fate that they sooner or later will be among the class they now spurn with contempt. The street-walker, too, cherishing her liberty, looks down on her sisters in their madames' establishments and calls them slaves, which indeed many of them are; these on the other hand despise the street-walker who must go her rounds to drum up customers.

The nationality of the girls is a matter of interest to any student of the social evil. Children of Irish or German or English parents many of them are. Girls of generous temperament and too trustful disposition have been betrayed by employer or friend, and have found no door open to them but that of a house of shame. There are many houses of a low order in which the girls are colored, and now and then one of higher class with colored girls whose patrons are exclusively white. The Jews are a race whose chastity is marked. Until lately there have been very few Jewish pros-

I have not mentioned drink as a cause of the social evil; but it deserves to be mentioned with tremendous emphasis. It is at the bottom of this as of most crime. Most girls are seduced when somewhat under the influence of liquor. It is certain, as they will confess to you, that they could not continue their bad life except as they fortify themselves with drink. And on the other hand it is true that men's lustful appetites are in ninety-nine cases out of a hundred aroused and sharpened by the cup. "Wine and women" are words that have been joined together ever since we have had a language.

Some are led astray by flash literature and pornographic pictures. Many attribute their fall to dancing. I need not dwell on that. But it is worth mentioning in passing that the merry-go-round, on Eighth Street near Vine, now rapidly taking the place of Applegate's Carrousel that was raided and closed up some time ago, has an iron gallery connecting its second floor with a dance hall in the building next door. The first floor of this next-door building is a cigar store, just as it is a matter of notoriety that the main entrance to Madame Evans' establishment is through a cigar store two doors below. In this fashion in scores of places, as well as in its issue of meretricious photographs, the cigar business lends itself to the promotion of the social evil.

The money returns furnish a very great temptation to girls to part with their virtue. Some fall because they cannot find work, some because they do not wish to work. Many a girl who is strong and healthy and comely and lazy, learns that there is a market for such as she, that she can earn more in a night by sin than she can in a week or a month by work, and she sells herself accordingly. Mr. Stead reminded the Woman's Club of Chicago, that the peculiar temptation of a woman is that her virtue is a realizable asset. This vice costs a man money, to a woman it yields money. Mr. Booth says that the number of young women who receive $2,500 in one year for the sale of their persons is larger than the number of women of all ages in all businesses and professions, who make a similar sum by honest industry. In sin the prizes come first, in honest callings only after long and painful toil. Even in the common houses on Bainbridge Street, at a fifty-cent rate, girls often make twenty dollars or more a week. Their board costs them half of that, and the madame usually contrives to get the rest of it for clothes and what not, so that the girls are tied to her by perpetual debt. But still they have the consciousness of having earned a much larger amount than any girl of their capacity could outside. For the first bloom of a girl's youth and beauty, of course, a much higher price is paid if the sale is discriminate. It is not long before disease and degradation and death follow, it is true. But these are lost sight of. Like all the rest of us, these fallen creatures remember only that sin when it is begun bringeth forth pleasure, and they forget that sin when it is finished bringeth forth death.

Many more are led astray by associates. Misery loves company, and one girl who falls is very apt to drag another down for the sake of companionship. And then the procuress is busy with her wily arts in Philadelphia, as in other large cities. I do not need to go into the sickening details of how the young and unwary are snared. Incoming trains are watched. Pretty girls out of work are discerned, and offered good paying places. Advertisements in the "Help" column of the papers lure others, and without knowing it they are in a brothel, and in a few days their names are announced as "missing." Sometimes an excursion on the part of the procuress to some country place yields an acquaintance with some comely girls, and opens the way to inviting them to paying employment in the city. Sometimes a cabman who is asked to take a girl to a boarding place delivers her to a fast house instead. Sometimes the head of a business firm is himself the means of a girl's ruin as he suggests the way by which she can eke out her paltry wages. Some time ago in a sermon in my own pulpit, I alluded in the most general terms to an Eighth Street house that had the reputation of making such "propositions." To my astonishment I found the name of the firm on everybody's lips; their information was as clear as mine, and in point of time preceded mine. There are a thousand ways in which the men and the women, whose business is to furnish recruits to fill up the vacant places in the brothels, disarm suspicion and induce the unwary to enter their toils.

When persuasion and fraud fail of their purpose, a little force may be used, and a girl whose only fault is ignorance finds herself an outcast for life. A member of my church, who with his sick wife lived on Vine Street above Fifth, one day saw a man and a young woman walking together on the opposite side of the street. They paused in front of a house of ill-repute. He tried to persuade her to enter; she hesitated. He urged; she refused. A man came out of the house, and the two men together forced her in. My friend watched for her while caring for his sick wife, but did not see her come out until two weeks later. Then her hair was cut short and she bore unmistakable signs of being a lost woman well started on the way to the river or a pauper's grave. One evening not long ago, after Friday evening service in my own church, I started up Fifth Street on my way home. On the corner of Locust Street I noticed two men of twenty-eight or thirty years talking to two girls of fourteen or fifteen years. I overheard some foul language as I passed. I slackened my pace and a moment later turned and saw one of the men with his arms about one of the girls dragging her by main strength into the private doorway of a house whose second floor is occupied by a young men's club. She made no outcry, and like many another silly child of her age may not have been altogether unwilling. I walked promptly back. My presence was all that was necessary; the man released her; she ran quickly away, and he slunk into the dark entry and shut the door.

Once despoiled, the way back to a virtuous life is exceedingly difficult. It is as easy to fall as it is hard to rise. To begin with, the brothel proprietor does not willingly part with a comely source of profit. Persuasion and attention are used to detain her, and if these fail there is no hesitation in using force. Stories of forcible detention are not mere hearsay. My family physician was attending a mission meeting in the slums, when one of the fallen girls in attendance called him by name and told him that in a certain house there was a young girl who would very much like to get away if she could. He asked whether she would grant him an interview, and was told that she would. He called at the house indicated and asked for her. She came down stairs with nothing on but a chemise, stockings and fancy slippers. He told her that he wished to go to her room that he might talk with her. They went, and he told her that he had come to take her out of that house of shame. She was more than willing. He bade her get her clothes. She replied that the proprietor had them. The man of the house was called, and the physician told him that he purposed taking the girl away. The man threatened to throw him out, but was assured that if any throwing was done it would probably be the other way about, since an officer from the Central Station was at the door. The man sobered. The physician asked for the girl's clothes. She had none, the man said. The physician sat down and said determinedly that he purposed staying there until the clothes were brought. They came promptly. The girl donned them, and departed with her deliverer, who sent her back to her home in Boston.

There are a score of influences about every such girl to hold her in her fallen estate; there are very few influences inviting her out of it. Not many people are willing to trust her. Not many Christian churches are anxious to have her in membership. We talk touchingly of the Magdalens whom our Lord forgave in Palestine nineteen hundred years ago. But it is not easy to give a warm welcome to our churches and homes to the penitent Magdalens of our day and neighborhood.

What are the available means of abating this evil? There are those who insist that the whole arrangement is necessary evil; that our daughters would not be safe on the streets but for these outlets for men's passions. If that be so, the fallen inmates of the brothel whom we affect to despise, should be honored as martyrs for the good of the race, as truly saving the bodies and souls of our dear ones by their vicarious sin, as Jesus Christ saved us by His vicarious suffering. If this claim is true, rather than have any womanhood dishonored, I should urge that we shut up, past all release, the bestial men whose passions so threaten society. If I believed such sin to be necessary, I for one never should preach again until a gospel were provided that should give what it professes to give, freedom from the power of sin as well as its guilt.

Others of somewhat the same temper as those who insist on the necessity of the evil, suggest that we limit the evil by licensing it. As has been well said, the proposal to license is a crime against woman and an insult to man,*— a crime against woman, for it proposes to legalize her sale for money for the basest uses; an insult to man, for it assumes that he is the slave to uncontrollable passions. A license and regular inspection might measurably prevent the disease which follows vice, but we need not be concerned to help men to sin safely. Moreover, any system of license is outrageously one-sided; a law which compels a woman to have medical certificates of health, should compel her customers to exhibit certificates as to their health.

A second suggestion is to make no attempt to restrict it. If let alone, some say, it will limit itself. But as the licensed and localized system has proved a failure in Tokio and Paris, so the unrestricted system has failed in London. The faulty operation of these systems elsewhere is the sufficient answer to any proposition to adopt them here.

The first thing to do, probably, is to arouse the people to a sense of the enormity of the evil as it exists among us. Mr. Stead's exposure of the traffic in girls in London not

---

* *The Outlook*, March 16, 1895, p. 433.

only moved all Great Britain but it was the beginning of an agitation for the raising of the age of consent all through the United States, and did a world of good in the better protection of girlhood. This healthful agitation took organized form in the W. C. T. U. convention in Philadelphia in 1886. Dr. Parkhurst's crusade has borne fruit already in a notable advance in New York legislation. A law has been passed and has been signed by Governor Morton making the age of consent eighteen years, and the penalty for violation, if in the first degree, imprisonment of not more than twenty years; if in the second degree, imprisonment of not more than ten years.

There is room for improvement in Pennsylvania's law. The age of consent here is sixteen years. A girl of that age cannot legally sell her toys; her consent to a virtuous marriage would not be valid. But she can legally consent to her own pollution, and if the villain who takes advantage of her can make a show of proving that she did not resist to the last limit of her physical strength, the law justifies him and he goes out scot-free. There is manifest room for improvement here. So there is in still another place. The penalty for violation of the age-of-consent law is fairly severe. Forcible violation of a maiden over sixteen years of age, or violation of a girl under sixteen, with or without her consent, is construed as rape, and is punishable with as much as one thousand dollars fine and fifteen years' imprisonment in solitary confinement. But if by hook or by crook any villain can persuade a child sixteen years and one day old to consent to her own dishonor, the crime is simply fornication, and the extreme penalty is one hundred dollars fine. The fine would be the same if a man were convicted of carnal relations with a hardened prostitute. There is a difference between persuading or compelling a virtuous girl of sixteen years and one day old to yield herself to pollution, and indulging in criminal intimacy with a public prostitute who offers her body for hire and solicits its use. But our law recognizes no difference. The law should be so amended as to define degrees of the crime of fornication, and attach imprisonment and not simply a fine to guilt of the first degree. The law as it now stands is an invitation to sin.

Another help in the dissipation of the evil would be the execution of the laws that we already have. The superintendent of our police force claims that there are no laws adequate to the closing of our brothels. The Act of March 31, 1860, reads: "If any person shall keep and maintain a common bawdy house or place for the practice of fornication, or shall knowingly let or demise a house or part thereof to be so kept, he shall be guilty of a misdemeanor and on conviction be sentenced to pay a fine not exceeding one thousand dollars, and to undergo an imprisonment not exceeding two years." The law would seem explicit enough. But it is only fair to recognize the great difficulty of producing evidence that is satisfactory to our courts of law. The law against massage parlors, for example, in Chicago, would seem sufficiently clear. They are simply houses of prostitution, which the law fosters rather than checks. Policemen have procured evidence against them by taking the "treatment." But the criminal code of Illinois says that no person can be convicted of a crime where the witnesses to the crime have been guilty of participating in the offence in order to procure the evidence necessary to convict.

We may recognize, then, the extreme difficulty of furnishing satisfactory evidence. It would seem as if open solicitation from doors and windows, a laying hold on strange men passing, and apparent efforts to pull them into the house, would be some sort of evidence. This sort of proof any one who wishes may secure by a visit to the streets where the houses swarm. But if this is not convicting evidence, and if one is not permitted to enter a house and secure further proof—if the evil must go on with the open and avowed cognizance of the police department, at least we should be delivered from the feeling that it goes on under police patronage. That such patronage exists one is apt to conclude, when he finds such houses fairly nesting under the eaves of police stations, or when he stands and watches policemen lolling against the open windows conversing with the abandoned inmates of the Bainbridge Street houses, or when he sees the policemen of the eighth district station house playing familiar with the prostitutes of Canton Street, or when he observes a policeman standing for half an hour at a time talking with the street-walkers on Eighth and Ninth Streets. All of this it has been my painful privilege to observe. I do not say that our police department profits by the impure lives of our lost women. But all signs indicate that if our police should undertake to join in prayer with us that the social evil might be abolished, the amen would stick in their throats. A little more diligent use of our police power would be an amazing help in mitigating this evil.

The best mitigation, probably, must come from our homes. Parents have been criminally negligent. Ignorant innocence leads most girls astray. A prudish silence lands many a girl in the brothel and provides her customers as

well. It ought to be possible to impart to our children some
instruction about these most important relations of life,
without mantling the cheeks of parent or child with a blush.
It is little short of criminal to send our young people into
the midst of the excitements and temptations of a great city
with no more preparation than if they were going to live in
paradise.

And I cannot escape the conviction that women hold in
their hands the key to the solution of this problem. They
are cruel in their severity toward their fallen sisters, but
they are criminally indulgent toward the men who cause
their fall. The woman sinner is reprobated. But the man
sinner is made a hero, is welcomed into respectable homes,
is permitted to marry a pure girl and make her the mother
of children, cursed before they are born with lecherous
appetites. Let woman's attitude be changed. Let the
fallen sister be won back to virtue by a kindly pity that can
forget the past and say as the Saviour did, "Neither do I
condemn thee: go, and sin no more." And let the godless
betrayer be spurned as he deserves; be turned down as
Colonel Breckinridge has been turned down by the women
of Kentucky and of the entire nation. Then you will have
put to work the most potent of forces for the suppression
of the social evil.

As a Christian minister, I do not need to say that I believe
that a more diligent use should be made of the gospel for
the reclamation of the lost. It has been said, I know, that
there is no use in attempting to reform a fallen woman.
The power of God did it nineteen hundred years ago; it can
do it to-day; it does do it. Mr. Crittenton's converts stay.
General Booth reports only a small percentage of failures.
The earnest workers in the rescue homes of Philadelphia
are encouraged by the results they see. But they need a
more diligent and general support from Christian people.
We ought for the sake of our own homes to feel deeply
about it. Mr. Crittenton estimates that there are two
hundred and thirty-two thousand prostitutes in our country
to-day. Their average life is five years. Every five years,
then, two hundred thousand pure girls must be dishonored
and spoiled to supply the demand of lust! Ancient and
heathen Athens used to go into mourning because every
nine years, seven youths and seven maidens had to be
furnished for the devouring Minotaur of Crete. How
ought we, then, as a nation to prostrate ourselves before
God in seeking deliverance from this monstrous evil
that every year devours forty thousand of our pure maidens
and pollutes two hundred thousand of our pure youths!

THE TELEGRAPH MONOPOLY.

BY PROF. FRANK PARSONS.

III.

EVILS OF THE PRESENT SYSTEM (*continued*).

In the fourth place the Western Union defrauds the public by *watering its stock.* This process, so much admired by corporations of every class, renders it impossible to reduce rates to a just level, the level of a fair remuneration for the labor involved and the capital actually invested.

The people must pay a profit on a large amount of capital that never was invested and on another large amount that was invested but is dead, as well as on the capital really alive in the plant and entitled to sustenance. And if the people wish to buy the telegraph lines they will have to pay for all the millions of water just the same as if they represented a real investment. A corporation may spend a million building its plant, issue five millions of stock, put its charges high enough to pay dividends on it all, and if the government exercises its power of eminent domain the courts will award the corporation five millions compensation, because the stock, or part of it, has been sold to persons who did not have anything to do with the overissue of stock and who are deemed by the law to be "innocent purchasers," although in nine cases out of ten they knew all the facts of the case. George Gould testified recently that corporations have to water their stock, or capitalists will not invest. This is not true of all capitalists, but the statement shows how innocent the majority of those who put their money into corporations really are.

The Western Union reports its stock at 95 millions, and bonds 15 millions—110 millions of capitalization It claims 190,000 miles of line, 800,000 miles of wire, and 21,360 offices. The figures, however, are false. Three-fourths of the offices are railway offices maintained by the railways. And the mileage appears to have been obtained by adding together the mileage of all the lines the Western Union has ever built, bought or leased, a large portion of which has long since ceased to exist, and another portion, consisting

of useless parallels constructed on purpose to be bought
by the Western Union, remains on its hands as mere lumber.
The total land plant in actual operation under Western
Union control is probably less than 100,000 miles of poles
and 400,000 miles of wire, and the larger part of this is not
in good condition. The total value of the plant, offices and
all, appears to be about 20 millions. Subtracting the 15
millions of bonds we have 5 millions of property which the
stockholders own after paying their debts—5 millions as
the total tangible basis of 95 millions of stock.[1] The evidence of all this is voluminous and convincing. Let us
examine it.

In 1860 a telegraph line was built from Brownsville, Neb., 1,100
miles to Salt Lake City. Charles M. Stebbins, a well known telegraph builder constructed 475 miles on the eastern end of the line, for
$67 a mile. The western end was more expensive, being built
according to Mr. Stebbins, at a large profit to the contractors. The
whole line cost $147,000, overcharge and all. On this expenditure
$1,000,000 of stock was issued in the name of the Pacific Telegraph
Company, which was owned entirely by men prominent in the
Western Union. This Pacific Company was then absorbed by the
Western Union, 2 millions of Western Union stock being issued to
pay for the 1 million of Pacific stock which was itself about all
water. After this the stock of the Western Union was trebled, so
that an original expenditure of $147,000 (half of which was itself a
fraud) came to represent 6 millions of Western Union stock.[2] The
Western Union is not satisfied with ordinary homœopathic dilution
of capital; they believe in the high potencies. The most amusing
part of it all, to the Western Union folks, is the fact that the expenditure of 147,000 was nearly three times repaid by a bonus of $40,000
a year from the United States government for a period of ten
years'—$400,000 in all, or more than 5 times the actual value of the
whole line,—$400,000 plus $6,000,000 of stock, or $6,400,000 that ought
not to have cost, and was not worth, over $75,000—84 parts water to
1 of solid.

In 1884 the Senate Committee on Postoffices and Postroads reported as follows on Western Union water:

"In 1863 its capital stock was only $3,000,000, and even of this
amount (small as it seems in comparison with the present [1884]
capital stock of $80,000,000) it is quite certain that at least five-sixths
consisted of what is known in stock manipulations as water. The
original line of the Western Union was from New York to Louisville,
via Buffalo, Cleveland, and Cincinnati, and was constructed at a
cost of about $150,000. It early acquired, by purchase at very low
rates, the property of embarrassed Western telegraph companies
owning lines from Buffalo to Milwaukee, and from Cleveland to

---

[1] Mr. Charles M. Stebbins told the Washburn Com. in 1870 that Western Union
stock had had *eleven* parts of water added to it (H. Rep, 114, p. 82), and it now seems to
have 18 parts of water to 1 of solid.

[2] Sen. Rep. 577, pp. 4, 5. Speech of Senator Hill in the U. S. Senate, Jan. 14, 1884.
The Voice, May 30, '95.

[3] Ibid.

Cincinnati, and built a line from Pittsburg to Philadelphia, but even then its actual cash investment is affirmed, by those who have carefully investigated the subject, not to have exceeded $300,000."[4]

"In 1863 the stock was doubled by a stock dividend, and during 1863–4, five millions were added to represent extensions and purchases of new lines paid for in stock. The capital being thus swollen to $11,000,000, was in 1864 again doubled by a stock dividend, and thereby made $22,000,000. The year 1866 was memorable for new consolidations, the stock having been increased to $41,000,000 by the issue of $19,000,000 of new stock. Since 1866 the stock capital has been carried up to $80,000,000 partly by the issue of stock for the purchase of new lines, but mainly by the three following stock dividends: In 1879, $5,000,600; 1881, $15,526,590; and $4,320,000, total, $25,807,190. It is not necessary to comment upon stock dividends, the nature and effect of which are well understood. In respect to the issues of stock for purchases of other lines, the prices paid have no relation either to the cost or to the earning capacity of the property. The purchases were influenced, in some cases, by the desire to get rid of competition, and in others by the fact that the persons controlling the management of the Western Union had large interests in the property purchased. The higher the prices paid, the greater were the gains of individuals in control of the Western Union."[4]

"In 1881 the Western Union paid $15,000,000 of its stock to buy the American Union Telegraph Company and $4,080,000 of its stock for all the stock it did not already own of the Atlantic and Pacific Telegraph Company. These purchases increased the Western Union property by only 3,975 miles of pole, 46,171 miles of wire, and 329 offices, the cost of which property must have been about $3,232,000. These purchases did not cause any accession to the business of the Western Union. . . . It is evident that the prices paid for competing lines were vastly in excess of either the cost or the earning capacity of the property acquired."[4]

"The swollen capitalization of the Western Union has created at one and the same time a cover, au inducement, and in some cases a necessity for excessive charges for telegrams."[5]

Here is the verdict of the National Board of Trade (Report of Exec. Com., Nov. 15, 1882):

"In 1858 the Western Union had a capital of $385,700. Eight years later the stock had expanded to $22,000,000, of which $3,322,000 was issued in purchase of competing lines, while nearly 18 millions were issued as stock dividends. This was the first attempt to spread out an increased paper capital which should hereafter afford a plausible pretext for imposing on the public an oppressive tariff of charges. The next step was the purchase of the United States Telegraph Company, for which purpose $7,206,300 of stock was issued, an amount alleged to be 5 times the true value of the property. Next came the absorption of the American Telegraph Company. The stock of that Company was almost as much inflated as that of the Western Union, and amounted, water and all, to $3,833,100; yet $11,833,100 of Western Union stock was issued to get possession of that line."

"Thus another illustration is furnished that in such enterprises

[4] Sen. Rep. 577, p. 4, et seq.

[5] Sen. Rep. 577, p. 7.

competition always ends in combination, and the public are ultimately obliged to pay for the construction of duplicate lines which
are not needed and are only constructed for the purpose of forcing
a divide of the enormous sums charged the public for a public service which is a natural adjunct of the postal service."

These are not the words of enthusiastic reformers, but
of hard-headed business men, thoroughly familiar with corporation methods from inside knowledge,—it would puzzle
even our best reformers, however, to outtalk these business
men on this subject of the telegraph. The report proceeds:

- "Later the 'American Union,' whose actual value was about 3
millions (franchise and all), was absorbed, together with the Atlantic & Pacific Co. (also worth about 3 millions franchise and all),
and in the consolidation the American Union was put at $15,000,000,
and the Atlantic Pacific at $8,400,000, while in order to absorb in
dividends the enormous earnings which they were levying on the
public, a further increase of $15,000,000 was made under the pre-
tense of issuing stock to represent surplus earnings previously
invested in the plant.

"Of course such evidence of what the public would stand in the
way of telegraph charges was immediately followed by a new strike,
in the form of a 'competing company,' 'The Mutual Union.' This
company was started on a basis of $600,000 capital, which almost
immediately increased to 10 millions without consideration, and as
appears from proceedings in court by a stockholder, the directors
made a contract with a Credit Mobilier construction firm in which
they were interested, by which 4 millions in bonds and about 10
millions in stock were guaranteed for constructing lines and plant
valued at 3 millions, and naturally things being developed thus far
negotiations were opened with the controlling spirits in the Western
Union for another consolidation and stock watering."

Subsequently the consolidation was arranged and there was a
further increase of stock amounting to 15 millions on account of a
plant the original cost of which did not exceed 3½ millions according
to the sworn testimony of the officers of the Mutual Union.[*]

The following statement of Western Union transactions
will give a good idea of their methods:

[1] TABLE I.

Original investment....................................$	150,000
Original capital (1852)................................	240,000
Capital stock (1858)..................................	385,700
Brownsville line worth $75,000, bought by issuing stock..	2,000,000
1863 W. U. plant worth $500,000, stock.................	3,000,000
Stock dividends (1863)................................	3,000,000
Total stock (1863)..................................	6,000,000
Stock to buy other lines.............................	3,322,000
Stock dividends......................................	1,678,000
Total (1864)....................................	11,000,000

[*] Blair Committee, Vol. 1, p. 120. See also as to all but the last step, Bingham Com.
Thurber's test, p. 26.

[1] See Sen. Rep. 577, N. B. T. and Blair Reps. above cited—also I. T. U. Hearings,
1894, the Bingham Rep., 1890, and the reports of the Western Union.

Stock dividends.. 11,000,000

Total (Jan. 1866)................................... 22,000,000
Stock to buy U. S. Telegraph Co. worth $1,443,000....... 7,216,300
Stock for Amer. Telegraph Co. worth perhaps $1,500,000.. 11,833,100

Total (1866)....................................... 41,049,400
Stock dividends.. 5,060,000
Stock for American Union and Atlantic & Pacific Co.'s
(worth together about $3,232,000 aside from the fran-
chises) over 23 millions, but as W. U. already owned
over 4 millions of A. & P. the new issue was only.... 19,080,000
Stock dividends.. 15,000,000

Total (1884)....................................... 80,000,000
Stock for Mutual Union worth about $3,000,000........ 15,000,000

Total stock (1895)...............................$95,000,000

Here we have a clear record of 60 millions of stock representing less than 10 millions of actual cost, and 35 millions
of other stock representing a value not ascertainable in
detail. This 35 millions chiefly consist of stock dividends,
and most of it is probably water. The National Board of
Trade evidently so regards it, and it stands to reason that
a corporation which issues 60 millions of stock for 10
millions of investment in the purchase department, would
not come any nearer to solid issues in the dividend department.

If the same principle—I beg the word's pardon for using
it in this connection—if the same rule has governed both
departments, the present capital stock of 95 millions would
represent a total expenditure of about 16 million dollars,
which added to the 15 millions of bonds,[8] would make a
grand total of 31 millions as the actual cost of the Western
Union system. Many of the lines, however, were utterly
useless duplications built solely to be bought off by the
Western Union,[9] and nearly all the lines are much depre-

---

[8] The bonds have been issued at various times to cover expenses that could not
be met with stock. It has sometimes required something more than Western Union
stock to buy competing lines and whenever hard cash has been needed in larger
quantity than that supplied by the regular income, an issue of bonds has been resorted to.

[9] For example, the American Union and the Mutual Union. Jay Gould used the
former company to fight his way to the mastery of the Western Union. Having control of the American Union he opened a vigorous war on the Western Union, reducing rates 30 to 60 per cent and damaging the old monopolists so much that they were
finally compelled to take the new pirate for their master, buying his property at several times its value, and guaranteeing 5 per cent on Gould's Atlantic Cable stock,
transactions which are said to have netted Gould 15 to 18 million dollars. (Blair Rep.,
vol. 2, p. 1272, testimony of D. H. Craig, a high authority in telegraph circles, and
thoroughly familiar with Western Union history).

ciated in value as we shall show pretty soon.   Let us first
determine what value the system would have if in good
condition.

In the United States we have evidence from the Western Union
and from outside of it.[10]   In his "History of the Electric Telegraph"
(1866) Mr. George B. Prescott, an officer of the Western Union Company places the average cost of the Western Union's lines at $61.80 a
mile.   As the Company had 2 miles of wire to each mile of poles in
1866, the division of cost was probably about $84 for the first wire
and $40 a mile for the second.   In his report for 1869, President
Orton says that $1,238,870 had been spent in three years for the
construction of 7,968 miles of poles and 18,127 miles of wire—about
$100 a mile of single-wire line, and $40 a mile of additional wire—
or less than $70 per mile of wire on an average of the whole.   For the
year ending June 30, '94, President Eckert reported the construction
of 1,300 miles of new poles and 22,000 miles of new wire, one half of
it copper, at a total cost of $557,021, or $21 a mile of wire.   In the
report of October, 1895, President Eckert says that $574,639 was
spent during the year in constructing 817 miles of new pole line, and
15,748 miles of new wire, two-thirds of it copper—about $75 per mile
of single line and $35 per mile of additional wire.   Colin Fox, a
Western Union builder, testified that he had built lines for the company from 1868 to 1876, constructing 500 to 800 miles of poles in
Michigan, (some of it 2- or 3-wire, but generally 1- wire line) at a cost
of $75 a mile, and $30 a mile of additional wire.[11]   Colonel John C.
Van Duzer, superintendent of construction for the United States
military lines has built 4,000 miles of single-wire telegraph line in
Texas, Indian Territory, New Mexico, Montana, and Dakota, since
the war, at a cost of $50 a mile for the materials; the troops did the
work, which would have cost, according to Van Duzer, $25 a mile.
An additional wire, he says, would cost $30 a mile.[12]   Mr. Charles M.
Stebbins, an experienced telegraph builder, told the Washburn Committee that he had built many hundreds of miles of one-wire line for
$50 to $75 a mile.[13]   In 1884 President Green testified that the average

---

[10] The cost of construction has been greater in Europe than in this country. In
France and Belgium the government built telegraph lines at a cost of $65 per mile of
wire, averaging about 3 wires on each line of poles. In Prussia the cost of 3-wire
lines was $70 per mile of wire. In Bavaria the cost was $71 per mile of wire. Even
in the mountains of Switzerland and across the wastes of Russia the cost is said to be
but $100 a mile on a 2-wire line. For European statistics of construction see H. Rep.
114, p. 88, and Sen. Rep. 18.

[11] Sen. Rep. 577, p. 6.

[12] Sen. Rep. 577, p. 6.

[13] H. Rep. 114, p. 81.   The details are as follows:

LENGTH.	LOCATION.	COST PER MILE OF ONE-WIRE LINE.
400 miles, from St. Louis to St. Joseph		$60
375 " " Jefferson City to Fort Smith		48
475 " " Brownsville, Neb., to Fort Sedgwick, Col.		67
(Had to haul poles in wagons 60 to 110 miles, and wire, insulators, etc., had to be so hauled 400 miles).		
475 miles, from Cheyenne, Wyo., to Sante Fe, N. Mex.		75
" This line was built when labor and materials were at their highest. The wire, insulators, etc., had to be hauled 600 miles in wagons, and the poles had to be hauled long distances."		

cost of the Western Union lines per mile of wire was about $45,[14] a bit of frankness for which I am very much obliged to him. In 1868, General Stager, the general superintendent of the Western Union Company, made a return under oath of the value of their property in Ohio to the commissioner of telegraphs for that state, in which he placed the worth of their lines at $35 per mile of wire.[15] During the year ending June 30, 1895, 2,684 miles of poles and 20,370 miles of wire that constituted the American Rapid Telegraph Company, has been bought by the Western Union for $550,000 in its stock at par, or $27 a mile of wire:[16] The actual market value of the stock payment was $22 a mile, and the Rapid lines were among the very newest and best the Western Union has ever bought. Let us apply these data to the 190,000 miles of line and 800,000 miles of wire now claimed by the Western Union.

TABLE II.

	Average cost per mile of wire.	Cost per mile of. single line.	Cost per mile of addit'nal wire.	Cost at same rate of the system claimed by the W. U.
Geo. B. Prescott, W. U. . . .	$62	$84	$40	$40,250,000
Pres. Orton's Report, W. U. . .	70	100	40	43,400,000
Pres. Green, W. U.	45			36,000,000
Pres. Eckert's Report, W. U. .		75	35	35,600,000
Colin Fox, W. U.		75	30	32,500,000
Colonel Van Duzer, U. S. . . .		75	30	32,500,000
Chas. M. Stebbins, N. Y. . . .		60	30	29,700,000
General Stager, W. U.	35			28,000,000
The Rapid Telegr. Purchase, W.U.	22			17,000,000
Pres. Eckert's '94 Report, W. U.	21			16,800,000

While I was studying this matter of cost, Judge Walter Clark of the North Carolina Supreme Bench, suggested to me the advisability of getting the valuation of Western Union property from the commissioners, treasurers, comp-

75 miles, from St. Joseph to Brownsville 50
85 " " " " to Kansas City 65
80 " " Booneville, Mo., to Brunswick 60
The first line and the last two crossed the Missouri River.
125 miles of second wire was put up from St. Louis to Jefferson City at a cost of $25 a mile. There is some extra expense in running through the streets of eastern cities, but the long hauls in the West probably offset this fully and make the average about the same for the country as a whole. " Before the war a good single-wire line could be built for $50 to $60 per mile, and additional wires cost from $20 to $30 a mile. . . . I have to-day received a circular quoting the best galvanized telegraph wire at 9 cents. That is only a trifle higher than it was before the war, and it will very likely go to a lower figure in a short time, so that telegraph lines can be constructed as cheaply as before the war."
This was written in 1870. To-day the telegraph wire in ordinary use costs only about $9 a mile; the poles cost the Western Union $1 apiece (10th Census); 25 to mile, $25; insulators, etc., $2; labor $25 = $61 a mile of single-wire line.

[14] Sen. Rep. 577, part 2, p. 227.

[15] H. Rep. 114, p. 38.

[16] U. S. Statistical Abstract for 1894, p. 363, and Western Union Reports, '94, '95.

trollers, etc., in the various states and territories. I drew up a circular letter, and Mr. Flower had a copy of it sent to the proper officer in each state and territory. Fifteen sent the desired information; some others replied to the effect that the facts requested could not be obtained. The successful reports are very interesting, and if it had been possible to get complete returns we should have discovered, not only the value of Western Union lines per mile, but also the *real number of effective miles* the company owns. Here are the results of the quest:

TABLE III.

	No. of wires per mile of line.	VALUATION.				METHOD OF VALUATION REQUIRED BY LAW.
		Per mile of line including all wire, office with furniture, instrumnts etc.	Per mile of poles with first wire.	Per mile of wire excess.	Per mile of wire average on entire system.	
Michigan . .	3		$31	$16		" True cash value."
Montana . .	3½		42	10	$21	" Full cash value."
Maine . . .	6½				26	" Value."
Missouri . .		$43				" Their value."
North Carolina,	3¾		30½	8½	15	" Real value," " True value."
New Hampshire,	3				39	" Full and true value."
Nevada . . .		52				" True cash value."
Kansas . . .			50			" True value in money."
Indiana . . .	5				*71	" True cash value " franchise and all.
Iowa	3				21½	
Idaho . . .	3		50	12½	25	" Cash value."
South Dakota.	2	50			22	" True and full value."
Tennessee . .		40				" Cash value."
Vermont . .	2½				28	
Wyoming . .	5½		50	15	20	" Full value."

*The valuation in Indiana includes the *franchise* as well as the physical plant. See Rev. Stats. Ind. §§ 8484 and 8485. In Mass. the assessment is based on stock values and no attempt is made to estimate the worth of the lines. The same no doubt is true in many of the other states that failed to send the data requested.

From these returns it would seem entirely fair to take $40 as the average value per mile of poles with the first wire, and $15 per mile of wire excess. This would make the lines claimed by the Western Union worth about 16¼ millions.

The truth is, however, that the claim of 190,000 miles of line and 610,000 miles of wire excess is not based on fact. The Western Union does not possess the system it claims. At the time of the Blair investigation the Western Union claimed 131,000 miles of line, 375,000 miles of wire, and 39,000,000 messages. D. H. Craig went carefully into the subject and proved to the committee that no such plant could be needed for the business reported—75,000 miles of good wire being ample to do the whole work over the territory occupied by the Western Union. He said the claim that 375,000 miles of wire and 131,000 miles of poles were necessary to transact the company's business was "a pure fiction," and that

"The only possible way in which the Western Union can figure its plant at 131,000 miles of poles and 375,000 miles of wire, is to assume that the company now uses all the old rattletrap lines it has bought or leased in its eagerness to wield a monopoly of telegraphing." It is true, beyond dispute, that a very large percentage of the many thousands of miles of posts and wires, leased or brought from opposing companies, were utterly or nearly worthless for practical work when they came into the possession of the Western Union Company, and were bought wholly and solely to be rid of a rival company. Whatever number of miles of line the Western Union has in its plant, it is very certain that not more than 75,000 or 80,000 miles of wire and 25,000 to 30,000 miles of poles can possibly be required to cover all the territory the company occupies. Among the extensive telegraph plants absorbed by the Western Union during the past ten years were the Pacific & Atlantic, the Southern Pacific, the Atlantic & Pacific, the Franklin, the Continental, the American Union, the Mutual Union, etc. Their many thousand miles of posts and wires were built parallel to the Western Union lines, but upon dirt roads, and therefore could have been of very little use to that company even if they had been well built. It is well known, however, that every one of the lines except the Mutual Union (and doubtless that also), was built expressly to be sold to the Western Union and built in the cheapest way possible. Being intended for annoyance to that company, they ran as close as possible to its wires, and therefore were of little practical use to the purchasing company. These seven companies drew from the Western Union not less than 40 millions of its stock, though it could construct a range of lines at a cost of 5 millions that would be far more useful and valuable than all of those speculative lines."[18]

These are the words of a very high authority, an organizer of telegraph companies thoroughly familiar with every detail of the

----

[17] Mr. Craig's testimony is confirmed by the letter of G. S. Thompson, a prominent telegraph builder of New York, to the Washburn Committee, in which he says: "It must be remembered that the estimate (in its report) of the quantity of lines owned by the Western Union has been predicated upon a computation made by simply adding together all lines that have ever come into its possession. Many of these wires have now ceased to exist, and others that are still standing are not in operation" (H. Rep. 114, p. 85).

[18] Blair Com., vol. ii, p. 1277.

business. His testimony is confirmed by Mr. Thompson, who told the Washburn Committee that the Western Union did not really operate more than 80 to 90 thousand miles of wire.

The Hon. Gardiner G. Hubbard, a man who knows the telegraph business from beginning to end, told the Bingham Committee (p. 13) that the Western Union "has a large number of wires that are not required. . . . They have probably twice as large a mileage of wires to maintain as is necessary, in consequence of the duplication of wires, bought of competing companies."

In 1887 the B. & O. system handled about 7½ million messages with 52,000 miles of wire, while for 47½ million messages the Western Union claimed to require 524,000 miles.[19] In 1889 Great Britain sent more messages with 175,000 miles of wire than the Western Union with its supposed 647,000 miles. In 1895 Great Britain handled 71 million messages with 35,000 miles of line and 215,000 miles of wire, while the Western Union wishes us to think that it needed 190,000 miles of line and 800,000 miles of wire to handle 58 million messages. These contrasts are interesting in connection with the testimony of the experts given above, but are not conclusive in themselves, because we cannot estimate exactly the difference in the length of circuits, nor allow precisely for the wires leased to newspapers, merchants, brokers, etc. The Western Union claims to lease 50,000 miles in this way. In England also many wires are leased out, but the mileage is not reported.

There is further evidence that the Western Union claims are too large, when we turn from the question of the *number* of miles in actual existence to the question of the *condition* of those existing miles of line and wire. Not only has the Western Union added together the mileage of the useless parallels it has absorbed, to make its plant appear 2 or 3 times as big as its effective working system really is, but it has allowed even its working lines to get considerably out of repair.

Mr. C. F. Varley, a distinguished English electrician employed by the Western Union some years ago to inspect their lines and report on their condition, said: "The insulating power of your lines is, on an average, but 20 to 25 per cent of the minimum allowed in England in the very worst weather." "The insulators even when new, are poor." "Your insulation is horrible in hot weather, and is getting worse. Take in hand those lines which earn most of your money, the Boston and Washington lines for example; reinsulate ½ or ⅓ of them, and I expect you will find them sufficient for your traffic."[20]

"This opinion of Mr. Varley as to the condition of the Western Union lines is concurred in by the electricians of this country, and confirmed by the best of authorities, the operators who work them. If this be the condition of the best wires, what must be the condition of the poorest?"[21]

Mr. Thompson said that at least one-third of the wires actually in operation, would require immediate renewal if the government should take possession of them.[22]

[19] Bingham Com., p. 76, D. H. Bates' testimony.
[20] H. Rep. 114, p. 42.
[21] Ibid.
[22] Ibid., p. 85.

On the whole it appears pretty clear that 80,000 miles of line and 300,000 miles of wire would be more than enough to replace the plant actually operated by the Western Union, including all the lines it leases from other companies, except the ocean cables. For the whole land plant then, including the lines leased to and by the Western Union, 100,000 miles of poles and 400,000 miles of wire is certainly a liberal estimate. At the rates returned by the states of Table III, the real plant would then be worth $10,000,000. And at the median rates of Table II (75 and 35), the Western Union's own data, the real plant would be worth $21,500,-000 if it were new. The first is probably too small, as the full value of property is rarely returned to the state officials no matter how strongly worded the law may be, and the second is too large because the operative plant is not new nor in first-class condition. It is certainly safe to take off at least one-third for depreciation, which leaves the actual value of the lines not above 14½ millions.[23]

---

[23] Senator Charles A. Sumner of California, a practical telegrapher and an earnest student of this whole subject, said in 1888, that "the lines of the Western Union and Baltimore & Ohio together are not worth $15,000,000. And for $25,000,000 sufficient first-class construction can be had for a postal telegraph reaching every postoffice in the United States" (Bingham Hearings, Thurber, p. 20). G. S. Thompson, after telling the Washburn Committee that many of the lines bought by the Western Union had ceased to exist though their mileage was preserved in the company's reports, went on to say: "It is also believed that this company, could they dispose of their present lines and build new ones, would devise a system that would much more perfectly meet all requirements, using therein perhaps less than two-thirds of the material now in their existing lines. It is therefore our purpose to urge upon your consideration the propriety of basing all estimates upon the presumption of entirely new lines, built in accordance with the latest scientific improvements, located according to a carefully digested system, believing that such new lines thus constructed, covering an area much more extensive than that now embraced in all existing lines of the Western Union, can be constructed for a sum of less than $10,000,000 " (H. Rep. 114, p. 86).

Mr. Charles E. Buell, one of the most experienced telegraph line managers in the country, wrote in 1885, "The entire property of the Western Union could be shown to be worth, not much, if any, over $10,000,000" (Sumner's speech in the House, Feb. 28, 1885, p. 6).

Taking the reported mileage without questioning its accuracy, it has been estimated that the Western Union system could be replaced for 25 to 30 millions. "The entire Western Union plant can be duplicated for 25,000,000" (I. T. U. 1894, p. 39). In the same hearing (p. 21), Gardiner G. Hubbard expressed the opinion that "A system substantially competing with the Western Union would cost 20 to 25 millions." John Wanamaker, taking the more conservative of the testimony before him, placed the cost of duplication with a new plant at $35,000,000 (Wan. Argument, p. 5).

Mr. Seymour, representing a syndicate of New York capitalists, told the Bingham Committee that they estimated the cost of duplicating the Western Union plant at 20 to 25 millions, using No. 10 copper wire, which is better and more costly than the iron wire which constitutes the bulk of the system now (Bingham Rep. 1890, Seymour's test. p. 8).

As for the other elements of the plant we have the testimony of President Green that the right of way cost the company nothing.[24] It forms no part of the investment; so far as it is an item at all, it enters into the running expenses, in the way of a rent paid by service. The patent values held by the company in recent years are said to amount to only about 16 thousand dollars. The company reports 21,360 offices. But more than three-fourths of its offices are really railroad offices, furnished and officered by the railroads.[25] The Washburn Committee (H. Rep. 114, p. 40) estimated the average cost of instruments, furniture, etc., at $80 per

---

John Campbell, a leader among telegraphers, told the Blair Committee (1883) that it was "the general impression of telegraph operators that 30 millions is a very high estimate for the Western Union system" (vol 1, p. 121); and the detailed estimates on which Mr. Campbell based his conclusion are higher than the cost shown by the actual records of construction cited in the text. Another witness before the same committee, Daniel S. Robeson of New York, telegraph engineer and contractor, said he should charge $1,000 a mile for an 8-wire line, which is certainly high enough to yield a comfortable profit even for a New Yorker; and yet this same Daniel Robeson said that for $30,000,000 he would be willing to undertake to reproduce, not merely the Western Union system, but the entire telegraphic facilities of the country, the whole telegraph system, Western Union and all, as set forth in the reports of the companies (Blair Com. vol. 1, p. 306). And this 30 millions would include the contractor's profit, which was not meant to be small as we can see by the gentleman's figures for an 8-wire line between New York and Chicago. One noteworthy circumstance about the testimony of the high-priced contractors is that they refuse to tell what the actual cost of construction would be, being unwilling to do more than state what they would charge, which leaves the listener in the dark as to their profit unless he has light from other sources.

One of the most amusing things in the history of Western Union affairs is the fact that the presidents have no idea what the plant did cost, so that when asked about it they have to compute the value, a process which produced results varying from 20 to 130 millions during the same investigation and from the same president (H. Rep. 114, p. 37). President Green a little later stated in a public address that the Western Union could not be duplicated for $150,000,000. What superb self-restraint must have been required to keep the stock down to $95,000,000!

When Mr. Sumner introduced his bill for a postal telegraph in 1885, stating that all the postoffices in the country could be connected for 25 millions, the report was industriously circulated that the Western Union system alone was worth 120 millions. When the inquiry began before the Senate Committee the claim dropped to 100 millions. When the statements came to be made in form for record by the reporters the estimate fell to 80 millions. Then an agent of the Western Union went over to the House Committee and said the system was worth 70 millions, — a spontaneous descent from 120 to 70 millions; and finally the Senate Committee reported that the Western Union lines were not worth over $30,220,960 (speech of Hon. Charles H. Sumner in the House, Feb. 28, 1885, pp. 5-7.)

[24] "Our right of way did not cost us any money cash down, we pay for it by service to the railroad companies." Dr. Norvin Green's testimony, Sen. Rep. 577, part 2, p. 227.

[25] Bingham Com., Hearing of Mr. Thurber, testimony of Mr. Wiman, a director of the Western Union, p. 22. See to same effect, testimony of President Green, Blair Com. vol. 1, p. 881.

office. Instruments are much less costly now than when that report was made. Colin Fox testified that it cost about $25 to fit up an office with a new set of instruments. Idaho reports them now as valued at $3.60 a set. North Carolina reports the batteries, instruments, furniture, etc., the whole outfit of 286 offices, as worth $7,206 or $30 an office. Any one who will examine the little offices in stores, hotels, etc., will see that $30 to $50 would be ample to cover the contents of most of them. In a large city office, perhaps $1,000 may be needed, sometimes more. If we put the average throughout the country at $100 an office, to be on the safe side, the office investment of the Western Union will amount to about $500,000. The company claims $4,979,533 real estate. As we cannot prove the incorrectness of this item we will allow it, and assume that it is all used as a part of the telegraph plant.

Adding all the items together we have about 20 millions as the real value of the Western Union plant.[26] Subtracting the 15 millions of bonds, we have 5 millions left as the basis of 95 millions of stock—18 water to 1 of solid present value not covered by the bond mortgage.

The bondholders own 15 millions of the plant, and 5 millions is all the physical value that is left for the stockholders. After paying 6% on the bonds the public should not be asked to pay the stockholders more than 6% on 5 millions, for that is substantially what they own of the plant above the mortgage, and they have no moral right to ask the public to pay interest on the franchise which was created by the public and is kept alive by its patronage. The expenses of the business including depreciation, plus a fair interest on the value of their investment, is all they have a right to ask. The public contributed the franchise on which a value has been placed of about 90 millions out

---

[26] And this includes all the land lines of which the Western Union is the lessee, and which are not a part of the property of the company. The New York Mutual lines are put down at 60,000 miles of wire, the Northwestern Telegraph Co., and the Gold and Stock Telegraph Co., etc., are supposed to bring the wire leased to the W. U. up to about 100,000 miles. A considerable part of the stock of these companies is owned by the Western Union, but the portion of the property still outside of Western Union ownership is quite large, as is shown by the fact that the company still pays over ⅓ of a million a year in rentals for the land lines that are leased to it. If the value of these lines still outside of Western Union ownership were taken into account, it would be seen that the basis of Western Union stock is even smaller than appears in the text. It is not possible, however, to ascertain the said value with any accuracy, because we do not know how much of these particular lines remain standing nor their condition; and the rental is no guide, for *a big rent on property owned by Western Union directors and leased to the Western Union is simply one way of hiding profits.*

of a total 110 millions, so that on the principles of partnership the public ought to get $9/_{11}$ of the profits.

This brings us to the *fifth* great evil of our telegraphic system—the *unjust profits* of the owners. Justice gives fair remuneration to labor, and a reasonable profit to the capital actually entering as a factor into present production. The ordinary corporation, however, cares nothing for justice.[27] It takes all it can get. For 1895 the Western Union reports $6,141,389 profit, and $1,578,584 paid in rentals for leased lines, part of it for ocean lines, leaving about 7 millions of profit for the land plant. Interest on bonds was $893,821, wherefore more than 6 millions remain as profit on less than 5 millions of property—the portion of the plant not covered by the bonds. One hundred and twenty per cent is a pretty good profit, but it is nothing for the Western Union. In 1874 the dividends amounted to 414 per cent—the investors got their money back four times in one year.[28] During the war when patriotic citizens were giving their lives and their money for the service of the public, the Western Union was squeezing the public with all its power and paying 100 per cent dividends a year,[29] not merely on actual investment but on the total stock, water and all. Since 1866 the receipts have been 440 millions, profits reported as such 137 millions, which rises to 160 millions with the profits put down under the head of rentals, and to more than 200 millions with the profits expended in buying rival lines that wouldn't take Western Union stock,—at least, President Green tells us that the com-

[27] Now and then there is a corporation with some lingering rudimentary ideas of justice; for example, the Chicago and Milwaukee telegraph company referred to in part II of this discussion, which ran two years on a 10-cent rate, paying back 90 % of their investment to the stockholders, then made a 5-cent rate or half a cent a word, and after deducting expenses and 7 % on the capitalization, gave back the remainder of the earnings to the patrons of the company, — said remainder amounting sometimes to 40 % of the gross receipts, and running continuously from 25 to 40 % of the entire business. It was wonderful for a corporation to give back to the patrons all above expenses and 7 % on the capitalization, and it would have approached complete coöperative justice if the capitalization had been true. But it was left at the original cost during the first two years of the surplus profit distribution, and afterward it was doubled, although the original cost had been almost wholly repaid to the stockholders before the profit-sharing began. Let us be thankful, however, for the record of a business corporation capable of manifesting so much of the mutualistic spirit, and hope that others may imitate and improve upon it. (For this story of the Milwaukee Company see Bingham Hearings, statement of F. B. Thurber, p. 23.)

[28] Statement of Hon. John Davis to the Committee on Postoffices and Postroads, 1894; I. T. U. Hearings, p. 59; see also p. 4, and Wanamaker's Argument, p. 5.

[29] Wanamaker's Argument, p. 5.

pany has spent more than 61 millions in cash to buy opposition lines,[30] and as the balance sheets show that these 61 millions did not come out of reported profits they must have come out of unreported profits except so far as provided for by the bonds. There are other additions to be made on account of new construction put down to operating expenses.[31] It is impossible to ascertain precisely the sum total of Western Union profits; even if all the items were reported it would not do to be too sure they were correctly stated, for corporation bookkeeping is a very flexible affair. There seems, however, to be good reason to believe that at least half the receipts have been profit. And these millions have in large part been received by men who put almost nothing into the plant. It is probably that the stockholders of the Western Union proper never paid in a half million dollars from first to last.[32] And John Wanamaker says that "An investment of $1,000 in 1858 in Western Union stock, would have received up to the present time, stock dividends of more than $50,000 and cash dividends equal to $100,000 or 300 per cent of dividends a year."[33] Think of it, getting your money back a hundred times in cash, and 50 times more in good interest-paying property!

It is probable that the total amount ever paid by stock-

---

[30] Bingham Com., p. 65.

[31] "We have built from 10,000 to 20,000 miles a year of new line out of our *earnings* all the time" (Sen. Report 577, part 2, p. 218). Yes, out of the earnings, not out of the profits. The reports say that the new construction has been provided for out of the surplus, but when you turn to the balance sheet you find that it is not true; the construction is included in expenses, and the surplus reported each year goes undiminished to the next.

[32] Sen. Rep. 577, part 2, p. 58. And see Bingham Com., testimony of Gardiner G. Hubbard, p. 5, where Mr. Hubbard says: "In 1858 the capital of the Western Union was $385,000. So far as my knowledge goes, and I believe I am conversant with the affairs of the Western Union" (the witness said he had every report the W. U. had ever issued, and he had evidently studied them carefully) — "so far as my knowledge goes, not one dollar of cash has been paid into the treasury of the company since that time."

[33] Wan. Argument, p. 5. Mr. Charles M. Stebbins, speaking of this subject, says: "At this time (about 1858) I think their expenditure had been about $250,000 to $300,000, but they soon after declared a dividend of more than enough to pay off their original investment in *cash* and *quadrupled* their stock. After that I think all their investments were paid out of their earnings *after paying dividends*, averaging 8%. They bought new lines, sometimes paying cash, but generally giving their own stock, making new issues as needed. . . . *They bought many lines very cheaply by first ruining the value of the line by competition or other means. They got many lines for nothing* by inducing railroad companies to pay all the expenses of construction and maintenance while the telegraph company received the benefits. They built other lines with the aid of subscriptions to be paid back in telegraphing at high rates, after the completion of the line. They absorbed many lines by giving their own stock— stock which, as I have said, has had 11 parts of water added to it " (H. Rep. 114, p. 82.)

holders into the treasuries of all the companies composing
the Western Union system does not exceed 16 millions.[34]
Of course there has been more money than that put into the
plant, but it has come from the profits and the bonds. The
system has been built up in four ways: First and least,
with money paid in by the original stockholders; second,
with capital put into competing companies which have
failed and been absorbed by the Western Union; third,
with profits, after payment of dividends which have been
used to construct new lines and extend the system; and
fourth, with money borrowed on mortgage of the plant.[35]
A reasonable merchant, manufacturer, or landlord is satisfied to pay for his property himself, and get 10% profit on
his capital, out of which profit or other capital of his own,
he expects to make any improvements his business may
require. The Western Union man, however, expects the
public to pay for his plant and all improvements upon it,
and give him 300% a year besides. How long are you going ·
to stand that sort of business, my brothers? And even this
is not quite all: the Western Union man likes to get a
bonus out of the government when he can without awaking
the people, and he has sometimes succeeded in getting a
· bonus that all by itself would pay 5 times the cost of the
line for which it was given.[36]

(To be continued.)

---

[34] Referring to this subject Gardiner Hubbard said to the Hill Committee: "I
think there has been of actual cash put in either by the Western Union or by other
companies about 5 millions" (Sen. Rep. 577, part 2, p. 58). The highest estimate I
have seen of the total amount paid in by all stockholders is that given in the Report
of the National Board of Trade for 1882, which says: "It is estimated by good judges
that there has never been paid in by stockholders 16 millions of dollars since the
beginning of the Western Union system, and that its present property represents
simply water and the amounts extorted from the public to extend the lines besides
paying dividends" (N. B. T., p. 11).

[35] I. T. U. Hearings, p. 16.

[36] H. Rep. 114, p. 82; Bingham Com., Hubbard, p. 10; Sen. Rep. 577, pp. 4, 5, etc.;
see notes 2 and 3 above. They also got a subsidy from the state of California. They
gave some service in return for the subsidies, but of insignificant value; even if
charged up at the high rates demanded of private patrons the said service would not
amount to a quarter of the subsidies received (Bingham Committee *supra*).

THE DESIRABILITY OF DISPOSING OF INFECTED BODIES BY CREMATION.*

BY J. HEBER SMITH, M. D.

The supreme simplifier of infection, as read from the experience of the ages, is fire. There is no noxa known to man that can withstand its fervor. Its heat gives back to the ground the elements proper to it, and restores to the fruitful atmosphere her own.

The belief in the efficiency of incineration of the dead for the safety of the living has been so general and so enduring that it would seem to have been developed in an age of experimental knowledge. Homer, in narrating an epidemic that struck Troy's foes like the shafts of an archer, killing "first the mules and swift hounds, and then the Greeks themselves," says that for nine days "the fires of death went never out." There is no more vivid picture of human interest · in all the language of necrology, though after the lapse of three thousand years, than this poet's recital of the burning of the body of Patroclus by his friend Achilles. Their ashes were mingled in one golden vase, and the promontory of Sigæum was said to have marked the place of their repose.

Fire from a funeral pile was one of the sacred sixteen commingled on the ancient Median altars. The corpse was pollution to a Mede or Persian, and running through all the minute directions for the treatment of a dead body, in their *Venidad, Fargard,* v-viii, is the idea of its utter impurity. Yet the fire in which a dead body had been burned was the most indispensable of all to the symbolical flame on their altars, for it was thought to have absorbed the fire in the human tabernacle, a spark of the divine Spirit. Though misrepresented as sun-worshippers, it is a fact that even the sun's rays were not allowed to fall on these sacred fires in their *Atish-kundars.* Such reverence, easily mistaken for idolatry, doubtless often became idolatrous. The media and symbols of the Omnipresent, in every age, are confounded with the Supreme Being himself.

* A paper read before the Boston Homœopathic Medical Society, by J. Heber Smith, M. D., chairman of the section on Sanitary Science and Public Health, Jan. 2, 1896.

Other motives besides fear of contagion may in part have
led to the diffusion of the custom of incineration, such as
the wish to place the remains of the dead beyond the reach
of desecration, or to possess in harmless form a revered
remembrance of those loved in life. The practice maintained its hold with inhumation in Greece and Rome, and
through the vast populations of Asia and northern Europe.
But though the influence of Roman, and especially Greek,
ideas and usages was most potential on the early Christian
church, she took her custom of earth burial from the Jews,
and after the lapse of eighteen centuries continues to regard
this election of the method of this "chosen people" as lending
a degree of sanctity to the practice of inhumation. But the
Jews, whatever may have been their method of disposing of
their dead in the early centuries of our era, are known to
have been adaptive to environment in their earlier history.
The law of Moses offered them no burial ritual. Always
rationalistic and practical, whether in palaces or in captivity, they practised burial, embalming, or incineration, according to outward stress. Their law, a law of life and not
for the dead, enjoined minutely observances for obtaining
"length of days" through keeping a pure mind in a clean
body. Even the word for death, *mut*, is omitted.

But funerary associations and rites, whether simple or
stately, are inherent in human nature. Their observance
antedates written history. In evidence I will simply cite
a translation of the memorial of Chnemhotep, one of the
earliest of the kings of Egypt, recently brought to light. It
reads:

I have caused the name of my father to increase and have established the place for his funeral worship, and the estate belonging
thereto. I have accompanied my statues into the temple. I have
brought to them their offerings of pure bread, beer, oil, and incense.
I have appointed a funerary priest, and have endowed him with land
and laborers. I have established offerings for the deceased on every
festival of the Necropolis.

But it may be said without irreverence, that customs,
however venerable, can be improved or set aside, through
enlarging knowledge of the conditions of life and death.

In the early part of the present century, there were evidences of the need of reformed methods of disposal of the
dead such as the present generation would scarcely believe
possible. But leaders of the medical profession were alive
to the necessity for relief from intramural interments. The
learned Dr. Jacob Bigelow, of Boston, in 1823, wrote an
influential paper entitled "The Dangers and Duties of

Sepulture, or Security for the Living, with Respect and Repose for the Dead." This appeal for reformed methods inaugurated a crusade against intramural interments that resulted, in 1830, in the establishment of Mount Auburn cemetery, the first of our rural cemeteries.

In London, with its immense population, the churchyard area, as late as 1849, amounted only to about 218 acres, within which were annually buried over 50,000 bodies. Such a number, according to the city's ratio of mortality, would cause this limited space to be filled each decade. The same condition of affairs was common all over Europe.

In this country the older graveyards were full to within eighteen inches of the surface. The stench from these cemeteries was sickening. During the cholera epidemic of 1849 the disease seemed to have a focus in their vicinity to such an extent that some were ordered closed against further interments. Would that all had been closed, and forever. But reforms move slowly against the forces of false sentiment, self-interest rooted in ignorance, and a hoary conservatism that is always more obstructive than corrective, and that halts humanity's heralds as though fearing to render account for its stewardship of unnumbered centuries.

Cremation, in its present most timely advent, comes forward as if Prometheus had freed his limbs from the chains of Strength and Force, to bring mankind once more the fire of the immortals. The torch, no longer inverted, but aggressively held, is helping drive from the city's heart the shadow of death.

But the dead, though borne farther away, continue to be little more than nominally buried, by reason of the interposition between them and the earth of such media as wood, lead and brick. Interment as still practised needs administrative reform, and, in the instance of infected bodies, abandonment of the practice in favor of incineration. The evils created by inhumation, in swarming cities, so vividly portrayed by perhaps over-zealous advocates of cremation, I am willing to grant are not inherent in the principle of earth-burial. My only apology for sustaining an opinion on this subject in any public way, is that I am absolutely sincere, and equally in earnest. But I do not go to the length of recommending that incineration, as a universal method of disposing of the dead, be made mandatory, or enforced with penalties for non-compliance. Every citizen, however, should favor the statutory correction of the faulty methods by which earth-burial is now effected.

The evils inhering in the practice of interment, as has been suggested, are independent of its principle, and are largely of man's own creation. After a thoughtful consideration of the subject, from every point, I candidly concede, although intending my own remains for the columbarium, that the natural destination of all the organized bodies that die on the earth's surface is the earth; and that the earth is fully competent, by its *unhindered* agency, to effect the resolution of all bodies committed to it. There is a remedy for the evils that threaten from burying the dead in sealed coffins, brick graves, and tombs, a practice that stores in our midst a multitudinous impletion of human remains in every stage of decay; the remedy, next to prevention, lies in a practical recognition of an obvious law of nature. The law referred to is the deodorizing and disinfecting power of natural soil over animal remains that are buried according to nature. The earth, whether wild pasture, or glebe of ecclesiastical benefice, is entirely competent to effect the resolution of its dead, under right conditions.

Do we not all know that if we look for a body that has been buried for five or six years (without inclosure) there is found only the inorganic part of it? The organic part has been resolved into its constituent elements, and reëntered the atmosphere.

In certain large cities of Europe such *carrion-troves* out-number by hundreds of thousands the living. They lie, incapable of further change, except through reformed legis-lation or a cataclysm of nature, a reproach to those responsi-ble for this state of things, and a source of danger for generations to come. Is it to be wondered at that our loved ones die in old-world capitals of unmanageable fevers, the exciting causes of which any government might eradicate at far less cost than the labor and treasure now expended on preparations for war?

Undeterred by the evils created by our progenitors, we are responsibly engaged in extending and perpetuating them. We, as citizens, should oppose the granting of privi-leges to corporations for the establishment of cemeteries too near our growing cities for the good of the public. Let us in every right way help do away with burial customs that are, in effect, a permanent tenure of land by the dead. The hand of death must not be suffered to hold the foot of progress.

The same great law applies to the body of the king as to the remains of the beggar; it must ever be a hurtful practice to bury the dead in sealed coffins, vaults, and tombs. Better to die at sea, and have some memory of us kept by cenotaph above an empty grave, than to imperil those who are to inherit our lands and name. Graves should not be reopened until ample time has been given for the complete resolution of their contents. Who would wish his remains so kept from the operations of nature that a laborer's pick, by a chance blow, might endanger society? In Xenophon's "Cyropædia," Cyrus the Elder is represented as saying, with a wisdom above that of our own vaunted civilization:

When I am dead, my children, do not enshrine my body in gold and silver, or any other substance, but return it to earth as speedily as possible; for what can be more desirable than to be mixed with the earth which gives birth and nourishment to everything that is excellent and good?

The common cemetery is not solely the property of one generation, now departed, but is likewise the common property of the living and of generations yet unborn. Some of the earliest records of the old English cathedrals and parish churches provide for the payment of larger fees for "chested buryalls" than for "unchested," but mention of coffins is nowhere made in the burial service of the Church of England. The coffin is of somewhat recent origin with our English ancestry, it appears, but it has become a costly and deplorable feature of the profusion which mars the rites with which we lay away our dead. As an illustration of the comparative imperishability of wood in ordinary soil, it is well known that, within a recent period, wooden coffins of the time of Charles II were removed from Holborn cemetery in as sound a state as those of recent burial. Wood in moist earth is nearly indestructible.

Burial has been conducted in a way so unnatural that the intramural graveyards offer a soil so saturated with animal matter that it can no longer be called earth. In granting privileges for the establishment of new cemeteries, suburban only for a year and a day with our rapidly encroaching population, are those who administer the laws exercising due care as to the kind of location selected, and as to the quality of soil chosen, and are they sufficiently assured that the same pollution of the ground and neighboring waters is not threatening to repeat and multiply the horrors of the older graveyards? Public health is purchased only by public vigilance.

No longer ago than 1875, in a report of the directors of the General Cemetery Company (of England), in recommendation of the plans which they were proposing for their future guidance, they say:

It has been found that seven acres will contain 133,500 graves; each grave will contain ten coffins; thus accommodation will be found for 1,335,000 deceased paupers.

A system of burial based on such a betrayal of humanity by decimals was at once inaugurated, and was suffered in this age of boasted intelligence to go into effect.

Surely, whichever way the minds of physicians incline on the question of cremation, they must unite in deprecating a continuance of the old régime. Our education and observation must compel us to oppose strenuously the accumulation in sealed inclosures of unresolvable animal matter, to the perversion of the earth from the exercise of its function, until, becoming supersaturated with death, it menaces the public health with exhalants laden with the potency of enteric disease and the slow tortures of malaria. An ideal civic administration will aim to preserve or provide an uncontaminated soil, pure water, and a pure atmosphere.

In the interest of sanitary science and of society I ask, Is there a surer and simpler way of disposing of infected bodies than that of modern cremation? Shall we not lend our influence to this method, and to other needed reforms in interment which need administrative enforcement, from this time, without division? But you will need, as physicians, to deal very thoughtfully with all who may oppose a change. Let us be very tolerant of feelings that have become entwined with the deep convictions of our fellow-citizens, and associated with the most sacred hopes and offices of religion, which to some appear in danger of profanation.

That incineration has a religious side none of us will deny. It is not for us to offer any censure for the quiet, but observant, conservatism of the church in relation to the increasing interest in cremation. But may we not venture to offer that this method of disposing of the dead seems, on careful thought, to comport with the purest ethical teachings of Jesus—the consideration of others as of ourselves?

Cremation is not opposed to the belief in man's survival of the dissolution of the physical body, nor to the lucid and generally accepted explanation of the doctrine of its resurrection given by the Apostle Paul. From his scholarly statement of man's upspringing from the state of physical death to a higher life, we are not called upon to dissent, nor should we throw the shadow of our positivism upon any light that can brighten the grave. The doctrine of the literal resurrection of the material. body is not the palladium of Christianity. Our choice of cremation must not be interpreted as an act of indifference to the position of the

Christian church. Despite the somewhat depressing influence of our study of death, and of our frequent and intimate relations with the dying, we cherish the hope common to humanity and older than Christianity, that when our work is finished, we shall depart like our fathers, crossing the valley of darkness, with all our faculties complete, our imperfections thrown off, clothed in a shining form, beyond this lower gloom ascending like pure flame, to achieve the perfection of a divine ideal.

But for one moment, let us consider just what is the real and present attitude of the Christian church toward the practice of cremation? What do her influential exponents say? The Very Rev. J. Hogan, S. S., in *Donahoe's Magazine* for July, 1894, writes:

Doctrinally the Church has nothing to oppose to it, for no divine law has determined the manner of disposing of the dead. Practically she is prepared to admit it in cases of necessity, such as those of war or pestilence, when a large number of decaying bodies may become a danger to the public health unless they are reduced to ashes. We go farther, and say that if we could suppose in some remote period the necessity to have become common, doubtless the Church would accommodate herself to it. But in the present circumstances she objects to the practice. She objects, first of all, because she is instinctively conservative, and dislikes all unnecessary changes, especially when the change would be a departure from what she has practised universally and invariably from the beginning.

After citing the several decrees of Rome in relation to questions of cremation referred to the Vatican, dating from September, 1884, to December, 1886, he continues:

From these rulings it is easy to gather the mind of the Catholic Church. She dislikes a change; she maintains her ancient customs, to which she is bound by many ties; yet she is ever ready to take into account the requirements of the day and the advent of new methods, so long as they are not introduced in a spirit of hostility to her faith. She clings to the past; yet she leaves to each individual bishop to decide in what measure it may be advisable to depart from it.

It is well known that the late Bishop Phillips Brooks was favorable to cremation. His successor, Rt. Rev. William Lawrence, addressed the annual meeting of the New England Cremation Society, on Dec. 19, 1893. He began by observing that cremation as a means of disposing of the bodies of the dead is worthy of the thoughtful consideration of Christian people. He further expressed his conviction that under certain conditions it merited adoption by them, for at least three reasons:

1. Cremation is in behalf of the living.
2. Cremation is a reverent method of disposing of the bodies of

School. This is the condition upon which the county commissioners themselves hold the property, and without this condition the transfer would be at once illegal and absurd. It is difficult even for Chicagoans to realize why this offer was not at once accepted, especially as, at the time it was made, the board of education was just upon the point of paying $20,000 for a scant acre of land in the immediate vicinity of that offered it for nothing. Incredible as it may appear, however, the board did hesitate long.

The real reason for this hesitancy is still more incredible to those, outside of Chicago, who are aware of the extraordinarily high standing, educationally, of the Cook County Normal School, which could thus be obtained free, with its faculty of picked specialists, its fine library, its well equipped manual training room, and its large gymnasium. The reason for the offer of this valuable public property is sufficiently simple. The school, although a county institution, stands well within the city limits. It cost the county board some $35,000 a year for its maintenance. The county is growing poorer, as the great city, growing steadily greater, annexes the county towns and diminishes the amount of the county taxes. Of course the county board must cut its garment to fit its cloth if it would remain solvent. The Normal School was a source of outgo, not of income to the county. It was a burden to the county commissioners but would be of great value to the city board of education. Hence the offer.

The hesitancy of the board of education over the acceptance of this offer was in part characteristic. It wished to be prudent, and it had a great distrust of the county commissioners—that distrust which a body of business men naturally feels for a body of politicians, a distrust which we shall sometime regard as shameful. There should be no such division between business men and politicians. This country was not designed to be governed by a class, but by all the people, and if a certain class does govern it, it is the fault, not of that class, who have simply taken up an idly relinquished privilege, but of those who have let the privilege drop. However this may be, the board of education whispered that this was a political scheme and must be looked into, and the more it was investigated the less it was liked.

For, although politically and legally the plan stood investigation well, educationally it revealed difficulty after difficulty. The Normal School is founded and maintained upon an entirely different plan from the city schools. To train the teachers there meant one of two things: either the teachers trained by its methods would inevitably change the city methods if brought into the city in any great numbers, or the school would have to be changed to conform to the city's requirements. It was well known that the Normal School was so strongly entrenched behind a barricade of the best sentiment of the community—indeed, of the whole country—that any attempt in this latter direction would inevitably precipitate a storm; while to train teachers after its methods would be to rouse all the conservative elements, now in the public schools, in vehement protest.

This, then, is the educational crisis in Chicago. The methods of Cook County Normal School, representing the new education more fully than any other school in the country, must be accepted or rejected. The issue cannot be blurred or blinked. Its acceptance means a declaration that Chicago has determined to educate her children according to the new ideals; its rejection means that she stands by the old. There is no doubt which way the decision will go if the people rouse in time and declare their will. Chicago's will, when she speaks in her proper person, is always upward bent, but she sometimes allows boards and small bodies of people to will for her, and then her decision is not so surely right.

Providentially the question of a reduction of teachers' salaries came up at this juncture, and the thousands of school teachers and their hundreds of thousands of friends made such a fuss about it, that all the newspapers began to talk of the importance of the teachers' work, and the iniquity of underpaying them; the pulpit thundered forth in the same strain; and the friends lobbied and gossiped and got interested in the schools. If the people once get to work on the matter, by whatever means, the issue will be met.

What is the difference between the new education and the old? Exactly the difference between a democracy and a despotism. As Colonel Parker, the principal of the Normal School and leader of the new movement, says truly, we are a democracy in form but as yet only so to a limited degree in spirit. We are far from being a self-governing people. We are governed largely by moneyed interests and political machines. We do not solve our questions of state by thinking, every man with his own brain, but by votes bought, sold, and exchanged. Patriotism is largely confined to the G. A. R. and the stump, and is not practical and sincere and simple enough to reach the primaries. All this is at once the cause and the effect of our public-school training.

A recent writer in the *Forum* said that the only argument for state education was the argument of self-preservation—which is true enough; but he spoiled it by adding that this object was attained when the child had learned to read, write, and cipher. If, he said, the state had money to spare after furnishing every citizen with these rudimentary requirements, it might, if it chose, put on the ornamental branches; but to do so before providing for the essentials was little short of criminal. This is, in brief, the argument of the old education. It assumes, without a shadow of doubt, that the essential for good citizenship is the ability to read, write, and cipher; and it does so in the face of the fact that our boodlers can all read and write, and are adepts in a certain kind of figuring; that very few of the inmates of our jails and houses of correction are without these accomplishments, and that an educated villain is far from unusual, except as to the unusual difficulty of catching and punishing him. This argument has based our schools upon the three Rs without a thought of inquiring into the soundness of the basic assumption. The scientific movement of the day has, in the prevalent system, found expression in a few high-school experiments, added to the curriculum, and, in the primary grades, a few talks about plants, insects, etc., called "nature study." The demand for a better physical development has been met by the installation of teachers of physical culture, and the regular grade teachers have been required to break up long hours of study with a few physical exercises. The awakened interest in art has been met, in Chicago at least, by the installation of eight special teachers of drawing, under Miss Josephine Locke, who have worked like giants and have subtly leavened the whole loaf, as Miss Lilian Whiting showed recently in the ARENA. Their work it is which has prepared the way for the coming of a greater good—the filling of the schools with teachers as full of power, earnestness, and wisdom as themselves.

Singing, fortunately, has never been in any great danger of being banished from the schools, a danger which only recently threatened drawing and physical culture in the Chicago schools. The love of music is stronger in us as a people than the love of art. We know better what it means.

But, although the public schools have taken on science and art and physical culture, they have retained their basis in the three Rs. To spell! What a noble thing it is! How well worth hours and hours of effort! What an imposing substitute for the ability to think! The whole point is, that the old education thinks spelling a good thing apart from the thing spelled. Did it ever occur to the worshippers at this shrine that the most objectionable books are admirably spelled, and that a state which really knew what it needed to preserve itself would put the desire to say the right thing before the ability to speak accurately, according to the laws of grammar? To cipher! Again, a noble thing, a triumph of the human reason! But did those who regard the arithmetic as second in sacredness only to the Bible, ever consider of what use to them in daily wrestling with the problems of life was the metric system, or the rule for extracting the cube root?

The new education takes a simpler ground. It assumes nothing, unless it be an assumption to suppose the child worth educating as a whole, and nature worth following as a guide. It begins by studying the child, and lays down as its fundamental proposition that any subject beyond the power of grasp of childish minds shall not be given those minds. It has as its aim the development of all the powers, mental, moral, and physical, of the child, with especial reference to their employment in actual life, for the benefit, not only of the individual, but of the society in which he lives.

From this point of view it becomes at once apparent that the three Rs are not the essentials of good citizenship. Indeed it may be doubted whether a criminally minded individual who cannot read or write is not a safer member of society than the same individual equipped with these dangerous weapons. The point of importance for the safety of the state is to see to it that he is not criminally minded. And in this connection may be cited a fact which cannot be too often repeated.

In San Francisco, some twenty-five years ago, were established the Silver Street Kindergartens. In them were trained, from the ages of three to six, the children of the poor—not the clean poor, but the slum poor. They were the children from whom are recruited the criminal classes. Ten thousand of these children were carefully watched, and records kept of their after careers. Only one of them was ever arrested, and he was discharged. No such showing can be made by the schools which give reading, writing, arithmetic, grammar, and geography as the bread of life. These kindergartens did not teach a letter.

The value of the power to read depends upon the thing read. The ability to read obscene literature has hastened many a boy into vice. It is absolutely essential to the self-preservation of the state that the taste for good literature be cultivated simultaneously with the power to read. Not one word should be taught except that with it be given the desire to use that word helpfully, not destructively. Practice in use of it must immediately follow its acquisition, and examples should be given in the form of verse, story, and history of its right and beautiful usage. From this point of view the study of literature becomes important to the state. Who could claim that "Is the cat on the mat?" and lists of such words as bat, rat, hat, sat, fat, etc., had any such value?

The new education recognizes that a thing apart from its meaning is valueless and potentially dangerous. Dirt is confessedly matter out of place; disease is misdirected energy in the human organs and tissues; similarly, ignorance is thought undeveloped, and viciousness mental and moral energy misdirected. The new education recognizes this, and seeks to develop thought, and so overcome ignorance; and to direct mental and moral energies aright, and so overcome evil.

The moral training in the Cook County Normal School, and the methods employed to secure it, may be illustrated by the following touching story. A boy who had attended the school some years was stricken down with scarlet fever. After his recovery, his mind was found to be clouded. The father came to Colonel Parker in great distress to ask about some asylum to which he could send the child.

"Never!" cried "the noble colonel," as his friends affectionately call him. "Send him right back here. We will take care of him. It will do every child in his room good. And, if anything will roll the cloud away from his mind, association with familiar scenes of mental activity will do so."

The child came; he was received by his mates as if nothing had happened. His recitations were nonsense, but nobody laughed at them; his writing was piteously vague, but no one reproached him. He taught every child in his room, more powerfully than a dozen books, the duty of the strong toward the weak. Tenderness, forbearance, and a chivalry more beautiful than any mere chivalry of sex,

bloomed in his path; and that which might have been a
curse proved a blessing. To-day the boy is in the highest
grade, sound of mind and body.

So little was this beautiful thing appreciated by the
adherents of the old system that a member of the county
board of education, now a member of the city board,
although the child's condition was explained to him, insisted on giving him a written examination, and pulled
down the reported average of the whole room thereby. He
did not think the divine lessons taught worth noting.

As an illustration of the scientific study of children which
is carried on at this school, the following instance is of interest. Two boys, twins, were brought there from a neighboring public school. Despite the identity in their ages,
one boy was in the eighth grade, the other in the third. No
one could tell why this boy did not get on. In action
he had never shown any lack of thought-power, but in
school he was simply stupid, and scarcely progressed at all,
although he evidently tried. As soon as Colonel Parker
saw him, he said to the mother:

"Madam, your son is deaf."

"Impossible!" cried the startled woman. "I should have
found it out in all these twelve years."

"I am sure of it," said the colonel, "from the way in which
he watches my lips when I am talking. However, we will
test him."

Sure enough, the boy was deaf; not stone deaf, but so
deaf that he had probably heard only about one-tenth of
the things said to him. The colonel put him in a schoolroom. He had not been there fifteen minutes before the
teacher discovered that he had astigmatism so badly that
he could not see a thing written upon the blackboard.
No wonder the poor lad had been "stupid" at school! One's
heart aches to think of the unjust markings and reproaches
he must have had to endure, and the strange, inexplicable
mess the world must have seemed to him; for, of course,
he was perfectly unaware of his own defects, having been
born with them. Now the boy is happy, and rapidly catching up with his more fortunate twin.

In short, the new education aims to build character, to
send forth well-rounded men and women, fitted to grapple
with life. It looks facts in the face, and argues from them,
not from theories or prejudices. It respects tradition only
as tradition preserves truth. It is, above all things, democratic. It sees in the association of human beings upon
a plane of absolute equality, the greatest educational power

in the world. "It is my aim," says Colonel Parker, "to have every child in my school as free as I am myself." And the colonel is uncommonly free—free from prejudice, and free from fear.

The new education recognizes that use not only exalts knowledge into wisdom, but that without use, even bare facts fail from the mind. It recognizes that the noble use of knowledge is even more essential to the well-being of the state than knowledge itself, and that habit and example are the two great agencies by which the child may become accustomed to use knowledge nobly. It recognizes that the legitimate function of the school is not to teach certain prescribed studies, but to increase the power to think wisely, to act forcibly, and to be righteous.

The new education stands ready to fit the children of this republic for the new era which is beginning to dawn. Chicago has been called upon first to face the issue practically. As she is nearly the centre of this continent, her example will count much, East and West, and, when she has proved that this education, at once more practical and more spiritual than the old, can be made a great factor in the regeneration of a city, other struggling communities will follow her example and rise up and call her blessed.

THE HUMAN PROBLEM ACCORDING TO LAW.

BY ABBY MORTON DIAZ.

Justice is the application of truth to affairs —*Emerson*.
Give them truth to build upon.—*Dante*.

In any bookkeeping if the accounts do not balance, the only way out of the confusion is to find the mis-take and rectify it. By the *miss* in taking, error has been made the basis instead of truth. Those interested waste no time in devising a remedy, still less in trying to so adjust affairs as to suit the outcome of error. They know that in regard to numbers exist fixed laws which if applied will themselves establish order.

Were the accounts of a community kept in great measure regardless of these laws—say two and two called other than four—and the results or "answers" applied in affairs generally, the consequence would be a widespread confusion, requiring corresponding effort in the way of adjustment. Though performed with all the zeal of self-consecration, such labor would still be adjustment—that and nothing more; something less for the adjustment could never be accomplished. It would become permanent, yet not, observe, as a legitimate work in and of itself, but as created by *unlawful* conditions which the people themselves had established. Even were those erroneous accounts carved in marble in letters of gold, and made the standard; were the consequent disorder supposed to be the natural state of things and therefore unchangeable; were it declared that under certain conditions two and two are not four, and that it is expected of figures to go wrong, still the "answers" so brilliantly wrought out would have in them nothing— no thing—because truth would not be therein; and the disorderly conditions would go on interminably, breaking out at intervals in contentions more or less violent.

Note, here, that as the unlawful figuring thus applied in affairs would work disaster in a countless variety of ways, there would *seem* to be required as many different kinds of remedy; but in reality, as the cause of all would be but one— breaking law, so the remedy would be but one—keeping law; and this only remedy would have to be applied, no matter how great the consequent changes.

Now as to our Human Problem, that there is fundamental

error somewhere becomes evident in two ways: First, by the prevalence of strifes, strikes, crime, pauperism, official corruption, private dishonor, the terrorism of trusts, the absolutism of money-power, and general distrust and in-harmony; second, by our numerous proposed remedies, in the shape of reforms, charities, philanthropies, missions, rescue works, tenement-house leagues, pauper institutions, watch and ward societies, good government societies, prison associations, prohibition schemes, and our innumerable legal and penal enactments.

The need of all these attempts at setting things right is sure proof of error in the foundation. Rightness needs no righting. In the real as in the supposed case, each different manifestation of error *seems* to require its special remedy,— we will say its special kind of adjustment. Hence all these various schemes devised with so much of thought and effort. A useless trouble! The remedy exists independently of human wisdom and human endeavor. It is—applied Law, according to the Creative Plan; *Order through Law.* Who-ever would solve our now complicated human problem should first recognize the fact that being a part of the uni-verse, the human world must come into line with the laws of the universe.

These laws are, first, Life. Everywhere life; no vacuity, no stagnation. To *live* is to fulfil—fill out fully—the inborn purposes of individual existence, as these are indicated by capacities. And the human "necessities of life" are what-ever, an all, this fulness of living may require.

The second law is *Oneness.* By this law any case of unde-veloped abilities for good or for use not only brings disaster to the individual, but the whole, as a whole, and as several, loses what the individual should have furnished. *Oneness* would so equalize opportunities that every possible career should be open to each, limited only by individual capacity, and by the same law the consequent gain would advantage all. Also, by the same law, none would seek profit through others' deprivation. This, indeed, would bring penalty. In a plant, for instance, were any single part to secure for itself more than its due share of light, heat, moisture, chemicals, thus making the mis-take of substi-tuting the selfhood rule for the Oneness rule, the penalty of broken law would affect the organism as a whole and also every individual member, the self-appropriating one included. This basic law, visible throughout Nature, holds with any organism, or organization; with a tree, with a human body, with a planetary system, with a country.

If other proof of Oneness as universal law be required, we will say that this law is divinely written on the heart. Neither man, woman, nor child will *respond* to selfness, like it, or in the least approve it, though many may practice it. The *response* is what tells. Oneness is the groundwork of science, of philosophy, and all of the leading religions. Christianity especially is based on it.

Our disastrous human conditions result naturally from law-breaking—are its penalty. The inequality of opportunities breaks the law of Oneness, and as to the law of Life, multitudes *of all classes* pass through existence without even a consciousness of their higher possibilities. Yet a complete living demands expression of these in the way of noble character, and of mental and spiritual development.

The penalty of this double law-breaking is seen in the general disorder whence has come oppression, repression, fierce competition, rivalry, dishonor, corruption, injustice, and unlimited self-seeking; all these causing worry, loss of health, poverty and the harassing fear of it, crime, the social evil; these, again, creating the need of continuous adjustment by charity, reform, palliation, alleviation, all now considered our pride and glory and merit, but the need of which is our shame and disgrace—because substituted for the justice of suitable opportunities—and none of which, as has been illustrated, is a legitimate work in itself, but one made necessary by the unlawful conditions which we have ourselves established.

The feet of Chinese women are undeveloped. Feet are made for walking, but people with useless feet have to be carried and in other ways attended to. With us, multitudes are allowed to grow up with capacities for use and for good undeveloped, and then they have to be carried and in other ways attended to.

The cause of our so prevalent disorder is one—law-breaking. The remedy is one—law-keeping. By the law of Life the best in every way of each would be educed. By the law of Oneness this full development in any could but work for the same in others, wherever lacking, and thus would be secured the prosperity of all.

Now whose business is it to see that human affairs are conducted according to Universal Law? Obviously those to whom the people have committed their affairs—as the enactment and enforcement of laws, public education, and the interests of the country in general. In one sense they are our servants, but by thus placing them in charge we put ourselves under their management. Collectively, they make a power we call the state. The right to legislate and to exact penalties, even unto death, implies the obligation of effective guidance. The responsibility of supporting, demands the economy of bringing out the full measure of capabilities.

At the head of the state stands the president. In times of danger from enemies he takes the lead. No enemy is more dangerous, more weakening—therefore destructive—than are sin and ignorance. Suppose, then, that as head of affairs and by the legitimate ways of Congress and the Bureau of Education, the president should call a convention of the wise and the good for planning a scheme of education which would bring out, in their fulness, *human values,* that is, the very highest and best in all—yes, in *all,* irrespective alike of wealth or poverty. For this need has no class distinctions, since selfness and ignorance and soul-poverty have none, and wherever these exist *there* are the "slums"; *there* is degradation. A state becomes grand only by human grandeur, and in this mere money-worth has no part. To educe the highest and best would do away with selfness, for that is neither high nor good. If self's *best* be developed into full activity, with all the more joy will self promote the welfare of others. For do but consider the meaning of *best!* It means Truth, Love, Justice—the germs of which are in every child—and in such presence their opposites would disappear as does darkness at the introduction of light. It does not have to be contended with; it simply *is not.*

Now form a mental picture of our world as it would be with Truth, Love, Justice, in entire control; mind awakened and stimulated; heart and soul enthused; the mechanical faculties in such activity as the general needs may require. *And this can be,* for every inborn high possibility is designed for use, otherwise that much of creation goes for nothing! This mental picture does but represent what may be—and will be. It will follow naturally from substituting the law of Oneness for the competition and rivalry of the *Selfness* now thought permanently established as a necessity of the case. It is not a necessity. Excellence for the sake of excellence, and the good of humanity are to be the leading aims.

Stamp out forever the falsity, so often asserted, that only through self-interest as favored by competition can be gained more and more of appliances for the world's advantage and advancement. Does it seem likely that the low is everlastingly to dominate the high?—that there are really times when wrong is right, when the royal qualities, Truth,

Love, Justice, should give place to the base and low? And our greatest acquisitions have *not* come through self-seeking, but from a desire to benefit the world. Witness the application of anæsthetics in the annihilation of pain; the persevering labors for inter-ocean communication; the self-sacrificing devotion to the interests of science; the efforts of the medical profession to discover specifics; the invention and unrestricted use of surgical appliances.

Let a grand purpose take hold of a man and he *must* work it out. A true poem *has* to be written; a fine picture *has* to be painted; science students are *compelled* to their studies. Think of Agassiz and others who "had no time to make money"; of the present experiments in aërial navigation; of the perilous voyages of discovery; of the years of antislavery effort in the cause of human freedom; of the hosts now working out innumerable schemes for the world's bettering! Is not, then, goodness a *compelling* force? These unselfish labors go to show the vast amount of it existing among the people, but more or less repressed by the unnatural restrictions which are degrading us, that is, bringing us below our rank as children and heirs of the Most High.

True, selfhood as a motive cannot at once be dropped. Why? This is why—because we have established conditions which demand it. It is as if a people had built their doorways and house-walls so low that entrance demanded stooping, and as a consequence stooping had become a prevailing posture. Should they be told to straighten up and walk erect, as they were made to, they would reply: How Utopian! Don't you see we *have* to stoop?

Subjects of a universe ruled by the grand Divine Laws, we have built up therein our little low-vaulted human world with its own belittling laws to match. This is rebellion. We must come under our rightful allegiance. The law of *Oneness*, working through the law of *Life* to bring out every high possibility—genius, talent, nobility of character, mental and spiritual development—would ensure the uplifting of the world; and thus, by the reign of *Law*, the Human Problem would be solved.

This will come by effective educational work; will come gradually, as shall be formed a public opinion which will demand an educational system requisite for the ends proposed. The way of forming such public opinion is to continually present the ideals and secure their recognition. This will be accomplished by thought-centres, established and to be established, and by continuous individual endeavor. A small part of the labor now spent on the merely remedial, or adjustive, would work that *prevention,* which is a thousand times cheaper, even financially. The present efforts deal chiefly with results, not with causes, supplying needs, not preventing them.

To be effective, this future education must come into line with natural law—nature's methods—and work from within out. She does not apply her efforts at the outside. The human working ground is the heart and the imagination. The future system will include kindergartens everywhere, and something else which it is a wonder has not yet been introduced, so very "practical" is its nature, namely, an advanced department of *Parenthood Enlightenment,* whereby children shall be better born and better reared. For the beginnings *must* be where human existence begins, in the home.

All this would require a very high order of teachers, a very much prolonged period of education, very many less pupils to the teacher, and—more money. But the gain would justify all this. Even if the general uplifting could not for long time be realized, yet it should be ever kept in mind, and worked for, as an aim to be accomplished, and suitable means devised. If our doorways and house-walls are now too low for our true stature, all the same educate the children with a view to it and they will do their building in grander style. Just think what one whole generation of children might thus accomplish!

And even if to thus educate for a complete living would require at the beginning the part support of families in absolute need of their children's earnings, yet in the long run it would be a much truer economy than our present yearly outlay of millions spent on pauperism and crime.

WHY THE SOUTH WANTS FREE COINAGE OF SILVER.

BY UNITED STATES SENATOR MARION BUTLER.

The South wants free coinage of silver because it is a great producing section and therefore suffers greatly when there is an insufficient supply of full legal-tender money that measures values. The West wants it for the same reason, and every section of our country wants it except where the money lender and speculator control.

Every man with common sense knows, and every man whose conscience is not smothered by greed or distorted by prejudice will admit, that the money of a country must increase as its business and population increase. This is the only way to keep a parity between products and money, between debtor and creditor, between the man and the dollar. When this safe and just rule is not followed, that is, when the volume of money increases faster or more slowly than the increase of population and business, then a great wrong is done by the government to a large portion. if not all of its citizens.

Let me illustrate: On the one hand, if the volume of money in any country is increased faster than the increase of population and business, then there is an over-production of dollars. This always stimulates and increases business, and hence business strives to increase fast enough to catch up, as it were, with the volume of money. But this is an unnatural stimulation and is often followed by a reaction, therefore it is not the safest course for a country to pursue. But there is another objection to this policy. When the volume of money increases faster than population and business, the dollar gets cheaper and prices rise. This enables a man to buy a dollar with less labor and products than before, therefore a man who owes a debt can pay the debt with less labor and products than he promised to pay. This helps every man who owes a debt, but helps him at the expense of the man to whom the debt is due. This policy always helps more people than it hurts, but nevertheless it is wrong.

On the other hand, when the volume of money does not

increase as fast as the increase of population and business, exactly the opposite happens. That is, there is an under-production of dollars. This always greatly stagnates and paralyzes business. Business gets dull, shrinks in volume, and draws in and contracts, as it were, to fit the decreased volume of money. This always causes a panic, a crash in the whole productive business of a country. Prosperous businesses fail, factories close down, labor is thrown out of employment, prices fall, and every bank that is at the mercy of the money centres is forced to close its doors and rob its depositors. The decay of civilization follows such a policy with the same certainty that night follows day. But there is another objection to this policy also. Let us see how it affects the debtor and the creditor. When the volume of money does not increase as fast as population and business increase the dollar gets scarcer and the prices of products fall. This forces the man who must get a dollar to buy it with more of his labor and products than he had to pay before; a man who owes a debt must therefore pay the debt with more of his products and labor than he promised to pay. This robs every man who owes a debt, and robs him for the benefit of the man to whom the debt is due. This hurts more people than it helps. This policy makes a million people poor to make one man rich. This policy accumulates the wealth of the country into a few hands and makes it impossible for the man who creates wealth or who is in debt ever to prosper. Such a policy means death to a producing section like the South.

If any class of the people of the country must be hurt for the benefit of others, then under the principle of the greatest good to the greatest number, is it not better to follow the policy that helps more people than it hurts? Hence, is it not better to have twice too much money than twice too little? But it is not necessary for any government to pursue a policy that will rob one class of its citizens for the benefit of another. Both of the above policies are wrong; they represent the two extremes—they are the Scylla and Charybdis of the financial problem; the ship of state should steer safely between the two.

The safe and just policy for any government to follow is for the money of the country to be increased year by year exactly in proportion to the increase of population and business. Under such a policy every citizen of the country would have equal opportunities. It is true that some would grow rich and some would remain poor, but in each case it would be the man's own fault and not the fault of the government. The condition of each citizen would be measured by his own industry or idleness coupled with good or bad judgment.

The above fundamental principles about the relations of money to man and business have always been fairly understood by the great masses of the people. Then the question arises, How is it that a people like ours, who are armed with a ballot, have allowed themselves to be robbed and bled through the instrumentality of the financial system enacted and perpetuated by our government? Why have not the people voted to change it? The answer is: Because our people have failed to appreciate what *was money*, and what *was not money*; that is, the difference between real money and token money, and the functions of each. So great have been the ignorance and misconception of the great bulk of our people on this vital point, that the South was almost ready a little while ago to accept state bank currency to be redeemed in gold in lieu of full legal-tender silver money coined on equal terms with gold. The misconception of our people on this very important matter has been almost as great among the lawyers, merchants and other professional and business men as among farmers and laborers. But the masses of the people of the South are just beginning to learn that the price of products is measured by the amount of real money in circulation and not by the amount of token money or bank currency and credits. It is standard money, full legal-tender dollars, and not bank paper that measures values and fixes the price of products. Any people who fail to understand the true significance of this great vital difference between real money and token money can easily be fooled, robbed and enslaved by the modern money changers.

The first scheme of the gold trust was to prevent the supply of money from increasing as fast as the increase of population and business. The second step was to substitute token money in the place of real money. The third step was to strike down half of the real money of the country at one blow. They cut the financial yardstick in two and prices fell one-half.

The fourth step in their scheme is now about to be perpetrated and may be summed up as follows:

1. To prevent any further coinage of silver into legal-tender dollars at the ratio of 16 to 1, and to bring this country to an absolute gold basis.

2. To have the silver dollars already coined robbed of

their legal power, so as to be only token silver money to be redeemed in gold, like token paper currency.

3. To destroy all silver certificates, treasury notes and greenbacks, and to issue and fasten upon this country gold interest-bearing bonds to the amount of the money and currency thus destroyed. The coin bonds of the government already issued will then be made payable in gold only.

4. To increase the power of the national banks by turning over to their management and control the entire issue of paper currency to be redeemed in gold.

The people of the South realize that if this scheme succeeds then gold (which is already scarce and getting scarcer) will be the only money—all values will be measured in gold. Silver will then be token money, that is, a silver dollar will have to be redeemed in gold just like a paper dollar that is not made a legal tender. If this scheme succeeds then prices will fall still further, debts will rise still higher, and all of the business of the country will have to be stagnated and contracted until they are measured by the small amount of gold that this country may be able to produce or get. Of course when this is done banks will issue a large quantity of paper currency, but every piece of it will have to be redeemed in gold, therefore no matter how much bank paper is issued, prices will not rise and debts will not be easier to pay; in fact, prices will continue to fall and debts get harder to pay, for with this increased demand for gold it will continue to rise in purchasing power. This will produce a condition of affairs horrible to contemplate.

The South is opposed to banks of issue. It wants all money to be coined or issued by the government and wants every dollar to be real money—every dollar to stand on its own bottom—every dollar to be a dollar without being redeemed in another dollar. A dollar that must be redeemed in another dollar is not a dollar. There is no excuse for the government to coin or issue two dollars and then require that one of these dollars shall be redeemed in another. Whenever this is done it is for the benefit of the money-lender and the gambler and at the expense of those who make the products that clothe and feed mankind.

It makes no difference how much silver may be coined and put into circulation, unless it is coined on equal terms with gold and given full legal-tender functions it is not money, and every piece of it so coined would have to be redeemed in gold just like so much bank paper. Therefore with silver demonetized and the legal-tender greenbacks retired, the real money of the country is reduced to gold, and all business and prices must contract accordingly, no matter how much token silver or token paper may be issued.

This means that it will take twice as much labor and products to pay taxes and twice as much to pay the salaries of the officers of the country, state and nation, and twice as much to pay the debt and interest which individuals, corporations and the government owe in Europe, as it would with a sufficient supply of real money. This means more panics, more business wrecks, more millions of people in poverty.

The South wants the free, unlimited and independent coinage of silver on equal terms with gold as it was before 1873, because this would make twice as much real money as if gold alone or silver alone were coined in full legal-tender dollars. If the full and free coinage of both metals should not make enough money to keep pace with our increasing population and business, then the South wants more legal-tender dollars made of something else furnished by the government (not by banks), and such additional money to be real dollars, every one to stand on its own bottom and not to be redeemed in other dollars. Any financial system that puts into circulation token money when there are not enough real dollars in circulation is a dangerous and dishonest system. The South wants as many dollars as the business of the country needs, and wants every one of them real dollars, each one of them standing on its own bottom. Anything short of this is dishonest and means robbery to the great majority of our people for the benefit of the few, and robbery of our own country for the benefit of foreign countries.

The South wants free coinage of silver so that our country can pay its bonds and debts to foreign countries in one-hundred-cent dollars according to the terms of the contract and not in two-hundred-cent dollars as we shall have to do under the gold standard. Every bond this government owes says on its face that it is payable in coin (gold or silver) at the option of the government. Now if we say by law that silver is not coin—is not money—then we change the contract so as to double our own debts. Will any sane man agree to do this? The indebtedness of this country to Europe is over five thousand millions of dollars. The annual interest on this debt is two hundred and fifty millions of dollars. We did not promise to pay this debt in gold, but these foreigners want us to pay it in gold. They promise to pat us on the back and call us "honest" if we

will pass laws that will make gold twice as dear and then
pay them in gold. They threaten to call us "dishonest"
if we persist in paying them just what the contract calls for.
Before we are fools enough to agree to purchase their
smiles (which would surely come coupled with their contempt), let us see what the result will cost us.

The output of gold in this country is nearly thirty-five
millions of dollars a year. This is barely enough to pay
one-seventh of the interest that we must pay to foreigners
each year. The output of gold for the whole world was
nearly a hundred and fifty millions of dollars last year. So
if we had all of the gold of the whole world each year it
would not pay half of the interest that we are bound to pay
and must pay each year to foreign bondholders and creditors, leaving half of the interest unpaid and not leaving a
single dollar of gold for circulation at home. Therefore
it is plain, and painfully plain, that we can never pay this
debt, not even the interest on it, with gold. On the other
hand, each year instead of paying our debts we shall be
getting deeper and deeper in debt; more bonds will have
to be issued each year with no prospect of paying them. Is
this the way to build up our credit abroad? Is this the way
to promote prosperity at home? What astonishing and
alarming folly. If we cannot pay as we go now, when shall
we ever be able to do so and pay in addition a large debt
and increasing interest?

But we can pay this debt and pay it honestly according
to the contract. How? We can, and we must pay it with
our products. We are the great producing nation of the
world, and the other countries must have what we raise.
We must, first, make our own people prosperous; we must
have a financial system that will enable our people to create
more products at less cost—a financial system that will
put our idle labor to work, at good wages, and set the
wheels of every piece of machinery turning at full speed.

India, Russia, the Argentine Republic and other countries that raise wheat and cotton and compete with us in
the markets of the world now have the immense advantage
over us, inasmuch as they, while selling their cotton and
wheat in the London market for gold as we do ours, yet
take their gold home and convert it into the money of their
own countries, which has twice the debt-paying power of
gold, while we take ours home and get no such increase,
therefore giving them nearly one hundred per cent the
advantage of us in raising these products for market.
Let me illustrate:

The price of a bushel of wheat in the Liverpool market for more than a generation has been an ounce of silver. The value of the two have remained in touch for more than a quarter of a century. As the price of silver went up or down, wheat followed. If we single out any one year, say 1892, we can estimate what the demonetization of silver has cost the wheat growers since 1873. The average London price for silver in 1892 was 87.1 cents per ounce. In that year an Indian farmer could ship a bushel of wheat to Liverpool, receive an ounce of silver for it, and have the silver coined into rupees at a ratio of 15 to 1, worth $1.37 in legal-tender money in India. An American farmer could also take a bushel of wheat to Liverpool, receive an ounce of silver for it, bring this silver home to the United States and sell it for whatever he could get, which was about 86 cents per ounce. Thus the Indian farmer realized $1.37 for his wheat delivered in Liverpool, while the American farmer received but 86 cents for his—a difference to the disadvantage of the American farmer of 51 cents per bushel.

But suppose we had the free coinage of silver in this country at the ratio of 15 to 1, then we should get $1.37 per bushel, and if at 16 to 1 then we should get $1.29 per bushel. The same is true of cotton and other products which we export and which come in competition with those of other free-coinage nations.

Senator Jones in his great speech delivered in the United States Senate on May 12 and 13, 1890, and again in the extra session of Congress, 1893, sets forth these same facts, and by taking the amount of wheat and cotton raised in this country each year and the price for which it sold, he shows that the demonetization of silver causes a loss to the American farmer of over one hundred million dollars a year on cotton, and over two hundred million dollars a year on wheat. He figures that the total loss to the American farmer on wheat and cotton alone since 1873 has reached the immense sum of four billions three hundred and eleven millions of dollars. He also shows clearly that nothing but the free and unlimited coinage of silver in this country at a ratio not lower than 16 to 1 will prevent South America, Mexico, China, Japan and other free-coinage nations from developing their agricultural resources at the expense of the farmers of the United States.

Our government by pursuing such a disastrous financial policy is not only each day increasing our debts but is at the same time reducing by one-half our ability to pay. In the light of these facts the demonetization of silver was the greatest crime ever committed against the people of this or any other country. This crime was committed by our own government, by congressmen and senators we voted for, by presidents of the United States who took an oath to see that even-handed justice was meted out between every class of our people and to guard and protect the interest of this country against foreign interference and foreign oppression. The perpetrators of this crime have during the last twenty years destroyed more property, desolated more homes, and caused more hearts to ache and bleed than have all the wars, pestilences and famines of a hundred years. They deserve to be branded with the deepest dye of infamy of all the ages.

The above are some of the fruits of a single gold standard. These evils can be remedied by our own government. Let our government furnish a sufficient amount of real money to meet the needs of our increasing population and business. The first great step to accomplish this is to restore silver to the position it held before 1873.

The people of the South are studying the science of money. The masses are studying for themselves and will not longer leave it to politicians and so-called financiers. The South knows what it wants and what is best for every honest citizen of our country, and it will never stop the fight until the great producing West and the great majority of wealth-producers, manufacturers, merchants and business men everywhere are joined together in one solid phalanx to rid this country of foreign debt and foreign dictation, and to reëstablish prosperity among our own people at home. The South also sees clearly the only way to secure these results, and that is to elect a president who is an honest man and an American patriot, a man who will be an independent president of the United States, who will guard and promote the interests of our own people and nation instead of one who is a tool and vassal of foreign money syndicates.

The South wants the free coinage of silver for the same reason that she wanted to throw off the yoke of British oppression in 1776.

THE SOCIAL VALUE OF INDIVIDUAL FAILURE.*

BY PROF. GEORGE D. HERRON.

I.

Jesus was brought to His death by those accounted the best and wisest of their day; by the religious teachers, and the prudent men of the state. While the Romans consented to His death, that they might be rid of an over-religious troubler and fanatic, the leading Jews demanded His crucifixion for blasphemy and treason. To the political and religious authorities His words had outraged, this death of shame seemed the fit ending of Jesus' life. They nervously thought themselves well done with the man, with their interests conserved and saved.

When He came from the tomb, to collect, commission and inspire His disciples, they were few in number. He plainly told them that their mission would render them worthless religious and social outlaws in authoritative opinion. The will of their Lord was to bring the disciples into unending conflict with the will of the world, causing them to be hated of all men and persecuted by all institutions.

If we should measure the life of Jesus by the notions of failure and success that prevail in both church and society, it would prove to have been a failure from beginning to end, mistaken to the point of moral insanity. He divided households, drew people away from their authorized teachers, and ruthlessly beat down the accepted religion of the day as an intolerable hypocrisy. He built no temples, and made no creeds; taught no system of theology, and organized no schemes of work. He was betrayed by one disciple, denied by another, and, in the crisis of his seizure, forsaken by them all. He was, says Dr. Young, "without a single complete example of success while He lived." His beloved nation, for which He conceived a universal mission, met His ardent patriotism with deadly rejection. His life was spent among the poor and wretched, the outcast and despised, the

* From an address given to the Religious Societies of Harvard College, and to the Twentieth Century Club of Boston.

diseased and vicious; and He expressed larger hopes for the
vile and ignorant than for the strictest observers of religious
ordinances. He had to go among the sinners to get a following; the religious would have none of him. He had small
entrance to what we call the better classes of society. His
manner of life was not respectable; in fact, to the religious
and social proprieties, His conduct was scandalous. The
most disreputable elements of society, the worthless and.
always discontented, the fanatical and revolutionary,
vagabonds and publicans, gathered about Him as their
leader. To the judicious and conservatively progressive, to
men of reasonable minds and wise methods, His denunciations of the order of things then existing were exaggerated
and outrageous beyond endurance. He came to be regarded
as the enemy of religion and government, of faith and
morals. His words were taken as inviting the rabble or the
mob to the overthrow of all that was sacred. He respected
not conservative reasoning nor official positions, neither had
He regard for organized interests or threats. It seemed that
nothing was safe so long as Jesus was left alive; His
presence was an increasing danger to both temple and
nation; from the standpoint of both patriotism and recognized religion, this man had to be made to die.

Withal, Jesus was the most wholly and intensely human
of men; no other man was ever so finely responsive to every
influence. He felt the horror of publicity which every nobly
sensitive spirit feels; only His exalted interest in His glorious undertaking, so intense as to make Him forgetful of
Himself, enabled Him to endure the public gaze and discussion, in which His offered life was a spectacle to the curious,
an opportunity to the religious debaters, an affront to the
official classes in church and state. As none of us can, He
suffered the sorrow of soul, the helpless ache of heart, which
comes with the absence of affectionate and intelligent fellowship with one's deepest life. One shrinks from simply
a momentary look into the holy pain of the enforced loneli-
ness that was His, even when thronged by the multitudes.
We cannot read the gospels sympathetically without seeing
how often and patiently, how eagerly and expectantly, He
tried to make Himself understood, and did ever man so completely fail? He was always seeking and waiting the
moment when He could take His near disciples into His full
confidence, which He was unable to do, even after the resurrection. His soul felt about for friends who could understand, and perhaps help Him to understand, His visions of
His own life, and of the world life, which He must often have

been tempted to doubt. Some of His appeals to His disciples reveal His great and unceasing hunger for sympathy with His strangely commissioned life.

Yet the life of Jesus was the most joyous ever lived among men. Unto the cross and even upon it, through all His measureless sorrows, He was the glad child of the universe. Compared with others, His life was a song of joy. His was the one free spirit, the gladdest heart, that has ever rejoiced our world which sin has troubled awhile. No one else ever so delighted in the spirit of nature, so rejoiced in the nature of spirit, so enjoyed the fulness of life, to which He opened His soul as the flower opens to the sun. Among all humans, Jesus is the one who sensed the sweetness of all life's elements, heard the music of its forces, and saw the beauty and concord of its movements. The life of the Christ was the music of God measured in perfect harmony to man. In His character were united the passion of a supreme sympathy for man with the peace of a faultless faith in God. Before Him was set the joy of perfect obedience toward God and perfect sacrifice in the service of man—the joy that swallows alike all joys and sorrows. He had no concern for His reputation, no anxiety for His individual future, but trusted Himself to the Father's keeping as unquestioningly as the babe rests in its mother's arms. His Father's will was the peace of His soul and the power of His work, so that He went about doing good with the expectant eagerness of a child at play. His deeds were done as the sun shines and His words spoken as the rain falls. He was free from all care of self, that He might pour His life into the impoverished lives of His brothers, to be their meat and drink, their healing and redemption. Thus, through the sacrifice and joy of human service, His life revealed God to men as their Father and revealed men to themselves as the Father's sons.

It is the human reality of Jesus' experiences that is slowly, yet more swiftly than we see, winning for Him the world's heart and confidence. The world is coming to believe in Jesus as the Christ of God, because it believes in Him as a man. His love and faith toward man are the witnesses that God is in Him. Because He came to His mission with the familiar garb and language of the people, a peasant born and bred, a carpenter and a carpenter's son, brave and joyous under the heaviest burdens, a partaker of the common lot and a sharer of the common life, through and through a man, we therefore believe in Him as the Son of God.

Had Jesus' experiences been different, escaping any of the trials and moral perplexities to which we are subject, He having spiritual resources not responsive to our faith, He could not have been the Saviour of man, because His life would not have been a fulfilment of our humanity. If His divinity had been essentially different from the divine nature and development of other men, His life would not have been the light of human life.

It was in the faith that man is the Son of God that Jesus met and overcame the worst that the world could do unto Him. He became in all things like unto His brethren; not some things. He was the incarnation of, as well as in, the common life; He accepted all the limitations of our humanity, and linked Himself with the widest human relationships. He was tried by our temptations, and learned obedience by our sufferings. He submitted to every kind of injustice, and died the most desolate of deaths. He had to conquer doubts that pressed in upon Him from without, and walk by faith, as we must walk. In solitary prayer, He had to dedicate Himself over and over again, sustaining Himself only through continuous consecrations, in order to bring Himself into unshrinking obedience to the Father's will. Three times He prayed in the garden, for the mysterious cup of the world's woe to pass from Him, before He arose serene and strong to meet His betrayer and pass on to His crucifixion. Day by day, He had to grow to the cross; grow in the knowledge of His Father's will, as all must grow. The gospels make it clear that He saw His way to the cross, step by step. We can see that His conception of His mission enlarged, and His wisdom deepened, with each new experience. There came no time when faith was not the spring to His action. There were things He did not know; He was amazed at the hardness of human hearts, and found it hard to understand the unbelief of His nation; He grieved over the conduct of His disciples, and marvelled at the slowness of their spiritual growth. It is evident that He had, in the early part of His ministry, expectations of the conversion of the Jews—expectations which were not realized, to His inexpressible sorrow and disappointment. Though His faith in the triumph of righteousness endured to the end, while His belief in the divine sonship of man was always deepening, and His vision of truth, with His power of love, continually increasing, the sin and shame of man yet broke His heart before His work was done.

II.

Jesus' nature was such that it was the necessity of His being that He should either make the strongest effort of which He was capable against organized wrong, or should exhaust the possibilities of His life in a service that would prove a universal moral revelation and attraction. His development had been so whole and human, with His interest so absorbed in righteousness as to invest all His life in its pursuit, that both His faith and His reason would have been left without foundation, had He long sought any middle course between directest antagonism and fullest sacrifice. It was His only possible self-expression, that He should make the most exterminating war against all the forms and structures of evil, sweeping with destruction the false religious institutions and their political hypocrisies and tyrannies, or else make the completest sacrifice by which the righteousness of God might be so redemptively revealed in human life as at least to draw all men unto it from the evil.

There are indications that Jesus met, in temptations beyond the power of our sympathy to interpret, the question of revolution. Civilization was a Roman dominion, making one vast splendid slave pen of the earth, with suicide the only escape for fettered, crushed and despairing lives. Roman virtues had been terrible. But when these virtues were dissolving in still more terrible vices, the earth became the arena of unmitigated suffering, seeming like the creation of devils. Could anything prevail against this exhausted system, save the attack of forces of its own kind—forces it could understand? Then there was the Jewish church, in which Jesus was born, which He never left, in which He was crucified. This church had become, perhaps not relatively more morally corrupt than ours, but a mere professional and official religion. Its teachers strained at gnats of traditional differences, and swallowed camels of social iniquity, laden with all manner of crimes against the nation. The church made merchandise of the truth, dealing out past inspirations as religious wares, while it was always rejecting the God of the living. It had thus come to stand for religiousness rather than righteousness, and had become an organized misrepresentation of God, making God seem a taskmaster and tyrant like unto the tyrants over the people. Could anything prevail against this apostate church, which had become the friend of oppressors and the mere patron of the oppressed, save fire and sword? How could God get

at the world through such misery in society and tyranny in
state, through such moral atheism in organized religion,
save in the revolution of terrific and destructive forces?
Could not a strong and intense character, with wide human
comprehension and sympathy, in almost any corner of the
earth, gather independent spirits about him, sufficient in
numbers and in politico-religious zeal, to overthrow both
the religious despotism of the Jewish church and the political despotism of the Roman state, and thus clear the way
for God to manifest Himself to the people as their deliverer,
and make them His people? The people, too, would accept
with universal acclamation and joy the advent and progress
of such a deliverance. And history has never dreamed of
such a revolutionist as Jesus would have been, had He taken
the sword.

But Jesus saw in Hebrew history and in nature, working
out the evolution of human society in a holy society, an
eternal force which man had not yet recognized. Perhaps
after years of prayer and noble waiting His brooding
thought perceived love to be the real constructive force
operating in the world of man, and throughout the universe
of God. In spite of the failures and expediences of unfaith,
and by the use of them, the love that was in God was evolving in man the heavenly moral kingdom. Jesus saw that
the kingdom of heaven, which He felt called to reveal and
realize on the earth, could be nothing else than the
organization of human life in the freedom of perfect love.
The establishment of a new civilization, upon what would
be merely a new religion, through the power of an appeal
to forces the world could then understand, in the place of
the order then existing and cursing the world, would have
been the failure of the kingdom of God, and a failure of the
freedom for which man was created. Even if He could
have scourged hypocrisy and tyranny to a judgment so terrible that they could never again rise in the old organized
religious and political forms, He saw that sometime the
beginning had to be made, never to be taken back, by which
human life would be consciously committed to love, with its
redeeming and perfecting law of sacrifice.

But, though God would give salvation through the spirit
and power of love, the world would have salvation through
the power of might. It was thus that by no other than a
life of entire moral failure, could Jesus accomplish His work
in perfect oneness with the will of God, and glorify God as
our Father. The will of God and the will of the world were
squarely antagonistic; in Jesus they met in mortal combat.

The attempt to make His life a fulfilment of both the will of the world and the will of God was the temptation which Jesus met at the beginning of His ministry, alone in the wilderness, and conquered in the faith that He was the Son of God. He must lose the world, and suffer death at its hands, before He could save it; He must fail in the eyes of the world, or the purpose of God in man would then fail. He saw that the failure of righteousness in conflict with the wrong is really the overthrow of wrong; that the inheritance of the world by the meek is both the natural law and manifest fact which the unbelief of power does not see. Between the contending passions of an overturning indignation against wrong and a saving love for the wronged and the wrong-doer, His spirit seems to have been often troubled and torn. Through faith and vision, through experience and suffering, He learned obedience to the sacrifice of service as the great law of redemption. Had not Jesus learned and obeyed this law, His ideal of the human world become a kingdom of heaven would have tormented Him to His own, and perhaps the world's destruction. Trusting that in committing Himself to this law He would commit humanity thereto, Jesus made the matchless adventure of His life.

Being so constituted that the making of His life the largest possible contribution to righteousness was His subjective necessity, and the existing order in which He found Himself being what it was, Jesus had to choose either the sword or the cross as the weapon by which He should undertake to deliver His nation, and establish God's royal reign in the world. Others, like Mahomet and Cromwell, have come to this choice, and have taken the sword. In one way and another, so long as the processes of redemption continue, all His true disciples will have to make His choice between the failure of success and the success of failure. Many are called to the cross, while still few are chosen. There may come a time, I can conceive it possible, in the social redemption of the world, when the faithful witnesses of Jesus will have to choose between the sword and the gallows. No man knows; but in an hour when we think not, the Son of Man may come to us in such a choice.

III.

Jesus committed Himself to sacrifice as love's revelation and law, in the faith that love is the mightiest force in the universe, and the ultimately triumphant and organizing force in human life. He would put this law to the test, through whatever experiences and to whatever end it might bring Him; though there should come the awful sense, as there did come when He cried from the cross to God as one who had forsaken Him, that He had been mistaken, His career a failure in reality. Sometimes strongly tempted to doubt what He did, struggling between the cross and the sword, Jesus accepted the full issues of the law of sacrifice to which He had committed Himself, in order that He might reveal it to men as the law of their common unity with God. It was thus that, in the face of the worst to be done to Him, Jesus made the holy assertion that He had accomplished the work given Him to do, and that He had so served man as to make His Father in heaven appear glorious on the earth; it was thus that He attached so high value to His service, in the face of failure and disgrace. The eternal value of His failure was the revelation of God in human life in terms of social sacrifice.

The crisis of civilization will call for its sacred victims; for such as shall be whole offerings in the social sacrifice, and shall fully manifest in themselves the love and law of the Christ. Doubt it not, there will have to be more dying of some sort, before the wrongs of this world are set right— the vicarious dying that is the resurrection of the world's divine life. Before civilization experiences its redemption, the Son of Man will somehow have to be lifted up in offered lives. We need not expect that we, in the midst of this exhausted yet sovereign industrialism, can be any more in accord with its social customs and religious opinions, and at the same time obedient to Jesus, than the disciples who followed Him through His conflict with Jewish religion, and then went abroad as His witnesses and martyrs in the Roman civilization, could at the same time obey Him and them. Sooner or later, they who stand for the social order of the kingdom of God, who believe and teach, in work and word, that the facts and forces of Jesus' life are wise and strong for the perfect organization of society, will meet the existing order of things in clearly defined lines of conflict. The Pilates of monopoly have already made friends with the Herods of the state, and the high priests of the church are blessing their union. The power of organized social wrong will exhaust itself in the wrath it pours upon the witnesses of the Christ order of society. It is no longer best to evade or conceal this. We must face the divine inevitable. The enemy of man is abroad in the world, filling the ruling social powers with every malignant device of diabolic inspiration, and will never permit the sons of man to become brothers without warring upon them, even unto the glorious disgrace and death of some of Jesus' friends. But their sacrifice will be the divine overthrow of the present evil order, by the faith and patience of love.

The full power of incarnate love has never yet been tried, save in Jesus. When it is finally tried, and we in any considerable measure learn how to love, we may begin to cease to have problems. As the legion of demons left the Gadarene, when confronted with the full vitality of the love of Jesus, so when there is a sufficient number messianic enough to commit themselves to the revelation of the social power and wisdom of love, with all the moral adventure and divine risk involved, what legion of social demons they may cast out no prophet can tell. In even the most disastrous failure, they would stir the world's blood to the purer life of a holy and undying discontent, and thus accomplish the work given them to do.

In committing Himself to failure, that He might reveal love as the basis of human life, Jesus committed humanity to love and its law of sacrifice. Call you this an experiment? Even so, the experiment is still on; yea, it is scarce begun. We must try it through to the consummation. That this love will triumph at last, and have the human future for its own, is the world's beatific hope that will not die.

Organized love is the manifest destiny of man. Love will yet inspire all motives, make all discussions, dispel all problems, and light all paths to knowledge. The governing of man will yet be done by love, become the inner substance and the outward power of the common life. Love will own all sources of production, organize all activities, and distribute earth's fruits and human products. The works of the world will be the harmony of love's social affections, with the fruits of the earth born of love's social sacrifice, and man's productions the sacred gifts which love bears from brothers to brothers. The great achievements of civilization will be the overflow of love's social gladness.

Then no man will any more call anything his own. As he has need, all things will belong to every man, who will add to all according to his powers. In the temple of the glorified humanity, the communion of saints will be realized in the consecration of all work to the fellowship of service. The children of the kingdom will break their bread with exultation and singleness of heart, praising God, and having favor with the whole people, their ransomed homes the living gardens of God in His full-come heavenly city.

BISHOP DOANE AND WOMAN SUFFRAGE.

BY MARGARET NOBLE LEE.

Bishop Doane of Albany recently contributed to the woman suffrage discussion, an article entitled "Why Women Do Not Want the Ballot." The reader is led to expect a recital of women's reasons for their presumed unwillingness to accept political rights. The "whys" adduced prove to be exclusively the bishop's own, coupled with an exhortation to both sexes to do all in their power to prevent women from ever obtaining the ballot.

At the outset the bishop classifies woman suffragists as follows:

Class one, "to be eliminated from the discussion because they fly into a frenzy . . . and are only vulgarly violent, with sharp tongues or sharper pens saturated with bitterness and venom."

Class two, "with whom one cannot deal without sacrificing self-respect or reverence, who revile Holy Scripture, holy matrimony, St. Paul, even our dear Lord Himself."

Class three, "a very different class of women and men, to whose sober second thought it is worth while to appeal."

This classification warrants the bishop's protest if it truthfully describes the general character of women who desire the ballot. But who are the women to-day identified with the suffrage movement? They include the Woman's Christian Temperance Union, who have as an organization enrolled in the cause; the Social Purity League, the White Cross Society, organized bodies of women wage-earners, and the majority of women engaged in the public-spirited, philanthropic, or mission work in every city; and, not least, growing numbers of young women in the Christian Endeavor Society, who are religiously pledged to good citizenship. To which of the classes do these women belong —brawlers, blasphemers, or the misguided? In which class do the great leaders of the movement belong—Mrs. Lucy Stone, Mrs. Elizabeth Cady Stanton, Miss Anthony, Mrs. Julia Ward Howe, Mrs. Livermore, Miss Willard, Rev. Anna Shaw? Either the bishop's classification comprehends these societies and individuals, or he has passed over the rank and file and their leaders, and turned his batteries upon isolated stragglers and camp-followers. The bishop deplores especially the godless drift of the cause; and yet in Wyoming, where woman suffrage has existed long enough to show its drift, polling places are frequently located in church parlors. Equally significant is the intuitive hostility to woman suffrage of saloons and allied forces, which foresee disaster in the success of the reform. Many such facts as these are inexplicable on the bishop's assumption.

The bishop's objections to woman suffrage are ranged under four heads, which he says he will not argue but merely assert. He asserts:

1. Suffrage is not a right of anybody. It is a privilege granted by the constitution to such persons as the framers of the constitution and founders of the government deemed best.

Looseness in the use of terms gives this assertion more explosive force than direction. To shift to the misty realm of metaphysics and fence with superfine sophistries concerning distinctions between rights and privileges has been the traditional tactics of equal suffrage opponents. In this contest the ground should be the constitution, lighted by plain common sense, and the weapons exact terms.

As to "anybody" having a right to suffrage regardless of place or qualifications, there is no such question at issue. No woman suffragist holds suffrage to be the right of the alien, the defective in mind, the criminal, or the juvenile classes. In order to differ from suffragists, the bishop's contention must be that suffrage is not the right of any citizen of the republic; further, inasmuch as woman suffragists do not claim the *legal* right of suffrage, he must mean precisely that suffrage is not the just, natural, and inherent right of any American citizen.

The constitution twice refers to the "right of citizens of the United States to vote," in one place providing a penalty for the infringement of that right, and in another declaring that it shall not be denied because of race, color, or previous condition of servitude. By thus providing penalities for the infringement of the right to vote, the framers of the constitution no more assumed to create and bestow that right than statutes for the punishment of theft assume to create the right of ownership. In both cases the enactment merely protects what it recognizes to be already in existence.

The fact is, the bishop is guilty of an anachronism; he puts the cart before the horse. The constitution is the effect and not the cause of suffrage. So far were the framers of that instrument from creating the "privilege of suffrage" that had not popular suffrage breathed into it the breath of life, the document would have remained absolutely impotent. On the bishop's hypothesis, whence came the "privilege" of the people to vote upon the adoption of the constitution—whence the right of the founders to frame a constitution? The bishop's foundation for suffrage has the same support as the fabled Atlas who upheld the world standing on the back of an elephant, which stood upon the back of a tortoise. In the critical period of the formation of the constitution, the people were in no mood to accept as a privilege from any body of men what they already enjoyed as a right. They had won self-government and political equality, and the ballot was the symbol of their freedom. Suffrage is inseparable from self-government, and the right to it is inherent in the citizens of the republic.

The justification of a republic lies in the nature of personality. Mulford in his profound work, "The Nation," says, "Personality has its condition and its realization only in freedom." While the bishop finds in his theory a reason for excluding woman from participation in the state, this philosophy admits her. Shut out from state membership, she is arbitrarily cut off from the first condition of self-realization. Her personality with which she is divinely endowed is forcibly restricted by human power.

The bishop asserts:

2. The old political proverb, "No taxation without representation," is utterly inapplicable to this question. It grew out of the tyrannical action of a government across the sea in which not one of all the people on whom the tax was levied had the faintest voice in the framing of the laws nor in the choice of the government. . . . But women who are taxed *are* represented by their relatives, by their potent influence, and by man's sense of justice.

The pith of this assertion is that our famous tax creed does not apply to women, for the reason that women who are taxed are represented by some or all of the three agencies deemed by the bishop equivalent to suffrage for women. While one is tempted to inquire whether the bishop would be willing to vest his vote in his relatives, merge it in his potent influence, or waive it, confiding to man's sense of justice, the point may be conceded that if women who are taxed can be proved to be represented, the old adage is inapplicable.

The claim that taxed women are represented involves the admission of their right to representation. It remains to determine in what way this is provided for and secured to them. Representation in any sense worth the name has as its essential characteristic the responsibility of the representative to those he represents, who on election day can bring him to strict accountability. Clearly the representation accorded to women by the bishop is not of this kind; it has no legal sanction; it is optional with the representative; it is a voluntary guardianship, such as the government extends to Indians *not taxed*. The colonists were favored with this mode of representation. They had relatives "across the sea"; they had "potent influence" in Parliament; they had "man's sense of justice" to rely upon. They refused to pay taxes; they rebelled. They knew that representation without responsibility is mockery.

Even if this *pseudo* representation were adequate, taxed women would be least assured of it, for the majority of them are husbandless, and their male relatives may have wives of their own to "represent" or may differ from them in political opinions. Tax-paying widows and single women thus comprise a class of political pariahs bearing the burdens of government but subject to the will of the governing caste. In New York State, for example, on an assessed valuation of a billion dollars, women pay in round numbers one million dollars in taxes, more money than the British government annually exacted from the colonists.

The theory of vicarious representation for women is founded upon the timeworn notion that the family is the political unit, that all women worth considering are married, and that the married woman is still a *femme couverte*, with neither personality, nor force in the state. But the family is not the *political* unit in any sense. A political unit has a single vote and retains that vote. A family may have one vote, may have many, or may have none. The voting strength of the family depends on the number of males in it, and families without male members are political wards.

Aside from its irresponsibility, its unequal distribution among women, its legal non-existence, political representation of one sex by another is in its nature impossible. A vote is the expression of a will; two wills make two votes, and if but one vote be cast, injustice is done either to the strength of two wills or the individual judgment of the one not expressed. If the will of the woman is not expressed, an affront is offered to the individuality of one whom the state has now recognized as a person and therefore entitled to expression. If the man change his vote at the persuasion of his wife, she is represented, but he is not, which is as unjust as the ordinary situation to-day, in which this evil is rare. As a matter of fact, comparatively few men tax their minds with delicate adjustments and balancings in order that their vote may represent the composite vote of two. The average man votes as he wishes and represents his wife as he wishes her represented.

The bishop asserts:

3. Equality does not mean identity of duties, rights, privileges, occupations. The sex differences are proof enough of this. The paths in which men and women are set to walk are parallel, but not the same.

This statement is absolutely sound; it is a truism. No amount of legal equality can do away with natural differences, and this holds between men and men as well as between men and women. The black man has legal equality with the white, but his "duties, rights, privileges, occupations," are not identical, and no law can make them so. All that women seek of the law is the equality granted to the negro, and they seek this because they realize that they have duties to the state which are *not identical* with those of men. The bishop fears that this equality would destroy the "equilibrium of society," and quotes the words of St. Paul, "If the whole body were hearing, where were the smelling?" This fear is groundless. Like the human body, the body politic is not "one member, but many"; and in the very chapter containing the passage quoted, St. Paul emphasizes the importance to the body of all its members, and condemns the disparaging by one member of the use or need of another. The trouble in the body politic has been that one member has assumed to be the whole body, and has arrogantly said to the other, "I have no need of thee."

The bishop is alarmed lest *political* equality may disturb *economic* laws. He pictures "overstocked professions, men and women crowding each other in and out of occupations, neglected duties, responsibilities divided until they are destroyed . . . if this unnatural idea be enforced." This figment of the imagination is "purely prophetic without the inspiration of prophecy." The bishop imagines woman's industrial freedom to be dependent upon her political emancipation. As a matter of fact woman is to-day as free in the choice of profession or occupation as the ballot can ever make her. The last census reveals the presence of women in almost every remunerative employment pursued in the United States, and yet we hear of no consequent friction in the shop nor misery in the home. If economic equality does not produce fratricidal competition in the labor world, how is political equality to bring this about? The bishop has again mistaken effect for cause. The suffrage movement is a result of industrial freedom, not its cause. And statisticians agree that the entrance of women into the business world, instead of producing the evils here conceived, has been a beneficent means in relieving the wants of homes.

The bishop asserts:

4. The theory of increased wages for women to be secured by giving votes to women workers, is equally preposterous. Wages, like work, are regulated by the unfailing law of supply and demand.

Women do not expect to force up wages by their ballots any more than men can now do so, nor do they think that their votes will ever work miracles; but they do count upon securing by their ballots equal pay for equal work in municipal, state, or national service, such as a statute of Wyoming provides for that state.

So much for the "fundamental and axiomatic truths" of the bishop's argument.

The bishop next proceeds with some personal objections to the enfranchisement of women. In his opinion, some of the bad results would be decadence of gallantry in men, increase of religious prejudices in political questions, multiplication of venal voters, and contention in homes. Loss of gallantry has been the favorite bogy of anti-suffragists to scare off women from this reform. It should be known by this time that if the issue involved a choice between justice and gallantry, suffragists would unanimously prefer justice. However, they hold American manhood in too high respect to believe its crowning characteristic of courtesy to women merely superficial, and they fail to note any diminution in the politeness of men towards themselves. The women of Wyoming boast of the chivalry of their men, which seems to have withstood the shock of being "jostled at the polls." Men may be jammed by women in street cars, crushed at receptions, elbowed in markets, made to take their turn at box-offices, but we are told that they will not be jostled at the polls.

By a curious process of reasoning the bishop discovers equally strong objections to the vote of women, in their goodness and in their badness. In one paragraph he applauds their native religious fervor, and in the next is horrified at the number of corrupt women that would be added to the electorate. Undoubtedly when admitted to the franchise, women will take their religion with them; but if it be deserving of the "infinite honor" with which the bishop regards it, it should preserve them against the bitter "religious" feuds he anticipates. At its worst it would stop short of the shedding of blood, which has marked recent theological differences of male political factions in a number of cities. And he insists that what damage injudicious good women may fail to do in government, wicked women will compass by the sale of their votes. If woman suffrage were yet a mere theory, such a prediction as this would be more pardonable; but wherever equal suffrage prevails, all parties agree that women as a sex cast pure ballots. At all events the same means adopted to deal with venality in men voters will be equally effective in the case of women.

In the equal-suffrage home, according to the bishop, either the wife must echo her husband or bedlam will break loose, and "in the heat and violence of party differences a new cause of dissension and alienation be added to the already strained relations in many families." The strife extends below stairs, kitchen arraying itself against parlor, and for days at election time, home life becomes a prolonged political broil. This jeremiad might affect timid suffragists, were it not in its nature a conclusion from an "imaginary premise," which the bishop elsewhere condemns as "illogical to the last degree." Under the same roof are now found differences in religious beliefs, frequently between husband and wife, and generally between mistress and maid, without destruction of domestic concord; and it is improbable that less vital differences will ruin homes otherwise happy. To the bishop's question, "Shall the cook leave her kitchen to cast a vote which shall counterbalance that of her mistress?" the answer is an emphatic Yes, just as the coachman does; and many mistresses might thus learn a needed lesson in political equality already learned by their husbands through the votes of their employees.

The bishop reaches the climax of assertion when he says:

There is no freer human being on earth to-day, thank God, than the American woman. She has all liberty that is not license.

Acting upon this theory Miss Anthony cast a vote at one election with her fellow-townsmen, and was fined one hundred dollars by a United States judge. Such an assertion finds its answer in the words of John Randolph: "That state in which any people is divested of the power of self-government, and regulated by laws to which its assent is not required and may not be given, is political slavery."

On the whole, opposition to woman suffrage is at present

on a somewhat higher plane than in the earlier days of the movement, when Dr. Horace Bushnell published his "Reform against Nature," for many years the opponents' classic. That celebrated theologian found a conclusive argument for man's monopoly of the ballot in "his heavy tread, his hard-knit frame, his thundering voice, his Jupiter-like air." He observed that all powerful forces of nature, such as tornadoes, thunder, and earthquakes were masculine, while breezes, dew falling, and grass growing were feminine. Again, commanding law was masculine; gospel which is "organized in submission and sacrifice" was feminine. "The subordination of woman," he declared, "is moral, and no condition of suffrage will take it away." She would find compensation, however, if she could only "conceive what it means to be the sex elected to patience." His ideal condition is one in which women will "keep their own pure atmosphere of silence and make a realm into which the poor bruised fighters with their passions galled, their hates and grudges, may come to be quieted and get some touch of the angelic." It never occurred to the doctor that the rational prophylactic for "galled passions, hates, and grudges" would be that those with the angelic touch should accompany the fighters to the political arena and there prevent them from reaching a bruised condition. But this would transform her into the voting woman, whose look the doctor tells us would be "sharp, the voice wiry and shrill, the action angular and abrupt; wiliness, boldness, eagerness for place, will become inbred." She was to be known by a "thin, hungry-looking, cream-tartar face, touched with blight and fallen out of lustre." Her stature would be "taller, more brawny, with bigger hands and feet"; she would be "lank and dry." In the face of this vision, he entreats women "in God's name, to save their beauty, for this is the power of the subject state." And he concludes, "If I were a woman in the present lot of woman, I think I should certainly wish to be a man," but assures them there are joys for them in the world to come.

This reference to a standard authority among early anti-suffragists shows the progress made by opponents. The old view regarded woman as a thing of beauty; from the bishop's standpoint she is an intelligent being entitled to the broadest knowledge and to her own opinions on all questions, and only forbidden to give expression thereto at the polls.

Both the doctor and the bishop have voiced the conservative sentiment of their day, always a useful element in social progress. It is statesmanship to consider well any fundamental political innovation before adopting it. It is not altogether unfortunate that legislators generally lag behind advanced sentiment. Consequently woman suffragists may be patient. Against every social reform existing custom, expediency, and a train of imagined ills have been invoked.

The political enfranchisement of women is grounded in justice, in science, and in the theory of the modern state. "Justice," declared Webster, "is the greatest concern of man on earth." Only through its application have the rights of individuals been conceived and acknowledged. Only through the possession of rights is moral growth in the state possible. This growth is the law of both sexes, and its development requires freedom. Men have won this freedom from the hands of tyranny, and on the ground of justice women demand it of them. On what principle can men withhold it? Has either sex the prerogative to determine the rights of the other sex? Such an assumption in any field but politics would meet with universal derision. Society makes progress along various lines—industry, culture, religion, and politics, the aim and object of all being the moral elevation of the individual and of the community. Each department of activity offers to the individual an opportunity for usefulness, and should be open to every responsible person so that according to his or her peculiar talents each may serve the great social end. Industry, culture, and religion are now open to woman, but she is still denied the opportunity to serve the state by the performance of political duties. But if man has the right to exclude her from this field, he has the same right to limit her in other directions. In that case he should prescribe her duties, in fact become the keeper of her conscience. Nature, then, has made an egregious blunder in giving woman conscience or will of her own. *Man either has complete sovereignty over woman, or his assumption of it in any province is usurpation.* As a matter of history, the arguments used to bar woman from state functions are of a piece with those formerly employed to keep her from business, education, and the professions.

In excluding woman from the suffrage man not only assumes political sovereignty over her but moral superiority as well. The exercise of the suffrage to-day is conceded to be a moral obligation. But it is urged that this obligation does not rest on woman. Who is to determine this? Are moral duties to be assigned by one sex to the other?

or by majorities? The essential feature of moral duty lies in each individual determining his or her own, so long as the rights of others are not interfered with. Woman cannot be a free moral agent while arbitrarily restricted in any sphere of moral action. And if the proposition of Burke that "The qualifications for government are virtue and wisdom, actual or presumptive," contains any truth, suffrage is as much the woman's moral duty as the man's.

A stock objection of opponents to equal suffrage is that woman has all she can do as mother of the race. Sociology demonstrates this objection to be without scientific basis. The evolution of the state has been from a military to an industrial plane. In warring societies and epochs, where mortality is great, the birth-rate has been correspondingly high, and the maternal function emphasized to the suppression of other capacities in woman. The same law holds in the animal kingdom. Spencer shows that species destined to heavy chance mortality meet the emergency by enormous reproduction. With increased life chances offspring are less numerous. Accordingly in industrial societies the birth-rate decreases, and quality replaces quantity as the criterion of the family.

The development of society from the military to the industrial stage has transformed the life of woman no less than of man. Smaller families, the general employment of servants, and the introduction into the household of labor-saving inventions and manufactured products now afford women time for new activities. Some of the sex are devoting their leisure to "pink teas" and other "social functions"; many, however, find in it an opportunity for larger usefulness, to themselves, to their families, and to society.

Enlarged contact with the world has forced upon the attention of some of these women social problems which centuries of Christian civilization guided and controlled by man have not solved. These problems in great part affect the family and the home, but women in their present status are powerless to cope with them. They have begun to realize that it is vain to expect virtuous and happy homes in great numbers while pernicious influences are so unrestrictedly at work in the state, counterbalancing more or less the effects of early training; and following their new opportunity they regard it as their duty to help guard the course as well as the source of life's stream. To do this they must extend their labors into the larger domain of the state.

It is useless to tell them to go back home and take care of
their children. They have come outside for this very purpose.
Their children are in state schools; they have an interest
in the composition of the school board, in the character of
the teachers, in the housing of pupils, and in all that constitutes our public-school system. Their children are necessarily on the streets and in public places; they must then
resist and combat every vice which spreads its snare for
the innocent. Indeed, to do their full duty as mothers of
the race they must extend·their power into the state, to
make it as tolerable a place as possible for their children.
No apprehension need be felt that woman will then neglect
her home duties. This was the agonized fear when she
sought an education. In that crisis the great Dr. Johnson
declared that woman "was better attending to her toilet
than using the pen." The only sphere hitherto freely conceded to woman has been religion with the Book of Job
underscored.

The theory of the modern state alone furnishes an adequate reason for the enfranchisement of women. The state
now assumes many functions once performed by the family
and other private agencies, and has greatly enlarged its
sphere for the promotion of the general welfare. It edu-
cates children, cares for the sick and the defective, enforces
sanitary regulations, reforms rather than punishes its
criminals, provides factory and tenement inspection, and
undertakes many other services for the common good.
The state as a police force existing only for the bodily protection of its citizens has become a social organism fostering the mental and moral as well as the physical well-being
of its members. In these new functions of the state, women
are fitted by nature and experience to coöperate with men.
Politics, it is true, are not at present inviting; but general
experience has been that with the advent of woman in the
shop, the office, the counting-room, the college, and wherever
she has gone, the moral atmosphere has improved. Her
mere presence at political meetings, to which she is now
cordially invited, has raised the tone of campaign addresses.
It is hardly probable that a different result would follow
her presence at the polls.

What does the ballot to-day signify? Is a vote an expression of so much physical power, and does a majority
indicate a preponderance of brute force? If this be true
"educational campaigns" and appeals to reason are senseless. Time was when voting was done by the clash of the
spear upon the shield. The ballot originally was a sub-

stitute for this demonstration, but now the state does not limit suffrage to warriors, and qualifications of voters are never physical. The ballot represents mere opinion, and law finds its validity in a majority of opinions. The basis of the modern state is intelligence. Why then should the state ignore the intelligence of half its citizens? The economy of human society demands that every factor should be used to the extent of its capacity.

Why do women stake so much on the ballot? Because it is at the root of every tax, every public institution, every choice of officials, every law; it frees government from arbitrary element, removes discontent, and affords to all full and equal political power. It is the door to self-realization. Its possession would make women responsible factors in the state; without it they are non-entities. Certain anti-suffragists protest that woman is morally superior to man, that she should exert an influence on the state, but that man should be the bearer of it. If this influence is desirable, why not introduce it directly into the state rather than filter it through a less moral medium? Women, however, do not claim the ballot on the ground of "moral superiority." The state does not need them more than they need the ballot.

Woman's emancipation has not been conceived in rebellion, brought forth on the battle field, made tragic by martyrdom. Woman has not trundled cannon over the land nor talked treason; she has not neglected her home nor family. She has studied and thought and reasoned away all opposition not founded in prejudice. Her purpose is fixed and her faith strong that her cause will prevail.

WEALTH-PRODUCTION AND CONSUMPTION BY THE NATION.

BY GEORGE B. WALDRON, A. M.

America's remarkable growth in material wealth has challenged the attention of the world. But that growth, with all the advantages it has brought, has at the same time developed conditions which unchecked may eventually work the ruin of the nation. It is probably not true that the poor as a class are growing poorer. Indeed, there are many indications that they are rather sharing in a measure the growing prosperity. But it is unquestionably true that the rich are growing richer; that wealth is more and more concentrating into the hands of the very few. On the one side are the millions whose many necessities and few comforts and luxuries absorb all, or nearly all, their incomes; on the other side are the few thousands who may have necessities, comforts and luxuries in abundance and still have a generous surplus which can be changed into capital yet more largely to swell their incomes.

A number of attempts have been made in recent years to measure this congestion of wealth, but little serious effort has been turned toward measuring the causes which lead to this growing intensity of conditions. It is the purpose of this article to blaze a pathway into this field by attempting (1) to measure the annual production of the country, (2) to distribute this production among the families of the nation according to their probable incomes, and (3) to show the final disposition of this product. The results of the first inquiry may be accepted as fairly accurate; there is room for some differences of opinion as to the second and the third; but it is believed that even these are sufficiently accurate to show the real trend of conditions and to shed light on the reasons for the increasing congestion of wealth. We come then to the first inquiry.

I. Annual Product of the Nation.

How much wealth does the nation produce annually? To be more explicit: What is the money cost during a single year of bringing the material products of the country from the farm, forest, mine or water through the various processes of manufacture, transportation and trade to the point of family or other consumption?

It is possible to answer this question with considerable accuracy for the census year 1890. The method adopted is based upon the number of persons actually engaged in productive work during the year. Census returns show that of the 62,622,250 people in the United States in 1890, there were 47,413,559, or 75.72 per cent over ten years of age. Of this possible number of workers 22,735,661, or 47.95 per cent were engaged in "gainful occupations." But not all in "gainful occupations" are direct producers of material wealth. The doctor, the minister and the teacher, for example, are valuable workers in society and indirectly, but not directly, productive of wealth, so such as they must be left out of consideration.

A careful analysis of the different occupations shows that in the census year there were 20,115,106 persons employed in occupations directly productive of some form of material wealth. These were further subdivided into groups as follows: On raw materials, 9,725,445 workers; manufacturing, 6,643,879; transportation, 1,557,721; trade, 2,188,061. Great care was taken to make these divisions as accurate as possible. Others might differ somewhat as to the classification of certain occupations. This would vary the estimates of production of different classes, but would not materially affect the total production. The following table shows in detail the method adopted of estimating the total annual production of the nation:

PRODUCTION BY THE UNITED STATES DURING THE CENSUS YEARS 1890 AND 1880.

1890.	Workers.	Value Produced.	Wages.	Gross Profits.	Produced per Worker.	Wages per Worker.
Raw Materials.						
Farm Products,	6,297,580	a $2,460,107,454	$1,385,467,600	$1,074,639,854	$391	f $220
Forest Products,	2,628,102	b 1,026,650,859	578,182,440	448,468,419	391	g 220
Mines	a 636,415	a 587 230,662	a 265,290,643	321,940,019	920	417
Fisheries . . .	a 163,348	a 44,277,514	35,936,560	8,340,954	271	g 220
Total.	9,725,445	$4,118,266,489	$2,264,877,243	$1,853,389,246	$423	$233
Manufacturing.						
Census Manufactures. . .	a 4,712,622	c $4,210,393,207	a $2,283,216,529	$1,927,176,678	$894	$484
Other	1,931,257	935,694,000	683,664,978	252,029,022	h 484	j 354
Total	6,643,879	$5,146,087,207	$2,966,881,507	$2,179,205,700	$775	$447
Transportation.						
Railroads . . .	d 749,301	d $1,051,877,632	d $416,544,135	$635,333,497	$1,404	$556
Water Traffic .	a 114,736	a 166,838,776	a 41,729,842	125,108,934	917	363
Express . . .	a 45,718	e 50,000,000	a 16,176,098	33,823,902	1,094	354
Telephones . .	a 8,645	a 16,404,583	3,060,330	13,344,253	1,898	h 484
Other	639,321	571,552,974	309,751,025	261,801,949	i 894	h 484
Total	1,557,721	$1,856,673,965	$787,261,430	$1,069,412,535	$1,192	$505

PRODUCTION BY THE UNITED STATES — *Continued.*

1890.	Workers.	Value Produced.	Wages.	Gross Profits.	Produced per Worker.	Wages per Worker.
Trade.						
Total	2,188,061	$2,519,904,205	$1,104,970,805	$1,414,933,400	$1,152	*k* $505
Aggregate . .	20,115,106	$13,640,931,866	$7,123,990,985	$6,516,940,881	$678	$354
Summary 1890.						
Raw Materials .	9,725,445	$4,118,266,489	$2,264,877,243	$1,853,389,246	$423	$233
Manufacturing.	6,643,879	5,146,087,207	2,966,881,507	2,179,205,700	775	447
Transportation.	1,557,721	1,856,673,965	787,261,430	1,069,412,535	1,192	505
Trade	2,188,061	2,519,904,205	1,104,970,805	1,414,933,400	1,152	505
Total	20,115,106	$13,640,931,866	$7,123,990,985	$6,516,940,881	$678	$354
Farm and Forest Products . .	8,925,682	3,486,758,313	1,963,650,040	1,523,108,273	391	220
All Other . . .	11,189,424	10,154,173,553	5,160,340,945	4,993,832,608	907	461
1880.						
Raw Materials .	8,667,997	$3,549,461,727	$1,749,308,421	$1,800,153,306	$409	$218
Manufacturing.	4,655,027	2,639,839,546	1,459,320,707	1,180,518,839	567	314
Transportation.	786,644	888,339,896	326,406,383	561,933,513	1,129	415
Trade	1,506,246	1,547,325,318	625,192,090	922,133,228	1,027	415
Total	15,615,914	$8,624,966,487	$4,160,227,601	$4,464,738,886	$552	$266
Farm and Forest Products . .	8,081,571	3,137,402,564	1,559,743,203	1,577,659,361	388	193
All Other . . .	7,534,343	5,487,563,923	2,600,484,398	2,887,079,525	728	345

a. Census of 1890.
b. Estimate of the Department of Agriculture for census year.
c. Total value of product ($9,372,437,283), less cost of materials used ($5,162,044,076).
d. Report of the Interstate Commerce Commission for the year ending June 30, 1890.
e. Estimated from census. Operating expenses of sixteen of the seventeen companies, $42,413,705; dividends declared by eight companies, $3,198,048.
f. The Agricultural Department estimates average farm wages without board (board furnished by the worker) for the United States in 1890 at $18.33 per month or $220 per year.
g. Estimated the same as farm wages.
h. Estimated the same as wages in manufactures.
i. Estimated the same as average product per worker in manufactures.
j. Estimated the same as wages of all workers.
k. Estimated the same as wages in transportation.

It will be noted that the products of all the workers are based on official figures (census for the most part), except for 1,931,257 workers in manufacturing, 639,321 in transportation and 2,188,061 workers in trade. Census returns for manufacturers do not include unorganized industries, such as most of the building operations in the smaller towns, nor organized industries producing less than $500 in the year. Under transportation those not included in the census returns are chiefly teamsters and small boatmen.

The principal difficulty was encountered in assigning the production of workers in trade. There was no official data for this class, so that it was necessary to rely upon private investigation. From estimates furnished by some twenty trade papers in nearly all the leading lines of trade in the country it was found to be a conservative estimate that the wholesale dealer on the average adds about ten per cent to the value of his goods when he sells them to the retailer, and that the retailer on the average adds about 25 per cent to his purchasing price when he sells to the consumer.

Take as a basis the $4,118,266,489 of raw material produced, and add the $5,146,087,207 of value given in the manufacturing process. This makes a total of $9,264,353,-696. Not all of this product goes through the hands of the wholesalers and retailers. Let us strike an average of three-fifths for wholesale and four-fifths for retail, making the average per cent added on the entire manufactured product 6 per cent for wholesale and 20 per cent retail. Without reckoning transportation from the factory to the wholesale house, or from the wholesale house to the retail store, a bill of goods costing $100 to the wholesaler, would be sold to the retailer for $106, and the retailer would sell at a 20 per cent advance, or for $127.20. This is 27.2 per cent advance on the price paid by the wholesaler. On the $9,264,353,696 of total manufactured product 27.2 per cent is $2,519,904,-205, which has been adopted as the value added to products through trade. This is an average of $1,152 per worker, about $40 less than the average value per worker in transportation. As trade and transportation are closely allied, with advantages on the whole in favor of transportation, the results may be taken as substantially correct.

From these figures the total product of the country is put at $13,640,931,866, which is $678 per worker, $217 per capita of total population, and $1,075 per family.

A similar process has been followed in determining the proportion of the product which has gone in wages. Most of the figures are official. The Department of Agriculture, after careful investigation in all parts of the United States, placed the average farm wages in 1890, when board was furnished by the worker himself, at $18.33 a month, or $220 per year. All farm products above this $220 per worker in the table are considered as profits. Wages in trade are assumed to be the same as in transportation. Following these estimates is found that of the total production of the country, $7,123,990,985, or 52.23 per cent, went in wages, and the rest in various forms of profit, either direct to the managers of the business or in rents, interest and dividends to owners of capital.

In a similar way were obtained the estimates of the total product, wages and gross profits in the four classes of production for the census year 1880. In that year the total production was $8,624,966,487, which was $552 per worker, $172 per capita of total population, and $867 per family. It is a striking fact that wages that year represented but **48.22** per cent of the total product, against 52.23 per cent in **1890,** so that labor has made a gain of four per cent on the total

WEALTH PRODUCTION IN 1890.

WAGES, 52.23 per cent.   PROFITS, 47.77 per cent.

TRADE $1,104,971,000	TRADE $1,414,933,000
TRANSPORTATION $787,262,000	TRANSPORTATION $1,069,412,000
MANUFACTURING $2,966,881,000	MANUFACTURING $2,179,206,000
RAW MATERIALS $2,264,877,000	RAW MATERIALS $1,853,390,000

TOTAL PRODUCT, $13,640,032,000.

WEALTH PRODUCTION IN 1880.

WAGES, 48.22 per cent.   PROFITS, 51.78 per cent.

TRADE $625,192,000	TRADE $922,133,000
TRANSPORTATION $326,406,000	TRANSPORTATION $561,934,000
MANUFACTURING $1,459,320,000	MANUFACTURING $1,180,519,000
RAW MATERIALS $1,749,309,000	RAW MATERIALS $1,800,153,000

TOTAL PRODUCT, $8,624,966,000.

production in the ten years. This gain runs through nearly every line of industry and to this extent is favorable to the workingman.

The ten years show small improvement for the farmer. In 1880 the average product per farm worker was $388; in 1890 it was $391, a gain of but $3. But the farmer had to pay more for his help in 1890, wages having increased from $193 to $220 during the decade. Nor is the farmer any better off in the ratio of the value of his product to his total capital invested. To produce the 2,213 millions gross value of farm products in 1880 required a farm capital, including live stock, implements and machinery, of 12,603 millions, so that the product was 17.6 per cent of the capital. In 1890 the 15,982 millions then invested produced 2,460 millions of gross product, or only 15.4 per cent on the capital invested.

II. Distribution of the Nation's Product by Families.

How is this 13,641 millions of wealth produced in the year, distributed among the families of the nation? The very full returns of the census of 1890 on the number of families owning and hiring farms and homes furnishes a basis for calculating family incomes. The table which follows divides these families into two classes: those who live largely or wholly on their wages and those whose incomes are largely due to the capital they own or use. On the lower side of the line are placed all families hiring farms or homes, families owning encumbered farms worth less than $25,000, or free farms worth less than $10,000; and families owning incumbered or free homes worth less than $5,000. The census gives the number of families owning encumbered farms and homes classified according to value. Upon this basis is calculated the number of families in each class owning farms or homes free. Among hiring farm families are included 214,949 families living in hired homes, but whose work is on farms. The aggregate incomes of these 4,856,554 wage-earning farm families, and of the 7,206,925 wage-earning home families are substantially as in the following table:

MAXIMUM INCOME OF THE POOR AND MIDDLE CLASSES.

CLASSES OF FAMILIES.	Number of Families	WAGES a.	PROFITS b.	TOTAL.
Farm Families:				
Hiring (including 214,949 home families)	1,839,382	$724,716,508	—	$724,716,508
Owing incumbered under $25,000	881,617	347,357,098	$209,032,483	556,389,581
Owning free under $10,000	2,135,555	841,408,670	662,584,769	1,503,993,439
	4,856,554	$1,913,482.276	$871,617,252	$2,785,090,528

MAXIMUM INCOME OF THE POOR AND MIDDLE CLASSES. — *Continued.*

CLASSES OF FAMILIES.	Number of Families	WAGES a.	PROFITS b.	TOTAL.
Home Families:				
Hiring	4,784,353	$3,951,875,578	—	$3,951,875,578
Owning incumbered under $5,000	671,129	554,352,554	$41,809,393	596,161,947
Owni'g free under $5,000	1,751,443	1,446,691,918	356,299,902	$1,802,991,820
	7,206,925	$5,952,920,050	$398,109,295	$6,351,029,345
Total above Families	12,663,479	$7,866,402,326	$1,269,726,547	$9,136,128,873
All other Families .	626,673	—		4,504,802,993
Total	12,690,152	—	—	$13,640,931,866

a. Farm wages, $220 per worker, or $394 per family of 1.7915 workers. Wages of home families, $461 per worker or $826 per family of 1.7915 workers.

b. Profits of farm families in proportion to value of farms less incumbrance. Profits of home families, 6 per cent of value of homes less incumbrances, if any; $100 added for each family owning home free.

From this table it appears that 12,063,479 families, or 95.06 per cent of all the families in the country, receive incomes amounting during the year to $9,136,128,873, which is 66.98 per cent of the total production of the nation, so that nineteen-twentieths of the families receive only twice as much in the aggregate as that received by the other twentieth. Assigning to the farm family of each class named the income which the farm of this value produces, and assuming that home families receive incomes equal to 60 per cent of the value of the homes they occupy, it is possible yet more completely to classify the families according to the incomes they receive, as in the table below. There may be some difference of opinion as to the amount of income to be assigned to each class, but that here accepted cannot be far out of the way:

ESTIMATED FAMILY INCOMES IN 1890.

INCOMES.	FAMILIES.				INCOME.	
	Farm.	Home.	Total.	Per ct. of Total.	Millions of Dollars.	Per ct. of Total.
Under $400	1,879,839	2,235,691	4,115,530	32.59	1,361	9.98
$400 to 600	1,153,298	1,469,118	2,622,516	20.67	1,300	9.53
600 to 900	920,518	951,330	1,871,848	14.75	1,375	10.08
900 to 1,200	684,532	697,678	1,382,210	10.89	1,400	10.27
1,200 to 1,800 . . .	218,267	929,132	1,147,399	9.04	1,650	12 10
1,800 to 3,000 . . .	—	903,976	903,976	7.12	2,050	15.02
Under $3,000 . . .	4,856,554	7,206,925	12,063,479	95.06	9,136	66.98
$3,000 to 6,000 . . .	125,574	330,090	455,673	3.59	1,800	13.19
6,000 to 15,000	— .	139,718	139,718	1.10	1,200	8.80
15,000 to 60,000 . . .	—	27,235	27,235	.22	670	4.91
60,000 and over . . .	—	4,047	4,047	.03	835	6.12
$3,000 and over . .	125,574	501,099	626,673	4.94	4,505	33.02
Total	4,982,128	7,708,024	12,690,152	100.00	13,641	100.00

It will be noted that 125,574 farm families have been assigned to the class receiving over $3,000 per year. Only a very small proportion of these families would receive such incomes from the farms upon which they live, but it is reasonable to suppose that owning at least $25,000 encumbered or $10,000 free most of them have other property bringing in returns.

If the figures given in this table are correct, then it is evident that over four million families, or nearly one-third of all the families in the country, must get along on incomes of less than $400 a year. More than one-half the families (53.26 per cent) get less than $600 a year; two-thirds of the families (68.01 per cent) less than $900; while nineteen-twentieths (95.06 per cent) receive less than $3,000 a year.

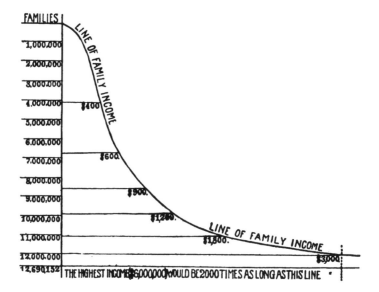

Among the upper five per cent there are at least 4,047 millionaires, according to the New York *Tribune's* list, to whom should be assigned incomes of not less than $60,000 per year. The highest incomes run up into the millions.

The late income-tax law, it will be remembered, laid a tax of 2 per cent on all incomes in excess of $4,000. There were about 300,000 families receiving such incomes in 1890, and their incomes aggregated some 3,360 millions of dollars. The exemption of $4,000 each amounts to 1,200 millions, leaving

2,160 millions to be taxed. Two per cent of this is $43,200,-000. The tax of two per cent on corporation incomes, which affected incomes of many families under the $4,000 limit, would raise the possible tax to about 50 millions of dollars.

III. Consumption of the Annual Product.

Another inquiry remains as to the final spending of these incomes. It has been shown that the 20,115,106 producing workers receive on the average $354 each in wages. If the 2,620,555 other workers in "gainful occupations" receive the same average, then the total wages of all the workers in the country in 1890 were $8,049,677,465. These include practically all the families in the country, many of whom receive more income, but in the form of profits, not wages. This 8,050 millions, in round numbers, may be taken as the amount required to supply all the families of the country with the necessities, comforts and luxuries of the average working family. At $354 per worker the average family wages (1.7915 workers to the family) are $634, which is somewhat higher than the average expenditures of 2,562 wage workers reported by Commissioner Carroll D. Wright in an investigation made by the United States bureau of labor in 1890. Using the 8,050 millions as a basis for expenditures and the percentages for the several classes of necessary expenditures revealed by that investigation, we get the results of the first part of the following table:

CONSUMPTION OF THE NATION'S ANNUAL PRODUCT.

ITEMS OF EXPENDITURE.	Millions of Dollars.	Per ct. of Total.	ITEMS OF EXPENDITURE.	Millions of Dollars.	Per ct. of Total.
Necessary Expenditures			**Expenditures pr Capital**		
Food (41.05 per cent.)	3,305	24.23	To Maintain Old Wealth	2,436	17.86
Clothing (15.31 per ct.)	1,233	9.04	Added Wealth	1,196	8.77
Furniture (3 96 per ct.)	319	2 33	Use of Foreign Capital	85	.62
Lighting (.90 per cent)	72	.53	Total per Capital	3,717	27.25
Fuel (5.01 per cent.)	403	2.96			
Other (9.54 per cent.)	768	5.63	**Expenditures per Gov't**		
Total Necessaries	6,100	44.72	Permanent products	176	1.29
			Department Supplies	64	.47
Luxuries	3,584	26.27	Total per Government	240	1.76
AGGREGATE EXPENDITURES				13,641	100.00

In this estimate of necessary expenditures the important item of rent (15.06 per cent) was not included, for the reason that rent is not consumed, but becomes a part of the income of the owner of the property. Upon the basis of the census estimates of the private wealth in the country in 1880 and 1890 it appears that the increase of productive wealth in 1889 was 2,568 millions, of which 2,287 millions was in real estate. But at a fair average 60 per cent of this real estate, or 1,372 millions, was in the form of land values, leaving 1,196 millions added by human toil. Estimating that it requires 3 per cent of their value to maintain buildings in their present value, and 10 per cent to keep in repair other wealth, the preserving of the wealth already in the country during the year took 2,436 millions. To these expenditures for capital we have added 85 millions sent out of the country for the use of foreign capital. This represents the balance between the total exports over imports for the year, including gold and silver.

Under government expenditures, national, state and local, are included only those of a permanent character, such as for buildings, bridges, roads, etc., and for such articles as are consumed in the several departments of government. A large part of the expenditures is in the form of salaries for

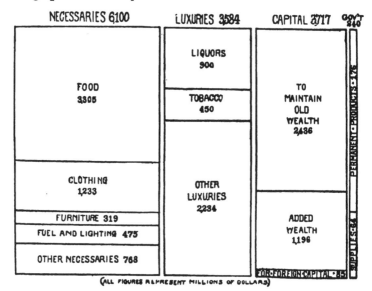

(ALL FIGURES REPRESENT MILLIONS OF DOLLARS)

services rendered, and spent, not by the government, but by the official.

It is a surprising fact that there is nearly as much left to be spent on luxuries (3,584 millions) as goes to the maintenance and increase of capital. A conservative estimate will place the consumption of intoxicating liquors at 900 millions for 1889, and of tobacco at 450 millions, so that these two luxuries consumed by both rich and poor, absorb fully three-eighths of all the luxuries,

We have shown the annual production of the country, how it is divided among the families according to income and how it is consumed at last. A final inquiry remains as to how this process affects the ownership of the permanent wealth of the country. The wealth added during the year is of two kinds—1,196 millions of net increase in values from labor and 1,372 millions of increase in the value of land, making a total of 2,568 millions. Drawing the line at $3,000 annual income, how much of this increase goes to the poor and middle families below this line, and how much to the 5 per cent of rich families above the line? The total income of the 12 million families receiving less than $3,000 a year is placed at 9,136 millions; how much of this is permanently "saved" to increase the possessions of this class? Remembering that millions are loaded down with interest-bearing debt, that many save for years only to have their savings swallowed up in misfortunes, that more than one-half the families are struggling along on incomes of less than $600 a year, that over one and a half million families are trying to pay for mortgaged farms or homes, and that thousands will lose their all in the attempt, that thousands and perhaps millions of families live up the limit of their incomes and many far beyond, that those who do save rarely succeed in saving more than 10 per cent of their incomes, it is certainly within the bounds of probability to place the permanent savings of the whole class at not more than 5 per cent of their total income, or 457 millions.

How much of the increased land values goes to this class? It is fair to estimate it in proportion to the real estate they own. Their total holdings of real estate in 1890, including the value of mortgages on their farms or homes, was 12,780 millions of dollars. On this the proportional gain of land values was 456 millions. This, with the 457 millions of permanent increase from savings makes a total of some 913 millions added to the holdings of the poor and middle classes during the year. Of the 2,568 millions of total added wealth, this leaves 1,655 millions, or 64.45 per cent, of increase for the rich. Little wonder, then, that the rich are rapidly growing richer, when, but one-twentieth of the families, they are absorbing one-third of the annual income and nearly two-thirds of the annual increase made in the wealth of the nation.

BETWEEN TWO WORLDS.

BY MRS. CALVIN KRYDER REIFSNIDER.

CHAPTER VII.

"Father, why are we so different in personal appearance from other people? My complexion, hair, and eyes occasion much comment, and I am frequently asked the question as to what nationality we belong."

Ruby and her father sat alone in the study. Callers had just departed, and Ruby's question was the outgrowth of the lady's inquiries.

"It may really interest you deeply to hear the story," her father replied, with a look of love upon her.

Ruby's heart gave a sudden bound of joy. At last her great wish was to be gratified. But as her father settled himself in his arm-chair, and she perceived the old quiver of pain for a moment convulse his lips, her heart smote her and she fain would have given up the great desire which she sometimes feared, after all, was born of unwise curiosity. Before she could frame another remark, however, her father proceeded in his usual calm tone, his eyes cast upon the floor, and his voice so low, but so full of painful memories, that she paused with parted lips and strained, eager eyes, to catch every word he uttered.

"There was a period in my life, my child, when the sun was darkened, the moon turned to blood, and the stars fell from the heavens. I cannot recur to that time without a shudder passing through my frame, nor would I do so were it not to show you how miraculously I was saved. During the time to which I refer I courted death as a happy relief. It would not come, and then, feeling myself forsaken of God, I looked into the wine cup when it was red, when it lifted itself erect, and found as all men do that at last it stingeth like a serpent, and biteth like an adder. Then days of repentance came, or perhaps more correctly, days of remorse. I suffered intensely from a sense of guilt, but weak and hopeless I turned and drank again. I loathed myself for this weakness, but I knew not where to turn for strength. I was disgusted with religion, for then I learned that many of the most alluring dramshops were

owned by so-called church members. I could not pray to
an angry God, an avenging God, and then turn again and
offend him. I had been educated to believe literally all
that the Bible contained. To what I did not understand
I closed my eyes in blind faith, and believed without comprehending.

"After many months of this kind of life I resolved once
more to try to live differently. I need not tell you that
I was prompted by a feeling that you might grow up to fear,
and at length hate me. You were only an infant then; the
only creature on earth from whom I might some day claim
a love I so much needed. And when I realized my great
responsibility I felt my own weakness and then I once more
groped blindly in the dark to find my God, and from Him
learn wisdom.

"One night after a long effort to calm my soul I laid me
down to sleep. The room was dark. I closed my eyes, and
there before me was the calm, benignant face of a man
dressed in the style of the last century, with long white hair,
and calm blue eyes. The face was the most spiritual that I
had ever seen. It was not an angel, but a man; and yet
he seemed to bring the peace of God with him and gave
me instructions what to do. When I opened my eyes the
room was quite dark and there was no one to be seen. The
substantial presence was gone, but the impression upon
my mind must remain forever.

"I drew, and afterwards painted in monochrome, the face
you see over my desk. I then set myself to work to discover who he was, if indeed such a person ever really lived.
I did not search in vain. I found, among the writings of
the last century, a book written by him, and a portrait of
this great spiritual philosopher. I bought the book. It
proved a spring of living water to my thirsty soul.

"At that time much was being said and printed about
the heresy of a famous minister of the old school. He
had been tried, condemned, and pitched out of the doctrinal ship, but once overboard he soon formed another and
better one, manned it with a faithful few, and was heard
from at more than one time as being too strong for his
adversaries. A desire to see this man caused me to make a
journey that proved a turning point in my life. I found him
and he welcomed me most cordially. I admired his courage
and was impressed with the purity of his life and purposes.
I became a student under him of the teachings of this wonderful, heaven-inspired philosopher, from whose teachings
he was building up a new church. Then I learned for the

first time that religion is one thing and religiosity another and quite a different thing; that religion is a vital thing, a life, not a creed. Religiosity is external, without internal religion, a creed without a corresponding life, ritualism without holiness; it is the result of false doctrines. We are Christians only as we love, live, think, feel, act, in a Christian manner. 'Christ liveth in me, and the life which I now live in the flesh I live by the faith of the Son of God.'

"Men may profess what faith they please but they have no more religion than that which always shows itself in every one of the minutest actions of their lives. We are what we do, for Christ declared, 'By their fruits ye shall know them.' I learned, too, that we are not saved by faith unless that faith be grounded in the truth; that truth obeyed makes us free; and if we are not free and enlightened, sanctified and saved, we have not obeyed the truth, or have been putting our faith in falsehoods and not in the truth.

"I learned to read the Bible for the first time correctly. My teacher furnished me the key to unlock the door that had been shut, barred, and bolted—the key of correspondence which opens the spiritual meaning of the word. I entered, I drank of the waters of life freely, and lived anew, for now I could worship the true God in spirit and in truth.

"I thank God that the light was given to me before it was my duty to teach you. But even then I realized the necessity of your seeing the false and the true, so I drew a picture of our Lord as taught by orthodoxy, and Him the new light revealed to me, and allowed you to choose for yourself. There was no hesitation; you said: 'This, father, this Divine Man is my God; not that great Judge demanding sacrifice, and worse than Shylock taking not the pound of flesh, but the whole life upon the cross, of His only Son for the crimes of others.' Then I taught you that it was not the death of Christ upon the cross that saved sinners but His life, and the death of His carnal nature inherited from His mother, Mary.

"Believing, then, that a man has just as much religion as he lives, that life as given in Christ's example must be made up of uses, I established my school of oratory and in the meantime determined with God's help to live according to the new light and rear you in the same; and furthermore to reconcile science and religion in our material bodies, so to speak. A pure mind means pure thought, a pure body pure blood, pure blood pure food,—the effect always faithfully indicating the cause. I began at the cause to produce the proper effect. As I ate of spiritual food, appropriating the purest truths I could find, so I studied and appropriated the purest of material food.

"I believed in regeneration from inmosts to outmosts, or ultimates, and I took the self-denying Jesus for my guide and in my puny, finite way I trod the path that He had trod. He was with me. In all my temptations nearer than at any other time. At length I no longer craved so much food, nor the same quality of food. I eschewed all stimulating food and drink, knowing that reaction is depressing, and finally I felt the one and only great stimulant necessary to virtue and strength bubbling up in a sparkling fountain within, an awakening of the spiritual force—medical men call it nerve force. It sustained me physically and mentally, while with all the aids known to reason and common sense, such as baths, exercise, and pure air, I aided the material part of myself to cast off the poisons that years of ignorance and almost wickedness (if ignorance were not called innocence) had accumulated. I kept my mind in a pure, healthy state. If dark thoughts came like shadows around me I resolutely chased them away. I placed mirrors about the walls that should reflect any change that occurred, to warn me of danger or encourage me, and gradually I perceived a more pleasant reflection. If the old thought of satan came, I said: "There is no evil or devil but man's antagonism to God. Evil is only good perverted, and I am a receptacle to receive all of that good which I desire. In its use I may become a perfect man, in its abuse a devil.'

"So I worked and lived and determined to rear you. Your food I chose with more care than your clothing, and strove to implant in your mind that sinful thoughts, words, or acts finally meant a diseased body. Thank God, I had the hearty coöperation of your nurse while you were young, and as you grew older my mind seemed to dominate yours and you grew into my beliefs on all subjects. I have endeavored to give you an interior education. The interior senses which are generally neglected, suppressed, and therefore dwarfed, furnish the real insight into things, give us true vision.

" 'We have a natural body, and we have a spiritual body.' Now our natural eyes cannot see spiritual things, nor can our spiritual eyes see natural things, but when our spiritual sight is opened we can discern spiritual things; thus were I to lay off my material body in death the resurrection of my spiritual body would immediately take place. Then were my Ruby's spiritual eyes opened she could see her father always, and death would not separate us at all. You could see me just as Mary and some of the disciples saw our Saviour after His resurrection, for no one whose spiritual sight was not opened ever saw Him after He was put into the tomb. And were my child to go before I could see her just as I saw that substantial or spiritual man whose visitation saved me from so many ills, who was sent to me from God just as He sent angels to men as recorded in the Bible.

"When I look about me in the crowded hall or street and see great animals called men and women eating and drinking with less wisdom than the lower animals manifest in such matters, I do not marvel that they cast strange glances at you and me and wonder from what strange land we came.

"That you might not be considered weak and ignorant as your youthful, almost infantile, expression would indicate, I have taught you difficult and abtruse things, exoteric and esoteric, natural, mental, and spiritual philosophy, and in every instance have found your mind receptive and retentive to a degree far exceeding that of the ignorantly fed student, male or female.

"We have seen every nation, every land on the habitable globe, and tarried in each long enough to familiarize ourselves with the people and their language. Earth, like heaven, is a kingdom of uses. Every faculty must be kept actively alive to become properly developed. Nowhere have we been idle. We have gathered startling facts among the so-called heathen to astonish Christian nations. We have gathered material sufficient, when put into simple, readable form, to enlighten many inquiring minds. Two hours every morning we devote to this pleasant task. Then these young lawyers, lecturers, and ministers must be trained to use their vocal chords. Do we not see a busy life before us, my child?"

"Yes, father, busy, useful, and instructive; such was the life of him you took so early for your guide. You are right, father; activity is life, inertia is death."

The recital was to Ruby like the reversal of a phonograph. She heard her father's voice rehearse his life purpose and labors, but the under-current of feeling, the subtle spring which had started the machinery, was not stirred, and she was again led away from the theme which contained the most vital interest for her. She had hoped to hear that she inherited her peculiar personal, physical, or mental traits from her mother; but no, all that she was she

evidently owed to God and her earthly father and to her
kind nurse. Alas, it must be true, she had never had a
mother.

When he ceased speaking he sat still, with closed eyes,
as though taking an interior view of himself in order to
convince himself that he had told the whole story in every
detail, or else he was busy putting that inner temple in
order again, rehanging old pictures that he had taken down
and hidden from her view.

The placid face in its serene, spiritual beauty fascinated
her. To a distant observer they might have appeared as
draped statues, so perfect was the entire repose expressed
in those two children of God.

(To be continued.)

THE VALLEY PATH.

A NOVEL OF TENNESSEE LIFE.

BY WILL ALLEN DROMGOOLE.

CHAPTER VI.

Down the road to Pelham a little cloud of dust arose. It came nearer; the eyes that had been feasting upon visions came back to earth, to see the familiar yellow mule that had trotted his first patient thither, again stop at the gate. The doctor slipped into his purple gown and went out to meet his visitor, half wondering what manner of prank he would attempt this time. But the man was clothed, even to the afflicted foot, and evidently "in his right mind."

There was something artistic about him, to the very swing of his body swaying gracefully with the movements of the mule. He was dressed in his Sunday best, a coarse, clean shirt and a suit of gray jeans. The inevitable slouch adorned his head; pushed back, it made a kind of shadow-nimbus for the short, clinging curls. Beneath the hat was a face, behind which was hidden a brain that would work out its own problems and stand or fall by its own blunders.

The doctor saw beneath the careless bravado with which his visitor swung himself down from the mule's back and came up the walk to meet him. The large foot touched the ground with positiveness, as if every step took hold upon the solid earth. His eyes were fixed upon the physician; evidently he was not altogether confident as to his reception; but there was that in his manner which said he meant to make the best of things at all events.

"Mornin', doctor," he said in response to the physician's cordial greeting. "I've come over here, Doctor Borin', to pay you a little visit. I'm Joe Bowen, from Pelham Valley down yonder."

The doctor eyed him carefully; it was equally clear to each that the other could scarcely refrain from bursting into laughter.

"Any more erysipelas down your way, Mr. Bowen?" inquired the doctor.

"Oh! say now, Doctor Borin'," said the mountaineer, "you

mustn't be holdin' a grudge against me 'count of that little
joke. I'm outright 'shamed of myself about that. Besides,
I was only aimin' to plague you a bit—you an' Lissy Reams.
Lissy she ware braggin' about you that peart I was afeard
betwixt you you might git a mortgage on the earth, let alone
Georgy. An' Lissy she talked so much that I laid a bet
with her as you couldn't tell snake bite from yaller ja'ndice.
So when the hornet stung me that mornin', while I was
hunt'n' the house over for my boot the coon had carried off,
why I"—— He broke into laughter in which the doctor
was forced to join. "It was *too* comical; it was too damned
funny for anything,—ter see you nosin' aroun' an' specticlin'
over that toe, an' tappin' of it like it might 'a' been a sp'iled
aig, an' allowin' you '*gentlemen* of the medical persuasion'—
ware it persuasion? or ware it *performance?*—Anyhow, you
smart Ikes called it 'erysip'las.'"

The mimicry was so ludicrously perfect the doctor could
not speak for laughing. The visitor, too, was enjoying the
recital of his smartness to the utmost; he had enjoyed it before, a score of times and more.

"And blame my hide," he continued, "if that ain't about
as nigh the truth as most of yer guesses come. But let
that pass. I've come over frien'ly, an' I hope you ain't holdin' no grudge ag'inst me, doctor."

The physician slipped his arm through the arm of his
visitor and led him into the house. Grudge? He was at
peace with all the world; he had discovered the secret of
content; he had awakened to new life, new joy, new hope,
"in his old age."

"Grudge!" said he, "grudge, hell! It was a sharp trick
you played me, young man. But I shall not refuse to see
the fun in it because the joke turned upon me. Come right
into my den; there are the pipes on the mantel, and there is
a chair for you. The occupant of that old sofa to your left
is my chum, Zip. Zip and I are old friends. Fill your pipe;
all mountaineers smoke. Most of them drink; if you are
ready for a toddy I'll mix one for you."

"I don't drink liquor," said Joe, "but I'll take a turn at
the pipe. An' I'm proper proud to make the acquaintance
of yer friend here."

He gave the terrier's ear a playful twitch that brought
him to his feet and then to the floor, where he stood regarding the visitor in an inquiring way, which sent that worthy
off in a peal of laughter.

"Peart pup, to be sure," he said; and as if the flattery had
indeed gone home the little terrier curled himself at the feet

of his new admirer and went to sleep. "No, sir," Joe went back to the previous question, "I don't drink liquor: I can't; it makes a fool of me. A man's an idiot to do that as makes a fool of him, an' beknownst to hisse'f too. But," he added with sudden thought, "I ain't got nothin' to say of them that do drink."

"I do not," said the doctor, smiling, while he pressed the brown tobacco into the bowl of his pipe. "I abstain for the same reason that you do; it makes a fool of me; I have no wish to be a greater fool than nature made me."

The mountaineer reached one long calfskin boot to touch the tail of the sleeping terrier:

"Oh, say now! I thought you ware the salt of the earth for smartness. Lissy Reams thinks you air, anyhows."

A smile flitted for a moment about the doctor's lips:

"Does she?" said he softly. "She is a smart guesser."

"*Does* she? Why, from the way Lissy talks I allowed you an' her would in an' about make a cha'ity hospital of the whole valley bimeby. Why, Lissy says the yarb doctor ain't *nowhar;* that you have got medicine that'll raise the dead out o' their graves—*if* the dead could be induced to swallow it."

The doctor gathered himself to resent the sudden turn the compliment had taken, reconsidered, however, drew in his breath and said, "*The dickens!*"

The mountaineer's eyes twinkled: "But then," he continued, "thar *air* some who say you air nothin' better nor a blamed fool, as never so much as heard of heavin."

He was looking straight into the doctor's eyes; the smoking pipe rested, the bowl in the palm of the broad brown hand. His face was aglow with the amusement he felt in reciting the opinions of his neighbors: amusement he saw reflected in the face of his listener, who again took breath and gave expression to a low, half humorous, "Hell!"

The mountaineer brought his foot down upon the floor with sudden vehemence:

"Say, doctor," he began, "you have heard o' one place, if you haven't heard o' t'other. The valley 'round here, an' the mount'n too, fur that matter, allows that I be the biggest sinner in the state o' Tennessee, or even Georgy hitse'f. But if you ain't toler'ble close behin' me then I ain't no Solerman. Why, they say you never heard o' Christ!"

The reply was low, earnest, and fraught with meaning:

"Then," said the physician, "they lie."

"Waal, now," the mountaineer leaned upon the arm of his

chair, his face close to the doctor's. The keen eye of the physician detected a fearless interest, an interest that was not assumed, under the careless, half-merry air with which he demanded, "What do you think of Him, anyhow?"

The doctor removed his pipe from between his lips, tapped the bowl of it gently upon his palm—the tobacco had ceased to smoke in the mountaineer's pipe—and set it upon the hearth, propped against the brass andiron, useless now save for ornament.

"I think," said he slowly, locking his white fingers loosely upon his knee,—"I think He is my elder brother—and yours."

"Great God!" the boy literally bounded; he gained his feet as if an electric shock had set him upon them. He stood perfectly still one moment, then gave his slouch a shove backward; shook first one leg, then the other, gave the terrier a kick with his calf-clad foot that sent it yelping from the room; then he began pacing up and down, pulling at the fireless pipe in long deep breaths, never conscious that no wreath of smoke responded to his drawing. Finally he stopped, looking down at the placid face of the man quietly twirling his thumbs, who had let drop that rank heresy as calmly as though he had expressed himself concerning a rise in Elk River.

"You mean to live *here*," he demanded, "an' preach *that* gospil? Here under the very nose of Brother Barry an' the Episcopers? An' you expect to come out of it whole—hide, horns, and taller? Great God! You'll find the valley hotter'n hell. You'd as well try to crack Cum'land mount'n wide op'n, as to try to crack the'r skulls wide enough to let in *that* doctrine!"

"I shall not try it," said the doctor. "I came here to get away from creeds and churches, not to build or to introduce new ones. I shall ask no man to think as I think. I shall neither question nor disturb any man's right to his own belief, and I shall claim the privilege of thinking for myself as well."

His visitor regarded him a moment in a kind of wonder, not without a touch of admiration. Then he extended his strong, brown hand, palm up. "Put yours thar," he exclaimed. "You have got spunk as well as spare-rib. Blamed if you haven't! Dad burn my hide if I don't jist *admire* the fellow that is too smart for Brother Barry. But Lord, you don't know *him!*"

"Yes, I do," laughed the doctor. "He called upon me one day last week, and the week before, and the week before that."

"Did he? Come in a mighty big hurry, I reckin; hitched that freckled-faced nag to yo' best apple tree, *I'll* be bound. Was in a *mighty* hurry an' fluster fixin' of the 'Master's bus'-ness'; but made out to let you put up his nag an' *prevail* upon him to stay all night. Oh, I know Brother Barry. He's too durned lazy for man's work, so he tuk to preachin'. An' the way he can preach, while the brethern lay to an' break up his fiel' for him, to keep his family from starvin'. I went over and plowed his gyarden for him las' spring; I done it to pleasure Lissy, more 'n anything else. An' when I was in an' about finished, parson he come out an' treated me with hell fire if I didn't get religion an' jine his church. You know what I done, Doctor Borin'?"

He stopped, lifted one calfskin and deposited it squarely upon the velvet cushion of the easy chair he had in his excitement vacated, and stood thus, leaning forward, his arm resting upon his knee, his face aglow with enjoyment of the discomfiture of the minister. "I reckin I am an awful sinner," he said; "the worst this side o' torment—thout'n it be you. When Brother Barry thanked me with his slap-jaw talk, I just got aboard o' my yaller mule, an' I says to that holy man, says I: 'Nex' time you wants yo' cussed fiel' broke up do you call on yo' fr'en' the devil to fetch out his spade an' shovel—I have heard he's got one—an ax him to break it up for you. An' if,' says I, 'if you ever come givin' o' me any mo' of yo' jaw I'll break yer darned neck,' says I. I ain't heard from mealy-mouth since then. I ain't lookin' for thanks, Doctor Borin'" (he brought his foot to the floor again), "an' I ain't begrudgin' nobody a little measly day's work at the plow. But I deny a man's right to *drive* a man, even into the kingdom of heaven. I don't believe he'd stay druv after he *ware* druv; sech ain't man natur'—leastwise it ain't my natur'. Nothin' won't be druv, if it's half sensed. My grandad druv a drove o' horses through this valley oncet, long ago. An' the last critter of 'em got back again whar they ware druv from. Well, after the cussin' I give him, I reckin he'll let me sa'nter on to ol' Satan at my own gait. I did cuss him; I have that to remember. I may die sometime an' go to the devil, but I have got the satisfaction of knowin' I did perform one good deed in the flesh anyhows."

"What did Lissy say to that?"

"Lissy?" He hesitated, cleared his throat, and blushed to the roots of his yellow hair.

"Yes, Lissy; what did she think of your performance—your one good deed?"

A softness crept into the bright fearless eyes, lowered now beneath the penetrating gaze of the physician.

"Doctor Borin," he shifted one great foot nervously, "I tell you, Lissy Reams air a good girl."

"Yes I know that. That's why I want to know how she received your reckless onslaught upon the church."

There was a moment's embarrassing silence. The clock on the mantel struck the half past twelve; the keen eyes of the physician were watching every change in the face before him. The mountaineer resumed his seat, awkwardly, and began tugging, with the fingers of his right hand, at the strap of his long boot. The doctor sighed and withdrew his gaze; he was satisfied with that he had discovered.

"Hit's a pity," speech had come at last, since those search- ing eyes were no longer upon him, "hit's a pity for Lissy to be made a mealy-mouth of. She's a girl of good sense. She ain't got her own consent to jine the church yit, an' I most hope she won't git it. Lissy is a quare gal, an' if she once takes a stand for the Methodis', thar ain't no tellin' whar it'll end, nor what sort o' fool notions she'll take into her head. She's tolerble heady for a sensible gal, sometimes. I air goin' to marry Lissy Reams, Doctor Borin'"——

Now it was his turn to look into the doctor's eyes; quick as a flash they fell. If the mountaineer saw anything, if there was anything to see, he gave no sign. "I'm goin' to marry Lissy, as soon as little Al's big enough to make a livin' for the ol' folks. I have got a good place t'other side o' Pel- ham. I can keep Lissy real comf't'ble. Al's fo'teen goin' on fifteen; Lissy's turned seventeen an' pritty as a pictur'."

Before the doctor could frame a reply old Dilce put her head in to say that dinner was ready—"raidy an' wait'n'."

It was always ready and waiting if once old Dilce got it on the table. The two men rose; the doctor laid his hand upon the arm of his guest:

"You are coming out to dinner with me," he said.

But the mountaineer shook his head:

"That's percisely what I ain't," he declared. "I'm not Brother Barry by a long sally. I'm goin' home. An' when you ain't got nothin' better to do, Doctor Borin', you come over to Pelham Valley; you can come the big road or you can keep the path all the way, an' see how a God-forsaken sinner manages to keep his head above water an' starvation. You'll find as pretty a lay o' land, an' as pleasant a pasture with the creek a caperin' through it as frisky as it capers for the biggest Methodis' in the state. An' I gits a shower, Doctor Borin', every blessed time my church neighbors gits one. An' if thar's a stint o' sunshine in the favor o' they-uns it didn't make itse'f known last July. You come over an' see."

"Will you send me off with dinner on the table?" asked the doctor.

The visitor hesitated, stared, seemed to catch a sudden idea, wheeled about, and tossing his hat into a corner said:

"Lead the way. Though God knows I do feel mightily like a Methodis'."

It was sunset when the yellow mule trotted leisurely down the road to Pelham. The physician stood at the gate, watching the big slouch bob up and down with the motion of the animal. When it disappeared in a strip of black gum woods, he placed his hand upon the gate latch, hesitated, dropped it, and turned back slowly toward the house.

He had thought of walking down to Lissy's in the dusky twilight. Instead he went to a little rustic bench under a giant beech and sat there, lost in thought, until Aunt Dilce called him in to supper. He rose slowly, his hands clasped behind him, and went in.

The lamps had been lighted, and as he stopped a moment in his sitting room to make some slight change in his clothing, his eye fell upon the dust imprint of a gigantic foot upon the velvet cushion of his easy chair.

He smiled and sighed with the same breath. Was he the thoroughly honest fellow he appeared, this young guest of his? It was odd: the visit, the unsought confidence, the breaking of bread in neighborly way. He had an idea the man had designed to put him on honor not to interfere so far as Alicia Reams might be concerned, in his love affair.

He sighed again and passed his hand over his brow as if to remove a veil that had fallen across his vision. His dream had been fast dispelled; life had put on her old gloom-garb again. And that when he had but just strangled all doubt, faced and overcome all fear—just at the moment when he was about to be happy. The golden apple had yielded bitter with the very first taste.

(To be continued.)

BOOKS OF THE DAY.

A BIOGRAPHY OF AMELIA BLOOMER.*

REVIEWED BY NEWELL DUNBAR.

When Edward L. Pierce published his "Memoir and Letters of Charles Sumner," he wisely let the subject of the biography so far as possible tell his own story. In books composed on this plan, from printed matter, letters, etc., of (or about) the subject, the author selects and arranges his material so as to give the history in order "from the original sources"; after that, his part is limited to comparatively little more than an occasional word or two of explanation, information or indication. He serves merely as a sort of showman; while the panorama, so to speak, unfolds *itself*. It is an admirable method in biography, and it is the one Mr. Bloomer has followed in this worthy memoir of his wife.

Those who in 1840, when Amelia Bloomer began her career as a writer, speaker and worker for temperance and woman's-rights reform, had come to years of thoughtfulness, who were her contemporaries, and followed with interest her course as it was run, are now necessarily few. They will, doubtless, welcome this volume and thank its author for the manner in which he has performed his task. His work will gladly be read, too, by a larger class, young when the more active part of Mrs. Bloomer's life was past, heretofore ignorant perhaps of her name and influence, or knowing of her indeed up to her death in 1894 as still on earth with themselves, but upon her lifework looking back as upon a tale told before they were born. For future generations, also, the book will have value. A life beyond most useful in its day, a life belonging in the choice number of those because of which the world perceptibly grows better, a life wedded to the larger realities, a life that seems to have been inspired above all things with a living sense of *justice*, is here rescued from tradition or oblivion and placed on enduring record. In the opinion, no doubt, of many a Biography of Amelia Bloomer was an unsupplied want; that want is now filled.

Amelia Bloomer was not a woman of great intellect, in the sense in which we use the word for instance of George Sand, George Eliot, or even Mrs. Humphry Ward. Indeed, perhaps, the impression

---

* "Life and Writings of Amelia Bloomer," by D. C. Bloomer, LL. D. With portraits. 12mo, pp. 387 ; price, cloth $1.25, paper 50 cents. Arena Publishing Company, Boston.

her Biography gives is that in spite of being editor, writer, lecturer, she was scarcely a distinctively intellectual person at all. On lines connected with the woman problem she seems to have come the nearest to a modern intellectual equipment. As with nearly all her sex, the strength of her character appears to have lain in her intuitions; these possessed unusual healthfulness and vigor, and of them her understanding was merely the servant—receiving their commands abjectly and just striving to get them carried out. One would imagine the impression received from personal intercourse with her might have been that which the late Bishop Brooks extolled as being the feeling produced by the best balanced and the most influential personalities he had known: viz., one of helpfulness and invigoration, without any thought occurring of their *having* any intellect. In a noble picture, the parts if possible are evenly opposed; at all events, the highest value holds first place.

The story of Mrs. Bloomer's outward life is soon told. Her father was a clothier by trade. Her maiden name was Jenks and she was born in Homer, N. Y., May 27, 1818. She received a district-school education probably limited to reading and writing, with a little grammar and less arithmetic. When about seventeen she taught successfully for a single term in a district school in Wayne County, N. Y. From nineteen to twenty-two she was a governess. At twenty-two she changed her name to the one by which she afterwards became famous, marrying Dexter C. Bloomer, who at that time was a young man twenty-four years old, of Quaker extraction, and one of the proprietors and editors of a Whig newspaper published in Seneca Falls, N. Y.; he was also engaged in studying law, paying considerable attention to politics. In later life, Mrs. Bloomer often dwelt with much satisfaction on the fact that the clergyman who performed the ceremony entirely omitted the word "obey."

Mr. and Mrs. Bloomer were both great readers. From letters received from his wife before their marriage Mr. Bloomer had formed an opinion highly favorable to her powers of expression and, persuaded by him, Mrs. Bloomer with great reluctance became a contributor on the social, moral and political questions of the day to the Seneca Falls newspapers; she wrote over different fictitious signatures, masculine as well as feminine.

Into the Washingtonian temperance reform of 1840–1 she threw herself heart and soul. When the woman's-rights movement was born in 1844–8 through the action or under the leadership of Ansel Bascom, David Dudley Field, Elizabeth Cady Stanton, Lucretia Mott and others, though she was interested in the agitation from the start. It was only gradually that Mrs. Bloomer was led to take an active part in it. The *Lily*, published at first in Seneca Falls, and of which for nearly six years (1849–54) she was sole editor, publisher and proprietor—being the first woman on record as having united in one person those responsible positions—she eventually made a woman's-rights in addition to its being a temperance organ. The circulation of the *Lily* reached over six thousand—which meant more in those days than it would mean now. Mrs. Stanton, Susan B. Anthony, Mary C. Vaughan and Frances D. Gage were among its contributors. Mr. Bloomer was appointed postmaster at Seneca Falls, 1849–53, and Mrs. Bloomer was his deputy. At the Rochester temperance convention of 1852, she began her career as a public speaker. In February, 1853, she spoke in New York City on temperance, the *Tribune* giving full reports of her addresses; in September of the same year, she spoke there again. During her life she lectured or delivered addresses on temperance or woman's rights, spoke as Fourth of July orator, etc., over New York state and widely throughout the West, and even spoke from the pulpit.

In December, 1853, Mr. and Mrs. Bloomer removed to Mount Vernon, O., receiving a public testimonial on leaving Seneca Falls. In her new home, she became the assistant editor of her husband's new journal; she also continued to conduct and publish the *Lily*, which she had transplanted with herself. She sold the *Lily* at the end of 1854, though she continued to contribute to its columns after that date. Early in 1855 the Bloomers removed again; this time to Council Bluffs, Ia., then possessing a population of only 2,000 or 3,000 and lying fairly in the wilderness. Here they continued to reside, growing up with the locality, until the time of Mrs. Bloomer's death, though in the interval she made numerous visits East and to Colorado.

In January, 1856, by formal invitation of a considerable body of its members, she appeared before the Nebraska house of representatives, and delivered on woman suffrage a lecture that all but made its subject an accomplished fact in that territory. Inspired by her arguments, embodying the principle she advocated was framed a bill that stood every chance of becoming a law; it had passed the house, and reached its third reading before the senate, when it expired with the term. Mrs. Bloomer was strongly anti-slavery in feeling, and during the Civil War her house was a centre for Union work; Iowa's contribution to the great sanitary fair held in Chicago in 1865 was collected largely through her efforts, and she herself was in attendance there three weeks. At this fair she met General Grant.

All through her life she served as delegate, on committees often at their head, as president, vice-president, secretary or treasurer of various organizations, meetings and conventions; when not able to be present personally she wrote letters: she conducted a voluminous correspondence, and contributed to or waged controversies in the press in different sections of the country; she was frequently interviewed by reporters; helped conduct and founded lodges; wrote the greater part of the chapter on Iowa in the third volume of Mrs. Stanton and Miss Anthony's "History of Woman Suffrage"; and her labors before and in societies small and large, at festivals, exhibitions, etc., for the promotion of causes she had at heart, sometimes raising very considerable sums of money, were unceasing. From 1867 to her death she was one of the vice-presidents of the National Woman-Suffrage Association.

At Seneca Falls, in 1843, with her husband she united with the Episcopal Church; of that church she remained a communicant, as well as a constant attendant upon its services, whether in the East or West, during the rest of her days—active in parish work and tireless in various parochial organizations and benevolent enterprises for a period of over fifty years. At Council Bluffs her house was the home of the clergy, of teachers and reformers, and she was a mainstay of more than one Christian denomination. It may be said here that, while a firm believer in the truths of Christianity, she "always insisted that certain passages in the Scriptures relating to women had been given a strained and unnatural meaning, and that the whole teaching of the Bible, when fully interpreted, elevated her to a joint companionship with her brother in the government and salvation of the race." Without children of her own, both at Seneca Falls and in the West she gave a home, sometimes for years, to many children of others. In Council Bluffs a brother and sister were adopted and brought up by her, the boy and his children after him taking her name. Throughout this life of effort, her health was seldom robust and she was frequently obliged to retire to sanatoriums, water cures, springs, etc., to recuperate. After two days of intense suffering she died Dec. 30, 1894, in her seventy-seventh year.

No life can be called in vain that, from the better element of the community in which more than one-half of it has been spent, has called forth words of commendation such as those contained in the two following tributes. The first is from a poem composed by a clergyman in Council Bluffs on the occasion of the celebration, in 1890, of Mr. and Mrs. Bloomer's "golden wedding." The poem was addressed to them both:

Foremost in every noble work, in every cause
  Where God leads on, where Light is seen, where Truth is heard,
There have you stood from first to last, the eternal laws
  Of Right obeyed. Where'er your lips could frame a word
To voice the thought, a hand could strike the great applause
  Of onward march, your helpful force has been conferred.

To you, this day, a grateful people tribute bring
  For all you've been to them, for all your steadfastness,

For all your words and deeds; for every noble thing,
　They would this day your true and honest worth confess;
They would a golden cup, filled from Affection's spring,
　Hold out to you and thus their gratitude express.

Take, then, the Crown.　Both heaven and earth proclaim it yours,
　The Sower's crown, the Reaper's crown, that glows with light,
That glows with light and love, and one that aye endures.
　The Evening Star, that hangs upon the fringe of night
And, like a lamp, the weary wanderer allures
　And tells him of his home afar, is not more bright.

Look round you, then, crowned as you are, and upward, too:
　Here shine the golden sheaves; there gleam the jasper walls;
Around you gather here the noble, good and true,
　With hearts aglow, and chant their tender madrigals.
Around, above, all things are wreathed in smiles for you,
　While on you, like a burst of sun, God's blessing falls!

The second tribute occurs in an article in one of the Council
Bluffs newspapers published two days after Mrs. Bloomer's death:

Her prominence in the woman-suffrage movement made her one
of the eminent American women of the century.　Her name has
become firmly linked with every reform movement for the uplifting and betterment of woman's condition during the last fifty years.
Her life was an intensely busy one, filled with many deeds of kindness and charity aside from the active part she always took in the
temperance cause and the advancement of her sex. . . . Her death
will be felt throughout the entire nation as an irreparable loss to
the cause she so warmly espoused. . . .　She will never be forgotten,
for her influence, with that of other good women, has *done more to
make the civilization of the West a possibility than the many inventions
of modern science* [italics the reviewer's].

Temperance and woman's rights were Amelia Bloomer's special
field of work—above all *woman's enfranchisement,* as the surest means
towards temperance amongst other things.　From 1851 to the end
this claimed her heart.　Her monument bears the inscription:
"A Pioneer in Woman's Enfranchisement."

Amelia Bloomer was a woman capable of achieving results from
her theories.　The glory of her life was the change effected in the
general life about her, into which her own had poured itself, which
it had helped reform, and the growing improvement in which it was
happily spared to see.　Says her biographer:

No colleges were then [1853] open to women.　No universities
offered her the literary advantages of their halls and lecture rooms,
and the general opinion was entertained among the mass of the people that the three studies of reading, writing and arithmetic were
enough for her.　So also there was little for women to do but to sew
and stitch, and occasionally teach school for wages far below those
paid to men.　There were no women lawyers, no women preachers,
except among the Quakers, no typewriters, no clerks in the stores,
no public offices filled by women.　Mrs. Bloomer in her lectures
. . . argued that the schoolroom, the workshop, the public office,
the lawyer's forum and the sacred desk should be opened to her

sex on entire equality with man. These were then unpopular doctrines to promulgate either in the public press or on the lecturer's platform; but Mrs. Bloomer was spared long enough to see her rather radical ideas on this subject brought into practical application, for at the end of 1894 woman's right to both education and employment on an equality with man had come to be almost universally recognized.—Pp. 130—1.

Again:

In 1880, she was enabled to write as follows: "The trustees of the public library of this city [Council Bluffs] are women, the teachers in the public schools, with one or two exceptions, are women, the principal of the high school is a woman, and a large number of the clerks in the dry-goods stores are women."

The revised Code of Iowa, promulgated in 1873, almost entirely abolished the legal distinction between men and married women as to property rights. As to single women there was, of course, no distinction. That code is still in force, and its liberal provisions in regard to the rights of married women have been still further enlarged. The wife may hold separate property, and may make contracts and incur liabilities as to the same, which may be enforced by or against her as though she were a single woman. So also a married woman may sue or be sued without joining her husband in matters relating to her separate property, and she may maintain an action against her husband in matters relating to her separate property rights. Their rights and interests in each other's property are identical. They may be witnesses for, but they cannot be against, each other in criminal actions.

It is not claimed that, for bringing about these beneficent changes in the laws of Iowa, Mrs. Bloomer is entitled to the sole credit. There were other efficient workers in the same field; but it is certain that her long residence in the state, and her continued and persistent advocacy of the principles of justice on which they are founded, contributed largely to their adoption by the law-making powers.—Pp. 240—1.

Further:

Mrs. Bloomer was spared to witness the triumph of many of the reforms she had earnestly advocated. The temperance principle in which her heart was so much absorbed made great progress during her lifetime, and the prohibitive features she so earnestly advocated were engrafted on the laws of her adopted state. She was not spared to see woman accorded a right to the ballot in all the states, but she was cheered by the wonderful progress in that direction that took place all over the world. In Wyoming and Utah women had voted for several years, and only a few weeks before her departure she learned with infinite satisfaction from . . . a favorite niece residing in Colorado, that the right of suffrage had been granted to women in that state. While therefore she was never herself permitted to exercise that inestimable right, yet she died in the full conviction that only a few years would elapse before it would be accorded to women in all the free countries in the world.—P. 244.

It is only just to say that, in the arduous and long protracted labors of Mrs. Bloomer's life, her husband appears to have given her all the sympathy and support the most exacting could have desired. They were worthy of each other. Miss Susan B. Anthony wrote in 1890: "I hardly believe another twain made one, where the wife belonged to the school of equal rights for women, have lived more happily, more truly one." Mr. Bloomer himself says: "She [his wife] was, in all her work of promoting temperance and woman's enfranchisement, aided and sustained by the cordial assistance and support of her husband. No note or word of discord ever arose between them on these subjects (and, indeed, very few on any other); *they passed their long lives happily trying to alleviate the sufferings and right the wrongs of their fellow-travellers through the journey of life* [reviewer's italics]." The portraits in this volume are appropriately of both.

Amelia Bloomer's career, side by side with that of her husband, may well stand as a rebuke and an exhortation to-day when throughout a large section of society pelf and domination are the most esteemed; helpfulness, beneficence and brotherhood bid fair to go out of fashion; and we are *all* threatened, as we have recently heard, with the advent of an age of "a competition keener than the world has yet known"!

The volume contains numerous and full extracts from Mrs. Bloomer's lectures, editorials, contributions to newspapers and other writings; and in the appendix is given in full her lecture on woman's enfranchisement, of which her biographer says: "It is believed to be one of the strongest arguments that has ever been written in favor of woman's right to the ballot." Not a few interesting anecdotes and facts largely new, also, will be found relating to Mrs. Bloomer's contemporaries, some of whom won a wider fame than she. Among these are Horace Greeley, Wendell Phillips, T. W. Higginson, Hon. William Windom, Elizabeth Cady Stanton, W. H. Channing, Gerrit Smith, the Cary sisters, Susan B. Anthony, George Thompson, Lucy Stone, William Lloyd Garrison, Mary A. Livermore, Antoinette L. Brown, Kit Carson, Anna Dickinson, Phœbe Cozzens, Frederick Douglass, T. S. Arthur, Abby Kelly Foster and others. Says the author:

Mrs. Bloomer was a great critic, and for that reason may not have been so popular with her associates as she otherwise might have been. Her criticisms, possibly, were sometimes too unsparing and too forcibly expressed. She had strong perceptive faculties and noticed what she believed to be the mistakes and failings of others, perhaps, too freely. No one ever attacked her, in print or otherwise, without receiving a sharp reply either from tongue or pen if it was in her power to answer. But no person ever had a kinder heart, or more earnestly desired the happiness of others, or more readily forgot or forgave their failings.

The *true* story of the origin, together with some of the early history, of, the great "bloomer" movement is here told. Recent innovations in athletics will, possibly, lend additional interest to this. At any rate, it is well it should be authoritatively on record.

THE THREE MUSKETEERS.*

REVIEWED BY B. O. FLOWER.

I remember reading, a few years ago, one of Louise Chandler Moulton's most delightful papers, in which she gave the expression of pleasure given by many leading contemporaneous writers on first reading the elder Dumas' most popular, of his many popular historical romances, and this paper called to mind the delight I had experienced when I first perused these works, then published in a cheap and unattractive form. I also remember how they interested me in the men and the stirring times of the period which they graphically depicted, so deeply that I renewed my acquaintance with the works of some leading French historians, and read much in historical and biographical literature which I might otherwise have left unread for years. This, it seems to me, is one of the chief points of value in historical romances, and when, as in the novels of Dumas, great fidelity to historical accuracy is observed, the work gains an added value—a value wanting in writers like Sir Walter Scott, who so frequently sacrifice history to the imagination or conceit of the author's brain in such a manner as renders the work confusing and frequently valueless to the general reader who desires to obtain historical facts in the pleasing form of romance.

Probably no writer of our century, who has essayed the field of historical romance, has taken anything like the pains in gaining the facts of history for the framework of his creations as has the elder Dumas. He was a romanticist of romanticists, and consequently has come in for wholesale criticism and condemnation from the ultra-classical writers on the one hand, and from the veritists on the other; but the fact remains that few French novelists have been so popular among the masses as the elder Dumas. "The Three Musketeers," which is generally accepted as his masterpiece, cannot bear comparison with that greatest of all works of fiction, "Les Miserables," produced by his friend and kindly critic, nor do I think it will bear comparison with several other popular works of fiction of our century; nevertheless, like "Les Miserables," its popularity continues to grow, notwithstanding the death of romanticism has long since been announced by the apostles of other schools of literature, who seem to imagine that romanticism has been buried and is wellnigh forgotten. It is difficult for man to see good in theories, ideas, or schools of thought with which he is not in accord, and there is no exception to this rule when we come to the world of literature; indeed, I sometimes think there is almost as little catholicity of spirit here as in the domain of dogmatic religion.

During the past few years a number of excellent English translations of "The Three Musketeers," published in a highly attractive

* "The Three Musketeers," by Alexander Dumas. Translated by William Robson. With an Introductory Letter from the late Alexander Dumas. With 250 illustrations by Maurice Leloir. In two volumes of 358 pp. each; price per set $4. D. Appleton & Co., New York.

manner, have appeared in this country, but none can compare with the superb two-volume edition, published by Messrs. D. Appleton & Company, containing two hundred and fifty characteristic illustrations by Maurice Leloir, and, with the exception of three or four drawings, which illustrate an escapade of D'Artagan, which, while probably true to the life of the time described, only serve to accentuate a passage which had been far better left out of the volume, the pictures are admirable. I regret that such pictures as these appear in so sumptuous a work, as I regret the presence of the description of the escapade which they illustrate, and other similar passages which do not make for morality.

The interest of Dumas' writings lies chiefly in their historical value, the quick movement, and the manner in which he seems to make one feel that his creations, no less than the historical characters he describes, have actually lived, moved, and acted as described; these characteristics render his works of absorbing interest to all who enjoy exciting historical novels of the romantic school.

The edition we are considering contains a touching Introductory Letter from the late Alexander Dumas, whose opening sentence runs as follows:

My Dear Father: In the world to which you have gone does memory survive and retain a recollection of things here below, or does a second and eternal life exist only in our imagination, engendered amid our recriminations against life by the horror of annihilation? Does death utterly annihilate those it snatches from us and is memory vouchsafed only to those who remain on earth? Or, is it true that the bond of love which has united two souls in this world is an indestructible tie not to be severed even by death?

These agnostic sentiments are followed by others more materialistic in character, though touching in the filial love expressed. The younger Dumas who has so recently passed beyond the curtain, like so many of his countrymen, seemed to regard the great problem of the hereafter as inexplainable and therefore as something idle to speculate upon. How different are his words and thoughts from the following lines from Victor Hugo, who viewed life from a vantage ground essentially loftier than that upon which the younger Dumas lived "life's little span":

I feel in myself the future life. I am like a forest which has been more than once cut down. The new shoots are stronger and livelier than ever. I am rising, I know, toward the sky. The sunshine is on my head, the earth gives me its generous sap, but heaven lights me with the reflection of unknown worlds.

You say the soul is nothing but the resultant of bodily powers. Why, then, is my soul the more luminous when my bodily powers begin to fail? Winter is on my head and eternal spring is in my heart. Then I breathe, at this hour, the fragrance of the lilacs, the violets, and the roses, as at twenty years.

The nearer I approach the end, the more plainly I hear around me the immortal symphonies of the world which invite me. It is marvellous yet simple. When I go down to the grave I can say, like many others, "I have finished my day's work"; but I cannot say, "I have finished my life." My day's work will begin the next morning. The tomb is not a blind alley; it is a thoroughfare. It closes in the twilight to open with the dawn. My work is only begun; I yearn for it to become higher and nobler, and this craving for the infinite demonstrates there is an infinity."

At one time Hugo tenderly said to a poor distracted mother, who mourned the loss of a child: "Console yourself, for it is only a departure, and that for us alone. The dead are not even absent. They are invisible, but every time you think of your little one he will be near you."

BLOSSOMS OF THOUGHT.*

REVIEWED BY B. O. FLOWER.

The author of this work is evidently an orthodox thinker, but one of those broad, fine souls who are not trammelled by dogma and creed, and who appreciate the new spiritual life of our time, which illuminates and warms without scorching, and elevates without carrying with it that soul-consuming influence of fear. The book consists of fifty "blossoms" in poetry and prose, which are well calculated to elevate, calm, and inspire the weary worker and the soul hungering for spiritual rest or "that peace which passes all understanding and which the world cannot take away." It is a book which can be taken up at any moment, opened at any page, and read with help and profit by those who are hungering and thirsting for spiritual assurance, and that sweet spirit of human love which has marked the most luminous sayings of Jesus, so precious to Christendom for over eighteen centuries.

I do not agree with the author in all her expressions, but the spirit everywhere present is the spirit which is yet to redeem the world, and I recognize that probably more bloodshed, persecution and misunderstandings have arisen through verbiage, or the use of words, than aught else; hence, when I see and feel a high, broad, true spirit permeating a book, it counts with me far more than the use of a few words which I would not have employed, because I think they have been so frequently mistakenly used in the past that they do not convey the meaning which the leaders of the new spiritual reformation desire to impress.

The work in its dainty and exquisite binding is in every way worthy of its fine, helpful contents.

---

* "Blossoms of Thought," by C. E. Russell. Extra cloth, cream, bird's egg blue, and sage green. Beautiful side design in gold. Gold back. Price 75 cents. Arena Publishing Co., Boston, Mass.

SAMANTHA IN EUROPE.*

Reviewed by B. O. Flower.

Miss Marietta Holley (Josiah Allen's Wife) has an immense *oli-entele*. Thousands of persons read with avidity the common-sense philosophy and the high religious and ethical teachings, which she clothes in such simple, quaint, and humorous garb, who could not be induced to consider the same vital thought if clad in more sober verbiage. Her latest book, "Samantha in Europe," is, in my judgment, by far her strongest work; it arraigns the criminal indifference of the church and state of our civilization exhibited in the presence of great crying evils in a spirit which is never flippant but always suggestive.

One seldom reads a stronger temperance story or hears a more telling appeal to the conscience than we find in the story of "Ellick Gurley" as told by Annie the "Contoggler." It is the simple story of misery wrought by rum, wherein a weak-minded young man yielded to the temptation set before him by his saloon-keeper brother-in-law who occupied a high seat in the church and was prominent as a worker in the "Association of Religious Bodies for the Amelioration of Human Woe." It is a story in which satire on church and state, tragedy and misery unspeakable, are set forth in homely fashion but as only a writer of Miss Holley's peculiar talent can portray. It is a common story; thousands upon thousands of cases more or less similar are occurring every year in our republic. We all know that such monstrous facts are stern reality—we all know that church and state close their eyes to these wrongs; but when they are individualized and brought home to the conscience of the individual they are apt to make one pause, and it is just such stories widely circulated which will aid greatly in bringing about the new reformation in which the religion of high, pure life will count more than dogma, form or creed.

The reading public is too familiar with the quality of Miss Holley's writings, replete with quaint but homely humor and true pathos which have given such popularity to the works of "Josiah Allen's Wife," to make it necessary to dwell on this phase of her latest work. I will merely say in passing that the rapid change of scene gives a variety, which, aside from the suggestive facts and the fund of information, will doubtless make this work the most popular of Miss Holley's books.

To me, however, two features of the work are peculiarly interesting; one is the high ethical teachings which are woven as threads of gold throughout the web and woof of the narrative—the sound

---

* "Samantha in Europe," by Josiah Allen's Wife; illustrated with one hundred and twenty-five artistic and humorous engravings; 8vo; pp. 727; price, cloth $3.50, half russia $4. Sold only by subscription. Funk & Wagnalls Co., New York.

philosophy and broad catholicity which characterize its pages, and the other is the striking fidelity displayed in her portrayal of marked types of life at the present time.

In Martin, "the self-made man who worships his maker," we have a vivid pen-and-ink sketch of the American *parvenu*. Such members of our mushroom aristocracy swarm to Europe every year spending a few hours where a man of culture and refinement would desire to spend months, but becoming weary and bored during these few hours and only going to places of note so as to affect superior knowledge and to appear to be "much travelled."

Al Faizi, the East Indian seeker after truth, represents in a very true way those in all lands to-day who are profoundly spiritual or deeply religious, using this much abused term in its high, broad, and true signification. These two characterizations are masterpieces as depicting types, while in a less pronounced way we see the essentially practical nature of Josiah.

The catholic spirit of the book is calculated to do much good at the present time, when the spirit of intolerance and persecution is constantly flaming forth from those who believe they are following that One who said, "Do unto others as ye would that they should do unto you." This broad and truly Christian spirit is illustrated in these lines in which Samantha reproves her "pardner" for wishing he had some thumb screws whereby certain deacons could be made less obnoxious to Josiah: "And, sez I, you see from Loyola and Cromwell down to Josiah Allen the carnal mind wants to punish somebody else for doin' suthin' different from what you wants 'em to do."

This book, while it doubtless will not hold any special attraction for those who are not interested in Miss Holley's style of writing, will be hailed with delight by the very large *clientele* who eagerly await all her writings, and it is safe to say that to these it will prove her most interesting and instructive work.

SIEGFRIED THE MYSTIC.*

Reviewed by E. H. Wilson.

"Siegfried" is a novel of uncommon interest. The characters are clearly conceived and distinctly portrayed. Siegfried the Mystic is a noble conception. This nonagenarian, endowed with a majestic presence and having a heart as wide-reaching in its sympathies as the needs of suffering humanity, known by many but understood by few, respected by the wealthy and the educated, loved by the poor, the downtrodden, and the despised, who found a refuge in him, kept a little old second-hand bookstore which was "the haven of the wretched, the hope of the weaklings, and a resting-place for all the

---

* "Siegfried the Mystic," a novel, by Ida Worden Wheeler. Pp. 295; price, cloth $1.25, paper 50 cents. The Arena Publishing Company, Boston.

weary ones who would come." He made these poor unfortunates feel that they had in him a true friend, a wise counsellor whose main purpose in life was to induce his less fortunate fellowmen to resolve "to be stronger, braver, truer, more loving, and more kind."

This gracious old man, whose daily life is a benediction to all who meet him, has acquired a remarkable influence over two young people of beautiful character—a young man, whose father is a leading merchant in New York, and a young woman of great personal beauty, whose origin is involved in mystery until the death of her uncle. Both these young people grew up under the beneficent influence of the old metaphysician, who had taught them that the only thoughts or acts that could bless them were the thoughts and the acts that aid others, and that the surest way to impede their own progress was to put stumbling-blocks in another's path. Two other young persons, equal to these in bodily and mental gifts, but lacking their sensitiveness of bodily organization and their responsiveness to spiritual influences, contribute largely to the interest of the story by their intensely human desire for the good things of this life. These five—four in the heyday of youth, two of the earth earthy and two rarely philanthropic natures given to mysticism, and the aged Siegfried who dignifies life by his high ideals, by his noble sentiments, and by his inspiring, uplifting thoughts—are the only characters that I shall notice in this review.

One day in Herbert Lord's early childhood, Siegfried, looking into his eager, boyish face, told him that he was "an eagle among a brood of hawks." This was the starting-point of a singular and most unselfish friendship. The ultimate effect of this friendship on the young man is described in part by the author as follows:

As Herbert's innermost consciousness, obeying the impelling force of his affections and his will, slipped its base from the sense to the soul plane, he became at once immeasurably broadened in intellect and in understanding. Eventually he found himself in touch with all life, sympathizing with all sorrow and failure and pain, rejoicing in all success, understanding all the complex mysteries of existence. He realized his oneness with nature and with humanity. He felt that he was no longer a lone unit, but an integral part of the universe of matter and spirit. He had lost his life from the little pool of self, but had found it again, intensified and glorified, in the shoreless ocean of the infinite.

Sherman Lord, however, had fondly looked forward to the time when his son, after the completion of his college course and a European trip, would join him in his business as his strong helper and become in process of time a worthy successor. But the son declined to accede to his father's wishes unless the business were put on a coöperative basis. The nature of the discussion may be understood from a brief extract:

"Well, think as you will, Herbert, but act sensibly. As to coöperation, as you call it, you must know that such talk in connection with

Lord, Son & Co. is preposterous. Look to your own interest. You have only your mother's few thousands at your command. I offer you a half-share in my business, and will not restrict your charities if kept within bounds. This will secure your future and at the same time enable you to experiment somewhat in your nationalism, socialism, or what you will. And if I have guessed aright it will provide accustomed luxury for the woman you love. It would suit me well that you and Diana should marry. Her mother was your mother's closest friend. Shall it be so?" He tried to speak lightly, but his spirit failed him a little, and he looked at his son appealingly.

Herbert felt that the supreme moment of an eternal choice was upon him. Before him he saw two roads: one, fair and enticing at the start, led to a waste of self-loathing; the other began darkly forbidding, but grew brighter and ever brighter as it neared self-conquest. One face—the face of her he loved—beckoned him in the ways of pleasantness, but at the entrance of the gloomier path stood his own higher self. His choice was made.

"Father," he said, "I would be unworthy of all good did I consent. It cannot be."

The son's decision was a death-blow to the father's hopes. The excitement attending the interview and keen disappointment due to the thwarting of long-cherished plans induced an attack of apoplexy. The son, summoned, hastens to his father's bedside only to find him speechless though conscious. Physicians administer an opiate and the son retires to the library to summon Siegfried by mental telegraphy. The old mystic responds to the summons and by his power as a thought-reader discovers the will of the dying man. Herbert Lord had broken his father's heart, and he was destined grievously to disappoint the woman whom it had been for years supposed he would marry, but he attained an illumined soul.

Only those who have themselves stood upon the heights where Herbert then rested can understand or even vaguely guess at the rare sensation of unity with nature and humanity and God which flooded the young mystic's physical, mental, and mortal nature with a rush of divinely vitalized life.

George Martin is a clear-headed young man who left his country home for New York where he intended to accumulate a fortune. Making Herbert Lord's acquaintance early in the story, he is drawn to him and finds delight in his companionship, though he cannot understand his mysticism. "Truth, love, wisdom, and all the grace of affectionate doing" may be the only realities, and amassing wealth by legitimate methods may be chasing a shadow, as Herbert says, but George Martin is convinced that nothing can be "better for a young man to gain than that which will give him independence, position, and power." So this money-making genius goes serenely and determinedly on his way, undertaking with courage and persevering with hope. His friends believe that he is endowed with the golden touch, for his every business venture turns a stream of gold into his coffers. He wins, too, the woman of his choice against great odds.

Diana Denmead, the adopted daughter of Sherman Lord, has no ordinary charms of person, and a face of surpassing beauty. She has grown up in close intimacy with Herbert Lord and has come to love him with all her heart and with all her soul. The author shows much skill in delineating the growing divergence in their characters until they are brought to declare their ideals of love. When Diana, perceiving a change in Herbert's attitude toward her, sought information of a psychic, she received this reply: "As you understand love, he loves you not." But though she had long turned this over in her mind, yet she was not prepared for Herbert's answer to her question: "Do you mean that you could bear to see me suffering, if it were in your power to interpose?"

"I do not think you understand me, Diana," Herbert said. "The man or woman who does me the greatest kindness is not he or she who gives me hysterical sympathy in my suffering, or who caters to my vanity and selfishness by flattery and gifts. The friend who is truly 'good' to me, is he or she who opens my eyes to higher truths, who inspires me with a desire for a cleaner and a more simple life, knowing that where spiritual wisdom lives, mental anguish may not enter.
"Yes, Diana," Herbert said, when Diana did not speak, "I mean that I could even bear to see you suffer; for I should know that you had, although perhaps unknowingly, keyed your life with discord, and that only through suffering could you be again attuned to harmony. I should know that pain had come to you, not as a monster of torture, but as a friendly teacher."

Suffice it to say that the conversation revealed to this "fair, slim, physically flawless young creature" that she required for her happiness a love less spiritual, less Platonic, less mystical than that proffered by this embodiment of perfected manhood.

Josephine, the beautiful psychic and Siegfried's "doubly endeared charge," is clairvoyant and clairaudient. Under the guidance of her aged friend and teacher her spiritual nature has been wonderfully enlarged and beautified by spiritual influences, until her outwardly unseen teachers and prompters have assured her that she is illumined and no longer needs their ministry, for she "could be trusted in my [her] normal state of consciousness to speak the right helping word to the right needy person, to do the right deed at the right season and in the right way."

This interesting story is well plotted and it holds the attention of the reader to the end. There are clear and strong portrayals of character. There are passages of almost dramatic interest. The morality of the book is unexceptionable. The moral trend of the volume may be perceived from the fact that it teaches that love is threefold in its nature—physical, mental, and spiritual; that perfect love is a blending of these three into one sweet whole, and that for this love alone is there an immortality; that while the unintellectual may enjoy physical love, the spiritually enlightened demand a still

more refined and sympathetic companionship; that married infelici-
ties are due to the fact that the married know each other externally
but not internally; that thought is responsible for all bodily ailments;
and that the discomforting circumstances of our lives are the
sequences of either wilfully or unwittingly mistaken thoughts that
have hardened into false beliefs.

"Your thoughts are alive, Josephine," Siegfried would say, impressively. "If your sight were but a little clearer you could see their
form, their color, and their size. Every thought is a fairy or an imp,
according as it is good or bad. Your body is really made up of an
aggregation of these little living creatures that are constantly
changing and shifting their character and position to accord with
the mood and will of your mind. When they are harmonious, you
are well. When you are unsettled and ill at ease or diseased, you
suffer pain. If you will have only brave, kind, and unselfish
thoughts you will never be ill, and you will grow to look like an
angel. But, Josephine, every bad thought is an ugly little thief that
steals away your beauty and your grace. If you entertain thieves,
you must suffer from their depredations. If you will think only of
goodness, you need fear no evil. Your thoughts are your real companions, Josephine, and the thought-world is the real world. Keep
your thoughts clean, strong, and trusting, and you will be healthful
and joyous. You will learn in this way to build for yourself a
spiritual mansion, where you may dwell with gracious fairies. This
is the only home, and these are the only friends that any person, or
any little girl can call her very own. Let me tell you a great, great
secret, Josephine. Thought is the greatest power in the wide, wide
universe. What can it do? Everything. It is supreme."

And again in his final words to his pupils, Siegfried says that he
can give them

"no deeper lesson in mysticism than this: Thought is the hidden
force called fortune or fate. You are not elected to suffer by any
other will or whim than your own. You are the effect of your past.
You will be the effect of your present."

Those who believe in occultism, in psychic manifestations, will
particularly enjoy the book. Mental scientists and healers will read
with pleasure this paragraph and those that follow:

"The philosophy of mental healing cannot be made clear to you in
a few words; but if you will lay aside all prejudice and follow me
closely, you will soon come to the conclusion that metaphysical cures
are pronounced impossible or miraculous, and the methods employed
supernatural, only because people in general are ignorant of spiritual
laws."

There is not a little wisdom in Siegfried's answers to questions
like these: "How to make an impression for good upon a naturally
weak and depraved brother man, whose heart is as hard as a rock?"
"How can he [a foul sinner] make amends?" "By what magic have
you accumulated so great a knowledge of human nature?" "Where
is the spirit world?" "How can we punish the rich and powerful
for their injustices to the helpless poor?"

The answers given to these and similar questions, which have to do with social, reformatory, psychic, moral, and religious problems that to-day engage the serious attention of beneficent philanthropists, of enthusiastic investigators, of profound scholars and thinkers, show that whatever else may be true, Siegfried was at home with himself and, knowing himself, knew man. The old seer's last word to his pupils may fitly conclude this review:

"Men and women can become all that they will to become. Life is worth living. It is worth while to live it after the pattern of your highest ideals. It is worth while to strive. It is worth while to hope. It is worth while to love. You can be well. You can find, and you can perform, your mission in life. You can be happy. Therefore, be of good cheer, my pupils, and be of completest cheer to know that, for the life and love of each individual soul. *There is no Death.*' "

UNCLE JERRY'S PLATFORM.*

Reviewed by E. H. Wilson.

This finely illustrated little volume contains three brief stories—"Uncle Jerry's Platform," "Pops," and "A Daughter of the Revolution." The scene of each of the stories is in Virginia. The first two stories and one or two incidents in the third remind us of the interest, the affection, the intense loyalty shown by slaves of the better class to the various members of their master's family. This feature of the book will commend it more particularly to those who in bygone days had an opportunity to witness the kindness of humane masters towards their heedless, helpless, and improvident dependents and the warmth of affection felt by the latter for the former.

The author's success as a writer of dialect may be seen from two or three brief extracts. Uncle Jerry describes his master's character thus:

"Nothin' mean 'bout Marse Randolph neider, eberyting open an' 'bove-board, an' nothin' underhand, cuz *I* knew all his ways. I was his body sarvent, an' what me an' Marse Randolph *was, we was;* what *oder people was, dey wasn't!* Now, Deacon Fisher tuk *his* toddy unbeknownst to nobody, an' neber axed a soul to jine him; an' ole Lawyer Corbin, he got on sprees when he wen' to town, an' kep' it moughty close; but dat was not de way wid me an' Marse Randolph; *what we was, we was; what we wasn't, we wasn't!*"

The Randolphs had six little girls but no boy to perpetuate the name. At last, however, on Christmas day the master rode down to the quarters and told Jerry to call all the hands out to drink the health of the fine boy that had come to make glad his parents. Uncle Jerry may tell how the negroes received the announcement:

"'Bless de Lord,' sez I, 'you don't say so!' sez I. 'Dat's a Christmus gif' to be proud of, sure 'nuff, an' right from de han' ob de good Lord Hissef! Here, Sam; here Dan'l; here, boys, come, 'gratilate Marse Randolph. Bring out your cups.'

* "Uncle Jerry's Platform, and other Christmas Stories," by Gillie Cary. Cloth; price 75 cents. Arena Publishing Company, Boston, Mass.

"Dey all crowded roun', an' Marse Randolph called little Jim,
who was totin' de big jemijohn, an' poured out a plenty for all, an'
den I giu' de toas': 'Three cheers for big Marse Randolph, an' three
cheers for leetle Marse Randolph; de los' is foun', de dead is cum to
life agin; le's kill de fatted cyarf.' An' Marse Randolph larfed right
hearty, he did, an' said, sez he, he hoped de baby wouldn't be no
prodigal son nohow.' "

"Marse Randolph" was wounded in the Civil War and brought
home to his Virginia estate to die. On his deathbed he charged
Jerry to take good care of his family, and particularly of his young
son "Ran."

" 'Jerry, I wants you to promise me to be good to your Miss Alice
an' de gyurls when I am gone, an' to remember to take special keer
of leetle Ran. I'm feard I hab loved dat boy too much, ole man,
an' 'dulged him too much for his good.'
"An' Marse Randolph groaned hard, an' lifted up his eyes to
heaben an' prayed de Lord to hab mercy upon de helpless ones; an'
den he hel' out his han' to me, an' squeezed mine hard, an' said, sez
he, 'Good-bye, my dear, faithful Jerry. God bless you, an' my good
Kitty too—I leab 'em all to you.' "

The heart-broken negro ran to the woods and, throwing himself on
the ground, wept long and bitterly, for in his own language, "Me an'
Marse Randolph had been frien's for thirty-odd year, an' neber a
cross word had he eber spoke to me."

"Ran" developed into a youth of such brilliant parts that his
instructors urged the duty of sending him to college. He inherited
from his father a taste for "dram-drinking," which terminated in
delirium tremens and suicide soon after his college days were over.
Uncle Jerry, who had been in the habit of taking his "toddy as
reg'lar as ole Marse hisself," took the death of his "Ran" so much to
heart that he adopted the following platform:

"And so, sah, ef yer com' to ax me 'bout my pol'tics, I can only say,
I am an ole man, an' gittin' on to de grabe, an' I kno' nothin' 'bout
your high-license an' your low-license, but I *do* kno' when I meet
Marse Randolph on de oder shore, I shall hab to tell him I tried my
bes' to take keer of leetle Ran, but—de whiskey was too much for me.
But ef dere's any oder poor boy like him to be saved, *mebbe* de only
son ob his mother, an' she a widder; an' so long as de Bible say 'Am
I my brudder's keeper'; an' so long as my poor Ran's blood cry to me
from out de groun', gemmen, you mus' 'scuse me, but ole Jerry feel as
ef nuffin' an' nobody can keep him from votin' de 'dry-ticket'
to-morrer."

"Pops," a young negro boy, was the playmate of his little white
charge. This interesting story, like the foregoing, shows the more
beautiful side of slave life in Virginia in the days before the war.
The story presents vividly the tender care and watchful solicitude of
"Pops," who finally sacrificed his life in rescuing little "Pil" from a
watery grave, as well as the beautiful way in which the latter in
after years manifested his gratitude for the sacrifice.

Incidentally the author gives us some notion of the crude ideas that prevail among negroes regarding such matters as "getting religion," what constitutes a proper funeral, and what qualifies one to inhabit the kingdom of heaven.

"A Daughter of the Revolution" narrates in a pleasing way the brave deed of a young French officer who belonged to the military family of General Rochambeau. He was nerved to the endeavor by his love for the heroine, Eleanor Page, whose birth, beauty, and devotion to the wounded and dying were such "that her very name was as a bugle's blast to numbers of brave souls"; and at the last moment he was strengthened and fortified for his perilous undertaking by the knowledge that his love was reciprocated. We will not detract from the reader's interest by giving an outline of the story. Suffice it to say that the story is well told and ends as it should.

The book is illustrated by V. A. Garber and Margaret May Dashiell. The illustrations are appropriate. The type and the binding are attractive specimens of art.

THE ARENA.

No. LXXVII.

APRIL, 1896.

THE LAND OF THE NOONDAY SUN — MEXICO IN MIDWINTER.

BY JUSTICE WALTER CLARK, LL. D.

Zacatecas is just within the tropics, as we passed the line of Cancer a few miles back near Calera, but the city is over eight thousand feet above sea level. This combination of low latitude and high elevation gives Mexico that magnificent climate which, never cold and never sultry, seems perpetual May.

In all the Mexican towns of any size there is a Plaza de Armas or Central Plaza in which the band plays nearly every night and whither everyone goes. On one side of this plaza is invariably the cathedral; on two of the other sides, if the town is a state capital, the governor's palace and the palace of the state legislature and supreme court, and on the fourth side large stores or handsome private residences. This was the case at Zacatecas, where on the night of January 2, in the open air, without overcoats or shawls, large crowds filled the seats ranged around the square, and while the band was playing the young men and maidens were promenading but never in company with each other.

According to the custom of the country, there was "an endless chain" of girls, in groups of two, three, or four, promenading in one direction, with a similar chain of young men going in the opposite direction, while the older people sat on the benches and seats. Thus every girl can be seen in succession by every young man in the other chain, and both parties make good use of their eyes. Where any mutual liking is evinced, or any encouragement shown, the girl's home is ascertained and then the smitten youth takes to "playing bear," as it is called. That is, he promenades at certain hours back and forth beneath the narrow balcony on which, in this delightful climate, the inamorata sits in

THE THEATRE, GUADALAJARA.

front of her apartment. He casts from time to time amorous glances, for he is not allowed to call at the house.

If he receives encouragement, or *thinks* he does (for there
are vain youths and feminine flirts in Mexico as elsewhere),
he contrives in some indirect way to transmit a letter.
The first letter is never noticed; it would be contrary to
the female sense of propriety to capitulate so easily. The
second letter is answered by means of the same underground
route, and in a non-committal way is calculated to terminate
or to encourage his suit. If the courtship proceeds favorably after a proper season of delay and hesitation, the matter
is "referred to papa." If he approves, the youthful parties
are then permitted to meet in the presence of some discreet
elderly person, but it would be deemed a great scandal if
they should be seen in public together, either riding or walking, until the marriage has taken place or at least until
the preliminaries have been settled and the engagement
announced. The marriage is not valid in law unless celebrated before the civil authorities, and as the women usually
insist on being married by a priest, the hymeneal knot is
thus usually twice tied in Mexico, as in France, and for the
same reason.

In Guadalajara, there is a double walk way around the
plaza. By tacit consent, on the outer one of these the
young men and maidens of the lower classes, the wearers

of the *scrapes* and *rebosos*, promenade, with their endless chains going in opposite directions, while at the same time on the inner walk, separated from the outer one by a row of seats, the young people of the upper classes do the same in their American or French costumes. In some other cities, this matter is tacitly arranged by one class promenading around one plaza and the other class around another. and in still other towns, by one class promenading on certain nights and the other on certain other nights.

What class a person belongs to or shall associate with, is settled in Mexico, as elsewhere, by a kind of tacit understanding, for there is no law or regulation, and in Mexico there is a total absence of those race distinctions which exist in the United States, or the caste requirements of India. All persons are not only equal before the law but equal socially—so far as race is concerned. There are social inequalities, and they are sharply marked as above shown, but the social distinctions arise not from

STATUE OF CUAHUTEMOC, MEXICO.

race but from the causes which create social distinctions in
any country where the people are of the same race, as in
France or England. Juarez, the greatest man Mexico has
produced, was a full-blood Indian; Diaz, the present able
president, is part Indian, while many of the most distinguished men have been of pure Spanish descent, a race
which is as white as the white race this side of the Rio
Grande.

The census gives ten thousand as the number of negroes
in Mexico, an infinitesimal number in the total population.
Indeed during my whole stay in the republic I saw only
six negroes, of whom four were Pullman car porters and two
were barbers. Three of the six were natives of the West
Indies, and one of the latter, it may be incidentally mentioned, was fluent in six different languages, due partly to
the fact, probably, that living in the seaport town of
Tampico his vocation as barber brought him in contact
with sailors and people of many nations,—still a negro
speaking six languages is something out of the ordinary.

The costume of the people of the upper and middle classes
has conformed very generally to our own, so that no difference can be observed, and very often it is impossible to tell
whether to address a person in Spanish or English. The
lower classes in some sections adhere altogether to their
former dress, but in other sections of the country in this particular they have to a large extent followed the example of
their superiors in social position. The distinctive features
of the former dress wherever retained, is for a man, a tall
cone-shaped hat of felt or straw, with a wide brim called a
sombrero, a pair of exceedingly tight-fitting pants, and a
gaudy blanket wrapped round the upper part of the body
and often held so as to conceal the mouth. This is called
a *zerape*. Often the sombrero is gaudily decorated, costing
sometimes fifty dollars or even more, and the pants are
decorated with lace on the seams. This is when the adherent to the old costume has some little means, in which case
he sometimes adds to his dress a jacket bedizened with great
quantities of gold lace or white braid. But these individuals are now very few in number. Often, especially further
south, the humble peon is content with a costume consisting
of a pair of coarse linen drawers, a coarse linen shirt and
a *poncho*, which last is a coarse blanket, with a slit in the
middle through which the wearer's head is passed. This
simple costume is completed by a cheap straw sombrero
with its high steeple crown, and a pair of sandals, unless, as
is most often the case, the sandals even are dispensed with.

BELEN CEMETERY, GUADALAJARA.

THE AQUEDUCT, QUERETARO.

COLLEGIATE CHURCH, GUADALUPE VILLAGE, ENVIRONS OF MEXICO.

ENTRANCE TO THE CHINAMPAS, ENVIRONS OF MEXICO.

The women of the upper and middle classes almost uniformly conform to our manner of dress save that the *reboso*—a kind of mantilla—is still often worn over the head in lieu of bonnet. The *reboso* is universally worn by the poorer classes, doubtless on account of its cheapness and durability as a covering for the head.

The police are very efficient, attentive to their duties, and very polite. At night every policeman carries a lantern, and this is set out in the street in front whenever he may happen to be on the sidewalk, so that looking down or up the street rows of these lanterns can always be seen. Step up to one of these men and ask him where your hotel is, and he will not only tell you but, unless you object, he will go with you to the next policeman who will in turn pass you on till you reach your destination. This is always done politely and without expectation of reward. In how many American cities would this happen? Not only in this respect, but in all others, and by all classes, the greatest politeness is the rule. It seems a part of the nature of the people of the country. They have their faults and as many of them as most nations, but boorishness or want of politeness is not one of them.

The railroads in Mexico, with the exception of one of the railroads between Mexico and Vera Cruz, known as the "Queen's Own" because built by the English, have been constructed almost entirely by Americans with American capital, supplemented by government appropriation, and are managed by Americans. They are as well managed as the railroads this side the border, and indeed the Mexican Central, which system controls some two thousand miles of track, is handled with unusual ability. The conductors and engine runners are nearly all, if not all, Americans. So are many of the station agents and other employees and all the higher officials.

As to speaking the language, one not understanding the native tongue will find less difficulty in travelling in Mexico than in France or Germany. It is almost impossible to enter a railroad car, or a hotel at which travellers stop, without finding Americans. They are everywhere and in every business and seemingly all prosperous; many of them have been wonderfully so. Then besides, as has been said, the conductors and many other railroad employees are Americans. The proprietors of the hotels where tourists stop, catering to their best customers, have either learned to speak English or have clerks who can. Then, too, there is everywhere a growing disposition with the classes that a traveller is likely to meet to learn our tongue. In fact, it is almost a "fad."

If one desires to strike out for himself the language is a very easy one to learn. Spain having been the remotest of the provinces of Rome when the barbarians made their irruptions, it was less submerged, and hence the Spanish tongue more closely resembles Latin than either Italian or French. It is a great aid in learning Spanish to have acquired a knowledge of Latin at school. But even to those who have not, the language presents few difficulties. It must be remembered that though an "encyclopedic," or "unabridged" dictionary contains over one hundred thousand English words, the number of words used by us in ordinary speech is said not to exceed five hundred. So in travelling in a foreign country the man who can memorize two or three hundred words and a few phrases can get along very well. It is true he could not make a speech or write an article or conduct a sustained conversation, but he can ask for information or anything else he needs and get it.

The pronunciation is easily learned and the accent and intonation also by a little practice. It is more difficult to understand a foreigner than to make him understand you, in speaking his language, because his words at first seem to run together. But so it is with us also. In conversation our words are not spaced as in writing or printing, but we speak as the old Romans and Greeks—more true to nature —wrote their books and inscriptions, i. e., without any space between words, using only the period at the end of a sentence. This digression is for the benefit of our countrymen who may feel deterred from visiting the country on account of the difference of language, but for the reasons above stated they will find far less inconvenience, if any at all, on that score than in travelling on the continent of Europe. Besides being spared the inconvenience of a sea voyage, the time from New York to the city of Mexico is now only a little over four and a half days *via* Laredo and indeed it is only three days from New York to the Rio Grande.

The appearance of a Mexican city strikes the eye at once as something very different from an American city. In the first place the houses apparently have no roofs, because their roofs are flat, with just enough elevation at one side to run the water off, and this top is entirely concealed by parapets. Then there are no chimneys; the climate does not require them. When it is unusually cool, they use, in the northern part of the republic, little brasiers containing burning charcoal to warm the hands, and in the humbler homes the fire that cooks the meal is sufficient. But even this has to be resorted to very rarely and only in the northern states. Certainly I did not see a chimney the whole time I was in the republic, nor did I see anyone who had ever heard of one. The cooking is usually done with oil or charcoal and on small stoves, and sometimes by cheaper devices.

The enforcement of the criminal law is far better than in the United States, for it is more efficient and more prompt. In our country year before last, by official returns, more than ten thousand capital offences were committed, out of which vast number one hundred and seven were executed by law and two hundred and forty-seven by lynch law. In Mexico, with its twelve million people, from the best data obtainable the capital offences committed are less than one thousand annually, and a case of lynch law is unknown. That the race is prone to homicide and the ignorant class to larceny is undoubtedly true, but a firm government represses and punishes with a promptness and certainty that deter. The manner of executing the law would not suit our people, but as a means adapted to the end, it is the best possible for the people and the country which have adopted it.

Brigandage has been entirely suppressed. The country is patrolled by picked troops, known as *Rurales*. These receive one dollar a day and are constantly on the alert to maintain order. The regular army is largely recruited from the Indian race and is paid much less. Whenever a train stops at a station a soldier in uniform, with sword or gun, is stationed on the ground near each car door. This is a relic of former days when this was necessary, and it is still useful to prevent petty thieves entering the cars. In some of the more northerly states, this seems dispensed with now in whole or in part, but in the greater part of the country this custom still prevails.

At Zacatecas I slept in a convent and in the city of Mexico in a palace, for convents and emperors having been abolished these buildings now serve more useful purposes as hotels. The Catholic churches are now all owned by the government and preaching in them is by permission. Under the old régime many more churches were erected than were actually needed and consequently some of them, though not many, are now used for secular purposes. I saw a convent that has been converted into a bull ring and more than one church that was used as a barracks for the soldiery.

The court system of Mexico is very similar to ours. Each

OLIVE TREES, STATE OF MEXICO.

state has its justices of the peace, its superior or circuit courts, and its supreme court. Then the federal government has its district courts, its circuit courts, and its supreme court; the latter is divided into three divisions, and meets as a whole only for the decision of certain important questions. The law is codified, the Code Napoleon, with some modifications, being adopted. As in France, the court renders decisions but files no opinions. Hence there are no shelves filled with volumes of law reports as with us, and the decision of a case, more or less similar, by another court, or by the same court on a previous occasion, cannot be cited as a precedent. This is equally the rule in all countries having the Code Napoleon for the basis of its law, and has at least this advantage, that an erroneous or unjust decision is not perpetuated as a rule to be always thereafter observed.

All civil actions are tried by the judges without the intervention of a jury. In criminal cases, the right of trial by jury is guaranteed by the constitution. A jury consists of nine, and six must concur to find a verdict of guilty. If as many as eight jurors agree to a verdict the judge cannot set it aside. The constitution prescribes a mode in which its provisions can be suspended, and the guarantee of trial by jury has been suspended as to persons guilty of throwing trains off the track, burning railroad bridges,

THE CARMEN GATE, SAN LUIS POTOSI.

and shooting into cars. In these cases the offenders are tried by court martial and if found guilty are shot within twenty-four hours. The brigand element was prone to this offence as they felt they were being destroyed by means of the speedy communication by train and the rapid concentration of troops. The brigands have been broken up, and this offence is now almost unknown.

GUADALAJARA, PANORAMIC VIEW.

COFFEE RANCH, STATE OF VERA CRUZ.

One great defect has been the want of education among the masses. But this is being remedied. Schools are established by law and are to be found everywhere. They have not only common schools and high schools, all secular, and maintained out of the public funds, but there is compulsory attendance. Not infrequently a policeman may be seen collecting a squad of truant children and marching them off to the schoolroom.

The signs over the stores rarely swing out across the sidewalk as with us, but the European mode of putting all signs flat against the wall is usually followed. This alone makes a marked difference in the appearance of the streets. Then, too, instead of the sign reading "John Smith & Co.," each store has, quite in Chinese fashion, a title, more or less fanciful, for example "The Paradise," "The Garden of Eden," "Aladdin's Lamp," "The Fifth of May" (a national celebration), "The Sacred Heart of Jesus," and the like.

In speaking of the houses, it may be added that they, especially the residences, look very plain from the street, for they have on the lower floor usually only a door, strong and substantially built, on the street side, and if there are windows always heavy iron gratings to them. This originated doubtless in the precarious and turbulent times of yore, but it is kept up in part for the reason that by excluding the light the rooms are kept cooler. On the upper floors, before each apartment, is a narrow balcony, and on these the family, especially young ladies, sit in the cool of the evening to see the world passing along beneath them and to reward their friends with a smile. But the interior of these residences belie their exterior. They are invariably built around an open courtyard, and around this courtyard runs a porch with floors for each story. Thus each room has its door opening on the porch, and the courtyard with its fountain and its flowers which bloom the year round presents a scene of color and life. The houses are built of stone, or *adobe*, i. e., sun-dried brick; if the latter, usually stuccoed. The walls are always very thick, and the pitch of the rooms very high and the floors tiled. This and the customary absence of windows keep the rooms cool and pleasant in summer and warm in winter. This mode of building also gives the most complete privacy. Evidently these people understand building for their own climate. An American wooden house, with its numerous windows and lower ceiling, and opening outwards would be unpleasantly warm in the glare of the tropical sun and too cool when the sun had withdrawn, and (besides its publicity) deprive the family of their courtyard, its fountain and flowers.

The *adobe*, or sun-dried brick, are usually about fourteen inches wide by twenty inches long and four or five inches thick. It is a very cheap building material and a house is built very rapidly. When the owner's means permit the adobe is stuccoed, otherwise not. The more substantial buildings, as well as the churches and public edifices, are usually constructed of stone. The stores on the public squares frequently have *Portales.* These are arcades running the entire length of the block and are constructed by making the sidewalks four times the usual width (they are ordinarily very narrow), thus moving the front of the stores back, and the second story is built over the entire sidewalk, giving a wide walk protected from sun and rain and inviting custom for the stores in inclement weather. The streets are usually paved with cobble stone, though some improvement on this has been attempted in some places. In the city of Mexico there are some streets with asphalt pavements. The names of the streets change with each block, or if the same name is retained, it is the first, second, or third of such a street according to the number of the block from the beginning.

The ordinary means of freight transport, exclusive of the new method by railroad, is by *burros*—donkeys—and by carriage on men's backs. It is astonishing what loads can be carried by both. The load on a man's back is usually sustained by a band passing around the forehead. The working women usually carry their infant children on their backs. The loads on the burros are divided and placed one-half on each side. Numbers of these animals singly, but more frequently in droves, can be seen at all times passing along without bridles and carrying loads much larger than themselves, and men can often be seen carrying loads so large that only the man's feet can be seen, thus resembling an animated hay rick or corn shock. When railroad construction began the native laborers would take off their *zerapes*, or blankets, load them with the dirt, then giving a twist they would fasten an end of the blanket around their foreheads and trot off with enormous loads. When wheelbarrows were prescribed, they would load the barrows up and place the loaded barrows on their heads and carry them off to empty. When made to roll them, they would still put the empty barrows on their heads to bring back. But this stage of development is now past, and the incident merely shows that the use of wheelbarrows, like many other things in our civilization, is not intuitive but acquired.

In all the cities and towns of any size they have street cars, electric lights, ice factories and other concomitants of modern civilization. These plants come from the United States and like the railroads are largely owned and operated by Americans. In respect to water works and sewerage the cities are as yet almost unprovided, with the result that with one of the healthiest climates in the world the cities on the great plateau of Mexico show a comparatively high death rate. This is especially true of the city of Mexico where the death rate is abnormally high. There a system of sewerage and drainage has been under construction some years and will be completed very soon, which will doubtless change all this. The signs and advertisements of our leading sewing machines are often met with and also the agencies of our great life insurance companies, though necessarily, from what I have said, there is small demand for fire insurance.

The religion of the country remains nominally Roman Catholic, for "The Reform" (as it is called), which confiscated all the church property was economic and political and had no religious element in it, thus differing widely from Luther's in Germany and Knox's in Scotland, and in some particulars, though not in all, more nearly resembling the confiscation of church property by Henry VIII in England. The women in Mexico are, as a rule, still devout Catholics. The men are said, by those who know them best, to have as a rule no religion to amount to anything, though probably the majority of them still lift their hats whenever they happen to pass a church door, were it fifty times a day. There are very few Protestants, as yet, among the native population, though the different denominations are represented by able and devout missionaries, all of whom, that I met, seemed to be hopeful and satisfied with the progress they are making.

In Mexico, as in all countries dominated by the Spanish-speaking race, Jesus is, as it was in ancient Judea, a not unusual name. I recall an incident I heard of a very sick man who on awakening from a troubled slumber was much terrified by finding on a chair in front of him a placard, "Call for Jesus." This happened to be the name of his nurse.

In appearance, the people of Spanish descent are white, and when dressed in American style, as most of them do, are not very different in appearance from Americans. Those of Indian or of Indian and white race mixed

"Wear the shadowed livery of the burnished sun."

They are a light yellow, and differ widely in appearance

from the sharp cheek bones and copper color of the Indians
of our plains. The Aztecs, Zapotecs, and Tarascons of
Mexico have a very remote kinship to the Cherokees, Choc-
tows, Creeks, Chickasaws, Sioux, Utes, Arapahoes, Chey-
ennes, and other Indian tribes of this country. The young
people of the wealthy classes are well educated, many of
them being sent to Europe and this country. Many of the
senoritas are exceedingly sylph-like and handsome, though
with a tendency to grow stout as they grow old. The
rhythmic tones of that "soft, bastard Latin which melts
like kisses from the female mouth" are musical indeed when
spoken by them, for their voices, like that of Annie Laurie,
are usually

> "Low and sweet, like summer breezes sighing."

Slavery has never existed in Mexico under the Republic.
Their laborers are said, by the Americans I met, to be faithful and efficient. On the haciendas, as the large farms are
called, large numbers of laborers are employed and are
called *peons*. On the estate or hacienda of Jaral twenty thousand peons, including their families, were formerly employed
and the owner of this hacienda furnished an entire regiment
of cavalry in the war of independence, but as is usually
the case with great wealth, on the side opposed to popular
rights. The peons are not slaves, nor attached to the soil,
but their wages not being more than sufficient to support
them and their families and having strong local attach-
ments, they usually remain from generation to generation in the employ of the same hacienda. Wages of labor
have always been very low in Mexico, the population being
in excess of the demand for labor and the opportunities
for its employment, but the dollar not having been enhanced
as with us, there has been no reduction in wages as with
us and hence no strikes in protest against such cuts. On
the contrary, owing to the new enterprises opened up and
the increasing demand for labor, there has been in certain
sections and in certain employments a decided rise in wages.
Still the laborer having been accustomed all his life to live
very cheaply and his wants in so mild a climate being very
few, wages are still much lower than with us. The fuel,
food, and clothing required by our more vigorous climate
could not be bought with the modest stipend of the Mexican day-laborer.

Travelling is mostly done on the railroads, but when
I had occasion to try the stage coaches I found them the
same conveyances, and exactly as uncomfortable, as with

us. I heard of this adventure, however. A traveller having bought a first-class ticket found many of the people around him had bought second- and third-class tickets. As all occupied similar seats and had the same accommodations he was puzzled to conceive where the difference came in, until the foot of a long, steep hill was reached, when the driver enlightened him by calling out (in Spanish), "Second-class passengers, get out and walk; third-class, get out and push; gentlemen (senores), first-class passengers, please keep your seats." On the cars, they also have three classes, but there is a distinction in the accommodations. The first class is like the first-class compartment in England, which it is usually said there "is used only by fools, Americans, and dukes." The second class has good accommodations and is used generally by people of means. The third class cars have four benches running the whole length of the car and are used by those who do not feel able to pay second-class fare. The rates of passenger and Pullman fare were fixed several years ago, at the average rate on our western railroads. At that time the Mexican and American dollar were of the same value. Since then the Mexican dollar has remained at the same value but the American dollar, by legislation designed for that end, has been doubled in value, requiring double the quantity of produce to buy it. The result of course is that while passenger fare and Pullman charges on both sides of the Rio Grande remain nominally the same, in fact travelling on our side costs about double. The same is largely true of freight rates, the reduction in these rates in the United States from competition being more than made up by the enhancement in the standard of value.

Above Zacatecas is the hill or mountain La Bufa (the buffalo), so called from its shape, and on that height a battle was fought in 1871 resulting in a victory for Juarez. From this summit, as also from the car windows as we leave for the southward, is one of the finest views in the world. The flat-topped houses, the domes, steeples, and the gulch in the mountain side in which the city is built lie spread out before you, with mountain after mountain rising above you to the north and valley after valley revealed to the south. There is a horse-car line from Zacatecas six miles down to Guadeloupe into which you roll, the whole distance, by the force of gravity; and the mules find cause for gravity on their part in pulling you back again. These two towns and their surroundings in many respects seem as if a bit of Palestine. The church at Guadeloupe is very old and

possesses peculiar sanctity. One is struck, however, with
the change time has made when he sees on each side
of the high altar a large Mexican flag, falling in folds from
ceiling to floor. The church is, like all others now, government property.

The town of Zacatecas has some seventy-five thousand
population, but it is compactly built and like all Mexican
towns it is without suburbs and covers not more than one-
fourth the space of an American town of the same population. Water is a comparatively scarce article in Zacatecas.
The fountains in the plaza are always thronged with people with their water jars, and as early as 4 A. M. women
and men of the poorer classes are at the fountain filling
jars with water which they sell to later arrivals at a centavo
(one cent) for four gallons—the quantity a jar holds. The
schools and the markets, the latter with their many varieties
of fruit unknown in our country, are very interesting.
Many of the vendors, spreading down a shawl on the pavement, divide their articles into sundry little piles, each of
which is sold for one cent. These sometimes consist of
cooked articles and many a passerby gets a meal for that
sum.

Mills are very rare in this country, and passing along
the streets, through the open door the mother of the family, or a young girl, can often be seen preparing the family
meal. Corn having been first soaked in a weak lye (as in our
Southern states it is prepared for "big hominy") is placed
on a flat stone over which a stone two inches diameter and
perhaps ten inches long is rapidly rolled by the hands of
the woman who is kneeling on the floor. The softened
corn is soon reduced to a kind of coarse paste, and is
flattened by hand into very thin wafers which are immediately baked. These are the *tortillas* which together with
the *frijoles* (in Bostonese, "baked beans") constitute the staple diet of the masses. Some of the tortillas are laid out for
dishes and plates on which to place the beans. Another
tortilla is twisted into a spoon, and when the beans have
been eaten, then the spoons, dishes, and plates are eaten,
and wiping their hands on a tortilla that is left, that is eaten
also. Thus the meal is over, the table cleared, and no dishes
or table cloth to wash.

From Zacatecas we roll southward, descending slowly
but steadily, and in forty miles drop down fifteen hundred
feet. Though it is January, the temperature is that of our
June, the trees are green and the flowers in bloom, and
the crops of all kinds are growing. To the right and left

..ie lofty ranges of mountains, with loftier peaks arising here and there. Away to the east like a mirror in an emerald frame shines Lake Pevernaldillo. The railroad runs through the middle of the great plain which extends hundreds of miles southward, and we come upon town after town as it were unaware, for there is no succession of houses becoming more and more frequent till the town is reached, as with us. The towns are compactly built, and extensions of town limits are made by building a new house just beyond the one last built, and not a mile or two out, leaving the intervening spaces to be filled in with other houses at leisure thereafter. Then, too, a town is generally a mile or so from the station, with which it is connected by a street-car line, but wherever you see the town there you will see church spires or domes rising far above everything else.

At Aguas Calientes ("hot waters") we come to a great health resort. The baths are very cheap and much frequented. On one side flows through a canal the surplus water from the springs, which is used gratis for bathing by those unable to pay the small charge of the bath establishment and by the washerwomen. There is a handsome *alameda* (or park) and *pasco*, as the grand avenue of these towns is called. The country around is very fertile and highly cultivated. A branch railroad runs to Tampico *via* San Luis Potosi, and on this road a few miles out at Salinas are the subterranean salt lake and the vast salt deposits from which thousands of tons of salt are shipped yearly. Several miles of side tracks are required to reach the vats and warehouses. The works support a town of five thousand people. Resuming our journey southward over the Mexican Central we pass large plantations of the maguey plant, and increasing quantities of the cactus plant, of which a new species begins to appear known as *organo* from its resemblance to organ pipes in the churches. This, besides its other qualities, makes an impenetrable and almost solid hedge. It needs no paint, is always fresh, and grows ready barbed. It fills the definition a North Carolina judge once gave of a lawful fence, for it is "horse-high, bull-strong, and pig-tight."

We cross a *barranco* near Encarnacion on a handsome iron bridge seven hundred and thirty-five feet long and one hundred and fifty feet above the stream. Passing Lagos and other towns we reach Leon, the "leather" town—as, a little further on, Irapuato is the "strawberry" town, Salamanca the "straw-hat" town, and Celaya the "candy" town. Leon is also a great manufacturing town and very thrifty. At nightfall, we reach Silao, the centre of a splendid agricultural region, whence a short branch road carries us to Guanajuato. It happened to be a *fiesta* (festival), and the streets were crowded. All around the cathedral, tents and booths were pitched in the streets, and in these every imaginable kind of gambling was going on, for the Mexican is especially addicted to this vice. Men, women, and children frequented the games and crowded the dealers on all sides. In substantial buildings close by were gambling rooms for those whose means required better accommodations. Throughout Mexico wherever and whenever there is a fiesta there the gamblers are always to be found in full force. They pay a license and their vocation is then considered lawful. Fifteen miles off, built in a narrow gorge, is the great mining centre and capital of the state, Guanajuato. It is built on the steep mountain sides, and every man could look down his next-door neighbor's chimney, except for the fact that there is not a chimney in the city. It would be a convenience to every man here if he could have one leg longer than the other. The city has a population of sixty thousand and is nearly seven thousand feet above sea level. It is unique in its appearance and does not resemble any other town in Mexico or elsewhere. The churches are very handsome, especially the Compania, commenced in 1747, the cost of cutting the shelf in the rock for the foundations of which alone was $100,000. It is an uncanny sight to visit the catacombs here with their collections of human bones reaching back perhaps two hundred years. It was at Guanajuato that Hidalgo in 1810 began the struggle for Mexican independence.

Again resuming our route southward on the Central we reach Irapuato, where we change cars for a trip over the branch line to Guadalajara and are instantly surrounded by the vendors of strawberries. The baskets of nice fruit are cheap enough, especially as the sellers are always willing to take half what they first ask. Their fruit, however, has been "deaconed"—as they say in New England—for inspection will show that by some coincidence the largest and nicest strawberries are always on top and the smallest ones always at the bottom of the basket. Irapuato has for its size—thirty thousand inhabitants—its full share of grand and venerable churches, plazas, fountains, large buildings, plain outwardly but handsome within, as residences for the wealthy, and long rows of squalid dwellings for the poor.

From Irapuato to Guadalajara, the branch railroad runs westwardly nearly two hundred miles through one of the most magnificent farming sections in the world, exceedingly fertile and well cultivated. Two crops of corn a year are readily made. When the corn is harvested by being shocked it is either stacked in long piles in the open field, or housed by being placed, out of the reach of stock, in the spreading limbs of scattered trees which grow in the fields and which seem especially intended for that purpose. No protection is needed from rain as none falls from November till May. When the corn is housed by being pulled off the stalk, instead of being shocked, the men throw the corn over their shoulders into baskets strapped to their backs and then pile it in the road for the bullock carts to haul it. It seems never to have occurred to them to drive the carts down the rows and throw the ears as gathered into the carts.

At Atequiza station we see a great hacienda, which possesses miles of wheat fields and hundreds of oxen and other animals, and has thousands of men at work. This hacienda, or plantation, has its own branch railroad and cars and a complete electric light plant. It is thought to be the place called "Miraflores" in Christian Reid's beautiful story, "A Cast for Fortune."

On the left, going west, we pass near Lake Chapala. This beautiful lake is something larger than the Lake of Geneva which it resembles in shape, and its shores some day will attract numbers of visitors and residents. To the right are the Falls of Juanacatlan, the Niagara of Mexico. It is reached by an electric railroad from El Castillo station. It may be mentioned that these falls furnish the electric lighting for the city of Guadalajara, fifteen miles away. The river Lerma is here five hundred and sixty feet wide and it pours the waters from Lake Chapala and an area of forty thousand square miles over the shelf of rock sixty-five feet at a single leap. There are smaller rapids above and below.

At Guadalajara we find a city of over one hundred thousand inhabitants, the second city in size in the republic. It is a substantially built town, for as in all Mexican cities a wooden building is almost unknown. In point of neatness it can be surpassed nowhere. The climate is as near perfection as can be found. From October to June, it realizes the poet laureate's dream of the island valley of Avalon,—

Where falls not rain, nor hail, nor any snow,
Nor ever wind blows loudly.

From June to October there are light, misty showers, two or three afternoons probably each week.

The public squares, public buildings, and institutions here are very handsome and on a large scale. On one of the government buildings is the scripture passage in Latin, "*Nisi Dominus custodierit civitatem, frustra vigilat qui custodit eam*" ("Except the Lord keep the city, the watchman waketh but in vain"). This reminds me that I saw a few days later inscribed over the cathedral door, at Coyoacan, the home of Cortez, another scripture text, also in Latin, which will be recognized at once as the memorable declaration of Jacob after his dream at Bethel, "Truly this is none other but the house of God and this is the gate of heaven."

The famous Hospicio at Guadalajara would be no discredit to New York. It is a very extensive charitable institution and has twenty-three patios, or open squares, bright, fragrant, and refreshing with fountains and flowers. The great city cemetery is surrounded by high walls within which roofed porticos run entirely around the enclosure with rows of pillars, colored and decorated. The appearance is unique and very striking. Within are many handsome monuments to the distinguished, or wealthy, dead. The climate in this state (Jalisco) and in the state of Michoacan, just south of it, is doubtless the best in Mexico, and probably is unsurpassed on our little planet. Returning to the main line at Irapuato we again proceed southward over the main line, passing through a country that is like a garden, by Salamanca, "the straw-hat" town, though it also exports kaolin and white clay and large quantities of leather goods, and then to Celaya, the "candy town," where Huyler would be nowhere. The *dulces* (candies) here are said to be made mostly from sugar and milk, and have been pronounced by good judges "the best in the world." The town was founded by the Spaniards in 1570, but for the matter of that the Spaniards had penetrated a thousand miles further north than this and founded Santa Fé in New Mexico, and over five hundred miles further than that and founded Monterey in California, before the English had established their feeble first colony at Jamestown in Virginia.

The next town to stop over to see is Querétaro, founded by the Otomite Indians in 1400, captured by a lieutenant of Cortez in 1531, and besieged in the Mexican Revolution of 1810, when it stood for the cause of freedom and suffered for it. "Many a tempest's breath and battle's rage has passed over" Querétaro. The latest was in 1867 when the ill-fated Maximilian was besieged here by General Escobedo. One afternoon, when taking his siesta, one of his followers, Lopez, whom the emperor had recently created a general, betrayed him by opening the gates to the enemy. Surprised, the emperor escaped to that hill over there northeast of the city, *Cerro de las Campanas* ("hill of the bells"), but on May 19 he had to surrender. He was tried by court martial and was shot thirty days later, on June 19, on the very spot of his surrender, together with his two leading generals, Miramon (who was an ex-president) and Mejia. Three square stones mark the spot where they stood, but these are said to be the third set, relic hunters having totally destroyed two former sets. In the museum in the state capitol at Querétaro are many mementoes of the siege and the execution, among others portraits of the leading officers on both sides. That of Maximilian is carefully labelled "Conde de Habsburgo, Archiduque de Austria," *not* "Emperador de Mexico," as he was once styled. His countenance indicates an amiable, weak man not "born to rule the storm." In the room, in execrable taste, is also preserved the rude coffin in which his remains were brought back to the town to be embalmed before being sent to Austria, the blood still showing in the bottom, and on the side is the full print of the back of his hand when in jolting it struck against the side of the coffin. His remains now rest in the lovely castle of Miramar, by the sounding Adriatic, which he left in his vain quest for imperial honors. Had he been content to wait for them, he would be the heir of his brother, the now childless Emperor of Austria and King of Hungary. The bodies of Mejia and Miramon were carried to Mexico and buried, beneath stately monuments, in the mausoleum of illustrious dead, in the Pantheon close by the church of San Fernando, and near them under a still handsomer monument, lie the remains of President Juarez, who refused to pardon them. Thus death is catholic and there are no rivalries in the tomb. Mexico doubtless deemed that death had expiated their errors, and rendered this homage to their earlier services to the republic.

"Fresh stands the glory of their prime,
The later trace is dim."

The remains of Miramon have been lately claimed by his native city of Puebla, the most republican of cities in those fighting days, and they have been reinterred there with great honors. The patriots were unable out of their scanty treasury to pay Lopez the $30,000 promised for his treason and presented him in lieu thereof, with a residence in the city of Mexico, where he lived abhorred by all.

In the public square of Querétaro is a monument to Columbus. On one side of this are the names of the distinguished men the city has produced, on another the names of those who deserve remembrance from their benefactions to the city, on the third side are inscribed the memorable events in the city history, with their dates, and on the fourth the elevation of the city above sea level, its latitude and longitude, its mean temperature, with its highest and lowest range, its rainfall, and similar information. The idea is not a bad one. I visited the Hercules Cotton Mill two miles south of the city. It is a large establishment with 20,000 spindles and 1,000 looms and is admirably managed. It has the latest machinery. I inquired the price paid for cotton and was told sixteen to seventeen cents at the factory. Up in the Mapimi country in Durango, where it was produced, the price was thirteen and a half to fourteen and a half cents, and later on at a cotton factory in the suburbs of Oaxaca, six hundred miles south of this, the superintendent informed me that they paid there eighteen to nineteen cents. In the U. S. Consular Reports for September last, our consul at Matamoros reports cotton selling to the factories at Monterey at sixteen to eighteen cents. On investigation I found all the prices about equalled thirteen cents in New Orleans, the tariff, freight, and charges making it cost sixteen to seventeen cents at Querétaro and eighteen to nineteen cents at Oaxaca, and they pay the local producer the New Orleans price plus these charges. Mexico does not produce enough cotton to clothe all her population. Her manufacturers buy in New Orleans the quantity the country fails to produce. A few years ago when their dollar and ours were equal, they paid on an average thirteen cents in New Orleans. Now they still pay thirteen cents in New Orleans and in the very same money, but owing to the enforced enhancement in the value of our money, by manipulated legislation, this thirteen cents instead of being still equal as it should honestly be to thirteen cents in our money is only equal to about seven cents of our "increased-value" money. The direct loss to the cotton planter of the South is, therefore, thirty dollars per bale or two hundred millions annual loss to the South on this one crop. The same is true of the wheat and corn of the West and all other crops, corn and wheat being one dollar to one dollar and forty cents per bushel in Mexico in their currency which has remained in value unchanged by legislation. The assertion about overproduction is a myth, as the countless thousands of half-clothed and half-fed people in the United States know only too well. The trouble is in the legislative increase of the value of the dollar made in order that those who live by clipping coupons from government, state, and other bonds, and on the public taxes, may be twice as rich as formerly without any additional exertion. They are twice as rich with the labor of clipping only the same number of coupons.

Leaving Querétaro we pass through Tula, a most interesting and very ancient city, which centuries before the coming of Cortez was the capital of Mexico. The interesting story of its ruins and antiquities is admirably told by Charnay. Further on we climb the mountain rim which encircles the Valley of Mexico, though rather it should be termed a double valley. Within it lie three lakes, Xochomilco, Chalco, and Texcoco. In the days of Cortez the waters of the latter encircled the city of Mexico, making it, though at the height of seven thousand five hundred feet above sea level, a western Venice. But frequent inundations and the difficulties in the way of proper sewerage rendered an outlet desirable. A canal known as the Pass of Nochistongo was begun in 1607 and work was prosecuted on it from time to time for nearly two hundred years. It is three hundred to six hundred feet wide, two hundred feet deep, and the length is nearly seventy thousand feet. Our railroad track runs along on the edge of the great cut, and we look down from the car windows into the yawning chasm below. This work lowered the ordinary level of Lake Texcoco so that its shore is now some three miles from the city, but it is still capable at times of invading the streets, and the city sewerage is very imperfect. A new canal has been begun in another direction, thirty miles long, twenty-six feet wide, and twenty feet below the main square of the city, and which is to discharge the waters through a tunnel seven miles long. This will probably be completed this year, when a good system of sewerage and water works can be put in and Mexico should become one of the healthiest cities in the world.

Now we have passed the last mountain barrier, villages become thicker and thicker, the country is a garden, the snowy cones of Popocatapetl and Ixticcihuatl wheel into sight, the tropical evening comes down, the mountains throw their shadows longer, the steeples and domes of a great city begin to rise up, now off to the right looms into view the castle of Chapultepec overlooking the valley and crowned with the Military Academy and the presidential mansion, now the long lines of electric lights begin to glitter, and now with clatter and a bang the long train stops and we are in—Mexico, once the Venice of the West.

"A thousand years their cloudy wings expand
Around me, and a dying glory smiles
From the far time when many a distant land
And subject state brought tribute" to Tenochtitlan's chief.

THE LIVING CHRIST.*

BY JAMES G. CLARK.

The Son of Man appears once more—
　The Christ who taught in Galilee
Proclaims His truth on every shore
　And walks the waves of every sea;
Unsullied by the taint of bribes
　He challenges the proud and great,
Rebuking Pharisees and scribes
　Who guard the doors of church and state.

He comes in signs, He "comes in clouds"
　Whose hidden lightnings bide their time;
He wanders homeless in the crowds,
　That Mammon drives to want and crime;
I see Him stripped and bleeding lie
　Beside the road to Jericho,
Where lordly bishops pass Him by,
　As in the ages long ago.

O! Christ, the tender, loving One
　In whom all deathless graces blend,—
The goal to which the cycles run
　In spiral paths to one vast end;
As torrents in their courses turn
　To mingle with the Mother-Breast,
All tongues and tribes and nations yearn
　For what is found in Thee expressed.

O! constant, patient Heart of Life,
　Whose warm pulse beats for all the zones,
While men still waste their powers in strife
　For gods of gold and petty thrones,—
I hear Thy voice amidst the roar
　Of trade and war on land and sea,
Repeat this message o'er and o'er;
　Take up the cross, and follow Me."

I see Thee smitten by Thy foes
　In courts of law and noisy marts,
While virtue from thy presence flows
　In healing streams to wounded hearts;
I see a drowsy priesthood—met
　In solemn form to watch and pray—
Who slumber while in bloody sweat
　Their Master waits the dawn of day.

* To Prof. George D. Herron, the John the Baptist of Applied Christianity.

I see those sad, reproving eyes
  Still search the cringing Peters through,
And One whom Pilate justifies
  Rejected by the church anew.
Again the robber is released,
  The saint to crucifixion doomed,
Again the Cæsar and the priest
  Conspire to keep the Lord entombed.

Again the surplice hangs revealed
  Behind the warrior's cassocked head,
Again the sepulchre is sealed
  Where Justice sleeps but is not dead;
But who can stay the awful birth
  Of Truth from out the age-long night?
Though all the armies of the earth
  Their legions hurl against the Light.

As rock-mailed shores submissive throw
  Their armors down upon the strand,
And towering summits plumed with snow
  Obey at last the tide's command,
So thou, O Christ! with love sublime
  Shalt draw all races to Thy breast,
And all the warring things of Time
  Shalt turn to Thee at last for rest.

THE EDUCATIONAL VALUE OF INSTRUCTIVE AND ARTISTIC ENTERTAINMENTS WHICH APPEAL TO THE NON-THEATRE-GOING PUBLIC.

BY B. O. FLOWER.

Slowly but surely the ideals of education which have been tenaciously clung to for generations are broadening on all sides. It is true that even the upholders of the old conventional book routine schooling are far in advance of the popular education of Colet's day, for it will be remembered that he created quite an innovation when he devoted the fortune left him to establishing St. Paul's Grammar School, where he announced kindness was to supersede brutality and where the children under his supervision, to use his quaint phraseology, were to "proceed to grow to perfect literature and come at last to be great clerks" for in that time, as one scholarly essayist has well observed, it was the all but universal dictum that "boys' spirits must be subdued" by merciless and oft-repeated beatings. Colet therefore inaugurated a real reformation when he established his humane institution, but his vision was limited, though indeed it is doubtful whether any more radical innovation would have taken root in his day.

There is something inexpressibly pathetic in the way in which even advanced apostles of learning have clung to the old methods which were happy innovations in 1512, but which should have long since been modified and revolutionized in a far greater manner than has characterized even our most progressive education. This is especially true of education in all its ramifications as carried on prior to the past generation, before the methods of Frœbel were popularized and a broad and magnificent outline of the "New Education" was promulgated by Prof. Joseph Rodes Buchanan, in which he showed conclusively that moral, industrial, and hygienic training should be emphasized as much as the intellectual,* which heretofore had been the chief concern of the teachers.

---

* "The New Education," by Prof. Joseph Rodes Buchanan, M. D., a volume of great merit but which, owing to the destruction of the plates, is now, we regret to say, out of print.

THE GRECIAN ART TABLEAU COMPANY.

He also emphasized the fact that education should be stimulative in character, that it should bring out and not restrain the thoughts and conceptions of the young, that it should encourage the imagination of the child to blossom, and thus develop genius instead of dwarfing the intellectual acquirements and wellnigh destroying the imaginative or creative faculty.

To-day we find a most hopeful change. Educators, and indeed the most enlightened persons who seriously think along the lines of human development, are coming to appreciate the fact that education should mean far more than simply book learning or chaining the imagination to the thoughts and ideals of the past. In this series of papers I propose giving our readers some thoughts on the "New Education." I shall strive to emphasize the more excellent way, nay, the necessity of beguiling the child into knowledge in various ways aside and beyond the instructions contained in textbooks.

The true teacher will flood the imagination with fine, high thoughts which must necessarily enrich the mind and quicken the imagination. He who points out to the child the beauty of the wayside flower, its richness of color, and the contrast presented by bloom, leaves, and roots wrought in nature's marvellous laboratory, who calls attention to the ever changing splendor of sunrise, sunset, the glory of the stars, and the beauty of nature, is in a very real sense a teacher, for he throws into the mind storehouse a fund of healthy food for the imagination upon which the soul feeds through life.

Broadly speaking, we may divide educational methods into two classes, the direct and indirect. At the present time I wish to deal with the new methods of enriching life through awakening the imagination, arousing the intellectual and bringing to it the enthusiasm which makes education a pleasure as well as a success in its true sense, in an indirect way, because the auditor is beguiled into a world where new knowledge, ideals, or suggestions of value are unconsciously absorbed while he imagines he is simply being amused or entertained.

There is no question in my mind but that the legitimate drama is a wonderful educator. Really great plays like those of Shakspere give the audience a world of information relating to the times, customs, and habits which are depicted, to say nothing of the educational value of the thought expressed; while plays so noble and pure as James A. Herne's "Shore-Acres" or "The Young Mrs. Winthrop,"

THE GRECIAN ART TABLEAU COMPANY.

and "Little Lord Fauntleroy" cannot fail to exert a wonderful and lasting influence for good on the mind and hearts of those who see them.   But, unfortunately, many plays are of a far different character, carrying an unhealthy, feverish, and in some cases injurious influence with them.*

* I have frequently greatly regretted the wholesale denunciation of the theatre indulged in by a large number of conscientious people, who, because of oldtime prej-

THE GRECIAN ART TABLEAU COMPANY — READING THE STARTLING INTELLIGENCE IN THE MORNING PAPER.

This fact, the cost of sustaining fine legitimate theatrical troups, and the oldtime religious prejudice on the part of a large class of thoroughly intelligent people, render de-

udice or because there is chaff among the wheat, fail to discriminate between the good and the bad, I believe that the legitimate dramas and plays which carry a high, noble purpose and are pervaded by a pure atmosphere are distinctly valuable from an educational and ethical point of view, while it is true here, as almost everywhere else in life, that discrimination, judgment, reason, and the conscience must be called into exercise.

sirable other forms of entertainments which appeal at once to the eye and the ear; when they are instructive, artistic, and pervaded by a high moral atmosphere, they are exceedingly helpful in a quasi-educational way, no less than as valuable influences in relieving the barrenness of life and affording food for the imagination long after the hour's entertainment is over.

Two incidents which occurred in my early youth stand out in my memory as if they happened but yesterday. To-day they seem simple and the reader will doubtless smile at their apparent triviality, and yet so positive were they in their influence on my young mind that they not only afforded much food for the intellect and imagination but they led me to further investigation and reading and thus greatly aided me in an educational way. They occurred when I was a very small boy in Southern Illinois. The first was a magic lantern lecture entitled "From the Orient to the Occident," if I remember correctly, and in exaggerated and somewhat sensational posters the wonders to be disclosed and discoursed upon were elaborately set forth. In those days the stereopticon had not been perfected, and the magic lantern show of that night would, I fancy, be considered a very crude and indifferent affair at the present time, and yet it opened a new world to me. It added a richness to life, and I have never come across scenes then depicted and described without their bringing up the oldtime lecture and the trains of thought which it awakened, thus giving a double pleasure to the scene. Hence, apart from its educational value this lecture stimulated my imagination and therefore enriched life.

The other instance was the impersonation of Shaksperean characters by a reader. I had always been taught to look upon the theatre as something necessarily bad, and as I was too small to read Shakspere, I knew little of the world's greatest dramatist and poet save what I had gleaned from snatches and short quotations in my father's library. This impersonator made a number of Shaksperean characters live before his audience. In a general way he explained the plays from which he read, and next proceeded to impersonate rôles from some of the best known passages in those popular dramas. It also opened a new world to me, and from that day I was not satisfied until I had read Shakspere's plays. Moreover, the reading of his historical dramas led me peruse histories pertaining to the times described. Since then, I have seen Edwin Booth, the elder Salvini, John McCullough, and many other really great Shaksperean actors, and though I now realize how commonplace, comparatively speaking, were the impersonations of the obscure reader of whom I am writing, I do not lose sight of the fact that that impersonator opened to me a new and wonderful vista and awakened unquenchable interest in

THE GRECIAN ART TABLEAU COMPANY.

THE GRECIAN ART TABLEAU COMPANY.

THE GRECIAN ART TABLEAU COMPANY.

the plays of Shakspere. I have cited these incidents merely to show how really educational and helpful are entertainments which stimulate the intellect and afford food for the imagination throughout future years, thus enriching life's barrenness.

The terrible pressure of social conditions during the past twenty-five years upon the vast army of wealth-creators and the rapid accumulation of wealth in the hands of the few have been exceedingly unfavorable for the success of entertainments outside of the moneyed centres of the country; but at length the people who while being buoyed up with hope have so long engaged in a struggle for a livelihood and a competence are finding out two things: (1) There is something more in life than food and raiment; the imagination, the brain, the heart, the soul, these must be appealed to and touched. (2) That until the voters change social conditions, the comparatively few who are already rich will grow richer, while the wealth-producers, the manufacturers, and the merchants (outside of the favored combinations) will grow poorer.

The apprehension of these momentous facts has greatly stimulated two things: (1) The desire for entertainments which appeal to the eye and ear and give the imagination food for sustenance, thus relieving the mind from the awful and continued strain due to the fearful struggle for a livelihood. (2) It has taught the people that after a quarter century in which they have been systematically deceived by the manipulators of the usurer classes and by their accepting opinions which have been manufactured for them by a venal press which has carried on a sham battle as ludicrous as anything in the narratives of Cervantes, were it not so tragic in its results, they are now beginning to perceive that they must think for themselves.

These and other reasons, which I have not space to enumerate, are producing a strong reaction in favor of a rostrum which shall be incorruptible and which shall address itself to the great principles of pure republicanism, the fundamentals of morality, justice, freedom, and fraternity; and coupled with this reaction in favor of a rostrum which will represent high, conscientious, and noble thought, we find a strong and growing desire for entertainments of a popular yet quasi-educational character, especially such entertainments as appeal to the eye and ear. On the lecture platform the unquestioned leader of these entertainments is Mr. John L. Stoddard. I have never had the pleasure

THE GRECIAN ART TABLEAU COMPANY.

of meeting this gentleman but I have greatly enjoyed his superb entertainments.*

Another kind of educational amusement which is proving exceedingly popular among the non-theatre-going

* There are numbers of other able thinkers who are utilizing the stereopticon in an educational way, but I have only space here to mention the Rev. R. E. Bisbee, whose lecture on "Soul Culture" has, I understand, proved very popular and which I judge from my knowledge of the man must prove helpful to all who are seeking a higher life. I would also mention Mr. C. O. Powers, who for two years has called the attention of thoughtful people to the pitiful condition of the slums and kindred topics.

classes, and which is at once delightful to the eye and imagination when rendered in a truly artistic manner and with due regard to the facts of history, is the tableau entertainment the scenes of which, being largely historical, mythological, or representative of the world's masterpieces of sculpture, interspersed with music and home or humorous scenes serve to relieve the mind and rest the imagination which have been insensibly educated and stimulated. Some time ago a fine tableau company of this character gave entertainments under the personal direction of Prof. Samuel R. Kelley of the New England Conservatory of Music. I understand, however, that the exacting duties of the Conservatory have compelled Professor Kelley to abandon, at least for the present, his tableau work. The tableau company which now stands in the same relation to tableau companies which John L. Stoddard occupies among those who deliver public illustrated lectures, is unquestionably Elizabeth F. Willis' Grecian Art Tableau Company. For this reason we have succeeded in securing a number of full-page illustrations, groupings, and arrangements as given by this company. The conscientious, persevering, and intelligent efforts of Mrs. Willis in designing and arranging her groups and producing striking situations illustrating historical and mythological scenes no less than pictures of home life and humorous groups, together with the general intelligence of the company and its fine equipments, have resulted in the production of entertainments which I think cannot fail to prove highly educational, beneficial, and uplifting in influence, and the addition of music in these entertainments has doubtless aided greatly in securing the well-merited success which has attended this company. I have referred somewhat at length to Mr. Stoddard's magnificent lectures and to the Grecian Art Tableau Company because they stand at the present time, in my judgment, in the very forefront of two kinds of quasi-educational factors which fill the mind with new ideals, while amusing, thus having a very real place in the new educational process which is silently (and unconsciously, so far as the large majority of the auditors is concerned) sowing seed-thoughts for a brighter day.

I believe the time has come when in every town and hamlet circles should be formed, subscriptions raised for a guarantee fund, and a course arranged which should be at once educational and entertaining. Let parents see that the imagination of the young be flooded with fine, high thought, and they will have done much toward making their

THE GRECIAN ART TABLEAU COMPANY.

offspring men and women of conscience and true nobility. I believe most sincerely in the great underlying principle of overcoming evil with good or driving out darkness with light as applied to the imagination. Give a child a fine ideal and it will work as leaven in the moulding process of his character. We have long fed upon the husks of materiality to the exclusion of the ideal, to which Victor Hugo aptly refers in these words: "The human mind has a summit—*the ideal.* To this summit God descends and man rises." And again he says, always referring, of course, to those noble conceptions which lift humanity, "The Ideal!— stable type of ever moving progress." It is the proud and august work of the new education to flood the imagination with high and noble ideals, to stimulate the intellect, to broaden and enrich life, to unchain the soul, and make man see that the quickened imagination and awakened conscience will accomplish far more toward redeeming civilization than is to-day imagined. To this end all means and measures of an educational nature must be called into requisition. The people need more sunshine in their souls, more light in their minds.

LIMITATION AS A REMEDY.

BY JOHN CLARK RIDPATH, LL. D.

I. LANDOWNERSHIP.

There was never before a time in which human society was so unstable and human life so greatly disturbed as at the present. Without doubt, unrest is the mood of the modern world. Every race, every people, every state, is in a condition of perturbation which threatens overthrow. Every man capable of comprehensive thought must see in the profound agitations of the existing order the unmistakable foresigns of catastrophe and reconstruction.

Let it not be said that one who points out this undeniable condition is himself a cause of it—a fomenter of the disturbance that is in the world. Some men by their constitution are distressed with the distress of others; they are discontented because their race is discontented; they suffer because society is in anguish; they complain because man is afflicted. It is rather the activity of sympathies, and the hope that a wholesome alarm may lead to peaceable and salutary change, that induces thinkers of the humane and philanthropic type to cry out from the watch-towers of the age and suggest remedies—however futile some of the remedies may be—for the evil that is abroad among mankind. Is it just that any human soul shall be condemned for hearing in the silence of the night the fearful cry, *La Patrie est en danger?*

It appears to me that a large part of the distress of the modern world is attributable to the fact that there are established in society and over man no salutary and accepted principles of limitation. There is no rational and welcome doctrine as to the rules of restraint under which society and the organic life of man ought to be placed. Civilization seems thus far to have allowed its products to grow and run and clamber as they will across all fields, over all barriers, and up all heights, without regulation or wholesome pruning.

If hitherto a limitation has been laid here and there upon the overgrowing exuberance of the organic life of man, it seems to have been laid in the wrong place, by the wrong hands, and with a wrong purpose. The restrictive gear which mediæval philosophers, priests, poets, statesmen, and social physicians have fixed on the race and its institutions, has only galled the shoulders, lacerated the withers, and made fractious the tempers of mankind. The products of society have by the means adopted been warped and curtailed of their fair proportions, and man himself, even the thinking man, has come to dread the law of limitation, as if it were the suggestion of slavery or anarchism—according to the disposition of him who thinks it.

To the philosophical mind, untempted by interest and unscared by threats, it appears certain that this whole question has to be thought out from the bottom; that the principle of salutary and scientific limitations applied to society and life has to be discovered, or at least to be stated anew; and that this principle has to be accepted and made constitutional before a peaceable stability can be attained among men and nations.

Let us, in the first place, agree that things cannot go on as they are now going in the world; that is, that they cannot continue without a catastrophe which is already imminent. It is certain, for example, that with the existing spirit and intelligence of men and nations one man cannot be permitted—and will not be permitted—to own the world and enslave the human race. It is certain that no organic combination of men can be—or will be—permitted to introduce in some revised form and aspect the dreadful social and industrial servitude of the past. In some way we have to be liberated and equalized. In some way we must be saved from the portent of universal servitude. Paradoxical as it may seem, it appears to me that the way of escape, the way of establishing universal liberty, is by the doctrine of limitations, laid not indeed upon the weak, who are limited too much already, but upon those high-up anarchical powers in society that have thus far refused to be limited at all.

The hints of limitation are to be found alike in man and nature. Man is naturally a limited animal. There is no part of him, no element in him, that is not by nature under limitations. He is not composed of infinities, but finities. His life is meted and bounded at every extreme. He begins in protoplasm and ends in dissolution. His entrance is an ascent and his exit a tumble down. All of his powers are naturally and wholesomely circumscribed; and the limitation is not such as he himself regards as slavery.

Take the case of the senses. The sight of a good eye reaches from one mile to six miles, according to the bigness of the thing seen. The finer sounds we do not hear at all, and the heaviest cannonade or thunder, beyond the horizon of a few miles, is mere silence. No animal can feel what it does not touch, or taste what it does not feel. Round about the nature of man there is drawn such a limit that his whole world of sense is not twenty miles in diameter. He does not fly; and his swimming is a fit subject for humor; he is a walker, or at most a rider. It takes time for him to go abroad, and other time most tedious for him to get home again. The young man full of hope, coming back from across the sea to the wicket gate of his adored, finds the last five miles a thousand. She for her part, leaning out of the window, reckons the last hour to be eternity. Both are limited; not even the exulting hope and bounding heart of youth can cancel time and space.

A large fraction of life—a third, they say—is spent in sleep; another fraction in eating and idling; another in the weakness of childhood and the weariness of old age; still another in sickness and accidents and the mistakes of avocation. A fifth fraction is expended in going about and in useless intercourse with others in like employment. The sixth and last fraction is consumed in marrying and in giving in marriage and in attending to the principal business of life—which in America is voting a party ticket! Certainly these limitations, partly natural and partly artificial, are sufficient to curb life within a narrow circle of activities.

The natural limitations of life, however, do not much impede us; and if we are sound and sane, they do not fret us at all. The fact is that we are used to them, and have been used to them for countless generations. They have become a law that does not gall, that does not vex, that does not enslave. The chambered nautilus sailing "the unclouded main" is not afflicted with its house of pearl. Why should the man-soul be hurt or annoyed with its necessary shell? A rational being is not worried in the exercise of his powers because of the restrictions that nature has put upon him. A man who is afflicted because he cannot fly over a mountain is not right; he who is envious of the sea-serpent is not normal in his desires. The normal man works in the harness of the natural world and does not feel it. He rises and eats and sleeps and conforms, breathing air, drinking water, seeing the world, attending the school of experience, acting by day and sleeping by night in a manner as rational as it is easy and necessary. Why should he not make laws, govern himself, organize institutions, let his neighbors alone, pay his debts, and serve society just as easily? But he does not; and there is the rub.

Nature—that strange aggregate of visible facts and invisible forces—is herself limited. The world is not infinite, but finite. It is not a great sphere, but a small sphere—a clod. After all, the Pacific is only a cupful; the Andes, only a ridge! The processes of nature are strictly circumscribed and defined. The flowers and grasses that come with the summer cease with the winter. It does not snow in Nicaragua—and cannot. Every month has it aspects and conditions. Man did not invent the calendar but found it in nature. The sun cannot illumine both sides of the earth at once, and the moon cannot be always ful No stream can flow back to its fountains in the hills. The Gulf of Mexico cannot freeze, and the Arctic Ocean cannot help freezing. The needle has to stand north and south— and never complains of it. The assassin Guiteau tried to raise walnuts on hickories; it was impossible! A body lighter than the air must rise, and a stone loosened from the brow of the precipice must fall. All things seem to be conditioned in nature, and as it were held in place by principles; and so far as nature is concerned there is no fretting, no peevishness, no discontent, no anarchism, no oppression on the one hand and no rebellion on the other.

Animal instinct and intelligence enter into union with the conditions of the natural world very gladly and happily. The creatures are absolutely unconscious of their limitations. The birds and beasts and fishes exercise their functions and perform their parts in perfect content. True, there is a clash of animal instincts. The eagle eats the dove, and the dove eats the cricket. Certainly it is not a pleasant thing to be eaten, but it is pleasant to eat, and it is pleasant to escape being eaten. Both the one and the other seem natural enough; and whatever is natural is accepted at length without complaint. There is a vast amount of animal content in the kingdom of nature, and nowhere a preponderance of unhappiness or symptom of insurrection.

It is enough to make happy even a miserable member of human society to look around him in the world, to walk abroad, to hear the songs of birds, the clamorous music of the cicada, the bark of the distant squirrel; to see the flight of many creatures, the swimming of some, and the scampering away of others. Though there is limitation upon them all—a limitation drawn around all activity and power as if with a geometer's hand—yet there is no complaint or anguish or hunting for change or symptom of revolt. Nature and the living creatures that inhabit her domain are all visibly and manifestly meted and bounded with principles and confines which may not be passed; and yet, taken as a whole, nature is an orderly place, well fitted for happiness, given to hospitality, and pervaded with much good cheer. The only creature that seems to be disorderly, troubled, vexed with cross purposes and unsound sleep, is the principal inhabitant. What is the matter with *him?*

There is much the matter with him; and his ailments are hard to define. On the whole, the trouble with mankind seems to be that the limitations demanded in order that society may exist and the individual be free have not been laid with the right intent, by the right authority, in the right place. They have been laid with wrong intent, by illegitimate authority, in the very place where they ought not to have been laid at all. They have been laid by power, by selfishness, and by organized tyranny, on the weak and unorganized elements of society, where there was no need of limitation or any suggestion of it except the suggestion to enslave. So much distress, so much confusion, have arisen from the misplacement of limitation that human beings have become distrustful of the *principle* of limitation; and as a result they find no stable equilibrium between the extremes of anarchism and slavery.

There is, we must admit, no well-ordered, well-defined, and well-established human society in the world.

> "The bird and the beast
> Have found, at least,
> By the land and the sea
> The way to be free;
> But the animal man,
> Capstone of the 'plan,'
> Possessing the earth,
> From the day of his birth
> Mopes, mocks, and complains,
> In the midst of his gains,
> And rebels, and has pains!"

Everything is slipping in the one direction or the other. Every human being seems to be pushing his neighbor either into slavery or into anarchy. Each elbows the other into one of the extremes of unhappiness and conflict. Nobody seems to stop to consider whether it is not possible that a social state can exist in which the limitations are so laid that life in it may be as easy and natural, as contented and perfect, as is the life of the irrational and unconscious orders of being that flourish around us. *They* live in easy perfection, and die without distemper or anguish. Why should not a man get through the world as well and as happily, as a rain crow, a bass, or a beaver?

Let none say that this view of prevailing conditions is merely academical and of no effect; that such a study of principles and facts granted to be true can have no practical value, no actual relation to society and to the progress of mankind. Why, here is a marvel. Would men have us believe that the condition of the world is devoid of reason, and that it is to remain devoid of reason forever? Are we to suppose that the principles of truth and philanthropy are to be everlastingly excluded from an influence in the affairs of men? Is society a product of unreason and of force? Does any human being suppose that any condition in the world is salutary or can be permanent when it cannot be justified by right reason and the soundest ethical analysis? To say so is to deny the supremacy of truth over the affairs of life, to put the better part of the aspirations of the man-soul under the incubus of the coldest pessimism, and to fling a mocking scoff into the awful ear of eternity. The fool-in-chief of the nineteenth century is he who wishes to put thought and conscience and truth out of the affairs of men, and to give over those affairs to the dominion of ignorance, caprice, and blind compulsion.

The two things which human beings most strongly desire and in which they appear to have the most abiding interest are *Property* and *Prerogative*. These are the things for which they strive, for which they compete, for which they pray, for which they fight. They are the two facts on which the modern world, so far as its endeavor is concerned, is based and builded. By property we mean whatever a human being may appropriate, may possess, may own, of the visible objects of desire. By prerogative we mean the outstretching of his influence and power over society. Certainly the greater part of all that men seek for in life belongs to one or the other of these classes of general motive and aspiration. Men desire to have, to possess, to own. They desire to exercise influence among their fellows, to have and to wield power. There is also a vague desire in man, very variable and unequally distributed, to rise in knowledge and moral character; and this, let us hope, will ultimately be the prevailing motive with our race.

It would appear that property, while it has been the source of a large part of the satisfaction of mankind, has also been its curse. Property has been the blessing and the bane of the human race. It has been the source of vast

happiness and of untold misery.   It has in a sense been the
foundation of the civilized life, and in another sense the
fountain of the river of anguish that has rolled through the
valleys of the world.   To the present day property has been
the chief end of human endeavor, and the chief menace of
human hope.   All that has been said by philosophers, poets,
and historians in praise of property may well be repeated;
and all that has been said by revolutionists, reformers, and
idealists in denunciation of property may be repeated also,
and verified.   Property is a two-headed creature, out of one
of whose mouths flow the living waters; out of the other
burst the lurid flames of destruction.

That men are happier and better for possessing property,
for having something of their own, for getting as a reward
of their toil a possession that they may enjoy, can no more
be doubted than that rain refreshes the fields and sunshine
makes glad the world.   That property is also the beginning
of that cruel strife which has converted the world into a
slaughterhouse and ultimately made every human being so
selfish that he can hardly any longer, by the utmost strain
of his powers, prefer another to himself, can as little be
doubted or denied.   Is it not possible that the doctrine of
limitations applied to property might rob it of its power to
curse and promote its power to bless?

It is not property moderated and limited, but only the
want of it, or the lawless excess of it, that curses the world.
It is the too-much or the too-little that blasts the hopes of
men.   There is a vast area of intermediate possession,
between the extremes of poverty and wealth, that is almost
an unmixed blessing.   A certain amount of property, we
think, tends strongly to happiness.   If it brings discontent,
it is only such discontent as is necessary to the proper
exertion of the human powers—such discontent as temperately stimulates the mind and promotes the healthful development of character.

We may note also that it is in this intermediate and wholesome region, between the extremes of want and surfeit, that
the genius of the world and all of its saving forces are born
and economized.   We are accustomed to say that genius
has its birthplace in poverty.   This opinion prevails because
in some conspicuous instances the children of the humble
poor rise to the godlike stature.   That anyone so born
should rise at all is a thing so remarkable as to attract the
attention of the world and to favor the opinion that only
the children of poverty can be great.   In a few instances the
children of the rich are born great also.   But the rule is that

the greatness and the power of human life proceed from the intermediate condition in which there is neither abject poverty nor abounding riches.

In this there is emphatic suggestion of the principle of limitation applied to property; and here the debate properly begins. If society could agree that property shall freely exist, that every man shall have for his part all that he earns by his labor and skill, *and no more,* men indeed would not be equal in their possessions, but poverty on the one hand would cease, and the glut of riches on the other hand would disappear. Those who have nothing—and starve—would rise into the vast and healthy body of society composed of those who have something and live. Those who have too much—and surfeit—would be drawn back from excess, and would be absorbed in the great body from which in an evil day they were permitted to escape.

Consider, then, the question of *Landownership.* This is the fundamental matter—the real bottom of all the issues about which men are contending and drawing the sword. The industrial, commercial, and even the financial controversies of the age have their roots deep in the soil; and the determination of man's relations to the ground must precede, we think, the solution of all other questions that rack and torment our epoch.

Thinkers, for a long time, have seen this truth with greater or less distinctness. As for back as the beginning of the sixteenth century, English writers, notably Sir Thomas More, pointed out the inevitable consequences of unlimited landownership. He demonstrated that out of this all other kinds of social despotism would arise—that man, cut off from free recourse to the ground, which is the true basis of all his exertions, and therefore the starting-point of civilization, must sooner or later land in servitude, ignorance, weakness, and degeneracy. The truth of this cannot be questioned; but it seems to be necessary to demonstrate over and over again the truisms of that contention which declares the principles of limitation on landownership to be the beginning of all reform.

The ground belongs in the beginning to mankind at large. No one at the outset has a right to exclude another from occupying and holding the ground and from possessing it to the extent of *use* and *occupation.* When society is organized and civilization begins, men fix themselves to the soil and get by prior occupation a prescriptive right thereto. They begin to own the ground. This right becomes, by consent, habitual ownership, and is at length recognized by the laws and constitution of society.

The natural right to take possession of the ground and to occupy it to the exclusion of others is not limited in the primitive stages of society—this for the reason that the necessity for limitation is not at first suggested by either convenience or social law. For a long time after the beginnings of the civilized life, there is no need for limitation; for the land, being comparatively free—at the first absolutely free—may be taken and possessed by whoever will. Under this rule, which is in the beginning a rule of custom and afterwards a rule of prescriptive right, a state of affairs supervenes that tends to make the right of ownership absolute; and absolute ownership once established refuses henceforth to concede a limitation.

This right of absolute ownership prevails at the present time. Civilized society at the close of the nineteenth century finds itself under the sway of such a right, and whoever denies it must attack the existing order. Absolutism always delights in such a condition of affairs; it fortifies itself and bids defiance to assault. The right of absolute landownership is conceded by society, is guaranteed, is defended, and is, as a rule, unchallenged. It is so in America. Our great country is in the grip of this principle, and it will not relax until it is cut either with the falchion of reason or the sword of battle.

As the case now stands, a man under the law and constitution may buy and hold in fee simple ten feet of ground, ten acres, or ten square miles, just as he will. Aye, more; he may buy a hundred square miles, a thousand, a hundred thousand, the whole Mississippi valley! He can buy it and hold it against all intending occupants. He can ward off the human race coming on for occupation, and can put mankind into the attitude of an invading force trenching upon his rights! He can build a stone wall five hundred feet high and thick as the buttresses of the Rocky Mountains around the Mississippi valley, with its two billion of cultivable acres, and can defy entrance into the domain by any human being other than himself and those to whom he concedes the privilege! He can put out ten million placards around the confines of his estate bearing the usual inscription, "No trespassing on these grounds"; and he can enforce the right under the constitution and the law, and with the persuasive energy of Gatling guns.

Mark what the principle of unlimited ownership has thus worked out as its result. The principle was sound to begin with. The man might well purchase, occupy, and hold ten rods or ten acres of ground. He might well own a farm and

fence it and put up his painted sign of "No trespassing on
these grounds." Civilization concedes him such a privilege.
The law concedes it, and right reason and human experience
concede it. But how about a man's owning the Mississippi
valley? It is as manifest as can be that no man has such a
moral right or ever can have it under the sun. Such a sup-
posititious right is an absurdity *per se*. The notion that one
man or many men in combination may by possessing the
earth make all other men their slaves or tenants-at-will is as
illogical as it is inhuman. Such a right conceded to the
individual, or to the corporation, or to any body or organic
power as against the original rights of man to possess the
ground and to use it as the source of his subsistence, is preposterous and, we must say, damnable.

What follows? It follows as the night the day that somewhere *between* the right to own an acre and to own the valley
of the Mississippi or the whole United States a line of limitation must be laid, over which no power known among men
may be allowed to pass. To pass this line is to prepare the
antecedents of the inevitable enslavement of mankind. It
is thus perfectly clear that a restriction on landownership
is a necessity of the situation which has supervened in
human society. The principle of unlimited ownership cannot be longer admitted if civil and industrial liberty is to be
maintained as a part of the rights of man. It is already
absurd to speak of unlimited landownership, or to attempt
to defend it. I doubt whether any man in his senses here in
the high light of the last decade of a great century will dare
to champion the supposed right of an individual or of a corporate body to own the five states of our great Northwestern
group, or to own one of them, or a quarter of one of them.
If there be such, he and I differ *toto coelo* and forever!

Precisely *how much* of the earth's surface a man may be
safely permitted to own is a question not here considered—
at least not with exactitude. The how-much is another
question. The argument is that a limitation lies *somewhere;*
and that the *principle* must be conceded in order that free
society may continue to flourish or even to exist.

The primary principles of land-limitation, however, are
easy to discover. The amount of the earth's surface that
may be rightfully owned by any one man or by several men
in combination ought to be determined out of the conditions
and circumstances of the case. The first use of the ground
is agricultural. He who makes this primary use of the soil
should be permitted to own *more* land than any other; his
purposes are more distinctly purposes of the soil than are

the purposes of any other. The manufacturer and the mechanic have certain needs of the ground, and on these needs there is a right of surface ownership; but the right of the manufacturer or the mechanic is less extensive than that of the farmer, though more extensive than that of the merchant. The merchant has greater need of the ground than the banker, and the speculator, who deals only in fictions and intangible things, has no need of the soil and *no right* to it at all; that is, in his character of speculator.

The age of the community will have much to do with fixing the limits of ownership. As the nation grows old and the people multiply and the powers of the soil are more fully developed, the limitation on land-possession becomes more and more narrow. The ratio of population to land-area is a powerful circumstance in determining the natural and rational limit of land-possession. There is, in a word, in nature and in social conditions, under all circumstances, at least a hint of the law governing the amount of real estate that may be equitably owned by any man.

The suggestions here offered may be easily followed to several applications. Real properties in a broken region are naturally divided into smaller parcels than on the prairie. Man dominates the plain much more easily than the mountain. Ownership may be more extensive in a great river valley than in a region of hills and knobs. Every man's pursuit viewed with respect to his environment suggests the limit of his land-possession. A tanner has need for so much ground, and no more. A brick-maker must have a considerable space. In the hunting stage of civilization, men as individuals do not own the land at all; but there is a tribal ownership. Every hunter plants himself where he will, and roams abroad unhindered. But when a town is built, even by aborigines, the limits of ownership are at once indicated, and are very soon greatly narrowed. In the civilized city the right to own ground is, or ought to be, reduced to the smallest possible compass. Some men appear to have no capacity, or indeed need, of the ground. The weather-beaten tramp, whether living or dead—poor product of a depraved society—has need of only a little earth, to which he contributes more than he will ever get out of it! A herdsman of the Llano Estacado may range over five thousand acres without hurt or injustice to society.

These suggestions are mere hints of the principles which should guide in determining the nature and logical limitations of landownership. I think it clear that the placing of the limitation will be determined in large measure by the somewhat nice distinction between ownership and possession. Under the existing order a man is permitted to *own* a great deal more than he can *possess*. If he were permitted to own no more than he could possess, the land question in a country like our own would be half solved already. As the case now stands, a man may go into Illinois and *buy* the Grand Prairie, and *own* it; but no man can *possess* the Grand Prairie, for the reason that he is not big enough. His faculties cannot, so to speak, spread over it, and if they could spread over it, such abnormal capacity ought to be curtailed in the interest of both the man himself and his fellow-beings. More exactly, the man's powers to use are not in such a case as great as the thing to be used, or if as great, they ought not to be. Unless in such a case he goes to work to organize a vast estate of tenants and subordinates, he cannot begin to cultivate, that is, to use, what he is said to own. As to all that part which he cannot cultivate or possess he is compelled to play, or at least is permitted to play, the part of dog in the manger. That portion of the earth's surface now owned *but not possessed* by the individual and corporate proprietors of the United States, if liberated from their control and surrendered freely to the people, would decentralize our population and restore the equilibrium of American industrial life. The engorged cities would discharge themselves of their overplus, and the human race, in our country at least, would substitute a home for a den.

Besides all this, the practice of unlimited landownership tends, in the main, to destroy the owner's character. He ceases to work with his own hands. He substitutes wit for exertion. He merely rides abroad, going about his fields and farms bossing others, overawing them and their families, conceding to them only a part of what they earn, and as it were "hogging the patch" without regard to a just economy or to the undemocratic and un-American conditions which he is fostering.

My judgment is that no man has a right to own the Grand Prairie, but only so much of it as he can possess; that is, so much of it as he can use with his own exertion, the exertion of his family, and possibly the exertion of certain employees whom he may justly hire. It seems to me that employees are natural and inevitable in the present order of the world; for many human beings are by nature so weak and unable as to prefer and strongly desire an attachment to some one stronger than themselves.

In suggesting the doctrine of limitation, however, we are

at once confronted with a general reluctance and alarm. The large landowner, even the moderate farmer, is likely to feel when the argument is presented that his interests and rights are endangered. He is scared at the proposition to limit his ownership to a certain area. He is perhaps offended at the suggestion of such a thing, and puts himself unwittingly, it may be passionately, into the absurd attitude of claiming the right to own the earth. Nor is his alarm wholly unreasonable. He does not know *where* the line of limitation is to fall. He cannot discover whether he is to be circumscribed to a section, to a quarter section, to ten acres, or to his house and lot. Therefore he flares up and cries out, *Socialism! Communism! Anarchy!*

All uncertainty in questions of property is an element of fear and distrust. We are all of this kind. We are alarmed at whatever is indefinite. If the doctrine of limitations were once known, accepted, understood; if the element of uncertainty were once eliminated from the problem, men, I think, would not only be contented with it, but would welcome it as a deliverance. Suppose that it were statutory throughout the Union that no *person* should own more than a section of land, and that no *corporation* should possess more than the actual necessities of its business may require, what cause would there be for fretting about it? The principle once established would become its own justification. I cannot discover in it anything of alarm or injustice or harm to the intending landowner, or to any member of society, unless it should be in the claim that the wholesome ambitions of the owner are removed and his energies paralyzed by the restriction.

But is it true that any reasonable ambition or wholesome energy would be abated by the limitation of landownership to a reasonable area? Such limitation would tend to a better development of the soil. It would absolutely abolish the holding of land merely for higher prices. It would prevent the holding of land against intending occupants. It might divert somewhat the energies of the landed proprietor into other channels; but such diversion would undoubtedly be to his own advantage and the advantage of the community. Some of the poorest examples of men that I have ever seen have been unlimited landowners. Possessing estates in a rich region of country, the ancestors of such people have handed down the lands for generations, adding to them and extending over them a certain coarse agricultural method, producing thereon the common grains and the grain-eating animals, without variation of industry, until the social, intellectual, and moral character of the occupants has sunk to the level of the earth.

The limitation of landownership to actual possession and use would vary the industry of every community, prevent stagnation, do away with intermarriage between the related offspring of families already injured by that method, and excite a wholesome revival of all the spiritual powers and aspirations of the given community. My notion of the ideal condition of human society is that in which the people, divided into families, reside on small estates, in proximity to large commercial marts, and cultivate those estates and beautify them to a high stage of perfection. Around these estates and homes shall be drawn by statutory enactment a limit of area which shall checkmate in advance that inordinate greed which left to itself will soon transform any country into one or a few vast estates, composed of fields under cultivation by peasant hands, stone walls and hedges produced by the many for the benefit of the one, and game-keeps in which a rabbit is more prized than the best young man, and a pheasant more regarded than the handsomest girl in the county.

The writer is not foolish enough to suppose that an ideal state such as that described above can be produced out of thought, transferred to paper, and thence converted into a reality; but it is the business of thinkers nevertheless to show what *ought to be* and what *might be*, and to indicate those conditions in society which being undeniably the cause of the social distress of mankind, undeniably antagonistic to justice and right reason, ought to be amended or wholly reformed and obliterated.

It was the misfortune of the great men who drew and adopted and defended the Declaration of Independence that they did not include in their list of inalienable rights the right of landownership; and it is something worse than the misfortune of the legislative power now in control of the destinies of our people that that power has not the intelligence, the discernment, and the courage to lay with a strong hand a limitation upon landownership in the United States so strict and rigorous as to reverse the tides of American population from the cityful to the countryside, offering thus a way for man into his native fields again, and substituting homes and industry and virtue for dens and idleness and vice.

MAN IN HIS RELATION TO THE SOLAR SYS·
TEM, A SUBJECT FOR SCIENTIFIC
RE-EXAMINATION.

BY J. HEBER SMITH, M. D.

PART I.

Mankind's knowledge and interests appear to move in
vast spirals of centuries, and once more we are seriously
confronted with the question of the truth or falsity of the
doctrine of planetary influences. It is a fitting time for the
concerted application to the remnants of the old astrology
of the modern methods of observation and induction. It
seems opportune to take up again the inquiry whether consequences are yet hanging in the stars, for the reason that
the scientists of this auspicious period are freed from superstition, and are distinguished for clearness of mental vision,
precision of method, unison of work, and independence of
restraints of every kind, as never before.

Let the vulgar pervert this knowledge if they will, and
seek to make the stars panderers to their vices, or guilty
of their disasters. Have we not recently seen them crowding to the sale of handkerchiefs which the venders declared
had been "blessed" by Schlatter? Only truth, knowledge
full-orbed, can reconvert the baser elements of human nature, and subdue in us the ape and the tiger. Until this
transformation, through pure knowledge, there is that in
us all that might infect even the north star.

In the study of mankind in relation to his remoter environment, the solar system, the theologies and philosophies
of the centuries need be neither courted nor repelled,
though they may yet be found related to our inquiries in
undreamed-of ways. Should zodiacal influence on the
physical, mental, and even moral, evolution of individuals
become a demonstrated fact to the scientific world, it will
be found so through natural laws already well recognized
in the realm of science.

A preliminary knowledge, somewhat more than cursory,
of the elements of astrology is necessary to guide the judgment, not only in nativities, but as well in estimating the

visible to the unaided eye at Alexandria were divided into six classes, according to their lustre ("magnitude"), from the brightest down to the least discernible. For upwards of fifteen hundred years no real improvement was made in the estimations of lustre by any of his successors in this field of research. Indeed it does not appear that by any unaided effort of the eye there can be estimated subdivisions of lustre exceeding those adopted by this still esteemed and often quoted astrologer.

These indisputable facts are mentioned, in passing, to indicate that the older astrologers were not such ignorant and blind gropers as it is customary to picture them. Neither will it appear on examination, that Cardan, Napier (inventor of logarithms), or Kepler was worthy of obloquy for having practised astrology. That the science fell into decay upon the Continent of Europe about the time of the Protestant Reformation, may be traced to whatever cause suits the prejudices or convictions of inquirers; it does not now concern us the least bit. It is the truth we are seeking. The insular position of England saved astrology from death among the so-called Christian nations. The survival of the science, even in England, appears one of the evidences of its marvellous vitality, for her laws have been ever hostile to its practice. But in this century, India has exercised a silent though potent influence in its favor over resident Englishmen. At the present time, there is seen to be a remarkable revival of interest in the science among even the most prominent Englishmen of the day—members of Parliament and leaders in the civil and military administration, at home and in the colonies. Drastic statutes, religious prejudices even, avail nothing against its brightening dawn. Again it may with truth be said, thanks to the encircling of the globe by England's predestined flag: "There is no speech nor language where the terms of the stars are not heard." They gem our most loved English classics, surviving the recent centuries of indifference and periods of efforts at suppression of all knowledge of the star-eyed science from sources that it is not now of consequence to mention.

It must be confessed that the real mystery of space lies still unsolved—incapable of solution for us, it would seem, as much now, despite the vast attainments of astronomy in its modern form, as it was in the prescientific ages. The cavilers at astral influences have illustrated science in the state of hypothesis rather than science in the state of fact. Let the ban of exclusion fall where it belongs, on mere hypothesis unsupported by observation, whether in astronomy or in astrology.

Many who hold a belief in the influence of the planets on human life and affairs are by no means certain or satisfied with much of the data available, and they yield to astrology only a provisional assent. I candidly confess that I am myself of this number. It is purposed, indeed, as the single object of these papers, to urge an investigation of the subject, a reëxamination in fact, by men trained to precise methods, and who can command world-wide opportunities.

It goes without saying that many absurd errors and radical misconceptions have become incorporated in astrology. But are not equal blunders being brought to light, also, in astronomy, geology, anthropology, and especially in history? Those who know but one science know none.

In the reëxamination of the relation of the solar system to all organized life on the earth, we require, next to a desire to know the truth amounting to an absorbing passion, a wide knowledge of correlative subjects, including the facts of astronomy. We may not secure depth, but we should take care that our knowledge is accurate so far as it goes, and need to recognize its true limits. Some knowledge is needed of the fundamental principles of electro-magnetism, the laws of motion, of energy, force, and heat, and also familiarity with the general principles of chemistry, studied as one of the prime agencies of nature.

At this point it may be well briefly to indicate some of the accepted principles of natural science on which a qualified belief in zodiacal influences can be presumed to rest, quite above the stigma of superstition. Science rests on what is proved, and of *matter* it assumes to know only that it is the elements and their compounds. Of its essence, nothing at present is known. There are sixty-five elements, having properties more or less understood, besides several recently announced, or supposed to have been isolated. Some exist as gases, such as hydrogen and oxygen; as liquids, like bromine and mercury; and as solids, such as carbons and the metals. But these physical states are not essential to their nature, and are dependent only on their existing relations to force, as light, heat, and pressure. Most of them can be made to pass from one state to another by altering the conditions of force.

There is evidence showing that the elements exist in the form of ultimate particles called atoms, possessing definite dimensions and weight. Their existence is not a mere hypothesis, but a deduction from well proved facts. The whole framework of the new chemistry and of the natural sciences is based on the atom, though it be infinitely small and beyond our powers of measurement or even of conception.

Whoever expects that the new astrology deals with ponderable bodies in space engaged in arousing the organism to ultimate resistance by stress applied in any gross way, has not begun to think profoundly on the problem of stellar influences. Our inquiry has to do with displacements occurring in the relative positions of the ultimate molecules of organized life, and their decomposition, by means of forces as fine as the rays that lie beyond the violet limit of the spectrum. When the image of the spectrum is thrown within a dark room, the captive ray of light has apparently expressed its power and beauty in the compass of a field of glorious colors running from red to violet. But let there be held some distance beyond the violet's outermost limit, where all seems black, a piece of uranium glass, and immediately it catches a beautiful opaline white glow. This experiment demonstrates the presence of an energy of light believed to possess incalculable potency. Every organism in the course of its history passes through two distinct and opposite phases by means of such subtile forces as this omnipotent white ray—a phase of evolution and a phase of dissolution; in these phases proceeding by their operation first from the diffuse or imperceptible into the compact and the perceptible, and secondly, from their farther operation, proceeding from the compact and the perceptible to the diffuse and the imperceptible. As frost-flowers form on the window-pane, through invisible force, geometrizing vapor in advancing lines of silver crystals, and then melt from view, so these bodies of ours are fashioned from elemental harmonies equally evocable and vanishing, under the operation of light-rays that to the opening perceptions of the reverent student of nature appear not only colors but musical chords.

It is probable that the so-called chemical rays have more to do with organized life than the heat-rays at the other end of the solar spectrum. Their modification in darkened abodes of squalor and filth favors the production of pathogenic germs, but, unquestionably, their concentration will yet be employed for the destruction of the microörganisms inimical to life. There will be employed the projection of cones of electric light whose rays will occupy areas sufficient to illuminate all the organs afflicted and to stimulate the reparative forces to the upbuilding of healthy tissue. The chemical action of light on atoms, it is admitted, seems proved. The decomposition of cell-structure can be affected by waves of ether set in motion by rays of electro-magnetic force either from the sun or an electric light.

The medium for the transmission of electro-magnetic phenomena is the same as that for the conveyance of radiations of light. The velocity with which an electro-magnetic disturbance is propagated, it would appear from different sets of data at hand, does not differ from the velocity of light in the air. We can suppose the constitution of the ether to be such that it is in a state of irregular and constant agitation;—indeed, Plato, in his Cratylus, derives its name, *aether,* from its supposed perpetual motion;—"always running in a flux about the air," Socrates is there quoted as saying.

From the experiments of Professor Crookes, now becoming so fruitful of world-wide interests, with the extreme vacua obtainable by means of the mercury pump (readily carried to the one-millionth of an atmosphere) there appears to be a *something,* filling all space, by which energy, as light, heat, etc., is transmitted, in which the elements appear to have undergone so complete a transformation, either into a non-atomic condition or into a more primal state, that it no longer answers to the fundamental definition of matter. It has no inertia, since it produces no friction or resistance to motion, and therefore does not absorb energy in transmission. It has no gravitation force, for it does not vary in density at varying distances from the bodies in space, and transmits light undisturbed.

Whatever be its essence, all systems of philosophy require this so-called ether. Let it be deemed as *one* ethereal substance transmitting the impulses of force; for this modern interpretation of phenomena is the most accordant with the facts needing explanation. But the mathematicians must not presume to apply the formulæ based upon the properties of matter to this entity, since our most certain knowledge of it is, that it does not possess these properties. We are obliged to suppose that this vast homogeneous expanse of isotrophic matter, through which light is transmitted, is something distinct from any transparent medium known to us, though it interpenetrates all transparent bodies, and will be made, in the immediate future, to subserve the uses of science yet farther in penetrating opaque bodies as well. The evidence of its existence has accumulated as additional phenomena of light and other radiations are being discovered, particularly those of the cathode, or X rays employed in Professor Roentgen's experiments in photograph-

ing through opaque media such as wood, etc. The properties
of this medium, as deduced from the phenomena of light,
have been found to be precisely those required to explain
electro-magnetic phenomena. "O divine *aether,* and ye
swift-winged breezes, and ye fountains of rivers and countless dimplings of the waves of the deep, and thou earth,
mother of all, and to the all-seeing orb of the sun,"—we appeal for more, and yet more, light.

A modern conception of the ether is well defined as matter
itself in the state of ultra-atomic motion which has formed
throughout space, and is ever forming, force-spheres, by
what is termed vortex-motion, whereon are aggregated
elemental substances in the process of world-building. It is
in accord with our present knowledge to presume that the
mutual attraction of the heavenly bodies is not a property
solely of their material part, but an expression in which
both their force-spheres and their material envelope take part.

Even the atom is to be regarded as a material body acting
as a centre of force. Distance is a merely relative and misleading term. It is already annihilated as a factor for the
exclusion of physical cause and effect, as well for the exclusion of solar magnetic storms (observed as if but simply
across a mill-pond) as of the projection of force-lines from a
grain of sand into space.

There is a fallacy in assuming the separateness of things
because of their distinctness. The all is one. Beyond the
inconceivable attenuation of matter, as we comprehend it,
mind, which we can call by no other name than *Being,* is still
the "Unmoved and the First Mover," as when this conception of the truth was so strongly grasped by one whom Dante
well calls "Master of those that know,"—the peerless
Aristotle.

The atoms of different elements differ by possessing one,
two, or more centres, or foci, of influence. It is believed
that the atoms of which matter is built up are not in absolute contact, but are separated by spaces (containing ether)
in which they move freely under the action of forces to
which they are susceptible. The atoms are held together by
attraction of force, called affinity, exerted across these
intervening spaces, through the agency of the ether. The
molecule, according to the strict meaning of the word, is
the smallest quantity of a substance which is capable of
separate existence as a free body, in which all the valencies
are satisfied, leaving the combined atoms to act as a whole
from one centre, so far as such forces as gravitation, cohesion, heat, etc., are concerned. Molecules held together by

high affinities require considerable force for their decomposition, and their separation may be considered as relatively. an elemental cataclysm, like the destruction of a planet.

From the smallest to the greatest the laws of nature are identical. The molecule represents on an infinitely small scale the solar system itself, which is built up of the several companies that move, each complete in itself yet all linked to one another, and forming a balanced whole. Mercury and Venus stand as monads, or single atoms; the earth, Jupiter, Saturn, Uranus, with their moons, resemble the compound atoms, or radicals of diatomic, triatomic, and quadrivalent attractions, so united as to play the part of a single atom in the mighty molecule which again forms but a relatively infinitesimal part of the sidereal universe, held together by forces acting across infinite space, as the molecules are called from viewless being and held together by the forces to which they are exposed.

The individual is formed by a complexus of forces so subtile that it seems truly presumptuous to attempt to divine the ego's future from the windings of his past (however it may seem revealed by the conditions attracting his re-birth) whether we consider as factors of the problem the processes of heredity or of the adductive stars.

Says Herbert Spencer, "I recognize no forces within the organism or without the organism, but the conditional modes of the universal immanent force." In this pregnant phrase, once so objectionable to orthodoxy, science has admitted through her ablest exponent, man's oneness with the all. And if one with the all, then he is moved by nature from her widest zones, and can himself some day discover how to move, in turn.

Man is the essence of all the elements, offspring of the universe and a copy in miniature of its soul. Whatever is or transpires in the universe exists or takes place in the constitution of man. Everything reflects itself in man and may come to his consciousness. On the recognition of this intimate relationship between the immeasurably great with the small depends the harmony by which the Infinite Being becomes at one with the finite, the fixed, eternal, and real with the collective aggregate of things in space called the external world.

In estimating the potency of the solar rays on the molecules that constitute all organized bodies on the earth, these special principles and laws thus hurriedly indicated, will be seen to have paramount weight. He who lightly denies the influence of man's larger environment is reminded, in closing, of the fact universally recognized, that all life on the earth of which we have any knowledge, higher or lower, is an organic unity, with its countless activities of nutrition and reproduction depending monentarily on the sun. From protoplasm to man the symmetry of being is continued by the great crystallizing forces of his light and heat. This effulgent orb, in truth, is the very heart of being, and the little heart of man beats in unison through its supply of solar energy as long as unstopped through the "darkening of the luminary" by some overmastering malific. The solar rays maintain all functional activities as unerringly as they accomplish the transits and occultations of the planets. And still, it must be confessed, there is but one simplifier of destiny, and that is the will of the Lord of Lights.

All of the material universe, all space, all time, are one; and man, that spark struck from inapproachable light, can best comprehend the greatest from a study of the laws that govern the most minute. In the abode of pure elementary force and of cell-life, the "Koph" of the old Talmudists, where dwell the microörganisms, are the hidings of the creating, sustaining, and destroying manifestations of the Absolute.

(To be continued.)

NAPOLEON BONAPARTE.

A Sketch Written for a Purpose.

BY HON. JOHN DAVIS.

CHAPTER VII.

Further Mistakes of Napoleon; his Downfall, Exile, and Dramatic Death.

One of the most effective expedients adopted by Napoleon in order to attain military success was unity of management. He claimed that, in the field, "One bad general is better than two good ones." Though the statement is not strictly true, yet it illustrates the general fact that in the management of an army there should be no conflicting plans when the time of action comes. Rather than admit an equal in the campaign of Italy he offered to resign his command. But unity of management must have a limit or it ultimately becomes a dictatorship, controlling both the armies and the government.

It became so in the case of Napoleon. At first he claimed and was granted the sole command of the army of Italy. From that he acquired such fame and power that he assumed control in Paris, and, through that, the command of all the armies of the republic. Then his power and egotism led him step by step from the consulship to the throne, when, brooking no equal, and neither asking nor accepting counsel of others, he fell into a thousand extravagances and fatal mistakes. Had he been willing to learn of others he would have adopted the Venetian or the English system of finance for war purposes; had he taken counsel of others he would not have adopted pillage and the general methods of the brigand for the support of his armies. Though an admirer of the great Gustavus Adolphus, he neglected to profit by his teachings and example in the matter of supporting his armies. The great military chieftain of Sweden, who fought for principle as well as for glory, said:

The choler and manhood that you have, score it, in God's name, on the fronts of your enemies, but stain not the honor of a soldier by outraging unarmed innocence. Live upon your means like soldiers, not by pilfering and spoiling like highway robbers. This if you do not, you will ever be infamous, and I, with such help, shall never be victorious.

Wherever Gustavus marched he conquered his enemies and multiplied his friends. Napoleon never increased his friends by his conquests. Nor would his supreme egotism permit him to learn of those who did. He took counsel of none, but aspired to be "the man without a model," oblivious of ultimate results. The policy begun as a successful military expedient in Italy, ultimately developed into one of his great mistakes. He could tolerate no equal in the governments of Europe, nor even in the world.

It was this egotistic aspiration which gave birth to his "Continental System," as developed and illustrated in his Milan and Berlin Decrees. He embarked in the absurd effort to close all the ports of the world against English commerce, with no power to enforce his mandates. His impracticable measures were most oppressive on all commercial nations, including his own dominions. So true was this that the emperor himself was compelled to violate his own decrees in order to obtain overcoats and other necessary supplies for his troops. And while in some parts of Europe fathers were shot for procuring a pound of smuggled sugar for a sick child, the great prince of smugglers in Paris was busy selling licenses at exorbitant rates for the violation of the decrees which others must obey at the risk of their lives. All the world protested, none more earnestly than the emperor's brother Louis, king of Holland. Russia at length ignored the French policy and opened her ports to British goods. To force Russia to submit was one reason for a renewal of the war, in 1812, which led to the ultimate dissolution of the French empire.

Another Napoleonic expedient was the control of the French press in the emperor's interest, and the censorship of all literature in the countries under his control. So complete was this censorship in France that, from 1807 down to the fall of Napoleon, Alison (vol. viii, p. 159) says:

No thought could be published to the world without having first been approved by the imperial authorities. . . . These powers were so constantly and vigorously exercised, that not only was the whole information on political subjects or public affairs, which was permitted to reach the people, strained through the imperial filters, but all passages were expunged from every work which had a tendency, however remote, to nourish independent sentiments, or foster a feeling of discontent towards the existing government. . . . The journals were filled with nothing but the exploits of the Emperor, the treatises by which he deigned to enlighten the minds of his subjects on the affairs of state, or the adulatory addresses presented to him from all parts of his dominions.

To enforce this censorship, authors were banished and booksellers were shot. The press had no other field or vocation but to breathe flattery to the great master to inflate his vanity and thus to become the promoter and bulwark of his imperial despotism. This might have been a happy expedient at first, but ultimately it was one of the Corsican's bad mistakes, contributing to his downfall.

I will illustrate the manner of enforcing the imperial censorship by two noted examples. Madame de Staël was a talented and brilliant writer much dreaded by Napoleon. She had long been forbidden to reside in Paris, but had not been forbidden to reside in France; when she wrote her work on Germany it was duly submitted to the imperial censors and officially revised and approved. Afterwards, when the author was "forty leagues from Paris," at a place where she had been residing for the purpose of reading the proof-sheets as they had come from the press, the entire edition of ten thousand copies was seized by the police, sent to the paper mill, and converted into cardboard, and the author herself was at the same time ordered to leave France within twenty-four hours. She wrote to the officers imploring a few days' delay, but without effect. As to the reason for the suppression of her book, the officer replied (Lanfrey, vol. iv, p. 321): "It seems to me that the air of this country does not suit you, and we are not reduced to the necessity of seeking models in the people you admire." The unhappy author was not only expelled from France, but was compelled to perform a winter journey from Switzerland, through the Tyrol, by way of Vienna, into Russia, for ultimate personal safety.

My second illustration is the case of the German bookseller, John Palm, who had in his possession for sale a pamphlet which exhorted the Germans to stand up for their country against the invader. Palm was a citizen of Nuremberg, a city not then subject to the French empire; yet Napoleon sent his emissaries, who, having arrested the offender, handed him over to a military commission, which had no alternative but to obey the imperial orders. The unhappy man was speedily condemned and shot.

Napoleon had one principal remedy in such cases, which is expressed by himself in a letter to Berthier: "My cousin, you have, I imagine, arrested the booksellers of Augsburg and Nuremberg. I intend them to be brought before a military commission and shot within twenty-four hours." It was a capital offence to write, speak, publish, sell, or distribute one word against the emperor. The military commissioners were obliged to condemn under pain of being themselves condemned.

Palm met his death with courage, and was very soon celebrated as a martyr in the patriotic songs which resounded throughout Germany, firing the hearts of the people with enthusiastic ardor against the tyrant. The result of this despotism showed itself most effectively in the campaigns of 1813 and 1814.

Thus did Napoleon coerce the press, the great palladium of liberty, into a most powerful instrument of bondage, by exhibiting through the literature of the time a series of false and delusive pictures and false statements to mislead the public mind; he completely excluded and suppressed the truth in every form. And yet he was not an enemy to literature when its style suited his taste. On the contrary, he delighted to distribute with his own hand the decennial prizes of the Institute for the encouragement of writers. The announcement of the distribution by the minister of the interior sufficiently indicates the style of language which was never suppressed by the censors. The minister said (Lanfrey, vol. iv, p. 326): "The decennial prizes are about to be given by the very hand of him *who is the source of all true glory*." The laureates must have been greatly pleased to be so near the topmost round of all human aspirations. But here are further illustrations of the favorite imperial style of literature, which never failed to meet the approving smiles of the censors. Alison (History, vol. viii, p. 152) says:

" We cannot adequately praise your Majesty," said Lacépède, the president of the senate; " your glory is too dazzling; those only who are placed at the distance of posterity can appreciate its immense elevation." "The only *éloge* of the empire," said the president of the Court of Cassation, " is the simple narrative of his reign; the most unadorned recital of what he has wished, taught, and executed, of their effects past, present, and to come." " The conception," said Count de Fabre, a senator, " which the mother of Napoleon received in her bosom could only have flowed from divine inspiration."

Such adulation, which sounds like burlesque and blasphemy to sensible people, pleased the low vanity of the emperor like sweetest music. It was the sycophantic fashion of the day, but it has been neither honored nor favorably remembered by posterity.

To show that such literature was pleasing to Napoleon, and not merely a matter of toleration on his part, I will give a specimen of the manner in which he spoke of himself. It is found in his proclamation (Alison, vol. iv, p. 617) at the time of the revolt in Cairo (1798). He said:

Sheiks, Ulemas, Orators of the Mosque, teach the people that those who become my enemies shall have no refuge in this world or the next. Is there any one so blind as not to see that I am the Man of Destiny? Make the people understand that from the beginning of time it was ordained that, having destroyed the enemies of Islamism, and vanquished the Cross, I should come from the distant parts of the West to accomplish my destined task. Show them that in twenty passages of the Koran my coming is foretold. I could demand a reckoning from each of you of the most secret thoughts of his soul, since to me everything is known; but the day will come when all shall know from whom I have received my commission, and that human efforts cannot prevail against me.

Thus spoke Napoleon himself. Is it any wonder that his tools and lackeys called him "the source of all true glory," and taught that his conception "flowed from divine inspiration"? With such a model, and all else suppressed, is it any wonder that the reign of Napoleon is a literary blank?

Closely connected with his harsh treatment of the press was the emperor's general cruelty towards all who were displeasing to him. The Duc d'Enghien was a brilliant young man of the Bourbon nobility, who, like thousands of his class, was an exile from France. He resided in Baden, apparently leading a quiet, inoffensive life. But Napoleon was not pleased with his proximity to the French frontier. A force was sent into German territory, the duke was arrested on a charge of conspiracy, conveyed to Paris, tried before a military commission, and shot. This inexcusable murder sent a thrill of horror throughout Europe, and caused the most inoffensive people to feel that their lives were not safe. About the same time General Pichegru, who had been arrested and imprisoned on the same charge, was found murdered in his cell. So plain and pointed were the facts and circumstances of the murder that no one seemed to doubt Napoleon's guilt, and in St. Helena he thought it necessary to defend himself against the imputation. These expedients seemed at the moment to strengthen the position of the tyrant, but the time arrived when they nerved and strengthened the sentiment of outraged Europe in the general struggle to overthrow him.

At the storming of Jaffa several thousand Turks surrendered on condition that their lives should be spared. The conditions were granted by the French generals, but were violated by Napoleon. The prisoners were all mercilessly shot. This treachery and inhumanity were a Napoleonic expedient for weakening and terrorizing the enemy, but in a few days it was seen to have been a bad mistake. At the siege of Acre not a Turk thought of surrendering, but all were resolved to sell their lives as dearly as possible. The siege was a failure, and Napoleon was not able to prosecute his invasion of Asia, but, on the other hand, was compelled to beat a hasty retreat into Egypt, leaving his sick and wounded in the hands of the Turks. If the prisoners of Jaffa had been humanely treated, the Turks defending Acre could have been induced to surrender when the defence became desperate. But when surrender means death, no man will consent to be taken alive. Napoleon bitterly mourned his failure at Acre. He complained that Sir Sidney Smith, who had charge of the defence, made him miss his "destiny."

Speaking of the savage massacre of the prisoners of Jaffa, Alison (vol. iv, p. 623) says:

The melancholy troupe were marched down, firmly fettered, to the sand hills on the seacoast, where they were divided into small squares and mowed down, amid shrieks which yet ring in the souls of all who witnessed the scene, by successive discharges of musketry. No separation of the Egyptians from the other prisoners took place; all met the same fate. In vain they appealed to the capitulation by which their lives had been granted; bound as they stood together, they were fired at for hours successively, and such as survived the shot were dispatched with the bayonet.

That act of unwise treachery and cruelty well illustrates the savagery of the eleventh century which Napoleon inherited from Corsica. Some writers attempt to justify it, claiming that Napoleon had no means of feeding the prisoners. That was not a good excuse, as they could have been released on parole. They would then have spread abroad the news of Napoleon's good faith and kind treatment, and it would not have been difficult to have obtained the surrender of Acre on the same promise given at Jaffa. But it is easy to show that the murder of the Jaffa prisoners was to gratify the savage nature of Napoleon, regardless of the wisdom or policy of the deed. Here is a case in point. After the revolt in Cairo (1798) he wrote to General Berthier (Lanfrey, vol. i, p. 284), saying:

" Order the commandant of the place, citizen general, to cut off the heads of all the prisoners who were taken with arms in their hands. Let them be taken to-night to the borders of the Nile between Boulak and Old Cairo; their headless corpses will be thrown into the river." Some days after, writing to Regnier, he said: " Every night we have about thirty heads cut off, and a great many chiefs; this I fancy will be a lesson to them." As the peasants in the neighborhood of Cairo had taken part in the revolt, a great number were seized and beheaded. One morning a troop of asses, laden with sacks and escorted by soldiers, arrived in the place Ez-Bekieh, the most populous quarter in Cairo; the inhabitants, attracted by curiosity, crowded round the convoy, and when the soldiers opened the sacks, the heads of peasants, with which they were filled, rolled upon the ground before the eyes of the terror-stricken multitude.

Such deeds of barbarism were doubtless expected to teach the simple people the divinity of the murderer, and of whom he "had his commission." What infatuation! Rather does it make us ready to believe all that Venturini has said, when he relates that, looking over the field of Borodino, next morning after the battle, strewed with eighty thousand men dead and dying, Napoleon hummed Italian tunes that astonished and disgusted his staff; "He was a great prince, like Satan, among the highest nobility of hell." Also at the crossing of the Beresina, Napoleon, being safely over before the fall of the bridge, was "seated like a chimera dire," enveloped in furs in his travelling carriage, and, viewing the struggling masses of men perishing in the icy waters of the river, or crawling about the wheels of his carriage, he laughed aloud and shouted, "See the toads!"

The Reign of Terror in Paris was scarce a suggestion in horrors as compared with the military régime of Napoleon. Yet there are writers of respectability who shout "Napoleon the Great," and have a thousand apologies for his unutterable atrocities! He had no conception of the moral sentiment of the world, and when by his cruelties he supposed he was destroying his enemies, he was multiplying them tenfold. This was a fatal mistake, which could only be made by a savage, bred and born, and educated in the ethics of Corsican barbarism.

All candid writers dwell with earnest grief on the horrors of the hospitals at Wilna, after the passage of the French army on its retreat from Moscow. The city was overwhelmed with sick and wounded men; contagious diseases were prevalent, and the mortality was great, among both the victors and the vanquished. Count Philippe de Ségur, speaking from the standpoint of a French soldier, who had accompanied the grand army to Moscow, describes the condition as follows (vol. ii, p. 337):

At Wilna more than sixteen thousand prisoners had already perished. The convent of St. Basil contained the greatest number; from the 10th to the 23d of December they had only received some biscuit, but not a stick of wood nor a drop of water had been given them. The snow collected in the courts, which were covered with dead bodies, quenched the burning thirst of the survivors. They threw out of the windows such of the dead as could not be kept in the passages, on the stair cases, or among the heaps of corpses that were collected in all the apartments. The additional prisoners that were every moment discovered were thrown into this horrible place. The arrival of Alexander and his brother at last put a stop to these abominations; and if a few hundreds escaped out of the twenty thousand of our unfortunate comrades who were there, it was to these two princes they owed their preservation.

Alison dwells more at length on the horrible situation

of the starving and dying men, literally rotting with
gangrene in the midst of filth, disease, and destitution.
When the Emperor Alexander arrived he removed the living
into the palaces of the city, which he converted into hospitals, where they were made comfortable and tenderly
cared for. Such of the French soldiers as were able to
travel were supplied with money that they might proceed
homeward. The dead, to the number of thirty thousand,
were collected and burned. The expenses of these changes
and alleviations were defrayed by Alexander out of his own
purse. When the sovereigns of Europe heard of the situation at Wilna, all who had soldiers there sent money to
Alexander to aid in the payment of expenses, *except Napoleon.*
The one man who, alone in all the world, had been the
cause of so much suffering, did nothing to relieve the situation! Surely no more need be said to illustrate the inherent savagery of the child of Mediterranean piracy. Napoleon's characteristic cruelty alone was a mistake of
sufficient magnitude to work his ultimate downfall, even
in half-Christian Europe, where absolute justice between
man and man has never had a permanent footing.

Not only was Napoleon a natural savage, but he gloried
in the fact, and chose the wild and savage lion of the wilderness as his favorite model. In St. Helena, "The emperor
remarked," says Las Casas (vol. iii. p. 40), "that the desert
always had a peculiar influence on his feelings. . . . His
imagination was delighted at the sight, and he took pleasure
in drawing our attention to the observation that Napoleon
meant *Lion of the Desert.*" After his return from Russia
and the defection of Murat, he said, "I suppose you are
among the number of those who think that the lion is dead;
if so, you will find you are mistaken." During the battle
of Leipsic, propositions for his surrender were sent to him
by the allies; he replied: "You are afraid of the sleep of
the lion, you fear that you will never be easy after having
pared his nails and cut his mane." In the entire career of
Napoleon one can scarce discern a single act springing from
a kindly motive or moral sentiment. Here was a huge void,
a fatal omission without remedy, in the man's inherited
nature; it could not fail to contribute to the ultimate downfall of this inhuman lion, this savage *megatherium* of the
wilderness.

There is one feature of Napoleon's conquests and political
policy which reveals the animus and weakness of the man
very fully. Although he designed to control everything as
the supreme master of all, yet, from the beginning to the

end, there appears no effort to combine and consolidate his conquests into one united autonomy. They were constructed into separate kingdoms for his relatives and dependents. These subdivisions were small and helpless in the hands of the one great emperor, easily mastered in case of revolt against his unmerciful conscriptions and levies of men and money. His was an empire constructed for despotic purposes, weak in its parts under the foot of a tyrant, but strong in the aggregate for the purposes of an imperial master. With such a policy it was impossible to construct an empire to last beyond the life of the founder. And yet, in the hope of accomplishing that impossibility, Napoleon divorced Josephine, married an archduchess of Austria, and tried to establish a legitimate dynasty. But on his downfall in 1814, while he carried with him to Elba the title of emperor, his alleged dynasty was swept aside as a mere cobweb, and this last master-expedient of this most impracticable of men, proved of no avail in preventing his overthrow.

Another mistake of Napoleon was his entire lack of confidence in the people, and his treason to all forms of government dependent upon the intelligence and the will of the people for their success. This blunder arose from the inherited nature of the man, and it affected his entire career. It caused him to scandalize and hurl back the cause of liberty in Europe for the space of two generations, and it gave to aristocratic writers a footing for their arguments against free popular government. Sir Archibald Alison never tires of ascribing all the atrocities of Napoleon to the evils of a "rapacious and unstable republic." He claims that the overthrow of monarchy and the abolition of a ruling aristocracy are the worst of evils and the most dangerous of policies. He argues that every effort at republican government, resting on the will of the people, must result, sooner or later, in either anarchy or military despotism. And he appeals to the French revolution and the subsequent career of Napoleon to sustain his position. Every mad enterprise and every cruel act of the despotic tyrant is charged up against the rapacity of the "military republic, resting on the will of the mob."

Even some American writers of prominence and influence have styled Napoleon the child of the revolution. Dr. Lyman Abbott, in the *Outlook* for Dec. 1, 1894, says: "He was at once the product and representative genius of his epoch. He embodied in a single person the spirit of the French revolution." No greater error as to the epoch or the spirit of the revolution can be uttered. The epoch from 1770 to 1825, in North America, in Europe, and in South America, was on fire with liberal ideas; and active revolutions in favor of popular liberty and republican government spread everywhere, resulting in immense progress for the human race. Napoleon represented the epoch of barbarism as it existed on the piratical coasts and islands of the Mediterranean prior to the days of Columbus, Copernicus, and Martin Luther, and he was the arch enemy of the "spirit of the French revolution" from the very moment that he attained sufficient power to exhibit his true character. All noble sentiments uttered by him before his elevation were gradually and treacherously abandoned; and his whole power, as fast as he attained it, was exerted for the reëstablishment of monarchy and an entire overthrow of the principles of the revolution.

I do not wonder that the learned writer speaks of Napoleon's character as "enigmatical." It must necessarily be so from his standpoint. Napoleon was not a child of the revolution, but a parasite upon it. He was no more a child of the revolution than the wolf is the child of the sheepfold or than the chintz bug is the child of the wheat plant. He appeared in his own character as a representative of the days of Alexander, Cæsar, Charlemagne, and William of Normandy. His origin, education, and entire career prove this. The revolution overthrew the monarchy and the nobility; Napoleon established another monarchy and created a new nobility. The revolution confiscated the great estates of the nobility and clergy for the benefit of the people; Napoleon restored them as far as he was able, placing the unsold lands beyond the reach of the people, but he dared not touch the homes of the new proprietors in cases where the lands had been sold. The revolution exiled the French nobles; Napoleon invited their conditional return. The revolution abolished slavery in the French colonies; Napoleon sacrificed an army of fifty thousand men in his effort to reëstablish slavery in San Domingo. The revolution was content to make war in self-defence only inside the boundaries known as the "Rhine, the Alps, and the Pyrenees." Napoleon changed that policy into one of conquest for the subjugation of the world. It was the policy of the revolution to encourage the establishment of European republics; it was the policy of Napoleon to change republics into kingdoms, and to place his brothers and relatives on the newly erected thrones. In no important particular did the spirit or the policy of Napoleon agree with the spirit of the revolution. He became an historic character in consequence of the revolution, but he was a parasitic enemy for its destruction and for the overthrow and reversal of all its principles. From this standpoint his character is not "enigmatical." When we would solve a problem we must start from correct premises and take into account all the elements necessary to the solution.

But at last the bad and most powerful influence of Napoleon's career as an argument against republican government is gradually wearing away. The halo of his name was greatly dimmed by the overthrow of Napoleon III, and the last of the dynasty perished a few years later in South Africa, wearing the hated British uniform.

And even the prestige of the first Napoleon, as *a brave man and an astute general,* is fading badly, as the calcium light of later history is dispersing the falsehoods of the Napoleonic bulletins and legends. The well established fact is now being considered that during twenty years of almost constant war, in which three million Frenchmen were swept from the earth, not one Bonaparte fell in battle. Although Jerome at Waterloo uttered the bravado, "Here every Bonaparte should fall!" and, Napoleon afterward admitted that he himself should have fallen there, yet no Bonaparte fell on that fatal field. Near the close of the battle Napoleon said to his staff, "We must save ourselves!" And, suiting the action to the word, they galloped off the field. In all his campaigns and battles Napoleon was very reckless of human life, and sacrificed men as mere toads of the puddle; but not one of the five brothers fell in battle or was captured on the battlefield. Whoever suffered, the Bonapartes were cared for.

Another well established fact is now coming up gradually for consideration: Napoleon never conquered a country where the inhabitants were united against him. His conquests usually succeeded as much by duplicity and treachery, or by some device or false hope which *divided the people,* or by the direct corruption of their commanders, as by military genius or heroism. Examples have been given to prove and illustrate these statements.

The prestige of the self-styled "architect of battles" is gaining nothing by later researches concerning his record. And as his prestige decreases, and the halo of his false glory is dimmed, men find themselves practising genuflections in the presence of an exploded meteor. It once dazzled and deceived, but the sunlight now illumines the horrible panorama of the tyrant's iniquities, and the power-

ful influence of his career against republican government, as
cited by aristocratic writers, is losing its force.

Everything must have an end. The career of Napoleon
was no exception to the rule. Having exhausted his every
resource for obtaining men and money, and every device of
duplicity and treachery; having undeceived the people as
to his loud professions in favor of liberty; and having
invoked against himself in every exasperated country the
"tactics of despair," the great "architect of battles" rapidly
went to the wall. His abdication in 1814 was a necessity.
The treaty of abdication was his parole of honor. The
prisoner was allowed the liberty of the island of Elba, as its
proprietor, with the nominal title of emperor. In 1815 he
violated his parole. Then came Waterloo and another surrender. The prisoner, a second time taken, had he been
tried by his own rules of war, so often enforced by himself,
would have been "shot within twenty-four hours." The
only excuse he ever offered for the butchery of the prisoners
of Jaffa was that "some of them" had violated their parole.
Whether he feared such a fate or not, certain it is that the
defeated chieftain made every effort to escape from Europe.
But the coasts were closely guarded, and there was no
alternative but to surrender. So, putting on a bold front,
he presented himself to Captain Maitland of the Beller-
ophon, *as the guest of the English people.* Writing to the
Prince Regent, he said: "I come, like Themistocles, to seek
the hospitality of the British nation." The British nation,
however, was not very poetic or sentimental at that particular moment; the surrender to Captain Maitland was considered *unconditional,* and the whilom emperor was in due
time informed that "the council of sovereigns" had decided
his status to be that of a prisoner of war in the custody of
the British government, and that his future abode would
be the Island of St. Helena. He was afterward transferred
to the ship Cumberland, in charge of Captain Ross, bearing
the flag of Rear-Admiral Cockburn. The British government permitted four officers and their families, one surgeon
and twelve members of his household, in all above twenty
persons, to share his exile.

Arriving at St. Helena, a residence was prepared for
Napoleon, known as "Longwood." It was situated on a
broad, elevated plateau, overlooking the ocean on the east,
with a background of hills and woodlands in other directions. The building was a long, irregular one-story structure, covering some six or eight thousand square feet of
ground. It was divided into about twenty principal rooms,

including dining-hall, library, billiard room, and the usual
necessary apartments, besides attics for servants' dormi-
tories. There were arrangements for twenty-three fires for
warming the building in cool or damp weather. The expenses of the establishment were defrayed by the British
government, and amounted to from eight to twelve thousand
pounds sterling per annum. The illustrious prisoner was
permitted the utmost freedom compatible with his safe
detention in the island, and was allowed the society of such
of his friends as had chosen to accompany him in exile. He
had books in great abundance, mainly of his own choosing;
writing materials and facilities; saddle and carriage horses
in profusion, and liberty to use them within a circuit of a
dozen miles. His table was abundantly and richly supplied,
including the choicest wines as his daily beverage.

What a contrast was this treatment of Napoleon in St.
Helena with his own treatment of others when in his power!
When Andreas Hofer, the Tyrolese chief, was captured,
Napoleon sent positive orders to have him "shot within
twenty-four hours." Hofer was guilty of no crime but
patriotism. On many occasions he had shown kindness
to French prisoners, and the French generals interceded to
save him. The order of Napoleon, however, was imperative,
and Hofer was judiciously murdered. By order of the
same tyrant General Toussaint, governor of San Domingo,
was murdered in prison by the slow tortures of cold and
hunger. The Chouan chiefs, after their surrender as prisoners, were shot by order of Napoleon. Cardinal Pacca,
also, was for months confined in a dungeon amid Alpine
snows, by special order of Napoleon.

But the list of his atrocities is too long to be recited here.
I will give but one other case. When Napoleon held the
pope a prisoner at Savona, he ordered him to be treated
with "the utmost rigor." His few personal comforts were
suppressed. "He was watched," says Lanfrey (vol. iv, p.
451), "and kept in sight, deprived of his carriages, forbidden
all communication or correspondence with the outer world,
his confessor and most special personal attendants were
imprisoned, his papers seized, his writing desks, pens,
breviary, and even a leather purse containing a few gold
coins were all taken from him. Finally, as a fit crown to
such insults, the Fisherman's ring . . . . was demanded
from him by the captain of the gendarmerie. Such were the
base and cowardly persecutions of an infirm and defenceless
old man by that same Napoleon who, at St. Helena, never
ceased in his complaints of bad treatment, though sur-

rounded by friends and supplied with every personal comfort. Herein is plainly seen the real littleness of the man of savagery, possessing no conception of a moral principle.

The prisoner's bounds were at first twelve miles in circumference, but he was so disgusted at seeing soldiers on guard wearing the "British uniform" that he refused to enjoy the freedom allowed him. The presence of guards and the loss of his title as "emperor" were perpetual grievances which embroiled him with the governor of the island at all times. But as the British government had uniformly refused to recognize his title of emperor during his reign, it was hardly to be expected that they would allow it to be bestowed upon him in his captivity. The thoughtful reader will not fail to be amused with the fact, already mentioned, that the last of the emperor's dynasty died in South Africa in 1879, wearing that British uniform which had so disgusted his father's uncle in exile. Such is the whirligig of time! The great emperor could not control future events, any more than he could be pleased with his wine or his dinner when quarrelling with his keepers and cooks in St. Helena.

On May 5, 1821, Napoleon died, and three days later his remains were interred with military honors in Slane's Valley, beneath the branches of a weeping willow, near a bubbling spring where the deceased had often rested in his walks.

This historic event may be illustrated by a notable contrast: A small brass tablet in the floor of Statuary Hall in the capitol at Washington marks the spot where fell John Quincy Adams, by a paralytic stroke which ended in death. His long and useful life closed as serenely as a sunset in the quiet days of autumn. The final words of the "old man eloquent were: "This is the last of earth; I am content."

Not so the Corsican. On a stormy evening, when the artillery of heaven seemed to bombard the rock of St. Helena like a repetition of the thunders of Borodino or Leipsic, and the windows of the skies were open to flood the earth with rushing torrents, Napoleon lay on his sick bed at Longwood. His strength was nearly exhausted, and a few faithful friends watched at his side. "As his strength wasted away." says Seward, in his picture of the scene, "delirium stirred up the brain from its long and inglorious inactivity. The pageant of ambition returned. He was again a lieutenant, a general, a consul, an Emperor of France. He filled again the throne of Charlemagne. His kindred pressed around him again, reinvested with the pompous pageantry of royalty. The daughter of a long line of kings again stood proudly by his side, and the sunny face of his child shone out from beneath the diadem that encircled its flowing locks. The marshals of the empire awaited his command. The legions of the old guard were in the field, their scarred faces rejuvenated, and their ranks, thinned in many battles, replenished. Russia, Prussia, Austria, Denmark, and England gathered their mighty hosts to give him battle. Once more he mounted his impatient charger and rushed forth to conquest. He waved his sword aloft and cried, 'Tête d'armée!' The feverish vision broke, the mockery was ended. The silver cord was loosed, and the warrior fell back upon his bed a lifeless corpse. This was the end of earth. *The Corsican was not content!"*

Thus died this child of savagery. Sorrowful to contemplate, yet dramatic in death as in life. The manner of departure reminds one of the barbaric régime of the eleventh century rather than the quiet enlightenment of the nineteenth. Napoleon was a child of the past. His education was in line with his ancestral and prenatal tendencies, and his life and death were true to his origin and tutelage. History suggests a tablet for his tomb. The epitaph of Robespierre is an appropriate model:

> Here lies Robespierre, let no tear be shed;
> Reader, if he had lived, thou hadst been dead.

That was proper for the Terrorist who caused the decapitation of less than ten thousand victims in Paris while he was master of the guillotine. But for the great "architect of battles" ten thousand murders are a mere figment, a suggestion. Look at Napoleon's single battles: Austerlitz, Jena, Eylau, Smolensko, Borodino, Essling, Wagram, Leipsic, Waterloo, and others, by the dozens and scores. It is estimated that the wars of Napoleon swept from existence three million Frenchmen. As many or more fell among his enemies, by the hand of that "star" of stupendous tragedies! And then the manner of the killing! The guillotine was mercy personified compared with the fatal manglings of musketry, bayonets, swords, grapeshot, and cannon ball on the battlefield, with the victims dying slowly under the hoofs and wheels of the charging cavalry and artillery. Ten thousand for Robespierre! Six million for Napoleon! The pupil must have the fuller tablet in order to imitate the truth. The language of man cannot do the subject justice. The following is far within the truth of history. Three or four of the titular epithets were chosen by the subject himself while living, and all are historically true.

HERE LIES NAPOLEON.

THE MAN OF DESTINY;
THE ARCHITECT OF BATTLES,
THE LION OF THE DESERT:
THE BRIGAND OF EUROPE
THE MASTER OF DUPLICITY;
THE PRINCE OF TREACHERY;
THE BREEDER OF WARS;
THE ROBBER OF TREASURIES;
THE MUZZLER OF THE PRESS;
THE ASSASSIN OF LIBERTY;
THE DESTROYER OF REPUBLICS:
THE BUILDER OF THRONES;
THE BREAKER OF TREATIES:
THE SHOOTER OF PRISONERS;
THE FRIEND OF SLAVERY;

DIED OF PERSONAL AMBITION AND
A VICIOUS FINANCIAL POLICY.

HERE LIES NAPOLEON; LET NO TEAR BE SHED;
READER, IF HE HAD LIVED, THOU HADST BEEN DEAD.

CONCLUDING OBSERVATIONS.

In looking over the ground of the foregoing discussions it will be seen that Napoleon's financial policy was the most comprehensive and far-reaching of his temporary expedients. It enabled France to treble the number of her troops, and thus to bring into the field a million men, while the burden of supporting them fell upon the conquered countries. This was a magnificent expedient while it lasted, but when the conquered countries were exhausted of their specie, it did not remain in circulation, but went into hiding. Hence, to recuperate his finances new conquests were necessary. This, as we have seen, drove him into foolhardy enterprises, which were charged up to his personal ambition.

When conquests ceased, his finances failed, and his downfall was certain and rapid.

Let me now mention a marvel of history: After the wars of Napoleon had ceased, England changed from her victorious paper and adopted Napoleon's vanquished metallic system. Alison's History (vol. xiv, p. 172), discussing the subject, says:

> By this means not only was the crisis surmounted without difficulty, but a hundred and thirty thousand combatants, with forty ships of the line, were assembled around Lisbon, which hurled back the French legions from the lines of Torres Vedras; and in the three last years of the war, while not a guinea was to be found in England, all the armies of Europe were arrayed in British pay on the Rhine and the Pyrenees. . . . It is remarkable that this admirable system, which may truly be called the moving power of the nation during the war, became, towards its close, the object of the most determined hostility on the part both of the great capitalists and the chief writers on political economy in the country.

The hostility of the English capitalists and the writers of the times towards the victorious English paper system, and their advocacy of the vanquished system of Napoleon, though a marvel in history, is now easily explained. The great bondholders who had loaned to the government cheap money during the war, desired to collect their interest in costly money, far more valuable than the money they had loaned. In 1807 British three-per-cent bonds were worth less than half their face value in coin or legal-tender paper. The bondholders now set about the abolition of paper money and the demonetization of silver, so that their bonds and the interest on them should be payable in gold only. The evil effects of currency contraction on the nation and the people did not disturb the nerves of those Shylocks. All they cared for was their "pound of flesh," even if it should drain the last drop of blood from the industry and enterprise of the people. In the same connection Alison argues the question as follows:

> Here, however, as everywhere else, experience, the great test of truth, has determined the question. The adoption of the opposite system of contracting the paper in proportion to the abstraction of the metallic currency, by the acts of 1819 and 1844 (followed as it was necessarily by the monetary crises of 1825, 1839, and 1847), has demonstrated beyond a doubt that it was in a system of an *expansive currency* that Great Britain during the war found the sole means of its salvation. And if any doubt could exist on the subject, it would be removed by the experience of the disastrous years of 1847 and 1848, during which, without any external calamity, and when at peace with all the world, the mere abstraction of eighteen millions of sovereigns to purchase foreign grain . . . produced universal and unexampled distress, and induced such a convulsion in the country as reduced the revenue, drawn with difficulty from twenty-eight millions of souls, to 51,250,000 pounds, and sent above two hun-

dred and fifty thousand emigrants each year out of the country; while in 1810, under a far greater abstraction of the precious metals, universal prosperity prevailed and 67,144,000 pounds was without any effort raised from eighteen millions of inhabitants, without any of them being driven to seek their bread in distant lands.

There were two errors in the British system of finances: (1) The paper notes were issued by the bank and loaned to the government. This created a class of bondholders who got their bonds at the mere cost of printing the notes. Instead of that the notes should have been issued by the government and paid out direct for the legitimate expenses of the nation. This would have put the notes into circulation without the intervention of the bondholders. The notes then being in circulation and money being plentiful, the people could have met most of the remaining governmental expenses by taxation.

(2) Then, if the currency circulating in the country during the war had not been retired, by converting it into interest-bearing bonds, there would have been no great public debt resting on the industry of the people. These wrongs in the management of the British finances came through the mistake of permitting an interested class of money-changers to manage the finances of the country. They controlled the issue of the bills in their own interest during the war, and then, after the war, caused the government to abandon the victorious paper system of England, and to adopt the vanquished metallic system of Napoleon on which to rest the bank paper.

These two blunders caused by the great financiers, who "sustain a state as the cord sustains the hanged," gave rise to the present great national debt of England, and placed its ultimate payment beyond the reach of the people. Now, as a lesson for Americans, it may be stated that the same brigand spirit and class interest which led the British government to adopt the metallic system in England, after its failure in the hands of Napoleon, is rapidly fastening the same barbarism and its resulting slavery on the American people, in the form of a bonded debt and "the single gold standard," which will make the debt perpetual.

The reader of history who learns no practical lessons from his studies wastes his time. The one great lesson of Napoleon's career useful to commercial nations is this: No nation is safe in time of war, or prosperous in time of peace, with a shrinking volume of money. Not even the sword of Napoleon, backed by the merciless barbarisms of the eleventh century and the most transcendent military genius, could reverse this inexorable law of finance. A money of shrinking volume and appreciating value congests in the banks and money-centres; if driven from those depositories by the dangers of military brigandage, it will burrow into the earth and beneath stone walls to escape circulation. The English system was better bcause it was expansive, yielding quick obedience to the military needs of the country; but the evils in the manner of its issue and of its contraction after the war should teach men the lesson that the bond-holder and money-changer should be eliminated from every system of finance. He is the same great brigand now that he was when the Saviour flogged him from the Temple in Jerusalem, and that he was in Wall Street when President Lincoln said, "I wish every one of them had his devilish head shot off!"

The brigandage of the bondholder and money-changer is as fatal to commercial prosperity and human progress as is the brigandage of the sword. It enacts, changes, manipulates, and violates laws in its own interest, and at every turn of the scale and tip of the beam the people are robbed. The brigandage of the sword is noisy, furious, and obvious, like the forays of wild beasts; and Napoleon, the greatest of military brigands, was consistent when he chose the wild lion of the wilderness as his model. The brigandage of finance is as silent as the grave, and as stealthy and dangerous as the serpent; and the nation that heeds its seductive whisperings, by favoring its schemes of contraction, bond issues, and gold basis, will find itself outside of paradise, with a flaming sword impelling its exit and forbidding its return.

My purpose in writing this sketch has been twofold: First, that the character and career of Napoleon may be better understood, and that he may be considered in a less degree the model of "all true glory" in military affairs; and, second, that his financial system may be appreciated as the flattest failure in history. If I have contributed to these ends, and aided ever so slightly in relieving the minds of my readers from that spirit of military hero-worship which is now being so industriously and powerfully nurtured by the plutocratic press of America; and if I have contributed something to save my country from the grip of that financial anaconda which stifles the industries and enslaves the people of the old world, and is now vigorously attacking the new under the delusive banner of "honest money," I have accomplished my purpose.

PROFESSOR HERRON.

BY HON. CHARLES BEARDSLEY.

My acquaintance with Rev. George D. Herron began in the summer of 1891. I was chairman of a committee of the Congregational church of Burlington, Iowa, charged with the duty of discovering and presenting the name of a suitable person to become associate of the pastor of the church whose term of service in that office had been continuous for nearly half a century. My attention was called to Mr. Herron by two or three individuals who had some knowledge of him, particularly through an address of his published in the *Christian Union* some months previously, entitled "The Message of Jesus to Men of Wealth"—afterwards widely circulated as a booklet and now as one of the chapters of "The Christian Society." I then read this address for the first time, and was astonished to learn that its author was the pastor of a village church in Minnesota. It occurred to me that a preacher who could write such a discourse as that would not lack invitations to wider fields. I wrote to him, not really expecting that anything would result from the correspondence, and learned later that, as I had surmised, he had already received a number of calls, some of them from large and wealthy churches, but from the first was disposed to look with favor upon that from the Burlington church, which he subsequently accepted. In the meantime he visited this church and preached from its pulpit, and conferred with its representatives.

He was under thirty years of age, of gentle ways, in person slender, a little above the average height, but somewhat below the average in apparent strength and vigor, yet with a fine public address and a tongue touched with the fire of a very earnest purpose, and a spirit all aflame in its zeal for righteousness and consecration to the truth. He spoke, indeed, as one having authority—not in his own right, but in the sure utterance of principles from which there could be no appeal.

It is not the purpose of this sketch to give a biography of Dr. Herron; but it is quite impossible to understand his unique position as a public teacher, his high and steady devotion to his calling, the significance of the message which he has to deliver, or his unsurpassed moral courage, without some knowledge of his parentage and the experiences which came to him in his youth and in the earlier years of his ministry. For this purpose nothing can be so good, nor so interesting, as his own history of himself, included in his confession of faith made to the ecclesiastical council which installed him as a pastor in Burlington, Iowa, on the 30th day of December, 1891. I will make, therefore, some considerable extracts from the paper which he read on that occasion, premising that hitherto it has had only a local publication, and that its contents will be new, with comparatively few exceptions, to the readers of the ARENA. Mr. Herron said to the council that he proposed to present them a confession of his Christian faith as it had grown out of his religious experience rather than an outline of theological opinions. He thought such occasions should be times of spiritual refreshment and the closer drawing together of a divine brotherhood, rather than times of discussion and criticism; and that it would be a great gain for truth if installation councils should meet in "so clear an atmosphere of sympathy that every nightmare of theological propriety might vanish in the light of an absolute spiritual honesty, shining from soul to soul." He pleaded for apostolic frankness and the examination of life more than opinion; for the sake of fulfilling his thought he was willing to be considered egoistic, and also was more ready to do this because certain inquiries had been made as to the spiritual experiences which lay behind some utterances of his which had gone abroad in the world. He continued:

While I find myself in accord with the evangelical theology of the day, with a growing tendency toward a conservatism of what I understand to be its fundamental doctrines, my belief in God and my thought concerning Him have not been formed by either the theology of the creeds or the philosophy of the schools. My theological beliefs have been cast in the mould of experience. My intellectual apprehensions of religious truth have their roots in spiritual struggles. My philosophy is the product of moral conflict. So that I believe in God the Father, who manifested himself in Jesus Christ as our Redeemer, who dwells in man as a life-giving spirit, because I know Him and have lived with Him.

I do not know when I began to live with God. I have never been without the inner consciousness of God's compelling and restraining presence. I cannot remember that the Eternal Word was ever silent in my soul. I know of no time when my life has not been subject, in some degree, to the profound conviction that it belonged to God.

I may have been converted before I was born. Through my father, a humble man who believed in the Bible and hated unrighteousness, I came from an unbroken line of Christian ancestors, reaching back to the days of Scottish Reformation. During the year preceding my birth my mother lived in an atmosphere of prayer, studying good books and brooding over her Bible. She asked God to give her a child who should be His servant. She received me as from God and gave me back to God as her freewill offering. She besought God to keep me upon the altar of a perfect sacrifice in the service of His Christ and her Redeemer. She told God of her willingness to have me drink of Christ's cup and be baptized with His baptism, if needful for my entire consecration to His purpose in my life. Her after years were crowded with trials, sorrows, and mistakes. She never again, nor had she before, reached the spiritual height upon which she walked with God during the year of my birth. But nothing has ever been able to separate her from the belief that in bringing me into the world she had fulfilled the purpose of her being, and she never doubted that I would be a messenger of God to my fellow-men. Of all this I knew nothing until after I had been preaching the gospel; nor have I ever spoken of this before, either publicly or privately.

Until I was nearly ten years of age it was nearly always a question whether I should live from one year to another. My mother was much of the time an invalid. I shrank from all companionship save that of my father. He taught me, very early, to read, and selected my books and directed my thoughts. We were seldom apart day or night. He drew out all there was in me and turned it Godward. Before my tenth year I had the history of the world, with God behind it, before my mind as a panorama. I had gone through the earlier edition of Bancroft and gathered from it something like a philosophy of history. The reign of God in human affairs was so wrought into all my thoughts that I could not form a conception 'from any other point of view. An accident, in the minutest detail of life, was a thing foreign to my comprehension. I was a slave, if I may so speak, to the idea of God. I knew little of childhood or play. But the Kingdom of God and its righteousness were tremendous realities. I could not disassociate a picket on a fence from the moral kingdom. God was my confidant. I never thought of myself as other than His child. I talked with Him over my books and on my walks. He answered my prayers. The words and deeds of His servants were my recreation. Joseph and Elijah and Daniel, Cromwell and John Wesley and Charles Sumner, were my imaginary playmates. Thus I grew up in the company of God, with a daily deepening sense of a divine call which sooner or later I must obey.

I think it was at thirteen that I first united with the church. I was then already working for my livelihood, in a printing office, amidst the most vicious associations. From thence to my twentieth year I encountered all manner of temptations. I sometimes looked upon sin lightly. I did much that was wrong. Yet I did not fall into the vile sins of my companions. In this fact, however, is no virtue. I seemed to be kept in spite of myself. I tried to fall into the depths and could not. When I would do evil good was present with me. Sometimes, I was so ashamed of my outward innocence that I pretended to be guilty of sin which I never committed, and my associates would not believe my pretensions. Again, when being led away into evil, a willing victim, upon my soul would close the awful grasp of an Almighty hand and I would bewilder my tempters with the sudden vehemence of my efforts to save them with myself. Then, alone in my room, would I, with bitter regret and fearful shame, entreat God to take me back and keep me evermore. And oftentimes, during those years of poverty and sickness, toil and trial, rebellious plans and wasted energies, hasty actions and crude efforts, oftentimes the glory of the Lord would cleave the darkness and envelop me, filling my soul with a joy I could not understand and giving unto me a quenchless faith. Strong mercy constantly encompassed me, and rendered me helpless to surrender to the sins that pursued me.

It was not until after I had been in the ministry, and other souls had professed Christ through the words spoken by me, that there came to me that profound self-revelation which our fathers called a conviction of sin. So far my Christian life, my religious thought, had been as much an inheritance as the fruit of experience. I had been more of a Hebrew than a Christian. I had been spasmodic and passionate in the pursuit of righteousness. But I had not yet personally realized the fact of redemption. I had also been largely influenced by the lives of the mediæval Catholic saints. I was fascinated with the spiritual charm of their ascetic piety and subtle devotion. God became to me a taskmaster, and I was constantly trying to fill up the measure of my misdoing with overdoing. I knew myself to be a sinner. I did not know myself as a lost and a redeemed soul. There came a time, however, when I stood face to face with the Infinite Holiness, oblivious to all else save my sin and God's righteousness. I saw the selfishness, the pride, the falseness, the absolute unholiness of my heart, until I could bear the revelation no more; yet was unconscious that there were depths of wickedness which the divine mercy had veiled from my eyes. I groped in that horror of darkness which settles down upon a soul when it knows that there is no sound thing in it and that it merits nothing but eternal death and endless night. The hopeless anguish of a lost life laid such hold of me that all the eternities seemed overwrought with speechless pain. I knew that nowhere had I an inch of standing-ground save the mercy of God, and the least of all God's mercies seemed too great for me. Jonathan Edwards' Enfield sermon was, at that time, the only thing real enough to answer to my experience. But out of this horrible pit I cried unto the Lord and He heard me, lifting me up and planting my feet upon the rock of his salvation. When neither body nor brain could longer endure the divine testing and searching of soul, God revealed to me His Christ, and I knew what it meant to be saved. I was now not only a child of God by birth and calling, but a redeemed child, bought by the blood of Christ, cleansed by the sufferings of God. I knew Christ no more merely as the historic Redeemer. He had manifested Himself unto me, and had shown me myself and the Father.

I know I am yet a sinner. But in Christ I behold God as the sinner's friend, and I have peace with God through faith in Christ. Not what I am, but what God has shown himself in Christ to be, is the ground of my immovable hope for my own future, and the future of the race. I am persuaded that nothing will ever be able to separate me, or the world in which I work, from the love of God which is in Jesus Christ my Lord. The footprints of Jesus upon the soil of this earth are the seal of God's eternal ownership. The blood of Calvary is the pledge of God's unchanging friendship for man. I know that I and my fellow-men must suffer and struggle. But I believe the God of peace, who has revealed His glory and manifested His power in Christ, will bruise Satan under our feet shortly. I see that the grace that shines from Christ is sufficient to light me home, where I shall be like Him. Gratefully and joyously I follow Him, pointing my brothers to Him as I go. I see nothing else to live for. I find His yoke of the Father's will easy, and His burden of love for

men light. Only one thing I fear: that I may sometimes reflect Him
darkly or falsely. I have but one wish: that Christ may work in me
the will of God.

As to my reasons for preaching the gospel, there is but one: I could
not help it. I dared not do else. The call to this ministry reaches as
far back as my memory. I seemed to awake to the consciousness of
this call as I awoke to the consciousness of my existence. It is as
real to me as my being. I did not want to preach. No one, not even
my mother, suggested that I should preach. Nothing seemed more
preposterous to my reason. I loved solitude and abhorred a crowd.
I shunned and distrusted people who were pious in their conversation and manner of life. I was silent in religious meetings. I gave
no expression to my inner and deeper life. To enter the ministry
meant the surrender of my tenacious ambitions for a life of literature. But events emphasized the divine call. Experiences of which
I need not speak, made it unmistakably distinct. In the still hours of
night I wept, and tried to believe myself deluded. I indulged in
many kinds of conscience-juggling in attempts to make terms with
God. I tried all the fine arts of getting away from God. And it
seemed to me unreasonable that God should give me both a frail
body and poverty and yet insist on my preparing for the ministry.
When through repeated failure of health I was compelled to relin-
quish my plans of study I rejoiced and thought myself free to go my
own way. But God went with me. The time came when I seemed to
have no choice save death or irrevocable self-surrender. I did not
much mind the matter of dying; for I cared little for my life. But I
was afraid to die without having preached the gospel. So, once and
for all, after a quick and intense struggle, during which God kept
near to me with His wondrous mercy, I let Him have His way; and
I went and preached according to His word. He has given unto me,
experience by experience, new and larger revelations of His truth,
and has shown me what he has for me to do. His joy is my strength
and He is my reward. His infinite purposes are my inspiration. To
show men the sufficiency of Christ in their personal lives, in the
reconstruction of society, in the problems of history, is my supreme
privilege, my consuming passion. I know of no words which can
express the depthless gratitude I feel for the privilege of presenting
Christ to human need.

Mr. Herron found no creed that contained the measure
of his faith. The best statement he could make of belief
was a simple confession of his "faith in Christ as God in
man and man in God." Nor did he see any theory of the
atonement that satisfied or even approximated his "estimate of the riches of God in Christ Jesus." He regarded the incarnation as the "coming of God within the
life of man to recreate and renew that life." "The incarnation brought forth the atonement. The life of Christ is
God's prophecy of the divine humanity which is to be the
fruit of that atonement. The incarnation is continuous and
the atonement eternal." He did not believe that Christ
was the Saviour of individuals only, but that His redemption comprehends the absolute subjection to His law of love
of all human affairs and institutions. "Capital and labor,

education and statesmanship, art and commerce, are as truly forms of communion with God as the most solemn prayer." As to the Scriptures he said:

I believe that the Bible is the inspired word of God. It is not the only word God has spoken or yet speaks. But it is the record of a progressive revelation of God to man, culminating in the incarnation of Christ and the redemption of the race. I accept the Bible as a divine rule of faith and practice, because I find in it the solution of all my problems and the answer to all my experiences. God speaks to me more surely from its pages each time I turn to them. My need of the Bible deepens, day by day. The more I feed my soul upon its messages the more I find it to be the word of God, and the more assurance and strength and joy I receive from its utterances.

The problems of eschatology did not trouble him. The reality of the future life was the ground upon which he walked. But he was face to face with the moral processes of the present economy, and here was his place and his work. "The adequacy of divine resources for human need; the relation of character to conflict; the work and joy of righteousness which is a triumph over sin,"—these demanded all his prayer and meditation, his energy and consecration. His business was to bid men "repent and receive the gospel." His commisssion permitted him to declare that "There is nothing in the universe for those who follow Christ to fear." "The cross is the manifestation of God's eternal attitude toward man," and "Christ His final judgment upon humanity."

Mr. Herron's Burlington pastorate lasted for seventeen months only. But the amount of work done by him in that time was surprisingly large. He preached Sunday morning and evening. Many of his sermons were reported for the daily press of the town, and subsequently appeared in permanent form in two or three volumes of published discourses. About thirty of his sermons, such generally as were not reported in full for the daily papers, appeared in a weekly journal. He organized among the young men of the congregation a Christian social union, and gave them a lecture each Monday evening; while Tuesday afternoon was given up to a like service in a similar organization of young women. These lectures were also frequently reported and given considerable publicity through the press. The mid-week meeting of the church of Thursday evening had his careful attention. He gave up most of the day to preparation for it, which included a prayer-circle with some young people in his study, at a designated hour in the afternoon. The Thursday evening meetings were exceedingly interesting and edifying. Mr. Herron's expositions of

Scripture were always fresh and luminous, and his general management of such social and devotional services was replete with a fine sense of the fitness of things, while his quiet and reverent demeanor was in itself a spiritual benediction. Those who entered into the spirit of those rare occasions can but remember and linger over them with delight. Under Mr. Herron's direction a sewing class for poor girls, meeting weekly in the church, and an evening school for indigent boys and young men who could not avail themselves of the advantages of the public schools, were set in motion. He thought the church should be open every day in the week for some beneficial service, including the missionary, benevolent, and other usual gatherings. He also took some time for pastoral visiting and a little personal recreation in rowing, tennis, etc., but Saturday night often found him with his Sunday morning's sermon unwritten, and to be struck off at a white heat long after those who were to be electrified with it were asleep. After a while a stenographer came to his relief and a private secretary became a necessity. Mr. Herron has good faculties for *extempore* speaking and could, if needful, let Sunday evening take care of itself, but for the most part he had a written discourse for that also. Of course during these busy days and weeks he had many calls for outside work, lectures, occasional sermons, writing for the press, etc. It will be inferred and should be mentioned that in the usual routine work of the church he had the valuable aid of the senior pastor, Rev. William Salter, D.D., so long known and so highly esteemed both in the church and in the community, though by mutual agreement the laboring oar was in the hands of the associate pastor.

In giving some account of the annual meeting of the church held the first week in January, 1893, the leading daily paper of the city said:

The coming of Rev. George D. Herron to be pastor of the Congregational church has been a happy experience in its history. During the year that he has been here he has secured the warm affection of his people, the respect and confidence of the community, and the admiration and gratitude of a constantly widening circle of readers and friends in this and other countries, who have been quickened and strengthened for good work by his published discourses. Dr. Herron's strength is probably greater than it was a year ago, and he begins the second year of his pastorate under very favorable circumstances.

One item of the year's work was a minister's retreat, suggested and conducted by Doctor Herron, which was held at Grinnell, the seat of Iowa College, a dozen or fifteen min-

isters, and perhaps a layman or two, coming together for a
week of prayer, conference, and serious consideration of
the deepest questions of faith and experience. In the following year or two the number attending this retreat was
increased to forty or more, including earnest and representative men from all sections of the country. But this attendance, I believe, was found too large for the most satisfactory results, and the number in 1895 was reduced to
about a score. These annual gatherings, it is understood,
have been greatly appreciated and very profitable to those
who have enjoyed their advantages.

In January and February of 1893, Doctor Herron (the
degree of D.D. had been conferred upon him in the previous
year) delivered a series of Sunday evening lectures on current problems, including the relations of capital and labor,
the questions of wealth and poverty, and kindred topics,
which were largely attended, particularly by workingmen.
These discourses awakened a great deal of interest in social,
business, and industrial circles, and were the subject of
animated debate in the columns of the local press. The
Trades and Labor Assembly of the city adopted resolutions
thanking Doctor Herron "for his noble and unselfish work
in behalf of humanity and a higher plane of Christianity,
and that he would ever be held in grateful esteem by its
members." Naturally there was more or less comment of
the opposite character, but Doctor Herron had by this
time become quite accustomed to find himself the subject
of adverse criticism, but apparently could say with as much
sincerity as any minister since the days of St. Paul, that
"none of these things move me." "I hold not my life of any
account, as dear unto myself, so that I may accomplish my
course, and the ministry which I received from the Lord
Jesus, to testify the gospel of the grace of God." While
of course Doctor Herron's life was not thought to be in
danger from violence, his most intimate friends more than
suspected that he was working at a pace that would soon
destroy the small amount of physical vitality which he
seemed to have. Perhaps his sureness of purpose and
serenity of mind under all circumstances have had something to do with his staying powers.

I have thus dwelt upon the Burlington pastorate because
it was an interesting and important episode in Doctor Herron's career, and a necessary stepping-stone to the wider
platform which he now occupies, and a preparation for the
increasing and commanding influence which his words and
personality have since acquired.

As to his transfer from the pulpit to the professor's chair, I cannot do better than to let President George A. Gates, of Iowa College, tell the story, as he told it to the Burlington church at the time of Doctor Herron's resignation, with an extract from the latter's letter; the two showing also the spirit in which the new work was undertaken, both on the part of Doctor Herron and the college. President Gates said:

My acquaintance with Doctor Herron began personally when he accepted an invitation made less than two years ago, to speak to our students on the day of prayer for colleges, which occurs on the last day of January. I had known something of him through his writings before that and was the more glad to invite him to that service and make his acquaintance. It was not very long before the thought came into my mind that I wished we could have just such a man connected with our college. He came to us a stranger on that day, but left some heart friends in that institution, for he did set the souls of our young men and women on fire with a high and holy passion, such as is not common in experiences of that sort. He has been with us since, and still I had not thought of the possibility of his coming to us permanently. Even before he came to you, an honored woman of this city, who has a long time been a friend of the institution over which I have the honor to preside, had a generous thought towards us and promised to give to us in her own way and time the endowment of a new professorship, the name and nature of which were to be determined in the future.

But up to six months ago the name of Doctor Herron and that professorship had never been associated in my mind, and I do not think they had in his, and I do not know that they had in Mrs. Rand's mind. Last January, when Doctor Herron came to us again on the day of prayer for colleges, he and I did have some conversation led by myself touching upon the possibility of some such thing as is now contemplated. After Doctor Herron's return here I brought the matter before our faculty, in order that I might be sure of my ground, and they said unanimously, we should very heartily welcome Doctor Herron to our company, and they sent me down here with that message in February. I laid the matter before the executive committee of the board of trustees who are charged with the responsibility of appointing the instructors of Iowa College; they said the same thing. When I came last February with the invitation to Doctor Herron to come and join us if he could I had the faculty and trustees in my invitation. He said "No." When I suggested the idea to Mrs. Rand that we contemplated stealing him away from this city to work with and for us, I have not often seen a more valiant expression of opposition than Mrs. Rand showed at that time. In short, this matter seems to have grown. It was no sudden thought on any one's part. But the course of events in the last two years seems to have set in that direction until the consummation was immediately before us. I have learned from what experience I have in life to have a vast deal more confidence in things that grow than in things that are born in anybody's own volition. The true principle of important events is suggested by the word evolution, a gradual evolving of events and plans each resting back of the other.

Without dwelling longer on the details of the history, I will say that at a meeting of the board of trustees of Iowa College, a special meeting called for May 9, this whole matter was discussed in all its bearings, the note constituting the full endowment of a new professorship to be called the E. D. Rand Chair of Applied Christianity was before us with certain conditions, and I am glad to say that the note with every condition was heartily and with absolute unanimity, every member voting, accepted by the board of trustees. The note carried with it the call to Doctor Herron to accept the professorship, and that vote, too, was with similar unanimity.

We have asked him there because we want him there to teach what we understand to be that for which Iowa College has always stood; that which Iowa College has always taught, teaches to-day, and, so God will, will always teach—the actual applicability of the principles of Jesus Christ to every department of the human life. We believe in Christianity and we believe that Christianity should be applied. We believe that the foundation of the new department in Iowa College is the opening of a wide door for the inculcation of the application of Christianity in every sphere of life.

Doctor Herron in his letter of resignation expressed himself as follows:

I resign to accept the E. D. Rand Chair of Applied Christianity in the Iowa College. The circumstances and outlook attending this call leave me no choice but to enter this new work as a door of urgent opportunity opened by the Son of Man, in whose name I preach, by whose strength I live. I should not dare to refuse the call.

I believe we are entering upon a supreme and momentous day in Christian history. I believe that unless the church grasps a new conception of Christianity, unless it comprehends that Christianity is a life to be lived as well as a doctrine to be professed both the church and nation can be saved only by fire. The church is lost and false if it continue as it now is. But it will not. The living Christ, who is among us in the problems of our day, calling the church to repentance, will prove Himself the strong redeemer of the church, our nation, our society. The kingdom of heaven is at hand in America. The lamb of God is bearing away the sins of our people in a new passion.

I believe God has sent me with this message of a new redemption through His Son. I must go as I am sent. The Chair of Christianity, endowed in memory of a noble and honored member of this church, opens the way for me to speak to the church at large. I do not resign one position to take another. I go to witness to the righteousness of Christ as the righteousness of society and the nation. I have no choice in the matter. I can do nothing else. I do not enter this open door because I expect to have an easier task. I go to toil as I never toiled. I go to suffer for the truth and the name of Christ.

It is not necessary that I should go into the particulars of Doctor Herron's more recent work. The ARENA has reviewed his books with intelligence and sympathetic appreciation. It has published a letter from him showing his catholicity of spirit, his desire to coöperate cordially with all who labor for the amelioration of human conditions; and the fine symposium in the September number of last year, relating especially to his recent California campaign, gives some glimpses not only of his quality and power as a public teacher, but also of the admiration, love, and confidence which his personality and unselfish aims inspire among those who can appreciate supreme devotion to the highest human service. It remains for me to give some estimate of Doctor Herron's character and work as formed from my four years of intimate acquaintance with him.

First of all, then, Doctor Herron is a preacher of righteousness—a rôle for which he has at least some preëminent qualifications. "Preaching," says George Macdonald, "is that rare speech of a man to his fellow-men whereby in their inmost hearts they know that he in his inmost heart believes." Measured by this standard Doctor Herron is a prince among preachers. No one who listens attentively and intelligently to his discourse can for a moment doubt that he in his inmost heart believes sincerely and profoundly in the divinity of the principles which he teaches and in their supreme importance to men in their individual and social relations. "Soul is kindled only by soul," says Carlyle; and "to 'teach' religion, the first thing needful, and also the last and only thing, is the finding of a man who *has* religion." Those who imagine that Doctor Herron is a mere political or social reformer wholly mistake him. Primarily he is neither. He belongs to the intensely religious type of men. His socialism and radicalism—using these words in their best sense—are the outgrowth of an intense religious feeling, a profound religious conviction, seeking to express itself in the actual terms of life. Next to the preëminent characters of the Old and New Testaments, the men who have most influenced his thought, as he himself would doubtless say, were John Calvin, who particularly influenced his earlier years, Cardinal Newman, the middle-age mystics, Frederick Maurice of England, Mazzini, and Elisha Mulford. Dr. Herron's work has been and is distinctly to take the religious consciousness, as it existed, for example, in the minds of such men as Edwards and Finney, and translate it into the social movement of our time.

Doctor Herron's experience in the earlier years of his ministry, as given by himself, exhibits the reality of a new birth—as it were, the recreating of a soul and sending it forward upon a new career and with unchanging purpose. Let no one think lightly of such a change as this until he has himself laid his whole being irrevocably upon the altar of a worthy consecration. "Except a man be born again he cannot *see* the kingdom of God." The greatest thing a man can do, says an eminent writer, is to *see* something

and tell what he sees. The true religious teachers of mankind must be men of vision—seers. Upon this prime and
essential quality of Doctor Herron's mind it is unnecessary
to dwell as it is universally recognized by those who know
him. His intellectual equipment is very strong. His
reasoning powers are good and he delights in logical composition, with which he might be supposed to have but
little sympathy. Hard reading has no terrors for him.
He is the master of an almost faultless literary style. He
has fine poetical gifts and tastes, and is a keen and admirable judge of human character. With quick intuition and
great sensibility, with a nature loving and greatly desiring
to be loved, he combines, as Doctor McLean has suggestively
pointed out, the most heroic and manly qualities. He was
born in the second year of the war, his father was a Union
soldier, and in his earliest years of memory he must have
been familar with the stories of the camp, the march, and
the field of battle, while, as he has told us, Savonarola and
Cromwell, Abraham Lincoln and Charles Sumner, were as
household words, and their moral heroism became the model
after which his own life was fashioned.

Six small volumes of Doctor Herron's discourses and
lectures have been published. It would be interesting and
profitable, if space permitted, to point out and by suitable
extracts to illustrate the more significant points of his
teaching found in these books. But it must suffice here to
suggest that probably the two sermons that are in a subjective sense the most autobiographical, revealing his outlook from within, more than any others, are the chapters
entitled "The Coming Crucifixion," in "The New Redemption," and "The Divine Method of Culture," in "The Call
of the Cross"; while the whole philosophy on which he
builds is best expressed, perhaps, in the first chapter of
"The Christian Society." His indictment of the existing
social order is well and somewhat elaborately given in
"The Christian State" on pages 88 to 97; and his complaint
against the church may be found in the chapter on that
subject in the volume last named.

It is pleasant to know that Doctor Herron's books are
having an increasing circulation at home and a very considerable influence abroad, particularly in England, India,
and Japan. The author is in receipt of many letters from
England. Some of the young men who are leaders in the
native Japanese religious movement, which promises so
much, are greatly taken with the view which Doctor Herron
presents of Christ, and one of them has already determined

to take a year's study with him, although he has had, as
I understand, two or three years' study in an American
institution of learning and considerable experience as a
pastor. Mr. Mozoomdar, of India, after reading one of Doctor Herron's books, writes in grateful recognition of its
value, saying: "Noble ideas are spread throughout your
book, and you press into the very core of the matter when
you say that Christ is God's idea of man. Every one who
can set us free from such a snare as the metaphysical Christ
is a deliverer of the race, and your book brings a message
of deliverance." Doctor Herron has recently prepared a
new course of lectures which he will deliver in various
cities during this winter and spring, and they will be afterwards issued as a book entitled "The Social Revelation of
Religion." This book will probably express his matured
thought more fully than anything he has yet given to the
public.

The attentive student of Doctor Herron's books can hardly
fail to notice what may be called the attitude of ardent expectation that pervades them and especially culminates,
evidently unconsciously and without deliberate plan, at the
close of nearly every one of his lectures. In the last two or
three pages of each chapter it appears as a refrain in the
eager anticipation of some great event, which will exert its
transforming influence upon the world. The language and
form of expression are varied, but the bright light of a great
hope illumines them all, and they are frequently carried to a
plane of noble and inspiring eloquence. Says Doctor Herron in one of these passages:

We are in the beginnings of a new redemption of the earth through
the application of Christianity to life. Society is being sprinkled
with the blood of Jesus. The redemptive is displacing the police conception of justice. Industry is on its way to Damascus. The Spirit
of Christ is coming to anoint the factory, the mine, the railroad, to
preach good tidings to the poor, and set at liberty them that are
bruised. Every school of thought is feeling the pressure of a new
and universal dispensation of moral energy. From Westminster
Abbey to the forests of Africa, from the Roman Vatican to the mining camps of western America, men are feeling the pain and expectation of a new social order. "We have arrived," as Mazzini once said,
"at one of those supreme moments in which one world is destroyed,
and another is created." Though what it shall be does not yet
appear, we who know in whom we have believed are sure that the
juster order, the changed world, will be like Him; that it will not be
a world of fragments, of individuals, of divisions, but of members of
the body of Christ.

GOVERNMENT BY BREWERY.

BY PRES. GEORGE A. GATES OF IOWA COLLEGE.

OFFICE OF THE —— RAILWAY,
Chicago, Illinois,
September 16, 1895.

Mr. ——, Agent, ——, Wis.

Dear Sir: Please note and return the inclosed papers.

The action of our employee at —— is, as you see, seriously affecting our business. The Brewing Companies are particularly touchy in regard to this matter.

We do not care to interfere with the private opinions of our employees, but in a case of this kind, where the Company's interests are affected, the employee should be given to understand that he is expected not to be specially active and obnoxious.

I do not know in what capacity Mr. —— is employed, but desire that you see him and explain our wishes to him, and request him to cease his activity in this matter.

Yours truly,

—— ——,
General Superintendent.

In a certain Wisconsin town of about two thousand people Mr. —— is an employee of the —— —— —— Railway. He is also a member of the city council, and voted for an anti-screen petition which was signed corporately by four churches and two temperance organizations, and later by a large number of individuals. He did not circulate the petition. Being on the ordinance committee he voted in favor of recommending to the council the passage of such an ordinance. He also voted with others in the council making a majority in favor of such an ordinance, and the screens of the saloons came down and have been down since that time. The Milwaukee brewing interests at once sent their representative to the town, who secured from the saloon people and their supporters many signatures to a petition addressed to the railroad company requesting the removal of Mr. ——.

The only astonishing thing about this document is that it should have got away. How the leakage occurred is unknown to me. But it seems to me worthy of serious thought. Let us see. In other words, every one of the nearly a million of railway employees in America is enjoined from taking part in the community in which he is a citizen, in movements which not only tend toward suppressing but even tend toward regulating the saloon business. How generous, that an employee may hold any opinion he choses, but instant decapitation awaits any expression by word or act of such an opinion! Why, I would almost be willing to have the devil a member of my household under those conditions.

This is the method of government in Russia and Turkey, but in those countries the conditions are better than these; for there it is an open ukase or firman, read and known of all men. The people can rise up and cut off Charles the First's head, for the head is visible and, when enough of the people desire it, accessible. But "our business" is private; only by some accident can a document like the above be published.

Let there be no misunderstanding. I am heaping no objurgations on the railroad companies nor on the brewers. Were this article dealing in personalities instead of discussing principles, names and places would appear in the blank spaces of the above letter. The purpose in calling attention to this matter goes very much beyond any personal criticism. This is simply one striking illustration of the general condition of American democratic life in the stage of development at which we now are. To understand the importance of the matter it is necessary to reflect how significant a place the railroad interests of the country occupy, especially in the great agricultural domains of the West where this correspondence took place.

The civilization of these vast prairies is a railroad civilization, and during the last twenty-five years it has been largely created by the railroads. They push ahead, open up the country, invite and cultivate settlement. In thousands of small towns the railroad factor is a very prominent one. For instance, it is a fact hardly doubted by anyone fairly informed that in the strongly Republican state of Iowa, Governor Boies, a Democrat, was elected by the railroad vote. Governor Larrabee, his opponent, had written a book sharply criticising railroad managements. That vote numbers anywhere from fifteen to twenty-five thousand, directly or indirectly controlled by the railroads. That is enough in most years to constitute the balance of power. If the railroad vote did not determine the election above referred to, then one of the most prominent railroad men of the country is mistaken, for he said to me, "We railroads determined that election."

Then, too, the saloon problem is one of the very largest in all parts of the country. It is more or less in the politics of every state. Politicians have made many attempts to get it out of politics, and have been to a greater or less degree and in certain localities, temporarily, successful. But we all understand that wherever the saloon exists it is becoming every year more and more a political power.

The above is an instance of these two great powers so vitally connected with the public life of our nation working in the nicest and sweetest harmony. The general superintendent of a great railroad is, in respect to certain matters, under the absolute domination, and subject entirely to the dictation, of brewers in a certain city on his line.

Of course a common carrier must be subject to the laws which govern common carrying. He is as much under obligation to carry the products of brewers as to carry church building material or transport teachers and clergymen on passenger trains. But has it come to this, that the American citizen must abrogate his common rights of citizenship; must shut himself out from the practical and ethical interests of his community; when great questions of public welfare are up for discussion he must keep silence; when the interests of his boys and girls, his home, are at stake, he must be as indifferent as an Egyptian mummy? In other words, he must repudiate his manhood in order to be considered competent to build a bridge or work on a section of a railroad that runs through that community.

What had this employee done? Had he in any way interfered with the obligation of a common carrier resting upon his employers? Had he hindered their doing their full duty to every public interest? Not in the slightest degree. He had simply cast his vote as an alderman in favor of good order in the community. He had done nothing directly to decrease the number of saloons nor to reduce by so much as one glass the beer transported by the railroad. The brewers evidently thought an anti-screen rule indirectly hostile to them. Being on the board of aldermen he had certain obligations arising out of that office; but here is a demand from a business interest in a distant city that he perjure himself with reference to his oath of office expressed or implied as alderman, certainly the oath he took before he cast his first vote as an American citizen. He is required by his employer to refuse to act conscientiously as an honorable and patriotic American citizen.

In other words, the brewers intend to run this country in their interests. In every community where "their business" is carried on they propose to make that community's

laws. They have men employed whose business it is to see
to it that no railroad which serves as carrier for their
products shall employ any man who desires even remotely
to exercise his rights of citizenship when those rights seem
to interfere with what the brewers consider a higher right
—their own private profit. Not only do they demand this,
which is a small matter, but they are able to enforce their
demands upon the railroads, which is by no means a small
matter. How any self-respecting railway superintendent
can write such a letter as the above is to me incomprehensible. The fact is, that letter is not self-respecting. It is the
abrogation of self-respect. It is the admission of a slavery
so abject that many a man would rather resign any salary
that any railroad could give him rather than sign his
name to such a letter.

The following is an example of another sort of railway
official:

The *Wine and Spirit Gazette* of New York publishes the following,
to which we call the attention of the brewers and jobbers who ship
goods to their customers by rail:

"The —— Railroad Company is enforcing most rigorously its new
rule forbidding its employees from indulging in wine, liquor, or beer.
It has a strong force of detectives employed watching the men, and
resorts to every artifice to catch them drinking. One young engineer
who was hauled over the coals protested his innocence and insisted
that he never drank. Thereupon a photograph was promptly produced showing the young man in the act of drinking a glass of beer.
The kodak had done the business and his head rolled in the basket.
An engineer who notoriously never touches liquor of any kind was
discharged for not reporting a subordinate who did. This is carrying
the business rather beyond the bounds of legitimacy. A company
may properly demand strict sobriety from its employees while on
duty, but it certainly has no right to interfere with them other times.
[Indeed!] Employees are not slaves!"

We have reason to know that the —— Railroad Company has no
use for papers published in the interest of the liquor trade, but freely
issues editorial passes to the prohibition papers in exchange for
advertising space. "A word to the wise."

The above slip was sent by a certain paper published in
the interests of the liquor traffic, to a prominent official of
the railroad named, accompanied by a threat to publish it
unless advertisements and passes were forthcoming. The
railroad official paid no attention to the communication;
which course seems to me infinitely more dignified and
worthy of the high position of the general manager of a
great railroad than the letter which stands at the head of
this article, with its shameful subserviency to the impudent
·dictation of the liquor traffic.

It is quite easy to understand that the business temptation

is great where hundreds of thousands of dollars in freight are the basis of the correspondence. In other words, all rights of American citizenship and self-respecting manhood are subject to the demands of business success. This is the generic principle. The specific result in this case is that business success in its turn is absolutely subject to the liquor interest.

It is no wonder that Mr. Roosevelt felt called upon to publish the statement that he was not deceived in his work in New York City into thinking that he was fighting somebody who wanted his beer on Sunday or the keeper of some seven-by-nine saloon who wanted to sell a few glasses more for what profit there was in it. He said:

> [Our opponents] know that we are fighting the richest and power-fulest organization that there is in this city; that this is an organization which has much money in its control and which will spend its money as freely as it can to defeat the effort to secure an honest government. I refer to the brewery influences. We are fighting them. You will understand that we have opposed to us the corrupting power of wealth.

So this series of facts, like most other social and industrial and trade matters in America, leads back to one root question: whether, whatever our fundamental intentions may be and however little doubt there is concerning the ultimate outcome, we are at present building chiefly a democracy or a plutocracy.

THE TELEGRAPH MONOPOLY.

BY PROF. FRANK PARSONS.

IV.

EVILS OF THE PRESENT SYSTEM (*continued*).

The sixth count in the indictment of the present telegraphic system in America, is the *illtreatment of employees,* and a general *abuse of the employing power,*—child-labor, overworked operators, long hours and small pay for those who do most of the work, short hours and big pay for those who manage and scheme, less wages to women than to men for the same work, favoritism and unjust distinctions between men in the same service, a settled policy of reducing wages and increasing work, denial of the right of petition, the right of organization, and the right to consideration because of long and faithful service, fraud, oppression, merciless discharge, blacklisting, boycotting, breaking agreements, treating men as commodities to be bought at the lowest market price and thrown away like a sucked orange as soon as the company has squeezed the profit out of their lives,—such are the items, or some of the items, under this vital count.

The employment of thousands of little boys twelve to sixteen years old is a very serious wrong. These children ought to be in school, not in the street. One of the best things about public business is that it does not impose the burdens of toil upon childhood. In the postoffice the carriers are men, not boys. There is no better measure of the difference in the spirit of national enterprise, and the spirit of a great private corporation, than is to be found in the contrast between the fine looking men who act as messengers for Uncle Sam 8 hours a day on salaries of $600, $800, and $1000 a year, and the little mind-starved, opportunity-cheated boys that act as messengers for the telegraph companies 10 to 16 hours a day on salaries of $2 or $3 a week.

The work of a telegraph operator is very exhausting.[1] He suffers from close confinement, cramped position, strenuous attention, and rapid work of brain and arm. President

---

[1] Testimony of operators, Blair Com. of the U. S. Senate, vol. 1, pp. 116, 125, 157, 193.

Orton of the Western Union testified that no operator should perform more than 6 hours' work per day.[2] Yet as a matter of fact the majority of operators are on duty from 12 to 13 hours,[3] and the day is often much longer than that. Victor Rosewater, himself an operator for many years, and for several years manager of the Western Union Telegraph Company at Omaha, told the Bingham Committee in 1890 that "At railroad stations 16 hours a day is a short day's work. I have worked 18 hours a day."[4] Hon. John Davis after telling the Henderson Committee in 1894 about the overworking of railway engineers[5] continued his testimony as follows:

"Telegraph operators, who, as you know, control the running of trains, are also overworked, and they are not competent for duty after a great loss of sleep. One train despatcher said that he sometimes had to work 20 hours a day, but sometimes found himself obliged to take some sleep in the meantime, though he made it as short as he dared."[6]

Worst of all, the *aim* of the companies is not to lighten the burdens of their workers but to increase them. The victory of the Western Union in the great strike of '83 gave the managers an opportunity for rearrangement which they improved to such purpose that Dr. Green, the president, is reported as saying:

"The several hundreds of thousands of dollars which have been lost in the strike I regard as the best financial investment made by the company. Hereafter General Eckert tells me that he will get one-third more work out of a man for a day's service, and the economy of such a step will retrieve the loss in less than six months."[7]

One-third more work in a day, though the men were already suffering from overwork, and paralysis, consump-

---

[2] Id., 125.

[3] Id., 119, 156. In the large city offices nine or ten hours constitute a day's work, but elsewhere the day is from 12 hours up, and even in the city operators are not seldom obliged to work 13 and 14 hours a day (p. 150).

[4] Bingham Rep., Rosewater, p. 6.

[5] I. T. U. Hearings, p. 59. The testimony about the engineers is so pertinent to the present subject of corporation ill treatment of employees that it seems well to give it in condensed form. Mr. Davis said that in many cases " Railroad engineers are worked 48 hours at a time without sleep"; also that "engineers have frequently told me that they have put tobacco in their eyes to keep themselves awake," and are sometimes obliged to leave the engine in charge of the fireman to get an hour's sleep, although it is dangerous to trust the fireman because his eyes are apt to be dazzled by the fire he has been replenishing at night, so that he cannot see well ahead for half an hour afterward and sometimes for several hours afterward.

[6] Ibid.

[7] Wanamaker's Argument, etc., p. 221.

tion, early disability, and death were common among them.[8] Even Dr. Green admitted that "there are some instances where the operators work very hard,"[9] and the operators themselves declared that " The Western Union has always been short of help, and it generally makes one man do the work of a man and a half."[10] And this is the way the Western Union succeeds in sending more messages per employee than is the case in England or Germany.

The systematic overworking of employees was one cause of the great strike of '83 in which the telegraphers demanded that 8 hours should constitute a day's work and 7 hours a night's work—very moderate demands in the light of the sworn testimony of President Orton and the uncontroverted statements of the men themselves,—but instead of less work they got more—"one-third more work out of a man for a day's service," Dr. Green said.

The dangers of this cruel system, not only to the operator but to the public, are well illustrated by the case of George Welsh, a young man of seventeen years who was telegraph operator at Plainfield, Conn., in 1892. On the 9th of July, after he had been on duty all day from 6 A. M. till 5 P. M., he received a train order to hold a passenger train, and immediately after receiving the order, he was "called up" by the chief operator at another station, who sent him a message ordering him to report at a neighboring town as soon as he was off duty at Plainfield, remain there on duty all night, and then to report back at Plainfield in the morning and remain there all day. The result was that the boy

---

[8] Blair Sen. Com., vol. 1, p. 193, operator's paralysis; p. 125, consumption. "The operators are frequently carried off by consumption, generally caused by close confinement and the positions they have to take while at their work. Owing to the peculiar nature of the business, drawing the attention of the mind to the instrument, and the rapid rate at which the sounds have to be distinguished and transcribed on paper, and owing also to the position a man must assume, sitting steadily and writing all day, the ordinary and proper exercise of the respiratory organs is prevented; and as a matter of fact you will find that when a man is what we call being 'rushed' he hardly breathes at all — respiration almost ceases " (testimony of J. S. McClelland).

Q.—What is the character of their work [operators] in respect to its exactions on the physical frame?
A.—It is very exhausting work. There are very few old men in the telegraph business.
Q.—Do you mean that the telegrapher dies young?
A.—Yes, sir; either he dies young, or he is compelled to quit the business in order to save his health. (Testimony of John Campbell, masterworkman of Brotherhood of Telegraphers. Blair vol. 1, p. 116.)

[9] Blair, vol. 1, p. 892.
[10] Ibid., p. 230.

mishandled the signals and a collision occurred which caused the death of three persons.[11]

While the Western Union is liberal in bestowing hours and burdens upon its employees it is very illiberal in the matter of wages. A few telegraph operators are well paid, but "nine-tenths of the operators employed by the Western Union are paid from $15 to $40 a month, and many educated, intelligent men, thorough in their profession, are being paid $50 a month."[12] President Green testified that the average salary of operators was $71.56 for men, and $36.75 for women, or a total average of $62 to $65.[13] But his estimates were made up from the New York offices alone (as clearly appears in the tables he gave the Bingham Committee), and his figures were reduced to the absurd on cross-examination as we have already seen.[14] The operators themselves testified that the average pay of operators even in the main office of the company was only $57;[15] that many operators employed in commercial telegraphing receive only $30, $35, $40, or $50 a month;[16] that for commercial operators, including the whole range, well-paid men and all, the average pay would not exceed $54, and for railroad operators $39;[17] that women get 35 to 40 per cent less than men for the same work;[18] that the company pursued a systematic policy of reducing wages by filling positions vacated by death, resignation, transfer, or discharge with new men at salaries $5 or $10 below the pay of the former occupants;[19] that the reduction had amounted to 40 per cent from 1870 to 1883;[20] that it had gone so far as to reduce the salaries of first-class operators in Chicago to $50 a month;[21] and that all the while the hours of labor were increasing, and the profits of the company growing larger. Senator Blair, the chairman of the Committee on Education and Labor, summed up the evidence in these words:

---

[11] Blair Sen. Com., vol. 1, p. 173.

[12] Wanamaker's Arg., p. 141.

[13] Bingham Com., p. 59; Blair Com., vol 1, p. 908.

[14] Note 5 to part II above.

[15] Testimony of John B. Taltawall, operator and editor of the *Telegraphers' Advocate.* Blair Com., vol. 1, p. 171.

[16] Blair Com., vol. 1, p. 103.

[17] Ibid., pp. 103, 192.

[18] Ibid., p. 116.

[19] Ibid., pp. 103, 125, 225.

[20] Ibid., pp. 103, 171.

[21] Ibid., p. 226.

"The operators who came here and testified, almost universally stated that for a long series of years there had been a constant reduction of salaries going on, and this while their efficiency was increasing and their hours of labor in many instances were also increasing, and more money was being made by the company."[29]

Such was the situation in 1883 when the men struck for 15 per cent increase of pay, no salary less than $50, the same pay for women as for men, and 8 hours for a day's work,—moderate demands, very, but the company did not accede to them. It would cost a million dollars or more, the managers said, and the company could not afford it. Poor company, only making 120 to 150 per cent on its investment; it could not afford to yield the men one-sixth of the profits the men produced. When you have read the following list of poverty-stricken individuals who constituted the board of directors of the Western Union and its chief owners, you will see why the company could not afford to pay fair wages to its men:

Jay Gould	William W. Astor	C. P. Huntington
Russell Sage	J. P. Morgan	John T. Terry
Fred L. Ames	P. R. Pyne	Cyrus W. Field
Sidney Dillon	Chauncey M. Depew	John Vanhorne
Thomas T. Eckert	George J. Gould	A. B. Cornell
Dr. Norvin Green	Edwin Gould	Robert C. Clowry
Samuel Sloan	Charles Lanier	Henry Weaver
George B. Roberts	Austin Corbin	William D. Bishop
Sidney Shepard	John G. Moore	James W. Clendenin
Erastus Wiman	Henry M. Flagler	John Hay

Mr. Thurber used this list in 1890 to answer the question why the public cannot have a postal telegraph, and it is an equally conclusive answer to the question why the men could not have moderate hours and reasonable wages. Every name represents some great interest—railway presidents, bankers, stockbrokers, millionaires by the ton; and you know a dollar is of much more importance to a millionaire than it is to a workingman. Gould, Sage, Astor, or any one of several others in the list could have given the men all they asked out of his own private income and never missed it if he had been of the ordinary mould of man, but being a millionaire the chances are it would have broken his heart. Some of the directors are fair-minded men perhaps, but the ruling spirits are wholly unfit to be trusted as employers with the mastery and management of human beings. More than two-thirds of them (all but the last nine) are on the *Tribune's* millionaire lists for the cities of New

---

[29] Blair Com., vol. 1, p. 892.

York, Boston, and Philadelphia, a number of them having fortunes of ten, twenty, thirty, fifty, even a hundred millions, and probably there are very few if any in the entire board so poor as to have but a single million; yet these men, or the majority at least, were willing to grow richer on the labor of men and women and boys and girls, receiving in many cases $8, $12, $20, $40 a month, and working often 12 to 16 or even 18 hours a day. A thousand dollars or the fair value of an average year of labor, put into Western Union stock in 1858 has brought its owner $3,000 a year ever since, or $114,000, and the investment is as good to-day as ever; but an operator who puts in a year of work on the wires gets on an average $500 for it and that is the end of it; if he wants any more he must work some more. The contrast between the results of a year's work put into capital by the employer and a year's work done by the employee is terrific. If the board were of a generous temper toward the people who earn their income for them or even the subjects of a just and righteous conscience, the dividends of the Western Union torn from the labor of overworked and underpaid employees would have burned a hole in their pockets and dropped back among the workers.

On the profiting-sharing principle of the Le Claire shops the men should have had 3½ millions of the 7 millions profit, and on the full coöperative or partnership principle the workers should have received over 5 of the 7 millions; but the company does not know anything about the principles of partnership or profit-sharing, it knows only of profit-getting.

After the strike—and the committee had listened to months of testimony about it—Senator Blair said to President Green:

"I have the impression very strongly that you could afford to give your operators more money, and now that you have got your own way about it I wish you would just come up and give those boys more money."[23]

In 1890, however, the evidence was that the average pay of telegraph operators was $40 to $45 a month,[24] that girls were employed in some instances as low as $12 to $15 a month,[25] and quite a number were paid no more than $20

---

[23] Blair Com., vol. 1, p. 891.

[24] Bingham Com., p. 30, testimony of A. B. Chandler, president of the Postal Tel. Co., and of D. H. Bates, formerly acting vice-president and assistant general manager of the Western Union, manager of the Baltimore & Oh. Tel. Co., etc.

[25] Bingham Com., pp. 30, 85, statements of Chairman Bingham, and of Mr. Beaumont citing reports of the Labor Bureau.

to $35,[26] while the president of the company drew a salary estimated at twenty-five to fifty thousand dollars.[27]

As a rule operators do not receive enough to enable them to marry[28] or to lay up anything for a rainy day[29]—they have little need to provide for old age if they stay in the business.

If the men apply for increase of compensation "the testimony is that universally, without a single exception, those applications (whether made by one individual or bodies of individuals) have been ignored.[30] The only notice the Western Union takes of petitions is to "spot" the leaders, discharge them, and blacklist them to prevent their obtaining employment elsewhere.

"Anything in the shape of getting up petitions for increase of pay has resulted disastrously to the ringleaders. They have either been dismissed from the service or discriminated against in many ways. Their names are placed on the black-list and managers all over the country are notified of it. When they apply for situations the managers tell them that they are on the black-list."[31]

A company that denies the right of petition, denies of course, with still greater emphasis the right of organization. It has repeatedly discharged and blacklisted men for joining the Brotherhood of Telegraphers and for activity in organizing their fellow workers.[32] This is the continuous

---

[26] Bingham Com., p. 30, statement of Mr. A. B. Chandler.

[27] On p. 84, Bingham Rep., Mr. Beaumont spoke of " the $50,000 salary of the president of the Western Union." Mr. Crain: "Is that his salary?" Mr. Beaumont: "There are some things a man knows that he cannot swear to. This is one of those cases." On p. 56 Mr. Anderson is reported as saying, "The salary of the postmaster-general is $8,000 a year, while it is generally known that the salary of the president of the Western Union is several times greater." To which President Green replied, "What matters $50,000 for executive salaries on 54,000,000 of messages?" Slight matter—only a matter of justice between man and man—insignificant indeed to the Western Union.

[28] Blair Com., vol. 1, p. 144. Those who do get married generally have to get something outside the regular work in order to obtain a comfortable living for their families (pp. 150, 194).

[29] Ibid., p. 152. Not 1 in a hundred accumulates anything. See also p. 192 as follows:

Q.—Excluding from the question men whose failure to save can be attributed to bad habits, I want to know what chance there is for a reasonably prudent and economical man to save a little money in the business of a telegraph operator?

A.—Well, there might be some chance for a man to do that if he cared to work 15 hours a day—that is, for a single man, but if he was a married man, or had a father or a mother or a sister or some other person dependent on him, it would be simply impossible for him to lay up anything without working extra hours.

[30] Ibid., p. 892, the words of the chairman, Senator Blair.

[31] Blair Com., vol. 1, pp. 113-115.

[32] Blair Com., vol. 1, pp. 115, 180. There is no doubt about the cause of discharge for it was distinctly avowed by the officers of the company to be as stated in the text,

policy of the company. It acted in this way long before the great strike of 1883. Nevertheless the men succeeded in organizing in secret, and finally sent a representative committee to confer with the officers of the company about the grievances of the men. The insulting treatment accorded this committee and the utter refusal to recognize any right of combination on the part of the men, was the main immediate cause of the strike.[33] When the strike was over the company refused to take the men back again except upon condition of signing an agreement not to belong to any organization that claimed to control their services or salaries as against the company,[34] which of course would uproot the Brotherhood or reduce it to impotence if the men regarded their contracts—which, however, they are not in the habit of doing in such cases. They sign an agreement not to belong to a trade union and the next day renew their allegiance to their fellow workmen. Thus does corporate oppression beget faithlessness in employees,—and it is hard to blame the men for ignoring the outrageous compact to forfeit their freedom and manhood which they are compelled by their necessities to sign. You cannot make a workingman see that it is all wrong for two or more telegraph operators to combine to secure fair pay and reasonable hours and yet perfectly right for two or more telegraph companies to combine to squeeze their employees and fleece the public—it takes a corporation official or a *laissez-faire* philosopher to see that.

The company does not hesitate to break its faith with employees if it suits its convenience, as in the case of the English operators who came to introduce the Wheatstone system on some of the Western Union lines, and were subjected to great annoyance and loss through the broken promises of Western Union officials.[35]

It is part of the policy of the company to prevent its men from securing employment in other places at better pay. Sometimes a man has travelled a long distance on the promise of $10 or $20 increase of salary, only to find at his

---

and no other cause was named; that was the sole cause, and in some instances the men were informed in plain English that they would be blacklisted. In a number of instances the witnesses make their testimony specific by giving the names of men discharged and blacklisted for connection with the Brotherhood.

[33] Blair Com., vol. 1, p. 122.

[34] President Green's testimony, Blair, vol. 1, pp. 896-7. After the great strike of 1870, the company took back some of the strikers on condition of their taking what was called the "iron-clad oath"—an oath to renounce their union and never again connect themselves with any similar organization. Blair Com., vol. 1, pp. 153, 199.

[35] Blair, vol. 1, pp. 157-8.

journey's end that Western Union influence had preceded him and shattered the promise.[36]

The meanness of the company is at times astonishing even to a student of corporation history. The Stager episode is an example. During the war General Stager was general superintendent of the Western Union and commander-in-chief of the military lines of the United States at the same time. Well, the salary of Anson Stager as colonel and assistant quartermaster and chief of the United States military telegraph corps was turned over to the Western Union, and he never got a cent of his salary as an army officer.[37]

There is very little chance of working up to a position of moderate work and reasonable income. Length of service is not taken into account.

"I asked my manager if length of service was taken into consideration in fixing a man's pay. He said, No; that that had no bearing on the question whatever, because there was always a new element growing up that could be engaged probably at less rates of pay than the old operators were getting" (Blair, vol. 1, p. 134); and again on p. 125 where a manager was asked "What encouragement there was for a man to remain steady and reliable and faithful to his duties," the answer was: "None whatever. If you get tired of this position we can fill it with another man at lower pay."

Favoritism and greed appear to be the factors that fix wages. The manager of another company testified that he had had daily applications from first-class operators in the Western Union who were working by the side of others no better in any way and doing the same work and who nevertheless received $10 to $15 a month less than the last named operators for no discoverable reason.[38]

"Favoritism seems to be one of the rules of the office. We know, as a fact, that sometimes the men who get the low salaries are capable of doing better work than those who get the large salaries." [39] Another witness said: "I saw that I was not receiving the wages due me in the position that I filled, and that on account of the drunkenness and imbecility of the man who was my superior I had his duties to perform as well as my own; and so as there was no probability of my ever getting any more wages, I left the company on short notice. I have been able to earn a living with opposition companies, but every absorption that has been made by the Western Union Company has resulted in a decrease of wages" (Blair, 228); and again (p. 231), "In the employ of the Western Union there is no hope whatever of promotion; that is, on a man's merits."[40]

[36] Ibid., p. 227.

[37] Bingham Com., testimony of Rosewater, an intimate friend of the general's.

[38] Blair, vol. 1, p. 231.

[39] Blair, vol. 1, p. 127, testimony J. S. McClelland.

[40] Testimony of A. H. Seymour, manager of the Mutual Union, and formerly with the Western Union.

No wonder John Wanamaker found that "One-third of all the telegraph operators are continually preparing themselves for other professions, and that the other two-thirds are continually thinking of doing so."[41] No wonder, either, that thoughtful operators universally favor national ownership of the telegraph.[42] The contrast of the telegraph service with the national postal service is indeed a striking one.

	TELEGRAPH OPERATORS.	POSTAL CARRIERS.	RAILWAY MAIL CLERKS.
Average pay per month .	$40 to $50.	$75.	$84.
Average hours	9 to 16.	8.	8.*
Promotion	For merit, rare.	For merit the rule.	
Length of Service	Not recognized as giving any claims to increase of pay, or continuance in employ.	Clearly recognized as giving a valid title to increase of pay, retention, and preferment.	
Tenure	Precarious,— dependent on individual whim and arbitrary power of an irresponsible superior.	" Freedom from removal except for inefficiency, crime, or misconduct."[44]	
Rights of petition, organization, etc.	Denied.	Accorded.	

* The daily train run of a railway postal clerk is 4 to 6 hours. (Postmaster-General's Rep., 1892, p. 523 *et seq.*), but the clerk is obliged to devote some further time to making reports, checking records, preparing supplies for the following trip, etc. In some cases the increase of correspondence has thrown an undue burden on some of the clerks, and then we find the postmaster-general doing all in his power to lighten their labors and increase their pay (Rep. 1892, pp. 501, 511-512, and 1894, pp. 391-2)—a line of conduct diametrically opposite to that pursued by Western Union managers. The facts as to wages of carriers and clerks are taken from the Postmaster-General's Reports, 1892, p. 815, and 1894, p. 407. A carrier receives $600 the first year, $800 the second year, and $1,000 the third. Between four and five thousand of the seven thousand railway clerks receive $1,000 to $1,400 each, and fifteen hundred more receive $900 each. The contrast with the telegraph becomes still more pronounced when we remember that the bottom round for a carrier or railway clerk in regular employment is $50 a month, while the telegraph bottom is not reached till you get to $12 or lower still if anybody could be found to work for less. The postoffice does not seek to buy labor at auction, but aims to pay as much as it reasonably can, regardless of the price of labor at forced sale in the markets of competition. The Western Union, on the contrary, aims to pay the least possible, makes the forced sale its standard, and takes a hand itself in depressing the rate by systematic and persistent reduction.

** Statement of Postmaster-General John Wanamaker, 1892 Rep. p. 501, not merely as the aim, but as the actual condition of the railway mail service, a condition which

[41] Wanamaker's Arg., p. 11; see also Blair, vol. 1, p. 227.

[42] Blair, vol. 2, p. 410, testimony of R. J. Hinton. " I have never found a working operator anywhere who has not been in favor (if he has thought at all of the question) of a government service instead of a private service."

had produced great improvement in the service. Postmaster-General Bissell, 1894 Rep., p. 395, says, "The civil service laws and regulations as applied to the Railway Mail Service accomplish all the most sanguine expected," and goes on to speak in the highest terms of the fine quality of appointments, the high efficiency, the permanence of employment, and the promotion for mei t, secured under the civil service rules.

It may be said that if the clerks in the fourth-class postoffices had been chosen for comparison the contrast as to tenure, hours, wages, etc., would not have been so strong in favor of public employment. The truth is, however, that the clerks in the fourth-class postoffices are not public employees. They are private employees doing public work. Uncle Sam lets out the fourth-class offices on contract and the postmasters hire their own help. The fourth-class offices are neither classified under the civil service nor nationalized. They are simply bits of private enterprise banded together to do a part of the nation's work under contract, and the clerks are no more public employees than the brakemen and conductors on the railroads that carry the mail under contract with the nation The postoffice has not yet applied its own principles to the whole of its own service. But it is moving in that direction and it is better to have good principles not fully carried out, than bad principles thoroughly carried out,—better to aim at heaven and take some years to get there, than to aim at h—l and get there right away.

The contrast with the telegraph service abroad is scarcely less marked than the contrast with the classified postal service here. In Great Britian appointments are made throughout the postal service by competitive examination, promotion is by merit, length of service increases pay, permanence of employment is assured during good behavior and efficiency, and provision is made in case of sickness, disability and old age.[43] After ten years' service the employee is entitled to a pension of $^1/_6$ of the salary and emoluments he was receiving; after twenty years the pension is $\frac{1}{3}$; after thirty years $\frac{1}{2}$; and after 40 years $\frac{2}{3}$ of the salary.[44] The hours of labor are 8 per day and 7 per night for six days in the week, all Sunday work being counted overtime. The salary of a first-class operator is $950 a year, or about $80 a month.[45] The most significant fact of all is the contrast between the *aims* of the telegraph management here and in England. Here the policy is reduction of wages as the business grows, so that the proportion of income

[43] Blair Com , vol. 1, p. 167. After 3 years' service an employee receives half pay during temporary sickness.

[44] Eleventh Rep. of U. S. Civil Service Commission, 1895, pp. 328-44. In Canada the pensions are larger still — one fiftieth for each year of service instead of one sixtieth as in England. For chief clerks the minimum salary is $1,800 which is increased annually by $50 up to $2,400. For second-class clerks the minimum is $1,100 increasing annually by $50 to $1,400, and for third-class clerks the minimum is $400 increasing annually by $50 up to $1,000. Women are employed in Canada on the same terms and conditions as men, but in England and most of the colonies their pay is slightly less being ⅔ to ⅞ of the pay of men in the same grade of service.

[45] Eng. P.-M. Genl.'s Rep., 1895, pp. 7, 11. The English operators who testified before the Blair Committee, said that a first-class operator received less pay in England than in America, but considering rents and prices as well as wages the English operator was better off than his American brother financially as well as every other way (Blair, vol. 1, pp. 165-6). The salaries of operators in England have risen since the years referred to by these witnesses.

that goes to labor is continually shrinking; there the policy is to raise the wage level, so that an ever-increasing proportion of the income shall go to labor. In 1870, only 39 per cent of the telegraph revenue went to labor; in 1880, 44%: in 1885, 52½%; in 1890, 58½%; in 1895, 72%.. The following table taken from Mr. Morley's returns to the House of Commons will show in greater detail the recent results of this admirable policy of the British postal management.

Year.	Percentage of Telegraph Salaries to Telegraph Revenue.
1870	39.13
1880	44.02
1885	52.64
1890	58.47
1891	61.30
1892	64.23
1893	67.96
1894	69.96
1895	72.18

During this period the revenue has risen from 4 millions to 13 millions a year, so that labor receives nearly 6 times as much as in 1870. The efficiency of employees—the amount of business per worker has of late years increased in a marked degree, and since '85 there has been no change of tariff, so that the increased percentage of revenue going to labor means a very decided addition to individual salaries.[46]

In France, as we have seen,[47] the average wage of telegraph employees has been for a long time above the average here even on the Western Union's own data. The French civil service is spoken of in the highest terms. It secures "perpetuity of tenure," "guarantees a constantly improving livelihood and in case of accident, provision for the families of employees," pensions as in England, and promotion for merit.[48] The great republic shows the breadth and sincerity of her belief in liberty and equality by paying women in the public service the same wages as men for the same class of work.[49]

---

[46] As a rule the salaries of telegraphers in England have been raised $150 to $200 each since 1881, and the hours have been shortened one-seventh (41st Rep. of the Eng. P.-M. Genl., 1895, pp. 6, 7, 11). This is fine, but the English public service is open to criticism in respect to its failure to recognize the full equality of women, and its employment of boys from 15 to 17 years of age.

[47] Notes 5 to 8 inclusive, part II above.

[48] Eleventh Rep. of the U. S. Civil Service Commission, pp. 354-8. Fraud or corruption of any kind is almost unknown in the public service (p. 355).

[49] Ibid., p. 358.

In respect to the contrast between our telegraph system and that of Germany under this head of the interests of employees, I cannot do better than to quote the pregnant words of Professor Ely who has studied the German system in its home:

"Experienced and tried men, with comparatively short hours, are employed in Germany, while in the telegraph offices of this country one finds very young lads, and they are frequently overworked. The fact that so few mature men are found among them shows that they have no secure tenure of office and no permanent employment. *One young generation of telegraph operators gives way to another.* They are employed frequently in dark, dingy and ill-kept rooms. The contrast with the class of operators employed in a country like Germany and the neat and attractive offices found in that country is painful, and it is really a disgrace to our own country."[80]

The italics are mine. I underlined that sentence because it touches a truth of tremendous import. "One young generation of telegraph operators gives way to another." Do you know why? Do you understand the meaning of that fact? Think back over the evidence collected in this article, and you will see what it means. It means that the telegraph system in America is a great press in which the youth and energy and life of thousands of men and women are coined into gold for industrial aristocrats. It means that as each new generation comes along, the telegraph management takes as large a portion of it as may be wished, puts it into the great press, rapidly squeezes the youth and freshness and beauty out of it, the best years, too often all the years, out of it, throws it away as a cider maker rejects the juiceless pulp, and turns to replace it with new victims, rosy, plump, and hearty, from another unsuspecting generation. It means that a colossal business is conducted in the interests of a few capitalists regardless of the welfare of the multitudes who do the actual work. It means the oppression of labor, the overworking of employees, the appropriation by the master of all they produce beyond a bare subsistence—the methods that slaveholders always follow, with the added viciousness of caring nothing for the life or health of the slaves because it costs the master nothing to replace them. Such is the meaning of our telegraph system on its working side—a perennial theft of youth and years, a systematic robbery of toil,—a meaning that ought to enlist every lover of manhood and justice in the cause of a National Telegraph.

(To be continued.)

---

[80] The ARENA, December, '95, p. 51.

PLANETARY FREEBOOTING AND WORLD POLICIES.

BY RICHARD J. HINTON

Great races have been great robbers, our own being no exception. Indeed, the Anglo-Saxon has been the champion bandit of the later centuries. Men shrug their shoulders and remark, "What has been will be." Rapine and robbery have marked the conflicts and indicated the catastrophes of all civilization. The martyrdom of Man has been an unceasing procession of horrors. Is there never to be a period of transfiguration—a lifting and remoulding of environment? Certainly there is not much now to indicate such changes, except that altrurian "cranks" are bolder and perhaps more numerous. Otherwise the horrors of Islamism, the reddened glare of past Roman marches, or the blackened embers of Spanish cruelty, with the grasping greed of Anglo-British statesmen and plunderers, fade into petty larceny and sneak thievery by the side and in the presence of the current planetary freebootage. That which is being planned seems likely to outrival for audacity in purpose and immorality in methods, the boldest dreams of conquering devastation that made drunken with blood and brutality, the mad ambition of an Alexander and the overpowering brigandage of a Napoleon!

The planetary robbery of our period fully befits the processes of the plutocratic policy that dictates its chief features. In the name of their god, Trade, John Bull and Herr Von Junker seize upon the larger part of the Dark Continent. Under the fasces of a republic, Chauvinism has been skilfully directed by the statesmanship of stockbrokerage, into avenues of plunder and channels of cheatery. France has stolen right and left in Asia, Africa, and the Indian Ocean. Everywhere, too, the temple has been made the plunderer's bazaar. The altar has sometimes served for a bargain counter, and its priests and missionaries have been efficient advance agents for Maxim guns and magazine rifles.

But John Bull, once the boldest of brigands, is now a

pattering fence playing the part of Fagin and seeking mainly to protect the plunder of the past. The Venezuelan braggadocio of Chamberlain and the Salisbury hectoring of the Turk on behalf of the Armenians, is part of the game to protect the East and hold Egypt. The Nemesis waits upon the "road to India!" Africa is used for a safety valve. The danger at home is in the discontent of those whom privilege steadily disinherits. Better for her that younger sons should be land marauders and mine robbers, against Kaffir and Boer, than remain at home to be Fabianized into socialism.

The German is a good trader, but a clumsy as well as brutal colonist.

France revels in buccaneering riot, bridling the dangerous temper by the discretion gained at Sedan and enforced in Paris. But this combination is fast making of her a fit ally of the crowned white terror, a servile serf to the bastard Byzantine pontiff and potentate whose ambition stretches dripping hands across two continents to find without open war the seat of a world's empire upon the shores of the Golden Horn, and the armed control of the planet's mid-oceanic waters!

Modern Russia is the most desperate and dangerous, then, of our planetary brigands. Her trumpets proclaim to European civilization the coming of Armageddon. She is strong enough to wait, and therein lies the secret of her terrible portents. Napoleon's prophecy, though belated, of Cossack or Republican, yet bids fair to become the living actuality. There is only one safe road out for Europe, and that is by way of a democracy founded on social equity, honest economics, and political justice. It must be moulded into a strong federation of republican states. It may be sooner than we now expect. The unexpected happens; the unforeseen often lifts the curtain of time. The womb of Russian statecraft is quickened by the desire to control the Asiatic Mongol and Turanian hordes and use them for its own purposes. It is a favorite sophism of the resplendent sciolists who seek to shape opinion through the press, to write of the northern empire as part of and not a menace to civilization and of its rulers as the protectors of peace. What Russia plays for is delay. What she proposes to achieve thereby is the control of continental Asia, free access to the sea by the Persian Gulf and the Pacific Ocean, thus flanking Great Britain, France (if need be), Spain, and Holland, in all their conquered realms in peninsular and island Asia. Constantinople can even wait for the completion of the Siberian railroad. The Mediterranean will readily become a Russian sea, and Asia Minor will pass under the control of a Greek Catholic pope.

With China in its toils, the Asiatic steppes and ranges for the almost unknown (to Europe) fields of organizing activity, it is within the range of possibility by the closing dates of the nineteenth century that we shall hear the movements of armies vaster than those of Cyrus or Tamerlane, rushed by steam, directed by electricity, equipped with guns carrying high explosives, and armed with magazine rifles that slay at long range. The patience of the Slavonian peasant and the fatalistic endurance of the Asiatic nomad, will be trained into machines with German drill and precision, while led as furies of slaughter and overthrow by the successors of Ghourko and Skoboleff. The Greek presbyter who taught Alexander III and controls Nicholas the Second, spins a powerful web for the enmeshment of the world's forces. The bomb that destroyed Alexander II created a new situation. The Treaty of Stefano and the Berlin Congress made imperative the new Byzantium propaganda, a strange and powerful policy of dissimulation and waiting. The Pope Sixtus of Russia sat behind the tutors and now fills the administrative desk of its orthodox church. Statecraft for ten years past has been directed to the gaining of time. All energies have been assiduously preparing for opportunity. Modern Europe knows less of Russian resources in men and money, in productiveness and staying force, to-day than it did when British and French guns thundered around Sebastopol. Opinion is in slavery. Intelligence seems broken and defeated. In religion and knowledge the fourteenth century and not the nineteenth rules in European Russia. The spirit of the Inquisition is enthroned. The only political church now existing as such, will have its apotheosis when the young czar is crowned in the Basilica of Moscow.

The revolution seems dead. Tolstoi alone, talks and—makes "shoes"! The leaders of nihilism are scattered. They have apparently no foothold at home. They have become, says Stepniak, "teachers of Europe." If so their lessons are meagre and show that the fountain of information is drying up. Are they ignorant or have pan Slavonian myths taken control, even of them? The world gets little evidence from that source, of the iron hand on the Russian Jew or protesting sectary. They tell little of the material progress making in Asia, or of the lax dealing with pagan and Mussulman by the same wily brain that drives the Jew to emigration and persecutes the Slavonian heterodox into silence, exile, or imprisonment and poverty. They do not tell us of the enormous wealth created for the secret treasury of the imperial household and diverted from the open doors of the public exchequer to the direct and unrestrained control of the czar himself.

The problems of planetary freebooting and the politics thereof, have been craftily shifted from the Golden Horn to the Yellow Sea. Only for the fanatical folly and frenzy of the Turk it would have continued unbroken on that line. But if Russia can make a catspaw of Armenia, she will not fail to sacrifice the Armenians to even Kurdish barbarism. "No war" is the checkmate she plays, at present. The Mediterranean of the near future is the Pacific Ocean, and she aims, as the Romans did, to be its ruler. British India may be the Carthage, Japan the Greece and Macedonia, and China the Egypt of the mighty struggle that impends. The greatest of modern Russians, Alexander Herven, who in 1861, proclaimed in the *Kolo-Kol* (The Bell)—his London revolutionary organ—the emancipation of the Russian serfs or the destruction of the empire, gave to the Pacific the historical title I have mentioned. Herven, who was a political seer, declared in a novel published in the early fifties, that a great world-contest was to be fought over an attempt to control the Pacific Ocean in the interest of a Slavonian imperialism. Bismarck and Disraeli both comprehended, each for his own purposes, that the unlocking and controlling of China by Russian efforts, might justify not only the rolling up of the map of Asia from the British standpoint, but that it would tend strongly also to the obliteration of present European lines and influences. All of northern and central Asia in Russian hands, means very much more than an open winter port on the Pacific. The direction of China, be it open or "under the rose," by the czar's agents will prove a Greek chorus the old world over—a dread signal of fate to all who fancied themselves secure.

What is the interest of the United States in such possibilities? Have we no part or parcel with that wonderful island-race whose superb isolation—which, unlike that of their Chinese neighbors, was never stagnation—we broke down? Even on the baldest of needs and for self-protection there must in public opinion as crystallized into formal national expression through the voice of Congress, be given a bold and dignified expression to wise policy and honorable comity. The cheap utterances and hints of a departing Russian diplomat, that fleets can lie in harbors to protect our cities, are to be valued only as the craft of a great despotism, unscrupulously pursuing its purpose of world-control. It is the law of such mighty forces that they rend their satellites when success intoxicates to the full. Are we to be such a satellite? Is there no distinction, internationally speaking, and vital to the life of democracy, between an empire like Russia and a federal republic like the United States? Are there no claims on us because thereof? What position are we to occupy in this world-embracing conflict which approaches so rapidly? Is there not, as represented by our own history, a power in the political ethics we are assumed to embody? The Monroe doctrine is not confined to shores that are washed by the Atlantic alone. In the growth of majestic international tendencies which have gravely and humanely affected the course of nations, during the passing two-thirds of a century, it is not too much to declare that the world owes the larger initiative therein to the American Union. From the Old World much is due to the New. Time waits on the Kibes of Daring. Opportunity swings forever its widening gates.

There is but one course for the United States. It is to maintain the Monroe doctrine of "hands off" from the American continents, and add to it a great international declaration and demand for the *neutralization of both the oceans*. The Atlantic is in many ways approaching the condition of a free world-highway. But, in the immediate interests of civilization and for the permanent security, too, of ourselves and the other American republics abutting upon the greatest of cosmical waters, the American people and government should begin at once to demand the neutralization of the Pacific Ocean. There is no possibility of undoing, if we were to wish it, the continental land-grabbing that characterizes the freebooting records of Great Britain, Russia, and France. But there is the grandest of duties and the broadest of occasions, to express as a matter of national record, our unquenchable hostility to the policy of imperial piracy, which make but a game of bowls of the lives and destinies of Asiatic and Oceanic races and countries.

Let us at least give new warning with simple, honest dignity, of the application of the Monroe doctrine to our western lines as well as our eastern borders. Let us put before the world in the interests of international justice and peace, and of commercial security also, the need of bringing under the rule of a world neutrality, the great ocean whose waters wash the shores whereon over one-half of the human race find their homes. Look with informing imagination at what such control must include, whether it is brought about by a fierce struggle to a single power or a composite control of political freebooters! Look also, for a brief moment, at the rugged conditions found on the lines of population, alone!

On our Western Hemisphere, the republics of Mexico, Guatemala, San Salvador, Costa Rica, Colombia, Bolivia, Ecuador, Peru, and Chili, besides our own Union, are all directly interested, by more or less maritime territory, in a free and neutral Pacific Ocean. That is to say, nations embracing over 90,000,000 of citizens—a population nearly as large as the semi-savage hordes and simple peasantry now ruled by the white czar—are to be left at the mercy of a European freebooter in regard to the future of commerce and the rights of free navigation.

In the purview of this article, the destiny and security of republican polity upon our hemisphere are also involved. Turning southward, the future of those young but superbly promising free commonwealths of Anglo-Saxon birth and conditions, that now arise in youthful majesty in the eastern limits of the South Pacific, are all involved and interblended. They are even now several millions strong, largely moulded from the same sane impulses that have made for these states a continental grandeur. But the issues that play ninepins with the future of 900,000,000 of the world's population are even greater and are not to be drooned over in a fat man's dream of diplomacy.

China has 300,000,000 people. Are they to be manipulated by Russia to be the crushing competitors of all other people's industries? Or shall they be the material for the terrific slaughter which the possible overthrow of Europe and the mastership of the world may demand? Are we to sit by dumbly fishing, while the island empire of Japan with its 40,000,000 people is subordinated to the military ambition of the ruler of 30,000,000 superstitious European peasants and traders and of 80,000,000 semi-nomadic Asiatics? Then, there are the Peninsular and island peoples of the Indian Ocean all facing and feeling the pulsations of the Pacific.

Great Britain alone claims 287,000,000 as its subjects. France has stolen the control of 15,000,000. The Netherlands hold 29,000,000 under a rather mild rule. Spain still flaunts its yellow flag above 9,000,000 on the Philippine and Ladrone islands. The Coreans number 11,000,000. Hawaii, our pledge to oceanic freedom, has but 100,000, while half a million more may possibly be found on the many score islands and archipelagoes of the Pacific Ocean.

Surely, then, the ambitions of the imperial and commercial freebooters who undertake to make over and remould at the nod of a Greek priest in the Winter Palace, by the orders of a council in India, or at the will of gamblers in the Paris Bourse, the destinies of over one-half of the world's people, have some live and alarming interest for a democratic nationality that looks forward in fancied security to see its commerce, white-winged and swift, sail or steam in freedom across the world ocean's paths. We seek no lands to conquer. But will this be true of others when the Russian holds the Pacific as its lake, or when continued conflicts make it red with blood and black with the flame of belching navies? There is only one remedy—one protection! That is, *neutralization in the interests and for the freedom of all!*

TELEPATHY.

BY CHARLES B. NEWCOMB.

The study of telepathy is a study of the tides and currents of mental forces. A knowledge of the laws that govern them would doubtless explain all psychic phenomena. This appears to be the pass key with which we could unlock all mysteries of hypnotism and all forms of mental healing, could understand communication between the seen and the unseen, and explain all the mysterious influences through which human minds dominate each other in the complex relations of life.

May we not fairly claim that the discovery of the *circulation of mind* is the greatest discovery of the nineteenth century, as that of the circulation of the blood was perhaps the greatest of the seventeenth? We are beginning to understand that not only are all men of one blood but that all are of *one mind*—not only that all are of one origin but are also of one destiny. The solidarity of the race is the great lesson of the day. Every human being is a *nerve centre* of humanity, a ganglion of the universal body, and sensitive to all the vibrations of the human system.

Is not then the study of telepathy the study of those subtle forces which telegraph sensation in the individual body between the brain, the organs, and the muscular system? Is it not simply an extended study of nerve force—communication between the *human sensoria* in the larger body? Will not a discovery in one field be found to be a discovery in the other, completing the analysis of the nervous system of the universe?

Science as yet has made us acquainted only with methods, and in all fields of discovery has failed to interpret causes.

We begin our march of progress with coarse tools, but after the work of the sappers and miners has been done, after the spade has turned up the earth and the axe has cut down the forest, after the geologist's hammer has broken the rock and the miner's pick has uncovered the vein, we complete the finer work of analysis in the laboratory, and with crucible and electric battery and microscope we penetrate farther into nature's secrets, and learn her processes of construction and operation. Progress is always towards simplicity. To-day we accomplish with simpler machinery and methods, more work in all mechanical fields than was possible half a century ago. This is in proportion as we have replaced muscle with mind.

Many such advances are preceded by examples of results without machinery, by the simple employment of mental forces. We discover the telegraph, and flash the cable signals under oceans that divide the continents. We apply the electric current to the telephone, and the human voice becomes audible between cities separated thousands of miles. We carry these applications of electricity to a higher development, and the range of the human vision is extended in the same way as the vocal and the auditory power. It is claimed that the latest discoveries in electric science make it possible to see to immense distances, and to photograph persons and objects far removed from the camera. Yet many of these results have already been obtained without the employment of any wires or batteries.

What, then, is the *fundamental law* by which these seeming phenomena are accomplished? Is it not *harmonious vibration?* Two violins are tuned to the same key; one is placed upon a table, and a bow is drawn across the strings of the other. The one upon the table responds and vibrates to every chord awakened by the player. This harmony appears to be the first condition of response in all mental communication. The subject and the operator must be in accord. It is often observed that people in close sympathy speak the same thought almost simultaneously, but it is not always possible to tell in which mind, if in either, the thought had its origin. The same inventions and ideas are often developed at the same time in different parts of the world. Thought waves appear to spread and widen in their vibrations very much as those of sound or light. They are also intensified in their power by being brought to a focus, as are the sun rays by a burning glass.

What, then, are the best conditions for projecting thought? Experiment in this field has been so limited, that, as yet, we have reached very few definite conclusions. It appears that the conditions which have produced the most satisfactory results at one time are by no means certain to produce the same results at another. From this it follows that this problem contains some undiscovered factors.

It appears, however, certain, first, that there must be *harmony* between the operators, to admit of reciprocal vibration and produce the best results; secondly, that the mind must be *free* from the disturbance of anxiety, and *confident* in its power to send and to receive thought-messages. It must also have developed the power of *concentration*, in order to obtain a focus of the mental forces and project the thought as sender, or perceive it as recipient.

How far the currents of the air, or ether, may facilitate or hinder thought-projection is perhaps an open question; also to what extent electric and magnetic forces have a part in the phenomena, and whether or not it is desirable to consider the points of the compass. We have good reason to believe, however, that mental force is the subtlest and most powerful of all elements yet discovered—that it can dominate all others and act with entire independence of them.

In an experiment I made some years ago for thought-transference between Chicago and Boston, the following conditions were arranged: The parties sat by appointment, making careful allowance for the difference in time between the cities. It was agreed that each should act alternately for fifteen minutes as sender and receiver. In order to assist concentration, each had placed before him a photograph of the other upon which he fixed his earnest attention. With a view to establishing magnetic relations, each held in his hand a lock of the other's hair. Pencil and paper were provided, and a careful record was made at both ends of messages sent and impressions received.

The experiment was particularly successful. Not only was the substance of the messages received, but with a precision that was remarkable. I had dwelt emphatically upon each word of my message in Chicago, repeating it many times in a low tone. My voice was actually heard in Boston, as though I had been calling through a telephone. In this case the parties had been in relation of operator and subject in a long series of hypnotic experiments, lasting many months, and relations of harmonious vibration had been well established.

Other experiments were made at closer range, several between Boston and New York, and always the substance of the message was received, though with varying precision. These experiments were always by appointment, though without the other conditions which were used in the Chicago trial. Sometimes the hour appointed would find me on the street instead of in the quiet of my room. In such case the required concentration was naturally more difficult, yet I do not recall any instance in which the signalling failed.

Upon several occasions I made the effort, without warning, to throw my subject into the hypnotic sleep, when we were separated by distances varying from one hundred to three hundred miles. In this I invariably succeeded. The influence would be immediately felt as a peculiar tingling sensation. This would be quickly followed by the hypnotic condition, which would sometimes last for several hours—in one case breaking up an entire morning's engagements, as I had neglected to throw off the influence. In these experiments careful note was always made of time, and the effects produced were always found to be at the exact hour of the trial.

Such experiments as these have certainly established as a scientific fact the conclusion that *thought can be projected* to great distances. It may be definitely recognized by the recipient, or its effects produced without the conscious recognition. The will of the operator is the projecting force. Time and distance do not appear as factors.

But there is another phase of telepathy which is still less understood than this we have considered, where conscious purpose exists in the mind of the operator,—viz., the *unconscious* field, in which the thought passes from one mind to the other at a distance, without intention, and registers itself in a resulting action. This is illustrated by the following experience. A gentleman in Chicago was sitting quietly in his room when he felt an inclination to yield his arm to automatic writing. A letter was thus written addressed to himself and signed with the name of a friend in San Francisco. Five days later the mail brought to him from San Fransico the original letter, of which the writer had unconsciously projected the duplicate at the time of writing. Here again appears to be the germ of the "auto-telegraph," operating without battery or wire.

From such experiences we may reasonably infer that every individual is at the same time a human dynamo, containing magnet and induction coil, receiving, generating, and transmitting mind-forces, consciously and unconsciously. Doubtless the largest field of operation is the realm of the unconscious.

This brings us to the recognition of the universal life through which these thought currents circulate. We perceive that not only is every individual a human battery of many cells, but that he is also only a single cell of the larger battery which includes all humanity, and perhaps an infinitely wider range of life of both higher and lower orders, seen and unseen. As "the wind bloweth where it listeth and we cannot tell whence it cometh nor whither it goeth," so is it true of the thought-life which pervades the race.

It is apparently the *circulation of a universal system.* It defies all efforts to trace it to its source, and at no point can we draw the line and say, "This is from incarnate mind and this from excarnate; this is from individual and this from associated minds." *All* life is "inspirational," and never was book written or line penned that could honestly claim the copyright of exclusive authorship.

Here is the great problem of life—to arrive at conscious development and control of these thought-forces, to purify them of every hurtful element and divest them of all destructiveness, and finally to apply them intelligently and with greatly loving purpose to the symmetrical construction of the Temple of Divine Humanity.

EASTER.

BY JOSEPHINE RAND.

The Easter sun had risen in splendor bright;
Earth lay enwrapped in shining robe of light;
There was a hush as if each living thing
Had caught the flutter of an angel's wing:
Heaven seemed so near, with but a veil between
The things material and the things unseen,
That as one gazed into the cloudless sky
'Twas but to feel one's immortality.
Beyond the veil the glad angelic host
Were praising Father, Son, and Holy Ghost:
An Easter anthem through all heaven pealed,
More and more joyous as One stood revealed,
White and all glorious midst the shining throng,
Yet sorrowful of face, as if the song
Pained the Great Heart which ages long agone
Broke on the cross of Calvary alone.
The singers' voices faltered: Christ their Lord,
Redeemer, King of kings, loved and adored,
Smiled not responsive to their hymn of praise,
But raised His hand and bade His angels gaze
Downward and earthward where the Easter sun
Was lighting up the new day just begun.
The singing ceased. The angels knew in part
The cross Christ carried still within His heart:
As much as angels may they shared the pain
Which crown of thorns entailed on Him again.
Was it indeed an Easter morn in heaven,
When He, to whom all glory had been given,
Stayed the glad music of the happy throng,
Silenced the hallelujahs of the song,
And with a wondrous light within His eyes
Beckoned His angels from the farthest skies
To follow Him, and earthward bend.their way,
And with the sons of men spend Easter Day?
Far, far behind they left the Heavenly Place,
Having no eyes but for the Lord Christ's face—
That face so full of pain, so white and still,
That none could gaze thereon without a thrill
Of agonizing sympathy and love
For woe like His, all other woes above.
All silently they took their shining way,
Making more bright and brighter still the day.
Men said: "How glorious is this Easter morn!
Was ever day so clear at early dawn?
How cloudless is the sky! Sure 'tis God's face
Smiling approval on the human race."
The Lord Christ heard, and bowed His kingly head:
"And there are witnesses of me!" He said.

"Lo! let us enter at this portal wide,
And hear the anthems of the 'saved' inside."
Through arch and nave exulting music pealed;
At Jesus' name devout ones humbly kneeled;
"The Lord is risen!" the salaried singers sang,
Paid "Hallelujahs" through the chancel rang;
The reverend rector in his priestly dress
Talked to his people of Christ's godliness,
Pointed to Him, who, on this Easter Day.
Stood for all nations as the Life, the Way.
Yea! Christ was risen: let all hearts rejoice,
Let men and angels sing as with one voice!
The Lord Christ heard: with white and pain-drawn face,
He beckoned to His host and left the place.
A moment lingered He outside the door,
Looking the massive structure o'er and o'er:
"And thus," He cried in bitterness, "my church
Rejoices in its Lord; forsakes the search
For those He came to succor and to save,
On whom still rests the darkness of the grave.
Yet is He risen!—Let us seek again
The power of resurrection among men."
Silent and swift the shining host passed on,
Waiting a signal from the Risen One;
Past gorgeous palaces and stately piles,
High monuments to business schemes and wiles,
Yet stayed He not, till in a noisome street,
Worn by the pressure of unnumbered feet,
Before a crowded tenement He stood
And gazed upon the purchase of His blood.
Children in swarms were playing near the door,
Unwashed, unfed, untaught, and needing sore
The love which only purity can shed
From two hearts blended and in true love wed.
And round them all such filth and utter woe;
Curses of men and shrieks of women low,
The vulgar speech of those who loved the night
Because their deeds were evil, whom the light
Had never reached in that dark vale of sin
Where hope they leave behind who enter in.
The Lord Christ stood and viewed the whole scene o'er,
As one might view a wreck upon the shore.
"It might have been!"—"It is!"—"It yet might be!"—
What would the verdict of to-morrow be?
"And this is Easter!" said He then, and sighed.
"'Tis for these children that I lived and died.
For such as these, the destitute and lost,
I counted life but cheap at any cost:
These, these, the ignorant of life's true way,
I came to pilot to eternal day.
Yet while the Easter anthems swell the breeze,
There lives no risen Lord for such as these;
While prayer and praise ascend to empty heaven
The heart of Him they call upon is risen:
Again the pains of Calvary He bears
In earthly sufferings and His children's tears.
My church! Why comes it not to haunts like these
Save to collect its rentals and its fees?

Yea, rentals from these very sinks of sin
Where it would stand appalled to enter in!
Why stand professed disciples dumb and still,
And let the wicked reign at their sweet will?
Why lift they not their hand against the power
That robs the poor man of his native dower;
That crushes opportunity; plants seed
Which brings forth but the flower of heartless greed;
That forces these, My babes, to bear the blame
And burden of a blasted life of shame;
That crushes out the semblance of a soul
By hunger, nakedness, and the long roll
Of penalties and fines the poor man pays
Unto his poverty through hopeless days?
Why stand they not to rid the honest poor
Out of the wicked hand, and to restore
The rights made equal to the sons of God
By Him who was, before the earth was trod?—
By Him who did create the sea and land,
Fashioned the round world with His mighty hand,
And gave the earth such power to produce
That food for all but waits upon its use?
Why stand they not against corruption's zeal,
Make sacred and secure the common weal,
Save these, My lambs, from ignorance and vice,
So that they make My paths of joy their choice?
Why? God in heaven, why!—"My heart doth bleed
When I look out upon My church's need."

He bowed His head, and all the angel band
Wept with Him o'er the darkness in the land.
Yea, Jesus wept again, as in that day
When o'er Jerusalem the night held sway.
He wept. Could mortals at His elbow's touch
Have dreamed that in their midst there stood One such,
Suffering with them, grief-stricken for their grief,
Methinks the knowledge might have brought relief;
Methinks it might have softened pain's hard edge,
And driven in the heart a mighty wedge
By means of which God's light should enter in
And cleanse the human dwelling of its sin.
Alas! they knew Him not; knew not He stood
With myriad angels near their poor abode.
So near help might have seemed! but now so far!
To them it was remote as farthest star.
Men drank to drown their woe, feed hunger's fire;
Women caroused—for them what was there higher?
Earth held no sweeter life for such as they;
Darkness and death the promise of their day.
The Lord Christ turned, and pityingly He laid
His hands upon the head of one wee maid;
A baby girl with far-off, searching eyes,
As if they read the mystery of the skies,
And pale, wan cheeks, sweet mouth that knew no smile,
Whose five short years had seemed a weary while.
What was there in that Touch that those sad eyes
Should suddenly light up with sweet surprise?
Whence came the halo round the childish brow?

Was life, so sad before, transfigured now?
Yea, let Him speak: 'tis His, the sweet decree;
"This day, dear child, in heaven thou shalt be."
The Lord Christ raised His eyes to heaven's dome
And said: "Thanks be to God there is a home
For all the weary and distressed of earth
Who have been robbed of sacred rights of birth.
'Tis not for long; grief lasteth but a night:
The morning cometh with its joyful light!"
He turned as to depart; but closer came
One of the angels in a garb of flame:—
"Dear Master, wilt thou bless but only one?
Shall there not more be freed ere set of sun?"
"Nay," said the Christ; "what could I give save death?
God's laws must be wrought out; and He that saith
'Work out your own salvation' waits to-day
To have His church discover the true way."
Again the shining throng pursued its way
Among the haunts of men that Easter Day.
They visited the dens and nauseous dives
Where were imprisoned precious human lives;
Souls which, degraded though they all might be,
Still held the germ of God's divinity.
Yea, on the head of even one of these
Christ placed His hand and said: "Say what they please,
This sinful woman is more near My throne
Than they who preach and pray, and *let alone*
The awful problems of the day and hour
Which cry aloud for workers and the power
Of righteousness and justice in the world
That Love's white banner be one day unfurled.
This woman sells her body—but for bread
That hungry child and mother may be fed:
She bears a cross; no eye like mine can see
The anguish of her soul—akin to me.
Let us pass on. I have a home in view
Which is this weary woman's rightful due.
She, the rejected, the despised, the lost,
Had been affianced to the genial host.
The old, old story once again as told,
Believed and trusted:—then, betrayed and sold,
She to her way into the world alone,
To bear the burden till her life be done.
While he, respected, rich, and blessed by Fate,
A shining light in church, pillar of state,—
Unworthy to pollute her garment's hem,
Yet represents a power which upholds them
Who feed upon her helplessness once more,
Hers and her fellowmen's the wide world o'er.
Landlord and speculator—such as he
Control the industry from sea to sea.
Upon his brow now burns the brand of Cain,—
The blood of helpless ones whom he has slain.
Here is his palace!—see ye o'er the door
Passover mark when I shall come once more?
Let us go in. I am not often here,
Though I am prayed at each day of the year.
See there his wife. Is she indeed his wife?

Let God be judge who gave a human life
In answer to the love of bygone years,
A love now quenched in misery and tears.
Yet sits she here as wife, mother as well,
Confessing to belief in heaven and hell,
Yet lifting not a finger to relieve
The dense, dark ignorance which none conceive
Save those who, gladly leaving joy behind,
Go forth to minister unto the blind:
Idly she sits, proud Fortune's petted doll,
Unwitting of the blow about to fall:
Yea, as God lives and sheds the Easter light,
Her soul shall be required of her this night.
Let us pass on—into the open street;
I hear the marching of triumphant feet!
See here My Army in Salvation's cause,
In whom the cultured pick so many flaws.
Here liveth Easter in the hearts of men!
Joy throbs exultant in My breast again!
Let us go forth and join them in the way,
Help swell the chorus of glad Easter Day!
Come ye, My angels, let your morning song,
Begun in heaven, once more ring loud and strong,
Give to the farthest spheres the joyful news
That Christ is risen; and these hearts infuse
With joy unspeakable and full of bliss
Who have remembered Me in ways like this:
Going about with Me to seek and save,
To love, to help, to succor from the wave,
Suffering with Me the poverty and shame,
From heartfelt love for the Redeemer's name.
Go back, My angels, to the God above,
And say His Son remains on earth for love.
Yea, let My throne in heaven empty be
Until I bring the last lamb back with me.
Let Me remain with these the faithful souls
Until through all the universe there rolls
The joyful tidings of a rescued race
Which turns its footsteps toward the Heavenly Place.
Christ shall indeed be risen, and Easter Day
Will light the nations with a matchless ray
When all men turn from darkness and false gods,
And every human creature is the Lord's.
A mightier song than ever yet was sung
Shall then reëcho all the worlds among.—
Ye may return. I am the Life, the Way:
My place is here, on earth, this Easter Day."
Once more arose the glad, triumphant strain
As the great host turned heavenward again.
The Lord Christ heard: but now upon His face
Shone glory suffering could not efface.
He lifted up His eyes to heaven and cried:
"Father, I claim each soul for which I died
I died for all; then give Me all, I pray.
And I am risen, indeed, this Easter Day!"

THE VALLEY PATH.

BY WILL ALLEN DROMGOOLE.

CHAPTER VII.

Summer drifted dreamily; the valley blossomed and budded and brought forth its treasures of harvest.

Alicia's peas "fulled" almost to bursting in their pale pods, and the shriveled vines were torn away to make room for a turnip patch, in order that "spring greens" might not be lacking when the season for them should come again. Still the physician tarried. Autumn, with its variant winds and restful skies, breathed upon field and flood; the water sang low in the Elk's bed, and the rebellious creek crooned the old, old slumber song of October; the wild grape hung in dusky bunches from the vine-crowned trees; the stealthy fox prowled along the river bluffs that were rich with the odor of the ripening muscadine; the mountaineer fed upon the opossum that had fattened upon the new persimmons. And still the doctor let fall no hint of returning to the city.

Autumn gave place to winter; the water rose in the river channel, and the foot log went scurrying off with the swollen waters of Pelham creek. The birds gathered in little frightened groups, made out a hasty route, and went south on very short notice. Only a dilapidated crow might be heard now and then, monotonously cawing from the tops of a denuded sycamore tree. There was an occasional dropping of dry nuts from the limbs where they had clung all summer, seeking the moist brown earth to wait until——. Ah! who knows when, how, what shall rise again?

At last the snow came; little drowsy dribbles that frosted the hills and put a crisp in the air. And still the good man lingered.

"Why should I go?" he asked himself. "I am contented here; am doing a little good, maybe, among the people here."

He scarcely knew himself that Alicia had anything to do with his staying; he scarcely understood just how he stood toward her.

He saw her almost every day; if she failed to call he hailed her when she passed, taking the nearer cut, the foot-path way to Sewanee. For in winter Alicia found something with which to tempt the appetites of the "Episcopers."

As for the doctor, his cheery call at the miller's gate had become as familiar as the click-clack of the mill itself. And so frequent were his demands for "more eggs" that granny fell to wondering "if the mad doctor were a feedin' of his cows an' horses on Lissy's hens' aigs."

It was one afternoon in November that he returned from a visit to a sick man down the valley. He was tired; his very eyes ached with the wind that had cut him unmercifully as he rode home in the teeth of it. He drew off his boots, stretched his chilled feet a moment before the fire, and thrust them into a pair of felt slippers with a sense of quiet rejoicing that he was home ahead of the snow cloud gathering over the mountain. The fire had never felt so good. Even Zip, as he curled up at his feet, his small head cuddled against the brown felt shoe, assumed vaguely the semblance of a friend.

He had scarcely had his first yawn when Dilce put her head in to say:

"Marster, dey's a 'oman sick up dar on de mount'n road a piece—mighty sick; en ole Mis' Reamses granddaughter wuz down here after you whilst you wuz gone. En she say she ud tek it mighty kin' ef't you'ud step up dar en see de 'oman what's sick. She say ef't you could come dis ebenin' she ud be mighty obleeged ter yer. But I tol' her you wan' gwine do no sich thing, not in dis col' en win'."

He tossed off his slippers but a moment before put on, and pointing to his boots still lying where he had but just left them said:

"Who is the sick woman? Did Lissy leave no name?"

"Naw, sir. I axed fur the entitlements but she didn't look lack she cud make up what dey wuz."

"No," said the doctor, "I suppose not; hand me my shoes, you villanous murderer of the king's English. Now tell me what the girl did say. You don't expect me to go tramping up the mountain, into the clouds, with nothing nearer than the stars for a sign post, do you?"

"She say hit's de fus' house on de road, after you tu'n de road by de big rock what hangs over hit, whar de S'wany boys hav painted de sun risin'. Mus'n' I git yo' supper fus' fo' you goes out again in de col'?" she asked, seeing him look about for his great coat. "I kin hab it on de table in a minute."

"No," he said wearily, "wait until I get back, or get your own, and keep mine back in the stove. I am going up by way of the foot path, but you may give Ephraim his supper and then send him with my horse around by the road."

"Marster?"

"Well?"

"Hadn' I better fix up a bite fur yer ter carry up dar?
Mis' Reamses daughter say dat de sick 'oman's folks is all
gone 'way, an' she wuz 'bliged ter g'long back up dar ter
knock her up somef'n ter eat. She say she got de mis'ry in
de side, mighty bad."

"You may get me a box of mustard and when Ephraim
comes send a basket of provisions up. You had better put
a bottle of blackberry wine in the basket also. And tell
Ephraim to get in plenty of wood; there is going to be a
snow storm."

The atmosphere cleared, however; the snow ceased to
fall; and although it was about the hour of sunset when he
reached the cabin on the mountain side, there was a deep,
half-sullen after glow in the west which brought out all the
more forcefully the otherwise cold gray of the heavens.

He found the sick woman to be old Mrs. Tucker, whom he
had met at the cabin where he met Alicia; he had bought
chickens of her more than once since then, and her son, a
listless, idle fellow with a young wife and a baby, had hauled
wood for the physician from the forests about the mountain.
He had no idea that he would ever be paid for his services,
if that payment depended upon the son. There was, however, something about the old woman herself, hints of those
peculiarly strong and admirable characteristics which flash
upon the comprehension with startling emphasis at times,
that had inspired him with faith as well as respect.

The tumble-down gate swung slightly ajar upon a broken
hinge; a tiny line of blue smoke was ascending from the low,
stack chimney, and in the woods across the road, a young
girl was gathering brush.

He did not recognize her at first in the half light, but
when she pushed back the shawl pinned about her head and
came to meet him, he saw that it was Alicia.

"I'm mighty glad you're come, Doctor Borin'," she said,
in her slow sweet drawl. "I was most afraid you wouldn't,
because Aunt Dilce said you were off to see some one
already. Come right on in, it's old Mrs. Tucker that's sick,
and her folks air all off visitin' down to Pelham."

She was trying to open the hanging gate by pushing
against it with her already burdened arms. The doctor put
her lightly aside.

"Wait, wait, young woman," said he. "Don't monopolize
the work I beg. Let me open the gate, or else carry the
brush."

It scraped along the frozen ground like a thing in pain, digging a long furrow in the light snow-crust as it went.

"Her folks air all gone off," Lissy was telling him as they walked toward the cabin, "else I reckin they wouldn't 'a' let me send for you. Jim he's mighty strong for the herb doctor, an' so is Lucy Ann; but I have heard Mrs. Tucker passin' compliments over you so many times that I up and went after you this evenin' without askin' leave of nobody, just on the strength of them compliments."

"Much obliged, I'm sure," said the doctor, "much obliged to both of you."

She did not detect the jest in his words, and her simple, "You are welcome," as she led the way into the cabin, was as genuinely sincere as it was quaintly simple.

She deposited her kindlings in the shed room, and returned to take her place with him at the bedside of old Mrs. Tucker.

To him there was no longer anything odd or incongruous in her being there. He had found her so often among the very poor and the suffering, so many times had they been thus associated together, that it seemed as much her proper place as it was his. She was as truly a physician to them as he.

"Had she been a poor girl, in a city, she would have been a trained nurse," was his thought; "had she been a rich woman, in the city, she would have been a patron of hospitals, with the afflicted indigent for a hobby. As it is, she ought to be a doctor's wife," he said; and so saying blushed to the roots of his gray hair.

Old Mrs. Tucker, however, received more of Alicia's attention than the general sick. The two had been real friends since Alicia, a little girl in short skirts, had made her first trip to Sewanee behind Mrs. Tucker on her gray mare. She had sold a mess of early beans that day, and with Mrs. Tucker's help had purchased a straw hat with the money. It was the very first hat she had ever owned; but since then so much from spring and fall vegetables was invested in a hat. The last winter's was a bright red felt, which the old grandmother declared made her look for all the world like an overgrown woodpecker. Mrs. Tucker liked it, however, and the face that peeped at Lissy from the little mirror over the bureau that had been her mother's was such a piquant, pretty face, under the red felt's brim, that she had worn it, in defiance of the woodpecker insinuation. The hat was in the second season now, but still retained its bright red color; so that when Lissy crammed it down upon her head and started up the mountain on a clear day in winter, it showed like a scarlet flag "plumb to the top of the mount'n," Mrs. Tucker was wont to declare.

Alicia seldom passed the cabin without stopping to ask after the health of the family. Thus it was that she found the old woman ill, with a chill upon her and alone.

"She was right glad to see me," she told the doctor, while she stroked the thin black hair back from the yellow forehead. "But I didn't ask her if I might send for you, Doctor Borin'. And if any harm comes of it the fault's all mine—if any harm comes to Mrs. Tucker."

The doctor caught his breath, looking up quickly to discover if might be whether the insult was of accident or of intent.

But the quiet face told him nothing; Alicia went on stroking the yellow temples as calmly as though she had not just put the physician on his honor to play no "infedel tricks," as her grandmother was wont to call his practice, upon the patient committed to his care.

Without replying he proceeded to examine the sufferer, who waked and recognized him, telling him that she was "much obleeged to him for trompin' up the mount'n ter see a ole woman die."

"Nonsense," said he. "You will bring me my Christmas turkey ten years from now, if Lissy will swing her kettle over the fire, and get some hot water to put your feet in. Then she must hunt me up a saucer in which to mix a little mustard, and get for me a bit of soft white cloth. I am going to put a plaster on your side and another on your chest. And I am going to give you a little powder out of this case,—it is called calomel. Lissy?"

She turned to him from the fire where she had been swinging the kettle upon an iron hook that was there for the purpose.

"Will you be here all night?"

"I reckin I'll have to be," she replied. "Though some one ought to go down to Pelham and let Lucy Ann and Jim know their ma is sick. I'll be obliged to run down the mount'n and feed my chickens first, because Al *won't* give 'em enough, and granny plumb forgets all about 'em. Then I can come back."

She sighed, standing with her hands folded, her profile against the blaze, her fine, clear-cut face and figure silhouetted against the firelight.

"It's mighty worrisome to know somethin' is left to your care; something that can feel, and suffer, and die; though," she added with a smile, "it be only a brood of chickens."

He went over and stood by her side, looking down into the earnest young face lifted to his.

"What if the something be human life?" he said softly: "what if it rested in your hand every day, almost every hour? What would you think of such a charge as that?"

Her lids dropped a moment; she hesitated, then looking at him with strangely glowing eyes said:

"Oh, it must be *grand, grand*, to help people to live—to know how to give 'em back their life. It *is* grand. It is like God, to be able to do that. To give back life, and to help people to live their life after they get it: I'd like mightily to be able to do that."

Her face was aglow with enthusiasm; the fine lights in her eyes sparkled like crystalline fires.

She was very near him, her hand resting upon the back of a splint-bottomed chair which stood between them. She leaned over, resting her elbows upon the chair, waiting for him to speak. He could feel her soft breath upon his hand, see the throbbing of her white throat, and the pretty bird-like neck, where the waist of her dark dress had been cut back to make room for a tiny ruffle of white muslin. He saw the rise and fall of her bosom; her gold-red hair brushed his sleeve. The firelight transfigured her; the dress of dark stuff, in the ruddy, uncertain light, became softest velours; the brooch of cheap glass at her throat became a glistening gem of rare worth. The fluffy bright waves of hair which crowned the well-shaped head were not for the rude caresses of the mountain stripling, Joe Bowen; they were his, the treasured tresses of his love, Alicia, his wife that might be.

His wife that might be for the asking. He knew her heart had not awakened; all the sweet beauty of life's richness was still there. It would never be called into being by Joe Bowen. The girl had a soul; Bowen's was not the voice that would sound its quickening. Yet unless he spoke she would marry him, and the great richness, the wonderful possibilities, would be lost, all lost.

He leaned slightly towards her, his hand rested upon hers; he felt the slender, flexible fingers close about his own.

"Alicia?" he said softly.

She started, and withdrew her hand. He knew then that her thoughts had been far away.

"Alicia, how would you like to help the world? in what manner, I mean? And where did you get your idea of being of service to your fellows?"

"At S'wany," she replied. "I was up here once of a Sunday. I didn't care much for the robe and fixin's of the

preacher—seemed like it was no use. But I remembered
what he said. He said we couldn't all be rich and smart, no
more could we all see our way clear; but we all could help
somebody to live their life, somebody not so well off as we
air. He said we could all do somethin', even if we couldn't
understand God; and He would count the good up to our
credit. He said we could make our fellow-men our religion,
and helpin' of them our creed. I got that much from the
Episcopers and I'm tryin' to live up to it. Doctor Borin',
I *have* thought that was true religion."

"It will do to steer by, I suspect," he replied. "But some
day I want to come over to your house and plan out a future
for you, more congenial than this life you have laid out for
yourself."

She laughed and lifted the steaming kettle from the hook
to the hearth. But her reply was foreign to his suggestion.

"Doctor Borin', if you could stay here a bit I could run
down and feed my chickens, and get back in no time."

Already her hand was extended for her shawl hanging
upon a wooden peg just within the cabin door.

"Child," said the doctor, "what are you made of? Rubber
or whit-leather? Talking of slipping down the mountain as
if you were a couple of cast-iron springs, and had only to
snap yourself in place. You have been down the mountain
once to-day."

She laughed and threw a handful of chips in the fire from
the basket she had filled for the morning's kindling.

"I have been down the mount'n *twicet* to-day," she said,
"but I can go again, I reckin. And I don't know but I *ought*
to go down to Pelham and tell Lucy Ann."

"Well, you'll not go to Pelham this night," said the
doctor. "My horse and boy will be around in half an hour,
and if you will direct him to the house where Lucy Ann is
stopping he can go down there and tell her that she is
needed here. You may go and feed your chickens, if you
are so sure nobody else can perform the service to your
satisfaction. Has Lucy Ann any way of getting home to-
night?"

"They went down in the wagon," she replied. "Jim he
had a load of straw to fetch up, for bed makin' and hen
nests; and he allowed Lucy Ann and the baby could ride
on the load well as not."

Half an hour later Ephraim had been sent upon his
mission, and Doctor Boring saw Alicia cram her old red felt
down upon her bright head, pin her shawl securely about
her shoulders, and run off down the little footpath that

wound past his own dwelling to hers at the foot of the mountain.

It was scarcely ten minutes until he heard her voice at the gate again, and through the curtainless window, he could distinguish in the fading light the slender, girlish figure leaning upon the low palings on the other side of which stood a tall, slender youth, whose erect carriage, and shock of yellow hair falling picturesquely about his shoulders and surmounted by the inevitable slouch, told him that it was Joe Bowen. His head drooped, ever so slightly, to meet the pretty face lifted to his. She was laying down instructions of some kind, for the giant nodded now and then, and her pretty gurgling laugh, half suppressed, in consideration of the sick woman, came to the ears of the physician, watching and listening, with a feeling half anger, half annoyance, in his heart, until the conference was ended and Lissy returned to her charge.

"Is she asleep?" she asked softly while she laid aside her things. "I met Joe Bowen yonder where the path forks, and he said he 'd go down and feed the chickens for me. Joe's a master hand at chickens, though he is a sinner."

She laughed, tucking the covers more securely about the feet of her patient. Evidently Joe's sins were not altogether unpardonable to her partial sense.

"But," she added naïvely, "I ain't so mighty good myse'f as I can be settin' myse'f in judgment on Joe. I ain't a perfessor; I ain't even clear in my mind that I believe all the Methodists say; nor the Episcopers either for that matter. I know there ain't any sense in all that talkin' back at the parson like the Episcopers talk, same as if he didn't know what he was sayin'; an' there ain't any call for him to put on them robe fixin's as I can see. And all of that about the dead risin' I know ain't so. For Joe opened an Indian grave last summer—there's a whole graveyard of 'em over yonder on Duck River—and there was the Indian dead and buried same as ever. And he must 'a' been buried a hundred years I know. Oh,"—she paused; a new idea had come to her,—"mebby the Indians don't count. The Book don't say anything about Indians, and neither does Brother Barry. Air you goin'?"

"Yes, I must get down the mountain while I can see the path. I am not as young as I used to be."

She laughed again, and toyed with the pewter spoon and coarse saucer with which he had prepared the mustard.

"You don't appear to be so mighty old as I can make out," she said.

The words pleased him. Age had never been unwelcome to him; in fact, he had scarcely felt that it had really come to him, until he crossed paths with this sweet young life. Her very next words, however, served to dash the little sweet with bitter.

"Are you afraid to remain here alone?" he asked. "If you are I will send Aunt Dilce up to stay-with you. Mrs. Tucker will not waken before midnight possibly; I have given her a sleeping potion."

There was the faintest hint of embarrassment in her manner as she replied:

"Joe said he'd come up and sit with me till Lucy Ann got here, and then he said he'd fetch me home again."

"Oh! he did."

There was a slight impatience in the words but she did not recognize it. She was innocent of intent to wound; too unconscious of offence, too entirely unused to the world and its ways, to understand that she could be in any sense a cause, however innocent, of contention—a thorn in the bosom of a man's content.

She gave him her earnest and entire attention while he explained the different medicines and gave directions concerning them, interrupting him now and then, if it might be called an interruption, with her simple "Yes, sir," "No, sir," "All right, Doctor Borin'." She even walked to the gate with him, and put the rusted chain over the post that held the broken fastenings; and called to him as he went off down the snow-dusted path:

"I'll fetch you a basket of fresh eggs to-morrow sure and certain."

And he had called back to her, "So do; so do," quite cheerily.

Yet there was an ache in his heart; the thorn had pierced home.

(To be continued.)

IRENE.

BY WILLIAM COLBY COOPER.

Come to my sheltering arms, Irene,
And pillow your head on my yearning breast —
Pillow it there and at last find rest,
Like a tired bird in its little nest,
    My beautiful fallen queen —
    My wayward, wand'ring Irene.

Come to my eager arms, Irene;
Fly from the tinsel and glitter and glare
That dazzle the soul, as they hide the snare
Spread for innocence everywhere,
    My beautiful fallen queen —
    My faded and jaded Irene.

Come to my open arms, Irene;
Spurned and despised, as you are, by all —
E'en by the wretch who caused your fall
And settled upon you this dreadful pall,
    My beautiful fallen queen —
    My saddened, maddened Irene.

Come to my outstretched arms, Irene;
Wearied you must be of sinful sights —
Tired and sick of the false delights
That fill up your days and delirious nights,
    My beautiful fallen queen —
    My hunted and haunted Irene.

Come to my hungry arms, Irene;
Oh! I am longing and longing to prove
To you, and the world, and the angels above,
The infinite reach of a spiritual love,
    My beautiful fallen queen —
    My trampled and tarnished Irene.

Then come to my lonesome arms, Irene,
And pillow your head on my waiting breast —
Pillow it there, and at last find rest,
Like a tired bird in its old-home nest,
    My beautiful fallen queen —
    My pitiful little Irene.

BETWEEN TWO WORLDS.

BY MRS. CALVIN KRYDER REIFSNIDER.

CHAPTER VIII.

"Were I in your place, surrounded by beauty, art, books, and music, I should never want to cross the threshold into the outside world," said Salome to Ruby as she seated herself in the Temple one Saturday morning to spend the hour before Ruby took her morning walk.

"Of what use would my life be then?" asked Ruby, looking at her with those penetrating eyes which Salome could never fathom, although she felt that they looked down into her very inmost being and penetrated her secret thoughts and motives.

"Could it not be a beautiful, peaceful one, sinless, in fact, since there would be no contact save with peace and purity here?"

"A hermit's life, however pure, could not benefit mankind. Our Saviour set us a different example. We must go among the ignorant and the poor and lift them up by giving them good thoughts and purposes," Ruby answered gently.

"And what thanks will you get for it?" almost sneered the sceptical Salome.

"Really, I had not thought of that," answered Ruby.

"Indeed! Then you're a queer Christian worker. The typical Christian workers are always trying to impress poor sinful humanity that they ought to be grateful. Grateful for what? Being poor, wretched, downtrodden, and for the visitors who come and tell them of it?"

"Perhaps you misunderstand the workers. Perhaps they are trying to teach the poor to be grateful for the fact that God is ever near them, ready to hear their first cry to Him for help; to strengthen the first resolve to turn to Him; to walk with them just as soon as they will suffer themselves to be led into the right path."

"They'd do better, in my opinion, to let people entirely alone; to attend to their own business. They are deceitful meddlers with only one general or particular motive; that is, to get their names in the daily papers for benevolent acts they never do, for charities they never give, for motives they never had. Ugh! how I hate them."

"If what you say is true, Salome, they harm no one but themselves."

"*Don't* they? I say they do! They cause others to hate them just as I do."

"Your hatred reflects back upon yourself, mars your young face, and scars your young heart," answered Ruby solemnly.

"My mother was a church member, and when my father was able to entertain all the preachers in the country she was 'Sister Blake.' When they, and other good friends, had eaten us out of house and home, they forgot all about her—the wretches," and the words came through Salome's teeth with a hiss that caused Ruby to recoil.

"So much the worse for them. So much the better for your mother, who entertained them in a spirit of love and generosity, and who, I doubt not, brightens many dreary moments with memories of what, to her noble heart, was genuine Christian love."

Had Ruby's silvery voice been a sharp steel dagger she could not have cut more deeply the proud, sensitive, rebellious Salome. For a moment she was silent. How did Ruby know this thing? For it was true—a memory of happier days was all that was left to little mother now. She did not think of the loss of her old friends as slights but as consideration for her that she could not afford to entertain them. But Salome would not yield the point. She was wretched, angry, jealous, and rebellious. She could not lay aside those old wrongs and leave them like seeds to spring up in the gardens of those who had sown them, as they surely would do, and let them reap their own harvest, but she fain would appropriate them as wrongs done to herself. Ruby, penetrating the feeling, said:

"Every wrong act, every unjust deed, every sinful thought, is impressed upon the person who does it."

"Do you mean to say that they do not affect the lives of others?" she asked with blazing eyes.

"Oh, no! certainly not. I might do you a grievous wrong from which you would certainly suffer but I should not go free from punishment. I might lie about you and that lie, being accepted as a truth by others, would have all the force of truth in wronging you, perhaps, temporarily, while I should in fact have made myself a liar, than which no other character is more detestable. Christ said the devil was a murderer from the beginning, and the father of lies. Does anything murder peace, honor, virtue, and happiness with such wholesale slaughter as the liar? The Lord permits nothing to happen that is not for our good."

"If you can show me how certain things that have happened me are for my good I would like you to do it. The environment of poverty that cripples all my faculties"——

"The very thing that awakened your courage, that gave you strength. From your own lips I learn that were you wealthy you would withdraw yourself from the world and sit down among books and music, flowers, pictures, and statuary, happy and content. Your chosen profession is a noble one, or, rather, one to be ennobled. You can reach a class of people that would not learn from priest or pastor. You can teach them moral lessons, religious lessons, that otherwise they might never learn. Like all good things the stage has been perverted. Half-dressed women, appearing in brazen and vulgar scenes, have lowered it; but beauty, modesty, and virtue may also be represented there. Unvirtuous women acting the parts of the courtesan will ever be demoralizing, but I cannot imagine you guilty of such things."

"If I could see the good to me—if I could believe in it."

"You will, you must. Salome, reflect upon this. So you have read ——, strong, passionate, and convincing, but her evil overshadows the good. The pen that can portray such characters is wielded by a diseased brain. Healthy minds can no more produce such characters in story than a good tree can bring forth evil fruit. Beware how you read them. Suppose you dramatize one of her tales. The heroine, the best and strongest part, should be played by one too vile to live. Were the women to-day such as she portrays, then would the sun indeed cease to shine, the moon turn to blood, and the stars fall from heaven."

Salome was silent.

Ruby invited Salome to accompany her upon her morning walk.

"Where are you going?" Salome asked, rising abruptly and sullenly tying on her broad-brimmed hat.

"I am going to —— Street to show a laborer's wife how to make a nice cheap dinner I promised her."

"Humph! That would be a charming operation to observe, and I must say changes my opinion of the refinement of your tastes. To leave this," with a wave of her hand indicating the Temple, "and go voluntarily into an untidy kitchen with ill-bred brats standing around scarce leaving you elbow room—no, thank you. I have enough of that at home. And I'll tell you what; I believe were you forced to live such a life you'd be ambitious to attain to something of this kind," again indicating their surroundings. "It is

the novelty of it that gives poverty a charm to you. It is
unnatural for a refined woman."

"Our Saviour left His heavenly kingdom and took His
place among them, taught them, showed them the way by
which they could reach His home in heaven. He loved
them and wanted them to have as good as He. I would to
God every living creature on this earth had just what I
have. I can show some of them the way to get it. In my
puny, finite way I want to follow the example He set me."

Her voice was low and sweet. As Salome followed her
out of the Temple she was puzzled. Was this Ruby an
angel or the direst hypocrite on earth? As they stood a
moment outside before they took their separate ways Salome said, with a sarcastic smile:

"I'll venture you would not stay and share that fifteen-
cent dinner—or how many in family? I'll divide by five
and say three-cent dinner—with thoughts of an elegant
repast at home."

"Salome, come with me. Do you suppose we live lux-
uriously in the sense of extravagance? Don't you know
if we did we should be living in direct opposition to our
teachings to the poor, and our sympathy with them? We
live most simply, but dear Goodie knows how to make
palatable the simplest food. She has taught me her cunning. I have found that much of the misery in the world
is caused through ignorance in not knowing how to properly
divide the poor man's earnings into food, shelter, and raiment. Little good comes to the poor in the way of advancement from drudgery until they know how to use their earnings. It resolves itself back into this: the more they earn
the more they spend and they get no further from hopeless
poverty."

They arrived at the tenement building occupied by some
dozens of families, and found the object of Ruby's solicitude
upon the fourth floor.

The mother was about thirty years of age, careworn, but
with traces of native refinement in her voice and manner.
She, her husband, and three children occupied two rooms
which were scantily furnished, and in the front room the
oldest child lay sick. Salome had come to observe Ruby.
She had no special interest in the family. Not that she was
hard-hearted, but it was a common sight to her, distasteful
in every respect, a thing from which her sole ambition
prompted her to get away.

After Ruby had talked with the children and brushed the
sick boy's hair, propped him up with pillows, and got him

interested in some picture books she had brought him, she
turned to the woman and said:

"It is high time we took a peep into our stock for dinner."

The woman led them into the next room where a couple
of cots, a goods box, which served for a table, a cupboard,
an old stove, and a few chairs composed the furniture.

She opened the cupboard and said: "We had boiled meat
and potatoes yesterday, as you know. This morning Indian
meal mush and coffee." She set each dish with its contents
upon the box as she spoke.

"Very well, you have a good start—cold potatoes, your
soup meat, and quite a lot of mush, which I see you have
cooked thoroughly, which when warm furnished a nice
breakfast with milk. Now, then, make your fire while I cut
this cold mush into thin slices for frying and slice the potatoes for the same purpose. Why, how smart your husband
must be," said Ruby as she heard a roar and saw the kindling blaze in the stove. "It is an old maxim that the woman
who makes a good fire quickly has a smart husband. Quick
now, hash your meat. We must economize fuel. Did you
get the eggs?"

"Yes, miss."

"Very well, we will have a French boullet."

Mrs. Wicks brought out a paper bag with six eggs, and a
pint of milk, and then set herself to chopping the meat with
an energetic hand.

"Those bits of stale bread and cracker if you please,
Salome, that you'll find on the upper shelf—thank you.
Now, then, the meat and bread crumbed and mixed well
with three eggs, fashioned into little balls and fried brown.
A nice dressing made of eggs and milk and a little flour.
Make your dish warm, lay on the balls, and pour the dressing over it. When finished, and the potatoes fried to a nice,
rich brown—the fried mush takes the place of bread to-day.
Quick, I hear footsteps on the stairs. All is ready. Clear
the table for the nice white cloth; only cotton—but it's
white and fresh. The dishes do not match but are washed
and rubbed till they shine.

"How do you do, Mr. Wicks?"

"I am hearty, thank you."

"And hungry too?" asked Ruby.

"Well, yes, a light breakfast and hard work makes a man
relish a lunch," and his eyes glistened as his wife put the
tempting meal before him.

Ruby was stirring something in a cup that looked more
tempting still.

"It is a custard for the sick child," she said in answer to the mother's glance.

"Oh, thank you, miss! He is so fond of a little sweet."

"Come to the table, Mr. Wicks, while your dinner is warm. Come, children, to your dinner"; and Ruby moved into the next room followed by Salome.

The sick boy's eyes brightened as she approached his cot. and he ate with a relish the dainty food she gave him.

As they passed out to go home while the family still sat at table, the workman spoke to her.

"My wife is learning fast, don't you think, miss?"

"Indeed she is."

"She was just telling me that this good dinner cost only a trifle and she knows what we are to have for supper already, afore it's supper time, and what it will cost. She says you writ her up a bill which is tacked on the cupboard door, and it calls for boiled milk and bread with a relish of some kind. Now, miss, I figure that we will be able to save up at this rate."

"Certainly you can."

"I believe we live now on what we once put into the slop pail when we had some left over, and starved at other times."

"There will be no more starving so long as you can earn even small wages, but comfortable clothing for yourself, wife, and children, added to enough to eat."

"I believe it, miss. I see as it can be done, and I tell my wife as you are the poor man's guardian angel."

"No, not that. I am only an instrument that God uses to show the poor man how to be happy and contented with poverty, and to teach him how to rise above it and at the same time to elevate his moral nature by making a square division of his earnings."

"You're right, miss, most poor folks eat up all they earn. It's a fact as sure as my name is John Wicks."

A pleasant goòdday, and a promise to call again, and Ruby and Salome were on their walk homeward.

"How many of those interesting people have you under instructions?" asked Salome.

"Quite a number, I assure you."

"I should think it very irksome if it came every day."

"It is the one useful act of each day that I can offer up at night to Him who gives so much to me. I can do so little for His wandering ones. At the end of this year I hope to see this family, and many others, able to buy comfortable cloth-ing and fuel, and have more comforts around them than they have ever known. I find them very teachable, and anxious, too, to learn, and it is true that they can have all the necessaries of life with no more outlay than it formerly took to feed them on what was not half so nutritious. The peasants of Germany live well on what the average American laborer's family throws away. We have taken pains to find the secret of poverty, and our life work is to dam the stream that is sweeping honest thousands into misery. Here we are at home. I would like to have you take luncheon with me."

"Not to-day, thank you, Miss Gladstone, another time I shall be pleased. I have spent the whole morning without so much as looking at my lesson. Your father will lose faith in me."

Salome's conscience pricked sorely. She had left the burden of the day's work upon her mother—not only that, but she had been ill-natured and unkind. Her mother required nothing of her, but had always treated her as a superior, and Salome had acted as though she considered herself such.

The morning lesson was brought forcibly to her mind as she sat down to the table at home. Food had been left in the stove to keep warm for her, and when she went to the cupboard to get a clean plate she noticed for the first time that of cold victuals that must be thrown out there was more than Ruby had used in making the poor family a nice dinner. On the table half that had been prepared was left untasted and would be thrown away. She did not make the observation with any idea of being benefited by it. The thing forced itself upon her, and had anyone suggested the comparison she would have said, "We are not so bad off as they, *yet*." But were they not on the road to reach that point?

Her little sister Lois scraped the dishes out at the back door for the dog and set about washing them, and Salome, after a word with her mother, who sat sewing industriously, went off to her room to memorize her lesson.

Now, as always after seeing Ruby, a great unrest was in her heart. But persuading herself that money would right all her wrongs, and promising herself that money she would earn, she walked the floor of her room reading aloud, and as she grew interested in her work she forgot Ruby, who had partaken of a tempting but simple repast with her father, and then walking into the Temple arm in arm with him detailed her conversation with Salome, their visit to the Wickses, etc.

"I am glad she went with you, my child, very glad. Poverty and unhappiness, like disease, are effects. Wherever possible we must learn the cause, and remove it, in every grade of life. You can easily reach the lower strata, but there is another grade above made impregnable by false pride and sensitiveness. In my lectures I try to reach and teach this grade, but I find you are making greater progress than I, in your daily rounds giving practical lessons. You say the majority are eager to learn and are advancing. I find a greater dissatisfaction among those who do not want to learn. They see others prosper and believe it to be by more fortunate surroundings. They will not admit it to be by their self-abnegation, their foresight and thrift. They will not deny themselves a pleasure simply because somebody else does not, who, perhaps, is more able to gratify it. They have longings and desires that are natural, perhaps right, but they do not understand the true method of attaining what they seek, but in the wrong pursuit of them bring misery instead of peace upon themselves.

"In every clime, in every country, it is the same. But here in this great land with room and to spare for all, with wealth untold in prairie, mine, and forest, with an understanding of the true principles of life all could be so happy and so blessed.

"Extravagance is the curse of the American people. The very air they breathe is infected by this pestilence. It is transmitted from father to son, from mother to daughter, like cancer or consumption, and indeed might be called the great American epidemic. It effects all classes alike, in different degrees, and beginning in the parlor finds its way to the kitchen. In no other land can a laborer off the street earn five dollars per day putting coal into a cellar. In no other country would cooks and house girls be allowed to wear silk and plush and oftentimes sealskin. More money, higher wages, oppression, is the cry. Money! money! money to spend! Money to waste! Money! Higher wages, less work, poorer work. They've drunk beer long enough, they aspire to wine and champagne. They have worn rhinestones too long, they must have diamonds. But no money for homes, no money to save; those who do save soon have their coffers full and overflowing from these poor diseased wretches who bring their money unsolicited and buy all the worthless things that moneyed people would not have.

"A young man earning a good salary must patronize the most fashionable tailor and pay double for goods no better than those sold by a less fashionable competitor. The most expensive furnishing house gets his orders. If he gets over one hundred dollars per month—and many do the same on less salary—he patronizes livery stables to a marvellous degree. If he takes a young girl out he must go in a carriage, for my young lady is dressed more expensively than foreign princesses of her age, and wears diamonds before she is twenty. She expects so much of her escort that he is penniless at the end of the month. Perhaps the young girl is the daughter of a widow with no expectations, or her father may be a salesman in a dry-goods store. Maybe he has risen a little higher and therefore his daughter must dress in the same style as the partner's wife. If the young man gets one hundred and fifty dollars per month, he launches upon still deeper waters. Girls go out with these young men, expecting, hoping, some day to be their wives. Common sense should teach both that they can never afford to marry. Men should know that, in their few moments of calm thought when oppressed by debt and care, they realize they can't afford it.

"Why don't sensible girls say: 'No thank you, we will take a street car. Save your money, and when I believe you can afford it I will drive in a carriage with you.' Why don't the young man say frankly: 'I would like to take you in the most approved style, but upon my honor I can't afford it. I want to own a home some day, and a carriage too. To do that I must patronize street cars for several years to come.'"

"Then there are flowers and presents of all kinds, improper to give, improper to receive. When will it end? Where does it end? In wreck and ruin to both young men and young women, fear and distrust of each other; and yet on, on, blindly they go upon that intoxicating road of extravagance, down into the dark valley of poverty."

"'Who has more right to ride in carriages than the honest breadwinner, or to wear diamonds than those whose hard earnings buy them?' said one indignant clergyman one day. Who? Who, indeed, but the man or woman who can afford it, being lifted above the possibility of want or oppression? Be honest with yourselves, is the lesson I try to teach them."

(To be continued.)

BOOKS OF THE DAY.

ETIDORHPA, OR THE END OF EARTH.[*]

By John Clark Ridpath, LL. D.

It would appear that Professor John Uri Lloyd, of Cincinnati, has won his laurel. He is not to be regarded as a candidate for literary honors, but rather as a wearer of them. His strange romance of "Etidorhpa: or The End of Earth," has come to us unexpectedly, and as it were out of the shadows. Of it we had not heard a word until the copy came with the author's compliments—an elegant example of the bookmaker's art, illustrated as if under the spell of an inspiration. To come directly to the matter, we are disposed to think "Etidorhpa" the most unique, original, and suggestive new book that we have seen in this the last decade of a not unfruitful century. We are all the more pleased with the work because it has come unannounced, because it is not formal, and not according to rule.

We confess that at first we did not know what to do with this literary apparition. We sat down with "Etidorhpa" incredulous, saying to ourself: "Etidorhpa? What is that? John Uri Lloyd? Who is he that thus obtrudes on the leisure of our reflective hour?" We had heard, not very definitely, of Mr. Lloyd as a man of science, a writer on pharmaceutical subjects, a chemist most expert in his art, a clever lecturer before scientific bodies; but reasoning dimly, in our dull manner, we had not supposed him skilful in literary art, and had not fancied him taking to flight; but had allowed him to remain imbedded in a poor deduction as one innocent—like most of the genus scientificum—of imagination and excursive power.

As to "Etidorhpa," we were not long in discovering that the word is simply an inversion of *Aphrodite*, name of the beautiful seaborn being of the Greeks. Moreover, we soon perceived that by a like inversion of method Aphrodite, or the Pure Love-passion of our race, lies hidden as the bottom principle and *motif* of this marvellous story. Let none read "Etidorhpa" without understanding that Etidorhpa *is* the End of Earth—not only in the author's theory of life, but to all of us forever. But of this we shall have something to say further on.

"Etidorhpa" is a puzzle—a literary mystery. It puts criticism at fault. Criticism delights in something that is according to pro-

---

[*] "Etidorhpa: or The End of Earth. The Strange History of a Mysterious Being and the Account of a Remarkable Journey," as communicated in Manuscript to Llewellyn Drury, who promised to print the same, but finally evaded the responsibility, which was assumed by John Uri Lloyd. With many illustrations by J. Augustus Knapp. Author's Edition, limited. Published by John Uri Lloyd, Cincinnati, 1895.

gramme, and is not measurable with the ordinary reed of the critic. We do not recall another book the sense of which is so difficult to seize and to interpret. We do not mean that it is hidden in a cloud of mysticism, but it is surrounded with shadows and obfuscation. The author appears to have had the *purpose* of putting us at fault. The very title leads us astray. We get into doubt as to who wrote the book, and then into greater doubt as to what it signifies. We become interested in a given part, and still more interested in the whole. We first think the parts fragmentary, but presently find them coalescing. The imagination gets beguiled with the story. The scientific studies are set in a chasing of fiction so realistic that the mind loses all distinction between the thing that is, the thing that may be, and the thing that is not. The fragments of "Etidorhpa" are nearly all in some sense independent literary entities; but there is a beautiful astral body, unseen to the eye of sense, that binds them all together in an organic unity which is as ideal as a Buddhistic dream or a piece of Hellenic art. Finally, we remark this peculiarity about the book, or the story incorporated in the book; and that is, that it is a sort of torso or *part*, like that other immortal fragment, the Venus of Medici, which, lacking much of physical completeness, lacks nothing of spiritual perfection. The story in "Etidorhpa" comes on like a play, upon the rendition of which we enter twenty minutes after the curtain has risen; and it goes away like a bas-relief or the epos of the Greeks; the drama does not conclude in its final passages, but simply ceases.

We know not whether to praise or to criticise Mr. Lloyd for his skill in leading us astray. In the prefatory part he makes up a fiction which to this hour we do not clearly apprehend. "Etidorhpa" pretends to be primarily the recital of a Mysterious Being called *I-Am-The-Man*. I-Am-The-Man is the myth of William Morgan *redivivus;* that is, of him whom the Masons were said to have abducted and destroyed in 1826 for his treason in publishing their secret lore. But he comes back again, vaguely, uncertainly, a man old and gray and venerable, a benevolent philosopher, a weird sage, who by some strange compulsion, as if under punishment, has made a remarkable journey, of which he has written and kept the history. On this journey he found, not indeed the end of the earth (reader, we pray you, read it not thus!) but the *End of Earth;* that is, the summation and final fact and principle of all that is to be sought for and desired in this human sphere; that is, I-Am-The-Man found *Etidorhpa,* the beautiful Spirit and Myth of Love.

All this I-Am-The-Man records, puts into a manuscript, and finally obtrudes it upon the attention of a certain eccentric and mythical chemist in the Cincinnati of the fifties. The name of this personage is Johannes Llewellyn Llongollyn Drury. I-Am-The-Man becomes the familiar of Drury, and haunts his study in the night. The sage reads to him from the manuscript of the mysterious journey, and finally leaves the document with him to be published after thirty years. Llewellyn Drury is a fiction. The author says of the name: "The reader of these lines may regard this cognomen with" little favor. . . . "Still I liked it, and it was the favorite of my mother, who always used the name in full; the world, however, contracted Llewellyn to Lew, much to the distress of my dear mother, who felt aggrieved at the liberty. After her death I decided to move to a Western city, and also determined, out of respect to her memory, to select from and rearrange the letters of my several names, and construct therefrom three short, terse words, which would convey to myself only, the resemblance of my former name. Hence it is that the Cincinnati Directory does not record my self-selected name, which I have no reason to bring before the public. To the reader my name is Llewellyn Drury." Now John Uri Lloyd is, as the reader will perceive, an anagram of Johannes Llewellyn Llongollyn Drury. It is the "three short terse words" referred to. So we begin in "Etidorhpa" with a Mysterious Being, who is a myth; with his manuscript, which is a fiction; with a remarkable journey, which never occurred; with the invented Llewellyn Drury, who never existed; and we end with the evolution of John Uri Lloyd himself and the story of "Etidorhpa"! The fiction is as perplexing as it is ingenious—we had almost said, funny.

The body of "Etidorhpa" is the content of the manuscript read by I-Am-The-Man to Llewellyn Drury and left with him for publication. Drury, according to the fiction, evades the responsibility, which is assumed by John Uri Lloyd. Lloyd becomes the editor instead of Drury, and "Etidorhpa" is the result.

In the beginning, I-Am-The-Man gives an account of his search for knowledge; how he became involved with a secret brotherhood; how he wrote a confession, or revelation, in the Stone Tavern, in Western New York; and how he was kidnapped and borne away to a block-house, where he found himself prematurely aged. Afterwards he begins his journey in search for the End of Earth.

By this stage in the manuscript, science begins to be injected into the narrative. There are little jets of dissertation flaming up here and there. Presently we have an account of the punch-bowl region of Kentucky, and a map of the country of the Cumberland. Near the junction of that stream with the Ohio is the region of the Kentucky caverns. Into one of these near Smithland (a most circumstantial and Defoe-like fiction this!) I-Am-The-Man enters, or is about to enter, when he is confronted by a singular-looking being, first of the many original marvels created by the author of "Etidorhpa." The singular-looking being is an eyeless and noseless cave-man, stark naked, moist as a fish, slimy but clean, dripping with the wetness of his cavern life, chaste as he is nude, a pure intelligence become

corporeal in the underworld. We do not recall from literature a creation more complete than this extraordinary being who, confronting
I-Am-The-Man, becomes his guide and counsellor in a journey more
mysterious and much more interesting and very much more in accordance with the scientific possibilities of the earth than anything which
Jules Vernes has invented.

To the mouth of the cavern at Smithland I-Am-The-Man had had a
companion of this upper world. After entering the cavern, he has
the sightless inhabitant of the nether world for his guide. The converse and experiences of these twain, the venerable and wholly
human I-Am-The-Man and the naked, chaste, silk-skinned, all-seeing
being of the subterranean sphere, constitute a great part of the
subject-matter of "Etidorhpa"; but the reader must remember that
the author of "Etidorhpa" uses the intelligence and inexperience of
I-Am-The-Man and the knowledge and experience of the naked guide
as the vehicles of what he, the author, wishes to communicate about
the scientific possibilities of our globe. By this means he sets forth
his views of the nature of things; the mysteries of matter and force;
new conditions and hints of scientific progress; the correlations of
mind and organization; the wonders of speculative research; the connection of the human organism with the elements in the assimilation
and effects of food and drink; the probable conditions and nature of
life in the interior of the globe; the predominance of gravitation over
all other forces and laws of being; and finally, on the spiritual side,
the almightiness of Love, which is the End of Earth.

This review is not intended to be exhaustive. The reader must open
"Etidorhpa" for himself. He must get under the spell of the narrative, if he would appreciate the merits of the work. I-Am-The-Man,
in charge of his eyeless guide, traverses the cavern and makes his
way further and further into the darkness of the nether world. The
sunlight fades behind them. The pupils expand, but the cavern
becomes more and more obscure. The two beings wade into the
water, until they come to a place where they must *dive under* and
emerge. Here the last ray of sunlight is left behind. The travellers
journey on, and presently come to a zone of light deep within the
earth. There comes a vitalized darkness, which appeals to the senses,
and presently the faculties of vision and perception are again in full
play under the influence of the earth-light of the interior of the globe.
All things begin to be intensely vital in the subterranean region. The
travellers come into a fungus forest, through which they pass in the
midst of such supplies of *natural food* as might never be consumed.

This episode enables the author to insert his chapter on the "Food
of Man," the first of the many dissertations of this kind. At length,
with the descent into the interior of the earth, I-Am-The-Man, being
human, begins to suffer alarms. Ever and anon he refuses to proceed,
but is induced to go on by the persuasions of the guide. Physical

problems of the vastest interest and importance are here presented. The laws of the equilibrium of liquids are discussed from a new point of view, and several startling experiments are recorded, such as that which demonstrates the rising of liquids above their level, with the possible explanation of artesian wells. The travellers continue onwards and downwards towards the heart of earth. They reach a point where I-Am-The-Man notices that his weight is disappearing. His step grows light. He skips, he bounds, he leaps down from precipices and falls like a leaf to safe landings below! Gravitation turns the other way, and this condition, which is not only scientifically probable, but wellnigh certain, gives opportunity to the author to insert the celebrated soliloquy of that great but ill-starred spirit, Professor Daniel Vaughn. His reverie, or soliloquy, on gravitation as recorded in Chapter xxiv of "Etidorhpa" embraces, according to our opinion, the profoundest speculations that have ever been uttered relative to the ultimate force of universal nature.

The reader must understand that I-Am-The-Man, who generally defines himself by the compound epithet of The-Man-Who-Did-It, did not read the whole of his manuscript to Llewellyn Drury at one sitting. The Mysterious Being on the contrary, came again and again to Drury's study, and there by night read the manuscript in sections. He would read and then leave his unwilling host to reflect and investigate. All this, being interpreted, signifies that the author of "Etidorhpa" has been considering scientific problems in groups, or sections, and that this book records the best of his deductive philosophy and the rarest of his speculations. Forget not that the author of the book is ostensibly Llewellyn Drury. It is *his* study that is visited by night, and out of such visitation the weird imagery and profound suggestions of "Etidorhpa" are evolved.

But returning to the narrative, I-Am-The-Man comes back from time to time and continues his reading. He next recites how he and the earth-man who is his guide, sightless, wet, and chaste, journeyed on to the central regions of the earth. They came to an interterrene sea, thousands of miles in extent, still as dreamless thought, clear as the air, profound as heaven, crystalline as an apocalypse. On the shores of this inworld ocean, a new class of problems arise for discussion. One of these is the origin of volcanoes. The sightless guide teaches The-Man-Who-Did-It how the distant volcano of Epomeo, in the island of Ischia, in the Tyrrhenian Sea, has its origin in the freshwater sea of the mid-world basin. This speculation is backed up with much satisfying proof. Again we note the absence of weight; for the eyeless guide picks up and carries a large metal boat as though it were a basket. We note also the existence here of new imponderable forces, by one of which the boat is propelled at an almost inconceivable rate across the waters of the crystal sea.

All the while the fish-man as cicerone continues to interpret nature.

He tells I-Am-The-Man about the true nature of sleep, and dreams, and nightmare. He instructs him in hitherto unsuspected physical paradoxes; how the ocean of the upperworld may have a sieve for a bottom and yet hold water; how the experiment is performed wherein water, by the action of nature only, rises above its own level. Then the guide teaches the Man-Who-Did-It to beware of the science of life. He contends that biology is a dangerous field of inquiry. He brings us to the verge of the psycho-physical mysteries, and finally suggests a scientific experiment by which we may see the convolutions of our own brain! The experiment is no fiction, but genuine. Certainly under the given conditions the experimenter may see something which is remarkably like the surface of his own brain. Whether it be that this internal spectrum projected before the vision is a picture of the retina, as some physiologists claim, or whether it is a visible transcript of the brain surface, as Professor Lloyd tentatively suggests, we do not know; but it is true in either case that the beholder, by the experiment described, may actually see a grayish surface traced with veins and nerves corresponding to the exterior of the brain or to the film of the retina as the case may be—a thing incredible in the absence of the demonstration.

Mr. Lloyd goes on to suggest the subdivision of colors and forces, and finally touches the fundamental problem of matter. Matter is defined as retarded motion, and a striking illustration is devised to show that it is nothing else! Retarded motion! Well, then; if matter be retarded motion, what is *spirit?*

We believe that the author here pauses; but the writer of this critique ventures to think that if matter could be demonstrably shown to be nothing other than retarded motion, then unretarded motion would be—spirit! This is to say that motion, being the total definition of nature, expresses itself in two forms; one retarded, and the other unretarded; that is, as matter and spirit! What does Professor Lloyd say to this application and extension of his scientific speculation?

I-Am-The-Man is conducted further and further by the corporeal intelligence of the inworld (who, by the way, we believe is sexless, as well as sightless) and comes to a region of other wonders. In the cavern world there are continents of fungi—that being the author's expression for such combinations of organic matter as are fitted by nature for food, without the modifying agency of the eater. At length the travellers come to the World of Drink. Here we have the wonderful dissertation on the drinks of man. Here we come to the drunkard's voice and to the drunkard's den. This part is an invention which would do credit to the genius of Dante. It is the author's idea that drunkenness *distorts.* He tells us that in the drunkard's den he saw "a single leg fully twelve feet in height surmounted by a puny human form which on this leg hopped ludicrously away. I saw close behind this huge limb a great ear attached to a small head and body; then a nose so large that the figure to which it was attached was forced to hold the face upward in order to prevent the misshapen organ from rubbing on the stony floor!" In this manner the horrors and distortions of the *spiritual* delirium are extended by the author into the *forms* of things. Nor have we disposition to tarry on the confines of the drunkard's hell as depicted in this extraordinary fiction. The appeal of the cave-man to The-Man-Who-Did-It is all the time, "Drink not, drink not, drink not!"

Thus through the inner region of the inworld sea the travellers journey on. I-Am-The-Man is tempted and tried in many ways. He comes at last to a scene of heavenly beauty. All that is gorgeous and fantastic opens up at one place in the underworld. Celestial beings gather in throngs. There are bands of spirits. There is music. There are phalanxes opening to right and left, and finally, "I observed," says the narrator, "a single figure advancing towards me." Here then was the end of earth. The being who came was Woman, beautiful and high. "My name," said she, "is Etidorhpa. In me you behold the spirit that elevates man and subdues the most violent passions. . . . Unclasp my power over man and beast, and while heaven dissolves, the charms of Paradise will perish. I know no master. The universe bows to my authority. . . . My name is Etidorhpa; interpret it rightly, and you have what has been to humanity the essence of love, the mother of all that ennobles. . . . I am Etidorhpa, the beginning and the end of earth."

Thus the Beautiful Vision discourses to the end of the apostrophe of Love. There is no finer soliloquy on the sublimest theme known to the soul of man. To The-Man-Who-Did-It she says, "He who loves will be loved in turn." To her he replies: "I give myself to you, be you what you may, be your home where it may, I give up the earth behind me and the hope of heaven before me; the here and the hereafter I will sacrifice." But she tells him also that for her he must be tempted as never before, and in particular that *he must not drink.* Finally she passes as a bubble of radiant vapor that breaks and is driven into mist. The scene of the underworld passes away, and misery comes in the place of the supreme dream that had wrapped the senses of The-Man-Who-Did-It.

The travellers of the nether world journey on, while the cave-man tells the human the mystery of "eternity without time"; also of the last contest. Then the pilgrims journey through caverns, which again recall to us the imagination of Dante. They pass through under worlds of flowers, about which gorgeous insects hover, and from which they gather the nectar.

The old man in the last section of his manuscript tells how he and his sightless guide, after crossing the subterrene sea, come to a land so near the centre of the earth that though life was highly exalted the

processes of life were all stayed and held in abeyance. The heart
stood still; and yet the possessor lived and thought. The old man
was alarmed. They came to a cliff higher than any of the upper
world. The guide took his companion in his arms and sprang from
the edge of the precipice into the abyss below. Here they floated to
the inner circle of the world, to the bottomless gulf where gravitation
and all things else stand still. Again, in the manner of Defoe, the
author would make all this real with a diagram. He inserts a section
of the earth carefully, even beautifully, drawn, to show the direction
and extent of the underworld journey of I-Am-The-Man and his guide.
They two, after leaping from the precipice, go oscillating through
space with the earth's shell above them. Weight is annihilated.
They float. They rest as well on nothing as on something. They pass
and repass through the central sphere, where the gravitating forces
pull counterwise and leave all matter in a state of indifferent equilibrium. So quiescent is the physical condition here that *wishing* is the
only force necessary to carry a living being from one side to the other
of the profound abyss!

Matter under such conditions becomes subservient. The body,
having no weight, is as a thought floating in a vacuum. So the
travellers come by force of will to a great reef on one side of the
abyss, and there *by moderation of their will* the human companion
alights, but the sightless man of the inworld continues floating,
receding, vanishing. I-Am-The-Man is left in charge of another, who
conducts him into the land of Etidorhpa, the Home of Love, from
which afterward he is taken again to the outer world. He comes
from the Unknown to the Known again. He produces the mysterious
written account of his journey in the inner sphere, but tells nothing
about the Land of Etidorhpa. He gives his manuscript to Drury,
under directions as to its final publication, and then bids him farewell. He holds out his hand to the chemist, who grasps it, and the
Mysterious Being gradually disappears from his gaze. The hand
which the scientist clutches melts into nothing, and he stands alone
in his room, holding the mysterious manuscript, on the back of which
is plainly written:

> "There are more things in heaven and earth, Horatio,
> Than are dreamt of in philosophy."

No mere sketch of what "Etidorhpa" is and suggests can do justice
to the variety, the originality, and the inspiration of the work. It
is a fiction that stands wellnigh alone, and constitutes a class by
itself. Here and there are suggestions that remind one of Verne; but
we imagine Professor Lloyd to have been indebted to his scientific
studies for *nearly* all of what is here delivered, and to his imagination
for the rest. Humorously, we might call "Etidorhpa" an alchemical
and cosmological romance of nature and of man, with episodes on
society, physics, and love. But philosophically the work is a pro-

found inquiry into those mysteries of material and immaterial things which in our age more than ever before seem to give strange hints of a solution to the inquiring soul of man.

Everything about "Etidorhpa" is unique. The author has produced only a private edition of a few hundred copies. The book was therefore written for the book's sake, as all books should be—and for art's. The work is illustrated in the manner of genius. J. Augustus Knapp has seized the spirit of the book, and has drawn its more striking parts with a fidelity to the text worthy of the highest praise. It is evident that the artist's imagination has been completely taken and enthralled by the spell of the recital. We should not be surprised if he believes as implicitly in the reality of The-Man-Who-Did-It, and of the manuscript which he brought, and in Drury who received it, as he believes in the verity of the hills around Harper's Ferry and the seals in Behring Sea!

Finally, as to the bottom significance of "Etidorhpa," we might be led to think it a scientific, and therefore a material, book. Certainly it is filled with materialities. Certainly a large part of the subject-matter is occupied with the abstruse and recondite parts of science. To the superficial reader it may well appear that Professor Lloyd, in so far as he has had a *purpose* in this book, has aimed to induct the thinkers of his epoch into the profound and mysterious avenues of physical speculation, where the laws of matter and force are adjusted and the possibilities of matter and life at least suggested as things rational and explicable. But whoever reads "Etidorhpa" in this sense and vein reads only the shallows and the surface of the sea. There is a profound depth in this book, else we might dismiss it with fewer words. That depth is suggested in the title. "Etidorhpa" is *not* a book of physical speculations, but is the story of a deep-down spirituality, so far below the surface, so mysterious and so sublime, as hardly to be discovered. This is a story of Human Love at its highest estate. It may have begun somewhere in the past with an actual love —most books begin so! But if so, the concrete example has disappeared by some process, and a spiritual revelation has come in its place.

It is not the business of the critic to make known out of an author's work what the author himself does not design to reveal. If it were the part of criticism to make out a story from the mystical pages of "Etidorhpa," we think we could produce at least the outlines; and we will go so far as to suggest that that story embraces an account of some love so great as wellnigh to have broken the vessels that contained it. Indeed, did it not break one of them? and did it not leave the other filled with a storm of clouds, pierced through with flashes of light and gilt on all the edges with a certain reviving and luminous hope which after years of subsidence has traced the shadowy image of itself in the weird pages of this book?

POLITICS FOR PRUDENT PEOPLE.*

REVIEWED BY FRANK PARSONS.

The author of this interesting but strangely inconsistent and illogical book, affirms that "Coöperation of any kind means decay," and at the same time defends and advocates trusts, combines, and monopolies, which derive all their advantages from the fact that within a certain area they turn competition into coöperation. He also commends in the highest terms, the advance towards complete coöperation in the business of defence, which will finally banish war from political life, but he is equally anxious that war should continue in industrial life.

The way in which the author arrives at the conclusion that coöperation means decay, is this (condensing his language somewhat for the sake of brevity): First step, "Accumulation of wealth is the only boon to the human race, the only means of raising the standard of living." Second step, "Coöperation lessens the incentive to exertion and gives a larger portion of wealth to the masses who consume all they get instead of saving as the rich do, thereby in a double way diminishing accumulation." Third step,————a leap in the dark the precise character of which is not recorded, but at the end of which the athlete finds himself in possession of the generalization that "Coöperation means decay." The ordinary mind may not possess sufficient elasticity to make the leap from the proposition, that "coöperation diminishes accumulation" to the proposition that "coöperation means decay." The fact that diminishing the rapidity of forward movement is a totally different thing from setting up a backward movement, that slowing the growth of a tree, but still letting it grow, is not quite like causing it to decay, and similar facts form serious obstructions in the path of the jump, which discourage the common mind, but a mind imbued with Phonocracy vaults easily over such obstructions.

The ordinary mind may even harbor a suspicion that the accumulation of wealth is *not* the *only* boon to the human race, and imagine that the wise *production* and *distribution* of the *great mass of wealth* that the nation *consumes*, is of more importance to humanity than the small portion that is saved and accumulated; that the wise distribution even of this accumulated portion is more important than its amount, since the people are no better off because of the accumulation of wealth, if the benefits of that accumulation are absorbed by a few; and that the growth of intelligence and character, the development of splendid manhood and womanhood are infinitely greater boons than any possible accumulation of wealth. A man may roll in wealth, yet live the life of a sensuous sot, or he may be poor, yet live the life of a Lincoln, a Whittier, or a Franklin; it is the same

*"Politics for Prudent People, or The Phonocrat." By Slack Worthington. Pp. 183, price, cloth $1, paper 50 cents. Arena Publishing Company.

with a nation as with an individual. But our author utterly ignores the intellectual and spiritual elements of life—never refers to them directly or indirectly throughout the book.

The ordinary mind may also suspect that coöperation does not diminish the incentive to exertion, but on the whole, increases it, since this is the observed effect in the coöperative cooper-shops of Minneapolis, the Pillsbury flour mills, the LeClaire paint shops, and everywhere else that coöperation, complete or partial, has been thoroughly tried. It is natural that it should act in this way because participation in profit is one of the greatest incentives to exertion, and under coöperation all will participate in the profits, whereas at present, this incentive applies to only a small portion of those engaged in industry. After a time, the practice of coöperation will evolve industrial patriotism just as coöperation in defence developed political patriotism, and men will work for their country with the same devotion that they fight for it now. Then, when the workers come to desire it, the yearly product of coöperative effort can be equally divided without diminishing the incentive to exertion, because new and higher motives will have taken the place of mere pecuniary incentive. But at first coöperation will pay in proportion to service and add for each and every worker the further incentive of an interest in the profits and in the control of the business in which he is engaged,—thus at every step adding new power to the incentives to exertion.

In respect to the distribution of wealth, our author says:

Either it is better that the property of a country be owned by one man, or by all men (which means public ownership), or by some number between one and all. It is perhaps better that those own it who do own it, for that condition is the result of all the agencies that bear upon it and they are infinite.

This seems conclusive—whatever results from an infinite number of influences must of course be right—that's what makes murder, theft, and slavery, the saloon and the brothel such commendable institutions. Our author continues:

Our industrial system is what it is because all influences considered, it is best. . . . We seek to make society different from what it is. Why not try to make astronomy different from what it is? . . . Men have no more rights relatively to their fellows, than the heavenly bodies have to their fellows. . . . We think each man has about his proper share [of wealth]. What is his share? All he can get relatively to the getting powers of his fellowmen.

The delicate ethics of these dicta would leave Jay Gould, Crocker, Tweed & Co. nothing to desire. But there is more:

Accumulated property re-invested is a benefit to society no matter by whom owned; only property that is squandered or held for exclusive private enjoyment, such as residences, private parks, country seats, seaside villas and the like, deprives society of anything beneficial to society. . . . It is estimated that 30,000 men own half the wealth of the United States or about 30 billions. This is not hurtful to society if said men give access to their wealth at current interest or rental rates. . . . It must ever be remembered that *the interest charge is the only difference between access by non-owners and access by owners.*"

This is the chief delusion of the book next to the fancy that "Accumulation of wealth is the only boon." It is true that wealth privately used may be more hurtful than wealth invested, but it is not true that wealth invested is equally beneficial to society, no matter who owns it, nor how it is invested. A man may use his invested wealth as a club to compel his fellowmen to yield up the larger portion of the wealth that justly belongs to them. It is not true that the interest charge is the only difference between access by non-owners and access by owners, although the author makes the statement in italics. A poor man cannot borrow money in effective quantities because he has no security to give, which is quite as necessary as the payment of interest. And he cannot leave the wealth in another's possession and have access to it on payment of interest, because that other will demand a profit on his investment over and above interest, and if he deals with the poor man he will expect him to be satisfied with the pay to which competition has reduced wages in his field, and will keep all the rest to make his profit as large as possible. And finally, it may be the poor man can neither borrow nor find employment, so that he cannot get access to accumulated wealth on any terms.

In respect to poverty, our author tells us that it will always exist, and that,

It cannot be too forcibly impressed upon the people that there is not yet enough wealth in the world to make everybody comfortable very long. . . . All the wealth in the United States in 1890 amounted to only about $1,000 per capita. The net gain for the previous ten years was only 3 per cent per annum. This means, of course, that if all wealth were divided, each inhabitant could receive an income of $30 a year, or less than 10 cents per day, more than he now receives.

This is one of the strongest illustrations of the author's chronic habit of ignoring the main facts of the case with which he is dealing. The equal division of the wealth that is *saved* each year would mean about $30 a year for each man, woman, and child—in the neighborhood of a hundred dollars a year for each worker—but the equal division of the *entire yearly product*, that which is consumed as well as that which is saved, would mean an income of about $1,000 for each worker, which would be entirely sufficient to make everybody comfortable. Our author forgets all about the distribution of the wealth that is consumed, which is far the larger item. It is nonsense on its face, to say there is not wealth enough to make everybody comfortable, when a day's labor produces tenfold, fiftyfold, and in some occupations one hundredfold, what it did four hundred years ago, when poverty was practically unknown in England, or a hundred and fifty to two hundred years ago, when poverty was practically unknown in Massachusetts. It is a question of the wise distribution of labor and of the yearly product, that is all. Yet the author repeats every little while throughout his book, this egregious fallacy that a division of "all wealth" would give "each inhabitant only 10 cents per day more than he now receives," and attempts to build his conclusions upon it, as if it were a solid rock instead of a bottomless chasm.

These are fair samples of the quality of the Phonocrat or Politics for Imprudent People. It is the richest mine of fallacies in which I have dipped my spade since the days of Herbert Spencer's "Social Statics," after the style of which a part of the illogic of the Phonocrat is patterned.

The author advocates a gold standard, opposes the movement to shorten the hours of labor, pronounces manhood suffrage a failure and advocates property suffrage, one vote for each $100 of residential rent and each $20 of residential taxation, and decides against woman suffrage, even on the property basis, arguing that if women invade the sphere of man's activity, the work that women do now will be left for men to do, which will entail a loss, for "we cannot admit," he says, "that men are as well adapted to bear and nourish children as women are." From the best information I can obtain I believe that he is right in this, and it settles the question of women's rights as conclusively as the other questions of the book are settled.

The author says that public ownership is to be discouraged, and the government confined to the duty of keeping order; that it wouldn't hurt anything if one man owned all the coal lands in America, nor if a syndicate could gain private title to air, sunshine, and midocean; that each man has a right to live as long as he can and get all he can and no other right; that "The tariff and the currency are not proper political issues," but adds,

There are, however, vital and pressing issues. These are: "Shall unrestricted democracy, Socialism, Communism, Populism, and the like, towards which there are strong tendencies, be permitted to destroy our republican institutions and convert our civilization into barbarism, or shall they not? Coöperation of any kind means decay.

Why the author should wish to stop these "strong tendencies," when he must know that the movement is the "result of all the agencies that bear upon it which are infinite," is difficult to understand until we remember that the author is not obliged to use all his axioms on every problem. What is the use of having principles and axioms if you can't choose each time the one that will give the answer you want? The author of the Phonocrat has followed this method throughout his book, with the additional felicity of creating and establishing whatever principles he needs by simply stating them in his pages.

I have not seen for a long time a more entertaining book. In some respects it resembles the Arabian Nights—in its use of fancy, its happy disregard of all troublesome facts, and its freedom from any allegiance to the laws of logic or nature; in other respects it reminds me of those correction exercises we used to have in English analysis where every second or third sentence contained an error, and the reader must keep his wits about him and be ready to supply what is missing and change the language into a truer form.

REGENERATION: A REPLY TO MAX NORDAU.*

Reviewed by B. O. Flower.

This thoughtful volume is written by a scholarly Englishman, and is worthy the careful perusal of all thinking persons, not merely because it ably points out in a most convincing manner the sophistry, unreliability, and fatal inconsistency of the brilliant but reckless German, but owing to the broad method of treatment, which is only eclipsed by the temperate spirit of the author. The American edition is accompanied by a carefully prepared Introduction by Prof. N. M. Butler, of Columbia College, in which we find the following thoughtful paragraphs:

The habit of reflective analysis, like letter-writing and other accomplishments that require much leisure, is slipping away from us under the pressure of our complex modern life. The newspaper, with its surges of insensate passion and unreasoned opinion, thinks for large portions of the community; and its thinking, like the amusements of the nursery, expresses itself in ways that appeal chiefly to the eye and to the ear. Information about things is too often mistaken for knowledge of things. . . . The music of Wagner, the dramas of Ibsen, the romances of Zola, the art of the pre-Raphaelites, the mystics, the symbolists, the Parnassians—who but a "decadent" would treat all these alike?—are passed in review and pronounced to be proofs of the decadence of mankind even more conclusive than those based upon physical measurements. All this is done in the name of Science, which, reversing the procedure of Saturn, thus hastens to devour the parent that begot it. Modern Civilization. . . .

Nordau is particularly prone to regard the small achievements of a certain school of alienists as having supplied him with a conclusive test of all excellence. Indeed, no part of his diatribe is more open to criticism than the use he makes of Science.

There is also hidden from Nordau's view that noble conception of the place and significance of Science to which Tyndall gave expression in the eloquent peroration of his Belfast address more than twenty years ago:

"Science itself not infrequently derives motive-power from an ultra-scientific source. Some of its greatest discoveries have been made under the stimulus of a non-scientific ideal. . . . The world embraces not only a Newton, but a Shakspere—not only a Boyle, but a Raphael —not only a Kant, but a Beethoven—not only a Darwin, but a Carlyle.

*"Regeneration: A Reply to Max Nordau." With Introduction by Prof. Nicholas Murray Butler. Cloth, pp. 312, price, $1.75. G. P. Putnam's Sons, New York.

Not in each of these, but in all, is human nature whole. They are not opposed, but supplementary—not mutually exclusive, but reconcilable. And if, unsatisfied with them all, the human mind, with the yearning of a pilgrim for his distant home, will still turn to the Mystery from which it has emerged, seeking so to fashion it as to give unity to thought and faith, so long as this is done, not only without intolerance or bigotry of any kind, but with the enlightened recognition that ultimate fixity of recognition is here unattainable, and that each succeeding age must be held free to fashion the mystery in accordance with its own needs—then casting aside all the restrictions of Materialism, I would affirm this to be a field for the noblest exercise of what, in contrast with the knowing faculties, may be called the creative faculties of man."

Why, then, should not literature and art and music enter and occupy the very field that the apostles of Science assign to them, without being exposed to the alienists' sneers for their symbolism and their mysticism? The truth is that Nordau is the slave of one idea, and that the logical outcome of his definition and conception of abnormality. Ribot described such a case perfectly when he said that "Nothing is more common or better known than the momentary appropriation of the personality by some intense and fixed idea. As long as this idea occupies consciousness, we may say without exaggeration that it constitutes the individual." Degeneration constitutes Nordau. He is himself an abnormality and a pathological type.

A fair idea of the scope of the volume may be gathered from the following subjects discussed: "Who is the Critic?" "Dusk or Dawn," "Mysticism and the Unknowable," "Symbolism and Logic," "The Bankruptcy of Science," "The Light of Russia," "The Real Ibsen," "An Ethical Inquisition," "Richard Wagner," "Vigorous Affirmations," "The Religion of Self," "Regeneration."

While not at all times agreeing with our author, I can recommend the volume as being on the whole a noble, helpful, and much-needed work. It is wholesomely optimistic, and far more scientific in its spirit, as well as its method of treatment, than the work of Nordau which it criticises.

A NOTABLE HANDBOOK FOR SOCIAL PURITY WORKERS.*

REVIEWED BY B. O. FLOWER.

The magnificent success of the first national congress of the American Purity Alliance was almost epoch-marking in its significance; coming during the confusion and turmoil of the great transition period which marks the closing decade of the nineteenth century, it was an event of special importance. That so successful a congress could be held, though due largely to the inde-

---

* The National Purity Congress, Its Papers, Addresses, and Portraits," containing fifty papers and addresses by eminent writers and speakers, covering many aspects of the purity question,—Rescue, Educational, Preventive, Legislative, Economic, and Religious. Edited by Aaron M. Powell, President of the American Purity Alliance. This volume contains sixty half-tone portraits, pp. 425. Cloth, price $2.50. American Purity Alliance, the United Charities Building, Fourth Ave. and 22d Street, New York, N. Y.

fatigable labor of Mr. Powell, President of the American Purity Alliance, and his sincere colaborers, indicates the awakening of the conscience of our nation to the imperative demands of the hour for brave, earnest, outspoken, educational agitation, that our civilization may be spared the awful fate which has attended every civilization of the past which has surrendered the high ideals of purity and justice to passion and injustice. So valuable, nay, so indispensable, do I feel this volume to be to social purity workers, and because I desire to give our readers a correct idea of its character, I give below the Table of Contents:

as Related to the Purity Movement," Mrs. Mariana W. Chapman—Address, Mrs. Mary T. Burt—Letter from Mrs. C. T. Cole—Address, "Rescue Work," Mrs. A. L. Prindle, Florence Crittenton Mission—Address, Mrs. Mary A. Livermore—Resolutions—Sermon, "Personal and Public Purity," Rev. Joseph May—Paper, "Relation of Poverty to Purity," William Lloyd Garrison—Paper, "Public Baths and Public Comfort Stations, and their Relation to Public Morals," William H. Tolman, Ph. D.—Address, "Demoralizing Literature," Anthony Comstock—Paper, "Equal Suffrage vs. Purity," Henry B. Blackwell—Paper, "Protection for Young Women in Stores, Factories, and other Places of Business," Isaac H. Clothier—Letter from Mrs. Laura Ormiston Chant—Paper, "The Canadian Law for the Protection of Women and Girls," with Suggestions for Its Amendment and for a General Code," D. A. Watt—"Regulation of Vice: Questions and Answers," Miss Harriet A. Shinn.

It is needless for me to say that personally I do not agree with all the thoughts advanced in a congress in which the great problem of social purity is discussed from so many points of view, any more than I would expect all thinkers represented to agree with me in all the positions I took; but this could not be otherwise, nor is it the iron law of conformity that earnest men and women with broad vision expect or aim at in the closing years of this century. That such a gathering of representative thinkers and earnest workers should be held, and that such able and outspoken utterances should meet with such approval as to demand the issuance in a large volume of the verbatim addresses is almost as hopeful and significant a fact as the general raising of the age-of-consent laws throughout the United States last year and the vigorous agitation now being carried on in states yet in the black-list. In his opening address President Powell thus outlined in part the objects of the congress:

We meet on this occasion in the First National Purity Congress held under the auspices of the American Purity Alliance. Our objects in convening this congress are, the repression of vice, the prevention of its regulation by the state, the better protection of the young, the rescue of the fallen, to extend the white cross work among men, and to proclaim the law of purity as equally binding upon men and women.

Purity is fundamental in its importance to the individual, to the home, and to the nation. There can be no true manhood, no true womanhood except as based upon the law of purity. There can be no security for the home, there can be no home-life in its best sense, except as it is based upon the law of purity. There can be no true prosperity, there can be no perpetuation of a nation, except as its life is based upon the law of purity. Impurity is destructive alike to the individual character, of the home, and of the nation.

Of the number of splendid addresses which no active worker in the field of social purity can afford to be without, I cannot refrain from speaking of the striking paper delivered by Rev. William F. Sabine, of New York, on "Social Vice and National Decay." It is a contribution of special value at the present time, as in it the scholarly author shows from unquestionable historical sources that in the great nations and civilizations of the past, social vice involved national decay. But among the scores upon scores of most thoughtful and excellent papers I find it impossible to dwell upon those which will prove indispensable to social purity workers. It is sufficient to say that the question of social purity has never been so ably discussed or considered from so many points of view. Perhaps it is enough to say that no person interested in social purity work can afford to be without this volume, which represents the best thought of many of the leading thinkers and specialists in America and Europe. Believing, as I do, that conscientious men and women who would save the republic and elevate manhood can no more afford to pursue the old policy of ignoring vice, lust, and immorality in all its forms, than a father can afford to sit idly by when his house is in flames and his children are in the house, I feel that this volume should have the widest possible circulation.

A DAUGHTER OF HUMANITY.*

Reviewed by Julia Dawley.

To readers of the ARENA, which for a year or more has been fairly black with records of Age of Consent Legislation and notices of books upon the unsavory subject of sex abuses and kindred evils, another book which sets forth in the form of a novel the dangers to which young, innocent and unsuspecting girls are subject, will be no surprise. This time, however, the story of lust of unprincipled men aided by feminine confederates in iniquity is narrowed down to two classes only, viz., the employers and the female employees.

Although the book deals with the same subject which is set forth in Helen Gardener's well known novels, it is by no means to be compared with them as a literary production, being in style and diction rather more like the sort of thing one finds in the story-papers, etc., thrown on doorsteps or hung on bell-pulls all through suburban streets. The book is "Sympathetically dedicated to every pure woman struggling to gain an honest livelihood," though it seems likely enough that very few of these will have time or inclination to read it, especially if the assertions made in it are true.

Briefly, then, the reader is at once introduced to a rich, noble-hearted young woman of Boston, of whom the author naively says: "Everyone acknowledged Miss Richmond to be handsome, so it was not strange that she was engaged to be married," from which it would appear that a plain girl's chance of such supreme felicity must be slight, even though an heiress. This young woman's attention having been called to the sad story of one poor country girl, whose funeral is the first scene in the drama to which the reader is invited, she

---

* "A Daughter of Humanity." By Edgar Maurice Smith. Pp. 317; price, cloth, $1.25, paper, 50c. Arena Publishing Company.

resolves at once to give up home, lover, and friends and under an assumed name to seek a situation in the same store where the aforesaid country girl had met her cruel fate. The simple girl, it seemed, anxious to earn money for her own support and to help those at home, had gone to New York, to work in a dry goods store for the munificent sum of four dollars a week. Failing, as of course she must, to keep body and soul together and the former clothed, upon this amount, she became a victim to the lust of the floor walker, whose time would seem to have been mostly devoted to intrigue of this kind, and died in childbirth.

So, moved by pity for her sister women, our daughter of humanity announces to her astonished lover her intention to investigate for herself, thus:

If, as you say, I occupy a pedestal of virtue, is it right for me to remain out of sight and hearing of those whom fate has made unfortunate? If my foothold is firm, if I am impregnable, should I hesitate to help steady the tottering steps of *a humble* [sic!] sister, who, as she stands on the brink of *her* pedestal, as precious and good as mine, hungers for food and cannot reach it unless she takes the irrevocable step downwards? Would her touch pollute me if, by leaning upon me, she were enabled to stand fast? Surely not.

Of course our heroine found the state of things even worse than she had expected, as most of us are sure to do, if we set out to look for evil, everywhere. The result of her investigations during seven months of servitude at —— and Co.'s, is thus summed up:

The proprietor will, for example, cast his lustful eye upon a good-looking girl in his employ. She avoids his advances for a while, but in vain. He persists, threatening her refusal with dismissal, promising to reward her surrender with increased pay. In desperation she seeks employment at other stores, but there are no vacancies. She is friendless and penniless. Live disgraced or die pure are the two alternatives she has to face. Sometimes she is brave enough to choose the latter course, but not often.

On the other hand, our heroine found among her new associates

The younger girls all appeared to flirt with men, and the questionable jokes made by one sex to the other often caused the blush of shame to mount into her cheeks. . . . She had imagined timid, retiring girls, subjected to the insults of brutal men who lorded their power over them; while the reality appeared to be quite the contrary . . . their manners were certainly more polite and polished than were those of the girls, who in many cases, invited familiarity.

Finally, having gained the necessary evidence; saved one poor, weak sister from suicide; helped another to a position as companion; ministered at the deathbed of the murderer, who died in hospital, and only thus was saved from trial for the attack upon the seducer of his intended wife; having found in the hospital surgeon a true and noble lover in place of the former one who could not endure to see his betrothed descend (?) to the position of a shop girl, this daughter of humanity, in her own proper person as the distinguished Boston heiress, delivered her first, and so far as we know, last lecture, before an audience of five hundred people. She arraigned all the offenders, the so-called helping hand societies, churches, and all the rest. The papers, full of reports of her lecture, reached thousands of readers; "public opinion veered about . . . and she had laid the groundwork for a certain reform." Some months after, Doctor Curtis and his gentle wife set on foot a plan of organization for rescue, to be known as "Daughters of Humanity," of which no doubt more will be heard.

So much for the book. Whether it will bring about an immediate reform in this line remains to be seen. That girls, and men too, in all sorts of employment, are ill paid and ground down to lowest living wages, is indisputable. That in department stores as in all places where hundreds of young women are employed among scores of men, there are many such instances as those recorded in this story, is no doubt true, human nature being much the same whether on social heights among the Mrs. St. Johns or the so-called lower strata of workers and mere vagabonds. Seduction, scheming, wrongs of all sorts, and oppression in all forms will be manifest so long as the preponderance of human thought, the drift of most literary effort, the trend of art, all are turned constantly in the direction of selfish greed, gratification of the senses, the lust of the flesh, and the pride of the eye; so long, in fact, as nearly all the sons and daughters of humanity live only in the *apparent* and lose sight of the *real* self.

One word more. There is probably no city of any size, where just such stories of life, wherever female help is employed, are not told. But any right-minded person would be sorry, I am sure, to believe that among the thousands thus employed none were virtuous or safe from insult and degradation, or that every male employer or person in authority is like those described in this book, descriptive of one among the many grave wrongs done to some daughters of humanity *because of a false estimate of human needs and human rights.*

James T. Bixby

THE ARENA.

No. LXXVIII.

MAY, 1896.

PROFESSOR ROENTGEN'S DISCOVERY AND THE INVISIBLE WORLD AROUND US.

BY PROF. JAMES T. BIXBY, PH. D.

The scientific world has been stirred and quickened, as rarely before, by the remarkable discovery of the power of the cathode rays, sent out through a vacuum tube, to give photographic prints of concealed objects, like the bones of the hands, coins locked in boxes, or bullets buried in the flesh. While the credit of this wonderful scientific achievement belongs unquestionably to Professor Roentgen of Würzburg, it is interesting to note that more than one physicist had been on the very verge of the same discovery. One of Dr. John W. Draper's favorite experiments, several years ago, was to lay a key on a sensitive phosphorescent surface, exposed to electrical action. After taking off the key, the plate was put away in the dark. On taking it out again and subjecting the plate to electrical action, the image of the key reappeared. In 1893, Doctor Lenard described before the Royal Prussian Academy of Sciences at Berlin, an arrangement by which these cathode rays were made to pass through a plate of aluminum.

But Professor Roentgen has given to these peculiar rays an immensely wider application and worked with them unprecedented and truly marvellous effects. Invisible to the eye, they pass through liquids, fleshy tissues, wood, and organic substances as if they were non-existent, however opaque to light they may be. But on the sensitized photographic plate or paper, though that also be boxed up securely, they leave a record of whatever article, non-conductible to their rays (as many of the metals are) may have been in their path. Through this discovery, the investigation of many diseases and the detection of flaws and alloys in metals will be wonderfully advanced. Many opaque substances are as translucent to these rays as glass is to light.

The scientific world is naturally interested in these strange phenomena. But to the religious world they are equally suggestive. They supply another of those stimulating intimations of an invisible world, which physical research has, in more than one domain, contributed to the encouragement of faith.

One of the popular cries of the day is that which laments the materializing tendencies of modern science. It is true that there is a numerous host who, intoxicated with the smattering of the new knowledge which they have obtained, have made an idol of physical nature and have fancied that every extension of law and every transformation of energy that was found out, expelled in the same measure the divine and the spiritual from the universe. Nothing (according to this pseudo-scientific scepticism) is to be credited, except what the eye can see or the finger feel. Influence and analogy, such as religion builds its temple with, are illegitimate methods of reasoning. Imagination and faith are but wings of Icarus that are sure to bring to destruction the man rash enough to explore with them.

But the real bearing of scientific research has not been thus antagonistic to faith. It has found that it can progress only by taking imagination as its guide and inference as its staff; and its greatest triumphs have been obtained by a courageous rejection of the sceptic's dictum, that the horizon of sense is commensurate with the limits of either possible existence or possible knowledge. What constitutes, according to science, one-half of the earth's crust, and eight-ninths of its lakes and oceans? Oxygen gas, the chemists assure us. But no chemist has ever seen, grasped, tasted, or smelled pure oxygen. It manifests itself, even when condensed to a liquid, only by its forces, the gravitative, repulsive, or chemic properties which it exhibits.

The more carefully science examines the senses, the more surely it demonstrates their limitations and of how small a part of the universe these fleshly organs can catch a glimpse. With the sirene, the physicist counts the vibrations of audible sound and finds that the ordinary ear can hear no note less than fifteen vibrations a second, nor more than 42,000; yet no one believes that when, with the increased revolutions of the wheel, silence comes to the human ear, the vibrations cease, or that they would not be heard, were our ear more delicate, as are those of ant, bee, and many other insects, who we have reason to believe do hear these finer sounds.

Similarly, with the prism, the physicist untwists the rays

of the solar beam and by delicate processes measures their velocity. Only those whose speed exceeds 399,000,000,000 vibrations a second or fall below 831,000,000,000 are visible to the eye. Yet the scientist has proved that the vibrations do not cease to exist, with the failure of the eye to perceive them. When at the extreme red end of the spectrum they cease to be visible, the thermopyle still detects them by their heat; and beyond the extreme violet, the phenomena of fluorescence or photo-chemical action disclose them as chemic force. Professor Roentgen's great discovery has indeed given a new extension and application to these invisible actinic rays, stretching beyond the last violet rays which the eye can observe. But for many years, they have been known to exist. Selenium swells in response to their passage. Bisulphide of carbon by special reactions testifies to their influence. The sensitized collodion film by the agency of these invisible rays, transmitted across immeasurable abysses of interstellar space, photographs nebulæ and galaxies, too faint for the eye, even with the aid of the best telescopes, to discern.

Thus scientific research, in these recent years, has disclosed to us sounds that we cannot hear, odors we cannot smell, light and various physical energies to which we are insensible, yet which, by their indirect action and effects, compel us as reasonable beings to recognize their existence. To supplement this infirmity of the senses, manifold ingenious mechanisms (telescope, microscope, microphone, thermopyle, etc.) have been invented; and in the borders of the world beyond the limits of each sense, a host of curious phenomena have been discovered. But even with the aid of the finest instruments, our senses are soon again brought to a halt. When the microscope has been so improved as to be able to show us specks a ninety thousandth part of an inch in diameter, sight has again found itself baffled.

But because not even the microscope could discern any finer structure, any more infinitesimal objects, have physicists admitted that nothing exists beyond this visible boundary? On the contrary, science has based the whole theory and explanation of one of the most important departments—that of chemistry—on the existence and interaction of infinitesimal components, as much smaller than the microbe as the microbe is smaller than the elephant. The solidity of matter, say the physicists, is a fiction. If our eyes were but microscopic enough, we should look through a block of granite as through the openings of a wire fence; and a ring of tobacco smoke would seem as little continuous as a flock of sparrows or the constellations of the skies. A cubic inch of air contains 21,000,000 molecules; and if closely packed, the whole solid substance of the sky, it is thought, might be comfortably stowed away in the Mammoth Cave of Kentucky. In the air bubble on a glass of water, 50,000,000,000,000 little bullets are flying about in all directions, bombarding our skin and coming into collision 80,000,000 times a second. With ceaseless oscillation they swing and revolve, every change in the heat or electrical force which they receive altering their paths from circular to elliptical, from elliptical to rectilinear, or vice versa. The things which naturally give us the highest conception of force and majesty are the great tidal waves, the vehement volcano, or the grand suns and planets that so irresistibly revolve through the skies. But all their energy is as nothing in comparison with these atoms, which build the worlds, which supply the earthquake and the lightning with their forces, which give to every material object its characteristic qualities.

And yet of these atomic units of matter, these primitive blocks of which the world is built, of this accepted basis of modern chemistry and physics,—how many of these atoms have been separately observed, weighed, touched, or isolated? Not a single one. Of these ceaseless motions, how much has been felt or seen? Of these constant clashes, how many have been heard? None at all. It would take, it is estimated, from a thousand to two thousand of the largest of them ranged in line to equal the width of the finest scratch which the most powerful microscope can discern. Nevertheless the scientific world constantly talks of them and uses them as established facts, not only in its theoretical reasonings but in its practical applications.

Thus scientific faith confidently pursues its way beyond the boundaries of the visible, from mote to molecule and from molecule to the still minuter and more undiscernible atom. Does it here make a halt and refuse to go farther? Ask any professor of optics, and he will tell you that the whole theory of his branch of science is conditioned on the existence of a substance still more tenuous and impalpable. In seeking for an explanation of the characteristic phenomena of luminous bodies, refraction, polarization of light, interference, etc., the *savans* of the present century have been forced to conceive of light as propagated by undulations. But light passes through the vacuum of an air chamber without the slightest retardation or diminution. It passes across the vast interstellar voids, with such complete retention of its characteristics that by its lines, as discerned by spectrum analysis, the very gases and metals in Sirius or Pleiades can be analyzed as readily as if we should put these orbs into our chemical retorts. A ray of light passing from one of these stars to our earth is thus a vibrating column, along which run countless waves, 30,000 to 70,000 in every inch. But to have such vibrations, there must be something to vibrate. The astronomers and opticians have thus been led unanimously to believe that wherever these light undulations pass, there, as the undulatory sub-stratum for them, there must be an exceedingly rare medium, which they call the luminiferous ether. It is infinitely more subtle than the thinnest gas, since it penetrates and pervades metals and crystals and plates of glass that shut out these gases; and yet it must be regarded as of the nature of a solid, because its vibrations are transverse, not longitudinal, as Fresnel showed. It must also be infinitely elastic, since light moves nearly a million times faster in it than sound does in air. The pressure of this, it is calculated, is many millions times that of gravity. It extends to the farthest visible star, and its magnitude is millions of millions of times that of all the solid matter of our giant sun and all its planetary attendants. We are wont to think of ourselves as living on the outer surface of this ball of earth round which there is an immense void. In point of fact, we are immersed in the depths of an ether-ocean, whose magnitude is so vast that if the whole planetary system were solid matter, it would be but one eleven-trillionth part of the sea of ether whose billows stretch to the nearest fixed star.

And now, if we inquire what warrant from observation science has for believing in this ocean of ether in which our globe floats as a tiny mote, our answer as before is—None. Though the medium of vision, it and its vibrations are farther beyond all visibleness than the tiniest atom. Though more tenacious than steel, we move through it without feeling it, and the movements of stars or planets are not measurably retarded by it. Though its pressure is many thousands of pounds to the square inch, no balance can weigh it. Though touching us on every side and penetrating us through and through, no touch of ours can perceive it. How, then, has its existence been established? Simply by the demonstration that by the supposition of such an ether and only by such a theory can the phenomena of optics be reasonably explained.

The discoveries of science are, then, daily reënforcing
the acute saying of Pascal, so many years ago, that all we
see of the world is but an imperceptible scratch in the vast
range of nature. And as natural philosophy is content to
accept the insight and satisfaction of the reason as good
proof of what no observation can verify, religion may, without condemnation, use a similar privilege. Outward and
visible phenomena are but the raw material of knowledge,
"the counters of the intellect," as Professor Tyndall used
to call them; and physical science, he pertinently added,
"would not be worthy of its name and fame, if it halted at
facts, however useful, and neglected the laws which accompany and rule phenomena." The first step in science is
to group facts about a thought. Geometry, algebra, and
astronomy are ideal constructions, and the fundamental
notions of modern knowledge are as transcendental as the
axioms of ancient philosophy.

"But halt a moment," doubtless, our modern materialists will at this point urge. "Though science accepts many
things actually beyond the scope of the senses, does she not
do it on the supposition that they are conceivably perceptible to sense, if only our senses were sharpened? Everything that positive science admits must belong to the realm
of matter, although the quantity of matter be very attenuated. Nothing really immaterial or supernatural is cred-
ible."

That is, indeed, the narrow and blind prejudgment of
materialism. But it is not the spirit nor the usage of science. Science both implies, and in many cases distinctly
recognizes, the immaterial. Think for a moment of the
fundamental conditions of all physical knowledge—time
and space. All objects exist in space; all events occur in
time. Now, sense may tell us of the finite extension of an
individual object; but sense never has told and never can
tell us of the infinite space which the apprehension of each
particular extension presupposes. From experience and
observation we may learn of the order and duration ·of
particular events; but from experience we cannot learn
of the eternal time, which is the implied condition of all
temporal things. They are not material things. Shall
space and time, then, be set down as fictions? But that
equally is impossible. They are, as all intuitively perceive,
the atmosphere which embraces all, the infinite ocean of
reality within which all float, the fundamental conditions
of experience. We can mentally think away everything
that is an object of sensation. But we cannot think away

space itself. Space is an integral part of all states of consciousness whatever.

Again, to explain the energies of nature, we must suppose the existence of the immaterial. For if we suppose no other kind of force in existence than that which is a property of material objects and seated in them, then the attraction of gravitation and cohesion, the repulsion of heat, the positive and negative forces of electricity and magnetism, are inexplicable. Immense voids separate star from star; yet the force of gravitation passes almost instantly from one to the other. Even between molecule and molecule similar interspaces, quite as large in proportion to their size, it is calculated, exist. For the hardest of substances are not absolutely incompressible; i. e., their molecules are not in direct contact one with another. One eminent mathematician has figured out that in a piece of dense metal the atoms would be as far apart as would a hundred men scattered evenly over the surface of England. I am quite willing to give up ninety-nine one hundredths of this claim, and still the intervals between the atoms are relatively immense. But if there be such interatomic voids everywhere, how do the waves of light and heat, the attractions and repulsions of chemic or electric power, get across? Think, e. g., of the extraordinary force with which a single gramme of hydrogen unites with the proportionate amount of chlorine (thirty-five and five tenths grammes) to form a speck of hydrogen chlorine—a force equal to lifting 10,000 kilogrammes to the height of a metre in a second. How can such a huge energy be compressed into a pinch of powder? How can it pass the huge voids that isolate it from its nearest neighbor? Diffuse, in the imagination, the luminous ether through all these interspaces,—still the problem is but pushed a little further back. For we have to invest this ether with absolutely contradictory properties, inconsistent with material substance. It must be rarer than hydrogen gas and more tenacious than steel, frictionless and yet with power to transmit motion and pressure with inconceivable speed and elasticity. If the ether has porosity and interspaces, then another finer ether must be conceived to fill these. If not, and space is absolutely filled with ether, then motion becomes impossible, and there arises a new lot of scientific conundrums to perplex us. In short, the supposition that the various physical energies are seated in matter and act only where there is matter, involves so many inconsistencies and difficulties that philosophers are accepting their immaterial character as the lesser improbability, and are resolving both atoms and ether into spherules or lines of force.

Certainly, when we see the vital force overruling the power of gravity and reversing the play of chemic affinities as it does; building up, out of inert and unconscious grains, sentient organisms, moulded according to ideal plans, and repairing intelligently its mechanisms when accidentally injured,—then we must recognize in it a power more than mechanical. Think of these marvels of heredity: the vanished loves or antipathies of the past, recorded in invisible ink in the instinct of the young creature, opening its eyes for the first time on the world; the newly hatched chick, aiming at its insect prey as dextrously as if it were a veteran, or running off in fright at the notes of the hawk that for the first time strike its untutored ear. Surely, for this, more is needed than certain arrangements of unconscious molecules.

In fact, in every commonest thought or exertion of the will there is a power which cannot be reduced to any sort of material property. It cannot be measured in foot-pounds. It has no extension nor form. This conscious mind moves and rules the body. It opens or shuts at will the window of attention to such feelings and thoughts as it chooses. Closely as it is connected with the bodily energies and changes, it feels itself to be of an entirely different nature. The more light the careful experiments of the physiologists have supplied on the material conditions of consciousness, the more they are compelled to see that none of these environments or conditions belong to its essence. Even to preserve the fundamental law of the conservation of energy and keep the chain of physical causation from falling to pieces, science has to admit that thoughts and physical energies do not transform themselves, one into the other, but move in parallel circuits. They constantly correspond, but they never interchange. Material as is its temple, material as are the instrument and process of every act, our consciousness belongs to an unseen world of its own and moves in a supermaterial sphere. What is there in inert matter to explain the vital architecture of the simplest grass-blade, the reproductive power of the humblest germ-cell? What is there in blind force or insentient atom to sift and order the medley of sounds and sights that strike the sense, to couple premise with conclusion, to turn its back on sweet sin and steadfastly follow painful right, through martyr fires? These things belong to a spiritual realm, which though the eye may see not, the soul recognizes as its native atmosphere. Does anyone say that this life and mind, like every other natural phenomenon, are also gifts and products of the universe? But the universe cannot give more than it previously owned. If it has given these supermaterial things, it must be because it is itself, at its heart, living, feeling, thinking; and that is but a more secular way of saying that it is a part or manifestation of that Divine Spirit whose stature is space, whose age eternity, and on whose azure robe nebulæ and galaxies shine as the golden embroidery of God's royal vesture.

The story is told of Raoul Pictet, the learned Swiss physicist, that once, having listened to a wholesale denunciation of science from an ignorant Catholic bishop, he went up to him and said, "Have you ever seen God?" "Of course not," answered the bishop. "Then," said the physicist, "I have this advantage as a researcher of truth over the theologians. For the longer *I* study nature, the more distinctly I see God in all nature's operations." That is the attitude which reverent scientists are everywhere beginning to take. That is the holy vision to the enjoyment of which men's eyes are daily more and more opened. In the natural world, close about us, on all sides, lie invisible realms, replete with marvels. Why, then, should we maintain such incredulity about the supernatural, because we cannot see its denizens? When the wonders of the material so overpass imagination, why should we deny the spiritual because we cannot comprehend it?

Certainly, it becomes not the men of science or those who accept it as their oracle, to shrug their shoulders whenever the church speaks of the unseen world. If eye and ear are too coarse to discern the finer manifestations of matter, why should spirit be obliged to certify itself to them or be dismissed as non-existent? If modern science, according to the accepted statements of its best trusted expounders, believes in an all-pervasive and eternally persisting Force, undemonstrable, but yet necessarily assumed, as the ultimate reality of the system of nature; and from the phenomena of light and electricity, science deduces the existence of an invisible but infinite ether, pervading space, why may not the theist, with equal justice, infer from the dynamic phenomena of the world and the rational arrangement of its parts, an invisible, omnipresent Will and Mind, as the cause and sustainer of all? And if the one view is not to be declared a mere figment of the scientific imagination because it rests, not on direct observation, but on inferential and analogical reasoning and the intuitions of consciousness, why should the other be rejected as a theological fiction because its foundations are of the same kind and order?

Even the materialists have to admit the spirit in the body, as something different from the body itself. But it is denied to be anything but a property sealed in the flesh, confined in its sphere of action to the nervous circuit, and perishing with the decomposing brain, as the piano's music perishes with the breaking of its wires.

But when we see, as in these cathode photographs, boxed-up metal and collodion film communicating through opaque envelopes, can we doubt the equal power of the mind to send its messages to neighbor minds, across similar gaps and barriers? The marvels of telepathy, of mind-cure, thought-transference, and clairvoyance have, for not a few years back, been admitted by the select circle of cautious investigators. With such analogies from the physical realm as these recent discoveries supply, ought they not to be generally acknowledged? And if the soul can thus send its mental telegrams and photographic images across land and sea, without wire or conductor, by its own spirit currents, is not the argument for its supermaterial nature and power to survive the shock of death and from the other shore to send back, on privileged occasions, some messages of comfort or help to the friends left behind, immensely strengthened?

"Where are your boasted mansions in the skies?" is the frequent sneer of those whose eyes are blurred with the dust of earth. "What does your God look like? What lancet has unsheathed the soul, what telescope caught sight of angel choirs in the skies or a brain structure in the galaxies of space?" To which we answer: He who fails to find them, does so because he looks with the wrong organs and instruments. He might as well try to grasp light with pincers, to photograph a thought, to weigh love with ounce weights in brazen scales. You look too far afield. If within the pores of the sponge there is a sea of invisible air, and between the atoms of the air a realm of unseen ether, why not within the interstices of the ether, another invisible and still subtler spirit-world? "In the discovery of this all-pervading ether," as has pertinently been asked, "is there not enclosed another revelation, the possibility of an imperishable form, hidden within us, which faithfully represents in every detail, the shape that we see?"

The ocean path of the ether reaches out to all points from which light radiates, even to the most infinitely remote nebula, whose existence not even the telescope, but only the photographic plate, can detect. The announcement of its outstretching pathway is as cheering news as that of the intelligence of a road opened through a wilderness to some distant settlement where our friends had gone before. "It makes the universe," as Mrs. Leighton says, "seem more homelike, and forever destroys that haunting terror of the imagination, the vast void that once suggested itself, with dreary anticipations of our whereabouts after death."

What reason have we to think that it is alone in the material and visible section of the universe that there is any life? Why should not this unseen realm that penetrates and envelops our visible world, be utilized as the home of conscious life? Our modern evolutionists have brought out overflowing illustrations of the struggle for existence, due to the crowded arena of creation. Darwin counted, on a single square yard of soil, 357 sprouting weeds of twenty different species. In Arctic snow-fields, in the heights of the Alps, in the depths of ocean, life battles its way. Every possible *habitat* has its corresponding form of existence. Why may not these unseen realms, these interstellar fields, forming almost the whole of space, have their inhabitants? "Is all sentient being confined to a few starry needle-points, while the rest is a desert, a void abyss vacant of all interest?" What astonishing prodigality, then, in the Creator who elsewhere is so economical of each smallest atom!

Everything visible we know is transient. If there be anything permanent it must be in the invisible sphere. In the progressive evolution of man, we see a continuous ascent from the material to the spiritual, a steady and fuller saturation of flesh by soul, until in man the process of development reaches a new plane, improving henceforth not the physical traits but reforming and elevating the mental and moral faculties. This new cycle of spiritual evolution in which man thinks the thoughts of God after Him and becomes a remoulder and finisher of the earth, a second creator, as it were, bespeaks for him a grander and more permanent future; bringing our race, as it does, into a closer union with the Author of our being, as the destiny and consummation of humanity. No less noble a sequel than this to the tragic story of to-day would properly interpret the struggles and pains of humanity or fitly conclude the drama of man's existence. Though the fleshly body decomposes at death and gives back to the earth the

dust it has borrowed for awhile, it is perfectly conceivable
that the soul that animated it has already organized for
itself some subtler, interior organism, ready with the decay of the grosser body to step out into the unseen world
where all its affections and hopes have long been centred.
When several vapors can occupy simultaneously a given
space, and the waves of ether can move through, and work
with, the coarser structure of solid or opaque bodies without disturbing either, then there is no improbability in the
coëxistence of such an ethereal body within the sheath
of the coarser flesh that enswathes it. It would be but
another illustration of the cosmic economy, which throughout nature builds up system within system, like the con-
jurer's nest of balls. Whether we regard the soul as
seated, according to the old view, in some subtle effluence
incarnated in the fleshly temple, or as scientific monists to-
day suppose, in some single superintending atom or royal
monad, enthroned in the brain, in either case it can organize about itself some firm atomic phalanx or indivisible
vortex ring of ether, equipped with which it may enter
on its new life with an organism equal to the demands of
its new destiny. Wherever life is nobly led there is constantly being evolved something which belongs not to the
dust of the body, a conscious personality more permanent
and unitary than the flux of the atoms which pass in and
out, a character whose attributes of reason, love, and righteousness have no explanation in any chemical properties.
As force is the preëminently persistent thing, this vital
force of the spirit, the highest shoot of the cosmic tree of
life, naturally persists. The rending of the flesh is but
the release of the soul.

> "Eternal process, moving on
> From state to state, the spirit walks.
> And these are but the shattered stalks
> Or ruined chrysalis of one."

When the opaque is being found transparent and an inch
of air to be the avenue for a multitude of diverse waves,
and streams of energies, of entirely different order, cross
and recross without the slightest interference, is it not
conceivable that this veil which separates us from the spiritual world may be after all a mere film, whose very thinness makes it appear so impenetrable?

"A turn, a change as slight as when the light pebble,
lying on thin ice, feels it melt and falls to the bottom, may
be all" (as Edwin Arnold suggests) "that is necessary to

lift the curtain of another and utterly transformed universe, which is yet not really another, but this same one that we see imperfectly with present eyes and think timidly with present thoughts."

The last utterance of the poet Wordsworth was, "Is that my dear Dora?" a daughter deceased, whom he saw as with open eyes. Such apparent lifting of the veil for brief moments is not at all infrequent, and there are many of these occurrences, free from all suspicion of delirium, that are abundantly certified. Approaching death, instead of enfeebling consciousness, as it should do if the mind were but a material effect, often seems to release it from the weakness of the body for a time. Dr. La Roche, a physician of Philadelphia, some years ago, published a treatise entitled, "On the Resumption of the Mental Faculties at the Approach of Death." He stated that the mind often becomes lucid just before death, even in cases where the brain is greatly diseased, "where inflammation of the coverings is present and even where there is change in the brain substance itself."

Doctor Brown-Sequard has observed that cholera patients often retain clear and active minds, even when the blood is becoming black and clotted, in the last stages of the disease. In cases of chronic insanity or life-long idiocy, where the lesions or imperfections of the brain were incurable, the normal self has reappeared above the wreck, for a brief period, setting a farewell signal of the soul's independence. Harriet Martineau reported in *Household Words* (vol. 9, p. 200), the case of a congenital idiot who had lost his mother when he was two years old and who could not subsequently be made cognizant of anything relating to her; who yet when dying at the age of thirty suddenly turned his head, looked bright and sensible, and exclaimed in a tone, never heard before, "Oh, my mother; how beautiful!" A friend in New York, a most intelligent and veracious woman, once told me how a short time before her young niece died, she expressed a fear of dying alone; but in a moment, her face lighted up and she said: "No, I am not afraid—for here is Charlie and George and grandpa" (mentioning those of her relatives who had already passed on). After a little while she said again, "Oh, it is beautiful, beautiful!" Similar experiences have been published by Doctor Clarke of Boston in his book called "Visions"; and in almost every town or large family circle some one can repeat some analogous occurrence. I have always been very slow in crediting the so-called revelations of the spiritualists and the visions of the hypnotic. But do not these significant visions of the dying, while still in full retention of their faculties, impress even the most cautious with the conviction that at such times the veil that separates the seen from the unseen world is really parted, for a moment, for a consoling glimpse to those so painfully bereaved?

Not infrequently when the curtain of night is drawn about you, you have been summoned to the telephone, and putting your ear to the receiving tube, heard familiar voices issue out of the darkness, guided by the slender pathway modern science provides. The friends were miles away, perhaps, or you did not even know at all where they were: you but recognized their voices, received their messages, and had no shadow of doubt about their continued existence. So when out of the cloud of mystery about us, significant voices and tender messages come to us by some strange telephony; prescient aspirations of the soul, comforting intuitions of the believing heart, marvels of the open tomb or the risen Christ, or modern miracles that demonstrate the superiority of mind to body and the thinness of the shell that shuts us out from the spiritual world, then let us receive them reverently and gratefully. We ought not to fear, but to rejoice in the advance of modern knowledge. This Saul of science has now become one of the prophets, for these latter-day miracles are daily making the hopes of religion seem less wild and fanciful. These fairy-tales that science is turning into everyday prose, are showing us how much more marvellous than any Scripture miracle are the realities of God's universe. The invisible forces are the mightest. Beyond the farthest range to which the telescope pushes the domain of the visible, stretches the invisible; and by its unseen energies, all this brave show that salutes the eye, is kept alive. In every inch of space, the fidelity of God, the wisdom of God, the power and love of God, are hiding. We rise to higher ranges of being as we match ourselves to these eternal rhythms and make our hearts the obedient conductors of these grander and invisible currents of force. It is incredible that God should intend that humanity's progress in knowledge should be only on the physical level. We may reasonably anticipate, therefore, a time when large fields of the spiritual shall open their secrets to us. Cheering rays of light, with most precious disclosures, already herald this dayspring from on high, which shall make the scepticism of to-day seem gratuitous doubt. In the light of nature's grandeurs and the weakness of the human mind, is it rational that the martyr faith and poetic visions of our race should outrun the realities of the universe and transcend the power of the Almighty? Prof. Stanley Jevons in his "Principles of Science" well says, "Science does nothing to reduce the number of strange things we may believe." And Prof. J. P. Cooke, so long professor of chemistry at Harvard, even more emphatically says, "There is nothing in science so improbable or inconceivable that it may not be realized."

The more we know of nature, the more replete we find it with treasured marvels and inexhaustible infinitudes. The more we learn of life, the more its sacred joys and duties overtop in august dignity all our dreams. As daily experience shows that all that is seen is temporal, we may rationally look to the realm of the unseen for whatever shall be eternal. As we review the history both of our individual lives and of the race as a whole, the steady movement disclosed is that of a continued transcendence in the reality of things to all our expectations. Here is the unshakable foundation for human hope, that life at every step leads on and on, to loftier heights, and the present no more plainly surpasses the past than the future is sure to surpass the present.

MAN IN HIS RELATION TO THE SOLAR SYSTEM, A SUBJECT FOR SCIENTIFIC RE-EXAMINATION.

BY J. HEBER SMITH, M. D.

PART II.

In the preceding chapter there have been cited certain accepted principles of natural science concerning the laws of matter, ether, light, and vibration, on which a qualified belief in the probability of stellar influences upon mankind may be supposed to rest on a foundation of reason.

Before attempting to offer claims for the recognition of astrology as, in any part, a body of experimental knowledge, or any farther plea for its reëxamination, I beg to refer briefly to certain other well-known natural laws, and to certain interactions and receptions of the ponderable bodies in space, quite generally acknowledged by scientists, which appear germane to our inquiry.

The Zodiac.—Were it not for the dazzling brilliancy of the sun we should see him against the background of familiar star-groups, passing seemingly (from the earth's motion in space) in a great circle through the constellations Aries, Taurus, Gemini, Cancer, Leo, Virgo, Libra, Scorpio, Sagittarius, Capricornus, Aquarius, and Pisces. This circle, full of human interests, pantheon of the old mythologies and path of vanishing heroes, is called the ecliptic. In the course of a year the sun is successively in every degree of this circle, which intersects the equinoctial at an angle of twenty-three and one-half degrees. A zone of the heavens extending eight degrees on each side of it is called the zodiac, and the just-named constellations, with which our inquiries have principally to do, are called the zodiacal constellations. The earliest astronomers had found a way of tracing among the stars this path of their "Lord of Lights."

The sun does not cross the equinoctial at the same points of the ecliptic, but a little farther west each year, and of course a very little sooner. This difference is only fifty minutes of longitude, but in 25,870 years it will make the equinoctial points revolve round the ecliptic. Polaris, the north star, will be at the centre of motion in the year A. D. 2000. In 2850 B. C., a star in Draco was pole-star. The present pole-star will one day be forty-seven degrees from the pole.

When the ecliptic was assigned in degrees, the circle was divided into twelve parts called signs, and each containing thirty degrees. The signs were named for the constellations they were then in, viz., Aries, Taurus, Gemini, etc. Since then, by the precession of the equinoxes, the signs have moved by the constellations from which they took their designations, but they have not changed their names. Thus, the intersection of the two great circles is called "the first point of Aries," though it is in the constellation Pisces, and on June 22 the sun is now in the constellation Gemini, and not in Cancer; and December 22 he is now in the constellation Sagittarius, and not in Capricornus. The same names being retained for both constellations and signs, it is necessary to be careful to understand which is meant, since they no longer coincide. When the terms are used in almanacs and in the ephemerides, in regard to the path of the sun or planets, the signs, not the constellations, are meant.

Have the signs changed their influences since the earliest astrologers, through this motion? Is their potency due to the constellations of great stars contained in each? Do the fixed stars, of which there are fourteen of the first magnitude visible all over the United States, influence us appreciably, either by light, heat, or in any other way? At present, who can answer? Most of them are no doubt enormous bodies, in many instances possibly transcending the sun in magnitude. But the greater number of them are a million times as remote as the sun, and, consequently, were the question of their effects one of the mere force of gravity, their attraction is so slight as to be inappreciable in the examination of zodiacal influences. Yet inasmuch as every body in the sidereal universe attracts, in some degree, every other body, it is supposable that the zodiac is the sum of these attractions, as the recipient of rays of force that have existed from innumerable ages, and for the purpose of our inquiry, practically each degree of this zone is a fixed quantity for transmission, singular and susceptible of perturbations. The passing of a slow-moving planet, like Uranus or Neptune, occupying the space of a single degree for many days, may send vibrations to the earth capable of modifying this fixed quantity by the very

process of its interference. The action of an intercepting
vibratory motion with another and practically fixed kind
would tend to neutralize or augment each the other by a
combination of opposite or like phases of motion, as in
diffraction by interference of rays of light,—or as a combination of two musical notes, of opposite phase, may produce comparative silence or greater intensity. Here is a
reason for belief in the influence of the zodiac, comporting
with the known laws of optics and acoustics; what reason
is there for a negation, equally cogent?

It seems pertinent, at this point, to refer to a novel tendency of astronomical research which Donati, a few days
before his death, characterized as the advent of a cosmic
meteorology, in which account should be taken of the mul-
tiple reactions of stars on each other, without limiting those
reactions to the habitual forces of attraction and heat.
It is sufficient to suggest that a deep study of the nature
and action of the stars tends to modify notably the attitude of cavilers at astrological belief, as well as to enlarge
our environment through the demonstration of the multiplicity of links that connect terrestrial existences with the
sidereal universe.

The present generation of salaried observers may laugh
in their watch-towers, should by chance these words ever
reach so high: *Ils mordront sur du granit.* The object for
which government observatories are erected, the improvement of navigation as a science, or to secure continued
time-measurements, magnetic data, and other information
for the guidance of seamen, precludes almost entirely the
pursuit of original researches in the far out-reaching fields
that some day, perhaps through private endowment, will
be traversed firmly by men whose discoveries will transcend-
ingly subserve the weal of humanity.

Agreement with fact is the sole and sufficient test of a
true hypothesis. That the zodiac is a spring of transmitted
influences modified by the transits of the swift-coursing
planets of our system, is an hypothesis that has not
yet been displaced by observed facts in the physical sciences. It would appear that many recent observations
go to sustain its probability. But it appears impossible, in the present state of knowledge, to apply to such
a far-reaching hypothesis, pregnant with consequences to
mankind, a sufficiently decisive *experimentum crucis* to either
negative or confirm it.

*The Angles of the Zodiac, and the Relation of Intersecting
Planes of Vibration to the Ecliptic.*—Hitherto we have been

referring to the interstellar ether as the medium for the transmission of rays of force as though pierced by lines not susceptible of deviation, and in themselves the sufficient excitants of phenomena. But as a matter of fact, physicists are knowing to the susceptibility of deviation of the cathode rays by the magnet, as one of their peculiar characteristics. The phenomena of light are accounted for by the theory of transverse vibrations, but it is possible that longitudinal vibrations exist in the ether, and according to the view of some physicists they must exist.

In the course of this research, for years I have ventured to suggest the concept that the earth acts as the armature of a great dynamo, and by revolving in the sun's magnetic field generates the so-called earth currents of electricity. And if the earth, why not consider the other planets equally, for the purpose of our inquiry, as dynamos influential in the deviation of the sun's forces? Faraday's well-known lines of magnetic force cause iron-filings to fall in curves according to the laws of electric induction, when brought under the influence of a magnet. Lichtenberg's electric figures suggested to Chladni the notion of discovering the state of vibration of plates, excited by the bow of a violin, acting on sand, freely scattered on their upper surface. As now exhibited in the class-room, this experiment is performed with a brass plate, usually round, of about twelve inches in diameter, pivoted at the centre, on which sand has been strewn; vibrations are induced by the violin bow drawn against the outer rim. The sand at once arranges itself in radii, falling into the non-vibrating parts of the plate's surface. These angles, though notably limited, are mathematically consistent, and exhibit definite portions of the circle, such as a semi-sextile, sextile, semi-square, or their multiples, as the trine or square. So far as this experiment goes, it appears to suggest that these angles, which are prime factors in an astrological figure, actually inhere in the natural workings of vibratory force in space. It is presumptive that the laws which call them into effect act in response to vibrations in areas of the ether, caused by planetary excitements exerted upon planes of the ecliptic.

The results and probable workings of a general natural law are shown by collective instances like these, when the curves and radii produced are of a precise and permanent character. admitting of exact measurement, as here, and it would seem that they furnish the principal present mode of approaching the question of the probable influence on

organized life of the vibrations excited by the movements
of the bodies in space. We have to deal, in our inquiry,
with definite periodic phenomena which, with the constant
and uniform change of the variable, return time after time
to the same value.

Periodicity and Mutuality of Planetary Action.—If one body
in space approaches by gravity towards another, they will
revolve round each other in an elliptic orbit and return
for an indefinite number of times to the same relative
positions. There would seem to be really no motion in the
universe which is not periodical. All motion, it is claimed,
is ultimately rhythmical. Rectilinear motion becomes on
examination purely hypothetical or infinitely improbable.
Though certain disturbances in the planetary system
seem to be uniformly progressive, Laplace is considered
to have proved that they really have their limits. After
an almost infinitely great time, the planetary bodies under
observation appear as if they might return to the same
original places, and the stability of the system be established. Is there such a thing in the universe as dissipation of energy? or do all occurrences manifested tend
to restoration? The occurrence time after time of some
unusual event strongly fascinates the attention of mankind. The rising of Venus in its brightest phase could
not have failed to excite the interest and admiration of
a primitive people. The attention given by early peoples
to the changes of the moon and the motions of the wandering planets began the first cyclopædia of physical science.
The Chaldeans must have understood periodical changes
of a somewhat complicated kind, because they were aware
of the cycle of 6,585 days, or nineteen years, which brings
round the new and full moon upon the same days, hours,
and even minutes of the year. The earliest efforts at scientific prophecy were founded upon such knowledge as this.
There are evidences remaining from the brutality of military destructiveness to show that not a few of the successful predictions in remote times commanded the wonder and admiration of men.

There is no apparent limit to the complication of periods
beyond periods, or periods within periods, which may ultimately be disclosed, attended by periodic variations on
which are probably superposed effects needing after consideration, the joint result presenting a very complicated
subject for investigation.

That the path of one planet is perturbed by the attraction
of another, and conversely, has for many years been recog-

nized as one of the most difficult problems which the astronomer has to encounter in the whole range of his science.
Such problems belong to the loftiest branches of mathe-
matics, yet though bristling with formidable difficulties, have
been successfully solved in the several important instances,
and in the others, as proposed within the solar system,
the limits of uncertainty have been reduced to as low a point
as may be desired. The famous "problem of three bodies"
moving freely in space has engaged the attention of mathematicians since the time of Newton. But if the number
of bodies be greater than three, as is the case in the solar
system, the problem of their mutual attractions becomes
hopelessly intricate, and, indeed, seems to defy solution.
Nothing in the annals of time seems so wonderful as the
fact that, in our own day, the planet Neptune was first revealed by profound mathematical research rather than by
minute telescopic investigation.

All investigations of the connection of periodic causes
and effects appear to rest upon a most important and general principle, demonstrated by Sir John Herschel, for
certain special cases, which has been thus formally stated:
"If one part of any system connected together either by
mutual ties, or by the mutual attractions of its members,
be continually maintained by any cause, whether inherent
in the constitution of the system or external to it, in a
state of regular periodic motion, that motion will be propagated throughout the whole system, and will give rise, in
every member of it, and in every part of each member, to
periodic movements executed in equal period with that to
which they owe their origin, though not necessarily synchronous with them in their maxima and minima." In
simple statement, the effect of a periodic cause will be
periodic, and will recur at intervals equal to the cause.
Whenever, therefore, we find any two phenomena which
proceed, repeatedly, through changes of exactly the same
period, there is a probability that they are connected.

From such reasoning it is probable that Pliny conjectured
that the cause of the tides lies in the sun and moon, "the intervals between successive high tides being equal to the
moon's passage across the meridian." This connection was
admitted by Kepler, and Descartes too, previous to Newton's demonstration of its precise nature.

The discovery by Bradley of the apparent motion of the
stars arising from the aberration of light, enabled him to
attribute it to the earth's annual motion, because it went
through all its phases in exactly a year.

But the most admirable instance of induction concerning periodic changes is that of the discovery of an eleven-year period in various meteorological phenomena. In 1826, Schwabe, of Dessau, began a series of observations of the sun-spots which has been continued to the present time. He was able to show that at intervals of about eleven years the spots increase both in size and number. Almost simultaneously with the announcement of this discovery, Doctor Lamont directed attention to a nearly equal period of variation in the magnetic needle as regards its dip or declination. The diurnal variations of the needle have been noted as not constant from one year to another; that they present maxima and minima, epochs of greatest and least activity; and that these maxima occur every eleventh year. The agreement of these phenomena cannot be accidental, as they have been traced through many such periods for nearly a century. By a comparative table of periods of the solar spots (supposed to be amplified whirlwinds of hydrogen) and of terrestrial magnetism, drawn by M. Wolf, of Zurich, it appears that even the slight anomalies that occur, in respect to the average period of one of these phenomena, are faithfully reproduced by the other, as simultaneously pointed out by Wolf, Sabine, and Gautier.

The occasional magnetic storms, or sudden irregular disturbances of the needle, were next shown to take place most frequently at the times when sun-spots were prevalent, and as aurorae boreales are generally coincident with magnetic storms, as first remarked by Arago, these phenomena were conclusively brought within the cycle, especially by the table drawn by Mr. Loomis.

It has been shown that the temperature of the earth's surface, as indicated by sunken thermometers, gives some evidence of a like period.

From the researches of Prof. Balfour Stewart, with Warren de la Rue and Loewy, there has been discovered a periodic change of 584 days in the solar spots, coincident with changes in the relative positions of the earth, Jupiter, and Venus, so that one of the most fascinating contributions to our inquiry is the mysterious part of these investigations which refers the phenomena to the planetary configurations as an ulterior cause.

From the researches of Doctor Kirkwood and others, it has been found probable that Schwabe's eleven-year period of the solar spots is due to the influence of the planet Mercury.

Forced and Accumulative Vibrations.—The temperature from the heating power of the sun's rays increasing with its height is greatest about noon; but the temperature of the air is an integrated effect of the sun's heating power, and as long as the sun is able to give more heat to the air than the air loses in any way, the temperature continues to rise, so that the maximum is deferred until about 3 P. M. The warmest day of the year falls, on an average, about one month later than the summer solstice, and, similarly, the seasons lag about a month behind the sun. The effect of the sun's, or moon's, attractive power in the case of the tides is never greatest when the power is greatest; the effect always lags more or less behind the cause. Thus the principle of forced vibrations holds true in all such instances.

Accumulated vibrations may sometimes become so intense as to lead to unexpected results. If the impulses communicated to any vibrating body are exactly synchronous with its vibrations, the energy of the vibrations will be unlimited, and may even fracture any body.

But it is important to our inquiry to know that many of the most important disturbances in the solar system depend upon the fact that if one planet happens always to pull another in the same direction in similar parts of their orbits, the effects, however slight, will be accumulated, and a disturbance of large ultimate amount and of long period will be produced. The long irregularity in the motions of Jupiter and Saturn is thus due to the fact that five times the mean motion of Saturn is very nearly equal to twice the mean motion of Jupiter, causing a coincidence in their relative positions and disturbing powers. The mutual perturbations of the planets distort their (approximately) elliptical paths.

We should hold in mind that a natural law may be generally accepted, and even proved to be correct a thousand times a month, and yet it cannot be weakened by the acknowledgment that certain other laws of much more limited range and infrequent action can coëxist. In this connection it may not seem inappropriate to quote from Cardan (b. 1501): "Life is short, Art long, Experience not easily obtained, Judgement difficult, and therefore it is necessary that a student not only exercise himself in considering several Figures, but also that he diligently read the writings of others who have treated rationally of this science, . . . but above all be a passionate lover of truth. The astrologer ought never to pronounce anything absolutely or peremptorily of future contingencies."

and their materials scattered along their orbit, forming at
last an elongated ring of dust. The Newtonian attraction
which subsists between the molecules of every body is by
no means to be confounded, or incorporated, with the electrical or magnetic phenomena of which that same body
may be the seat, or with the repulsive action due to heat.
Repulsion by heat, even in vacuo, and independent of
currents of air, has been shown by Professor Crookes to be
decided and energetic. Under these conditions he found
that the repulsion by a beam of sunlight resembles that produced by the impact of a material body, even causing
danger to the apparatus employed for the test.

Electrical Qualities Inherent in all Kinds of Matter.—It appears, from certain electrical and magnetic phenomena,
needful to assume for atoms of all kinds of matter of
which we have any knowledge, electric qualities which are
as inherent in them, as are the qualities of mass, elasticity,
and gravity. For the modern explanation of chemical reactions it is now held that they represent transforms of
electrical energy. No chemical action can occur when the
conditions do not allow of electrical changes. The basis
of physiological activity of every kind, it is now believed,
is electro-magnetic, and electro-magnetic conditions regulate all of the functional activities of organized life. The
tuneful soul, viewless monad, pauses for the brief space
of an incarnation, in its house of transparent flesh, an electrical organ incomparable for refinement of adjustment.
As in music, it would appear of these bodies of ours, that
the smallest curves of external accessory vibrations are
superposed on the larger ones, and every influence, though
apparently simple, is in effect a system and an assemblage
of an infinity of partial impulses that compose a total in
which no confusion is remarked. The principle of life can
select, does select, the pulse of these undulations with which
it is able to vibrate in unison, and from which, constructing
as it were a free aerial reed, it raises them to the dignity of
harmonies immortal though often unheard.

(To be continued.)

WHY THE WEST NEEDS FREE COINAGE.

BY C. S. THOMAS.

The question which the editor of the ARENA desires me to answer is in no sense a sectional one. It relates to a subject of national concern, and affects the interests and the welfare of all classes and conditions. Whether it be considered from the standpoint of morality and justice, of necessity, or of expediency, the problem absorbs or overshadows all the incidental and involved issues with which politicians and the beneficiaries of existing conditions are so earnestly endeavoring to obscure it. Like the passage of celestial bodies between the earth and the sun, they may for a brief period intercept the fulness of his rays, but when he again looks upon us with eye undimmed, we soon forget the transient moment of eclipse.

There are some reasons peculiar to its resources and environment which justify the desire of the West for free silver. If there were no others, or if these could be satisfied only by retarding the growth and impairing the prosperity of other sections of our country, the West would not ask for free coinage. It would protest against the adoption of a system which must operate for the welfare of one portion of the body politic at the expense and to the injury of the rest. Its patriotism is broad enough to prevent its acceptance of benefits under such conditions; and its comprehension is clear enough to teach it that true happiness and prosperity can be secured only by methods which benefit the masses of the people everywhere. The West, therefore, is primarily in favor of the free coinage of gold and silver at the ratio of 1 to 16, for the same reasons which impel it to believe in the virtues of local self-government, of trial by jury, of *habeas corpus*, or of the Monroe doctrine. The history of constitutional government, the teachings of our fathers, and the experiences of the past all demonstrate their possession as indispensable to the enjoyment of "life, liberty, and the pursuit of happiness."

"The West" is one of the commonest of general expressions. It is used to designate a great political and geographical division of the republic. If one were asked to define its limitations, his answer would be largely influenced by his environment. To the citizen living east of the Alleghanies, the term comprises everything west of Pennsylvania and north of the Ohio River to the Pacific Ocean. To the man of Chicago or St. Louis it includes a dominion tributary to and west of these great centres. To those living beyond it, the "Big Muddy" forms the line of separation from the East. Whatever allowance may be made for such limitations upon its extent, the fact remains that the term comprises by far the vaster portion of the Union, teeming with unbounded natural resources, and occupied by millions of enterprising and industrious people. The story of its occupation and development has been and will be the story of the nation's industrial rise, progress, and prosperity.

An enumeration of the resources of this vast domain would exhaust the limits of a magazine article. Conceded to be the granary of the world, it is at once the metallic treasure-house of the nation and the principal source of food supply. Its annual yield of grain, live stock, wool, and metals, measured by the existing scale of low prices, is far in excess of two billion dollars. The cotton of the South and the oil of the Rockefellers excepted, it practically supplies the sum total of our exports. It furnishes the great lines of transportation with the bulk of their business and equips our manufactories with much of the raw material essential to their continued operation. It is emphatically the source of production; and as producers its citizens can only prosper through an active and continued demand for their products at prices sufficiently remunerative to balance their cost and leave a fair margin of profit. Without these conditions industry must languish, the development of the country is arrested, debt increases, energy is palsied, and ruin becomes inevitable.

There was a time, not very long ago, when mining, agriculture, and stock-raising in the West were profitable pursuits. The miner, the farmer, and the ranchman thrived apace. Markets were active and constant. Employment was furnished to all who cared to work. The varied occupations to which our vigorous and complex civilization have given rise kept pace with the progress and development of our leading industries. Immigration was attracted by the temptations of reward which the great West offered to labor, sobriety, and intelligence, and was warmly welcomed in a land where people were scarce and opportunities were abundant. The Mississippi, the Missouri, the Plains, the Sierras, each in turn became and ceased to be the frontier, and then the frontier itself became a memory. The valleys gave their harvests and the plains their flocks to the sustenance of the people, and the mountains yielded their silver and their gold to be coined into money whose value was kept steady and constant by the restrictions of nature upon the sources of supply, and whose volume swelled in harmony with the growth of product and of population. The muscle and enterprise of the western people became an efficient lever for the development of the country, using capital borrowed in the current money of the realm as its fulcrum. Manufactures came in their turn; railways penetrated the farthest reaches of the national domain, and content smiled upon a section which seemed blessed with all that nature and free government could bestow.

But these conditions were not destined to long duration. Nature continued to be as bountiful as before; man's energy and capacity for toil flagged not; the sower still reaped his harvest; the herds of the stock-grower increased and waxed fat; the mines yielded their continued measures of metallic wealth. The universal need for all these productions was undiminished. Wealth and population increased, and statistics revealed the steady expansion of commercial pursuits. Yet prices fell, markets dwindled, exchanges became stagnant. Grain could not be sold for the cost of production; live stock would hardly pay the cost of transportation; corn became a substitute for coal. But barter could not be made to supersede the functions of money. The yearly balance appeared on the wrong side of the ledger. The torpor of hard times retarded everything save taxes and interest on the mortgage; these thrived apace, and their persistent demands for payment compelled resort to fresh loans and increased rates of interest. Hard times were upon us; from whence or why they came, or how long they would continue, were questions asked by all which few could answer. High tariffs, home and foreign markets, over-production, improved facilities for production, cheap transportation,—these and similar causes were assigned for the general depression. Some of them had doubtless contributed to the result; but the great and underlying primary cause of these forced and unnatural conditions was the radical transformation of our monetary system in 1873, and the ultimate demonetization of silver.

"The benumbing influences" of a shrinking circulation are conceded by all students of monetary science. A steady and constant fall of prices is its surest and deadliest symptom. A steady and constant rise in the purchasing power of money is but an expression of the same thing. The dry rot of this all-pervading evil has been our sore affliction for many years, and it must continue until the knife is applied to the root of the evil. Apologies and explanations will not effect a cure; nor can the demon be exorcised by angry denials of its existence.

The demonetization of silver was intended to enhance the value of primary money by lessening its quantity and limiting it to a metal small in bulk and easy to control. Gold is such a metal. It is unfit for coins of small denominations, and therefore cannot circulate as money of the people. Silver, on the other hand, is unfit for coins of large denominations. The dollar is its largest representative, and as fractions of the dollar it finds its way into the hands and pockets of all classes. This makes it emphatically the money of the people, and beyond the power of any combination to gather it in and store it away. It was therefore marked for destruction, although its actual value exceeded that of gold when the blow fell upon it.

But the fundamental purpose of those who encompassed its overthrow was postponed of its full accomplishment by the passage and operation of the Bland Act. Its two millions of dollars per month, accompanied by an increase of public revenues and a renewal of industrial and commercial activity, postponed if it could not avert the catastrophe. Meantime there were other methods of currency contraction, and resort was had to all of them. National bank circulation was retired, and time contracts were made payable in gold, while silver could be rejected when offered in settlement of clearing-house balances, until congressional action should inhibit the practice. Besides, agitation could disturb the financial situation, and the cautious and the timid could thus be impelled to hoard their treasures. Finally, by the cunning interpolation of a "parity clause" in the act of 1890, a construction was secured which not only did violence to itself, but perverted the entire purpose and meaning of the law whereby greenbacks became redeemable in gold only at the option of the holder and silver discredited by the government. The sacred reserve, with no law for its being and no necessity for its existence, became subject to pillage by the devotees of honest money. The object lesson of the New York bankers, the coincident closing of the India mints, the presidential proclamation, the submission of an obsequious Congress, and the deed was done. The adverse times which had so long buffeted the West reached their climax in a commercial convulsion without parallel in the history of mankind. Gold mono-metallism became the order of the day. All commerce and industry are founded upon it, and public and private debts, the annual interest upon which is equal to its volume, have become payable in that metal and that only. The citizen who protests against this appalling situation is a lunatic and a robber; the patriot who demands a return to the system of the fathers is an anarchist to be exterminated with or without due process of law.

The people of the West, prostrate under these conditions, desire the free coinage of gold and silver at the old ratio, because they are honest and want to pay their debts. In times past they have borrowed large sums of money and agreed to return the same with interest. It was legally and morally a part of their agreements that they should return these loans in money similar in kind and value to that which they had received. Without such an equitable and just understanding, borrowing and lending would have been impossible. With it as an element of the contract, borrowing and lending were mutually profitable. But between the date of the loan and the date of payment money has become the equivalent of gold. That and that alone can now satisfy the covenant of the bond. As a consequence, the obligation has become doubly onerous. The effort to discharge its superadded burden is unavailing; property has shrunken in value, and the debtor is becoming bankrupt. This is cruelly unjust to him. He feels and has a right to feel that his government has allied itself with his creditor for his undoing, and he protests against its disregard of the sacred purposes of its creation and existence. He realizes that though he has paid two-thirds of the national debt of 1865, with interest exceeding the principal sum, it nevertheless requires more of his products to pay the remaining third than was originally necessary to pay it all. He realizes that the sum of the public and private debts of his section of the Union is vastly greater than the national debt ever was, and that the annual interest account can only be paid by fresh borrowings. He reads the romantic treasury statements of the erstwhile champion of bimetallism, but his personal knowledge of the slender monetary circulation of the country is too keen to enable him to enjoy the humor of their conclusions. He does not believe in an unlimited irredeemable paper currency, which is the alternative of bimetallism. He sees but one remedy for himself and for his country—the restoration of silver, the indiscriminate use of both metals as money of redemption, and government issues of paper money based thereon. Given this sort of a currency system, he can pay his creditor in dollars which are worth each one hundred cents; the price of his products will yield him a profit; the mortgage will cease to be his principal ornament, and the old days of thrift and happiness will come again.

The West desires free coinage because the unrestricted use of gold and silver coined by the public mints makes contraction difficult and the cornering of the money volume impossible. Silver, as we have said, can only be used for coins of small denominations. It does the work of the common people; it goes to and remains among them; it is the measure of their small but innumerable transactions. It does not seek the great financial centres of the land to be held in reserves or utilized in the adjustment of balances, but does the monetary work of the world, when specie is used at all. It cannot be gathered by the few and stored away to the disaster of peoples and the confusion of governments. It is not popular with those advocates of "sound money" who confound soundness with scarcity. It cannot be utilized by syndicates for sale to panic-striken debtors or to governments which they first control and then debauch. The demand for it in the form of coin rises superior to that for gold, even when administrations and financiers are leagued together for its monetary destruction. Its use relieves the pressure on gold, and like a true helpmeet it bears with the latter the common burden of the hour. It enables the people to look upon the ebb and flow of gold without fear or apprehension. It places the total of primary money at a figure adequately commensurate with the needs of the world, steadies values, makes a secure basis for paper circulation, and prevents the acquisition by private interests of the sovereign power to furnish the people with such kinds and amounts of money as in their judgment may be necessary or expedient, to be expanded or contracted at their pleasure.

The West desires the restoration of silver money because it is opposed to the further expansion of debt, and sees no other way to avoid it. The annual interest charge upon the nation is enormous. Two hundred and fifty millions of dollars are needed to liquidate that part of it which accrues to the foreign creditor and which must be paid in specie or in commodities whose price is fixed by the competition of the nations. More than thrice that sum is needed to liquidate the remainder. This must be earned or borrowed to reap its meed on interest in turn. Only net earnings are available for interest charges, and borrowing cannot go on forever. The creditor clamors for honest money or money of redemption. He has loaned honest money, the money of the land. We can be secure from future borrowings; we can perform our contracts and discharge existing burdens, by placing silver upon its ancient pedestal as the coëqual of gold. Why should we beg for loans from the accumulated treasures of Europe when we can dig from the hills the silver and gold from which money has from time immemorial been coined? Why should we pay tribute to Cæsar for the bounties with which nature has endowed us, but whose blessings we spurn at the behest of avarice and greed? With the restoration of its money function to silver and its admission to the mints on equal terms with gold, in accordance with the spirit of every national political platform which has spoken upon the subject, this republic would begin a career of commercial and industrial glory without parallel in its past and with no limit to its future.

The West needs the gold and silver coinage of the constitution, because with the South it bears the greater portion of the public burdens. Taxes bear heavily upon its people, and the infamous bond issues of the present administration have grievously increased them. Taxes must be paid by industry; for such is the edict of the Supreme Court. Realized wealth cannot be made to share the public expenditures, although it asserts the first right to governmental protection. The decisions of a century have been blown away like chaff; the great principle of equality and uniformity of taxation has been swept aside; the existence of a privileged class has been judicially recognized; the nation is impotent to enforce its sovereign power against the strongholds of wealth and affluence. It may levy war and control commerce; it may coin gold and suppress insurrection; it may vindicate the Monroe doctrine and sell bonds. But it cannot coin silver, nor lay its hand upon the sacred income!

It would seem but reasonable that if industry and commerce must bear between them the weight of the public revenues, the channels of circulation should be quickened by the infusion of a new and healthy current into their stagnant waters. Enterprise should be encouraged and labor given employment and reward. The marts of trade and exchange should be made to renew their oldtime life and bustle. These changes can never come with shrinking money volume and falling markets, with bond issues in times of profound peace, and gold and greenbacks the chief subjects of bargain and sale. Nor can they come from wild resort to the opposite extreme. A wise but homely statemanship may discern from the experiences of the past the necessities of the present, and, by a return to the monetary system of our fathers, enable the producers of wealth to meet with serene composure all the burdens which the new régime of judicial construction has shifted upon them. They must succumb at last if those who are exempt from national taxation may also dictate the character and control the volume of our monetary supply.

The West demands the restoration of silver money, because the fall in the exchange value of silver with gold has placed it at the mercy of its silver-using competitors in the markets of the world. This fall has placed a bounty upon all the staple products of Asiatic and South American countries, against which the farmer of the Mississippi Valley contends in vain. It enables the Indian wheat-grower and the Argentine shepherd to sell their surplus commodities at gold prices nominally below the cost of production, and reap their profit through the exchange of gold for silver. The bounty increases as silver falls, and the price of American grain and wool and food-stuffs, regulated of necessity by the foreign market, is therefore measured by the rise or fall of silver bullion in the city of London. What wonder that the grain acreage of India and Argentina has quadrupled in recent years, while that of the West has steadily diminished; that the sheep-grower of South America is thrifty, while his competitor of the Western plains bewails his unhappy lot, and in his misfortunes mistakenly reviles the Wilson bill as the source of all his woes? What wonder that agriculture, the greatest of the four pillars of prosperity, languishes like a stricken thing; that farm lands are passing into the hands of mortgagees; that a tenant class is rapidly supplanting the independent yeomanry of the nation? Until the reunion of silver with gold, until the hemispheres shall be reunited in the bonds of bimetallism, there can be no true prosperity for the great producing classes of the West.

The West wants free coinage, because the premium which the gold value of silver offers to the producer in silver-using countries operates as an embargo upon the manufacturer in gold-using countries. If Asia and South America can sell in foreign markets with profit, they must buy in the same markets at a loss. The gold price of their commodities, when exchanged for silver, gives a large return. But the same price when exchanged for European and American goods represents only what these goods will bring at home. There the markets have not experienced substantial change. Prices are regulated upon a silver basis. Variations in exchange between silver and gold must result in loss to the importers of Japan or Mexico, unless they can buy at lower rates in gold or sell at higher rates in silver. The first is difficult and means loss to the exporter. The last is impossible, for the customer will not buy at all under such conditions. There remains but one of two alternatives: Japan and Mexico must go without the manufactured products of Europe and the United States or make them at home, —or, submitting to necessity, use them as sparingly as possible until they can be made at home. They seem to have chosen the latter course. Exports from England and the Continent of manufactured products to silver-using countries, machinery excepted, are decreasing. On the other hand, manufactories in silver-using countries are multiplying. They are learning to supply themselves with common but necessary wares and are beginning to supply themselves with all grades of manufactured products. The causes which discourage their purchase of foreign goods discourage also their purchase of the raw material from which these goods are made. China now furnishes Japan with most of the cotton for her looms, and the coal of Japan supplies her own and the needs of adjacent countries. Mexico is becoming an exporter of manufactured products to Asia and South America, and her raw material is supplied from her own vast natural resources.

If these serious conditions only portended destruction or disaster to the foreign commerce of gold-using nations, the people of the United States, or those of them who look upon a prohibitory tariff as the last, best gift of God to man, might view them without apprehension. They might indeed regard them with satisfaction, since they must operate to diminish the commercial importance of Great Britain, and furnish a practical answer to some of the theories of the Cobden Club. But what will be said of the complaint of the German Monetary Commission that imported Indian yarns are supplanting those made at home? Of the fact that the jute mills of India and not those of Great Britain are supplying the foreign markets? Of the Malaccan boast that silver at fifty cents per ounce must close the mines of Cornwall, and give the Straits Settlements complete control of the tin product? Of the fact that twenty-one cotton mills in Osaka, Japan, paid an average dividend of eighteen per cent in 1894, while sixty-three cotton mills at Oldham were operated at a loss of £366,800 for the same period? Of the warning which the Yokohama Board of Trade has sounded to the manufacturers of Europe? Of the cheerful circumstance that so many believers in "sound money" are investing their capital in manufacturing enterprises in silver-using countries? Of the extreme probability that without relief through bimetallism, the Orient will become the supply source of manufactured commodities for Europe and North America? If the hearts and consciences of the people cannot be enlisted in the great cause of monetary reform, surely the baser instincts of selfishness should rouse them to action.

For the wages of labor, always cheap and plentiful in Asia, in South America, and in Mexico, have not been affected by the dislocation of the bond between gold and silver. Quoted in gold, they are nevertheless fifty per cent cheaper than they were twenty years ago. The advantage thus given to the manufacturer in these countries is incalculable. The same may be said of the cost of raw material. Skilled labor and machinery are expensive, but at the outset only. Against such competition we cannot last. The tide of foreign goods will soon begin to reach our shores. The flood to follow must inundate the land. Protection to American labor has long been the battle cry of the few who demand that the government shall load their tables with its bounty that the many may scramble for the crumbs which perchance may fall to the ground. Protection to foreign labor is the unpardonable sin of legislation. The party which would even suggest encouragement to such an idea would melt in the fierce blaze of popular condemnation. And yet by our insensate policy of gold monometallism, we give to the teeming millions of the far East a royalty upon the product of their looms and foundries before which the duties of the McKinley Bill are as nothing. We grant them absolute protection against our home competition, and unite them to take possession of the markets of the world. The protection thus extended is absolute. It knows no free list; it makes no exemptions; it forces the American laborer to come to the level of the cooly. It requires the manufacturer of Pittsburg and of St. Louis to scale down his wage list and his price list to that of Osaka and of Hong Kong, or go out of business altogether. And yet we are told that the gold standard alone will keep us above the level of Mexico and Argentina!

The influx of a hundred thousand Chinese has aroused our gravest apprehension. Wherever they have appeared in considerable numbers they have supplanted the white man and taken possession of his pursuits. Centuries of toil have seasoned them to every hardship. Their endurance overcomes all in the struggle for existence. They work by night and by day, and live in luxury upon a city's vermin. No race whose higher civilization makes family the centre, the pursuit of happiness the object, and physical and intellectual improvement the necessities, of existence can contend against them. Labor has cried out against their presence; patriotism has demanded their expulsion. Government, realizing the danger, has sought to avert it by forbidding further immigration under penalties which pass the verge of subsisting treaties, and has justified the rigor of its action by pleading a necessity which knows not law. The great republic, home of liberty and asylum for the oppressed, cannot survive if Mongolian hordes shall overrun its valleys and its mountains, if the dragon of Confucius shall supplant the banner of the cross.

But of what avail shall be our feeble barrier to Chinese immigration, if China and Japan shall become the manufacturing centres of the future, and deluge the world with their products? What are the few thousand Chinese of San Francisco to the swarming millions of the Flowery Kingdom? What is a protective tariff to a destructive bounty? The menace to our homes, our hopes, our posterity, our institutions, and our country which this crisis involves, seems to me to be as grave as any that ever confronted the progress of a nation. Our statesmen are issuing bonds; our financiers are buying them with eagerness; our journalists are fulminating diatribes against the opponents of "sound money"; our merchants are lending their influence to the crusade against silver, and our manufacturers are clamoring for protection, instead of rousing themselves to the peril of the hour and providing against it. Like the seamen in the storm, they content themselves by being as devout as possible, and show their zeal by taking up a collection.

The West believes in bimetallism as a national policy. It knows that there was no serious disturbance between the mint and market value of silver until by legislation its right to coinage and legal tender was destroyed. It knows also that with the restoration of that right, bullion values will return to their old place. It knows that there never was such a thing in the United States as a fifty-cent dollar;

that no silver coin turned out of our mints ever failed to
circulate at par with gold, that no creditor ever lost a cent
whose debt was paid in silver. It realizes that gold monometallism was suggested and afterwards established in
the interest of lenders and investors to the detriment of borrowers and producers. It recognizes that the spirit of protection also played its part in the selection of gold and the
exclusion of silver as the so-called standard of value; and
that cheap silver for its silver-using subjects could be secured from its commercial rivals by Great Britain only
through its demonetization. If the figures of the director
of the mint be reliable, the combined annual silver product
of all the gold-standard countries is less than that of the
United States, while the combined annual gold product of
all the silver-standard countries is less than half that of
Great Britain and her dependencies; a fact of which the
gold-standard members of the British Monetary Commission made good use in their celebrated report.

The West repudiates the charge that her "silver barons"
are seeking by unjust legislation to debauch the national
currency, or that sordid motives of personal gain prompt
all the agitation in silver's behalf. Silver-mine owners are
interested in the question, just as the gold-mine owners are,
and have a right to be. The charge involves an admission
of the falsity of the assertion that free coinage cannot exalt
the bullion value of silver. An enchancement of its value,
while personally beneficial to the miner, is incomparably so
to every industry in the land, if there be any truth in the
economic maxim that an increasing and stable circulation
raises prices and stimulates business. As it is, the profit
derived from silver mining largely goes to others. For
example, the silver-mine owners of the world realized less
profit on the output of 1892 than did Great Britain upon
her purchases of that year from the United States and
Mexico at a ratio of 23 to 1, which she either coined or
deposited in fine bars at a ratio of 15 to 1 for her Indian
subjects; a profit realized at our expense and by the operation of laws evidently made for her benefit. Did her dependencies produce silver instead of gold, every advocate of
"sound money" in either hemisphere would denounce the
cheap and nasty yellow metal and all who advocated its use
in the monetary work of the world.

It is true that our gold output is increasing. So is the
percentage of its consumption in the arts and industries.
So are the hoardings of the great military powers and
bankers of Europe. So is the absorption by Great Britain

of an undue proportion of the world's stock of gold. So is the insatiate demand of the creditor for gold. So is the absence of it from the treasuries of debtor nations and the pockets of their people. In 1891-2 the gold coinage of Great Britain at her London and Australasian mints was greater than that of the rest of the world. Her *per capita* gold coinage was three times as great as that of the United States. She is reaching out and seeking by force or fraud to acquire dominion over gold-mining countries everywhere, and divert all their product into her capacious maw. We, her only rival, her superior in all that makes a nation great and independent, shape our course to suit her purposes, and accept her policy to the end that she may utilize our powers and resources to our own undoing. She has but to suggest that our wisdom and statesmanship are inferior to her own, that her monetary system is the perfection of human reason, that her supremacy is caused by the color of her money, that philanthropy has been the lode-star of her wondrous career, and that she can be eclipsed only by imitation, and our rulers become the passive creatures of her scheming ambition.

No country producing half as much gold as the United States ever established silver monometallism. No country producing half as much silver ever established gold monometallism. None but a creditor country ever began the scheme of demonetizing either. The success of such a scheme is only possible through the coöperation of its victims. Its overthrow is essential to the lasting independence and prosperity not only of the great West, but of every section of the Union.

The mother country is the great creditor nation. Whatever enhances the value of money redounds to her benefit. Her dependencies produce about twelve per cent of the world's annual yield of silver. She purchases seventy-five per cent of the amount annually offered for sale. Whatever diminishes its gold value redounds to her benefit in proportion as it diminishes the amount she must pay for its acquisition. Ours is the great debtor nation. Our creditors unjustly demand payment in gold. Whatever enhances its value increases the burden of our obligations and operates correspondingly to our injury. We produce forty per cent of the world's annual yield of silver. Whatever adds to its value increases our capacity to pay the principal and interest of our debts, lightens the load we have been carrying so long and so patiently, relieves us from the dependence which debt always imposes, and promotes

even-handed justice in giving to the holders of our securities
that which is nominated in the bond and whose value has
neither been increased nor diminished by the manipulations
of cunning financiers and dishonest legislators.

Finally, the West desires free coinage of both metals
that the deportation of gold from our shores may cease,
and with it the public apprehension it excites. Gold, in
obedience to the law of demand and supply, goes where
it will bring the greatest return to its owners. Of late it
frequently crosses the ocean that speculators may call it
foreign, but in general it emigrates because it can do better elsewhere. With silver doing duty as primary money
the demand for gold diminishes, as it is divided between the
metals. Half a dozen cars on a city tramway crowded to
overflowing cannot supply the traffic by rapid running to and
fro. Increase the number of cars, and the public are accommodated, safety is promoted, and the strain on the slender
equipment is relieved. Gold stays with us only when silver is coined at the mints and enjoys the attribute of legal
tender. In 1878, when the Bland Law became effective,
our stock of gold was estimated at $118,000,000. Contrary
to the predictions of statesmen and financiers the supply
steadily increased as silver dollars fell from the mints,
until in 1890 the figures exceeded $665,000,000. It was only
when Secretary Foster in 1891 suspended silver coinage,
and announced that under the parity clause of the Sherman
Law he was compelled to redeem all government obligations save silver certificates in gold, that the treasury holdings began to decrease. Wall Street dictated that ruling,
and at once acted upon it. Mr. Carlisle, a good Democrat
in theory, but a better Republican in practice, continued
the policy of his predecessor, ignored the discretionary
powers with which the law invested him, and continued to
pay out gold. The redemption of greenbacks or treasury
notes according to the requirements of the law, the coinage
of silver for that purpose and for the needs of the people,
would give us all the gold we need. The anxiety with
which the public watches the departure of gold from our
shores, a constant disturbance to business and traffic, would
cease to be. But our sound-money patriots prefer to deplete the treasury. They alone are in the business. Bonds
have been sold again and again for fresh supplies of gold,
and the cheerful work goes merrily on. The administration
and its friends the bankers long ago assured us that repeal
of the purchasing act would turn the tide of gold toward
us. It was repealed, yet gold persisted in leaving us. We

are now told that the pestiferous greenback forces its
departure, and it must be captured and destroyed. That
accomplished, our silver certificates will become in turn
the offenders, and they too must be removed. Their retirement will bring us face to face with the obstacle of
coined silver; these plebeian dollars need not expect that
patrician gold will make the republic its abiding place so
long as they are given any monetary privileges. They
must be melted down and sold to Britain. Then the
bankers will give us all the money we deserve, for government must abdicate its right to coin metal or issue legal-
tender notes. This power acquired by the moneyed class,
the dearest object of its crafty and calculating ambition
will have been achieved. It is a power sovereign among
sovereigns; it is the *ultima thule* of the crusade against the
silver dollar; it is the magician's wand whose owner may
with it reduce all things to his possession; it is the ensign of
unlimited authority. Monarchs and magistrates, presidents
and parliaments, are its vassals. Once secured by those
who seek it, the rights of man will become an idle phrase,
equality before the law an obsolete idiom of the past.

Between the beneficiaries of this colossal iniquity and its
realization stand the advocates of a constitutional system
of national metallic currency, the defenders of the bimetallic principle, the citizens who demand that the government shall be the sole depositary of the power to regulate and control the coinage and the issue of all forms of
monetary circulation. The enemy realizes that our defeat
is absolutely essential to the accomplishment of his purpose. We must be destroyed utterly, or the republic will
retain and continue to exercise this its supreme function.
Every scheme which cunning can contrive or malice ex-
ecute will be utilized for our destruction; no motive too
vile, no falsehood too black, to serve the purposes of avarice
and greed. Execrated as traitors and swindlers, reviled
as idiots and lunatics, denounced as enemies of mankind
and destroyers of the public weal, we shall fight a good
fight and keep the faith. Our cause is the cause of justice,
of liberty, of humanity. If there be virtue, if there be courage, if there be intelligence, if there be vigilance, if there
be patriotism, if there be integrity, if there be love of posterity still remaining in the hearts and the consciences of the
American people, "the gates of hell shall not prevail
against us."

THE LAND OF THE NOONDAY SUN — MEXICO IN MIDWINTER.

BY JUSTICE WALTER CLARK, LL. D.

Until the advent of railroads, the opinion prevailed among the great majority of Mexicans that the people inhabiting the United States were a rude, semi-civilized race, presuming on their numbers and brute force. Nor was this opinion unnatural, since they based their conclusion upon those specimens of our people at that time most generally to be found there, rough frontiersmen, needy adventurers, and that class of gentry who went to Mexico because it was no longer entirely safe for them to live north of the Rio Grande. The advent of railroads has changed all this. Large numbers of our people have gone to Mexico, and among them the great majority are thriving, energetic, honorable business men, who are developing the country while they are also making fortunes for themselves. The result has been to elevate this country immeasurably in Mexican estimation, and they too have risen in our scales when better known and judged more correctly. But many of the tourists who go to the country, unlike the intelligent men who go there to invest, so conduct themselves as to earn the dislike of the people. The following extract from a letter just received from an intelligent American now resident in Mexico sums up many similar complaints I heard while there:

"In the last two months we have had several excursion trains pass through here loaded with Americans. These trains are specials and stop at all places of importance. Generally the people on them seem to think they are down here among a lot of savages or rather uncivilized people, and that everything is open for their inspection and criticism. Some of them make perfect guys of themselves by combining Mexican dress with that of their own country, and some of them will even put Mexican sandals over their shoes and parade the streets in that style. Where these people come from I don't know. I have never met them in the States and I take very good care to keep shy of them here. I should certainly tell them what fools they are making of themselves. No wonder Mexicans have a dislike for Americans. I could not understand it at first, but I do now."

I heard many almost incredible instances of rudeness and lack of refinement on the part of members of these large travelling parties (though of course the great majority of them are ladies and gentlemen there, as they are at home), which serve to bring odium upon the American name. It is the more shocking since politeness is a striking characteristic of the Mexican people, and a lack of good manners is, in their eyes, the deadliest sin in anyone claiming to be a gentleman. It is very certain that if members of an excursion party of Mexicans were to behave in one of our large cities as some of those tourists think they are privileged to behave in Mexico, the next carload would be hooted out of the town by the boys.

The time must come, and that at an early day, when the great central plateau of Mexico will be to the teeming millions of the United States and Canada what the south of France and the Riviera are to the people of England and of Northern Europe. The scenery and the climate of Mexico, for a winter resort, are incomparably superior to the shores of the Mediterranean. All that is lacking, besides a better knowledge of the country, is a few of the magnificent hotels which have been erected in Florida. The hotels in Mexico generally are said to be far better than they were formerly and are still improving, but much is yet to be desired. The only hotel in the whole country which has an elevator is the "Iturbide" in the city of Mexico, and the short hours of service of that have caused it to be said that "It is like a ballet dancer's costume—begins too late and leaves off too soon."

The most striking building in the city of Mexico is the famous cathedral, with its twin towers and graceful dome, on the north side of the Plaza Mayor. Begun in 1573, it took ninety-odd years to build it and the cost was many millions, the walls alone costing two millions. It is built on the spot where the great Aztec temple or *teocalli* stood, on whose summit, upon the great sacrificial stone (now in the museum close by), twenty thousand beings were annually offered in sacrifice, the sacrifices being made hourly. The ancient temple was pyramidal, one hundred and fifty feet high, and was served by five thousand priests. The towers of the cathedral are each over two hundred feet high, and in the western one is the great bell, named Santa Maria de Guadeloupe, nineteen feet high and which is probably the largest in the world next to the great bell in the square of the Kremlin at Moscow. That was cracked and rendered useless by the great fire which drove Napoleon out of the Russian capital, whereas this is in daily use. The cathedral is four hundred feet long by two hundred wide. Quadruple pillars, each thirty-five feet in circumference, support the roof, which is one hundred and seventy-five feet from the floor. The railing of the choir, made in China, cost, it is said, one and a half million dollars. Much of the former equipment of the church has gone into the possession of the government, notably the solid gold candlesticks, each heavier than one man could lift, the statue of the Assumption, also of solid gold and inlaid with diamonds and rubies, and many other costly articles. A genuine Murillo and a Michael Angelo are among the paintings on the walls. Here Maximilian and Carlotta were crowned in 1864, and here behind bronze gates, in one of the side chapels, the soldier-emperor Iturbide "sleeps the sleep that knows no waking."

From the summit of the towers at set of sun is one of the loveliest views it was ever given to man to see. Beneath us rolls along the ceaseless, moving, human tide of a city of four hundred thousand people. Around us, bordering the horizon, are the gigantic purple-hued ranges of mountains completely encircling the valley; to the south are Popocatapetl and Ixtaccihuatl, each thousands of feet higher than Mont Blanc, their snow-crowned summits glistening like diamonds in the rays of the departing orb of day; between them lies the mountain pass through which Spaniard and American, Cortez and Scott, marched to the conquest of the city, while nearer us are the sunlit mirrors, the great lakes of Chalco, Xochomilco, and Texcoco. The distant fields of maguey, mathematically regular as lines of soldiery on parade, the verdant patches of alfalfa, the luxuriant meadows, and the groups of grazing cattle, give variety to the scene. To the north rises the holy hill and church of Guadeloupe, the Mecca of Mexico. Around us in every direction are the suburban towns which dot the great valley, Tacubaya, San Angel, Santa Anita, Castaneda, and many another. There to the southwest lies Coyoacan, the home of Cortez, and in the south and west Contreras, Cherubusco, Casa Mata, Chapultepec, Molino del Rey, Belen and San Cosme, fields illustrated by American valor. Due west, at the city's extremest verge, towers the lofty hill of Chapultepec crowned with the presidential mansion and the Military Academy, the West Point of Mexico, while lying darkly between in the growing shadow is the great Paseo with its colossal statues, and the Alameda, and the La Viga canal

with its flower-crowned boats, and the spires and domes of
a hundred churches. All these combined make a panorama
which Humboldt pronounced the finest on which the human
eye has ever rested. Once seen it can never be forgotten.
The rarefied atmosphere causes each distant object to stand
out with a distinctness and a coloring unknown elsewhere,
and the golden flood of the sun's latest rays encircles the
whole in a framing of amethyst and amber.

> "So sinks, more lovely ere his race be run,
> Along Morea's hills the setting sun,
> Not, as in northern climes, obscurely bright,
> But one unclouded blaze of living light."

On the eastern side of the same Plaza is the National
Palace which covers an entire square and has a frontage of
seven hundred feet on the Plaza. It is occupied by the
presidential offices and the departments of state, treasury,
and war. Many of the rooms are magnificent, notably the
Hall of Ambassadors, which is over three hundred feet in
length, with its walls decorated with portraits of the most
distinguished men of the republic, Hidalgo, Morelos, Juarez,
Diaz, and many others, besides a striking portrait of Washington. The National Library, with over two hundred thousand volumes, the National Museum, the School of Fine Arts,
the Mint (and in Mexico some four thousand millions of the
world's money have been coined) and many another building
claims the attention and would justify a full description,
but space forbids.

A visit to the La Viga canal and the Chinampas, or floating
gardens, is exceedingly interesting. Here in midwinter
flourish in tropical profusion the fruits and flowers to be
found in Florida in midsummer. When the lake came up to
the city in ancient times the people built osier frames on
which they laid dirt and thus raised their vegetables and
flowers, hence the designation "floating gardens"; but
merely the title has been retained, for the floating gardens
of this day are simply the rich alluvial land left by the
receding lake, which is intersected every few feet by numerous canals. The little patches are watered from the canals
by hand and beneath the tropical sun produce at all seasons
the flowers and fruits formerly raised on the osier floating
gardens.

The numerous lines of street cars take one not only to all
parts of the city but to all the suburban towns and the battle
fields, for all of Scott's battles except the skirmish at the
National Bridge and the stout fight at Cerro Gordo, down
below Jalapa, were fought in this valley in sight of the city

walls. A visit to the field of Cherubusco will forcibly remind those who have been on the field of Waterloo of the contest for the similar wall-surrounded enclosure of Hougoumont. At Chapultepec, which was also carried by our troops, a visit to the National Military Academy and the rooms of the presidential mansion is very interesting. From the east windows the president looks down upon the great city and the lovely valley and up to the encircling range of mountains and the snow-covered peaks. No monarch in all Europe has so magnificent a location for his castle, palace, or chateau. At the foot of the hill is a touching memento, a tall shaft to the memory of the boys, the young cadets of the military academy, who fighting for their homes "perished here," so the inscription reads, "in the northern invasion, 1847." In such a case, God alone can adjust the responsibility. With the sleeping moonlight lying athwart the white shaft and the green mound, the thought must come that somebody, not these gallant youths, was to blame.

The great street leading west from the north end of the cathedral is the one along which Cortez retreated on the terrible night of June 30, 1520, during which he lost three-fourths of his men. The street was then intersected by canals the bridges over which had been broken down by the Aztecs. A flying leap taken by his lieutenant Alvarado over one of these gave the name of "Alvarado's Leap" to the spot, which is still pointed out, though there are now no canals, but solid pavement. At another point where the slaughter was especially fearful, a church stands to commemorate the event and that masses may be still said for the dead, who perished on that memorable and fearful retreat. Further along the present street, which has now firm land on each side, was then a narrow causeway intersecting the lake in which the canoes of the Aztecs swarmed to assail the retreating line of Spaniards. Cortez lost eight hundred and eighty-seven Spaniards (three-fourths of them), four thousand allies, all his artillery, treasure, and wagons, and when he reached the end of the causeway, he sat down and wept beneath a great tree which is still standing and called the tree of *Noche Triste* (*anglice* "Dismal night"). Well might he weep, for he had of his Spaniards only some two hundred and fifty left, not one of them unwounded, and was in the midst of a mighty empire which had risen against him. Every foot of his succeeding retreat was harassed, and at Otumba, a few miles off, it is related that he cut his way with his little band through two hundred thousand hostile soldiers. After making all allowance for our receiving the history of these events from the conquering side only, enough remains to show that this conquest of the millions of Mexico by Cortez with his few hundred Spaniards was one of the most marvellous events in all history. He had magnificent "staying qualities," for notwithstanding this terrible disaster he came back in December of the same year and after a siege of eight months, with the aid of one hundred and twenty-five thousand Tlascalans whom he had persuaded to help him, and a small reënforcement of Spaniards, he retook the city and completed the conquest of the country. Some American tourists having injured the historic tree by cutting relics from it, it is now surrounded by an iron fence and guarded. The street-car line to Tacuba runs close by it.

Notwithstanding the great work of Cortez, the immense slaughter which this man of "blood and iron" committed in order to strike terror into the subject millions has not been forgotten. A large portion of the Mexican people being of Indian descent, not a town, hamlet, or street in all Mexico preserves his fame; no monument in all the republic has been erected to his memory, while on the Paseo, the great avenue leading to Chapultepec, stands a colossal bronze statue of his victim, the last Aztec emperor, Cuahtemoc (*anglice* Guatemozin)—one of the revenges of history. Cortez died in Spain, but his remains having been brought back to the country whose name is forever linked with his fame, reposed here long years, but when Mexico became free these remains had to be secretly removed at night to prevent their being thrown into the lake, and were carried back to Europe, where they now rest in the family vault of his descendants, the dukes of Monteleone in Sicily.

At the head of the Paseo is the equestrian statue of Charles IV of Spain, a splendid piece of art and said to be the largest equestrian statue in the world ever cast in a single piece. One of the most contemptible of men, the subservient tool of his wife's paramour, at whose bidding, to thwart his son, he delivered up his kingdom to Napoleon, Charles owes this statue to the fact that he happened to be king of Spain when it was cast. The republic has retained the statue but has been careful to add, "Preserved by the Mexican Republic only on account of its value as a work of art." It is immensely more valuable than the original and all of his tribe.

In the Panteon, by the church of San Fernando, not far off, in which rest so many of the illustrious men of the republic, is another handsome work of art, but this time art could not surpass the merits of its model. Under a marble **canopy is** seated a marble statue of Liberty weeping who **holds in her** lap the head of "Juarez Dying"—a marble likeness **of the** great statesman and patriot. A Zapotec Indian, of the **pur-** est blood, born in a little Indian village near Oaxaca, **in** Southern Mexico, till twelve years of age he had heard **not a** word of Spanish. He bound himself out as a servant **in order** to learn that language, won an education, became governor of his state, chief justice, and president of the republic **during** its stormiest era, from 1857 till his death in 1872, overthrew the gigantic political power of the church, confiscated all its property, amounting to nearly half of the total in Mexico, resisted the French invasion, had the foreign emperor shot, reëstablished order, and started Mexico on the upward path which she has trodden ever since. In an age and country where the military is the first of professions he was not a soldier, and though of stoical courage he showed no desire to earn a warrior's prestige. With the power of the church against him and no sympathy from military leaders, he won because he leaned for support upon the masses, for whom he unselfishly labored and who instinctively and thoroughly understood him. He died after so many toils and so many perils in the full flush of success. Daunted by no danger, depressed by no defeat, hopeful when all others had ceased to hope, he, this Zapotec Indian, lived to see his country redeemed by his efforts alike from the invader from without and the more deadly money power within, and climbed to that pinnacle where he justly takes his stand by George Washington and William of Nassau. Such men belong to no race, no time, and no country, but are the common property of all mankind and the glory of all the ages.

The street-car line that passes by the tree of Noche Triste goes through the Garita (gate) San Cosme, and the church is pointed out to whose steeple, when the Americans assaulted this gate, U. S. Grant, then a simple second lieutenant, had a cannon raised and efficiently aided by its fire to take this entrance to the city. This he did without orders, inspired only by his military instinct. He tells the story very modestly in his autobiography.

The top of Popocatapetl is a vast crater filled with sulphur which is brought down and sold by its owner, a wealthy Mexican. The summit, which is not easy of ascent, is said to present a glorious view, and well it may, being so much taller than Mont Blanc, and this rarefied atmosphere permitting such clearness and distinctness of vision. It is much to be desired that some enterprising company shall run a funicular or cogwheel railroad to its summit or to the top of Orizaba. Electricity has reduced greatly the difficulties of operating such roads. The road to the top of the Righi pays admirably, as does the hotel on the summit, though owing to the rigors of the Swiss climate that railroad and hotel can be used only four months in the year. Here they could be used the year round and would attract thousands of visitors. If such a railroad can be built in no other way, all the railroads centring in the city of Mexico might unite for the purpose and would doubtless find a profit in the greatly increased travel over their own lines in addition to the profitableness of the enterprise itself.

In the numerous churches in Mexico is always to be found excellent music, and many instruments are used which are not common in our churches, among them violins, bass viols, etc. At times there may be heard tunes astonishing to our ears as, "After the Ball is Over," "When Johnnie Comes Marching Home," and "Sweet Violets"; church orchestras will play "Garryowen" in a style that would have moved an Irishman and "Wilhelmus von Nassauen" as it is played by the brass bands along the streets of Amsterdam. Doubtless these tunes have different names here and are set to most orthodox words.

On a bright January morning, seeming, however, like June in this land of eternal summer, I left for Vera Cruz, intending to go down to that "city by the sea" over the Mexican railroad (called commonly the "Queen's Own," because built with British money), and return by the Interoceanic, for there are two railroads between the capital and its seaport. Passing out between the lake, and the hill and church of Guadeloupe, the railroad presents scenes of interest at every turn. At San Juan Teotihuacan are the two famous pyramids of the sun and moon. The former, two hundred and sixteen feet high, is half as large as the great Cheops of Egypt. Between the two pyramids is a causeway called the Street of the Dead, visible from the cars. At Otumba we pass the field of the battle between Cortez and the Mexicans, fought July 8, 1520, during his retreat after the defeat of Noche Triste. We pass through thousands and thousands of acres of the immense plants which would be called in this country "century plants," out of which the pulque is made. It is planted ten feet apart and always with mathematical regularity and each plant is in line eight different ways. At Soltepec all four of the great peaks, with their snowy summits, are in view—Orizaba far to the east, and nearer Malintzi and the two great peaks of the

Valley of Mexico which we are leaving behind us. A few
miles beyond Apizaco we reach the highest point on the line,
8,333 feet, and at Esperanza we are at the edge of the great
central table-lands and begin to descend toward the *Tierra
Caliente* or tropical lowlands of the coast. The only use of
steam now is to hold back the train which descends for many
miles by the force of gravity.

The scenery on both these roads in passing from the table-
lands of Central Mexico down to the *Tierra Caliente* is grand
beyond description. Above the little village of Maltrata, the
train crawls around the side of an almost perpendicular
precipice twenty-five hundred feet above the village into
which we could almost toss an orange, and the churches and
houses look like toy houses, and the people like pigmies, and
the track by many a devious turn and twist passes then
over twelve miles before we get down to the village. Take
the scenery along the two roads as they descend, and I have
seen nothing to equal it in the Highlands of Scotland, in the
Swiss Alps, or in California. It is well worth a trip here to
see this alone. For instance, I stopped over one afternoon in
January at the little town of Orizaba, nearly half way down
the mountains. From one window of my room I could see the
grand summit of Orizaba, over eighteen thousand feet high,
the tallest peak on this continent (and a full half mile higher
than Mont Blanc, the highest point in Europe), his head
covered with the snows that never melt, while around me
the roses were blooming and the strawberries were ripening in the open air, and the little children were playing bare-
footed in the streets; and far away to the right stretched
out at our feet the vast plain of the fertile *Tierra Caliente*,
where the sugar cane was green, and the corn tasseling, and
the mango trees and bananas were swaying in the breeze
down to where eighty miles away and five thousand feet
below us could be seen the shore line of the Gulf, the white
houses of Vera Cruz, and the big ocean steamers resting
like ducks on the water and seemingly, even in this clear
air, not much larger. So looked Italy with "her fatal gift of
beauty" as she lay smiling at the feet of her mountains when
Goth and Vandal gazed down upon her and when Hannibal
and Napoleon poured down their troops like Alpine torrents
from the mountain passes. The healthfulness of Orizaba is
perfect, and long centuries ago it was a health resort. It
was a favorite residence of Maximilian.

It is strange that Americans should go to Europe when
here close at hand and without the discomfort of ocean
travel is far more magnificent scenery. Travel offers more

novelty here, in every way, than in the beaten pathways of Germany and France, and the expense is not one-third so much.

At Orizaba I had the fortune to meet President Diaz, the remarkable man who with a firm and true hand has for so many years been guiding Mexico along the path that leads to order, peace, and prosperity under a government "broad based on the people's will." A swarthy man, with unmistakable firmness and executive capacity stamped upon his countenance, he has been the providential man for Mexico. A fine organizer, he has news by telegraph laid before him every morning from his agents in every township of the republic. He has been quick to utilize the agency of the railroad and the telegraph, and by his promptness of action he has for many years made brigandage and revolutionary uprisings impossible. Not overgiven to observing the forms when the substance of liberty was at stake, his has been a "hand of iron in a glove of velvet." At his touch order appeared out of chaos, and hard upon her footsteps in this fertile land came prosperity and contentment. When the people become better educated, by experience in the art of self-government, a less governing president may accord better with the requirements of the presidency, but for the needs of the hour Mexico could have found no man better fitted to establish that order and peace which is the foundation of a nation's prosperity than the soldier and statesman, President Porfirio Diaz. He had come down to the next station (Nogales) to bring an invalid relative for the benefits of this delightful clime, and so, having missed him in the capital, I met him at Orizaba. From there he went on to Vera Cruz, where he was received with great rejoicings and display, and thence by sea to the northern terminus of the Tehuantepec Railroad, which railroad he wished to inspect. Nothing escapes him, and he is the best posted man in Mexico as to everything which concerns in any way the welfare of the republic.

Passing over a bridge one hundred and forty feet high, with a sheer precipice above and below, with the mountain stream rolling in a cascade down the ravine, we passed through the frightful-looking cañon known as Infernillo, i. e., "little hell," from Nogales to Orizaba. From Orizaba the railroad runs through cane and coffee fields. Six or seven miles further on the line enters the Barranca de Metlac, and a thousand feet below in the bottom of the chasm almost under our car windows rushes along the Rio Metlac until at last an immense horse-shoe

curve takes the track over a curved bridge of nine
spans to the other side. At Cordoba, where pineapples
sell for a cent apiece and oranges six for an American
cent, we are in the tropics at last, the temperate zone
being left well behind; and amid profusion of flowers and
blossoms and blooms the train rolls eastward to Vera Cruz.
Here in January, we found the scorching heats of August.
Passengers in the cars appeared in their shirt sleeves, and
the rolling of the blue waves of the Gulf was the only reminder of coolness. San Juan d'Ulloa lay out in the harbor,
a sullen reminder of more warlike times, and steamers and
vessels crowded the roadstead which is to be protected by a
breakwater now under construction. But the port has
always been poor and can never be made satisfactory,
and owes its importance solely to the fact that it is the port
of the city of Mexico, but Tampico, since its harbor has been
deepened by the Eades jetties, is far superior, and when the
railroad thence to the city of Mexico shall have been completed the glory of Vera Cruz will be eclipsed. A little
north of the city Cortez landed April 21, 1519, more than
a century and a year before the Mayflower sighted Plymouth
Rock, and a little south of the city General Scott and the
American army landed in 1847, and from this city both generals marched on the capital by practically the same route
via Jalapa. Vera Cruz has many churches and some handsome public buildings, but the intense heat and the frequent
visits of yellow fever render it undesirable for a residence
or a lengthened visit. It has, however, a really efficient set
of street commissioners, who are so diligent in cleansing the
streets that a penalty of five dollars is incurred by killing one
of them. They are styled *zopilotes* here, but in Charleston,
S. C., where they are equally diligent and effective, they are
called simply turkey buzzards. In these hot lands the railroads use iron cross ties. They are of sheet iron and mere
shells. The hollow side being put downwards takes a firm
hold and thus makes a solid roadway. Iron telegraph poles
are also used, as vermin are very destructive to wooden ones.

Leaving Vera Cruz over the Interoceanic railroad, the
road runs through the tropical country, beneath the palm
trees, passing near the National Bridge and the field of
Cerro Gordo. The track along here is a wonderful piece
of work. There are a hundred horse-shoe curves, and at the
famous Huarumbo cutting, the deepest cut in Mexico, the
line makes almost a complete loop. Climbing, still ever
climbing, and turning to right and left as we climb, we reach
Jalapa. This is one of the oldest and quaintest towns in the

republic, a bit of the sixteenth century clinging to the side of the mountain—nothing modern save the railroad, the electric lights and street cars, and the hotel which has the comforts of New York. But once inside the hotel you will find that you are not in New York, for there is not a chimney, and never any need of one, and the house, like all hotels and private residences hereabouts, is built around an open courtyard where the fountain plays and flowers and roses are blooming—in January. Jalapa has a medicinal reminiscence, as *jalap* came from hence, but you would never know it here for the people pronounce the name of their city *Halap'per*. It is indeed very ancient. When Cortez three hundred and seventy-six years ago (nearly ninety years before the settlement at Jamestown), made that dare-devil march with four hundred men to take the city of Mexico with its half million of people, and *took* it, he passed through Jalapa, and it was already then a city of importance. The two principal churches here were built by the Spaniards long years before Sir Walter Raleigh made the first attempt at an English settlement on this continent at Roanoke Island.

And forty-nine years ago Jalapa saw another army come up from the seaward, from the white walls dimly discerned where nestles Vera Cruz by the deep waters. And the bugles rang out full and free, and the drums rolled and the long blue lines came marching through, and in their ranks, but unnoted then, were young captains and lieutenants— Robert E. Lee and U. S. Grant and Stonewall Jackson and Sherman and Meade and Thomas and Longstreet and many another whose names have passed into history now and are

> "written high
> On the dusty roll the ages keep."

They had first met the enemy and driven him back at the National Bridge, which we passed a station or two back, and then at Cerro Gordo (*anglice* "round hill") the conical-top mountain which lifts its head out yonder. Sharing the same fare, following the same leaders, drinking from the same canteen, they passed by the door of this hotel, up that street yonder, through the pass that opens beyond, up the mountain, on and on, ever on and upwards till now they live amid the stars.

And down this same street rode since at the head of a retreating army, with the tricolor floating over him and the imperial eagles of a Napoleon borne before him, a marshal of France who left a reputation behind him to find the infamy of an Arnold on the green and golden slopes of Lorraine—Bazaine, the only man in all history who has ever surrendered an army of 175,000 fighting men.

And so Jalapa, with her bright sunshine and her narrow streets and her pretty women and laughing children and bubbling fountains, has seen history pass by her, and she remains unmoved and unchanging as Orizaba, which stands out yonder, the monarch of this republican continent, with his slumbering fires beneath and his unmelting snows above, the sentinel of the ages, unchanged, while generations of men and empires pass by and disappear like fleecy clouds melting into the infinite azure of the past.

Jalapa was the birthplace of President Lerdo de Tejada, and his banishment from the country has not prevented his statue from being erected in the Plaza, and a plate affixed to the house records the locality and date of his birth. A tram road carries us out to Coatepec, a little village embosomed amid coffee haciendas. The coffee trees are evergreens, as are all trees hereabouts, and the coffee is gathered continuously the year round. It grows on trees which bear fruit very much resembling cherries, each cherry containing two seeds which are the coffee grains. The business is very profitable, as coffee is raised here at a cost of from six to eight cents and is sold in San Francisco at twenty-two and one-half cents in gold, which, at the present enhanced value of our standard, is equal to forty-one cents here. In some sections the coffee trees require to be irrigated during the dry season, but here there is moisture enough the year round. The profitableness of coffee raising is carrying a great many Americans to Mexico. The merits of Mexican coffee are now well established, and it is said to be not surpassed by the best Mocha.

Leaving Jalapa westward we begin to climb the mountains. The track, especially on reaching the edge of the great plateau, runs through lava beds for many miles, showing that the great central plateau of Mexico was in some remote age lifted up seven thousand feet by the titanic forces beneath. When this was done the corresponding depression was made which is now the Gulf of Mexico. The views from the ascending train are marvellous. Mountain ridges and valleys unroll themselves like a panorama, and a full hundred miles away are the ships and white walls of Vera Cruz—while first before, and then behind, us as we turn, now this way and now that, are the white-capped Orizaba and the coffer-shaped Cofre de Perote, looking like a gigantic square box on the top of a truncated cone. We pass also the old castle of Perote, where formerly a large garrison was kept to patrol the National Road, running from Mexico to Vera Cruz. The Interoceanic is nearly one hundred miles longer than its rival road, the "Queen's Own," from the capital to the sea, and follows very closely the track of the former National Road, which in turn was substantially the route taken by both Cortez and Scott.

We stop over at Puebla, whose history is romantic and historic, and whose name originally was the City of the Angels. Like Queretaro, Puebla has seen much of the vicissitudes of war. It was captured by Iturbide 1821, by General Scott 1847, by Zaragoza May 5, 1862 (hence one of the national holidays), by the French the 17th of the same month, and recaptured from the French by Gen. Porfirio Diaz (now president) in 1867. It is surrounded by the ruins of forts and the remains of breastworks. The city lies in the centre of a great plain with the four snow-crowned peaks in full view—Orizaba and Malintzi to the eastward and Popocatapetl and Ixtaccihuatl to the west. The city has 100,000 population, and is the third in size in the republic. The great cathedral is three hundred and twenty-three feet long by one hundred and one feet wide, and one of the towers cost $100,000. In this is placed a chime of eighteen bells, the largest of which weighs twenty thousand pounds. The altar alone cost $110,000.

Six miles west of Puebla and reached by both railroad and street-car lines are the remains of the ancient city of Cholula, whose origin outdates tradition as well as history. Cortez counted here four hundred temples, but the former great city, in which he massacred so many thousands of people, has now dwindled to a village of five thousand people. Its point of attraction now is the great pyramid of Cholula, which is one hundred and seventy-seven feet high, with its summit, formerly crowned with the sacred fires and the stone on which human victims were sacrificed, now occupied by a Catholic church. The base of this pyramid is half as large again as the great pyramid of Cheops on the banks of the Nile. From this summit there is a beautiful view of one of the loveliest plains in the world. It is generally understood that this immense pyramid is built of sun-dried brick, and it is considered one of the marvels of the world—and so it is; indeed, Ignatius Donnelly has written to prove that it is the remains of the tower of Babel. But if it is not presumption in one who does not claim to be a *savant* or to speak *ex cathedra*, I will say that it is my opinion that neither this nor the great pyramids of the Sun and Moon at San

Juan Teotihuacan (already referred to) are wholly artificial. I think they are mostly natural hills, like many others in the plain not far from both places. These more nearly approximated the four points of the compass and a pyramid in shape. They were, therefore, doubtless selected and exactly oriented, and made pyramidal by artificial means. This required an enormous amount of work and was enough to make them marvels, but exacted nothing like the superhuman labor which would have been required to erect the structures from the base. At Cholula, not only was the hill oriented and shaped into an exact pyramid, but a road winding round the four sides to the top was built of sundried brick, the pavement of which was tiled, and probably all the sides of the hills also were plated with brick to make the pyramidal shape perfect. I come to this conclusion, by seeing on both these plains other hills close by which with some labor could be trimmed into pyramidal shape and their four sides made to correspond to the points of the compass, and from the consideration of the enormous labor and length of time requisite to have built these pyramids out of brick, and the absence of any depression whence the material for so large a mound, if artificial, could have been taken. To have constructed these pyramids from their bases would have been an overwhelming and entirely useless task.

The city of Oaxaca lies three hundred and fifty-eight miles southeast of the city of Mexico. The route to it is *via* Puebla over the Mexican Southern Railroad, which is intended to be a link in the great Inter-Continental Railway line connecting North and South America when it shall be built. This road is completed to Oaxaca, with its immediate objective point at Tehuantepec on the Pacific, some one hundred and fifty miles further south. It penetrates one of the best agricultural and mineral sections in the republic. Unlike all other railroads in Mexico the Southern runs neither across plains nor along mountain sides, but follows up the valley, and for the last fifty miles it runs through a deep and narrow cañon like the Yosemite in California, though the latter is only seven miles long. From the track for miles we look two thousand feet up the almost perpendicular sides of the mountain walls on either side of the little river whose sinuous banks we follow, first on one side the stream and then the other. At Tomellin we get a most admirable dinner at a hotel kept by two of those cosmopolitans, the Chinese. They spoke English, French, Spanish, German (and it is to be presumed Russian and Hindoo) like natives of those countries, and talked to each other in Chinese. Years ago when I visited the famous Yosemite it was considered one of the world's wonders, but here we have it duplicated but many times longer and with a railroad running the whole length. Along the stream we could see the natives rocking gold out of the yellow sands. The magnificent valley of Oaxaca was granted to Cortez and from it he derived his title of Marquis of the Valley. In the city of Oaxaca President Diaz was born (which fact is marked in European fashion by a *plaque* on the walls of the house) and Juarez was born in a little Indian village close by. The city is the capital of the state of the same name and has its fair share of grand churches and handsome public buildings with its Plazas and a Zocalo. It has a population of thirty thousand. The railroad descends from seven thousand feet at Puebla to five thousand feet here.

From Oaxaca it is usual to go out by stage to the wonderful ruins of Mitla, twenty-five miles off, but as there was no one else to go that day, I went on horseback accompanied only by an Indian *mozo* or servant. It was a delightful bracing ride in this elevated atmosphere, albeit the sun was rather trying for January, seeing that we were within seventeen degrees of the equator, about the latitude of Khartoom, Aden, and Bombay, and some hundreds of miles further south than Cairo (in Egypt), Delhi, or Calcutta. A few miles out, we stopped to see the big tree of Tule. While not so tall as the big trees in the Mariposa or Calaveras groves in California (though some one has said it took two looks to see to the top) it is larger round, and in fact is probably the largest tree in the world, being one hundred and fifty-five feet in circumference, measured at a height of six feet from the ground. It stands in the churchyard of Santa Maria del Tule. On the east side of the tree is a wooden tablet signed by Humboldt in 1806 which is now partly overgrown and imbedded in the tree. Stopping at Tlacolula for dinner and at other villages to rest and see the customs and novelties of this far-off country, Mitla was reached early enough to see the wonderful and mysterious prehistoric ruins before sunset, for towards the equator winter days are longer and summer days shorter than with us. No one knows when and by whom these solid granite buildings with such elaborate carvings were erected. In the entablature are chiselled hieroglyphics which might tell the story, but as at Belshazzar's feast no one has been prompt to decipher them, and the mystery remains unsolved. No bilingual tablet has been discovered, and the "dead past has gone down to the

dead." The mountains and the valley and the sky are still
here, as beautiful and as smiling as on that far-away day
when these buildings came forth fresh from the hands of the
builders. What glorious name were they intended to hand
down to future ages, what great deeds to commemorate?
Earth and sky make no reply, and the breeze gently blowing
passes by and no man knows whence it came or whither it
goes.

At night, the glorious stars are glorious indeed in the
translucent air of these cloudless skies. Larger and
brighter, apparently nearer and more numerous than at
home, we see among them new constellations. Far to the
north is still the pole-star and a part of the Great Bear, while
to the southward shines the Southern Cross. Here, as in
crossing the Andes, it is said that those travelling by night
will hear the Indian guides cry out at midnight, "*The cross
begins to bend.*" And at sunrise and sunset what coloring
in the sky and on the lonely mountain tops,—

> "Hues that have words
> And speak to ye of Heaven."

Returning to Puebla, a short run on the railroad brings
us to the station of Santa Ana, whence a tramway of six
miles through beautiful woods, well-cultivated fields (the
hedges on either side of the road covered with wild flowers
filling the air with perfume), and through the quaint little
town of Pablo Apetitlan brings us to Tlaxcala. This is
one of the most interesting places in Mexico, and its very
name is redolent of antiquity and the conquest. Cortez
met in battle an army of a hundred thousand warriors of this
brave little republic, and then deeming it better to make
friends, marched with them to Cholula which he turned
over to their uncovenanted mercies. It was only by the
aid of the Tlascalans that he conquered Mexico. Then they
in turn fell into subjection, and its three hundred thousand
inhabitants have now dwindled to four thousand. Here
is a museum of interesting antiquities, and the oldest church
on the continent, begun in 1521, the very year of the conquest, and the pulpit in which the gospel was first preached
this side of the great waters. Here too are the state buildings, and the governor and the supreme court were seen,
for in deference to its history Tlaxcala is the capital of a
state of that name, though the smallest in the republic,
having only fifteen hundred square miles, somewhat larger
than Rhode Island but smaller than Delaware. The population of the little state is one hundred and fifty thousand.

The ancient town was built in an amphitheatre in the foothills. The present town is not exactly on the old site.

Returning again to Puebla, the route then leads us back to the city of Mexico over the Interoceanic Railroad, through one of the richest and most highly cultivated sections in all Mexico. At Nanacamilca the track reaches an elevation of nine thousand feet. At Calpulalpan and at Otumba we pass through two famous battlefields. A little further on we have one of the best views of the valley of Mexico. Far and near are the gleaming roofs of busy towns, the green groves of olives and other trees, and amid apparently fathomless depths of air sleeps the great lake. Here the railroad turning almost back on its track but on the other side of the mountain range, we roll southwards past Texcoco, once the rival of Mexico and the place at which Cortez launched his bergantines for the taking of the latter city, along the eastern side of Lake Texcoco, then turning west we pass through the valley with Lake Texcoco on the right and Lakes Xochomilco and Chalco on the left, then along the Viga canal with its boats, then under a double row of willows lining the tracks, with Chapultepec to the left looking down upon us and the mountains all around, and halt at San Lazaro station in the city of Mexico. As in Italy all roads lead to Rome, so in Mexico all roads lead to the capital.

WHAT IS AMERICA'S RELATION TO ENGLAND?

BY EVELEEN LAURA MASON.

The war before us is but a call to arms for brains and for straight shooting at facts. The time for ambush fighting, even between intellects, is over. For "a conspiracy of silence" concerning antagonisms never creates peace.

It is interesting that while Britain has aroused from self-satisfaction sufficiently to see that she has made herself disagreeable to America and the rest of the world, she yet tries to persuade herself that America's antipathy is only based (as some writers for the British cause suggest) on "the policies of government for which England stands," "free trade" and the "gold standard." The British do not seem to know that on these points the conglomerate American mind takes different individual views, and that the antipathy is based on the difference between the principles for which America stands and the conduct of England. And this difference is, that America stands for the principle, "Liberty to all and license to none"; while England's practice is "Liberty to none and license to England." Therefore the relation is, in the nature of things, as antipathetic as peace and war, heaven and hell!

When using the name of the chosen symbol of the British in speaking of their chosen policy, we leave out of the discussion those individuals whose intelligence has outgrown the symbol and the policy. And when we speak of the Goddess of Liberty, we do it, realizing that not all Americans are yet imbued with the power to practise that "Liberty to all and license to none" which we theoretically delight to honor. Yet we must continue to lay stress on the names of "goddess" and "lion," because we know that a people's ideals are to them wings or weights. And we claim that our national ideals of personal liberty and self-sovereignty are as the wings on which people will mount to moral heights as yet unattained by any of us, while the polity symbolized by the lion is a weight, pressing its adherents to a plane of violence and stupidity.

But the stolid inability of the lion to understand these facts constrains the goddess to emphasize her wish that he would understand, and puts her in no frame of mind to say to him, "Roar me gently, good beast." On the reverse, its intrusions oblige the goddess to reaffirm, "America's relation to England is that of a conqueror to a foe vanquished in 1776, and with whom America will have no entangling alliance, and· as little traffic until the lion is transhumanized."

Meanwhile, as distance gives perspective, it is probable that the goddess knows England better than England knows herself, for she stands too admiringly near to herself to get right perspective of her past history and present intentions. She does not realize that America is a great reader, and that, as her citizenship is conglomerate, her language.is polyglot, which puts her in the way of knowing past and present, with the result that, "in all the affliction of" the nations on whom British violence, rapine, and slaughter have fallen, America "has been afflicted." For America is the nations of the earth, and the nations are America. America, not England, is the motherland; for the maternal principle of "Liberty to all and license to none" is the Comforter come to lead our citizenship into all knowledge through peace. It is not good form for the lion to intrude his old-fashioned bloodthirsty ways on America! He should be restrained and made to see that the goddess is beautifully busy, and cannot turn from her business of bringing her men and women into right relations with one another for the full practicalization of her principles; but that meanwhile, it would be right in the line of evolution for England to stay at home and teach her lion to change his methods, and to climb up from brute to human, and from human to the divine level where stands the goddess whose principles we emulate.

True, in the course of the evolution of each succeeding world-epoch wars have been. For in every immature age the common majority of men have been fighters, not thinkers, and so seem to have been weights on progress. But always these fighting methods have been antipathetic to the principles of goddess and eagle, both of which are very old ensigns of the supreme principles which America has set herself to demonstrate in popular practice.

England does not want to hear that America's great concern is to *sustain right relations with her own principles* whatever becomes incidentally of England, whose plans have no more bearing on the question than have the plans

and interests of France, the donor of that ideal statue of
Liberty which lights our harbor and the world's people as
they enter that harbor—Germany, Spain, Russia, and the
rest. England cannot see these facts, and does not want
anyone else to see them; for she knows that if at this
crisis America should put herself into right relations with
her own principles she would be invincible, and that, England forefends. For the more absolutely America stands
upon her own high level, the further she separates herself
from British methods to-day. So that if America were
true to herself, she would rise to eyrie heights, which are
above ordinary faith and ordinary fear—and where
British force would have no more power than the nerves
of a dead man. But when America descends from her
right level and puts faith in, or has fear of, British methods,
she then clothes England in a power not her own. England needs and desires to be so clothed, and she is *trading
on her assumption of oneness with America*, and thereby is
bringing upon America the dislike that France and Spain
rightly have for the methods of their age-long enemy, England. Hence England insists upon making it appear that
she is the mother of America, who therefore would be
supposed to have faith in England and a fear of her, and
to be at one mind with her in all her enmities, wishes, and
ways. This, she already has gotten into the minds of Spanish colleges, and has confused the dignity of our flag with
the indignities of her lion; embroiling us in her old quarrels with our friends, the relatives of our citizens. We long
since came to a point at which we declared we would have
no part in England's quarrels. If we go a step further now,
and say to her definitely, "We have no faith in *your methods,*
and we will stand by our own principles and our own citizens." England intends to be ready to answer: "*Fear* me,
then! I have your bonds and here are my guns. As I am
doing in Egypt, so will I do in America!"

And all this because America has—false to her principles
—entered into an entangling alliance with England, to
the amount of "five thousand million dollars, the annual
interest of which is two hundred and fifty million dollars,"
and thus has unfittingly complicated the independence of
her right relations, by adding to them that of *debtor to the
"Constable of Egypt."* But America is not Egypt, neither
are the people Egyptian fellaheen! So, besides being
herself, America has the advantage of Egypt's experience
of British ways. But all will be plain work, if the people
will but swiftly study up the situation, and then put them-

serves in right relations with their own principles, regardless of instructions from the enemy. This will make them
invincible; and, of course, release them from England's
specious claims and *rouge et noir* sort of money speculations;
a game at which, as readers know, whoever loses, the bank
wins. For, notwithstanding the incidental financial complications, the question of America's relation to England
to-day, is but of the same importance as that of her relation to any and every other nation; and is first, independent,
and next—well?—friendly, but by no means intimate, till
the pressing needs of her own national family are adjusted.

For what is "England"? It is within proof that the
British nation is far from being English; and that, if it
were English the lion would not be its symbol, nor would
its policy be that to which the British now adhere. This
sounds farcical; but a swift review of British history will
show that neither the sovereigns nor the methods of Britain
are particularly English, and that the British lion is the
English people's worst enemy. As is well known, near
the time of the establishment of the Saxon Heptarchy just
after the Roman army of occupation was withdrawn from
Britain about the middle of the fifth century, a horde of
fighters pressed in to take advantage of the fine conditions
with which ancient Rome had filled the island. So the
Saxons invited the Angles from Southern Denmark to
come to their help. But these Angles entered into the
business so well, that they took possession, reducing the
inhabitants to submission or driving them to retreat to the
mountains. *"From these Angles or Engles was derived the
name of Angleland or England."*

The Danes then succeeded to the throne. But the
Danes are kindred of the Saxon, and belong to the same
great Teutonic family, having a similiar language and
religion, says history. Yet the Danes and the Angles of
Southern Denmark are not necessarily the same people,
as is shown by Knight, an intelligent historian, who says,
"After the death of Hardicanute, the English people (however composed of *English, Danes, and Saxons*) went on with
their national songs and traditions under Athelstan, Alfred,
and Edward,"—thus emphasizing the fact that, to the fighting force of Teutons—Saxons and Danes—was added the
permeating influence of the tradition-keeping, Angle element. Let us hunt up this elusive element. Edward the
Confessor was brought up in Normandy, educated as an
illuminati, familiar with the customs and language of other
peoples, and was a lover of studious cloister life rather than

built up the British nation, and is admired by those who think that is the chief thing to be done, at any cost of cruelty to all the rest of the world.

But an effigy of Edward II of Cærnarvon in the Gloucester Cathedral shows him with his feet on a coiled-up dead or dying lion lying on its back, and with a staff, sur-mounted by conventionalized wings, in his right hand, and the globe in the other. Edward III's seal shows him with the globe in his hand, surmounted by the cross, and the *plant et genet* rising large above him, and falling on his shoulder. At his feet are two lions, half rising, not under his feet. While a statue of St. George of England, which is at Dijon, shows him with his sword above his head in one hand, and his visor raised to look down on the dragon under his two feet, into whose mouth he is thrusting his long sword.

There is much to show that the so-called British lion was brought to England as a symbol by the Norman Crusaders, and that this, which appears as the British standard to-day, is but a debased form of a spiritually significant sym-bol. The casual study of the seals of the kings, shows that reigns which made for the advance of higher life, were sym-bolized by the presence of the bird token.

When we come to the time of the division of the Plan-tagent family into the branches of the House of York and the House of Lancaster, the fight goes on under the name of the "War of the Roses" white and red, which is a significant name from the fact that "while in most cases the rose of the poet and the botanist are one and the same kind, yet popular usage has attached the name, rose, to plants whose kinship with the rose no ordinary botanist would admit." The Rose Spinosissima (the Scotch This-tle?) and the Rose Marinus (rose of the sea, or water lily) which plays an important part in folk-lore, are interesting on that score; while mythologically, the white lily (Juno's rose) was taken in the middle ages as the symbol of heav-enly purity, and was contrasted with the red rose of Aphrodite. So the true inwardness of the War of the Red and White Roses would repay research, and would show that the same principle was at stake as that symbolized in the "golden lilies of France," which were a variety of the *plant et genet's* blazing yellow blossoms.

So when in 1485 Henry VII married Elizabeth, grand-daughter of Edmund Tudor, descended from the wise man Owen Tudor of Wales, the branches of York and Lancaster united in the red Tudor rose; bringing forward, who shall say how much of the rose-cross mysteries over which the knights of the various secret orders and of the "ancient and accepted Scottish rites of Masons" have toiled through the ages. From this house of Tudor came the scholarly Elizabeth, who, among other good things, knew how to appropriate for England's benefit, the discoveries which the Portuguese navigator had made and the enterprises which the Italian Columbus aided by Spain's Isabella, carried forward.

The reign of the Scotch House of Stuarts followed, which, lasting fifty-four years, was one struggle between sovereigns and people for power.

And the Angles had not only appeared among British dominants and not of them, but had secured recognition as the people who had rights which the king was bound under seal to respect. Did their prophetic souls realize that that which was in part should be done away when the whole should have come? And did they know that their charter was but like the wail of a babe, "crying in the night and with no language but a cry," compared to the shout which sent across the world the announcement that kings had no rights which "the people" are bound to respect, except the right to be respectable? And did they know that their *Magna Charta* would lead the way for that *Maxima Charta*, the constitution of these United States of America, which declares universal liberty to all, without distinction of color or former condition of servitude; even of that most humiliating and race-destroying sort of servitude to which licensed animalism has subjected the mothers of men? It was no cry, but the spirit of a shout which in 1775 drove from these shores that lion symbolical of a government that to-day can relish a thirteenth-century charter, and with pap-spoon in one hand and a gun-fuse in the other, is at our door trying to administer the drugged dose to our goddess.

This is plain from the fact, that even Sir William Harcourt, Liberal leader of the House though he is, said the other day, that "the points of difference between Great Britain and the United States are insignificant, and could easily be settled between the two cabinets; but if the populace" (mark "populace," for he does not know that this is the government of a people, by a people, and for a people) "if the populace on both sides were *allowed* (?) to raise the excitement of the *real matters at stake*, there would be great danger of strife."

Now if English language means anything this English means: The matters at stake must be star-chambered by the two cabinets; for if English people and American people are *allowed* (?) to know what we are about, the excitement of the real issues at stake would drive the people to make war against—what? Why, against something, of course, which is not the people, but is the would-be masters of the people, that Sir William Harcourt puts before the imagination under the name, "*the two cabinets.*" That is the style of doing business into which the British are already lassoing the English people and the American self-sovereigns; *vide,* the methods which are obtaining in our national Congress to-day, and in "the House" on the Hill, concerning which, someone justly asked through the *Transcript,* "Have we a House of Lords?"

So "I sing arms" which America bears in her *Charta* of American liberties, from which British practices, as here demonstrated, are as far removed to-day, as in 1215 King John's ideas were from those of the real English people whose name (but not whose principles or nature) the British-lion-lovers still bear. And I affirm the British lion is always treacherous, whether *rampant* or *couchant;* and warn, when he *crouches* be prepared for his death-grip.

Cut short was the 1694 attempt of the Angles "to gain and retain that full personal liberty in which the Commons voted to abolish the House of Lords as unnecessary, burdensome, and dangerous alike to the liberties, safety, and public interests of the people." In eleven years the project was thrust back, although the republican form of government was established and a council of state was appointed of which John Bradshaw was president, and John Milton, the poet and extreme republican, was secretary.

Then again came in the Stuarts who, whatever else can be said of them, were firm believers that laws were made for subjects, not for kings.

In 1730, the Elector of Hanover came in as King of England, under the name of George I. He was followed by his son, George II, also a Hanoverian, so that George III was the first of this House of Brunswick who was born in England. Then came George IV who was succeeded by his brother, Duke of Clarence, with the title, William IV; and William's niece Victoria (the daughter of the Duke of Kent) succeeded William IV, in 1837 and, in 1840, married Prince Albert of Saxe-Coburg-Gotha. During all this time, the Teutonic Empire was building up by marriage alliance and force of arms, and the English people were ruled by good Teutons—first and last—with an interregnum of Danes, Normans from Jerusalem and elsewhere, Spanish (?), Welsh,

Scotch, and Dutch sovereigns. But as conglomerate as were the families of the kings, quite as conglomerate became the so-called English people; as they carried also in their veins whatever the ancient Romans and their armies through four hundred and seventy-five years, had contributed from *their* blood, gathered up as *that* was from all the nations of that ancient time, when greater Rome was mistress of now buried civilizations.

In view of all this, what does it signify that such a heterogeneous mass are called English? If their birth, lineage, or kings are not preponderably even of the English language (though that is an utter conglomerate), is it some *hidden ideal*, some *essentially* Anglo-*intellectual influence*, which gives permanence to the name of that people of whom we first hear, in this review, as having come from Southern Denmark? "There is something" sweet "in Denmark," or the name of "the people" of its south would not have adhered to the British nation.

Conglomerate America is a keen spectator of conditions, and looks with the eyes of the twentieth-century civilization into the eyes of other people as conglomerate. For it has nearly come to pass, Of all bloods is each nation of the earth; which is but another way of saying, "Of one blood are all the nations of the earth." This binds us all up in one bundle of life, and does away with talk about "one language" and "one blood" as a basis of alliance of the few as against the many. The chief interest is that in whatever language we speak we should succeed in saying something of profit to those who have to hear us; and it is of interest that the "one blood" should be full of good nerve-force, instead of being devitalized to the verge of *invalidity* or insanity by family doings. And we must all know that the development of a strong intellectual purpose and an identity of actuating moral principles do not come by chance, but are the outcome of generations of spiritual development carried on by individuals who, at last, do attain to a makeup of this kind, and that those individuals may be of any or every nationality. And so we must see that no nationality, in itself, places the bar-sinister on any escutcheon.

Yet, on the 17th of February, a Chicago audience heard a British preacher explain that "People of unhistoric minds, little development of reason or conscience, and no religious depth of nature may get themselves into a belief that certain surface interests may be promoted by a war between English-speaking races." They also heard, "Looking in the direction of an abiding union between all **English**-speaking people as being the most desirable of all things practicable, let us consider the past history of England"; and then the lecturer went back a little way, as far as King John's transaction with the Angles and the Charter, in support of the British international scheme of we two, England and America as against the rest of the world.

Now with such a worldwide work as America has taken in hand, why should a gentleman make such remarks? As if any people ever restrained themselves from war because of the language spoken! Have the British ever been so restrained in all their long history of constant fighting within their own island? Has England ever kept her guns off of America because some Americans speak English? And supposing they did all speak English, what is English but the conglomerate climax of all languages, welded into an ever-changing form of utterance, not yet at its best and most permanent. So what can it matter to a hoipolloi nation like the British, whose honorable queen is German and whose princes and princesses are everything good in the way of language, and whose parliament and whose Londoners at home and colonists abroad send up to Heaven a clatter of tongues like that which arose from Babel—what can it matter to such a polyglot Bedlam that America's "English" is not much worse?

Have the British disabled themselves from dispassionate thinking? Has the love of fighting and—other things given them delirium, as they look toward "the surface interests which will be" for them "promoted," if America will but give up war of words and weapons and come into alliance with them as against the rest of the world, and meet their convenience in the matter of land syndicates, money bonds, the gold-standard, free trade, etc.? For then we two would be one, and that one would be—Angles? We are not half sure of that. We should be, simply what we are now, a conglomerate people, but with our heads thrust into the noose of a thirteenth-century contract as to what king and parliament might allow (?) to the populace of both countries, and with the things of the *Pall-Mall-Gazette* style established as the conditions to be fixed upon American womanhood.

The Angles are a most elusive element in the British conglomerate, and the British nation is wide away from being truly English. If it were English, its policy would not be such an one as is that to which the British adhere, nor would the lion be its symbol. For "the lion's whole organization

·is that of a creature modified to fulfil in the most perfect degree yet attained, an active, predacious mode of existence." And it is the English people's worst enemy.

Two thousand years ago, pagan (?) Rome had dominated Egypt, the Mediterranean, and the East, gathering up into its personality the wealth, learning, and skill of the world, and bringing them in the person of Cæsar, the Roman army and consulates to Britain, which was thereafter held as a Roman colony for four hundred and seventy-five years. British history did not begin even then, when, 55 B. C., Cæsar entered the country. Cæsar himself knew that he had come not to destroy but to fulfil purposes older than Rome; and to plant with the Britons, before Rome should fall, Rome's ancient policy and methods of extending dominion through the earth by force of arms, and to establish the influence which inhered in the act of *setting up the standard of the eagle.* For it is known that to the standard of the eagle all nations will gather. Cæsar knew that the Carthaginians and Phœnicians had been in Britain (then called Albion) generations before he first came in 55 B. C., and that they had settled Britain for the exact purpose of planting there the truly human teaching the love of which must be born in people, or they cannot delight themselves on the plane of living which this teaching sets for occupancy.

The ancient Britons whom Cæsar found, had a principle of coöperation in their industries, as in their studies and religion. They cremated their dead, which gave rise to the vulgarly popular assertion that they "burnt their victims in iron cages." In the religion of the Gauls (French) and the Britons, there was no difference. "For Albion was once believed to have been part of the Continent," as Richard Verstegan says, and supports the opinion with "sundry pregnant reasons." He says, "that our Isle of Albion had been continent with Gallia, hath been the opinion of divers." And a century earlier one very satisfactory reason was pleasantly imagined by Sir Thomas More: "Howbeit as they say, and as the fashion of the place itself doth partly show, it was not always encompassed about with sea. But King Utopus whose name as conqueror, the Island beareth, even at his arriving and entering upon the land forthwith obtaining the victory, caused fifteen miles space of uplandish ground where the sea had no passage, to be cut and digged up—and so wrought the sea about the land!" Now if he "wrought the sea *about* the land," then he and his tremendous army (who together did as great things all along their

line of march, as the commentaries show) not only cut
through the English channel but must also have cut,
blasted out, and annihilated the land where to the east
of the British Isles, the North Sea now is—the North Sea,
which, being there, sunders Denmark, Germany, Holland,
Belgium, and that part of France from the land now called
the British Islands. By doing this Utopus (whoever he
was) shut up as in a schoolroom the people of the "snug
little, tight little, right little island," and prepared it for
Cæsar and the Empire to put over these people for four
hundred and seventy-five years, those worldwide-educated
teachers, the Romans.

If this were so, then it is easy to see how the land of
Bretagne in France, and Britain in Albion, with the "fifteen miles of uplandish ground" between, might all have
been one land, and the two people one in speech and religion;
and how it chanced (?) that in the district of Stonehenge in
Britain and Carnac in Gaul (France) there are still to be
seen the remains of the stupendous work of the Druidical
age, in the four thousand immense stones which are associated with the legends of their antique worship. If those
two regions once were one, then probably the fifteen miles
of what is now British Channel was covered with great
temples and halls of learning of the Druids. For Cæsar
in his Commentaries reports, that "once a year the priests
of Britain used to come in boats to say mass over the remains of an engulfed city, where great blocks of stone,
held to be relics of buried Druidical temples, were to be
seen at low water."

Were the teachers and lawgivers surrounded by a few
votaries of learning? Says Cæsar in the Commentaries:
"The population is very great, and the buildings very
numerous. Their instruction was oral. They held that
after death, the soul does not perish. They believe in
the transmigration" (reincarnation?) "of souls. They discoursed of the heavenly bodies and their motion; and of
the extent of the world and of the peoples of other climes."
"They were very learned; and very simple in their manners
and modes of living," said Diodorus Siculus, a contemporary of Cæsar. "Their passions were under subjection to
their intellectual leaders; and, not only in peace but in
war with other nations, not friends alone but even enemies
defer to them, and to composers of verse." For they had
bards who sang the praises of their heroes, who were
heroes in the sense of having gained victory over their own
lower natures. "Frequently during hostilities, when

armies are approaching each other, with swords drawn and lances extended, these men, rushing between them, put an end to their contentions, taming them," into a love for some mysterious link of attachment which was more powerful than was the opposing force which, for the time, had deluged them in fury.

Ptolemy the geographer, who flourished about a century and a half after Cæsar became acquainted with the ancient inhabitants of Britain, describes them as "building temples of gigantic proportions and raising earth works that rival the wonders of modern engineering"; which, as they wisely cremated their dead, were probably not sepulchres, but were more probably great covered roads, by means of which they were able to transport themselves and their great hosts invisibly from point to point, or, go into absolute seclusion, at need, and for any great national purpose. "For their priests were lawgivers and teachers; and the most *perfect elements of learning* were considered to have existed in Britain." And those who wished to be more accurately versed in the occult, power-giving mysteries went to Britain in order to become acquainted with them.

This is the genuine ancestry of the genuine Angles. Knight says, that, in the time of Alfred, "the darkness began to break, and the people who had been lost to view as Britons, began to appear as the English people," or Angles. Not that all the Angles were necessarily there, but that some of the widespread wisdom-lovers were there, working wonders; as others of them were in Egypt, Jerusalem, Greece, India, China, Japan, and, even then, were in *ancient America*, as a better knowledge of our Spanish and our Toltec and Aztec civilizations in America will reveal to us.

These were "the people" whom Cæsar found. And he knew that their principle of "close association" was for the protection of their ideals. It would seem that the Saxon Heptarchy attempted to symbolize "the white religion" of Albion, "the white isle," with "the white horse." But the Danes held to the symbol of the bird, and perhaps it was in the struggle and the defeat of that higher ideal that the Danish bird came finally to appear as "the black raven," whose sad-colored plumage and whose cry became a thing of terror to those who loved better to follow the ways of the good brute. And, as in all past time, the full discussion of these principles was driven into cloistered retreat because of the violence with which the lovers of less intellectual method fight against these better ways, so the Angles of Southern Denmark may have gone into seclusion till need summoned them to action. So it was with the Julian family. Julius Cæsar's mother's family had always held to the practice of a principle which is back of the philosophy of brain-building, a philosophy which is half revealed and half concealed in the story of the phœnix, which, at every great world-period, rises out of the ashes of the altar, flies forth, lays an egg, and returns to its soli- tude and deathlike self-obliteration.

The symbol of the bird, conventionalized, has marked the standard borne in battles and affixed to seals and to the coat-of arms of those who aspire to be of this kind, in contra- distinction from the type who love better to follow the beast, wherever it leads.

The history of each succeeding æon is but a repetition of the methods which in a preceding æon, were brought to bear on society for its unfoldment through the faithfulness of the individual to his principles. When such an unfold- ment is attained by any individual, he or she belongs to the world; as did Julius Cæsar, who was *Pontifex Maximus* of Rome before that Jesus of Jerusalem was born, from whose birth we date the Christian era. Like the fabled phœnix, each such individual goes forth, doing what must be done to perpetuate in the earth Phœnixian deeds and doers of such deeds: deeds, which when recorded in his- tory are not believable by ordinary minds, and so are com- monly relegated to the realm of fable. Thus it was at Rome's beginning when Romulus and Remus there found a solitude in which to *plant themselves* and their ideal methods of abstemious life according to that principle of liberty to all, which excludes license or special privilege to any.

Thus the illumined ones of the Phœnixian type have become saviours in time of need, as did Cæsar, who was not sundered from his personal principles, which were those of the eagle, nor from his polity of national practice, which was that of ancient Rome.

The polity and practice of Rome was to plant her in- stitutions as far as possible in her colonies, and to furnish from her own numbers the chief officers of government and administration. And this policy is ingrained British practice to-day. But the British polity is Rome's polity minus the eagle and plus the lion. *Vide*, every country where they plant their guns when they go to obtain gold mines and other things, on whatever claims they can man- age, while the government does the rest. The Angles of old Albion were the Phœnicians of the world, who, history shows, were driven from place to place, while endeavoring, here and there, to plant their principles, carrying, in sealed symbolism, the oral teachings of "the white religion," which gives a "white world" (as the Welsh say) to those who attain to the practice of its peace-making principle, "Liberty to all, special privilege to none." The symbol of the Phœnicians is the phœnix; and the symbol of the phœnix is the eagle. This symbol the British have forsaken because of their affinity for the lion. But as about three thousand years ago the eagle appeared in historical prominence as the Roman standard of attainment, so now since 1776 the eagle has figured as the American standard toward which for a hundred and a quarter years the nation has been struggling, and struggling under the disadvantage imposed upon it by a disfranchised womanhood; who, in their condition of political degradation, can hardly become the mothers of the Phœnixian type of man. For it is on the full practicalization of its principles by all the people (and women are people) that America depends, as she looks to—not gather to her support the opposer of all other lands but—see every nation of the earth set up within its own borders this standard: that each, who "knows," may teach the one who knows not, the dignity of human individuality and the delight of life.

Then the descendants of Foulke, King of Jerusalem, or of Solomon or David, would be allowed to go home, and under the winged symbolism of the cherubim of their Shekinah-mystery, enjoy again Hiero-salem, the hidden peace, thus relieving the British of a burden they are not competent to carry. And if the real Angles would sympathetically discuss with Ireland its history and the meaning of the Ionian dove, the angel of the harp of harmony, as of old, bardlike, would bring peace, and release the British from all further anxiety on the score of that "turbulent people." And Germany and Russia, France and Spain, Italy and the Asiatics and Africans, in a conclave of exact truth-telling would find themselves at one mind; and would proclaim peace for the reason that peace reigns wherever the eagle nests. For to its standard gather men and women filled with the knowledge of the arts and sciences and the best grace of life. The learning of the Alexandrian and Greek schools is borne on the wings of the eagle. And it empowers with wings those who honor its standard.

It is supposed that Westminster Abbey now stands on the former site of the temple of Apollo; and it is said, St. Paul's Cathedral is very properly erected on the spot where the

Romans had set up a temple to Diana, the goddess of chastity—a virtue without the practice of which nothing is possible to the very ancient philosophy of high life.

It is related that once in passing through a market-place in Rome, Gregory saw some British slaves for sale, noticeable for their fair complexions and beauty. "Who are these?" he asked. "Angles," said the merchant. "Not Angles, but angels shall they be," said Gregory.

In our scientific gropings after the spirit-principle of Life, we talk of "persistence of type," which is one way of saying, "The spirit does the body make." And that is absolutely true of the spirited-blood of the Phœnixian type of people which appears here and there in the self-recreating, self-resurrecting kind. Such are born of mothers who have freedom to live according to the law of the goddess, "Liberty to all and license to none." This is the inherent law, characteristic of the true Angle, and secures high heredity.

"The gods are to each other not unknown," and men and women of this kind, in whatever land they live, will have no feud with America for driving from the goddess "the beast," who otherwise "would devour the child," divine humanity, "or ever it could be born." And their standard is that of the mystical phœnix, figured forth to-day in the American eagle upborne by the hand of the Goddess of Liberty. For to this war of principles Phœnixians are summoned in this continent, whose wealth consists not alone in the abundance of its bimetallic medium of exchange, called gold and silver money, but in the released industries which will start up on every side, as the *treasures* in the heart of Mother Earth and the skilled labor of the hands and brains of her sons and daughters work together for the creation of new forms of life, of knowledge, and of beauty.

THE TELEGRAPH MONOPOLY.

BY PROF. FRANK PARSONS.

V.

EVILS OF THE PRESENT SYSTEM (*continued*).

Strikes are among the serious evils of a private telegraph system. They result from the ill-treatment of employees. In the last quarter of a century there have been two tremendous telegraph strikes extending from ocean to ocean and causing enormous loss and inconvenience. The Western Union officially stated its own loss by the strike of 1883 as being $709,300.[1] The loss to the employees and the public in general cannot be estimated precisely, but the *total* loss was not less than a million, probably much more. The strike lasted about one month.

We never hear of any such declarations of war on the part of public employees either here or abroad, for the reason that as a rule the comfort and prosperity of employees is a matter of solicitude with the management, and in those cases where, for some temporary reason, full justice is not done them, the employees affected know they possess an effective remedy of a peaceable nature, whereas the employees of a private monopoly find themselves crushed beneath the irresponsible power of a management that cares nothing for men but everything for gold,—petition disregarded and the petitioners blacklisted and discharged,—no hope of any quick relief but by rebellion.[2]

---

[1] Blair Com. vol. 2, p. 59.

[2] There was a time when if B stole the property of D the latter had no redress but retaliation or battle. He was at perfect liberty to knock B down if he could and trample on him till he was willing to do the square thing. This was inconvenient in several ways,—it disturbed the peace and harmony of society, and was not quite reliable as a means of justice even between B and D, for B might prove the stronger and squeeze the life out of D as well as absorb his property. For these reasons society ordained that individuals should not fight out their quarrels among themselves but should take them into courts of justice where they could be settled without a breach of the peace, and with a clearer sense of justice than either party to the squabble could be expected to possess. So much for war between man and man; but when a corporation and its employees get into troub'e they are left to the primitive plan, because it disturbs society so much less, I suppose, to have a couple of battalions fighting in the streets than to have a row between D and B, or perhaps the corporation doesn't want any court interference and is able to wield a greater influence with society than

Apropos of the strike of '83 the Washington *Sunday Herald* said:

"A country that leaves its most vital means of intercommunication, the very nerve of thought, in the grasp of a Jay Gould, deserves to have a strike every week that will paralyze correspondence, railway traffic, governmental operations (signal service, etc.), and everything else until it learns sense in the school of experience."

The following strong words are taken from *Harper's Weekly:*

"Such interruptions as those arising from the strike produce not only incalculable inconvenience, but loss, and it is only for the people to decide whether they shall be tolerated. They will be always possible and imminent under the existing conditions of vast counter-organizations of labor and capital. . . . A general strike of the telegraphs and railways would in a very short time cost the government and country very much more than the construction of a telegraph."

Poor service is another evil in large part due to abuse of the employing power. It manifests itself in slowness, inaccuracy, insufficient facilities, failure to guard the secrecy of messages, etc.

The Chicago *Tribune* long ago called attention to the fact that while the Western Union service between the stock exchanges was very prompt and reliable, yet "when we step outside the isothermal lines of speculation we find a sudden drop in the efficiency of the telegraph."[3] The

the little thief B could obtain. There is no doubt that a court established to do justice between employers and employees and substitute impartial equity for the gage of battle would accomplish much good. It could fix general principles of action, as has been done in respect to the other relations in which men stand to one another. It could, for example, affirm the principle that $50 per month should be the minimum reward for the services of man or woman in the telegraph service, and that any agreement to the contrary should be void as unconscionable and against public policy. No system of arbitration, however, whether voluntary or compulsory, could ever remove the antagonism of interest between owners on the one hand and employees and the public on the other—an antagonism which is the cause of all the evils of the telegraph system and which will cause evil in some form so long as it continues to exist. Only public ownership can remove this antagonism, wherefore public ownership is the only complete remedy for the evils of the present system. To illustrate by a concrete case: if the Industrial Court declared that $50 should be the minimum pay permitted by public policy (except, of course, where the service is a labor of love and friendship), the Western Union would immediately advance the price of telegraphing, and they could easily adjust their books in agreement with the Postal Telegraph Company so as to give the appearance of necessity to any price they chose to adopt. Moreover they would arrange with employees to pay back a part of their salaries, and discharge and blacklisting would await anyone who complained. If this were met by legislation we should have another effort at evasion, and so on in endless succession, an eternal struggle to outwit and defeat the public and the employees; we have all seen it and we know only too well how largely it succeeds. Nothing but public ownership (or a marvellous conversion of the telegraph managers) can secure good wages to employees together with low rates for service and earnest efforts on the part of the management to conduct the business in the interests of the people as a whole.

[3] Issue of Nov. 23, 1883.

New York *Herald* calls the Western Union service "poor and irregular"; the New Orleans *City Item* says, "The service is slow, bungling, and expensive";[4] *The Manufacturer* says: "The service is by no means what it ought to be. In a large percentage of dispatches errors of vexatious and hurtful character are made."[5] Poor service is one of the standing complaints of that portion of the press which dares to criticise the Western Union, and its defenders have little or nothing to say in rebuttal,—only the president of the company attempts to maintain that the service is good, relying for his proof on illustrations taken from the transmission of dispatches to and from the stock exchanges or smaller gambling dens.

Professor Ely calls the service "defective and irregular," and says that he "has sent a telegram a distance of some four hundred miles and has given the telegram a start of twenty-four hours, then taken a train and arrived at the destination of the telegram on the same day on which the telegram was delivered. This is by no means an isolated experience."[6]

It is no uncommon thing for a person or letter to outstrip a telegram and reach the common destination ahead of it, though starting later than the electric message.

"Two years ago the 22d of February I was visiting Mr. Powderly on business. As we sat in his house at eleven o'clock at night the door bell rang. When the door was opened, a reporter from the *Irish World* in New York walked in. After taking his seat, he inquired of Mr. Powderly if he had received his dispatch. He replied that he had not. 'Why,' said he, 'I sent you one, just before getting on the train at New York, notifying you that I would be here at 11.' Just at that moment the bell rang again; when the door was opened, the Western Union messenger boy walked in, and the reporter had the pleasure of seeing Mr. Powderly receipt for the message that he had sent from New York. He had beaten his own message, by train, fifteen minutes. For fear that the gentlemen present representing the Western Union may think that is so long ago that it is barred by the statute of limitation, I have here another one. This one was sent to my colleague on the committee from Florida. On the face of it, it says it was received in Washington 12.10 A. M. I saw him receipt for it at 11 A. M. It had taken them eleven hours to get it from the Western Union office to my office, five blocks away. Why, only last night I received a letter from Philadelphia by special delivery. It arrived in Washington by train, at 9.25 P. M., and at 10.15 I receipted for it, only forty minutes to get it through the postoffice and up to my office, the same distance as the Western Union."[7]

A few years ago some relatives of mine telegraphed from

---

4 Wanamaker, 1890, pp. 42, 204.

5 Issue of April 1, 1890 (Philadelphia).

6 December ARENA, 1895, p. 50.

7 Bingham Com. p. 86, testimony of Mr. Beaumont.

Atlantic City about 10 A. M. to their home in Mount Holly eighteen miles east of Philadelphia. At 3 P. M. they took train for home which they reached that evening. Next day the telegram came, announcing that they were coming. At the time of sending the message they inquired if it would go right through and were assured that it would.

There is plenty more of the same sort:

"It is within the experience of every business man that messages might sometimes have been sent by hand on one of the two-hour trains from Philadelphia to New York with a fair chance of reaching the destination as quickly as if they had been sent by wire. The service between the large cities is, however, better than that to the smaller towns. Not far from Philadelphia is a town of six or seven thousand inhabitants, having great industrial interests. It costs but little more to send a messenger thither from the city by rail than to use the wires, and ordinarily such a messenger can go out and return before a telegram sent in one direction will reach the person to whom it is addressed. No telegrams are delivered in the town after eight o'clock in the evening unless it is of vital importance. The operator is the person who estimates its importance, and he rarely fails to give the benefit of the doubt to the legs of his boy. If the postoffice gave such inefficient service in the matter of letters, it would be compelled by public opinion to improve its methods." [8]

"It is simply wonderful, the delay in many of these dispatches. One of the leading and most responsible commercial travelling men of this city makes the proposition to wager any sum from $100 to $1,000 that he will file in the telegraph office in this city, any day in the year, a dispatch to ———, and after filing and paying for the dispatch, he will step across the street and hire a livery team and drive to ———, a distance of thirty-two miles from here, and his wager is that he will reach ——— in advance of his telegram." [9]

The company's appetite for slowness is not always content with finite delay,—the message is sometimes laid away and never sent at all.[10]

The exercises are also varied by transmitting to the wrong destination, misspelling the name of the addressee so that no delivery can be made, omitting essential words or altering the terms of the message so that misunderstandings arise, occasioning serious losses to persons innocent of all fault except that of relying on the telegraph. Hundreds of pages of legal text are required to discuss the cases in which suit has been brought against the telegraph companies for damages caused by inaccuracy of transmission, delay, or total failure to transmit,[11] and the cases in which suit is brought are but a small part of the total num-

---

[8] *The Manufacturer* (Philadelphia), April 1, 1890.

[9] Wanamaker 1890, p. 139.

[10] Sprague v. Western Union, 6 Daly 200; s. c. 67 N. Y. 590; Candee v. W. U., 34 Wisconsin 471, etc.

[11] See Croswell's Legal Text Book on Telegraphs, etc., Little, Brown & Co., 1895.

ber in which injurious errors occur. It may be interesting to note the facts in one or two cases.

In the Landsberger case[12] a telegram to Landsberger, 28 Broad street, New York City, was transmitted "Lammeyer," failing thereby to reach the plaintiff. The address was inquired about over the wires, but before the error was corrected the time limited in the contract made by the sender of the telegram had elapsed and he had lost $900 by failing to fulfil a bona tide agreement for the sale of merchandise. The company was held not to be responsible because the damage was a loss of *profit*.

In the Lowery case a telegram to "send $500," was changed so that it read "send $5,000." The plaintiff sent $5,000 and the consignee absconded with it. Western Union not responsible.[13] So if the message is in cipher the company is not responsible for errors in transmission, however careless and injurious,—so it is held by the U. S. Supreme Court and others of high authority, on the ground that as the company cannot understand the message it cannot contemplate any damages, which appears to me to be nonsense, but is none the less law, except in Alabama, Georgia, Florida, and Virginia.[14]

Suits have been brought in considerable numbers even by the brokers whose work the Western Union boasts of doing so perfectly, and the general public can calculate with certainty on a large percentage of error. The following testimony of a wide-awake postmaster in the city of —— tells the universal story of Western Union service.

"Many of the actions of the Western Union Telegraph Company in regard to business connected with the mail are inexcusable. Take, for instance, as an illustration, last Friday; I received, as postmaster here, three dispatches from commercial travelling men ordering their mail forwarded to three different points. Not merely one of these dispatches, but *all three* of them were transmitted wrong; that is, the initial of the name was wrong or the name spelled so badly it was absolutely impossible to decipher it. Of course there was some similarity in names or initials so as to give me some clue as to who it was meant for, but a postmaster is not safe in guessing at these matters. I was confident they were wrong and refused them and asked the telegraph company to have a second transmission. They did so, and in each case of the second transmission the names and initials were absolutely correct; but the second transmission did not get here until the next morning, and as a consequence thereof the mail for these gentlemen was delayed in forwarding from twelve to twenty-four

---

[12] 32 Barb. N. Y. 530.

[13] 60 N. Y. 198.

[14] See Croswell § 590 *et seq*. In one case the plaintiff's loss was $20,000, but the Western Union kept its millions of profit free of contribution for the wreckage caused by its employment of illtrained, overworked operators.

hours. I mention this particular date because it is fresh in my mind, but I could give you many others of like character; in fact it is a frequent occurrence at this postoffice."

"Some two years ago I had a personal experience which cost me $40. I sent a telegram to the third assistant postmaster-general ordering 20,000 No. 5 2-cent envelopes, first quality, white. The envelopes came but were not first quality and were not white. An investigation showed that the telegraph company in transmitting the message left the words 'first quality' and 'white' out of the message, and the order was filled exactly as the message reached the third assistant postmaster-general with these words left out. The result was that I could not use the envelopes and the department simply redeemed them for their face value in postage stamps. The only thing for me to do was to grin and bear the loss. Of course the telegraph company 'were sorry,' so they informed me." [15]

Do not imagine that the Western Union's program of bad service is completed by slowness, inaccuracy, and failure to transmit. There are other threads in the fabric of their disrepute as carriers of intelligence.

"Grave difficulties have arisen from time to time between the government and the telegraph companies which have declined and still decline to furnish such facilities as are deemed essential to the perfect success of the signal service." [16] Hannibal Hamlin stated the insufficiency of the public service afforded by the telegraph companies, as one of three emphatic reasons which impelled him to advocate a government telegraph. [17]

The Western Union is not always satisfied with mere insufficiency of facilities for the public business. On the 4th of March, 1871, it suddenly terminated the transmission of weather reports over all its lines because of a misunderstanding as to the power of the federal authorities over the telegraph under the law of 1866, and it was nearly four months before it could be persuaded to resume business and allow the sailors, farmers, travellers, and general public to be informed as usual of coming storm or sunshine, thaw or freeze. [18]

---

[15] Wanamaker 1890, p. 139.

[16] P.-M. Genl. Creswell Nov. 15, 1872, p. 27.

[17] Congressional Globe 42d Cong. 2d sess. p. 3554. The three reasons were: 1st, for the sake of the signal service which the Western Union does not properly serve although the government pays it $250,000 a year; 2d, for the sake of the low rates all the rest of the world enjoys, and 3d, for the sake of the postoffice system which may at any time be depleted by a strong telegraph in competent private hands.

[18] The Committee on Commerce, Senator Chandler chairman, reported that "The sudden cessation of the telegraphic reports extending in their consequences to so many interests threatened to prove disastrous " (Sen. Rep. 223 42d-2d, June 1, 1872). Other companies helped the government out some, and finally on June 24, 1871, after a good deal of discussion the Western Union kindly consented to permit the P.-M. Genl. to fix the rates for government dispatches as is provided by the law under which the Western Union holds its right to do interstate business.

Another sort of insufficiency in our telegraph service is strongly stated by Victor Rosewater, for seven years the Western Union manager at Omaha and a high authority as we have already had occasion to state in these papers.

"One of the most significant facts in regard to the present condition of the telegraph service in this country, is that only one-fourth of the telegraph offices in this country are commercial offices, and the other three-fourths are railroad offices. The telegraph companies will not maintain offices at points where the income does not cover rent and the salary of the operator. The consequence is that the people in thousands of American towns are obliged to depend upon a service where the wires are constantly busy with the transmission of railroad service messages. The railroad operators are, as a class, not competent to handle commercial business, and the dispatches transmitted through railroad offices are frequently subjected to errors and ruinous delays. Now, in Great Britain and other European countries, the reverse is true. I found that there are three postal-telegraph stations to one railroad-telegraph station. In fact, the railroad wires are seldom used for commercial business. In nearly every village where there is a postoffice there is also a postal-telegraph office." [19]

Our telegraph service is also poor because it is not properly coördinated with the telephone service, because old methods are used instead of the newest and best, because it is marred by unjust discrimination, and because it divulges the secrets entrusted to it. The first three points will be dealt with hereafter, but a word about the last may be useful here. If you impart a secret to a doctor or a lawyer professionally, you need not fear for its safety, but if you give it to the Western Union you might almost as well tell it to the town gossip or the new reporter on a city paper whose position and wages depend on the amount of sensational matter he can collect.

Speculative operations largely depend on telegraphic reports from Liverpool and New York. On the strength of dispatches men buy wheat by the hundred thousand dollars' worth. This is not commendable business, but it is none the less an outrage to take money from A for a private dispatch to himself when the information contained in it has already been peddled out to others. Yet this has been done not once merely but many times. "An operator in Chicago claims to have paid out $400 a week for dispatches from the Old World, and the wheat markets of this; and not long since he discovered that others had been getting the benefit of these dispatches before himself, and at much less cost than he was subjected to. In an attempt

---

[19] *The Voice*, New York, Aug. 29, 1895, p. 1. For the reasons of the insufficiency of the ordinary railroad office for prompt and accurate commercial service see Bingham Com. 1890, Rosewater, p. 6.

to solve the mystery of these dispatches, a decoy was sent to Chicago from Milwaukee, instructions having been previously given by letter. At the Chicago office the dispatch was evidently given into other hands, for wheat advanced 3 cents a bushel at once, and the parties who secured the telegram lost $300,000 by their sharpness. A gentleman who knows whereof he speaks tells us that the contents of dispatches sent from this city by wheat men to the Northwest are frequently given to rival buyers who operate upon them."[20]

Loud complaints have been made about the disclosure of political messages, and government business, even military dispatches in time of war. In 1894 Mr. Wilson said: "Suppose I transmit a confidential telegram relative to political matters of importance to myself. In the general judgment of the people of the West, such news as that now leaks like a sieve."[21] At the time of the Hayes canvass the governor of Florida complained that messages were exposed at Tallahassee to a leading Democratic politician.[22] In 1889 the Western Union received $88,000 for selling election news to pool rooms, theatres, etc.,[23] the news being abstracted from messages sent over its wires by third parties, just as if the postoffice should select information of special interest from the letters that pass through its hands and sell it to pool-rooms, theatres, etc. Of the insecurity even of orders sent to the troops in time of war a flagrant instance was referred to by Mr. Albright in the second session of the 43d Congress. Important government dispatches ordering certain movements of Union troops were sent by Major-General McDowell to Captain Mills and other officers. Twenty-four hours before the dispatches were delivered to the addressees the contents of the messages had been given to the public in a garbled form for the sake of political effect, and the contemplated movements of the troops had to be countermanded.[24]

The contrast between our telegraphic service and that of Europe is not at all pleasing to American pride. President Francis Walker of the Massachusetts Institute of Technology told the writer that he found the service in England and Germany much better than in the United

[20] H. Rep. 114. pp. 11, 12.

[21] Henderson Committee I. T. U. Hearings, p. 41.

[22] Blair Com., vol. 1, p. 901.

[23] Bingham Com. Rosewater. p. 3.

[24] Congressional Record 43-2, p. 1422.

States. Professor Simon Newcomb says that the telegraph service in the United States is the poorest in the world.[25] And Professor R. T. Ely says, that " the contrast between the service in this country and the service in Germany is most painful to one who has lived in both countries,"[26] and he specifies the facts that the offices are so frequently closed, that none exist in rural districts, that transmission is irregular and unreliable, and that inaccuracy in greater or less degree is the rule rather than the exception, all of which is the exact contrary of his experience with the German telegraph. Other evidence of the superior efficiency of the public telegraphs across the sea will be adduced when we come to speak specifically of the foreign telegraph.

Now and then an individual worker will make a mistake or commit a wrong even when all the employees are chosen with care, well-trained, well-paid, and well-treated, but the multiplicity of errors, discriminations, delays, etc., that characterizes our telegraph service and distinguishes it in so marked a manner from the public service abroad, is due to the very nature of a selfish private monopoly.

A private telegraph does not aim at service. It wants cheap labor, and that means inefficient labor. It abuses its employees, and they are consequently out of sympathy with their work, do not put their hearts into it nor give as good service even as they know how to give. The long list of imperfections in Western Union service results from the ill-treatment of employees, the lack of proper care in the use of the employing power, the policy of suppressing inventions, the absence of needful facilities, the false distribution of those that exist, and the ruling thirst for gain regardless of the public good. For every count in the indictment the management of the company is responsible.

[25] Harvard Quarterly Jour. of Economics, July, '93.
[26] ARENA, Dec. '05, p. 59.

(To be continued.)

REPRESENTATIVE WOMEN ON VITAL SOCIAL PROBLEMS.

Is the Single Tax Enough to Solve the Labor Problem?

The opportunity to say a "last word" in answer to this question is offered me.

On re-reading the papers of the symposium I find that the socialists answer "no," mainly because they cannot see:

1. That taking economic rent for common expenses will, by opening land to free settlement, raise the wages of labor at the margin of cultivation to a point ensuring comfort and leisure for itself, the base of the pyramid of human effort, and consequently for its whole superstructure.

2. That the relation of man to land on which and from which he must live, is the basic relation, and that no other problem relating to his material welfare can be rightly and permanently solved until that basic relation is justly established; that the problems involved in the private ownership of the ways for the transportation of persons and property and the transmission of intelligence will be solved by such just establishment; and that the money question is of secondary importance, and is one which will largely settle itself after the single tax has secured to the laborer the wealth he earns.

3. That the relation of labor to land remains the same under all systems of production, from the simplest to the most complex; the application of labor to land producing all wealth, first, by means of the bare hands of man, then with the aid of those first forms of capital, the pointed stick and sharpened stone, and finally by the marvellous modern machine.

4. And that, failing to understand this persistent relation, they cannot see how the making of it free and perfect will by natural process compel the just distribution of wealth, but are forced, in order to justify the unnatural distribution which they propose, to deny to men their place in the universe as conscious moral units, and to introduce a fourth factor into production by separating brain- from hand-work and calling it "ability."

I note, also, that it is made a reproach to single taxers that they do not agree on the money question and that, while some of us assert that the single tax is enough to solve the labor question, other of us "prudently fail to affirm" that it is.

The lack of comprehension of these points is owing, it seems to me, to lack of earnest consideration of the course of reasoning which supports our economic statements, and further, to the failure to carry that reasoning into the domain of morals, and the consequent failure to understand the body of doctrine grouped under the name of "single tax" as a *philosophy*, and not merely a fiscal measure having its beginning and end in the proposition to tax into the public treasury for the support of government the annual rental value of land in lieu of all other taxes.

It is impossible, in the space granted me, to offer reasons for the belief that under the single tax system of land tenure (and all which that implies in the way of lessened taxation, sure and steady markets, just transportation rates, etc.), the worker at the margin of production, be he farmer, miner, cattle-ranch man, lumberman, fisherman, or other, will earn enough to command comfort and leisure, and will pocket his earnings; but I will point to one fact, and ask one question in connection with him. Fifty or sixty years ago the farmer, for instance, was an independent and prosperous man. With the causes which have changed his condition removed by the single tax and his productive power increased, as all admit it has been, by discovery, invention, and the specialization of labor, what is to prevent his condition being not only as good under the single tax but better? There is nothing in political economy to teach us that the worker at the margin of cultivation is not abreast of his age. In fact, no man can live his life "à la Robinson Crusoe" in a civilized country; he must coöperate or perish.

As to the second point. The private ownership of common ways created monopoly of the right of way, a land monopoly pure and simple. This kind of land monopoly built up the power of the Standard Oil Company by means of the secret rebate, a species of highway robbery being more or less rapidly applied to other branches of trade. Single taxers say (with few exceptions, I believe) that these common ways should be treated as our streets are now, namely, that they should be owned and policed by the community and used by individuals as long as free competition in such use is possible. When from the nature of the use made of them monopoly is involved, as seems to be the case in the gas and water supplies and perhaps others, then the community should operate as well as own them.

In regard to the third and fourth points I will only ask a question or two. Granting for the sake of argument that the "rent of ability," "the additional wealth created by the use of machinery in combined labor," exists, and that it must be taken by the community in order justly to distribute wealth and ensure the well-being of all, I would ask, At what point in the history of production does the rent of ability begin? Surely the primeval hunter by means of sharpened stones and with the help of his family created wealth over and above what he could have produced alone with bare hands. And surely the miller and his assistant by their wind or water wheel produced more flour than the wife of the primeval hunter by means of her round and hollowed stones and handful of grain. Land, labor, capital—are not their relations fixed for all time, the same now in the fur and flour industries as they were in former days, the same always in complex as in simple methods of production?

When a fundamental moral principle as incontrovertible as this, namely, that all men have a natural, inalienable, equal right to the use of the earth, is found to underlie the money question, and when a great thinker has built up by a series of logically inseparable steps a plan by which that principle may be put in practice, then single taxers will be a unit on the money question, and not till then.

And this brings us to the last and most important point, —most important, because the statement, that some of us "prudently fail to affirm" that the single tax is enough to solve the labor problem, involves a charge of intellectual dishonesty most unjust to a body of men and women whose attitude of mind toward their economic belief is serious even to solemnity. Nevertheless, it is true that sometimes we say, "The single tax is enough," sometimes we say, "It is not enough." This is not due to the difference in our views of the single tax philosophy, but to the different meaning we attach to the words "labor problem." When we are considering the "labor problem," technically so called, i. e., our present low wages and lack of employment, we unhesitatingly say, "The single tax is enough." But when we are discussing with socialists the merits of our opposing conceptions of man in his relations to his fellow and the universe, our imaginations take a wider flight. We think of the labor problem of the ages, of the welfare, the progress, the fate of mankind; and we say as unhesitatingly, "The single tax is not enough." What is enough? When the eternal answer is given, will there be one to record it? For with perfection development ceases, and without change can man exist?

Meanwhile, will socialism help toward a solution? Yes, possibly, in its day and generation, *if* in the process of evolution, society develops more and more complex forms of evil side by side with more and more complex forms of good. Yes, if another system of slavery is in the natural order.

That socialism involves slavery a little thought will show. The appropriation by some of the earnings, i. e., the results of the bodily and mental exertions of others, is the essence of slavery. It is also the essence of socialism of every brand. Witness the two kinds represented in this symposium, that which would confine its robbery to the "additional wealth created by the use of machinery in combined labor, or, as it is called, the "rent of ability," and that which would take all wealth, distributing "our common product for free consumption," and justifying this course by denying the individuality of the man, reducing him to the level of a "cell in a relation of coördinate activity," saying, "a man has no own labor." Deny in practice that a man has "own labor," deny his right to himself, his own powers, and the results of their exercise, and slavery ensues as surely as it does when he is denied equal access to the earth with all other men,—the earth, that storehouse of nature,—to enter which the race has an inalienable right for all time.

But if, on the other hand, we have reached one of those periods when man may take a stride forward towards liberty and hold his ground, then the single tax will be the next help toward the solution of the time-long problem. And man, from the eminence it has helped him to attain, may take a breathing spell between possible oppressive phases of the problem and establish the "vast coöperative commonwealth" of Mr. George, wherein free competition in production, exchange, and transportation, including those more subtle forms of production, discovery, and invention, will raise society to heights material and moral yet unattained and perhaps unsuspected. And this without changing human nature, which, I beg the writers of the symposium to remember, will not be affected in its fundamental attributes by either socialism or single tax.

SARAH MIFFLIN GAY.

FOUNDATION AND FELLOWSHIP.

The besetting danger is not so much of embracing falsehood for truth as of mistaking part of the truth for the whole.— John Stuart Mill.

Our discussion of the sufficiency of the single tax to solve the labor problem quickly outran the original intention. A few questions and misconceptions remain. There may be some "failure to understand" and "lack of comprehension" on both sides of the discussion: but probably there is more substantial agreement than appears at a glance. For instance, I think we are all agreed that "*The relation of man to land is a basic relation,*" *and there can be no solution of the labor question which does not involve the establishment of the principle that all men have a natural, equal, and inalienable right to the use of the earth.*

I think we all believe that since physical life cannot exist without land, but can exist without the use of money or railroads, the financial and transportation questions are intrinsically of secondary importance. Yet these "secondary" questions are now demanding immediate attention, if we would escape great increase of subtle forms of slavery. The nation is being "held up" in open day and systematically robbed by a class which is using every means to increase its power of legal robbery. We are in the midst of the war for industrial freedom, with small chance to carry out ideal plans of campaign. "New occasions teach new duties."

Again, "the *vast co-operative commonwealth* of Mr. George," mentioned respectfully by the last writer, is probably not very different from "national coöperation" advocated in this discussion. The statement of one writer that "a man has no own labor" seems harmonious with the declaration of the last writer that "he must coöperate or perish." No one could assert that "slavery is the essence of all socialism" who thinks of the root-meaning of the word—*socious*, a companion. It is the principle of companionism, fellowship, equality—crudely conceived and imperfectly embodied at first, but gradually leavening the whole lump of humanity as a saving principle or evolving ideal. Whatever is tyrannical or unjust cannot be true socialism. It has been said that the creed of communism is, "to every one according to his need"; of socialism, "to every one according to his deed"; of individualism, "to every one according to his greed." The ideal of national coöperation is "economic equality," not communism: this principle to be applied, like the keystone of an arch, when the full coöperation of all productive and distributive labor has gradually been accomplished, instead of the concentration of monopolies and trusts now threatening us with a plutocratic oligarchy having the people at its mercy.

We are told that the "farmer was prosperous fifty years ago." Was the prosperity of the *average* farmer then such as would satisfy you and me, for ourselves and families, to-day, with its endless round of hard labor and its close pinching and monotonous life? It is asked, "With the causes which have changed his condition removed by the single tax, and his productive power increased, as all admit it has been, by discovery, invention, and the specialization of labor, what is to prevent his condition being not only as good under the single tax but better? There is nothing in political economy to tell us that the worker at the margin of cultivation is not abreast of his age."

Much is taken for granted in putting this question, but never mind. Fifty years ago rapid transportation and communication had not placed the farmer in competition with all the world; his prices are now largely determined by the cheap labor of India, Russia, Egypt, and other foreign countries, and his home markets mainly in the power of trusts and corporations. Steam machinery had not been applied to agriculture, requiring for its successful use great tracts of land and great capital; the conditions described by Mr. George showing that the small farmer must be driven out, since "with great capital nothing can compete save great capital."

The productive power of the bare-handed individual is little greater than that of his grandfather—is often less. The power of labor has increased enormously by the increment of those "mighty forces," steam and electricity: but this immense increase in the power of labor can no more be averaged among individual workers as the personal ability of each, than the increased land values of New York state can be divided by the number of acres to set the price of each acre. I do not see how the worker at the margin of cultivation, unable (because of location or poverty) to take advantage of latest improvements or best markets, can possibly be "abreast of his age" in respect to labor. Great numbers of these, too poor to compete or coöperate successfully, would form an American peasantry.

Invention is the gift of God to the race, to bestow leisure for higher culture and enjoyment; but its capitalistic monopoly increases the numbers of the idle rich and the idle poor, saving the latter from labor by turning them adrift.

A striking instance of labor-saving, since steam and electricity stimulated invention, is found in the new iron works of Mr. Edison. The ore is drilled from the ground in great blocks of earth, hoisted by derricks and carried through many processes in the forty-one contiguous buildings, till it is packed as iron bricks on cars ready for shipment, to be used in the manufacture of steel—all this without any expenditure of muscular exertion, the twenty-four men employed for a daily output of one thousand tons simply cleaning, oiling, and tending the machinery. It is said that Mr. Edison makes a profit from these works of sixty-nine hundred dollars daily. Did God love Mr. Edison better than other men?

We are told that in the cotton industries one man and two boys now do the work that employed 1,110 spinners not long ago; and in weaving, one man takes the place of forty men; while in the fields the cotton-picker has now come to displace ninety workers. I read the other day that ships are now unloaded by machinery, one man taking the place of 2,000 men. This is the tendency everywhere—meant for the blessing of the race. Ability, the unearned increment of the power of labor, has so increased that the work of the world must be done by a comparatively small part of the population, or the great gift of leisure and the opportunities for culture and enjoyment which leisure implies must be shared equally among all by coöperation.

Just look at the situation. Great multitudes of our fellows are in compulsory idleness, surely and unavoidably degenerating and increasing the numbers of defectives and criminals; while those who, by our bad management, have been allowed to accumulate standing orders on all wealth and tribute rights against labor, as landlords or bondholders or monopolists of one kind or another, are coolly skimming the cream from everything and setting up as superior beings in consequence. Yet statistics are said to be capable of proving that the whole work of the nation could be done—if the great powers and best inventions were applied coöperatively with coördination of all industries—by less than two hours' daily labor of all the men between the ages of sixteen and fifty, or less time if women helped. Tesla, the great electrician, says the work of the future will be mainly "touching electric buttons" to set automatic machinery in motion. An equal sharing of the annual labor values (in the form of equal credit on the national stores and services—to be used according to personal taste and judgment) would result in such freedom and independence as we hardly dream of now. All this is possible. Those who think it is not desirable have not enjoyed Mr. Howells' "Traveller from Altruria" as I have.

Formerly the rent of ability seemed to be reflected in land values, but this cannot be seen in (for instance) the introduction of linotype machines in the newspaper offices, throwing three-fourths of the printers out of work. Some of the proprietors of the greatest inventions are taking rent of ability literally, refusing to sell the machines but renting them out for immense sums and keeping them under their own strict supervision.

"When does rent of ability begin?" Let me answer by asking, When does economic rent begin? Morally, whenever there is inequality of opportunity. In the family there seems no "slavery" in "bearing one another's burdens, so fulfilling the law of Christ." In a "vast coöperative commonwealth," taking advantage of all the organization and equipment which would be impossible to small societies, the truth of Mr. Bellamy's statement in the *Contemporary Review* would be obvious: "Nine hundred and ninety-nine parts out of the thousand of every man's produce are the result of his social inheritance and environment." Mr. Kidd quotes this in "Social Evolution," and adds, "This is so; and it is, if possible, even more true of the work of our brains than of the work of our hands."

Free competition between individuals has become almost impossible, and it can be regained only by giving up the great inventions which offer the human race leisure and freedom from the strife and slums of the present, and going back to the primitive methods. Free coöperation is better than free competition. Competition now means fierce battling for supremacy between great corporations, with constant tendency to end the wasteful strife by uniting in one great monopoly—perhaps the "military despotism" which Herbert Spencer a few years ago foretold as our destiny.

The people do not know their danger. The public mind is kept in a partially asphyxiated condition by a press mainly controlled by the bankers and a monopolized telegraph. Wendell Phillips warned us in these words:

The great question of the future is money against legislation. My friends, you and I shall be in our graves long before that battle is ended; and, unless our children shall have more patience and courage than saved this country, republican institutions will go down before moneyed corporations. Rich men die, but banks are immortal and railroad corporations never have any diseases. Our fathers, when they forbade entail and provided for the distribution of estates, thought they had erected a barrier against the money power that ruled England. They forgot that money could combine; that a moneyed corporation is a succession of persons with a unity of purpose. Now, as the land of England in the hands of 30,000 landowning families has ruled it for six hundred years, so the corporations of America mean to govern; and, unless some power more radical than ordinary politics is found, will govern inevitably. The survival of republican institutions here depends upon a successful resistance of this tendency. The only hope of any successful grapple with this danger lies in rousing the masses, whose interests lie permanently in the opposite direction.

FRANCES ELDREDGE RUSSELL.

A BAREFOOT BOY WHO WAS ALSO A DREAMER.

BY B. O. FLOWER.

" Blessings on thee, little man,
Barefoot boy, with cheek of tan!
With thy turned-up pantaloons,
And thy merry whistled tunes;
With thy red lip, redder still
Kissed by strawberries on the hill;
With the sunshine on thy face,
Through thy torn brim's jaunty grace;
From my heart I give thee joy,—
I was once a barefoot boy!"
— *Whittier's "Barefoot Boy."*

" I think at the age of which thy note inquires, I found about equal satisfaction in an old rural home with the shifting panorama of seasons, in reading the few books within my reach, *and in dreaming of something wonderful and grand in the future."*
— *Whittier to a youthful correspondent.*

John Greenleaf Whittier was born on the 17th of December, 1807, in a typical New England farmhouse a short distance from the town of Haverhill, in Massachusetts. His father was poor; rigid economy and incessant toil on the part of all members of the household were required in order to provide life's necessities and lift a debt which hung over the dear old homestead. If, however, the little Quaker boy was schooled in poverty, it cannot be said that he was poor in any other sense than that he possessed little of that which gold may purchase. As a matter of fact, few children enter the arena of life so dowered with inestimable riches as the little barefoot boy who was destined to become New England's poet of home life and America's prophet of freedom. Behind him were generations of pure, high-minded and sturdy ancestors. In his parents we find united the rare charm which marks the life of the consistent and profoundly religious Quaker and the sturdy, almost austere morality of the Puritan shorn, however, of that harsh, unrelenting and intolerant spirit which not unfrequently shadowed and made repulsive the otherwise noble lives of the early Puritans.

Nor were the hereditary influences and prenatal conditions more favorable than the environment that enclosed his early years. Biographers have frequently deplored the poverty of Whittier's parents, which prevented the youth from having access to many books adapted to the young;

but I am by no means convinced that this apparent misfortune was not a blessing rather than an evil. Many of the men who have accomplished most for the moral uplift and enduring progress of the race have had access to but few books in youth. Indeed, the studious child who possesses few books soon assimilates their contents and unconsciously acquires the habit of retaining the facts which have been drawn from their pages, in a manner quite unknown to those who are surfeited with literature and who early learn to skim over rather than carefully peruse a printed page; and this early acquired habit of retaining facts remains with the person throughout life. Again, the thoughtful and ambitious child whose literature is so limited that he soon masters the knowledge contained in the books within his reach early turns his mind in other directions in search of knowledge; he becomes a close observer of nature and, if possessed of imagination, the sky, earth and sea, the changing seasons, the forest and the flowers, the birds and bees—each of these bears a message to his brain. We must also remember that the child who from early youth has been surrounded by books comes to rely too much on the opinion and thoughts of others and loses an originality in idea and expression which has never been properly fostered by educational processes. This, fortunately, Whittier escaped; what he lacked in booklearning was more than made up by—

> Knowledge never learned of schools,
> Of the wild bee's morning chase,
> Of the wild-flower's time and place,
> Flight of fowl and habitude
> Of the tenants of the wood;
> How the tortoise bears his shell,
> How the woodchuck digs his cell,
> And the ground-mole sinks his well;
> How the robin feeds her young,
> How the oriole's nest is hung;
> Where the whitest lilies blow,
> Where the freshest berries grow,
> Where the groundnut trails its vine,
> Where the wood-grape's clusters shine;
> Of the black wasp's cunning way,
> Mason of his walls of clay,
> And the architectural plans
> Of gray hornet artisans!

Nature teaches those children who will hearken to her words, and she is never false in word or note or picture. If the literature of the Whittier family was very limited, she was prodigal with treasures which appealed to the eye, ear and imagination of the Quaker boy.

I was rich in flowers and trees,
Humming birds and honey bees;
For my sport the squirrel played,
Plied the snouted mole his spade;
For my taste the blackberry cone
Purpled over hedge and stone;
Laughed the brook for my delight
Through the day and through the night,
Whispering at the garden wall,
Talked with me from fall to fall;
Mine the sand-rimmed pickerel pond,
Mine the walnut slopes beyond,
Mine on bending orchard trees
Apples of Hesperides!
Still as my horizon grew
Larger grew my riches, too.

Whittier never lost sight of the treasures which were his
amid what men of to-day would term biting poverty. On
one occasion in casting a retrospective glance over the long
vanished past, he thus characterized his early lot:

A farmer's son,
Proud of field-lore and harvest-craft, and feeling
All their fine possibilities. How rich
And restful even poverty and toil
Become when beauty, harmony and love
Sit at their humble hearth, as angels sat
At evening in the Patriarch's tent; when man
Makes labor noble!

The old homestead of the Whittier family has been endeared to the nation by the many bits of descriptive verse
which the poet has woven into his poems of New England
life. It was a large frame building somewhat better than
the average farmhouse of the period. Around it grew a
variety of hardy trees such as maple, walnut, butternut
and the picturesque Lombardy poplar. In one of his
prose sketches the poet thus describes the site of the
old home:

It was surrounded by woods in all directions save to the southeast,
where a break in the leafy wall revealed a vista of low green meadows
picturesque with wooded islands and jutting capes of upland; through
these a small brook, noisy enough as it foamed, rippled and laughed
down the rocky falls. By our garden side wound silently and scarcely
visible a still larger stream known as the Country Brook.

Rising abruptly almost from the Whittier garden was
Job's Hill, a high eminence from which a magnificent view
of the surrounding country could be obtained, although
not so favorable in this respect as Great Hill, a little distance further. It was on the slope of Job's Hill that the
young poet when quite small suddenly found himself con-

fronted by great peril, from which he was only saved by
what in a human being we should call presence of mind,
on the part of a favorite ox named Old Butler. Mr. Samuel
T. Pickard, whose "Life and Letters of Whittier" is the
latest and most authoritative utterance on the life of the
poet, thus describes this interesting incident:

One side of Job's Hill is exceedingly steep — too steep for such an
unwieldy animal as an ox to descend rapidly in safety. Greenleaf went
to the pasture one day with a bag of salt for the cattle, and Old Butler
from the brow of the hill recognized him and knew his errand. As the
boy was bent over, shaking the salt out of the bag, the ox came down
the hill toward him with flying leaps, and his speed was so great that
he could not check himself. He would have crushed his young master,
but by a supreme effort, gathering himself together at the right moment, the noble creature leaped straight into the air, over the head of
the boy, and came to the ground far below with a tremendous concus-
sion and without serious injury to himself.

The same author gives an additional anecdote about this
favorite ox, as related by Mr. Whittier:

Quaker meetings were sometimes held in the large kitchen at his
father's house. One summer day, on such an occasion, this ox had the
curiosity to put his head in at the open window and take a survey of the
assembly. While a sweet-voiced woman was speaking, Old Butler paid
strict attention, but when she sat down and there arose a loud-voiced
brother, the ox withdrew his head from the window, lifted his tail in
air and went off bellowing. This bovine criticism was greatly enjoyed
by the younger members of the meeting.

The most important room in the old homestead, as it was
lovingly called by the poet, was the kitchen, immortalized
in "Snow-Bound"; but besides this room, on the ground floor
were other apartments, one of which was always regarded
somewhat as a sanctuary by the children and was known
as "mother's room." On the second floor were several
chambers which hold special interest for lovers of the poet.
In one of these the young poet made his experiment in
lifting, which Trowbridge has so aptly described in one
of his delightful little poems. The story is as follows: One
day during the working hours young John, musing on the
fact that he found no difficulty in lifting his brother Matt,
and that his brother had also frequently lifted him, came
to the conclusion that if the two lifted together both would
simultaneously rise. This conclusion, it will be seen,
though plausible on its face like so many things in life
which involve factors that have not been considered, was
destined to prove a disappointment to the youthful experimenter. The poet imparted his deductions to his brother,
who thought them reasonable, and forthwith the experiment was tried in their room. Somehow it did not work,
but as Trowbridge observes:

'Twas a shrewd notion none the less,
And still, in spite of ill success,
    It somehow has succeeded.
Kind Nature smiled on that wise child,
    Nor could her love deny him
The large fulfilment of his plan;
Since he who lifts his brother man
    In turn is lifted by him.

. Whittier was an ethical philosopher rather than a scientist, and the idea he conceived was neither false nor unphilosophical in the ethical realm, or world of conduct, as his own life illustrates.

Many of those most delightful pictures of New England life which were indelibly impressed upon the sensitive plate of his brain at this time when nature taught the artless boy, hold for us a special charm, due to their revealing the secret hopes, loves and disappointments which entered into his life. While it is probable that Whittier does not reproduce in detail actual experiences when he reveals to us love welling high within his heart—for pictures of this character are usually held sacred and carefully guarded from an unsympathetic world, even when the profound emotions which they awaken lend power to imagination's flights—there can be little doubt but that he experienced every emotion which he so simply and beautifully depicts. Thus, when we read the following exquisite lines from "My Playmate," we see behind the moaning pines on Ramoth Hill, the falling blossoms eddying in the fitful breeze, the melody of the robin's song or the gay plumage of the oriole, beyond the violet-sprinkled sod, beyond the graceful waving branches of the birch, beyond all these beauties and melodies of nature, the workings of the human heart; we catch a glimpse of something which is always sacred, something in the presence of which "the soul kneels though the body may remain erect," and that something is the Holy of Holies of the human heart from which the poet for a moment lifts the veil:

The pines were dark on Ramoth Hill,
    Their song was soft and low;
The blossoms in the sweet May wind
    Were falling like the snow.

The blossoms drifted at our feet,
    The orchard birds sang clear;
The sweetest and the saddest day
    It seemed of all the year.

For, more to me than birds or flowers,
    My playmate left her home,
And took with her the laughing spring,
    The music and the bloom.

She kissed the lips of kith and kin,
  She laid her hand in mine:
What more could ask the bashful boy
  Who fed her father's kine?

She left us in the bloom of May;
  The constant years told o'er
Their seasons with as sweet May morns,
  But she came back no more.

She lives where all the golden year
  Her summer roses blow;
The dusky children of the sun
  Before her come and go.

There, haply, with her jewelled hands
  She smooths her silken gown—
No more the homespun lap wherein
  I shook the walnuts down.

I see her face, I hear her voice —
  Does she remember mine?
And what to her is now the boy
  Who fed her father's kine?

What cares she that the orioles build
  For other eyes than ours, —
That other hands with nuts are filled,
  And other laps with flowers?

O playmate in the golden time!
  Our mossy seat is green,
Its fringing violets blossom yet,
  The old trees o'er it lean,

The winds so sweet with birch and fern
  A sweeter memory blow,
And there in spring the veeries sing
  The song of long ago.

And still the pines of Ramoth wood
  Are moaning like the sea,—
The moaning of the sea of change
  Between myself and thee!

Again, these simple but natural lines have won their
way into the hearts of English-speaking people, because in
them our poet in picturing a boyhood scene has imbued it
with sentiment so delicately expressed and so true that the
heart of humanity, being one, responds to that which recalls
youth's young dream, when for the first time all things are
glorified with the indefinable rapture of love's awakening:

  Still sits the schoolhouse by the road,
    A ragged beggar sunning;
  Around it still the sumachs grow,
    And blackberry vines are running.

Within, the master's desk is seen,
  Deep scarred by raps official;
The warping floor, the battered seats,
  The jackknife's carved initial;

The charcoal frescos on its wall;
  Its door's worn sill, betraying
The feet that, creeping slow to school,
  Went storming out to playing!

Long years ago a winter sun
  Shone over it at setting;
Lit up its western window panes,
  And low eaves' icy fretting.

It touched the tangled, golden curls
  And brown eyes, full of grieving,
Of one who still her steps delayed
  When all the school were leaving.

For near her stood the little boy
  Her childish favor singled,
His cap pulled low upon a face
  Where pride and shame were mingled.

Pushing with restless feet the snow
  To right and left, he lingered,
As restlessly her tiny hands
  The blue-checked apron fingered.

He saw her lift her eyes; he felt
  The soft hand's light caressing,
And heard the tremble of her voice,
  As if a fault confessing:

"I'm sorry that I spelt the word;
  I hate to go above you,
Because,"—the brown eyes lower fell,—
  "Because, you see, I love you!"

Still memory to a gray-haired man
  That sweet child-face is showing.
Dear girl! the grasses on her grave
  Have forty years been growing!

He lives to learn, in life's hard school,
  How few who pass above him
Lament their triumph and his loss,
  Like her, — because they love him.

But of all the poems descriptive of child life and New England scenes and incident which were absorbed by his plastic brain while he was still a boy and destined to be marvellously developed in later years, none equals that superb idyl of the old-time New England winter, "Snow-Bound." In this creation we have some wonderfully faithful pictures, almost photographic in quality, although to a certain extent idealized. "Snow-Bound" was written in 1866; it was the first imporant work by the poet after he had exchanged the helmet of the aggressive reformer for the robe of the poet-priest of nature. And in this counterfeit presentment of his childhood's home during that memorable New England winter we see a subtle and almost indefinable idealization which might be compared to the purple mantle which rests over the distant hills at eventide. Here we see the power of the poet in describing home life, in depicting character; and here, too, we see the moralist and philosopher.

Whittier was first of all a teacher; to him duty was august, her commands imperative. This did not please the *dilettanti*. It has always offended those who fail to see the highest and divinest mission in art. The teacher, the philosopher, the moralist—these must be sneered down. They are disquieting; they compel us to think; they startle our conscience; they compel us to boldly take sides in the great battle of progress which is being waged, or win the contempt of our better selves. It is not pleasant to break with conventionalism, it is also perilous to do so; let us remain as we are; let us parley with wrong if we cannot ignore it, but do not compel us to join the maligned and slandered minority. Such is the voice of conventionalism. But the true prophet cannot heed the smooth tongue of the charmer. He has a mission; God's hand has touched his eyes; he sees the enormity of the injustice on every hand; he beholds the splendid possibilities which lie beyond humanity's conquest of animality or selfism. He cannot remain silent; he cannot prophesy pleasant things. He is an optimist, and therefore he refuses to allow the hideous wrongs to fester when health and happiness lie within the grasp of humanity the moment shortsighted selfishness is exchanged for wisdom. Whittier was always a teacher, always a moralist. If in the later years he came to some extent under the spell of conventionalism and ceased to be the aggressive reformer he had been in early manhood, he never ceased to be a teacher.

Here is one of those rare glimpses embalmed in descriptive verse which reveal the artist power in the poet and which constitute one of the chief charms of many of Whittier's pictures of life in old New England. As the reader will quickly recognize, it is taken from "Snow-Bound":

> As night drew on and, from the crest
> Of wooded knolls that ridged the west,

The sun, a snow-blown traveller, sank
From sight beneath the smothering bank,
We piled, with care, our nightly stack
Of wood against the chimney back,—
The oaken log, green, huge and thick,
And on its top the stout back-stick;
The knotty forestick laid apart,
And filled between with curious art
The ragged brush; then, hovering near,
We watched the first red blaze appear,
Heard the sharp crackle, caught the gleam
On whitewashed wall and sagging beam,
Until the old, rude-furnished room
Burst, flower-like, into rosy bloom.

* * * * *

Shut in from all the world without,
We sat the clean-winged hearth about,
Content to let the north-wind roar
In baffled rage at pane and door,
While the red logs before us beat
The frost-line back with tropic heat;
And ever, when a louder blast
Shook beam and rafter as it passed,
The merrier up its roaring draught
The great throat of the chimney laughed,
The house-dog on his paws outspread
Laid to the fire his drowsy head.

Next we find the reminiscent poet becoming the moralizer, as was his wont, and the great problem of the future, ever present when he gave himself up to serious musing, challenges his attention, as it does more than once in subsequent lines of the same poem:

What matter how the night behaved?
What matter how the north-wind raved?
Blow high, blow low, not all its snow
Could quench our hearth-fire's ruddy glow.
O Time and Change! — with hair as gray
As was my sire's that winter day,
How strange it seems, with so much gone
Of life and love, to still live on!
Ah, brother! only I and thou
Are left of all that circle now,—
The dear home faces whereupon
That fitful firelight paled and shone.
Henceforward, listen as we will,
The voices of that hearth are still;
Look where we may, the wide world o'er,
Those lighted faces smile no more.

* * * * *

Yet Love will dream, and Faith will trust,
(Since He who knows our need is just),
That somehow, somewhere, meet we must.
Alas for him who never sees
The stars shine through his cypress trees!

Who, hopeless, lays his dead away,
Nor looks to see the breaking day
Across the mournful marbles play!
Who hath not learned, in hours of faith,
   The truth to flesh and sense unknown,
That Life is ever lord of Death,
   And Love can never lose its own!

We come very near to the heart of that memorable little circle as we read these lines in which some members of the group are described in Whittier's frank, graphic and simple manner:

We sped the time with stories old,
Wrought puzzles out, and riddles told.
     *   *   *   *
Our mother, while she turned her wheel
Or run the new-knit stocking-heel,
Told how the Indian hordes came down
At midnight on Cochecho town,
And how her own great-uncle bore
His cruel scalp-mark to fourscore.
Recalling, in her fitting phrase,
   So rich and picturesque and free
(The common unrhymed poetry
Of simple life and country ways),
The story of her early days,—
She made us welcome to her home;
Old hearths grew wide to give us room;
We stole with her a frightened look
At the gray wizard's conjuring-book,
The fame whereof went far and wide
Through all the simple country side;
We heard the hawks at twilight play,
The boat-horn on Piscataqua,
The loon's weird laughter far away.
     *   *   *   *
Our uncle, innocent of books,
Was rich in lore of fields and brooks,
The ancient teachers never dumb
Of Nature's unhoused lyceum.
In moons and tides and weather wise,
He read the clouds as prophecies,
And foul or fair could well divine,
By many an occult hint and sign,
Holding the cunning-warded keys
To all the woodcraft mysteries;
Himself to Nature's heart so near
That all her voices in his ear
Of beast or bird had meanings clear,
Like Apollonius of old,
Who knew the tales the sparrows told,
Or Hermes, who interpreted
What the sage cranes of Nilus said;
A simple, guileless, childlike man,
Content to live where life began.
     *   *   *   *   *

Next, the dear aunt, whose smile of cheer
And voice in dreams I see and hear,—
The sweetest woman ever Fate
Perverse denied a household mate,
Who, lonely, homeless, not the less
Found peace in love's unselfishness,
And welcome wheresoe'er she went,
A calm and gracious element,
Whose presence seemed the sweet income
And womanly atmosphere of home,—
Called up her girlhood memories,
The huskings and the apple-bees,
The sleigh rides and the summer sails,
Weaving through all the poor details
And homespun warp of circumstance
A golden woof-thread of romance.

* * * * *

Through years of toil and soil and care,
From glossy tress to thin gray hair,
All unprofaned she held apart
The virgin fancies of the heart.

* * * * *

There, too, our elder sister plied
Her evening task the stand beside;
A full, rich nature, free to trust,
Truthful and almost sternly just,
Impulsive, earnest, prompt to act,
And make her generous thought a fact,
Keeping with many a light disguise
The secret of self-sacrifice.
O heart sore-tried! thou hast the best
That heaven itself could give thee,—*rest*.

* * *

As one who held herself a part
Of all she saw, and let her heart
  Against the household bosom lean,
Upon the motley-braided mat
Our youngest and our dearest sat,
Lifting her large, sweet, asking eyes,
  Now bathed within the fadeless green
And holy peace of Paradise.

* * * * *

With me one little year ago:—
The chill weight of the winter snow
  For months upon her grave has lain;
And now, when summer south-winds blow
  And briar and harebell bloom again, . .
I tread the pleasant paths we trod,
I see the violet-sprinkled sod
Whereon she leaned, too frail and weak
The hillside flowers she loved to seek,
Yet following me where'er I went
With dark eyes full of love's content.

* * * * *

I cannot feel that thou art far,
Since near at need the angels are;
And when the sunset gates unbar,
    Shall I not see thee waiting stand,
And, white against the evening star,
    The welcome of thy beckoning hand?

An incident in the life of the aunt referred to above was frequently related by Whittier when talking over psychical and spiritual matters with friends greatly interested in such subjects. The main points in this story, which is interesting alike to students of psychical phenomena and to lovers of romance, are as follows:

The poet's aunt was betrothed to a young man who was absent in the state of New York. One winter evening the Quaker maiden had lingered over the great wood fire in the spacious kitchen until the others had retired. At length she rose and, turning to the window, beheld without in the clear moonlight which fell on a landscape wrapped in snow her lover approaching on horseback. She hastened to the door, noticing as she passed the window that he had reined in his horse as if to leap from the saddle. On opening the door, however, no one was visible. Then a great fear fell upon her which grew into a nameless terror; she called her sister and related the strange vision and expressed her forebodings. In vain did the sympathetic sister try to reason away her apprehensions, suggesting that she had been dreaming; the maiden only shook her head, affirming that she had never been more thoroughly awake. Some days later a letter came to her written by a stranger telling of the death of her lover at the very time when she had beheld his apparition.

To his mother, lovingly described in "Snow-Bound," Whittier owed more than to any other person for his success as a poet. While the father, a plain, prosaic and matter-of-fact man, frowned upon his verse making and discouraged him, the mother lent him sympathy and encouragement. She also stored his mind with legends and stories which he later immortalized in his simple and heart-reaching lays. This mother was a very superior woman, and the moulding power which she exerted over her son cannot be overestimated. Her influence and the poetry of Burns were far more to the poet than the benefits he received from the district school or the academy at which he spent a short time. Burns was a real educator to Whittier; he fulfilled the function of a true teacher in calling out or developing the latent power in the poet's mind, and teaching him how to appreciate the beauty in the commonplace things of life. He was fourteen years old when a copy of the Scotch poet's works fell into his hands. In his autobiographical notes Whittier thus refers to his introduction to Burns:

When I was fourteen years old, my first schoolmaster, Joshua Coffin, the able, eccentric historian of Newbury, brought with him to our house a volume of Burns' poems, from which he read, greatly to my delight. I begged him to leave the book with me, and set myself at once to the task of mastering the glossary of the Scottish dialect at its close. This was about the first poetry I ever read — with the exception of that of the Bible, of which I had been a close student — and it had a lasting influence upon me. I began to make rhymes myself, and to imagine stories and adventures. In fact, I lived a sort of dual life, and in a world of fancy as well as in the world of plain matter of fact about me.

Robert Collyer, in relating a conversation which he had with the poet, quotes Whittier as follows:

Burns is to me the noblest poet of our race. He was the first poet I read, and he will be the last. . . . I read Burns every moment I had to spare. And this was one great result to me of my communion with him: I found that the things out of which poems came were not, as I had always imagined, somewhere away off in a world and life lying outside the edge of our own New England sky — they were right here about my feet and among the people I knew. The common things of our common life I found were full of poetry.

It is the true teacher who so instructs the childish mind that it learns to apprehend the beauties and truths which lie around it, who stimulates the imagination and awakens the noble sentiments of the soul, who succeeds in calling into independent action the reasoning faculties, and centres the youthful thought upon the vital problems of life as they affect the peace, happiness and elevation of man.

Whittier inherited a deeply poetic nature; his imagination was limited, but within its bounds it was compelling in its power. He also inherited a deeply spiritual nature. On one occasion when in conversation with a friend, he described a sense of awe and almost oppressive solemnity which suddenly came over him one evening as he was driving home the cows—he was only seven years of age— when the thought, "Why am I different from those cows, what have I got to do in life, what is life?" swept in upon his startled mind.*

"He never lost the impression of that hour," observed his friend. "It affected his whole life."

He was a born dreamer. In reply to a little girl who wrote him of his childhood, he said: "I think at the age of

* "Whittier with the Children": by Margaret Sidney.

which thy note inquires, I found about equal satisfaction in an old rural home with the shifting panorama of seasons, in reading the few books within my reach, and in dreaming of something wonderful and grand in the future." In reminiscent moods the poet often related how when a boy his imagination carried him far away from the work in hand and, lost in dreams, he would lean upon his hoe or spade until his father, "a prompt, decisive man," would call out, "That's enough for a stand, John."

The work on the farm was ill suited to one so delicate as Whittier and, when seventeen years of age, he sustained from overexertion injuries from which he never fully recovered. Yet this apparent calamity was not an unmixed evil, as it helped to gain for him his father's consent to his going to the Haverhill Academy. Heretofore the only regular schooling the poet had enjoyed had been received in the district schools, which were very indifferent in character. He had written many verses which his sister Mary had highly complimented. One day this sister, who had always occupied a very large place in the poet's heart, sent one of his poems to Garrison for the Newbury *Free Press*. The poet knew nothing of the submitting of the lines, and the editor was ignorant of the authorship. However, on reading them, Mr. Garrison promptly published the poem. Whittier was spell-bound when he found his stanzas in print. In referring to this experience Mr. Pickard observes:

His heart stood still a moment. Such delight as his comes only once in the lifetime of any aspirant to literary fame. His father at last called to him to put up the paper and continue his work, but he could not resist the temptation to take the paper again and again from his pocket to stare at his lines in print. He has said he was sure he did not read a word of the poem all the time he looked at it.

Garrison found out by inquiry who the youthful poet was, and forthwith drove out to the Whittier homestead to meet the young author. On the editor inquiring of the father for his son John, the worthy Quaker became much agitated, fearing that his boy had in some way got into trouble or disgrace; when, however, the facts were made known, the old gentleman was much relieved, but he frowned upon Garrison's suggestion that the boy be encouraged in his literary aspirations. "Poetry will not bring him bread," exclaimed the old man, a fact which Garrison could not then gainsay.

The visit, however, fanned anew the ambition of the dreamer boy. He importuned his father to let him go to the academy about to be opened in Haverhill. At length it was agreed that, if Whittier could earn sufficient money by working nights to pay his way, he might go. The youth made shoes during the winter evenings and thus earned enough for his first six months at the academy. Subsequently he taught school for a short time and assisted in posting books, and in this manner earned enough for his second term.

Thus, with the slight profit derived from the district school and two terms in the academy, Whittier went forth to play upon the heartstrings of his fellow-men, and touch the conscience of a nation in a manner seldom equalled in this century. He entered upon the aggressive warfare that marked his early manhood without the polish which lent grace to the work of several of his contemporaries; but he also escaped the benumbing influence of soulless conventionalism, whose skeleton fingers extend from a dead past and too often crush originality and silence the voice of conscience in aspiring youths while they are pursuing the curriculum of our conservative educational institutions. If he lacked in polish, he possessed what were of far more importance—a heart aflame with love of justice, a nature pure and simple, and a brain stored with "knowledge never learned in books and schools." His boyhood days, if uneventful, were far from uninteresting; and the pictures he has given us of old New England life, no less than the hopes, joys and sorrows which filled the horizon of his boyish world, are dear to our people, and will continue to be a source of pleasure and inspiration for many generations to come.

Ah! thou little barefoot dreamer boy, who wandered over the hills and vales round thy native home, revelling in the beauty and fragrance of our wild flora, charmed by the matchless music of the forest's feathered orchestra, awed by the sublimity of nature in her grander manifestations, thou child of pure and honest parents, had we more lives like thine, the curses of our day and generation would lose their power, and in the place of feverish hate, misery, poverty, drunkenness, debauchery, bigotry, intolerance and woe, we should see peace, love, prosperity, purity, and nobility open their blossoms on every side; earth would put on Eden-like beauty, and humanity with great strides would sweep onward and upward toward the sun-bathed plane of perfect civilization. And all peoples, even as the voice of one man, could unite in these words from thy song of triumph:

The airs of heaven blow o'er me;
A glory shines before me
Of what mankind shall be,—
Pure, generous, brave, and free.

A dream of man and woman
Diviner but still human,
Solving the riddle old,
Shaping the Age of Gold.

The love of God and neighbor;
An equal-handed labor;
The richer life, where beauty
Walks hand in hand with duty.

*　　*　　*　　*　　*

I feel the earth move sunward,
I join the great march onward,
And take, by faith, while living,
My freehold of thanksgiving.

MYSORE, OR A GLIMPSE OF AN EAST INDIAN STATE.

BY JNANENDRA NARAYAN GHOSE, M. D.

Mysore is one of the feudatory states of India governed by an Indian prince. It is situated in the southern part of India, and has an area of 27,936 square miles, with a population of 4,943,604, of whom 4,639,127 are Hindus, 252,973 are Mohammedans, and 38,135 are Christians. It is larger than West Virginia, but with the advantage of having more than six times the population of that state. The importance of Mysore does not lie in its size or population, but in its representative system of government, its railways, telegraphs, educational institutions, irrigation works, good roads, sanitation, and the prosperous condition of its people. Mysore is to-day not only one of the most prosperous states of India, but it can be favorably compared with any other civilized country of the world.

The administration report of the last year is just out. We have very meagre materials at our disposal to give an adequate idea of its good government. We have before us *The Sanjibani*, a Bengalee weekly paper published in Calcutta, containing a brief review of the last fourteen years' government of his highness, the late maharajah, Sir Chama Rajendra Bhadia Bahadur.

From 1830 to 1880 Mysore was governed by the British government. The story of Mysore of this period is a very sad one. A British officer was appointed chief commissioner. The Public Works and other departments were under the control of the British officers—in fact, British officers were everywhere, and they were highly paid. "They had the country to deal with after the most approved British fashion." The seasonal rains failed in 1876, 1877, and 1878 in Mysore as well as in other places of India, and the result was that one out of every four persons died for scarcity of food. Such was the forethought and precaution of the English officers. There could never have been a famine in Mysore had the officers in charge of the Public Works department been careful; for so complete and admirable is the tank system of Mysore that famine was an impossibility.

There are tanks in Mysore varying in size from small ponds to extensive lakes, 38,000 in number, and are dispersed through the country, the largest being forty miles in circumference. Some of the anicuts on the river are as old as one thousand years, while the most recent were constructed three hundred years ago. And these, by the negligence of the officers in charge, were out of repair and were useless for storage of water.

There were Rs. 10,000,000 in the treasury when the English took the government of Mysore. In the year 1880 Mysore was found in debt of Rs. 8,000,000, after spending the money in the treasury. The British government was baffled to find means to save Mysore from bankruptcy. And the last resource was to reduce the official staff, which, instead of improving, made the matter worse. And this was not all. When the government of Mysore was handed to the late maharajah, Rs. 1,000,000 were added to the British government to his annual tribute.

When such was the condition of Mysore the Marquis of Ripon, the then viceroy of India, than whom India has never had the fortune of having a better governor, installed the young maharajah on March 25, 1881. The maharajah, though then only eighteen years old had received a sound education and possessed a rare executive ability and judgment, which made him, later, one of the most enlightened and efficient rulers of the day. But unfortunately for India and the people of Mysore, the maharajah, after a brief but very successful government of thirteen years and nine months died in Calcutta, Dec. 28, 1894. During this short period, under exceptional difficulties, his highness did not only make many improvements in Mysore, but raised its people to a condition of prosperity equalled by few other people in India. We shall in this paper roughly endeavor to give a brief review of his thirteen years' government.

After assuming the government, the maharajah's first thought naturally was, how to save the people from another such terrible famine, which had already swept away about one-fourth the population of Mysore. His highness directed his attention to building railways and improving the tanks that were in a condition of disrepair, and if possible to dig new canals. But from where was the money to come was the question. A man of his highness' calibre was not to be daunted even by such a difficulty. He began the railway works, repair of the old tanks, and dug some new canals. During the first three years the expenditure was more than the income. And he had to borrow Rs. 2,000,000 from

England. In four years one hundred and forty miles of railways were completed. And he saw three hundred and sixty-five miles of railways completed in Mysore before he died. For repair of tanks, digging wells and canals, from 1881 to 1885, Rs. 1,800,000; from 1885 to 1889, Rs. 3,400,000; and from 1889 to 1894, Rs. 8,100,000, were spent. The result is that, though for years there may be no rain in Mysore, it will be impossible to have another famine throughout an area of 1,558 square miles.

Then the maharajah directed his attention to reform the government. As the prime minister was at the head of all departments, and could not pay equal attention to all, his highness divided the government into the following departments, and appointed a secretary at the head of each: Land Revenue, Legislation, Public Works, Education, Police, Mining, Forest, and others.

In 1881, when the maharajah first assumed the government, the expenditure was more than the income, and for three years there was no possible way to improve this condition. In the fourth year there was another famine for want of rain, though this was not so bad as the former one. The expenditure of this year was even more than the previous year. The railways and the irrigation and repairing works were not yet quite completed, but by this time the people appreciated the benefit of these works. At this time Mr. William Digby, C. I. E. and late member of Parliament, wrote the following about the condition of Mysore:

At this moment, in spite of the strenuous efforts of a wise Indian statesman, the late Runga Charlu, C. I. E., and the earnest attempt of the present minister, Sir Sheshadri Ayer, the state is on the verge of bankruptcy. It is safe to assert that, had an Indian minister of the calibre of Sir Madhab Rao, or any other of a dozen who could be named, been in charge of Mysore during the maharajah's minority, the famine notwithstanding, the state would at this moment have been among the most prosperous in the whole continent.

At the end of ten years it is very gratifying to note that, under the wise ministry of Sir Sheshadri Sekhar Ayer, Mysore is to-day one of the most prosperous states of India. Since 1885 there has been every year a gradual increase in the income. The income in 1881 was Rs. 10,300,000, but in 1894 to 1895 is Rs. 18,050,000. In fourteen years there has been an increase of 75.24 per cent without levying any fresh tax, while, on the other hand, millions of money have been spent to better the condition of the people.

Mysore is a hilly country, and many parts are covered with forests. There were only 6,154 square miles of cultivated

land; whereas now, since the improvements in irrigation ɛ
the building of railways, there are 9,863. Land revenue]
also increased from Rs. 6,900,000 to Rs. 9,600,000.

There has been an improvement in the administration
the forest department, the income being double what it ʋ
ten years ago. The area of the protected forest is now 1,ʲ
square miles, against 643 square miles in 1881. Valua
trees have been planted in thirty-five square miles. ꓶ
rent was decreased on the land suitable for coffee plantiɪ
and there has been an increase of twenty-eight square mi
of coffee plantation. Income has also increased.

During the maharajah's government a gold mine was ɗ
covered in Mysore. The mining work began in 1886. Lɛ
year Rs. 15,000,000 worth of gold was mined. The reven
received from the mine by the Mysore government w
Rs. 703,000. Geologists and mining engineers have be
appointed to discover new mines. They are now engag
in work in different parts of Mysore. There has been ɛ
increase of income in every department. The income of t
excise department has increased four times; from stam
and registration, 65 per cent and 124 per cent respectively.

An agricultural bank has been founded for the farmeɪ
They deposit money in it, and can draw in time of nee
receiving a nominal interest. Better laws have beɛ
enacted so that the people can easily sell and purchase land

The number of government and aided schools hɛ
increased in thirteen years from 866 to 1,796; the number
male scholars from 39,413 to 83,390, and of female schola
from 3,000 to 12,000. Three times as much money
spent now as in 1881. During his highness' rule 800 pɪ
mary and grammar schools, 50 middle-class English schooꟾ
30 Sanskrit colleges, one English college for arts aɪ
sciences, one English college for the higher education
women, and three colleges for Oriental languages have beɛ
founded.

Mysore has a small army of about 3,500 men, consistiɪ
of both infantry and cavalry, which is equipped with tꟾ
latest improvements. An efficient police force has beɛ
organized. The state is divided into sixty-six districɬ
having municipal and district boards. All the importaː
districts have been connected by telegraph lines. All tꟾ
towns and important villages have post offices. Letters aɪ
delivered by the postman, no one having to go to the offɪ
for the letters, as is the case in the small towns of the Unitɛ
States. Rs. 6,800,000 have been spent for the public road
besides the money spent by the municipalities and the dꟾ

trict boards. There are now 5,107 miles of good roads, against 3,930 miles in 1881.

Sanitary arrangements have been improved. All the towns and villages have been supplied with pure drinking water at the government expense. Schools have been founded for the scientific training of midwives. Of the sixty-six districts of Mysore, sixty-three have midwives appointed by the government. In 1881 there were only nineteen hospitals, and the number of patients treated was 130,-000; but now there are one hundred and fourteen hospitals, and the number of patients treated last year was 706,000. There are special hospitals for women and children. From 1881 to 1891 there had been an increase of 18.34 per cent of population, while in the surrounding British districts the increase has been much less.

A system of competitive examination has been inaugurated for the civil service of Mysore. The privilege of competing in this examination has been extended to the graduates of the different Indian universities, whether born in Mysore or in British India. Anyone who holds the degree of B. A. and is under twenty-five years of age can compete for this examination. The whole policy of the late maharajah's government was to secure the best men available to improve the condition of the people. His highness was a patron of all that is good. Trade has flourished and commerce has increased in Mysore during the last few years.

The following, we believe, are the crowning glories of his highness' short but brilliant government:

1. The granting of the representative system of government to the people.

2. The abolition of child marriages by law.

3. The foundation of a college for the higher education of women.

Every student of history knows what a hard struggle it has been for peoples to obtain free institutions and a representative system of government. England boasts herself to be the mother of parliaments. What a hard and continuous struggle it was, not to mention the length of time it occupied, to get these rights and privileges which the free Britons now enjoy! The history is almost the same everywhere. No emperors and monarchs yielded to the demands of the people very easily. But the history of Mysore is different. His highness, unasked, granted this boon to the people of Mysore. Three hundred men are elected for a term of three years from the different districts as representatives of the people. They assemble together and discuss the annual

budget and other important matters of the state. **This is**
by no means a very perfect form of representative **govern-**
ment. But the experiment has worked well. It is **now**
acknowledged by all to be an important institution.

In social reformation the maharajah accomplished **what**
the British government has not yet been able to do. **The**
British government, with its usual policy, has always **been**
careful not to interfere with the social customs and religious beliefs of the people of India. The same policy **was**
manifested when the suttee (burning of the widows) **was**
abolished in the beginning of this century. The progressive
Hindus, at the head of whom was the late Rajah Ram Mohan
Roy, the founder of the Bramah Somaj, who has been called
by Prof. Max Müller "one of the greatest benefactors of
mankind of this century," had to fight hard, and then the
government made a law prohibiting this monstrous custom.
Some years ago the English government with great reluctance passed the bill raising the age of consent.

We admire this policy of the British government. We **do**
not believe in unnecessarily interfering with the social customs and religious beliefs of a people when governed by
a people whose social customs and religious beliefs are different. Nevertheless we believe that a government ought to
protect its people from such social customs as are morally
wrong and harmful to society, especially when there are
people in the same society who demand reformation. This
is what the maharajah of Mysore did. His highness first
took a census of the number of child marriages each year,
and then consulted some of the prominent men of Mysore,
and finding that there were men who wanted reformation,
his highness, two years ago, with the assistance of the representatives of the people, passed a law prohibiting child marriage forever. The maharajah knew the evil effects of child
marriage, so common in India, especially in southern India.

The third important event of his government was the
foundation of an English college for the higher education of
women, where now more than four hundred native women
are studying literature, arts, and sciences.

After such an enormous sum of money had been spent for
the welfare of his subjects, we notice that at the end of 1892
there were Rs. 9,004,000 in the treasury.

The maharajah left two sons and three daughters. The
eldest son is about eleven years of age now, and he has been
recognized by the British government to be the heir. Her
highness the maharanee, who had always been a companion
in all the good works of the late maharajah, has **been**

appointed regent during the minority of the present maharajah. There has been no change in the government. The British government, appreciating the good work done by the Indian officials, did not think proper to interfere in any way.

What the British government, with an able staff of English officers, failed to do, an Indian prince accomplished with purely Indian officials, who at the time of his installation was only eighteen years of age, and at the time of his death was only thirty-one. The people of Mysore to-day are one of the most prosperous and happy communities in India.

We cannot close this paper without saying a few words about His Excellency Sir Sheshadri Sekhar Ayer, the prime minister of Mysore, without whose wise council and help the maharajah, perhaps, could not have brought Mysore to such a prosperous condition. The ability of a minister who can achieve such a result without any increase of taxation, and yet leave the people better off than they were thirteen years before, and more prosperous than corresponding classes in British territory, is unquestionable, and surely he is a statesman of no mean order. In recognition of the valuable services rendered to the Mysore government, his excellency was knighted by the British government two years ago. The maharajah was very fortunate in the selection of his officials. There is no corruption among the Mysore officials. High or low, every one is devoted to his duty and to the bettering of the condition of the people.

Yet it has been flippantly asserted that the Indians have no capacity for self-government. Give them a chance, they will perform what Sir Salar Jung accomplished in Hyderabad, Sir T. Madhab Rao in Baroda and Travancore, and Sir Sheshadri Sekhar Ayer in Mysore. India during this century has produced statesmen like Sir Salar Jung, Sir T. Madhab Rao, Raghunath Rao, Nilambar Mukherje, Kristo Das Pal, Purneah, Sir Dinkur Rao, Rungacharhi, Tantia Tope, Shahamut Ali, and a host of other such statesmen whose names cannot be mentioned here, "who have" to quote Mr. Digby, "under exceptional difficulties, accomplished feats which no European ministers of this country have excelled."

This is a short though imperfect review of what an Indian prince accomplished with Indian officials in India.

While this is the condition of Mysore and such other feudatory states, what is the condition of the people of India under British rule? Let an Englishman speak. Says Mr. William Digby, who was an honorary secretary, Indian famine relief, 1877–78, in his "India for the Indians—and for England":

The effect of English rule in the ordinary Indian district may be illustrated by the definition given of gout as a pain in comparison with rheumatism. Put, it is said, your hand in a blacksmith's vise, and turn the screw till you can bear no more; that is rheumatism. Give the screw an additional turn; that is gout. Likewise, consider a state of existence whereby a vast proportion of the people barely keep body and soul together, and do not know what it is from one year's end to another to have as much to eat as they want. This is the condition of the Indian people under the collectors in our provinces. Then, once every four years, in one part of India or another, a famine occurs, and those insufficiently-nourished subjects of ours die by hundreds, by thousands, and in extreme cases, say, once in ten years, by millions. This is an accurate statement of our rule in India. Such is the general effect of the picture seen through clear glasses and with eyes which look straight. Here and there in British districts the keen observer finds incidents of a pleasing character; a little closer investigation and the rosy gleam is lost in a dark ray of gloom quivering with suffering. Of the Indian-ruled states such experiences are not recorded. In those territories the people are uniformly prosperous and are wholly contented and loyal.

Why is the contrast so great between India ruled by the Indians and India ruled by the English? The reason is not far to seek. While the money obtained by taxation in the feudatory states remains in the country and is spent for the prosperity of its people, the money collected by the British government by taxation, goes out of India and is spent in paying pensions to the retired civil and military officers and in providing for an enormous army, while the people die of starvation. Nowhere in the world are officers so highly paid as in India. The viceroy of India gets three times as much as the president of the United States, the governors of Bombay and Madras each more than twice as much, and the lieutenant-governors of Bengal, Northwest Provinces and the Punjab each twice as much, in addition to travelling expenses; and each of them is provided with two palatial houses, one for summer and another for winter. The Chief Justice of the Calcutta High Court gets four times as much as the Chief Justice of the Supreme Court of the United States. No use of multiplying cases. Hindus from British India migrate to the adjoining feudatory states, while no Hindus from a feudatory state have ever been known to migrate into a British province. The Hindus under the English government are to-day, perhaps, the most highly taxed people in the world in comparision with their average income.

It is a melancholy fact, and there is no use in disguising it, that while the people of India are so poverty-stricken and are dying of starvation, millions of money are drawn, every year, from that unhappy country to England, where the people are already living in wealth and luxury.

DIVINE HEALING OR WORKS.

BY EUGENE HATCH.

There are people who consider the Bible as inspired and so authority upon all questions that come within its province, but there are many who only accept it upon its own merits as a human production. Those who do not accept the Bible as authority can hardly fail to recognize the fact that it is a great reservoir of truth, containing the treasured wisdom of past centuries.

Jesus Christ stands out prominently as the grandest, purest, and most attractive character, not only in Biblical, but in all history. It is a well-established historical fact that He lived in Palestine near nineteen hundred years ago and taught the people a new system of truth, and that He performed many strange and wonderful works. It is also true that a reasonably clear record of His life, teachings, and works has been preserved in the New Testament against the ravages of time.

The truth that Jesus revealed to the world is always true and in harmony with all other truth, whether taught by science or religion. Truth, from the fact that it is truth, is always true, everywhere and in all relations. If changeable or false in any of its relations it is not truth. Truth is like the sunlight, everywhere and always the same and unchangeable. We may alter our relations to truth through a better understanding of it, but we can never alter truth any more than we can change the sunlight.

In the Book of Revelation we read, "I will give unto him that is athirst of the fountain of the water of life freely" (Rev. xxi, 6). It is unto those who are thirsting for truth that the Divine Presence is not only ready but waiting an opportunity to supply it. That divine, all-inclusive life, whose kingdom Jesus says is within you, is able, willing, and ready to give the water of life to whomsoever thirsts for or desires it. But we must seek if we would find, and if we will seek earnestly and with the whole heart we shall not seek in vain. The mistake that is commonly made is to think that we are seeking the light of life when we are in fact not seeking truth at all. Living as we do in our old beliefs, we seek to confirm them. We think they are true

and so try to explain or understand everything in keeping
with them. This keeps us in error. We are too apt to
allow our mistaken view of the great questions of life to go
ahead and decide for us without a full and fair investigation.
Our disposition is to oppose any new question rather than
to seek the light. People are not prejudiced and do not intend to be, but they are misled by their own false beliefs.

There is but one right way to search for truth, and that
is to bear in mind the fact that our old firmset opinions
are liable forever to lead us astray, and to lay them aside
and seek for truth and truth only for truth's sake. A spiritual willingness and desire to be led right, to be led by truth,
is necessary before it is possible for the spirit of truth to
lead us.

> "Great truths are dearly bought. The common truth,
> Such as men give and take from day to day,
> Comes in the common walk of easy life,
> Blown by the careless wind across our way.

> "Great truths are greatly won; not found by chance,
> Nor wafted on the breath of summer dream;
> But grasped in the great struggle of the soul,
> Hard-buffeting with adverse wind and stream."

Job says, "There is a spirit in man: and the inspiration
of the Almighty giveth him understanding. Great men,"
he says, "are not always wise: therefore I said, Hearken to
me." Jesus Christ saw that He that made that which is
within made that which is without also, and that life in all
its relations is one. This is a great truth and one not commonly understood or appreciated. The author of the life
of man is the author of the body of man. God, the Indwell-
ing Life, is the Sole Cause, the All in all in all things and
all men. Jesus from His spiritual perceptions was enabled
to do His mighty works; from His understanding and conviction of truth, His word was with power. Whatever He
did and whatsoever He said were at one with eternal, unchangeable truth. He lived and spoke the truth from the
centre of life and says, "If I do not the works of My Father,
believe Me not," but He says, "If I do, though ye believe not
Me, believe the works." His works were His credentials,
they proved His words; but if the world declined His teachings He wanted it to accept His works for the good there
was in them. "Believe for the work's sake."

In Matthew we read how He went about all Galilee,
"healing all manner of sickness and all manner of disease
among the people." And again how he "went about all the
cities and villages . . . healing every sickness and every

disease among the people." It is not strange that "they marvelled and glorified God which had given such power to men." Christ is still saying to the world, "If ye believe not Me believe the works."

The testimony of the Bible as to the disciples and others doing like works as Christ, and especially the teachings and very commandments of Jesus Himself, are plain. They are so plain that he who runs may read and understand, if he will, that a part of the Christ ministry is to heal the sick. "These twelve Jesus sent forth, and commanded them, saying, As ye go, preach, saying, the kingdom of heaven is at hand. Heal the sick, cleanse the lepers, raise the dead." Or, as again expressed, He sent them to preach the kingdom of God, and to heal the sick. And they departed and went through the towns, preaching the gospel, and healing everywhere." "After these things" it is related how "the Lord appointed other seventy also," and sent them forth saying, "Go your ways; and into whatsoever city ye enter, and they receive you, heal the sick that are therein, and say unto them, The kingdom of God is come nigh unto you." Again we read, "Go ye into all the world, and preach the gospel to every creature. . . . And these signs shall follow them that believe . . . they shall lay hands on the sick and they shall recover."

These commands, or rather this one command several times stated in different ways or different words, is plain and specific. Jesus sends out His disciples, His followers, the twelve, the seventy, and all them that believe, to give His glad tidings to the world, and to heal the sick. They were to teach what He had taught them, the way to health and happiness, to live the life He lived and do the works He did. Teach this gospel to every creature, and these signs shall follow them that believe, they shall lay hands on the sick and they shall recover.

We see, in the first place, that Jesus sent out the twelve to preach the kingdom of God and heal the sick. In the second place, we see that He sent out the seventy to heal the sick and say unto those that would receive them, "The kingdom of God is come nigh unto you." In the third place we see that "these signs shall follow them that believe: they shall lay hands on the sick, and they shall recover": or, as Christ again says in the Gospel of John, "Verily, verily, I say unto you, He that believeth on Me, the works that I do, shall he do also."

The last two verses in Matthew contain the only other record of Jesus' charge to His followers, and in them He

says, "Teach all nations . . . to observe all things whatsoever I have commanded you: and lo, I am with you alway,
even unto the end of the world." Among the things "whatsoever I have commanded you," healing cannot very easily
be forgotton. There are no other commands or teachings
of Jesus that conflict with those given. There is nothing
between the covers of the Bible that teaches a contrary
doctrine. There are scores of passages that support gospel
healing but not one against it.

The disciples are then sent out to teach the new way and
to put it into practice—to heal "all manner of sickness and
all manner of disease among the people"; and they went
forth "healing everywhere." The disciples carried out the
whole command to teach and heal, and who can, or has a
right to say, that one part of the command shall be accepted
and the other part rejected? Christ says to all believers,
"Follow thou Me." The Christ gospel is a gospel of works
as well as words. The command is, "Say and do, teach and
heal."

The works were signs rather than miracles. They seemed
miracles or wonders because the principle upon which they
were based was not understood. They were signs that the
workers had the truth. They were signs that the Christ
truth was the true healing agent. They were signs of
present salvation. "Ye shall know the truth and the truth
shall make you free." Jesus says, "These signs shall [not
may] follow them that believe the truth." To believe error
does not set free but to know the truth does. The works
are the ever living signs of the truth of Christ. A want
of works, a lack of signs, is proof of error, if not in doctrine
then certainly in life; and as Jesus says, "If I do not the
works of the Father believe Me not." So if works do not
follow a teaching we need not believe it.

There are many passages in the Old Testament showing
that divine healing was known and practised long before
the times of the apostles: "I make alive . . . and I heal."
"I am the Lord that healeth thee." "I will take sickness
away from the midst of thee." "My son, attend to my
words; incline thine ear to my sayings. Let them not
depart from thine eyes; keep them in the midst of thine
heart. For they are life unto those that find them, and
health to all their flesh." "I will restore health unto thee,
and I will heal thee of thy wounds, saith the Lord." "Fools,
because of their transgression, and because of their iniquities are afflicted. Then they cry unto the Lord in their
trouble, and He saveth them out of their distresses. He

sent His word, and healed them, and delivered them from their destructions." "Bless the Lord, O my soul, and forget not all His benefits: who forgiveth all thine iniquities; who healeth all thy diseases." The fame of Elisha as a healer was so great that Naaman, captain of the host of the king of Syria, came to him and was healed of leprosy; and he even raised from death the son of the good Shunammite woman. Many other passages might be given showing that healing was known and practised in the Old as well as the New Testament.

There are many material methods in the practice of the healing art, the allopathic, homœopathic, and others but all are based on the same fundamental error, that of medicating or treating symptoms or effects as seen in the body. The science of Christ teaches healing through mind or spirit. The Scripture records show plainly that one way is not in keeping with divine truth, as is manifest in the following passages: "In vain shalt thou use many medicines." "Thou hast no healing medicines." "Why shouldst thou die before thy time?" "Ye are all physicians of no value." The following is a plain and pointed statement from Second Chronicles: "Asa was diseased in his feet, until his disease was exceeding great; yet in his disease he sought not to the Lord, but to the physicians. And Asa slept with his fathers and died." In the New Testament is recorded the case of the woman who "had suffered many things of many physicians, and had spent all that she had, and was nothing bettered but rather grew worse," who was healed the Christway. Was not this last, like the case of Asa, recorded for a purpose? They show the Christ-way right and the other ways wrong.

The Christ-way of healing is based on truth. Jesus gave it to His followers and the world, and it was not overlooked and left unrecorded—this truth that Jesus and His followers proved true over and over again by the marvellous works they performed.

This is the principle as given by Mark. He says, "And when He had called all the people unto Him, Jesus said unto them, Hearken unto Me, every one of you, and understand; there is nothing from without a man that, entering into him, can defile him; but the things that come out of him, those are they that defile the man." "If any man have ears to hear, let him hear." "And when He was entered into the house from the people, His disciples asked him concerning the parable. And He said unto them, Are ye so without understanding also? Do ye not perceive, that whatsoever thing from without entereth into the man, it cannot defile him; because it entereth not into his heart, but into the belly, and goeth out into the draught, purging all meats? And He said, That which cometh out of the man, that defileth the man. For from within, out of the heart of men, proceed evil thoughts, adulteries, fornication, murders, thefts, covetousness, wickedness, deceit, lasciviousness, envy, blasphemy, pride, foolishness; all these evil things come from within, and defile the man."

This is the true cause of all sickness, and the statement of this principle has been standing here for nearly nineteen hundred years. Now it is being proved true by scientific experiment under government supervision at Washington by actual chemical test. It has always been known that fear and wrong belief have a deleterious influence on the body. Sudden and great grief and fright have been known to bring on sickness, insanity, and even death. This line of thought is now receiving attention by scientific men. Prof. Elmer Gates, by chemical tests, proves cause to be in mind. "To illustrate," he says, "suppose half a dozen men are in a room; one feels depressed, another remorseful, another ill-tempered, another jealous, another cheerful, and another benevolent. It is a warm day; they perspire. Samples of their perspiration, on examination, reveal all these emotional conditions. Each bad emotion produces its own peculiar poison and has a deleterious physical effect. For each bad emotion there is a corresponding chemical change in the tissues of the body, which is life-depressing and poisonous, while every good emotion makes a life-promoting change." Again Professor Gates says, "This new science does not pertain to the realm of the visionary. Its conclusions are based on facts." So the trouble comes, as Jesus says, from the heart, or as Professor Gates is proving, from the emotional conditions. Revelation and material science coincide.

Professor Gates speaks of the putting a person through a course of mental lessons and the benefit that would result. This would do great good, but as wrong mental conditions are legion and do not always produce sickness at any particular time, a system based on physical facts alone is incomplete and insufficient in rendering the help humanity wants. What the world wants is a full mental renovation not only in harmony with physical but moral and divine truth, regardless of the present state of health, and this will insure permanent health and abiding happiness. This is the truth that Jesus Christ gave to the world. Professor

Gates has touched the hem of the robe of man's divine rightness, and as the world believes so generally in physical facts and physical sciences these discoveries will do great good.

The body and spirit are so intimately interwoven that they are as one, and what affects the mind through the mind affects the body. In the mind is the cause, in the body the effect. Jesus says, "The light of the body is the eye; therefore, when thine eye is single, thy whole body is full of light. But when thine eye is evil thy body, also, is full of darkness. Ye fools, did not He that made that which is without, make that which is within, also?" He that made the body made the mind; and when Professor Gates finds that thoughts are the cause of physical conditions he only proves the truth of Christ by material science.

It has been aptly said, "Had the demonstrations of the Master only extended to reforming sinners, He could never have said, Be ye whole; He could only have said, Be ye half whole and take this prescription of drugs for the other half."

We read that Christ did not many mighty works in His own country because of their unbelief. He was without honor in His own country; His own people refusing to believe on Him, His teachings, and His works. Unbelief, or lack of faith and trust, is the only obstruction to a full and free manifestation of His presence and power; "Lo, I am with you alway, even unto the end of the world."

We know in reason that Peter states what is true when he says, "I perceive of a truth that God is no respecter of persons," and that "God is the same yesterday, to-day, and forever, without variance or shadow of turning."

Truth is always and in all relations true. All we need is to know, live, and speak it and the Divine Presence will do the works. "The Father who dwelleth in Me, He doeth the works."

John the Baptist, while in prison, hearing of the marvellous things Christ was doing, sent two of his disciples unto Him to learn the truth about Jesus. The messengers, coming to Him, made their mission known, and "in that same hour Jesus cured many of their infirmities and plagues, and of evil spirits; and unto many that were blind He gave sight. Then Jesus answering said unto them, Go your way, and tell John what things ye have seen and heard; how that the blind see, the lame walk, the lepers are cleansed, the deaf hear, the dead are raised, to the poor the gospel is preached. And blessed is he whosoever is not offended in

Me." After John's disciples make their errand known to
Jesus, and before He gives them His answer, He performs
His works of healing before them, that they may go and tell
John what they have actually seen. He healed the sick
and taught the gospel to the poor, and again we have healing
and teaching united and by the Great Physician Himself.
These are the glad tidings He sent to John and, as He said
to the messengers of old, His spirit is saying now, at all
times and to all men, "Blessed is he, whosoever shall not be
offended in Me."

Christ says, "Judge not according to the appearance."
Here is where we make our mistake. We judge according to
appearances and our conclusions are wrong. We see the
surface of things, but do not see the moving cause. God
is Spirit, and Spirit is everywhere and acts from within.

In answer to the Pharisees as to when the kingdom of
God would come, Jesus says, "The kingdom of God cometh
not with observation; neither shall they say, Lo, here, or
Lo, there, for, behold, the kingdom of God is within you."
This is only a part of Jesus' answer. In a fragment in
Second Clement He is recorded as saying in reply to this
same question, that the kingdom of God will come when
"Two are one and when that which is without shall be as
that which is within."

When our outer life and thought is in harmony with
the kingdom of divine life in our inner spiritual nature the
kingdom of God is come. The inharmony between the
outer life and thought or acquired mental condition and our
inner spiritual nature is the one first cause of all sickness,
pain, and death. The various effects which Professor Gates
finds in the blood and perspiration express the nature of
the thought or belief at the time active in the mind; if one
of these effects manifests inharmony it is called poisonous;
if it shows harmony it is called helpful.

This universe is the product of Omniscient Wisdom and
all truth is one. The manifest and the unmanifest, the
within and the without, are one grand unity. Error and
discord cast shadows while they last, but "Ye shall know
the truth and the truth shall make you free."

So the kingdom of God is not a place or locality, but is an
inner, spiritual state in the mind of man. "Ye are the
temple of God and the spirit of God dwelleth in you." Then
omnipotence is within the mind of man, and it is from
within, through the mind, that Jesus and His followers
did their mighty works. The same truth is endued with
the same power now that it was nineteen hundred years

ago, as truth is unchangeable and God is no respecter of persons.

Jesus Christ understood man, his nature, and his needs, and His teachings were to free man from sickness and misery by freeing him from the cause of his sickness and his misery. He says, "I came that ye might have life and that ye might have it more abundantly." He knew that for man to lay aside the errors of life would free him from their consequences and bring into his consciousness that more full and abundant life which is health and happiness.

Christ-truth is to save men from error, from all wrong mental conditions, and not from punishment, and now and here in this world is the time and place. "Seek and ye shall find," but we must seek where it is. The kingdom of heaven is within and there we must seek. "Knock and it shall be opened," but we must knock in the right way. Truth stands at the door and knocks, the door of our mental consciousness. If we will open this door to the truth it will come in and sup with us. "Ask and ye shall receive." Jesus has pointed out the way. What is it that we may ask and receive? "All things whatsoever ye desire," for we are heirs of God, "joint heirs with Christ." We are all branches of the one vine of Life which in its inner spiritual nature in man as the divine Ego is pure and perfect and present possessor of every good thing. The only worthy object of life in our oneness with God and one another is to assist in making the without as the within in all men. "He that hath done it unto the least of these hath done it unto Me."

BANK MONOPOLY — SPECIE CONTRACTION — BOND INFLATION.

BY ALBERT ROBERTS.

One of the strongest presentations of the evils of the interest liabilities being forced upon the tax-payers of the United States through the continued and unnecessary issue of national bonds is contained in an article in the ARENA of March, 1894, by Mr. I. W. Bennett, on "The Cause of Financial Panics." He claimed that it was susceptible of mathematical demonstration that the average interest charge for the last decade upon the various kinds and character of bonds, including national bonds, more than absorbs the entire yearly increase of wealth in the United States, and that "the very foundation principle of our industrial system leads us to recognize obligations which we can never pay." He shows that during the last decade the country's wealth increased about twenty-two billion dollars and during the same period the interest charges were thirty billion dollars. Thus every ten years the assets of the country's citizens fall eight billion dollars below their liabilities. But when there is added to interest on national, state, county, and municipal bonds, the expenses of these various governments, we have, according to Mr. Bennett, $16,970,000,000 as the sum which our assets fall behind our liabilities every decade. The writer's condemnation of interest-taking applies with force to the proposition of Mr. John Sherman and President Cleveland in the scheme of unlimited inflation of the interest-bearing paper in order to facilitate the compound-interest-bearing device of the national bank system.

An equally strong presentation of the evils of interest-taking is given in the chapter on "Usury" in Mr. Arthur Kitson's work, "A Scientific Solution of the Money Question," comprehensively reviewed in a recent issue of the ARENA. Both of these papers are worthy the thoughtful consideration of patriotic citizens of the United States.

The foundation of all our commercial distresses and losses for the past quarter of a century may be laid to the charge of the interest-takers and usurers. The National Bank system was the most brilliant and audacious scheme of usury ever devised in the cunning brains of able and far-seeing financiers.

The political press throughout the country teems with discussions of the metallic standards, but significantly ignores the national banks of issue. President Cleveland, with a coincidental significance, in every executive message or utterance on the money question since his inauguration in 1893, has studiedly ignored the one plank in the party platform upon which he was elected demanding the repeal of the ten-per-cent tax, enacted, not for revenue, but as a protection to the monopoly to which, it is alleged, he owed his nomination and election.

Address a direct question to the newspapers comprising the Associated Press, requesting a categorical answer as to their views on the national bank system, and the result will be a golden flash of silence and an increased vehemence in the denunciation of free-coinage heresies. How consistently to discuss the currency question and persistently avoid even a reference to the instrument which creates and distributes the currency, is a problem. The opponents of the single gold standard do not seem to realize that the political Poloniuses, who do the dirty work for the bank monopoly, are fooling them to the top of their bent. The censors of the subsidized press in bank parlors adroitly direct the discussion to the metallic excitement and away from the fundamental issue. It is suspected that at the proper time they will concede the free-coinage demand, but only when they shall have secured the perpetuation of their beautiful interest-making and interest-taking system, the national banks of issue, based upon bonds. They encourage and provoke the metallic-standard agitation, but they know well that with the abolition of that system the gold-standard question dies by inanition and desuetude. For the only interest they have in contending for the gold single standard (having destroyed silver as specie of resumption) is that it is the means by which an involuntary issue of interest bonds can be forced upon the country.

That the private bank of issue scheme, the gold, or specie-cornering scheme, the bond-forcing scheme were part and parcel of one colossal scheme of usury and interest-making, goes without saying, and cannot be successfully refuted. The object of issuing bonds was to create a debt, whereby a few would be enabled to accumulate the representation of wealth, without working for it or producing it. It is estimated that the bond-holders have received in twenty-eight years profits amounting to $3,048,972,903.77. This they received without taxes on their bonds, and it was drawn from the taxes of the people. The English bankers, in col-

lusion with others in the deal, in the United States, sent
over in 1862 the "Hazzard Circular," which, while favoring
the abolition of chattel slavery as a mere owning of labor
carrying with it the care of the laborers, was for capital
to control labor by controlling wages, and this secured by
control of the money. Said this infamous circular:

> The great debt that capitalists will see to it is made of the war
> must be used as a measure to control the volume of money. To
> accomplish this, the bonds must be used as a banking basis. We
> are now waiting to get the secretary of the treasury to make this
> recommendation to Congress. It will not do to allow the greenback,
> as it is called, to circulate as money for any length of time, for we
> cannot control that.

Thus the debt was created, and has been growing ever
since, not to borrow money, but to be used as a measure to
control the volume of money. The system was introduced
by London bankers, adopted by an American Congress, and
favored by two secretaries of the treasury from Ohio, Sal-
mon P. Chase and John Sherman, as essential preliminaries
to the National Bank Act, which became the law in March,
1863. E. G. Spaulding, in his "Financial History of the
War," says:

> No national bank currency was issued until about the first of Janu-
> ary, 1864. After that time it was gradually issued. On the first of
> July, 1864, the sum of $25,825,695 had been issued; and on the
> twenty-second of April, 1865, shortly after the surrender of General
> Lee, the whole amount of national bank circulation to that time, was
> only $146,927,975.

It will therefore be seen that comparatively little direct
aid was realized from this currency until after the close of
the war. All the channels of circulation were well filled up
with the greenback notes, compound-interest notes, and certificates of indebtedness to the amount of over $700,000,-
000, before the national bank act got fairly into operation.
This bank issue was, in fact, an additional inflation of the
currency.

The Hazzard circular was followed later by a circular said to have been sent out by the National Bank
Association to bankers. It, substantially, urged them to
support such daily and weekly newspapers, especially the
agricultural and religious press, as would oppose the issuing
of greenback paper money and withhold patronage or favors
from all applicants now willing to oppose the government
issue of money. The same practice is pursued to-day in the
buying up of papers opposing the bank monopoly, and in
the distribution of gold-standard literature over bank counters. The provincial bankers were advised that the issue

of more greenbacks would furnish the people with money and "therefore, seriously affect your individual profit as bankers." The convenient and impecunious press, carried by national banks, were prompt to denounce the greenback as "rag money" and "the rag baby." Yet during the war, according to Spaulding's History, "the greenback was indispensably necessary and a most powerful instrumentality in saving the government and maintaining the national unity." The government had no money and could get none except by creating it. Greenbacks were paid out to the soldiers and for supplies, paid back by taxation, and would have continued to circulate, but for legislation dictated by the bank combine against the people. The issue of treasury notes in 1862 was made legal tender for all debts, public and private, except interest on the public debt and duties on imports, and exchangeable for six-per-cent bonds redeemable after five years. The act shows that they were issued for funding the floating debt, not to borrow, but to destroy, money. It was to give the usurers opportunity to exchange non-interest-bearing greenbacks for untaxed, interest-bearing bonds.

In a little brochure published by I. C. Vallette, of Norwich, Conn., he shows the absurdity of the proposition that the first bonds were issued to borrow money, when the government issued more than $830,000,000 of seven-thirty treasury notes, made them a legal tender, and within three years' time they were all destroyed and bonds put in their place. The efforts of the money power were directed against the government issue of greenbacks. The only reason for opposing greenbacks was because the government was furnishing the people with money without interest and they could not control it. Mr. Vallette shows, by high official authority, that a large part of the bonds were issued after the war was closed and the soldiers and contractors had all been paid. Of the $1,854,736,150 issued from 1862 to 1868, only $603,262,250 were issued before Lee's surrender, and $1,251,473,900 after it. There are many people in the United States who yet believe the bonds were issued to carry on the war.

To further this colossal scheme of debt-making and interest-gathering, the banking association procured legislation which was a long series of shameless repudiation of honest money. They repudiated United States treasury-note obligations in 1862 by inserting the exception clause as to import duties, to give coin-hucksters a chance to make "honest money." They repudiated greenbacks in 1863 and substituted national bank notes based on interest-bearing bonds, by making the greenback non-receivable for bonds after July 1, 1863. They repudiated our fractional currency of 1864 by substituting in 1865 fractional coin at an annual cost of two and a half million interest on bonds sold by bullion. They repudiated treasury notes in 1869 by making them payable in coin, contrary to the law creating them, by which they were redeemable exactly as gold and silver fiat money was redeemable in debts due the government save the one cunning exception as to duties; and finally they repudiated the silver specie of the constitution in 1873–4. Said Professor Lumley, of Wheaton College, in his little work on "National Suicide":

In corruptly repudiating just obligations to the people, they have destroyed thousands of millions of value of other people's property and are, before God, responsible for the loss of thousands of human lives of men who have died by suicide because of their losses; and for much of the intemperance, poverty, crime, misery, and idleness that now make every thoughtful patriot tremble for his country.

If no more bonds are issued before 1907, the maturity of those outstanding will put an end to the present unsatisfactory national bank system, and with the fall of that system the necessity for the gold-standard monopoly and the necessity for a prohibitive tax upon competing bank circulation, will not exist. Of the bonds available for the use of national banks, the most numerous are the four-percents, of which there are some $559,605,700 outstanding. These are not due until 1907. Long before that time it will be necessary to improvise a new banking system and the plans may as well be inaugurated now as later. The present system was established in 1863 while the war was raging, and when gold was held in the East, affording that section the opportunity to reap the greatest measure of profit from it. Mr. Goldsmith, of Georgia, describes thus the *modus operandi:*

Greenbacks were worth forty cents on the dollar, and United States bonds the same price. Now, see what these shrewd people did with the $4,000 in gold. A decided he would establish a national bank. He had $4,000 in gold, his entire capital. He borrowed from his friend B, for a few days, $90,000 in currency. With this $4,000 in gold he bought $10,000 in currency. He went to Washington, bought $100,000 of government bonds with his $100,000 in currency, and applied for a national bank charter. The government took his bonds as collateral and handed him $90,000 in national bank bills. He returned to his friend B the $90,000 in bills, so that he was out only $4,000 in gold. The minimum rate of interest paid by the government on the bonds was four per cent. At this rate the government has paid $120,000 for the use of his $4,000 in gold. It was paid semi-annually and frequently in advance. Just after the war, interest was high, and the man who had ready money could get almost any price he chose to ask for it. This interest paid him each six months $2,000. He has loaned easily at ten per cent per annum for the average time. What do you suppose it amounts to? $736,915.86. Deduct from this the $4,000 invested and the interest on it at the same rate, and he has a net profit of $732,738.86.

Of course this profit has all been "taken out" of the pockets of the people by direct taxes, tariff taxes, revenue taxes, etc. Is it any wonder that 30,000 people in the United States own more property than 64,970,000, that they are getting richer each day, until they will own all the property and the 64,970,000 will own none? The national banking laws have been a great thing for them; and is it to be wondered at that they should advocate their continuance, and that they should spend millions of dollars in perpetuating the system?

No warrant of the constitution ever authorized a congress to give to holders of bonds the exclusive right to bank, and monopoly control of the circulating medium of the people. By this monopoly land and real estate are denied all bankable value; bonds and stocks were the only collaterals and the monopolists held the bonds and stocks, and the borrower must buy them at the holders' price to hypothecate. The prices of these collaterals were churned up and down in the stock exchange, which has always been a convenient appendix to the banking combine. They act in concert. The banks lend on stocks and bonds, and the exchange gambles in them. The gamblers, by "wash" sales, mark the collaterals up and down, and the banks will accept no other price than this fictitious one. And yet, great as is the contractile power of the banking monopoly, it is weak at the base. Says Col. Thomas M. Norwood, of Georgia:

It is a seeming paradox in physics and dynamics that the claw of a crab which can pinch to the bone, is so highly articulated that a baby can break it off. This banking system, so powerful to crush, is so weak at its base that a few small depositors in New York, by concert of action last year, could have forced every bank to suspend. So sensible were the officers of this result that they had to turn back to back to prop themselves up, and took refuge or safety in refusing to pay out currency, and in using certificates of credit. Even depositors had to use these certificates.

By this system of robbery the banks themselves are handicapped by their inactive reserves from which they earn no interest, and the people are burdened with an interest-bearing circulating medium which costs them twenty millions a year in unnecessary taxation—some estimates making it from thirty to forty millions. These are bank reserves $571,000,000 at five per cent, making $28,550,-000, and treasury reserve of gold $100,000,000 at five per cent, making $5,000.000 more, and a total loss to the people of $33,550,000. And this to make the government pretend to do what it does not and cannot do for itself, viz., currently redeem $1,200,000,000 of currency notes. Instead of adding to local circulation under this system, we really send out from a state $6,000 more money than we receive in return for every national bank of $100,000 capital started in that state. Hence the more invested in United States bonds as a basis for circulation, the greater the loss to the banks—the greater the drain upon the actual money circulation of the state. Hence an inflation of capital, but contraction of currency. In short, we are banking upon the debt of the country instead of upon its wealth.

The only way to break the backbone of this crushing monopoly is to give emphatic voice at the ballot-box against the further issue of bonds. It will also be necessary to quit sending to Congress bank presidents and bank directors to make our financial laws. That the founders of our government had a salutary dread of the bankers' influence making itself felt in shaping legislation on national finance was shown in the adoption of this resolution in the Third Congress, Dec. 23, 1793: "Any person holding stock in any institution of the nature of a bank for issuing or discounting bills or notes payable to bearer or order cannot be a member of the House whilst he holds such office or stock." This resolution was signed by President George Washington. At that time there were only three banks in the whole country. The three banks of 1793 had grown to over 3,000 in 1894, and the banking interest had at one time within the past twenty years 189 representatives in Congress—the next largest representation being that of the legal profession. Any party—yea, even the Republican party—espousing the cause of the abolition of interest-bearing bonds, the abolition of specie redemption primary money, the abolition of national banks based upon bonds, and the abolition of an interest-bearing circulating medium, would sweep the country from ocean to ocean. Not only this, the party so determined would give to the United States twenty-five years at least of unprecedented prosperity, and would save the Union from dismemberment or revolution and the national debt from repudiation. The demand for the repeal of the ten-per-cent tax on bank circulation other than that of national banks, by many opponents of the tax, was less a desire to return to the old system of ante-bellum state banking than it was a protest against the present national bank system. The repeal of the prohibitory ten-per-cent tax was regarded as an essential preliminary step toward breaking the monopoly behind which the national bank system had entrenched itself.

In a well-considered paper by William Knapp in the *American Journal of Politics* for August, 1894, these evils of the present banking system are vividly and pointedly presented. Briefly summarized, they are "the power conferred for the prevention of the use of the currency so as harmfully to contract its volume." Mr. Knapp holds that all banks should, as individuals, be required to do business upon their own resources, and exercise no control over the currency, except in their legitimate current business transactions, and on equal terms with all the people, for whose use and benefit it is created. The principal injustice inflicted upon the people by the present system is the great power of its organization to monopolize and contract the currency and divert its use by all alike. In furtherance of this, he shows how the policy of the creditor class is "to keep the volume of currency for actual use as small as possible all the time, regardless of its volume," and of course, of the much vaunted large per capita of circulation, a few individuals holding and withholding the per capita from distribution.

The radical and fundamental defect of the present banking system is the theory of "doing business upon the money of depositors, with a nominal capital." Why, indeed, should not banks, like individuals, do business upon their own resources? Why should paternalism furnish an interest-bearing debt to be used as a basis for circulating notes, and exempt this circulation from taxation? "To allow them to do business upon the funds of depositors, and not upon their own capital, or from the avails of the sale of stock, and not even utilize the surplus funds for this purpose," is certainly an extraordinary privilege to be extended to a private association of individuals.

BETWEEN TWO WORLDS.

BY MRS. CALVIN KRYDER REIFSNIDER.

CHAPTER IX.

They sat in the morning room of the chapel. Salome had called, as was her wont, to get herself in condition to begin the day. Poor girl! They both welcomed her, and with words of love and encouragement strove to help her into the right path. They understood that the trouble lay within her own young heart; the older woman felt that nothing is so bitter as the aspirations of a proud heart conscious of inability to reach its goal. She longed to see the mother, to thus learn the source, but every effort to learn anything of this girl's home life was unavailing. At times she alluded to her mother with great affection and always with a genuine respect; but a kind of shame, fear, or horror accompanied any allusion to her home, and they noticed that after one of these conversations she would sometimes remain away for days and then appear again and seem to studiously avoid broaching any subject that would lead them into that channel, until it became tacitly understood that it was dangerous ground. But she never avowed a sentiment that did not give them a clew to her unhappy surroundings, mysterious as they were, for she evidently had been reared with care and by a woman of superior mental and moral attainments. Her neatly fitting clothing was most beautifully made, with every evidence of taste and skill, and she sometimes alluded to the fact that her mother was her dressmaker.

This morning the question of envy and jealousy was broached in some incidental way. In a moment Salome was on fire.

"A woman without envy, jealousy, or any of the baser passions of the human heart—I would like to see her," Salome said with the most withering scorn.

"Do you not believe there are such women?" asked Mrs. Goode, raising her calm eyes to the excited face of the young girl.

"No; woman is woman's natural enemy. Who so heartless to woman as woman?"

"Do you believe that they are worse than men?"

"I believe that if a woman needs a friend she must never expect to find one among those of her own sex. Man was created to protect and befriend her."

"But do you not observe that men are sometimes as treacherous as you claim women are?" persisted the good old lady.

"To men, yes. If a man wants a sure, reliable ally he chooses a woman."

"Then you do not believe the sexes are true to themselves? Is that it?"

"Yes, that is what I mean."

"Then, Salome, my dear, listen to me. You must feel that you are not a true woman; you feel that you have never seen one, and that you have never seen a true man; if you were right in your own heart you would believe in a true womanhood, exalted above all the petty jealousies and meannesses of which you speak; one who from her throne of purity and truth could reach out a helping hand to all her sister women; strong in her own strength of noble purpose she could know no fear that others might outstrip her and could praise them if they did for a true woman will accord honor where honor is due"——

"Ah, that is it; but a woman cannot see merit in another woman, it is impossible. She may acknowledge success where it would be bad taste not to do so. For instance, all women must agree upon the beauty, power, pathos, of ——'s voice, yet they would do it with a slur upon her virtue. I've heard them do it. They cannot leave out the personality; they cannot separate the art from the woman."

"How is it with yourself in regard to her?"

"I could listen to her and forget all else about her but her voice; and how God has favored her with that divine gift of song. I care not what she is nor who she is, the tones she sends forth awaken within me a new life; inspire me with fresh courage, and I thank God for the privilege of being able to comprehend the possibilities of the human voice, a thing of which I never could have had any conception had I never listened to her."

Mrs. Goode's face brightened. "There, you express no envy, but only wonder and admiration; you do not know if the evil things said of her are true or not, and you do not care; you freely acknowledge her talent and her genius, not only that, but her physical beauty, perhaps; you feel elevated and inspired to emulate her in your own divine gift. Humph—do you suppose you are the only woman who feels just the same?"

Salome was a little abashed.

"But I have only heard the unkind things said."

"That is true. Great people never say little things; the unkind criticisms are always made by little souls; the kind ones by great ones. You have really done credit to woman by your praise of this one; believe me there are many women who feel just as you do. Meanness is the product of a narrow, little soul. Who knows her sin? Who knows any other's sin? If we would allow within ourselves a counsel for the accused and permit him to ask questions, how few of us would bear witness against our neighbors. 'How do you know his sin?' 'I saw it.' 'Ah, then you were there, right in the same sphere, on the same level; or else you are judging without knowing—you are lying.'"

In all these conversations between Salome and Mrs. Goode Ruby sat apart, listening with quiet attention, never venturing a remark unless directly appealed to, and then answering by asking another question, as if thus appealing to this strange girl's reasoning power, or rather trying to awaken it.

That in her art Salome had talent, Ruby knew; that she had genius she had yet to prove, for the difference is a difference between the head and the heart. The actor upon the stage who has talent only, seldom wins distinction; if he has genius he may, but the two combined override all opposition in every direction. In music it is the same; talent produces the great bassos, baritones, and contraltos; genius the great sopranos and tenors. Talent charms the public, genius wins the people; talent shows ability, genius true power; the one skims along the earth, the other soars up towards heaven.

"One question to you, Miss Gladstone, before I go; you put so much stress upon the physical that at times I have questioned whether in spite of the contradiction in your own physical appearance you are not more than half materialist."

"Then I must correct a false impression unintentionally given. Papa's lesson to me is that we have no means of manifestation of our thoughts but through speech, action, and writing. If the machine is out of order its work is indifferent, therefore I believe in keeping the physical machine in perfect order. 'Materialism that claims that matter is all is not true; idealism that claims that thought is all is not true; but a dual realism is true.' You seek self-reliance. There is no such thing to be found. You must

work and look to God for the result. Self-derived intelligence that will sustain you is a treacherous ladder, hooked
upon a phantom wall that will fall and leave you broken
and dismembered on the earth. If blind ask God for sight
and He will make clay with spittle and anoint your eyes and
bid you go wash in the pool. If your physical condition
were harmonious you would not only feel well but you
would look well, and you would always be able to say
just what you mean. As it is you do but imperfectly what
you aim to do, and express but feebly what you think, or
else make yourself entirely misunderstood and not infrequently misunderstand others. But you are improving
rapidly. It cannot all come in a day.

"The unrest of life, the lack of appreciation of home,
parents, friends, all comes from an abnormal physical condition, brought about by unwholesome diet, irregular hours
for rest and nourishment. We see the woman in her
luxurious home more miserable than the very servant who
scrubs her steps. The whole fabric of life is wrong. Men
become drunkards, women use narcotics and try to forget
what should be their daily joy. Where shall we begin?
Politically we are wrong, socially we are wrong, and all
because physically we are wrong. Revolutionize medicine
and you will revolutionize theology. Revolutionize theology and you will change the whole fabric. There are
too many churches, too few Christians. Too many doctors,
too little skill. I am not a materialist, but I insist upon
it the natural man is the expression of the spiritual man.
The physical must be harmonized."

Salome said good-morning and was passing out of the
door. Her feet seemed tired and heavy, and she moved
apparently like one in pain.

"I come and come again," she said, "to learn the secret
of you two who have it but will not part with it. I want
to know how to live, how to make others happy and thus
be happy with them."

"Salome," said Ruby rising, "I give you freely the only
power I know. It is no secret. It is but this; live to-day;
I mean, live in the Present, the living, breathing moment;
it is all we have. The past is gone, and with it our failures and mistakes; the Future is what the Present makes
it. To-day is ours, is yours—our time to love, our opportunity to do good, to bind up wounds, to wipe away tears
from sad eyes about us. To make our faces bright with
smiles, to cheer the faint-hearted. Oh, one to-day is worth
a thousand yesterdays, for it can weave the golden thread

of a thousand joys for the to-morrows yet to come. Don't forget a loving word for your mother to-day, to-morrow may never come. To-day, now, this moment, fill it with sunshine, let it be too precious to permit one cloud to fall upon it, and O, Salome! this world will grow so bright. If you have a flower for your mother, give it to her to-day, don't wait to plant it on her grave."

"You can well say this with your Present; I must live in the Future; I dare not for a moment pause to think of the Present, else my strength would fail me—I would have no heart to go on. It is a thought of the Future that makes the Present endurable. I try to close my eyes when night comes and forget the day that is done; to let it be a dead thing whose ghost will not, I hope, rise up against me somewhere and tell me that I have murdered it. Work, work—hope, hope. Ah, Miss Gladstone, you may live to-day, I will live next year, or in five years, perhaps—I am dead to-day."

The smile she forced upon her pale lips was sad indeed, and she repressed her tears and walked hastily from the room.

"The poor child! She is too sentimental; she has some real sorrow, but she is her own worst torment, I am sure. I pity her poor mother; what a cross such a child must be. But, like your father, I believe there is great good deep down within her. I would like to know something of her child-hood, say from infancy to the present time, then I could judge what her womanhood would be. 'The internal of thought is from the life's love and its affections and consequent perceptions; while the external is from the things which are in the memory, and which are subservient to the life's love for confirmations and for means to attain its end.' "

The quotation Mrs. Goode made only half audibly, but Ruby's quick ear caught it.

"Goodie, your frequent reference to this subject causes me to examine myself almost daily to recall all the early impressions of my childhood, then my heart's longings and desires, to thus endeavor to ascertain what my life's love or trend really is."

"In childhood, from infancy, we involve, and impressions for good and evil are stamped upon the memory, or sink into the heart, to be evolved later in life, for it is certain that nothing can be evolved which has not first been in-volved."

While Mrs. Goode and Ruby discussed the subject Salome

walked slowly and mechanically homeward. Her thoughts
were turned inward; she was resolving to turn over a new
leaf; to begin that very day; to forget her own misery, to
crush down her own longings and desires, her own hopes
and ambitions, to take hold of the things near at hand, to
help her mother with her toils and care. With this feeling
in her heart she reached the uninviting place called home.
Her little sister had put away the dishes and stood unkempt
in the open doorway watching for her, while her mother
sat near the window at the sewing machine.

"Mother," said Salome, tossing aside her hat, and without pausing she called her sister to her as she took up a
brush and began to arrange the disordered mass of curls,
"mother, I have been wondering if it would not be best to
give up this plan of fitting myself for the stage and to just
content myself to spend my days teaching. As a substitute I have been successful and next year can have a
permanent position in one of the best public schools. The
principal tells me that I am a born teacher—do hold still,
child; it is tangled dreadfully and you only make it worse.
When I was your age I could comb and braid my own
hair."

This last was an unfortunate remark. The mother had
looked up with surprise at Salome's first remark, but her
words to her little sister touched an old wound in the delicate, overworked mother's heart, and flushing painfully
she said:

"When you were her age we had servants to do the
drudgery and I could give you some attention; now I must
do what half a dozen servants did, besides helping to earn
a living; I have no time to give to the children, and you
prefer leaving the house and spending your morning in
better company to sharing the duties that a more affectionate, or. I should say a more natural daughter would do,"
and with a sniff and a few tears the mother rose, took the
brush from Salome's hand and proceeded to curl the little
girl's hair.

Little Lois felt that she had made a mistake; she wished
that nothing had been said about her tangled hair, for she
well knew it had begun an unpleasant day, and all children
dread unpleasant days at home. Mother would pout, Salome would go off to her room alone, and she would have
to look after her little brother when he awoke. She was
a true prophetess; without one word Salome started to
leave the room, but the irritated mother would fain learn
more of this half-formed resolution which made her ill

at ease, for she was proud and fond of Salome but had never learned how to manage her.

"I suppose you imagine that my heart is set upon your being something and somebody is the reason why you take a notion all at once to be a nobody."

Salome paused and maintained a respectful silence. Ruby's words came like the echo of silver bells: "Remember to have a loving word for mother to-day; to-day, now, this moment; fill it with sunshine, let it be too precious to let one cloud fall upon it."

As her eyes filled with tears and her lip quivered she would fain have dropped upon her knees and cried, "O mother, let us begin all over again," but a memory of being once repulsed and the love of her young heart turned aside, held back the words.

"Don't shed any of your crocodile tears about me," said the mother, turning her face away from her and apparently giving her whole attention to the child's hair. Salome hesitated no longer; she turned and walked proudly away and up the dark stairway to her little gloomy room, and throwing herself upon the bed burst into a passion of tears.

Here then is a question for philosophers to solve. Why did this mother, who loved her child, who put forth each day all the strength in her puny frame to bring comforts to her children, and insisted that Salome's earnings as a teacher should be expended wholly upon herself, thus turn the channel of this same child's love into stony places, away from herself, and send her away in bitterness of spirit from her? Where lay the trouble? Here is one of the inconsistencies of love. Who is to blame? Where shall we go to find a remedy for these domestic ills, the root and bane of social life, for as the home and family is, so must the nation socially and morally be. We ask again "Who hath sinned, this girl or her parents?" and we might go further and ask "Her parents or her grandparents?"

Mrs. Blake's mother had a large family, the eldest a daughter who married at an early age leaving her mother with a large family of boys and a little daughter of seven years; the father owned a business to which he had apprenticed all his sons, for he belonged to one of those old Virginia families who held to their forefathers' maxim that every man should have his own legitimate trade. Mrs. Blake's mother was a thorough housekeeper; she superintended the spinning, the weaving, the knitting, the darning, but did very little of it herself. She recognized a treasure in her little daughter, who was expert with scissors and needle, and at an early age, only a child, she was head of the workroom where the sewing for a large family of boys, as well as half a dozen negro servants, was done. The child's pride was flattered by the dignity of her position, and the praises she received from all the old ladies of the town and surrounding country. The married sister sometimes suggested to the mother that little Mary might "overdo" herself, but the good mother with the Roman nose knew better than all the daughters in the world, and so little Mary queened it over all other girls like the fairy princess in the tale, who spun the wonderful amount of flax; but poor little Mary had no fairy godmother to bring her help; she cut and sewed, and stitched and felled, and soon it was found that she was so rapid that the outside help could be reduced to half, and next year two-thirds, and at last little Mary, who bid fair to be always little Mary, sat alone in the workroom day in, day out, earning with weeks of toil a visit to her sister or to some one of her brothers' wives who had folded away many a package of linen or lawn that no scissors but those in little Mary's hand could invade, and no hand but hers should cunningly fashion into a robe for some mysterious angel, nameless still, whose advent was expected sometime when little Mary would be too busy to make these preparations, so it must be done during her holidays. So she worked, and was so rapid that she turned it all off before it was time to visit the next brother, for whom half a dozen linen shirts were to be made that only little Mary knew how to do; besides, he was no longer a journeyman; he had been to college and was just granted a license to practise law; another brother was studying medicine, and little Mary saw them all rising out of the workshop into professions.

Beaux by the score came to this busy bee, but the Roman nose was ever on the alert. No ordinary man could aspire to the hand of little Mary. Who was ordinary? Why, a poor clerk, a man of no means, even though it was whispered that little Mary wept in secret over one tall young clerk who believed, and expressed the belief, that she was most shamefully imposed upon, and who did not care if her brothers did give her prettier clothes than any of the village girls could wear; he vowed that with less work she could earn better, and would not be laying the foundation for a life of misery and ill-health as she was then doing. It was believed that little Mary would never have thought of such a thing as that she was imposed upon if this young gentleman had not suggested it, and that he only wanted to win her for some selfish purpose of his own; so he was forbidden the house, and little Mary could think of no other means of avenging her wrong than to at once receive the attentions of young Blake, whom her mother pronounced a most eligible match, for he had money, plenty of it. So little Mary then had servants of her own to sew for, a house to care for, guests to entertain, and yet did most of the sewing for her mother's family, which was smaller of course, and for the brothers' wives and children, and found time to help her neighbors. Her husband was a generous man, fond of company, as all those good old Virginians are to this day, and nothing pleased him better than to have a house full of young folks around. His wife's cares he lightened by adding now and then another servant; but as time went on the love of company took him from home, and from the innocent pleasures of home and company he sought the gaming table and more exciting scenes.

Then little Mary's sorrow began indeed. This was when Salome was a very young child. Petted, praised, spoiled, and neglected by turns, she grew up among the changing crowds of visitors which filled her father's house until she was sent away to school. She was delicate and nervous, but like her mother a worker, though in a different line. Her mother had taught her to sew and thus relieve her in some measure; no other child wore such beautiful clothing as Salome; handsomely embroidered merinos, lawns, and swiss; all of her mother's work with now and then a piece from her own deft hands. Salome loved her mother. She was a tender-hearted, impressionable child, whose heart threw out its tendrils in all directions for love and sympathy. Her mother's expression of love was in her work—in the beautiful clothes, so faultless in fit and workmanship, so exquisite in their dainty frills and almost priceless embroidery. Sometimes 'the child was ill; the mother's love shone forth then in tenderness and untiring care, so that the little one almost enjoyed her pains soothed by the presence of her beautiful mother. She was timid and did not like to mingle with children in general at school, so she drew to herself, by a peculiar magnetism of her own, what she believed to be a true heart now and then and loved it with a worshipping idolatry until she was disappointed in it by some act of slight or rudeness too plain to be mistaken. It took her a long time to understand that her pretty clothes, her liberal allowance of pin-money, attracted some and turned others from her in jealous rage; but when she did learn the lesson she shrank within herself, fell to work with her books to study or to read things scarcely wholesome for so impressionable a nature, too much inclined to dreamy sentimentalism already. She loved and would have been demonstrative to the last degree to one who loved her unselfishly; but she found no such love. If she won a prize in school she was praised and given presents, when a caress or words of love would have fed her starving heart to satisfaction. If she made some childish mistake she was scolded or punished with unwonted severity. She was looked upon as precocious beyond her years, while in truth she was immature in many things. While she stood at the head of her class among boys and girls many years her senior, she was as ignorant of things in which they were already graduated, as her little sister at her mother's knee. Love; love for somebody, something; she had wasted more love on her beautiful wax doll in one lonely hour than had ever been shown to her in all her life. She had poured out in gushing, fervent kisses, and in the tender twining of her poor little bony arms about her baby sister, more love than she perhaps would ever know in this world, live she never so long. She had hung upon a word of praise spoken by her mother's lips longer than any lover would ever dwell upon any avowal of hers. Her mother would sometimes say: "Kissing love does not amount to much; if you love me prove it by being a truthful, honest, industrious child, and then we can dispense with the hugs and kisses." Her mother had not wholly neglected her soul; she had taught her the Lord's prayer and the first chapters of St. John, and from her old nurse she had learned "Now I lay me down to sleep." These Salome repeated every night as she lay upon her little bed. and the sound of merry. grown people's voices floated through the open windows. In those days children were taught to be seen and not heard, and truth was, then as to-day, that when children are not heard they are seldom seen by the class of pleasure-seekers that filled Mr. Blake's house. Therefore it was best after having her supper, consisting of anything she chose, to seek her little bed. But Salome could not always sleep, and it happened frequently that she lay looking up at the sky and wondering about strange things, among others if she was always to live here, in this very same place, and see these same people. She wanted to go away to school and be a great lady and a clever one, for even into that tiny breast crept the spark of ambition that years of sorrow, neglected love, and disappointment fanned into a flame. It was a laudable ambition at first, a wish to be good as well as great, and a visit to a theatre at this time perhaps was the decisive point in Salome's young life. Her father had promised her such a treat. The actress was the reigning star of that period, and the play was one which took hold upon the impressionable child with great and lasting force. It never left her. She would be an actress; she avowed the intention to her horrified grandmother, who scolded Mr. Blake, as only a mother-in-law can scold; he responded with a mocking laugh that could only emanate from an obdurate son-in-law, that Salome should choose her own career, and that of an actress would please him above all others.

Little Mary loved her children, loved her home, and gave that love expression through her untiring energy. Now we may condemn her that she did not manifest it in caresses. Did she have the time? There is a limit to the endurance of every human being's strength; we condemn the society woman for neglect of her children; when we think of the demands made upon her, by herself as well as by others, how can we blame her for having no more time to give to her children than to her own soul; both must go neglected or be cared for by others.

Mr. Blake became a confirmed drunkard while Salome was still a child, and she had grown up in an atmosphere hateful, revolting to the delicate, sensitive nature she inherited from her mother. Liquor had almost brutalized her father; he became coarse, profane, almost cruel to his wife and children, and what she had suffered through shame, fear, and mortification, God only knew. All her sympathy was for her mother, all her love. She would gladly have seen them separated, but little Mary was of the olden type that had a horror of divorce. Oh, no, she might be disgraced by her husband's conduct but not by herself. Seeing all hope cut off in that direction, Salome resolved to get away from home and every hateful memory of it. Alas for Salome!

(To be continued.)

THE VALLEY PATH.

A Novel of Tennessee Life.

BY WILL ALLEN DROMGOOLE.

CHAPTER VIII.

The patient was asleep and Alicia busy putting things to rights in the shed room, when Joe tapped against the window. Carefully she opened the door to admit him, and drew back, laughing noiselessly at the figure he presented. His arms were filled with hickory sticks he had cut in the forest; his very chin was invisible; only a mass of tawny hair, a slouch, and a pair of restless blue eyes appeared above the "lumber pile."

"I fetched you up an armful of wood," said he. "I'll pile it back here by the fireplace handy for you. I reckin it won't come amiss in the mornin', nohow."

"Set it down careful, Joe," said Lissy, "so's not to disturb Mis' Tucker. It was certainly thoughtful of you to fetch it up for—Lucy Ann."

"Lucy Ann be"——

"Heish," laughed Lissy, nodding toward the sick room.

"Waal," said Joe, "I didn't fetch it for *her*, though I knew in reason she'd use it. I reckin I'd better take the pail and run down to the spring for some water. It's goin' to be mighty dark outside, an' toler'ble cold. Yes, I lay I'll fetch a pail o' water—for Lucy Ann."

Alicia left the dishes she was arranging on some shelves and came and stood by him resting her hand lightly upon his sleeve.

"You're mighty good, Joe," she said, "an' mighty thoughtful o' others."

He looked down into the pretty uplifted face so near his shoulder. It was very pleasant to have the face there—very pleasant.

"I'm a-feard it's only you I'm thinkin' of, Lissy," he admitted. "A feller don't deserve much praise for tryin' to pleasure the girl he loves, I reckin. But"—he hesitated; it was pleasant to hear from Alicia's pretty mouth that he was "good"; he would like her to say it again, to have her think it always; but his natural honesty spurned the deceit. "Shucks!" he said, "I ain't 'good.' You know I'm the biggest sinner on this earth, maybe in Georgy, too. Ask old mealy-mouth if you misdoubt it,—he'll tell you, Brother Barry will. Shucks! I say I'd ruther be a sinner o' the deepest dye 'an ter be like him: he's the darndest"——

She laid her hand lightly upon his lips:

"Heish!" The laughter in her eyes belied the sternness in her voice. "You're mighty wicked, that's certain; and I ain't any better. I reckin we're about give over to Satan alike—me and you, and Doctor Borin', too."

There was a momentary flash in the eyes fixed upon her. If she saw it, it was gone so quickly she doubted it had been there; his voice was friendly enough when he asked quietly:

"Has he been here, the mad doctor?"

"Why, I went after him," she replied, "and he wasn't there, but he come up and fixed a plaster out o' mustard, and mixed somethin' in a teacup, for Mrs. Tucker to swallow; and then he went home again. O Joe, I just wish you could hear him say—" she glanced over her shoulder, drew closer to his side, and put her lips to his ear—" 'Hell!' when things don't go to pleasure him."

"I heard him say a hornet sting ware erysip'las," said Joe, mollified by the nearness of her face, "an' if I rickerlict right hit ware me as said 'Hell' that time."

"I'll be boun' it was," said Alicia. "When compliments o' that kind air passin' I'll be boun' you'll get in a say. What's become o' the pail o' water, Joe? I reckin I'll need it about knockin' up somethin' for Lucy Ann and Bob to eat, 'gainst they get here."

"Plumb forgot it," said Joe. "But I'll go now, if I can get my own consent ter tear myse'f away ter the spring an' leave you a-standin' here by yourse'f when I might be a-standin' with you."

She glanced up with sudden inspiration.

"Why, Joe," she said, "I'll go with you. Wait till I peep at Mrs. Tucker."

She drew the covers gently about the sleeper, noiselessly laid a stick of wood on the fire, and as noiselessly slipped back to Joe, the cedar water bucket in one hand, her old shawl in the other.

"I'll have to hurry back and get you a mouthful to eat," she said, as they started briskly off together.

"Don't you be worryin' about me," said Joe. "I come over here ter he'p you, not to be makin' of more work for you-uns;

I can jest as well wait till the rest have their supper as not, an' waitin' will make less work for you, Lissy. My! this gate *is* a bother; I'll come over ter-morrer an' mend it if the Lord spares me, seein' as that lazy Bob won't. Now then! see who'll git ter the spring first."

They swung the bucket between them, and started off, like two children, in the crisp, cold air, down the road to the spring under the bluff's side. It was a short run, for there was no moon and the stars were straggling in the west, clouds were gathering, and when they turned off the road into the footpath, the way was too narrow and the rattling dead undergrowth too close and thick, for further racing. They tarried but a moment, for the night was cold; yet they returned slowly, and their talk was serious, their voices low, as if that had been said at the spring under the bluff which had touched the stronger chords and awakened the deeper feelings of the heart. In his right hand Joe carried the bucket; his left lay upon his heart, and Lissy's right slipped through his arm was snugly folded within it.

"I'm a comin' sometime, *sometime*," she was saying, "just as soon as they can spare me. When you talk about the little chickens and the lambs, and the cows waitin' to be milked, I want to go real bad, and he'p you with 'em, Joe. I like little chickens; and I never hear a lamb bleat but I want to pick it up in my arms and rock it to sleep. But"——

She hesitated, and resting her head against his arm sighed.

"Do as you see best, Lissy," said Joe. "I'm a-tryin' not ter worry you. But it do seem to me as you air mighty give ter puttin' off."

"I know it," she admitted. "I know it, Joe. Granny's tellin' me about that constant; and Brother Barry."

"Oh, damn Brother Barry! What's old mealy-mouth got ter do with you-uns? I know I do despise the groun' he tromps on. An' I tell you now, Lissy, I ruther hear that ole sinner down yander, the mad doctor, as don't know heaven from hornet—I'd ruther hear him draw his breath in and shet his teeth, an' say one good honest 'Hell!' like he says it, as to hear Brother Barry hallaluyahin' for a month. Thar's more religion in it, ter *my* notion. An' ther' aint no sneak about him, nuther. He's ready ter own up, fair and square, if a feller gits the best of him. Why, he told it all over the mount'n about that hornet-sting joke —told it up ter S'wanee even; let on he ware plumb sold.

It was only a little runt of a joke anyhow, but blamed if
he didn't stan' up ter it like a man."

"I reckin we're all mighty wicked," said Lissy, ignoring
the bringing of the doctor into the conversation; "but
somehow I can't bring myse'f to think like Brother Barry.
I can't make God out to be as brother Barry makes Him.
He preached to the people over at Goshen last fall that
God killed Ike Jordan last September, because Ike drove
his sheep up the mountain on Sunday. Everybody knew
the lightnin' struck him when he was bringin' Mrs. Tucker's
warpin' bars home for her, because she wasn't able to go
down to Pelham to get 'em, and there was nobody else at
home to go, unless it was Lucy Ann's baby that hadn't
learned to walk yet. And he told at Jim Tyler's funeral
last spring that the Lord had need of Jim and took him
home. I'm a-thinkin' as there must be a mighty dearth
of hands in heaven if such a no-'count as Jim Tyler was
needed to fill out. Truth is, Jim fell off the bluff when he
was drunk and broke his own neck after gettin' lost goin'
home from Tracy. He was a professin' member, however,
and so maybe his sprees were overlooked, and he really
had a call to come up higher.

"I'm a sinner—I can't set myse'f up in judgment. Though
it always seemed to me as there ought to be, as there *must*
be, some better way o' savin' folks than by threat'nin' of
'em, an' killin' 'em off with lightnin' and such. Seems like
it ain't right: it makes God most like a—wild beast. I
reckin that's why I can't love Him; I'm 'fraid of Him. An'
I won't be druv—I can't. But I would truly like to know,
for certain; I'd like to know what be the truth. Sometimes
I almost get my own consent to ask Doctor Borin' to tell
me."

The arm upon which her hand rested gave a sudden jerk;
the owner of it stood free of her, and although it was too
dark for her to see his face she understood that Joe was
angry; the jealousy that had been brooding in his heart
suddenly burst forth.

"Do!" he exclaimed, "do ask him; he knows; he knows
ever'thing. He's smart—he's smart as God, I reckin; since
he knows the plan o' salvation so peart. Keeps it corked
up like he does his doctor stuff, in a bottle, I reckin. Oh,
yes! go ask the mad doctor to save yo' soul; he can do it.
He'd like mighty well to have you saaft-so'derin' him like
the *sisters* saaft-so'der Brother Barry. An' it ain't so clear
ter my mind but you'd enjoy it 'bout as much as old
erysip'las would."

"Joe Bowen!"

Her voice was full of surprise, indignation, shame. Had he been calmer, more himself, he would have known that he alone had suggested Doctor Boring as something more than the truly benevolent friend, the lonely old man, the thoroughly good physician. He would have detected in her simple, startled exclamation, her inability to find words with which to deny his unseemly charge, the very first intimation of the doctor's regard for her that had ever so much as hinted itself to her unsuspecting heart. But he was too angry to see anything, or to heed what he did or said.

"Oh, I know you, Lissy," he broke out fiercely. "You're mighty careful not ter set a day for marryin' me; I'll lay you wouldn't find it so hard ter fix a time for marryin' him, if he asks you. I know you. It's all mighty well ter be runnin' over the mount'n nussin' of the sick, as ain't no manner o' kin ter you, an' got no manner o' claim, when you know *he'll* be thar, ter pass complimints over you, an' send you off ter breakfast at *his* house, ridin' *his* horse. An' happen he ain't thar you must up an' *sen'* for him ter *mix mustard*, an' dose out *qui-nine*, an' do a lot o' rubbish as ain't got neither sense nor savin' in it. Darn his hide! if he don't leave this valley I'll shoot him. An' you may tell him so with my complimints. Shucks! it's easy as eatin' ter see he's in love with you."

They had reached the door of the shed room; Lissy stood with her hand upon the latch-string, afraid to draw it lest the loud, angry voice disturb the sick woman in the next room. Yet she was terribly angry; angry enough to go in at that door and leave him there on the outside, and on the outside of her life forever. She had made no reply to his outbreak other than the simple exclamation of surprise. While she stood there, waiting until he should finish his tirade, she heard Mrs. Tucker calling to her to come in: "she wanted her special."

"Mrs. Tucker's 'wake and wantin' me," she said quietly. "Good night, Joe. You can leave the pail outside, I sha'n't need it." And giving the latch-string a pull, she went in and left him there in the darkness, with the door shut fast between them.

He had planted a thought in her heart which might never be cast out; had accomplished that which of all things he would not have done. He had awakened her wonder, drawn for her a comparison between himself and the man sleeping at that moment the sleep of one who feels that he has met a burden and lifted it,—he had lifted many burdens for the poor, the last for the old woman to whose need he had responded at the sacrifice of his own comfort and inclinations. Joe, too, had offered his shoulder to the burden; but ah, the difference of motives. He admitted that difference to his own heart as he rode through the valley toward his home. But he was ungenerous enough to hope that Alicia would not see it in the same light.

But Alicia scarcely thought of him. At another time, girl-like, she would have sat down and cried over the ruin of her pretty dream; but now, having explained to Mrs. Tucker that Joe had "got mad and gone home," and having given her the medicine as she had been instructed to give it, and having seen her patient drop into a gentle slumber, Alicia went back to the shed room, made a pot of coffee for Lucy Ann and Jim, and otherwise proceeded to "have things ready 'gainst their comin'."

But that night when her work was done and the pretty head lay upon its pillow in Mrs. Tucker's close little rafter room, sleep, heretofore so easily wooed, refused to come. Still, her thoughts were not of Joe, so much as of Joe's words. *Did* the doctor care for her? She felt the red creep to her temples. She had never thought of such a thing; but now—since Joe had thought for her—his touch had been always gentle, his voice kind; he had always a smile for her. "And he was so good, he never went off at a tangent and railed out upon folks. If he loved a woman, and knew someone else loved her better, he would close his lips for all words but the very kindest. He would never fault a girl because someone else found her good and pretty."

And although no word was spoken, Joe lost by the comparison.

"It did look bad, perhaps, her always meeting him when there was sickness; but she had always helped this way. Most of the neighbors did who had nothing to prevent. Still, it did look bad; she had never thought of it before, but now that she did think, it looked decidedly queer. She would not do it again. Doctor Boring might think bad of it his own self—might think she was trying to meet him. And she wouldn't go over there as free as she had been going; he might think bad of that. But no: he was good; had sense; he was too good to think bad of anybody. And he liked her to come, ordered eggs just to make her come —perhaps." And with a smile upon her lips, as if the thought might be not altogether unpleasant, Alicia fell asleep.

CHAPTER IX.

There was trouble in the wind. The old trust and quiet sense of oneness that had existed between Joe and Lissy had received a shock. As the weeks went by and the quarrel was not made up, Joe began to grow sullen and morose. He had never known Lissy as she appeared to him during those weeks. Light, gay, careless, she seemed to care no more for his anger than she cared for his suffering. He had expected to teach her a lesson, to force her to sue for forgiveness; failing in that, he sought to play upon her tenderness, to reach her by his own sadness and regret.

His first call after the rupture was ostensibly upon the old people. He brought a turn of corn to the mill, and while waiting "allowed he'd step up ter the house an' see how granny was comin' on."

Lissy saw him coming up the mill path and, blushing, rose to receive him. After all, she liked Joe, and regretted the quarrel; had he asked her to do so, at that moment of surprise and pleasure, she might have received him again into her trust and affection.

But he merely gave her a careless "Howdy, Lissy," and asked to see her grandmother.

The next time he called she was careful to meet him at the door, and, calling to her grandmother that he was there, went quietly on making her preparations for carrying some fresh butter to the boarding house on the mountain. He had the chagrin of seeing her adjust the red felt upon her head with more than her usual care; she even tied a bit of bright ribbon into her hair; he noticed how perfectly the red adornment blended with the color in her cheek; and he noticed, in the same mirror that had reflected the laughing girlish face, his own hollow eyes that told the story of sleepless nights and weary vigils. She made no apology for leaving; on the contrary she tossed him an offhand defiance by calling to Al to bring her the basket of eggs for Doctor Boring.

"I'll stop as I go by, and see if anybody's sick and needin' me," she said. "I'm gettin' my hand out since Mrs. Tucker got up and about. Though I'm glad she's well, goodness knows. Well an' singin' the praises of the mad doctor like the woods afire."

Granny unconsciously added fuel to the flame jealousy had kindled:

"Though she's a wonderin' some whar the pay air ter come from, for the powders an' stuff he give her. It do

beat my time, the hold the infidel air gittin' on the valley.
He even tol' Lissy thar as he'd make his nigger plow her
gyarden an' plant it in the spring. Servin' ter destruction,
I tell Lissy, but seems like her an' her grandad can't see
it so."

Joe could do nothing but see her go off with that contented look upon her face, and a basket on either arm.

But his visit lost its flavor when she was gone; he had
exhausted himself upon the new colt he had bought and
meant to "break ter a side saddle," before Alicia left; the
horse was mean and valueless enough when it dawned upon
him that the rider he had intended should occupy that
same side saddle might never mount it after all—might
marry the mad doctor, just to spite *him;* for it never occurred to him that she could love the man old enough to
be her father. Still she might marry him; women were
guilty of very foolish acts sometimes, and Lissy was a
woman. So he reasoned, and the more he reasoned the
more angry he became; until, unable to sit tamely there
with the knowledge that she was at that moment at his
rival's house, sitting opposite him at the fire perhaps, with
that same motherly sweetness in her face that had been
there when she spoke of rocking the little lambs to sleep in
her arms, he got up, said good by, and struck out across
the mountain. He meant to meet her somewhere upon the
way, or to wait for her if she tarried, and to have it out
with her. They must either "make it up" or "fight it out,"
he declared; meaning that she was to understand that she
couldn't play fast and loose with him.

By the time he reached Mrs. Tucker's cabin his anger
had cooled somewhat; he was quite willing to make up.
If Alicia would agree to marry him without further "foolishness," or would even "fix a day," however distant, he
would let "bygones be bygones and say no more about it."
So he hung about, talking to old Mrs. Tucker, and inwardly
fretting because Alicia tarried at the doctor's.

When at last she did come she would have passed him
without a word, without so much as a nod of recognition,
but that he went down the road a little distance to meet
her. Then when her eyes were lifted to his he saw that
she had been weeping; the lids were instantly dropped,
refusing to meet his.

Old Mrs. Tucker from her window could see, without hearing what was said, that Joe was angry. She saw, too, that
which Joe failed to see—that Alicia was not feigning indifference.

As they drew nearer her sharp old ears caught a threat the jealous young lover let fall; not the whole of it, but enough to convince her that the doctor was in danger of his life.

"Land o' mercy," she exclaimed. "Air Joe Bowen drunk? Or air he out of his head? *Or* air he just a nat'ral fool? Jealous of the mad doctor! Well, I'll be beat. What air we-all a comin' ter, I wonder. Thar! if Lissy ain't comin' in, an' just leavin' him ter preach ter the gate post an' the horse block. I don't wonder. I ain't forgot how he talked that night I ware so sick, an' I called the child in so's he couldn't jaw the life out of her,—though he didn't know I heard his threatn'n', an' no more did Lissy."

How easy it would have been to set him right; yet Alicia refused to speak the consent he asked, or to explain her tears and agitation. She had meant to tell him, to be kind to him; but he had given her no opportunity; now she said "He might go."

She gave Mrs. Tucker a quiet "Good mornin'," and as that woman wisely refrained from speaking of the quarrel it was not mentioned.

After awhile she said "Good mornin'" again, and went back down the mountain, home, and sent Al to carry the butter to Sewanee. Once alone in her own little room with its white naked walls and muslin curtains, Alicia buried her face in the pillows of her bed and burst into tears. For the moment, Joe became dear; the sense of loss made him so. But the next day she went about her duties as usual; the storm had passed. Of his threats she had little fear. She had known him a long time, almost all her life, and she had never known him do a cowardly or an unprincipled thing.

Mrs. Tucker, however, was not so sure of him. No sooner had Alicia gone home than the old woman tied the strings of her black sunbonnet under her chin and went down the mountain. She did not, however, follow the footpath leading to the physician's house from the rear, but took the little trail to the right which would cross the "big road" at a point where she knew he often walked mornings, going as far sometimes as Pelham Creek.

When she reached the top of a little bluff where there was a clearing she, saw him coming down the road, flecking with his cane at the long dry grasses either side. His head was dropped forward in the attitude of one lost in thought. And indeed he had abundant cause for meditation; he was half tempted to close his house and go back to the city, as his first plan had been, and remain there until summer. Joe Bowen was beginning to annoy him considerably. He had been disappointed in Bowen; he had not been the friend a first acquaintance with him had promised. Of late, indeed, he had been quite unfriendly; had displayed a touch of meanness even, in shooting a fine colt of the doctor's that had broken out, and found a way into Joe's pasture.

"I ought to sue him and make him pay for it," said the doctor, "and I would only that I believe he is trying to provoke me into a quarrel."

Since the killing of the colt, that sense of littleness, the sure effect of a cowardly deed, had kept him at a distance. What had he done, he wondered, to so arouse the animosity of the young fellow? If he had wronged him he was more than willing to make atonement if he only knew wherein the wrong consisted.

He was soon to be enlightened; the enlightenment, or the bearer of it, was calling and signalling from the bluff above the roadside.

"Doctor Borin'," she called, "O Doctor Borin'! wait thar a minute if you please, Doctor Borin'; I am comin' down by the path to speak ter you-uns."

Nothing loath, he seated himself upon a great gray boulder at the foot of the bluff and waited, while Mrs. Tucker ran down the path to meet him.

She stood before him at last, breathless, panting, and although she made an effort to disguise it he saw that she was excited.

"Doctor Borin'," she said, "I want ter have a settlemint with you-uns, for doctorin' of me whenst I ware took sick last month. I want a settlemint."

Accustomed to humanity in many phases, he saw at once that she was manœuvring.

"A settlement?" he replied. "Well, bring me half a dozen chickens. I'm not going to skip the country yet and I don't believe you are."

The worried expression in her face did not leave it, as she said, "Doctor Borin', you air a good man; you have been mighty clever ter me an' mine."

"Much obliged, madam," said the doctor, a twinkle in his eyes. But she gave no heed to the interruption.

"I wish you well, Doctor Borin'; I ud' hate mighty if anything ware ter happen to you-uns."

"Well," he said, "am I in any danger, Mrs. Tucker?"

The amusement left his face; an expression of annoyance came in its place.

"Yes, Doctor Borin', I'm afeard you air. Leastways—
won't you take t'other path home? I ain't a-sayin' anybody
ud be mean enough or sneak enough or coward enough ter
hurt you unbeknownst. But I wish't you'd take the
mount'n path home, 'stid o' the valley path."

Her solicitude touched him keenly. But there was no
coward taint in his blood; the man who had braved creeds,
religious and social ostracism, was not the man to quail
before a physical danger. He hesitated, but only in order
to shape his language into a form not to wound her.

"Neither shall I," he said, "be small enough or weak
enough or coward enough to turn my back to a hidden danger. Madam, no coward ever sees the old doctor's heels!"

"Then won't you go, t'other way I mean, for me? Jest
ter pleasure an ole woman who air obligated ter yer, an'
who wishes you well?"

She laid her hard old hand upon his sleeve; in the faded
eyes tears were starting; the thin lips twitched in a way
that was almost painful to witness. Watching her, there
stirred in his heart a feeling which had slumbered for years.
Before him, between the yellow old face and his own, another face arose, his mother's; gentle, wistful, the tears
in the sad fathomless eyes, the white lips a-quiver with
pain as they pleaded with him to renounce his "heresies"
for *her* sake. He had tried, for her sake, and had failed;
but for her sake he would "pleasure" this humble old woman
who had come to him in his mother's stead.

"Well, well," he said, "if it will be any gratification to
you I will take the path down the mountain and go home
by the back way. But you must know that I am not afraid
of dangers that hide in the bush, because I am not afraid
of death; it is life that makes cowards of men, not death.
I hope you are not going to ask me to put on your sunbonnet."

He was laughing again, as he walked by her side, up the
mountain to a point where her path met the path leading
to his cabin.

"Naw, sir, I sha'n't ask you to do that," she replied; "but
Doctor Borin', if you meet Lissy Reams on the way, I wish't
you wouldn't stop ter talk ter her."

He gathered himself together, looked her full in the eye,
and said, "Hell!"

"I knowed that ware just what you would say. But I wish
you would mind what *I* say. I'm goin' up this way now;
I'll come down an' fetch the chickens to-morrer, maybe this
evenin'; good day, Doctor Borin'."

Her black sunbonnet appeared now and then, bobbing above the laurel where her path wound among the short stunted growth. He watched it a moment, the tail flapping in the breeze like the wings of a great crow about to alight among the bushes. Then he turned and went slowly down the mountain. He forget the wrinkled old face under the sunbonnet's shade; to his vision appeared only the sublimity of gratitude, in an earnest, simple heart. She had tramped all that distance to warn him of a fancied, perhaps a possible, danger.

When she had eaten her dinner she caught six of her best young pullets, and, tying their legs securely with strips of old cotton, set off down the mountain again. All her fears were reawakened. She had seen Joe ride by with a rifle flung across the saddle bow.

How he laughed at her, the odd, death-defying old man.

"Why, my good woman," he said, "I am no more afraid of Joe Bowen than I am of you. He will never shoot me, don't you believe it; not if I can get a word with him before he pulls the trigger. If he does he will have to shoot me in the back, and Joe Bowen isn't a coward, whatever may be his faults."

"He's crazy," she insisted. "He's ravin' mad, a-thinkin' as how you-uns air tryin' ter keep company with Lissy Reams. I told him myself that he was a fool, an' little better than a idiot, ter s'pose you ware thinkin' o' that chil'. An' you ole enough ter be her gran'father, a-mighty nigh."

He colored, and dropped his eyes; the folly of his thought had been brought home to him many times during the day. Strange he had not seen it himself. Yet if he chose—that pure, wax-like nature——

He put the temptation aside; he would put a thorn in no man's content.

"You are very good to think of me," he said. "And Joe is very foolish to hold such ideas. Yes, I am an old man —an old man. Old enough to be her father; yes, quite so, quite so."

He had forgotten her presence, and sat with his head dropped forward, and his eyes fixed upon the fire. The vibrant clearness of her voice when she spoke again, quite startled him. "Can't we have a settlemint now, Doctor Borin'?"

He glanced up quickly:

"Bring me another half dozen chickens," he said.

He sat there long after she had gone, his head drooped upon his breast, his eyes fixed upon the glowing coal bed.

The gold of the afternoon faded; the gray twilight set in, and then the night, starlit and cold. Ephraim came in and built up the fire, but the physician did not stir. At last old Dilce called him to supper, and he got up, exchanging without thought his coat for the purple dressing gown.

As he stood before the mantel he caught a glimpse of his face in the little mirror above it. His head had never looked so white, his eyes so wearily heavy. "Old enough to be her father," he murmured, resting a moment against the mantel.

"De supper am gittin' col', marster."

"Yes, yes, I am coming. I forgot all about it, I am afraid." Then softly, "An old man; old enough to be her father; quite so, quite so."

Yet he remembered that she had said, "You don't appear to be so old."

(To be continued.)

THE WONDERFUL CITY.

BY EMMA GHENT CURTIS.

Have you heard of the tale of Alvarez
  Of the city he found in the wild,
Where Mexico's mountains climb highest
  In masses forbiddingly piled?
He tells us that this city's pavements
  Have never by white men been trod,
And that in a tall teocatli
  Men still worship Gautemozin's god.

They drove him away from the city,
  For they dreaded the white man's sway;
And the path was lost on the mountains
  As night is forgotten in day.
So Alvarez can tell us no story
  Of this people secluded and lone,
Who laugh at intending invaders
  In their natural fortress of stone.

But I wonder, when thoughts of this city,
  Crowd into and dwell in my mind,
Whether its rulers and wise men
  Are great and observing, or blind.
I wonder if its little children
  In hunger and pain droop and die,
All unpitied by fortune's lieutenants
  Who heed no unfortunate's cry.

Has it shops, this mysterious city,
  Where from dawn until star-bedecked night,
Pale girls droop like sun-withered flowers
  Crushed down by the fierce heel of might?
Has it mills, where the swift turning spindles
  Hold many a wight's thread of life?
Has it mines where men's souls are buried
  In greed's awful and pitiless strife?

Are the blessings of life in this city
  Given o'er to the homes of the few?
Are the doors of its dungeons closed tightly
  On the noble, the fearless and true?
Are its workingmen sunk in dejection?
  Are its lawmakers cruel and stern?
Are its women compelled to grovel in shame
  The means of existence to earn?

Or is it the oft-sung Elysium
  Where love is from interest free;
Where noble works earn not contumely,
  And where Right need not cower or flee?
Are its citizens strong, fearless freemen
  Who refuse the slave's collar to wear?
Are its poets and singers such minstrels
  As to sing the truth valiantly dare?

If the latter is true, O strange City,
  Then happy we know are your days,
And gladsome and blithe are your children.
  And kind seems the god that you praise.
But if the former conditions
  Have into your midst been hurled,
Then wide fling your gates; you are only
  A part of the great unjust world!

BOOKS OF THE DAY.

THE CENTURY OF SIR THOMAS MORE.*

REVIEWED BY MARGARET CONNOLLY.

Emerson says that, properly speaking, there is no history, only biography; and in "The Century of Sir Thomas More," the latest and most brilliant work of that versatile and prolific writer, B. O. Flower, this will be, to a large extent, verified to the thoughtful reader. In writing a review of this work for the pages of the ARENA it were superfluous to dwell on the personality of its author, already so well known to readers of this magazine by his soul-stirring and inspiring words in the articles, essays, and editorials which, month after month, pour from his pen, which seems, verily, to be touched with fire from heaven in its tireless energy for the cause of humanity and a higher and nobler civilization.

Every age has its heroes, its great men—poets, prophets, sages, saints—the men whom that age needs as pioneers in the vanguard of progress; for as it is with the individual, so it is with nations: to stand still is to retrograde; we must either progress or deteriorate, and it is only by holding the torchlight up to the past, profiting by the experience of those who have gone before, drawing inspiration from the noblest and best that it has to give us, while avoiding its errors and excesses, that we can take another step forward in the evolution of the race. And in tracing the events of this most momentous epoch in the history of modern civilization, 1450–1550, in bringing out its lights and shades, passing in review before us the colossal figures who have left their mark for good or ill on its pages, Mr. Flower has accomplished a work which is destined to be a factor of immense value in the further enlightenment and progress of this our century, so fruitful in scientific discovery, in invention, and in research along every line of thought. Indeed, "The Century of Sir Thomas More" is no mere record of historical facts, to be coolly read over and stored away in the memory, cataloguing important events chronologically, and religiously remembering dates for future reference. It is a work palpitating, throbbing with human interest; it carries us back to this wonderful century; we live in it; we forget we are reading history; it is a great drama enacted before us, so vividly and impressively are the commanding personalities and the important and far-reaching events of this marvellous age brought

" * The Century of Sir Thomas More," by B. O. Flower. Cloth, pp 293; illustrated with numerous portraits; price $1.50. Arena Publishing Company, Boston.

before us. The object of the work is to arouse the thoughtful to an appreciation of the importance of the many-sided crisis through which civilization is now passing, on the ethical, the moral, and the spiritual planes; to point out the marked similarity of the century of Sir Thomas More to our own, and to show how gloriously the nineteenth century may enrich itself if it will only profit by the example of the sixteenth century, and so make this one of the proudest and most exalted periods in the annals of time.

The volume is divided into thirteen chapters with the following suggestive titles: Western Europe during the Century of Which We Write, 1450-1550—The Reformation and Some of Its Leading Spirits—A General Survey of the Italian Peninsula during the Renaissance—Some Fatal Figures of the Italian Renaissance—Some Bright Lights of the Italian Renaissance—The Spanish Peninsula during the Century of Sir Thomas More—The France of this Period —The England of Sir Thomas More—The Life of Sir Thomas More— The Utopia of Sir Thomas More, Part I—The Utopia of Sir Thomas More, Part II—Historical Parallels Presented by the Lives of Seneca and Sir Thomas More—A Survey of the First Century of Modern Times.

The book opens with an Introductory Note, in which Mr. Flower describes in the following terse and cogent sentences the century of More and the conditions which mark our own at the present time:

It [the century of More] was a period of transition, when civilization passed with pain and anguish from an outgrown order to a freer state; and the battle which was waged during that century is, to a great extent, being fought by us at the present time. We, to-day, are in the midst of a struggle much the same as that which marked the century of More; the same velvet-tongued sophistry is heard now from scholarly special pleaders for the old order as was heard in that elder time. For gold, fame, and the praise of the powerful the prophets of conventionalism are actively endeavoring to lull to sleep the newly awakened conscience of civilization. But the struggle has gone too far; the forces of the new time are too numerous and too powerful to be beaten back. A new social order is inevitable.

Then follows a brief but lucid sketch of the conditions prevailing in Western Europe during this time, which, in the author's brilliant characterization, was

an epoch of unrest and growth, of dazzling surprises and momentous achievements. It was an era of exit and entrance, witnessing at once the eventide of the Middle Ages and the dawning of modern times; a century in which the glory of former ages seemed to flood the receptive vision of chosen spirits, revealing at once the beauty of the past and unveiling new heights of attainment and nobler ideals than the preceding ages had conceived. This century broadened and deepened the ethical and spiritual impulses of the German and Anglo-Saxon peoples; it crowned Italy with immortal glory in the realm of art; it gave to Spain the sceptre of Western domain; it brought forth Colet, Erasmus, Sir Thomas More, Savonarola, Luther,

Calvin, Zwingli, Knox and Melanchthon; it was the age of Angelo, Titian, Correggio, Da Vinci, and Raphael. During this period Columbus gave to Europe a new world, and Copernicus revealed a new heaven.

Mr. Flower points out how the general awakening of this century affected the different nations; how the peoples north of the Alps, especially the German and English races, were affected on the ethical, religious, and philosophical side, while south of the Alps art or the æsthetic nature was appealed to, and "All for beauty" became the dominant thought of Italy; to the westward, the awakening being more on the physical plane, man was actuated by the spirit of avarice, the greed of conquest, and the lust for gold, "which," he observes, "furnished the money for Columbus' expedition and which nerved the Portuguese to weather the Cape of Good Hope."

In this remarkable work, which is as notable for profound spirituality and loftiness of thought as it is for brilliant scholarship and intellectual and critical research, the author never loses an opportunity of arousing the soul to a consciousness of its own dignity and inculcating the fundamental principle of the divinity in man, as the following quotation will serve to illustrate. After rapidly reviewing the causes which led up to the Reformation, he thus describes its moral effect:

The Reformation demonstrated the essential heroism which dwells in the soul of man, whether he be peasant, priest, or noble. It held before the mind's eye of those who hungered for a higher life and an exemplification of religion purer than was to be found in the conventionalism of the day, an exalted though austere ideal which awakened a deep response, causing men, women, and children to sink all thoughts of present happiness, comfort, or even life, rather than yield what they believed to be the eternal truth. It illustrated anew the wonderful power which an idea or conviction may exert in transforming human lives. As though a trumpet-blast had called them to come up higher from a plane of sordid selfishness and license, or a condition of sodden hopelessness, a multitude of highborn souls in various European lands became living examples of a purer conception of religion. To the student of human nature nothing is more instructive than the constantly recurring illustration of the transforming power of ideas or ideals which appeal strongly to the imagination, and the Reformation furnishes a striking illustration of this truth, which when appreciated by civilization will render a redeemed humanity an assured fact instead of a persistent but elusive dream.

Brief sketches are given of the leading lights of the Reformation, but entering more into detail with the most prominent figures, Luther and Calvin, while we have impressive pen pictures of Erasmus and of that John the Baptist of the Reformation, the noble and godlike priest, statesman, prophet, martyr, Savonarola.

While every chapter abounds in suggestive lessons, perhaps the most suggestive and important for patriotic Americans and all lovers of the great republic and of republican institutions in general, is that dealing with the Italian peninsula during the Renaissance, in which is outlined the causes which led to the downfall of the three republics, Venice, Florence, and Milan, which at one time were the pride and glory of Italy. At the present time, when many of the causes which conspired to the ruin and enslavement of these states are existent among us, when the toiling masses of the United States are being crushed under the iron heel of wealth, and a small but powerful minority, dominated wholly by the lust for gold, seems to have complete ascendancy in the council halls of the nation, nay, even in her very institutions of learning, all lovers of liberty may well linger over this chapter and take to heart the warning it conveys. Equally suggestive is the history of the Medici family (chapter IV), because, in the author's own words,

it illustrates the manner in which the usurer class and the acquirers of wealth subvert liberty, trample upon justice, and, while maintaining the shell and name of free institutions, exercise a despotism as baleful in its influence over the masses as it is progressive in its character; a despotism which subtly advances step by step, through controlling the opinion-forming organs of society, and later by controlling legislation from behind the scenes, until the wealth-producers of a city, nation, or civilization become in reality, though not in name, the bond slaves of the acquirers and manipulators of unearned wealth.

The history of the Papal See, and the scandalous corruption of the church is touched upon; the life and writings of Machiavelli, that prince of conscienceless politicians; the growth of art in Italy, including short sketches of the life and work of some of her greatest artists and sculptors—Michael Angelo, Da Vinci, Correggio, Raphael, who with other bright geniuses of this period "wrought on canvas and in stone dreams and conceptions which made this period the golden age of art," and the startling contrasts which marked the Renaissance in Italy—the beauty and refinement, the coarseness and sensuality, the luxury and riotous profusion, the degradation and misery, are brought into bold relief. A graphic picture is drawn of the Spanish peninsula during this century, with its awakened appetite for gold and power, its blind religious dogmatism and fanatical persecutions, the fall of Grenada and the reëstablishment of the fatal Inquisition, the conquests of Cortez in Mexico, Columbus' discovery of the New World, and Magellan's circumnavigation of the globe. The France of this period is also reviewed, showing that while she was affected by the general awakening experienced in Germany, Italy, and Spain, she was not a leader in any direction; a very interesting sketch is given of the great satirist, Rabelais, one of the giant intellects of the age.

The most interesting portion of the volume, however, is devoted to a consideration of the life and work of one of the greatest of England's statesmen and philosophers, and of the England of his time. **After** a brief but comprehensive outline of the general political and **social** conditions in England at the time of Sir Thomas More's **entrance** upon active life, when the Hundred Years' War with **France had** just been ended and the War of the Roses had terminated **in the** overthrow of Richard III and the accession of Henry VII, **the author** observes:

Like all revolutionary or transition periods, it was a time characterized by wonderful activity, undaunted hope and far-reaching misery. . . . It was a period of unrest for the brain of man. Profound moral, spiritual, and intellectual agitation was visible everywhere. It was an age when daring ideas were conceived and great thoughts were born. It was this century which laid the solid foundation for the golden age of Elizabethan literature.

But, on the other hand, turning to a contemplation of the condition of the masses, he observes:

We find that for the poor man this century was essentially tragic. Feudalism, as has been intimated was rapidly giving place to a new social order, and as a result the retainers and the hosts of humble laborers who had long been a part of the feudal organism—depend. ents upon the various noble houses—were cast adrift. Large areas of farming lands were being turned into pastures for sheep, as wool growing was less expensive and more remunerative than farming. The very poor were the prey of the landlord and the capitalist.

How admirably does this last sentence describe the condition of the toiling millions in our own land to-day. This condition of things it was which called forth More's "Utopia," which Mr. Flower criticises in detail; and it may be said in passing that his admirable analysis of this wonderful work of the great English humanitarian will render it far more interesting and intelligible to many who may not yet have read it, and perhaps to many who have read it but may not have grasped its full import. The seeming incongruities and inconsistencies in the life and conduct of Sir Thomas More, its magnificently altruistic and progressive author, will also be made clear by his sympathetic and intuitive comprehension of the opposing influences which beset the great statesman, and which caused him on more than one occasion to run directly counter to the teachings of his immortal work, whose lessons, alas! are as much needed to-day as they were in that far less favored time. And well would it be for our nation if "The Century of Sir Thomas More" were to be made the "Utopia" of this century, and that its lofty teachings instead of falling on dull and unheeding ears, as did the teachings of Sir Thomas More three centuries ago, might kindle a flame which should never die until one more height had been gained, one more forward step taken in the march of humanity toward a diviner ideal. And, indeed, it is shame to the nineteenth century that with the experience of more than three centuries behind her and the key to the knowledge of the ages within her grasp she should still lag so far behind that if the spirit of Sir Thomas More were to come amongst us to-day he might imagine, that he had only fallen asleep for a short time and awakened in his own England, at least so far as the condition of the masses is concerned, as will be seen by the following quotation of Mr. Flower's from "Utopia":

The rich men not only by fraud, but also by common laws, do every day pluck away from the poor some part of their daily living. Therefore, when I consider all these commonwealths which nowadays do flourish. I can perceive nothing but a certain conspiracy of rich men procuring their own commodities under the name and title of the commonwealth. They invent and devise all means and crafts, first how to keep safely without fear of losing that which they have·unjustly gathered together, and next how to hire and abuse the work and labor for as little money as may be. These most wicked and vicious men by their insatiable covetousness divide among themselves those things which would have sufficed for all men.

And again, how vividly do these sentences of More's bring to our minds the condition of a large proportion of our agrarian population to-day:

Therefore, that one covetous and insatiable cormorant may compass about and enclose many thousand acres of ground together within one pale or hedge, the husbandmen be thrust out of their own, or else by cunning and fraud or by violent oppression they be put beside it, or by wrongs and injuries they be so wearied that they be compelled to sell all: by one means, therefore, or by another, by hook or by crook they must needs depart away, poor wretched souls, men, women, husbands, wives, fatherless, children, widows, and woeful mothers with their young babes. Away they trudge, out of their known and accustomed houses, finding no place to rest in. All their household stuff they are forced to sell for a pittance, and when they have wandered abroad till that is spent, what can they then do but steal and be hanged, or beg and be cast into prison as vagabonds because they work not when no man will give them work though they ever so willingly proffer themselves thereto? *Thus the unreasonable conclusion of a few hath turned that thing to the utter undoing of the island in the which thing the chief felicity of the realm did consist.*

Another point alluded to in "The Century of Sir Thomas More" will be of especial interest to students of occultism and those who are interested in psychical research, namely, the widespread interest which existed at that time of general intellectual awakening in the study of astrology and occult phenomena. Very suggestive are the quotations from "Utopia" in this connection.

It is impossible, however, to give any adequate idea of the profound significance and absorbing interest of that portion of the volume which treats of Sir Thomas More and his "Utopia." It must be read to be appreciated. The last chapter is devoted to a luminous review of the whole century, 1450–1550, with suggestions as to the kinship of great eras of civilization and a recapitulation of the many parallels offered by the century of More and the nineteenth century.

In literary excellence, historical accuracy, and concise compre-
hensiveness "The Century of Sir Thomas More" is a masterpiece,
and places its author among the first rank of writers to-day. Shorn
of all unnecessary detail, yet omitting nothing that would help to a
better understanding and clearer comprehension of the ethical,
political, and religious revolutions and the social conditions of that
century, it will be invaluable to students, teachers, and thinkers.
Adorned with passages of poetic beauty and bursts of impassioned
eloquence, and pervaded throughout with a magnificent spirit of
optimism, which inspires hope and fills the soul with enthusiasm
for the ushering in of that new time of which Mr. Flower is so
ardent a prophet, it will be enjoyed by the millions who are longing,
hoping, praying, for that better time which will surely come. But
in order to hasten its coming it is necessary that we should realize
how much depends upon the individual, and that, "There can be
no progress by people or nations without obedience to the laws of
healthy development of the best part of our nature; a steady, persistent struggle after more light; the earnest desire for truth; an
invincible determination to leave the world better than we found
it; and onward and upward progress achieved by knowledge of the
laws that cause success, and the faithful observance thereof."

Such are the lessons which Mr. Flower constantly seeks to
impress upon his readers, whether his theme be ethical, religious,
social, political, or historical; and while he is outspoken and unflinching as Thomas Carlyle in his denunciation of sham, fraud, and all
forms of injustice, tender and sympathetic as Victor Hugo for the
sufferings and hardships of the poor and downtrodden in humanity's
field, yet he ever holds up the ideal of a truer and nobler civilization, which each one of us has the power to advance. And while
"The Century of Sir Thomas More" is a profound historical study,
the production of a master mind, a monument of scholarly and
critical research, this central thought is never for a moment lost
sight of.

The mechanical part of the volume is in keeping with the contents. It is handsomely bound in cloth, printed on heavy plate paper,
with wide margins, and illustrated with many portraits of the leading
men of the century written of, that of Sir Thomas More forming the
frontispiece.

STUDIES IN THE THOUGHT WORLD.*

REVIEWED BY B. O. FLOWER.

The more I study the scholarly works of Henry Wood, the more I
am impressed with the conviction that he is the legitimate successor

---

* "Studies in the Thought World," by Henry Wood, author of " Ideal Suggestion,"
" God's Image in Man," " Edward Burton," "The Political Economy of Natural Law,"
etc. Cloth $1.25, Lee & Shepard, Boston.

of Ralph Waldo Emerson in so far as progressive idealistic conceptions are concerned. As Charles Darwin, Alfred Russel Wallace, and Herbert Spencer were successors of Lamarck and Erasmus Darwin, not in literary style but in taking up and elucidating the thought which they enunciated, so Henry Wood is accentuating and placing in a more definite and scientific manner the noble ideas more or less vaguely put forth by the great New England transcendentalist. Both must be classed as apostles of idealism, but Mr. Wood is far more positive, aggressive, and scientific than was the Sage of Concord; hence, in a sense he cannot expect the popularity at the present time which is being bestowed upon Emerson. The fact, however, that his works are in great demand speaks well for the author and also indicates how firmly the revolutionary ideas which he presents in so scholarly a manner are taking root in the minds of thinking people. The literary style of Ralph Waldo Emerson and Henry Wood is very unlike; indeed, it would be difficult to compare Mr. Wood's style with that of any author with whom I am acquainted. The general impression given to the mind by his writing, due doubtless to the wealth of imagery, is that the author is to be classed among florid writers; but the moment one analyzes his work he is struck with the singular absence of superfluous words, the conciseness of expression, and wealth of imagery which are rarely found in modern literary works, but in these excellences Mr. Wood excels. One is charmed with the beauty of his writings even though he may not be ready at all times to agree with him, while the presence of the discriminating or scientific spirit, added to felicity of expression, renders all his writings delightful in the extreme.

Probably no work from the author's pen, however, will do so much to establish him as a foremost thinker among the scholarly metaphysicians and idealists of our time as his new volume, "Studies in the Thought World, or Practical Mind Art." Some of the chapters of this volume have appeared in the ARENA but the greater number will be new to our readers. Among those which impress me as being of special interest, owing to the scholarly and suggestive treatment they have received and the new and comprehensive manner in which they are discussed, I would mention the following: Has Mental Healing a Valid Scientific and Religious Basis?—The Evolutionary Climb of Man—Mental and Physical Chemistry in the Human Economy—The Education of Thought—The Vital Energy and Its Increase —The Nature and Use of Pain—The Psychology of Crime.

So excellent is the work in its masterly treatment of the various subjects discussed, and so charming and engaging is the author's style of expression, that this book is, in my judgment, justly entitled to a position in the very forefront among the scholarly metaphysical and idealistic works of recent years.

A DAUGHTER OF HUMANITY.*

REVIEWED BY B. O. FLOWER.

Nothing is at once more striking, suggestive, and hopeful than the efforts visibly exerted on every hand for the hastening of a new birth of civilization. The battle being waged by those who believe in a religion of life as against an obsequious conservatism, which is as busy enlarging its phylacteries and cringing before wealth and power as was the pharisaism of the days of Jesus is scarcely less marked than the activity in the world of invention, which under the guidance of the altruistic spirit enunciated by the great Galilean in the Golden Rule, would transform the world, changing present-day misery, starvation, and degradation to a condition marked by harmony and goodwill no less than enduring progress. In the domain of social, economic, and political thought change is written on every hand; the larger ideals of evolutionary philosophy have acted on the brain of man much as the discovery of the New World acted on the thought of European civilization in the closing decade of the fifteenth century and the opening half of the sixteenth century. But this is not all. In the domain of ethics, our civilization apprehends as never before the august demands upon the individual. We are coming to see that the interdependence of the units is such in our civilization that every impure, unholy, or immoral act affects society as a whole and what is more it extends its baleful poison to generations yet to come. The realization of these stupendous facts is day by day taking root in the minds of the oncoming generation in a manner which has probably never been equalled in the history of the world before. We are coming to see that the religion of life demands (1) temperance and the return to a simpler mode of living; a life less artificial, in which excesses will be unknown for the reason that enlightened understanding and an illuminated conscience will rule where passion, appetite, and selfishness have so long held sway; (2) more justice, more toleration of others, more of the spirit of fraternity and love; (3) patient, scientific, sympathetic investigation of all those things which give clews and hints of another life; (4) social purity, or a white life for two. This last idea is taking possession of the minds of thousands of our young men and women. It is manifesting itself in various ways,—in educational agitation, in higher ideals, in the teachings enunciated by physicians and clergymen, in essays, and scientific discussions, and in that tremendous engine of modern educational agitation, the novel.

In "A Daughter of Humanity" we have a simple story simply told, of the temptations and perils of shop girls in too many of our great stores, where starvation wages are paid and where the poor girl too

---

* "A Daughter of Humanity; A Novel Dealing with the Temptations and Trials of Poor Girls in Our Great Cities," by Edgar Maurice Smith. Pp. 318; cloth $1.25, paper 50 cents. Arena Publishing Company, Boston.

frequently falls into the toils of lecherous men or procuresses. I think no one conversant with the facts relating to this painful subject will accuse the author of overdrawing his picture. If any one imagines such to be the case let him read "If Christ Came to Chicago," by William T. Stead (Laird & Lee, Chicago); "The White Slaves of Boston," by Rev. Louis Albert Banks, D. D.; "Traffic in Girls and the Florence Crittenton Homes," by Charlton Edholm (Woman's Temple, Chicago), and other works dealing more or less specifically with these terrible conditions. Of course it should be remembered that the pictures drawn by Mr. Smith do not prevail everywhere; but low wages, an overcrowded market for labor, the lightness with which immorality is treated when the offenders are men, and especially if they occupy high stations in church or state or are possessed of great wealth,—all conspire against the poor girl where the heads of the houses are not men of sterling worth and men who seek to throw a protecting arm around their employees.

"A Daughter of Humanity" represents a wealthy Boston heiress while on a summer vacation coming face to face with one of those common and inexpressibly sad tragedies which are too frequent, and of which the world knows comparatively little. The facts in this case are so terrible that the young lady determines to seek and to save such victims, and also to make known to the world the hideous truth after she has obtained indisputable evidence. The man to whom she is affianced opposes her plan and the engagement is broken off. Many difficulties naturally beset her, which are only equalled by what she is called upon to witness and endure as a poor shop girl.

Of her revelations and their results, and of the noble aid she finds in a broad-souled young physician, who learns to love her as a poor shop girl, because of her devotion to humanity's cause, it is not my purpose to speak. Suffice it to say that, while written in a simple manner, the volume deals delicately with awful crimes *which do exist*, and the high and noble purpose of the author is evident throughout. It is another voice in the call to conscience, to man's higher self—the demand for a nobler civilization.

INDEX TO THE FIFTEENTH VOLUME OF

THE ARENA.

e do not take possession of our ideas but are possessed by them.
They master us and force us into the arena,
Where like gladiators, we must fight for them."—HEINE.

EDITED BY

B. O. FLOWER.

TABLE OF CONTENTS.

NA PUBLISHING COMPANY, BOSTON, MASS.:

PIERCE BUILDING, COPLEY SQUARE.

ntano's, 17 Avenue de l'Opera; The Galignani Library, 224 Rue de Rivoli.

SOCIAL, POLITICAL AND ECONOMIC SUBJECTS:

WHY THE WEST NEEDS FREE COINAGE, by Hon. C. S. Thomas, Democratic National Committee; MEXICO'S PROSPERITY AND SILVER, by Justice Walter Clark, LL. D.; THE TELEGRAPH MONOPOLY, by Prof. Frank Parsons; SPECIE CONTRACTION AND BOND INFLATION, by Albert Roberts.

THE WORLD OF BOOKS.

Two little volumes well worthy of perusal have just been added to the Round Table Series: "Under the Shadow of Etna: Sicilian Stories from the Italian of Giovanni Verga," translated by Nathan Haskell Dole, and "The Starling," by Norman MacLeod, D. D. (Joseph Knight Company, Boston; price, cloth, gilt tops, 75 cents each).

"Under the Shadow of Etna" contains admirable translations of six among the best of the short stories of the famous Italian novelist Giovanni Verga: "How Peppa Loved Gramigna," "Jeli the Shepherd," "Cavalleria Rusticana," "The Story of the St. Joseph's Ass," and "The Bereaved." The pictures presented in this little volume are full of the pathos and tragedy and the infinite sorrow of human life, and are utterly destructive of the pretty pastoral ideas yet entertained by many in regard to peasant life in the sunny South. "Jeli the Herdsman" is one of the best stories in the book, and gives a general and comprehensive idea of Sicilian peasant life, some special phase of which, however, is illustrated by each sketch. "The Story of the St. Joseph's Ass" is a second "Black Beauty," with which all are familiar, while "Cavalleria Rusticana" and "La Lupa" have been enjoyed by many in their dramatic form, and will doubtless be enjoyed by many more in the form of the original stories upon which the operas are founded. "How Peppa Loved Gramigna" is pathetic, dramatic, and humorous, all in one, and is interesting beyond any of the other sketches, in that it contains a confession of the author's literary creed, of which it is also an exemplification. The whole collection is marked by great variety and contrast, and shows the great Italian novelist at his best.

"The Starling" is a reissue of well-known story of Dr. Mac which for power and pathos an tense human interest is unrivalle the work of any Scottish author. deed, after the reader has once t up the book he will find it difficu lay it aside until he has read it cover to cover. The touching of the noble and beautiful life of Sergeant Mercer, his love for starling with all the consequ which it brought upon him, the ous phases of character dealt with reformation of the poor outcast Hall through the love and kindne the old sergeant, and the outcom it all, showing how all-powerful is divine influence of love, make this volume one of surpassing inte While depicting different phases Scotch character with a master h it appeals to all the noblest imp of the soul.

"Stella, and An Unfinished C munication: Studies of the Unse by C. H. Hinton, A. B. (Macmilla Co., New York, cloth, price $1 has something the same effect upon reader in stimulating thought arousing interest as Mr. Hint "Scientific Romances," in noticing first of which, "What is the Fo Dimension? Or Ghosts Explain the *Pall Mall Gazette* says: "It exh a boldness of speculation and a po of conceiving and expressing even inconceivable, which rouses one's fa ties like a tonic."

In "Stella" the author puts f theories which at first seem inconc able, and which the mind cannot e accept, but in which the reader beco thoroughly absorbed, and is car away even in spite of himself by Hinton's clear and earnest reaso in support of his theories. In the

face to this work he remarks that our age is a happy one, in that "all doubt, all disputation about the higher world can be discarded—there is scope for all our energy in obtaining the necessary faculties of perception, just as the study of the minute or the very large requires microscopes, telescopes, and other apparatus, so for the study of the higher world we need to form within our minds the instrument of observation, the intuition of higher space, the per ception of higher matter." The story arouses thought and interest in a marked degree, and will prove especially interesting to occult students.

"An Unfinished Communication" is mystical, allegorical, rich in the suggestion of progression through trial, and emphasizing the fact that we must rise step by step into the higher life, to which we can attain only by conquering self and living the life unselfish.

This work will form a valuable addition to the occult literature of to-day, strongly imbued as it is with the thought which makes for right living and unselfishness, teaching the lesson that "being is being for others," and that through our trials and sufferings only can we progress to the higher life.

I hope at an early date to be able to give an extended notice to Mr. H. C. Lea's very scholarly work, the first volume of which has just appeared, entitled "History of Confession and Indulgence in the Latin Church." This volume is invaluable to students of history owing to the temperate spirit which pervades it no less than the fact that the author confines himself for the most part to authentic data within the church. The following brief notice from the Boston *Advertiser* will be interesting to our readers:

Mr. H. C. Lea, whose history of the Inquisition published a few years since won for itself a wide reputation as a scholarly historical work, has just brought out (Lea Bros. & Co., Philadelphia), the first volume of a new work entitled "History of Confession and Indulgence in the Latin Church." The work is to be completed in three volumes. That just issued treats of the

theory and practice of the prim church, the successive beliefs as to pardon of sin, the rise and develop of the power of the keys, the intr tion of auricular confession and its tablishment as an obligatory d Mr. Lea is well known for his schol research, and in his desire to be im tial and dispassionate he has avo Protestant authorities, confining self to Catholic writers and ori documents. The work is one of historical value.

Of the last issue of Roberts Broth unequalled edition of the novels Balzac (library edition, half moro price $1.50), the Boston *Advertiser* serves:

The latest number in the Ro edition of Balzac's works is that w is publised under the title of "The lery of Antiquities." This volume contains the story of "An Old Ma a character which figures in the fo story. In both of these novels Ba has rendered the main theme in con tion • with the old war between masses and the classes, between the tocracy and the radical element, an usual in most of the great French no ists' works the sympathy of the re seems almost insensibly developed favor of the nobility. The "Gal of Antiquities" does not present strongest episode in the "Human C edy," but nevertheless it has that p liar charm and interest which al every novel issued by Balzac posses The character of the two main figu the steward Chesnel and Mlle. D grignon, are vigorously drawn the pen that has had few equals in picting French character which, a all, is but human character under p liar environments.

The Boston *Transcript* gives the lowing interesting notice of a new n which is attracting general notice. titled "The Man Who Became a age":

Mr. William T. Hornaday, the aut of this somewhat remarkable story. be remembered by many readers as writer of a volume which creat strong impression at the time it published, a dozen years ago— Years in the Jungles." Mr. Ho day was bred on a Western farm. uated from a Western college. trained as a naturalist in Roches New York. He has, we are told. cessively achieved success as a coll

ing naturalist, taxidermist, a founder of zoölogical gardens, a business man, and an author. As a traveller he has penetrated the jungles of Venezuela and British Guiana, hob-nobbed in Cuba with both Spaniards and Cuban prisoners during the insurrection of 1875, studied both science and art in the museums and galleries of Europe, and for three years consorted with wild beasts in the jungles of India, Ceylon, the Malay peninsula and Borneo. And it was his acquaintance with the mild-mannered head-hunters of Borneo, his publishers tell us, that led to "The Man Who Became a Savage." In this book the author tells the story of a man whose sense of right and justice was so constantly outraged by the acts of men in office that in a fit of disgust he makes up his mind "to find some decent savages, and live with them a few years, at least." He settles upon Borneo as the proper place, and the story deals with his adventures on the way and after getting there. These occasionally get to be quite exciting. But the book has a purpose beyond the mere entertainment of the reader. An attempt is made to give a clear idea of what the country and people of Borneo really are, for the author had ample opportunities for studying both during his wanderings among the Pacific islands some years ago. The text is very well illustrated. Published by the Peter Paul Company, Buffalo, N. Y.

In the same journal we find the following critical notice of "Armenian Poems" (Roberts Bros, Boston, price $1.25):

It is a timely volume which is offered to the public in these translations from the Armenian by Alice Stone Blackwell. At an hour in the history of Armenia when the sufferings of her people impress the world, as yet too much in vain, this book appears to reveal to all readers something of the soul of this nation, of these people; simple, devoted and possessed of much delicate fancy, as well as of much vigor of spirit. A number of these poems appeared in these columns. In the preface to her volume, Miss Blackwell disavows any attempt to reproduce the metres used by the Armenian poets. She has adopted simple English forms to interpret the meanings set down for her in prose translations by several Armenian scholars. Her gift of sympathy, her passion for right and justice, as well as her own admirable poetic endowment, are made to serve the cause of the freedom of Armenia as well as to give

some of her literary treasures t world. Many of the poems are t and graceful, many more valian ringing. The translator is a true who adds such stanzas as these t wealth of international literature:

Armenia's life shall not become ex
The heavens are full of that life-g
    flame.
While the all-conquering cross of C
    shall reign,
So long shall live her name.

Why are you fearful? See you not,
    lime
Above your heads, the shadow o
    rood?
Of old your fathers with that
    sign
Mingled their sacred blood.

Anchor your hope, too, on the c
    Have faith!
The light will shine, since you
    are true.
It was your nation's bulwark,
    still
Weapon and flag to you!

The Richmond (Va.) *Evening* thus reviews Prof. Frank Par convincing pamphlet on street rail

"Public Ownership of Street ways," by Professor Frank Pars counsellor at law and lecturer on law jurisprudence in the Boston Univer and author of "Our Country's Nee "The Philosophy of Mutualism," Boston: Arena Publishing Comp

A strong and unanswerable little v by one who is fast becoming an aut ity in economics—a man every in scholar and heart and soul in symp with the new political economy.

Professor Parsons shows that a cent fare in our large cities is suffi to pay all expenses of trolley transp tion, including insurance, taxes, de ciation, and interest on the actual vestment. A three-cent fare w yield a large profit. Under muni ownership and operation, with a partisan board and genuine civil ser rules, the system could be made sustaining at a one-cent fare.

Political corruption is an almost versal incident of the private owner of street railways in our large ci Watering stock is a favorite pas with street-car companies. The ide to issue several times as much st as will be needed to build the r then to sell part of the said stock, k ing enough to retain control of the r The roads are then built with part of funds so obtained and the rest pocke

Bond the roads for all they are worth and put the cash in your pocket. Charge high rates and if the people object, why, it is clear you cannot reduce the fare because you have to pay dividends on all that stock and interest on all that debt. And the courts won't interfere, because some of the stock and bonds are in innocent hands. And the legislature and council won't interfere, because you have given them some of the surplus stock, and you have paid them well for allowing you to issue the said stock and perform the rest of your financial feats, and you will pay them well again if they behave with due docility. An ample issue of stock has another advantage. It acts as a check upon efforts for public ownership. If the people buy they must pay hard cash for the water, every drop of it, unless they were wise enough to reserve the power of purchasing at the actual cost of the plant, as in Philadelphia.

Employees get no more sympathy from the railways than the public. The treatment of motormen is especially unfair. No city has a right to call itself civilized so long as it permits its motormen to whiz through the winter, fourteen hours a day, and in some cases longer, unprotected, as are our motormen.

Another grievance remains worse than any matter of pay or exposure. The men are not free. They are political as well as industrial slaves. They must work and vote for the company's candidates. The penalty for violation of these unwritten laws is discharge on the first flimsy pretext that presents itself.

Public ownership is the only real cure for the ills of our street-car systems. It is the only means of unifying the interests of owners, employees, and patrons, and so removing the antagonism of interest which produces those ills. It will enable the people who ride in the cars to say how they shall be run. It will make the employees part owners, with a voice in the management, and a certainty of better hours, better pay, better protection from the weather, better treatment in every way. There will be seats for all, because the people who hang on the straps to-day will own the roads then. For the same reason the cars will be comfortably filled. Fares will be reduced. The dangerous net of ugly wires will be removed. The watering of stock and doctoring of railway accounts will cease and the most prolific source of municipal corruption will be destroyed, and all without danger of creating new evils, if solid civil service rules are made a part of the plan, as they must be in order to have a real ownership by the people. Civil service is a vital part of public ownership. You may put the legal title in the people and call it public ownership, but if you omit the civil service principle you will have public ownership only in name and boss ownership in fact. The roads should be put under a non-partisan commission (one member from each political party) similar to the one that has been so successful in the management of the railways in Australia. And it should be made a part of the organic law that appointments and promotion shall depend on merit determined by fair examination and faithful service, and that dismissal shall not be made except for cause, judicially ascertained if the employee sees fit to use his right of appeal to the courts.

BOOKS RECEIVED.

"The Return of the Native," by Thomas Hardy. Paper, pp. 465, price 50 cents. Published by Lovell, Coryell & Co., New York.

"Observations of a Bachelor," by Louis Lombard. Paper, pp. 151, price 50 cents. Published by L. C. Childs & Son, Utica, N. Y.

"History of Confession and Indulgences," Vol. I, by Henry Charles Lea, LL. D. Cloth, pp. 523. Published by Lea Brothers & Co., 706–708 Sansom St., Philadelphia, Pa.

Columbian Knowledge Series: "Hand Book of Arctic Discoveries," by A. W. Greely. Cloth, pp. 257, price $1. Published by Roberts Brothers, Boston, Mass.

"A Gray Eye or So," by F. Frankfort Moore. Paper, pp. 314. Published by Rand, McNally & Co., New York, N. Y.

"The American Plutocracy," by M. W. Howard. Cloth, pp. 246. Published by the Holland Publishing Co., 1287 Broadway, New York, N. Y.

KANSAS.

ANTHONY. H. Llewelyn Jones.
GARDEN CITY. Brown, Bierer & Cotteral.
GREAT BEND. Clarke & Russell.
HARPER. Sam. S. Sisson.
HUTCHINSON. Johns, Winnie & Fairchild.
KANSAS CITY. Clogston, Hamilton, Fuller & Cubbison, Husted Building.
OBERLIN. S. M. McElroy.
OSBORNE. E. F. Robinson.
OSKALOOSA. Marshall Gephart.
OSWEGO. Case & Glasse.
SCOTT CITY. L. V. Craveres.
STOCKTON. W. B. Ham.
TOPEKA. Douthitt, Jones & Mason, Bank of Topeka Building.
WICHITA. Sankey & Campbell, corner Douglas and Market Sts.
KANSAS CITY. Walter W. Davis, 1041-3, N. Y. Life Building.

KENTUCKY.

BARBOURVILLE. James D. Black.
HARRODSBURG. O. S. Poston.
HENDERSON. Montgomery Merritt.
LOUISVILLE. Rowan Buchanan, 418 Centre St.
MORGANFIELD. H. D. Allen.
MT. STERLING. Wood & Day.
"   O'Rear & Bigstaff, Maysville St.
PADUCAH. Thomas E. Moss.

LOUISIANA.

HOUMA. L. F. Suthon.
MONROE. Franklin Garrett, cor. Wood and St. John Sts.
NATCHITOCHES. D. C. Scarborough.
NEW IBERIA. Andrew Thorpe.
NEW ORLEANS. Harry H. Hall, 173 Common St.
"   "   Moise & Cahn, 21 Commercial Pl.
ST. JOSEPH, TENSAS PARISH. Clinton & Garrett.

MAINE.

PORTLAND. Strout, Gage & Strout, 52 Exchange St.
"   Clarence Hale, 39 Exchange St.

MARYLAND.

BEL AIR. Septimus Davis.
HAGERSTOWN. Frank W. Mish.
ROCKVILLE. William Veirs Bouic, Jr.

MASSACHUSETTS.

ATHOL. George W. Horr.
BOSTON. Walter Church, 65 Albion Bldg., Beacon and Tremont Sts. Special attention to recovering estates and finding heirs.
"   Southard & Baker, 27 School St.
GREAT BARRINGTON. O. C. Bidwell.
NEWBURYPORT. Charles C. Dame, 59½ State St.
PEABODY. Chas. F. Hoag.
PITTSFIELD. E. M. Wood, 9 Bank Row.
ROCKLAND. Geo. W. Kelley.
SALEM. William H. Gove, Post Office Building.
SPRINGFIELD. Edward H. Lathrop, Room 18, Fuller Block.
WORCESTER. Rice, King & Rice, 6 P. O. Block.

MICHIGAN.

COLDWATER. John S. Evans.
EAST SAGINAW. Herbert A. Forrest
GRAND RAPIDS. Clark H. Gleason, 53 Pearl St.
HASTINGS. James A Sweezey.
KALAMAZOO. Wm. Shakespeare, 130 W. Main St.
MUSKEGON. F. A. Nims.
PORT HURON. Sparling, Law & Moore.
SAND BEACH. Chas. L. Hall.
SAULT STE. MARIE. Jno. A. Colwell.

MINNESOTA.

BLUE EARTH CITY. Geo. W. Buswell.
DULUTH. R. R. Briggs, 501 to 503 Chamber of Commerce.
"   Alfred Jaques.
JACKSON. T. J. Knox
MINNEAPOLIS. Dwinell & Prior.
"   James O. Pierce, 21 4th St., So.
SAUK CENTRE. N. H. Miner.
ST. PAUL. Ewing & Ewing, 716 Pioneer Press Bldg.

MISSISSIPPI.

BATESVILLE. L. L. Pearson.
BROOKHAVEN. R. H Thompson.
CANTON. F. B Pratt
FRIARS POINT, COAHOMA CO. D. A. Scott.
GREENWOOD. Jas. K. Vardaman.
JACKSON. Frank Johnston
MERIDIAN. Cochran & Bozeman, formerly R. F. Cochran
"   McIntosh & Williams.
EDALE. Chas. & A. Y. Scott.

MISSOURI.

APPLETON CITY. W. W. Chapel.
BETHANY. J. C. Wilson.
KANSAS CITY. Brown, Chapman & Brown, 4
"   "   W. W. Davis, 515 Main St.
LOCKWOOD. W. S. Wheeler.
PARIS. Temple B. Robinson.
ST. LOUIS. Henry C. Withers, 711 Odd Fel Illinois Business.
"   Chas. Claflin Allen, Laclede Bu
"   Edwin S. Puller, Com'l Probate Law, 320 Commercial Bldg.
"   Seneca N. Taylor, Rooms American Central Bldg., Locust and

MONTANA.

BOZEMAN. Luce & Luce.
HELENA. Massena Bullard, Room 8, Gol Main St.

NEBRASKA.

ARAPAHOE. J. A. Dudgeon.
KEARNEY. John E. Decker.
NORTH PLATTE. William Neville.
OMAHA. J. H. Burchard, N. Y. Life Bldg.,
PLATTSMOUTH. H. D. Travis.
YORK. George B. France.

NEVADA.

VIRGINIA CITY. W. E. F. Deal.

NEW HAMPSHIRE.

EXETER. Charles H. Knight, Ranlet's Block
GREAT FALLS. Wm. F. Russell.
PETERBOROUGH. R. B. Hatch.

NEW JERSEY.

BELVIDERE. John H. Dahlke.
CAMDEN. Herbert A. Drake, 127 Market St.
JERSEY CITY. Wm. C. Gebhardt, Fuller Buil
NEWARK. W. C. Damron.
NEW BRUNSWICK. James H. Van Cleef, 391

NEW MEXICO.

ALBUQUERQUE. Bernard S. Rodey.
LAS VEGAS. A..A. Jones.

NEW YORK.

BUFFALO. Wm. W. Hammond, Erie Co., Jud
ELMIRA. Denton & McDowell, 335 E. Water
ELLENVILLE. John G. Gray.
FULTON. C. H. David.
ITHACA. David M. Dean.
KINGSTON. John E. Van Etten, 49 John St.
MALONE. J. C. Saunders.
MIDDLETOWN. Dill & Cox. Formerly Charles
NEWBURGH. John M. Gardner.
NEW YORK CITY. Theodore R. Shear, Drexe corner Wall and Broad Sts.
PORT JERVIS. Wilton Bennett, St. John's Bloc
POUGHKEEPSIE. John H. Millard, 52 Market
PRATTSBURG. Jay K. Smith.
SYRACUSE. Smith, Kellogg & Wells.
THERESA. D. Bearup.
WHITEHALL. O. F. & R. R. Davis.

NORTH CAROLINA.

LOUISBURG. F. S. Spruill.

NORTH DAKOTA.

FARGO. Newman, Spalding & Phelps.
"   Fred B. Morrill.
VALLEY CITY. Frank J. Young.
WAHPETON. A. M. Berseth, Divorce Law.

OHIO.

BATAVIA. A. T. Cowen (Late Common Pleas
CANAL DOVER. John A. Hostetler.
CLARION. Reed & Wilson.
CLEVELAND. Harvey Keeler, 236 Superior St.
"   John O. Winship, Room 10, Bla Building.
"   W. E. Ambler, 963 The Arcade.
CINCINNATI. Wm. Houk, N. E. corner Wal Canal Sts.
"   Orris P. Cobb, S. E. cor. Main and
"   Pogue, Pottenger & Pogue, Unit Bldg.
FINDLAY. J. Frank Axline, 222½ South Main
GALION. J. W. Coulter.
LIMA. Josiah Pillars.
MANSFIELD. Donnell & Marriott, 43½ No. M
PAULDING. Seiders & Seiders.
SANDUSKY. Hewson L. Peeke.
TIFFIN. Lutes & Lutes.

ALVA. Jesse J. Dunn.

OREGON.

PORTLAND. Woodward & Woodward, Abington Building.
SALEM. Seth R. Hammer.

PENNSYLVANIA.

CLARION. Reed & Wilson.
NEW BLOOMFIELD. W. N. Seibert.
NEWCASTLE. E. T. Kurtz, 81 Pittsburg St.
PHILADELPHIA. W. J. Shaeffer, Broad and Arch Sts.
PITTSBURG. Marshall Brown, 157 Fourth Ave.
SCRANTON. Edward Miles, 225 Washington Ave
SHAMOKIN. Addison G. Marr.
TAMAQUA. J. O. Ulrich.
WARREN. W. M. Lindsay
WILKES BARRE. W. L. Raeder.
WILLIAMSPORT. T. M. B. Hicks, Cor. Fourth and Williams Sts.

SOUTH CAROLINA.

DARLINGTON. E. Keith Dargan.

SOUTH DAKOTA.

ABERDEEN. H. H. Potter.
CHAMBERLAIN. James Brown.
PIERRE. D. F. Sweetnd, Law and Real Estate.
"   Coe l. Crawford,
"   Albert Gunderson.
RAPID CITY. Edmund Smith.
SIOUX FALLS. U.S.G. Cherry, Com'l and Divorce Law.
"   J. M. Donovan, Com'l and Divorce Law.
WOONSOCKET. S. A. Ramsey, Attorney at Law.

TENNESSEE.

CHATTANOOGA. Clark & Brown.

TEXAS.

ALBANY. A. A. Clarke.
AUSTIN. Z. T. Fulmore.
CAMERON Henderson & Streetman.
"   W. T. Hefley.
CLARKESVILLE. H. B. Wright.
CLEBURNE. S. C. Padelford.
DALLAS. James B. Simpson.
DALLAS. W. B. Merchant.
FORT WORTH. Oliver S. Kennedy.
"   "   Newton H. Lassiter.
LA GRANGE. R. H. Phelps, Masonic Building
LAREDO. Dodd & Mulally
LONGVIEW. Edward O. Griffin.
MASON. Holmes & Bierschwale.
PEARSALL. R. W. Hudson.
ROCKPORT. W. H. Baldwin.
SAN ANTONIO. Cassius K. Breneman.
WACO. Edward A. Marshall, *Land Lawyer and Notary Public.*

UTAH.

SALT LAKE CITY. Maurice M. Kaighn, Rooms 4, 5, & 6, Old Tribune Building.
SALT LAKE CITY. Cherry & Cherry.
"   "   Richard B. Shepard, Rooms 37-40, Commercial Block.

WASHINGTON.

SEATTLE. Hugh Clark, Rooms 76-81, Safe Deposit Building.

VIRGINIA.

CHARLOTTESVILLE. Micajah Woods.
DANVILLE. Withers & Withers.
HILLSVILLE. D. W. Bolen.
LAWRENCEVILLE. N. S. Turnbull.
LEXINGTON. Letcher & Letcher.
LYNCHBURG. J. E. Edmunds, 807 Main St.
PEARISBURG. J. D. Johnston.
PORTSMOUTH. Wm. H. Stewart, " Land Specialty."
STAUNTON. Braxton & Braxton.
TAZEWELL COURT HOUSE. A. J. & S. D. May.

CHARLESTON. Brown & Jackson.
PARKERSBURG. J. G. McCluer.
WHEELING. George W. Shinn, Room 10, City Building.

WISCONSIN.

BARRON. Fred B. Kinsley.
DARLINGTON. Orton & Osborn.
GREEN BAY. Wigman & Martin.
LA CROSSE. E. C. Higbee, Rooms 3 & 4, 305 M
MILWAUKEE. Winkler, Flanders, Smith, Bott Vilas, 37 Mitchell Building.
NEW LONDON. G. T. Thorn.
NEILLSVILLE. O'Neill & Marsh.
OSHKOSH. Charles W. Felker.
"   Hooper & Hooper, Room 9, Al Building.
RACINE. John T. Wentworth.
STOUGHTON. Luse & Wait.
SUPERIOR. D. E. Roberts.
"   Carl C. Pope.
"   E. B. Manwaring.
WEST SUPERIOR. Reed, Grace & Rock, Rooms 14, First National Bank.

CANADA.

QUEBEC.

MONTREAL. Burroughs & Burroughs, Nos. 61 614 New York Life Building, Place d'Armes

ONTARIO.

PEMBROKE. James H. Burritt.

THAT ROMANIST

BY
ADELLA R. MᴬᶜARTHUR·

The Arena Publishing Co.'s List of New and Forthcoming Books.

DAME FORTUNE SMILED, the Doctor's Story.

By WILLIS BARNES.   *Cloth, $1.25; paper, 50 cents.*

"Dame Fortune Smiled" is a plain story with no attempt at literary excellence. The author assumes that millionaires should regard their great wealth as a public trust to be used for the benefit of those who have helped them to accumulate it; and that, by so doing, they would themselves derive uncommon pleasure from giving large sums to charity in their lifetime, and do much toward solving the difficult problem of equalizing capital with labor for the moral and social benefit of the masses. The book contains medical suggestions of great value for those who work under high nervous tension. Mental suggestion as a therapeutic agent and the development of one's second-self are incidental features of the story.

THE CENTURY OF SIR THOMAS MORE.

By B. O. FLOWER.   *Cloth, price $1.50.*

With frontispiece, full page portrait of Sir Thomas More, and numerous pen and ink drawings of leading personages of his century, among whom are Gutenberg, Columbus, Erasmus, Luther, Calvin, Zwingli, Knox, Melanchthon, Michael Angelo, Raphael, Correggio, Titian, and Da Vinci. This work deals with the first century of modern times. It contains the following chapters:

I. Introduction.

II. A Glimpse of Western Europe During the Century of Which We Write.

III. The Reformation and Some of Its Leading Spirits.

IV. The Italy of the Renaissance.

V. Some Fatal Figures in the Italy of This Century.

VI. Bright Lights in Italian Life During the Renaissance.

VII. The Spanish Peninsula.

VIII. The France of This Century.

IX. The England of Sir Thomas More.

X. The Life of Sir Thomas More.

XI. Utopia Considered. (Part I.)

XII. Utopia Considered. (Part II.)

XIII. The Lives of Seneca and Sir Thomas More Compared.

XIV. A Brief Survey of the Century of Sir Thomas More.

Handsomely Bound, with gilt side and back dies. Published only in cloth.

For sale by all booksellers. Sent postpaid on receipt of the price.

Copley Square.   *Arena Publishing Co., Boston, M*

WHOSE SOUL HAVE I NOW?

By MARY CLAY KNAPP.   *Cloth, $1.25; paper, 50 cents.*

The author believes that the material age is passing away; that the present is the age of spirit, of love, of giving and doing all for the sake of humanity; and that only through suffering do we rise to the soul's height. She holds that the life of the heroine of the story proves that the perfect woman exists only when the material development equals the higher mental and spiritual, and that by intimate association with such a woman a man who is purely material and selfish may through the triumph of his sense of justice become a humanitarian and bless the world by pure and disinterested service.

BIRKWOOD.

By JULIA A. B. SEIVER.   *Cloth, $1.25; paper, 50 cents.*

Attention is directed to the intellectual, moral, and physical qualifications that should be required in those who are about to contract marriage in view of the obligations resting upon parents to see to it that their children shall be well born. The author believes that the proper generation of children will obviate the necessity for regeneration; and it is therefore called " the foundation-rock of *true* human progress." She also enforces the importance of teaching children early in life to recognize the beauty of purity and truth. The varied incidents of the interesting story will satisfy, also, even the exacting reader of novels.

KING MAMMON AND THE HEIR APPARENT.

By GEORGE A. RICHARDSON.   *Cloth, $1.25; paper, 50 cents.*

This book is an attempt on the part of the author, who believes that genuine progress can be made only when intelligence reigns, to educate the people to true views regarding the following social problems: "How to give more equal opportunities, or at least some approach to equal opportunities; how to prevent wealth-tyranny; how to break up the luxurious idleness and the predatory viciousness of certain rich men; and how to lessen the ignorance and vice and destitution of the lower levels, and to remove at least a portion of the enforced idleness of men who want work and cannot find the opportunity of working." He argues that "In the law of successions lies the root of the wealth-evil " and that society is continuing wrong by permitting the individual power of making bequests; "Succession to wealth is purely a matter for society to determine with justice to all its members." The privilege of making wills should be abolished and a maximum limit set to inheritable wealth, and all wealth beyond the inheritable limit "should escheat to public ownership — in this country, to the United States government." Intelligent people should seek to transmit to their children, not a heritage of wealth, but a " heritage of safe government under just conditions and equal opportunities."

For sale by all booksellers.   Sent postpaid on receipt of the price.

Copley Square.   *Arena Publishing Co., Boston, Mass.*

PERSONS, PLACES, IDEAS.

B. O. FLOWER. *Cloth, Price, $3.00*

A magnificently illustrated volume of miscellaneou$ essays. This
lume is printed on heavy enamelled paper, and contains over thirty full-
ge illustrations, with numerous smaller pictures. The edition is limited
one thousand copies. It is richly bound in colored cloth, with gilt side
d back dies, gilt top and uncut pages. The following is the table of
ntents :

Fancy cloth, gilt side and back dies, gilt top, uncut edges. Published
ly in cloth.

BLOSSOMS OF THOUGHT.

C. E. RUSSELL. *Cloth, 75 cents; paper, 25 cents.*

" Blossoms of Thought," as the title implies, is not a book for con-
uous reading, but one to be opened at random in brief moments of leisure
r a suggestive and helpful thought, that may serve to sweeten toil. The
m of the author is to assist others to find Him who is " the way, the truth,
d the life," that thereby they may enter " the pathway of eternal progress."

r sale by all booksellers. Sent postpaid on receipt of the price.
Copley Square. Arena Publishing Co., Boston, Mass.

A DAUGHTER OF HUMANITY.

By EDGAR MAURICE SMITH. *Cloth,* $1.25; *paper,* 50 *cents.*

"The whole book, from cover to cover, has been written with a view to illustrate in a small degree the temptations and trials that the average working-girl is forced to suffer—silently and without sympathy." The story tells what reasons induced Helen Richmond, a Boston heiress, to enter a New York dry-goods house in the guise of a shop-girl, what trials she underwent, how bravely she endured till her purpose was achieved, and what happiness crowned her endeavors.

LIFE AND WRITINGS OF AMELIA C. BLOOMER.
With Portrait.
By D. C. BLOOMER. *Cloth,* $1.25; *paper,* 50 *cents.*

Mrs. Bloomer's prominence in various reform movements—temperance, anti-slavery, woman's rights, and reform-dress for women—and the friendship of Horace Greeley, Susan B. Anthony, and Elizabeth Cady Stanton gave her a world-wide fame. Her recent death opens the way for her biography which her husband has supplied in a very happy and satisfactory manner. This volume contains a full account of her life, which is told mainly in her own words. Copious extracts from her writings are given. The book is a storehouse of information and anecdotes concerning contemporary reform and reformers. All interested in the reform movements of the last fifty years will welcome the appearance of this volume.

HILL-CREST: A Novel.

By JULIA COLLITON FLEWELLYN. *Cloth,* $1.25; *paper,* 50 *cents.*

Hill-Crest is the homestead of an Irish-American family, consisting of father, four motherless daughters, poor but proud, and an old maiden sister-in-law. A beautiful and fashionable young lady cousin is a disturbing element. The principal hero is an ideal young clergyman. The interest of this well-written love story centres in three love affairs that end in happy marriages. This narrative is marked by fine feeling and pervaded by a strongly religious and moral tone.

HIS PERPETUAL ADORATION: The Captain's Old Diary.

By Rev. JOSEPH F. FLINT. *Cloth,* $1.25 ; *paper,* 50 *cents.*

This extremely interesting and realistic war story is told in the form of a diary left at his death by a veteran who had been a captain with Grant at Vicksburg and with Sherman on his march to the sea. Two or three of the great events of the war are told in stirring fashion, but the narrative deals mainly with the inside life of the soldier in war-time, and its physical and moral difficulties.

UNCLE JERRY'S PLATFORM AND OTHER CHRISTMAS STORIES.

By GILLIE CARY. *Extra cloth, beautifully illustrated, 75 cents.*

This beautifully illustrated little book, containing three stories — "Uncle Jerry's Platform," "Pops," and "A Daughter of the Revolution" — is gotten up in very attractive style for the Christmas trade. The first, a well-told story in dialect, shows the tender care and loving solicitude of the better class of slaves for the members of their master's family. The second describes the supreme devotion of "Pops" to his little white charge and the gratitude the latter felt toward the former. The third story narrates a thrilling event that took place at Yorktown, Christmas, 1781.

NICODEMUS.

An appropriate gift book.

By GRACE SHAW DUFF. *Extra cloth, 75 cents.*

A short poem in which Nicodemus describes the impression made upon him by Jesus on "that last great day of the feast; when the golden glory of a rising sun decked roof and dome, and edged with lustrous line the gently swaying palms." Of the effect of the words of Jesus he says:

> " When He spoke, His words
> And voice seemed fitted parts of some great psalm. "

And of His look:

> " But as He turned
> I looked again into His eyes, and in
> Their depths my soul met His — and then I knew
> In very truth — He was the Son of God."

SONG BLOSSOMS.

By JULIA ANNA WOLCOTT. *Cloth, $1.25.*

A beautiful book of verse in many moods; for old and young, grave and gay. The poems are arranged in ten groups. Some of the groups are: Riverside and Meadow; Among the Hills; At the Fireside; In Lightsome Mood; and In the Sanctuary. The book contains Christmas poems. It is attractively bound in handsome cloth. The design and lettering are in gold. Especially suitable for a holiday gift.

THE LEAGUE OF THE IROQUOIS.

By BENJAMIN HATHAWAY. *Cloth, $1.00; red line, $1.50.*

It is instinct with good taste and poetic feeling, affluent of picturesque description and graceful portraiture. — *Harper's Magazine.*

Has the charm of Longfellow's "Hiawatha." — Albany *Evening Journal.*

For sale by all booksellers. Sent postpaid on receipt of the price.

Copley Square. *Arena Publishing* Co., Boston, M

TWO IMPORTANT SOCIAL BOOKS.

THE COMING REVOLUTION.

By HENRY L. CALL.   *Cloth,* $1.25; *paper,* 50 *cents.*

This is an economic study that holds the reader in a grip of fascination from the first page to the last. It takes up the tangle of modern industrial society, and unravels it web by web, and shows the anomalies, inconsistencies, falsities and criminality and injustice which we accept as an unalterable economic law, because it dates from Adam Smith — is something over one hundred years old! The author of "The Coming Revolution" first touches upon the ferment everywhere existing in the minds of men upon all questions of public concern, and then systematically examines the economical doctrines and social conditions that have made labor, the creator of all wealth in its application to the resources of nature, the slave of its creature — the product, wealth. He deals in turn with "The Struggle for Existence"; "The Curse of Privileges and Class Legislation"; "The Fruits of Privilege"; "The Plea of Privilege"; "The Law of Freedom"; "Inheritance"; "Land"; "Money"; "Transportation"; "Trade"; "The Corporation"; "The New Republic"; "The Conflict."

The author deals with the various aspects of modern industrial society with a clearness and perspicuity that is so rare in this department of literature as to deserve the name of genius, and "The Coming Revolution" will reveal the fundamental falsities of existing economic conditions to many who have been merely befogged by the economics of the orthodox schools, which split hairs for the express purpose of mystifying their students and blinding them to the fundamental laws of inexorable nature and justice. The Revolution he treats of is not a social upheaval of violence, but a revolution in economic and political thought.

THE HISTORY OF BROOK FARM.

By Dr. JOHN T. CODMAN.   *Cloth,* $2.00.

The wonderful little group of great men whose names are associated in American biography and literary history with the Brook Farm experiment will always make it a fascinating subject for American readers. The real inner, intimate history of Brook Farm should find a place in the library of every student of American literature and social movements. This is precisely the niche in our literary annals that Dr. Codman's book admirably fills. There has been a good deal of scrappy, reminiscential writing on Brook Farm, but no adequate and complete history. Dr. Codman's book will be the standard history of the subject. He gives the complete historical record, with the fascinating touches of an intimate knowledge of all the men and methods and aims and daily incidents of the community. Dr. Codman is one of the few living men who were on the Farm, so that his book has an immense value for the new generation about him, and will be the standard authority for the social thinkers and writers of the coming generation.

This book is one for which the student of social experiment should be very grateful. The kindliness, the breadth of view, and the large space given to the social life of Brook Farm, will give the book a deep and abiding interest. Dr. Codman deserves great praise for having reproduced the Brook Farm life with vividness and simplicity. Its very artlessness is in its praise as a book of sketches, and it supplies a gap in our literature which has been deplored, but which no one else of all the brilliant people who had to do with Brook Farm has filled. — *Boston Herald.*

For sale by all booksellers. Sent postpaid on receipt of the price.

Copley Square.   *Arena Publishing Co., Boston, Mass.*

THE KEYS OF FATE.

By HERMAN SHORES.   *Cloth, $1.25; paper, 50 cents.*

This story has a purpose not expressed as in a tale with a moral, but in its life-like presentations. The scene of the story is laid in New England, and it is a tale of incident and romance. It deals with some of the current questions of reform, and the thoughtful reader perceives that chance has much to do with the drift and attraction of one's thoughts and sympathies ; in fact to what an extent, under the proper conditions, good character and generous ideals are " catching." It is a suggestive and attractive story.

OVER THE OLD TRAIL.

By L. B. FRANCE (Bourgeois).   *Cloth, $1.25; paper, 50 cents.*

" Over the Old Trail " takes the reader back some thirty years to the picturesque scenes of a Colorado mining camp, just after the close of the war. This pictures a phase of life that is rapidly disappearing throughout the domain of the States, except on the extreme frontier, and it does so with that touch of certainty and sincerity which shows that it has all been lived by the author. The main interest of the story, however, is a delightful love story, which gives us the old sweet and perpetually charming sentiment of old-fashioned lovers. Incidentally the story touches the question of woman suffrage and kindred topics. The book has so much charming literary art and delicious sentiment that it promises to become as popular as Mr. France's other books, "Pine Valley," "With Rod and Line," "Mr. Dide," etc. Of these the critics have been almost unanimously enthusiastic.

KERCHIEFS TO HUNT SOULS.

By M. AMELIA FYTCHE.   *Cloth, $1.25; paper, 50 cents.*

A story of Bohemian life in Paris, full of vivid pictures of the fascinating Latin Quarter, in which the reader is introduced to several interesting and memorable characters. It shows the trials, difficulties and temptations to which a pretty English governess is exposed in the gay environment of Paris, among students and artists and writers. The purpose of the book, as far as any purpose is revealed in this story of love and incident, may be said to lie in pointing out the dangers of marriages for love and passion, without intellectual and moral affinity. The heroine makes an unfortunate alliance, for love, which almost wrecks her life. Her husband deserts her, upon a base legal technicality, and after other embittering experiences she returns to America and makes a marriage of reason.

THE VISION OF THYRZA.

By IRIS.   *Cloth, 75 cents.*

A dramatic poem in blank verse. It is an invocation to the gods, a fine revival of the classical form, after the manner of Swinburne's " Atalanta in Calydon," appealing to them in the name of despairing humanity to visit the earth and reform the follies and vices of society.

For sale by all booksellers. Sent postpaid on receipt of the price.

Copley Square.   *Arena Publishing Co., Boston.*

MONEY WARS.

By SAMUEL LEAVITT.   *Price, paper,* 50 *cents; cloth,* $1.25.

Have you a copy of MR. SAMUEL LEAVITT's "MONEY WARS" in your library? If not, you should immediately procure this most valuable history of American finance.

CRITICAL PRESS AND PERSONAL OPINIONS.

A monument of learning. . . . One cannot but be more than pleased with the history, and admire the immense industry. — *N. O. Picayune.* Valuable for purposes of reference. . . . He is not unknown to us, for we happen to have read his "Peacemaker Grange," etc. . . . Quite worth careful perusal. . . . Gives us good reading matter. — *N. Y. Herald.* There is no question of the value of the facts that he has digested and arranged. — *San F. Chronicle.* An epitome of information. . . . Leaves none of his facts unverified. . . . Exceedingly useful. . . . Unquestionably right in many of his arraignments. — *San F. Call.* Mr. (Coin) Harvey was joined in his denial by another financial oracle who was visiting him at the time; Mr. Samuel Leavitt, author of "Money Wars," an encyclopedia on the money question. — *Chicago Inter-Ocean.* The financier of financiers. — *W. H. Harvey.* The benefit that this work will be to the scientific student of value, will be enormous. — *N. Y. World.* The most remarkable book on finance of the century. — *Arena.* This book contains much very valuable matter that was in danger of being lost. — *Gen. A. J. Warner.* It is a valuable compendium of just the kind of information that is being needed to-day. I have constant inquiries for such information from correspondents of mine, and will take great pleasure in calling their attention to your work. — *Henry D. Lloyd.* No romance of Hugo, no tragedy of Shakespeare, ever stirred the blood as does this infamous record. — *Tom Watson of Georgia.* It is acknowledged the *Ultima Thule* of the finance question, and must stand undisputed in the forefront for years to come. — *Chicago Searchlight.* Just the book we have been awaiting for twenty-five years. — *Henry Carey Baird.* Has created considerable discussion. — *Chicago Times.* Does not hesitate to place the blame where, in his opinion, it properly belongs. — *Philadelphia Daily Item.* The American system of money rises, like Solomon's temple, without the blow of a hammer, in the magnificent sequences of this history. — *H. E. Baldwin, in Arena.* The book is a great one. Entitles him to the gratitude of every searcher after economic truth. — *Editor of Nonconformist.* It will be the standard for quotation and authority. — *J. H. Ferriss, in Arena.* The most important volume yet issued for the cause of the people. — *Junction City Tribune.* The most valuable financial work that has come to our notice. — *Farmer's Voice.* The most complete, accurate and valuable work issued on the subject it treats. — *A. C. Fisk, Pres. Pan-Am. Bimetallic Ass'n.* Comprehensive, exhaustive, systematic, clear and condensed. — *San Francisco Star.* No one of our acquaintance is more competent to write an intelligent, truthful and impartial work on the actual occurrences connected with finances. — *Western Rural.* Will be of incalculable value to speakers and writers. — *Chicago Express.* Your book is a whooper and no mistake. — *C. C. Post.* I will positively affirm that no man in this whole country is so well qualified to write such a book. — *Editor New City, N. Y.*

For sale by all booksellers. Sent postpaid on receipt of the price.

Copley Square.   *Arena Publishing Co., Boston, Mass.*

A COMPLETE CATALOGUE

OF THE

ARENA PUBLISHING CO.'S WORKS

HISTORY, BIOGRAPHY, AND TRAVEL.

ALBERT BRISBANE. A Mental Biography.

By REDELIA BRISBANE. This work, in the form of an autobiographical recital, covers many of the most important events of the century. Mr. Brisbane's unique experience as a student, a traveller, and a philosophic observer, together with his rare power of original thought, invests with peculiar interest every subject touched upon,—prominent among which is a vivid picture of the social movement from the days of St. Simon down to the present in which he played an active and prominent part. Cloth, $2.00.

THE HISTORY OF BROOK FARM

By JOHN T. CODMAN. The standard history of the famous social experiment by one of the few survivors who participated in it.
Mr. Codman deserves great praise for having reproduced the Brook Farm life with vividness and simplicity. Its very artlessness is in its praise as a book of sketches, and it supplies a gap in our literature which has been deplored, but which no one else of all the brilliant people who had to do with Brook Farm has filled.—Boston Herald. Cloth, $2.00; paper, 75 cents.

ALONG SHORE WITH A MAN-OF-WAR.

By MRS. MARGUERITE DICKINS. This is a more than usually entertaining book of travel and of countries which the people of the United States are to know more intimately in the near future. Heretofore commercial relations with South American countries have scarcely been encouraging and never cultivated. The United States has awakened from such commercial blundering none too soon. The author is the wife of Commander Dickins, of the United States Navy, and has shared with him a sailor's life in many parts of the world. The story takes the reader to nearly every interesting place along the South American coast.—Chicago Inter-Ocean. Cloth, $1.50.

GERALD MASSEY: POET, PROPHET, AND MYSTIC.

By B. O. FLOWER. Gerald Massey will be better known to the English-speaking people fifty years from now than he is to-day. His genius is only just beginning to be recognized, and Mr. B. O. Flower has done the world a service in his critical monograph, "Gerald Massey, Poet, Prophet, and Mystic." It is a true tribute from the heart to a true prophet of freedom, fraternity, and justice, ever loyal to the interest of the oppressed.—New York World. Cloth, $1.00.

LESSONS LEARNED FROM OTHER LIVES.

By B. O. FLOWER. Hudson Tuttle writes in the "Golden Gate," of San Francisco: "There are countless writers who are able to write elegantly, whose sentences are faultless in construction, and charm by the rhythm of their cadence; but there are few who combine with beauty and sweetness of diction a thorough and comprehensive knowledge, and earnest and conscientious desire to impart it to others. Mr. Flower has not only a charming style, but his whole soul is engaged in the subject he has under consideration, and he impresses the mind of the reader with his own sympathetic fervor. No youth can read these pages, so replete with lessons of fortitude, endurance, and noble purpose, without receiving a strong incentive to imitate the character portrayed." Cloth, $1.00; paper, 50 cents.

THE RISE OF THE SWISS REPUBLIC.

By W. D. McCRACKAN, A. M. The Rt. Hon. James Bryce, M. P., writes to the author; Duchy of Lancaster Office, London, W. C., Oct. 27, 1892. "It seems to me that you have happily blended the picturesque treatment which some parts of Swiss history demand with the object of bringing out the political lesson of the last thirty or fifty years. I trust your book may do much to show our people, as well as yours, how much is to be learned from a study of Swiss affairs."
Good as gold; a work that should be treasured by the thoughtful student; a book to take the place of honor on the book shelf; to be read once, twice, thrice, and afterwards used for the purpose of reference as often as need be.—The New York Herald. Cloth, $2.00.

SULTAN TO SULTAN.

By M. FRENCH-SHELDON (Bébé Bwana). A thrilling account of a remarkable expediton to the Masi and other hostile tribes of East Africa, which was planned and commanded by this intrepid woman. A sumptuous volume of travels, homely illustrated; printed on Coast paper, and richly bound in Africa silk-finished cloth, $5.00.

SOCIAL, ECONOMIC, AND POLITICAL WORKS.

HOW SHALL THE RICH ESCAPE?

By Dr. FRANK S. BILLINGS. Dr. Billings has written a very strong book.—B. F. Underwood.
Dr. Billings is an audacious writer. The most remarkable book I ever read.—Hon. James Whitehead, Nebraska. Cloth, $2.00.

THE COMING REVOLUTION.

By HENRY L. CALL. "A revolution is upon us; the fountains of the great deep are broken up," says General Francis A. Walker, and the widespread interest among thoughtful men of all classes in economic problems is shown by the enormous demand for any and all studies of our present social condition. The latest, by Henry L. Call, called "The Coming Revolution," is a scientific, cold-blooded, mathematical analysis of modern industrial society in which the tangled web of economic falsities, inconsistencies, and anomalies is shown with the clearness of demonstration of a professor of anatomy. Its great value is that it gives a comprehensive survey of social conditions as a whole, a view of the entire field, while other works are devoted to particular phases — money, land, and the like. The book holds the reader from the first line to last, and it is not necessary to accept all of Mr. Call's conclusions to admire his excellent work.—New York World (April 15, 1895). Cloth, $1.25; paper, 50 cents.

CIVILIZATION'S INFERNO.

By B. O. FLOWER. Merits the careful attention of all students of social problems, especially those pertaining to our great cities. The volume is one of remarkable interest and power.—The Traveler, Boston. Cloth, $1.00; paper, 50 cents.

THE NEW TIME.

By B. O. FLOWER. The New York World says: "It is in every way practical, everyday common sense, dealing with facts and not theories."
The Chicago Times says: "Candor is a marked characteristic of the author's treatment of the various economic subjects touched in the course of the book. Mr. Flower is one of the prominent 'reform' writers of the day. He has done more, perhaps, than any other one writer for the advancement of his fellow men and the improvement of their condition. His plans, if put in practical operation, would be productive of good to all." Cloth, $1.00; paper, 50 cents.

A SCIENTIFIC SOLUTION OF THE MONEY QUESTION.

By ARTHUR KITSON. Books on the money question are multiplying, but "A Scientific Solution of the Money Question," by Mr. Arthur Kitson, is the latest, is one well worthy the study, and the careful study, of every person who wishes to take an entire survey of the field occupied by the science of economics of which the subject of exchanges is a branch . . . Few readers of Mr. Kitson will accept all of his views, but his work is original, thoughtful, honest and conservative.—New York World. Cloth, $1.25; paper, 50 cents.

DIRECT LEGISLATION.

By J. W. SULLIVAN. This book demonstrates the possibility of the universal republic. It has convinced hosts of Ameri-

cans that middlemen in law-making m go. It has afforded at least one fun mental proposition on which all ac voting social reformers may unite. It induced many citizens, partisans and partisans, conservatives as well as cals, to believe that a common work men of all classes lies outside of p Cloth, 75 cents; paper, 25 cents.

POVERTY'S FACTORY.

By Rev. STANLEY L. KREBS, M. A. is an excellent study of the social lems of our day written by a though liberal clergyman, who is animated sincere sympathy for the industrial ions. It endeavors to present the que fairly and fully, and to do justice to sides. It traces the bulk of mo poverty to unjust laws. Paper, 25 cen

THE WOMAN SUFFRAGE MOVEM IN THE UNITED STATES.

By A LAWYER. A review of the Wom Suffrage movement by an orthodox Cl tian of the strictest sect of the faith opposes the movement on Scriptu social, and political grounds. Cloth, cents; paper, 25 cents.

OUR MONEY WARS.

By SAMUEL LEAVITT. Samuel Lea has compiled, under the title of " Money Wars," an encyclopedia of facts relating to our monetary legislat These have never been brought toget in a single volume, and Mr. Leavitt spent twenty years in collecting and v fying the details gathered from thousa of books, official reports, and files of ne papers accessible, and indeed kno only to one who had made such labor life's object. The benefit that this w will be to the scientific student of va will be enormous.—The World, New Yo Cloth, $1.25; paper, 50 cents.

WOMEN IN THE BUSINESS WORLD

By ONE OF THEM. It points out the portance of pecuniary independence, t how business efficiency may be secu and discusses many of the business tions now filled by women, explain their advantages and disadvanta their demands and rewards. The styl the book is good, its fund of wis large, and it will be of wide and per nent value. Many Sunday School librai would be the better for it.—The C gregationalist, Boston. Cloth, $1. paper, 50 cents.

SOCIOLOGY. Popular Lectures before Brooklyn Ethical Association.

By Rev. JOHN W. CHADWICK, ROBERT ECCLES, M. D., Prof. JOHN FISKE, Pr GEORGE GUNTON, Dr. LEWIS G. JAN JOHN C. KIMBALL, Miss CAROLINE LEROW, HUGH O. PENTECOST, WILLI POTTS, Z. SIDNEY SAMPSON, Prof. RU SHELDON, JAMES A. SKILTON, DAN GREENLEAF THOMPSON, Mrs. M TREAT, JOHN A. TAYLOR and C. ST LAND WAKE. Cloth, $2.00.

THE WOMAN QUESTION.

By ISAAC N. TAYLOR. A very interest survey of the special texts of the Testament and the New, and the ar ments deduced from them to support theory of the divine subordination of man according to Scriptural injuncti The author maintains the negative of orthodox view of this question, and claims that an examination of Moses and Paul does not support the opposite. Cloth, 30 cents.

RAILWAYS OF EUROPE AND AMERICA.

By Mrs. MARION TODD. An excellent alignment of the arguments which are urged in favor of State control of railways. It comprises extended extracts from the publications and from political documents, and presents the essential figures condensed from many railroad reports at the cost of enormous labor on the part of Mrs. Todd. The work is strong and creditable.—The Times, Boston, Mass.

A very complete and exhaustive work upon an important subject.—The Flo Times-Union, Jacksonville, Fla. Cl $1.25; paper, 50 cents.

LABOR AS MONEY.

By JOHN O. YEISER. The theory of writer of this book is to demonetize gold and silver, and all existing mo and to create instead an exchange upon human labor power as co distinguished from the product of particular labor. The exposition of theory is so plain and simple tha readers, even those who have never a study of economic questions, will come interested. Cloth, $1.25; paper, cents.

POPULAR SCIENTIFIC WORKS.

TEMPTATIONS, HABITS, CHARACTER.

By Dr. WILLIAM M. CAPP. This is a very useful little brochure on the difficulties which beset the young about the dangerous period of adolescence, and it treats the matter on such a high moral and common-sense physiological plane that it will serve admirably in the place of, or lead up to in a natural and wholesome manner, that personal explanation so many parents dread. Paper, 25 cents.

HYPNOTISM. How It Is Done. Its Uses and Dangers.

By JAMES R. COCKE, M. D. A complete survey of the subject, experimental and historical, of hypnotism to the present time.

The subject treated of in this book is certainly one of the very few vital topics of the day, the study of which is a matter of profound interest to the intelligent laity as well as to members of the medical profession. In other words, the subject appeals with a peculiar force to all thinkers, both in and out of the medical profession, and the author's object is the difficult one of writing a book sufficiently technical to satisfy the trained medical mind, and yet not so scientific as to repel the lay reader. The author is to be congratulated on his good fortune in succeeding so admirably in accomplishing his object.—The New England Medical Gazette. Cloth, $1.50.

ÆDŒOLOGY.

By SYDNEY BARRINGTON ELLIOT, M. D.

Prenatal influence is the influen physical, mental, and moral, which, act through the parents, affects the un child, not only during actual pregna but for some time prior to it. The au has clearly demonstrated that ha well-born children is within the reac almost all parents. The physical, mei and moral development are each s rately considered. It is shown how impart good physique, strong vital o and desirable mental and moral qual even under unfavorable circumstan Cloth, $1.50.

EVOLUTION. Popular Lectures before Brooklyn Ethical Association.

Papers dealing with various phases Evolution, Physical, Social, and Mo by Rev. JOHN W. CHADWICK, Prof. E. COPE, Dr. ROBERT G. ECCLES, Dr. LE G. JANES, STARR H. NICHOLS, WILL POTTS, NELSON C. PARSHALL, ROSSI W. RAYMOND, Ph. D., JAMES A. SKIL7 Rev. MINOT J. SAVAGE, Z. SIDNEY SA SON and GARRETT P. SERVISS. Cl $2.00.

MAGNETISM. Its Action and Poten with Suggestions for a New Cosmograp

By GEORGE W. HOLLEY. The auth theory is that the all pervasive fo which binds the forces of nature in un is magnetism, following up a hint of F day's. Cloth, $1.25; paper, 50 cents.

RELIGIOUS WORKS.

EVOLUTION AND THE IMMANENT GOD.

By Rev. WILLIAM F. ENGLISH. The author accepts the doctrine of evolution in the belief that it affords important aid to the apprehension and elucidation of Christian truth.

It is well written and candid. . . . readable and suggestive.—The New York Observer. Cloth, $1.00; paper, 50 cents.

CHRIST THE ORATOR.

By Rev. THOMAS ALEXANDER HYDE. No one who reads this book can fail to be convinced that its author has thoroughly

studied his subject, knows how to to the chords of human nature, is conve with the best methods of oral add and has well presented the Christ as One who not only perfectly unders all these things, but was Himself Model Orator. It is a very sugge and refreshing book.—The Treasur Religious Thought, N. Y. Cloth, $1.

THE SUPREMACY OF THE SPIRIT1

By Rev. EDWARD RANDALL KNO L.L. D. A discussion of the intr and important problem of the nature of matter from the standpoint of a believer in Christian orthodoxy. A philosophical discussion of very deep questions. The author's claim is that, accepting as incontrovertibly proved the existence of an all-pervading ether, it is equally necessary to recognize the fact that this single, universal medium is not only omnipresent but immaterial, and hence not of the material existence and its conditions and laws, but spiritual, and therefore there must be a Divine Will and an Eternal Spirit.—Public Opinion, New York.

This book of Dr. Knowles, clearly treating the ultimate nature of matter, the essential nature of electricity, and making original and important researches of a most vital character concerning invisible powers of the universe, will cause the author to rank with the most notable discoverers of this progressive age.—The Globe, Boston, Mass. Cloth, 75 cents.

A NEW DEPARTURE.

By W. K. M——. The aim of this remarkable book is to give what the author believes to be the true symbolic or spiritual interpretation of the Bible, including the Apocalypse. The work is evidently the outcome of years of patient research, study, and reflection; and every one who holds that there is an inner, esoteric meaning to the Biblical text, will do well to study carefully the conclusions arrived at in the present work. Cloth, $1.25; paper, 50 cents.

THE GOSPEL IN PAGAN RELIGIONS.

By An Orthodox Christian. The author seeks to find and recognize the truth to be found in all religions, and especially that part of truth which belongs to the Gospel. It is a very fair work, as well as an able one.—The Christian Advocate, Pittsburg, Pa.

It contains much fresh and true thought excellently well expressed.—The Advance, Chicago.

The work is a scholarly one, presenting its arguments in a pleasant, convincing way, evidencing at every point the deepest research and the most careful consideration.—The Times, Boston. Cloth, $1.25; paper, 50 cents.

WIT AND HUMOR OF THE BIBLE.

By Rev. Marion D. Shutter. Dr. Shutter is widely known to American Universalist Christianity as pastor of the First Universalist Church of Minneapolis. "Wit and Humor of the Bible" is a worthy literary study of those elements in the Scriptures and is a summary several years of investigation. Dr. Shutter is certainly a pioneer in the field he has done his work in a reverent sympathetic and masterly way.—The view of Reviews, New York. Cloth, $1

THE IRREPRESSIBLE CONFLICT TWEEN TWO WORLD THEORIES.

By Rev. Minot J. Savage. This is most powerful presentation of the evolution versus orthodoxy that appeared in the whole field of scient theological literature. Mr. Savage sta in the van of the progress of moral, mane, and rational ideas of human soci and religion, which must be inextrica commingled in the new thinking, an stronger word for moral and intellec freedom has never been written t "The Irrepressible Conflict." Cl $1.00; paper, 50 cents.

THE RELIGION OF THE FUTURE.

By Rev. S. Weil. The Rev. Samuel is the author of a very earnest volu "The Religion of the Future." It gi an outline of the modern spiritual p osophy. It is rich in personal experien and in arguments based upon them. T clergyman has found in the occurren of modern spiritualism the "satisfact proofs" of a life beyond this present o which Herbert Spencer fails to find any of the religions and theologies of day. It is a remarkable narrative.— Times, Hartford, Conn. Cloth, $1. paper, 50 cents.

THE WORLD'S CONGRESS OF RELIGIONS.

The object of this volume is to state c cisely and clearly—and as nearly as p sible in the exact language of the emin men of all the denominations—what th creeds and beliefs are. It is intended serve no creed or sect but to give eac hearing upon its merits. The volume printed in neat style, cheap, to be wit the reach of the masses.—The Inter-Oce Chicago. Cloth, $1.50; paper, 50 cent

---

PSYCHICAL RESEARCH, METAPHYSICS AND OCCULTISM.

THE SPHERICAL BASIS OF ASTROLOGY.

By Joseph G. Dalton. A comprehensive Table of Houses for Latitudes 22° to 56°. With rational views and suggestions, explanations and instructions, correction of wrong methods and auxiliary tables.

A much-needed beginning of some rational, honest, and careful study of what lies so debased and obscured by ignorance, folly, and pretence in all books on the subject. It is the condensed result of many years' close thought, computation, and observation, pursued originally with the sole view of testing privately by exact methods the doctrine of nativities in astrology.

If there is any truth in astrology, it worthy of study as part of the Word God in nature. It can be studied righ only by a systematic and scienti method. This never yet has been ev attempted. The present work is a la able endeavor toward that end, and p vides a sure and broad foundation intelligent pursuit of this abstruse a cloudy subject.—The Boston Transcri Cloth, $2.00.

A GUIDE TO PALMISTRY.

By Mrs. Eliza J. Henderson. A co plete manual on the subject. Cloth, cents.

Psychical Research, Metaphysics and Occultism.—Continued.

THE ASCENT OF LIFE.

By STINSON JARVIS. This is one of the most important contributions to psychical science which have appeared in this decade of scientific activity. The author is an evolutionist in natural philosophy, and he applies the method and the principles of evolutionary science to an investigation of such psychic phenomena as are well authenticated and within common knowledge. The work has been enthusiastically received by the press and has been endorsed by the Theosophical Society of New York. Cloth, $1.50.

SON OF MAN.

By CELESTIA ROOT LANG. The author seeks to place the Christ-principle or theory of divine incarnation, of which Jesus is an example, on purely scientific grounds, making it an orderly sequence of psychic evolution, and eliminating here, as elsewhere, the idea of supernatural intervention. For this work the author claims, and we think justly, that it is thoroughly consistent with the spirit of the teachings of Jesus and the evolution theory. Her citations from Scripture are wonderfully apt. Indeed she presents many of Jesus' sayings in an entirely new light, apparently justifying her claim to an interpretation of Christianity from a higher plane of spiritual insight.—Literary Digest. Cloth, $1.25.

PSYCHICS: FACTS AND THEORIES.

By Rev. MINOT J. SAVAGE. Dr. Savage is

universally recognized as the lead thinker of the liberal wing of the U tarian clergy, and his experience speculations will command respect attention everywhere. This volume is tensely interesting, containing as it doe marvellous line of well authentica ghost stories, and vivid portrayals various psychical phenomena, which as interesting as fiction, although in ev instance they are fortified by evidence the most convincing character.
It is an unprejudiced, very candid pre tation of the case, by a particularly petent investigator, who seeks the Tru first and always, no matter what may its bearings on his own previous beli The interest and value of the cases relates can hardly be overestimated.— Times, Hartford, Conn. Cloth, $1 paper, 50 cents.

THE LAW OF LAWS; or, Origin, Natu and Destiny of the Soul.

By Prof. S. P. WAIT. In this rema able work no theory is offered, but a tion is invited to the operation of ce principles that are as fixed, orderly, enduring as the laws of any scie This book will put the Bible for many an entirely new light. The Over-shad ing power of God is set forth as the of Laws, the involuntary principle w is the cause of all phenomena of so-ca natural evolution, thus supplying missing link which makes science re lous and religion scientific. Cloth, $1.

ESSAYS.

J ACTS AND FICTIONS OF LIFE.

By HELEN H. GARDENER. Helen Gardener is at her best in the most difficult literary channel, that of the essa_'st. She says more in fewer words than any writer of the day.—Louisville Courier-Journal. Cloth, $1.25; paper, 50 cents.

MEDITATIONS IN MOTLEY.

By WALTER BLACKBURN HARTE. Mr. Harte is a litterateur of the light and humorous sort, with a keen eye for observation, and an extremely facile pen. He has some original ideas and always an original way of putting things.
The writer if not quite a genius, is very closely related to one. There is a sly and quiet humor everywhere present, and bits of sarcasm scattered here and there, which provoke a quiet smile. On the whole, we give a warm welcome to the volume, and hope that the author will

soon sharpen his quill for more work the same kind.—New York Herald. Clo $1.25.

ESSAYS AND POEMS.

By THOMAS BABINGTON MACAULAY. Th vols. Cloth (for set), $3.00.

THE REIGN OF LUST. A Satire.

By THE DUKE OF OATMEAL. This is remarkably clever burlesque or satire o well-known work written by, and on tain doctrines attributed to, a promin Scotch nobleman and British libe statesman, who is thinly disguised un the title of "the Duke of Oatmeal." "lust" the author means greed, and object is to show that, by following t Duke's line of argument, lust or greed c be proved to be the great ruling force the universe. Cloth, 75 cents; paper, cents.

POETRY.

SONGS.

By NEITH BOYCE. Illustrated. A collection of dainty poems in white and gold, bound in heavy paper, $1.25.

THE FINISHED CREATION AND OTHER POEMS.

By BENJAMIN HATHAWAY. Mr. Hathaway

might be glad to borrow. His songs real songs, always forceful and noble, always and intensely lyrical.—Bos Times.
A true poetic quality, a delicate insig and exalted thought.—Boston Budg Cloth, $1.25.

THE LEAGUE OF THE IROQUOIS.

of picturesque description and graceful portraiture, and its versification is fairly melodious.—Harper's Magazine.
Has the charm of Longfellow's "Hiawatha."—Albany Evening Journal.
Of rare excellence and beauty.—American Wesleyan.
Evinces fine qualities of imagination, and is distinguished by remarkable grace and fluency.—Boston Gazette. Cloth, $1.00; red line, $1.50.

VISION OF THYRZA.

By IRIS. A dramatic poem in blank verse. It is an invocation to the gods, a fine revival of the classical form, after the manner of Swinburne's "Atalanta in Calydon," appealing to them in the name of despairing humanity to visit the earth and reform the follies and vices of society. Cloth, 75 cents.

FOR TO-DAY. Poems.

By FRANCES M. MILNE. The noble aim of all Mrs. Milne's writings, combined with their great literary merit, should commend them to all. What Whittier was to the anti-slavery movement, Mrs. Milne is to this greater movement of to-day, which is based on "equal rights for all, special privilege to none," which means freedom not alone for the black man, nor the white man, but for all mankind.—The Star, San Francisco. Cloth, $1.00.

THE AZTECS.

By WALTER WARREN. Uniform with "Columbus the Discoverer."
Mr. Walter Warren is a man evidently in warm sympathy for his kind. His play is gorgeous with the local color of Mexico in the fifteenth century, and replete with fine thoughts, which, however, he acknowledges might not have come to Aztecs, although, again, he alleges they might. Its plot is a noble conception.—The Commonwealth, Boston. Cloth, $1.25.

COLUMBUS THE DISCOVERER. A Drama.

By WALTER WARREN. A spirited drama in five acts. Mr. Walter Warren makes a psychologic rather than a historic-though not unhistoric—study of the character of Columbus, as manifested and developed in connection with his experiences before, during, and after his discovery of America. In dramatizing a story in this fashion, one gains a better insight into the personality of Columbus than is possible from the merely abstract narratives.—The Boston Herald. Cloth, $1.25.

CECIL THE SEER.

By WALTER WARREN. In peacock blue and silver, uniform with above.
A strong drama from a literary point of view. This is not the author's first attempt at drama but his most ambitious one. It is rich in metaphysical thought stated in the tersest way. Epigrams abound and they have the Shakespearian vigor.—The Sentinel, Indianapolis, Ind. Cloth, $1.25.

SONG BLOSSOMS. Poems.

By JULIAN ANNA WALCOTT. It is a book of sweet, tender, and wholesome poetic thought throughout.—The Times, Boston, Mass. Cloth, $1.25.

FICTION.

Stories Dealing with the Double Standard of Morals.

A MORAL BLOT.

By SIGMUND ALEXANDER. The world of novel readers has always felt the fascination of the strong lights and shadows of the world of Bohemia. It is into this world of picturesque figures, generous thinking and kindliness, of youth and beauty and talent, ambition and joys and sorrows, all keen and vivid and fleeting, that Sigmund B. Alexander introduces us in "A Moral Blot." Cloth, $1.25; paper, 50 cents.

IS THIS YOUR SON, MY LORD?

By HELEN H. GARDENER. It is the opinion of some of the best contemporary critics that this is the most powerful American novel written in this generation. No braver voice was ever raised, no clearer note was ever struck, for woman's honor and childhood's purity.—The Vanguard, Chicago.
It comes very close to any college man who has kept his eyes open. When we finish we may say, not "Is This Your Son, My Lord?" but "Is It I?"—Nassau Literary Magazine, Princeton. Cloth, $1.00; paper, 50 cents.

PRAY YOU, SIR, WHOSE DAUGHTER?

By HELEN H. GARDENER. "The civil and canon law," writes Mrs. Elizabeth Cady Stanton, "state and church alike make the mothers of the race a helpless and ostracized class, pariahs of a corrupt civilization. In Helen Gardener's stories I see the promise of such a work of fiction as shall paint the awful facts of woman's position in living colors."
Every legislator in every state should read it and ask his conscience whether if such iniquitous laws are on the statute book of his state, he should not hasten to move their repeal.—Public Opinion. Cloth, $1.00; paper, 50 cents.

THE FORTUNES OF MARGARET WELD.

By Mrs. S. M. H. GARDNER. The book is an interesting contribution to the social problem which has for its solution the better adjustment from a social point of view of the status of the man who sins and that of the woman who sins with him. There is a moral in the book and one which it is to be hoped will not escape the reader. The story teaches the lesson of kindness and charity towards an erring woman in a manner which should go far to impress it permanently upon the minds of all who read it.—The Evening Item, Philadelphia. Cloth, $1.25; paper, 50 cents.

UNVEILING A PARALLEL.

By ALICE M. JONES and Mrs. ELLA MERCHANT. "Unveiling a Parallel: a Romance," by Two Women of the West, is

Fiction. Stories Dealing with the Double Standard of Morals.—Continue

the latest of the Arena Publishing Company's issues. It minutely describes, with mingled strength and delicacy of touch, a visit to the much-studied planet of Mars. Entertaining as the story is, it is but a vehicle for conveying the most advanced thoughts in regard to the crying evils of the time, and advocates a wholesome human doctrine of reform.—Boston Transcript. Cloth, $1.25; paper, 50 cents.

THE STRIKE OF A SEX.

By GEORGE N. MILLER. I wish every thoughtful man and woman in this republic

would read it. The author has looke to the heart of woman, and with uns able love for both sexes has writter truth.—Kate Field's Washington. P 25 cents.

AFTER THE SEX STRUCK, or Z sent's Discovery.

By GEORGE N. MILLER. The seque "The Strike of a Sex." This is writte response to a great demand to know v was Zugassent's Discovery, the quer Mr. Miller's first book. Paper, 25 cen

Fiction of Purpose, Dealing with Social, Economic, and Political Problem

WHO LIES?

By EMIL BLUM and SIGMUND ALEXANDER. This is unquestionably the most vivid and realistic exposé of the sham hypocrisy and lies of conventional society which has appeared since the publication of Max Nordau's "Conventional Lies of Civilization."
This is one of the boldest, most radical and realistic works of the decade. It is unconventional as it is unique, and will unquestionably call forth criticism in quarters where its shafts enter.—Illinois State Sentinel. Cloth, $1.00; paper, 50 cents.

EARTH REVISITED.

By BYRON A. BROOKS. Mr. Brooks is an earnest man. He has written a religio-philosophical novel of the life in the coming century. . . . Social and scientific and religious evolution have in a hundred years contrived to make an almost irrecognizable world of it. Human nature is changed; altruism is fully realized; worship has become service of man; the struggle for wealth and social rank has ended. Mr. Brooks' book is worth reading by all sincere people, and in particular by those interested in Christian socialism and applied Christianity.—The Outlook, New York. Cloth, $1.25; paper, 50 cents.

MOTHER, WILL, AND I.

By MILTON COIT. A skilful psychological analysis of character. It depicts the possible revolt of certain spiritual elements in civilized society from idealism to materialism and anarchy. It shows how society creates its own spectres. Cloth, $1.25; paper, 50 cents.

CHRIST THE SOCIALIST.

By the author of "Philip Meyer's Scheme."
This is a novel and interesting story of a New England manufacturing town. It tells the story of the conversion of a minister from the errors of his social philosophy to a more Christ-like view of human needs and life and destiny. The means of this slow change of life-long and unquestioned convictions is an old Scotch schoolmaster, who is an open and avowed socialist. Cloth, $1.25; paper, 50 cents.

AI; A Social Vision.

By Rev. CHARLES S. DANIEL. One of the most ingenious, unique, and thought-provoking stories of the present generation. It is a social vision, and in many respects the most noteworthy of the many remarkable dreams called forth by the general unrest and intellectual activity of the

present generation. Cloth, $1.25; pa 50 cents.

CÆSAR'S COLUMN.

By IGNATIUS DONNELLY. A story of twentieth century and the downfall plutocratic civilization. The one hund and eightieth thousand; thirteenth tion.
As an example of the highest literary f it deserves unstinted praise.—Card Gibbons.
A very extraordinary production.- Rev. Henry C. Potter.
The book is a plea and a striking Its plot is bold, its language is force and the great uprising is given terrible vividness.—Public Opinion, York. Cloth, $1.25; paper, 50 cents.

JUST PLAIN FOLKS.

By E. STILLMAN DOUBLEDAY. The p people have always fought freedo battle. So here—the author takes common work-a-day characters that brush against every hour, and shows their hopes, fears, aspirations, their cesses and defeats, in most vivid man The story appeals to the great throbb heart of humanity. It is strong, earn masculine, yet at times touchingly ten and pathetic.—Editor of The Are Boston. Cloth, $1.25; paper, 50 cents.

A THOUGHTLESS YES.

By HELEN H. GARDENER. The te edition of these stories is now publis in a new and attractive form. The York Tribune says: "Marked by a qu philosophy, shrewd, sometimes pung reflection, each one possesses eno purely literary merit to make its way hold its own. 'The Lady of the Club indeed a terrible study of social abu and problems, and most of the others gest more in the same direction." Cl $1.00; paper, 50 cents.

PUSHED BY UNSEEN HANDS.

By HELEN H. GARDENER. The for edition is now ready.
Must add to her already enviable rep tion.—Boston Traveller.
The book is clever, dramatic, and l literary sense has much merit.—New Y Times.
Fascinating to the imagination.— Orleans Picayune. Cloth, $1.00; paper cents.

A SPOIL OF OFFICE.

By HAMLIN GARLAND. Radically un ventional, and doubtless the truth of Western life that

American fiction.—Commercial Advertiser, Detroit, Mich.
A work which possesses a fascinating interest for the superficial reader, and many excellent suggestions for the thoughtful student of the economic questions of the day—a rare combination.—Books and Notions, Toronto, Can. Cloth, $1.00; paper, 50 cents.

MAIN TRAVELLED ROADS.

By HAMLIN GARLAND. This volume has become one of the standard works of contemporary fiction.
"Main Travelled Roads" contains six American pastorals. not eighteenth-century, Dresden-china types, but real idyls of the farmer. Its characters are alive—individuals, not types, that the author's skill has made catholic in their appeal to the reader.—Review of Reviews, London, Eng. Paper, 50 cents.

JASON EDWARDS: An Average Man. A Story of City and Country Life among the Toilers.

By HAMLIN GARLAND. Garland is a fresh, vigorous, and original writer. He has lately leaped into fame, and promises as much as any contemporary American writer.—Toronto Globe. Cloth, $1.00; paper, 50 cents.

THE STORY OF A CAÑON.

By BEVERIDGE HILL. This story may be looked upon as a literary agate, in which the varied threads of mining life are clustered and outlined like the mossy threads in the preserving stone. It shows the daily life of the hardy mountaineers and miners of the highlands of Colorado, and touches upon their view of the silver question. Cloth, $1.50; paper, 50 cents.

THE TROUBLE OF LIVING ALONE.

By F. R. HOFMAN. A new novel portraying political life and ambition by a new writer who tells a good story for the story's sake. It deals with questions of the day, and phases of American life which are now much in men's minds. The author has a suggestive style, and he tells his story freshly. Cloth, $1.25; paper, 50 cents.

ARISTOPIA.

By CASTELLO N. HOLFORD. "Aristopia" is an original conception, and the picture it gives of the founding and development of an ideal republic in Virginia in the seventeenth century holds that subtle verisimilitude to fact that so few Utopian imaginations can impart to their fantastic creations. Cloth, $1.25; paper, 50 cents.

THE CHRONICLES OF BREAK O' DAY.

By E EVERETT HOWE. This is a story of varied life in the West. The hero is a "hired man." and he has an abundance of adventures—more, perhaps, than fall to the lot of the average "hired man" on a farm, but surely none too many to please the lover of a good story told for the story's sake

The volume abounds in descriptions scenery, studies of men, women, events, and underlying all is a quiet l story. In descriptive writing and an sis of motive Mr. Howe seems to b strength. The villany of certain c acters is not overdrawn, nor are virtues of others overestimated. In and treatment the "Chronicles" imp one as a record of daily life.—Det Journal. Cloth, $1.25; paper, 50 cents.

ONE THOUSAND DOLLARS A DAY.

By ADELINE KNAPP. Of this book famous poet Joaquin Miller has "Great stuff! Capital stuff! Full of points, well put."
A forcible, earnest writer and a woma brains; her work never declines fro certain established mark of excellenc The Saturday Press, Oakland, Cal. Cl 75 cents.

WHICH WAY, SIRS, THE BETTER?

By JAMES M. MARTIN. A story deal with the industrial question. It tells story of a great strike and shows one out of the difficulties of this probl Cloth, 75 cents; paper, 25 cents.

MUGWUMPS.

By ONE OF THEM. A vivid story political life behind the scenes in Bost It shows how a promising young la could have been a "statesman" if he sacrificed his principles and worked "machine." His democratic opinions sturdy independence also cost him heiress. It is a rattling good story American life. Cloth, $1.25; paper, cents.

YOUNG WEST; a Sequel to "Loo Backward."

By SOLOMON SCHINDLER. This is only a supplement to, but the com ment of, the famous nationalistic d ment, "Looking Backward." "Yo West" describes his own eventful ca from his first awakening to consciousr to his age of threescore and ten, t picturing life in its various phases, a will be acted out by a citizen of United States of America in the twen second century. Cloth, $1.25; paper, cents.

SALOME SHEPARD, REFORMER.

By HELEN M. WINSLOW. Miss Winsl does not enter idly into discussions wh she cannot ably and righteously uph Her book is strong, keen, and power and her ideas are so expressive that t meaning is clearly conveyed. — Bo Herald.
There is, however, not a dull page in book, which has already been favor compared with Charles Reade's works.—Boston Journal. Cloth, $1. paper, 50 cents.

Fiction Dealing with Psychical, Metaphysical, and Occult Subjects.

AN APOCALYPSE OF LIFE.

By W. T. CHENEY. This is a metaphysical work of great importance, imbued with the new hope and the new thinking. The one great basal fact of the author's philosophy, the foundation of his book, is the truth of a higher spiritualism, which necessarily classes man as a spiritual entity with spiritual powers and attributes of being, and a spiritual destiny resulting therefrom that links him with the Infinite Spirit. Cloth, $1.25; paper, 50 cents.

PILATE'S QUERY.

By S. C. CLARK. This is one of the strongest and most convincing books setting forth the claims and data of spiritualism ever written. The work is put in the form of a novel, and it portrays the soul history of a young man and his wife. The title of the book is taken from the New Testament, Pilate's famous question, "What is Truth?" It examines Theosophy, Unitarianism, and Spiritualism. Cloth, $1.25; paper, 50 cents.

DR. JOHN SAWYER.

By Mrs. ELVINA J. BARTLETT. A story of psychic phenomena. Cloth, 75 cents.

THE DOUBLE MAN.

By F. B. DOWD. This is a story of spiritualistic phenomena and hypnotism. It is a study in the complexities of the moral nature of man and presents two startling types in contrast—the spiritually aspiring mind and the carnal and selfish mind. It shows that intellect alone cannot fill the demands of the soul. The mind and life must be spiritualized. The hero's journeyings in the spiritual world, which follow the drama as it is played out on earth, will be interesting to all who are adherents of spiritualism or students of this and other occult theories. Cloth, $1.25; paper, 50 cents.

BROTHER OF THE THIRD DEGREE.

By WILL L. GARVER. This is a story of occultism, and its events are supposed to transpire in the twentieth century. The Brothers who give their name to the story constitute a strange society, in which those admitted pass through various spiritual experiences and temptations. The object of the society is the development of the highest morality and the capacity to live in the pure spirit, and its members attain the most wonderful occult and clairvoyant faculties and powers. Cloth, $1.25; paper, 50 cents.

BETWEEN TWO FORCES.

By FLORA HELM. This is a strange and brilliant book by a new writer who will surely take a high place in the literary world. She is widely read in psychic philosophy and physics. In this fascinating story she shows in one small circle of life the perpetual conflict between passion and aspiration which has always rent the world, and still rends it. In her development of the character of Younod Rencliffe, who has discovered the secret of incorruptible psychic life, even in the flesh, by the complete elimination of human passion and emotion and affection, the author displays a very real literary power, which will have to be reckoned with by those who seek to estimate the progress and quality of our contemporary literature. Cloth, $1.25; paper, 50 cents.

THE DREAM CHILD.

By FLORENCE HUNTLEY. A fascinat romance of two worlds.
Although simple and unvarnished w any inflammable descriptions, enth the mind to the exclusion of ot thoughts, until reluctantly the rea closes the last page.—Minneapolis Sun Times. Cloth, $1.00; paper, 50 cents.

FORBES OF HARVARD.

By ELBERT HUBBARD. The sketches character and the bits of philoso give charm and value to the whole. philosophy of the love letters is no idealistic yet simple, practical rather t abstract, and the letters of Honor in ticular exhibit the beautiful aspiration the tenderness of a strong nature. I worthy's tales of college pranks and se comic love rhapsodies supply the fun, there is a suggestion of adventure n the end.—The Boston Traveler. Clo $1.25; paper, 50 cents.

MARGARET SALISBURY.

By MARY HOLLAND LEE. The setting the story is vivid and picturesque, bri ing the period of our Civil War, and touches upon New England and Virg life are full of local color, provin phraseology and dramatic power. N Lee strikes the note of heredity firm and the most tragic complication of plot hinges upon the unlawful use hypnotic power. The sad struggles of great rebellion are incidentally set for Cloth, $1.25; paper, 50 cents.

THE MYSTERY OF EVELIN DELOR

By ALBERT BIGELOW PAINE. "The M tery of Evelin Delorme," a hypno story by Albert Bigelow Paine, deals w the curious phenomena of a dual per ality. The author has made a good sto with this idea as a basis, and ended it a grand climax.—Detroit Free Pre Cloth, 75 cents.

THE PASSING OF ALIX.

By Mrs. MARJORIE PAUL. A story sh ing the perils which are too often incld to alliances between American girls members of the European nobility, which one seeks a title and social am tion and the other money. Cloth, $1. paper, 50 cents.

ZENIA THE VESTAL.

By MARGARET B. PEEKE. In this w the author tells us upon the title page has been assisted by the Brotherhood by order of the Hierophant Egyptian Alcantra of Granada, under direction the Algerine. It is certainly a very markable volume of ancient and mod lore, skilfully blended in the alembic o narrative of life that passes from actual into the supernormal and magi The vehicle of strange teachings is a st of contemporary social life, in which characters are mostly American. main purpose of the book, however, is embodying in proper relation the occ laws of spiritual development, as given the wise men of other lands and tim Cloth, $2.00.

THE OPEN SECRET.

By A PRIEST. A wonderful story of munication with the planet Mars. Scie in the dress of fantastic fiction. O 75 cents.

Fiction. Dealing with Psychical, Metaphysical, and Occult Subjects.—Conti

IT IS POSSIBLE.

By HELEN VAN ANDERSON. The author shows wonderful insight into child-life, and the story is delightful.

"It Is Possible," by Mrs. Helen Van Anderson, is a story written evidently by a thinker of more than usual ability.—Inter-Ocean, Chicago.

"It Is Possible," by Mrs. Helen Van Anderson, is a work deserving of a large sale and of being widely read. No one can read the book without partaking, in some measure at least, of the intense spirituality which pervades the story.—American Farm News. Cloth, $1.25; paper, 50 cents.

THE RIGHT KNOCK.

By HELEN VAN ANDERSON. An extraordinary story dealing with psychic forces and the science of healing as practised by the Christian Scientists.

If a book comes from the heart, it will contrive to reach the heart.—Carlyle.

"The Right Knock" is presented with no other apology than this, it has come from the heart.—Author's Preface. Cloth, $1.25.

LIFE.

By WILLIAM W. WHEELER. A story of unusual vigor and imagination, and ten with fine literary art.

In the form of a novel, called "L William W. Wheeler has put before public some of the clearest statemen logical ideas regarding humanity's pre aspects, its inherent and manifest pot and its future, that we have ever

The book is strong, keen, powerful; ning over with thought, so expressed to clearly convey the author's ideas; et thing is to the point, nothing superflu —and for this it is especially admirabl The Boston Times. Cloth, $1.25; pa 50 cents.

REST.

By WILLIAM W. WHEELER. A v strange and bizarre story.

The title of this curious and interest work gives only a faint idea of its port. It will be found especially inte ing to those who understand the spirit philosophy, inasmuch as it is a very genious attempt to show what may be possiblities for man in other spheres advanced knowledge and consequ power over material elements, such spiritual phenomena already give a mens of in the materializing and de terializing of objects.—The Religio-F osophical Journal. Cloth, $1.25; pa 50 cents.

Historical Novels.

AN UNOFFICIAL PATRIOT.

By HELEN H. GARDENER. This is a story of the war, but it is the first story of its kind that has appeared in our literature.

Is in many ways the most remarkable historical novel of the Civil War which has yet appeared. The story is filled with strong dramatic incidents, and there is a bit of charming romance. Mrs. Gardener has produced a book that will take very high rank in the historical literature of the War of the Rebellion; for although presented in the form of a novel, its historical value cannot be questioned.—Boston Home Journal. Cloth, $1.25; paper, 50 cents.

ENEMIES IN THE REAR.

By Rev. FRANCIS T. HOOVER. Promin among the forces with which the natio government had to contend in the while the Southern armies were in front were the Knights of the Gol Circle, otherwise known as the Sons Liberty.

In "Enemies in the Rear" an effort made to preserve the history of some the doings of this most dangerous org zation. In the form of a popular st Mr. Hoover presents to the reader an side iew of the workings of the Knig of the Golden Circle. Cloth, $1.50; pa 50 cents.

Miscellaneous Fiction.

BORN IN THE WHIRLWIND.

By Rev. WILLIAM ADAMS, D. D. The plan of the work is admirable, sometimes even bold and striking, its plot ingenious and well sustained, its tone lofty and pure, its motive and moral suited to stimulate lofty aspirations and to make duplicity and revenge hateful in our eyes. The style, moreover, is very fine.—Christian Observer, Louisville, Ky. Cloth, $1.25; paper, 50 cents.

WHERE THE TIDES MEET.

By EDWARD PAYSON BERRY. The plot of "Where the Tides Meet" is very strong, and the story is told in such simple yet graphic language that the interest is held at a high pitch from the first chapter.—The Topeka Advocate. Cloth, $1.25; paper, 50 cents.

UNION DOWN.

By SCOTT CAMPBELL. In "Union Down" the author writes in his most interesting vein. It is an affecting story powerfully told, replete with vivid pictures wh boldest outlines are softened by an arti mingling of light and shade. It is a st of passion and pathos, of love and w love will do, of woman's patience man's erring, of remorse, repentance, self-sacrifice—a story which should ment the author's not undeserved rep tion. Cloth, $1.25; paper, 50 cents.

REDBANK.

By M. L. COWLES. This book abounds delightful descriptions of old South "dining-days," of free, joyous ri through the pines, of child-life on plantation—of all things, in short, t make up the real South, known only the Southerner and never portrayed m faithfully, more graphically, more cha ingly, than by Mrs. Cowles. Cowles is a fairer representative of So ern culture, a far better exponen Southern feeling and customs, than other writers of that section. All So erners who feel an interest in the aut of the South, all Northerners who d to obtain an insight into real Sou life, should read this valuable and thoroughly delightful novel.—Public Opinion, New York. Cloth, $1.00; paper, 50 cents.

OVER THE OLD TRAIL.

By LEWIS B. FRANCE. "Over the Old Trail" takes the reader back some thirty years to the picturesque scenes of a Colorado mining camp, just after the close of the war. A delightful love story, which gives us the old sweet and perpetually charming sentiment of old-fashioned lovers. The book has so much charming literary art and delicious sentiment that it promises to become as popular as Mr. France's other books, "Pine Valley," "With Rod and Line," "Mr. Dide," etc. Cloth, $1.25; paper, 50 cents.

KERCHIEFS TO HUNT SOULS.

By M. AMELIA FYTCHE. A story of Bohemian life in Paris, full of vivid pictures of the fascinating Latin quarter. It shows the trials, difficulties, and temptations to which a pretty young American girl is exposed in the gay environment of Paris, among students and artists and writers. The purpose of the book, as far as any purpose is revealed in this story of love and incident, may be said to lie in pointing out the dangers of marriages for love and passion, without intellectual and moral affinity. Cloth, $1.25; paper, 50 cents.

A MUTE CONFESSOR.

By WILL N. HARBEN. A stirring romance of a Southern town.
Full of beauty and strength combined; an ideal union.—Boston Ideas.
If knowledge and insight and the flawless taste of the artist can make a popular novel, "A Mute Confessor" will be one of the season's literary successes.—New York Home Journal. Cloth, $1.00; paper, 50 cents.

ONE DAY.

By ELBERT HUBBARD. Elbert Hubbard has given us in "One Day" a tale of the prairies as exquisitely cut as the finest cameo. It is perfect in conception and construction.—The World, New York. Cloth, 75 cents.

EDITH : A Story of Chinatown.

By HARRY M. JOHNSON. The object of this well told and interesting story is to draw attention to a moral evil that is allowed to flourish in the Chinese quarter of San Francisco. Cloth, 75 cents; paper, 25 cents.

A JOURNEY TO VENUS.

By GUSTAVUS W. POPE. This romance, by a writer who may well be called the American Jules Verne, gives a most entertaining and exciting account of a trip, by a combined party of Terrestrials and inhabitants of the planet Mars, to the planet Venus by means of the "ethervolt," which enables them to traverse the interplanetary spaces at a speed far greater than that of the earth in its orbit. The exploration of Venus which the party makes is full of exciting adventures, hairbreadth escapes, and perilous vicissitudes. Cloth, $1.50; paper, 50 cents.

THE CHILDHOOD OF AN AFFINITY.

By KATHARINE E. RAND. A striki study of psychology of child life in form of a story. Love has hitherto considered solely as the passion of turity. But here we find the revela that the attraction of sex exercises subtle influence at a very tender among little men and women, and we love in pinafores. Cloth, $1.25; paper, cents.

ONE OF EARTH'S DAUGHTERS.

By ELLEN ROBERTS. "One of Eart Daughters" possesses the strongest fem sketch that has been sent out in the son's fiction. The style is easy, ra common sense, and graceful, and is un cumbered by useless or flowery verbiag The Minneapolis Tribune. Cloth, $1. paper, 50 cents.

DAVID AND ABIGAIL.

By B. F. SAWYER. "David and Abiga is, notwithstanding its biblical title, story of modern days. It is a wholeso story; it will be read around the even lamp. Men will smile, women may c all will be better for the reading. Clo $1.25; paper, 50 cents.

THE KEYS OF FATE.

By HERMAN SHORRS. This story ha purpose not expressed as in a tale wit moral, but in its life-like presentati The scene of the story is laid in N England, and it is a tale of incident romance. Cloth, $1.25; paper, 50 cents

A WEDDING TANGLE.

By FRANCES CAMPBELL SPARHAWK. name of Miss Frances Campbell S hawk is not unknown to American r ers, and this new volume from her will attract hosts of fresh admirers to already long train of followers. Ther a vivid sense of reality throughout Wedding Tangle" which carries us b to old colonial times. The effort is, b ever, to untangle a wedding problem threatened to mar the happiness of principal actors in this drama.—The ton Herald. Cloth, $1.25; paper, 50 ce

ZAPHRA.

By JOHN P. STOCKTON, Jr. A stri story of social conditions in the east of New York by a new author, John Stockton, Jr., who, however, comes f good literary stock, for his uncle is famous Frank R. Stockton. The s also touches incidentally on the deve ment and progress of psychic scie Cloth, 75 cents; paper, 25 cents.

A MARKET FOR AN IMPULSE.

By WILLIAM WHITTEMORE TUFTS. Thi a very charming love story. The dialo is especially smart and natural and sp ling, reminding the reader here and t in its bright, epigrammatic turns George Meredith's playful cut and th It glides lightly over the deeper spi of human thought and conduct, and veals as few contemporary writers the dramatic intensity of the psycho tragedy of life beneath its surfaces of monotony. Cloth, $1.25, pa cents.

Fiction. Miscellaneous Fiction.—Continued.

BEHOLDING AS IN A GLASS.

By VIRGINIA D. YOUNG. This is a clever and vivid story of life in the middle West, which will attract as much attention as Miss Wilkins' New England stories or

Will Allen Dromgoole's Tennessee stories on account of the skill and fidelity with which the provincialisms and peculiar characteristics and customs of the people of that great section are depicted. Cloth, $1.25; paper, 50 cents.

COPLEY SQUARE SERIES.

Works on Economic Problems.

(Published only in paper.) Price 25 cents.

A BETTER FINANCIAL SYSTEM; or Government Banks.

By GEORGE O. WARD. Price, 25 cents. A valuable exposition of the financial situation. The work of a strong, keen, logical thinker and student. This book should be in the hands of every man with a vote and a mind.

BONDHOLDERS AND BREADWINNERS.

By S. S. KING of the Kansas City Bar. Price, 25 cents. President L. L. Polk, National F. A. and I. V., says: "It should be placed in the hands of every voter of this country."

ESAU; or The Banker's Victim.

By Dr. T. A. BLAND. Price, 25 cents. It is a most thrilling story of war, love, and tragedy. It is in a new line, and will fill a new channel of thought and prove a most valuable campaign book. In writing it you have served well your country.— Hon. John Davis, M. C.

Per hundred, $10.00.

FREE SILVER.

By SIDNEY DELL. Price, 25 cents. The central idea of the author's argument is that the panic of 1893 was caused by the rise in gold through money contraction by foreign nations, and that the resulting confiscation in falling values can be defeated by the United States Congress by

restoring free coinage and full legal tender power to the old silver dollar.

INDUSTRIAL FREEDOM.

By JOHN DAVIS, M. C., Gov. LIONEL A. SHELDON, C. C. POST, and C. WOOD DAVIS. Price, 25 cents. Strong articles by able writers.

MONEY, LAND AND TRANSPORTATION.

By C. WOOD DAVIS, HAMLIN GARLAND, and R. B. HASSELL. Price, 25 cents. A new declaration of rights. The sub-treasury plan. The railroad problem.

OUR COUNTRY'S NEED.

By Prof. FRANK PARSONS. Price, 25 cents. The author is well known to students of law and lawyers in the East as a counsellor-at-law and master of the science.

SWISS SOLUTIONS OF AMERICAN PROBLEMS.

By W. D. McCRACKAN, A. M. Price, 25 cents. All who are interested in good government, good citizenship, a pure ballot, real political and social freedom, will find the crystallization of their ideas in this remarkable little document.

ARENA PUBLISHING CO.

COPLEY SQUARE, BOSTON, MASS.

FOR SALE BY

ALL NEWS DEALERS

AND

THE ARENA PUBLISHING CO.

COPLEY SQUARE, BOSTON, MASS.

ADDENDA.

LIFE AND WRITINGS OF AMELIA C. BLOOMER.

By D. C. BLOOMER. The author allows Mrs. Bloomer to tell her life so far as possible in her own words. Copious extracts from her writings are given. Her intimacy with Horace Greeley, Susan B. Anthony, and Elizabeth Cady Stanton, and her prominence in various reform movements gave her a world-wide fame. As the book abounds in anecdotes and information concerning contemporary reform and reformers, it should meet and satisfy a long felt want. Cloth, $1.25; paper, 50 cents.

BEAUTY FOR ASHES.

By KATE CLARK BROWN. "What becomes of the souls that do not pass through the 'pearly gates'?" The author offers a speculative solution of this mysterious problem in a story that contains passages of much pathos and dramatic power. The old moral that man is purified by suffering, and will reap what he sows, is very cogently inculculated in this remarkable story. Cloth, 75 cents; paper 25 cents.

UNCLE JERRY'S PLATFORM.

By GILLIE CARY. This beautifully illustrated little book contains three stories, — "Uncle Jerry's Platform," "Pops," and "A Daughter of the Revolution." The first is a well told story in dialect in which a telling argument is made for "Temperance." The second sets forth the supreme devotion of a young negro boy for his little white charge. The third describes a thrilling rescue made Christmas, 1781, and the sequel. Cloth, 75 cents.

THE HEART OF OLD HICKORY.

By WILL ALLEN DROMGOOLE. Eight charming and popular stories by this gifted young Tennessee writer are collected in this beautiful volume. These stories are studies of different phases of human character and each study is a work of art. Raciness, strength, vividness, and felicity of expression characterize the author's style. The author is a literary genius. Cloth, $1.25; paper 50 cents.

NICODEMUS: A Poem.

By GRACE SHAW DUFF. In this fine blank-verse poem is given in autobiographic form as from the lips of Nicodemus himself a poetic account of the two episodes between that ruler of the Jews and Jesus as related in the third and seventh chapters of John's gospel. The poem is full of local color, and opens with a striking description of sunrise on the morning of the last day of the feast of Passover in Jerusalem. The book is beautifully printed and is finely illustrated. Cloth 75 cents.

HIS PERPETUAL ADORATION; or, The Captain's Old Diary.

By Rev. JOSEPH F. FLINT. This is an extremely interesting and realistic war story, told in the form of a diary left at his death by a veteran who had been a captain in the Northern army, with Grant at Vicksburg and with Sherman on his march to the sea. Two or three of the great events of the war are told in stirring fashion, but the narrative deals mainly with the inside life of the soldier in war time, and its physical and moral difficulties. Cloth, $1.25; paper, 50 cents.

HILL-CREST: A Novel.

By JULIA COLLITON FLEWELLYN. Hill-Crest is the homestead of an Irish-American family, consisting of father, four daughters, poor but proud, and an old maiden sister-in-law. A beautiful and fashionable young lady cousin is a disturbing element. The principal hero is an ideal young clergyman. The interest of this well-written love story centres in three love affairs that end in happy marriages. The narrative is marked by fine feeling and pervaded by a strongly religious and moral tone. Cloth, $1.25; paper, 50 cents.

THE CENTURY OF SIR THOMAS MORE.

By B. O. FLOWER. With frontispiece, full-page portrait of Sir Thomas More, and numerous pen and ink drawings of leading personages of his century, among whom are Gutenberg, Columbus, Erasmus, Luther, Calvin, Zwingli, Knox, Melanchthon, Michael Angelo, Raphael, Correggio, Titian, and Da Vinci. This work deals with the first century of modern times. It contains the following chapters:

I. Introduction.
II. A Glimpse of Western Europe During the Century of Which We Write.
III. The Reformation and Some of Its Leading Spirits.
IV. The Italy of the Renaissance.
V. Some Fatal Figures in the Italy of This Century.
VI. Bright Lights in Italian Life During the Renaissance.
VII. The Spanish Peninsula.
VIII. The France of This Century.
IX. The England of Sir Thomas More.
X. The Life of Sir Thomas More.
XI. Utopia Considered. (Part I.)
XII. Utopia Considered. (Part II.)
XIII. The Lives of Seneca and Sir Thomas More Compared.
XIV. A Brief Survey of the Century of Sir Thomas More.

Handsomely bound, with gilt side and back dies. Published only in cloth. Price, $1.50.

PERSONS, PLACES, AND IDEAS.

A magnificently illustrated volume of miscellaneous essays by B. O. Flower. This volume is printed on heavy enamelled paper, and contains over thirty full-page illustrations, with numerous smaller pictures. The edition is limited to one thousand copies. It is richly bound in colored cloth, with gilt side and back dies, gilt tops and uncut pages. The following is the table of contents:

I. Charles Darwin: A Character Sketch. With full-page portrait of the great scientist.
II. An Idealistic Dreamer, Who Sings in a Minor Key. With full-page portrait of Louise Chandler Moulton.
III. Mask or Mirror. A discussion of the difference between Artificiality and Veritism on the Stage. With four illustrations.
IV. A Poet of the People. With full-page portrait of James G. Clark.
V. After Sixty Years.
VI. Chester on the Dee. With full-page illustrations.
VII. Strolls Outside the Walls of Chester. With full-page illustrations.
VIII. Winter Days in Florida. With full-page illustrations.
IX. Religious Ideals of Colonial Days as Mirrored in Poetry and Song.

Fancy cloth, gilt side and back dies, gilt uncut edges. Published only in cloth, price

HE PAST.

ION MORE. This interesting and in-
book sets forth in the nature of an
he unending conflict between good
The story gives in outline the possi-
a Brahmin; his views of the conduct
of wives; the origin of *sute* or *suttee*
the wife with the corpse of her hus-
the reason for it. Thought trans-
lso, is touched upon in a new and
g way. The story is full of incident,
ptions are graphic, and the style is
Cloth, $1.25; paper, 50 cents.

S OF THOUGHT.

USSELL. Cloth, 75 cents; paper, 25

AND PATRIOTISM.

SCHULTZ. This book should be read
red by all who desire to be well in-
the literature of the day that has
a more intelligent grasp, on the part
ple, of the corruption in politics that
he endeavors of reformers. The evils
sent system are set forth and reme-
ested. If people at large were pos-
the facts presented by the author,
oubt rings and bosses would be rapidly
l from our political system. Cloth,
er, 50 cents.

D OF NADA: A Fairy Story.

G SCOTLAND. This fairy story should
aed by those who are in search of a
g book for children. There is in it
a philosophy which older heads can
consider. It is gotten up in beau-
. Cloth, 75 cents; paper, 25 cents.

TER OF HUMANITY.

t MAURICE SMITH. "The whole book,
er to cover, has been written with a
ustrate in a small degree the tempta-
trials that the average working-girl
to suffer — silently and without sym-
The story tells what reasons induced
ichmond," a Boston heiress, to enter
rk dry-goods house in the guise of a
what trials she bore, how bravely she
till her purpose was achieved, and
oiness crowned her endeavors. Cloth,
er, 50 cents.

OWS OF YESTER-YEAR : A

ERTINE TETERS. The interest of this
and powerful novel of character

analysis centres mainly in "the Madame," as
the heroine is called throughout the story,
which is written with remarkable insight into
character. The incidental discussions are so
original and clever that the reader's interest is
held enchained from the beginning to the very
end. Cloth, $1.25; paper, 50 cents.

POLITICS FOR PRUDENT PEOPLE.

By SLACK WORTHINGTON. The author aims to
establish the propositions that "mankind can
be substantially benefited only by the increased production and conservation of
wealth"; that "wealth is necessary to the
progress of civilization"; and that "mankind
is benefited by wealth, if it be reinvested and
not consumed, whosoever owns it." The book
is a substantial contribution to the literature
that deals with legislative and governmental
problems. Cloth, $1.00; paper, 50 cents.

DAME FORTUNE SMILED : The Doctor's Story.

By WILLIS BARNES. This volume attempts to
present a practical solution of the problem that
confronts those that regard their great wealth
as a public trust. It suggests to overworked
men and women, who are struggling with this
world's problems, the correct and feasible plan
for the equalization of capital with labor for
the moral and social benefit of the masses.
Cloth, $1.25; paper, 50 cents.

BEYOND.

By HENRY SEWARD HUBBARD. The author
declares that he has been away and that he has
become acquainted with the conditions that
follow death. His aim is to convince "those
who seem constitutionally unable to perceive
the reality of this other world, although willing
and anxious to be convinced," that "the truths
that pertain to the superior life do not conflict
with common sense, however they may rise
beyond the perfect grasp of that power of the
mind." Cloth, 75 cents; paper, 25 cents.

SIEGFRIED, the Mystic.

By IDA WORDEN WHEELER. This story is
written to acquaint the public with psychic
and occult phenomena. The central figure is
Siegfried, the mystic, whose main purpose in
life is to better the condition of his less fortunate fellowmen, chiefly by inducing them to
resolve to be stronger, braver, truer, more
loving and more kind. The book will give
pleasure to many who care naught for occultism, psychics, and Christian science. Cloth,
$1.25; paper, 50 cents.

TITLE INDEX.

15

The Next President Must Be an American In Fact as well as Name.

The American voter should demand either the immediate and unconditional repeal of the dark-lantern act by which silver was demonetized or the demonetization of gold by our government and the issuance of national greenbacks, full legal tender for all duties and taxes, *to a sufficient extent* to enable the business of this country to be carried on on practically the cash basis. The demonetization of gold by our government would bring England to her knees before the great republic, and we would hear a general clamor from over the water for speedy consummation of international bimetallism. The prosperity of every wealth-creator in the republic no less than the dignity of this government demands that we cease the miserable, servile, cringing policy, fawning at the feet of England, that we cease to imitate India and Egypt. Patriots of America, awake! The tocsin has sounded; the battle is on. There is not a moment to lose. The next president of the republic must an American in something more than name.

The Gold Ring must be Broken.

There can be neither happiness, progress, nor morality among a people where industrial slavery obtains; and precisely in proportion as the agrarian population are pushed to the wall through low prices for products and excessive charges for transportation of their products, the artisan will suffer, and later the merchant, the manufacturer, and all men engaged in creating wealth and carrying on legitimate business will find themselves caught between the upper and nether millstones of the British gold power

and the Wall Street gamblers.
fact will appeal to the conviction every thinking man who is not blin by prejudice or guided by a bl subserviency to a partisan press demagogues who betray the wea creator for place or profit.

The Battle of the Bank of England the American Tories against Am ca's Wealth Creators.

The interest of the manufacturer merchant is no less at stake than t of the farmer and artisan, but t may feel the general stagnation sioned by low prices less quickly the latter classes. But such is th terdependence of the units in thi public that what affects favorabl unfavorably any considerable clas wealth-producers must necessa sooner or later, affect in like ma all classes engaged in legitimate b ness, though in some instances pr may be *artificially* maintained fo little time. The gradual and ste ascendency of the financial polic England and the American tories the gold ring of both countries, s 1872, the result of which at first most heavily on the agrarian p tion, is to-day being felt in all bran of productive industry, and the s ing in selling prices, brought abou this English rule, is not only rap reducing one of the greatest we producing nations of the globe to a pendent condition and affording same conspiracy of English financ and American tories an opportu to saddle the nation with an imm bonded debt in a time of profc peace, but it is being felt more or severely by all legitimate and pr tive business throughout the r The battle of 1896 will be a ballots, cast by patriots against the power which more openly and less successfully assailed us in 1776.

~~~~~~~

The Talk of International Bimetallism, until the United States forces Europe to Come to Our Terms by Our Repealing the Demonetization Act, is Simply a Snare and Delusion of the Usurer Class, and should Deceive no Thinking Man or Woman.

All talk of international bimetallism is a snare and a delusion. It is part of a deliberate plan of the gold ring to divide the forces of progress, prosperity, and plenty. The only way in which international bimetallism can be brought about is by *the unconditional repeal by our government of the law which demonetized silver and all subsequent legislation which has directly or indirectly affected the ancient constitutional standing of silver.* This move would unquestionably (1) force the gold power to sue for international bimetallism; (2) it would turn the course of commerce of the world's great silver nations from England to America; (3) it would raise the prices of the *real wealth* of the nation and start into operation the wheels of business; (4) it would lend new energy to the arm of industry; (5) it would inspire our industrial millions with new hope; (6) it would bring the Bank of England and the tory class of America to a sudden halt, and place those who have so long subtly waged a winning battle against American independence and the prosperity of the wage-earners upon the defensive. The mighty uprising of the people against the gold ring, and the election of sturdy, incorruptible patriots next autumn will mean a far greater victory for republican institutions and the happiness and prosperity of our nation than the victory at Yorktown. There must be no faltering, no division, no lukewarmness among patriots or lovers of America from now till the polls close next November; nay more, not until the inauguration of an *American* president on the fourth of March, 1897.

Patriots of America.

"The Patriots of America" is t name of a recently instituted non-pa tisan political organization which rapidly growing in the West and Sou and also extending its influence ea ward. William H. Harvey, the we known author of "Coin's Financi School" and the successful opponent Roswell G. Horr in the celebrate financial debate of last summer, is the head of the order. The first lod was organized in Chicago late in D cember, and on March 10 about on hundred and fifty lodges had been o ganized in twenty-nine states and ter tories. The order is especially stro in Illinois, Michigan, and Missour but in nearly every Western stat reaching to the Pacific Ocean, there a lodges, and even Connecticut has or that is full of vigor. The growth this new order has been purely spont neous; no organizer up to the date March 10 had been sent into the fiel the propaganda being so far solely d pendent on a book issued by M Harvey in December last, which co tains the constitution of the organiza tion, its principles and purposes, an instructions as to formation of lodge

The order teaches the fundament principles of a people's government an inculcates the purest sentiments o true patriotism. It holds that th rights of humanity are paramount t selfish property interests or the di tates of any political party. It er deavors to impress upon its member the noble ideal of good citizenship s tersely expressed by Thomas Jefferso in the sentence, "Man serves himsel best by promoting the common good, as also the truly democratic declara tion of Abraham Lincoln that th government of this country is, o should be, "a government of th people, by the people, and for th people." In various cities and town public meetings under the auspices o this order have been held and the ain of the organization widely advertised

There is no mystery about the order and except that the lodge meetings ar held as executive sessions, from whic

cratic newspapers against this organization reminds one of the denunciations of the whiskey ring against
Benjamin Bristow for his service to
the republic when he brought so many
thieves to justice. Wherever there
is a lodge, any good citizen who will
subscribe to its principles may become a member of the "Patriots of
America." Neither the place of birth,
religious faith, nor the political party
affiliation of an applicant is any barrier to membership.

Senator Vest Resents the President's Calumny of the West.

Perhaps in recent years there has not
occurred anything more grotesque than
the invitation to Grover Cleveland to
address the Presbyterian Home Mission meeting, unless we except the address of Mr. Cleveland on that occasion. The insult he went out of the
way to give the West was as amazing
as it was wholly uncalled-for and untrue in fact and implication. It is not
strange, therefore, that it should be
resented in both branches of our government. Senator Vest of Missouri,
in the course of some remarks in the
Senate, made the following observations, as reported in the New York
World. In referring to this calumny
against the West by the president,
Senator Vest said:

"He stood with the ghastly light of
the hell-holes and the rumsellers of
New York blazing upon him, and cant-
ingly said home missions must be used
to civilize and christianize the West."

Continuing, the Democratic senator
from Missouri observed:

"There is a disposition on the part of
the present administration to treat
the Western people as though they
were in a condition of tutelage, as
though they needed correction and
guardianship and guidance. Even the
president of the United States, lately
on a missionary occasion," continued
Mr. Vest, "spoke of the West as a land
of immorality and crime. Our presi-

which we have heard so often in
childhood:

"From Montana's sinful mountain
 From Utah's wicked plains,
They call us to deliver
 Our land from error's chains."

There was long and loud laughter
Mr. Vest repeated the lines in tones
intense sarcasm.

"We are told," continued the senat
"by high ecclesiastical authority tl
his excellency has lately laid down
honors at the feet of Jesus. I am gl
to know it. It has been the gene
impression of the Democratic pa
that the mugwumps and incense bu
ers have got all those honors and inte
to keep them. I have great respect
the Christian religion and missions
home and abroad, but the presiden
statements are a slander upon the n
who with rifle in one hand and an a
in the other have gone out and bla
the pathway of civilization in th
Western wilds. I say to our presid
now that if he will interrupt hunt
ducks in North Carolina and sil
Democrats in Kentucky long enou
to come out West, we will show hi
God-fearing, self-respecting, law-ab
ing people; we will show him churcl
in which there is real and unaffect
piety. We will show him happy a
Christian homes where the son, t
husband, and the father pray. O
spires may not go as near heaven
do those of Eastern cities; we may n
have organs that roll delicious ton
along the fretted aisles, but we have
people who fear God and observe t
law and all the commandments as th
are given unto them.

"And, in comparison with this hu
ble but real worship, I am tempted
quote those beautiful lines of t
Scotch poet:

"Compared with this how poor rel
 ion's pride,
In all the pomp of method and of a
When men display to congregatio
 wide,
Devotion's ev'ry grace, except t
 heart.

"This is what we have come to at la
that the president of the United Stat
in his official capacity says to the pe
ple of the whole world that in one p
tion of this country their surroundin
are such that missions, home missio
are necessary in order to bring them
the proper knowledge of what is
and true,"

High Rates of Interest in the West where Men can Ill Afford to Pay.

In the ARENA for December, 1894, George Wilson, the Lexington, Missouri, banker, in answering the article of David A. Wells in the *Forum* of October, 1893, denied the statement of the latter that interest has been low in the United States for a number of years past. Mr. Wilson showed that the crops of the South and West are produced under the payment of a very high rate of interest. Mr. Wilson informs me that a man who used to lend money in Nebraska gave him the following facts: "I used to lend money to the farmers in Nebraska, most of my customers being hard-working, honest Swedes who always paid their interest promptly. I would lend a man in this way: would take his note for a certain sum and give him three-fourths of the sum named in the note, thus making a discount of twenty-five per cent to start on. Then he would pay me interest monthly at the rate of three per cent a month on the sum named in the note. Thus out of a note for $100 I would get $25 at the start and by the end of the year $36 more, or sixty-one per cent a year on my money."

It is not likely that the Swedish corn-growers and cattle-feeders of Nebraska would agree with Mr. Wells that money is cheap and plenty.

The Futility of a Plutocratic Press in its Act of Traducing an Honest Man.

The shameless manner in which the plutocratic press has misrepresented Senator Tillman for exposing the corruption and base betrayal of the wealth-creators by the gold ring, has exposed a tremendously significant fact, which, if these subservient tools of the bank of England and the Wall Street gamblers were more far-sighted they would appreciate, namely, that the people are thinking for themselves and are losing all faith in the partisan organs which have carried on sham battles for the past quarter of a century while the same ruinous financial

policy has been steadily carried o both parties irrespective of the sol pledges given in the platforms an the supposed representatives of people. The tens of thousands of ters which have been sent congra ting Senator Tillman, from sincere triots *who think and who are tir being echoes of a parrot press,* great number of papers which published his speech verbatim, are 'a few of the indications which s how thoroughly the people aroused. It is too early to predict will be the representative of the ple's Party or whom the silver fo and the defenders of an American tem of finance will nominate for presidency; but if reason and judg rule and the true reformers unite a our patriot fathers against the ag sion of England and the tories of R lutionary days, I believe no power prevent the triumph of American 1 ions for the restoration of the repu To me it seems of paramount portance that the South and the \ bear the standard of the we creators.

A Man Among Men Entirely Unfit for Presidency of a Free People.

The erstwhile railroad attor Thomas B. Reed, in his contempt treatment of the members of the 1 ple's Party in Congress represen over one million and a quarter vo or 6,000,000 people, proves beyond adventure, if such proof was nec (after his similar treatment of Democratic party when form speaker), the small nature of man, his total lack of broad, sta manlike qualities, and his total lac any conception of the ideals of rept can government. Thomas B. F should have been born four hunc years ago; his arbitrary and es, tially despotic rulings, none the repulsive because veiled behind smile, render him one of the n dangerous men that we can conce of to be honored with a respons position in a republic. From the \ the gold organs and mugwump sh are singing his praises, it is evident the gamblers of Wall Street and the Bank of England's representatives would greatly rejoice to see him nominated. On January 10 Mr. Bell of Colorado made a short but statesmanlike appeal for *simple justice* in Congress, during which he pointed out the fact that he belonged to a party which cast a million and a quarter votes, but that so far as committees were concerned the People's Party had been assigned no important position on any committee of the House. Speaking of the rules which control the House Mr. Bell said:

These rules give control of the House to less than half a dozen men—the five forming a committee on rules—the dictates of whom a majority will obediently obey. The rules of this House give the power of the American Congress to a half dozen states. Take the state of Maine, with 600,000 inhabitants, and it has the greatest power of any state in the Union here. I know one county in Colorado that contains more innate wealth than can be found in all of the state of Maine, and this whole state is without recognition in any committee concerning her chief resources under these sacred rules. Maine, with four representatives, occupies *four of the best positions in this House* and directs and controls more legislation than all the members of the western states from Colorado to California, inclusive, and we are told this is in accordance with these sacred rules.

SAMPLE SPEAKER FROM PARTY OF "MORAL ID
From *Puck*, March 5, 1890, by permission

Continuing, Mr. Bell observed:

We, as Populists, as also the Republican members, have app time and again in this House for r nition. The few Populists who here have permitted you to come i the Republican and on the Democ side and pass your bills by unanim consent. But under your present here are seven members, represen

THE GORILLA AND HIS PREY.
From *Puck*, February 12, 1890, by permissio

a constituency of over a million an quarter of voters and over 6,000, people, who have had no recognitio this House, who are not even regar as a part of the minority. To the re sentatives of this vast constitue are given little positions upon com tees that do not deserve to be dignl by the name of committees. They not given a single position on a g committee anywhere. I speak of in answer to the argument of the tleman from Iowa who last spoke. suggested that we have the rw debate on measures coming fr committees. I want to say to

A PARLIAMENTARY DESPOT
From New York *World*, Jan. 24, 1890.

the members of the Populist party are on no committees, and the same may be said of new members of the Republican party from the West. Therefore I gladly second the generous effort of the gentleman from Iowa [Mr. Hepburn] who first spoke in favor of amending these autocratic and despotic rules.

It is needless to say that the impassioned appeal of a sincere patriot met with no just response from the man who, "clothed in a little brief authority," wields the speaker's gavel to the injury of the nation. For a man who is so small and unjust in his conception of statesmanship cannot fail to prove injurious to the best interests of the nation, no matter what position of authority he holds.

~~~~~~~

The Modern Honest-Money Pharisees who Devour Widows' Houses and for Pretence Enlarge their Phylacteries and Make Long Prayers.

The desire of the gold rings which have robbed the people of their prosperity and weighted the republic with a monstrous bonded debt to label themselves "honest-money" men reminds one of the pharisees of old, who for a pretence made long prayers in public and enlarged their phylacteries while they devoured widows' houses, and the terrible denunciation of those hypocrites by the great Galilean was not more applicable than is the same to the men who seek to increase the misery of the industrial millions, continue stagnation of business, and add to the wretchedness of the wealth-creators by playing into the hands of the world's octopus, and who to divert attention from their criminality label themselves *honest-money men.*

~~~~~~~

National Prosperity Versus Bankruptcy, or Why the Mexican Republic Prospers While Our Nation Resorts to Bonded Indebtedness and all Industries are Stagnant — Some Telling Words from the Mexican Herald.

The *Herald* of Mexico City, in an editorial noticing one of Justice Clark's able papers on Mexico, after quoting the following from Justi Clark in the ARENA,—

Mexico has not made the mistake contracting her currency, and hen being untrammelled in her progres has marched on by leaps and boune in her development during these latt years, while the United States, owir to a contrary policy, has been suffe ing under the blight of a long-endu ing depression,—

makes the following observatio which the great Eastern dailies da not publish, as they are muzzled I the gold power so effectually that the will give no space to speak of fe the cause of real honest money and just American financial system whic would bring the republic greater pro perity than that which to-day mar our sister republic. Says the *Mexic Herald,* in the editorial to which refer:

The distinguished gentleman entirely right in his premise ar the conclusion he draws from Mexico has wisely refused to enterta the idea of going upon a gold basi *and her wisdom is now justified in t vastly increased internal commer and industrial activity of the countr* which yields, through a most equit ble form of taxation, a continually i creasing revenue to her treasur *Had she contracted her currency going on a gold basis, she would, t day, be a stagnant country, and Ame ican capital, seeking escape fro hard conditions, would not be flowir in here. Her tropical agricultu would not have expanded so marr lously.*

The gold power has succeeded paralyzing the prosperity of our gre republic, in fastening upon it a enormous bonded indebtedness in hour of profound peace, and has e riched alien nations and their agen in this country at *a terrible expen to life, property, prosperity, and happ ness to the wealth-creators.* A chan in our national policy must be acco plished. The double-headed go power must be broken, or the doom ancient Rome will be repeated in t history of this once *prosperous* public. *Men of thought and action, t hope of the gold power lies in diri ing the forces of reform and misleadi the voters by the same false pretences which have been systematically employed with such terrible effect for three decades.* Every man has a solemn duty to perform in order to rescue his home, his loved ones, and his country from the grasp of plutocracy. It will not do to merely "turn the rascals out." Honest men who will be loyal to an honest American financial system, and who cannot be bought by the honest-money (?) rogues of Europe and their allies among the gamblers of Wall Street, must be elected next November. Let every patriot understand two things. First, a greater and more solemn duty confronts him than that which confronted the patriot army during the darkest hour of the Revolution. Second, that the people can bring about prosperity by voting down and out the two "Organized Appetites" which are governed by English gold and Wall Street wealth; on the sturdy wealth-creators, as upon the forlorn hope of Washington's command during the winter of Valley Forge, depend the freedom and happiness of their children and the glory and prosperity of their nation.

The Step-By-Step Plan.

If a besieging army should be encamped about a city protected by several lines of fortifications, while it might be deemed wise to shell the enemy, no capture of the inner lines of fortification or storming of the city could be successful until the outer breastworks should have been carried. So in politics, the success which has marked the work of the Fabian Society in England during recent years has been due to two things: (1) a systematic educational propaganda along many lines of reform, (2) the union or concentration of their strength at the polls upon the one issue on which the people were best educated and which was most urgent at that time,—never, however, relaxing one whit their educational work, so that as soon as the point upon which they had concentrated their efforts had been carried they could bend all their energies to

the carrying of the next point. Now, omnibus platforms, while they may be almost ideal in their demand when viewed from the vantage ground of the highest altruistic principles, fall before the sophistry of the enemy, because the points upon which the people are not educated or the planks unpopular in certain directions are seized upon and emphasized so as to obscure the issues upon which the rank and file are thoroughly in accord, having been educated up to them. Hence, while I yield to no man in my allegiance to the principles of national, state, and municipal ownership of natural monopolies, and while I believe the land problem to be fundamental in character, and also am a most sincere believer in the principles of direct legislation, yet I realize that upon these issues as well as other root problems in social science and political economy, there is much diversity of opinion and still greater ignorance on the part of the rank and file of voters as to what constitutes these questions, owing largely to their being systematically misrepresented by organized plutocracy. Now this is not true of the money question, for while many reformers believe in a national scientific currency not based on commodities, a vast majority of them realize that the increasing of the money of the people through the restoration of silver would immensely aid the wealth-creators by raising prices, stimulating all legitimate business, and enabling the wealth-creators to pass out of the Egypt of industrial slavery. Hence, here we find the first step upon which the industrial masses, the wealthy manufacturers and merchants, the farmer and the artisan, can unite. It will be carrying the *outer redoubt of the enemy.* But I should not favor this move if it were to be regarded as the ultimate. My idea is that our duty now is to unite and conquer while we carry on the educational campaign as vigorously as possible, so that the moment the first doubt is carried we can push for

ye down of
the splendid imaginations of such philosophers and prophets as Plato and Sir Thomas More. The present is no time for dividing forces; every vote is needed, and the enthusiastic support of the forces of progress will ensure a victory which will enable our wealth-creators to push forward the work of social and economic progress.

McKinley's Only Hope of Election Would Lie in His Secret Pledge to the Gold Power.

There is something amazing in the assumption of ignorance on the part of the people which characterizes the action of the political wire-pullers who are trying to delude America's industrial millions into the belief that Major McKinley honestly favors restoring silver to her ancient constitutional position by the only method whereby this can be accomplished, viz., independent action on the part of the great Republic. In the rôle of Mr. Facing-Both-Ways the Ohio tool of the millionaire street-railway magnate Hanna cannot be said to be a success. McKinley's record in Congress on the financial question is such that no friend of an American financial system, no believer in *real honest money*, no wealth-creator, no man who would forward the prosperity and increase the happiness of America's millions, could for one moment think of casting his vote for this man, whose record has been so largely tainted with the gold influence and who has not the courage to speak out his convictions on the money question—a man who would go before his party convention on a state plank which represents the despicable straddle which has so frequently characterized the tactics of unscrupulous politicians and demagogues who have deceived the people the interests of plutocracy. The that Senator Sherman strongly

merican, y unwort
of the support of honest men the ballot box. In this connecti a dispatch to the New York *Journ* from Cleveland, Ohio, dated Mar 27, in which ex-Secretary of t Treasury Charles Foster had hims interviewed, is of interest. The qu tion was put to this henchman McKinley as to whether the financ question would figure prominently the campaign, and he replied:

"No, I don't think it will; and if chance it should, it will be entire subservient to the greater and mo vital issue of protection. I am f sound money, of course, and I wou favor the incorporation of a pla embodying that idea into the Repub can national platform. Yes, I re the plank adopted by Morton's su porters, but it amounts to just t same thing. When you sift the tv down the Ohio and New York plan are practically identical."

The Tool of Hanna.

Even if Mr. McKinley was accept ble to patriotic American citizens a had proved himself to be a fran honorable, outspoken statesman i stead of an "artful dodger," there a facts connected with his candida which would be absolutely fatal his election should the Republic party be blind enough to nomina him. In the first place it will be membered that when Mr. McKinl became bankrupt the street-railw magnate, Mr. Hanna, arranged f the payment of Mr. McKinley's deb thus placing the Ohio politician fo ever under obligation to him. At th time it did not appear that Mr. Hann had political aspirations; it now a pears that he rather than the litt man from Ohio proposes to pose a Napoleon in the political arena. B it is safe to say that the thoughtf industrial millions of America are n going to support a man who would the nature of the case be the to of a millionaire street-railway ma nate, any more than they will su port a man who faces both ways on the great question of finance which is uppermost in the minds of all thoughtful people, when no thinking man can disguise the fact that the coming campaign is to be a campaign for free silver and industrial freedom or for the triumph of the Bank of England's policy and industrial serfdom. The gold power of New York would not for one moment support McKinley with the funds that would be needed to carry the states in the Northeast which would be essential to him, unless he would make pledges to them to follow their bidding, while the free silver men of the Northwest, the West, and the South, after being systematically deceived by the two great parties in their platforms and in their candidates for more than a quarter of a century, are in no mood to stand longer the "artful dodger" methods of Major McKinley. It is safe also to say that the nomination of Major McKinley would mean a Waterloo to the Republican party.

The Standard Oil's Protege.

The persistency with which William C. Whitney denies being a Democratic candidate, and the persistency with which he professes favor for the white metal in the face of the fact that he declared only a short time ago that Grover Cleveland, the greatest enemy silver has ever had in the presidential chair, was the best person the Democratic party could nominate for the presidency, will not deceive the Democracy of the South or West. Mr. Whitney may be an astute politician, but the people have been too long deceived to allow themselves to be longer hoodwinked by the protégé of the Standard Oil Trust.

The Great Banker, Jay Cooke, who Floated the Government Bonds in '61, Denounces the Gold Ring and the Parasites of England, and States that an Honest Supreme Court would Declare that the Closing of the Mints to Silver was Unconstitutional.

Only now and then will an Eastern daily paper allow its columns to be opened to the most eminent authorities or the most careful economists and students when they speak for free silver and prosperity for the nation, so great is their terror of the ring of men who are called financiers, who have systematically plundered the nation and the wealth-producing millions for more than thirty years. Recently, George Alfred Townsend, better known in the newspaper world as "Gath," interviewed the great banker, Jay Cooke, who, it will be remembered, floated the government bonds in '61, and whose utterances, in this instance were they part of the hired harangues of the attorneys for the gold power, would have appeared in every great daily in the East in large headlines. This interesting interview was published in the Boston *Globe*, of March 29, in Townsend's regular weekly letter, but placed in an out-of-the-way position, and from the reading of it one would infer that a portion of the letter was not printed, as for example, in one place in this letter Mr. Cooke says, "One of the newspaper publishers here who has recently taken up silver as his specific tempted me to write a letter which I will read to you as a beginning." But no extract even of this letter is given to the reader of the *Globe*. On the contrary, the next question is, "Have you any interest in silver in any way, Mr. Cooke, as a producer or dealer?" to which the veteran banker replied, "None." I have space only for an extract from this letter, but I feel that it will be of exceeding interest to our readers; and as the gold press will not allow their readers to be informed as to the facts which have brought about the great stagnation, the misery, the suicide, and industrial slavery under which we are to-day groaning. I make the following extended quotations from this letter:

Philadelphia, March 27, 1896.—This is how it happened: Having known Jay Cooke, the seller of the government loans during the war, since he began that work in 1861, and having in recent correspondence discovered that he was not on the side of bankers as to disestablishment ver, I went to his office by appointment and spent from 10 o'clock in the morning until 2 in the afternoon, obtaining his argument, together with interesting reminiscences of his great banking career.

Jay Cooke is 75 years old. He has the beautiful eyes of the pilgrims at Plymouth, from whom he is descended, and which are repeated in the pictures of Priscilla Alden. Mr. Cooke has red cheeks, is to this day an active fisherman, and his hair and beard are all white.

"I have tried," said he, "not to figure as a disputant on this question. Letters come to me from all over the country since you printed the fact that I was dissonant with the banking world on the silver question, but I am too old to neglect my remaining business to lead any public cause. I don't want to get angry at my time of life, and I am sorely tempted to feel so. One of the newspaper publishers here, who has taken up silver as his specific, lately tempted me to write a letter, which I will read you as a beginning."

"Have you any interest in silver in any way, Mr Cooke, as a producer or dealer?"

"None.

"Dr. Lindermann, the chief of the mints at Washington, came from this state. About the time of this demonetization he went to London. He was particularly susceptible to the sort of flattery they throw around American officials. He went to many dinners, and was made to feel that he ought to fall in with the English standard. Had the American people, in their political conventions, or in congressional debates, come to this question openly, they never would have consented to leave silver out of our coin standard. Lindermann had the revision of the money laws under his control. It was done without anybody's knowledge, and, notwithstanding the demonetization, even after it became known, silver continued to appreciate until the constant war against it by these railroad bankers, by the government, and the excessive energy of the silver-producers started its decline. We have, therefore, cut off an immense source of our wealth, as well as of our currency. Do you mean to tell me that any nation but this on the globe, possessed of such ample silver mines, would have disparaged that species of wealth voluntarily? And I tell you, sir, that it is going to make a great issue before the people. You can't keep it down. ere is a letter from the state treas-

urer of Missouri, received in morning's mail, telling me that people out there are overwhelmi for silver restoration. I get let all the time."

"In a word, Mr. Cooke, you w restore silver at the old ratio o to 1?"

"Yes unless we should wish to ob France and take her standard of to 1."

"Do you find silver a drug?"

"Just the contrary. I stayed at lantic City a part of the winter, an leaving there yesterday to have portrait painted for my famil, wanted to get some silver quar to give the servants. All they c raise in the house was a dollar in ver in small pieces. Why don't government use its mints and turn quarter dollars?"

"Then you hold at least one of questions sure to appear in the con campaign is silver?"

"Silver and the tariff. They bel to each other. In both cases dropped our Americanism and w misled by the parasites of Engl and her insidious policy, and in o to maintain the credit of railro more or less broken already, we running into debt, and with all unfriendliness to silver are get every day in a worse condition. ' country is just ready for busin Look at these splendid facilities, s as these office buildings. Do you pose that the men who framed government out there would l tamely acquiesced in the British standard of money?" (He pointed Carpenter's hall, which I now served to be right behind me, h courtway.) "There the Contine Congress met in 1774, with Washi ton one of the delegates.

"Men of that character," said Cooke, "would rise out of their gra if they had the power, to reprove state of things we see at Washing Instead of putting the people on t feet and giving them money and cations, they are trying down there throw us into a war, first with E land, next with Spain. I consi President Cleveland's Venezuelan n sage to have been next to a crimi attempt to disguise to the Ameri people the absolute failure of his saults upon the tariff and upon money."

"You think this country w free silver coinage could easily han all that coin?"

"Of course."

"Have you ever seen gold at a count, Mr. Cooke?"

"Why of course I have. Many a dollar have I made by shaving gold and sending it over to New York by special messenger. I have seen the two Drexels—Tony and Frank—bringing on their own shoulders over to our banking house of Clark & Co., bags of gold which we allowed them mercantile paper for."

"I suppose you have seen silver also lugged around in bags?"

"Why, in the days of Spanish and Mexican quarters, fips, levies, etc.,— for we rarely coined any dimes and half dimes—I have bought kegs of silver to be sent out to China for tea, silk, etc."

"How do you account for Germany's attitude?"

"Germany has always been a parasite of England. For centuries the Germans were subsidized by the British to fight British wars on the continent."

"They say that wages are going up in Japan, Mr. Cooke, on account of the skilled labor there getting the trades union wink."

"That is not true to any great extent. Wages started up a little in Japan and then they fell back again. These college professors and smart boy experts on the gold press will have to make a great many assertions of the kind to prove their syllogism.

"In the East in the large communities is the place to do missionary work. If I had a newspaper press, as I had in the civil war, when I advertised the public loans and paid every bill without shaving it, paid the copperhead papers just as well as the union papers, why, I could have done anything in this country on a question like silver; it would have been the very easiest of all ques-

tions to convert men upon, thr the press."

"I think you dropped the idea now about the unconstitutionalit demonetizing silver, or rather, of standardizing it?"

"Yes, I believe that if we ha honest supreme court it would d that closing the mints to silver co was unconstitutional."

Western Farmers Travelling Back Age of Barter.

The editor of one of the mos fluential papers in Nebraska w me under date March 27:

You cannot conceive the a poverty of the people in every tion of this state. I received ye day a letter from a prominent cit in the northern part of the state ing that hundreds of farmers l not had one cent of money in pockets for weeks. What few th they can buy are procured by tra eggs or small farm products at country store. They are trave back to the age of barter.

I am receiving many such le from various portions of the S and West. A tremendous gro swell is upon us, and notwithstan the attempt upon the part of "parasites of England" and minions to protect the people in great cities *against intelligence* to suppress all free speech in re to the monetary system at the best of the gold power, the da reckoning is at hand.

The Close of Volume XV of the Arena.

With this issue we close Volume Fifteen of the ARENA with a much larger circulation than this review has enjoyed at any previous time in its history; and what is more valued by us, the possession of the warm, we might almost say passionate love of a large proportion of our tens of thousands of subscribers. Almost every mail brings in letters' from all parts of our land, from Europe, Asia, and Australia, all expressing an intense love and loyalty to the ARENA which we believe is exceptional among reviews. Here, for example, is an extract from a young lady's letter from Switzerland: "You do not know how eagerly I await the coming of the ARENA. I am among society people here, and the shallowness of life makes me sick at heart until your great review comes bringing stores of real live thought, fairly palpitating with moral life, and then I take courage." From Melbourne, Australia, come these lines: "It must be no unusual thing for you to get letters from all parts of the world. Your brave and fearless courage is attracting daily increasing interest, so you must be overwhelmed with questionings and inquiries from all quarters. I have been a constant reader of the ARENA since its first appearance and have an intense admiration for its exposure of injustice, corruption, and villany wherever these are found to exist. How few, alas, are courageous enough to face the odium and censure which attaches itself to all those who endeavor to reach the *causes* which are at work, producing the most awful and calamitous moral evils the world has ever known, and unless the tide is stemmed surely there must be a more terrible fate awaiting our modern Christian (?) civilization than which befell pagan Rome. It is such as you who proclaim the 'Repent ye' that the workers of world depend as captains of cause of freedom, righteousness, justice. *Silence* as to *causes* is watchword of the press. *Effects* as murder, infanticide, abortion, in drunkenness, outrages on child divorce, etc., are drawn attention t startling and exaggerated headli but a timidly or cautiously worded gestion as to the *causes* which are ducing these effects ensures volley abuse. Men and women who call a sp a spade suffer here as they do elsew It is an immense help to us to ha magazine such as is yours. It is n use of on all sorts of occasions an almost every meeting on reform wo

We might multiply similar extr by the thousand from recently ceived letters, but our purpose in q ing these typical extracts from let daily received is to show how re place the ARENA has in the affec of thinking, earnest people who conscientiously and persistently la ing to bring about a higher condi of life.

<hr/>

Volume XVI of the Arena will be Un ally Strong.

Our arrangements are such that feel justified in promising our reac that our appreciation of their lib support during the past will be she by *a volume which will eclipse all predecessors in ability, variety, general interest.* The reduction of price of the ARENA has placed within the reach of tens of thousa who prior to this year could not a it, but we are constantly receiving ters from parties asking us if ARENA is reduced to $3, for in case they wish to subscribe, hence we urge our friends everywhere to call the attention of thinking men and women of conscience to the reduction in price, to the fact that it is the largest original monthly review now published, and that almost every issue contains choice illustrations. The June ARENA will contain two or three magnificently illustrated papers, and with the exception of the present issue every number of this volume has contained exceptionally fine illustrations made expressly for the ARENA. During the summer months we propose to publish a number of very *richly illustrated papers*. In a word, it is our determination to make Volume XVI of the ARENA surpass in excellence and general interest any review published in the republic.

More than Doubling Its Sales — The Voice of Denver.

A short time ago we published a letter from the Armstrong News Agency of Boston, showing that they had increased their monthly sales of the ARENA one hundred and forty copies since the reduction in price. Jones News Company of Portland, Oregon, have increased their sales fifty copies a month. We are constantly receiving similar letters. Here are a few from the leading newsdealers and booksellers of Denver, Colorado:

KELLY & WESTLING,
Booksellers and Stationers,
727 16th St.   Denver, Colo.
March 23, 1896.
To the Arena Pub. Co.:
Our sales of the ARENA since the reduction in price have been MORE *than doubled.*
KELLY & WESTLING.

E. BESLY & CO.
Wholesale.
Booksellers and Stationers.
Denver, Colo., 3/23/96.
Arena Pub. Co.:
I desire to say that since the reduction in the price of your Magazine our sales have MORE THAN DOUBLED.   E. BESLY & CO.
G.

CHAIN & HARDY.

Book, Stationery and Art Co.
Denver, Colo.
1609–1615 Arapahoe Street,
Denver, Colo., 3/23/'
The Arena Pub. Co.,
Gentlemen: We judge that the mand for the ARENA Magazine about *doubled* since the reduction price, and the sale seems to be *stea increasing.* Yours respectfully,
CHAIN & HARDY C

HAMILTON & KENDRICK

Books, News, Stationery,
906–910 Seventeenth St., Denver,
March 23, 1
Arena Co., New York City,
Dear Sirs: Since your reductio price of the ARENA from 50 c to 25 cents per copy WE HA DOUBLED OUR SALES AND TH ARE STILL ON THE INCREA
Yours respectfully,
HAMILTON & KENDRIC

Some Strong Features of this Issu the Arena.

In this issue of the ARENA ap many very notable papers of sp interest to thinking men and wome conviction. I would especially call tention to " *Professor Roentgen's covery and the Invisible World Aro Us*," by PROF. JAMES T. BIXBY, PH. " *Man in His Relation to the Solar tem,*" by J. HEBER SMITH, M. D.; " *Telegraph Monopoly,*" by PROF. FR PARSONS of Boston University Scho Law; " *Why the West Needs Free C age of Silver,*" by HON. C. S. THOMA the National Democratic Commi "*The Land of the Noonday Sun,*" by TICE WALTER CLARK, LL. D.; " *R sentative Women on Vital Social P lems,*" by SARAH MIFFLIN GAY FRANCES E. RUSSELL; "*What Is A ca's Relation to England?*" a ti paper by MRS. EVELEEN LAURA MA the well-known author and essa These are a few of the notable cont tions which will appeal to thinking and women in this issue of the ARE

Miss Dromgoole's Powerful Sto Tennessee Life.

In "The Valley Path" goole is demonstrating that

much at home in the creation of a powerful novel as she has proved herself to be a master in the production of brilliant short stories. "The Valley Path," while incidentally emphasizing the difference between the religion of life and conventional theology, is a powerful and faithful picture of the life with which the author deals. This work alone is so strong, vigorous, and meritorious that had she written nothing else it would place Tennessee's gifted author high in the world of letters. The South has just reason to be proud of Will Allen Dromgoole.

Between Two Worlds.

The June ARENA will contain a brief synopsis of the preceding chapters of "Between Two Worlds," and also a number of exceptionally fine illustrations of this remarkable psychical story.

Divine Healing and Works.

Eugene Hatch, the author of one of the ablest works I have had the pleasure of reading on the New Testament Teachings and Divine Healing contributes a very thoughtful paper to this issue of the ARENA, which will read with special interest by those who believe that a recognition of spiritual supremacy is the key to health, happiness, and success.

The Barefoot Boy who was also a Dreamer.

In this issue I give a sketch of the boyhood of Whittier, trusting it may prove an inspiration to the young, for seldom have we had a life at once so pure and inspiring as that of the poet of New England. Reared as he was under very hard conditions, the story of his early struggle will prove helpful, I trust, to other youths who aspire to something nobler than an acquisition of gold or gaining a merely intellectual education.

Dr. Ghose's Paper on Mysore.

Very interesting is Dr. Ghose's paper on one of the semi-independent states of India, and full of suggestions to patriotic Americans of to-day when it is remembered that the United States is year by year becoming more and more a debtor nation to England. Mysore under England's rule, like Egypt and many states where the merciless power of Britain has been exerted, sank to the brink of ruin more terrible than can be pictured, but since her partial independence this state, as shown by the statistical reports, has evinced a progress which has been little short of marvellous. If there is any nation on the face of the earth which ought to take the part of LEADER instead of supinely contenting itself with being a camp follower of other nations, that country is this republic; yet for a quarter of a century we have yielded to the domination of British financial policy and have hearkened to the Wall Street gamblers who, posing as financiers, have proved veritable blood suckers of national prosperity. The clock has struck the hour for a change. *The next president must be an American, and the Bank of England's policy, the Tory class in the government, and the Hessians of plutocracy must be routed all along the line.*

tion THE

THE FINISHED CREATION
AND OTHER POEMS.

THE AZTECS.

Cloth, $1.25.

Uniform with "Columbus the Discoverer."

Mr. Walter Warren is a man evidently in warm sympathy for his kind. His play is gorgeous with the local color of Mexico in the fifteenth century, and replete with fine thoughts, which, however, he acknowledges might not have come to Aztecs, although, again, he alleges they might. Its plot is a noble conception. — *The Commonwealth, Boston.*

COLUMBUS THE DISCOVERER. A Drama.

Cloth, $1.25.

A spirited drama in five acts. Mr. Walter Warren makes a psychologic rather than a historic — though not unhistoric — study of the character of Columbus, as manifested and developed in connection with his experiences before, during, and after his discovery of America. In dramatizing a story in this fashion, one gets a better insight into the personality of Columbus than is possible from the merely abstract narratives. — *The Boston Herald.*

CECIL THE SEER.

Cloth, $1.25.

In peacock blue and silver, uniform with above.

A strong drama from a literary point of view. This is not the author's first attempt at drama but his most ambitious one. It is rich in metaphysical thought stated in the tersest way. Epigrams abound and they have the Shakespearian vigor. — *The Sentinel, Indianapolis, Ind.*

At all Bookstores, or mailed, postpaid, on receipt of price.

ARENA PUBLISHING COMPANY,

Copley Square, Boston, Mass.

A charming narrative pervaded by a strongly religious
and moral tone.

HILL CREST~

by JULIA COLLITON FLEWELLYN.

ARENA
PUBLISHING Co.

Cloth, $1.25;   Paper, 50 Cents.

Published by

The Arena Publishing Company,

COPLEY SQUARE, BOSTON, MASS.

Mr. Charles S. Patterson, the publisher of *Newspaperdom*, says that it is not often that he gets so enthusiastic as he does over Ripans Tabules. Almost with the regularity of clockwork he used to feel, at about eleven o'clock, that something had gone wrong with his breakfast; especially was this true if he had had a restless night, as is no uncommon thing with head-workers. " My stomach," said Mr. Patterson, " is under the standard as to strength, and it seems at these times to act only indifferently, and finally to stop. Clouds come before my vision and a slight nausea is felt. Then I reach out for my Ripans. (Years of the sort of thing related have made me know the symptoms as well as my name.) Down goes one of the blessed little concentrated boons, and in a few minutes the visual clouds lift, discomfort passes away, stomach apparently resumes operations, and at 12.30 or 1 o'clock I go out for my usual rather hearty luncheon — all in delightful contrast with my former practically ruined afternoons — that I sought to escape by fasting and various doses."

Sam Rivers of Keyser, N. C., is an old colored man who is very influential with his class, and the colored people are numerous in that section In an interview with Fred W. Saunders, a local reporter, on the 10th of June, 1895, the old gentleman said: " For a long time I have been annoyed with dyspepsia and indigestion (man's two worst evils).

Ripans Tabules having been tested (many others had failed gave me perfec lief. I rec mmen l them to all my who are afflicted with these or kindred eases. " Signed), SAM RIVERS, D.

Mr. Xeno W. Putnam, a literary man a student of advertising, residing at H burg, Pa., under date of June 3, 1895, as follows: " Not long since I came upo ' Knight of the Road ' taking something f a small vial, a circumstance that I wo hardly have noticed had not my eye f upon the well-known Ripans label. The was interested, and proceeded to intervi him. ' What do I take 'em fur? ' he answe my query. ' See here, young fellow, what ye take yer swag fur? Fun, ain't it? Yer when a fellow's liver and stomach is out whack ther ain't much fun in my biz; gets these here pills and then I have fun. fellow can have lots o' fun trampin' if stomach's in good order. So that's wha takes 'em fur; just fun. Where do I li Usually about where I happen ter be. see, I live there because I hain't happened die there yet, thanks ter these little fello holding up the vial. Partly in a spirit of I told him it might be considerably to his vantage to give some address where he mi be reached. ' I don't take no advantages,' answered sagely, ' I just take these 'er pills travel.' The circumstance was so unique t I decided to report it to you."

RIPANS TABULES are sold by druggists, or by mail If the price (50 cents a box) is sent to the RIPANS CHEMICAL COMPANY, No. 10 Spruce Street, New York. Sample Vial, 10 cents.

When writing please mention THE ARENA.

OLD MEXICO . . .

SPRING TIME ALL=THE=YEAR=ROUND.

A land of sunshine and flowers, of of grand old cathedrals and pictur civilization dating back centuries.

It is only three or four days' travel between any of the principal c of the United States and the City of Mexico via Laredo, and the Mexi National R. R. "Laredo Route" is the Short Line, the Bee Line, tween the United States and the principal cities of Old Mexico,

MONTEREY, SALTILLO, SAN LUIS POTOSI, SAN MIGUEL DE ALLENDE, CELAYA, MORELIA, PATZCUARO, TOLUCA, CITY OF MEXICO . . . .

The "Laredo Route" offers to travelers scenery unsu through Pullman Buffet Drawing-Room Car service between Laredo the City of Mexico. The Company controls the restaurants at meal tions and assures their excellence.

Time tables, guide books and all information desired will be furnished on applicatio nearest ticket agent, or to

W. E. THURBER,	**B. W. THACHER,**	**W. B. RYAN,**
General Western Agent,	General Passenger Agent,	General Eastern Agent
⁀⁀0 Quincy Building, Chicago, Ill.	City of Mexico.	353 Broadway, New Y

When writing please mention THE ARENA.

No one concern makes the best Bicycles in the world ❧ ❧ ❧ ❧ ❧ ❧ ❧

No one make of bicycle has a monopoly of quality or superior devices. Some excel in one particular, others in another. There are many grades of bicycles, and grade is not to be determined by price ❧ ❧ ❧ ❧ ❧ ❧ ❧ ❧

The **Waverley** Bicycle

is the peer of any bicycle on the market at any price. This product of a modern factory, unequaled in its appointments, employing the highest mechanical skill and the best materials obtainable, is sold at

$85 <u>A FAIR PRICE</u> $85

and strictly at one price to all ❧ ❧ ❧ ❧ ❧ ❧

INDIANA BICYCLE COMPANY
INDIANAPOLIS, IND.
EASTERN WHOLESALE BRANCH, 339 B'WAY, NEW YORK

Catalogue free by mail

When writing please mention THE ARENA.

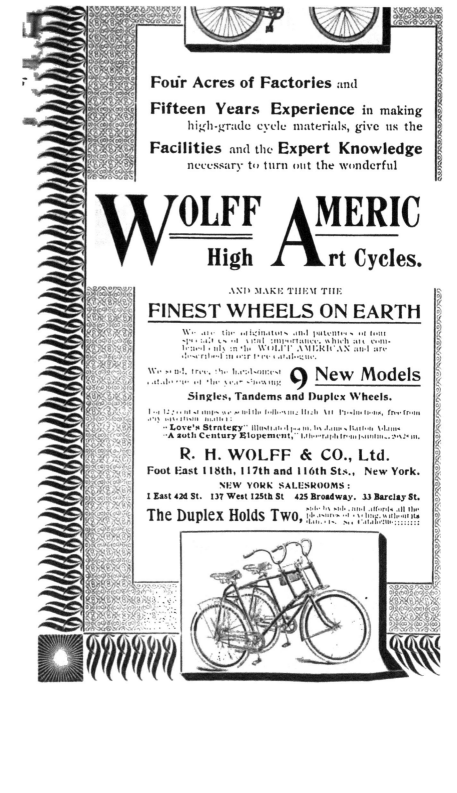

Lightning Source UK Ltd.
Milton Keynes UK
UKHW011216051118
331792UK00012B/2416/P